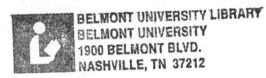

International Directory of
COMPANY
HISTORIES

International Directory of

COMPANY HISTORIES

VOLUME 20

Editor

Jay P. Pederson

ST. JAMES PRESS

AN IMPRINT OF GALE

DETROIT • NEW YORK • TORONTO • LONDON

STAFF

Jay P. Pederson, *Editor*

Miranda H. Ferrara, *Project Manager*
Joann Cerrito, Nicolet V. Elert, Tina N. Grant, Kristin Hart,
Margaret Mazurkiewicz, Michael J. Tyrkus, *Contributing Editors*
Peter M. Gareffa, *Managing Editor, St. James Press*

The paper used in this publication meets the minimum
requirements of American National Standard for Information Sciences—
Permanence Paper for Printed Library Materials, ANSI Z39.48-1984.

This book is printed on recycled paper that meets Environmental Protection Agency Standards.

Library of Congress Catalog Number: 89-190943

British Library Cataloguing in Publication Data

International directory of company histories. Vol. 20
I. Jay P. Pederson
338.7409

ISBN 1-55862-361-2

Printed in the United States of America
Published simultaneously in the United Kingdom

St. James Press is an imprint of Gale

Cover photograph: Floor of the American Stock Exchange
(courtesy American Stock Exchange)

10 9 8 7 6 5 4 3 2 1

CONTENTS _____

Company Histories

PREFACE

The St. James Press series *The International Directory of Company Histories (IDCH)* is intended for reference use by students, business people, librarians, historians, economists, investors, job candidates, and others who seek to learn more about the historical development of the world's most important companies. To date, *IDCH* has covered over 3,000 companies in 20 volumes.

Inclusion Criteria

Most companies chosen for inclusion in *IDCH* have achieved a minimum of US$100 million in annual sales and are leading influences in their industries or geographical locations. Companies may be publicly held, private, or non-profit. State-owned companies that are important in their industries and that may operate much like public or private companies also are included. Wholly owned subsidiaries and divisions are profiled if they meet the requirements for inclusion. Entries on companies that have had major changes since they were last profiled may be selected for updating.

The *IDCH* series highlights 10% private and non-profit companies, and features updated entries on approximately 35 companies per volume.

Entry Format

Each entry begins with the company's legal name, the address of its headquarters, its telephone and fax numbers, and its web site. A statement of public, private, state, or parent ownership follows. A company with a legal name in both English and the language of its headquarters country is listed by the English name, with the native-language name in parentheses.

The company's founding or earliest incorporation date, the number of employees, and the most recent sales figures available follow. Sales figures are given in local currencies with equivalents in U.S. dollars. For some private companies, sales figures are estimates. The entry lists the exchanges on which a company's stock is traded, as well as the company's principal Standard Industrial Classification codes.

Entries generally contain a *Company Perspectives* box which provides a short summary of the company's mission, goals, and ideals, a list of *Principal Subsidiaries*, *Principal Divisions*, *Principal Operating Units*, and articles for *Further Reading*.

American spelling is used throughout *IDCH*, and the word "billion" is used in its U.S. sense of one thousand million.

Sources

Entries have been compiled from publicly accessible sources both in print and on the Internet such as general and academic periodicals, books, annual reports, and material supplied by the companies themselves.

Cumulative Indexes

IDCH contains two indexes: the **Index to Companies**, which provides an alphabetical index to companies discussed in the text as well as companies profiled, and the **Index to Industries**, which allows researchers to locate companies by their principal industry. Both indexes are cumulative and specific instructions for using them are found immediately preceding each index.

Suggestions Welcome

Comments and suggestions from users of *IDCH* on any aspect of the product as well as suggestions for companies to be included or updated are cordially invited. Please write:

The Editor
International Directory of Company Histories
St. James Press
835 Penobscot Building
Detroit, Michigan 48226-4094

ABBREVIATIONS FOR FORMS OF COMPANY INCORPORATION

A.B.	Aktiebolaget (Sweden)
A.G.	Aktiengesellschaft (Germany, Switzerland)
A.S.	Atieselskab (Denmark)
A.S.	Aksjeselskap (Denmark, Norway)
A.Ş.	Anomin Şirket (Turkey)
B.V.	Besloten Vennootschap met beperkte, Aansprakelijkheid (The Netherlands)
Co.	Company (United Kingdom, United States)
Corp.	Corporation (United States)
G.I.E.	Groupement d'Intérêt Economique (France)
GmbH	Gesellschaft mit beschränkter Haftung (Germany)
H.B.	Handelsbolaget (Sweden)
Inc.	Incorporated (United States)
KGaA	Kommanditgesellschaft auf Aktien (Germany)
K.K.	Kabushiki Kaisha (Japan)
LLC	Limited Liability Company (Middle East)
Ltd.	Limited (Canada, Japan, United Kingdom, United States)
N.V.	Naamloze Vennootschap (The Netherlands)
OY	Osakeyhtiöt (Finland)
PLC	Public Limited Company (United Kingdom)
PTY.	Proprietary (Australia, Hong Kong, South Africa)
S.A.	Société Anonyme (Belgium, France, Switzerland)
SpA	Società per Azioni (Italy)

ABBREVIATIONS FOR CURRENCY

DA	Algerian dinar		M$	Malaysian ringgit
A$	Australian dollar		Dfl	Netherlands florin
Sch	Austrian schilling		NZ$	New Zealand dollar
BFr	Belgian franc		N	Nigerian naira
Cr	Brazilian cruzado		NKr	Norwegian krone
C$	Canadian dollar		RO	Omani rial
RMB	Chinese renminbi		P	Philippine peso
DKr	Danish krone		Esc	Portuguese escudo
E£	Egyptian pound		SRls	Saudi Arabian riyal
Fmk	Finnish markka		S$	Singapore dollar
FFr	French franc		R	South African rand
DM	German mark		W	South Korean won
HK$	Hong Kong dollar		Pta	Spanish peseta
Rs	Indian rupee		SKr	Swedish krona
Rp	Indonesian rupiah		SFr	Swiss franc
IR£	Irish pound		NT$	Taiwanese dollar
L	Italian lira		B	Thai baht
¥	Japanese yen		£	United Kingdom pound
W	Korean won		$	United States dollar
KD	Kuwaiti dinar		B	Venezuelan bolivar
LuxFr	Luxembourgian franc		K	Zambian kwacha

International Directory of

COMPANY HISTORIES

All American Communications Inc.

808 Wilshire Boulevard
Santa Monica, California 90401-1810
U.S.A.
(310) 656-1100
Fax: (310) 656-7410
Web site: http://www.aacom.com

Public Company
Incorporated: 1991 as All American Television
Sales: $236.5 million (1996)
Employees: 321
Stock Exchanges: NASDAQ
SICs: 7812 Motion Picture & Video Tape Production
   Services; 7922 Television Program Producers; 7389
   Recording Studios

All American Communications Inc. is a major global producer and distributor of television programming and other entertainment media including music and motion pictures. An outgrowth of the Scotti Brothers record label and record production company, All American rose to prominence in the competitive U.S. syndicated television production industry in the early 1990s when it began producing and distributing a little known one-hour action show named *Baywatch* after it had been canceled by NBC. Soon a hugely popular and profitable television property around the world, *Baywatch* generated the income to allow All American to diversify into game and talk shows, movies, and other syndicated television productions through the acquisition of U.S. and international entertainment companies. In 1996 an estimated 100 million viewers watched *Baywatch* each week in more than 110 countries around the world.

In 1996, All American ranked as the 15th largest firm in the U.S. motion picture and video production industry, behind industry leaders Sony USA, Walt Disney, Time Warner, and Universal Studios, among others. All American is the world's largest supplier of game show programming in terms of variety of formats and number of local language versions, and it is the owner of *The Price Is Right*, the longest-running game show in

the U.S. television history. Its portfolio includes some 32 television series, about 30,000 game show episodes, 145 motion pictures, and many children's and special documentary television shows. In 1996, its recorded music and merchandising segment, whose major artists included James Brown and "Weird Al" Yankovic, contributed about 11 percent of the company's total revenues. In 1996, All American maintained administrative offices in California, New York, London, Athens, and Germany as well as production studios in Marina del Rey, California, and Hurth and Koln, Germany.

From Valley of the Dolls *to All American Television: 1967–1990*

In 1967, Anthony J. Scotti was a struggling actor whose claim to fame was an appearance as "Tony Polar," the heart-throb protagonist of the popular film version of Jacqueline Susann's bestseller *The Valley of the Dolls*. For all the boost the part gave his Hollywood career, Scotti found the actor's life dull—long hours of waiting punctuated by a few moments of real work. As he later told *Forbes* magazine, "I had come to the conclusion that acting was the most boring God-awful thing a human being could do." Acting on that sentiment he abandoned his film career in 1971 and joined the record production arm of film studio MGM as a senior vice president.

With three years of entertainment experience under his belt in 1974 he joined forces with his brother Ben to form Ben Scotti Productions, a music marketing firm that went on to handle such artists as the Electric Light Orchestra, Eddie and the Cruisers, and Survivor. In 1979, the brothers branched out into the television business, producing a pop music show called *America's Top Ten*, which featured Casey Kasem in the emcee role. In 1981 the show's success led the Scottis to enlist Joseph E. Kovacs, a seasoned entertainment industry executive, to form a new entity, New York-based All American Television (AATV), to distribute television shows and sell commercial time to advertisers (the company's name derived from Anthony Scotti's success as a football hero during his high school days). In 1982, the team was expanded to include George Back, the founder of a small but profitable television syndicator in New York City, and

Sydney Vinnedge, a veteran of television and radio advertising with the J. Walter Thompson and Grey Advertising agencies.

In 1985 Kovacs spearheaded the company's decision to go public, and AATV began trading as a "pink sheet" on the over-the-counter (OTC) market and then the New York Stock Exchange. By 1986, the firm was posting a net income of $485,000 and—after a loss of $850,000 in 1987—enjoyed another profitable year in 1988. By 1989, All American's net income had risen to an all-time high of $635,000, and the Scottis decided to merge AATV and their still privately held Scotti Brothers Entertainment Industries.

"Baywatch" and Ratings Heaven: 1991–92

In early 1991 Scotti Brothers Entertainment Industries and AATV finally merged in a stock swap that created the television/music recording core of what would eventually become All American Communications Inc. Anthony Scotti became CEO, and in January 1991 he recruited Myron Roth, a former executive with MCA Records and CBS Records West Coast, to become All American's president and chief operating officer. Syd Vinnedge was named senior executive vice president and Ben Scotti was named executive vice president of the records group. In 1990 the Scotti Brothers record operation signed an agreement with the Bertelsmann Music Group (BMG) for the worldwide distribution of its recordings until 1996, but despite sales of $8.8 million All American's net income for the year fell to $255,000.

Over at network giant NBC, however, a little appreciated one-hour "action drama" show named *Baywatch* was reaching the end of its first—and, it appeared, last year in prime time. Led by David Hasselhoff, the 42-year-old star of the mid-1980s TV hit *Knight Rider*, *Baywatch* dramatized the adventures of a well-chiseled team of co-ed lifeguards on a southern California beach who were regularly assaulted by gunmen, boating mishaps, near drownings, predatory sea life, and troubled lovers. As AATV executive Syd Vinnedge later recalled, "The [*Baywatch*] property was recognizable and distinctive, whether you liked it or not. . . . There was a buzz about it and we built on that."

Unhappy with the show's ratings, NBC canceled it in 1990, but All American, noting the canceled show's already remarkable popularity overseas, decided the sandy soap held promise as a first-run syndicated vehicle and acquired its rights in late 1990 through LBS Communications Inc., an advertising barter sales company. A traditional "strip" syndicated television show is a previously seen block of network shows (with at least 65 total episodes) that is distributed by companies like All American to independent broadcasting companies around the nation for airing on a five-day-a-week schedule. The independent distributor or "syndicator" tries to sell the show to enough local television stations so 70 percent of the entire U.S. television market is covered. Once this "clearance level" is achieved, the syndicator can sell national advertising time to big sponsors like MCI, Kellogg Company, or Proctor & Gamble. The syndicator may receive cash from the local TV station for the block of shows or—in a "barter syndication" arrangement—it may receive the advertising time allotted to the program, which it can then sell for a profit to national advertisers.

Baywatch would have been a typical syndicated product for All American except that with only 23 episodes already shot new episodes had to filmed before the start of its first syndicated season in September 1991. As an NBC commodity, *Baywatch* had been an expensive item. Produced for the network by Grant Tinker/Gannet Entertainment, a typical episode took seven to eight days to film at a cost of $1.2 million, an all too typical price for most network programs in the 1990s. To ensure that the new syndicated version would be profitable, All American insisted that it be produced quickly and cheaply. Its ace in the hole was the show's star, Hasselhoff, who had been named one of the show's four executive producers and, like the show's other actors, offered a cut of its profits. Hasselhoff immediately became one of the most fervent supporters of the show's new stripped-down production strategy, which included less wastage of film, the use of cheap locations and accommodations, the streamlining of the approval process for changes and decisions, the use of smaller production staffs, and the agreement with industry labor unions to permit flexible work rules.

All American and the Baywatch Production Co. were also helped in no small part by having raised $10 million in presales production, advertising, and distribution revenue from overseas broadcasters. Between May and November 1991 the 22 episodes of the show's first syndicated year were shot at a cost of $775,000 an episode. By November 1991 *Baywatch* had already become the most popular American show in Great Britain and had been sold to every major TV market in the world (except Brazil) under such names as "Alerte a Malibu," "Guardianes de la Bahia," and "Mishmar Ha-mifratz." At home, All America's *Baywatch* partner LBS Communications had sold it to 147 U.S. stations, or 90 percent of the total market.

With its sales moving briskly toward $35 million, in March 1991 AATV officially changed its name to All American Communications Inc. (All American) and pursued the acquisition of its *Baywatch* distribution partner, LBS Communications, which, bloated by debt, had declared Chapter 11 bankruptcy. As *Baywatch*'s first successful syndicated season wound down, All American attempted to demonstrate its independence from its beach-centered cash cow by airing its own two-hour documentary on the JFK assassination, "The JFK Conspiracy," the first of many attempts to establish an identity independent of bikinis and surf boards. To raise capital it made a 750,000-share public offering of stock in May, generating some $6 million, and in October announced its long-awaited merger with LBS Communications. Anthony Scotti decided to name LBS's founder, Henry Siegel, All American's new president, and Henry's brother Paul Siegel became All American's new president of international and ancillary markets. The distribution rights of *Baywatch* and the game show *Family Feud* reverted to All American in the agreement, and with All American's sales plowing ahead to almost $60 million, *Baywatch* began filming its second season with a new cast member, a young Canadian blonde named Pamela Anderson, who became a global sexual icon and helped lift the show to even greater popularity. By the end of 1992, All American's Scotti had been profiled in *Forbes* magazine and the company's first big attempt to clone its *Baywatch* success—an action series called *Acapulco H.E.A.T.*—had been sold to half the U.S. independent television market.

The "Baywatch Franchise" and After: 1993–94

The *Baywatch* juggernaut continued to almost singlehandedly propel All American's revenues and stock price throughout 1993 and 1994. By July 1993, All American was marketing a special new *Baywatch* package for a strip (Monday-through-Friday) rerun syndication for the 1995–96 season that would include the first 23 NBC episodes of 1989–90 and the 88 new episodes already filmed or to be shot through the end of the 1994–95 season. By the beginning of its third syndicated season, *Baywatch*'s ratings had climbed from a respectable 4.4 in 1990–91 to a very healthy 7.7, and All American's revenues were eclipsing the $70 million mark.

Baywatch was among the top three syndicated first-run action dramas in the United States by early 1994, and at an industry conference in France in April, All American executives announced that Hasselhoff had signed a multiyear, multiproject contract with the company to star in *Baywatch* through the end of the 1995–96 season and to develop a son-of-*Baywatch* action series that he would star in and produce. Whenever—if ever—*Baywatch* ceased production, the show's international distributor estimated it would continue to earn money for All American for at least another 10 years.

All American management continued to attack the widespread Wall Street perception that the company was wholly dependent on *Baywatch* for its rising position in the entertainment industry. Thus, in December 1993 All American's Scotti Brothers Records operation announced a new urban/rap subsidiary named Street Life Records that in later years would feature such African American urban artists as Skee-Lo, Comrads, and Craig Mack. In television, the popular *Family Feud* game show was being readied for its sixth season of syndication in early 1993, and in July All American announced the impending rollout of a live-action animated children's show named *Bots Master* for the 1994–95 season.

Moreover, production of the *Baywatch* spinoff *Acapulco H.E.A.T.* began in Mexico in July 1993, and in September All American announced another *Baywatch* offshoot: a beach-based athletic competition show named *BeachQuest* that would pit four athletic young men and women each week against a team of "Hard Bodies" in a series of events staged on the beaches of California. Universal Television immediately protested that the *BeachQuest* name was an infringement of the

seaQuest DSV TV series produced by Steven Spielberg. All American's Paul Siegel called the resemblance "purely coincidental" but within a year the show had been renamed *BeachClash*. Finally, in November 1993, All American announced that—in hopes of repeating its good luck in rescuing *Baywatch* from NBC's cancellation bin—it was acquiring the 13 episodes of a canceled "femme fatale police show" named *Sirens* from ABC for syndication beginning in September 1994.

Branching Out: 1994–96

Despite sales of almost $115 million in 1994, All American found itself once again fighting its image as a "one-show wonder" when it was forced to pull the plug on *Acapulco H.E.A.T* after half a season and *Sirens* after a disappointing first year. Amid rumors that Henry and Paul Siegel were being shown the door because of their dissatisfaction with All American's decision to drop *Acapulco H.E.A.T.*, in July 1994 All American acquired a stake in international game show producer Fremantle Group from New York-based advertising giant Interpublic Group for $63 million in cash and stock. (Fremantle had handled the overseas distribution and format sales of All American's *Family Feud* for several years.) In exchange for a 20 percent interest in All American, Interpublic would give All American some of the programming rights to Fremantle International's 93 game shows, which included local language versions of American game show stalwarts like *The Dating Game*, *Family Feud*, *Divorce Court*, *The Honeymooners*, *The $25,000 Pyramid*, *The Price Is Right* (called *Le Juste Prix* in France), and *Let's Make a Deal* (*Geh Aufs Ganze* in Germany)—all highly popular in their foreign markets. As an All American executive told *Forbes* magazine, "In markets where programming is scarce, nothing sells better than game shows. They are cheap, easy to produce and outrageously popular." Although the formats of the shows followed the basic formats of the American originals, the hosts and guests were all natives of their country, and the shows were so closely tailored to their markets that viewers of the French version of *The Price Is Right* were sometimes known to express outrage that the Americans had tried to copy the show for American TV audiences. The move opened large profit opportunities in the growing international game show industry and finally gave All American another revenue leg to stand on.

A month after the deal was struck Fremantle International's former chairman, Larry Lamattina, replaced Henry Siegel—the man who had rescued *Baywatch* from oblivion—as president and CEO of All American Television. Siegel was invited to stay on in a nonpresidential role but later left to form Seagull Entertainment Inc., while his brother Paul remained at All American as president of international and ancillary operations. Anthony Scotti's determination to lessen All American's reliance on *Baywatch* continued in July 1994 when All American announced that 52 episodes of its new childrens' series, *Superhuman Samurai Syber-Squad*, would be available for distribution to TV stations. Similarly, in November it launched two "reality strips" (nondramatic series for five-day-a-week broadcast)—*The Richard Bey Show* and *Thanks a Million*—and announced that it was considering developing an animated version of *Baywatch* for Saturday mornings and a movie network to feature first-run made-for-television movies. Meanwhile, 32 foreign countries were negotiating for the broadcast of All American's *BeachClash* show, which had also reached the 70 percent clearance level in the U.S. market.

With *Baywatch* continuing to generate millions a year, in October 1995 All American took another step toward balancing its sources of revenue by acquiring, for $50 million, the assets and library of Mark Goodson Productions, the producers of more than 40 classic game show formats, including *Password, Match Game, Concentration,* and *To Tell the Truth* (as well as *The Price Is Right* and *Family Feud,* whose foreign distribution rights All American had acquired through Fremantle). "The Goodson acquisition is an important element in our strategic plan to produce and distribute programming for every country in the world," Scotti told the press. With 1995 sales of $228.8 million, All American could claim a revenue growth rate for 1991–95 of more than 60 percent, but its acquisitions had larded it with debt, and in October 1995 it announced a $45 million public stock offering. With *Baywatch*'s worth alone estimated at $74 million, however, some Wall Street analysts still wondered if All American, despite its diversifying moves, had truly escaped the "one-trick pony" label.

Hasselhoff's new project had become *Baywatch Nights,* an action-oriented drama starring Hasselhoff as a kind of beach detective in a vehicle All American advertised as an "unbeatable blend of nonstop action and fast-paced humor" with a "strong appeal to [the] young adult audience." Its ratings proved to be only adequate, however, and, more ominously, *Baywatch*'s own ratings in the 1995–96 season—its sixth— were 22 percent lower than the year before. Still, its sale into rerun syndication in 1995 had added a whopping $33 million to All American's coffers, and the company had successfully licensed it to cable provider USA Network, ensuring even more future revenue. An agreement with the Gerber Company, headed by former Columbia Pictures television executive David Gerber, contracted Gerber to develop programming for All American, which hoped he would be able to deliver a blockbuster like the shows *thirtysomething* and *In the Heat of the Night* that had established his reputation. In August 1995, Gerber was named president of All American Television Distribution.

All American's next attempt to capture the fickle interest of the TV market was a one-hour live action series named *The Adventures of Sinbad,* which hoped to duplicate the success enjoyed by such mythology-based action series as *Xena: Warrior Princess* and *Hercules* when it debuted in September 1996. Meanwhile, *Baywatch* was readied for its seventh syndicated season and *Baywatch Nights* won the go-ahead for its second season. In March 1996, Scotti Brothers, which since 1982 had released some 142 albums, officially changed its name to All American Music Group and announced a new distribution deal with Warner/Elektra/Atlantic that promised to increase its penetration of the crowded pop music market. "Weird Al" Yankovic, a parodist of pop hits, had emerged as the most lucrative of the 17 artists on its 1996 roster, but the label was also balanced by the recordings of Count Basie and Sara Vaughan as well as several soundtracks (including, naturally, that of *Baywatch*).

In April 1996, All American paid Interpublic Group $25 million for its stake in the previous year's acquisition of Mark Goodson Productions, giving it total control over the Goodson library of game show formats and recorded episodes. Two months later Scotti expanded again, purchasing international talk show producer and distributor Orbis Entertainment Co., which was rechristened All American/Orbis Communications. The acquisition significantly bolstered All American's shift into international television production and distribution and led to All American's second domestic foray into the talk show niche in the fall of 1997, *Arthel and Fred.* Its first attempt, the lowbrow *The Richard Bey Show,* fell below the 50 percent national TV market "clearance" and was axed in November 1996. Further, in July, All American acknowledged the growing importance of the product spinoffs spawned by the popularity of its TV series by creating an in-house licensing and merchandising division to increase its control of *Baywatch* and other merchandise lines.

In late 1996, *The Adventures of Sinbad* was displaying sufficiently positive ratings to encourage All American's management to believe it had finally escaped the *Baywatch* limitation with a new vehicle that might survive on its own. In November, Tribune Entertainment withdrew from a short-lived partnership with All American to produce the game shows *Card Sharks* and *Match Game* for the U.S. market, and in December Pamela Anderson Lee disclosed she was leaving *Baywatch* at the end of the season to pursue other projects. All American announced that it intended to press on with domestic game show production for the 1997 season to exploit a perceived shift in viewers' interest from daytime talk shows to game shows like *Family Feud.* "We're committed to game shows," Syd Vinnedge announced, "our enthusiasm is undeterred." Moreover, in January 1997, All American announced another new tack: a weekly "science-fiction anthology" series narrated by Rip Torn and featuring two stories per episode. All American's long struggle to prove it was more than "just the *Baywatch* company" was finally winning the agreement of industry observers. In February 1997, the *Wall Street Journal* noted that the company "is quietly emerging as a diverse and disciplined international entertainment company." "We have built a business," CEO Scotti triumphantly commented, "right under the nose of Wall Street."

Principal Subsidiaries

All American Television, Inc.; All American Television Production, Inc.; All American Entertainment, Inc.; All American Fremantle International, Inc.; All American FDF Holdings, Inc.; All American Goodson, Inc.; All American Orbis, Inc.; All American Consumer Merchandising Group, Inc.; All American Netherlands B.V.

Further Reading

"All American to Join in Strategic Alliance with Interpublic Unit," *Wall Street Journal,* July 7, 1994.
" 'Baywatch' and More for Hasselhoff," *Broadcasting & Cable,* April 25, 1994, p. 34.
"Beach by Any Other Name," *Broadcasting & Cable,* July 4, 1994, p. 14.
Benson, Jim, "All American Nears Goodson Deal," *Variety,* April 24–30, 1995.
——, " 'Baywatch' Enjoys Week in the Sun," *Variety,* August 7–13, 1995.

"Beyond the Valley of the Dolls," *Forbes*, October 12, 1992, p. 150.

Borzillo, Carrie, "Scotti Bros. Gets New Moniker Along with New Distribution Pact," *Billboard*, March 9, 1996, p. 5.

Freeman, Mike, " 'Baywatch' Hits Street as Off-Net/Off-First Offering," *Broadcasting & Cable*, July 12, 1993, p. 33.

——, "Battling on the Beach," *Broadcasting & Cable*, September 27, 1993, p. 32.

——, "Sirens Is Revived," *Broadcasting & Cable*, November 22, 1993, p. 24.

——, "All American Stake to IPG," *Mediaweek*, July 11, 1994, p. 6.

——, "All American Sinks 'Sirens,' " *Mediaweek*, April 17, 1995, p. 9.

"Games Are Afoot," *Broadcasting & Cable*, May 13, 1996.

Gubernick, Lisa, "Media Hype," *Forbes*, April 22, 1996, p. 118.

Hofmeister, Sallie, "Paramount Bets on Game Shows," *Los Angeles Times*, December 5, 1995, p. D5.

"Interpublic Group, All American to Buy Mark Goodson Assets," *Wall Street Journal*, October 13, 1995, p. B5.

Kim, June Bryan, "Syd Vinnedge," *Advertising Age*, June 26, 1995, p. S-12.

LaFranco, Robert, "Long-Lived Kitsch," *Forbes*, February 26, 1996, p. 68.

McClellan, Steve, "Lamattina in for Siegel at All American," *Broadcasting & Cable*, July 11, 1994, p. 16.

——, "All American Readies Reality Strips for Launch," *Broadcasting & Cable*, November 14, 1994, p. 32.

McDougal, Dennis, "Surf's Up Again for 'Baywatch,' " *Los Angeles Times*, November 28, 1991, p. F1.

Mitchell, Emily, "Worldwide Wave," *Time*, September 25, 1995.

Peers, Martin, "All American, Interpublic in Buying Game on Goodson," *Variety*, October 16–22, 1995, p. 32.

——, "All American Trades on 'Baywatch' for Fresh Coin," *Variety*, November 27–December 3, 1995, p. 26.

——, "All American Buys Out Goodson," *Variety*, April 15–21, 1996, p. 192.

"Siegel Starts Seagull," *Broadcasting & Cable*, July 18, 1994, p. 19.

"Siegels to Stay Put," *Mediaweek*, July 4, 1994, p. 2.

—Paul S. Bodine

Altron Incorporated

One Jewel Dr.
Wilmington, Massachusetts 01887-3390
U.S.A.
(508) 658-5800
Fax: (508) 988-0900
Web site: http://www.altron.com

Public Company
Incorporated: 1970
Employees: 1,085
Sales: $165.25 million (1996)
Stock Exchanges: NASDAQ
SICs: 3613 Switchgear & Switchboard Apparatus; 3672
   Printed Circuit Boards

Altron Incorporated is a leading contract manufacturer of advanced electronic interconnect products, including surface mount assemblies, custom-designed backplanes, and multilayer printed circuit boards. The company also manufactures total systems, which include these components as well as card racks, power supply, and housing. Altron principally targets the mid-volume original equipment manufacturer (OEM) interconnect market, providing value-added services such as original design and engineering, prototype engineering, and pre-production and full production capabilities. The company generally works closely with its customers to develop components for customer products ranging from cellular telephones to magnetic resonance imaging equipment.

Altron's customers are typically high-growth electronics OEMs in the telecommunications, data communications, computer, industrial, and medical systems industry. Altron's list of more than 125 customers includes Motorola Inc., which accounts for approximately 13 percent of revenues, General Electric Co., Hewlett-Packard Co., Silicon Graphics Inc., Lucent Technologies, 3Com Corporation, Cabletron Systems, Inc., Cascade Communications Corp., Cisco Systems, Inc., Data General Corporation, EMC Corporation, Johnson and Johnson, Inc., KLA Instrument Corp., and U.S. Robotics Corp. Altron's

value-added contract manufacturing activities account for nearly three-quarters of the company's revenues; the remaining portion of the company's sales comes from its manufacturing and sale of printed circuit boards.

The company's emphasis on value-added services during the 1990s has enabled the company to triple sales in the first half of the decade, from $53 million in 1990 to $165 million in 1996. The largest share of company revenues are typically generated through sales to the data and telecommunications industries, which account for more than half of Altron's revenues. Sales to high-end computer manufacturers, such as Hewlett-Packard and EMC, generate approximately 30 percent of revenues. Altron is led by company cofounder Samuel Altschuler, who serves as chairman, president, and CEO. Another founder of the company, Burton Doo, is executive vice president, and president of the company's subsidiary, Altron Systems Corporation. The Altschuler family controls more than 18 percent of the company's stock.

Headquartered in Wilmington, Massachusetts, Altron operates a 200,000-square-foot manufacturing facility there. The company also operates three ISO 9002-registered production facilities, a 104,000-square-foot plant and a 30,000-square-foot plant, both in Woburn, Massachusetts, and a 70,000-square-foot facility in Fremont, California. These facilities are part of the company's more than $50-million investment strategy in state-of-the-art electronics manufacturing, engineering, and design equipment, including capital-intensive surface mounting machines for soldering microprocessor chips directly to circuit boards.

Altron provides service-oriented, vertically integrated manufacturing capabilities, including the manufacturing of most of the printed circuit boards used in the company's total system products, surface mount assemblies, and custom-designed backplanes. Vertical integration enables the company to control not only quality, cost, and delivery of its products, but also to offer a broad range or high-technology prototype assembly and other high value-added services. A key component of Altron's business strategy is its pursuit of partnership-type contracts with its customers, providing design and engineering support to early product design stages, as well as quick turnaround times and just-in-time inventory management and delivery. Through such partnership contracts, Altron seeks to build long-term relationships with its customers, providing its value-added manufacturing services for a range of customer products and across multiple product generations.

Altron has positioned itself to take advantage of the growth in demand for multilayer printed circuit boards as developments in technology have created components requiring greater performance and speed, and more compact size than can be achieved with previous two-sided printed circuit board designs. The multilayer boards are composed of three or more layers of printed circuit boards. By laminating together several layers of printed circuit boards and interconnecting the layers with holes lined with conductive material, the multilayer boards provide increased density and reduced size of printed circuit packaging, greater power and ground distribution, and higher circuitry speeds. In 1996, multilayer printed circuit boards, which represented 80 percent of industry-wide printed circuit board production, accounted for 94 percent of the company's total printed circuit board sales. Altron also uses surface mount assembly technology (SMT) to solder, rather than insert using pins, semiconductor components directly onto circuit boards. SMT enables a greater density of components, increases in interconnect leads, and reduced size, as well as the ability to manufacture two-sided circuit boards.

Altron's custom-designed backplanes, also known as "motherboards," use the company's two-sided and multilayer printed circuit boards to assemble pins, housings, and other components. Backplanes house power supplies, component interconnects, processors, and fittings for additional printed circuit boards and cards. Altron produces backplanes ranging in complexity of up to 32 layers of printed circuit boards, thicknesses up to 0.300 inches, and dimensions of nearly two feet by three feet. In additional to these components, Altron also provides custom-designed total systems meeting the design and engineering specifications of its customers. Total systems feature components such as power supplies, backplanes, printed circuit board assemblies, and card racks and component housings.

The Slow Road to Growth in the 1990s

Together with Doo and two other partners, Altschuler formed Altron in 1970. Altschuler, who held a bachelor's degree in electrical engineering and a master's degree in business administration, had been working larger firms in the electronics industry when he saw a need for supplying high-quality printed circuit boards. These would remain the company's primary

product through the 1970s. The company posted slow but steady growth based on its printed circuit boards, concentrating on building long-term relationships with its customers. A child of the Depression, Altschuler, who would serve as president and CEO from the company's inception into the 1990s, avoided taking on debt, preferring to maintain sufficient cash reserves to weather the cyclical downturns in the semiconductor industry.

By the end of its first decade, Altron was still only a $15 million company. In 1979, however, the company began manufacturing multilayer printed circuit boards. Over the next decade, buoyed by increases in technology and the growth of the computer and electronics industries overall, the company would more than triple the size of its revenues. Altron remained profitable during the early 1980s, despite the national recession and a severe downturn in the computer industry. By 1985, the company posted a net income of $1.7 million on nearly $30 million in revenues. The following year, however, the computer industry's troubles caught up to Altron. Sales slumped to $25.6 million, and the company recorded a net loss of more than $3.7 million. Altron was forced to close a manufacturing plant in Puerto Rico, write off inventory, and sell off some of its real estate. In 1987, as the electronics industries began to pick up again, the company managed to boost sales to $31 million, and cut its losses to just over $1 million, aided by the sale of its Puerto Rican plant.

By 1988, Altron was back in the black again, posting a net income of $26,000. But sales were rising rapidly, reaching $42 million for the year and climbing to $53 million in 1989. By then, Altschuler had already moved to diversify the company's operations. Altron added an in-house engineering design department, and began investing in equipment to give the company the capability of manufacturing complete electronic systems. The company's new strategy was to place itself in the position to take over more and more of its customers electronic engineering design and production. Meanwhile, Altron continued to avoid costly advanced research activities. As Altschuler told *Investor's Business Daily*, "We haven't fallen in love with technology for technology's sake. You have to be at the leading edge of technology. But not so far ahead that there's no business behind you . . . . We don't have an 'R&D' budget. We have a 'D' budget. We're doing applied development to solve customers' needs."

Altron's move to vertically integrated production capacity came at the right time for the electronics industry. As the 1990s began, major OEMs, which had previously looked in-house for their printed circuit board, backplane, and other electronics production, began to look for third-party manufacturers to supply them. By turning to value-added contract manufacturers like Altron for these products, the OEMs were able to reduce their own capital investment—on the rise as both production and product technologies were making significant advances—while refocusing their resources on their core technologies. Freeing up these resources enabled the OEMs to compete more effectively in the tight margins and stiff rivalries of the electronics industries. Contracting out to third-party supplies enabled OEMs to maintain access to cutting-edge production technology, while reducing inventory costs, particularly by shifting to on-demand delivery and just-in-time inventory systems. In turn, the third-party suppliers offered a greater flexibility and shorter turnaround times for their customers orders. This became particularly important into the 1990s, when product life-cycles became progressively shorter, and also during the early years of the decade, when OEMs were faced with a worldwide recession. Between 1991 and 1996, the electronics industry underwent a dramatic shift in production of printed circuit boards. Where only 66 percent of the printed circuit board market was shared among third-party manufacturers in 1991, these manufacturers, including Altron, held more than 85 percent of the printed circuit board market, valued at nearly $8 billion, by 1996.

In the early 1990s, Altron put into place the capacity to most of the components of a single electronic system, including the circuit board and assemblings, disk drives, ventilation fans, power supplies, and casings. With this capacity, the company's revenues posted strong gains, particularly among communications OEMs, but also among computer makers, such as Sun Microsystems and Hewlett Packard, and makers of electronics-based medical equipment. In 1991, the company added surface mount technology to its production capacity, bringing the company fully into the contract manufacturing business. By 1992, the company's annual sales had jumped to $68 million.

In 1994, after signing an agreement to act as a value-added reseller for AT&T Microelectronics Power Systems, designing and manufacturing custom-designed power supply systems using AT&T power supply components, Altron made its first-ever acquisition, buying Astrio Corp. of Fremont, California, for a purchase price of $4.6 million, including $3 million in cash and the balance in Altron stock. The addition of Astrio to the company's Altron Systems Corp. subsidiary combined the latter company's card cages and systems assembly production with the former company's printed circuit boards, surface mounts, and data board assembly production. As Altschuler told the *Boston Business Journal*, the acquisition "greatly expanded capacity and capability to better serve our growing customer base in Northern California." Doo, serving as president of the Altron Systems subsidiary, stated that adding Astrio's production capacity would provide Altron with a "real presence on the West Coast," a crucial market for the third-party suppliers to the computer and electronics industry.

Altron continued to deploy its "value and build" strategy, turning its ISO 90002-certified plants to include backplane assembly and testing, multilayer manufacturing up to 32 layers, card cage design and assembly, surface mount assembly, and the design, assembly, and testing of complete systems. In addition, Altschuler looked forward to increasing the company's share of its customers' business, eventually to taking on distribution of completed products. As Altschuler told *Fortune*, "we want to supply the total system and ship it to our customers' customers." The Altron strategy was working. After posting a revenue increase to $104 million in 1994, which generated more than $8 million in net earnings for the company, Altron saw its sales jump past $143 million, for more than $14.5 million in net earnings in 1995.

The growth of the company's value-added services has steadily reduced its dependence on sales of printed circuit boards, from primarily all of the Altron's revenues in the 1980s to just 39 percent in 1994 and 27 percent in 1995. Under Altschuler, the company had built long-term relationships with many of the leading "blue-chip" OEM electronics companies, building a strong position within the highly fragmented—and competitive—value-added contract manufacturing market.

Principal Subsidiaries

Altron Systems Corporation.

Further Reading

Alster, Norm, "Altron Inc.," *Investor's Business Daily*, December 5, 1995, p. A6.
——, "Altron's Sam Altschuler," *Investor's Business Daily*, May 21, 1996, p. A1.
Labate, John "Altron," *Fortune*, October 31, 1994, p. 238.
Schreiber, Yoav, "Altron Buys Astrio Corp.," *Boston Business Journal*, June 17, 1994, p. 5.

—M. L. Cohen

Aluminum Company of America

Alcoa Building
425 Sixth Avenue
Pittsburgh, Pennsylvania 15219
U.S.A.
(412) 553-4545
Fax: (412) 553-4498
Web site: http://www.shareholder.com/alcoa

Public Company
Incorporated: 1888 as The Pittsburgh Reduction
 Company
Employees: 76,800
Sales: $13.06 billion (1996)
Stock Exchanges: New York American Basel Brussels
 Frankfurt London
SICs: 3334 Primary Aluminum; 3341 Secondary
 Nonferrous Metals

The largest aluminum manufacturer in the world, Aluminum Company of America (Alcoa) produces aluminum and alumina for the packaging, automotive, aerospace, construction, and other markets. Alcoa's primary operations included bauxite mining, alumina refining, and aluminum smelting. Its principal products included alumina and its chemicals, automotive components, and beverage cans. During the late 1990s, the company was organized into 21 business units, with 178 operating locations in 28 countries.

Origins

Alcoa was founded in 1888 in Pittsburgh, Pennsylvania, under the name The Pittsburgh Reduction Company. Its founders were a coalition of entrepreneurs headed by Alfred Hunt, a metallurgist who had been working in the steel industry, and a young chemist named Charles Martin Hall. Pittsburgh Reduction's sole property was a patented process for extracting aluminum from bauxite ore by electrolysis, which Hall had invented in the woodshed of his family house in 1886, just one year after his graduation from Oberlin College. Hall's discovery had promised to make aluminum economical to produce for the first time in history. Later in 1886, Hall had taken his process to a smelting company in Cleveland, Ohio, but left in 1888 after it showed little interest. One of his associates there, who had also worked with Hunt at another company, introduced the two men, and Pittsburgh Reduction was started as a result of their meeting.

Despite its relative abundance, few practical uses existed for aluminum because it was so expensive to extract. By 1893, however, Hall's process allowed Pittsburgh Reduction to undercut its competitors with aluminum that had been produced at a lower price. The company then faced two challenges: to generate a larger market for aluminum by promoting new uses for the metal and to increase production so that it could cut costs even further through economies of scale. Efforts in the former area proved most successful in the manufacturing of cooking utensils, so much so that the company formed its own cookware subsidiary, Aluminum Cooking Utensil Company, in 1901. Aluminum Cooking Utensil adopted the Wear-Ever brand name.

Pittsburgh Reduction also began the process of vertical integration, insuring itself against the day when Hall's patent would expire and it would no longer have a monopoly on his process. In the mid-1890s, it began acquiring its own bauxite mines and power-generating facilities. This process continued after the death of Alfred Hunt, who had served as president since founding the company. In 1899 Hunt, an artillery captain in the Pennsylvania militia, was sent to Puerto Rico with his battery during the Spanish-American War and succumbed to malaria there. He was succeeded by R. B. Mellon of the Mellon banking family, which had loaned the company much of its start-up capital and controlled a substantial minority stake. The Mellons, however, had been content to let the engineers run the company. Arthur Vining Davis, a partner who had joined Pittsburgh Reduction only months after its founding, acted as president during this time, and the Mellons formally ceded power to him in 1910. In 1907 The Pittsburgh Reduction Company changed its name to Aluminum Company of America. In 1914 Davis became the company's last surviving link to its early days when Charles Martin Hall died, leaving an estate with an estimated worth of $45 million.

Company Perspectives:

Our safety performance is important in its own right, but at Alcoa it has implications far beyond safety. In the process of demonstrating that we have the ability to produce a team result such as this—that is directly relevant to each employee—we have developed and integrated the ideas and tools that are necessary to superior achievement in all that we do: manufacturing, finance, logistics, environment. We have made progress in all of these areas, but we are far from finished; and we will never be through with our efforts to achieve and sustain zero injuries. At root, this is a profound change in culture, a transformation from old habits of settling for the "inevitable" (accidents happen . . . costs go up . . . markets get glutted . . . strikes are a fact of life) to the belief that a company can seize the initiative and shape its own future. This emphasis on creating our own fate has changed us as a company. If you go any place in Alcoa's twenty-eight country universe you will find safety is the first internal commitment. And on this safety backbone we have been building excellence in all things we do.

Post-World War I Expansion

Alcoa had virtually created the market for aluminum, and its only competition came from foreign producers, who were hindered by high tariffs. Alcoa also benefited from rising demand from the automobile industry; by 1915, 65 percent of all new aluminum went into automotive parts. The outbreak of World War I ended the threat from foreign producers, and Alcoa even became an exporter. Annual production rose from 109 million pounds to 152 million pounds between 1915 and 1918, with much of it going to Great Britain, France, and Italy. At home, the vast majority of Alcoa's output was used for military applications.

The export boom that the war had fostered made it seem natural that Alcoa should expand its overseas operations once hostilities ended. Throughout the 1920s, the company acquired factories, mines, and power-generating facilities in Western Europe, Scandinavia, and, most prominently, in Canada. Late in the decade, however, the difficulty of managing far-flung operations, combined with a rising tide of economic nationalism abroad, made Alcoa's position overseas increasingly untenable. In 1928 it divested all of its foreign operations except its Dutch Guiana bauxite mines, spinning them off as Aluminium Limited, based in Montreal and headed by Edward Davis, A. V. Davis's brother. Aluminium Limited was renamed Alcan Aluminium Limited in 1966. In 1929 Arthur Vining Davis retired as president and became chairman. He was succeeded by Roy Hunt, the son of Alfred Hunt.

At home, the general economic boom carried Alcoa with it, but between 1929 and 1932, during the early years of the Great Depression, sales fell from $34.4 million to $11.1 million. Alcoa laid off half of its work force in this time, slashed wages for those who remained, and cut back its research-and-development budget. Demand for aluminum did not recover until 1936.

Even so, Alcoa's market share remained unchallenged, as it was still the only aluminum smelter in the United States thanks to its technological lead and economies of scale—a position that had not gone unnoticed.

Aluminum Company of America had been having antitrust run-ins with the Justice Department since 1911, but all of the blows had glanced off of it until U.S. Attorney General Homer Cummings filed suit in 1937, charging monopolization and restraint of trade on Alcoa's part. The trial lasted from 1938 to 1940 and was the largest proceeding in the history of U.S. law to that time. A district court ruling in 1942 found in favor of Alcoa, but the government appealed. In 1945 an appeals court sustained that appeal. In his decision, Judge Learned Hand ruled that although Alcoa had not intended to create its monopoly, the fact remained that it had a monopoly on the domestic aluminum market in violation of antitrust law and it would be in the nation's best interest to break it up. Hand's decision became a landmark in the history of judicial activism, although it did leave open the question of how Alcoa's grip on aluminum was to be broken.

Meanwhile, of course, the United States had entered World War II. Demand for aluminum skyrocketed. Alcoa, however, proved to be unable to keep up with the increases in demand, disappointing the War Department. During the war the government financed new plants that were built and run by Alcoa, but also encouraged the development of other aluminum producers. As the tide of the war shifted in favor of the Allies in 1944, the U.S. government began deliberations on how to dispose of these plants, which would soon become surplus capacity. As a result, a solution to the problem of how to carry out Hand's ruling became apparent. The Alcoa plants that the government had financed would be sold off to two new rivals: Reynolds Metals Company and Permanente Metals Corporation, owned by industrialist Henry Kaiser. Reynolds and Permanente were to buy the plants at cut-rate prices. In effect, this divestiture created an oligarchy where there had formerly been a monopoly. In 1950 a district court decree carved up the U.S. aluminum market between the three: Alcoa would get 50.9 percent of production capacity, Reynolds 30.9 percent, and Kaiser Aluminum & Chemical Corporation, as Permanente Metals was renamed, 18.2 percent.

Roy Hunt retired in 1951 and was succeeded by Irving Wilson. During the 1950s, Alcoa's share of U.S. production capacity declined as it expanded more slowly than Reynolds and Kaiser. Faced with increased competition, Alcoa also found itself without any brand-name recognition on which to capitalize in the consumer products arena; Reynolds, by comparison, had established a name for itself quickly with its Reynolds Wrap aluminum foil. Nevertheless, booming demand for aluminum, the result of successful wartime experiments in using the metal to build military aircraft, helped compensate for decreased market share. Despite increased competition, Alcoa remained the industry's largest member and its acknowledged price leader.

Davis retired in 1957, ending his 69 years of service with Alcoa. He was succeeded by Wilson, and Frank Magee became president and CEO. Alcoa came out of the brief recession of 1957–58 by realizing that it would have to internationalize and diversify in order to ensure its future. In 1958 Alcoa joined with Lockheed and Japanese manufacturer Furukawa Electric Company to form Furalco, which would produce aluminum aircraft parts for Lockheed. Also that year, Alcoa became a player in what was then the largest takeover battle in British corporate history when it negotiated a friendly acquisition of a stake in struggling British Aluminium, Ltd. The acquisition was aborted, however. Alcoa had been approached by British Aluminium chairman Lord Portal, Viscount of Hungerford, who had neglected to consult his major stockholders before closing the deal. Thus, when Reynolds and British manufacturer Tube Investments made a substantially sweeter bid, a bitter struggle ensued. Institutional investors sold their shares to the Reynolds and Tube venture and Alcoa lost out. The fight over British Aluminium became a sensation in Britain not only because of the sheer spectacle of foreign interests vying for control of a major domestic corporation, but also because hostile takeovers were considered a breach of etiquette in British finance. What came to be known as The Great Aluminium War split British investment banks between the old-line, established houses that backed Alcoa and Portal, and the upstart firms that supported Reynolds and Tube.

Undeterred by this setback, Alcoa went on to spread its mining operations into other parts of the world, re-establishing an international presence it had not had since it spun off Alcan. Back home, the company moved aggressively into producing finished aluminum products. In 1959 it acquired Rome Cable and Wire Company. The next year, it purchased Rea Magnet Wire Company and Cupples Products Company, a manufacturer of aluminum curtain walls and doors. Both Rome and Cupples eventually had to be divested, however, because of antitrust objections.

When John Harper became president and CEO in 1963, Alcoa found its profit margins squeezed by increased competition, high overhead, and a generally low market price for aluminum. One of Harper's solutions was to move more aggressively into manufacturing finished products, which provided higher returns than smelting. On his initiative, Alcoa began producing sheet metal for aluminum cans, which became more popular among beverage consumers in the 1960s after the invention of the pop top, and aerospace parts. In 1966 the company posted a record profit, finally exceeding a mark it had set ten years before.

1970s: Recycling and Diversification

High labor costs, dramatically high energy prices, unpredictable bauxite prices, a slower national economy, and new competitors trying to break up the aluminum oligarchy all conspired against Alcoa in the 1970s. Sales and other operating revenues grew from $1.8 billion to $4.6 billion between 1972 and 1982, but profits as a percentage of gross income remained below historical levels. High interest rates forced Alcoa to slow its expansion and concentrate on paying down existing debt. In 1972 the company also decided to sell its technology to other manufacturers on a large scale, something it had been loath to do in the past.

W. H. Krome George succeeded John Harper as chairman and CEO in 1975, and Aluminum Company of America began to

show new signs of life. In the late 1970s it seized upon recycling as an alternative to the high cost of smelting, although somewhat later than rival Reynolds. By 1979 Alcoa was reprocessing 110 million pounds of scrap aluminum. By 1985 that figure would rise to over 500 million pounds and recycling would account for 19 percent of the company's aluminum ingot capacity. George, who was more scientifically oriented than his predecessors, also led Alcoa into expansive research into high-tech applications of aluminum. By the time George retired in 1983, he had started the company on the path once again to developing new high-strength alloys for use in the aerospace business. Other areas of research and development, often pursued as joint ventures with other companies, included alumina chemicals, satellite antennae, and computer memory discs.

George's successor, Charles Parry, took over in 1983, and was even more committed to diversifying Alcoa. His goal, he said, was that half of the company's revenue should come from non-aluminum sources by 1995. Immediately, Alcoa began scouting around for companies to acquire, particularly in high-tech fields. At the same time, however, Parry's vigor in attempting to reshape the company was not well-received in all quarters. He was attempting to radically change corporate thinking in a short period of time even as he continued the layoffs and plant closures that George had begun in an effort to cut costs, and employee morale suffered. Many did not see how he could create new business worth between $7 billion and $9 billion from scratch in less than 10 years. Although Alcoa made only minor acquisitions during Parry's tenure, which ended in 1987, the directors became concerned that the deals that Parry proposed to make would not fit in well. Some worried that the risks involved were more appropriate to a young company just starting up, not a major corporation nearing its centennial.

Even George became uncomfortable with his successor, and in 1986 he led the search for Parry's replacement. Aware of his board's discontent, Parry took an early retirement in 1987. He was replaced by Paul O'Neill, former president of International Paper Company and deputy director of the Office of Management and Budget during the administration of President Gerald R. Ford. O'Neill's appointment was largely George's doing; the two had met because of the latter's directorship at International Paper.

1990s

Under O'Neill, the first outsider ever to run Alcoa, the company slowed its diversification and refocused on its core aluminum business. In 1990 it formed a joint venture with Japanese manufacturer Kobe Steel, Ltd. to make sheet metal for aluminum cans and parts for automakers for the Asian market. O'Neill had also sought to revitalize employee morale and ensure product quality by emphasizing safety as a primary concern, and by instituting a profit-sharing plan.

Combined profits for 1988 and 1989 more than doubled Alcoa's total for the first eight years of the decade, providing an early sign that the changes instituted by O'Neill were working. By 1991, the revitalization of the aluminum business under O'Neill's watch had achieved great strides. A billion-dollar program to modernize its plants was finished that year, long-term debt had been whittled down, and the company's research and development budget had been increased significantly. Important changes in the structure of Alcoa also were underway during the early 1990s, as O'Neill pursued his agenda of "reinventing" the venerable aluminum giant. Two layers of corporate management were stripped away, including the company's presidential post, exposing 24 business units that were ceded autonomous control over their respective operations. Each of these business units reported directly to O'Neill, who exerted considerable sway over the company's operations despite his desire to give the business units an unprecedented amount of power.

Two developments outside Alcoa's control affected the early years of the 1990s, however, hampering the company's progress under O'Neill's decisive rule. The collapse of the Soviet Union had a disastrous effect on the world aluminum market, causing prices to fall to the lowest in history. The Soviets exported an average of 250,000 metric tons of aluminum a year before the Berlin Wall came down, but when revolution swept communism aside and left Russia in a precarious financial position, aluminum shipments exported from the former Soviet Union increased exponentially. In dire need of cash, Russia was shipping an average of 1.2 million metric tons of aluminum per year during the early 1990s, flooding the market and drastically reducing the price of aluminum. Aluminum, which sold for $1.65 a pound in 1988, was priced at $.53 a pound by 1993, the lowest price ever recorded.

To make matters worse, a worldwide recession settled in during the early 1990s as aluminum prices plummeted. The effects of the recession had a more lasting hold on Alcoa's fortunes than the fall of the Soviet empire. The company trimmed its payroll by 2,000 in 1992, the first major layoff since 1986, as depressing financial totals were tallied at the company's headquarters. Alcoa lost $1.1 billion in 1992 and recorded a paltry $4.8 million gain in 1993. Despite the bad news, O'Neill remained steadfast to his revitalization plan and focused his attention on reducing the company's healthcare costs, which were rising by 11 percent a year and costing the company nearly $200 million annually. "Our productivity improvements," he declared, "are effectively being eaten up by health care costs."

By the mid-1990s, O'Neill's reputation for running a tight and efficient enterprise had helped Alcoa realize a full recovery from the ills of the early 1990s. Alcoa's net income rose from $4.8 million in 1993 to $375.2 million in 1994 and up to $790.5 million in 1995, while annual sales increased from $9 billion to $12.5 billion. As the company charted its course for the late 1990s and the new century ahead, O'Neill continued to hold a tight rein on spending, vowing to cut $300 million from Alcoa's annual sales and administrative costs by the end of 1997, which would produce a savings of 25 percent. O'Neill also planned to relocate the company's headquarters to a $50 million facility along the Allegheny River. The move was expected to take place in 1998, and with construction underway in 1997, Alcoa embarked on its future course, reigning as the preeminent aluminum producer on the globe.

Principal Subsidiaries

Alcoa Brazil Holdings Co. (79%); Alcoa Aluminio S.A. (Brazil, 74.8%); Alcoa-Deutschland GmbH (Germany); Alcoa Generating Corp.; Alcoa International Holdings Co.; Alcoa Manufacturing (G.B.) Ltd. (U.K.); Alcoa Minerals of Jamaica, Inc.; Alcoa Nederland Finance B.V. (Netherlands); Alcoa Properties, Inc.; Alcoa Recycling Company, Inc.; Alcoa Securities Corp.; ALCOA/TRE, Inc.; Capsulas Metalics, S.A. (Spain, 80%); Grupo Aluminio, S.A. de C.V. (Mexico, 44%); Halco Inc. (27%); H.C. Industries, Inc.; H-C Industries, Inc. of Mississippi; Inversiones Alcoa, S.A. (Venezuela, 42%); Moralco Limited (Japan, 75%); Shibazaki Seisakusho Limited (Japan, 51%); The Stolle Corp.; Suriname Aluminum Co.; Tapoco, Inc; Texas Engineered Products Co., Inc.; Yadkin, Inc.

Further Reading

"Alcoa, the Microcosm," *Financial World,* June 25, 1991, p. 76.

Carlisle, Anthony Todd, "Alcoa's Steely Course Prevails," *Pittsburgh Business Times,* December 30, 1996, p. 1.

Klebnikov, Paul, " 'Absolutely Trashed,' " *Forbes,* April 12, 1993, p. 86.

McGough, Robert, "The Spoiler," *Financial World,* February 18, 1992, p. 22.

Plishner, Emily S., *Financial World,* October 24, 1995, p. 26.

Regan, Bob, "On Road Dead Ahead O'Neill Sees 'Black' as Others See 'Red,' " *American Metal Market,* October 13, 1993, p. 1.

Schroeder, Michael, "The Quiet Coup at Alcoa," *Business Week,* June 27, 1988.

Smith, George David, *From Monopoly to Competition: The Transformation of Alcoa, 1888–1986,* Cambridge, Cambridge University Press, 1988.

Stewart, Thomas A., "A New Way to Wake Up a Giant," *Fortune,* October 22, 1990.

—Douglas Sun
—updated by Jeffrey L. Covell

American Business Products, Inc.

2100 RiverEdge Parkway
Suite 1200
Atlanta, Georgia 30328
U.S.A.
(770) 953-8300
Fax: (770) 952-2343

Public Company
Incorporated: 1967 (formed to acquire Curtis 1000 Inc.,
   incorporated 1882)
Employees: 3,520
Sales: $631.6 million (1996)
Stock Exchanges: New York
SICs: 2671 Paper Coated & Laminated—Packaging;
   2677 Envelopes; 2678 Stationery Products; 2732
   Book Printing; 2761 Manifold Business Forms; 2789
   Bookbinding & Related Work

American Business Products, Inc. (ABP), a Georgia-based company, manufactures and distributes specialty custom printed information products and services. It is one of the nation's leading suppliers of printed business supplies, principally envelope products, custom labels, and custom business forms. Additionally, ABP manufactures and distributes books for the publishing industry and performs specialty extrusion coating and laminating of papers, films, and nonwoven fabrics for packaging and other products. Almost all of ABP's products are sold within the United States, but it is also a joint venture partner with a company operating in Europe. After over half a century of higher sales year after year by ABP (and its predecessor Curtis 1000 Inc.), in the mid-1990s ABP's sales leveled off and the company began a general restructuring and a consolidation of its manufacturing facilities.

Origin and Founder

ABP was born in 1882 as Curtis 1000 Inc., a family-owned printing business based in St. Paul, Minnesota. In 1942 Henry Curtis VI joined the company, then led by his father. By 1948 he had learned the workings of the business and had opened a new division based in Atlanta. He was named president of Curtis 1000 in 1958, but soon decided that there was potential for Curtis 1000 to become a larger, publicly owned business. In 1968 Curtis 1000 Inc. became a subsidiary of a new company, American Business Products, Inc., with Curtis as its president and chairman. The company made a public stock offering the following year.

Curtis remained as president until 1973 and as chairman until 1983. In 1989 he retired from the board after 47 years with Curtis 1000 and then ABP. During those years he guided the business from a small company with $13 million in annual sales, to a national corporation with five operating companies, a European joint venture, and annual sales of over $387 million. Just before retiring as chairman he chronicled the growth of his business and his philosophy in *An American Adventure*. Henry Curtis VI died on March 1, 1997.

Chief Products and Operations

The cornerstone of ABP is its business supplies printing operation, which traditionally has accounted for almost three-quarters of its total sales. Its wide variety of products includes business envelopes and labels, express and lightweight packaging products, business forms, and records management systems. Discount Labels, Inc. (New Albany, Indiana), an ABP operating company acquired in 1993, is the largest supplier of short-run custom labels in the United States. The outstanding feature of this operation is its 24-hour turnaround of orders. ABP has made a commitment to customer service in this area, with a sophisticated ordering system and more than 60 specialized presses that ABP developed itself.

ABP also claims to be the world leader in production of envelopes made from Tyvek@, through another operating company, the International Envelope Company (Exton, Pennsylvania). Tyvek@ is noted for being a strong, almost unrippable material made largely from recycled materials. One of IEC's chief customers is the U.S. Postal Service, which uses Tyvek@ envelopes for its priority mailers. IEC also produces lightweight shipping envelopes made from SHIP-lite@ (which in turn is produced by another ABP company, Jen-Coat) and heavyweight specialty paper envelopes and filing products.

Curtis 1000 Inc. (Atlanta, Georgia) still exists as an ABP operating company. Its product line includes on-demand digital printing, custom labels, envelopes, forms, color brochures, presentation folders, and fine business stationery. While digital printing is considered a huge growth area, ABP also continues to emphasize production of traditional business stationery.

ABP's operating company BookCrafters USA, Inc. (Chelsea, Michigan) specializes in orders for printing of books in quantities from 500 to 100,000 copies. Many of the books printed by BookCrafters are in specialty areas (for example, travel, cookbooks, university press publications, and books about computers). BookCrafters also handles digital media projects, another growth area. It maintains two distribution centers capable of holding more than a million books, one in Chelsea, Michigan, and the other in Fredericksburg, Virginia.

Through its operating company Jen-Coat, Inc. (Westfield, Massachusetts), ABP produces many familiar items: backing for peel-off postage stamps; sugar, salt, and pepper packets; fast-food sandwich wrappers; liners for juice cans; and material used to make surgeon's gowns.

ABP carries on a joint venture with a European partner, Curtis 1000 Europe GmbH, headquartered in Neuwied, Germany, with other facilities in Poland, England, and Luxembourg. This operation produces and markets Tyvek@ and paper envelopes in several European countries, with the plant in Poland serving eastern European countries such as Hungary and Czechoslovakia. In 1996 Curtis 1000 Europe GmbH introduced a product still in demand even after the end of the Cold War: a protective envelope for top secret government documents.

Technological Innovations

ABP's Discount Labels operation utilizes a sophisticated order-processing system to provide 24-hour turnaround on custom label service to 55,000 dealers. These customers also can receive round-the-clock status reports on their orders. In 1997 ABP planned to begin using the Internet to allow dealers to design and place label orders online.

ABP has concentrated a great deal of attention on developing innovative printing processes. It uses more than 60 specialized presses developed by the company itself. By the mid-1990s ABP also had launched digital printing operations, for printing of materials such as sales manuals, directories, product catalogs, handbooks, and business forms. This process allows ABP to produce only the quantity actually needed at any given time, so that there is no need for storage facilities for an inventory of printed objects. In 1996 the BookCrafters operation received almost half of all of its projects in digital format.

ABP's Jen-Coat operation likewise utilizes technologically advanced equipment in its production processes, including fiber optics communication and extremely sensitive gauges. In 1996 and 1997 ABP expanded its capabilities by installing four-color printing equipment for the packaging products manufactured by Jen-Coat.

Key Acquisitions and Divestitures

Jen-Coat, Inc. was acquired in 1990, and its laminating operations quickly became a major asset for ABP. In 1992, then-president Thomas R. Carmody attributed ABP's record sales for the previous year to the performance of Jen-Coat. In 1996, Jen-Coat accounted for over $100 million of ABP's sales for the first time.

Discount Labels, Inc. was acquired by ABP in 1993. Since then, Discount Labels has become the leading short-run custom label manufacturer in the country, and has continually brought in increased sales. In 1996, Discount Labels had double-digit sales gains and record sales once again.

In 1995 ABP's subsidiary Vanier Graphics, a producer of business forms and supplies, acquired Electronic Form Systems, a producer of electronic forms, for almost $10 million. Vanier brought with it a product line of electronic forms software, custom form services, and on-site training services. However, this partnership with ABP was short-lived. In December 1996 Vanier in turn was sold by ABP to the Reynolds and Reynolds Company, a leading provider of information management systems to the automotive, healthcare, and general business markets for $47 million. Although Vanier was profitable, long-term operations would have required major investments by ABP in order for Vanier to compete against the major competitors that had emerged in the forms industry. ABP president Robert W. Gundeck saw the divestiture of Vanier as part of an overall strategy to concentrate on ABP's core custom printing business.

Industry Consolidation in the 1990s

The printing industry in the United States had a dismal time during the early 1990s. One industry expert, John J. Serrell, predicted in a 1994 *Printing Impressions* article that industry consolidation was the best hope for bringing about profitable operations once again. Through the 1990s, consolidation in the industry became standard practice. The cost of equipment and facilities needed to operate a company made it difficult for small companies to survive, and lenders became hesitant to extend credit. The growth of electronic printing technology provided a new and continually changing menu of expensive equipment.

Some companies made major investments in new equipment, only to find it obsolete soon after its purchase.

Adding to the problem was the history of the industry. Many printing companies were set up after World War II as family-owned businesses, and their original owners were ready to hand down these businesses by the 1990s. However, the market made it extremely difficult for such family-owned businesses to survive.

Figures provided in 1994 by PIA, an industry organization, indicated that there was significant overcapacity in the industry as well, further cutting into profits for the remaining companies. The end result was that the largest companies (such as ABP) had the highest profits and the best likelihood for survival.

Given this scenario, ABP opted to restructure and consolidate its operations in the mid-1990s. As stated by Gundeck in Serrell's article, "Larger firms have the ability to specialize in their markets. This adds value and enhances customer loyalty." Divestiture of the Vanier Graphics operation in late 1996 was a key part of this restructuring process.

ABP also decided to close numerous production facilities, beginning in 1995. By the end of 1996 ABP had closed 13 facilities, combining their operations into several large regional centers. It also committed about $30 million to modernizing and expanding its remaining business operations. Much of this investment was targeted for redesigning and automating order processing systems, particularly those at the Curtis 1000 facilities in which most of the plant consolidation also occurred.

Financial Performance in the 1990s

American Business Products had steadily increasing sales for almost 60 years between the late 1930s and 1995. In the early 1990s, sales grew dramatically: $463.5 million in 1992; $486.1 million in 1993; $563.1 million in 1994; and almost $634 million in 1995. However, sales dropped slightly to $631.6 million in 1996. During the same five-year period, employment at ABP also rose significantly, but dropped sharply when ABP began to close numerous facilities in 1995 and 1996.

According to the ABP annual report for 1996, the $563.1 million in sales in 1994 were at record levels, rising almost 16 percent over the previous year. Sales in the business supplies area were up 20 percent, with the acquisition of Discount Labels the previous year contributing both to this increase and to the companywide increase in sales. The book manufacturing operation also did extremely well, with a 12.4 percent increase in sales. In 1994 76.2 percent of sales were from business supplies products; 8.8 percent from book manufacturing and order ful-

fillment operations; and 15 percent from extrusion coating and laminating operations.

Sales for 1995 were likewise excellent, totalling $634 million and increasing 12.6 percent over 1994. Sales in the business supplies segment rose 11 percent; the book manufacturing segment saw a 17.7 percent increase; and the extrusion coating operation had a 17.6 percent increase. By business division, 75.2 percent of sales came from business supplies products; 9.2 percent from book manufacturing and order fulfillment operations; and 15.6 percent from extrusion coating and laminating operations.

However, according to the same report, sales in ABP's business supplies segment fell 1.8 percent in 1996 even though the custom label market grew rapidly. ABP attributed the drop to lower material prices that were passed on to customers, "processing bottlenecks" caused by the company's restructuring program, and "distractions caused by the Vanier sale." Sales in book manufacturing fell 6.1 percent, due to lower levels of demand from customers. The one growth area was in the extrusion and laminating operations, where sales rose 10.1 percent. As a result ABP devoted additional resources to expanding this operation. During 1996, sales by division were: 74.1 percent of sales from business supplies products; 8.6 percent from book manufacturing and order fulfillment operations; and 17.3 percent from extrusion coating and laminating operations.

Principal Subsidiaries

Curtis 1000 Inc.; BookCrafters USA, Inc.; International Envelope Company; Jen-Coat, Inc.; Discount Labels, Inc.; Curtis 1000 Europe GmbH (Germany).

Further Reading

"American Business Products Expects Another Banner Year for Sales," *Atlanta Constitution*, February 13, 1992, p. F5.
"Back to the Basics: It's ABP's New Credo," *Atlanta Constitution*, February 16, 1988, p. C1.
Curtis, Henry, *An American Adventure*, Atlanta: American Business Products, 1981.
Serrell, John J., "Only the Strong Survive; US Printing Industry to Consolidate With Fewer and Larger Companies," *Printing Impressions*, May 1994, p. 64.
"Vanier Graphics and EFS Merge; Is Acquired by American Business Products for $9.8 Million," *Printing Impressions*, October 6, 1995, p. 6.
Walker, Tom, "Office Products Firm Expecting Better Days Ahead," *Atlanta Constitution*, March 20, 1997, p. F4.

—Gerry Azzata

American Pad & Paper Company

17304 Preston Road
Dallas, Texas 75252
U.S.A.
(972) 733-6200
Fax: (972) 733-6298

Public Company
Incorporated: 1992
Employees: 4,105
Sales: $583.86 million (1996)
Stock Exchanges: New York
SICs: 2600 Paper and Allied Products

American Pad & Paper Company manufactures and markets paper-based office products, excluding copier paper. An industry leader in North America, the company daily manufactures more than fifty tons of paper every hour. American Pad & Paper is also a market leader in the largest and fastest-growing office-products channels. The company offers a broad assortment of high-quality products. American Pad & Paper's product line comprises nationally recognized brand names and private label writing pads, file folders, envelopes, machine papers, and other paper-based office supplies. Its major brands in 1996 included Ampad, Century, Embassy, Evidence, Gold Fibre, Huxley, Karolton, Kent, Peel & Seel, SCM, Williamhouse, and World Fibre.

The company's Ampad Division is one of the largest suppliers of pads and paper-based writing products, filing supplies, machine papers, and retail envelopes serving large office-product distributors. The Williamhouse Division, also a leading supplier, provides paper merchants and distributors with mill-branded, specialty, and commodity business envelopes and machine papers.

As one of the larger participants in the highly competitive paper-based office products industry, American Pad & Paper vies with many regional and local companies for customers. Its sheer size, however, allows the company to be a national presence that benefits from economies of scale, a diverse product line, strategic acquisitions, consolidating distribution channels, and a strong management team.

A Century Ago

The current company formed in June 1992. Formerly the Ampad Holding Corporation, American Pad & Paper was created as a holding company to purchase Ampad Corporation. Originally established in the 19th century, Ampad invented the legal pad in 1888. Since then, it has been a prominent supplier of pads and paper-based writing products. In 1986, Ampad found itself a subsidiary of Mead Corporation. It remained so until July 1992 when Bain Capital, Inc. and the management of newly formed American Pad & Paper Company purchased the subsidiary from Mead. Since its inception in 1992, the new company has seen net sales grow at nearly a 53 percent compound annual rate through 1996, increasing from $8.8 million in 1992 to $200.5 million in 1996. In July 1996 American Pad & Paper became a public company, a surprising move for such a well-established private enterprise.

National Scale and Service Capabilities

Upon its formation, American Pad & Paper consolidated its 13 manufacturing and distribution facilities into six in 21 locations in the United States. It maintained more than 3.7 million square feet of production and warehouse facilities in California, Colorado, Georgia, Illinois, Massachusetts, Mississippi, New Jersey, New York, Ohio, Pennsylvania, Tennessee, Texas, Washington, and Wisconsin. This network of strategically located manufacturing and distribution centers provided the company with the means for rapid and efficient order fulfillment and advanced EDI capabilities for executing automated transactions.

The company's national reach and service capabilities ensured its purchasing advantages and economies of scale. For more than 30 years, American Pad & Paper maintained strong, long-term relationships with paper mills. It consistently ranked as one of the larger buyers of principal paper grades used in manufacturing and continued designated mill relationships with recognized paper mill brands, including Hammermill, Hopper, Neenah, and Strathmore. The relationships helped the company to achieve consistently a broad price point coverage.

Paper Prices

Paper, the principal raw material for American Pad & Paper, influenced the direction of the company perhaps more than any other external factor. Since 1989, the average paper prices increased less than 1 percent annually. Nevertheless, the prices of some commodity papers were much more volatile than that. In 1994 paper costs and supplies required that American Pad & Paper modify the prices on some product lines without prior notice to customers. Beginning in 1995, the company instituted new pricing policies that set product prices consistent with the cost of paper at the time of shipment.

These paper purchasing and distribution advantages—in addition to modern, efficient manufacturing technology and a high-quality work force—allowed American Pad & Paper to achieve low-cost operations. From 1992 to 1996, for example, the company's fixed marketing costs decreased from 7.4 percent to 5 percent of its net sales. Similarly, American Pad & Paper's selling, general, and administrative expenses fell from 10 percent to 8.2 percent of net sales during the same time period.

Innovation and New Products

American Pad & Paper offered customers an extensive product line and a multitude of brand names, notably the Ampad and private-label brands. The company quickly became one of the largest manufacturers of pads and paper-based writing products. By 1996 American Pad & Paper offered more than 2,400 SKUs (store-keeping units) of writing pads, notebooks, and specialty papers. Its products appeared in multiple sizes, paper grades, colors, and bindings (for example, glued, perforated, or wire bound).

New products also differentiated American Pad & Paper from other suppliers and increased its profitability. During 1992 to 1996, new products accounted for $155 million of the net sales for 1996. Some new items introduced included Gold Fibre classic and designer notebooks, Papers with a Purpose, World Fibre ground-wood writing pads, and Peel & Seel envelopes. Since 1994, American Pad & Paper also initiated innovative packaging for its customers, including bulk and crate packaging for warehouse clubs.

Growth Through Acquisitions

In July 1994, American Pad & Paper acquired SCM, a hanging folder and writing products company. Though this acquisition brought increased potential to the company, it also brought some strife. When American Pad & Paper attempted to bring work rules and costs at the newly acquired plant in Indiana in line with market labor agreements, workers there balked. In September, plant employees initiated a strike, resulting in American Pad & Paper's closing of the Indiana plant in February 1995. By the following July, all machinery and equipment moved from the plant to another production facility.

Undaunted by these events, American Pad & Paper pursued a second acquisition about a month later in August 1995. The company purchased selected file folders and products from the Globe-Weis office products division of American Trading and Production Corporation. The acquisition of these brand names bolstered American Pad & Paper's position in filing supplies, making the company one of three large filing supply manufacturers in North America. By 1996, American Pad & Paper offered its customers more than 800 SKUs of filing supplies, including file folders, hanging files, index cards, and expandable folders. American Pad & Paper focused on large retail customers and contract stationers to expand its market share until it achieved status as the leader in filing supplies. Although the company's right to use the Globe-Weis trademark on a nonexclusive basis would expire in 1998, American Pad & Paper expected no adverse effects from the loss of the name.

American Pad & Paper's $300-million acquisition of WR Acquisition and Williamhouse-Regency Division of Delaware, Inc., a wholly owned subsidiary, in October 1995 positioned the paper company as the largest manufacturer of envelopes for paper merchants and distributors and for office products superstores. In particular, American Pad & Paper established a specialization in envelopes manufactured from mill-branded paper; that is, paper unique in color and texture to a mill with an identifying watermark.

When the company acquired Williamhouse, a leader in mill-branded, specialty, and commodity business envelopes and machine papers, it greatly enhanced its role as an envelope manufacturer and supplier. Williamhouse historically sold materials to paper merchants and distributors. After the acquisition, American Pad & Paper became the designated manufacturer for 33 mill brands—double that of its closest competitor—including Hammermill, Strathmore & Beckett, Hopper, Neenah, and Gilbert.

American Pad & Paper sold the Regency Division of the newly acquired Williamhouse for close to $48 million in gross proceeds in 1996, the year that the company acquired Niagra Envelope Company, Inc., for $53 million. Niagra Envelope Company supplied mill-branded, specialty, and commodity envelopes to paper merchants and distributors through four manufacturing facilities in Buffalo, Chicago, Dallas, and Denver. In 1995 Niagra's net sales totaled $106 million, and its operating income was $8.5 million. The acquisition of this company strengthened American Pad & Paper's distribution in the Midwest and added to its manufacturing capabilities.

After buying Williamhouse and Niagra Envelope, American Pad & Paper offered approximately 30,000 SKUs of envelopes. Important envelope products included standard-size and specialty envelopes from commodity paper, pressure-sensitive Peel & Seel envelopes, and giant, X-ray, and remittance envelopes. American Pad & Paper also supplied Tyvek envelope products, such as those used in booklet and catalog mailers and metal-clasp or button-and-string envelopes. (Tyvek—a high-density, polyurethane-based substance—is manufactured by DuPont.)

In February 1997 American Pad & Paper acquired Shade/ Allied, Inc., for nearly $50 million. Based in Green Bay, Wisconsin, Shade/Allied supplied continuous forms to paper manufacturers and distributors and to retail customers. It maintained manufacturing facilities in Green Bay, Seattle, Atlanta, and Philadelphia. In 1996, Shade/Allied earned $90 million in net sales.

The purchase of Shade/Allied established American Pad & Paper in its fourth major product category. The acquisition made American Pad & Paper one of the leading manufacturers of machine papers such as ink-jet papers, printed formats, fine papers (including cotton-content and laid papers) and continuous forms. American Pad & Paper also became one of the larger manufacturers of invitations, announcements, Christmas and holiday cards, and presentation folders in 1997. The company sold this product line to paper merchants and distributors, to personalizing businesses such as the former Regency Division of Williamhouse, and to wholesale outlets throughout the United States.

Consolidation in Distribution Channels

The mid-1980s brought major changes in channels of distribution for office products. New channels of distribution emerged, notably national superstore chains, national contract stationers, and mass merchandisers. Since approximately 1994 national superstores such as Office Depot and Office Max presented a new avenue for paper-based office products. Much consolidation also occurred within distribution channels. For example, in 1987 there were more than 13,000 office products distributors. By 1994 the number dropped to 6,800. The remaining paper merchants—companies accounting for 30 percent of the envelope market—grew larger through the consolidations. National contract stationers—Boise Cascade Office Products, for instance—likewise enjoyed rapid growth from the acquisition of smaller companies.

Together these events caused American Pad & Paper to target its customers carefully, concentrating on those entities that drive consolidation in retail, commercial, and paper-merchant distribution channels. The company also sought customers that needed a supplier with a broad product line and with innovative, value-added merchandise. American Pad & Paper further capitalized on its national distribution capabilities, its low-cost manufacturing, and its reputation for reliable service when courting potential customers. With this strategy, the company maintained a well-positioned and diversified customer base since its establishment.

American Pad & Paper built a strong relationship with Wal-Mart and other mass merchandisers, warehouse clubs— including Sam's Warehouse Club—office products wholesalers such as S. P. Richards and United Stationers, and independent dealers. As Charles G. Hanson III, American Pad & Paper's chairman of the board and chief executive officer, explained in an April 1997 news release: "Our ability to offer broad product lines, higher value-added products, national distribution capabilities, low costs, and reliable service gives us a competitive advantage and strengthens our position as supplier of choice to giant customers. The validity of our offering is clearly demonstrated at Wal-Mart. Two years ago we became their legal pad supplier. In June we will significantly expand our distribution by becoming their supplier of home and office envelopes, filing products, and certain machine papers in 50 percent of their locations."

American Pad & Paper became attractive to other large customers as well, particularly office products superstores. Key customers in this segment in the 1990s included Office Depot, Office Max, and Staples. In fact, Staples alone accounted for 10.8 percent of net sales in 1996.

Sales to the four largest paper merchants and distributors also increased in the first four years of American Pad & Paper's existence. In 1992, the company sold about $75.6 million worth of products to Nationwide, ResourceNet, Unisource, and Zellerbach. By 1996 the total sales to these paper merchants and distributors increased to $118.4 million. In addition, American Pad & Paper's sales through its Williamhouse Division to large contract stationers—notably Boise Cascade Office Products, BT Office Products, Corporate Express, and U.S. Office Products—remained strong.

A Team Built

The success of American Pad & Paper has been attributed to the strength of its management team. Headed by president and chief operating officer Russell M. Gard, the team had more than 85 years of experience in management in the paper industry in 1996. Gard worked in the paper industry for more than 26 years, in the past managing some of the largest paper-products facilities. Executive vice president Tim Needham joined American Pad & Paper with the Williamhouse acquisition, bringing 14 years of experience in paper products, and chief financial officer Kevin McAleer worked as an executive at public companies for 15 years before joining American Pad & Paper. According to a statement by Charles G. Hanson III, chairman of the board and chief executive officer of American Pad & Paper, in the 1996 annual report: "Together this team is tough to beat. We have shown that we can make tough decisions in a tough business. We have become tough to beat because we perform. We will continue to focus on accretive acquisitions, the development of new products through acquisition and innovation, and on maximizing efficiencies at all levels of the company. These efforts make it tough to deny the bright future of American Pad & Paper."

Speculation about the Future

In 1997, the team's strategy for the future was to maintain and strengthen the company's leadership position. First, American Pad & Paper would continue its expansion by concentrating on the largest, fastest-growing distribution channels for office products. In 1996 the company expected its business with large customers to grow 15 to 35 percent in the upcoming five years. The plan also focused on serving industry leaders as American Pad & Paper's customers by increasing the importance of the company's national scope and broad product line as its customers consolidate further. The executive team envisioned new products that would offer greater selection for customers, as well as improved profitability of those product lines.

American Pad & Paper anticipated future acquisitions of companies that would expand or complement its product lines.

The company also expected to enter new markets by acquiring established companies. "Our acquisition pipeline is full," explained Hanson in 1997. "We will continue to drive growth through accretive acquisitions and are evaluating opportunities in both new product lines and add-ons to our existing product lines. We will pursue companies that fit our acquisition strategy of strong distribution channels, a strong product base, and the workforce and facilities necessary to serve our existing customers."

Hanson also revealed a desire to broaden American Pad & Paper's product distribution through the sale of newly acquired product lines. In the past, the company successfully sold the envelope product lines acquired in the Williamhouse and Niagra mergers under the Ampad and private-label brand names using Ampad's distribution channels instead of paper merchants and distributors. Another such arrangement would be highly desirable for the company, as would maintaining American Pad & Paper's position as a low-cost manufacturer. In all, "we remain confident in our business strategy going forward," said Hanson, "and believe we are strategically positioned to achieve our long-term goals."

Principal Subsidiaries

Ampad Division; Williamhouse Division.

Further Reading

"American Pad & Paper Company Announces First Quarter Results" (news release), New York, NY: Morgan-Walker Associates, Inc., April 21, 1997.
Grunwald, John, "IPOs: Look out Below!," *Time,* July 22, 1996, p. 60.

—Charity Anne Dorgan

American Safety Razor Company

Razor Blade Lane
Verona, Virginia 24482
U.S.A.
(540) 248-8000
Fax: (540) 248-0522

Public Company
Incorporated: 1875
Employees: 2,100
Sales: $260.6 million (1996)
Stock Exchanges: NASDAQ
SICS: 3421 Cutlery; 3841 Surgical and Medical
Instruments; 3842 Surgical Appliances and Supplies;
2211 Broad Woven Fabric Mills, Cotton; 3423 Hand
and Edge Tools; 2844 Perfumes and Cosmetics; 2841
Soap and Detergent

American Safety Razor Company (ASR) is a leading manufacturer and marketer of brand-name and private-label personal care products, and the largest manufacturer in terms of units of private-label and value-brand shaving blades and razors in the United States—accounting for 66 percent of their net sales. In addition to shaving blades and razors, the company primarily produces fiber and foot care products, custom bar soap, bladed hand tools and blades, industrial and specialty blades, and medical blades. These products provide a value-priced alternative to other premium national brands, generally selling 25–35 percent below competitors' prices. Products are sold under a retailer's own store label or under ASR's brand names such as Personna, Gem, Flicker, PFB, Treet, GEM Blue Star, and Pal, and are marketed to major national mass-merchandise, drug and supermarket chains such as Wal-Mart, Kmart, Walgreen, Rite Aid, Kroger, and Safeway. ASR also ranks as the largest manufacturer in terms of revenue of both premium and value-priced bladed hand tools and blades, sold primarily under the Personna, American Line, and Ardell brand names—products which include carpet knives, utility knives, and paint scrapers, which are sold through home-improvement centers, retail paint chains, and hardware stores such as Home Depot and Sherwin-Williams. ASR is the second largest manufacturer in terms of revenues, of cosmetic/skin care, bath, pharmaceutical, and specialty custom bar soaps, sold under the company's brand names such as Kensington, Lavender & Old Lace, and Sandalwood. As one of the largest specialty soap manufacturers in the world, ASR's custom bar soap is sold by Johnson & Johnson, Estée Lauder, and Neiman Marcus.

ASR also serves a variety of industries including food-processing, fiber cutting, automotive and printing, in addition to its consumer products. These specialty blades that perform the cutting, chopping, and slicing functions involved in manufacturing processes are sold to companies such as DuPont and Ford. Voluntary Hospitals of America and Baxter International buy carbon and stainless steel surgical blades, disposable scalpels, and surgical prep blades under the Personna brand name.

The American Safety Razor Company originally produced straight razor blades for the shaving public, but profited due to the frustration of a traveling salesman, who lamented the dull edge on his traditional razor. King Gillette imagined a new type of razor, one with a double-edged, disposable blade. He employed the skills of a machinist, William Nickerson, who had been educated at the Massachusetts Institute of Technology, to develop the tools and processes needed for blade production. Before long several companies were producing disposable blades, and Gillette changed the name of his company to The Gillette Safety Razor Company, and began a decades-long competitive race with The American Safety Razor Company.

By this time ASR was well established in the blade market and in January 1920 the company turned over all of its foreign assets and a substantial amount of cash to The American Safety Razor Export Corporation, incorporated in Delaware, giving the export subsidiary sole license for the use of American Safety Razor trademarks and patents throughout the world.

From Burma Shave to Buyout: 1925–63

Blade manufacturing diversified into the production of soaps and shaving aids. Burma-Shave was a brand of shaving cream developed in 1925 by Minnesota entrepreneur Clinton Odell from his father's liniment made of camphor, cassia, and cajeput oils—a recipe reputedly offered to his grandfather by an old sea captain. Beginning in 1926, Burma-Shave advertising became popular along American roadsides, made memorable by signs placed in sets of six spaced at 100 feet apart, each sign containing silk-screened jingles aimed at capturing the attention of male drivers: "He played/A sax/Had no b.o./But his whiskers scratched/So she let him go." In the 1930s and 1940s the small red signs were visible on most rural highways. During World War II signs were visible in places as far away as the South Pole, upon request by the U.S. Navy to help boost the morale of officers stationed in Antarctica. By the 1950s there were more than 7,000 sets of signs throughout the U.S., but faster driving and television advertising left the Burma-Shave campaign in the dust. Phillip Morris bought the company in 1963 and discontinued the then-famous advertising signs and later dropped all Burma-Shave trademarks, until they were re-registered by American Safety Razor—then a division of Phillip Morris—in 1979, one year after ASR bought the Burma-Shave Division from Morris. Leonard Odell, the mastermind behind the signs, became president of the new ASR division, which continued to produce a limited supply of the shaving cream.

More Owners, 1970s–80s

Bic Pen Corporation bought out ASR in the 1970s, competing with companies like Gillette for the blade market, until Phillip Morris took the company over. Then, in 1989 ASR was acquired for $140 million in cash by John W. Jordan, seven years after he set up the Jordan Company and entered the leveraged buyout business. After graduating from the University of Notre Dame, Jordan began his career in the trust department of the First National Bank in Kansas City, Missouri. Finding the Kansas City business climate too slow for his ambitions, he moved to New York and for ten years worked for Carl Marks & Company, a Wall Street Investment firm. He amassed a portfolio of 25 companies during that time—before quitting his job to form the diversified industrial holding company, Jordan Industries, Inc., along with David Zelaznick who had worked with him at Carl Marks & Co.

In January 1990, the Anti-Trust Division of the U.S. Justice Department filed a complaint against ASR and its wholly owned subsidiary, Ardell Industries, Inc., alleging that the acquisition of Ardell by ASR in April 1989 violated antitrust laws through the combination of the two companies' industrial blade businesses. The suit was settled in 1990 and the ASR was required to sell certain equipment and terminate a non-compete agreement. Litigation expenses cost ASR approximately $1.7 million, and Ardell lost a substantial portion of its customer base and encountered operational difficulties at its facilities. During 1992 Ardell's business was consolidated with that of its parent, adding restructuring expenses of approximately $2 million.

Complicating their legal and financial difficulties, in June 1992 ASR was faced with a patent infringement suit brought against them by Warner-Lambert Company. The suit was filed in regard to ASR's alleged use of a water soluble lubricating strip on certain of its shaving products. As part of the $12 million settlement, ASR was permitted to manufacture and sell razor blade cartridges with lubricating strip attachments throughout the world. The company also obtained a non-exclusive license to patent rights in exchange for the payment to Warner-Lambert of $1.4 million over 2½ years.

ASR Goes Public, 1993

Following Jordan Industries' acquisition of ASR, the management team had determined that going public should become a major objective since capital was needed to reduce debt. The company sustained net losses of $4.1 million in 1989, $5.2 million in 1990, $39.8 million in 1991, and $3.6 million in 1992. In June 1993 the company sold 5,000,000 shares of common stock in its initial public offering, receiving net proceeds of $54.8 million. Finally, by the end of 1993 ASR was in the black, and positioned to focus on long-term objectives: developing new products, establishing an international presence, and improving its branded shaving product business. Increased operating income allowed the company to expand manufacturing in Europe and to transfer more production assembly to their facility in Obregon, Mexico.

In response to the health care industry's concern for safety in preventing possible HIV infection, ASR introduced the disposable Personna Safety Scalpel, which has a protective shield that covers the blade when the scalpel is passed between doctors and nurses. Sales of specialty medical blades almost doubled between 1988 and 1992. The growth of a more health-conscious public also affected the specialty-soap business. Particularly among the elderly, soaps using pH-sensitive materials were gaining ground. A new soap manufacturing facility was opened in Columbus, Indiana, expanding soap making capabilities for pharmaceutical, skin care, and cosmetic soaps.

Big Strides in 1995

ASR produced the Moving Blade Cartridge (MBC system) as described in a 1995 annual report: "We developed our MBC system for sophisticated consumers who look to technology to deliver a close, comfortable and safe shave. This system offers a level of technical sophistication that draws on several patents to allow the shaving blades to adjust to the contours of a man's face. The system's flow-through design quickly rinses away soap residue and whiskers for easier cleaning, and a closer shave." Counting on value-pricing and the nostalgia of older shavers, ASR relaunched its Burma Shave line with its pungent, soapy smell. Another innovation, the Bump Fighter, was a shaving system designed to meet the "unique shaving needs of African-American men." A shaving condition called pseudofolliculitis barbae (razor bumps or ingrown hair) affects over half of this population of men, which can be remedied by using the patented Bump Guard, a blade that shaves whiskers at a precise length to help prevent razor bumps. The product includes an accessories line including a shaving gel, cleanser, beard relaxer, and skin conditioner. The female systems market is the fastest-growing segment of the shaving category. Lady MBC, which uses the same patented moving blade technology to protect a woman's sensitive skin, was introduced in 1995. Strong sales in this segment—$13. 2 million in 1996, led to emphasis on other female products including the March 1997 introduction of the Revlon "Perfect Finish," a shaving system marketed under a license agreement with Revlon.

By 1995 sales and operating income were the highest in the company's 120-year history. The company began expanding in the consumer products sector, accounting for 82 percent of total sales. Price increases in raw materials challenged management to seek greater manufacturing efficiencies and to further reduce costs. Having previously acquired Megas Beauty Care Inc., ASR then acquired Absorbent Cotton Company, another manufacturer of cotton balls and puffs, cosmetic pads, swabs, foot care products, and pharmaceutical coils—and consolidated the manufacturing, sales and distribution, and administrative functions of the two. In April 1997 ASR completed its acquisition of The Cotton Division of American White Cross, Inc. for $9.8 million. In 1996 ASR expanded its shaving razor and blade manufacturing capabilities when it acquired Bond-America Israel Blades, Inc., manufacturers and distributors of private-brand and value-brand shaving razors and blades.

The Present and the Future

ASR's first quarter of 1997 showed record financial results over previous first quarters, with sales of domestic private-brand shaving products and international shaving products experiencing double-digit increases. A modest decline in domestic branded shaving products was attributed to inventory adjustments. The company was optimistic about the performance of its newer products which have been well received by the retail trade. The acquisition of Bond-America Israel Blades, Inc. was an investment aimed at enhancing ASR's distribution system by utilizing that company's existing channels, and with the intention of broadening the line of products to these markets. The company is already an established presence in the U.K., Europe, and Canada, and looks toward growth in international markets such as Asia, Africa, the Middle East, and Latin America.

Principal Subsidiaries

American Safety Razor of Canada Limited; Ardell Industries, Inc.; Autenticos Sistemas de Rasurar de Mexico, S.A. de C.V.; The Hewitt Soap Co., Inc.; Industrias Manufactureras ASR de Puerto Rico, Inc.; Personna International de Republica Dominicans, S.A.; Personna International Limited; Personna International UK Limited; Personna International (Deutschland) GmbH; Megas Beauty Care, Inc.; Sterile Products, Inc.; Bond-America Israel Blades, Ltd.

Further Reading

Cuff, Daniel F., "Jordan's Founder Adds American Safety Razor," *New York Times*, April 19, 1989, IV, pp. 4–5.
Kansas, Dave, "Safety Razor Firm Planning to Make Initial Public Offering," *The Wall Street Journal*, April 5, 1993, p. B7D (E).
"Patent Lawsuit Withdrawn Against American Safety Razor," *The Wall Street Journal*, February 23, 1996, p. B11.
"Sales Climb at American Safety Razor," *Supermarket News*, August 9, 1993, p. 20.
Weathersby, William, "120 Years and No 'Knockoffs,'" *Washington Post*, January 14, 1995, p. A24.

—Terri Mozzone-Burgman

Ark Restaurants Corp.

85 Fifth Avenue
New York, New York 10003-3019
U.S.A.
(212) 206-8800
Fax: (212) 206-8845

Public Company
Incorporated: 1983
Employees: 1,942
Sales: $76.8 million (fiscal 1996)
Stock Exchanges: NASDAQ
SICs: 2051 Bread and Other Bakery Products, Except
Cookies and Crackers; 5461 Retail Bakeries; 5812
Eating Places; 5813 Drinking Places (Alcoholic
Beverages); 6719 Offices of Holding Companies, Not
Elsewhere Classified

Ark Restaurants Corp. is a holding company that, through subsidiaries, was operating 26 restaurants, 2 bakeries, and 2 corporate dining facilities in 1996. The bakeries and 20 of the restaurants were owned by the company. Although Ark's restaurants had no single format, most were in New York City and offered a wide range of moderately priced food. Many were big, open spaces that could seat a large number of diners. In 1997 the company opened a group of restaurants in a new Las Vegas hotel and casino that were capable of feeding as many as 25,000 people a day.

Ark Restaurants to 1989

Michael Weinstein, a law-school dropout, was a young New York City investment banker when he invested $6,000 to open, with two friends, the Museum Cafe near his home on Manhattan's Upper West Side in 1975. When the partner running the restaurant became sick, Weinstein took over the management and fell in love with the business. He followed this up with other restaurants, including Perretti—also on the Upper West Side—in 1977 and the Metropolitan Cafe in midtown in 1982. Wein-

stein and Ernest Bogen formed Ark Restaurants in 1983 as a holding company for four restaurants and took it public in 1985, at a time when it had nine restaurants and $19 million in sales. The two partners reserved about one-third of the stock each for themselves, but Bogen sold much of his investment in 1987.

In 1982 Ark opened its biggest restaurant yet, 300-seat Ernie's, located on the Upper West Side and specializing in Italian food. Two years later Ark opened Albuquerque Eats (which later became Canyon Road), serving Southwest cuisine on the Upper East Side, and 350-seat America near Union Square Park, which with its later Center Cafe satellite could accommodate 700 patrons. Ernie's proved popular, and America, featuring regional American food, became the company's biggest hit, accounting for about one-fourth of Ark's revenues at the time.

In 1985 Ark Restaurants, flush with cash from its initial public offering of stock, ventured into the metropolitan area's New Jersey suburbs, opening an Albuquerque Eats in Englewood, America Eats in Paramus, America's Diner in Verona, and an Ernie's in Hackensack. But within a year of their opening, the first three had closed, with the company taking a $1.5-million writedown. (The New Jersey Ernie's, also in the red, later closed as well.) Betty Brown's Broadway Dining, an East Village diner featuring "retro" food like meat loaf and mashed potatoes, also failed. Ark's common stock, first offered at $7.50 a share and trading as high as $12.25 in 1986, dipped to $3.25. "But I learned several things from it," Weinstein later told a *Nation's Restaurant News* reporter. "You can't go into the suburbs with a New York value system. It's too competitive out there, and we did not know how to get people out of their cars."

Unfazed, Ark Restaurants expanded its holdings to 14 restaurants by the spring of 1987. The five 1986 openings, all in Manhattan, included another Albuquerque Eats on lower Third Avenue; Big Kahuna, a bar with a surfing theme and limited food service on the former site of Betty Brown's; B. Smith, a trendy cafe in the theater district; and the Ritz Cafe on lower Park Avenue, featuring Cajun-Creole seafood. These were followed, in 1987, by the Western-style Rodeo Bar on the location of the Third Avenue Albuquerque Eats. Company revenues reached $24.4 million in fiscal 1986 (the year ended in September 1986). Ark also revamped and began managing three restaurants in Boston's Faneuil Hall for developer Ben Thompson.

Ark Restaurants, which lost $284,000 in fiscal 1986, rebounded the following year, earning $699,000 on sales of $26.7 million. By then it had earned a reputation for cost control, reducing its food and beverage tab to 30 percent of net sales, and keeping its rental bills low by locating in Manhattan neighborhoods that were rundown but being discovered by yuppies. Ark negotiated long-term leases for most of these locations and sometimes even persuaded landlords to pay part of the construction costs.

Expansion Between 1989 and 1993

Early in 1989 a partnership brought Larry Forgione's esteemed An American Place to the site of the former Ritz Cafe. *New York Times* restaurant review Bryan Miller reported that "Mr. Forgione has carried many of his signature dishes downtown" and "tables are well spaced and (how rare in New York!) generous with elbow room." During the summer Ark opened K-Paul's New York on the site of the former Big Kahuna in partnership with Paul Prudhomme, celebrity chef of K-Paul's Louisiana Kitchen in New Orleans, which had been largely credited with the vogue for Cajun-style cuisine. In April 1989 Ark established a catering division that drew on the resources and kitchen staff of other restaurants in the chain, and by June the company had opened Gonzalez y Gonzalez, a Mexican restaurant, across the street from K-Paul. Waiters and waitresses were required to speak Spanish at all times, and a strolling eight-member mariachi band entertained customers.

Also in 1989, Ark opened a 17,000-square-foot version of America in Union Station, the refurbished Washington, D.C. railroad terminal whose innards had been transformed into a retail center. In 1990 Ark launched its first megarestaurant, 1,000-seat Sequoia, in a huge vacant space overlooking Washington's Potomac River waterfront where another restaurant had failed in 1987. The setting did more to lift *Washington Post* reviewer Phyllis C. Richman's spirits than the food, but by 1993 Sequoia was grossing $9.5 million a year. In 1991 Ark opened a second Sequoia in Manhattan's South Street Seaport historic district and the Beekman 1766 Tavern in Rhinebeck, New York. The K-Paul joint venture ended in 1992, with Ark remodeling and reopening the restaurant as the Louisiana Community Bar and Grill.

After earning net income of $848,000 in fiscal 1988 on revenues of $28.1 million, Ark Restaurants lost $43,606 on revenues of $29.1 million in 1989. The following four years, however, were all good ones. Revenues rose from $39.1 million in 1990 to $56 million in 1993, and net income from $753,000 to $1.9 million. By the end of 1993 Ark had 26 restaurants in its stable, including the Whale's Tail, acquired in Oxnard, California, that year. Although Ark's lack of a single identifiable concept for its restaurants troubled investment analysts, by refusing to adopt any one formula the company also opted not to accept any limit on its potential market appeal.

Willingness to locate in marginal Manhattan neighborhoods and hard bargaining with landlords was still helping to hold Ark's costs in check, allowing prices to remain the same on most items for six years. A computerized system was in use for buying in quantity 3,000 food and beverage items a year for the company's 140,000 weekly patrons. Dining-out reviewers were less impressed, and the editor of *Restaurant Business* told the *Wall Street Journal,* "Mr. Weinstein is known more for his success with themes and concepts, decor and ambiance, than he is for stunning food." Former *New York Times* food critic Mimi Sheraton added that Ark's restaurants tended to be "places where food is the prop; you want to be there and therefore you eat something."

New Venues, 1994–96

During 1994 Ark Restaurants ventured into fine dining for the first time since becoming a partner in An American Place by purchasing Lutèce, one of the world's best-regarded French restaurants, from its proprietor-chef, André Soltner, for an undisclosed sum. Lutèce remained at its East 50th Street location in Manhattan and retained its four-star rating under Soltner's successor, Eberhard Müller. The company also opened two new Washington-area properties in 1994: a second B. Smith's in Union Station and a third America in McLean, Virginia, plus the Lorelei Restaurant and Cabana Bar in Islamorada, Florida. By then it also had formed a travel-and-tourism division to book groups into its restaurants. Ark Restaurants ended fiscal 1994 with reduced earnings of $1.1 million on net sales of $60.4 million, which Weinstein blamed on bad weather and higher corporate overhead due to a beefed-up management team and rising salaries.

Also in 1994, Ark Restaurants converted Poiret, a restaurant on the Upper West Side's Columbus Avenue, into a bakery supplying its restaurants and also selling at retail coffee, baked goods, and prepared foods on a takeout basis or for on-premise consumption. A second Columbus Bakery opened in 1995, adjacent to the Metropolitan Cafe.

That same year Ark opened its biggest eatery yet, in Manhattan's midtown Bryant Park, just south of 42nd Street and west of the New York Public Library. The complex consisted of Bryant Park Grill, which could seat 220 in a small building and had room outside for 300 more patrons. In season, a roof terrace could accommodate 200 and the casual outdoor Bryant Park Cafe another 700, allowing the complex to serve as many as 4,000 customers on a summer day and evening. *Nation's Restaurant News* reported in the fall that the complex "has played to a relentlessly packed crowd ever since its debut." A hard winter, however, included the cancellation of many parties scheduled for the year-end holiday season.

Ark ended fiscal 1995 with net sales increasing to $73 million but net income holding at $1.1 million. The company gained an important corporate client the following year when it began managing the cafeteria of Universal Studios in southern California. Also in 1996, it purchased two Manhattan restaurants, Jim McMullen and Mackinac Bar and Grill, which it had been managing. Before the year was out, however, Ark sold the latter, plus the Rodeo Bar and the Museum Cafe—Weinstein's initial establishment—for $1.5 million, below book value.

Interviewed about the sale by *Nation's Restaurant News,* Weinstein pointed out that "managing larger facilities makes more sense, and they are more economically efficient.'' Robert Towers, the company's treasurer and chief operating officer, stressed that small restaurants would continue to play an important role in Ark's evolution, but added ''that other operators are better at running these smaller restaurants, and it's hard to compete against them.'' Ark chose to sell these properties below cost rather than make a profit by pursuing competitive bids because, according to Weinstein, ''It was more important to us that we put them in the right hands, people who appreciated the asset. We had a responsibility to our landlords and our employees that there be no business interruption.''

Ark Restaurants was known for a paternalistic policy in a high-turnover industry, offering medical benefits to anyone working at least three shifts a week and giving its staffers, many of them artists or actors, time off for a theater role with a guaranteed job on return. When Ernie's had to be shut down for an eight-month remodeling after the building collapsed, he kept the entire 325-person staff on the payroll. In exchange, Weinstein said, he received employee loyalty in an industry plagued by petty thievery. Nevertheless, after storms during the harsh 1995–96 winter forced the cancellation of many holiday-season parties for the second straight year, Ark Restaurants began paring its payroll through attrition and layoffs. Its net income fell to $788,762 in fiscal 1996 on net sales of $76.8 million. The long-term debt, only $761,000 at the end of fiscal 1994, reached $6.4 million at the end of fiscal 1996.

Gambling on Las Vegas in 1997

Ark Restaurants was taking on debt for its largest project: operating restaurants, a food court, room service, and employee dining for the New York-New York Hotel & Casino resort in Las Vegas, which made its debut in 1997. In addition to opening a 450-seat around-the-clock America and a second Gonzalez y Gonzalez, Ark introduced a branch of midtown Manhattan's Gallagher's Steak House and built a quick-serve food court with Little Italy, Greenwich Village, and other New York themes for the hotel-casino, each of whose 10 towers duplicated a famous Manhattan skyscraper. Ark invested $15 million in the project, which covered 100,000 square feet and was capable of feeding 20,000 to 25,000 people a day.

Principal Subsidiaries

Ark Boston Corp.; Ark Bryant Park Corp.; Ark Operating Corp.; Ark Parties, Inc.; Ark Potomac Corporation; Ark Union Station, Inc.; Las Vegas America Corp.; Las Vegas Festival Food Corp.; Las Vegas Restaurant Corp.; Las Vegas Steakhouse Corp.

Further Reading

Blumenthal, Robin Goldwyn, ''Ark Restaurants Differ in Looks, Earn Big Profits,'' *Wall Street Journal,* December 29, 1993, p. B1.
Edwards, Joe, ''Ark Plugs 'Leak,' Plots New Ventures,'' *Nation's Restaurant News,* March 6, 1987, pp. F30, F32, F34.
Fabricant, Florence, ''We'd Like to Make a Reservation: Table for 1,000 Please,'' *New York Times,* May 17, 1995, pp. C1, C6.
Frydman, Ken, ''Ark Restaurants Launches Gourmet Catering Division,'' *Nation's Restaurant News,* April 3, 1989, p. 3.
Gambon, Jill, ''Restaurant Group on Expansion Arc,'' *Crain's New York Business,* August 29, 1994, pp. 3, 20.
Hall, Trish, ''Urban Dining: An Empire Built on Savvy and Intuition,'' *New York Times,* May 11, 1988, pp. C1, C5.
Hilzenrath, David S., ''Washington Harbour Pact Reached,'' *Washington Post,* August 12, 1989, pp. F1, F14.
Kamen, Tobin, ''Profits Set for Higher Ark After Group Weathers Storm,'' *Crain's New York Business,* March 25, 1996, p. 67.
Miller, Bryan, ''Lutèce. A Bastion of Classic French Cuisine, Is Sold,'' *New York Times,* October 12, 1994, pp. B1, B2.
Prewitt, Milford, ''Ark to Bring Taste of the Big Apple to Las Vegas,'' *Nation's Restaurant News,* October 2, 1005, pp. 3–4.
——, ''Ark Downsizes NYC Holdings, Focuses on New Ventures, *Nation's Restaurant News,* November 18, 1996, pp. 3, 67.
——, ''Michael Weinstein: The Ark Restaurants President Reigns Over a Flood of Prosperous Business Ventures,'' *Nation's Restaurant News,* January 1997, p. 222.

—Robert Halasz

Asahi Breweries, Ltd.

23-1, Azumabashi 1-chome
Sumida-ku, Tokyo 130
Japan
(03) 5608-5112
Fax: (03) 5608-7111
Web site: http://www.mediagalaxy.co.jp/asahibeer/
home/homee.htm

Public Company
Incorporated: September 1, 1949
Employees: 4,274
Sales: ¥1.21 trillion (US$10.44 billion) (1996)
Stock Exchanges: Tokyo Osaka Nagoya Kyoto
SICs: 2082 Malt Beverages; 2086 Bottled & Canned Soft
Drinks & Carbonated Waters; 2834 Pharmaceutical
Preparations; 5812 Eating Places

Asahi Breweries, Ltd. is the second-largest brewer in Japan; its 35 percent share of the Japanese market trails only market leader Kirin Brewery Company, Limited, which holds about a 47 percent share. Asahi also boasts the top-selling beer in its home country, Asahi Super Dry. In addition to its brewery operations—which account for more than 75 percent of the company's net sales—Asahi also manufactures and markets soft drinks (headed by the flagship Mitsuya Cider) and food products (mainly brewer's yeast extracts and related products), sells pharmaceuticals, and runs restaurants. Asahi is very active overseas and has built a network of alliances with such major brewers as Molson and Miller in North America and Bass and Löwenbräu in Europe, as well as making aggressive moves to capture a major share of the emerging market in China.

Early History

The history of Asahi Breweries is linked with that of virtually every other brewery in Japan. The first brewery built by the Japanese was a government enterprise; it was established in the early days of the Meiji restoration on Hokkaido, the nor-

thernmost of the islands of Japan. In the 1880s the government sold its Hokkaido brewery to private interests—and thus the Osaka Beer Brewing Company, Japan Beer Brewery Company, Sapporo Brewery, and Nippon Brewing Company all came into being. In 1888 Hiizu Ikuta was sent to Germany by Osaka Beer Brewing Company to study brewing at the famous School of Weihenstephen in Bavaria. He returned the following year and was appointed manager and technical chief of the Suita Brewery, one of the individual breweries controlled by Osaka. Three years later, in 1892, his creation, Asahi Beer, was released for sale.

In 1906 the Osaka Beer Brewing Company, Sapporo Brewery, and Nippon Brewing Company were amalgamated into the Dai Nippon Brewery Co., Ltd. Asahi, now a separate division of the new company, began a long history of producing nonalcoholic beverages as well as beer. Asahi pioneered the soft drink industry in Japan with both Mitsuya Cider and Wilkinson Tansan, a mineral water. Mitsuya Cider was released for sale in 1907, 17 years after Asahi Beer had first been introduced to the market.

Asahi Breweries, Ltd. Formed in 1949

In 1949, as a result of the enactment of the Excessive Economic Power Decentralization Law, Dai Nippon Brewery was divided into two parts—Asahi Breweries, Ltd. and Nippon Breweries, Ltd. In 1951 Asahi introduced Wilkinson Tansan mineral water to the Japanese market. That year also saw the introduction of Japan's first fruit-flavored soft drink, Bireley's Orange. In 1958 the company launched a canned version of Asahi Beer, Japan's first canned beer. Asahi's first plant exclusively devoted to the production of soft drinks was opened in Kashiwa in 1966. Six years later another Asahi soft drink plant began production in Fukushima. By the mid-1970s soft drink sales accounted for 35 percent of the company's total sales.

Asahi also enjoyed other kinds of success. Its Central Research Laboratory, charged primarily with quality control, also developed new products, including "Ebios," a day brewer's yeast renowned in Japan for its medicinal properties; the company introduced Ebios in 1930 and has been manufacturing it ever since. In 1965 laboratory staff invented the world's first outdoor fermentation and lagering tank (the "Asahi Tank");

Company Perspectives:

Established in 1889, Asahi Breweries, Ltd., is Japan's leading innovator in the beer industry. Asahi Super Dry commands a leading share in Japan's beer market. Asahi boasts fully integrated production, inventory control, and marketing systems that operate under the Company's Fresh Management principles to ensure timely supply of products to consumers. Our corporate philosophy is based on meeting the needs and fulfilling the expectations of consumers with products of the highest quality.

the West German beer plant construction firm of Ziemann soon negotiated with the company for a license to build the tank.

The early 1970s saw Asahi take its first serious moves outside Japan and in the area of importing. In 1971, in a joint venture with Nikka Whiskey Distilling Company, Asahi established Japan International Liquor to import foreign liquors, primarily Scotch whiskeys (Dewars and King George IV). Also in 1971, Asahi was the first Japanese brewery to have its beer produced overseas under license when it concluded a technical assistance agreement with United Breweries of New Guinea, and a brewery was subsequently constructed at Port Moresby. Two years later Asahi began to import French and German wine. In January 1986 a technology transfer agreement was reached with the San Miguel Corporation of Indonesia for the local production of Asahi beer. Another technical transfer agreement had previously been reached in 1979 with this same company for the use of Asahi's automatic beer gauge system for beer fermentation at other plants under San Miguel control. This system had been jointly developed by Asahi and the Toshiba Corporation.

Asahi entered the restaurant business in the early 1980s. Subsidiary companies—Asahi Kyoei and New Asahi—managed more than 100 restaurants in western and eastern Japan, respectively. The company also entered into a joint venture with the American company Pizza Hut to establish Pizza Hut restaurants in Japan.

Market Share Decline Turned Around in the Mid-1980s

In October 1981 Asahi Chemical Industry (despite their similar names, the companies were not previously related) acquired 22 million shares of Asahi Brewery. An agreement was concluded between the two companies concerning relations involving personnel, technology, and sales. Asahi Chemical eventually held about 10 percent of Asahi stock, making it one of the brewer's ten largest shareholders.

Another of Asahi's important shareholders at this time was the Sumitomo Group, which held about a 12 percent stake. Over the preceding decades, Asahi's share of the Japanese beer market had declined significantly, from a peak of 36 percent in 1949 to 10 percent in 1981. Among Japanese brewers, Asahi was a distant third, trailing both Kirin and Sapporo Breweries

Ltd. Executives at Sumitomo Bank had been placed into the president's office starting in the early 1970s, but they were unable to stop the decline. Then in January 1982 another Sumitomo Bank executive, Tsutomu Murai, was sent to Asahi to take over. Murai specialized in turning around troubled companies and had previously helped to rescue Mazda Motor.

Murai began with a reorganization aimed at improving communication between company departments. He then concluded a series of licensing agreements with foreign companies. In 1983 the company entered into an agreement with the Löwenbräu Company of West Germany to produce Löwenbräu Beer under license in Japan. Asahi also gained needed technical know-how by signing contracts with American, British, and German brewers to obtain technology. In 1984 Asahi's soft drink division concluded an agreement with Schweppes, which led to Asahi manufacturing several Schweppes brands in Japan—Tonic Water, Golden French (an apple and ginger drink), Passion Orange, and Grapefruit Dry. Asahi entered into other partnerships, notably to import foreign beers and wines into Japan. Asahi in 1985 formed a partnership with the Australian wine company Lindemann's, after which Asahi sold Australian wine under the "My Cellar" brand.

Perhaps most importantly, Murai pushed the company to become more attuned to its customers. One byproduct of this was a renewed attention to quality. Asahi abandoned its policy of buying most of its wheat and hops in Japan, and began to buy the best raw materials available, regardless of cost or origin. The company also made moves to ensure the freshness of its beer, such as having salespeople visit stores where they would throw out any Asahi beer older than three months.

In 1985 Murai ordered a series of market surveys. Of most significance was that 98 percent of the beer drinkers surveyed advised Asahi to change the taste of its beer; consumers said that they wanted a beer that was rich but left no aftertaste, a combination that the company's technicians said was not chemically possible. Murai insisted that nothing was impossible and Asahi subsequently developed and introduced in 1986 Asahi Draft, a full-bodied beer with a crisp taste. Then in March 1987 Asahi introduced Japan's first dry beer, Asahi Super Dry, which became a blockbuster hit. Super Dry, a cold-filtered draft beer, contained slightly more alcohol than other Japanese beers—5 percent compared to 4.5 percent—but less sugar and was thus lighter. The brand became particularly popular among younger drinkers and helped Asahi's market share increase to 17 percent just one year after its introduction.

So successful was Super Dry that Murai had to abandon a planned diversification, which aimed to derive half of the company's revenue from nonbeer operations. Instead, beer increased in importance, making up 80 percent of sales in 1988.

Marketing Innovations and Globalization in the Late 1980s and 1990s

By the end of the 1980s Asahi's market share had surpassed the 20 percent mark and the company leapfrogged Sapporo into second place among Japanese brewers. In addition to the new brands, Asahi's success in the late 1980s and early 1990s was also attributable to changes in marketing. In Japan, most beer was traditionally sold in small liquor stores by the bottle. Asahi targeted nontraditional customers by producing more of its beer in cans and packaging it in six packs, and by sending the canned beer into supermarkets and convenience stores. The company also became much more aggressive in its pitches to retailers who sold beer. Asahi continued to emphasize the freshness of its product and by 1995 was able to deliver beer to stores just 10 days after brewing. By 1996 Super Dry had dethroned Kirin's Lager brand from the top spot among Japanese beer brands and the following year Asahi's overall market share hit 35 percent.

From the late 1980s into the mid-1990s, Asahi continued to be active in importing but at the same time stepped up its export activities. A technological agreement was reached with the U.K.-based Bass Brewers Ltd. in 1988, whereby Asahi began to import the Bass Pale Ale brand. In 1996 the two companies entered into a new agreement which called for Bass to produce and market Asahi Super Dry in the United Kingdom and elsewhere in Europe.

In 1990 Asahi gained further access to manufacturing and marketing channels outside Japan by purchasing a significant stake—which stood at 20 percent in 1992—in Foster's Brewing Group Ltd., based in Australia and then the fourth-largest beer company in the world. In the succeeding years Asahi expanded its own system of overseas operations so that the purpose of the tie-in with Foster's grew less important. Asahi consequently reduced its stake, then in mid-1997 sold its remaining 14 percent stake back to Foster's.

A 1994 license agreement with Molson Breweries brought Super Dry into the Canadian market. Asahi then targeted the two largest beer markets in the world—the United States and China. In 1995 a wide-ranging alliance with the Miller Brewing Company commenced, which initially featured the introduction of the Miller Special brand in Japan—a brand brewed specifically for the Japanese market—and the Super Dry brand in the United States. In September 1996 Asahi and Miller introduced Asahi First Lady, a beer targeted toward women, in Japan and the United States.

On the Chinese front, in 1994 and 1995 Asahi acquired shares in and began managing five Chinese brewing companies in Beijing, Yantai, Hangzhou, Quanzhou, and Jiaxing. Initially four of the companies sold a beer called Asahi Bichu, then in 1997 production and sale of Asahi Super Dry began at two of the breweries. Asahi's Chinese partners sold 1.5 million cases of beer in 1996 and aimed to double that for 1997.

In addition to growing market share in Japan and an increasing presence in Europe, North America, and China, further proof of the brewer's resurgence came in 1996 when Asahi posted record net sales, operating income, and net income. In mid-1997 the company finished construction of a new research and development center in Ibaraki Prefecture, and was confidently building its ninth brewery, the Shikoku brewery, which was scheduled to be completed in March 1998. Asahi Breweries seemed certain to remain a leading Japanese brewer and to increase its stature internationally.

Principal Subsidiaries

The Nikka Whisky Distilling Co., Ltd. (58.2%); Asahi Beer Pax Co., Ltd.; Asahi Beer Malt, Ltd. (91.9%); Asahi Beer Winery, Ltd.; Nippon National Seikan Company, Ltd. (51%); Torii Pharmaceutical Co., Ltd. (51%); Asahi Soft Drinks Co., Ltd. (97.2%); Asahi Beer Food, Ltd.; Asahi Beer Pharmaceutical Co., Ltd. (99.7%); Asahi Cargo Service Tokyo, Ltd.; Asahi Cargo Service Nagoya, Ltd.; Asahi Cargo Service Osaka, Ltd.; Asahi Cargo Service Kyushu, Ltd.; Asahi Beer System, Ltd. (75%); New Asahi, Ltd.; Asahi Beer Pizza Studio, Ltd.; Asahi Beer Garden, Ltd. (81.3%); Asahi Beer Restaurant Service, Ltd.; Asahi Beer Real Estate, Ltd.; Asahi Building Management, Ltd.; Asahi Beer Finance Co., Ltd.; Asahi Beer Communications, Ltd.; East Japan Asahi Draft Beer Service, Ltd.; West Japan Asahi Draft Beer Service, Ltd.; Chuo Advertising Shinsha, Inc. (53.3%); Asahi Beer Information System, Ltd.; Asahi Breweries U.S.A., Inc.; Asahi New York, Inc.; Asahi Beer International Holding (Australia) Ltd.; Asahi Beer France S.A.R.L.; Asahi Beer International Finance B.V. (Netherlands); Buckinghamshire Golf Company Limited (U.K.); S.A. du Golf International de Grasse Claux-Amic (France).

Further Reading

"Asahi Flattens Kirin's King of Beers," *Nikkei Weekly*, July 8, 1996, p. 9.

Jameson, Sam, "Team Spirit: The Case of Asahi Breweries Illustrates How Bank Rescues of Struggling Firms Help the Japanese Economy. But There Is No Guarantee of Success," *Los Angeles Times*, December 8, 1988, pp. 1, 11.

Miller, Karen Lowry, "Can Asahi Brew Up Another Blockbuster?," *Business Week*, March 4, 1991, p. 41.

Moffett, Sebastian, "High and Dry: Asahi's Deft Moves Win Over Japan's Beer Drinkers," *Far Eastern Economic Review*, October 3, 1996, pp. 98–99.

Tomioka, Katsuhiko, "The Secret Behind Asahi's Growth: Interview with Yuzo Seto, President of Asahi Breweries," *Japan 21st*, November 1996, pp. 12–13.

Yamamoto, Yuri, "In Beer Battle, Kirin Goes Flat while Asahi Barrels Ahead," *Nikkei Weekly*, March 3, 1997, pp. 1, 19.

——, "Japan's Brewers Tapping Chinese Market," *Nikkei Weekly*, October 7, 1996, pp. 1, 21.

—updated by David E. Salamie

Asanté Technologies, Inc.

821 Fox Lane
San Jose, California 95131
U.S.A.
(408) 435-8388
Fax: (408) 432-1117
Web site: http://www.asante.com

Public Company
Founded: 1988
Employees: 197
Sales: $67 million (1996)
Stock Exchanges: NASDAQ
SICs: 3577 Computer Peripheral Equipment, Not
    Elsewhere Classified

A fast-growing but young company, Asanté Technologies, Inc. is a leading producer of computer networking products for graphic and image-intensive applications used by departmental and workgroup networks, otherwise known as Local Area Networks (LANs). The company makes Ethernet products for Macintosh and PC computers, including bridges, hubs, and routers, facilitating information transfer over the most popular networking protocol. The company also offers LAN switches and web-based network management software and network acceleration tools. The company's adapters (including EtherPaC, MaCon, and NetDock) connect Macintosh and IBM-compatible computers and peripheral devices to Ethernet networks. The company's network interconnect devices include hubs and bridges (NetStacker, AsantéHub, and NetExtender), network management software, and networking products (AsantéFAST scrics) for the high-speed Fast Ethernet technology. Asanté's target market is small to medium-sized companies and departments within larger corporations. Products are marketed through distributors in 36 countries, value-added resellers, system integrators, and independent sales representatives. In addition, a direct sales force targets higher education customers.

In 1988, Asanté was founded in the corner of a small Silicon Valley warehouse. Cofounders Jeff Lin and Wilson Wong, both 37, were electrical engineers who had immigrated to California before the age of 30. Lin, from Taiwan, and Wong, from Hong Kong, met at a Chinese Christian Church in Mountain View, California, in 1983, when both were working as electrical engineers. They went on to work together at a since-defunct networking company in Mountain View. Together, thcy left their jobs, created their company and christened it Asanté (from a French toast meaning "to your health"), choosing the name because it begins with the letter "A," and would therefore be placed at the beginning of catalog listings. In the early days, Lin and Wong—both workaholics—often brought sleeping bags to their warehouse office in Sunnyvale, California, working 24 hours straight, napping briefly, and then working 12 more hours.

The cofounders' business goal was to provide services and products to make computer networking easy and affordable, by designing, manufacturing, and marketing Ethernet networking products. Originally, Asanté found its niche through manufacturing products for the Macintosh, connecting Mac computers in networks much faster than the Macs' built-in LocalTalk. The computer networking industry had largely focused on linking various IBM-compatible networks, and had not emphasized Macintosh networking. The company's cofounders chose to focus on Macintosh to achieve better profit margins, aiming to be number one in one segment, rather than number three or four in several PC segments with hundreds of competitors. In 1989, Asanté shipped its first Ethernet adapter card for Macintosh computers, and in that fiscal year, the company brought in $94,000 in net revenues. In 1990, the company shipped its first non-intelligent Ethernet hub. In these first years, Asanté's primary market was educational, with universities comprising 85 percent of sales.

By 1991, Asanté was thc top manufacturer of Macintosh adapters in the world. Apple Computer was both a partner and a competitor for Asanté: the company manufactured the products which made Asanté's Ethernet adaptors necessary, but at any moment Apple could decide to provide connectivity internally, choking Asanté's sales. Asanté's market share was 34.5 percent in 1991, with Apple at 23.5 percent. Flexing its competitive muscle, Apple presented a major challenge to the company in

Company Perspectives:

Asanté Technologies, Inc. is a leading provider of high-performance, end-to-end intranetworking solutions for graphics and image-intensive applications. The company's goal is to provide services and products to make computer networking easy and affordable, by designing, manufacturing, and marketing Ethernet networking products. Asanté sells its products through distributors and supports this distribution channel with marketing and promotional programs and a network of direct sales and service personnel. The management and Asanté team are focused on realizing milestones to meet the challenge of growing the Company as a premier supplier of high-speed Intranet switching solutions.

October of 1991, when it began shipping its high-end Quadra computers with Ethernet cards installed.

Forced to compensate for the decreased demand for Ethernet products by consumers of new Macintosh computers, Asanté diversified. In 1991, the company assembled a hub engineering team to design products for IBM-compatible computers, in order to generate additional revenues for the company. In 1992, it entered the PC market with Ethernet adapters, while continuing to maintain its Macintosh business. Following a marketing plan spearheaded by vice president of sales and distribution Ronald Volkmar, the company garnered its resources toward the development of new market products, shipping hubs, network management software, and PC Ethernet cards between 1992 and 1994. The addition of the line of PC products made Asanté one of the industry's most complete providers of families of Ethernet adapter cards for both PCs and Macs. The company moved its headquarters from Sunnyvale, California, to a much larger space in San Jose. Sales for 1992 were $47.5 million, over 500 times greater than revenues achieved only three years earlier in 1989.

The company went public in 1993 with fiscal year end sales of $67.2 million and income of $2.1 million. That year, Asanté was the first company to support the new Macintosh computers, continuing to lead the Macintosh Ethernet connectivity market while making parallel inroads in the PC market. The company's efforts that year were directed toward entering the realm of networking enterprise systems with thousands of nodes (work stations), where it would compete with major players such as SynOptics, Cisco, and IBM. Continuing to introduce leading new products, the company advanced the smallest Small Computer Systems Interface (SCSI) Ethernet adapter, for Apple Powerbooks. A 72-port intelligent Ethernet hub (a hub capable of monitoring networks and network management software for LANs) was debuted, and the U.S. Department of Commerce named the company "Minority Manufacturer of the Year" for 1993.

In March 1994, the company introduced NetStacker, the industry's first "stackable chassis." Asanté entered the remote local-area net access market with its NetConnect-Remote Ac-

cess Server that year. The company continued to garner public acclaim, rating 19th on *Business Week*'s 1994 "Best Small Company" list and 29th on *Fortune*'s "Fastest Growing Company" list. Sales in 1994 continued to leap forward, increasing 16 percent to $79.9 million with a $1 million surplus. The company brought in Ralph Dormitzer, of Digital Equipment Corp., as president and CEO, with the goal of bringing sales to $100 million.

Despite such success, the company suffered from a drop in market share due to increased competition in 1995, bringing a 24 percent decline in sales to $60.9 million and a net loss of $3.7 million. The competition that spurred the sales loss was primarily due to Apple Computer's incorporation of Ethernet connections into the motherboards of more Macintosh and Powerbook computers. To address this problem, Asanté streamlined operations, lowered some of its prices, and began to offer lifetime warranties on hub and adapter card products. New products introduced in 1995 included AsantéFAST 100 Hub (the industry's first stackable Fast Ethernet managed hub) and ReadySwitch (Asanté's first switch product).

In 1995, sales to wholesale distributors made up 45 percent of the company's revenues. Cofounders Jeff Lin and Wilson Wong each owned 16 percent of the company, while Eugene Duh, of Orient Semiconductor Electronics in Taiwan, owned 14 percent. Seventy-two percent of sales were within the United States, with 16 percent in Europe and 12 percent in Canada and the Pacific Rim. The company settled a lawsuit, which had been filed by Synoptics in 1994 alleging violations of federal securities laws, entering an agreement that cost $2.6 million, with $520,000 paid for by the company's insurance. Specifically, Synoptics had charged that some of its former employees, since employed at Asanté, had implemented SynOptics's software code into Asanté products. Due to the large portion of the settlement which was picked up by Asanté's insurance, the settlement had no major impact on revenues.

The company seemed to be on the road to recovery in 1996, with a 10 percent gain. The increase was primarily due to a large number of shipments of Fast Ethernet and new switched products, as well as stackable and unmanaged hubs. The company also expanded its efforts to sell to original equipment manufacturers (OEMs), and courted larger OEMs for contracts. Management was strengthened, with the appointment of a new CFO and vice president of sales, as well as a new vice president of engineering. Despite the loss in 1995, Asanté was ranked the 10th fastest-growing (networking) company of 1990–95 by *NetworkWorld* Magazine, and the company received the Top 50 Award (for the second consecutive year) from Deloitte & Touche as one of the fastest-growing companies in the Silicon Valley.

New product development and market segment entry continued, as the company moved into the switched Ethernet market with several workgroup and segmentation switches. The company also serviced publishing and prepress markets with networking solutions via its combined Fast Ethernet and Net Doubler network acceleration tools. IntraSpection, an innovative, Intranet-based network management program for Windows NT servers became the industry's first open software system or Intranet-based network management. IntraSpection allows network managers to initiate device queries that set off Simple Network Management Protocol-based polling of their networks or to view graphical maps that are automatically updated as network changes occur.

All told, sales reached $67 million in 1996, and the company was ranked the Number Five Fast Ethernet hub provider in the country by the Dell'Oro Group. However, revenue growth was less than the company's increased operating expenses, and the year ended with a small loss of $457,000 on a 10 percent increase in revenues. After its setback in 1995, Asanté had backtracked and regained, more or less, its revenue position at the time of its public offering in 1993. The ratio of U.S. to foreign sales was consistent with previous years, at 23 percent (as compared to 28 percent in 1995 and 22 percent in 1994). In the third quarter of 1996, the company added to its international sales offices in the United Kingdom, Taiwan, and Canada, establishing a new location in Japan.

By the second quarter of 1997, Asanté again reported strong sales results, with net income of $448,000 on $21.2 million in revenue, an improvement over a loss of $520,000 on $14.8 million for the same period the previous year. Sales figures for the first six months of fiscal 1997 were equally improved, with a 24 percent increase over the previous year. The improvement was attributed to a new line of switches and Web-based network management software.

A Look to the Future

The company has identified four trends affecting the future growth and success (or vulnerability) of its business in the late 1990s: 1) the adoption of switched Ethernet technology, 2) the adoption of Fast Ethernet products, 3) the use of "Intranet" software technology in corporate LANs, and 4) the gains in market share of Microsoft Windows NT. Future success will depend on the ability of the company to respond to the markets corresponding to these trends, and to accurately forecast sales and assembly lead time so as not to lose sales to competitors. Such predictive powers are essential competitive tools, because the distribution of the company's products in its first decade of existence has been characterized by rapid change, consolidations and financial problems suffered by distributors, and emerging alternate distribution channels. At the same time, high

competition means that distributors may stop marketing the company's products at any time at their own discretion, and without notice to the company. Declines in average selling prices and improvements in product features and performance enhance the competitive environment, in which many of the company's challengers are more established and have more resources and name recognition. For this reason, Asanté must always keep on its toes, one step ahead of the market and its competition. In the mainstream market, the company's primary competitors are Cisco Systems, Bay Networks, 3Com, and others.

Another potential threat to the company's continued success is the unpredictability of actions by Apple Computers. As it did in 1991, when it made Ethernet connections available in its computers for the first time, Apple can steal business from Asanté with no warning through new products which increase the availability of Ethernet on the motherboards of new computers. While Asanté has achieved successful penetration of the PC market, it continues to depend on Macintosh users, and such aggressive strategies on the part of Apple computers would adversely affect sales in the future, threatening the profitability of the company. If the company can manage to simultaneously maintain a competitive edge in both the Macintosh and PC markets, it will continue to maintain its status as a fast-growing and flexible winner in the Ethernet connection market.

Further Reading

Campbell, Monica, "Asanté, Global Up; Farallon Down," *MacWEEK*, May 5, 1997, p. 41.

Clark, Tim, "Asanté Needs New-Product Push," *Business Marketing*, June, 1993, pp. 38–9.

Davis, Beth, "Management Made Easier," *Informationweek*, November 4, 1996, p. 83.

Dunlap, Charlotte, "SynOptics Sues Asanté Over Key Software Code," *Computer Reseller News*, February 14, 1994, p. 199.

Kaufman, Steven B. "Affordable Mac Networking," *Nation's Business*, August, 1994, p. 17.

MacAskill, Skip, "Remote Access Starts Year with Bang: Asanté, Cayman Announce Servers," *Network World*, January 10, 1994, pp. 21, 24.

Paul, Frederic, "Firm Unveils Mini Adapter for Notebook," *Network World*, March 15, 1993, p. 13.

—Heidi Feldman

Asplundh Tree Expert Co.

708 Blair Mill Road
Willow Grove, Pennsylvania 19090
U.S.A.
(215) 784-4200
Fax: (215) 784-4493
Web site: http://www.asplundh.com

Private Company
Founded: 1928
Employees: 18,000
Sales: $900 million (1996)
SICs: 0851 Forestry Services

Asplundh Tree Expert Co. is the world's leading line clearance and tree-trimming company. While most of the company's business is in the United States and Canada, it also has operations in Australia, France, New Zealand, England, and Ireland. Asplundh's primary business, accounting for about 60 percent of its sales, is trimming trees for telephone and electric utility companies and municipalities. Its divisions and subsidiaries also keep railroad rights-of-way clear, inspect and maintain telephone poles and dock pilings, read meters, clean and repair street and traffic lights, install underground lines and cables, and sell automobiles. The third generation of Asplundhs manages the company and all board members are family members.

The Early Years: 1928–45

Griffith (Griff) Asplundh was seven years old when his Swedish immigrant father died in 1903. His brother Lester was two, his brother Carl an infant. "Asplund" in Swedish refers to a grove of aspen trees, so perhaps it is not surprising that, 25 years later, the boys decided to make trees the family business. They got their training working for their big brother Oswald E. (O. E.) who started a nursery and tree-trimming company to help support his widowed mother and his seven siblings. Griff, Lester, and Carl trimmed trees to pay for college, with Griff majoring in forestry at Penn State, Lester in electrical engineering at Swarthmore, and Carl in finance at the University of Pennsylvania.

In 1928 they decided to combine their talents and go into business for themselves, setting up shop in Glenside, Pennsylvania. Not wanting to compete with O. E.'s residential business, the Asplundh Tree Expert Co. focused on business customers—the fast-growing telephone and electric companies whose overhead lines needed to be kept clear of tree branches. The first customers were Philadelphia Electric Co., Public Service Electric & Gas, Co., Jersey Central Power & Light Co., Pennsylvania Power & Light Co., and American Telephone and Telegraph.

Their decision proved a wise one, as the telephone and electric companies continued to expand, despite the Great Depression. In 1934, the company moved to larger quarters in Jenkintown, and in 1936, O. E. left his nursery business and joined his brothers, helping them move into new territory. While Griff oversaw the trimming and Carl kept the books, Lester concentrated on research and development to bring the latest technology to the company and its customers. Able to offer the first power saws (operated by two men) and hand-cranked aerial platforms, Asplundh attracted more customers. By the end of the decade, the company had employees working throughout the Mid-Atlantic region, in the Carolinas and Georgia, in the Midwest, and as far west as Texas and New Mexico. To keep in touch with their far-flung workforce, the company introduced *The Asplundh TREE*, a quarterly magazine, in 1940. Business slowed significantly during World War II as workers left to join the military and rationing made it difficult to buy fuel, tools, and supplies.

New Services, New Technology: 1946–59

The Asplundh brothers thought the "chemical brush killers" developed during the war might prove useful for clearing rights-of-way and, in conjunction with American Chemical and Paint Co., tested these new herbicides. Liking what they found, Asplundh developed special formulae and, in 1946, began offering brush control services for utility rights-of-way, the company's first step in diversification. To make it easier and faster to clear and dispose of brush, Lester invented the first wood chipper and the company began assembling these at its growing Equipment Division. The demand for electricity mushroomed to supply the housing developments and apartment complexes being built for veterans and their families. To meet that need, utility companies had to expand their rights-of-

34

way networks in order to erect new transmission towers. This meant clearing and cutting lots of brush, bushes and trees. In 1956, the brothers created their first subsidiary, the Asplundh Brush Control Co., to handle the right-of-way clearing work.

Lester was elected president in January 1949, following Griff's death, but stepped down from that position in 1952 because of a health problem. Carl became president and Lester continued to use his engineering skills to expand Asplundh's capabilities. His next project dealt with the company's core business, tree trimming.

By the early 1950s, the technology of tree-trimming had progressed from ladders and ropes to a vehicle called a turret or ladder truck. A tree worker still climbed a ladder, but that was attached to the back of the truck, making it easier to reach branch ends. Then came the introduction of the hydraulic aerial lift, called a "Skyworker." Asplundh started leasing the lifts in 1953, but found their insulation poor. Lester used a new material called fiberglass in designing a stronger and better insulated lift which the company began producing in 1958 through its new manufacturing division. That same year the company established its Pole Maintenance Division for treating and reinforcing utility poles.

In 1954, Asplundh sent crews to help restore service in Mid-Atlantic states following Hurricanes Carol and Hazel. As a result of those experiences, the company produced a formalized storm emergency procedure for its crews and customers. Seven members of the second generation, sons of the founders, completed college and began training in the field and home office. The company began participating in a research project to study the safe use of herbicides along utility rights-of-way and initiated its supervisory training program for general foremen. Company operations spread throughout New England.

The early 1960s saw Asplundh continue to extend its operations—into Florida and the Pacific Northwest—and to expand its services as it offered underground utility construction. In 1967, the company pioneered commercial thermographic/infrared inspections to detect "hot spots"—short circuits, overheating and equipment failures—in a power distribution system and prevent power outages. In 1968, Barr Asplundh, Griff's son, was elected president and all second generation family members working for the company became board members. That same year, the company established the Asplundh Utility Services Ltd. subsidiary for the start-up of its Canadian operations and formed Asplundh GMC, its own commercial truck dealership.

New Markets: 1970–89

The company continued to grow and diversify during the next two decades. Street lights seemed a logical place to use its lifts, and Asplundh began cleaning, inspecting, and repairing street lighting and traffic signals for utilities and municipalities.

In 1975, the company opened its first One-Call Center in New Jersey. Initially called the Underground Location Communications Division, the center served as a link between excavators and utilities with underground lines. Before beginning to dig, a contractor could call the center and describe where the work was to be done. Personnel at the center would notify member utilities with facilities in the work area so they could mark where their underground cables and pipes were. Within 20 years the company had eight such centers around the country using computers and specialized software.

Also in 1975, the company established its Railroad Division, turning its vegetation sprays on the weeds, brush, and trees along railroad tracks. Asplundh began working on large railroads east of the Mississippi, using three spray trucks equipped with Hy-rail wheels which could run on both highway and railroad tracks. To meet the special needs of its new clients, Asplundh designed new equipment, including a high-production spray train car that could operate while attached to a train. In the early 1980s, the division began offering rights-of-way clearing as well as vegetation management, putting Hy-rail wheels on aerial lifts and chippers to trim and remove trees. Soon the equipment shop facility was designing and building specialized equipment including brush cutters that ran on a railroad track and had arms spanning the line, clearing an area 56 feet wide along the track. Both services proved popular and the division was soon working on railroads of all sizes, from coast to coast, from Canada to Mexico.

During the 1980s, Asplundh expanded into western Canada through several acquisitions; bought a Buick franchise which it combined with its GMC truck operations; began its first "overseas" line clearance operations in the U.S. Virgin Islands; expanded line clearance operations to serve Hawaii (thus working in all 50 states); created the Municipal Tree Division for trimming trees for cities and towns; and established Asplundh Canada, Inc. to serve Quebec and eastern Canada. The decade also saw the introduction of a self-propelled, portable backyard chipper developed in the company's Alabama region and the acquisition of Florida-based American Lighting & Signalization Inc.

One of the company's greatest strengths was evident following the disruption in telephone and electrical services caused along the East Coast by Hurricane Gloria in 1985 and in the Caribbean and North and South Carolina by Hurricane Hugo in 1989. Asplundh could shift large numbers of employees (1,500 for Gloria and 1,600 for Hugo) to the damaged areas to repair lines and restore service, augmenting the crews of the local utility companies. These emergency storm services, providing quick mobilization of trained crews and specialized equipment, proved to be an important marketing tool for the company and led to the establishment of a weather center at Asplundh's headquarters which monitored every storm in the country. As president Chris Asplundh explained in a 1995 *Forbes* article, "Santa Ana winds in California, that's our problem. Nor'easter in Boston, that's our problem; ice storm in Minnesota, that's our problem."

In 1987 the first of 13 third-generation Asplundh family members completed the Family Management Development Program. An Asplundh must graduate from college, spend three years working outside the company, and then be recommended by three family members, including at least one board member, before being accepted for the eight-year training program. Once in the program, the young Asplundh works in the field as a crew foreman, general foreman, supervisor, and then manager, moving around the country with each promotion, before coming to work at headquarters. In 1989, members of the second generation began to retire.

More Services, Global Markets—1990 to the Present

Asplundh started the 90s with a buying spree. In 1990, it acquired New York-based B&J Maintenance Co., to increase its utility line construction activities in the Northeast; L. Fulcher Electric, a traffic signal contractor, which became a subsidiary of American Lighting & Signalization; and four small line clearance firms in France. The French companies retained their names and management and operated as partners of Asplundh's French subsidiary, Robert S.A., named for Chairman of the Board Robert Asplundh, who helped negotiate the business arrangements. Located in different regions of the country, the firms' primary client was the government-owned power company, Electricite de France.

Later that year, Asplundh formed a joint venture with a large electrical and engineering contractor in New Zealand. The new company, Electrix Asplundh, offered line clearance tree maintenance, right-of-way clearing, mowing, and spraying to municipal councils and electric supply authorities.

Training had long been a tradition at Asplundh, beginning with informal training schools for crews. The Supervisory Training Program for general foremen was initiated in 1953, and the Supervisory Skills Seminars started in 1986. As a regional manager stated in *The Asplundh TREE*, "Our people have become more professional. This is especially true of crew personnel. They used to be considered 'just tree trimmers.' Now they have Commercial Driver's Licenses, Pesticide Applicator's Licenses, better first aid training, arborist training. . . ." In 1990, the company established Professional Line Clearance Training Crews who came in and provided two-weeks, hands-on training to crews working on utility properties. That training experience was in addition to the normal on-the-job training crews received.

Equipment development was another company tradition, and 1991 witnessed the unveiling of the manufacturing division's LRIII-55, an aerial lift with a reach of 55 feet, well beyond anything then available.

The year 1992 was busy as all Canadian operations came under the company's Asplundh Canada, Inc. subsidiary; the Asplundh Manufacturing Division was sold to Altec Industries, Inc.; Christopher Asplundh, the youngest member of the second generation took over as president; and some 3,000 workers from seven states helped clean up and restore service in Florida and Louisiana after Hurricane Andrew. During the year the company began a new service, reading meters on the property of Chattanooga Electric Power Board, and, in cooperation with the Philadelphia Electric Co., Asplundh promoted its Philly Foam, a low-volume foliage spraying system that made it easier for a sprayer to see what had been treated, thus reducing skips and misses. On the international scene, the company formed a wholly owned subsidiary in Australia and acquired Read & Co., a long-established firm in England. Asplundh financed the firm's restructuring to help it expand in England and Wales and offer services to the newly privatized electric utilities in England. Late in the year

Asplundh bought Ginnifer Tree Care Service in the Republic of Ireland. A commercial/residential tree service company, Ginnifer broadened its services by clearing lines for Ireland's Electric Supply Board around Dublin.

Asplundh's 65th year of business began with the mobilizing of more than 1,300 crews to restore power all along the East Coast following the Blizzard of '93 in March. The company continued to expand. B&J Maintenance was renamed Asplundh Construction Corp. and began to move beyond its Northeast base and Asplundh bought the assets of five subsidiaries of Southeastern Public Service Company, one of its line clearance competitors. By 1995, the company's revenues had grown from $100 million in 1984 to $850 million. Four of its original five customers were still doing business with the company and some 20 utilities had been using Asplundh crews for 40 or more years.

In the last half of the decade, Asplundh turned several of its divisions into wholly owned subsidiaries. Underground Utility Locating, Inc. assumed the responsibilities of the One-Call Division; the relatively new meter reading operations became Utility Meter Services, Inc.; the renting and leasing of equipment and vehicles was placed under Compass Equipment Leasing, Inc.; and the division handling pole maintenance became Utility Pole Technologies, Inc.

According to Randall Lane in his *Forbes* article, much of the company's recent growth and service expansion has occurred to provide more opportunities for family members in the company. With 65 members in the fourth generation, and the eldest ones in college, the company may not be big enough to hold those who complete the family training program. The other potential problem raised by Lane was the issue of dividends. Most of the company's earnings have been put right back into the business, allowing it to operate with no long-term debt. But the growing number of family shareholders may want more than the book value of their shares paid by the company. Asked by Lane if he might take the company public, president Chris Asplundh replied, "Then we'd just have money. That isn't what this family is about." Instead, Asplundh appeared to be making the most of the outsourcing needs of deregulated public utilities and cost-conscious municipalities.

Principal Subsidiaries

Asplundh Canada Inc.; Robert S.A. (France); Electrix Asplundh Co. Ltd. (50%) (NZ); Asplundh Tree Expert (Australia) Pty. Ltd.; Read & Co. Utility Services Ltd. (England); Ginnifer Tree Care Services (Ireland); American Lighting and Signalization, Inc.; Asplundh Brush Control Co.; Asplundh Construction Corp.; Asplundh Motors Co.; Compass Equipment Leasing; L. Fulcher Electric; Underground Utility Locating, Inc.; Utility Meter Services, Inc.; Utility Pole Technologies, Inc.

Further Reading

The Asplundh Tree, 65th Anniversary Issue, Asplundh Tree Expert Co., Willow Grove, PA, 1993.
Lane, Randall, "Let Asplundh Do It," *Forbes*, October 16, 1995, p. 56.
"Whacking Weeds with Water," *Railway Age*, July 1994, p. 57.

—Ellen D. Wernick

ASTRA

Astra AB

S-151 85 Södertälje
Sweden
46 (8) 553 260 00
Fax: 46 (8) 553 290 00
Web site: http://www.astra.com

Public Company
Incorporated: 1913
Employees: 20,000
Sales: SKr39 billion (US$5.4 billion) (1996)
Stock Exchanges: Stockholm London New York
SICs: 2835 Diagnostic Substances; 2834 Pharmaceutical
Preparations; 5047 Medical and Hospital Equipment

Astra AB is the leading pharmaceutical company in Scandinavia. Long recognized by the Swedish scientific community for its strong emphasis on research and development, the company burst onto the international scene in the early 1990s with a new leader, Håkan Mogren, and an aggressive new marketing strategy. The CEO has been credited with transforming Astra from ''a cautious, slow-moving outfit'' into ''a true global player.'' Sales multiplied from SKr 6.1 billion in 1988, Mogren's first year at the helm, to SKr38.4 billion in 1996. By this time, Astra's drug portfolio included the world's best-selling drug, the peptic ulcer treatment Losec (known as Prilosec in the United States), which alone generated US$3.5 billion in annual sales. Other drugs in the company's stable included Naropin, a derivative of the local anesthetic Xylocaine; anti-asthma drugs Pulmicort and Oxis (as well as a CFC-free delivery device, Turbuhaler); and the Plendil heart treatment. Though Europe accounted for well over half Astra's revenues, the United States was its biggest single market.

Early Twentieth-Century Origins

Prior to 1913 Swedish law limited the manufacture of pharmaceuticals to registered apothecaries. With the ratification of an amendment to the statute in 1913, it became possible for industrial companies to manufacture drugs. Astra was formed by the initiative of more than 400 doctors and apothecaries who joined together to establish the company and to become its first shareholders.

Principal among these early participants were a number of accomplished men who also assumed leadership positions in the new company. Prof. Hans von Euler, who was later to be the recipient of the 1929 Nobel Prize in Chemistry, joined Astra as its scientific adviser. Dr. Adolf Rising, a former employee of Ciba, the Swiss pharmaceutical concern, became Astra's first production manager. Dr. Sven Carlsson, owner of another Swedish company, provided financial support and secured a production site, a factory manager's house in Södertälje. Carlsson eventually assumed the chairmanship of the company.

Two products—Digitotal, a heart medication, and Glukofos, a nutritional supplement—emerged from Astra's facilities in 1914, and the company began to prosper. When the apothecary Hjalmar Andersson Tesch joined Astra in 1915 as the company's new president he brought with him a number of his own pharmaceuticals; Astra's product line now comprised a variety of medicines and chemical compounds. Government wartime restrictions on imports created a demand for Astra's products, and the company bought new factory buildings to meet that demand. By the end of World War I Astra was reporting handsome profits.

Interwar Difficulties

The years following the war proved less successful. In an attempt to create a company of international stature, the Swedish chemical company AB Svensk Färgämnesindustri acquired Astra's entire capital stock. The directors of Svensk incorrectly assumed that the shortage of raw materials during the war would persist in the postwar years. They invested in equipment for the manufacture of artificial sweeteners (a lucrative product for Astra during the war) and acetylsalicylic acid, the chemical base for aspirin. But prices for raw materials dropped as war shortages disappeared. The company faced imminent bankruptcy as its manufacturing costs grew larger than the prices its products could command in the marketplace.

Company Perspectives:

Our Vision. Astra's values and way of working make it a special company. Established in 1913 in the small town of Södertälje, Stockholm, Astra today is hardly recognizable from its early origins. Yet many of the values that characterize Astra remain fundamentally the same. These include: a commitment to excellence and safety; a strong belief in research; an enterprising, innovative spirit; an emphasis on hard work, and respect for the individual.

*This has proved to be an enduring formula for success. At the same time, the world is changing rapidly. Only the best will continue to prosper and grow. If we want to stay successful we will have to set new goals and take on the challenges of a dynamic future. Our vision can be summarized in four main points: **To Stay a Step Ahead.** Reductions of health-care spending and rising research costs will force many companies out of the market. Only the best companies will survive and Astra intends to remain one of them, through strength in research, with first-rate products and excellent people. **To Expand our Global Influence.** Astra aims for the top. This means that we will need to continue expanding our influence and attain leading positions in many more markets by the turn of the century. **To be Better Where we are Already Good.** Building on our core business is the right strategy for the immediate future. We should aim at being worldwide leaders in our chosen therapeutic areas by the year 2000. **Individual Performance is the Key to Our Long-Term Success.** Our future is critically dependent on the skills, motivation and commitment of Astra's staff. Astra's rapid expansion presents a major management challenge. We must continue recruiting high-caliber, skilled employees.*

A solution seemed possible when Sweden's first socialist government announced plans to create a nationalized pharmaceutical monopoly. Despite harsh criticism from the apothecaries, the press, and opposition members of parliament, the government authorized the state liquor monopoly to purchase Svensk Färgämnesindustri. Dr. Ivan Bratt, former leader of that monopoly, became Astra's new chairman, and the company seemed ready to assume a major role in the proposed pharmaceutical monopoly. Yet, within months, the socialist government fell, and its successor was staunchly opposed to the new monopoly. From 1921 until 1925 the government sought a private buyer who would release the state from its responsibilities—even the employees of Astra were approached as potential buyers. A purchaser was finally found in the form of a private consortium, and Astra became an independent company once again. Meanwhile, Astra's running deficit had cost the state millions of kroner.

The company's new board members included Erik Kistner and Richard Julin, a merchant and a banker respectively, whose business acumen helped to stop Astra's seemingly endless losses. In 1927 Bîrje Gabrielsson became company president; he remained in this position until 1957. The new hierarchy reorganized many of Astra's operations. The most important of

these changes allowed for the formation of the company's own distribution network. In just a few years the company was again profitable.

With the establishment of research and development facilities in the 1930s, Astra began to create more innovative products. Hepaforte, marketed in 1937, offered treatment for sufferers of pernicious anemia. Another important drug to emerge from Astra's laboratories was Nitropent, a medication for angina pectoris.

Astra's growth during the years prior to World War II resulted not only from its development of new products but also from its aggressive expansion and acquisition strategy. By 1940, company subsidiaries were operating in Finland, Latvia, Stockholm, and Hässleholm.

Restricted imports and shortages of raw materials during World War II placed Astra's products at a premium, and once again profits increased. The company constructed a new modern central laboratory and established a subsidiary to supervise the management of, and distribution to, Astra's numerous branch offices. The company established new subsidiaries in Denmark, Argentina, and the United States.

Development of Xylocaine Spurs Post-World War II Growth

In the postwar years a number of successful pharmaceuticals emerged from Astra's laboratories. Ferrigen, an iron preparation, and Sulfadital, a sulfa medication, were two products of many that were well received in the marketplace. The most important of all Astra's products developed during this period was Xylocaine, a local anesthetic that even today remains one of Astra's most popular products. Yet Xylocaine might never have happened if it had not been for Astra's strong relationship with the academic community and its commitment to research.

In 1943 two chemists from the University of Stockholm, Nils Lofgren and Bengt Lundqvist, approached Astra with a discovery they thought worth further investigation. The chemists had offered their compound to other companies, but only Astra demonstrated the ultimate interest of financial support. After five years of clinical testing in Astra's laboratories, Xylocaine appeared on the market, and its immediate success confirmed the chemists' and Astra's belief that they had produced the best local anesthetic available. Xylocaine's quality was soon recognized in foreign markets as well, and Astra's reputation as one of the world's most important pharmaceutical manufacturers grew accordingly. By 1984, local anesthetics constituted 24 percent of Astra's total group sales, with Xylocaine alone contributing SKr 696 million.

The worldwide production of Xylocaine began in earnest during the 1950s, and during that decade Astra broadened its overseas activities with an international network of subsidiaries and foreign licensees. Domestically, Astra consolidated its holdings to forestall the problems usually associated with quick growth, overhauled its pharmaceutical line to remove any unprofitable products, and confined all drug manufacturing to the Södertälje plant. The company continued to modernize its facilities and increase the size of its sales organization. By far the most important of Astra's measures during this period was its significant increase in research and development spending. As a result of this commitment, the company produced a number of successful new products throughout the 1950s, including Secergan (an anti-ulcer medication), Ascoxal (a treatment for oral infections), Jectofer (an injectable iron preparation), and Citanest (another local anesthetic).

Global Expansion in 1960s, 1970s

Throughout the 1960s Astra continued to expand both at home and abroad. The company acquired a manufacturer of nutritional products and a distributor of medical supplies. It created and built new operations in Western Europe, South and Central America, and Australia. It joined with England's Beecham Research Laboratories in an attempt to develop synthetic penicillins. By 1983, 80 percent of Astra's sales were generated from overseas markets.

By the 1970s Astra's diverse activities required the company to form separate divisions. In addition to the variety of drugs developed in the past, the pharmaceutical division now manufactured cardiovascular and anti-asthmatic drugs. The chemical products division produced agricultural products, nutritional products, cleansers, and recreational items. The varia division was responsible for medical equipment and rust prevention products. By the end of the decade, however, Astra announced that it would henceforth concentrate solely on the production of pharmaceuticals and, as a result, the company sold all of its other holdings.

Re-Emphasis on Pharmaceuticals in 1980s

With a renewed commitment to the manufacture of pharmaceuticals, Astra's unique and highly efficient research units emerged as the company's strongest assets. One notable pharmaceutical to emerge from Astra's laboratories in the 1980s was Seloken, now a very successful medication for heart disease. By 1984 Astra's three most important products—Seloken, Xylocaine and Bricanyl (a bronchodilator)—grew to generate over half the company's revenues; specifically, Seloken would become Astra's best-selling drug as well as one of the best-selling medications in the world.

The development of several new drugs to treat viral infections, gastrointestinal agents, and the central nervous system helped propel Astra's pre-tax earnings over the one billion kroner mark in 1985. Sales of the asthma drug Pulmicort helped propel total revenues to over SKr6.2 billion in 1988, by which time pre-tax earnings had risen to SKr1.5 billion.

Though Astra's financial performance was beginning to attract the attention of investors around the world, a core group of stockholders remained dissatisfied. Sweden's well-to-do Wallenberg family, which owned a 10 percent stake in Astra, launched a search for a replacement for CEO and President Ulf Widengren. In 1988, they hired an unlikely candidate: 44-year-old chocolatier Håkan Mogren. Mogren turned the company's former marketing program on its head, rescinding licenses and instead beefing up Astra's own distribution and sales organization. He established subsidiaries where there had previously been licensees, and added nearly 1,000 sales representatives worldwide by the end of 1990. Mogren also led a fundamental

shift in the corporate culture. As he told *Forbes* magazine's Richard Morais in 1997, "We had to turn from an inferiority complex—where we licensed out [drug inventions]—to self-confidence and the ambition to be a true global player. It was an emotional change."

Mogren chose a tough market for his first outing, launching the anti-ulcer drug Losec in competition with Glaxo Pharmaceuticals's best-selling Zantac. The battle between these two drugs was waged in doctor's offices and regulatory agencies as well as research labs, as salespeople, lobbyists, and scientists from the two companies dueled for sales and market share. Fortunately, Astra enjoyed a close relationship with longtime U.S. distributor Merck, which became an important ally in the competition, playing an especially vital role in convincing the U.S. Food & Drug Administration to approve Losec as a first-tier ulcer treatment. In his first two years at the helm, Mogren boosted sales by nearly 50 percent, from SKr6.3 billion to SKr9.4 billion, and increased pretax earnings by SKr1 billion. It was only the beginning.

Transformation Under Mogren in Early 1990s

The new leader intensified his transformation of Astra in the early 1990s, propelling the company into the ranks of the pharmaceutical industry's fastest growth vehicles. Mogren more than doubled the sales force from about 3,000 in 1990 to nearly 7,000 by mid-decade and boosted the company's roster of subsidiaries to 40 nations worldwide. These assertive moves succeeded in increasing the company's sales and income at a truly astonishing rate. Total sales quadrupled, from SKr9.4 billion in 1990 to nearly SKr39 billion in 1996, while pre-tax net mushroomed fivefold, from SKr2.5 billion to over SKr13 billion. Though the employee roster burgeoned from about 8,800 to nearly 20,000 during the period, productivity at the "self-confident" multinational grew even faster. As measured in terms of annual sales per employee, productivity doubled from SKr1 million to SKr2 million.

Losec became the world's top-selling drug in 1996, with an estimated 200 million prescriptions and US$3.5 billion revenues. Astra hoped to double the drug's market share by the end of the 1990s. But with the ulcer treatment's patents nearing expiration (termination dates ranged from 2001 in the United States to 2010 in other nations), Astra ramped up its research and development budgets from less than SKr2 billion in 1990 to over SKr7 billion in 1996. The investments paid off with six new pharmaceuticals scheduled for launch in 1997, including the Oxis Turbuhaler asthma treatment; Naropin, a derivative of Xylocaine that merged a local anesthetic with painkilling qualities; MUSE, a treatment for impotence; and the anti-hypertensive Atacand. While continuing to pursue its historically successful drug derivation strategy, Astra also aimed to add new therapeutic concentrations to its repertoire—gastrointestinal, respiratory, cardiovascular, pain control, anti-infective, and central nervous system—by 2010.

Principal Subsidiaries

Astra Arcus AB; Astra Draco AB; Astra Hässel AB; Astra Pain Control AB; Astra Pharmaceutical Production AB; Astra Production Chemicals AB; Astra Production Liquid Products AB;

Astra Production Tablets AB; A.S.P. S.A. (France); Astra S.A. Productos Farmacéuticos y Químicos (Argentina); Astra Pharmaceuticals Pty Ltd. (Australia); Astra Ges.m.b.H. (Austria); N.V. Astra pharmaceuticals S.A. (Belgium); Astra Química e Farmacêutica Ltda. (Brazil); Astra Pharma Inc. (Canada); Astra (Wuxi) Pharmaceutical Co. Ltd. (China); Astra Danmark A/S (Denmark); Suomen Astra Oy (Finland); Laboratoires Astra France; Astra GmbH (Germany); Astra Hellas S.A. (Greece); Astra Pharmaceuticals (HK) Ltd. (Hong Kong); Astra Pharmaceuticals (Ireland) Ltd.; Astra Farmaceutici S.p.A. (Italy); Astra Japan Ltd.; Yoshitomi-Satra Ltd (50%); Astra Luxembourg S.A.R.L.; Astra Pharmaceutical (Malaysia) SDN BHD; Astra Mexico S.A. de C.V.; Astra Pharmaceutica B.V. (Netherlands); Astra Pharmaceuticals (New Zealand) Ltd.; Astra Norge AS (Norway); Astra Pharmaceuticals (Philippines) Inc.; Astra Protuguesa Lda; Astra Pharmaceuticals (Singapore) Pte Ltd.; Astra Korea Ltd. (South Korea); Laboratorio Astra España, S.A.; Astra Läkemedel AB; Draco Läkemedel AB/Tika Läkemedel AB; Hässle Läkemedel AB; Astra Pharmaceutica AG (Switzerland); Astra Pharmaceutical (Taiwan) Ltd.; Astra (Thai) Ltd.; Astra Pharmaceuticals Ltd. (United Kingdom); Astra USA, Inc.; Astra Export & Trading AB; Astra Pharmaceuticals, s.r.o. (Czech Republic); Astra Pharmaceuticals Kft. (Hungary); Astra Pharmaceuticals (Poland) Sp.z.o.o.; Astra Pharmaceuticals (Pty) Ltd. (South Africa); Astra Tech AB. *Principal Affiliates:* Astra Merck, Inc. (United States) (50%); Astra-IDL Limited (India) (26%).

Further Reading

"Astra Adds Muscle in the U.S.," *Business Week,* November 14, 1994, p. 47.

Blackledge, Cath, "Glaxo/Astra Plot Courses for Success," *ECN-European Chemical News,* November 20, 1995, pp. 26–27.

Blanton, Kimberly, "New Astra CEO Makes Changes," *Boston Globe,* May 14, 1996, p. 39.

"Harassment Suit Against Astra Chief Is Dismissed," *New York Times,* May 29, 1997, p. D3.

Moore, Stephen D., "Astra's Successful Ulcer Drug May Become Bellyache," *The Wall Street Journal,* November 26, 1996, p. B4.

Morais, Richard S. "The Confidence Man," *Forbes,* May 5, 1997, pp. 116–17.

Stevenson, Richard W., "A Certain Glow on Sweden's Astra," *New York Times,* November 22, 1992, pp. 3–13.

"Too Much Acid," *The Economist,* March 30, 1991, pp. 82–83.

—updated by April D. Gasbarre

Authentic Fitness Corp.

6040 Bandini Boulevard
Commerce, California 90040
U.S.A.
(213) 726-1262
Fax: (213) 721-3613
Web site: http://www.speedo.com

Public Company
Incorporated: 1990 as Authentic Fitness Corp.
Employees: 2,008
Sales: $309.6 million (1996)
Stock Exchanges: New York
SICs: 2329 Men's/Boys' Clothing, Not Elsewhere
    Classified; 2339 Women's/Misses' Outerwear, Not
    Elsewhere Classified; 5651 Family Clothing Stores

A market leader in the swimwear industry, Authentic Fitness Corp. manufactures and sells swimwear through its own stores and to other retail operators, deriving the bulk of its sales from its widely recognized Speedo label. For years, Speedo was owned by women's lingerie maker Warnaco Group, but in 1990 Speedo and the rest of the Warnaco Group's activewear division was sold to Linda J. Wachner and other investors. The result was Authentic Fitness Corp., an offshoot company with Speedo at its core. Wachner, who also served as chief executive officer of Warnaco while she headed Authentic Fitness, transformed Speedo into a retail concept, opening a chain of stores throughout the United States and in selected foreign locations. As the number of Speedo stores proliferated, Wachner strengthened Authentic Fitness by acquiring other swimwear labels such as Cole, Catalina, Oscar de la Renta, and Anne Cole. By the late 1990s, Authentic Fitness operated roughly 150 Speedo stores.

Wachner and Authentic Fitness's Formation

The formation of Authentic Fitness represented one astute accomplishment in a long series of shrewd business moves effected by the company's creator, the lionized Linda J. Wach-ner, who made an indelible mark in an area of the business world predominantly populated by male executives. Wachner, in fact, was alone in the upper echelons of corporate America, standing as the only female CEO in the *Fortune* 500 and the only female to preside over two New York Stock Exchange companies. Not surprisingly, Wachner ascended to such lofty heights by acting aggressively, demonstrating a high degree of determination and decisiveness that sparked her unprecedented rise in the apparel industry. Her singular distinction in an exclusively male domain was a function of her will to win. She was a "savvy negotiator," pundits noted. A "shrewd operator," others remarked. "Wachner," one fashion consultant said, "is like Alexander the Great—she's chosen a very weak marketplace to become the big player."

Wachner, described by a member of the business press as the "diminutive, gray-haired apparel veteran," registered her first major coup in 1986 by taking over the floundering Warnaco Group. It was from this bold move that the foundation for Authentic Fitness's birth was gained. Wachner, who had started her career as an assistant department store buyer during the 1960s, held considerable sway by the 1980s, enough to launch a hostile takeover of the Warnaco Group. Warnaco, which manufactured, among other apparel products, women's lingerie and men's shirts, was in deep trouble at the time, staggering under the suffocating weight of $600 million of debt and sporting a balance sheet that translated into a negative net worth. Despite its myriad problems, Warnaco was Wachner's prize, and she took to her commanding position over the fortunes of the company firmly resolved to turn the struggling enterprise around. This she promptly did, orchestrating a turnaround that earned the accolades of industry analysts. Warnaco's debt was whittled down and its $425 million in sales were boosted up during the ensuing decade, transforming a beleaguered business into a billion-dollar corporation. Wachner achieved her remarkable results by expanding internationally and significantly broadening the distribution channels of Warnaco's business, thereby freeing the company from its dependence on department stores for sales and opening up avenues of growth in the mass market. As this push overseas and into new distribution channels was underway, Wachner also superintended a massive overhaul of Warnaco's many businesses, shedding those properties that were unprofitable and divesting those that could give the company much-needed cash. It was during this exodus of Warnaco businesses that the stage for Authentic Fitness's entrance into the business world was set.

As the 1990s began, the economic climate in the United States was beginning to display the anemic characteristics that would pock the early years of the decade as a time of economic recession. Credit was increasingly hard to come by, and Warnaco needed cash quickly to meet maturing debts. One by one, a procession of Warnaco businesses made their exit, but the company's board of directors and Wachner disagreed on the fate of one business, Warnaco's money-losing swimwear business. With Speedo swimwear at its core, Warnaco's swimwear business was grouped within Warnaco's activewear division, a facet of the overall Warnaco enterprise that the company's directors deemed dispensable. Wachner disagreed, deciding that the swimwear business still had enough potential to keep. Unable to convince Warnaco's directors to retain the swimwear business, Wachner enlisted the financial support of General Electric Credit Corp. and venture capitalists Pentland Ventures Ltd. and in 1990 purchased Warnaco's entire activewear division for $85 million.

The activewear division, which included Speedo and White Stag skiwear, was christened Authentic Fitness Corp. in 1990. Wachner served as CEO of both the newly formed Authentic Fitness and its former parent Warnaco, guiding each toward recovery in distinct directions. For Warnaco, Wachner's panacea was geographic expansion and a headlong move into the mass market; for Authentic Fitness, Wachner's prescription was different, its essence revealed when she took the activewear manufacturer public one year after taking Warnaco public. Authentic Fitness debuted on the New York Stock Exchange at $7 per share in June 1992, when Wachner announced her plans to transform the widely recognized Speedo label into a retail concept. Initially, Wachner's plans for opening Speedo retail outlets were relatively modest. Five stores were to be opened during a six-month span that began in November 1992 when the first Speedo store opened. Wachner's plans quickly escalated after initial success, however, and the ensuing years would witness a prodigious spate of Speedo store openings throughout the United States and on foreign soil.

Speedo Retail Begins in 1992

The first Speedo outlet opened in Los Angeles, an 1,800-square-foot store that featured a complete line of Speedo swimwear and Speedo Authentic Fitness, a new line of activewear designed to be worn in or out of water. Inside, diving mannequins, a seven-foot cascading waterfall, and ceiling decor that replicated an upside-down swimming pool—complete with pool markings, ladders, and tile—lent an aquatic theme to the store. Patrons quickly lined up in front of the Los Angeles Speedo store, the first of five units to be opened by June 1993. Each of these five units were to serve as, in the company's words, "merchandising laboratories" for Authentic Fitness's wholesale division, providing executives with up-to-date information on the buying patterns of the public.

As work was underway to establish five Speedo stores during the first half of 1993, Wachner displayed her talents as a

dealmaker by adding important new lines of apparel to dilute Authentic Fitness's overwhelming dependence on the Speedo label to drive sales. The company by this point derived roughly 80 percent of its sales from the sale of Speedo swimwear through its handful of retail outlets and to department stores, but by the end of 1993 the company could also look to other well-known labels for sales support. In August 1993, Wachner signed a licensing agreement with Oscar de la Renta Ltd. for a line of swimwear bearing the designer's label. The following month, Wachner added three strong properties, acquiring the Cole, Catalina, and Anne Cole swimwear labels, each at bargain prices obtained out of bankruptcy court. Also in September Wachner signed an exclusive licensing agreement to be the official sponsor at the 1996 Summer Olympics in Atlanta, rounding out a highly productive month for the 46-year-old CEO.

The string of momentous events in September 1993 did not come to end with the announcement of the Summer Olympics deal, however. While new labels were being added to Authentic Fitness's portfolio during the month, Wachner developed decidedly more ambitious expansion plans for Speedo specialty shops, resolving to open 100 mall-based retail stores during the ensuing two years. The expansion plans called for 10 new stores by the end of October 1993, 40 more stores by the end of 1994, and another 50 stores by the end of 1995, which was expected to provide additional sales of more than $100 million on top of the $133 million collected in 1993.

Month by month, new Speedo stores opened, each adorned with the same decor as the company's first store in Los Angeles. As planned, the increased exposure of the Speedo name through store openings breathed new life into the venerable yet struggling Speedo brand Wachner took charge of in 1990. By the spring of 1994, when there were 15 Speedo stores in operation, the Speedo swimwear line held a hefty 50 percent share of the market for competitive swimwear and its men's water shorts garments held 30 percent of the department store market, up from the 20 percent market share held in 1990. Wachner's strategy was working. She was gaining a dominant position in what characteristically had been a weak marketplace through resolute expansion, and Authentic Fitness was the instrument she used to establish jurisdiction. As the company entered the mid-1990s, it was growing by leaps and bounds.

Between 1993 and 1995, when the frenzied rush to open 100 Speedo stores was underway, Authentic Fitness's revenues doubled as Wachner displayed the qualities that elicited her comparison to Alexander the Great. She was stealing market share from smaller competitors in the fragmented swimwear market by assembling a broad collection of brands that covered nearly every segment of the market. By early 1996, there were 100 Speedo stores in operation, fulfilling the objective Wachner had laid out in late 1993, but she did not stop there. The expansion of Speedo stores continued after the 100th unit was opened. Meanwhile, Wachner set herself to the task of completing her next bold maneuver, and that was the reunion of Warnaco and Authentic Fitness into one corporation.

Failed 1996 Merger

Separated since 1990, Warnaco and Authentic Fitness had each recorded meaningful growth under the stewardship of

Wachner, blossoming into vibrant enterprises that were textbook examples of the strength of astute marketing. By early 1996, Wachner wanted to reunite her two success projects under one corporate banner, declaring that the merger would put together "two powerful growth stories and provide the benefits to shareholders." In June 1996, the first step toward the merger was taken when Warnaco proposed an exchange of stock worth an estimated $500 million for Authentic Fitness. The following month, the board of directors of each company agreed to the proposal and a merger agreement was signed that designated Authentic Fitness as a future wholly owned subsidiary of Warnaco. Before the month of July was through, however, the merger was terminated, shelved indefinitely as Authentic Fitness was forced to deal with an unexpected problem.

The merger agreement was terminated because of financial difficulties experienced by Authentic Fitness during the summer of 1996. The company's largest customer, Herman's Sporting Goods, had declared bankruptcy in May 1996 and consequently tarnished the luster Authentic Fitness exuded. As the merger grew imminent, it became clear that Authentic fitness was headed for a financial loss for the fourth fiscal quarter, and the merger was aborted as a result. Although the loss of the company's largest customer was sufficient to scrub the plans for the merger, the financial loss was only a hitch in Authentic Fitness's otherwise glowing record of growth. As the company plotted its course for the late 1990s, with Wachner at the helm, moving past the temporary setback caused by Herman's Sporting Goods' failure occupied the attention of Authentic Fitness executives. The expansion of Speedo stores continued on and the company's commanding market share remained intact, fueling confidence for the years ahead.

Principal Subsidiaries

Speedo Authentic Fitness, Inc.

Further Reading

Barman, Sharon, "Wachner Takes on the World," *Working Woman,* February 1995, p. 11.

Brown, Christie, "The Body-Bending Business," *Forbes,* September 11, 1995, p. 196.

Fiedelholtz, Sara, "Authentic Braves the Waters," *WWD,* November 3, 1993, p. 10.

Kellin, Dana, "Speedo's First Fitness Store to Open in Los Angeles," *WWD,* December 2, 1992, p. 13.

Monget, Karyn, "Speedo Means Speed at Retail," *WWD,* May 25, 1994, p. 11.

——, "The Consensus on Wachner: She's Doing OK," *WWD,* December 16, 1996, p. 8.

Rutberg, Sidney, "Warnaco, Authentic Fitness Eye Becoming One Again," *WWD,* June 7, 1996, p. 2.

Ryan, Thomas J., "Wachner Sees New Growth for Warnaco, Authentic Fitness," *WWD,* April 20, 1994, p. 18.

Seckler, Valerie, "Warnaco Sweetens Offer, Authentic's Board OK's It," *WWD,* July 15, 1996, p. 2.

——, "Warnaco-Authentic: What Went Wrong with Wachner's Deal," *WWD,* July 31, 1996, p. 1.

Serwer, Andrew E., "A Wachnerian Soap Opera: Linda W. Hunts for CEO, Loses Accountant: What Gives?," *Fortune,* May 12, 1997, p. 22.

Siegel, Jeff, "Authentic Fitness Sets Big Retail Expansion Plans," *Daily News Record,* September 24, 1993, p. 3.

—Jeffrey L. Covell

Autologic Information International, Inc.

1050 Rancho Conejo Blvd.
Thousand Oaks, California 91360
U.S.A.
(805) 498-9611
Fax: 805) 499-1167
Web site: http://www.autoiii.com; http://autologic.com

Public Company
Incorporated: 1996
Employees: 450
Sales: $86.2 million (1996)
Stock Exchanges: NASDAQ
SICs: 3555 Printing Trades Machinery; 2791 Typesetting

Autologic Information International, Inc. (AIII) is a world leader in the design, manufacture, marketing, distribution, and servicing of computer-based document production and publishing systems that automate the pre-press production steps of newspaper and magazine publishers, commercial printers, and other printing and publishing facilities. Based in Thousand Oaks, California, AIII is the result of a merger between two long-time leaders in pre-press and publishing systems, Autologic and Information International. Under the merger agreement, finalized in January 1996, former Autologic parent Volt Information Sciences, Inc. retains 59 percent ownership in AIII. Volt CEO and chairman William Shaw also serves as AIII's chairman and CEO. Dennis Doolittle, former president of Autologic, serves as AIII's vice chairman and COO, while Alden Edwards, former Information International president, fills the presidency of AIII.

The combined company posted sales of $86 million in 1996, its first year of operation. In addition to its Thousand Oaks corporate headquarters, AIII operates headquarters in England, serving Europe, in Australia, serving the Asia-Pacific region, and in Rio de Janeiro, serving Latin America.

AIII designs, manufactures, and distributes a range of equipment targeted at two main branches of the printing and publishing industry, publishing pre-press and ad or document distribution. The company offers an integrated line of products designed to meet the variety of speed, size, output, and quality needs from the largest publishers to smaller commercial printers and in-house publishing facilities. AIII's line of integrated products enable the tracking and control of output systems, provide centralized data storage and management, and translation of the various data formats used in the printing and publishing industry. Products include raster image processors (RIPs), capstan and drum recorders, large-format color imagers, workflow management systems, including advertising management and output systems, electronic document delivery and distribution systems and other network management systems, and computer-to-plate (CTP) and press systems. The integrated, modular design of AIII's products allows the company to design company-specific, networked pre-press printing and publishing solutions.

AIII's APS Grafix RIP family, designed to operate through the Windows NT operating system running on Intel Pentium or Digital Alpha chips, as well as on Apple's PowerMac operating system, apply PostScript-language interpretation to raster image processing. The APS Grafix RIP allows for simultaneous ''ripping'' and imaging, and compressed image queuing, prioritizing, and online previewing. APS Grafix RIP documents may be routed through AIII's APS 32 Port Imager Hub to any of over 25 output platforms, including laser printers, DTP imagers, color drum recorders, and wide-format imagesetters, enabling a wide selection of resolution capabilities. The Imager Hub features 32 ports that can be configured with nearly any combination of input and output connections, from a single input/31 output setup to a 31 input/single output setup. The Imager Hub can also be configured to enable remote transmission up to 1.5 kilometers via fiber optic cables.

AIII offers a variety of imagers to meet the range of needs in the publishing and printing industry. The APS 3850 Laser Color Imager family features high-performance capstan laser imaging for large-scale production environments. The APS 3850 color imager family—which includes the APS 3850, the APS Aspen, the APS Aspen SST, and the APS Sierra—support color and black and white output resolutions ranging from 800×800 dots per inch up to 3600×3600 dots per inch. Output page sizes support widths up to 112 picas (18.6 inches) and lengths of 28 inches. Imaging can be performed at very high speeds, ranging from 24 inches per minute at 1000 × 1000 dots per inch to 70 inches per minute at 1000 × 1000 dots per inch.

The company's APS Colormaster Series, including the APS Colormaster HS, the APS Colormaster Magnum, and the APS Colormaster Mercury, are high-speed laser imagers specifically designed for high-end commercial-quality color output. Image areas range from 20 inches by 26 inches to 32.3 inches to 47.2 inches. Speeds range up to 18.8 inches per minute, on resolutions ranging from 1270 dots per inch to 5080 dots per inch. Other imagers in the AIII line include the APS 84ACS Laser Imager, which provides black-and-white and color output in resolutions ranging from 600 × 600 dots per inch to 3000 × 3000 dots per inch, pages widths up to 84 picas (14 inches), at speeds up to 22.5 square inches per minute at 1200 × 1200 dots per inch. The APS Typhoon 16 Laser Printer and the APS BX II Laser Printer provide black-and-white output at 600 × 600 dots per inch for the inexpensive printing of plain paper proofs, and are capable of printing up to 16 letter-sized pages per minute, with a rated capacity of 30,000 images per month. Other proof-quality imagers in the APS family are the APS Prosetter 1000, and the APS Oce Thermal Printer. Another member of the APS family is the APS Platemasters, which offer multiple-resolution laser printing to aluminum and polyester printing plates and silver halide-coated graphics arts film.

The company's workflow management tools include its Ad Manager and Output Manager software products. AIII's APSCOM automated workflow system is designed specifically for the pre-press industry, providing multi-format, multiple-site document delivery.

In addition to these products, AIII continues to add to its product offerings. In March 1997, the company, in conjunction with Harlequin, a software provider to the pre-press industry, announced the conclusion of a successful test of the new TIFF/IT-P1 (Tag Image File Format for Image Technology) data file format, designed to supplement or replace the PostScript format. In June 1997, AIII signed an agreement with Israel-based Scitex Corporation Ltd. to distribute that company's Dolev 4news imagesetter as the APS 4news Laser Imager. AIII also announced a September 1997 release date for an interface linking the APS 4news with the company's standard imaging architecture.

Merging Pre-Press Pioneers in 1996

Both Autologic and Information International had roots going back to the early days of electronic pre-press publishing systems before the two companies agreed to merge in January 1996. Autologic had operated for much of its history as a subsidiary to Volt Information Sciences, Inc., a conglomeration

of companies, including temporary employment services, publishing, and computer services, led by founder William Shaw. In the 1950s, Shaw, graduated from Brooklyn College, and brother Jerome went into business producing technical manuals for the U.S. military. The brothers originally outsourced page makeup and typesetting to another company. That company, however, was failing, and, in order to maintain their own business, the Shaws bought the other company. In 1964, the typesetting business was incorporated as Autologic, Inc.

Information International had incorporated two years earlier. Operating since the early 1950s, the company had been involved in the development of cathode ray tubes, and then became among the first to adapt CRT technology for use in typesetters and scanners for the publishing industry. By the 1960s, the printing and publishing industry had begun to incorporate newly emerging digital technology, replacing previous typesetting technologies. Cold type, representing the first generation of the new technology, used matrices to reproduce characters on photographic negatives on acetate film, replaced the 'hot metal' system, which required the setting of individual type characters. The second generation of typesetting technology also used photographic negatives, but introduced digital technology to create the type characters. Using computers, characters were scanned in and displayed as dots and lines on CRTs, which could then be outputted to paper.

By the mid-1960s, the industry evolved into the third generation of typesetting technology. The first to be fully digital, the new technology did away with the use of photographic images and instead used disk-based characters and symbols that could be created and reproduced entirely within the computer, before being displayed to CRTs for reproduction on paper. The new technology allowed a much wider range of typesetting faces and sizes, at speeds up to 10 times faster than the previous generation. Autologic quickly came to dominate the third-generation typesetting technology, supplying machinery to the country's largest newspaper and magazine publishers. The third generation machines soon switched to minicomputer platforms, introduced in the 1970s. They remained extremely expensive—with prices ranging as high as $1 million—and were thus available only to large-scale publishers.

Autologic continued to lead the industry through the 1970s. In the mid-1970s, advances in microcircuitry, produced by Intel Corporation, led to new opportunities in typesetting equipment. In 1979, the company introduced its groundbreaking APS-Micro 5 CRT digital typesetter. The Micro 5, which incorporated Intel's 86/12A single-board computer based on the 8086 microprocessor, represented one of the first machines to be priced under $25,000, placing the digital typesetter technology within reach of small and medium-sized printing operations. The Micro 5 was powerful, capable of inputting at speeds up to 10,000 characters per second and outputting set type at 1,000 lines per minute, while offering resolutions of more than 3,600 lines per inch.

By 1983, the company had sold more than 350 Micro 5s and had sales offices located across the country. Customers included such papers as the *New York Times,* the *Los Angeles Times,* and startup *USA Today.* However, a slump in the computer industry in the early 1980s soon caught up to Autologic, and in 1985 the company was forced to cut back on its employment. The following year, Autologic introduced a new line of imaging systems, the APS Micro 6, which included page image processors and laser images, providing text and graphic processing. The APS Micro 6 line proved quickly successful, and, added to the APS Micro 5 and the earlier, larger APS 4, sales of Autologic systems reached more than 1,000 by the end of the decade. While Autologic was building its typesetting and imaging business, Information International was recording its own successes, including building a leadership position in the introduction of early facsimile systems, and pioneering the use of workstation technology for the use in display advertising production.

Meanwhile, a new technology was finding its way to the publishing industry. The arrival of the first personal computers introduced the new era of desktop publishing. Autologic, however, responded only slowly to this new market, allowing other companies, such as Micrographix and Linotype to take the lead in this market. At the time, Adobe Inc. was introducing a new type format, called PostScript, which soon became an industry standard. In 1989, Autologic received licensing rights to use Adobe's PostScript interpreter for its newspaper typesetting and other laser imaging systems. The following year, Autologic introduced a line of integrated products, adding its PostScript Page Image Processor and Graphics Integrator to its APS Micro 6 systems. Information International also began shifting its products, which included the 3850 Grafix imager family, from a proprietary format to the standardized PostScript language around this time.

At around this time, Volt, Autologic, and Information International began discussing a possible merger of Autologic's and Information International's imaging operations. These early talks proved fruitless, yet pointed toward a move toward consolidation within the industry. In 1992, Autologic entered negotiations with DuPont Co. to purchase that company's Camex Inc. subsidiary's display ad systems and customer business. The two companies reached agreement for Volt to purchase all outstanding shares of Camex in December 1992, with the Camex operations to be grouped under Autologic. That deal, however, collapsed just two weeks later, at the beginning of January 1993. Then, at the end of that month, Information International announced that it had agreed to purchase Camex.

Both Autologic and Information International had been hit by the worldwide recession of the early 1990s; in 1992, Information International had been forced to reduce its staff. Competition in the industry was heightening, with the shift to PostScript formats tightening profit margins. At last, in July 1995, Volt and Information International reached an agreement to merge Autologic's operations into Information International. The merger called for Volt to receive around 59 percent of Information International's stock, effectively making the new company, called Autologic Information International, a subsidiary of Volt. In keeping, William Shaw was named chairman and CEO of the company, while former Information International CEO Charles Ying was named to the new company's board of directors. As Information International had been a public company, AIII remained public, trading on the NASDAQ stock exchange. The merger, worth about $35 million, was completed in January 1996.

The new company had combined 1995 revenues of $104 million. In February of that year, AIII began a restructuring designed to eliminate redundant products and staff, and to streamline expenses, freeing up resources for research and development. The first phase of the restructuring resulted in a layoff of nearly 100 employees, reducing the company's payroll to 450. Plans also called to consolidate the combined companies operations at the former Autologic headquarters in Thousand Oaks. By the end of 1996, with much of the consolidation of the two companies' operations completed, AIII posted revenues of more than $89 million.

Principal Subsidiaries

Digiflex; Xitron.

Further Reading

''Digital Technology Is Slashing Cost of Typesetting Machines,'' *New York Times*, September 8, 1980, p. 5.

''Integrated Pages for Newspapers,'' *Graphics Arts Monthly*, June 1990, p. 104.

Jones, John A., ''Volt Information Sciences Shaping Up in Communications,'' *Investor's Business Daily*, February 21, 1995, p. B14.

McNatt, Robert, ''Economy on Mend Giving Firm Voltage,'' *Crain's New York Business*, February 8, 1993, p. 3.

''Microcomputers Boost Typesetting,'' *Graphics Arts Monthly and The Printing Industry*, March 1983, p. 106.

Rosenberg, Jim, ''Autologic, Triple-I Merger Complete,'' *Editor & Publisher Magazine*, February 24, 1996, p. 36.

——, ''Autologic to Merge With Triple-I,'' *Editor & Publisher Magazine*, July 8, 1995, p. 28.

—M. L. Cohen

AUTOTOTE

Autotote Corporation

750 Lexington Avenue
New York, New York 10022
U.S.A.
(212) 754-2233
Fax: (212) 754-2372
Web site: http://www.autotote.com

Public Company
Incorporated: 1979 as Autotote Systems, Inc.
Employees: 935
Sales: $176.2 million (fiscal 1996)
Stock Exchanges: American
SICs: 7372 Prepackaged Software; 7373 Computer
    Integrated Systems Design; 7999 Amusement and
    Recreation Services, Not Elsewhere Classified

Autotote Corporation provides computerized wagering equipment, computer software, facilities management, and satellite broadcast services for parimutuel wagering at horse and dog racetracks, jai-alai frontons, government-sponsored lotteries, and legalized sports-betting facilities on four continents. It was, in 1996, the leading provider and operator to the racing industry. In 1993 Autotote became the exclusive licensed operator of almost all off-track wagering in Connecticut. The company suffered heavy losses in the mid-1990s, forcing it to sell its manufacturing facilities in 1995 and its casino/sports-wagering service business in 1996. In early 1997 it signed a letter of intent to sell its European lottery business.

Autotote Before 1992

Autotote Corporation began as Autotote Systems, a firm established in 1979 by Thomas H. Lee, a Boston venture capitalist and specialist in leveraged buyouts who purchased Autotote Limited from ATL Limited of Sydney, Australia. Based in Newark, Delaware, Autotote Systems designed, engineered, manufactured, marketed, and operated computerized parimutuel wagering systems in the form of totalizators, or tote boards, which calculate and display odds and potential payouts for racetrack bettors. The company maintained a warehouse and manufacturing facilities as well as its offices in Newark. It also had manufacturing facilities in Hatfield, Pennsylvania, and a sales office in Konstanz, West Germany. Net sales rose from $5.4 million in fiscal 1980 (the period from the firm's inception in May 1979 to June 30, 1980) to $10.2 million in fiscal 1982. Net income increased from $124,000 to $970,000 over this period.

Autotote Systems had revenues of $36.2 million in fiscal 1989 and was supplying wagering equipment to some of the largest racing associations in the United States and more than 50 racetracks abroad when it merged in 1989 with United Tote, Inc. By this means United Tote, though smaller than Autotote, acquired all of Autotote's outstanding shares for $87.8 million in cash and securities. Together the two companies commanded almost half of the $92-million-a-year U.S. market for the manufacturing and servicing of totalizators. United Tote's owners thought they would run the business, but Autotote's owners conceived the transaction as a back-door method of taking their company public. Since Lee and his partners held the largest share in the combined company—36 percent—the president of Autotote, James H. Pierce, became president of United Tote.

The deal quickly unraveled when, despite assurance by lawyers from four major firms that there would be no problem with the merger, the U.S. Department of Justice filed suit against United Tote for violation of antitrust law. While the suit was in the courts it became impossible to integrate the operations of the two firms, except to discuss essential financial information. Moreover, one of the lenders who had made a bridge loan to finance the cash portion of the deal refused to refinance it when it ran into legal difficulties, and no other lender would step in to complete the transaction. Largely because of legal costs, increased interest payments, depreciation and amortization expenses from the acquisition, and delays in international sales, United Tote posted a loss of $2.7 million in fiscal 1990 (the year ended October 31, 1990) on revenues of $69.2 million.

A federal court decision in 1991 forced the dissolution of United Tote. Autotote Corp., founded in 1992, retained operations accounting for about 59 percent of the consolidated company's revenues, consisting of the principal totalizator unit and a Nevada sports/race-wagering business. A. Lorne Weil, a director and consultant to Autotote Systems since 1982, became chief executive officer of Autotote Corp., which assumed about $50 million of the consolidated company's long-term debt.

Expanded Operations, 1992–95

In fiscal 1992 Autotote had revenues of $48.4 million—two-thirds in the United States—and net income of $5.7 million. It was providing about 60 percent of the tote boards in the United States, receiving a percentage (about .5 percent) of the sum of wagers placed. Moreover, Autotote had become the leader in the field not only in on-track but also intertrack betting. In 1992 it won a contract to provide on-site betting parlors for all three major California racetracks, so that between races at one track patrons could bet on races being held at the other two. And the company was poised to introduce a new system, called Probe, that was the first fully integrated system not only for parimutuel betting but also video lotteries, keno, nonracing-sports betting, and any other form of legal betting involved with odds.

In 1993 Autotote was selected to operate Connecticut's off-track betting (OTB) system, which was being privatized. The company, which already was providing systems for keeping track of the Connecticut OTB bets, now took over operation of the betting parlors as well, paying the state a flat fee of about $20 million and making annual payments based on total dollars wagered. In the spring of 1995 it opened a $9-million, Las Vegas-style New Haven emporium called Sports Haven, where patrons could view and bet on races throughout North America and also patronize a bar wrapped around a cylindrical aquarium stocked with exotic sharks, dine at an upscale restaurant, dance the night away at a discotheque, or shop for sports memorabilia.

Autotote also was adding to its significant level of operations abroad. It signed a contract in 1992 to supply 10,000 lottery terminals to an Italian lottery based on horse racing. In June 1993 Autotote acquired the ETAG Group of Switzerland, a leading supplier of European computerized wagering systems, for $10.5 million, and in September of that year it completed its acquisition of Tele Control GmbH, an Austrian company providing lottery systems in Germany, Austria, the Netherlands, and Switzerland, and wagering systems for racetracks in Germany and Austria. In fiscal 1993 the company had net income of $9.5 million on revenues of $84.9 million.

In 1994 Autotote acquired Marvin H. Sugarman Productions Inc. and its affiliate, Racing Technology Inc., for 500,000 shares of common stock. Sugarman Productions was the largest simulcaster of live horse and greyhound racing events to OTB patrons in North America. And in January 1995 Autotote acquired certain assets of IDB Communications Group Inc.'s broadcast division for $13.5 million in cash and subleases for satellite transponders, or channels. A spokesman for Autotote said the transaction would allow it to telecast simultaneously races from more than 60 horse and dog tracks in North America.

Heavy Losses, 1994–96

By this time, however, Autotote was clearly sailing into troubled waters. Although its revenues climbed to $149 million in fiscal 1994, it lost $22.2 million and doubled its long-term debt to $144 million. Management cited, as factors contributing to the loss, charges of about $3.8 million resulting from closing the Newark manufacturing facility and discontinuing certain product lines; a $4.3 million writeoff of certain assets principally related to domestic and overseas projects; costs of $2.8 million attributed to a strike by employees of a subsidiary; and an extraordinary noncash writeoff of $4.2 million associated with the company's repayment of its prior senior bank credit facility, as well as payments for the acquisitions made in 1993 and 1994.

Autotote's stock fell from a year-long high of $26.50 a share to a low of $4.50 in February 1995, when the company admitted it was not in compliance with its credit covenants. Nine banks refused to lend the company additional funds for violation of these covenants in lending agreements. Several shareholders filed a class-action suit in federal court, charging that Autotote's officers and directors had violated certain securities laws. A settlement in 1996 for $11.8 million in cash and preferred stock did not require any admission of guilt on the company's part.

Thomas DeFazio was appointed chief financial officer of Autotote in May 1995 and president and chief operating officer later in the year. He restored the company's relations with its creditors and launched a restructuring program expected to save the company some $15 million by closing its North American lottery headquarters and its plant in Ballymahon, Ireland. In October DeFazio persuaded Autotote's subordinated debtholders to accept company shares instead of $2.2 million in interest payments that it could not meet.

Nevertheless, Autotote lost $49.9 million in fiscal 1995 on revenues of $153 million. The company attributed $11.6 million of the loss to a restructuring charge taken for the closing of the support facility for lottery operations in Owings Mills, Maryland, and the scaling back of certain international activities, including the closing of the Irish plant. The company also wrote off $6.6 million in investments and assets, including $2.7 million attributable to its Mexican video-gaming-machine contracts and $2.6 million attributable to European wagering terminals. Its long-term debt swelled to $166 million.

During fiscal 1996 Autotote reduced its long-term debt by $6 million and cut its loss to a still-substantial $34.2 million on revenues of $176.2 million. Its costs included a $6.6 million litigation-settlements charge. Autotote's stock dropped below $1 a share at one point during the year. In October 1996 the company sold its Autotote CBS Inc. sports-wagering subsidiary, which had provided systems to 107 of the 113 Nevada casinos and to the leading operator of sports-wagering facilities in Mexico. Three months later Autotote signed a letter of intent to sell its European lottery business, Tele Control, to Scientific Games Holding Corp. for a price estimated at between $25 million and $30 million, using the proceeds to pay off bank debt.

Autotote's Operations in 1996

In 1996 Autotote's parimutuel wagering systems processed approximately two-thirds of the estimated $20-billion total racing-industry handle (betting volume). Its wagering systems and/or related equipment were installed at more than 100 racetracks in North America, including 10 of the 15 largest, and in more than 800 OTB betting parlors. These company systems were also in use in many of the largest racetracks and OTB parlors in Europe—including all French, German, and Austrian racetracks—Latin America, the Far East, and New Zealand, also in eight Atlantic City casinos. In addition, Autotote had installed about 1,300 video gaming machines in racetracks in West Virginia and Manitoba.

Autotote also was simulcasting live horse and greyhound racing events to approximately 50 racetracks and more than 850 OTB parlors throughout North America as well as in Atlantic City casinos. In its simulcasting operations, the company leased satellite transponders and owned decoders used to unscramble the transmission signal. Prior to its decision to sell its lottery operations abroad, Autotote was providing terminals for a nationwide Italian lottery based on horse racing and, with a European partner, designing and installing computer-based lottery systems in six German states. It had also been selling central processing systems and/or terminals for lotteries in Austria, Switzerland, the Netherlands, and Israel. In the United States, Autotote was operating the Connecticut lottery and providing services to the Massachusetts state lottery.

Of Autotote's revenues in 1996, services accounted for 78 percent and sales contracts for wagering equipment and software for the remaining 22 percent. The parimutuel group (including wagering and simulcasting systems, the Connecticut OTB, video gaming, and casino/sports wagering) accounted for 73 percent of revenues and lottery operations for the remaining 27 percent. The company's long-term debt was $159.7 million at the end of fiscal 1996. Officers and directors held about 26 percent of Autotote's common stock, with director Thomas H. Lee controlling nearly 13 percent.

Principal Subsidiaries

Autotote Communication Services, Inc.; Autotote Enterprises, Inc.; Autotote Keno Corporation; Autotote Management Corporation; Autotote Mexico, Ltd.; Autotote Products, Inc.; ETAG Electronic Totalisator AG (Switzerland); ETAG Electronic Totalisator GesMBH (Austria); Marvin H. Sugarman Productions, Inc.; Racing Technology, Inc.

Further Reading

"Autotote Selling Off European Lottery Business," *New York Times,* January 15, 1997, p. D4.

Benson, Barbara, "Exec's Focused Course Improves Firm's Odds," *Crain's New York Business,* November 13, 1995, p. 15.

Berman, Phyllis, "Home on the Range," *Forbes,* November 9, 1992, pp. 113–14, 116, 118, 120.

Siklos, Richard, "Autotote Gambles on High-Tech High-Rollers," *Financial Post,* May 25, 1995, p. 5.

Simmons, Jacqueline, "Autotote Corp. Appoints New Finance Officer," *Wall Street Journal,* March 24, 1995, p. B4.

Welling, Kathryn M., "No-Name Stocks," *Barron's,* December 14, 1992, p. 15.

—Robert Halasz

Axel Springer Verlag AG

Axel-Springer-Platz 1
D-20350 Hamburg
Germany
49 40 347-22884
Fax: 49 40 347-25540
Web site: http://www.asv.de

Public Company
Incorporated: 1985
Employees: 12,646
Sales: DM4.14 billion (US$2.9 billion 1995)
Stock Exchanges: Frankfurt
SICs: 2711 Newspapers; 2721 Periodicals; 2750
Commercial Printing; 2731 Book Publishing; 2741
Miscellaneous Publishing

Over the course of its more than 50 years in business, Axel Springer Verlag AG has evolved from a publisher of local radio transcripts into Europe's largest publisher of newspapers and magazines. By the late 1990s, the company's media and communications holdings also included interests in radio; broadcast, cable and digital television; book publishing; premium telephony; and electronic information as well as a vast German distribution system. The company is an enduring monument to its founder, Axel Springer, who was an influential and controversial figure in German public life for nearly 40 years. Since his death in 1985, the company has been guided by his widow, Friede Springer, who with his family owns just over 50 percent of the company. Rival German media mogul Leo Kirch owned 35 percent of the conglomerate plus one share in 1996.

Post-World War II Origins and Early Development

Born in Hamburg in 1912, Axel Springer brought a lifetime of experience to his eponymous company, having worked in his father's firm, Hammerich & Lesser, a publisher of local newspapers, until it was closed by Joseph Goebbels in 1941. At the war's end, Springer was among a select group of well-con-nected publishers who were not stained by Nazism. In fact, Springer's politics would become a hallmark of his media empire. With permission from the Allied occupation leaders, Springer began in 1946 to publish the *Nordwestdeutsche Hefte*, a monthly magazine made up of transcripts of broadcasts on the radio station Nordwestdeutsche Rundfunk. In the same year he followed up with *Hîr Zu!*, a more populist publication providing radio program listings alongside articles for a family audience, which has since become a television listings magazine. In 1948 he launched his first newspaper, Germany's first evening daily, the *Hamburger Abendblatt*. Within just two years, the daily had grown to become Hamburg's top paper.

Springer was happy to take ideas from any source if they seemed likely to be workable and profitable. His most famous innovation, the daily *Bild Zeitung*, was launched in 1952 and was similar to the U.K.'s *Daily Mirror* in its tabloid style but not in politics. It soon became, and has remained, the largest selling daily in Europe, with a circulation of about six million at its zenith. Springer was careful not to over-specialize, and in 1953 balanced *Bild Zeitung* by acquiring the quality daily, *Die Welt*, which had been established in April 1946 by the British occupation authorities. Heinrich Schulte, who joined *Die Welt* as publishing manager in 1948, had begun to diversify by printing other publications, including Springer's *Hîr Zu!* But with circulation falling and debts mounting in the early 1950s, *Die Welt* sought a buyer, and in 1952 found Axel Springer more than willing. Not coincidentally, it was the sudden withdrawal of Springer's printing contracts with *Die Welt* that had precipitated the crisis; his bid was made in secret and was anywhere from DM2 million to DM6 million; and it is widely believed that what tipped the scales in his favor was the intervention of the Christian Democratic Chancellor Konrad Adenauer. The British allowed the deal to go through on condition that Springer share ownership with an independent trust. In any event, the trust never had more than 25 percent of the shares, and was abolished in 1970.

Springer's choice as chief editor was Hans Zehrer, who had been editor of the extreme right-wing, but not Nazi, paper *Die Tat* before World War II, and who had been prevented from becoming editor in 1946 after protests from the U.K.'s Labour government and from the Social Democrats then governing Hamburg. Springer concentrated on building up *Bild Zeitung*, launching its Sunday version, *Bild am Sonntag*, in 1956. Under Zehrer's control, *Die Welt* began publishing a Berlin edition in 1955, and promoted the notion that Germany could be reunified as a neutral state at peace with both East and West. Perhaps surprisingly, this divergence from the 1950s Cold War consensus did not damage circulation, which rose from 165,000 in 1954 to 217,000 five years later. Heinrich Schulte still retained some influence at the paper, and resisted Springer's pressure to push the paper toward being a vehicle for Springer's views right up until his death in 1963.

By 1959 Zehrer's enthusiasm for neutrality was wearing off in the face of Soviet intransigence, and Springer himself, who had always been staunchly anti-communist and had always insisted that his publications place quotation marks around the term "German Democratic Republic," began to get more involved in the paper. That year saw the laying of the foundation stone for the Springer group's new offices in Berlin, in the heart of the prewar newspaper district, intended as a symbol of the continuity of German culture in the face of the Soviet threat. The move to Berlin was not purely idealistic, but reflected the takeover in the same year of the publishing group Ullstein, which had been founded in 1877 and which published two local daily papers, *Berliner Morgenpost* and *B.Z.* (originally *Berliner Zeitung*), as well as books. The Springer group's headquarters continued to be in Hamburg, rather than Berlin, until 1967. Throughout the crisis over the building of the Berlin Wall, Springer and his papers were active in demanding a strong response from the West, including a ban on exports from the federal republic to East Germany, a proposal his Christian Democrat friends in the federal government did not carry out.

Ascent to Dominance in 1960s

By 1964 Springer controlled more than 40 percent of daily papers sold in Germany, more than 80 percent of Sunday papers, 45 percent of magazines for young people, and 48 percent of radio and TV listings publications. *Bild Zeitung*'s circulation rose to 5.3 million under its new young editor Peter Boenisch and *Die Welt* was at the height of its influence and circulation—290,000. Its reputation as a highly partisan right-wing organ was further enhanced by the appointment of Dr. Herman Starke as editor after Zehrer's death in 1966, as allegations about his past record of pro-Nazi and anti-Semitic views led to an international scandal.

From 1967 onward, the "Extra-Parliamentary Opposition" (APO) began protesting against the American incursion into Vietnam and the conservative values that dominated West Germany. Springer's delivery vans were blocked, turned over, or set afire and the APO demanded that Springer be expropriated. The protests reached their peak in April 1968 when the most famous APO leader, Rudi Dutschke, was shot and seriously injured by a deranged reader of *Bild Zeitung*, and discount sales of *Die Welt* to students collapsed, along with sales to teachers, so that by 1970 the paper was losing money for the first time since Springer had taken it over. Springer's own reaction to the campaign, in a speech he gave in 1972, was to claim that the radicals had been inspired by the East German leader, Walter Ulbricht—whom Dutschke and his comrades

hated as much as they hated Springer—and to portray his company as the guardian of the federal republic's economic and political freedoms. It might be noted at this point that both Springer and his enemies have always overestimated the importance of his newspapers and magazines. Although, for instance, one-third of the *Bild Zeitung*, the day before the 1972 elections, consisted of anti-government advertising, the Social Democrats stayed in power, albeit in coalitions through to 1982.

Springer announced in 1967 that his papers would adhere to the following four principles, which were written into the company articles in 1985 and included in every Springer journalist's contract: the peaceful reunification of Germany; reconciliation of Germans and Jews and support for Israel; rejection of totalitarianism or extremism; and support for a free market economy. For almost all citizens of the federal republic the first two were uncontroversial. The fourth sounded a little ironic, in view of Springer's monopoly position: indeed, he sold off several of his titles in the late 1960s in order to keep his total share of the print media market just below the 40 percent threshold which would attract the attentions of the Federal Cartel Office. As for opposing dictatorships, the Springer papers, led by *Die Welt*, hardly mentioned the reign of terror that followed Ugarte Pinochet's coup in Chile in 1973, their journalists accepted fees from the Greek colonels' junta to write favorable stories, and they cooperated with the Shah of Iran's secret police to the extent of publishing reports on opposition activities taken straight from their files. Springer's real target was the Soviet Union. He saw the 1970 treaty with the Soviets as a blow to any hopes of unification, since it made permanent the borders created after the war. He was so convinced of the likelihood of a Russian invasion that he invested most of his considerable wealth outside the federal republic, mostly in North America.

Vertical Integration and Diversification Via Acquisition in 1970s

Starting in 1972 with the building of Germany's first offset printing plant for newspapers, Springer, along with its rival Gruner & Jahr, led the way in establishing vast new printing centers, taking advantage of the new technology and the chance to cut labor costs. Unlike their largely non-unionized colleagues in the United Kingdom or the United States, German journalists refused to undertake composition on video terminals, thus helping to save at least some jobs which elsewhere have been lost. Throughout the 1970s the group expanded its holdings in local newspapers and specialist magazines, including a majority stake in Gilde-Verlag, publisher of *Rallye Racing* and *Sportfahrer* (1975); the new Springer publications *Tennis Magazin* and *Ski Magazin* (1976); and a majority stake in the Kunst und Technik Verlag of Munich (1979), which has since been renamed Weltkunst Verlag GmbH and now publishes the fortnightly art magazine *Weltkunst*. In 1976 another new subsidiary, Cora Verlag, was created to publish translations of the romantic fiction published by the Canadian company Harlequin. Springer was determined to keep abreast of changes in tastes and leisure interests in Germany, a policy confirmed by the launches of new magazines for women—*Journal für die Frau* (1978) and *Bild der Frau* (1983).

By 1974 *Die Welt*'s sales had fallen to 196,000 and its annual losses were over DM20 million. In 1975 the paper's offices were moved from Hamburg to Bonn and the Berlin edition was closed down. From 1979 to 1981 Springer experimented with allowing a guarded shift to the left in *Die Welt*'s editorial policy, under Peter Boenisch, who led the paper into a more critical approach to the Shah of Iran and a more supportive view of détente with the Soviet bloc, but then Springer returned control to the "cold warriors," Herbert Kremp, Wilfried Hertz Eichenrode, and Matthias Warden, in spite of the protests of the staff. Staff feelings were expressed in their arranging the headlines in the paper, on the day Boenisch was fired, to read: "The Good Times Are Over; Big Setback for the World; The People Don't Back the Junta; Decree from the Top." Once again the paper swung into action against the peace movement, the Greens, and the left, in tandem with *Bild*. Between 1970 and 1985 the paper lost more than $100 million, and its circulation remained below 250,000. The changes at *Die Welt* were accompanied by the first breach in Springer's almost complete control of the company, as continuing financial problems forced him first to offer a majority shareholding to his rivals in the publishing business, the brothers Franz and Frieder Burda, in 1981, and then, when the Federal Cartel Office vetoed the plan, to sell them 24.9 percent instead, in 1983.

In 1970 Springer had become one of the first of the European press barons to enter the electronic media, establishing a subsidiary, Ullstein AV Produktions—und Vertriebsgesellschaft, which was renamed Ullstein Tele Video (UTV) in 1981. One of the main obstacles to Springer's further expansion into the field of television was the constitutional provision that placed broadcasting under the control of the *Lander* (states) rather than the federal government. No one state was willing to give up its powers over television and radio to any commercial interests, least of all to such a threateningly large organization as Springer. Accordingly Springer had to enter a consortium set up in 1983 by the leading German newspaper publishers to finance the satellite ECS 1, from which the commercial television station SAT 1 has been broadcast since 1987. Until then the station was limited to the cable network owned by the German postal authorities, and made no money for its investors. In 1985 Springer took stakes in the cable television company Teleclub, specializing in showing films, and in two Munich radio stations, as well as 35 percent of the shares in SAT 1's news service.

Management Transition Begins in Mid-1980s

In 1984, after nearly 38 years in charge of expanding and diversifying an empire, Springer went into semi-retirement, handing over the running of the group to his wife Friede and to Bernhard Servatius, Ernst Cramer, and Günter Prinz, who sat on the supervisory board of the group alongside the Burda brothers. The group was restructured in the summer of 1985 via an initial public offering of 49 percent of the shares in Axel Springer Verlag by the holding company, Axel Springer Gesellschah für Publizistik KG, founded in 1970. The sale was heavily oversubscribed, but the 7,000 new shareholders found themselves holding registered voting shares, with the provision that any sale of a holding of more than 0.5 percent could not go ahead without the board's approval. Thus Springer's personal holding fell to 26.1 percent, but his, and therefore his heirs', control covered 75.1 percent. It was also arranged that a majority of 80 percent would be needed to alter the four principles the

founder had laid down for his publications. The official reason for these arrangements was to preserve the company's independence, although it was not being threatened at the time; in addition, the Springer family wanted to minimize the payment of death duties when Springer died.

Axel Springer died in September 1985, having ensured that his empire would remain in the hands of his chosen successors, including his second wife, Friede, whom he had married in 1978, his daughter, his younger son, and his two grandchildren, who were directed in his will to keep their holdings together for at least 30 years. Servatius and Cramer received holdings of 3 percent each in the Springer holding company, while Peter Tamm became chairman of the executive board, having been chief executive since 1968.

In 1985 the Springer group accounted for 29 percent of the domestic newspaper market. Expansion did not stop with Springer's death. The 20 book publishing divisions acquired over the years were reorganized in 1985 into Ullstein Langen Müller, the third-largest publisher of general books in the federal republic, while a particularly successful new magazine was *Auto-Bild* (1986), from which have developed, via joint ventures or franchising, similar magazines in the United Kingdom, France, and Italy.

A dispute developed in March 1987 between Tamm and his deputy, Günter Prinz, over the future of Springer's stake in SAT 1, which was then running at a loss, and of the new magazine *Ja*, which had been an expensive flop. At first Prinz appeared to have won his case for closer supervision of Tamm's executive board by the supervisory board. However, in May Prinz was dismissed and Tamm was free to press on with expansion of the television business; the closure of *Ja*; new investments in the Spanish company Sarpe, which publishes women's magazines; a new Austrian newspaper, *Der Standard*; and a joint-venture printing and publishing firm in Hungary.

The boardroom rows that broke out in March 1988 were more serious, since they involved threats to Springer's elaborate arrangements for protecting the shareholding pattern established just before his death. Leo Kirch, the owner of an enormous feature film library, had built up his own stake in the Springer group to 10 percent, and had some influence over another 16 percent. Having arranged in 1987 to cooperate with the Springer executors, he now sought to gain overall control by forming an alliance with the Burda brothers against them. The outcome, in April 1988, confirmed the determination of the Springer executors, led by Servatius and Friede Springer, to keep control of the group: they bought the Burda brothers out for DM530 million—as compared to the DM255 million the Burdas had paid five years before. They were by no means out of danger with regard to voting control, however; by the end of the decade, Kirch had accumulated a 35 percent stake in Springer, including right of first refusal to seven percent of the family's shares.

These financial battles did not prevent the group from achieving its highest ever profits in the 1987–88 financial year. In 1989 the group took a 60 percent share in Capitol Film + TV International, created to buy and sell films, TV series, and TV productions, including those of Springer's own production subsidiaries Commerzfilm, Multimedia, and Cinecentrum. It also bought the New York-based Medical Tribune Group, a leading publisher of medical and health-care literature worldwide.

The 1990s and Beyond

The 1990s brought continued challenges to Springer's second generation of owner/managers. The long-awaited reunification of Germany in 1990 left a dramatically changed environment in its wake. Like its fellow competitors among the nation's "big four"—Gruner & Jahr, Bauer, and Burda—Springer wasted no time in moving into this market. *Bild Zeitung's* circulation in the east had already reached one million copies per day by the spring of 1990. But rival Burda's May 1991 inauguration of its own daily tabloid, *Super! Zeitung,* burst Springer's bubble; *Bild's* sales in the former East Germany were halved by the end of the year. Furthermore, declining circulation forced the closure of three Springer papers in the former East Germany in 1991.

Early in that year, Springer chairman Peter Tamm ended his bitter and often personal feud with Leo Kirch by resigning to take a position with rival Burda. Gunther Wille, formerly of Philip Morris, was appointed to succeed Tamm and Gunther Prinz returned to Springer's editorial board after a six-year hiatus. Kirch's growing influence over the Springer management team was felt again in 1994, when new supervisory board chairman Bernhard Servatius and Friede Springer ousted three longtime members of the managing board over the protestations of Axel Springer's son and grandchildren. Jürgen Richter emerged as executive chairman, president, and CEO that July and continued to serve in that capacity into 1997.

Despite frequent shifts in upper management, Axel Springer Verlag's annual turnover grew rapidly in the early 1990s, advancing from DM2.8 billion (US$1.87 billion) in 1989 to DM4.14 billion (US$2.9 billion) by 1995. Losses at *Die Welt* and SAT.1 were offset by new magazine launches in Eastern and Central Europe, boosting net income from DM65 million in 1990 to DM142 million in 1995. And although the company had purchased significant stakes in everything from Internet access services to digital television, newspaper and magazine revenues continued to contribute 87 percent of total sales.

Principal Subsidiaries

Bergedorfer Buchdruckerei von Ed. Wagner (GmbH & Co.); BERLINER WOCHENBLATT Verlag GmbH; Cora Verlag GmbH & Co. KG; Koralle GmbH & Co. Vertriebs-KG; Erich Lezinsky Verlag und Buchdruckerei GmbH; Medical Tribune International GmbH; Medical Tribune Verlagsgesellschaft mbH; "top special" Verlag GmbH; Ullstein Anzeige Marketing GmbH; Ullstein Buchverlage GmbH; Ullstein GmbH; WBV Wochenblatt Verlag GmbH; Weltkunst Verlag GmbH; Alpenländische Medienverwaltungsgesellschaft mbH & Co. KG (Austria); Buch-und Zeitschriftenverlagsbeteiligungsgesellschaft mbH & Co. KG (Austria); Intergraphik Ges.mbH (Austria); Medienagentur West (MA-West) Ges.mbH (Austria); Moser Holding AG (Ausria); Schlüsselverlag J.S. Moser Ges.mbH (Austria); Schlüsselwerbung Moser Ges.mbH & Co. OHG (Austria); Schlüsselwerbung Moser Ges.mbH (Austria); Tiroler Tageszeitung Medienholding Ges.mbH (Austria); TT-Verlags-und Managementges.mbH (Austria); AXEL SPRINGER-RUDAPEST GmbH (Hungary); Axel Springer-Ungarn GmbH (Hungary); Népújság GmbH (Hungary); Petöfi Zeitungs-und Buchverlag GmbH (Hungary); Axel Springer Japan Publishing Inc. (Japan); Axel Springer Polska Sp.zo.o. (Poland); GRUPO AXEL SPRINGER S.L. (Spain); "Medical Tribune"-AG (Switzerland); AS TV-Produktions-und Vertriebsgesellschaft mbH; 'Axel Springer Verlag' Beteiligungsgesellschaft mbH; Axel Springer Verlag Vertriebsgesellschaft mbH; CompuTel Telefonservice GmbH; Hamburger Abendblatt · Die Welt Reisebüro GmbH; "Overbruck" Spedition GmbH; VVDG Verlags-und Industrieversicherungsdienste GmbH; Wulf & Hölter Spedition GmbH; Z.Z.-Verlagsservice Eichberg GmbH & Co. KG; Leipziger Verlags-und Druckereigesellschaft mbH & Co. KG; Ostsee-Zeitung GmbH & Co. KG; OZ-Lokalzeitungs-Verlag GmbH.

Further Reading

"Axel Springer Names Surprise CEO-President," *Advertising Age,* July 25, 1994, pp. 37–38.
Fondiller, David S., "Ich Bin Ein Mogul," *Forbes,* December 19, 1994, pp. 98–100.
Frederick Studemann, "Germany's Paper Tigers," *International Management,* November 1991, pp. 58–60.
Müller, Hans Dieter, *Press Power,* London, Macdonald, 1969.
Our Product—The Living Word, Berlin, Axel Springer Verlag AG, 1989.
Springer, Axel, *Aus Sorge um Deutschland,* Stuttgart, Seewald Verlag, 1980.
Walker, Martin, *Powers of the Press,* London, Quartet Books, 1982.

—Patrick Heenan
—updated by April D. Gasbarre

Back Bay Restaurant Group, Inc.

284 Newbury Street
Boston, Massachusetts 02115
U.S.A.
(617) 536-2800
Fax: (617) 236-4175
Web site: http://www.great-food.com

Public Company
Founded: 1983
Employees: 2,600
Sales: $87.8 million (1996)
Stock Exchanges: NASDAQ
SICs: 5812 Eating Places

Back Bay Restaurant Group, Inc. owns and operates full-service, upscale restaurants in Massachusetts, Connecticut, New Hampshire, New York, New Jersey, and Washington, D.C. Of the 34 locations operating as of mid-1997, 14 served Northern Italian cuisine under the Papa.Razzi name. The remaining 20 restaurants offered American-style menus under various names including Charley's Eating & Drinking Saloon, J.C. Hillary's, Joe's American Bar & Grill, Famous Atlantic Fish Company, and Hillary's. By using different restaurant concepts with similar menus, Back Bay is able to operate several locations in popular restaurant markets.

Early History, 1965–75

From the opening of his first restaurant, Boraschi's Cafe, in 1965, Charles Sarkis wanted to make dining out attractive and exciting, and he wanted to reach the young, upscale customer. "Our aim has always been to put out great food, quality service, and a great environment at a very reasonable check average," he explained in a 1991 *Restaurant Business* article.

By 1968, Sarkis had decided on the concept he thought would attract that clientele: American food served in a "saloon" setting. That year he opened the first Charley's Eating and Drinking Saloon on Newbury Street in Boston's Back Bay

area. The restaurant was decorated with lots of dark wood, etched glass, brass, and fabrics of burgundy and hunter green. The menu had five sandwiches, a salad, four entrees, two soups, and two appetizers. As he told Kevin Farrell in a 1988 article, "We did a lot of things first that are taken for granted now. In the late 1960s, we served shrimp by the piece. We prepped french fries from scratch. We put top-grade mustard on the tables. We offered gourmet hamburgers. And we had waiters introduce themselves to their customers using their first names." That practice was so important that a waiter who did not introduce himself stood to be disciplined.

New Concepts, 1975–89

Charley's became the flagship concept of The Westwood Group, Sarkis's company. But it was not the only concept. In 1975, Sarkis introduced a Victorian-themed dining room, which he named J.C. Hillary's Ltd. He opened three of these that fall, two in Boston (including Back Bay) and one in Dedham, Massachusetts, joining the Charley's in the region. That step was to become a Sarkis trademark, adding an entirely new restaurant concept, not just opening another location.

In 1983, Sarkis expanded outside of his base, buying five restaurants in Florida and opening them as J.C. Hillary's locations. He also incorporated the restaurants business, naming it the Westwood Restaurant Group, Inc.

The next years were busy ones for Sarkis as he updated menus and introduced new restaurant concepts. In 1984, he opened Joe's American Bar & Grill in Back Bay, five blocks from the original Charley's on Newbury Street. The new location was an urban, upscale restaurant with a club atmosphere and a menu that featured grilled fish and meats, pasta, and seafood. It also offered a lighter menu in a separate dining room.

In 1985, he introduced The Famous Atlantic Fish Company, a concept that combined a bistro and raw bar and featured a wide variety of fresh seafood. Westwood Restaurant owned the restaurant's name and expansion rights, but Sarkis retained the original bistro separately, as he did with J.C. Hillary's. In 1986,

Company Perspectives:

To provide each guest the "Perfect Guest Experience," which we define as fine food and drink, artful service and remarkable hospitality.

Hillary's opened in Wayland, Massachusetts, a more formal, upscale version of J.C. Hillary's.

But while business was doing well in New England, the company was having problems with its locations in Florida. Those five sites had never done as well as Westwood Restaurant expected them to, and it put most of the restaurants up for sale. Despite that problem the company, with 19 restaurants, had annual sales in 1987 of $30 million. At the end of the year Sarkis sold the privately-held restaurant business to the Westwood Group, of which he was the majority shareholder. In addition to the restaurant business, the Westwood Group owned and operated Wonderland Dog Track, a greyhound racing facility in Massachusetts. The merger was viewed as a means of helping to infuse money into the track, which had seen its revenues fall.

By 1988 there were eight Charley's in Massachusetts, New Hampshire, and Connecticut. With seating for 108 people, the average per-person check was $10.50, and each unit averaged $3 million in volume a year. The menu had been expanded over the years, and while still the narrowest among the five concepts, it included nine appetizers, four salads, 24 entrees, four hamburgers, deli sandwiches, individual pizzas, and a variety of desserts.

The three J.C. Hillary's remaining in the company had checks averaging $8 at lunch and $12 at dinner. The sole Hillary's unit was slightly more expensive, $8.50 for lunch and $15 in the evening. The prices were similar at the three Famous American Fish Company bistros. Meals at the two Joe's American Bar & Grill were the most expensive of the concepts with lunches averaging $9 and dinners $17. Each of the units served liquor and had a bar, and all were open seven days a week for lunch and dinner. Four of the restaurants were within a five-block radius of each other in Boston's Back Bay. The others were located in regional shopping malls.

Despite the problems experienced in Florida, Sarkis was still interested in expanding beyond the New England region. He recognized he needed some help to do that, and went outside the organization to hire people with experience operating larger chains. He also began developing a new dining concept in response to the growing demand for moderately priced, light, healthy Italian food.

Introducing Papa.Razzi, 1989–93

Papa.Razzi, the company's Northern Italian bistro concept, was unveiled in Back Bay in November 1989, during the depths of Massachusetts' economic depression. As he had in building a new management team, Sarkis went outside the company in developing his new concept. The menu was more sophisticated

than those of the other concepts and required more skill in the kitchen. Along with veal chops, chicken dishes, and roast beef tenderloin, dinner customers could select pastas that ranged from spiral tubes with roasted egg plant, smoked mozzarella, tomatoes, basil, and romano to hollow straws with Italian bacon, hot peppers, onions, and tomato sauce. Or they could select the seafood pasta of the day. Among its more than a dozen pizzas, which ranged in price from $6.75 to $10.95, customers could choose one with fresh tomatoes, eggplant, smoked mozzarella, and basil, or with ham, mushrooms, artichoke hearts, mozzarella, oregano, and tomato sauce instead. Lunch customers could also order individual pizzas and Italian-style sandwiches with a salad. The restaurant was decorated in earth colors with marble and light wood accents. The first location featured a wood-burning pizza oven and a food display case, to emphasize the importance of food preparation at the restaurant. This was a shift from the earlier concepts, where the decorating emphasis had been on the dining room.

The concept was a hit from the beginning and the company had two more operating in Massachusetts by the end of 1991 and four more, including one outside New England in White Plains, New York, in 1992. The second location reached the original's $3 million plus annual sales level after being open only three weeks. The Papa.Razzi locations tended to be larger than the Westwood's other restaurants, from 4,000 to 12,000 square feet, with seating for between 200 and 350 people. By the end of 1994, there were 13 units, with two located as far south as New Jersey.

Sarkis was not satisfied with just one new concept, however. In 1990, he renovated a Florida location and reopened it as Rayz Riverside Cafe. Funkier and more casual than the other concepts, Rayz was decorated in a nautical/beach style, complete with menus shaped like suntanning reflectors. The menu included many of the dishes from the other restaurants, but also offered its own specialties: soft shell crabs in season, Maryland crab cakes, and rotisserie-grilled ribs and chicken. That November he opened the second Rayz in Cambridge, Massachusetts. At the end of 1990, the restaurant division had 21 units, with total annual sales of $50 million.

In April 1991, Sarkis reincorporated the Westwood Restaurant Group, Inc. as the Back Bay Restaurant Group, Inc., a wholly owned subsidiary of The Westwood Group. For the first time, Westwood began publicizing that its various restaurant brands had a common ownership. As Sarkis told *Restaurant Business*, "I used to think people might have negative associations if they saw us as a chain. But since 90 percent of our customers have a good experience, why shouldn't we want to let them know about our other restaurants?" The concept of clustering the different concepts together had worked well in the Back Bay area, with the company reporting doing $15 million worth of business from its five different units there, compared to $5 million by a single-location competitor. Back Bay expected to follow that strategy as it expanded beyond New England.

In March 1992, Back Bay went public. The company, with 26 locations, ended the year with sales of $59.6 million and net income of $2.6 million.

Even as the company grew, Back Bay continued to stress its traditional standard of quality. Management trainees had to complete a 10-week course, during which they learned about the operations of the entire restaurant (kitchen, bar, and dining room) as well as food quality, customer service, employee relations, and issues related to liquor liability. The training made it relatively easy for managers to move among what the company was now calling its American concept restaurants or from one Papa.Razzi location to another.

In 1993, Back Bay sold the remaining Florida property to the U.S. Department of Transportation for $4.7 million and formally separated from the Westwood Group. More units were opened, bringing the total number of locations by the end of the year to 31. Sales reached over $74 million, with profits of nearly $3.5 million. But trouble signs were developing. Average sales in the units had dropped slightly and same-store sales rose less than one percent compared with their revenues the year before.

1994 to the Present

The company continued to expand, reaching a peak of 37 restaurants at the end of 1994, with a total customer count of 5.3 million people. But that growth and increased competition took their toll as profits fell 86 percent from 1993, even though sales were up 16 percent, to nearly $86 million. David Loeb, a restaurant analyst with The Chicago Corp. in Chicago, put it succinctly to Robin Lee Allen of *Nation's Restaurant News* in a 1995 article, "As someone at Shoney's said to me, 'In casual dining, the seats are growing faster than the fannies to fill them.'"

To attract customers, Back Bay initiated a Preferred Guest Program in September. Under the program, a customer received a $20 certificate good at any of the company's restaurants each time their account reflected $200 in food and drink purchases. By March 1997, the program numbered some 18,000 members.

The company also closed several older sites and slowed its development plans. It did open new Joe's American Bar & Grill units, in towns where a Papa.Razzi already existed, and, in February 1995, opened a Papa.Razzi in Georgetown in the District of Columbia.

Despite these efforts, same-store sales, particularly for the 17 Papa.Razzi units, continued to drop during 1995 and by mid-year the company was reporting a net loss. Back Bay countered by starting a summer radio campaign for Papa.Razzi in the Boston area, a break with the company's traditional dependence on word-of-mouth publicity. The company also sent its Papa.Razzi concept chef to Italy where he spent nine weeks studying regional cuisine. In September, the trattoria's five-year-old menu was expanded with the addition of dishes from southern Italy. The restaurants began using fresh pasta instead of dried, and new entrees ranged from a broiled veal chop served with linguine tossed with wild mushrooms in a Marsala wine sauce to whole-wheat pasta with sausage, roma tomatoes, arugula garlic, and fresh parsley. Olives, capers, and artichokes appeared in more dishes as well. The total customer count increased 8 percent during the year, and the company had record sales of over $93 million. However, Back Bay and its 33 units operated at a loss for the year due to charges against closed restaurants and abandoned projects.

The new year did not begin well, as the Blizzard of 1996 dropped more than 100 inches of snow in Back Bay's major market. However, as the year passed, each fiscal quarter showed year-to-year earnings improvement. In September the company opened its first new restaurant in more than a year, a Joe's American Bar & Grill in Braintree, Massachusetts.

The financial picture improved during 1997, with the company reporting net income of just over one-half million dollars for the first six months, compared to a net loss for the period in 1996. In January, Back Bay announced it had purchased the Cornucopia restaurant, located atop pilings in Boston Harbor. The company's eighth Joe's opened on the site in May, offering "American fare with a distinct seaside flair." During the summer the last Rayz closed, but customers could still get a taste of the sun as some of the concept's specialties were added to the menu of the nearby Papa.Razzi. And Sarkis had not run out of concepts. The company announced on its new web site, the introduction of Waldo's, a rhythm and blues club, offering music and food three nights a week above the J.C. Hillary's in Back Bay.

Further Reading

Allen, Robin Lee, "Papa.Razzi: Now That's Italian!" *Nation's Restaurant News*, May 16, 1994, p. 97.

——, "Back Bay Still Plagued by Competition, Operational Difficulties," *Nation's Restaurant News*, May 8, 1995, p. 11.

——, "Papa.Razzi Adds Southern Touch to Menu," *Nation's Restaurant News*, September 11, 1995, p. 7.

"Back Bay Acquires Cornucopia in Boston Harbor," *Nation's Restaurant News*, January 13, 1997, p. 2.

Casper, Carol, "Rayz of Light in New England," *Restaurant Business*, December 10, 1991, p. 92.

Farrell, Kevin, "Charles Sarkis's 'Front Door' Style," *Restaurant Business*, April 10, 1988, p. 130.

Fiedler, Terry G., "An Eat-and-Run Merger: Dog Track Owner Buys Restaurants to Nurture Profits," *New England Business*, April 6, 1987, p. 44.

Grunwald, Michael, "Sarkis Blasts Critics," *Boston Globe*, December 18, 1993, p. 67.

"New Stock Listings," *The Wall Street Journal*, March 23, 1992, p. C4.

—Ellen D. Wernick

Barclays PLC

54 Lombard Street
London EC3P 3AH
United Kingdom
(0171) 699-5000
Fax: (0171) 699-2460
Web site: http://www.barclays.co.uk

Public Company
Incorporated: 1896 as Barclay & Company, Ltd.
Employees: 85,200
Assets: £186.00 billion (US$318.06 billion) (1996)
Stock Exchanges: London New York Tokyo
SICs: 6082 Foreign Trade & International Banking
　　　Institutions; 6712 Offices of Bank Holding Companies

Barclays PLC, a one-bank (Barclays Bank) holding company and the United Kingdom's largest bank, has it origins in the 18th century. Although located in the heart of London's commercial district, the bank became identified with the agricultural and fishing industries through mergers, an identification it retained through much of the 20th century. Steeped in tradition, Barclays manages operations that include U.K. retail banking, the BZW global investment banking unit, an asset management group, and a network of banks—primarily retail—in continental Europe, Africa, and the Caribbean.

Early History

Barclays takes it symbol, the spread eagle, from the Quaker goldsmithing and banking firm founded by John Freame in 1728. In 1736, James Barclay, Freame's brother-in-law, became a partner in the Black Spread Eagle. When two more of Barclay's relatives joined the firm—Silvanus Bevan in 1767 and John Henton Tritton in 1782—the banking firm took the name by which it would be known for more than a century: Barclays, Bevan & Tritton. While fledgling joint-stock banks outside London struggled to establish themselves in the late 18th and early 19th centuries, Barclays, Bevan & Tritton was still occu-

pied with the well-established and highly lucrative commercial life of London.

A series of legislative changes completed in the late 19th century created a new banking climate that threatened the existence of private banks such as Barclays. First, the Bank Charter Act of 1826 allowed banks with more than six partners to be formed only outside London. In 1833 the geographical restriction was removed. Stockholders of new joint-stock companies were granted limited liability for the first time in 1854. Finally, in 1879, existing joint-stock associations were allowed to convert to a limited-liability structure.

Series of Mergers in Late 19th and Early 20th Centuries Created Modern-Style Barclays

As a result of these legislative changes, provincial limited-liability joint-stock companies started picking off private banks. After lengthy negotiations, three of the largest Quaker-run banking firms—Barclays (which had become Barclays, Tritton, Ransom, Bouverie & Company after a merger in 1888), Jonathan Backhouse & Company, and Gurneys, Birkbeck, Barclay & Buxton—and 17 smaller Quaker-run banks agreed to merge and form a bank large enough to resist takeover attempts. Barclays took its modern form in 1896 when the 20 private banks merged to form Barclay and Company, Ltd., a joint-stock association with deposits totaling an impressive £26 million. This marked the beginning of Barclays's tradition of service to farmers and fishermen.

Francis Augustus Bevan, grandson of Silvanus Bevan, served as the new bank's first chairman for 20 years. The company's structure and course, however, were directed for its initial 40 years by Frederick Crauford Goodenough, as first secretary, until 1917, and then as chairman after Bevan's retirement until his own death in 1934. Goodenough was the only chairman recruited from outside the original founding families until 1987. Recruited from the Union Bank of London, Goodenough remained aloof from family controversies and quickly proved his merit.

Goodenough's first task was to meld the constituent banks into a single enterprise. He took a decentralized approach that was to be Barclays's hallmark for most of the 20th century. Each member bank was independently operated under the control of its own board of directors. Senior partners of the constituent banks were given a seat on the Barclays board. In this way, longstanding relationships between each member bank and its customers were maintained, and the new company took advantage of the knowledge and experience of its leaders.

At the same time, Goodenough initiated a series of mergers which eventually made Barclays one of the largest banks in Great Britain. In its first 20 years, Barclays acquired 17 private banks throughout England, including Woods and Company of Newcastle upon Tyne in 1897, Bolitho Bank in Cornwall, and United County Banks, its first joint-stock bank acquisition, in 1916. The bank's merger with the London, Provincial and South Western Bank in 1918 made it one of the Big Five British banks. During this period, Barclays merged with 45 British banks and its deposit base grew to £328 million.

This era of banking amalgamations came to an end in 1919, when the Colwyn Committee recommended, and banking authorities unofficially adopted, limitations on previously unregulated bank mergers. The committee suggested that thenceforth the Bank of England and the treasury approve only those mergers that provided important new facilities to customers or secured significant territorial gains for larger banks. Mergers were no longer approved if they resulted in a significant overlap in the areas served by constituent banks without countervailing benefits to customers or if they would result in "undue prominence" for a larger bank. After the Colwyn Committee report, mergers were increasingly difficult to justify, and the consensus was that mergers among the Big Five would not be approved.

International Expansion in the 1910s and 1920s

After Barclays's expansionist phase ended, Goodenough turned his attention to international banking operations. Barclays's first international venture took place in 1914 when it established its French subsidiary, Cox & Company. Goodenough had a vision of a network of Barclays banks spanning the globe to the greater glory of the British Empire. As early as 1916, he started preparations for worldwide banking by acquiring the shares of the Colonial Bank, established in 1836 to provide banking services in the West Indies and British Guiana. The Colonial Bank's charter was extended by special legislation to British West Africa in 1916 and then worldwide in 1917.

Immediately after World War I, Goodenough began negotiations with the National Bank of South Africa Ltd. and the Anglo-Egyptian D.C.O., operating in the Mediterranean. Despite the opposition from the Bank of England, which feared Barclays would become overextended, Goodenough engineered the 1925 merger of the two banks with the Colonial to form Barclays Bank (Dominion, Colonial & Overseas), later renamed Barclays Bank (D.C.O.). Although Goodenough never realized his dream of establishing banks throughout the British Empire, for decades Barclays was the only British bank to combine domestic business with a widely dispersed international branch network.

A contemporary of Goodenough's speculated that the chairman became interested in expanding Barclays's international operations because domestic growth was very limited. Despite this stagnation and later the Great Depression, Goodenough's plan did not result in a disastrous overextension of the bank's assets.

Barclays survived the Great Depression relatively intact to take its place as a leading wartime financier. Goodenough died in 1934 and was replaced by William Favill Tuke, who was in turn replaced in 1936 by Edwin Fisher. Fisher saw Barclays through the boom years of World War II. When Fisher died in 1947, he was replaced by William Macnamara Goodenough.

In 1951, Anthony William Tuke, the son of William Favill Tuke, became chairman following William Goodenough's retirement that year. A. W. Tuke was essentially conservative but encouraged innovations, even those he personally disliked, which were potentially beneficial to the bank. Under Tuke's leadership, Barclays became Britain's largest bank, surpassing the Midland Bank in the late 1950s. Barclays was also a leader in introducing new banking technology: Barclays was the first British bank to use a computer in its branch accounting, in 1959; introduced the world's first automatic cash-dispensing machine; and started a plastic revolution in Britain by introducing the Barclaycard in 1966.

Entered U.S. Market in 1965

In the late 1960s and early 1970s, when most competitors were struggling to establish international operations, Barclays enjoyed an enormous head start, since its operations in former British colonies in Africa and the Caribbean were well-established. The economies of many of these countries, however, were precarious. To offset its high exposure in developing countries, Barclays decided to enter the U.S. market. It first established Barclays Bank of California in 1965, and then in 1971 formed Barclays Bank of New York. Together these two banks gave Barclays the unique advantage of having retail banking operations on both U.S. coasts. Another advantage Barclays enjoyed was an exemption from 1978 legislation barring foreign banks from operating branches in more than one state.

In 1967 British banking authorities clarified their position on domestic mergers. The National Board for Prices and Incomes stated that mergers would be allowed to rationalize existing networks and that further reduction in the number of independent banks would not be viewed as inherently anticompetitive. Barclays quickly took advantage of the change in policy by merging with the venerable Martins Bank, in November 1968. Martins Bank began as the Bank of Liverpool in 1831 and had merged with more than 30 smaller banks by the time it was acquired by Barclays. The most important of these mergers was with Martin's Bank of London, founded by Sir Thomas Gresham, chief financial adviser to Elizabeth I and founder of the Royal Exchange. The merger with Martins Bank, the sixth-largest in the country, brought Barclays more than 700 branches, mostly in northern England.

In 1973 A. W. Tuke was succeeded as chairman by Anthony Favill Tuke, William F. Tuke's grandson. A. F. Tuke served until 1981, when he left Barclays to operate a British mining company. His tenure was most notable for Barclays's expansion in North America. In May 1974 Barclays Bank International acquired the First Westchester National Bank of New Rochelle, New York. In the late 1970s, Barclays opened a series of branches and agencies in major U.S. cities. By 1986 North American operations had extended to 37 states. In the early 1980s Barclays Bank International diversified into commercial credit, acquiring the American Credit Corporation, renamed Barclays American Corporation (BAC), in May 1980. Later that year BAC acquired 138 offices from subsidiaries of Beneficial Finance and the operations of Aetna Business Credit Inc.

Restructuring in Early 1980s

In June 1981 Timothy Bevan became chairman of Barclays and immediately, with the assistance of United Kingdom Chairman Deryk Weyer, set about restructuring domestic operations. The system of local control initiated by F. C. Goodenough had become outdated as the bank expanded and diversified. Senior managers' responsibilities were not clearly defined, and, although technically higher in authority than regional bank directors, in practice the senior managers were subject to the regional officials' control as board members. Moreover, the original structure of the company tended to produce dynasties. Weyer's strategy was to establish three basic divisions to represent Barclays's most important markets—the large corporate market, the middle market of small- to medium-sized businesses, and the traditional individual-customer and mass-consumer market. Bevan and Weyer moved cautiously, however, avoiding wholesale reorganization of the company so that the relationships of local managers with large customers were not disrupted.

Further changes in the structure of the company followed. Barclays had converted from a joint-stock bank to a public limited company in 1981, and it assumed its present name in 1984. In 1985 Barclays became a holding company and all of its assets were transferred, in exchange for stock, to its operating subsidiary, Barclays Bank International Ltd., which was simultaneously converted to a public limited company and renamed Barclays Bank PLC.

In 1986 Barclays acquired Visa's traveler's check operation, becoming the third-largest issuer in the world with 14 percent of the market. That same year, in preparation for the deregulation of the British securities market, Barclays Merchant Bank Ltd. de Zoete and Bevan and Wedd Durlacher Morduant & Company merged to form Barclays de Zoete Wedd (BZW), a new investment-banking enterprise.

Faced Challenging Environment in Late 1980s

Chairman John Quinton, appointed in May 1987, faced a number of challenges in the late 1980s. Domestic banking had always been Barclays's strength, but the bank faced increasing competition. National Westminster Bank edged out Barclays in assets. The building societies, by offering high interest on savings, threatened the bank's traditional deposit base. Finally, American and Japanese banks entered the commercial-lending market and began to pose a threat to British banks. Barclays fought back with two formidable money-generating enterprises,

Mercantile Credit and the Barclaycard, which generated about 20 percent of Barclays's domestic profits. The bank also continued to rationalize its branches to better serve the three major banking-service markets. In addition, Barclays planned to spend more than £500 million on technological advances, including the introduction of the first electronic debit card in the United Kingdom.

Barclays's future in international banking was less certain. It was dealt a number of setbacks in the late 1980s. In 1986 Barclays divested its 148-year-old, wholly owned South African subsidiary, Barclays National Bank (Barat), in response to a disastrous drop in the subsidiary's earnings from 1984 to 1986 and to losses in the lucrative student market in Britain as Barclays's presence in South Africa became more unpopular at home. Also, the steady deterioration of African economies posed a hazard because the bank's African involvement was so heavy. Barclays decreased its African investments where possible, but had difficulties in removing profits and proceeds from Africa. In addition, Barclays's Hong Kong and Italian operations both suffered large losses in the 1980s, and the performance of Barclays's American operations was consistently disappointing. In the early 1980s, Barclays expanded very rapidly and tried to build earnings quickly through an aggressive lending policy. As a result, branches picked up a large volume of low-quality loans. Bad-debt ratios were very high, costs were difficult to control, and American operations only started to show a profit in the late 1980s (only 4 percent of Barclays's profits were from U.S. operations, while 15 percent of the bank's assets were invested there). As a result, Barclays began offering specialized services in the United States in an attempt to improve its position there. Nevertheless, after years of trying to make it profitable, Barclays sold its California banking subsidiary in 1988 to Wells Fargo. And the following year, Barclays sold its U.S. consumer finance unit to Primerica (later known as Travelers).

On the positive side, Barclays's investment-banking operations showed promise. BZW expanded its operations by purchasing 50 percent of Mears and Phillips, an Australian brokerage firm. Barclays also formed a new bank in Geneva, Barclays Bank S.A., to develop capital markets with BZW.

1990s and Beyond

Although Barclays began the 1990s in an expansion mode, the bank was soon forced into retreat. In 1990 Barclays acquired Merck, Finck & Co., a German investment bank, and L'Europeenne de Banque, based in Paris. But extended recessions on both sides of the Atlantic led to numerous bankruptcies in the early 1990s, and many banks—including Barclays—suffered huge losses from bad loans. Barclays was forced to set aside £1.55 billion in 1991 and £2.5 billion in 1992 against these bad loans. Profits, already hurt by continuingly high operating costs, plunged as a result. Barclays, in fact, posted a pretax loss of £244 million in 1992.

The bank's difficulties led to the early—and forced—departure of Quinton, who had been expected to stay on for a couple more years. Andrew Buxton, who had worked his way up through the ranks since joining Barclays as a trainee in 1963 and was a descendant of one of the company founders, became

CEO in April 1992 and then added the chairmanship at the beginning of 1993. Although a Barclays tradition, the dual appointment provoked controversy as institutional shareholders voiced concerns that the bank had grown too large for such an arrangement. Subsequently, in the fall of 1993 Barclays took the rare move—for Barclays—of tapping an outsider when it appointed Martin Taylor as CEO, with Buxton remaining chairman. Taylor had most recently led a turnaround at U.K. textile firm Courtauld Textiles, a turnaround that involved closing factories and restructuring the business.

In the midst of these management changeovers, Barclays began a retrenchment—which continued into the mid-1990s—whereby it reduced its far-flung operations, at least in selected countries and regions; undertook a massive cost-cutting program; and once again restructured its domestic retail banking operations. Barclays dramatically reduced its troubled U.S. operations, starting with its exit from U.S. retail banking in May 1992, through the sale of its remaining branches and assets to Bank of New York Co. In late 1994 Barclays Business Credit, a firm that offered asset-based lending to U.S. companies, was sold to Shawmut National Corp. for US$290 million. In 1996 Barclays's U.S. mortgage unit, Barclays American Mortgage Corp., was sold to Norwest Mortgage Inc. In addition to these American divestments, banking operations in Israel were sold off, and Barclays's Australian retail banking subsidiary was sold in 1994 to St. George's Bank of Australia.

The most visible aspect of the cost-cutting program were the 18,000 jobs eliminated between 1990 and 1995. The majority of these cuts were made in the United Kingdom, most notably as a result of the restructuring of the bank's domestic retail branches. By late 1994 Barclays's domestic branch network had been cut to 2,080, a reduction of 21.5 percent since 1989.

Like most U.K. banks, Barclays benefited from the improved economic conditions of the mid-1990s and as a result the bank was able to enhance its loan portfolio. Barclays only had to set aside £396 million in 1995 and £215 million in 1996 for bad loans. The bank's reduced foreign and domestic operations and cost-cutting moves in concert with the improving economic environment led to healthy before tax profits of £2.08 billion in 1995 and £2.36 billion in 1996. Nevertheless, during these two years, Barclays continued to restructure, this time concentrating on its Asset Management Group. In 1995 the bank bolstered its presence in the Asia-Pacific region by purchasing Wells Fargo Nikko Investment Advisers, which was integrated into the Asset Management Group. Two years later Barclays sold its global custody business to Morgan Stanley Group Inc.

Barclays neared the turn of the century (and its 275th anniversary in 2003) in its strongest position in years. Although it will continue to face serious competition at home, the bank's restructuring of its domestic retail banking network seemed to be a success. As Europe slowly moved toward integration, Barclays smartly divested many of its non-European operations while seeking opportunities for continental expansion. At the same time, Barclays had retained some geographic flexibility by maintaining an international presence in investment banking through its successful BZW unit.

Principal Subsidiaries

Barclays Bank PLC.

Principal Operating Units

UK Banking Services; BZW; Asset Management Group; International and Private Banking; Businesses in Transition.

Further Reading

Bailey, Martin, *Barclays and South Africa*, Birmingham: Haslemere Group, 1975.

Bray, Nicholas, "Barclays Pursues Shrinkage to Achieve Solid Returns: Round-the-World Presence Is Played Down in Favor of U.K. Retail Banking," *Wall Street Journal*, October 31, 1994, p. B4.

Caplan, Brian, "Is Martin Taylor's Halo Slipping?," *Euromoney*, March 1996, pp. 54–58.

Crossley, Julian Stanley, *The DCO Story: A History of Banking in Many Countries, 1925–71*, London: Barclays Bank, 1975.

"The Davidson Interview: Martin Taylor," *Management Today*, April 1996, pp. 40–44.

"The Eagle Preens Itself," *Economist*, June 25, 1988, pp. 84–85.

Great Britain Commission on Industrial Relations, *Barclays Bank International, Ltd.*, London: HMSO, 1974.

Green, Edwin, *Debtors to Their Profession: A History of the Institute of Bankers, 1879–1979*, New York: Methuen, 1979.

"Half Way up to the Top of the Hill: Barclays Bank," *Economist*, August 13, 1994, p. 71.

"Is Might Right?," *Economist*, April 16, 1988, pp. 97–98.

"The New New Look: Barclays Bank," *Economist*, December 12, 1992, p. 86.

"The Shake-Up in the Barclays Boardroom," *Economist*, April 25, 1992, p. 83.

Tuke, Anthony, and P. W. Matthew, *History of Barclays Bank Limited*, London: Blades, East & Blades Ltd., 1926.

Tuke, Anthony, and R. J. H. Gillman, *Barclays Bank Limited, 1926–1969: Some Recollections*, London: Barclays Bank, 1972.

Valdmanis, Thor, "No Sacred Cows: Former Industrialist Martin Taylor Whips Barclays Back into Shape," *Financial World*, May 9, 1995, p. 34.

Watkins, Leslie, *Barclays: A Story of Money and Banking*, London: Barclays Bank, 1982.

—updated by David E. Salamie

BIG O TIRES.

Big O Tires, Inc.

11755 E. Peakview Ave., #A
Englewood, Colorado 80111
U.S.A.
(303) 790-2800
Fax: (313) 782-3333

Public Company
Incorporated: 1962
Employees: 242
Sales: $142.1 million (1995)
Stock Exchanges: NASDAQ
SICs: 6794 Patent Owners and Lessors; 5014 Tires and
Tubes; 5013 Motor Vehicle Supplies and New Parts

Big O Tires, Inc. is the largest and fastest-growing independent tire and auto service operation in North America. In 1996 Big O became a subsidiary of TBC Corporation—one of the nation's largest marketers of automotive replacement products. Marketed through their more than 400 existing franchised and company-owned retail stores in 18 western and midwestern states as well as Canada, Big O offers a complete line of their branded tires and related products for passenger, light truck, and RV vehicles. Company retail stores provide brake, alignment, shock/strut work, lubrication, oil changes, and front-end repair services in addition to tires. Big O owns and operates three distribution centers located in Boise, Idaho; New Albany, Indiana; and Henderson, Nevada. Their tires are manufactured by Kelly-Springfield, but their dealers also offer brand names such as B.F. Goodrich, General, Dunlop, Goodyear, Michelin, Uniroyal, and Yokohama. Big O was ranked by consumers as "Best Overall Replacement Tire in Customer Satisfaction for Passenger Vehicles" by J.D. Power and Associates' 1995 Replacement Tire Study (an international marketing information firm specializing in measuring and analyzing consumer opinion and behavior). *Entrepreneur Magazine* ranked Big O number 82 in their 1997 Annual Franchise 500 study.

Promoting Travel in the 1950s

The prosperity of the 1950s brought growth to all segments of the American economy including the automobile industry, which in turn effected a positive impact on the tire industry. Augmented by automobile advertising, the 1956 Interstate Highway Act promoted more long-distance travel, while motoring for leisure became more appealing, and the growth of suburbs meant driving farther to work. Tire replacement sales rose as a natural consequence of the travel boom, increasing sales from 45 million tires sold in 1952 to 78 million sold within the next decade. Increased sales resulted in increased competition, favoring major manufacturers' companies over those of independent dealers. From one of the early successful retail chains—OK Rubber Welders—emerged the new Big O Tires company. OK Rubber Welders was founded in the 1930s by Nebraskan Harold V. James, an inventor who created an electric machine designed to repair tires without the "bump" that had always accompanied tire repairs in the past. His franchise organization maintained an advantage due to the technical superiority of his patented machine over the techniques of his competitors. OK dealers were linked merely by James's machine and the OK brand name, but as they became more focused they organized a system of dealer interaction, whereby they later tested newfound information. The OK franchisers solidified their ranks and their businesses soon took on a similar appearance and identity. They established a communications network system, or "Committee System" still central to Big O's philosophy today. One of their innovations, the concept of "Outside Merchandising," was born—dealers had noticed that the more tires they moved outside of their small garages, the more they sold. Then Harold James had a new idea. Since rubber was being rationed during World War II he reasoned that in addition to repairing punctured tires he would find a way to salvage treadless casings, and soon developed the "rubber welder," a retreading machine that kept more cars on the roads while saving on precious rubber—and making his company the largest tread rubber account in the nation. They added their own brand of new tires but, unfortunately, the company officials did not reduce prices as competitors gained significant business and technological strides, refusing to upgrade with the times, which

61

Company Perspectives:

Exceed your customers' expectations, and they will have no reason to shop anywhere else. Providing customer satisfaction boils down to fundamentals so simple that they never occur to some companies: select the right site, choose the right franchisee, provide the right training, and give the right kinds of ongoing support. These principles have been driving objectives at Big O Tires since nine founders created the company in 1962. With our concept, we believe we can deliver a superior product and superior service, thus giving superior customer satisfaction and achieving superior business success for our franchisees.

ended in internal company disputes that caused a split into dissenting factions—the more progressive group, which included one of the founder's sons, Milliard James, broke off from OK Rubber Welders in 1962 and regrouped as Big O Tires (Salvaging the "O" from OK Rubber).

A New Beginning in the 1960s

Big O began as a simple buying cooperative, with dealers pooling their inventories to secure volume pricing. Millard James became president of the co-op, but within a year the company was incorporated in the state of Colorado, and Norm Affleck became the new president. Affleck had the idea that customers were waiting too long to have their tires mounted. So he introduced the idea of the "speed lane" to their retailing industry, creating a drive-through area where well-trained technicians worked together to move cars through at a record pace. The idea proved extremely profitable with dealers making up to $10,000 in a single day. The company then decided to offer a free replacement warranty on their top-of-the-line private brand tires, in anticipation of an advertising edge over other retailers.

Growth was minimal until 1968 when a dealer incentive program was instituted, giving leading dealers in each geographical zone a percentage of sales, while encouraging new dealers to join the system. By the early 1970s Big O grew to approximately 200 stores and the company offered their first Big O brand tire in 1974. Made by Uniroyal, the tires were an immediate success, and the company went on to produce an entire line of tires through a variety of manufacturers whose products were continued, or not, based upon customer satisfaction.

The 1980s Marketplace Required New Leadership

During the volatile mid-1980s the tire industry underwent major repositioning with competitors Uniroyal and Goodrich merging, General Tire's acquisition by Continental, Firestone's acquisition by Bridgestone Armstrong, then acquired by Pirelli, and then Uniroyal-Goodrich acquired by Michelin. By 1984 Big O recognized the need to change with the times and turned the company leadership position over to Steven P. Cloward, who had begun his career as a territorial sales representative for Michelin based in northern California. Big O had been one of

his accounts and he soon became assistant to the Area Director of Big O Tires of Northern California. Cloward also accepted the position as president of William B. Thomas Enterprises, the largest of the area tire distributors, and shortly thereafter he orchestrated the merging of "his" two companies. Experienced management was added after Big O's going public, in preparation for rapid growth. In order to implement more efficient distribution, eleven warehouses were consolidated into five, and an aggressive franchisee recruitment program was launched. By this time 40 Canadian stores operated under the Big O banner, and by 1994 total stores numbered over 400.

A commitment to training induced the formation of "Staker University," a Big O training school located in Mesa, Arizona, with courses structured around customer-related programs and business approaches developed by Big O dealers. They became a franchisee training school—recognized as an industry leader in training. Big O also decided to provide a staff of regional trainers traveling to individual stores, giving sessions on everything from accounting to sales techniques, brake work, and undercar care. According to company records, Cloward reasoned that "The better job you do at conveying your genuine interest in a customer, the more customer inventory base you're going to build, the more repeat business you're going to get, the more positive word of mouth—the net result is a more successful business. The times may change, but the basic needs to satisfy customers will not."

Deflated Price Margins of the 1990s

Increased competition and slimmer margins led to Big O's emphasis on promoting professionalism in every aspect of their business. Relentless price-slashing by chains like Discount Tire Co. and Wal-Mart forced Big O to lower its prices in an effort to lure customers away from competitors. Their "Cost-U-Less" program contributed to increased revenues of $122.9 million for 1993, up approximately $4.7 million over the previous year. The company announced in 1992 that it was switching to U.S.-produced tires for all its stores because of difficulty in receiving adequate supplies of tires from companies such as Kumho and Hankook of South Korea. In 1995, lagging performance prompted shareholders of Big O stock to approve a resolution requiring Big O to hire an investment banker to investigate a possible sale of the company. A dissident investor, Kenneth W. Pavia, owning 9.6 percent of Big O stock, forced Big O management into a proxy fight over his proposal of either hiring an investment banker, or considering a merger or sale. He complained that in addition to an unacceptable return on assets, the Big O board was riven with conflicts of interest. Following several years of problems with one of its manufacturers, the company had terminated its supply contract with Ohio-based General Tire, Inc. (a subsidiary of Germany's Continental AG, the world's fourth-largest tire maker), which had contributed to staggering tire-warranty costs—$4.6 million in 1993 alone—due to manufacturing defects. General Tire continued to provide and sell tires to Tire Marketers Associates, a division of Big O that supplies tires to distributors predominately based in the eastern United States, as reported in *Rubber World*. A previous private-label supplier had racked up $3.9 million in net warranty expenses five years earlier. The problems mounted.

According to Elliot Blair Smith of the *Knight-Ridder/Tribune Business News*, "Investment cheats at the now-defunct Haas Securities exploited the prior scenario to manipulate Big O's laggardly stock price throughout the late 1980s, leading to three criminal convictions in 1989 against brokerage principals. Big O management was an unwitting victim of the scheme."

Pavia lobbied company shareholders and gained a 46 percent vote in favor of the initiative to hire an outside investment adviser, and PaineWebber Inc. was chosen for the job. Big O management advised shareholders that their new business strategy was a viable one, while they continued to pursue acquisition opportunities. Anaheim, California-based AKH Co. Inc., a family-owned discount tire retailer, stepped forward to discuss a possible merger. Big O was then valued at $15.875 a share, with a company purchase price beginning at $52 million. According to Smith of *Knight-Ridder/Tribune Business News,* "President Cloward told industry newspaper *Tire News* last week that any merger probably would produce the reverse of its intent: a substantial number of store closings considering that our franchises are in close proximity to most of AKH's stores." At a Las Vegas dealers meeting, embittered president and CEO Steven Cloward resigned from his duties, but only to rescind his resignation after dealers rallied to his side. After failed negotiations between the two companies, an insider group headed by Cloward, senior managers, and franchised dealers, bid $61 million or $18.50 per share to acquire the company, hoping to return it to private ownership; however, they were unable to secure financing. This news sent the stock down to $14.25 and the group dropped its bid. The company named Cloward and John E. Siipola, Big O's chairman, to share the new office of chief executive.

By March 1995 the insider group again expressed interest in acquiring Big O, stating that the price needed to be lower than $18.50 per share, offering $53 million, or $16 per share, subject to financing and, "to participation of at least 80 percent of the shares held by the company's employee stock-ownership plan, which holds a 17.2 percent stake in the company; and to participation of dealers operating at least 85 percent of the franchised locations," according to a *Wall Street Journal* report. News of the rebuffed bid caused Big O stock to fall 12.5 cents to close at $13.75 a share. The insider group made a third offer, raising their bid to $54.7 million, or $16.50 a share. The group disclosed that it had sent proxy materials to their 10 largest shareholders, recommending that the company abolish its shareholder-rights plan and begin a "good faith" consideration of the $16 per share offer. In July 1995, Big O announced that it had signed an agreement, subject to shareholder approval, with

BOTI Holdings Inc., headed by Cloward, for $54.7 million. Blaming a time lag in consummating the deal, Big O finally changed its course and merged with TBC Corp., a Memphis, Tennessee marketer and distributor of automotive products, settling on an approximate value of $56 million.

The company continues to focus on customer satisfaction, and statistics provided by Cloward in *Franchising World* show that 89 percent of customers who purchased Big O tires as replacements said "they 'definitely' or 'probably' would purchase the same brand in the future. This compares to a national loyalty level among all brands of just 37 percent."

Principal Divisions

Tire Marketers Associates.

Further Reading

"Accord Is Signed to Buy Big O Tires of Colorado," *Wall Street Journal*, March 15, 1996, p. B4.

Anton, Maria, and Osowski, Stephanie, "Big O Tires, Inc. Ranked #82," *Entrepreneur Magazine*, January 1997.

Big O Tires Company History, Englewood, CO: Big O Tires, Inc., 1962–present.

"Big O Tires Gets Bid From Group Including Officials, Franchisees," *Wall Street Journal*, April 7, 1995, p. B3.

"Big O Tires Insiders, Led by President, Lift Bid to $54.7 Million," *Wall Street Journal*, June 6, 1995, p. B4.

"Big O Tires Names Mehlfeldt to New Post," *Wall Street Journal*, February 17, 1995, p. B2.

"Big O Tires Rejects Second Takeover Offer from Insider Group," *Wall Street Journal*, April 14, 1995, p. A5.

"Big O Tires Says Inside Group Dropped Bid to Buy Company," *Wall Street Journal*, February 9, 1995, p. B13.

"Big O Tires Signs Supply Contracts with Kelly-Springfield and General Tire," *Rubber World*, April 1992, p. 11.

"Big O Tires, Inc.," *Wall Street Journal*, March 10, 1995, p. B16.

Brennan, Brian C., "Big O Big Foot AT and XT," *4x4 Mechanix*, May 1996, pp. 1–3.

Cloward, Steven P., "Big O's Big Goal," *Franchising World*, May/June, 1996, pp. 1–3.

"General Tire to Discontinue Marketing Agreement With Big O," *Rubber World*, March 1994, p. 12.

"Insider Group Will Acquire Group for $54.7 Million," *Wall Street Journal*, July 26, 1995, p. A4.

Smith, Elliot Blair, "Rebounding from Bad Luck Colorado-Based Big O Tires, *Knight-Ridder/Tribune Business News*, November 21, 1994, p. 112102.

Steers, Stuart, "Big O Returning to Private Hands," *Denver Business Journal*, March 3, 1995, p. 3A.

—Terri Mozzone-Burgman

BLACK&DECKER®

The Black & Decker Corporation

701 East Joppa Road
Towson, Maryland 21286
U.S.A.
(410) 716-3900
Fax: (410) 716-3318
Web site: http://www.blackanddecker.com

Public Company
Incorporated: 1910 as The Black & Decker
    Manufacturing Company
Employees: 29,200
Sales: $4.91 billion (1996)
Stock Exchanges: New York Pacific London Frankfurt
    Zürich Basel
SICs: 3423 Hand & Edge Tools, Except Machine Tools &
    Hand Saws; 3425 Hand Saws & Blades; 3429
    Hardware, Not Elsewhere Classified; 3432 Plumbing
    Fixture Fittings & Trim; 3452 Bolts, Nuts, Screws,
    Rivets & Washers; 3524 Lawn & Garden Tractors,
    Home Lawn & Garden Equipment; 3545 Cutting Tools,
    Machine Tool Accessories & Machinists Precision
    Measuring Devices; 3546 Power Driven Hand Tools;
    3553 Woodworking Machinery; 3559 Special Industry
    Machinery, Not Elsewhere Classified; 3634 Electric
    Housewares & Fans; 3635 Household Vacuum Cleaners

The Black & Decker Corporation is the world's leading maker of power tools and accessories—and is the firm most responsible for the creation of the post-World War II consumer market for power tools. Black & Decker (B&D) also leads the world in the production of electric lawn and garden tools, specialty fastening systems, glass container-making equipment, steel golf club shafts, and security hardware (locks and locksets). The company is also the largest full-line supplier of small household appliances in North America. B&D products are sold in more than 100 countries and are manufactured in plants located in 14 countries.

Early History

Alonzo G. Decker and S. Duncan Black, two industrial tool designers and engineers, formed The Black & Decker Manufacturing Company in September 1910. With $600 from the sale of Black's second-hand car and a loan of $1,200, they set up a machine shop in a rented warehouse in Baltimore, Maryland. Black was the president of the company. In their first years the partners contracted to manufacture industrial products invented and sold by others, such as a milk bottle cap machine, a cotton picker, and machinery for the U.S. Mint.

In 1916 Black and Decker began to design and manufacture their own electric-powered tools. The German-made electric tools then available were heavy and difficult to operate, and, as a result, had not been commercially successful. Black and Decker designed a universal motor—the first for electric-tool use—which employed either alternating or direct current, and a trigger switch modeled after the mechanism in the Colt revolver. The first tool incorporating these innovative elements was a ½-inch portable drill with the innovative "pistol grip and trigger switch" that have remained standard for electric drills ever since. The drill was comparatively light at 21½ pounds, and it was considered inexpensive at $230.

B&D grew consistently during the 1920s, as businesses bought labor-saving devices to deal with rising labor costs. In 1917 the company was awarded patents for its pistol grip and trigger switch and constructed a factory on the outskirts of Towson, Maryland. By 1918 sales surpassed $1 million. Immediately after World War I, more portable electric tools were introduced, including a ⅜-inch drill, a grinder, and a screwdriver. To accommodate demand the Towson plant was expanded three times by 1927. A Towson headquarters building was also constructed in 1924.

Black & Decker used aggressive salesmanship and product services to build its client base. The company's first service centers were opened in Boston and New York in 1918. B&D also organized clinics to teach distributors how to use and sell the tools; demonstrators toured the country in two buses. At the end of the 1920s the company even outfitted a monoplane to

Company Perspectives:

We are the world's largest producer of portable electric power tools, residential security hardware, and electric lawn and garden tools. We are the world's largest supplier of power tool accessories and specialized, engineered fastening and assembly systems in the markets that we serve. Our household products business is the leader in North America and a major global competitor in the small electric appliance and premium portable lighting industries. Our plumbing products business is the third-largest faucet manufacturer in North America, and we are the worldwide leader in golf club shafts and glass container-forming and inspection equipment.

showcase its tools. In addition, the firm began its first mass-media campaign in the *Saturday Evening Post* in 1921.

With its initial success The Black & Decker Manufacturing Company expanded outside the United States, marking the beginning of its development into a global business. During the last year of World War I, burgeoning overseas sales led the company to establish representatives in Canada, Great Britain, the Soviet Union, Australia, and Japan. Canada was the site of B&D's first foreign subsidiary, started in 1922. Three years later a London sales and service subsidiary was formed. In 1928 the British company began manufacturing operations at a leased facility in Slough, outside London. The British company eventually built its own plant at Harmondsworth, Middlesex, in 1939. In 1929 an Australian subsidiary was established in Sydney. Until the 1950s the British subsidiary remained Black & Decker's only foreign manufacturing operation. It was the most important of B&D's many foreign operations after World War II.

In the latter half of the 1920s Black & Decker expanded its U.S. operations through several acquisitions. In 1926 the Marschke Manufacturing Company of Indianapolis, Indiana, a maker of grinders, was purchased. Two years later the Van Dorn Electric Tool Company of Cleveland, Ohio, was acquired. In 1929 B&D purchased the Fleming Machine Company of Worcester, Massachusetts, and the Domestic Electric Company of Cleveland. Fleming Machine made wire brushes, saws, and grinding stones, and Domestic Electric was a major producer of electric motors. In addition Black & Decker acquired the Loadometer Company, from which it previously had bought the rights to a portable truckweighing scale.

Like other businesses, The Black & Decker Manufacturing Company experienced great difficulties during the Great Depression. Despite huge layoffs, including Alonzo Decker's son, the company nearly went bankrupt. Employee loyalty—some workers continued to work although the company could not pay them—and a large influx of capital from outside investors kept Black & Decker afloat. The Marschke Manufacturing Company acquisition did not prove successful, and that company was sold in 1932. Black & Decker continued to develop new products. In 1930 and 1931 the firm marketed a portable circular saw, an adjustable-clutch electric screwdriver, and a new, streamlined housing for its drills. A line of power tools using the new induction motors, the High Cycle line, was introduced in 1935. As the decade ended there was a cascade of new B&D products, including an electric hammer, an industrial vacuum cleaner, a portable metal cutter, a portable trim saw, and the Shorty series of drills.

Successful Marketing to Postwar Consumers

When the United States entered World War II Black & Decker switched to the production of fuses, shells, and other products to contribute to the war effort. Alonzo Decker and S. Duncan Black were determined to avoid the problems that had followed World War I. They believed that the key would be postwar consumers. Although the company had developed an inexpensive ½-inch drill in 1923, and introduced the Cinderella washing machine in 1930, its forays into the consumer market had not been successful. In 1942 the Black & Decker Post-War Planning Committee was established. This group developed plans for Black & Decker to manufacture power tools for do-it-yourselfers and homeowners. The committee believed B&D could provide cheaper tools using new, less-expensive plastic housings to tap this unexplored market.

In 1946 The Black & Decker Manufacturing Company introduced the world's first power tools for the consumer market, the inexpensive Home Utility line of ¼-inch and ½-inch drills and accessories. In the first five years, one million ¼-inch drills were produced. This success led to the addition of other products to the Home Utility line. A set of circular saws was introduced in 1949, and a finishing sander and jigsaw in 1953. Black & Decker also continued to market new tools for professional users, including an impact socket wrench introduced in 1949 and two heavy-duty routers introduced in 1957. As a result of great demand, the company began construction of a large new plant in Hampstead, Maryland, in 1951; by 1955 this facility had been expanded to more than four times its original size. The old Towson plant ceased production in 1965, although the site remained Black & Decker's headquarters.

In the 1950s and 1960s B&D resumed the overseas expansion begun in the 1920s. Manufacturing operations were organized in Australia and South Africa in 1956. During the 1960s production facilities were built or acquired in West Germany, France, Italy, Spain, Canada, and Mexico. In addition, sales and service subsidiaries were established in many other countries. The U.K. subsidiary successfully expanded into other European markets, and, as a result, a new plant was built at Maidenhead in 1962. Three years later this factory was expanded, and another plant was opened in Spennymoor, Durham. By 1969 43 percent of B&D's sales and earnings came from its foreign operations.

Despite personnel changes, The Black & Decker Manufacturing Company remained under the leadership of the Black and Decker families during the 1950s and 1960s. In 1951 president and cofounder S. Duncan Black died at age 67. Black was succeeded as president by his partner, Alonzo G. Decker, who also took on the new post of chairman in 1954. Two years later, however, Decker died at age 72. Robert D. Black, S. Duncan Black's brother, succeeded Decker. In 1960 Decker's son, Alonzo G. Decker Jr., was named president. The 54-year-old

Alonzo Decker Jr. had started at B&D as a floor sweeper in the early 1920s. In 1964 he replaced Black as chief executive officer.

Diversified Product Line in 1960s and 1970s

Although Black & Decker enjoyed healthy profits, by the late 1950s the company was not increasing beyond its 20 percent share of the U.S. market. To generate growth the company branched out into other types of labor-saving machinery. The Master Pneumatic Tool Company of Bedford, Ohio, maker of portable pneumatic tools, was acquired in 1959. Production of portable air tools was begun at a new facility in Solon, Ohio, in 1960. The Value line was introduced in 1967 to offer standardized, less-expensive models. The pneumatic tools business remained a minor part of B&D's operations, until that sector was sold in 1986.

In 1960 Black & Decker purchased DeWalt of Lancaster, Pennsylvania, makers of radial arm saws and other woodworking equipment. An improved line of radial arm saws was introduced in 1966. To expand the woodworking operations Black & Decker bought the Carbide Router Company of Moonachie, New Jersey, in 1970 and the Wisconsin Knife Works of Beloit, Wisconsin, the following year.

Black & Decker also entered the garden- and lawn-care field in the late 1950s. It introduced electric lawn edgers and hedge trimmers in 1957. The first electric lawn mowers were unveiled in 1966, and a cordless model went into production three years later. In 1973 the business was expanded by the purchase of McCulloch Corporation, a manufacturer of gasoline engines and chain saws. During the mid-1970s production of certain outdoor-tool models was scaled back because of the unpredictable nature of their sales. Sales of outdoor tools depended upon weather conditions and seasonal buying patterns. McCulloch performed very well during the energy crisis of the early 1970s, which spurred the use of woodburning stoves, thus popularizing chain saws, but in the early 1980s the subsidiary began losing money. In 1983 the chain-saw business was sold.

Black & Decker power tools continued to enjoy success during the 1960s and early 1970s, as prices were cut and products improved. The cost of B&D's ¼-inch drill was reduced in increments from $15.98 in 1963 to $7.99 in 1970. A research-and-development task force brought out dozens of new tools each year, maintaining Black & Decker's status as an industry innovator. The Workmate portable worktable and accessories were first marketed in England in 1973, and soon proved very successful around the world. Beginning in 1964 Black & Decker also made extensive use of television advertising. Sales surpassed $100 million in 1964, $200 million in 1969, and $500 million in 1974. To accommodate the new demand the company built two plants in North Carolina, at Fayetteville and Tarboro, in 1966 and 1970, respectively. In 1974 a plant also was constructed in Easton, Maryland.

In 1975 Decker retired as chief executive officer, to be replaced by Francis P. Lucier who had been named president in 1970. Although Decker remained chairman, this marked the end of the founding families' executive control of the company. In 1975 B&D also experienced its first break in postwar growth,

and many employees were laid off. The firm's future looked dim in the face of growing competition from Japanese and German toolmakers. Offering lower-priced, high-quality tools, the Japanese firm Makita Electric Works steadily gained on Black & Decker. By the early 1980s Makita had nearly equaled Black & Decker's 20 percent share of the world market in professional tools. High turnover among the top executives also contributed to Black & Decker's woes.

Restructurings and Major Acquisitions Highlighted 1980s

Promoting a program of globalization, 48-year-old Laurence Farley was promoted to president and chief executive officer in 1983. The new head of B&D was determined to develop a world market for standardized consumer goods, including housewares. He implemented a sweeping reorganization scheme, closing five plants in England, Ireland, and the United States. Two years later more plants were closed in the United States, Brazil, Mexico, and Canada. Farley also integrated the global operations of Black & Decker, in the process firing 25 European managers and closing the European headquarters in Brussels. In 1985, to help bring home the reorganization, The Black & Decker Manufacturing Company revamped its hexagonal trademark and changed its name to The Black & Decker Corporation. The name change was meant to give greater emphasis to the marketing and sales side of the company.

Black & Decker's new path under Farley grew out of the firm's earlier development of cordless technology. In 1961 Black & Decker had introduced the world's first self-contained cordless electric drill. This tool and others that soon followed were powered by nickel-cadmium batteries, which failed to deliver the necessary performance. Nevertheless, the firm developed a cordless minimum-torque-recreation tool and a lunar surface drill, both of which were used by NASA on several space missions.

Using this earlier experience, Black & Decker introduced the Dustbuster cordless vacuum cleaner in 1978. This product was an immediate success, establishing B&D as the leader in the hitherto untapped small-appliance niche market. The Dustbuster was followed by the Spotliter rechargeable light and other cordless appliances. To put Black & Decker squarely in this new business, Farley paid $300 million in 1984 for the small-appliance operations of General Electric (GE). By purchasing the largest U.S. producer of irons, toaster ovens, portable mixers, coffee makers, and hairdryers, Black & Decker was able to gain a large chunk of the market immediately, without risking the loss of Black & Decker hardware shelf space to its housewares. Farley also believed production costs would be lowered by integrating the research and production of power tools and housewares.

During the two years following the 1984 purchase, Black & Decker undertook a $100 million brand-transition program. Meanwhile, the company also developed its own upscale light appliances, such as the Spacemaker series, a line of under-the-cabinet kitchen appliances. Black & Decker also introduced more cordless appliances, including a mixer and an electric knife. Farley began marketing the company's small-appliance line overseas. In Britain, where B&D had long enjoyed considerable name recognition, the first Black & Decker appliances were introduced in 1985. Other markets soon followed. In addition, GE's expertise in manufacturing electric motors enabled Black & Decker to design more efficient power tools using a smaller and more powerful 47-millimeter motor.

Yet Black & Decker's sales performance remained unspectacular, and fears that Laurence Farley was not sufficiently committed to product development, contributed to his replacement as president by Nolan D. Archibald. A year later Archibald also was named chief executive officer and chairman of the board of Black & Decker. Archibald came to The Black & Decker Corporation from Beatrice Company, where he headed the consumer durables group. Bringing in his own management team, the new B&D chief cut 3,000 jobs by 1987 and spurred product development. The company's worldwide operations were restructured into product groups. In 1986 the household-products group introduced a number of successful products, including the Cup-at-A-Time coffee maker. Greater efficiency at Black & Decker led to record sales of $1.9 million and improved profits in 1987.

Once he had returned Black & Decker to efficiency and profitability, Archibald set out to expand the company's operations through acquisition. In January 1988 he attempted to purchase American Standard to obtain its line of plumbing fixtures, but American Standard escaped through a leveraged buyout. Archibald then acquired Emhart Corporation, a conglomerate, in early 1989 for $2.7 billion. With its True Temper lawn and garden tools, Kwikset locks, GardenAmerica sprinkler systems, Price Pfister faucets, and various fastening systems, Emhart's product line—at least parts of it—complemented Black & Decker's own products. Archibald combined the two companies' distribution and sales networks.

Debt Burden Plagued Early 1990s

Unfortunately, Emhart, whose $2.7 billion in revenue exceeded B&D's own $2.3 billion, turned into a bit of a nightmare after the economy moved into recession in the early 1990s and the market for asset sales dried up. B&D's debt had increased to more than $4 billion as a result of the highly leveraged acquisition and Archibald had planned to sell Emhart's numerous noncomplementary operations—about $1.8 billion worth—to reduce this debt burden. With the go-go years of the 1980s over, however, Archibald ran into difficulty finding buyers and in getting the kinds of prices he needed to quickly pay down the debt. By 1991 several Emhart businesses had been sold, including Bostik chemical adhesives and Arotronics nondomestic capacitors, but only for a total of $762 million. Debt still stood at $3.2 billion and annual net interest expense was about $300 million.

Meanwhile the recession hit the housing market particularly hard, reducing demand for power tools among both professional builders and do-it-yourselfers. As a result company sales declined sharply in 1991 and increased only marginally in 1992. B&D's net margin was less than one-half percent in 1991, then B&D posted a loss in 1992 thanks to a $135 million restructuring charge primarily associated with its Dynapert operations. Dynapert, which made equipment used in the assembly of printed circuit boards, had been acquired with Emhart and

slated for sale but a buyer had yet to be found. Clearly, Emhart was dragging Black & Decker down.

Savvy Marketing and Innovative New Products Spark Mid-1990s Turnaround

A company turnaround had its start during 1992 with the launch of the DeWalt line of high-end power tools. This was actually a relaunch since B&D took the existing line of Black & Decker brand professional power tools, improved their quality, guaranteed 48-hour service center repair, *increased* their price (to be slightly *higher* than the competing Makita brand), and resurrected the 1960-acquired DeWalt brand, which was still highly respected by contractors. The company was now able to offer the low-end Black & Decker line of power tools aimed at do-it-yourselfers and the high-end DeWalt line aimed at professional contractors. This brilliant strategy—in part the brainchild of marketing whiz Joseph Galli, who soon headed B&D's entire worldwide power tool group—was immensely successful. The company's share of the domestic professional power tool market increased from 8 percent in 1991 to more than 40 percent in 1995. Sales of the DeWalt line increased from less than $30 million during the launch year to more than $600 million by 1997. In 1993 a similar high-end/low-end strategy began to be employed in B&D's security hardware group, when the Titan line of locksets were added to complement the Kwikset line.

Increased cash flow from these introductions helped Black & Decker decrease its debt load. During the record revenue year of 1994, when sales hit $4.37 billion, total debt was reduced to $2.39 billion. Reinvigorated new product development resulted in several successful 1994 introductions, most notably the VersaPak interchangeable battery system used in a new line of consumer cordless power tools and SnakeLight, a flashlight with a flexible base which became the fastest-selling product in company history.

Meanwhile Archibald was also able to further reduce debt by belatedly selling off additional Emhart businesses. In 1993 B&D sold the Corwin Russwin Architectural Hardware unit to Williams Holdings for $80 million, and Dynapert's through-hole circuit business for $28 million. In 1995 Archibald was finally able to sell the PRC information technology and services businesses in three separate deals totaling $520.5 million.

To further strengthen its financial health, Black & Decker also closed several plants in Europe in 1994 and restructured its consumer businesses in 1996, eliminating about 1,400 jobs and incurring an after-tax charge of $74.8 million. In 1995 efforts also began to further expand Black & Decker internationally, through joint ventures in India and China and the debut of the DeWalt line in Europe and Latin America.

Black & Decker seemed back on track heading into a new century. By 1996 sales neared the $5 billion mark and total debt was down to $1.71 billion. Although earnings were reduced because of the restructuring charge, the net margin of 3.2 percent was a significant improvement over that of the dark days of the early 1990s. Although there remained some Emhart operations to divest, notably True Temper recreational products, Black & Decker had revitalized itself through the development of innovative new products and the savvy and aggressive marketing of those products.

Principal Subsidiaries

Black & Decker Inc.; Black & Decker (U.S.) Inc.; Black & Decker Funding Corporation; Black & Decker Group Inc.; Black & Decker Holdings Inc.; Black & Decker Investment Company; Black & Decker (Ireland) Inc.; Black & Decker India Inc.; Black & Decker Investments (Australia) Limited; Black & Decker (Puerto Rico) Inc.; Corbin Co.; Emhart Corporation; Emhart Credit Corporation; Emhart Far East Corporation; Emhart Glass Machinery Investments Inc.; Emhart Glass Machinery (U.S.) Inc.; Emhart Glass Research, Inc.; Emhart Inc.; Emhart Industries, Inc.; Kwikset Corporation; Price Pfister, Inc.; Shenandoah Insurance, Inc.; True Temper Sports, Inc.; Black & Decker Argentina S.A.; Black & Decker (Australasia) Pty. Ltd. (Australia); Black & Decker Distribution Pty. Ltd. (Australia); Black & Decker Finance (Australia) Ltd.; Black & Decker (Malaysia) Sdn. Bhd.; Black & Decker, S.A. de C.V. (Mexico); Price-Pfister de Mexico, S.A. de C.V.; BD Power Tools Mexicana S.A. de C.V. (Mexico); TECHNOLOCK, S.A. de C.V. (Mexico); Nemef B.V. (Netherlands); Black & Decker (Nederland) B.V. (Netherlands); Black & Decker International Holdings B.V. (Netherlands); Black & Decker (New Zealand) Limited; Black & Decker (Norge) A/S (Norway); Sjong Fasteners A/S (Norway); Black & Decker de Panama, S.A.; Black & Decker International Corporation (Panama); Black & Decker Asia Pacific Pte. Ltd. (Singapore); Emhart Fastening Teknologies Korea, Inc. (South Korea); Black & Decker Iberica S.C.A. (Spain); Aktiebolaget Sundsvalls Verkstader (Sweden); Black & Decker AB (Sweden); Emhart Sweden AB; Emhart Sweden Holdings AB; Emhart Teknik AB (Sweden); DOM AG Sicherheitstechnik (Switzerland); Black & Decker (Switzerland) S.A.; Emhart Glass SA (Switzerland); Black & Decker (Thailand) Limited; Black & Decker ITHALAT Limited SIRKETI (Turkey); Aven Tools Limited (U.K.); Bandhart (U.K.); Bandhart Overseas (U.K.); Black & Decker Finance (U.K.); Black & Decker International (U.K.); Black & Decker (U.K.); Black & Decker Europe (U.K.); Emhart (Colchester) Limited (U.K.); Emhart International Limited (U.K.); Emhart (U.K.) Limited; Tucker Fasteners Limited (U.K.); United Marketing (Leicester) (U.K.); Black & Decker de Venezuela, C.A.; Black & Decker Holdings de Venezuela; Emhart Foreign Sales Corporation (U.S. Virgin Islands).

Further Reading

"A.G. Decker of Black & Decker," *Nation's Business*, December 1969.

Brown, Warren, and Sandra Sugawara, "Wall Street Worries over Black & Decker: Buying Emhart Corp. Caused Debt Difficulties," *Washington Post*, February 5, 1990, p. WB5.

Flack, Stuart, "All Leverage Is Not Created Equal," *Forbes*, March 19, 1990, p. 39.

Highlights of Progress, Towson, Maryland: The Black & Decker Corporation, 1987.

Huey, John, "The New Power in Black & Decker," *Fortune*, January 2, 1989, p. 89.

Schifrin, Matthew, "Cut-and-Build Archibald," *Forbes*, September 23, 1996, pp. 44–48.

Sellers, Patricia, "New Selling Tool: The Acura Concept," *Fortune*, February 24, 1992, pp. 88–89.

Weber, Joseph, and Brian Bremner, "The Screws Are Tightening at Black & Decker," *Business Week*, September 23, 1991, pp. 61, 64.

—Neal R. McCrillis
—updated by David E. Salamie

Black Box Corporation

1000 Park Drive
Lawrence, Pennsylvania 15055
U.S.A.
(412) 746-5500
Fax: (412) 746-0746
Web site: http://www.blackbox.com

Public Company
Incorporated: 1988
Employees: 600
Sales: 193.4 million (1996)
Stock Exchanges: NASDAQ
SICs: 5961 Mail Order Houses; 6719 Holding Companies

Black Box Corporation is a leading direct marketer of computer communications and networking equipment. They also offer technical services and solutions to businesses, large and small. In 1996 they offered over 6,000 products in 77 countries, through catalogue and other distribution sources, targeting business professionals, purchasing agents and resellers who make computer design decisions. Black Box emphasizes their superior customer and technical support over that offered by their competitors. Their broad end-user base consists of educational institutions, federal, state, and local governments, small organizations, and many of the world's largest corporations. Black Box's 1996 annual report lists their private label products which include: "PC communications and accessories, cables and connectors, tools and racks, testers and equipment protection, video and mass storage, switches, printer devices, converters, line drivers, modems, CSU and DSUs, muxes, and local area networks." Over 90 percent of the company's sales are private-label brands under the Black Box brand name, along with branded offerings from companies such as Intel, Bay Networks, Cisco Systems and U.S. Robotics. Black Box's products are primarily voice, data, and connectivity-related, with more than 250 suppliers providing products for their private label, ensuring source diversification.

The company was distinguished as the first U.S. direct marketer to be ISO 9001 certified (by the International Organization for Standardization) for quality assurance and management systems, important in part because many overseas companies will only buy from ISO Certified companies. Their subsidiary and joint venture countries include Australia, Belgium, Brazil, Canada, France, Germany, Italy, Japan, Mexico, Netherlands, New Zealand, Spain, Switzerland, the United Kingdom, and the United States.

Networking in the 1970s

Black Box (previously Expandor, Inc.) evolved from Micom Systems, a company organized in 1973 to supply a wide range of networking equipment. Founders E. R. Yost and Richard Raub combined talents gained in sales experience, with engineering experience in the printing industry, respectively. Their first catalogue listed six products. The Black Box division concentrated on sales of mail-order data communications products and accessories, and performed very well until the mid-1980s when the telecommunications equipment business slowed. In 1988 two of Micom System's shareholders brought suit against that company in an effort to stop a takeover bid from the MSI Corporation—a company formed for the purpose of acquiring Micom, by Odyssey Partners, a New York investment group intending to sell off parts of the company: Micom Digital Corporation and Micom-Interlan. The suit alleged that the price offered to shareholders ($16 per share) did not reflect adequate compensation over the market share value of $15.62, stating that "If the total assets of Micom were sold in whole or in part, the company's common stockholders could realize an amount substantially in excess of the proposed transaction price. The defendants, listed as MSI, Micom, and nine of Micom's directors, intend to appropriate these assets for themselves," the suit claimed. They also stated that the sale came at a time when the company was entering a growth phase, according to Daniel J. Lyons of *PC Week*. Company officials advised stockholders that the merger was in their best interests, and to tender their shares. The $334 million sale came about as the result of an internal dispute within the board of directors concerning the future strategic direction of Micom Systems.

Entering the 1990s with Debt-Load

By 1990, following Black Box's reorganization, the catalogue business had developed into a thriving enterprise, and the

---

Company Perspectives:

The mission of Black Box Corporation is to grow profitably as the leader in providing quality connectivity solutions and support services through a combination of state-of-the-art technical and direct marketing skills to all the customers we serve on a global basis.

---

company moved its headquarters from Simi Valley, California, to its main facility in Lawrenceville, a suburb of Pittsburgh, Pennsylvania. Despite growing revenues, the company defaulted on a leveraged loan put together by Odyssey Partners and other financiers, forcing the company to make public offerings at a time of market uncertainty, and to refinance. The Micom buyout had been heavily reliant on debt, partly financed by a $138 million revolving credit loan. According to Anne Newman of the *Wall Street Journal*, Manufacturers Hanover Trust Company "issued $110 million in senior subordinated increasing rate notes, which carried a rate of $16.19 percent. An additional $34 million came from selling various preferred shares. Despite the sale of three subsidiaries, Black Box owed the revolving credit line $80.5 million as of July 1990." Even with revenues for the year at $107 million, the notes became due and the interest payment was not met—interest expenses grew to $26.7 million, resulting in a loss applicable to common stock of $33.9 million for the year. Black Box filed a pre-packaged bankruptcy that primarily affected note and equity holdings. A public offering was made in 1992 by MB Communications, a holding company comprised of Black Box and Micom. Black Box became a stand-alone company in 1994 when the company distributed all of the outstanding shares of common stock of Micom Communications Corp. to all holders of the company's outstanding common stock who held shares on the date of distribution. It had been decided that Black Box and its wholly owned subsidiary, Micom, supported two very diverse and incompatible product lines, attracting opposing types of investors to the organization. Black Box's lucrative and predictable income invited investors in search of stable gains, while the less-stable Micom tended to attract risk-takers.

Another public offering in September 1996 created a marketplace for Odyssey stock, owners of 49 percent of the company at that time. The buy-out tactics of Odyssey Partners had been portrayed in less than favorable terms in a *Wall Street Journal* article by Jereski and Pullman, warning that Odyssey advertised their 20-year buyout record of 37 percent average returns, but added that "while Odyssey may have excelled, other investors have been hard-pressed to do as well. Odyssey has sold stock to the public in less than one fifth of the partnership's 90-odd buyouts. But several of those companies have floundered in just a few years after Odyssey's public stock sales." All of Odyssey Partner's holdings in the company were sold in the offering, with none of the proceeds of the sale going to Black Box, although the sale did allow the stockholder group to expand substantially, according to a 1996 Black Box annual report.

In the meantime, the business of generating income through catalogue sales continued to preoccupy managers. It became

policy to invest in the technology Black Box uses to run its own business. The company put out at least three catalogues per year and has concentrated efforts on streamlining the production, ordering, and inter-company communications systems, having learned from their early utilization of new technology in the form of fax equipment, for example, that the fastest and easiest communications could make a far-reaching difference. The machines allowed moment-by-moment reviews of catalogue pages in progress, diminished the chances of disagreement between Black Box and vendors, who previously ordered via telephone, simplified technical application inquiries and requests, and allowed for efficient product review—services deemed important for a competitive company whose bottom line is customer service. All aspects of its business have been managed by information systems that "monitor sales trends, make informed purchasing decisions, perform statistical analyses of its customer database and provide product availability and order status," according to company reports. The company began listing its products and services on the Internet in 1995.

Growing Optimism in the Late 1990s

Black Box is on the leading edge of technology, although basic hardware such as cables and connectors comprise the largest portion of Black Box revenues. The company offers products such as fast and easy-to-use Global Teleconnect Kits that contain adapters and tools to connect a portable PC for modem links to various international power systems; it also offers Modem Splitters, high speed units with cables which allow three-way sharing of a single modem, and all sorts of component and user connectors. The 24-hour, 7-days-a-week certified technical support experts answer questions pertaining to all aspects of product use, in addition to more general consumer questions not directly related to Black Box products, and claim that most questions are solved within 20 minutes. The company promotes the technical education of the consumer through its phone, fax, video, and online support systems. Black Box provides a 45-day return or exchange policy, warranties of at least one year and lifetime warranties on many products—90 percent of the orders received are repeat customers. The company also stresses the speed at which they deliver, citing in its 1996 annual report the example of an exhibit scheduled to open within 24 hours at the largest amusement park in Sao Paulo, Brazil, at which the display videos were not working: "They called Black Box where technical support quickly gave them the right solution, then immediately hand-delivered the product to the amusement park. The exhibit opened on time."

Guided by the success strategies of their past, Black Box worked to increase its market share in countries where it was already established, with particular attention placed on its subsidiaries in Japan, the U.K., France, and Brazil. Japanese revenues increased by 59 percent in fiscal 1996, and 30 percent in the U.K. International revenues increased overall by 32 percent. The company opened a new subsidiary in Mexico, which achieved break-even results by the fourth quarter. Black Box tripled the number of new products introduced from the previous year to more than 1,000 in 1996, and increased the circulation of its specifically-targeted publications. A steady rise in revenues increased from $142 million in 1994, to $193.4 million in 1996—with selling, general, and administrative expenses accounting for 33.2 percent of that figure. Their long-term debt was reduced to $41.1 million, and New York analysts from Southcoast Capital Corporation predict that the company should be debt-free early in calendar 1998.

Black Box performed consistently well in the early 1990s. In May 1997 the Black Box board of directors announced that it authorized management to buy back the company's stock, depending on market prices and other factors. Due to rapid growth of the data communications industry, competitively-priced distributors such as Black Box stand to prosper. They are distributors, not manufacturers, and as such they avoid substantial risks, while providing competitively priced products and offering a high level of service in a broadening international market.

Principal Subsidiaries

Black Box de Mexico, S.A. de C.V.; Black Box de Brazil Industria e Comercia Ltda.; Black Box Japan Kabushiki Kaisha; Black Box United Kingdom; Black Box France; Black Box Netherlands; Black Box Belgium; Black Box Switzerland; Black Box Australia; Black Box Canada; Black Box Germany; Black Box Italy.

Further Reading

"Black Box Corp. (New Securities Issues)," *The Wall Street Journal*, September 20, 1995, p. C16 (w), p. C18 (e).

"Black Box Corp. (Who's News)," *The Wall Street Journal*, December 19, 1995, p. B6 (w).

"Black Box Corp. (Who's News)," *The Wall Street Journal*, May 30, 1996, p. B16 (w).

"Black Box Corp. (Who's News)," *The Wall Street Journal*, November 10, 1995, p. B3(w), p. B18 (e).

"Black Box Expects to Post Earning Rise for Fiscal 4th Quarter," The Wall Street *Journal*, May 8, 1996, p. B 10B:5.

"Black Box Unit Starts Operations," *The Wall Street Journal*, May 25, 1995, p. B6:5.

Gianturco, Michael, "The Affordable Black Box," *Forbes*, January 31, 1994, p. 114, vol. 153.

Jereski, Laura, and Pulliam, Susan, "Odyssey's Lemons Have Become Lemonade, But Leave Sour Taste," *The Wall Street Journal*, September 25, 1995, p. C1:5.

Ramirez, Anthony, "Hot-Wiring Overseas Telephone Calls," *The New York Times*, January 9, 1992, p. C1 (n), p. D1 (l).

Rowinsky, Walt, "Black Box Corp.: Power Control Center SP200A," *P.C. Magazine*. January 29, 1991, p. 309.

—Terri Mozzone-Burgman

Black Hills Corporation

625 Ninth Street
Rapid City, South Dakota 57709
U.S.A.
(605) 348-1700
Fax: (605) 348-4748
Web site: http://www.blackhillscorp.com

Public Company
Incorporated: 1941 as Black Hills Power & Light
   Company
Employees: 403
Sales: $162.6 million (1996)
Stock Exchanges: New York
SICs: 4911 Electric Services; 1221 Bituminous Coal &
   Lignite—Surface; 1311 Crude Petroleum & Natural Gas

A public utility holding company, Black Hills Corporation is involved in three principal businesses: electric utility service, coal mining, and oil and gas production. These businesses were operated by Black Hills Power & Light, Wyodak Resources Development Corporation, and Western Production Company, respectively. Black Hills Power & Light, the original business of the company, operated public utility electric operations that served roughly 55,600 customers in 11 counties in western South Dakota, northeastern Wyoming, and southeastern Montana. Wyodak mined low sulfur sub-bituminous coal from the Powder River Basin near Gillette, Wyoming. Western Production, operator of 277 oil and gas wells during the mid-1990s, produced and explored for oil and gas in the Rocky Mountain region, Texas, and California. In addition to these primary businesses, Black Hills also owned Daksoft, Inc., a customer information system software marketing company, and held 50 percent interest in Enserco Energy Inc., a national marketer of unregulated energy and energy services.

Origins of Black Hills's Growth

When General George A. Custer led a U.S. Calvary scouting party into the Black Hills of Dakota Territory in 1874 there could be no anticipation of the momentous events that would follow. The year was 1874, 15 years before the region surrounding the Black Hills would become part of South Dakota, and the discovery made by Custer and his scouts would do much to justify the territory's admittance as the nation's 40th state. Statehood and a series of other signal developments in U.S. history all sprang from the cataclysmic discovery of gold in the Black Hills, the finding of which sparked the Battle of the Little Bighorn, fueled the financial ascension of the nation's most powerful publishing family, and gave the United States its primary source of gold for the next century.

When news of Custer's discovery spread throughout the western territories, waves of prospectors poured into the Black Hills, with the attendant manifestations of a gold rush— saloonkeepers, bankers, merchants—close on their heels. Burgeoning communities quickly flowered, each born from the bustling prospecting and mining activity pervading the Black Hills. Towns such as Deadwood, a hotbed of entertainment for prospectors and miners where Wild Bill Hickock and Calamity Jane met their deaths, turned into thriving, tumultuous hubs of activity, the sudden emergence of which did not settle well with the resident Sioux. Tensions between the Sioux and the encroaching whites flared, finding hostile expression in the Battle at the Little Bighorn in 1876, when Crazy Horse and Sitting Bull led Sioux and Cheyenne warriors in their defeat and demise of Custer.

Hostility between the Sioux and the whites was not resolved, at least militarily, until the massacre of the Sioux at Wounded Knee in 1890, but the years of aggression between the natives and the settlers were not enough to stop the growth of communities surrounding the Black Hills. White colonization rallied inexorably forward, spurred by gold production and its largest producer, the Homestake Mining Company. One of the investors in the Homestake mine, a claim that included what ranked as the largest gold deposit in the United States, was George Hearst, father of publishing magnate William Randolph Hearst. With the profits earned from the production of the Homestake mine, the Hearst family was enriched, enabling William Randolph Hearst to purchase the *San Francisco Examiner* in 1887 and begin the development of the world's largest publishing empire.

Hearst, Homestake Mining, and the residents of South Dakota were beneficiaries of the discovery of gold in 1874—gaining where Custer and the Sioux lost—but there was also another beneficiary, Black Hills Power & Light, a utility whose existence was owed to the economy and population engendered by the discovery of gold. The events that precipitated Black Hills Power & Light's formation occurred more than a half-century before the company came into existence, but as the utility in charge of serving the area surrounding the Black Hills, the company was indebted to the developments that gave it its foundation. Homestake Mining would become Black Hills Power & Light's largest customer, and the gold company's presence in the Black Hills would speed the development of communities surrounding it, including the advent of electricity. The region gained its first utility company in 1893, and by the turn of the century power and lighting were being supplied to four Black Hills communities. With the Homestake mine advancing the economy at an accelerated pace, denizens of the region enjoyed technological luxuries well before residents in neighboring areas. In 1911, for instance, the streets in Deadwood and Lead were lit by electricity for the first time, long before others in adjoining areas, and as time marched forward, the region's infrastructure and utility companies expanded, spurred by the riches wrought by gold production.

1941: BHP&L Is Born

By the end of the 1930s, following the 1935 Public Utility Act that assigned utility companies to serve geographic regions, there were two major utility companies that served the Black Hills region, General Public Utilities, Inc. and Dakota Power Company. It was from these two companies that Black Hills Power & Light Company's founder, J. B. French, acquired the properties and assets to form Black Hills Power & Light in August 1941. French sold shares to the public, offering $100 per share for preferred stock and $16.50 for common stock, and the new utility commenced business several months later, supplying all of the Black Hills region except Hot Springs and Edgemont, South Dakota, and Newcastle, Wyoming. One year after commencing business, the utility began filling the few holes in its service area, purchasing an electric plant in Edgemont, and in 1946 a plant in Newcastle.

Expansion through acquisition continued in the 1950s, including the utility's purchase of an electric distribution system in Keystone, South Dakota, in 1952, but Black Hills Power & Light's most important acquisition by far during the decade was a deal struck with its largest customer, Homestake Mining. In 1954, the utility acquired Homestake Mining's Wyodak Coal Company, from which the utility would gain all the coal it needed to generate electricity. The addition of Wyodak, which in 1956 became a subsidiary named Wyodak Resources Development Corporation, stood Black Hills Power & Light apart from other, small utilities in the country, giving it a singular and stable source of low sulfur sub-bituminous coal and presence in a business outside of electric service. Additional steps outside the power generation business would be taken in later years, but the acquisition of Wyodak represented the first, setting the tone for Black Hills Power & Light's future involvement in mining, oil, and gas.

As these acquisitions were being completed, Black Hills Power & Light set itself to the task of promoting its mainstay product. Classes were offered throughout the 1950s and 1960s to encourage residents to use electrically-powered appliances, then somewhat of a novelty in rural areas of South Dakota. As these efforts were underway, the utility benefitted from a growing list of industrial customers. Aside from Homestake Mining, the Black Hills region was home to Ellsworth Air Force Base, a vital part of the Strategic Air Command and a heavy user of electric power. During the 1960s, the utility also benefitted from plant expansion by several industrial customers, giving it a solid and flourishing customer base to support its business. Wyodak, after a decade under Black Hills Power & Light's control, owned or had under lease more than 180 million tons of recoverable coal, enough to supply all of the utility's coal needs and offer reserves for sale to other companies.

During the 1970s, Black Hills Power & Light's service area stretched across 9,300 square miles, embracing much of South Dakota and parts of Wyoming and Montana. The utility's service area included a population of roughly 165,000, not large when compared to other more densely populated regions in the country, but Black Hills Power & Light was not solely dependent on electric service for its income. Wyodak contributed roughly half the income produced by the utility's electric business, and forays into the development of oil, gas, and uranium represented promising avenues for future growth. Still, viewed exclusively as a utility, Black Hills Power & Light occupied a stable and enviable position within the utility industry. The composition of the utility's customer base was well-balanced, with residential and commercial customers each accounting for one-third of electric utility revenues, while large industrial customers such as Homestake Mining and Ellsworth Air Force Base accounted for the balance. The even distribution of its electric load helped the utility record growth throughout the 1970s that exceeded the pace of growth registered by the electric utility industry as a whole. Black Hills Power & Light, nearing its 40th year of business, exited the 1970s having paid dividends to its shareholders every year since 1941.

1980s Diversification

The 1980s witnessed changes as defining as those experienced during the 1950s for the small, Rapid City-based utility, as Black Hills Power & Light's involvement in businesses outside the utility industry deepened. Diversification was the means by which the utility brought about these changes, but before Black Hills Power & Light's directors embarked on the acquisition trail the utility recorded successive years of robust growth, fueling confidence for the bold moves completed midway through the decade. Revenues increased from $52.7 million in 1979 to $85.2 million in 1983, while the utility's net income more than doubled, reaching nearly $14 million in 1983. As these encouraging figures were being tallied, the utility's management chose to enter into the trucking business, diversifying under the auspices of Wyodak. In 1983, Wyodak acquired Universal Transport, Inc., an interstate and intrastate trucking company involved in bulk commodity hauling. With a fleet of 45 tractors and 90 trailers, and terminals in Rapid City and Fort Collins, Colorado, Universal Transport hauled cement, coal, bentonite, sand, lime aggregates, and limestone in North Dakota, South Dakota, Wyoming, and Colorado. This initial foray into trucking was followed by the 1987 acquisition of Les Calkins Trucking, Inc., a small bulk commodity trucking company, but one year after the Les Calkins acquisition was completed Black Hills Power & Light's management decided to exit the trucking business entirely. In September 1988, Universal Transport and Les Calkins were divested. By this point, a more lasting acquisition had been completed, one that represented an integral component of Black Hills Power & Light's business during the 1990s.

In June 1986, Wyodak acquired Western Production Company, an oil producing and operating company with interest in an oil and gas processing plant. The purchase of Western Production added a third arm to Black Hills Power & Light's business, giving it oil and gas holdings to go along with mining and electric utility services. With the addition of Western Production, the utility matured into an energy services company, and acknowledged as much by changing its name several months before the Western Production acquisition was completed to Black Hills Corporation.

With Black Hills Power & Light, Wyodak, and Western Production each operating as wholly owned subsidiaries, Black Hills Corporation moved forward in pursuit of strengthening its role as an energy services company. Only modest annual growth could be realized through its utility service, with such growth largely dependent on the expansion of the economy and population within its service territory—factors outside the company's control. Consequently much of Black Hills's future growth was dependent on the success of its mining and oil and gas activities.

A decade after its acquisition of Western Production, Black Hills stood strongly positioned in its new role as an energy

services company. Western Production, which had extended the company's geographic reach into Texas and California, recorded its best financial year in 1996 since being acquired through Wyodak, reaching $12.5 million in revenue for the year. Wyodak, for its part, also made substantial gains during the year, signing a contract with Kerr-McGee that increased its coal reserves by 73 percent for a total of approximately 300 million tons. Black Hills also carved niches into new business areas during the mid-1990s. In 1994, the company formed Daksoft, Inc., a customer information system software marketing company. In 1996, Daksoft entered into a joint venture with Montana-Dakota Utilities to market a multi-utility customer information system to other utilities. That same year, Black Hills helped launch a start-up company named Enserco Energy Inc. to market unregulated energy and energy service on a national basis. Black Hills's 50 percent interest in the company, which was based in Lakewood, Colorado, was expected to provide access to markets previously unaccessible and to strengthen the company's core businesses. With these businesses providing promise for the future, Black Hills prepared for the 21st century, intent on developing into a nationally recognized energy services company.

Principal Subsidiaries

Black Hills Power & Light Company; Wyodak Resources Development Corporation; Western Production Company; Daksoft, Inc.; Enserco Energy Inc. (50%).

Further Reading

Campanella, Frank W., ''Dakota Dynamo,'' *Barron's,* January 7, 1985, p. 46.
——, ''Coal Power: Black Hills Power & Light Is Counting on It for a Profits Rebound in 1980,'' *Barron's,* October 29, 1979, p. 42.
''Excellent Area Conditions Prompt Optimism at Black Hills Power,'' *Investment Dealers' Digest,* April 18, 1966, p. 29.
Smith, Mike, ''Black Hills Power and Light Company,'' *Wall Street Transcript,* February 12, 1979, p. 53,380.

—Jeffrey L. Covell

Brite Voice Systems, Inc.

7309 E. 21st Street, North
Wichita, Kansas 67026
U.S.A.
(316) 652-6648
Fax: (316) 652-6800
Web site: http://www.brite.com

Public Company
Incorporated: 1984
Employees: 751
Sales: $110.4 million (1996)
Stock Exchanges: NASDAQ
SICs: 7371 Computer Programming Services; 7375 Information Retrieval Services; 7372 Prepackaged Software

Serving the fastest-growing market in the world—the telecommunications and information services industry, Brite Voice Systems, Inc. is a global leader in the deployment of speech recognition for the wireless industry, and offers systems that integrate voice response, voice recognition, voice/fax messaging, electronic information, and audiotex systems (audiotex involves access to recorded, computer-stored information over the telephone). The company introduced voice dialing to the industry in 1993. Brite offers services to a wide variety of companies and communities, including wireless carriers, financial and health-care institutions, public utilities, telephone companies, newspapers and government agencies. Brite is a leading supplier of communications and information products and services in high-growth markets worldwide, including South America, the United Arab Emirates, South Africa, Asia, and the Middle East. European sales are made through Brite's subsidiaries, BVSGL (Manchester and Cambridge, England), Brite Voice Systems Group, GmbH (Wiesbaden, Germany), Brite Voice Systems S.p.a. (Rome, Italy), and Brite Voice Systems A.G. (Zurich, Switzerland).

Brite's Founder Links with the Computer Revolution of the 1970s

Described by an investment analyst as "one of the better visionaries," Brite's founder, president, and original chief executive officer, Stanley Brannon, initially tapped into the computer and information processing explosion of the late 1970s. According to David Dinell of the *Wichita Business Journal*, prior to founding Brite, Brannon tested his entrepreneurial abilities when he invested $1,400 of his personal savings to form Mycro-Tek Inc., which he later sold for $10 million—and which eventually went bankrupt under the new management. Assisted by five employees, the Wichita, Kansas native founded Brite in 1984. After going public in 1989, the company began its aggressive strategy of establishing alliances and partnerships in an attempt to expand its technical services and geographical positioning. Aiming to be less vulnerable to market trends or a single technology in an industry defined by extremely rapid shifts, Brite set its sites on diversifying products and services, while continuing to invest approximately 10 percent of sales on research and engineering.

The company entered the European market when it negotiated a deal with Ferranti Business Communications in Manchester, England, and acquired the assets of their voice systems group operating division. In 1993 Brite bought Perception Technology, adding additional products and expertise in the area of interactive voice response (IVR) and computer telephony integration (CTI). IRV and CTI applications use voice processing systems to link callers to various mainframe computer databases. Callers enter information through their touchtone keypad or with voice commands, and can retrieve or change information by following prerecorded instructions. Examples of IRV and CTI include telephone calls to obtain an account balance, transfer funds, check on the status of a shipment, order a pay-per-view movie or enroll in a college class.

1990s Phone Shopping

Shopping by phone exemplifies another interactive system made possible by Brite technology, allowing consumers to place orders by using the buttons on their touchtone phones, or utilizing the option to talk directly to a customer representative. The world's largest electronic retailer, QVC, Inc., contracted Brite to install their BT III Voice Processor to automate the ordering process, increasing their order-taking capacity to over 40,000 calls per hour, and cutting by three times the expense of

---

Company Perspectives:

Brite is committed to helping its customers prosper with voice processing systems and services that increase revenues or decrease costs. The collective expertise of customers, partners, and more than 700 Brite employees worldwide, will continue to be leveraged to create the solutions that bring people and information together.

---

using the traditional operator-driven system. QVC handled almost 20 million calls automatically in 1994.

In addition to installing, maintaining, and repairing systems, through a geographically dispersed field service staff, Brite provides software support and a help desk for their customers. Customers are further supported by a training department which provides beginning and advanced training sessions for customers and employees in areas of software and technical development, product orientation, programming, and system operation. Brite's systems contain built-in modems, allowing convenient diagnostic back-up via remote communications between Brite's staff and its customers. Expertise is offered by company-sponsored technical/engineering consulting, made available to assist in the designing, engineering, procuring, and implementing of telecommunications services, networks, and equipment.

Cantel, the Canadian cellular company, implemented a Brite system that allows multiple language voice dialing, becoming the first cellular carrier in North America to offer their services with the option of either of their national languages, English and French. The two companies, Brite and Cantel, entered into a creative business partnership centered on new product development and revenue sharing. Representatives from both companies agreed to meet quarterly to assess technological developments and possibilities for improvements in cellular service. Brite instigated a similar relationship with Cellnet, the United Kingdom's leading cellular network operator. Cellnet installed a Voice Services Director providing a range of subscriber voice messaging services on Cellnet's Global System for Mobiles. Subscribers can access these services in 17 European countries outside the United Kingdom.

Managed Services, Brite Visions of the 1990s and Beyond

Envisioning a wider and more profitable market, the company shifted toward providing more managed services, i.e. custom audio information, a telephone-based system that is fed by satellite to newspapers, telephone companies, and others. According to company reports, "To support its electronic publishing customers, Brite has developed the industry's largest information services group to create content for audio, fax, and the Internet. Brite broadcasts audiotex programming over the industry's first digital satellite transmission network, ensuring crystal-clear audio quality." The company boasts the development of more than 600 new programs daily for English and Spanish audiotex networks. The report explains that "Outsourcing all technical requirements to Brite offers many advan-

tages. Customers avoid using their capital on technical systems. They eliminate time-consuming budget approvals and equipment selection processes. They can create and offer new services without adding new staff."

Using Brite's products, *Voice Directories* and *CityLine*, publishers of Yellow Pages directories and newspapers offer categories of information at no cost to callers (revenues are generated by selling advertising sponsorships to advertisers), such as sports scores, weather, stock quotes, gardening tips, horoscopes, soap opera updates, and business news. Audiotex, Connect, and Select Series systems allow "talking Classifieds" providing readers and advertisers with efficient methods of researching, buying, and selling. Select Series provides an ideal consumer profile to advertisers via phone or fax. For example, Select Series connects the prospective car buyers "Ideal Wheels Profile" with the advertisers "CarSelect," narrowing the list of potential purchases to match appropriately-matched products offered. Similar systems coordinate house buyers with sellers, through "HomeSelect," and apartment-searchers with available rentals, through "RentSelect." Over 5,000 categories of information are produced with the help of Brite staff writers, editors, and broadcasters who create and load information into the system. Key customers and alliances include GTE, Sprint, the *Washington Post,* the *New York Times,* the *London Financial Times,* Tribune Newspapers, Fleet Services Corporation, Chemical Bank, Bank of Hawaii, PageNet, Airbourne Express, Intel, MCI, 3M, and many others. Company Audiotex revenues increased from zero to $1 million a month by 1994 according to their annual report for that year. Managed services largely accounted for a 42 percent soaring of overall Brite revenues, up from the previous year's sales of $46.9 million to a record $66.3 million—liberating the company from all debt.

Brite expanded its IRV and CTI capabilities in April 1995, when it acquired Touch-Talk Inc., a Dallas, Texas-based company which specialized in custom software and application development tools. This move expanded Brite's operations to include the telecommunications, financial, government, and wireless providers markets, and provided Brite customers a single vendor for all of their voice response requirements.

In July 1995 Brite acquired Internet Resources Corporation, another Wichita company and one that provided local access to the Internet. Internet Resources Corporation was founded in 1994 by Stan Marekl, a former vice president of new technology for Brite, according to Dennis Pearce in a *Knight-Ridder/Tribune Business News* report. The move sped the company into the Internet services sector, and within months the company bought a group of telecommunications companies, valued at more than $60 million. Comprising the group were Telecom Services Ltd. (TSL), Telecom Services Ltd. (West), TSL Software Services, and TSL Management group. Pierce explained that the companies provided service to several large enterprises such as J.P. Morgan & Co., Bank of New York Co., and Smith Barney Inc. Telecommunications services include billing verification to audit telephone rates, tariffs, taxes, surcharges, and other charges billed by telecommunications carriers and vendors. The company verifies that the client pays only for the services, circuits, and equipment it actually uses and for which it has been contracted; ensures that the proper rates are applied for taxes, tariffs, rates and surcharges; corrects billing discrepancies and prepares claims; and negotiates and collects refunds.

Billing verification generally saves costs for the company's clients. Eight U.S. states and the federal Office of Veteran's Affairs began using Brite's utility billing verification, estimated to save 5 to 15 percent on their operating costs.

Added to their Internet access capabilities, Brite Internet services include search engine development, secured transactions, server usage, real-time audio via Iwave, complete digital audio production facilities, server-push animation software, forms processors, and audio/video services.

Brite's domestic sales are primarily made through a direct sales force, specializing in either industry, territory, or product line, with offices in Wichita, Kansas; Canton, Massachusetts; Dallas, Texas; New York City; Parsippany, New Jersey; and San Francisco, California. North American sales climbed steadily from $60.3 million in 1994, to $69.9 million in 1995, to $71.3 million in 1996. Companies such as Alltel, Amarex Technology, Inc., Digital Data Voice Systems, Intecom, Quotient Software, Inc., Southwestern Bell Telecom, and United States Advanced Networks utilize Brite hardware platforms for their integrated systems or services.

International sales rose more dramatically, from $19.6 million in 1994, to $27.14 million in 1995, to $39 million in 1996, amounting to between one quarter to one third of total revenues for those periods. Non-European out-of-country sales are made through the U.S.-based sales force, distributors, and local agents. Brite has speculated that Europe offers significant growth potential due to a lesser degree of audiotex and IVR systems penetration—and less competition—in that market. According to Brite's 1996 annual report the company's European subsidiaries "concentrate its efforts on five different vertical markets: telecommunications, home shopping, travel and transport, finance, and utilities. The company also relies on indirect distribution of its systems through prominent PBX manufacturers such as Philips, Ericsson, Telenorma and S.E.L." European sales of IVR and audiotex systems increased 95 percent between 1995 and 1996, and the company anticipates continued growth. In a March 1996 interview with David Dinell of the *Wichita Business Journal,* Brannon said that he predicted that the "company could grow to the $300 million to $500 million range in annual sales within five years." He explained that with stiffer competition in the United States, he expected the strong international markets to provide the growing edge. Dinell's article explains that, "In Europe, for example, the concept of consumer information through the yellow pages is still a new idea. Brite helped Telecom Italia set up an audiotex advertising product that is already common in many U.S. cities. That type of growth potential is ripe throughout the world, say Brite officials."

In the highly competitive market for voice processing systems Brite contends with companies such as Edify, Intervoice, Periphonics, Syntellect, and larger companies like IBM, Lucent Technologies, and Digital. Mail order providers such as Boston Technology, Comverse Technology, and Octel compete in the European arena. In the telecommunications management market competitors range from small localized companies to nationally-known firms such as AT&T, Electronic Data Systems, and IBM. Brite feels that its specialized expertise and reputation favor its standing in the marketplace, although increased competition from larger companies with greater resources than its own could affect future performance.

In a December 1996 interview Brannon told Molly McMillan of *Knight-Ridder/Tribune Business News* that he felt the need to hire a new Brite CEO, someone with experience broader than his own. He favored David Gergacz, the chief executive and president of Cincinnati Bell Telephone and founder of Sprint Corporation—primarily responsible for developing the first global fiber-optic network—and a member of Brite's board of directors. Gergacz is considered to have strengths in the technical and marketing aspects of telecommunications, someone who can also contribute his own network of sales and management contacts. In his short stint at Cincinnati Bell the stock rose from about $30 to $57 a share. Brite's stock had been dropping in the latter months of 1996 due to soft sales, but had risen slightly by the end of the year. Brannon plans to remain as chairman of the board, expecting to focus in areas where he feels comfortable—in new product development and acquisitions.

By July 1997 Brite planned to be moved into new headquarters in Heathrow, Florida, a suburb of Orlando, lured by $1.5 million in tax credits, easy airline access, and the advantages of close proximity to other high-tech companies such as AT&T and Sprint. It is estimated that only 30 to 35 top administrative, marketing, and management jobs would be moved, and the rest of the 240 Wichita employees would remain at the Kansas headquarters, which is the international headquarters for the company. The new location will include a Product Demonstration Center, designed to increase the company's sales effectiveness and leverage its existing worldwide sales growth. The company is reorganizing in an attempt to narrow its focus, increase its ability to serve existing customers, and allow Brite to lower costs while providing new products. In an April 1997 Brite news release Gergacz stated, "The combination of consolidating in a more strategic location and eliminating unprofitable ventures will position Brite to better capitalize on the many opportunities being presented in the rapidly growing global telecommunication and information market." He continued, "These actions, while detrimental to short-term results, are necessary in order to improve our long term prospects." First quarter of 1997 net income was $1.3 million, or 11 cents per share, compared to $2.7 million, or 23 cents per share, in the first quarter of 1996. Revenues from telecommunications consulting and customer-premise equipment sales fell below expectations, and the reorganization and relocation is a Brite strategy aimed at improving future financial results.

Principal Subsidiaries

BVSGL (England); Brite Voice Systems Group (Germany); GmbH; Brite Voice Systems S.p.a. (Italy); Brite Voice Systems A.G. (Switzerland).

Further Reading

Boulton, Guy, "Brite Voice of Wichita, Kansas, Seeks Site for Headquarters," *Knight-Ridder/Tribune Business News,* August 24, 1995, p. 8240192.
"Brite Voice Systems Inc. (Executive Changes)," *New York Times,* December 3, 1993, p. C3(N), p. D3(L), vol. 143.
"Brite Voice Systems Inc. (To Purchase Perception)," *The New York Times,* September 9, 1993, p. C3(N) & D3(L).

"Brite Voice Systems, Inc. (To Merge with Perception)," *The Wall Street Journal*, September 3, 1993, p. A8(E).

"Brite Voice Systems, Inc. (Who's News)," *The Wall Street Journal*, December 5, 1996, p. B10 (E).

Cox, Bob, "Brite Voice Systems, Inc. Leaves Wichita, Kansas for Orlando," *Knight-Ridder/Tribune Business News*, April 24, 1997, p. 424 B1106.

"Dial 1 for More Options," *PC Week*, December 23, 1996, p. E5, vol. 13.

McMillin, Molly, "Founder Has High Goals for Brite Voice Systems," *Knight-Ridder/Tribune Business News*, December 5, 1996, p. 1205B1108.

Pearce, Dennis, "Brite Voice Acquires Internet Resources Corp.," *Knight-Ridder/Tribune Business News*, July 3, 1995, p. 7030125.

—Terri Mozzone-Burgman

British Sky Broadcasting Group Plc

6 Centaurs Business Park
Grant Way
Isleworth, Greater London TW7 5QD
England
(44) 1-71-705-3000
Fax: (44) 1-71-705-3453
Web site: http://www.sky.co.uk

Public Company
Incorporated: 1988 as SkyTV and British Satellite
    Broadcasting
Employees: 4,025
Sales: £1 billion (1996)
Stock Exchanges: London
SICs: 4833 Television Broadcasting Stations

With nearly 6.5 million subscribers by mid-1997, world-leading satellite television provider British Sky Broadcasting Group Plc, better known as BSkyB, has captured the attention of England and Ireland's television-viewing audience. Beaming from leased transponders on the Astra satellites, BSkyB's mix of some 40 "channels"—many of which are not broadcast full-time but instead offer targeted program segments at specific times of the day or week—has helped the company gain a 10 percent share of the total British viewing audience. BSkyB's programming strength lies particularly in its sports and film offerings. In addition to exclusive live broadcasting rights for the English Premier Football League and the U.S.'s National Football League, the company also has exclusive first-time broadcast rights with many of the leading film producers, including the Top 50 box office performers, for a total offering of some 7,000 films per year. BSkyB also features many of sister company Fox Broadcasting's programs, including hits such as "The Simpsons," "The X-Files," and "90210," as well as broadcasting agreements with major subscription-based channels such as the Disney Channel, the Playboy Channel, the Discovery Channel, VH-1, and Nickelodeon U.K. Since 1996, the satellite service has also been broadcasting pay-per-view programming.

BSkyB plans as well to begin offering digital television broadcasting services in 1997—with an increase in channels to as many as 200 or more. In May 1997, BSkyB joined with partners British Telecom, Midland Bank, and Matsushita Electric to form British Interactive Broadcasting Ltd. (BIB), and independent company planning to bring digital interactive television services to the UK market in 1998. This follows the termination of BSkyB's digital television joint venture with Germany's Kirch Gruppe in March 1997.

The bulk of BSkyB's more than £1 billion in annual revenues comes from subscription fees—ranging up to £25 for the full array of premium services—from its 3.3 million satellite dish subscribers and 2.2 million cable subscribers (who receive BSkyB programming through third-party cable television providers). Only slightly more than £100 million of the company's revenues come from advertising, although that figure has been rising as BSkyB increases its penetration of the British television market. BSkyB is also solidly profitable, posting earnings of £257 million for the year ended June 1996, with expectations of more than £350 million in net earnings for the 1997 fiscal year. Led by Samuel H. Chisholm—the New Zealand-born architect of BSkyB's success and, with a compensation package worth some £9 million per year, one of the highest paid television executives in the world—BSkyB is 40 percent owned by Rupert Murdoch's News International Corp. Other principal shareholders include television programmer Granada (11 percent), and the French television company Chargeurs (17 percent). Twenty percent of BSkyB's shares are traded on the London Stock Exchange.

British Satellite Birth Pains in the 1980s

The 1990 merger of bitter satellite rivals SkyTV and British Satellite Broadcasting to form BSkyB caught the U.K. television industry by surprise, but the company's roots already reached back to the early 1980s. In 1983, Rupert Murdoch's News International set up Sky Channel, a European-based satellite-to-cable broadcaster providing a mix of English-language sports and entertainment programming to much of Europe's cable television systems. Sky Channel proved less than successful, however, generating under $20 million per year in advertising revenues, and by the mid-1980s, Murdoch was already looking to evolve the Sky concept toward the newly emerging direct satellite broadcasting technology and to focus the television subsidiary on the British market. Rather than paying for the rights to beam Sky's single-channel signal to cable providers, which in turn supplied the channel's programming to subscribers, direct satellite broadcasts presented the opportunity of providing multichannel programming directly to subscribers' homes via small satellite dish and decoder packages.

Satellite television represented a significant step in British television history. By law, broadcast television was restricted to just four channels—the two license-fee backed BBC channels, and two advertiser-supported channels, ITV and Channel 4. Cable television, meanwhile, was nonexistent in the United Kingdom (the country's cable infrastructure would be completed only toward the mid-1990s). If the Australian-born Murdoch, who had already become a dominant player in the British newspaper market, as well as a key figure in the U.S. newspaper and television market (taking on U.S. citizenship to satisfy FCC television network ownership requirements for the nascent Fox network), hoped to step into the British television market, satellite appeared his sole opportunity. But when regulators handed out the satellite broadcasting license, Murdoch's SkyTV concept, wholly owned by his News International Corp., was denied, due to British law that limited foreign ownership in television networks to 20 percent. Instead, the exclusive British satellite license was awarded to British Satellite Television, a consortium launched by media giants Reed, Pearson, Granada, and Chargeurs.

BSB, as it was known then, was established in 1988 and announced plans to begin broadcasting in mid-1989. Rather than making use of existing satellites, the company determined to build and launch its own satellites, dubbed Marco Polo, and to broadcast using a new technology, called D-MAC, to a Philips-designed receiver dish known as a "squarial." BSB proposed five channels, including a premium movie channel supplied through exclusive rights for more than 2,500 films from such major distributors as Paramount, MCA, MGM/UA, Columbia Pictures, and Orion Communications, purchased at premium flat-rate prices totaling £500 million. Technical problems with the system delayed BSB's launch for more than nine months, until April 1990; even after starting up, BSB was confronted with a shortage of squarials. And by then, BSB no longer had an exclusive on the British satellite market.

Murdoch had not abandoned his British satellite designs. Denied the British license, and rebuffed in an attempt to join the BSB consortium, Murdoch pushed ahead with his SkyTV concept. By renting space on the Luxembourg-based Astra satellites, Murdoch circumvented British ownership laws. Formed in 1988 and using the existing PAL broadcast technology, SkyTV began broadcasting four channels of programming in 1989, including an upgraded version of the original Sky Channel, called Sky One; Eurosport, a joint-venture between the European Broadcast Union and News International; Sky Movies, a fee-based all-film channel; and Sky News, a 24-hour news channel. Start-up costs reached £122 million; losses for its first year of operations were £95 million.

By the time BSB finally launched its service in April 1990, SkyTV had already placed 750,000 satellite dishes. Six months later, SkyTV had extended its reach into more than 1.5 million homes, against BSB claims of 750,000—figures that included cable-based subscribers. Actual sales of satellite dishes told a different story, with nearly one million SkyTV dishes sold compared to less than 120,000 of the BSB squarials. Both services were hurt, however, by consumer reluctance to commit to satellite dish purchases (of £650 per unit) before a standard was reached between the two competing—and incompatible—satellite receiver systems.

Meanwhile, engaged in a bitter rivalry for the home satellite market, both companies were hemorrhaging badly. Murdoch's investment in SkyTV already totaled some £400 million, while the satellite company was losing more than £2.2 million per week. Yet, with a break-even point of 3 million households expected to be reached in 1992, SkyTV still appeared in better shape than BSB. That service had already spent some £800 million by November 1990, with a break-even point projected for 1993, at the earliest. That point seemed more and more unlikely as the weeks went by, given that each week was costing the BSB partners more than £8 million. Nonetheless, it was early days in the British satellite market, with its television viewing potential of more than 20 million households. And despite SkyTV's early subscriber lead, BSB held the financial edge, with its powerful parent companies prepared to plow as much as £1.3 billion into the company—compared to Murdoch's growing struggles to meet the interest payments on News International's debts of more than £4.5 billion. In the end, Murdoch's financial problems determined the next phase of the British satellite television industry.

The two companies caught the British television industry by surprise when they announced their intention to merge in November 1990. Talks between the services had begun informally in July of that year, during a dinner meeting between Murdoch and Read CEO Peter Davis. Without reaching any agreement—Murdoch was uninterested in selling, given SkyTV's early lead and its good chances of reaching its break-even point—but the pair agreed to keep in touch. As pressure from Murdoch's banks mounted, however, the pair met again in October. This time, Davis and Murdoch sketched out a merger agreement, which was finalized after two weeks of intensive, secret meetings by the beginning of November.

The newly merged company, now known as British Sky Broadcasting, or BSkyB, represented a 50–50 ownership between Murdoch and the four BSB investors. The two sides agreed to put up £100 million in working capital, with the BSB side contributing £70 million and Murdoch adding the remainder. The agreement also included a scale of dividend payments: after reaching profitability, News International would receive 80 percent of the first £400 million in dividends, which would then be split 50–50 for 12 years until 2008, at which point BSB would receive 80 percent of the next £400 million. The merger was met with resistance from Britain's television regulators, an issue again subverted by plans to broadcast the new BSkyB from the Astra satellite group—and later mooted altogether by a redrafting of the British Broadcasting Act. The company would abandon the BSB D-Mac technology—and its two satellites—and convert its combined subscriber base of 2.3 million wholly to the SkyTV receiver system. The combined nine channels would be narrowed to just five, including two premium-fee movie channels, one each from

BSB and SkyTV. Within the company itself, the former SkyTV staff quickly dominated the workforce, virtually replacing all of the former BSB managerial and other staff.

Reborn in the 1990s

Perhaps the most significant change for the newly merged company, however, was the appointment of Sam Chisholm as the broadcaster's CEO. Born to a well-to-do farming family in New Zealand, Chisholm started his career as a floor wax salesman. Moving to Australia at the age of 25, Chisholm joined that country's Channel 9, where, as a protégé of the station's founder, he worked his way up the ladder, finally becoming its CEO at the age of 35, making him the youngest chief executive in Australia's television history. Chisholm remained at Channel 9 for 15 years, building it into the country's largest and most profitable television station, while establishing a reputation as an aggressive, even abrasive personality, an uncompromising but effective leader, and a lavish spender. Recruited by Murdoch in September 1990, Chisholm was placed in charge of repairing the damages at the merged company—which posted a loss of £14 million in its first week of operations. These losses would continue for some six months, forcing Murdoch and partners to arrange a refinancing package, worth some £700 million, to keep the company afloat.

Chisholm pushed through an extensive series of cost-cutting procedures, which included firing most of the former BSB staff—total staff dropped from 4,500 to just 1,000—and returning the BSB's fleet of luxury cars, managing to reduce the company's losses to just £1.6 per week by the summer of 1991. Chisholm next turned his attention to BSkyB's programming. His first step there was to renegotiate the expensive film rights contracts the company had inherited from BSB—and the rivalry between the two former companies had resulted in both companies bidding as much as £1 million for the rights to a single film—releasing the company from the flat-rate fee structure and instead linking fees to subscriber levels—effecting immediate savings of some £100 million per year. Next, Chisholm scored a programming coup when, with BBC backing, he offered £304 million, outbidding rival ITV, for the exclusive rights to broadcast the plum Premier League's live football (soccer) matches. With these broadcasts added to its sports lineup, Chisholm converted this channel to a premium, subscription-backed, scrambled broadcast—a gamble that quickly proved successful, generating more than one million subscribers within months after implementation, while also attracting new subscribers to the satellite service.

By March 1992, BSkyB was showing its first operating profits, of £100,000 per week, fully a year ahead of schedule. Subscription revenues reached £3.8 million weekly, while advertising revenues added another £1 million each week. The company continued to post operating profits through the year, and by the end of the company's 1993 fiscal year BSkyB was posting an operating profit of nearly £186 million. A large part of the company's rise in fortune was Chisholm's and Murdoch's decision to convert the company to an entirely fee-based, multichannel concept. Launched in September 1993, Sky Multi-Channels initially featured 14 channels (and would grow to 40 channels), including Sky One, Sky News, Bravo, Discovery, BBC-owned the Children's Channel and UK Gold, the Family Channel, U.K. Living, Nick at Nite, VH-1, and MTV, as well as the Viacom-BSkyB joint venture Nickelodeon U.K. and a BSkyB partnership with the QVC home shopping network.

As BSkyB expanded its multichannel offerings, often accompanied by subscription fee increases, the company's virtual monopoly on the British satellite television market continued to bring in new subscribers, passing the critical three million mark in 1993, and topped 3.5 million households by mid-1994, Chisholm—by then leading Asia's StarTV satellite network, 64 percent of which Murdoch had purchased for $525 million in 1993—prepared to lead BSkyB into a public offering. Completed in January 1995, the offering of 20 percent of the BSkyB's shares valued the company at £4 billion. The stock flotation, which reduced Murdoch's holding to 40 percent, raised £825 million, cutting the company's debt in half. Bringing the company public also proved enormously profitable to Chisholm, who saw himself become one of the world's most highly paid television executives.

While BSkyB's fortunes continued to rise—with revenues topping £1 billion and pre-tax profits of £257 million by year-end 1996—the company has also hastened to join the next, and perhaps greatest, revolution in television history: digital broadcasting. With the capacity of offering as many as 500 channels, as well as interactive services such as video on demand, and telephony applications, the dawn of digital broadcast technology was quickly making BSkyB's analog equipment appear obsolete. BSkyB first announced its intention to join a consortium with European media giants Bertelsmann of Germany, and CanaPlus and Havas of France, to form a digital television alliance. When that fell through, BSkyB next attempted to form a joint-venture partnership with Germany's Kirch Gruppe. This deal, too, fell through. Finally, in May 1997, BSkyB announced the formation of British Interactive Broadcasting (BIB), an independent company owned by BSKyB and British Telecom (each with 32.5 percent), Midland Bank (20 percent), and Matsushita Electric (15 percent). With initial funding of £265 million, BIB promised to bring BSkyB—and the United Kingdom—firmly into the new era of interactive digital television and telephony services.

Further Reading

Clarke, Steve, "BSkyB: The Second Coming," *Campaign*, April 26, 1991, p. 24.

Fallon, Ivan, "How They Kept the Secret of TV Deal," *Sunday Times*, November 4, 1990.

Groves, Dan, "BSkyB Takes Sky-High Bamble with Pay TV," *Daily Variety*, September 6, 1992, p. 23.

Lynn, Matthew, "BSkyB Partners Play Shrewd Flotation Game," *Sunday Times*, October 4, 1994.

Reed, Stanley, "Murdoch's British Sky Is Looking Brighter," *Business Week*, February 24, 1997, p. 16.

Snoddy, Richard, "Sky Bruiser Who Relishes the Fray," *Financial Times*, September 11, 1995, p. 10.

——, "Day of the Dish for BSkyB," *Financial Times*, August 22, 1996, p. 17.

Thomson, Richard, "Thunder Behind the Blue Sky," *The Independent*, November 20, 1994, p. 8.

Thynne, Jane, "Murdoch Aims for the Sky and His Press Rivals," *Daily Telegraph*, September 2, 1993, p. 4.

—M. L. Cohen

Brothers Gourmet Coffees, Inc.

2255 Glades Road, Suite 100E
Boca Raton, Florida 33431
U.S.A.
(561) 995-2600
Fax: (561) 241-0139
Web site: http://pwr.com/bean

Public Company
Incorporated: 1992
Employees: 436
Sales: $72.58 million (1996)
Stock Exchanges: NASDAQ
SICs: 2095 Roasted Coffee

Brothers Gourmet Coffees, Inc., ranks first among U.S. distributors of gourmet coffees to supermarkets, grocery and drug stores, coffee bars, military commissaries, warehouse stores, mass merchandisers, and specialty stores. An integrated sourcer, roaster, and wholesaler, the company sells high-quality gourmet coffee products throughout the United States. As one of the leading U.S. wholesalers of gourmet coffees, Brothers Gourmet earned a reputation for consistently offering high-quality and the freshest possible products. Brothers Gourmet's goals historically have been twofold: to develop brand franchise and customer loyalty to its products and to increase the company's activity in wholesale channels of distribution.

More than three million cups of Brothers Gourmet Coffees were served each day in the United States in 1996, which amounted to 15 million pounds of coffee beans. That year Brothers led all other suppliers of branded gourmet coffees. The company, in fact, was the largest supplier of gourmet coffees to the U.S. grocery channel. Its products were available to 50 percent of all supermarket shoppers in the United States. In addition, the company supplied more gourmet coffees to U.S. military commissaries than any other provider, as well as operated as a major supplier in the specialty wholesale market. In 1996 Brothers was the only wholesaler in the United States totally dedicated to gourmet coffee.

Coffee Business Percolates

Coffee traditionally has been one of the larger traded commodities in the world, though its supply and price are volatile—dependent on weather, politics, economics, and other uncontrollable variables. In 1985, 50 percent of all Americans considered themselves coffee drinkers. Ten years later, the number remained stable, but coffee drinkers' preferences changed. Now more consumers were grinding their own coffee beans instead of buying ground and canned coffee. About 20 percent of retail coffee was roasted bean, a 7 to 10 percent annual increase in whole-bean coffee.

Historically, the coffee industry entailed three market segments: commercial ground-roast, mass-merchandised products; premium coffee products of national roasters; and gourmet coffees. Gourmet coffees—the super-premium, specialty coffees sold in supermarkets, gourmet-food stores, and specialty-coffee stores—were manufactured from the highest quality arabica beans. Superior to the robusta beans used in commercial ground coffee, arabica beans came from Hawaii, Columbia, Brazil, Kenya, Indonesia, Mexico, Costa Rica, Guatemala, and other Central American, South American, Asian, and African nations. Arabica beans offered a richer taste, lower acidity, and lower caffeine content than other coffee beans.

Though part of the overall coffee market, the gourmet coffee market was always somewhat fragmented, with most of the competition concentrated locally or regionally. Since 1986, gourmet coffee consumption grew dramatically, and industry analysts suggested that by the year 2000 half of all coffee sold would be of the gourmet variety—about a $3 billion market. "You ever see a black-and-white TV?" Dennis Boyer, president and chief executive officer of Brothers in 1994, asked when explaining the popularity of gourmet coffees for the *South Florida Business Journal.* "My view is that when people switch from the black-and-white version of coffees to the color versions they don't go back. The small difference in price allows people to see this as an affordable luxury."

Three companies played major roles in the gourmet coffee industry: Sark's Gourmet Coffee Company, a subsidiary of Nestle S.A.; Millstone Coffee, Inc., a subsidiary of Procter &

Company Perspectives:

Brothers Gourmet Coffees has adopted a six-point Gold Quality Standard that touches every aspect of our business. We are committed to: The best in green coffee bean sourcing; testing each coffee bean lot to ensure that it meets the highest standards of aroma and flavor; excellence in bean processing for visual appearance, consistency, and flavor; excellence in package design to assure customers they are getting superior quality products; maximizing the freshness of our coffees by enhancing merchandising rotation; confirming our superior quality through a detailed program of random sampling of finished goods. We do coffee—that's all we do. . . . Our leadership role in the gourmet coffee category comes from the reality of our product quality and innovations and our dedication to the wholesale gourmet coffee business.

Gamble Company; and Brothers Gourmet Coffees, Inc. Unlike the other two, Brothers sourced, roasted, packaged, and marketed its own product to ensure that its coffees were of the highest quality possible. The company bought green arabica beans, roasted the beans under the strictest standards, and tested for quality at each stage of its operation. As Terry Olson, vice president of marketing/sales for Brothers, observed in a press release: "We've renewed our commitment to quality at a time when our competition is finding a way to cut corners. Our green beans are the world's finest specialty and premium grade coffees according to the standards set by the Specialty Coffee Association of America."

Brothers offered consumers 75 varietals, blends, and flavors of coffee under several brand names. The company sold its Brothers brand nationally through supermarkets. In addition, Brothers marketed several regional brands to supermarkets under the names of Hillside Coffee, Cafe du Jour, and Country Mill. Its Fairwinds brand sold to specialty stores, and the company also maintained a private label program. The company had three avenues of distribution, notably direct store delivery or direct shipments, customer warehouses, and specialty food distribution.

Getting Started

Sam and Dennis Boyer were the brothers behind Brothers Gourmet Coffees. Their father operated an institutional coffee company in Denver, so they were familiar with the business from him but initially pursued independent interests. During the 1980s the brothers established their own coffee company in a 20 by 20 foot office in Denver. They had three employees. Their company operated on a regional basis until merging with Specialty Coffee Holdings of Concord, New Hampshire, in December 1992. The merger created a privately held company with four sales territories, 13 regional sales offices, and manufacturing and distribution facilities in Denver, Concord, and Pittsburgh.

Thus, the current company formed in 1992 with a recapitalization and merger with Brothers Gourmet Products, Inc., and Boyer's International, Inc., both established in 1988. Collec-

tively the two companies were the leading wholesaler of gourmet coffee products in the Rocky Mountain region. Two wholesale gourmet coffee distributors—Nicholas Coffee company (founded in 1919) and Elkin Coffee, Inc. (founded in 1933)—were predecessor companies of Brothers Gourmet Coffees.

After the merger Brothers Gourmet Coffees became the largest wholesaler of gourmet coffees in the United States. Brothers was now the major supplier of gourmet coffees to grocery stores in the United States, as well. Dennis Boyer explained the appeal of Brothers to supermarkets in the *Tea & Coffee Trade Journal:* "We have the infrastructure to deliver to our markets as well as advertise our various brands. . . . [W]e can assure quality and freshness from roaster to store." The company distributed its Brothers brand, Cafe du Jour, and Nicholas Gourmet Coffees to more than 6,000 grocery stores and its Fairwinds gourmet coffees to 3,000 gourmet stores. With product in all 50 states, the company became a national presence. Dennis Boyer explained in *Supermarket News:* "Our combined resources will enable us to continue our shared corporate visions to offer our customer the very best gourmet coffees as we compete in the national marketplace."

In 1993 Brothers Gourmet Coffees acquired Hillside Coffee of California, a West Coast wholesale coffee roaster and distributor. The company paid $38.5 million in cash for the subsidiary of Chock Full o' Nuts Corporation, in addition to offering $1.5 million in Brothers common stock and assuming $22 million in Hillside obligations. Hillside Coffee was to operate as a wholly owned subsidiary of Brothers. As Dennis Boyer explained at the time in *Supermarket News:* "We're in the business of providing a gourmet coffee experience to as many consumers as possible. The acquisition allows us to advance this objective by strengthening grocery store distribution and securing the fine Hillside operations."

Moving South

From 1989 through 1993, Brothers enjoyed a 2,000 percent increase in sales, so the Boyer brothers were ready to make some changes. First, the Boyers moved the company from Denver to Boca Raton, Florida, in order to be closer to the coffee bean trade. Then they positioned the company in a second channel of distribution: The brothers brought the company into retail coffee outlets. Feeling that grocery store and coffee bar sales were not mutually exclusive, the Boyers realized that grocery-store customers would buy the coffees that they sampled at coffee bars. To finance the purchase of retail outlets, the company initiated its first public stock offering of 4.2 million shares in 1993. Brothers then purchased 200 Gloria Jean's Gourmet Coffees outlets in 1993 to move into mall-based retail operations. In 1994, the company also opened retail coffee stores in urban settings under the Brothers name.

Improving Plant

In addition to relocating its headquarters and moving into the retail business, Brothers improved its manufacturing plant in Denver. The company installed new and faster auger fillers for the one-pound can line and reconfigured its line. Output at the plant doubled after adding computerized controls for filling, check weighting, seaming, labeling, and capping machinery.

The company saved $60,000 annually in labor costs, and sales increased by 40 percent, allowing Brothers to realize $25 million in sales from the upgrade.

During this time, Brothers also acquired a 250,000-square-foot coffee roasting and packaging facility in Houston from Procter & Gamble. The company completed a $1 million-upgrade of this facility in 1994.

Positioned as the Largest and Fastest

Brothers was the largest roaster of gourmet coffees in the United States in 1994. The company distributed more than 130 varieties of coffees under several brand names. At this time it converted some supermarket brands to the Brothers name. Beginning in 1994, 50 percent of Cafe du Jour brand was renamed, then 25 percent of Hillside products. At this time, Brothers distributed coffees to 195 retail outlets, 3,200 specialty stores, and 8,000 supermarkets.

Listed on *Inc.* magazine's list of the fastest-growing small companies in the United States, Brothers became a significant presence in both the wholesale and retail segments of coffee sales by the end of 1994. The company commanded 25 percent of the wholesale gourmet coffee market. It sold whole-bean coffees, ground coffees, cocoa, and flavored non-dairy creamers to 11,000 supermarket and specialty stores. It had a line of iced coffees under development, and Brothers had about 230 retail coffee bars in operation in malls and urban settings when the Specialty Coffee Association projected by-cup sales of gourmet coffee to be $1.5 billion annually by the year 2000.

Financial Woes

Yet, the company began to founder financially. For the year ending December 30, 1994, the company showed a net profit of $2.4 million, but the year after that was not profitable. So Brothers reviewed its retail operations closely. After careful study, the company decided to end retail operations to focus on its wholesale business. Brothers sold its Gloria Jean's coffee bars to Second Cup Ltd. for $30 million and the Brothers Gourmet Coffee Bars to various buyers, including Diedrich Coffee and Foster Brothers.

To recover financially, Brothers planned to align its cost structure with the wholesale business by decreasing the number of sales, management, and administrative personnel and by consolidating roasting, packaging, and warehousing facilities. The company announced a corporate restructuring in 1995. Dennis Boyer—the last brother at the company—left in August. The new chief executive officer David Vermylen stayed a mere five months before leaving for an executive position with Keebler. Despite the short time of his tenure, Vermylen, cut management staff by one-quarter and consolidated production at the Houston plant after closing the Pennsylvania production facility. (The roasting facility in Denver closed shortly thereafter as well—in January 1996.)

When Vermylen left, Brothers appointed executive vice president and chief financial officer Donald Breen as president, chief executive officer, and a director of the company. The company charged Breen with restructuring the company, fin-

ishing the closing of the retail business, and establishing a plan to concentrate on the wholesale business again. Breen told the *South Florida Business Journal:* "We've laid the groundwork for what we want to accomplish, and we're working on it." Nevertheless, the company posted a net loss of $53.5 million in December 1995.

Working Toward Tomorrow

In 1996, Brothers explored new avenues of distribution for coffee. It became the "preferred provider" of trial-size and gift-packs of coffee for Hallmark Cards Gold Crown retail outlets. Continental Airlines—which brews four million pots of coffee each year—also signed Brothers as the primary provider of gourmet coffees. The airline served the popular supreme roast coffee Foglifter on all its domestic and international flights. As Continental chief operating officer Greg Brenneman explained in a press release: "We conducted extensive taste tests among our passengers before we made our selection—and Brothers was clearly the favorite."

In addition to increasing customer awareness of Brothers products through new distribution channels, the company also expanded its supermarket presence by selling to chains, to grocery and warehouse stores, and to mass merchandisers that were not its customers in the past. Brothers hoped to expand its presence in specialty stores in the wholesale distribution channel, as well as to explore other distribution opportunities in the wholesale market.

Brothers also worked to command more shelf space in stores of current customers. The company renewed its sales agreement with Publix Supermarkets of Lakeland, Florida, in 1996. Publix Supermarkets—one of the world's 30 large grocery retailers—was Brothers' largest customer that year with 525 stores in four southeastern states. Under the new three-year agreement, Brothers supplied a full coffee program to the stores, including bulk whole-bean gourmet coffees and pre-measured packages in state-of-the-art display units.

The company introduced new sizes and types of packaging for customer convenience in 1996; for example, an eight-ounce can and a 1.75-ounce mini can as a trial size. Brothers also redesigned all packaging in eye-catching jewel tones. "Our new packaging says it all," said Olson in a press release. "We wanted to put product on the shelves that tells the story of our business this year—it's a brand new company with a bright future."

Brothers also introduced an enhanced product line in 1996, including new gourmet flavors and supreme roasts. The company repositioned its Brothers, Fairwinds, and Hillside brands in different markets with different price points. As Olson observed in a press release: "We know that today's coffee customer is looking for higher quality and unique items, and we moved quickly to answer that call."

Although the company reported a net loss of $10.2 million in 1996, Brothers management felt it was positioned for success in the future. As Breen wrote in the 1996 annual report: "Nineteen ninety-six was a year of fulfilling promises. We set a product strategy and established a firm financial foundation. We improved customer service levels and renewed our commitment to quality. Our next step is to improve profitability by becoming the undisputed leader in at-home gourmet coffee products nationwide.''

Further Reading

"Brothers, Specialty Coffee Merge," *Supermarket News,* February 1, 1993, p. 20.

"Brothers Taps President, CEO," *Supermarket News,* February 19, 1996, p. 34.

Brown, Suzanne J., "Who's Tending the Beans?," *Tea & Coffee Trade Journal,* May 1994, p. 46.

Busetti, Max, "Coffee Is Hot," *Prepared Foods,* October 1994, p. 34.

"Filing and Labeling Can Boost Efficiency for Coffee," *Packaging Digest,* January 1994, p. 50.

Hutchinson, Julie, "California Firm to Swallow Brothers, Java City," *Denver Business Journal,* February 9, 1996, p. 1B.

Kuhn, Mary Ellen, "Fast Track!," *Food Processing,* December 1994, p. 20.

Moukheiber, Zina, "Oversleeping," *Forbes,* June 5, 1995, p. 78.

Phillips, Dana, "New Deals Brewing for Brothers Bars," *South Florida Business Journal,* February 23, 1996, p. 1A.

——, "Wall Street Weak on Brothers' Brew," *South Florida Business Journal,* March 4, 1994, p. 1A.

Saxton, Lisa, "Brothers Gourmet Buys Hillside," *Supermarket News,* November 8, 1993, p. 3A.

——, "Randall's and Brothers in Specialty Coffee Tie," *Supermarket News,* June 13, 1994, p. 45.

—Charity Anne Dorgan

Brown Group, Inc.

Brown Group, Inc.

8300 Maryland Avenue
St. Louis, Missouri 63166
U.S.A.
(314) 854-4000
Fax: (314) 854-4274
Web site: http://www.browngroup.com

Public Company
Incorporated: 1881 as Bryan Brown Shoe Company
Employees: 11,500
Sales: $1.53 billion (1996)
Stock Exchanges: New York Midwest
SICs: 3143 Men's Footwear, Except Athletic; 3144
Women's Footwear, Except Athletic; 3149 Footwear,
Except Rubber, Not Elsewhere Classified; 5139
Footwear; 5661 Shoe Stores

Brown Group, Inc.—known through most of its 100-plus years as The Brown Shoe Company—is a leading footwear retailer and wholesaler. The Brown Group wholesales many popular brands of women's, men's, and children's shoes—such as Connie, Naturalizer, Life Stride, and Buster Brown—to department stores, specialty retail stores, and mass-merchandisers. The company operates about 800 Famous Footwear stores (which comprise the largest U.S. branded family shoe store chain) and about 450 Naturalizer specialty stores in the United States and Canada. Founded as a U.S. shoe manufacturer, Brown Group now imports all the shoes it sells, about 78 million pairs a year, with most of the sourcing handled by a division—Pagoda Trading Company, Inc.—with offices in Brazil, Italy, China, Hong Kong, Taiwan, and Indonesia. Another division, Pagoda International, markets footwear to retailers in Europe, Latin America, and the Far East. The Brown Group was involved in retailing a variety of products from the 1970s into the early 1990s, including children's furniture and play equipment, rubber balls, women's clothing, rifle sights, equestrian accessories, and fabric, but by 1995 all of these operations had been divested.

Early History

The company began as a shoe manufacturing concern. George Warren Brown moved to St. Louis from New York in 1873 to work in his older brother's wholesale shoe business. While working as a traveling salesman, George Brown came to see great potential in the St. Louis area for shoe manufacturing. At that time, shoes were primarily manufactured on the East Coast. Skilled workers in New England factories made shoes that were then shipped to jobbers at points west. George Warren Brown believed that shoes could be made more cheaply in St. Louis than in the established East Coast factories. After working for four years in his brother's wholesale business, Brown had accumulated enough capital to test his idea. With two other investors, Alvin L. Bryan and Jerome Desnoyers, Brown founded Bryan, Brown and Company to make women's shoes. Brown paid five skilled shoemakers from Rochester, New York, to come to St. Louis and start the factory. The company grew rapidly. In its first year, 1878, the company had sales of $110,000. By 1885 sales were up to $500,000 and growing. In 1881 the company incorporated as the Bryan Brown Shoe Company. In 1885 when Bryan sold his interest, the name was changed to Brown-Desnoyers Shoe Company. In 1893 Desnoyers retired, and the name was changed to The Brown Shoe Company. Brown shoes were sold all over the Midwest, at prices lower than those of the older New England shoe firms. By 1900 the company was growing at a rate of $1 million a year, and St. Louis was becoming known as a major shoe manufacturing center.

In 1900 Brown Shoe contributed $10,000 to the St. Louis World's Fair, a gala event that put a spotlight on the Missouri town. The company put up a model shoe plant at the fair, and this exhibit won Brown a grand prize. Another exhibitor at the fair was the cartoonist R. Fenton Outcault, creator of popular comics "The Yellow Kid" and "Buster Brown." A young Brown executive, John A. Bush, made a lasting contribution to his company by buying the rights to the Buster Brown character. The little blond boy and his dog Tige became the emblem of the Brown Shoe Company children's line. In addition to printing the Buster logo on its shoe boxes, the company hired 20 little people to dress as Buster Brown and tour the country. Buster and Tige played in theaters, shoe stores, and department stores across the country, to much popular acclaim.

While some youngsters were applauding the Buster Brown little people, others were at work in Brown Shoe factories under deplorable conditions for extremely low pay. Because the cost of plant equipment and materials was relatively fixed, Brown Shoe had to make its profits by keeping its labor costs as low as possible. As manufacturing became more mechanized, shoe factory jobs became less skilled. Increasingly, shoe manufacturing jobs were filled by women and children, who could be paid less than men. For example, a 1911 survey of St. Louis shoe workers found more than half to be between the ages of 14 and 19. Some 84 percent of the women and close to 70 percent of the men were under age 24. An average wage for a girl under 16 was less than $10 per week. More shoe manufacturers had followed George Warren Brown's example and set up shoe factories in St. Louis, making the industry extremely competitive. Under these conditions, the wage paid to shoe workers spiraled down.

By 1902 Brown Shoe was operating five factories in St. Louis. In 1907 the company started its first "out of town" plant, in nearby Moberly, Missouri. Several St. Louis shoe companies began manufacturing in surrounding rural towns because of the cheaper labor available in those areas.

In response to the poor working conditions at Brown and in other St. Louis-area shoe factories, workers formed unions. The first was the moderate Boot and Shoe Workers Union; the second was the more radical United Shoe Workers of America, associated with the International Workers of the World. Bitter strikes led to increasing militancy among St. Louis shoe workers. George Warren Brown responded by becoming a local leader of the Citizens Industrial Association, a nationwide antiunion propaganda organization that maintained blacklists against union sympathizers. The best way to fight the unions, however, proved to be to leave St. Louis.

The small towns around St. Louis offered many advantages to the Brown Shoe Company. It was standard at that time for a town that wanted a shoe factory to offer to build one for a company, and exempt the company from paying taxes. In return, the company would agree to pay out a certain amount of money in wages over a five- or 10-year period. After the stipulated amount of wages had been paid, the company had no more obligation to the town. There were always more towns willing to subsidize a new shoe factory. While Brown's management remained headquartered in St. Louis, the company opened factories in many rural towns in Missouri and Illinois. Each town's economy became dependent on the shoe factory, and pro-company sentiments within the factory towns created a hostile climate for union organizers. The distance between the factories also made union organization more difficult than it had been in the condensed St. Louis shoe district.

Regardless of worker discontent, the Brown Shoe Company grew. In 1907 the company moved its headquarters to a stately building in downtown St. Louis. In 1913 Brown was listed on the New York Stock Exchange. With the entrance of the United States into World War I in 1917, Brown Shoe won large, profitable army contracts.

The company stumbled in 1920, however, when a sudden change in women's fashions caught Brown by surprise. Hemlines went up, and Brown was left with an overstock of sturdy high-topped shoes that did not go with the new look at all. John Bush, who had bought the Buster Brown logo rights and then worked his way up to president in 1915, when George Warren Brown became chairman of the board, had to go to Boston before he found a bank that would give the company credit. After this crisis, however, Brown Shoe boomed until the stock market crashed in 1929 and the Great Depression set in.

Labor Strife Reached Peak During Great Depression

During the Depression, Brown Shoe struggled to keep its costs down, which meant that workers' wages suffered. A National Labor Relations Board investigation at Brown's Salem, Illinois, plant found that workers were sometimes drawing checks for as low as $2.50 and $3.00 for a 60-hour week. Workers protested worsening conditions in Brown's factories, but the company's management grew more abusive. U.S. President Franklin D. Roosevelt drafted the National Industrial Recovery Act in 1933 to force industries to standardize wages and prices and thus alleviate the workers' downward wage spiral. Two years later, the Wagner Act guaranteed all U.S. workers the right to organize into unions and to strike. Brown's management, however, remained adamantly anti-union. When workers at the Vincennes, Indiana, factory struck for recognition of their union in 1933, Brown closed the plant. William Kaut, the company's general manager in St. Louis, declared that "The intention of the Brown Shoe Company is to do as much for their help as any shoe industry in the United States . . . and when Brown Shoe Company does its part and even more and if the help are then not satisfied, there is only one thing left to do and that is to close the mill.'' What the Brown Shoe Company was doing for its help, however, reportedly included physical intimidation of union organizers, spying on and infiltrating workers' organizations, and hiring a notorious strike-breaking agency, in addition to its policy of closing down "troublesome" plants.

Eventually, Brown attracted national attention when a union representative in Sullivan, Illinois, narrowly escaped being tarred and feathered in September 1935, and the Illinois Federation of Labor forced a grand-jury investigation. No indictments resulted, but the Regional Labor Board in St. Louis later issued a complaint, citing Brown for unfair labor practices and for using officers and agents of the company to intimidate employees. The hearing that followed revealed that John A. Bush had hired the A.A. Ahner detective agency in 1934. Bush testified that he did not know that Ahner was a strike-breaking agency, but Ahner was in fact known as such in St. Louis. In 1929 he had been implicated in an attempted bombing connected with antiunion work. Although Ahner himself claimed he was not hired to break unions, a report in the *Nation* on January 29, 1936, noted that termination of Ahner's connection with the shoe company coincided with the dissolution of most of the locals of the Boot and Shoe Workers' Union in Brown plants.

It was not only physical threats and the economic threat of plant shut-down that led many union locals to disband. The Labor Board hearings revealed that Brown had kept a paid spy in its Sullivan factory. The spy turned out to be the former head of the union local. After urging workers into an ill-timed strike, he then incited his union's members to burn the union charter and disband. He was later overheard telephoning Brown headquarters to report his success. Attacked from within and without, most of the Boot and Shoe Workers Union locals at Brown plants folded, because workers were desperate to hang on to their jobs. Brown sometimes closed its plants temporarily, later to rehire only workers who had had no union involvement.

The National Labor Relations Board cited Brown in 1936 for violating the Wagner Act in connection with the dissolution of the Salem local, but the company refused to reinstate strikers and workers who had been fired for union activity. The workers who had not lost their jobs at Brown were finally given some help in their struggle for decent wages when the Fair Labor Standards Act of 1938 established a minimum wage in the United States. The labor shortage during World War II finally gave a boost to union organization, although unrest continued to some degree.

In 1941 Brown opened a new plant in Dyer, Tennessee. A Brown executive, Monte Shomaker, who was later to serve as Brown's fourth president, urged the move south. Shomaker worked to modernize Brown's factories after the war, and to relocate many of them in the traditionally nonunion South. At the same time, Brown's third president, Clark Gamble, was taking steps to move the company into retailing.

Expanded into Retailing Through 1950s Acquisitions

Gamble assumed the presidency from John Bush in 1948, and in 1950 he initiated a merger with Wohl Shoes. Wohl was a 35-year-old wholesale and retail shoe business with headquarters in St. Louis. Wohl had annual sales of $33 million, 90 percent of which came from women's shoes. Brown had provided only 10 percent of Wohl's shoes before the merger, and the merger provided a large new market for Brown. Wohl wholesaled shoes through 2,500 stores throughout the United States, Canada, Mexico, and Cuba, and operated several hundred retail stores and leased department store shoe salons. With this first major acquisition, Brown took a giant step toward integrating its operations into both manufacturing and retailing.

The Wohl merger was followed by Brown's acquisition of another large retail chain in 1953, Regal Shoes. When Brown acquired G.R. Kinney Corporation in 1956, the company had gone far toward assuring itself of both manufacturing and retailing capabilities. Brown was then the fourth-largest shoe manufacturer in the United States, and Kinney the largest operator of family shoe stores. A U.S. District Court in St. Louis, however, found Brown guilty of antitrust violations in 1959, and ordered the company to divest itself of Kinney. The judge in the case concluded that the Brown-Kinney merger seriously limited the ability of independent retailers to compete with company-owned retail outlets, as well as limiting the market for indepen-

dent manufacturers. In 1962 the Supreme Court upheld the lower court's ruling. By that year Brown had taken the number-one spot in the shoe industry. Brown subsequently sold Kinney to F.W. Woolworth.

Monte Shomaker took over the presidency of Brown from Clark Gamble in 1962. Despite the setback of the Kinney ruling, Shomaker was able to continue Brown's expansion. In 1959 the company had acquired Perth Shoe Company, a Canadian firm with wholesale, retail, and manufacturing operations. In 1965 Brown bought the Samuels Shoe Company, a high-fashion women's shoe company, and in 1970 Brown acquired a men's shoe importer, Italia Bootwear, Ltd.

Began to Diversify Beyond Shoes in the 1970s

Brown's earnings rose each year in the 1960s, until a flood of imports swamped the U.S. shoe industry in 1968. The company's earnings plunged 25 percent in 1969. A new president, W. L. Hadley Griffin, took over that year. Griffin decided to do what other large shoe companies had been doing for years, that is, to diversify into nonshoe areas. Brown quickly acquired retail fabric chains, the Eagle Rubber Company, Kent Sporting Goods, and a luggage sales company, among others. In 1972 The Brown Shoe Company changed its name to Brown Group, Inc., to reflect the company's diversification. By 1973 close to 20 percent of Brown's sales were coming from its nonfootwear subsidiaries. The Brown Group continued to diversify through the 1970s, buying up companies in two main areas: children's products, and sports and recreation.

In 1979 W. L. Hadley Griffin moved up to chairman, and B. A. Bridgewater became the new president. Bridgewater had worked in U.S. President Richard Nixon's Office of Management and Budget, where he set fiscal priorities for the State Department, the Defense Department, and the Central Intelligence Agency. Bridgewater introduced cost-cutting measures at Brown, including reductions in the workforce and cutbacks in executive perquisites. Bridgewater's first year was a record year for the Brown Group, with sales up 16 percent and earnings up 25 percent, and with net income of $41 million. Increased costs, and foreign competition, however, led Brown to close its St. Louis warehouse in 1980.

Heightened Competition Led to 1980s and 1990s Restructurings

Pressure from cheap imports led to more competitive conditions in the U.S. shoe market throughout the 1980s, and President Bridgewater had to constantly adjust the Brown Group's business strategy. In the 1970s diversification into nonshoe areas had proved essential, but in the 1980s, slimming down the company and concentrating on shoe retailing seemed to be the right thing. In 1982 Brown's recreational products division sagged, and Bridgewater ordered a restructuring, which included plant closings and changes in marketing and management. In 1985 after a very poor third quarter, the company announced it would divest itself of all its recreational products operations. The divestiture left Brown with about 75 percent of its business concentrated in shoe manufacture and retailing. The other 25 percent represented various other retail operations, such as Brown's line of fabric stores, specialty women's clothing stores, and the Meis chain of department stores.

In the mid-1980s, Brown bid to keep its shoe business competitive by moving more strongly into shoe importing. Brown acquired Arnold Dunn, Inc., a women's shoe importer, in 1984. That year Brown established an importing division, Brown Group International, and in 1986 it acquired the Pagoda Trading Company, a Far-East importing firm. Importing proved far more profitable than manufacturing. The company closed several U.S. shoe plants, but at the same time improved the efficiency of its remaining factories. By 1988 Brown was able to produce almost as many shoes as in 1980, in spite of a 40 percent reduction in the number of plants it operated. The company also opted to concentrate on marketing its well-known brands such as Connie, Naturalizer, and Buster Brown, and discontinue its marginal lines.

Ultimately, over the course of the early and mid-1990s— and under the continuing leadership of Bridgewater—Brown dramatically restructured itself into a footwear retailing and wholesaling company, with shoe manufacturing almost entirely jettisoned and all nonfootwear businesses divested. In 1989 the company sold off all of its remaining nonfootwear specialty retail operations with the exception of the Cloth World retail fabric chain. The following year, the Pagoda International division was formed to market footwear to retailers in Europe, and eventually in Latin America and the Far East. Brown closed six of its fast-dwindling domestic shoe plants in 1991 and 1992. And the following year it began to shutter its troubled Wohl Leased Shoe Department operation, which managed 500 shoe departments in 26 department store chains.

Brown's restructuring efforts reached a peak in 1994 and 1995. All of the company's remaining U.S. shoe factories were closed, leaving Brown with only two manufacturing plants in Canada. More than 100 company-owned Regal and Connie specialty shoe stores and 50 Naturalizer stores were closed. Three of the company's five headquarters buildings were sold. And the company sold its Cloth World chain to Fabri-Centers of America, Inc. for $65.7 million, thereby returning to a pure focus on footwear. More than 8,500 jobs were eliminated as a result of these moves, about 35 percent of the overall workforce.

Freed from several burdensome operations, Brown began to bolster its core businesses through acquisitions and licensing deals. In 1995 the company acquired the Larry Stuart Collection, an upscale women's shoe brand. Brown beefed up its offerings in the hot athletic shoe segment with the 1995 acquisition of the le coq sportif brand (a century-old brand popular in Latin America, Europe, and the Far East) from Adidas AG and with 1996 license agreements through which Brown would market athletic footwear under the Russell and Penn brand names. Pagoda International, meanwhile, built up an impressive list of famous brands that it licensed for use on shoes sold to children outside the United States, including Barbie; Star Wars;

Disney's 101 Dalmatians, Hunchback of Notre Dame, and Mickey for Kids; and Warner Brothers' Looney Tunes, Batman, and Space Jam.

By 1996 Brown Group's extensive and lengthy restructuring had begun to show signs of paying off. The downsized company's sales of $1.53 billion were still well below the levels of the late 1980s and early 1990s, but when adjusted for discontinued operations sales were on the rise. Profits—$20.3 million in 1996—were recovering as well. In possession of an impressive—and expanding—assortment of brands, Brown looked to step up its advertising in order to further increase sales with $21 million (8 percent of sales) slated for brand marketing in fiscal 1997. The company was also expected to continue to aggressively pursue overseas sales, which although on the increase still comprised less than 1 percent of overall sales.

Principal Subsidiaries

Brown Shoe Company; Pagoda Trading Company, Inc.; Brown Shoe Company of Canada, Ltd.; Laysan Company Limited (Hong Kong); Linway Investment Limited (Hong Kong); Brown Group Dublin Limited (Ireland); Moda Universal S.A. de C.V. (Mexico; 50%); LCS International B.V. (Netherlands).

Principal Divisions

Famous Footwear; Branded Marketing (Brown Shoe Company); Pagoda (Brown Shoe Company); Naturalizer Retail (Brown Shoe Company); Canadian Wholesale; Canadian Retail.

Further Reading

Brown Group: The First Hundred Years, St. Louis, Missouri: Brown Group, Inc., 1978.
Byrne, Harlan S., "Brown Group: Prosperity Following a Shakeout," Barron's, March 15, 1993, pp. 46–47.
Feurer, Rosemary, "Shoe City, Factory Towns: St. Louis Shoe Companies and the Turbulent Drive for Cheap Rural Labor, 1900–1940," Gateway Heritage, Fall 1988.
Harris, William, "Buster Brown Lives," Forbes, July 19, 1982, p. 50.
Heiderstadt, Donna, "Brown Group Puts Growth on Value, Traditional Bases," Footwear News, August 9, 1993, p. 24.
Ludington, Callaway, "Brown Group Strides Toward Recovery," St. Louis Business Journal, August 6, 1990, pp. 1A, 11A.
Macdonald, Laurie, "Far Reaching Restructuring Under Way at Brown Group," Footwear News, January 17, 1994, p. 1.
Quick, Julie, "Bridgewater Shakes Brown's Cobwebs," St. Louis Business Journal, January 13, 1992, pp. 1A, 10A.
Sahm, Cathy, "Brown Enters Athletic Shoe Race," St. Louis Business Journal, March 25, 1991, pp. 1A, 19A.
Sender, Isabelle, "Brown Factory Closings Lead to $8.4M Qtr. Loss," Footwear News, September 11, 1995, p. 1.

—Angela Woodward
—updated by David E. Salamie

Browning-Ferris Industries, Inc.

757 North Eldridge
Houston, Texas 77079
U.S.A.
(281) 870-7632
Fax: (713) 870-7844

Public Company
Incorporated: 1970
Employees: 37,000
Sales: $5.77 billion (1996)
Stock Exchanges: New York Midwest Pacific London
SICs: 4953 Refuse Systems; 5093 Scrap & Waste
   Materials; 8748 Business Consulting Services, Not
   Elsewhere Classified

The second-largest waste disposal company in the world, Browning-Ferris Industries, Inc. (BFI) collects, processes, disposes, and recycles solid waste for commercial, industrial, and residential customers. From a one-truck operation established in Houston, Texas, in 1966, BFI grew with phenomenal speed into the waste industry's second-largest corporation, active throughout the United States and in international markets as well. Like its bigger rival, Waste Management, BFI offered a full range of waste, recycling, and sanitation services. During the late 1990s, BFI operated in nearly 800 locations in Asia, Australia, Europe, the Middle East, New Zealand, and North America. The company's North American operations included 104 solid-waste landfill sites, 32 medical-waste treatment facilities, and 125 recycling facilities.

1960s Origins

Browning-Ferris's extremely rapid growth was made possible by the wholesale change that overtook the waste-disposal industry in the 1960s. Prior to that time, waste was known as garbage, and usually was transported by municipalities or small local collection firms to a distant plot of land and there dumped or incinerated. Regulations were few and the industry was completely fragmented, a typical company consisting of no more than a few trucks and the family that owned them.

This was the situation in Houston in 1964 when a young accountant named Tom Fatjo Jr. began keeping financial records for a number of local garbage collectors. Fatjo became intrigued with the wide-open business, and in 1966 bought a truck and opened his own garbage collection company, one of the 17 small firms at that time working in the Houston area. At the time, national legislation designed to tighten regulation of both collection and disposal services had recently been enacted. This legislation would change radically the nature of garbage treatment in the United States. Henceforth, collection trucks would have to meet higher standards of sanitation, while for reasons of air pollution the incineration of garbage would give way increasingly to landfill burial. Both changes would require large capital investments on the part of waste operators, most of whom were in no position to raise the sums involved. The situation was ripe for the creation of a large, multi-city company capable of spending the money needed to establish the garbage business as a modern, sanitary, technologically competent industry. The days of one-horse garbage hauling were over.

Tom Fatjo accordingly began looking for ways to expand his Houston company. After beginning with residential waste collection, he added accounts in the commercial and industrial sectors such as shopping malls and small factories. In 1968 he branched into the disposal end of the business, winning a large landfill contract from the city of Houston. At about this time Fatjo, his eyes trained on a much larger, regional organization, became partners with Louis A. Waters, then a vice president of corporate finance for a New York securities brokerage. The two of them decided to embark on a program of acquisitions designed to weld together scores of the tiny collection and disposal companies operating across Texas and the South. To help raise the capital needed for so ambitious an undertaking, Fatjo and Waters in 1969 gained control of Browning-Ferris Machinery Company, a publicly traded manufacturer of garbage trucks and landfill equipment, among other things. Not only did Browning-Ferris offer an obvious match for the two partners' collection business, it also allowed them to issue stock for the purposes of working capital and equity swaps.

Thus fortified, Fatjo and Waters went to work over the next three years buying up small operators at the rate of one a week. By consolidating its acquisitions, most of which were in Houston; Memphis, Tennessee; and Puerto Rico, Browning-Ferris, renamed Browning-Ferris Industries, Inc., was able to take advantage of the basic axiom of the collection business: the more adjacent stops made by each truck, the greater the return on equity. It is much more profitable to collect waste, for example, from ten large apartment complexes in a row than to collect from the first, fifth, and tenth buildings and then be forced to move elsewhere for the next pickup. Therefore, as BFI bought up the businesses of rival collectors in Houston or Memphis, its costs per customer dropped sharply and profits accordingly rose, paving the way for further acquisitions. In the meantime, growing public pressure for environmental protection prompted a continuing flurry of new regulations affecting every aspect of the waste industry. Compliance with such legislation was expensive, in terms of either equipment or knowhow, which in turn made it easier for BFI to buy out financially strapped, smaller competitors. BFI bought out competitors as fast as the contracts could be written. Most owners of the acquired companies stayed on as managers.

By 1975 BFI's revenues had climbed to $256 million. The company operated 2,800 trucks in 131 different cities, employed 7,700 workers, and had accumulated 60 landfills. The latter would prove critically important, as further regulation and public anxiety made it nearly impossible to create new landfills and raised the costs of operating those already in existence. Dumping charges skyrocketed, adding a new source of bottom-line funds to BFI's resources; more importantly, the scarcity of landfill sites discouraged new competitors from jumping into the business. Those companies such as BFI and Waste Management that got into garbage early, stayed in and grew at prodigious rates; those that came later found the industry nearly locked up. BFI expanded its landfill holdings whenever possible, and also began handling a new form of waste variously labeled as chemical, toxic, or hazardous. Although toxic waste would later play an important role in BFI's history, in the mid-1970s the company had just begun to explore the complex and notoriously litigious field, chiefly in the form of waste-oil treatment.

In 1976 Tom Fatjo withdrew from BFI to run an investment company of his own, leaving Louis Waters in charge of the firm's finances and Harry Phillips, Sr. as its chief operating officer. Phillips had owned a number of the garbage collection companies in Memphis acquired by BFI, and his hands-on experience made him invaluable to the company's founders, neither of whom knew intimately the day-to-day problems of the garbage business. Phillips remained chief operating officer and served as chairman from 1979 until the appointment of William D. Ruckelshaus in 1988, and even then continued as chairman of the executive committee.

1970s: Diversification and Expansion

Aside from its core business in solid waste, by the mid-1970s BFI had developed a number of peripheral interests. It was one of the earliest companies to experiment with the recycling of paper waste, using its own collection supply and also buying paper from thousands of users that could then be treated, shredded, and sold to papermakers. A sharp recession in the paper markets in 1975 threw BFI's paper division into the red, however, and in the following year its paper recycling assets were spun off to shareholders in the form of a separate company. Of greater importance was BFI's first foreign contract, a 1973 agreement to provide sanitation services in parts of Spain. The business of international waste services grew rapidly during the 1970s, particularly after rival Waste Management signed a contract in 1975 to clean the city of Riyadh, Saudi Arabia, for five years, and it seems that despite its early success in Spain, BFI was generally slow to pursue the many opportunities overseas. As a result, Waste Management won most of the lucrative international contracts, while BFI only established its presence in Europe and the Far East markets in later years, winning the Riyadh contract back from Waste Management in the next round.

Harry Phillips proved to be an outstanding leader for BFI. His background in operations enabled him to keep a tight lid on costs even as the company continued to expand at breakneck speed through the early years of the 1980s. Thus, not only did BFI's revenue double between 1978 and 1983 to $843 million, its operating margin also increased dramatically, from just under 31 percent to 35.8 percent. The latter was due to BFI's economies of scale, by which a greater number of pick-ups translated into a larger bottom line; to a large and highly motivated sales force expected to bring in scores of new customers every year; and to Phillips's ability to coordinate the day-to-day complexities of a rapidly growing corporation.

It was also during this period that chemical and toxic waste became a more important factor at BFI. In 1976 Congress passed the Resource Conservation and Recovery Act, a piece of legislation designed to tighten control of all forms of potentially dangerous landfills. By the time the law was fully implemented in 1980 it had sharply increased the difficulty and cost of chemical and toxic disposal, giving much additional business to companies like BFI with some experience in the field. By 1983 chemical waste provided 10 percent of BFI's revenue and was projected to be a mainstay of the company's future, as it became more difficult to find opportunities for expansion in the solid-waste sector. About half of the company's toxic-waste business was the result of the 1983 purchase of CECOS International Inc., one of the industry's leaders, along with the smaller Newco Waste Systems. The CECOS acquisition brought with it two toxic disposal sites—giving BFI a total of eight—and opened up the important New York and Ohio markets. With the Environmental Protection Agency (EPA) about to begin distributing billions of dollars from its Superfund to clean up toxic waste, and BFI's 400-person sales force aggressively on the march, the company had every reason to expect hazardous disposal to become a second major revenue stream.

Difficulties During the 1980s

As it turned out, however, it was primarily those two elements that caused BFI much grief during the next five years. BFI's sales force was not only large and aggressive, rival firms and a number of grand juries alleged, it also engaged in predatory pricing. As of 1984 the company was under investigation in seven states for suspected monopolistic practices such as price-fixing, charges that it denied but often settled out of court for amounts totaling $15 million by 1989. The monetary damages were relatively minor, but such publicity hurt the company's image with customers and with the increasing group of governmental, environmental, and industrial parties involved. The problem was intensified in 1985, when a BFI toxic dump in Williamsburg, Ohio, was repeatedly closed by both state and federal environmental authorities. A grand jury also brought criminal charges against BFI, claiming the company had contaminated a nearby creek. Amid the attendant turmoil, BFI's hazardous division as a whole dropped into the red for the first half of the year.

While the company's solid-waste business continued to grow profitably and its first few waste-to-energy plants opened in New York and New Jersey, the comparatively minor hazardous-waste division became a major liability. Company-owned toxic landfills in New York, Ohio, and Louisiana were found wanting when BFI applied for permit extensions near the end of the 1980s.

Concerned that the company might be permanently shut out of these three sites, and generally in need of a face-lift, BFI in October 1988 announced that it had hired William D. Ruckelshaus as its new chairman and chief executive. Ruckelshaus brought with him a reputation for integrity, first established during the Watergate scandal when as deputy attorney general he refused President Richard Nixon's order to fire special prosecutor Archibald Cox and later burnished by his second term as head of the EPA following the scandalous reign of Anne Gorsuch Burford in the early 1980s. Ruckelshaus was respected by the business community, environmentalists, and public servants, and it was thought that he could salvage BFI's hazardous-waste contracts.

1990s: Recycling and Revival

Ruckelshaus was very much an outsider at BFI, however, and his arrival as the company's chairman struck observers as a public relations ploy. The company's relationship with the federal and state environmental agencies was strained beyond the point of immediate repair, and despite the presence of Ruckelshaus, BFI was unable to win approval for any of the three dumps in question. BFI announced in the spring of 1990 that it was withdrawing from the toxic-waste business, citing poor profit margins as the source of its decision. The company took a $452 million pre-tax charge against earnings to cover the cost of devalued assets, pushing fiscal 1990 into the red and sending a clear signal that in the battle between BFI and Waste Management for the industry's top spot, BFI would at least temporarily settle for second. Despite the legal liabilities inherent in toxic waste, the field is extremely profitable and is certain to grow indefinitely; in the year of BFI's withdrawal, for example, Waste Management earned $176 million in that segment of its business.

Once BFI exited the hazardous waste business, Ruckelshaus led the push toward recovery by focusing on what he called "managing the middle." His objective was to reduce operating costs wherever he could, and in this effort Ruckelshaus left no stone unturned. In addition to slashing the maintenance costs associated with operating the company's fleet of bulldozers, trucks, and other equipment, Ruckelshaus made smaller and less

obvious cuts, including the doughnuts served at staff meetings and his own airline ticket expenses. Although the savings realized by flying coach rather than first class amounted to little for a multi-billion dollar corporation like BFI, the across-the-board overhead reductions added up, enabling the company to trim operating costs by nearly 15 percent in a few short years. Further profit gains were made by acquiring landfills, thereby improving operating margins by avoiding third-party landfill fees.

Productivity and efficiency improved in the wake of these measures by Ruckelshaus, giving him the power to move in the direction he perceived BFI should take in the future. From Ruckelshaus's vantage point, BFI's best chance for long-term financial health was in recycling, but few at BFI shared his view. "Ruckleshaus brought the vision of recycling with him," Harry Phillips related to *Forbes* magazine. "Most of us who had been in the business took a dim view of it." Despite his detractors, Ruckelshaus moved headlong into recycling, resolving to concentrate on paper, which accounted for 45 percent of the U.S. waste stream and soon would represent 85 percent of BFI's recycling business. By receiving a fee for collecting waste paper, sorting and baling it and then reselling it directly to papermakers, BFI gained a new, powerful, revenue-generating engine, one that drove sales upward at an encouraging rate and provided great promise for the future. BFI's recycling division recorded less than $10 million in 1990; by 1995 the company's recycling efforts were bringing in $675 million annually.

Increased operational efficiency coupled with a focus on recycling proved to be the restorative financial salve BFI needed to rebound from the massive loss in 1990. After overhead costs had been reduced and the foray into recycling began in earnest, BFI mirrored the strategy employed during its inaugural years of business by executing an ambitious acquisition spree. In 1993, as the regulatory environment in the waste-disposal industry made it increasingly difficult for smaller companies to survive, BFI swallowed up many of its more diminutive competitors, spending nearly $140 million to acquire more than 100 companies. The following year, when sales eclipsed $4 billion, BFI acquired 115 companies, including a 50 percent interest in Otto Waste Services, a German solid waste services company, for $375 million. The pace of expansion slackened only marginally in 1995 when BFI added $267 million in revenues through the purchase of 103 companies.

The actions taken by BFI during the first half of the 1990s pointed to the direction it would take during the second half of the decade and most likely into the foreseeable future. Recycling, which accounted for 11 percent of the company's total revenue volume midway through the decade and was growing exponentially, was expected to account for 35 percent of BFI's revenue total by the beginning of the 21st century. Likewise, further progress was expected to be made on the acquisition front, as BFI pursued the waste-disposal industry's smaller competitors. Acquisitions and recycling, accordingly, represented the operative words describing BFI's future in the massive and increasingly important business of waste disposal.

Principal Subsidiaries

A.B.C. Disposal, Inc.; Atkinson Enterprises, Inc.; CECOS International, Inc.; Cotecnica, C.A.; Dave Systems, Inc.; Dooley

Equipment Corp.; Eastern Disposal Inc.; Empire Sweeping Co.; Empresa Nacional de Residuos Ltd.; Environmental Equipment Corp.; ESI, Inc.; Geneva Waste Services, Inc.; Heavy Equipment Leasing Services Co., Inc.; Hennepin Transfer, Inc.; HL-NIW, Inc.; Indoco, Inc.; International Disposal Corp.; Joe Ball Sanitation Service, Inc.; Land Reclamation, Inc.; Landfill, Inc.; Lanham Waste Control, Inc.; Louis Kmito & Son, Inc.; Lyon Development Co.; Multi-Packer Inc.; National Disposal Service, Inc.; Newco Waste Systems, Inc.; Pine Bend Landfill, Inc.; Prince William Trash Service, Inc.; Removal, Inc.; Residential Service, Inc.; Risk Services, Inc.; Rot's Disposal Service, Inc.; Servicos Metropolitanos, C.A.; Waste Disposal, Inc.; West Roxbury Crushed Stone Co.; Westowns Disposal Systems, Inc.; Woodlake Sanitary Service, Inc.

Further Reading

Bailey, Jeff, "Trash Troubles: Browning-Ferris Fails to Boost Its Business by Hiring 'Mr. Clean'," *The Wall Street Journal*, May 14, 1991.

Hackney, Holt, "Browning-Ferris Industries: A Pure Play in Trash," *Financial World*, February 1, 1994, p. 17.

Lucas, Allison, "BFI Hauls in the New York Market," *Sales & Marketing Management*, October 1995, p.14

Miller, William H., "Cashing in on Trash," *Industry Week*, February 16, 1976.

Sullivan, R. Lee, "Garbage In, Earnings Out," *Forbes*, December 5, 1994, p. 96.

—Jonathan Martin
—updated by Jeffrey L. Covell

BVLGARI

Bulgari S.p.A.

Lungotevere Marzio, 11
00186 Rome
Italy
39 6 68 81 01
Fax: 33 6 68 81 04 01

Public Company
Founded: 1884
Employees: 573
Sales: L385.3 billion (US$237.6 million) (1995)
SICs: 3911 Jewelry, Precious Metal; 2844 Toilet
Preparations; 5944 Jewelry Stores; 5122 Drugs,
Proprietaries, and Sundries; 6719 Holding Companies,
Not Elsewhere Classified

Bulgari S.p.A. is one of the world's leading manufacturers and marketers of luxury goods. From its traditional emphasis on the highest-quality jewelry and watches, the company has expanded into perfumes, silk scarves, and eyewear. Bulgari sells its fine wares via 31 company-owned stores and 18 franchisees as well as thousands of perfumeries, department stores and duty free outlets. Though the company went public in 1995, brothers Paolo and Nicola Bulgari—grandsons of the founder—continued to share a controlling 61.8 percent share of its equity. Their nephew, Francesco Trapani, has served as chief executive officer since 1981.

Company Origins Stretch Back to 19th-Century Greece

Company founder Sotirio Boulgaris was born in 1857, the lone heir to an apparently long line of itinerant Greek silversmiths. Fleeing the violence and banditry endemic to mainland Greece at the time, Sotirio and his parents moved to Corfu, where they established a shop in the late 1870s. The young metalworker soon sought to find his own way in the world, and in 1880 settled in Rome, Italy. After operating a short-lived partnership, Sotirio founded a variety store featuring silver belts, buckles, bracelets, and buttons as well as tableware and antiques in 1884. By the turn of the century, the enterprising businessman had established outlets in St. Moritz, San Remo, Naples, Bellagio, and Sorrento. He Romanized the family name to Bulgari, and in 1880 bestowed that name on his bride, Eleni. Though he was putting in long hours to make the business a success, Sotirio found time to father two sons, Costantino and Giorgio in 1889 and 1890, respectively.

Around the turn of the century, Sotirio sold his budding chain of shops in order to concentrate on a single jewelry and silver business. In 1905 he purchased a shop at no.10 Via Condotti in Rome, a location that would remain the Bulgari headquarters for the duration of the 20th century. The new outlet offered a more upscale selection of goods ranging from embossed and engraved silver serving pieces to decorative ceramics as well as gold and silver jewelry, often set with gemstones. Over the course of the first two decades of the 20th century, Bulgari gradually took on a more cosmopolitan air. Giorgio and Costantino had their first involvement in the family business during this period. By the time the Bulgaris resumed business after the interruptions of World War I, the company had completed its shift from an emphasis on silver to pricier bejeweled pieces.

The Second Generation Takes the Helm in 1930s

After Sotirio died in 1932, his sons undertook an extravagant remodeling of both the interior and the exterior of the Via Condotti store and formally changed the company logo to "BVLGARI," an application of the traditional Roman alphabet. The L2 million project took two years and featured the pink and beige Italian marble that would become the worldwide hallmark of the firm's retail outlets. Giorgio's global gem-sourcing travels exposed him to the latest fashions in the then-Paris-based jewelry industry, while Costantino's penchant for collecting ancient silver wares would later be a source of inspiration for the company's adaptation of classical themes.

Having latched onto style trends emanating from Paris, Bulgari continued to follow the lead of what was then the world's jewelry capital throughout the first half of the century. In the 1920s, Bulgari embraced Art Deco themes. In the 1930s, the company concentrated on diamonds set in platinum. Wartime

Company Perspectives:

Bulgari is on the attack. In Italy, we're a legend—we don't need to aspire to be anyone else because we're at the top, but our goal is to expand both in quantitative terms and qualitative terms. The quantitative goal is easy: We want to sell more and be more profitable. But the qualitative goal is perhaps foremost. We have a prestigious role in the luxury goods industry and we want to become even more important in this sense. Our goal is to have a mix of products that will enable us to be present in several different markets.

restrictions and a general climate of austerity was reflected in a dearth of jewelry designs of the 1940s. When the company did produce a piece, it often featured yellow gold and few or no precious jewels. Though highly regarded for their craftsmanship, the Bulgari brothers continued to follow, rather than set, trends after World War II. In the prosperous years of the immediate postwar era, the jewelry house produced lavish settings of diamonds, emeralds, sapphires, and rubies in platinum. Floral motifs, many featuring *en tremblant* settings that moved with the wearer, were especially popular during this period.

The store's marble-decked façade would be the backdrop of many a paparazzi photo in the postwar era, as celebrities from around the world were drawn to the Bulgari shop. The expanding clientele, which prior to the 1960s included Italian nobility; South American political figure Evita Peron; American businessmen like Nelson Rockefeller and Woolworth's founder Samuel Henry Kress; and U.S. Ambassador to Italy Clare Boothe Luce, reflected Bulgari's growing stature among the world's high-class jewelry houses.

BVLGARI Style Emerges in 1960s

In the 1960s, Italian jewelers in general and the Bulgari brothers in particular began to break away from France's fashion dictates to establish their own recognizable styles. The Bulgari mode of design that emerged over the ensuing decade departed from the French in several respects. In place of large, faceted diamond centerpieces, Bulgari began to substitute colored gemstones in a smooth, domed cut known in the industry as ''cabochon.'' Diamonds—often brilliant cut and/or pavé set—became the supporting actors in these color plays. When choosing its stones, the jewelry house shunned the traditional emerald-ruby-sapphire trio, and instead began to choose gemstones based more on their artistic contribution to the piece than their financial contribution. Smooth outlines and highly stylized forms in yellow gold would complete the Bulgari look. In their 1990 essay on the firm for *The Master Jewelers*, Charles M. Newton and Omar Torres aptly noted that ''The symmetry and proportions of Bulgari products are based more upon art and architecture than on nature—a factor which distinguishes the Bulgari jewel from that of the French masters.''

The family's third generation, represented by Giorgio's three sons Paolo, Gianni, and Nicola, took the helm in 1967. Eldest son Gianni earned a law degree and favored a playboy lifestyle—complete with a stint as a racecar driver—but was soon drawn into the family business and served as chief executive into the early 1980s. Paolo, the artist of the trio, has been called ''one of the world's foremost jewelers.'' *The Master Jewelers* noted that ''One of his greatest talents is his ability to translate his understanding of his family's traditions into recognizably Bulgari jewels while continually moving forward with new and exciting forms and ideas.'' Though Nicola, the youngest, has been characterized as the businessman of the family, he was also responsible for an important design contribution. An avid collector of ancient coins, in the late 1960s he revived their use in jewelry, dubbing them *Gemme Nummarie*, or ''Coin Gems.'' Bulgari's most popular treatment featured coins set in heavy, open-linked, yellow gold chains, but the firm also produced rings, earrings, bracelets, and even tableware and gift items on this theme. The juxtaposition of patinated coins and highly polished precious metals would become a Bulgari hallmark.

International Expansion Begins in 1970s

The brothers established their first international outlet in 1970 in New York's Pierre Hotel on Fifth Avenue. By the end of the decade, they had launched locations in Geneva, Monte Carlo, and even Paris. Bulgari's jewelry designs of this decade were strongly influenced by the exhibitions of the treasures of Tutankhamen's ancient Egyptian treasures. Indian motifs, particularly the ''boteh'' (leaf), were also prevalent in the 1970s. The company's purchase of a collection of carved Indian jewels, which were remounted to create new treasures, was a key to this in-house trend.

Though the company had made and sold pocket, lapel, and wrist watches throughout its history, Bulgari did not introduce a major collection of timepieces until the late 1970s. The simple lines of the ''BVLGARI-BVLGARI'' wristwatch, which featured a black face encircled by a gold band, would become the company's most-recognized and highest-selling watch. Another important design was Bulgari's snake watch, which evolved from the jewel-encrusted, Art Deco snake of the 1920s (its hinged head concealed a watch face), into a highly stylized coil bracelet set with an exposed face.

The 1970s were a period of great success for the company, a time when Bulgari enhanced its ranking among the world's greatest jewelers through innovative designs. The firm's patronage grew accordingly, expanding to include celebrities like Sophia Loren, Audrey Hepburn, Kirk Douglas, and perhaps the house's best-known client, Elizabeth Taylor. Royalty from around the world shopped at the company's showcases. Perhaps most tellingly, lesser jewelers began to copy Bulgari designs. At the end of the decade, outside observers pegged the company's annual sales at US$50 million.

Bulgari in the 1980s

Bulgari's growth came to a halt in the early 1980s. According to published estimates, annual revenues remained at the US$50 million level through 1985, and the company did not open a single new retail outlet during the first half of the decade. Some sources blamed squabbling among the three brothers, and indeed, eldest Gianni resigned the chief executive office in 1985. Two years later, Nicola and Paolo bought out their brother's one-third stake and prohibited him from using the Bulgari trademark. (Giorgio went on to chair global footwear giant Fila S.p.A.) In the meantime, they had asked a nephew, Francesco Trapani, to revitalize the business. The new CEO, who had first joined the company in 1981, guided an aggressive strategy for growth, opening new retail outlets in Milan (1986), Tokyo (1987), Hong Kong, Osaka, Singapore, and London (all 1988). Before the decade was out, the company had also launched new stores in Munich and New York. Bulgari returned to Sotirio's old summer haunt, St. Moritz, in 1990. Trapani also hired new designers, boosted advertising, and reacquired some franchised stores during this period of rapid growth.

Though the company remained firmly ensconced in the high end of the jewelry market, designs from the 1980s on were noteworthy for their increased "wearability" and the development of design themes. Before he departed the company, Gianni Bulgari reflected on this strategic shift, asserting in a 1981 interview for the *International Daily News* that "We are trying to change our image from one of a business only for the very rich to one designed for those of discerning tastes. You don't have to be rich to like quality." These two concepts fused to form a strategy that allowed Bulgari to expand its potential audience while maintaining the highest quality of design and execution.

The jewelry house introduced the first of several collections based on modular designs in 1982. "Parentesi" (parenthesis) featured several bracket-shaped elements arranged in a pattern. The individual elements could be combined in a seemingly infinite variety of ways to form rings, bracelets, watches, necklaces, and earrings. Bulgari made more or less expensive pieces of jewelry based on this design by executing the parts in more or less valuable materials ranging from polished steel and coral at the low end to fine gemstones and gold or platinum at the upper end. The point, however, was not necessarily to manufacture less expensive pieces—price tags averaged US$3,000 and ranged up to US$1 million in the mid-1990s—but to make fine jewelry that could be worn from day into night.

Trapani reflected on the strategy in a 1996 article for fashion magazine *WWD*, commenting, "We are becoming a jeweler that sells products for everyday use, not just special occasions. This is what has been driving our growth." Periodic launches may also have introduced an element of planned obsolescence, as evinced by the parade of thematic collections that followed. In the 1980s these included "Doppio Cuore" (double heart, 1983), "Boules" (beads, 1986), "Gancio" (hook, 1987), and "Alveare" (beehive, 1988). These strategies succeeded in tripling Bulgari's sales in the latter years of the decade, reaching an estimated US$150 million by 1989.

Diversification into Other Luxury Goods in 1990s

The firm continued to launch collections of modular jewelry in the early 1990s, introducing "Saetta" (thunderbolt) and "Spiga" (ear of wheat) in 1990; "Naturalia," which featured stylized fish and birds, in 1991; "Celtica," based on ancient Celtic motifs, and "Doppio Passo" (classical ballet) in 1993; "Chandra" (Sanskrit for moon) in 1994; and "Trika" (braid) in 1996. These patterns were virtually instant status symbols, highly recognized as Bulgari pieces.

Though Bulgari had long emphasized jewelry and watches, it had from the outset sold other goods, including silver tableware and giftware. In the early 1990s, CEO Trapani followed the lead of other major luxury goods companies that had parlayed their well-recognized and highly-respected brand names into highly profitable growth vehicles. It was not a foolproof process; Trapani had to take care that he did not devalue the venerable Bulgari cachet while seeking a wider clientele. After two years of research and development, the company launched its first fragrance, Eau Parfumée, a unisex scent based on green tea. BVLGARI pour Femme followed in 1994 and BVLGARI pour Homme in 1995. By the end of 1996, perfume was contributing 14 percent of annual sales and generating an estimated US$40 million (L63 billion). Bulgari launched silk scarves and neckties in 1996. That same year, the firm licensed its trademark to fellow Italian firm Luxottica for use on a line of sunglasses and optical frames. A collection of Bulgari leather goods, including handbags and other accessories, was slated for 1997.

New store openings increased Bulgari's retail concentration in Europe (including the countries of the former Soviet Union), the United States, and Asia, and broadened its geographic reach to include the Middle East and Australia. From 1990 to 1996, the company added more than two dozen new shops. Trapani confidently forecast that the company would increase its distribution points to 70 company-owned boutiques, 300 independent watch retailers, and 5,000 perfume sales outlets by the end of the 20th century.

Bulgari's sales increased from L154.3 billion in 1991 to L448.8 billion (US$268.9 million) in 1996, while after-tax net grew from L6.9 billion to L57.7 billion (US$34.6 million). The company went public on the Milan exchange in July 1995, selling out a 32.1 percent stake in only two days. Its stock performance reflected the rapid expansion of its bottom line. Shares rose from an offering price of L8,600 (US$5.32) to L36,000 (US21.44) in mid-1997 before a four-for-one stock split that June.

CEO Trapani was by this time the unquestioned leader of Bulgari. Beginning in 1996, the astute strategist was awarded for his service to the family company with a significant stake in its equity. And at just 39 years old in 1997, he seemed assured of the top position at Bulgari for years, and perhaps decades to come. Trapani was not at a loss for new growth ideas, either. In September 1995, he told *WWD* that Bulgari anticipated a strategic acquisition, noting that the firm sought "a company with a well-known name which might have fallen on hard times," ironically adding, "We don't want to pay a lot of money for it." Industry analysts speculated that the purchase would focus on the high end of the apparel industry.

Further Reading

Bentley, Logan, "Rome's Gianni Bulgari Hangs the Right Stuff Around the World's Richest Necks," *People*, May 8, 1981, p. 104.

Conti, Samantha, "Bulgari Slates Major Expansion," *WWD*, September 26, 1995, p. 9.

Forden, Sara Gay, "Bulgari's World-Class Plans," *WWD*, August 16, 1993, pp. 8–9.

"Gianni Bought Out of Bulgari," *WWD*, January 15, 1988, p. 7.

Hessen, Wendy, "Bulgari's West Coast Barrage," *WWD,* October 7, 1996, p. 16.

Mascetti, Daniela, and Amanda Triossi, *Bulgari,* New York: Abbeville Press, 1996.

The Master Jewelers, New York: H.N. Abrams, 1990.

Newman, Jill, "Bulgari: Going All Out in New York," *WWD,* November 3, 1989, p. 14.

Seckler, Valerie, "Bulgari: Luxe Goes Public," *WWD,* February 26, 1996, pp. 20–22.

Torcellini, Carolyn, "Peacemaker," *Forbes,* March 5, 1990, p. 154.

Warhol, Andy, "Nicola Bulgari: Wearable Wealth," *Interview,* November 1980, pp. 62–63.

—April Dougal Gasbarre

For the way you live

Bush Industries, Inc.

One Mason Drive
Jamestown, New York 14702
U.S.A.
(716) 665-2000
Fax: (716) 665-2074
Web site: http://www.bushfurniture.com

Public Company
Incorporated: 1959 as Bush Brothers Products Corp.
Employees: 2,200
Sales: $256.3 million (1996)
Stock Exchanges: New York
SICs: 2521 Wood Office Furniture; 2599 Furniture and
    Fixtures Not Elsewhere Classified; 2511 Wood
    Household Furniture; 2512 Upholstered Household
    Furniture

Bush Industries, Inc. is the third largest manufacturer of ready-to-assemble (RTA) furniture in the United States, and the 12th largest furniture maker overall. With an emphasis on innovative design and cutting-edge technology, and the ongoing acquisition of companies that add to its manufacturing capabilities and product lines, Bush has grown significantly faster than the RTA industry as a whole. With continuous product development and annual sales increases since the early 1980s, Bush has firmly established its position as a leader in the furniture industry.

Founded in 1959

Bush Industries began in 1959 as Starline Housewares, a maker of towel racks and toothbrush holders in western New York State. Future corporate president and CEO Paul Bush, a 1957 mechanical engineering graduate of Rensselaer Polytechnic Institute, joined several family members in starting the business, which soon changed its name to Bush Brothers Products Corp. Paul Bush initially served as a sales representative for the company, but by 1967 had assumed operating control. The company's output during the 1960s consisted mainly of metal-plated and plastic bathroom products, including a clothes hamper that required some assembly by the purchaser.

In 1970 Paul Bush bought out the remaining family members and took over sole control of the management of Bush Products. The early 1970s saw the introduction of chrome and glass end tables and a plastic television table which was made to resemble wood. This product quickly became a success, and led to an increasing focus on the manufacture of furniture. The company changed its name to Bush Industries in 1975.

In the late 1970s, Bush sold its metals and plastics manufacturing facilities, using the proceeds to expand its furniture manufacturing operation. Bush began to make wood products, primarily stands for televisions, microwaves, and other consumer electronics goods, including some items requiring assembly. The success of its RTA products led the company to focus exclusively on RTA goods after 1979. Typically, such items were made from one-inch thick particle board with a plastic laminate covering, or sometimes wood veneer. The public perception of RTA furniture at this time was somewhat negative, due to a reputation for limited durability, unappealing design, and difficulty of assembly. Though estimated by Bush to account for as much as 40 percent of the European furniture market, RTA was much less popular in the United States. By studying the responses of consumers and looking at European and Japanese manufacturing models, Paul Bush began to improve what the company was offering at a time when consumer demand was beginning to increase dramatically.

Rapid Growth in the 1980s

By the end of the 1970s, Bush Industries was still a small company, with annual sales of around $7 million. But the expanding interest of consumers in such electronics goods as videocassette recorders and microwave ovens began to fuel rapid sales growth for Bush, especially in its lines of economically priced furniture designed to house these products. Bush's wares were being sold largely in discount outlets, including Best Products and Service Merchandise, as well as alongside electronics goods in Sears, J.C. Penney, and Montgomery Ward stores. The relative price of a ready-to-assemble piece of furniture was a third to a half less than that of preassembled goods, and retailers saved greatly on storage costs and space. A downturn in the economy also contributed toward many consumers taking another look at RTA furniture which they had previously spurned, and many found they now liked what they saw.

By 1984, with annual sales increasing dramatically each year, Bush moved into a new 350,000-square-foot plant near Jamestown, New York, consolidating its manufacturing operations and replacing plants at Gowanda, New York, and Bradford, Pennsylvania. Its corporate headquarters were also relocated to Jamestown from its finishing/packaging plant in Little Valley, New York. In 1985 the company went public, with shares offered on the American Stock Exchange. Paul Bush, who was named corporate chairman, kept controlling interest in the company, limiting the shares on the market to 20 percent of the total. The company's annual sales for 1985 stood at a record $41.6 million.

In the late 1980s, the rise of the personal computer gave Bush a new niche to fill, and its products designed to accommodate computers sold well. Consumers appreciated the convenience of being able to purchase a computer and stand all at once, then take it home in the car with them, rather than waiting for the stand to be delivered later. Another successful line of goods was home entertainment centers, which could hold a television, videocassette player, stereo system, and various tapes or CDs. The company also began to market ready-to-assemble bedroom furniture. Among the design innovations from Bush in the 1980s were the use of soft forms with smooth, rounded edges and products that combined oak veneers with solid oak components. In 1989 Bush inaugurated its "Furniture on the Move" sales program, a product display for use in traditional furniture stores with signs and kiosks giving information about the products. Bush furniture was positioned in the middle to upper end of the RTA marketplace, pricewise, with industry leaders O'Sullivan and Sauder selling more to the lower end. Bush products continued to find space in the 1980s in more large retail chains' stores, in some cases with pieces designed specifically for a particular client. By 1990 annual sales had climbed to $110.3 million.

Continuing Growth and Acquisitions in the 1990s

In 1990 Bush Industries purchased two furniture manufacturing companies, Case-Casard and Eric Morgan. The former was a maker of lower-priced RTA products, while Eric Morgan manufactured preassembled furniture for the more expensive end of the market. The company integrated these acquisitions into its structure, continuing to use the product names and maintaining the manufacturing operations in Tijuana, Mexico (for Eric Morgan), and Greensboro, North Carolina (for Case-Casard). Bush now had products that sold at both ends of the price spectrum, as well as in the middle. In 1991, Bush sued competitor O'Sullivan Industries for alleged design-patent infringement, but the suit was dismissed "for obviousness." The company purchased the manufacturing equipment of a former competitor, Gusdorf, Inc., in 1993, and added 450,000 square feet of manufacturing capacity at a site in Jamestown in 1994, plus a distribution center in Saybrook, Ohio, the same year. In July 1994, Bush's stock began trading on the New York Stock Exchange.

The RTA market, which had grown by leaps and bounds in the 1980s, had slowed a bit by the end of that decade, with Bush's annual sales increases leveling off in 1989–90. But they soon took off again, fueled by the increasing demand for home and commercial office furniture, a new market for "home theater" products, and by a lucky avoidance of problems faced by several competitors such as lawsuits and restricted manufacturing capacity. Bush products were being marketed in such office superstores as Staples by the mid-1990s, with Bush becoming a leader in commercial office furniture sales with the 1995 introduction of its Office Pro Collection. The office furniture segment of the RTA market had increased to almost a third of the total by the late 1990s.

The company continually sought new ways to improve its product line and keep the customers happy. One successful idea was the addition of a toll-free help line, available 24 hours a day, year-round. Customers with missing or damaged parts, or with problems assembling their furniture, could call and get immediate help. If needed, replacement parts would be rush-shipped to them. Paul Bush also demonstrated a commitment to his employees and the community of Jamestown. The plant installed a state-of-the-art ventilation system which removed wood dust and compacted it into pellets which could be used as fuel. Bush Industries strove to obtain the raw materials for its vertically integrated manufacturing operations from the surrounding area, shipping them directly to the factory in Jamestown.

New Developments in the Mid-1990s

In 1995, Bush Industries acquired controlling interest in The ColorWorks, Inc. of North Carolina, a company which had the American and partial foreign master license for a process called HydroGraFix. This manufacturing process, developed in Japan, gave Bush the ability to attach sheets of printed material to oddly contoured surfaces, giving Bush's designers a cutting-edge tool for future design innovations. In 1996, the company broke ground on a 500,000-square-foot manufacturing and distribution facility in Erie, Pennsylvania. The new facility would give the company a total of approximately 2.5 million square feet of manufacturing capacity. Once the distribution part of this plant was finished, Bush closed its distribution operation in Saybrook, Ohio, transferring its functions to the closer-to-home Erie location. Bush also had showrooms by this point in Jamestown, San Francisco, and High Point, North Carolina.

The company experimented with a site on the world wide web in 1996, though problems with the service provider led it to be shut down after three months. Later, the company developed a web site in-house, going online in mid-1997. The site was to include product information, links to noncompeting furniture manufacturers and suppliers, and online assembly assistance. The complete line of Bush products was also available from a separate online furniture distributor. Also in 1996, Bush was selected by The Associated Volume Buyers, a group of over 1,000 independent retailers, as its primary source for RTA furniture products. Bush was to supply the retailers with a ''turnkey'' package of marketing tools, display materials and products for their stores. Bush's annual sales in 1996 stood at $256.3 million, over 35 times what they had been at the beginning of the 1980s, and outstripping the growth rate of the RTA marketplace as a whole.

In 1997, Bush announced the intent to purchase 51 percent of Rohr Gruppe of Germany, the 10th largest German furniture manufacturer. The company formed a subsidiary called Bush-Viotechnik GmbH to market Bush's surface-finish products to Europe. Bush products were already being sold in 40 countries, but this marked the largest expansion to date onto foreign soil for the company. Another development in 1997 was the creation of a distribution partnership with Thomson Consumer Electronics, makers of RCA and GE products, to sell Bush furniture through smaller retailers serviced by Thomson. Bush would design some models to specifically be compatible with products made by Thomson.

Bush Industries, Inc., following a sustained period of sales growth during the 1980s and 1990s, continued to build on its strengths while moving forward into new territory as the opportunities arose. With a strong position as an innovator and with a steadily increasing share of the market in the growing ready-to-assemble furniture industry, the company should see continued success to the end of the 1990s and into the 21st century.

Principal Subsidiaries

Bush-Viotechnik GmbH (Germany); The ColorWorks, Inc.

Further Reading

''About Bush Industries, Inc.,'' Jamestown, New York: Bush Industries, Inc.

Allegrezza, Ray, ''Lucky Seven: Bush Stays on its RTA Sales Roll,'' *HFN*, April 22, 1996, pp. 15–17.

——, ''Bush ColorWorks Buy Final,'' *HFN*, June 17, 1996, p. 17.

——, ''Buying Group Picks Bush as Primary RTA Supplier,'' *HFN*, September 30, 1996, p. 22.

——, ''Bush Set to Purchase German Manufacturer,'' *HFN*, April 21, 1997, p. 17.

Anderson, Manley J., ''Bush Named Entrepreneur of the Year,'' *Post-Journal*, June 26, 1993.

——, ''Upward Climb: State-of-the-Art Facility Has Bush Industries at Top of Game,'' *Post-Journal*, October 8, 1995, p. 1.

Campbell, Tom, ''New Company to Give Bush a Bigger Name,'' *Business First-Buffalo*, July 23, 1990, p. 8.

——, ''Not an Ordinary Stick of Furniture,'' *Business First-Buffalo*, July 29, 1991, p. 10.

——, ''There's a Bush Product for Every Computer Need,'' *Business First-Buffalo*, August 18, 1986, p. 23.

Cook, James, ''A Better Mousetrap?,'' *Forbes*, March 7, 1988, p. 96.

Debo, David, ''Screwdriver in Hand Worth Hefty Gains for Bush,'' *Business First of Buffalo*, January 17, 1994, pp. 1–2.

Hartley, Tom, ''Sales Growing Piece by Piece at Jamestown Furniture Maker,'' *Business First of Buffalo*, September 23, 1996, pp. 1–2.

Hazard, Hap, ''Jamestown to Have its First Feature Film Premiere Since '56,'' *Buffalo News*, November 16, 1994, p. B5.

Jones, John A., ''Bush Industries Expands Home-Assembled Furniture Sales,'' *Investor's Business Daily*, May 15, 1994, p. B14.

Lagnado, Ike, ''RTA: Assembly No Longer Required,'' *HFN*, April 18, 1996, p. 10.

Marks, Robert, ''Bush Aims to Double Sales: Restructures Management, Expands RTA Line,'' *HFD*, March 20, 1989, p. 12.

——, ''O'Sullivan Wins as Court Dismisses Suit by Bush Charging Design Infringement,'' *HFD*, September 23, 1991, p. 18.

——, ''Bush Burgeons; Grows in Innovation, Diverse Product Offerings and Service, Making RTA Accepted as 'Furniture,' '' *HFD*, December 14, 1992, p. 14.

——, ''Talking Shop (Ready to Assemble Furniture),'' *HFD*, January 3, 1994, p. 13.

McCarthy, Sheila, ''Lucy Museum to Open with Renamed Festival,'' *Buffalo News*, March 25, 1996, p. B1.

Much, Marilyn, ''Leader's Success—Furniture Maker Paul Bush: Broadening the Appeal of Ready-to-Assemble Furnishings,'' *Investor's Business Daily*, December 10, 1993, p. 1.

''New Stock Listings,'' *The Wall Street Journal*, July 18, 1994, p. C15.

''1993 Entrepreneur of the Year Awards—Paul Bush: Bush Industries, Inc., Jamestown,'' *Business First-Buffalo*, June 21, 1993, p. B8.

''Ranking Places Bush Near Top,'' *Post-Journal*, March 20, 1994.

Robinson, David, ''Bush Industries' New Orders 'Well Ahead' of Record Pace,'' *Buffalo News*, June 17, 1994, p. A12.

——, ''Bush Industries' Profit Increases 10%; Firm to Buy Controlling Interest in German Furniture Maker,'' *Buffalo News*, April 11, 1997, p. C-9.

——, ''Bush Industries Says 1997 Looks Like Another Record Year,'' *Buffalo News*, May 2, 1997, p. A11.

Saunders, Tina, ''Ready to Assemble Furniture,'' *Atlanta Constitution*, September 17, 1993, p. 1.

Stouffer, Paul W., ''Bush Industries Sees Growing Sales, Net From Its Do-it-Yourself Furniture Kits,'' *Barron's*, March 16, 1987.

Youssef, Jenni; Allegrezza, Ray; Beatty, Gerry; and Olenick, Doug, ''Homing in on the Net: Four Vendors' Distinct Journeys in Cyberspace,'' *HFN*, April 8, 1996, pp. 82–3.

—Frank Uhle

Caere Corporation

100 Cooper Ct.
Los Gatos, California 95030
U.S.A.
(408) 395-7000
Fax: (408) 354-2743
Web site: http://www.caere.com

Public Company
Incorporated: 1976
Employees: 272
Sales: $54.53 million (1996)
Stock Exchanges: NASDAQ
SICs: 7372 Prepackaged Software; 3577 Computer
    Peripheral Equipment, Not Elsewhere Classified

Caere Corporation is a worldwide leader in the design, production, and distribution of optical character recognition-based (OCR) information management hardware and software products. Capturing more than 50 percent of the global OCR market, Caere's core product line revolves around its flagship OmniPage software family, including OmniPage Professional, OmniPage Limited Edition, and OmniPage Direct. Together with WordScan Plus, the OmniPage family accounts for approximately three-quarters of the company's annual sales. The company also designs and distributes Recognita Plus, acquired in January 1997, which adds to the company's OCR product base with a text recognition capacity of more than 100 languages. Cacrc's OmniForm, developed in conjunction with Colorado-based Formonix, which the company acquired in April 1997, applies OCR technology to the scanning and creation of electronic forms. Caere extended the OmniForm line with the February 1997 release of OmniForm Internet Publisher, which allows users to convert paper-based forms to Internet and Intranet ready electronic forms such as invoices, purchase orders, expense reports, and questionnaires.

While software has become the company's primary revenue generator, Caere has also built a line of OCR hardware products, including hand-held and slot-reader systems, sold largely to the original equipment manufacturer (OEM) market. Caere's hardware products are directed toward high-speed transaction processing applications, such as bar code systems and magnetic stripe readers. The company's 800 Series Combo Reader integrates OCR, bar code, and magnetic strip reading to provide remittance processing, banking, point-of-sale, routing, and payment processing for government and military agencies, post office use, public utility use, and private wholesale and retail use. The Model 1200 Travel Document Reader, introduced in 1996, enables the reading of passports, identity cards, and other travel documents. The company's 1500 Series Document Processor is a desktop reader/sorter for high-speed document processing.

The second prong of Caere's hardware line is its bar code readers, including the Easy-Scanner 1000 and 2000 Series bar code systems, which cater primarily to the high-end of this market. The Model 1731 Integrated Laser features Caere's bar code processing technology combined with a hand-held laser scanner developed by PSC Inc. Caere also designs and distributes document processing support hardware and software, such as its M/Series II OCR Accelerator Board, which can add document processing capacity of up to 750 pages per hour.

OCR has retained a relatively small niche in the global computer market since the first OCR systems were developed in the 1970s. However, a new generation of low-priced, highly accurate scanners introduced in the mid-1990s, and a surge in interest in OCR capability, driven in part by the rapid growth of Internet and World Wide Web activity, promises to carry OCR into the mainstream and home computing markets. Through software bundling agreements with scanner manufacturers, which package upgradable 'light' versions of Caere's software, the company has positioned itself to capture a share of these markets. In 1996, Caere shipped more than two million bundled units, double the year before. These shipments have translated into increased upgrade purchases of the full version of Caere's OmniPage and other software products, and to rising revenues for the company. In 1996, Caere, led by chairman and CEO Robert Teresi, recorded $54.5 million in sales.

Founded by Robert Noyce in 1976

Caere was founded by Robert Noyce in 1976. Noyce was by then already a legend. After working at Shockley Semiconduc-

---

tor Laboratory in the early 1950s, Noyce, with Shockley colleague Gordon Moore, formed Fairchild Industries in 1957, where Noyce led the invention of the integrated circuit. In 1968, Noyce and Moore—famous for the prescience of his Moore's Law, which posited that chip performance would double every 18 months—cofounded Intel, soon joined by another former Fairchild employee, Andy Grove. Noyce later went on to form and lead Sematech, the U.S. government-backed consortium created to secure U.S. dominance of the worldwide semiconductor industry.

In the early 1970s, however, Noyce became interested in the practical application of the newly robust computer processor technology. Noyce focused on developing methods of automating data entry. In 1973, he founded Caere Corporation to develop products based on recently developed OCR technology. OCR enabled computers to 'read' documents by converting text and graphics images into digital code. OCR equipment worked much like copy machines, taking a picture of the document and, instead of reproducing it on a sheet of paper, recreated it for manipulation by computer software. Early applications of OCR had already been implemented in the bar-code systems being introduced in the early 1970s. In 1977, Caere brought out its first series of products, hand-held and slot reader OCR systems. These early systems were expensive—costing $50,000 or more—and required user programming to ''teach'' its software to recognize characters. Nonetheless, OCR offered the promise of enabling the treasured dream of the ''paperless office.''

In 1983, Caere debuted a second line of products, its 200 series of bar code scanners. These were compatible with many of the common computer interfaces, including minicomputers, serial terminals, and the young IBM personal computer line. Bar code readers had quickly found popularity in a variety of industries, applications, and environments, from the shop floor, to warehouse and inventory control, to administrative and accounting functions. OCR, meanwhile, while steadily developing its capability, remained priced beyond mainstream reach. Scanning remained limited to a small range of typefaces, and suffered from poor accuracy levels on lower-priced equipment. Yet OCR technology had begun to find its way into such document-intensive business as law firms and insurance companies. Caere's growth paced the limited growth of the OCR industry. By 1986, the company's net revenues had only reached $9.68 million. Caere was profitable, however, posting earnings for the year of $1.5 million.

New Products and New Success for the 1980s

Caere's position—and OCR acceptance—rose dramatically in 1988 when Caere introduced the first in its OmniPage software family. Introduced first for the Apple Macintosh and a few months later for the IBM PC and compatibles market, OmniPage featured artificial intelligence that enabled scanners to read entire pages of text and graphics, recognize columns and tables, and, using complex algorithms, interpret a variety of typefaces and type styles—even several different typefaces in a single document—without first being taught to recognize them. OmniPage also allowed the user to manipulate the scanned text file's columns, tables, and graphics, edit the text, convert text into a variety of word processing applications, and search the document for missing words. Initially priced at under $800 for the Macintosh version (the PC version was bundled with a controller card, for a cost of less than $2,000), OmniPage opened up the OCR and scanning market to a new range of users, include the growing desktop publishing market. OmniPage also posted industry-leading accuracy rates of more than 99 percent, making it a practical, and financially attractive, alternative to typist-based data entry.

The effect of OmniPage on Caere's revenues was immediate. By 1989, sales had jumped past $19.5 million. Based on the national attention earned by OmniPage, Caere went public in 1989. In that year, the company attempted to build on its success by introducing a dedicated OCR computer scanning system, the Caere Parallel Page Reader. Priced at around $10,000—a competitive price at the time when OCR scanning system costs ranged from $40,000 to $250,000 —the computer system, which featured four 386-based processors working in parallel, was originally developed for the Securities and Exchange Commission, as that agency prepared to implement the digital submission of financial reports. The Parallel Page Reader, for which the technology behind OmniPage had been developed, boasted word recognition rates, which had previously been the bottleneck of OCR scanning systems, of up to 2,500 words per minute, making it possible for near simultaneous scanning, recognition, and output.

Several months later, however, Caere introduced another new product that would go a long way towards building mainstream penetration of scanning technology. In August 1990, the company debuted its hand-held Typist scanner. Priced at under $700, the Typist featured a five-inch wide scanning surface that could be moved over a document, capturing up to two inches of text per second, and automatically transferring text to the user's word processing, database, or spreadsheet application. Using the company's AnyFont recognition software, the Typist easily converted document text into the typeface and type size in use by the word processing software, eliminating the need to reformat scanned text. Caere's revenues reached $27.6 million in 1990. Founder Robert Noyce died in that year, and Robert Teresi took over as chairman and CEO.

Led by Caere, the OCR scanning market underwent its first real boom. Scanner sales reached 420,000 in 1990 and climbed to 640,000 in 1991. Caere's sales for that year raced past $50 million, and the company posted net earnings of some $7 million. The following year, when Caere opened a sales office in Germany to promote European distribution, sales continued to grow, nearing $60 million. By then, other companies were entering the hardware side, including Hewlett Packard and its popular, low-priced ScanJet line, and MicroTek, already a leader in color scanning.

A New Business Model for the 1990s

Caere's growth stopped short, however, in 1993. Coupled with the effects of the worldwide recession, which suppressed computer, software, and peripheral sales in general, a new trend was emerging among scanner product purchasers. Advances in scanner hardware technology, and steadily dropping prices for computer equipment in general, led buyers to upgrade their scanning equipment, rather than updating with new software. Lower prices for scanners also attracted a wider range of first-time buyers, particularly among the burgeoning small office/home office (SOHO) market. But a new software 'bundling' trend had emerged in the personal computer and peripheral market, in which purchasers of computer equipment would find software, and often several programs, packaged with the equipment. While the bundled software was generally a limited version of an existing program, users, having become familiar with the basic program, were encouraged to upgrade to the full version. Caere's competitors had reached the bundled market first. While the company held onto its dominance of the OCR software market, its revenues slid for the 1993 year below $50 million. Earnings, too, dropped precipitously, to $352,000. Caere was also hurt by its failure to enter another quickly growing category, that of facsimile software; in 1993, the company discontinued its FaxMaster product.

Caere fought back hard the following year. By mid-1994 the company had developed a new business model, focused on its flagship OmniPage software family. Caere stepped up its research and development expenses, designing new software and upgrading its existing software. The company also lowered its prices, enhancing its appeal among the swiftly widening pool of home scanner purchasers. The lowered prices helped increase the company's retail store sales, boosting year-end revenues to $59 million. And, by December 1994, these purchasers were likely to find a "light" version of OmniPage Pro, called OmniPage Limited Edition, inside the box with their new scanner, as Caere adopted the software bundling approach. The limited edition version of OmniPage gave the user an introduction to the capabilities of the professional version. Customers were also offered lowered upgrade prices to encourage their migration to OmniPage Pro.

The immediate effect of the new business model was to depress Caere's software revenues, despite an increase in total software shipments of more than 100 percent. At the same time, Caere exited the hand-held scanner market, crimping its hardware revenues. Meanwhile, the continuing economic crisis in much of Western Europe was hurting the company's international sales, which shrunk below 30 percent of total sales. The company was forced to cut back its employee base, which dropped from 300 employees to 220. By the end of 1995, sales had slipped back to $52 million.

In that year, however, Caere began a drive to acquire competing and complementary scanning software companies. The company first acquired Calera Recognition Systems, in a 2.5 million share stock-swap deal, adding Calera's popular WordScan OCR software family to Caere's OmniPage. Caere shipped new versions of both programs in 1995; in August 1995, with the launch of Microsoft's Windows 95, the company

also announced development of a Windows 95 version of the OmniPage family. The company's bundled software shipments topped 1 million in 1995; meanwhile, the company also expanded its retail sales network, adding the 450-store OfficeMax chain in the United States, and adding another important reseller, Vobis, the largest computer retailer in Europe.

Continuing its drive to expand by acquisition, Caere reached an agreement to acquire ViewStar Corp. and its client/server workflow and document management software. That agreement fell through in early 1996, however. Caere also invested $2.4 million in ZyLAB International, giving it a 20 percent stake and an option to acquire complete control of that company and its full text indexing and retrieval software. ZyLAB failed to meet its planned targets, however, and Caere wrote off its ZyLAB investment in 1996. In the beginning of 1997, the company found an acquisition that fit, paying $4.7 million for Hungary's Recognita Rt, the world's third-largest OCR software designer. In April of that year, Caere also acquired Formonix Inc., which had been developing a new product for Caere, called OmniForm. The acquisition involved an exchange of stock worth about $3.2 million.

The end of 1996 brought good news to the company. Corporate revenues had begun to climb, despite a slump in hardware sales, to $54.5 million, representing the success of Caere's software seeding moves. Shipments of bundled software had doubled over the year before, and, importantly, the company saw a 116 percent increase in its upgrade revenues. The introduction of the Windows 95 version of OmniPage and WordScan also helped drive total software sales up 67 percent for the year. Importantly, 1996 saw the first true surge in popular and corporate interest in the Internet and especially the World Wide Web, which helped spur scanner sales. At the same time, Caere began preparing its OmniForm software, which enabled the conversion of text-based forms into electronic forms for web page publishing. OmniForm began shipping in early 1997. Given the growing interest in commercial applications of the World Wide Web, the demand for OCR forms capacity appeared a highly promising market. After nearly two decades as a niche market, OCR seemed ready finally to move into the mainstream. And Caere was poised to hold onto its position as the OCR market's dominant player.

Further Reading

Bellamah, Pat, "OmniPage OCR Software Snares PC Users' Attention," *PC Week*, January 9, 1989, p. 27.

Belsie, Laurent, "Makers of Computer Scanners Plan to Crack the Office Market," *Christian Science Monitor*, August 16, 1991, p. 8.

Clark, Don, and Ken Siegmann, "Caere Scanner Could Give It Long-Awaited Recognition," *San Francisco Chronicle*, August 9, 1990, p. C3.

Eames, Richard, "Is Hungary Developing a Silicon Puszta?" *Budapest Business Journal*, January 13, 1997, p. 10.

Jacobs, April, "Turning to a New Page," *Computerworld*, July 15, 1996, p. 69.

Lewis, Peter H., "If a Laser Printer Ran Backwards," *New York Times*, March 4, 1990, Sec. 3, p. 8.

——, "A Scanner in Hand, Worth Several Typists at Desks," *New York Times*, August 12, 1990, Sec. 3, p. 7.

Miller, Michael J., "OCR Technology Comes a Long Way in a Short Time," *InfoWorld*, February 27, 1989, p. 65.

—M. L. Cohen

Cagle's, Inc.

2000 Hills Ave., NW
Atlanta, Georgia 30318
U.S.A.
(404) 355-2820
Fax: (404) 351-4552

Public Company
Founded: 1945
Employees: 3.500
Sales: $353.1 million (fiscal year ended March 1997)
Stock Exchanges: American
SICs: 0250 Agriculture Production—Poultry; 5133
   Wholesale Trade—Poultry and Poultry Products

Cagle's, Inc. is a regional poultry operation located in the southeastern United States. With its wholly owned subsidiary, Cagle's Farms, Inc., the company breeds, hatches, and raises chickens, slaughters them, processes and reprocesses the meat, markets, and distributes fresh and frozen chicken products. The company slaughters over two million birds a week at its three processing plants and ranks eighth nationally in pounds produced. About half of the chickens are deboned, as Cagle's markets 85 percent of the birds as value-added products. These deboned, cut, marinated, and breaded products are sold primarily in the United States to supermarkets, national fast-food chains, food processors, restaurants, schools, and other institutions. The Cagle family owns over 50 percent of the company stock.

Background on the Chicken Industry

In 1923, Mrs. Wilmer Steele ordered 500 chicks for her farm on the Delmarva Peninsula, east of Chesapeake Bay. She sold the 387 birds that survived to reach two pounds for 62¢ a pound (approximately $5 a pound in 1996 dollars). According to John Steele Gordon's history of the U.S. poultry industry in *American Heritage*, Mrs. Steele was the first person on the peninsula to raise chickens solely for market. Before her entrepreneurial enterprise, farmers' wives sold whatever chickens were not needed at home. Few people, and certainly none of the agricultural experts, thought things would change. After all, what industry could compete with a system in which the labor (the farmers' wives and children) and the feed (table scraps and grain spilled by other animals) were free? The problem the experts had was that they were looking at the big, prosperous livestock and grain farms in the Midwest, which led the nation in egg production.

The truck farms on the Delmarva (*Del* aware, *Ma* ryland, and *V* irginia) Peninsula were in a different situation. They needed to develop a steadier supply of products for their markets in Baltimore, Philadelphia, New York, and Washington, D.C. Mrs. Steele's efforts were quickly copied. Two years later, Delaware produced 50,000 chickens for market, and in 1926, that number had reached 1 million.

Changes occurred quickly as the new industry grew. Hundreds of companies began developing special feeds for chickens since production in those numbers could not depend on table scraps. Adding cod-liver oil to the feeds meant that the chickens did not have to depend on sunlight to synthesize vitamin D, and this allowed farmers to put the chickens indoors where diet and temperature could be controlled for maximum weight gain. In 1933, a chicken had to eat 6½ pounds of feed to produce one pound of broiler meat. Ten years later, it took only 4 pounds of feed to get that same amount of meat. During this period, another major change occurred as egg production was separated from chicken farming to become an industry all its own.

During World War II, the War Food Administration took all the Delmarva chickens, 90 million a year, to feed the Armed Forces. As a result, non-military customers had to look elsewhere for their chickens, and the southeastern states, with their many small farmers, became the center of chicken production. The success of the industry in the South, according to John Steel Gordon, was largely due to a man named Jesse Dixon Jewell, the father of the modern contract growing farm.

Jewell ran a small feed store in Gainesville, Georgia. To earn more money during the Great Depression, he bought chickens and eggs from local farms and took them to Atlanta to sell. Most of the farmers could not afford to buy his feed and could not even buy more chicks to raise to sell, even though there was a demand for them. Jewell made a deal with a feed company to buy the feed on consignment and then got a loan from a bank to buy day-old chicks. As Gordon described it, "He placed these chicks with the farmers, taking back a note secured by the chickens, and supplied the feed needed to raise them to market weight. When the chickens were ready for sale, Jewell would buy them, and he and the farmers would settle accounts."

The business expanded quickly, with Jewell placing chickens with more farmers and then starting his own hatchery and processing plant. In 1954, J. D. Jewell put its own feed mill in operation, becoming a completely integrated poultry company. It operated as an independent company for the next 25 years, when, in 1979, it was bought by Cagle's Inc.

Cagle's Early Years, 1945–69

George L. Cagle was a Georgia farmer. In 1945, he set up a poultry shop in downtown Atlanta, selling chickens to retail customers and to hotels, hospitals, and restaurants. Eight years later, in 1953, he incorporated the business. That year George's son, Douglas, became a company director after having worked in the shop as a teenager. Ten years later the company began expanding into a vertically integrated organization. It acquired through mergers Strain Poultry Farms, Inc.(which was renamed Cagle's Farm's Inc.), Georgia Poultry Feed Mills, Inc., and several affiliated companies. In 1969, Talmadge Farms, Inc. was merged into the company. Other poultry companies in the region were also growing. Between 1947 and 1960, broiler production in the region increased by 365 percent. The competition within the industry was great. During the 1950s large regional operators such as Don Tyson in Arkansas and Frank Perdue in Maryland began reaching for a national market. The price of chicken fell dramatically.

That production growth led the Kennedy Administration, at the urging of Agriculture Secretary Orville Freeman, to set up the National Broiler Stabilization Advisory Committee to examine the feasibility of controlling prices and stabilizing production. Although the committee gave the Secretary the authority to regulate the supply of hatching eggs and therefore the supply of chickens when they hatched, the effort to regulate the industry died shortly thereafter.

The mid-1960s saw the beginning of another long-term change in the poultry business—automation. As producers spent more to automate their plants, productivity in processing plants began to increase. Between 1963 and 1985, according to the *Monthly Labor Review*, hourly output by employees increased an average 2.9 percent each year. In addition, the demand for poultry, especially chicken, started growing dramatically due both to lower prices and greater consumer concern about cholesterol and healthy eating.

Growth During the 1970s and 1980s

The company began the 1970s with Douglas Cagle being named CEO and continued to broaden its operations. In 1971 Cagle's bought a poultry distribution operation in Florida where it conducted business as Cagle's of Florida, Inc. The Florida operations grew with the purchase of June Dairy Co. and the

broiler division of Modern Foods Inc. in 1972. In 1978, Cagle's bought J.D. Jewell, Inc., for $1.4 million, and in 1979, it acquired Plumbrook Farms for approximately $1.35 million. The consumption of poultry continued to increase, with double-digit growth occurring during the late 1970s and early 1980s.

Perhaps in response to that demand, Cagle's concentrated its efforts and capital on the production business. During the 1980s, the company eliminated its retail operations and sold its poultry processing equipment division and its interest in Select Laboratories Inc. of Gainesville, Georgia.

The foundation of Cagle's entire operation were the breeder flocks owned by the company and maintained on 60 contract farms in north Georgia. The company also had contract grower farms for replacement breeders. A breeder chick was sent to one of those 41 farms when it was a day old and reared for about 18 weeks. It was then moved to one of the breeder farms where, at 25 weeks old, it began producing eggs. Each breeder produced eggs for about 40 weeks.

The eggs were set in incubators at one of Cagle's two hatcheries in Georgia, where in three weeks, baby broiler chicks were hatched. On their first day, the chicks were removed from the incubator, separated by sex, vaccinated, placed in the specially designed Chick Bus and transported to one of approximately 285 contract grow-out farms in Georgia, Tennessee, and Alabama.

While the chicks were at the farm, Cagle's paid for the feed and all veterinary costs, and owned the birds themselves. The farmers provided the housing, equipment, utilities, and labor. They made their money based on the weight of the live bird with a guaranteed minimum rate. That minimum was increased with various incentives that took into account the farmer's performance compared to other farmers whose birds were marketed during the same week. The chicken's feed came from Cagle's three feed mills. The mills were all located in Georgia and had the capacity to produce over 800,000 tons of feed a year. The corn for the mills came primarily from the Midwest.

The chicks stayed at the grow-out farm for six to eight weeks, depending on how large a chicken was desired. Since male and female birds have different growth rates and nutritional needs, the chicks were grown separately by sex to provide the exact size requirement required by various customers. Once the broilers reached the desired weight, they were sent to one of the company's three processing plants, located in Macon and Pine Mountain, Georgia, and Collinsville, Alabama.

The Early 1990s and Further Expansion

Poultry sales, particularly for chicken, continued strong as the decade began. The U.S. Department of Agriculture reported Americans were eating 90.1 pounds of poultry per person in 1990 and predicted that amount to rise to 95 pounds in 1991. By 1992, Americans were eating over 50 percent more poultry than they had in 1980.

The company began expanding again during the decade, becoming one of the fastest-growing poultry producers. In 1990, Cagle's bought 50 percent of a grain elevator corporation and in March 1993, announced a 50–50 joint venture with

Executive Holdings L.P., one of Cagle's major customers, to own and operate the Cagle's processing plant at Camilla, Georgia. The joint venture, named Cagle Foods JV, was created by Cagle's contributing its former south Georgia and north Florida operations. Within two years of its establishment, the joint venture built a new hatchery and a new processing plant. With these additions, Cagle Foods JV had the capacity to produce approximately 1.4 million birds a week, a major portion of which was sold to the company's largest customer, Equity Foods.

In 1993, Cagle's reentered the retail market with individually quick-frozen chicken pieces, joining the industry's movement toward value-added, convenience products. In addition to frozen chicken, new retail products soon included deboned breast and thigh meat and cut-up marinated and breaded chicken for barbecues. The industry recognized, and was responding to, consumers' diminishing interest in, and time for, cooking whole broilers.

Those same consumers were also eating out much more, and Cagle's produced cuts that ended up in sandwiches and other chicken meals at fast-food restaurants. The company's largest customer, Equity Foods, turned much of the meat it bought from Cagle's into chicken nuggets for McDonald's.

Bad weather caused grain prices to rise during 1993, but the strong demand for chicken products helped keep prices at profitable levels. Cagle's sales in fiscal 1994 grew 12 percent to $312.7 million from $280.1 million, with income up 66 percent to $8.65 million after an accounting change. As feed costs declined in 1994, the company ended fiscal 1995 with sales of $349.8 million. That year the company reported it ranked 11th nationally in terms of pounds produced.

During 1994, Cagle's announced plans to construct a new broiler complex planned in Franklin, Kentucky. The company anticipated spending $30 million on the facility which was to include a feed mill, hatchery, and processing plant). Of that amount, $17 million was to come from working capital.

1995 to the Present

Fiscal 1996 was a difficult period for Cagle's. In June 1995, the Pine Mountain processing plant was destroyed by fire. The cause of the fire was believed to be an electrical short in an ice-cream vending machine, and 600 workers were laid off. The company decided to delay construction of the new facilities in Franklin and to concentrate on rebuilding the Pine Mountain plant. That was accomplished in record time, and the rebuilt facility, double the size of the old one and state-of-the-art, was back in production in November 1995. In December, Cagle's acquired a one-third interest in a company that financed poultry houses for growers in South Georgia. The growers receiving the financing were under contract to Cagle Foods JV, the company's joint venture.

In March 1996, the year-long rally in corn futures finally appeared to scare away users. The three largest poultry producers announced they were cutting back hatches between 7 to 8.5 percent, citing the high cost of feed corn. For Cagle's, the production loss caused by the fire combined with record grain prices and export uncertainties resulted in a drop in earnings for the year. Sales declined by $41 million compared to fiscal 1995, to $308.8 million. Even so, the company was ranked ninth nationally in terms of pounds produced.

By the fall of 1996, feed prices were almost 43 percent higher than the year before. But some relief appeared to be in sight when, in November, commodity experts predicted a bumper corn crop of an estimated 9.2 billion bushels. The dropping price was expected to lead to greater demand from beef, pork, and poultry producers.

In an interview with *Supermarket News*, representatives from the four biggest poultry companies (Tyson Foods, ConAgra Poultry, Perdue Farms, and Gold Kist) expected chicken consumption to continue to increase, although more slowly than the 5 percent rate experienced in mid-decade. The key appeared to be the industry's consumer-oriented emphasis of offering convenient, easy-to-prepare products. These now included refrigerated pre-cooked chicken parts (breast quarters, half-birds) that took under five minutes to put on the table. A related trend was to include chicken in prepared items such as ready-to-heat pasta salads. In 1996, the U.S. Department of Agriculture announced new labeling regulations that prohibited labeling as ''fresh'' poultry that was previously frozen.

With the expanded Pine Mountain facility back in full production, the company had the capacity to process 31,800 birds an hour. Sales for fiscal 1997 increased to $353.1 million, and the company moved up to the number eight ranking nationally in pounds produced. However, Cagle's continued to face health and safety violations in its Macon plant. In 1996 it paid a fine of $88,000 and in 1997, the Occupational Safety and Health Administration ordered the company to pay $1.3 million, citing over 20 violations of federal safety rules at the plant. Cagle's settled that citation for $608,000.

In fiscal 1997 and beyond, the company was carrying a higher than average level of debt as a result of rebuilding and expanding the Pine Mountain plant. However, with the added capacity and the continued high demand for convenience chicken products, Cagle's expected to continue in the tradition of Mrs. Steele and Mr. Jewell.

Principal Subsidiaries

Cagle's Farms, Inc.; Cagle Foods JV, L.L.C. (50%).

Further Reading

Ahmed, Ziaul, and Mark Sieling, ''Two Decades of Productivity Growth in Poultry Dressing and Processing,'' *Monthly Labor Review*, April 1987, p. 34.

Blamey, Pamela, ''New Directions for Poultry,'' Part I, *Supermarket News*, September 25, 1995, p. 19.

——, ''New Directions for Poultry,'' Part II, *Supermarket News*, October 2, 1995, p. 24.

''Cagle's Must Pay Fine for Safety Violations,'' *Atlanta Business Chronicle*, March 31, 1997, http://www.amcity.com/atlanta/stories/033097/weekinbiz.html.

''The Cold Hard Facts About 'Fresh' Poultry,'' *Tufts University Diet & Nutrition Letter*, December 1996, p. 2.

Gold, Donald H., ''Corn Explodes on Export Report; With No Rain, Wheat Flies,'' *Investor's Business Daily*, March 8, 1996.

——, "Corn Swoons to a 16-Month Low After Forecast of a Bumper Crop." *Investor's Business Daily*, November 6, 1996.

Gordon, John Steele, "The Chicken Story," *American Heritage*, September 1996, p. 52.

Hetrick, Ron L., "Why Did Employment Expand in Poultry Processing Plants?" *Monthly Labor Review*, June 1994, p. 31.

Jones, John A., "Cagle's Builds for New Growth in Strong Poultry Industry," *Investor's Business Daily*, December 12, 1994.

Kuhn, Mary Ellen, "Poultry Producers Crow About Value-Added Offerings," *Food Processing*, April 1995, p. 33.

Linsen, Mary Ann, "Poultry Packs a One-Two Punch," *Progressive Grocer*, May 1991, p. 201.

"Livestock, Dairy and Poultry Situation and Outlook," *Frozen Food Digest*, December 1996, p. 13.

McCutcheon, Stephen, "Time to Hold Cagle's, Coca Cola," *Georgia Trend*, November 1996, p. 68.

Robinson, Bill, "Poultry Plant Fire May Have Started in Vending Machine," *Atlanta Constitution*, June 26, 1995, p. C2.

Shaw, Russell, "Seeing Poultry Trend Called Key," *Supermarket News*, January 30, 1995, p. 25.

"Very Versatile Variety," *ID: The Voice of Foodservice Distribution*, May 15, 1995, p. 61.

—Ellen D. Wernick

Caradon plc

Caradon plc
Caradon plc

Caradon House, 24 Queens Road
Weybridge
Surrey KT13 9UX
United Kingdom
(01932) 850-850
Fax: (01932) 823-328

Public Company
Incorporated: 1985
Employees: 21,500
Sales: £2.11 billion (US$3.61 billion) (1996)
Stock Exchanges: London
SICs: 2761 Manifold Business Forms; 3089 Plastic
   Products, Not Elsewhere Classified; 3354 Aluminum
   Extruded Products; 3432 Plumbing Fixture Fittings &
   Trim; 3433 Heating Equipment, Except Electrical &
   Warm Air Furnaces; 3442 Metal Doors, Sash, Frames,
   Molding & Trim; 3499 Fabricated Metal Products,
   Not Elsewhere Classified; 3643 Current-Carrying
   Wiring Devices; 3699 Electrical Machinery,
   Equipment & Supplies, Not Elsewhere Classified;
   5074 Plumbing & Heating Equipment & Supplies;
   6719 Offices of Holding Companies, Not Elsewhere
   Classified

Caradon plc is a U.K.-based supplier of building products to the construction and home improvement industries, with 80 percent of sales being generated from these operations. Among other company activities, Caradon's security printing division is one of the leading printers of checks and business forms in the United States. Active primarily in Europe and North America, the company derives more than 60 percent of sales and profits outside the United States.

Although Caradon plc was founded only in 1985, thanks to a confusingly complex series of mergers, acquisitions, and divestments in the 1980s and in the early 1990s, the company actually traces its origins to those of Metal Box PLC, a pioneer in the British tinning industry and eventually a giant in packaging in general. In 1989 MB Group (the former Metal Box) merged with Caradon (which was formed in 1985 as a spinoff from Reed International) to create MB-Caradon PLC. Then in 1993 MB-Caradon divested itself of its packaging roots and soon underwent another name change, becoming Caradon plc.

Early Roots of the Tinning Industry

The canning of foods, or "tinning" as it is often called in Britain, has been a common method for preserving food for about a century. Before that time, all foods had to be purchased fresh, salted, or dried. The industry that developed to produce these cans, or "tins," in Britain was originally controlled by numerous family firms, each with a small tin can making factory in which workers could turn out 200 cans in an hour. These family concerns were small, profitable, and only mildly competitive in such a large market.

One of the family can makers was initially a printing business established in 1855 by Robert Barclay, a Quaker. His main customer was Barclay's Bank (owned by distant relatives) for whom he printed checks. Barclay's brother-in-law, John Fry, joined him as a partner in 1867, and their company, Barclay & Fry, became Britain's largest check printer. With the help of some technical information sold to him by an early industrial spy in France, Barclay developed the process of offset lithography and tried to sell it to many other firms. He died of a stroke in 1876 before any sale could be finalized.

The new printing process ended up being leased to Huntley, Boorne & Stevens, tin box makers for the biscuit company Huntley & Palmer (the two Huntleys were also related). Huntley & Palmer was the first manufacturer to use the offset process to print designs on their own tins; prior to that their tins had been hand-painted. Soon, Carr's Biscuits were also using printed tins; these were manufactured by their Quaker relatives, Hudson Scott & Sons. Sometime during the 1890s, Barclay & Fry decided to use their offset process themselves, but they remained primarily stationery printers.

Decorated biscuit tins were very popular throughout Great Britain and many homes had quite large collections of them.

Company Perspectives:

Caradon plc is a major international group of some 30 companies organized into five product divisions, operating across Europe and North America. The Group employs 21,500 people.

The Group's main activity is the supply of building products to the construction and home improvement industries. In the UK and Continental Europe, Caradon brands include Catnic, Twyfords, Terrain, Everest, Friedland, Stelrad, Henrad, Weru, Ideal, Mira, and MK Electric; in North America, Better-Bilt, Peachtree, Thermal-Gard, and Indalex.

Caradon's portfolio also includes companies such as Clarke American serving the financial services industry.

There were Alice in Wonderland designs, tins to commemorate every grand occasion, and tins resembling miniature cottages or featuring birds, books, or beauty spots. The tin making industry grew and since labor costs were low, profits were high. Soon, the Trade Boards Act required tin manufacturers to improve worker conditions and wages, and this caused some of the employers to form the British Tin Box Manufacturers Federation in order to protect their interests.

Metal Box Founded in 1921

World War I brought more business to the industry; a new product had to be manufactured—the ration tin used by British troops. Due to government restrictions on tin, many of the companies in the Federation cooperated closely, and after the war, in 1921, four of these tin box makers, Hudson Scott, F. Atkins & Co., Henry Grant & Co., and Barclay & Fry, formed the Allied Tin Box Makers, Ltd. A year later they changed their name to Metal Box & Printing Industries. From the beginning it was understood that each of the member companies would remain private, but that all would cooperate in controlling the market and making acquisitions.

Before long, however, the group's comfortable control of their market was threatened by the importation of an American method of semiautomatic can making that could produce 200 cans every minute. G. E. Williamson's family firm, which had refused to join the manufacturers' group, purchased the new American machinery in 1927 and began to produce cans for the government's Fruit & Vegetable Research Station in Gloucestershire. The research organization was interested in advanced canning methods in order to increase the markets for British farm produce.

Inevitably, with its superior technology, the U.S. canning industry quickly became interested in the British market. American Can moved in first by purchasing a small independent company and renaming it the British Can Company, Ltd. It then attempted to acquire Metal Box & Printing Industries. In its determination to resist a takeover, however, Metal Box arranged a partnership that not only kept it independent, but defined and nurtured its growth. The company signed an agreement with American Can's U.S. rival, Continental Can. The two

firms exchanged stock shares and Metal Box was given the exclusive right in Great Britain to purchase canning machinery, technical advice, training, and patent licenses from Continental Can. This effectively eliminated the competition as no other British company was able to purchase the technology. In little more than a year, British Can was in disarray. Metal Box agreed to buy it out on the condition that American Can stayed out of Great Britain and Ireland for the next 21 years.

These deals, illegal under the business laws of later decades, had been arranged by Metal Box's Robert Barlow. Still under 40, Barlow was now the head of Britain's canning monopoly and determined to make it even larger. But his aggressive managerial style alienated most of the old family leaders of the group's companies, and many resigned from the board of directors. Barlow wanted to bring all member companies under one authority and ignored those on the board who opposed him. He set up an executive committee with two others, Hepworth and Crabtree, to make policy decisions and, essentially, to circumvent the board.

In 1931 Barlow's committee instituted a single accounting system for all member companies in an attempt to force some kind of uniformity on them under a newly created head office. The managing director of Barclay & Fry tried to have Barlow fired, but Barlow called a meeting of the entire board and convinced them that his plan would make the company stronger still. As Barlow consolidated his position he banished some of his detractors to plants in South Africa and demanded the resignations of others. By 1935 he was in complete control of Metal Box and had largely succeeded in centralizing sales and supplies, and rationalizing production functions, for all the company's plants.

Succeeded in Spite of the Great Depression

Metal Box experienced nothing but success during the Great Depression. As smaller canmakers collapsed, the company purchased them, and by 1937, Metal Box was selling 335 million cans a year. Following the American example, Metal Box had begun to manufacture the equipment needed to seal the cans on-site and sold this machinery to its customers. Metal Box was not interested in expanding into the field of food production, but it did open a publicity department to increase interest in canned foods. Whenever there were difficulties, either with suppliers or customers, Metal Box considered a takeover. For example, inefficient management at a tin plate supplier in South Wales led Metal Box, with the help of Continental Can, to purchase the company.

Surprisingly, Metal Box's income from security check printing combined with turnover from machine manufacturing and interests in mining, etc. was double that of its income from the cans themselves. Profits rose dramatically for Metal Box in the 1930s—from £103,480 in 1931 to £316,368 in 1939.

Throughout the decade Barlow had maintained a strong interest in foreign markets. Partnerships or subsidiaries had been formed in France, the Netherlands, Belgium, India, and South Africa. Continental Can was still Metal Box's mentor and main partner and the two essentially divided up the world markets between themselves. Metal Box was to expand within

Europe and the British colonies, while Continental Can would develop interests in the rest of the world.

In the late 1930s, the innovative company planned to produce new forms of packaging such as card containers with metal ends and cans with wax lining for beer. The onslaught of World War II, however, curtailed new production in favor of equipment for the troops. Containers for gas masks were easy to make in tin box factories, and Metal Box produced 140 million of them for the government. The paint tin production lines were adapted to produce casings for antitank mines. Shell casings and ration tins were also produced by the millions. Even so, due to strict government controls, company profits fell to £242,428 in 1945.

Expanded into Other Forms of Packaging Following World War II

In 1943, as the war turned in the Allies' favor, Barlow established a committee to plan new forms of packaging that could be exploited as soon as the war was over. Consequently, Metal Box was an innovator in the field, quickly moving toward paper, foil, and plastic container products as the postwar economy began to improve. But Metal Box still dominated the British can and carton market. Between 1941 and 1961, eight new factories were built or purchased, and by the 1960s, Metal Box was the leading packaging supplier to some of the largest companies in the world, including Unilever, Nestlé, Heinz, Imperial Tobacco, BAT, ICI, Hoechst, and Shell.

After the war, Metal Box was more than ready for further organizational changes. The accounting department was restructured and a financial comptroller was appointed. Additionally, administrative functions were more clearly defined and brought under central control, and subsidiaries were also made more accountable to central management. Barlow retained his position as executive chairman, but in 1946, he brought in D. W. Brough as his managing director. Brough had been in charge of operations in South Africa; nevertheless, he lasted less than two years. Barlow replaced him with two executives, G. S. Samways and D. Ducat, and these two men served as joint managing directors until Samways's resignation in 1954; Ducat then served alone, but Barlow still maintained overall control until his retirement in 1961.

In the late 1940s, the U.S. Department of Justice had filed an antitrust suit against Continental Can and began to investigate its arrangements with Metal Box. The two companies hastily modified their agreement in 1950 and cooperation between them was restricted to machinery and technical information; all mutual ventures and attempts at market controls were dropped. The modified agreement was renewed and slightly expanded in 1970 and was slated to continue until 1990.

Up to 1970, Metal Box had continued to expand both at home and abroad. In Britain, Wallis Tin Stamping Co., Brown Bibby & Gregory, and Flexible Packaging were all acquired, widening Metal Box's product line to include plastic film, aerosols, central heating, and engineering. The company established facilities or subsidiaries in Italy, Malaysia, Tanzania, Japan, and Iran, and upgraded the older plants in India, France, and South Africa. Even so, Metal Box still conducted three-quarters of its business in the United Kingdom.

In 1967 the Board of Trade referred the British can industry to the Monopolies Commission which ruled that Metal Box was operating a monopoly—supplying 77 percent of all metal containers, 63 percent of aerosols, and 80 percent of open-top cans. Nevertheless, the Commission concluded that the company's monopoly did not harm the public interest and did not find Metal Box lacking in efficiency, innovations, or service. Its report even praised Metal Box for passing on savings to its customers. But the company was instructed to terminate all of its exclusive arrangements, both with customers and with suppliers. Thus, in one stroke, Barlow's market control procedures were ended.

Diversified Beyond Packaging in the 1970s

The 1970s were a decade of significant changes for Metal Box. Under the direction of chairman and chief executive Alex Page, the company began to make serious moves to diversify outside of packaging, a mature industry unable to support long-term growth. The company's diversification was a measured one, however, and the areas targeted—although seemingly far removed from packaging—were nonetheless considered similar in terms of the manufacturing technology involved. Thus the company had by the mid-1970s begun to build—primarily through acquisitions—significant operations in the manufacturing of radiators used in central heating systems as well as a machinery building group. In late 1975 a company reorganization highlighted the importance of these new ventures when they were placed into a new diversified products group, alongside a packaging group that included Metal Box's traditional businesses. Also in 1975 the company moved its headquarters from central London to Reading. And sales reached the US$1 billion mark in 1976.

As the 1970s progressed, Metal Box's packaging unit faced a climate of increasing competition at home and abroad. The company opened itself to further competition in 1978 when it abandoned its licensing deal with Continental Can, which immediately began to build a plant in Wales to make two-piece aluminum cans. By this time, two-piece cans were considered state of the art because they used 40 percent fewer raw materials in their manufacture. Metal Box had moved to set up its factories to make two-piece cans, but was initially thwarted by its workforce which balked at the continuous production process needed for the manufacturing to be most efficient. Eventually, in 1982, Metal Box had to abandon two-piece manufacturing at one of its plants and decided to close another one, but did manage to initiate two-piece production at other plants.

While dealing with these troubles at home, the company increasingly looked overseas for opportunities for growth. In 1979 Metal Box opened a two-piece can plant in Carson, California, that would eventually supply Pepsi-Cola with 625 million cans a year. The company also acquired Risdon Manufacturing, a maker of cosmetics packaging based in Connecticut. In Europe Metal Box sought to build on its existing operations in southern Europe (which were primarily in Italy, Greece, and Portugal), by entering into a licensing agreement with France's Carnaud, whereby Metal Box provided equipment and expertise for a two-piece can plant near Brussels to be built by Carnaud. Cans from the plant were to be sold in the Benelux countries and parts of France and West Germany. As a result of these overseas moves, the portion of Metal Box profits derived outside the United Kingdom increased from 41.4 percent in 1977 to 55.5 percent in 1980. By the end of the 1970s revenues had reached US$2.7 billion.

Blockbuster Deals Marked 1980s

Metal Box barely survived through a very difficult period in the early 1980s, ravaged by a recession and hampered by a management team that lacked the kind of forward thinkers needed in an environment marked by ever more increasing competition. By the mid-1980s Dr. Brian Smith had been brought in as chairman; he had previously helped to turn around ICI. In January 1988 Murray Stuart became chief executive of the newly named MB Group, after having joined the company as finance director in 1981. Smith and Stuart would by the end of the decade engineer deals that completely transformed the company.

The name change reflected a desire to deemphasize the company's tinning roots. By the late 1980s MB Group had steadily built up its nonpackaging operations to the point where it was Europe's largest manufacturer of central heating radiators, through its Stelrad unit; it had developed a bathroom products business with the Stelrad Doulton brand; and its Clarke Checks subsidiary—built through a series of small acquisitions—had become the fourth-largest printer of checks in the United States. Stelrad was boosted further in 1988 with the acquisition of the leading producer of radiators in continental Europe, Henrad Beheer of Belgium.

Smith and Stuart next surprised many observers when they agreed in October 1988 to merge MB's packaging operations with those of Carnaud to form CMB Packaging SA, based in Brussels. CMB, of which MB initially held a 25.5 percent stake, immediately became the third-largest packaging company in the world and was better able to compete on the global stage than MB packaging could on its own. Carnaud gained management control of the new company but more important to MB was the £240 million in cash it received from the merger, money it could use to further bolster its nonpackaging units. MB did just that in September 1989 when it acquired American Bank Stationery Co. for £193.7 million, beefing up its U.S. security printing operations.

Another blockbuster deal for Smith and Stuart came only one month later. After a year of negotiations, MB acquired Caradon plc in a £337.6 million reverse takeover, with half the amount in cash and half in Caradon shares converted to those of MB. Caradon had been founded in 1985 through a £61 million management buyout of the U.K. building products division of Reed International, the U.K. publishing giant. Caradon, which had gone public in 1987, was a perfect fit with MB's central heating and bathroom products since its top brands were Twyfords bathroom and sanitary products, Mira showers, Terrain plastic pipes, and Celuform plastic timber. Following the acquisition, Smith retired and the newly named MB-Caradon PLC was headed by Stuart as chairman and Peter Jansen, Caradon's chief, as chief executive and in charge of day-to-day operations.

1990s and Beyond

Not surprisingly, MB-Caradon next sold its stake in CMB (at the time known as Carnaud-Metalbox), and thus divested itself of its Metal Box roots. The £467.5 million (US$700 million) generated by the April 1993 sale was used almost immediately when MB-Caradon paid £800 million (US$1.2 billion) for RTZ Corp.'s RTZ Pillar industrial products group in August of that same year. Pillar brought with it construction, general engineering, automotive, and aviation operations. Yet another name change followed on the heels of this acquisition when MB-Caradon became Caradon plc.

By 1994, through these and other deals, Caradon had established itself as a leader in doors and windows, with its other operations being plumbing products, electrical products, structural and engineering operations, and security printing. That year, sales nearly doubled, having reached £1.61 billion, while operating profits were a record £205.4 million.

The following year Caradon acquired a 43 percent stake in Weru A.G., a German leader in doors and windows. Later in the year, however, profits suffered as sales of doors and windows in the United States fell sharply, the cost of raw materials used to make plastic products rose, and the U.K. building industry suffered a general depression. Operating profits fell as a result, to £127.1 million and sales increased only 6.4 percent.

In response Jansen launched a restructuring late in 1995: 1,600 jobs were eliminated, a layer of management was jettisoned so that the directors of the five divisions reported directly to Jansen, and noncore businesses began to be divested. In December 1996 Caradon sold off 18 businesses for a total of £220 million (US$360 million), including most of its European engineering and distribution operations. Meanwhile the company spent £48.2 million (US$75 million) for another 30 percent of Weru, bringing its total stake to almost 80 percent.

The 1996 divestments were in many cases long overdue (some dated back to the merger of MB Group and the original Caradon; others came with RTZ Pillar) and were a key to a possible company turnaround. More divestments were certainly possible, and the North American engineering and security printing units were the leading candidates. Caradon was also likely to make further acquisitions in the late 1990s to beef up its already considerable building products operations, which accounted for 80 percent of overall company sales in 1996.

Principal Subsidiaries

Caradon Inc. (U.S.A.); Caradon America Inc. (U.S.A.); Caradon Limited (Canada); Caradon Bathrooms Limited; Caradon Ideal Limited; Caradon Mira Limited; Caradon Stelrad Limited; Caradon Terrain Limited; Hendrickx Radiotoren NV (Belgium); Caradon Stelrad BV (Netherlands); Caradon Stelrad GmbH (Germany); Stelrad Radiatorenwerke GmbH (Austria); Caradon Doors and Windows Inc. (U.S.A.); Caradon Doors & Windows Limited; Caradon Everest Limited; Weru AG (Germany; 79.87%); Caradon Gent Limited; Esser Sicherheitstechnik GmbH (Germany); Caradon Friedland Limited; Caradon MK Electric Limited; Caradon Trend Limited; Novar Electronics Corporation (U.S.A.); Brampton Foundries Limited (Canada); Caradon Catnic Limited; Fabricated Steel

Products Inc. (Canada); Indal Technologies Inc. (Canada); Checks in the Mail, Inc. (U.S.A.); Clarke American Checks, Inc. (U.S.A.).

Principal Divisions

Plumbing; Doors & Windows; Electrical; Structural & Engineering; Security Printing.

Further Reading

Bowditch, Gillian, "Caradon Agrees £337m Deal with MB Group," *Times* (London), October 4, 1989, p. 31.

Campbell, Colin, "MB Ties Up Packaging Interests with Carnaud," *Times* (London), October 27, 1988, p. 25.

Foster, Geoffrey, "The Remaking of Metal Box," *Management Today,* January 1985, pp. 43–51.

"Metal Box Aims to Kick Continental Can," *World Business Weekly,* September 1, 1980, pp. 10–11.

Oates, David, "Metal Box Re-Packages Its Operations," *International Management,* May 1976, pp. 10–13.

Reader, W. J., *Metal Box: A History,* London: Heinemann, 1976.

Urry, Maggie, "Bold Deal Soothes Anxious Onlookers," *Financial Times,* August 26, 1993, p. 19.

—updated by David E. Salamie

Cash America International, Inc.

1600 W. Seventh Street
Fort Worth, Texas 76102-2599
U.S.A.
(817) 335-1100
Fax: (817) 335-1119
Web site: http://www.streetlink.com/pwn

Public Company
Founded: 1983
Employees: 2,635
Sales: $281 million (1996)
Stock Exchanges: New York
SICs: 5932 Used Merchandise Stores

Cash America International, Inc. is the world's largest and only international pawn company. In addition to providing secured non-recourse loans (pawn loans) to individuals, the company provides check cashing services through its Mr. Payroll Corp. subsidiary and buyer financing arrangements through its affiliate, Express Rent-a-Tire, Ltd. As of June 1997, the company had 392 locations in the United States, Great Britain, and Sweden.

Getting Started, 1983–89

Jack Daugherty, the chairman and CEO of Cash America, opened his first pawnshop, in Texas, in the early 1970s and was so successful he moved into the oil business. When that industry went bust, he returned to pawnshops, founding the company in 1983, and incorporating it the following year as Cash America Investments, Inc. Daugherty took the company public in 1987, making it the first pawnshop company to be publicly owned. The initial offering raised $14.5 million, with 5 million shares sold. Using the money to expand, Cash America acquired the Big State chain of 47 pawnshops later that year. The company continued to grow, primarily through acquisitions. In 1988, five years after its founding, the chain opened its 100th location.

The stores in the Cash America chain did not fit the dark, dingy image of a storefront pawnshop. Daugherty's strategy was to provide big, well-lit stores, to computerize the inventory and to centralize management. The company established a three-month training program for new employees that included classroom and on-the-job training in loans, layaways, merchandise, and general administration of store operations. More experienced workers received training in the fundamentals of management and managers went through a year-long program that dealt with recruitment, merchandise control, income maximization, and cost efficiency. Each store had a unit manager who reported to a market manager responsible for about ten locations. The market manager in turn reported to a division vice president.

"Cash America is bringing modern management to a backward industry," Prudential analyst John D. Morris told Ellen Stark of the *Wall Street Journal.* And investors, including some of the nation's largest banks according to Michael Hudson of *The Nation,* appeared to like it. In 1988, the company sold an additional 4.92 million shares, raising $24 million to finance its expansion.

Cash America used the term "non-traditional borrowers," to refer to its customers. These were people not willing or unable to use a credit card or get a bank loan to cover the cost of repairing their car, paying a utility bill or other short-term need for cash. Many did not have a checking account and usually conducted their business on a cash basis.

Customers brought in items of personal value—wedding rings, silver tea sets, televisions, firearms, bicycles, radar detectors, weed wackers—to use as collateral for an immediate loan of money. Using sources such as catalogues, blue books, newspapers, previous similar pawn loan transactions, and his or her own experience, the Cash America employee determined the estimated value of the item and the amount to be financed.

The Cash America customer received a computerized pawn ticket that gave a detailed description of the collateral, amount loaned, and identifying information about the customer (address, age, driver's license number). The average Cash America loan was for under $100 and was outstanding for less than two months. The customer redeemed the item by paying the loan amount and service charge. About 70 percent of the company's loans were repaid. For those that were not, the collateral became the property of Cash America and could be sold.

The company's gross revenue was calculated by adding the amount received from the sales of unredeemed items plus the amount earned from service charges. Sales were generally around 70 percent of the gross revenue. But when the cost of the sales was subtracted, service charges accounted for at least half the net revenue each year.

The pawnshop industry has long been an extensively regulated activity. States determined the process to be followed in applying for a pawnshop license, what records had to be maintained and whether the local police could inspect them or whether transactions had to be reported to local law enforcement officials, how old a customer must be to be served, and what hours the business could be open. States also established the range of loan amounts and the maximum annual service charge for each range. In Texas, for example, in 1997, the most a pawnshop could charge was 240 percent per annum, and that only for loans of $1–$132. No pawn loan could be more than $11,000, for which the maximum annual rate was 12 percent. Oklahoma also had 240 percent as the maximum annual rate, but for loans of $1 to $150. Loans in that state could not exceed $25,000, with a maximum annual rate for that amount of 36 percent. Other states, including Florida and Georgia, allowed a maximum of 25 percent of the loan for each 30-day period of the transaction, with no breakdown by loan amount.

Growing Fast, 1990–95

By 1990, Cash America was operating 123 company-owned locations. That year the company was listed on the New York Stock Exchange and the stock split 3 for 2. In 1992, a 4.6 million stock offering raised $45 million, the stock split 2 for 1, and the company opened its 200th store, in Mission, Texas. It was at this point that Daugherty decided to take his company international. He acquired Harvey & Thompson, a U.K. chain with over 100 years in the pawnshop business. Harvey & Thompson was based in London and had 26 locations in England and Scotland. The pawnshop business in the United Kingdom was essentially the same as that in the United States. However, pawn loans generally were secured only by jewelry and gold or silver items and the average loan was larger, approximately $120. Additionally, for loans larger than about $40, unredeemed items were sold at auction. Finally, the Consumer Credit Act of 1974 prohibited pawnbrokers from entering into "extortionate credit bargains" with customers and Cash America charged a rate of around 6 percent per month.

The company continued to expand in the United States as well, opening more stores, buying the 18-store Express Cash chain and entering Alabama and Missouri in 1993. At the end of the year the chain operated 280 locations. In 1994, Cash America opened its 300th store and had over 1,800 employees. That same year it bought shares in Mr. Payroll, a check cashing franchise operation and also acquired the 10-store Svensk Paantelåning, one of the oldest operating pawnshop chains in Sweden. As in the United Kingdom, the pawnshops in Sweden handled primarily jewelry and precious metals, catering to a more affluent customer. Under a new pawnbroking act passed in 1996, loan terms were not to exceed one year, but the act set no maximum interest rates for pawn loans and did not authorize local boards to regulate those rates as the statute had in the past. Also as with Harvey & Thompson, unredeemed merchandise was sold at public auction, although pawnbrokers could sell items they purchased at auction to the public from their pawnshop. The average loan amount in Sweden was approximately $300. In both Sweden and the United Kingdom, loans generally were outstanding for 180 days or less and forfeiture rates were one-third less than in the United States. At the end of 1994, the company had gross revenues of $221.9 million and $15 million in net profits.

During 1995, the company faced increased competition in the United States. Several companies, including EZ Corp. Inc. with 240 locations, and First Cash, Inc. with 50 operating units, completed initial public offerings and announced plans to expand through new locations and acquisitions. A number of smaller companies also entered the market.

The competition affected the company's Cash America VIP program which offered discounts on unredeemed merchandise to frequent shoppers in an effort to attract bargain shoppers. Cash America turned to its proprietary loan and inventory tracking system to analyze the problems. The system linked all its U.S. stores to coordinate and manage thousands of loans and over a million different items of inventory. Using information from that system, Daugherty found that inventory was too high, that unredeemed items were not being turned over quickly enough despite the discounts. He also decided that too much emphasis was being placed on retail to the detriment of the actual loan business.

1996 to the Present

The company established two goals for 1996: to reinforce U.S. operations on the importance of successful lending at the unit level and to sharpen the emphasis on cash-on-cash returns at every level of the organization, both domestic and foreign. Cash America also decided to slow its rate of growth, with a net gain of 9 units during the year, for a total of 382.

But the refocus did not stop Daugherty from moving into another alternative financial business. By December 1996, Cash America had purchased all the shares of Mr. Payroll, which then had about 160 locations in 21 states. Mr. Payroll was started by John Templer in 1988 as he lay in a hospital bed in High Plains, Texas, after battling Guillian-Barre, a rare neurological disease, for two years. Templer and his partner, Michael Stinson, began by cashing checks for nurses at the hospital, using an armored car. Running the armored car two days a week, they also cashed checks for workers at two nearby manufacturing plants.

Mr. Payroll expanded to Amarillo in 1989, putting check cashing booths in eight Toot'n Totum Food Stores. People kept calling Templer, wanting to open booths in other towns, and he decided to franchise the concept. By the time it became a wholly owned subsidiary of Cash America, national companies such as Texaco, Circle K, and Diamond-Shamrock wanted to be franchisees. In Shreveport, Louisiana, for example, Mr. Payroll built eight locations for Circle K. "They want it. It adds value to them. They take the cash out of the store and recycle it through checks they cash and the customers spend the money in the store. That's a big advantage to the stores," Templer explained to the *Amarillo Business Journal*.

The acquisition was also advantageous to Cash America in its efforts to serve the non-banking segment of the population and become, to quote the 1996 Annual Report, "a broader based, specialty financial services entity." Neither Mr. Payroll nor the company's affiliate, Express Rent-a-Tire, Ltd., contributed to earnings in 1996.

Cash America's income from its domestic operations increased in 1996 after dropping in 1995. Loan balances increased 23 percent while inventory levels dropped by 14 percent. The company ended the year with an all-time high average domestic loan balance of $190,000 per location and a year-end inventory level of $145,000 per location, the lowest in several years. Daugherty credited the company's ability to respond to a stronger than expected demand for loans, with the increase coming from more loans, not larger loans. This was evidence that the company was increasing its customer base and market penetration. For the first time in its history, Cash America had more than $100 million in outstanding loans.

In November, the company announced a "Dutch Auction" to buy back 4.5 million shares. Under that process, shareholders tendered shares at prices between $7.00 and $8.50 and Cash America then determined the single share price within that range that would allow it to purchase 4.5 million or fewer shares. In December the company purchased 4.5 million shares at $8.50 per share. In January 1997, the Board of Directors was authorized to repurchase up to one million shares on the open market. In May 1997, Cash America acquired Rothchilds Sales & Loans, the largest pawnshop chain in Utah with five locations in and around Salt Lake City. That same month, Mr. Payroll expected to have its first self-service check-cashing and automated teller machines up and running in three towns in Texas. With the TrueFace technology used in the machines, customers would be able to cash any check in less than a minute without showing any photo identification. Instead, the technology verified a customer's identity by recognizing the contour of his or her face.

The company's earnings continued to grow during 1997, with its loan balance standing at over $100 million and its inventory down 12 percent at the end of the first quarter. While law enforcement officers remained concerned about customers pawning stolen property, the company stated that stolen property accounted for less than one-half of 1 percent of property pawned with the chain.

In June, Daugherty announced a new franchise program. Under it, selected independent pawnshops would be franchised under the Cash America brand name starting later in 1997. "By joining forces with hundreds of other quality and service-minded pawnbrokers, we will be able to reach markets beyond those served by our existing and planned company-owned stores," COO Daniel Feehan explained.

According to Mike Rapoport, an analyst with Dabnehy/Resnick, in addition to Cash America's successful pawn business, the company was among the nation's largest gold producers. It sold gold melted down from unredeemed, unsold jewelry on the metals exchange as bullion. "This thing makes money," Rapoport told the *Sun Sentinel*.

Principal Subsidiaries

Mr. Payroll Corporation.

Further Reading

Bowser, David, "Business Cashes in By Cashing Checks," *Amarillo Business Journal, Amarillo Globe-News Online*, February 12, 1997.

Falkner, R. Jerry, "Research Profile: Cash America International, Inc.," RJ Falkner and Company: Crested Butte, CO, May/June 1997.

"Fact Sheet—March 31, 1997," Cash America International, Inc.: Austin, TX.

Glover, Scott, and Evelyn Larrubia, "Want a Piece of Shops? Try Wall Street," *Sun Sentinel*, November 25, 1996, http://www.sun-sentinel.com/news/1664.htm.

Hudson, Michael, "Cashing in on Poverty: How Big Business Wins Every Time," *The Nation*, May 5, 1996, http://www.thenation.com/issue/96520/0520huds.htm.

"Pro Forma Historical Financial Information," Cash America International, Inc.: Austin, TX, February 2, 1997.

"Retailers and Consumers Benefit From TrueFace Technology," PRNewswire, April 15, 1997, http://www.prnewswire.com.

Stark, Ellen, "You Can Hock the Silverware to Buy This Stock," *Time*, February 1995, p. 57.

"Time Line—1983–1994," Cash America International, Inc.: Austin, TX.

—Ellen D. Wernick

CASTLE & COOKE, INC.

Castle & Cooke, Inc.

10900 Wilshire Boulevard
Los Angeles, California 90024
U.S.A.
(310) 208-3636
Fax: (310) 824-2159

Public Company
Incorporated: 1894
Employees: 42,000
Sales: $4.1 billion (1995)
Stock Exchanges: New York
SICs: 6552 Land Subdividers & Developers; 7011
Hotels, Motels; 5148 Fresh Fruits & Vegetables; 5149
Groceries & Related Products, Not Elsewhere
Classified

Castle & Cooke, Inc. has two core businesses, including real estate development and hotel management, and food processing. The company owns vast residential real estate properties in Hawaii, California, and Arizona, and also holds commercial and industrial properties in the same locations. Castle & Cooke also own and manages office buildings, apartment complexes, shopping centers, luxury resort hotels, luxury vacation homes, and golf courses. Yet the company is best known for its ownership of Dole Food Company which is famous for its Dole Pineapple. Castle & Cooke, Inc.'s real estate revenues amounted to approximately $308 million in fiscal 1996, but its food operations brought in an astounding $3.8 billion in sales.

Early History

In 1837 Samuel Northrup Castle and Amos Starr Cooke landed on Hawaii, then known as the Sandwich Islands, as part of the Seventh Reinforcement of the American Board of Commissioners for Foreign Missions, to begin their lives as lay missionaries. Castle's assignment was to order, unload, and distribute supplies for the mission depository. Cooke's job was to teach the ''natives''—he taught the children of the royal families who then ruled the various islands for many years.

Over the years Castle, who felt Cooke's accounting abilities would help the depository, kept trying to convince his friend to join him. Cooke firmly declined until 1849, when his schooling of the royal children was complete. He needed to make a living since monetary support from Missions headquarters had been discontinued.

That year Castle suggested to Cooke that they set up a partnership to take over the operation of the depository as a private enterprise. Money could be made by trading with the community at large, while mission posts could be supplied at cost. They took up the matter with the Mission Board in Boston, which, after two years, decided to release the partners from the mission and pay each a yearly salary of $500. On June 2, 1851, their partnership began, and a sign reading ''Kakela me Kuke'' (''Castle & Cooke'') was installed at the entrance to the Honolulu depository.

Business began with a bang. In their first year in business, profits came to nearly $2,000. In 1853 a branch store was opened downtown, to be closer to the considerable action the California Gold Rush brought. Also in 1853, Castle and Cooke purchased their first ship, the *Morning Star* to ship produce to California. By 1856, the partners elected to sell the depository, located on the outskirts of Honolulu, to concentrate on their burgeoning downtown business.

In 1858 Castle and Cooke first ventured out of the mercantile business to make an investment in the new sugar industry. In the late 1860s they branched into the shipping business, handling shoreside business for a number of transpacific schooners and several inter-island vessels. Despite these diversifications, however, the mercantile portion of the business continued to provide the bulk of the profits.

As time went on, Joe Atherton, Cooke's son-in-law, handled more and more of the day-to-day business while Castle devoted most of his time to public affairs. On July 14, 1894, 10 days after the Republic of Hawaii was proclaimed, Samuel Castle died at the age of 86.

On December 28, 1894, the Castle & Cooke partnership was incorporated and Joe Atherton was elected president. At this time the company was just coming out of a financial slump caused by its 1889 investment in a sugar development called Ewa Plantation on the island of Oahu. To provide the huge amount of money needed to fund the project, Castle & Cooke had sold a large part of its holdings, including its valuable interests in the Haiku and Paia sugar plantations on Maui. The company continued to believe in the profitability of the Ewa Plantation and the risk paid off. By 1898, its production totaled 18,284 tons of sugar; in 1925 it reached 50,000. To add to the abundance, when Congress annexed Hawaii in August 1898, sugar prices rose.

Also in 1898, the original merchandise business was sold. Diversification did not stop, however. In the ensuing years Castle & Cooke involved itself in an (unsuccessful) automobile company, the Hawaiian Fertilizer Company, and a big but short venture into the sugar refinery business with the Honolulu Sugar Refining Company. Although C & C had been in the shipping business for 50 years, a 1907 agreement with William Matson to be the agent for his Matson Navigation Company greatly increased the business in this area. The agreement endured for 56 years, most of them profitable.

In 1916 Edward Davies Tenney, a Castle nephew, became chairman of Castle & Cooke and a year later president of Matson Navigation upon William Matson's death. He held these posts for more than 30 years, until his death in 1934. Tenney became chairman just as the United States was entering World War I. Hawaii was a long way from the war zone; the only real effect of the war was to drive up the price of sugar, increasing Castle & Cooke's profits. Within a few months after the war, Tenney began to act on his prewar decision to diversify. He acquired for the company an assortment of stocks and bonds, including shares in the Bank of California, Pennsylvania Railroad, California Telephone and Light, Poulsen Wireless, Santa Cruz Portland Cement, and Sterling Oil & Development.

His next big project was the company's entrance into the travel business. In 1925 a group of entrepreneurs decided that the travelers on their luxury cruise lines needed a glamorous place to stay during their trip to Hawaii. As president of the Territorial Hotel Company (almost half of the directors worked for Castle & Cooke) Tenney oversaw the building of the $2 million Royal Hawaiian. In the long run the hotel was a flop, but news of its glamour ranged far.

The company's growth continued when Matson bought the Los Angeles Steamship Company to ward off its taking over his luxury steamship trade. Castle & Cooke, along with Matson Navigation, was now the largest steamship system in the Pacific.

The Great Depression and World War II

The Depression was less severe in Hawaii than on the mainland. Although Castle & Cooke never missed a dividend payment, the year-end bonus in 1931 included a warning that it probably would not be repeated. In April 1932, salaries and pensions were cut. By the time Alexander G. Budge became president in 1935, Castle & Cooke was already making a rapid recovery, in large part due to its 1932 purchase from Jim Dole of a 21 percent interest in his Hawaiian Pineapple Company. The Waialua Agricultural Company (part of Castle & Cooke) had already acquired a one-third share of Hawaiian Pineapple in

a 1922 lease agreement. The purchase caused hard feelings between Dole and Castle & Cooke. After the reorganization, Dole was made chairman of the board, but was immediately sent on a "well-earned rest" from which he was never recalled. When he finally returned in 1933 he found his office moved to a storeroom.

World War II had a much more immediate effect on Castle & Cooke than the first war had. The military requisitioned most of the canned fruit that Hawaiian Pineapple and other companies produced, the cannery was blacked out completely, and chunks of acreage were converted to potatoes and other vegetables to help feed the military and local populations. Equipment and manpower were also commandeered; the labor force was cut in half, and key officials were given wartime jobs. Even so, sugar plantations stayed at close to normal production levels and with careful planning, enough vessels were made available to carry some crops to the mainland.

Growth in the Postwar Era

As life returned to normal after VJ day in 1945, the question of statehood for Hawaii resurfaced. During and just before the war, articles had appeared in the mainland press criticizing what were termed feudal practices in Hawaii, especially by the Big Five companies there, which included Castle & Cooke. Many in Hawaii, especially heads of the bigger corporations, felt that this problem was hindering Hawaii's acceptance into statehood. The heads of 15 Hawaiian companies employed a New York public relations firm to make a study of the island's industry and social structure and tell them what to do. The report recommended that the leading island companies divest themselves of stock in rivals and foster real competition. Budge had already done this, limiting himself to positions on the boards only of the seven companies in which Castle & Cooke held a large financial stake. The company also disposed of holdings in agencies that were its competitors; Matson followed suit and several big estates were broken up and distributed among the heirs.

The labor movement also picked up again after the war, and Castle & Cooke's operations were involved in several disputes. In late 1946 the International Longshoremen's and Warehousemen's Union (ILWU) led a strike of 28,000 workers on 33 sugar plantations. The strike lasted 79 days; all over the islands irrigated cane dried and lost its sugar-bearing juice, resulting in a loss of some $20 million of sugar. Then in April 1949 the union called out 2,000 longshoremen, cutting off all of Hawaii's supplies completely: nothing could come into the islands and nothing could be shipped to the mainland. This remarkable strike lasted 179 days and in the end the union lost its major demands, but it gained rank and file solidarity. During the strike, no goods could travel on the Pacific coast, but cargoes could and did use Gulf and Atlantic docks, giving Hawaii's economy links to the Atlantic coast for the first time in almost a century.

As the Hawaiian Pineapple Company suffered losses due to another strike in 1952, Budge kept pushing for diversification to end the firm's dependence on sugar and pineapple. In 1946 Hawaiian Tuna Packers had been purchased for this reason, and in 1948 Castle & Cooke organized the Royal Hawaiian Macadamia Nut Company as well.

Throughout its history, Castle & Cooke had only owned real estate indirectly, as an investor in agricultural businesses. In 1958 that changed: Helemano Company, Ltd. was merged into Castle & Cooke, adding 27,000 acres of land to its holdings.

Finally, in 1959, Hawaii became a state. Also in 1959, Malcolm MacNaughton became the president of C & C. He believed that an entirely new corporate structure was needed to promote the company's growth.

Through the years, Hawaiian Pineapple had been run independently, but in the late 1950s frictions reached a point of no return. Henry White, who had run the company for many years, had made some decisions about diversification that Budge had strongly disagreed with. As Hawaiian's profits fell, White was moved out of his position and in 1961 the company was merged into Castle & Cooke, adding another 15,000 acres to C & C's holdings.

The same year, Columbia River Packers (renamed Bumble Bee Seafoods, Inc.) was merged into Castle & Cooke, making the company an important player in the food industry, along with its shipping, stevedoring, and merchandising businesses.

By this time, Castle & Cooke owned 155,000 acres of land in Hawaii and a ranch in California. To manage and develop this property, Oceanic Properties was formed as a wholly owned subsidiary. The subsidiary's projects have included new towns, golf courses, apartment and medical buildings, and downtown development worldwide.

International development became a reality when Dole Philippines was organized in 1963 to farm 18,000 acres on the island of Mindanao. The decision to farm abroad was made when management felt that costs, especially labor, were too high.

Castle & Cooke then turned to bananas. With cash from the sale of Matson (in 1964) and Honolulu Oil, Castle & Cooke purchased a 55 percent share of Standard Fruit and Steamship Company of New Orleans; the rest of the stock was purchased in 1968. By 1973 Donald J. Kirchoff, C & C's executive vice president on the project, had made Castle & Cooke the U.S. leader in the banana market.

Restructuring and Transition

By the beginning of the 1970s a decision was made to bring the various companies together, tightening the loose-knit corporate structure. In 1972 a complete corporate revamping took place. Kirchoff, now president, felt that C & C had always just evolved rather than grown according to a plan. Now the company was a group of unrelated businesses, including a 26-store retail chain, a plate glass company in the Philippines, a drainpipe company in Thailand, and a quarry in Malaysia. The first step was to centralize food marketing and corporate financial administration in San Francisco, with headquarters to remain in Honolulu. This move eliminated overlapping assignments and allowed for a 30 percent reduction in corporate staff. Tight central controls were established over budgets and results reviewed quarterly against performance. All food activities except sugar were brought into a single group, Castle & Cooke Foods. Real estate activities and manufacturing and merchandising were organized into two additional groups. Rather than buying companies, "just because the numbers looked good," Kirchoff used planned diversification, buying companies in fast-growing niches of the food market.

Over the next several years, Kirchoff's plan worked extremely well. Between 1972 and 1978, earnings rose about 20 percent a year. The bubble burst, however, in 1979. Besides bad luck with the weather, some critics claimed that the expansion program was just too ambitious; for example, C & C's movement into the European banana market ended up causing an oversupply.

C & C's problems persisted into the early 1980s. In July 1982, Kirchoff resigned and Henry Clark assumed interim responsibilities. The company tried moving in directions that would not be as cyclical—regional preparation centers to prepare vegetables for fast food restaurants, for example. When Ian Wilson became president, he concentrated on three main areas—fresh produce, packaged foods, and real estate. In 1983, he purchased the A & W root beer business, and at the same time placed more emphasis on marketing and advertising. Castle & Cooke's current logo for Dole brands was introduced as part of a drive to establish itself as a premier marketer of fruits around the world.

The next few years were turbulent ones for Castle & Cooke. The company was the subject of several takeover bids, by Houston investor Charles Hurwitz in 1984, then by Minneapolis investor Irwin L. Jacobs, and finally by David Murdock, who merged C & C with his Flexi-Van Corporations in July 1985 to keep the company from going bankrupt.

Murdock, who installed himself as chairman and CEO of his new company, took firm control of Castle & Cooke, reorganizing it into a holding company for three separate operations: Flexi-Van, Dole Food, and Oceanic Properties, and relocating its headquarters to Los Angeles. Prospects began to brighten immediately and kept improving.

By the late 1980s, Castle & Cooke's Dole Foods had become the world's largest pineapple marketer, ranked second in banana sales, and also became a leading purveyor of iceberg lettuce, celery, cauliflower, broccoli, and other vegetables. The company owned vast amounts of land around the world: 28,000 acres in Honduras, 12,000 in Costa Rica, 18,400 in the Philippines and 5,000 in Thailand, as well as approximately 46,000 acres in the United States. Through Oceanic Properties the company also owned 151,000 acres, including virtually the whole Hawaiian island of Lanai, extensive property in Oahu, and 5,200 acres in California.

Almost immediately after his takeover of the company, Murdock let it be known that Dole Foods was for sale. As a result, he began to shop the food operation of Castle & Cooke to the highest possible bidder. However, as Dole Foods continued to bring in larger and larger amounts of revenue, Murdock changed his mind and, by the late 1980s he was adding to the Dole Foods product line.

Itching for something to do, Murdock then decided to develop Lanai island, traditionally known for its pineapple growing, into a lavish resort for tourists. He built two luxury hotels in

1991, and added a second golf course in the same year. Unfortunately, the entire project cost $550 million and the venture lost $117 million during the first two years of its operations.

Undeterred, Murdock went headlong into other expensive real estate development projects. During the mid-1990s, he began to develop the swanky Sherwood Country Club & Estates located in Los Angeles, California. Taking money from Dole Foods to convert a washed-out gully into a luxury golf course and tennis club, the corporate raider also spent hundreds of thousands of dollars on transplanting 1,500 California oak trees to create beautiful fairway for golfers. Yet the development project bled Dole Foods dry and, as a result, Murdock began to use some of his own personal resources in the project. Yet Sherwood failed to show a profit and Murdock personally fell into debt and began selling off shares of his Dole Foods stock.

In spite of these circumstances, Murdock seems committed for the short term at least to keep both Castle & Cooke and Dole Foods in good running order. Although the real estate development projects of Castle & Cooke are at the whim of Murdock, the continued success of Dole Foods will keep Murdock's real estate dreams alive.

Principal Subsidiaries

Flexi-Van Corp.; Castle & Cooke Fresh Fruit, Inc.; Castle & Cooke Fresh Vegetables, Inc.; Castle & Cooke Kabushiki Kaisha, Limited (Japan); Castle & Cooke Worldwide Limited (Hong Kong); Intercontinental Transportation Services, Limited (Liberia); Dole Philippines, Inc. (Republic of the Philippines); Dole Thailand, Ltd. (Thailand); Kohala Corporation; Oahu Transport Company, Ltd.; Oceanic Properties, Inc.; Pina Antilana, S.A. (Honduras); Produce Continental, Limited (Bermuda); Produce International A.B. (Sweden); Standard Fruit and Steamship Co.

Further Reading

Barrett, Amy, "Dole's Stunted Harvest," *Business Week,* February 7, 1994, pp. 116–17.

Biesada, Alexandra, "Castle & Cooke's Dole Strategy," *Financial World,* February 5, 1991, pp. 14–16.

"Castle & Cooke May Sell Its Crown," *Business Week,* December 17, 1990, p. 52.

Machan, Dyan, "Busted Millionaire?", *Forbes,* April 21, 1997, pp. 76–78.

Marcial, Gene G., "There's Big Money On Castle & Cooke," *Business Week,* March 3, 1986, p. 106.

Siwolop, Sana, "Castle & Cooke: Murdock's Next Move," *Financial World,* February 21, 1989, p. 16.

Taylor, Frank J., et al. *From Land and Sea: The Story of Castle & Cooke of Hawaii,* Chronicle Books, San Francisco, 1976.

Zweig, Jason, "Pineapples Anyone?", *Forbes,* November 27, 1989, p. 286.

—updated by Thomas Derdak

Cattleman's, Inc.

1825 Scott Street
Detroit, Michigan 48207
U.S.A.
(313) 833-2700
Fax: (313) 833-7164

Public Company
Incorporated: 1972 as Eastern Market Beef Processing
    Corp.
Employees: 340
Sales: $125.3 million (1996)
Stock Exchanges: NASDAQ
SICs: 5147 Meat and Meat Products; 5421 Meat and Fish
    Markets

From beef briskets and chuck steaks to hamburger and ribs, Detroit-based Cattleman's, Inc. annually converts over 100 million pounds of beef into packaged steaks and other custom cuts for the wholesale market, while also offering the patrons of its retail outlets a healthy supply of fresh fruits and vegetables on the side. Through its wholly owned subsidiary, Cattleman's Meat Co., located in Detroit's Eastern Market area, the company packs and markets beef to almost 400 fresh meat distributors, institutional food service clients, hotels and restaurants, and other large retailers in the U.S. as well as in Canada, the Caribbean, Mexico, Taiwan, and the Far East.

Because of the variety of grades, sizes, and cuts of beef requested by its many customers, Cattleman's fills a unique market niche: The company is able to offer a wide range of fresh beef products in a prompt manner. Cattleman's buys its beef carcasses from three of the largest slaughterhouses in the United States on a non-contractual basis, thereby purchasing only what it needs to fill existing orders. The company provides a service to these slaughterhouses, which can use only beef of exact specifications in terms of size, shape, fat content, and color to run through their own meat packaging plants. Those carcasses that do not fulfill a particular packing-house's exacting requirements are sold to Cattleman's, which in turn can furnish its own regular wholesale customers with a wide variety of specialty

cuts. Turn-around time for many of the company's orders is overnight; the company processes over 2 million pounds of beef per week in its Eastern Market plant.

Established as Processing Plant in 1970s

Cattleman's was established in 1972 as the Eastern Market Beef Processing Corp. Company founder Markus Rohtbart was a survivor of Auschwitz who had immigrated to the United States from Poland with his family in 1948. By the early 1950s Rohtbart had established a wholesale meat business in Detroit; he would experiment with several other business ventures before moving to the city's busy Eastern Market district as a beef "fabricator," purchasing beef carcasses which were then cut, vacuum-packed, and shipped to wholesalers and retailers throughout the East and Midwest.

Purchasing beef by the "swinging trailer-load"—quartered carcasses suspended on hooks—Cattleman's produced both packing-house style boxed beef and trimmings, which it further processed into hamburger and sausage. The company's central packing plant and warehouse facility consists of a company-owned building of approximately 56,500 square feet. The company employs 340 full-time workers, most of whom are represented by the AFL-CIO-affiliated United Food and Commercial Workers Union. In keeping with federal regulations, regular inspections of the company's Eastern Market processing plant have been undertaken by the United States Department of Agriculture since Cattleman's first opened.

Expands into Retail Market in Late 1980s

During the 1970s and 1980s, Rohtbart gradually expanded his market, gaining wholesale customers throughout the South as well as in western states and north into Canada. In 1987, at the urging of his son, David Rohtbart, Markus agreed to enter the retail business. David, who had been involved in the family business since 1976 and was employed by Detroit meat distributor Osten Meat Co. during the mid-1980s, saw that by eliminating the middleman and retailing its meat products directly, the company could obtain a competitive advantage in the retail market. To finance the development of its new retail operations in the Eastern Market location, in 1988 the company merged with Arrow Point Resources, an inactive public corporation located in Utah and later moved to Delaware. Markus was named director and chairman of the board, while David was named chief executive officer and president.

In June 1991 the company changed its name to Cattleman's, Inc., and opened its first outlet store in Eastern Market. In addition to the company's own beef, the retail outlet sold pork and poultry to its customers. While efforts to establish a strong retail presence in the metro Detroit area were aggressively pursued through significant television and radio advertising, the retail sector of the business continued to grow slowly, with two more stores opening up between 1991 and 1994. Produce was introduced in the third store, although sales were sluggish. Company products were promoted by accentuating their low price, the store's no-frills atmosphere—shoppers at the outlets, which were open seven days per week, selected their meat while walking through huge, refrigerated coolers—and their high quality. Main competitors to Cattleman's retail outlets were high-volume supermarket and grocery store chains able to buy in bulk to keep meat prices down, and small-scale specialty meat markets that could provide local customers with custom cuts of beef at a location convenient to their home.

As Cattleman's expanded, it began to adopt a more sophisticated structure for its increasingly complex business. Management introduced a vertical integration strategy and treated its greater investment in employee training and job satisfaction as central to its overall success as a retailer. Employees on all rungs of the company ladder received training, support, and opportunities for increasing both their job and interpersonal skills. Such efforts the company perceived as crucial to fostering new and improved customer relations. At the close of fiscal 1991 company sales had been $108 million against net income of $200,000; the following year they had risen to $123.82 million against net income of $499,921.

Company Goes Public in 1993

To finance its expansion into the retail market, Cattleman's went public in 1993, combining a stock split of all existing Arrow Point shares with the issuance of new shares to result in over 3 million shares outstanding. The father-and-son team of

Markus and David Rohtbart continued to control more than 80 percent of the company's total shares; in April 1993 Markus was appointed treasurer while David became assistant treasurer of the company.

In August 1993, in an effort to boost consumer awareness of the company as a produce, as well as meat, retailer, Cattleman's acquired Oak Farms Market, a produce company that operated two fruit and vegetable markets in metropolitan Detroit, in exchange for 90,000 shares of Cattleman's stock. The former Oak Farms retail locations were remodeled and renamed Cattleman's Markets, and by December 1994 the company had five retail locations in operation around the city. In addition, a new warehouse was opened to accommodate the company's expanding product lines. Late in 1993 Cattleman's also changed accounting and law firms, contracted with a new advertising agency, and became a Securities and Exchange Commission reporting company.

By the end of fiscal 1993 Cattleman's was able to post $134.4 million in sales against $1.3 million in net income—a banner year. While 1994's sales figures would be higher—$143.7 million—net income would fall by almost 60 percent to $47,532 due to accounting for the costs of purchasing and remodeling the Oak Farms Market outlets, as well as the costs associated with registering with the SEC in preparation for the company's listing on the NASDAQ over-the-counter market. The drop in net income was also a result of a nationwide downturn in the cattle market, which saw a decline in the price of boxed beef beginning in March 1994. The downward pressure that this downturn created on wholesale and retail beef prices was reflected by the company's pricing adjustments; however, these price decreases resulted in greater overhead costs in proportion to sales.

Retail Outlets Experience Slower Than Expected Growth During 1995

By 1995 the company employed over 300 people in operations at its central packing plant and its five Cattleman's outlet stores in metropolitan Detroit. Outlet stores, which ranged in size from 4,000 to 18,000 square feet, now all offered fresh produce, dairy products, and a variety of meat cuts at prices 10 percent to 40 percent lower than those of area supermarkets. Although outlet sales continued to climb, their sluggish ascent continued to frustrate management. In an effort to reacquaint Detroit consumers with its changing product line, the company hired consultants to help plan a fresh marketing strategy. Among other changes, the decision was made to add the "Farmers' Market" name to each of the Cattleman's retail outlets in 1995.

Now with its five retail locations bolstered by a new image, a new, aggressive sales campaign designed to both increase sales and counteract a spate of negative local media coverage of fresh food retailers in general, and with plans still underway to open a sixth Metro-Detroit Cattleman's Farmers' Market store, the company watched its retail outlet sales gain momentum. Outlet sales, which had accounted for 11.7 percent of total sales in 1994, jumped 30 percent to 16 percent of company sales in fiscal 1995. Unfortunately, this increase was not enough to bolster losses from other operations. Taken as a whole, company sales decreased by 12.2 percent between 1994 and 1995, cresting at only $126.3 million against a net loss of $353,761 by the end of fiscal 1995. The company attributed the loss to the 7.1 percent decrease in the wholesale price of beef products nationwide, a market condition that had prompted them to reduce production by 9.6 percent in terms of total tonnage.

Company Successfully Weathers
Adverse Media, Sluggish Retail Market

In fiscal 1996, 17.4 percent of total sales would come from Cattleman's Farmers' Market retail establishments—an increase of 8.3 percent over 1995 levels. In addition to this continued slow but steady expansion of its market in the retail arena, Cattleman's continued to broaden its wholesale customer base. The company's eastern distribution network accounted for 32 percent of total sales by 1995, with sales of cut and packaged beef in its home state of Michigan running in second place at 26 percent. The remainder of the Midwest scored sales of 18 percent, with southern states accounting for 14 percent, and western states 5 percent. Foreign sales accounted for only 2 percent of the company's 1995 gross sales.

Sales for fiscal 1996 totaled $125.3 million, although the company would post a net loss of $161,159 for the same period due to both the continuing lower-than-average market price for boxed beef products and Cattleman's continuing efforts to expand the sales of its retail operations. The year would also prove to be lackluster for the Detroit meat packager because profits made from its expanding wholesale and retail sales were eroded by increased payroll and payroll-related costs as a result of union contracts made two years earlier. The company's labor contracts with both retail and processing division employees run for four-year periods; they would not be scheduled for renegotiation until November 1998.

While operating in the red for the second year in a row, Cattleman's nonetheless posted a 1996 net loss that was half what it had been during 1995; this fact was attributed by management to the improved performance at Cattleman's Farmer's Market stores. However, cognizant of the fact that further expanding retailing of its product would not materially improve the company's overall profitability in the near future, the decision was made to halt plans to open a sixth retail outlet.

Halfway through fiscal 1997 the company was rocked by the kind of news that can prove fatal to a business in the food industry. In November it was reported in the media that one of Cattleman's Metro-Detroit outlets was the source of an outbreak of Legionnaire's Disease. The reports were later verified by investigations made by Michigan state officials, who traced a small outbreak of the disease to an evaporative condenser in the heating and cooling unit operating at Cattleman's Farmer's Market in Farmington. Over half of the 30 known victims of the outbreak had visited the market prior to exhibiting symptoms of Legionnaire's, while others maintained that they had been to locations near the outlet store. Cattleman's was vehement in contesting the state's findings, and ultimately proved successful in riding out the barrage of negative media. Net income for the 39 weeks ending in January 1997 was $550,000, a 29 percent increase over the same period during 1995–96 that showed the confidence in Cattleman's product held by its growing retail and wholesale customer base.

Principal Subsidiaries

Cattleman's Meat Co.

Further Reading

Wernie, Bradford, ''Firm Beefs Up Its Menu,'' *Crain's Detroit Business,* August 23, 1993.

—Pamela L. Shelton

Cemex SA de CV

Avenida Constitucion 444 Poniente
P.O. Box 392
64000 Monterrey, Nuevo Leon
Mexico
(8) 328-30-00
International Telefax: 52 (8) 345-20-25

Public Company
Incorporated: 1906
Employees: 18,000
Sales: $3.3 Billion (1996)
Stock Exchanges: Mexico City
SICs: 3241 Cement-Hydraulic; 5032 Brick, Stone &
   Related Materials

Cemex SA de CV is the largest cement producer in the Northern Hemisphere, and ranks third in the industry globally. Within Mexico, the company holds the distinction of being the fifth largest publicly held, non-state-operated company in terms of market capitalization. Operating in 22 countries, Cemex is made up of several subsidiary companies located in Mexico, the United States, Spain, Venezuela, Panama, and the Caribbean. Its primary markets are in countries with a great need for infrastructure and a growing demand for housing. In addition to cement, the company produces and distributes ready-mix concrete and aggregates. One of Cemex's goals is to participate in construction at all levels, from the largest projects to the most humble dwelling. The company was listed on the Mexican bolsa (stock exchange) in 1976.

1906–85: Third Generation Zambrano Begins Leadership Role

Operating successfully in its traditional capacity within Mexico for 80 years, Cemex saw its future as a cement supplier and distributor dim in the 1980s when the governments' relaxation of protectionist policies posed a considerable challenge to Cemex's market position. Fortunately for the company, the savvy, Stanford University-educated M.B.A., Lorenzo Zam-brano—whose grandfather reorganized the company in 1920 (and whose family owns about 30 percent of Cemex)—was named chief executive in 1985. He had spent his teenage years at the Missouri Military Academy in Mexico, Missouri, and later earned an industrial engineering degree from the Institute Tecnologico in Monterrey, Mexico's version of MIT, according to *Forbes* writer Claire Poole. He returned to Monterrey after earning his M.B.A., and took a job with Cemex, where his uncle sat on the board, and proceeded to climb the corporate ladder for 18 years before becoming Cemex's CEO. Undaunted by the changing market climate, Zambrano began the implementation of an ambitious expansion plan, giving the company a near-monopoly in Mexico, where cement is the primary building material, beginning with the purchases of several smaller Mexican cement companies, including the purchase of Empresas Tolteca, his biggest domestic competitor. Cemex also diversified into other Mexican industries, such as tourism and hotels, but decided by the late 1980s to divest its non-cement holdings and concentrate on geographic diversification.

Gaining almost 5 percent of the U.S. cement market, Zambrano spent heavily to acquire marketing facilities all over the southwestern U.S. Awakening to the Cemex threat, U.S. producers, including eight cement companies and two labor unions, filed an antidumping suit against Cemex, claiming "they had unfairly deflated cement prices and hurt the American companies' expansion plans in the Southwest and Florida," according to Poole. Zambrano was hit with a 58 percent countervailing duty when the International Trade Commission ruled that the U.S. producers had been hurt by the prices Cemex and other Mexican producers were charging—despite the fact that cement in Arizona and California was selling for the same price that Cemex charged. Zambrano reduced exports to the U.S. by 30 percent because the 58 percent import duty substantially affected Cemex profits. Zambrano held on to his U.S. market share in areas where the company could remain competitive due to higher prices. A GATT (General Agreement on Trade and Tariffs) later ruled that the antidumping duties levied by the U.S. Department of Commerce on imports of cement from Mexico were unfounded. Cemex owns Sunbelt Enterprises, a subsidiary made up of Sunbelt Corporation, the firm controlling Cemex's holdings in the U.S. The company bought the Western

---

Company Perspectives:

Cemex's strategy for success can be explained by seven guidelines: professional and modern management to reorganize acquired companies and the ability to adapt to changes in circumstances; concentration on traditional business lines (cement, concrete and concrete block); and a solid and well-capitalized financial structure. In addition, the company's principal markets are located in countries with a strong need for infrastructure and a growing demand for housing. Finally, Cemex has an efficient and low-cost structure of operations, a balance in its sources of income through geographically diversified operations, and leadership in growth markets.

U.S. affiliates of Blue Circle Industries and two Houston companies, Houston Shell & Concrete and Gulf Coast Cement. Due to the close proximity and language/cultural similarities, Cemex continued to develop ties within the mini-trade zone between northern Mexico and southern Texas, California, Arizona, New Mexico, Kentucky, Florida, and even as far north as Minnesota.

Pouring Pesos into Mexican Infrastructure: Early 1990s

The economic situation was becoming more lucrative at home, where Mexico's president, Carlos Salinas de Gortari, a Harvard-educated political economist, initiated public works programs for infrastructure modernization, increasing the demand for cement, as well as increasing the government-set price for cement. The government gradually allowed cement prices to rise from $46 per ton to $72 per ton. The production costs of about $30 per ton at Cemex's Mexican plants were the lowest in North America. By 1990, the company reached sales of approximately $1.2 billion, and accounted for 66 percent of Mexico's cement market, gaining the attention of investors who also appreciated Cemex's operating margins: 27 percent vs. 9 percent for U.S. rival Lafarge. Ten years after Mexico's debt crisis, the ratio of government debt to annual gross domestic product was down to about 40 percent, vs. 60 percent in the U.S. Zambrano was an outspoken proponent of the North American Free Trade Agreement (NAFTA), although he admitted that the opening of the Mexican economy would be damaging to many of their industries not well-prepared in the areas of managerial expertise, technology, and marketing. Cemex invested heavily in robots and computers, giving them a far-reaching efficiency edge. Their main competitor in Mexico was Aspasco, left with a 20 percent market share—a company controlled by Holderbank of Switzerland.

In 1992 Zambrano negotiated a bridge loan from Citicorp, among others, for the acquisition of majority holdings in two Spanish cement companies, spending $1.84 billion, causing Cemex stock to plummet due to investors' fears that the company was expanding too rapidly. The move into Europe pitted Cemex against world leaders such as Switzerland's Holderbank and France's Lafarge Coppee. Zambrano told Joseph L. McCarthy in *Chief Executive*, "Every time we acquire a company,

we are told that we paid too much, that we are buying at the wrong time, and that we are crazy. Our critics know a lot about Mexico, but not enough about the cement industry." Cemex had paid less than half of what Cemex's competitors Lafarge and Ciment Francais (now part of Italcementi) paid for smaller Spanish cement companies in 1989. Critics worried that Cemex was taking on too much debt, and questioned whether or not the company had sufficient international management expertise. Cemex repaid a large portion of the loan by reselling nonstrategic assets in the Spanish cement companies. Justifying his ambitious expenditures, Zambrano explained to McCarthy that, "We had to become one of the biggest global companies. If we didn't, someone undoubtedly would have acquired us." The two Spanish companies were combined into Valenciana de Cementos, becoming Spain's largest cement producer. In 1994 Valenciana's net profit jumped to $95.5 million, up from $37.7 million in 1993. Cemex operated 10 plants, four grinding units, and 23 distribution terminals in Spain, both maritime and land-based. *The Economist* reported that Cemex almost doubled the operating margin of its Spanish plants by firing a third of its workers there, adding that the purchase enabled Cemex to bypass anti-dumping duties imposed by the Bush administration to protect American cement producers, whose costs averaged a third more than Cemex's. Despite NAFTA, the Clinton administration maintained the duties (until a later ruling), which Cemex compensated for by exporting from duty-exempt Spain.

The company bought a cement plant located in New Braunfels, Texas, from Lafarge Corporation, which included four cement terminals and 52 percent of Parker Lafarge Inc., which is an aggregate plant producing an annual capacity of 820,000 metric tons. During this period Cemex had 18 cement production plants and 36 distribution terminals strategically located in Mexico and the U.S. The company's first quarter 1994 American sales increased by 45 percent over the previous comparable quarter.

Mexico's economy began to decline and private investors were discouraged by the uprising in the south and the murder of the ruling party's candidate. Cemex's foreign operations gave the company a hedge against the weakening peso, down 7 percent against the dollar in the first half of 1994. The recession had the affect of paralyzing mortgage loans in Mexico, which in turn affected the housing sector and the demand for cement. Still, net sales dropped only 2.27 percent, offset somewhat by a decline in the costs of sales and operating expenses derived from lower fuel and electric energy prices (a major expenditure in the cement industry), a decrease in personnel, and a 23 percent increase in worker productivity. To strengthen Cemex's presence in Latin America, Zambrano bought 60 percent of Vencemos, Venezuela's largest cement company, for $550 million, partly in preparation for export to places such as northern Brazil, Panama, and the Caribbean. In the Caribbean, Cemex completed negotiations for the acquisition of 50 percent of Scancem Industries, Ltd., a company which operated in five countries in the area. The transaction enabled the company to market half a million metric tons of cement to the region, accounting for approximately 50 percent of the imported cement consumption there. At a Panamanian government-held auction, Cemex was awarded Cementos Bayano of Panama, for a price of $60 million, furthering the consolidation of its Caribbean market. Cemex was pursuing its ambitious plan to provide raw materials for the large infrastructure projects developing in Spain, Asia, Africa, Europe, and other Latin markets. Within seven years the company had tripled its global production capacity.

Emerging Markets Throughout the 1990s

Chief financial officer Gustavo Caballero Guerrero told Victoria Griffith of *CFO Year* that "the company's main commitment is in emerging markets, and future purchases are likely to take place either in Asia or Latin America. Emerging markets have a number of advantages. First, they will grow much faster than the First World in the long run, and strong economic growth is essential in the cement market. Second, emerging markets view cement not as a commodity, like the First World, but as a brand-name product. It's much easier to differentiate ourselves in emerging markets from our competitors." Cemex established a sales office in Hong Kong, hoping to enter economies of scale necessary to beat its competitors, while also diversifying its sources of borrowing. Caballero explained that their financing of eurobonds, convertible bonds, and other sources of credit made raising money easier for Cemex than for other Mexican groups, but that financing is still expensive compared with international competitors. He admitted to one disadvantage of operating in Asia having to do with cultural and language differences, unlike their commonalities with Spain, the Latin countries, and the border with the U.S., but acknowledged that Asia usually moves in different cycles from Latin America, which could be a significant overall market-equalizing factor. Cemex crossed a major milestone in 1995 when non-Mexican operations accounted for 51 percent of the company's $3 billion in annual sales, balancing declining cash flow from Mexican operations. In that year the company exported 2 million tons of cement products to Taiwan, Thailand, and Indonesia.

Into the 21st Century as Industry World Leader

Company officials credit Cemex's competitive abilities to its on-line information system. A network of satellite dishes, leased lines, and microwave communications link all of the company's offices in Mexico and abroad. A Cemex competitor noted that their network is phenomenal, giving the company flexibility, for example, of where to bring in their product. Caballero told Jim Freer in *Latin Finance* that "Carrying our laptops is like carrying our telephones around. We do about 90 percent of our communications through e-mail," making global interactions instantly possible, and even acting to reduce the hierarchy, for example, because anyone can shoot off an e-mail to anyone else in the company. Cemex sets the curve for Latin technology users, and attributes its successful global expansion efforts to its hands-on approach. Cemex was the only Mexican company named in *Computerworld*'s 1995 "Global 100" listing of the world's most outstanding users of information technology. A company official stated that he was surprised that Cemex's competitors have next to no computers. Cemex began by using technology to reduce costs and improve efficiencies, but improved on that functional view, and transformed the way they delivered to the market. Their system keeps a constant log of the chemical composition of the cement it produces, of the reasons for kiln problems and shutdowns, and of the delivery routes of the company's trucks. Cemex's information technology department is maintained by a staff of 25, who work with Cemtec, an engineering technology division to provide and develop information access. Gelacio Iniguez Jauregui, the company's director of information technology told Freer that Cemex will continue to build on its record of developing information technology, "not just for the sake of having information, but for using it, sharing it, and providing access to it."

One of Zambrano's proudest achievements, according to Daniel Dombey, writing for *Industry Week*, is Cemex's Tepeaca complex—probably the most modern cement plant in the Americas, located two hours outside of Mexico City. Situated among green fields, the unassuming-looking plant filters out pollutants via bags of glass fiber that "filter out smoke before it reaches the open air; pollutants are gathered at 60 points throughout the complex," according to Dombey. Its emissions are far below legal requirements, attributable to a system financed by 10 percent of the total cost of the plant. With more capacity than any other kiln on the continent, Tepeaca supplies one-fifth of the Mexican market and is the lowest-cost cement producer in the world.

It is estimated that Mexico's cement industry will grow between 6 to 8 percent in 1997, due in part to an increasing population and a profitable countrywide economic expansion. Having survived the worst recession in memory, Zambrano, while entrenched in Mexico, does not wish to place too much emphasis on operations there—it was foreign revenues that kept Cemex's top line growing during 1995–96, when Mexico's gross domestic product tumbled by more than 6 percent. Cemex's debt is at an enormous $4.8 billion, making it Latin America's biggest corporate debtor, restricting the company's cash flow and causing Zambrano to put a hold on major expansion moves. He is particularly interested, according to Dombey, in markets such as Indonesia and Malaysia. The company authorized a 1997 plan to buy back as much as $200 million worth of stock in an effort to convince investors that the company's operations generate enough cash to pay debt, fund its expansion program, and set a buyback program. Cemex shares are traded in Mexico City and over the counter in New York as American depository receipts (ADRs). In February 1997, stock prices declined to $3.33, down from $9.40 at the end of the previous November. With the peso's devaluation and doubts about Cemex's ability to meets its debt, investors grew concerned. Roberto Carillo, who tracks Cemex for Baring Securities, Inc. of Mexico City, expressed confidence in Cemex's abilities to manage its rising hard-currency revenues from abroad as a cushion. He told Geri Smith and Stanley Reed of *Business Week* that "These guys know what they're doing—they know how to finance things."

Principal Subsidiaries

Cementos Mty, AS de CV; Tolmex AS de CV; Grupo Empresarial Maya SA de CV; Sunbelt Enterprises, Inc.

Further Reading

Brown, Elicia, "Tolmex: Repaving Mexico's Roads," *Financial World*, July 23, 1991, pp. 18–21.

"The Children with the Magic Powder," *The Economist*, May 21, 1994, pp. 76–79.

Dombey, Daniel, "Well-Built Success," *Industry Week*, May 5, 1997, pp. 32–39.

Ellis, Junius, "Five Stocks to Buy on the World's Hottest Market," *Money*, September 1992, pp. 153–56.

Freer, Jim, "Check the Voltage, Please," *Latin Finance*, March 1996, p. 62.

Griffith, Victoria, "Not a Mexican Company," *Latin Finance*, September, 1995, pp. 24–26.

Hernandez, Janine, "Cementos Mexicanos," *Latin Finance*, July–August 1994, pp. 46–48.

Holland, Kelly, "Citicorp Leads 1.2 Billion Bridge Loan for Cemex," *American Banker*, August 14, 1992, pp. 1–2.

Luxner, Larry, "Taking the Plunge," *Pit & Quarry*, February 1996, pp. 26–29.

McCarthy, Joseph L., "Lorenzo Zambrano (CEO of Cementos Mexicanos)," *Chief Executive*, September 1993, p. 27.

Pearson, John, and Smith, Geri, "Cemex: Solid as Mexico Sinks," February 27, 1995, pp. 58–62.

Poole, Claire, "Cement Wars," *Forbes*, October 1, 1990, pp. 99–102.

Weeks, Scott, "Solid Sale: Cemex Converts in a Difficult Market," *Latin Finance*, November 1994, p. 68.

—Terri Mozzone-Burgman

Champion International Corporation

One Champion Plaza
Stamford, Connecticut 06921
U.S.A.
(203) 358-7000
Fax: (203) 358-2975
Web site: http://www.championinternational.com

Public Company
Incorporated: 1893 as Champion Coated Paper Company
Employees: 24,379
Sales: $5.88 billion (1996)
Stock Exchanges: New York
SICs: 2435 Hardwood Veneer & Plywood; 2436
 Softwood Veneer & Plywood; 2621 Paper Mills; 2631
 Paperboard Mills; 2656 Sanitary Food Containers,
 Except Folding; 2677 Envelopes; 2678 Stationery,
 Tablets & Related Products; 2679 Converted Paper &
 Paperboard Products, Not Elsewhere Classified

Champion International Corporation is a leading U.S. maker of paper products, specializing in paper used for business correspondence, commercial printing, publications, and newspapers. Champion also manufactures pulp, beverage containers, plywood, lumber, and studs. The company, one of the largest private landowners in the United States, owns or controls more than 5 million acres of U.S. timberlands, and also owns or controls—through subsidiaries—significant timber acreage in Canada and Brazil.

Early Misfortunes Led to Competitive Edge

Champion Coated Paper Company was founded in Hamilton, Ohio, in 1893 by a retired greeting-card and valentine printer, Peter Thomson. Thomson was an energetic businessman, keenly competitive and ambitious. His aggressive quick thinking turned some of his company's early misfortunes into successes. In December 1901, the paper mill at Hamilton was destroyed by fire. In 1913, a flood of the great Miami River followed by fire again destroyed the Champion mill. Both times new mills were built and new machinery installed. These natural catastrophes turned out well for Champion, as the new equipment gave the company a considerable edge over competitors who were using older, less productive equipment.

Through much of its history, the company was owned and managed principally by members of the Thomson family. In 1906 Peter Thomson's son-in-law, Reuben B. Robertson, Sr., founded the Champion Fibre Company in Canton, North Carolina. Robertson's company provided the Hamilton mills with a supply of wood pulp, the raw material from which paper is made. Family members thus were in control of both ends of Champion paper production. The two companies were nominally separate entities until 1935, when they merged to form the Champion Paper and Fibre Company. Peter Thomson's two sons, Alexander and Logan, joined the family business, as did Reuben Robertson and Peter Thomson's other son-in-law, Walter D. Randall. Peter Thomson instituted the rule of primogeniture for his corporation, stipulating that only one son from each of these four families, preferably the eldest son, would be allowed to enter the business. In 1932, nearly 73 percent of Champion's stock was owned by members of the Thomson family. In 1960 that figure was still close to 42 percent.

In the 1910s and 1920s, Champion made its reputation by always offering the lowest prices in the industry for its coated papers, papers with smooth surfaces that can be imprinted. Champion was able to offer a consistently low-priced product for several reasons. Champion's stockholders were principally family members, so there was no need to offer high dividends to please Wall Street. Profits were quickly reinvested into new and better mill equipment. Champion avoided the notoriously volatile newsprint industry. It instead made magazine and book paper, paper for cigarette packages and gum wrappers, coffee bags and tobacco pouches, postcards, and pickle labels. Because of the size of Champion mills' booming production, they were among the hardest hit in the industry in the 1921 recession that followed World

War I. Champion recovered quickly, however, and continued to churn out a high volume of coated paper into the next decade.

Pioneered Use of Scientists in Papermaking in the 1920s

In 1926 Champion instituted a technical research division, a relatively new concept in the paper industry. The craft of papermaking is' an ancient one, and few papermakers in the United States had scientific training in the field. In 1926, problems with the alum that was used to make the coating on the paper led Champion's president to hire a chemist from Du Pont. After only a week of research, this chemist, a veteran of the chemical warfare service in World War I, found a cheap additive to the alum that eliminated the problem. Champion's management was convinced of the financial gains possible by having research chemists as permanent staff. Within a few years, Champion had 40 chemists in its research laboratories. The investment in the laboratory paid off markedly. Champion's paper went up in quality and down in cost. It was also able to develop profitable byproducts from its mills, such as tanning extract, turpentine, and cleansing powder.

During the Great Depression of the 1930s, Champion continued to pull in a profit and to plow money into new equipment. Champion mill production ran well ahead of industry averages throughout the Depression years. The mills actually continued to expand their output, in spite of reduced markets for the industry as a whole. One factor that contributed to Champion's well-being in these competitive times was its forced sale of some of its North Carolina timberland in 1931 to the government, which used 90,000 Champion acres for the Great Smoky Mountains National Park, and paid $3 million for them. Between 1929 and 1932, Champion spent $4 million on new equipment or improvements to existing equipment. Champion opened a new mill in Houston, Texas, to capture profits from cheap southern pine.

The company forced pay cuts on its workers twice between 1929 and 1932, to keep down its expenses. Champion mills were not unionized at the time, but workers were said to have high company loyalty, and they had steady work six days a week. The Thomson family prided itself on its care of the Champion mill workers, who usually earned 15 percent higher pay than industry averages. Company policy was to not hire black workers or new immigrants, preferring second or third generation Americans of German or Anglo-Saxon descent.

The paper industry took a sharp upward turn with the entrance of the United States into World War II. Wartime demands for paper were high, and Champion continued to expand. After the war, the Champion Paper and Fiber Company was near the top of the industry in its coated white book paper sales. The company diversified its product line, to make bag paper, cardboard, and milk cartons. To prepare for more competitive conditions in the postwar economy, Champion began to buy timberland and paper-marketing outlets. Champion wanted control of its raw material—timber—as well as the distribution of its finished products. Champion had used this strategy, vertical integration, to some extent since 1906, by operating the pulp mill in Canton, North Carolina, to supply the Ohio paper mills. With its investments after the war, Champion was continuing an

earlier successful policy. The company liquidated its subsidiary chemical company in 1947, and in 1951 sold another chemical laboratory. The company continued to invest in expensive machinery at its U.S. plants and opened a pulp plant in Brazil as well. Growth in the paper industry throughout the 1950s was slow. The decade ended in a recession. With Champion's high costs, profits were too low to keep the company healthy. By the end of fiscal year 1959, Champion's net income had fallen dramatically to less than $8 million, from a high two years earlier of more than $14 million.

Era of Thomson Family Control Ended in the 1960s

In March 1960 Champion's president, Reuben B. Robertson, Jr., died. He was the grandson of Champion's founder, Peter Thomson. His father, Reuben B. Robertson, Sr., resigned the chairmanship of Champion in the wake of his son's death. For the first time in the company's history, a person outside the Thomson family attained the office of president. With the company in serious financial trouble, the new president, Karl Bendetsen, took unprecedented measures. The former chairman, Reuben Robertson Sr. had operated the company in a paternalistic fashion. Bendetsen, on the other hand, realized that in many ways the family style of management had hurt the company. He fired 20 percent of Champion's employees within a year of taking office and extensively reorganized the corporation's management.

Champion had been producing more than 100 different grades of paper. Bendetsen dropped all but the top 20 bestsellers. Many executives took early retirement, and Bendetsen sold off the company's fleet of seven private jets. These cost-cutting measures were rapid and severe, and Bendetsen was not popular in the company's home base, Hamilton, Ohio. Bendetsen boasted in a *Business Week* report of June 26, 1961, two years later, that Champion was "no longer paternalistic in any sense of the word." The Thomson family gradually withdrew from Champion's board of directors. By 1967 the company's profits had gone up by 41 percent, and *Forbes* declared in its March 15, 1967 issue "one of the best managed companies in the entire paper industry."

In 1967 Champion merged with United States Plywood Corporation, a large lumber manufacturer. The merger was seen as equally beneficial for the companies. Both companies used timber, each to make different products. added its forest reserves in the western United States to Champion's large holdings in southern pine. The new combined company was expected to make more efficient use of its joint timber resources, to cut its costs substantially, in general, and to gain some protection from the volatility of business cycles in both industries.

At the time of the merger, the new company was given the name U.S. Plywood-Champion Papers, Inc. Karl Bendetsen and U.S. Plywood's president, Gene Brewer, were to share the running of the corporation. During the first year of the merger, however, the plywood division fared much worse than expected, and Bendetsen was elected chief executive officer, outranking Brewer. A year later, Brewer resigned. Within three years, most of U.S. Plywoods remaining executives had also left the company. In 1972 the company changed its name again, to

Champion International Corporation. Although profits rose, the company was still not doing as well as anyone had hoped.

Management problems plagued Champion International in the 1970s. Karl Bendetsen reached the age of mandatory retirement in 1972. Passing over all of Champion's top executives, Bendetsen hired a man from outside the company to take over as chief executive. Bendetsen's successor, Thomas Willers, had been through a merger similar to the U.S. Plywood-Champion merger. He had been chief executive of Hooker Petroleum when it was bought by Occidental Petroleum. Bendetsen thought Willers would be able to pull Champion out of its postmerger stagnation.

Sigler Began Long Leadership Reign in 1974

Willers took Champion in a new direction by diversifying its products even further. The company bought into the home-furnishing and carpeting industries under Willers's leadership. Although Karl Bendetsen was officially in retirement, he was so alarmed by the tack Willers was taking that he used his influence with Champion's board to force Willers to resign. Willers was with the company less than two years. A former head of Champion's timber division, Andrew C. Sigler, was then named president and chief executive officer in December 1974. Under Sigler's management, the company focused more on its original product line. In 1977 Hoerner Waldorf Corporation, a paperboard and corrugated-box manufacturer, merged into Champion. This strengthened Champion's stance in the domestic paper market, but heavy reinvestments in new mills and equipment and a long slump in the building-products industry continued to keep Champion's profits down into the 1980s.

In 1984 Champion bought the St. Regis Corporation for $1.8 billion. It was an overnight deal that rescued St. Regis from a hostile takeover by Australian newspaper magnate Rupert Murdoch. St. Regis had been one of the largest U.S. producers of magazine paper and newsprint. The St. Regis acquisition doubled to 6.4 million acres the holdings of timberland owned or controlled by Champion, making it one of the largest private landowners in the United States. Afraid that Champion itself would be vulnerable to a takeover attempt after the St. Regis merger, Chairman Sigler instituted a sweeping debt reduction plan. He shut down seven wood-product plants in the western United States and sold off assets in Champion's packaging and building-supply divisions. In the next two years, Champion continued to narrow its product scope to mostly newsprint and white coated papers, selling off subsidiaries in brown paper packaging, envelopes, cardboard boxes, and wood products. In 1987 two mills in Texas were sold, while 1988 saw the divestment of a specialty paper plant in Columbus, Ohio.

An upswing in the economy helped Champion's net income rise after the St. Regis acquisition, but the paper industry slumped suddenly in 1989. Wall Street saw an end to the latest high cycle in the paper industry in 1989, and Champion stock continued to drop. Profits began to fall in 1990, reaching the nadir in 1993 of a $156 million net loss. As the company was weathering this latest cyclical industry downturn, it also invested heavily in capital improvements in order to be ready for the next upturn. Over an eight-year period ending in 1993, Champion poured $5.5 billion into adding capacity company-

wide as well as into environmental overhauls of some of its mills. While the additional capacity was expected to eventually improve company cash flow, Champion also took more immediate steps to generate cash by selling off a large portion of its U.S. timberlands. In 1991 and 1992 the company sold off its holdings in California and Oregon; the following year 867,000 acres in Montana were sold to Plum Creek Timber Co. for $260 million. These sales made additional strategic sense for Champion since none of the company's mills were located within easy reach of these holdings.

In a controversy dating back to the mid-1980s, a $5 billion class-action lawsuit was brought against Champion charging that the company had dumped pollutants—including dioxins—into the Pigeon River from its mill in Canton, North Carolina. Following a 1992 mistrial, Champion reached an out-of-court settlement in 1993 that called for the company to pay $6.5 million in compensation. Three years later, the company agreed to pay $5 million to settle a $500 million class-action lawsuit filed on behalf of waterfront property owners in Alabama and Florida who alleged that Champion's Pensacola, Florida, mill had polluted Perdido Bay with dioxins and other toxic substances.

Foreign Operations Became Increasingly Important in the 1990s

Paper prices swung sharply higher in 1994 and 1995 and Champion, just as planned, bounced back impressively, especially in 1995—the company's best year ever—when it posted net sales of $6.97 billion and net income of $772 million. In January 1996 timberland holdings near the company's Quinnesec, Michigan, mill were bolstered with the purchase of Lake Superior Land Company and its 288,000 acres of hardwood forest in Michigan and Wisconsin. In July of that same year, the company's Canadian subsidiary, Weldwood of Canada Limited, became a wholly owned Champion subsidiary. Weldwood, whose operations were centered in the provinces of British Columbia and Alberta, was a manufacturer of pulp, plywood, and lumber.

Champion did not fare as well in 1996 as it had in 1995, primarily because paper prices had once again fallen. Sales fell to $5.88 billion and net income to $141 million. Nevertheless, the company was able to point to its foreign operations as continuing bright spots. In addition to Weldwood, Champion also had a highly successful Brazilian subsidiary, Champion Papel e Celulose S.A. Between them, Weldwood and Champion Papel accounted for 85 percent of the company's consolidated pretax income and 91 percent of consolidated net income. In November 1996, Champion Papel's landholdings were bolstered with the purchase of 438,000 acres of land, 183,000 of which were in pine plantations. Also purchased with the land were a chip mill and an Amazon River port site from which Champion began exporting chips to Europe and Japan. Following this deal, Champion Papel owned or controlled nearly 1.4 million acres of Brazilian timberlands and savannah; the subsidiary also continued to operate a paper mill in southeastern Brazil which manufactured uncoated paper for export to almost 50 countries worldwide.

In October 1996 Sigler ended his 22 years of leadership when he retired. Richard E. Olsen, a 29-year Champion veteran, stepped into the roles of chairman and CEO. Although his company was still vulnerable to the cyclicality of the paper industry, Olsen could take at least some comfort in Champion's proven ability to be very profitable during upturns (shown in 1995) and in the very strong subsidiary operations in Canada and Brazil. Despite these strengths, Champion's stock continued to lag and rumors of possible mergers with Weyerhaeuser or Georgia-Pacific—fueled by a spate of paper industry mergers during the mid-1990s—periodically hit the press. Champion, itself the product of a series of mergers, thus faced a somewhat uncertain future as a new century approached.

Principal Subsidiaries

Champion Recycling Corporation; Weldwood of Canada Limited; Cariboo Pulp & Paper Company (Canada; 50%); Champion Papel e Celulose S.A. (Brazil).

Further Reading

Bartlett, Richard A., *Troubled Waters: Champion International and the Pigeon River Controversy,* Knoxville: University of Tennessee Press, 1955.

Benoit, Ellen, "Champion Int'l: Squeeze Play?," *Financial World,* October 30, 1990, p. 19.

"Champion International: $5.5-Billion Expansion Prepares for the Future," *Pulp & Paper,* April 1994, pp. 32–33.

"Champion Paper," *Fortune,* January 1949.

"Competition Not Cartelization," *Fortune,* October 1932.

Gubernick, Lisa, "Scouting the Tall Timber," *Forbes,* December 17, 1984, p. 226.

McGough, Robert, "Champion International: Patience, Patience . . . ," *Financial World,* March 3, 1992, p. 16.

"The Merger That Wasn't Made in Heaven," *Forbes,* March 15, 1967.

Oliver, Suzanne, "The Day They Booed Andy Sigler," *Forbes,* May 11, 1992, pp. 46–48.

Sandler, Linda, "Champion International Swings into Action As Merger Pressure Rises in the Paper Industry," *Wall Street Journal,* May 12, 1997, p. C2.

Smith, Kenneth E., and Debra A. Adams, "With St. Regis Merger Complete, Champion to Be Top Producer," *Pulp & Paper,* November 1985, p. 113.

Vogel, Todd, "Tisch and Buffett May Help Champion Turn the Page," *Business Week,* October 22, 1990, p. 73.

—A. Woodward
—updated by David E. Salamie

Cheung Kong (Holdings) Limited

Cheung Kong (Holdings) Limited

China Building
29 Queen's Road Central
Hong Kong
(5) 526 6911
Fax: (5) 845 2940

Public Company
Incorporated: 1950
Employees: 16,000
Sales: HK$13.20 billion
Stock Exchanges: Hong Kong
SICs: 6552 Subdividers & Developers, Not Elsewhere
   Classified; 6512 Nonresidential Building Operators;
   6513 Apartment Building Operators

Cheung Kong (Holdings) Limited is among Hong Kong's leading property and investment development companies. It has expanded its network into North America and Europe, consolidated its holdings, and begun building a portfolio of contracts and interests in China as Hong Kong prepared for its transfer to Chinese government in 1997. Cheung Kong is the flagship company for the property-to-telecommunications empire built up in Hong Kong by Li Ka-shing, who started his meteoric rise in business around 1960 by making plastic flowers. The company's collection of more than 100 subsidiaries and joint ventures are organized principally under four main listed companies. In addition to flagship Cheung Kong, the company's major holding is Hutchison Whampoa Ltd., of which the company owns nearly 50 percent. Hutchison is one of Hong Kong's major "hongs," or conglomerates, with holdings ranging from retailing to container terminals to telecommunications, energy, and property and financial investments. Cheung Kong Infrastructure (CKI) Holdings Limited, organized in October 1996 and led by Li's eldest son and likely successor, Victor Li, groups Cheung Kong's infrastructure subsidiaries and interests, primarily in road-building, toll roads and bridges, and power plants on the Chinese mainland. The final piece of the Cheung Kong empire is its stake in the electric monopoly Hong Kong Electric (HKE). In January 1997, Cheung Kong restructured its

business, providing, among other features, for a full takeover of HKE by Cheung Kong.

From Plastic Flowers to "Superman"

Known to his colleagues as K.S. Li, the Hong Kong tycoon was born in Chiu Chow, in southern China, in 1928 and later emigrated to Hong Kong. In 1950, Li set up Cheung Kong as a business manufacturing plastic flowers. But the company's real growth started in the late 1960s, when Li bought his first building. In less than 30 years, Li built an empire controlling, through a series of interlocking stock market holdings, over 14 percent of stock registered on the Hong Kong exchange. Besides residential property developments, Li owns a land bank of 22.5 million square feet.

Cheung Kong (Holdings) also includes highly profitable cement, quarrying, and ready-mixed concrete operations. At the end of 1972, after its first year on the Hong Kong stock market, the company had a total of 40 sites in its property portfolio, with a total floor area—after development—of about 2.4 million square feet of residential and commercial space.

Among the projects Cheung Kong had onstream were a number of residential developments. Typical of these was the development of the Castle Peak Hotel, in the colony's New Territories. Originally occupying a site of over 84,000 square feet, the former hotel was doubled in size and turned into several six-story, expensive blocks of flats with a total floor area of over 167,000 square feet.

The company also planned to develop a number of warehouses and factories, as well as offices. Recognizing the static nature of the Hong Kong property market in 1973, Li Ka-shing informed his shareholders that his company would look to increase its supply of regular rental income from its properties, to protect their interests.

This increased effort at boosting rental income paid off a year later in 1974 when Hong Kong's property market slipped into depression. Cheung Kong's development plans continued undeterred, with a 10 percent rise in profits to HK$48.2 million, against profits of HK$43.7 million a year earlier.

This improved performance was encouraged by rent reviews which boosted income. One example was Regent House, on Queen's Road Central. Cheung Kong had planned to redevelop the property, but put back plans after the rental income increased to HK$4.6 million, from about HK$3 million, per year. Because it would take three years to develop the site, and would cost HK$16 million, a loss of some HK$13.8 million from leaving the building vacant was not thought feasible, particularly when depressed conditions in the colony made the prospects of any future developments doubtful.

The continuing downturn in fortunes hit Cheung Kong's profits in 1975, which dipped 6 percent to HK$45.6 million. In that year, the company saw the fruits of a joint venture into which it had entered the previous year with the Canadian Imperial Bank of Commerce. The joint venture, Canadian Eastern Finance, acquired for HK$85,000 a site along the Hong Kong harbor of some 864,000 square feet. On 53,000 square feet of the site, the company planned to build ten expensive residential units, each 24 stories high, and a car park. On the rest of the site, recreation facilities—including a swimming pool and sports ground—were planned.

At the end of 1975 Cheung Kong had some 5.1 million square feet of commercial and residential space. This property portfolio jumped by more than 20 percent in size over the next year to stand at a total of 6.35 million square feet at the end of 1976. Of this space, 3.62 million square feet were said by the company to be in residential property, while 1.04 million square feet and 1.65 million square feet were bound up in commercial and industrial space, respectively.

Improving market conditions in Hong Kong in 1976 helped boost the company's profits that year to HK$58.8 million, a rise of 29 percent over the previous year. The renown Li Ka-shing was gaining in the Hong Kong financial community was confirmed a year later, in 1977, when Cheung Kong announced its profits up a further 45 percent to HK$85.55 million. This improvement coincided with a 38 percent rise in total space in the company's property portfolio, to 10.2 million square feet in size.

Among the company's new properties was the celebrated Tiger Balm Gardens, a site of 150,000 square feet originally developed by the inventor of Tiger Balm, an ointment used to cure a number of minor ailments. Cheung Kong bought the site with the aim of building high-class residential units, a practice for which it was becoming widely known in the colony.

In 1977 the company also diversified into the hotel trade. It acquired Wynncor Limited, which owned the 800-room Hong Kong Hilton Hotel and shopping arcade, and nearly all of the 400-room Bali Hyatt Hotel.

While Hong Kong's local property market was improving, Li Ka-shing warned in 1977 that various restrictions from the emerging European Common Market, based in Brussels, which included anti-dumping measures against Asian electronic products, were affecting export prospects for Cheung Kong. The reason was that Hong Kong's industry sector was felt to be tied in fortunes to that of the local property market. When the first failed, the second was certain to feel the effects.

In 1978 the company's profits continued to rise. Total profits for the year reached HK$132.6 million, a 55 percent increase over the previous year. In that year, Cheung Kong sold a number of properties not producing sufficient rental income, including sites in the Kwun Tong region of Kowloon, and on Hennessy Road. The company was now gaining wide reputation throughout Hong Kong, as demonstrated by the publicity given to each pre-let of its completed properties. The value of rents reached by each pre-letting—the practice whereby a property developer signs up a tenant for the building or property he is about to build—would give the local property market an indication of the going rates to follow.

As Li Ka-shing told his shareholders that year: "In both prestige and business expansion, the group has entered a new era, and it is my opinion that 1978 has been an exceptionally important year in the group's development." Li cautioned that the effects of high interest rates in Hong Kong and abroad would affect the local property market. He added, however, that mortgages and property developments would provide a useful hedge to investors against threatened inflation. Also in 1978, Cheung Kong took a 22 percent stake in Green Island Cement, increasing its holdings on the construction side.

In 1979 the company saw a 91.6 percent rise in profits to HK$254.1 million. Among the developments then under construction was a joint-venture project with four other property companies to build an office development on the Hong Kong Macau Ferry Pier. With a 20 percent interest in the Shun Tak Centre, due for completion in 1984, the final complex was to include a total 1.5 million square feet of office space.

In the same year, Cheung Kong purchased a substantial share stake in Hutchison Whampoa, a group whose interests included electricity, communications, wholesaling, and distribution. Hutchison was also involved in manufacturing, quarrying, and concrete markets.

The initial stake in Hutchison was for 90 million shares in the group, or 24.4 percent of outstanding shares, bought for HK$693 million. The company increased its stake in Hutchison to 30 percent by the end of the year.

At the same time, Li Ka-shing warned shareholders that continuing high interest rates in the colony, and emerging rent control restriction, led him to believe that the local property market was showing signs of leveling off. Continuing economic difficulties in the Hong Kong economy continued to color the business climate for Cheung Kong in 1980. Li Kashing, nevertheless, maintained an optimistic air. "There is a slight slackening in the property market," he told shareholders. "But this phase will pass with a lowering of interest rates and an upturn in trade. I am, therefore, cautiously optimistic about the future of the Hong Kong property market."

The 1980 profit rise of 176 percent, to HK$701.3 million, gave grounds for this optimism, but also reflected first-time profit contributions from Hutchison Whampoa and Green Island Cement. In addition, the Hong Kong Hilton Hotel increased its profits for 1980 by 34 percent, compared with the previous year.

During 1981 Cheung Kong began amassing an overseas portfolio that would grow over the coming years. Overseas investments totaled HK$125 million in value, or 3 percent of the group's total assets. These included a number of commercial buildings in the United States with 950,000 square feet of space, and a shopping center with over 370,000 square feet of freehold space. This growing overseas portfolio was motivated by continuing recessionary conditions in the Hong Kong property market, and anxiety about any fallout from fears of 1997, when control of the colony would revert to China.

At the time, Li Ka-shing signaled to shareholders that it would be difficult, given the current trading conditions, to maintain in 1982 the same high level of profit recorded in 1981. In that year, profits were raised 97 percent from the previous year's level, to HK$1.38 billion.

Li Ka-shing's profit warning turned out to be timely. A decline was suffered across the board by the company at the end of 1982. Overall profits declined by 62 percent to HK$525.6 million. Profits at the Green Island Cement company tumbled by 65 percent, and were affected, according to the company, by a slowdown in the colony's construction industry, bad weather, and large imports of Japanese cement. Even more difficult problems were projected for 1983.

Hutchison Whampoa, on the other hand, increased profits by 20 percent. Yet even here Cheung Kong forecast reduced profits for its subsidiary in 1983. At the Hong Kong Hilton Hotel, profits were 10 percent lower than in 1982, reflecting strong competition from new hotels coming on stream in the colony, and a fall in the worldwide tourist trade owing to recessionary pressures in Europe and the United States.

Li Ka-shing had few words of consolation for his shareholders at the time. As he saw the local property market during 1982, "Property prices plunged and hesitation on the part of investors combined with generally weakening purchasing power left the market in a very depressed state from which appreciable recovery is unlikely in the short term."

Matters did indeed deteriorate still further in 1983. The speculator-led boom in property prices and rents of the previous few years came to an abrupt halt, curbed by high interest rates and political tensions surrounding the future of the colony. As a result, Cheung Kong's annual profits fell 22 percent to HK$408.8 million. Green Island Cement became loss-making as the Hong Kong construction industry faced depression conditions.

Investors in Hong Kong were maintaining a wait-and-see attitude as conditions in the United States and European markets began to improve. At the same time, the property market was expected to lag behind as lower interest rates allowed for growth worldwide, and therefore investment in commercial and residential properties throughout the colony would be delayed.

This situation was confirmed by Cheung Kong's 1984 profits of HK$213.5 million, a fall of 47 percent compared with a year earlier. The company at this time was making fewer property acquisitions than usual for future developments. Two notable acquisitions were a site of 12,600 square feet on Queen's Road Central, destined to become a 130,000-square-foot office complex; and an 18,000-square-foot site in Repulse Bay, which was to provide space for a 12-story luxury residential complex.

A long-awaited improvement in earnings for the company came in 1985 when profits reached HK$551.7 million, 158 percent higher than the previous year. The effects on earnings from the three-year-long recession appeared to be over. The

company insisted that prices for residential property were on the rise, although the demand for commercial and industrial holdings had not yet meant substantially higher prices.

At this time, Hong Kong appeared to throw off some of the anxiety that had gripped the colony after the signing of the Sino-British joint declaration in December 1984, signaling a return to Chinese sovereignty in 1997. Many Hong Kong residents had been hesitant to buy homes or rent offices until the ink on the newly signed agreement was completely dry.

For Li Ka-shing, fears over investing for the future in Hong Kong were partly allayed by his influence among Chinese leaders in Beijing. The entrepreneur was not a man to be ignored when, for example, Hutchison Whampoa imported each year 850,000 tons of coal from China, or 14 percent of the country's annual output. Li Ka-shing was also at this time working with China International Trust and Investment Corporation, China's investment bank, to build a US$10 billion electricity plant in China's eastern province of Jiangsu.

Large profit gains resulted in 1986, when Hong Kong's economy grew by 9 percent over the year. Cheung Kong reported earnings of HK$1.28 billion, an increase of 128 percent on the year before. The improvements were helped by the completion of a number of developments, and by the company's sale of Hong Kong's Hilton Hotel for HK$1.03 billion to Hongkong Electric, which Li Ka-shing also owned.

Cheung Kong announced at this time a reorganization of its management structure. In particular, Hongkong Electric's utility and non-utility businesses were to be split. The non-utility holdings—including the Hong Kong Hilton Hotel and a 43 percent stake in Husky Oil of Canada—were to become part of a new firm, Cavendish International Holdings.

The Cheung Kong/Hutchison/Electric group had by now become very important in Hong Kong. Shares in Li Ka-shing's empire accounted for 15 percent of all shares traded on the Hong Kong stock market.

Cheung Kong moved ahead in 1987, producing profits of HK$1.58 billion, 23 percent over earnings posted a year earlier. The number of properties for development that the company was acquiring continued to increase. They included an 8.8 hectare site and a 15.5 hectare site which together would require up to HK$9 billion in investment before yielding more than 17,000 residential units, and two large shopping centers with total floor space of 1.22 million square feet. Profits at Hutchison Whampoa reached HK$2.62 billion. The property market in Hong Kong suffered slightly from the effects of the worldwide stock market crash of October 1987, but the underlying strength of the Hong Kong economy helped steady the local property market and increase demand for residential and office space.

A shortage of office space in Hong Kong contributed to strong profits for Cheung Kong in 1989. Earnings were posted at HK$2.09 billion, a 33 percent increase over the previous year. On the strength of improved earnings, the company announced that it would purchase all outstanding shares in Green Island Cement (Holdings) not already owned by Cheung Kong. Li Ka-shing told his shareholders in his 1989 accounts that he was optimistic about the outlook for the colony's property market, and that demand and prices for properties were likely to hold up.

The Hong Kong government announced the building of a new airport for the colony, for which Cheung Kong received lucrative contracts. In 1989, the company posted profits of HK$2.77 billion, 33 percent up over earnings a year earlier. At the same time, Li Ka-shing saw the colony's property market entering a period of consolidation. This was reflected in profits for the first six months of 1990 when Cheung Kong's earnings rose only 3 percent to HK$948 million.

Around this time, Li Ka-shing, nicknamed "Superman" in the colony, made a HK$484 million profit when Cheung Kong sold its 4.8 percent stake in Cable and Wireless, the U.K.-based telecommunications giant. The company, having bought the stake in 1987, profited from a rising Cable and Wireless share price, and the relative strength of sterling in the intervening period. By the beginning of the 1990s, Li's overseas holdings amounted to some 20 percent of his companies' assets, with forecasts to raise that stake to more than 30 percent. Meanwhile, Li, together with son Victor, ventured into satellite broadcasting, founding Star TV. In 1993, Li sold two-thirds of that company to Rupert Murdoch for US$525 million.

Preparing for the Chinese Handover in 1997

As the 1990s began, Li pledged to remain in Hong Kong after the colony's handover to China in 1997. Cheung Kong's strategy leading to that event seemed to confirm this, as Cheung Kong stepped up its investments and projects on the mainland. In 1995, Li transferred more than 30 percent of the company's assets to the Cayman Islands; this move, however, was largely seen as a means to avoid Hong Kong's inheritance tax as Li prepared to hand over the company to his sons. In the year before, Victor Li was named a deputy manager of Cheung Kong, while younger son Richard, engaged in building his own conglomerate in Singapore, was named a deputy manager of Hutchison Whampoa.

In 1993, Cheung Kong strengthened its economic, as well as political position by teaming up with CITIC Pacific, the Hong Kong arm of the Chinese government-owned investment vehicle led by Larry Yung, son of China vice president Rong Yiren, in a HK$9.65 billion takeover of Miramar Hotel & Investment Co. At the same time, Li hedged his political bets by joining with Deng Zhifang, a son of the late Deng Xiaoping, and Shougang, the third-largest steelmaker in China, to take over Kader Investment. Another investment, with China National Non-ferrous Metals Corp., allied Li with Deng's son-in-law, Wu Jianchang, a vice president of that company. These deals helped boost Li's Chinese investments to nearly HK$20 billion. On the basis of these and other deals, Cheung Kong's profits surged past $16 billion for 1993.

After adding the HK$2.2 billion purchase of the 665 King's Road North Point site in 1994, Cheung Kong announced plans the following year to redevelop the colony's Hilton Hotel, as well as a purchase of 40 percent of the colony's last walled village, a 50,000-square-foot site targeted for redevelopment. Next, again working with CITIC Pacific, Cheung Kong won a HK$7 billion contract to develop the Tsing Yi airport railway station near Kowloon. In late 1995, Cheung Kong, in a joint venture with Hutchison Whampoa and the Kowloon-Canton Railway Corporation, was awarded the property development

rights, worth as much as HK$8 billion, for the Hunghom area. Cheung Kong's earnings were rising steadily, climbing to HK$10.11 billion in 1994 and to HK$11 billion in 1995.

While Cheung Kong showed no signs of slowing down in 1996—the company won the rights to build the Tuen Mun River Terminal, a project worth HK$1.14 billion; the company also received an exceptional gain of more than HK$4 billion after the public listing of Hutchison Whampoa's UK mobile and telecommunications subsidiary Orange—Li also took steps to restructure the company for the impending handover. In June 1996, the company spun off its Hong Kong and mainland infrastructure holdings as a separately traded subsidiary, CKI, under leadership of Victor Li, which raised more than HK$3.6 billion through sales of nearly 300 million shares. Then, in January 1997, Li restructured all of the holdings of the Cheung Kong Group in a series of ownership shifts among its four principal subsidiaries.

Under the restructured holding company, CKI became principally specialized in the company's Chinese infrastructure projects, including a nearly completed 140-kilometer toll highway running south of Shantao. Cheung Kong's share of Hutchison, meanwhile, advanced past the halfway mark, to 50.2 percent, while Hutchison's share of CKI moved up to 84.6 percent. This meant that Hutchison also added CKI's 35 percent of Hong Kong Electric, triggering a mandated takeover bid for full control of HKE. The restructuring was widely regarded as a shrewd repositioning of the company in the final months leading to the Hong Kong handover. Meanwhile, Victor Li's role as a principal architect in the restructuring signaled the coming to an end of Li Ka-shing's reign as Hong Kong's "Superman." The elder Li, who had previously suggested that he would retire prior to the July 1997 handover, instead indicated that he would step down in January 1998. In any event, the Li family's financial dominance of Hong Kong was expected to continue long after the colony's transition to Chinese control.

Principal Subsidiaries

Hutchison Whampoa, Ltd.; Cheung Kong Infrastructure; Hong Kong Electric; The Green Island Cement (Holdings) Limited Group; Anderson Asia Quarry Group.

Further Reading

Hamlin, Kevin, "Superman in a Navy Suit," *The Independent*, January 5, 1992, p. 9.
Hewett, Gareth, "Full Steam Ahead for Li's Flagships," *South China Morning Post*, October 25, 1996, p. 25.
"Li Builds Ties to Safeguard Future," *South China Morning Post*, June 27, 1993, p. 2.
"Li Ka-Shing Stays Ahead of the Game," *Financial Times*, January 7, 1997, p. 20.
"Li Ka-shing: Preparing for China," *The Economist*, January 11, 1997, p. 58.
Lucas, Louis, "Infrastructure Spin-off Helps Lift Cheung Kong," *Financial Times*, March 27, 1997, p. 24.
Sito, Peggy, and Josephine Ma, "CKI to Raise Mainland Profile After Reshuffle," *South China Morning Post*, March 4, 1997, p. 14.

—Etan Vlessing
—updated by M. L. Cohen

Chic by H.I.S, Inc.

1372 Broadway
New York, New York 10018
U.S.A.
(212) 302-6400
Fax: (212) 819-9172

Public Company
Founded: 1923 as Honesdale Manufacturing
Employees: 3,350
Sales: $318.8 million
Stock Exchanges: New York
SICs: 2330 Women's, Misses, and Juniors Outerwear;
2339 Women's, Misses, and Juniors Outerwear,
Not Elsewhere Classified; 2325 Men's and Boys'
Separate Trousers and Slacks; 6794 Patent Owners
and Lessors

With a concentration on the budget segment of the denim market, Chic by H.I.S, Inc. ranks among the top producers of jeans in the United States and Europe, churning out more than half a million articles of clothing every week. The company designs and manufactures women's and girls' apparel—mostly jeans, denim shorts, and cotton-blend slacks—for sale under the Chic (pronounced ''chick'') brand in the U.S. In the early 1990s, Chic was the fourth most widely recognized jeans trademark behind Levi's, Lee, and Wrangler. The company also licenses its name to manufacturers of over 160 products, including sportswear, accessories, lingerie, and hosiery.

The revived h.i.s label is used to promote men's and boys' clothing in North America and women's jeans in Europe. By the mid-1990s, overseas operations contributed over one-fourth of total sales and proved the company's most profitable business segment. Chic's sales increased from $267.8 million in 1990 to over $376 million by 1995, then declined to $318.8 million in 1996 when a noticeable slackening of the American retail clothing market left the company with excess production capacity and inventory. Costs associated with a major staff reduction and

transfer of production to Mexico translated into a $25.6 million net loss for Chic in the latter year. Company insiders own over 50 percent of the apparel maker's stock, which was offered on the public markets in 1993.

Origins in 1920s

The company was founded by Henry I. Siegel as Honesdale Manufacturing in 1923. Headquartered in New York but with production in Tennessee, the company specialized in private-label work clothes and jeans for men and boys. These articles were distributed through such department stores as J.C. Penney and Montgomery Ward and sold under the stores' own labels. By 1940, when Henry's brother Sam joined the business, the company had three plants in Tennessee.

Honesdale's homefront contribution to America's World War II effort included the manufacture of field jackets for the armed forces. When Henry died unexpectedly in 1949, his 19-year-old son, Jesse, assumed control of the firm. A recent graduate of Columbia University, Jesse Siegel brought a new emphasis on fashion to the family business, at first making slight modifications to its existing line of functional clothing. A 1966 *Forbes* article noted that ''Siegel was the first to take khakis, an old-time favorite in work clothes, put a buckle on the back, and aim it toward the youth market.'' The shift doubled sales from $9 million in 1949 to over $18 million by the mid-1950s.

Hoping to tap into the burgeoning consumer market of the postwar era, Siegel launched the company's first brand, H.I.S (a play on his father's initials), in 1956. The company's line of branded casual wear targeted teen and college-aged baby boomers with denim jackets, corduroy pants, shorts, sportcoats, and suits. By the mid-1960s, Siegel ranked among the nation's top manufacturers of sportswear for young men. Sales multiplied from $18.5 million in 1956 to $42.1 million in 1964, with the H.I.S brand contributing three-fourths of revenues by the latter year. Though the creation of a national brand allowed the company to command higher profit margins than it had generated with private-label goods, Siegel continued to concentrate on making clothes for middle-market customers.

Company Perspectives:

As we enter the challenges of the 21st century, we at Chic by H.I.S recognize our responsibilities to our customers, our employees, our communities, and our stockholders. In an effort to fulfill these responsibilities we commit ourselves to: Creatively maintaining our goal of being a leading domestic and international supplier of fashionable family apparel. Having a corporate sense of responsibility to our customers, our communities, and our environment. Insuring a long-term growth of profits through a commitment to customer satisfaction. Continually seeking to improve our products, in quality, in service, and in value. Honoring an atmosphere of honesty, integrity, and trust in our fellow workers, which encourages a spirit of shared responsibility and commitment. Individual recognition of each person's creative ability to perform successfully and with merit. Setting standards of ethical responsibility to enhance the culture of our company, the prosperity of our people, and the continual pursuit of excellence.

Initial Public Offering in Early 1960s

Jesse Siegel honored his father's memory more directly when he engineered the firm's initial public offering as Henry I. Siegel Co. in 1962. In an effort to capitalize on the popularity of its now lowercase h.i.s brand men's jeans—and at the urging of Jesse's wife, Barbara—the company launched ''h.i.s for Her'' women's wear in 1964. With women increasingly wearing slacks and other formerly ''man-tailored'' garments, it was a relatively easy and logical transition. Within just two years, the new line was selling $4 million and had achieved profitability. Companywide sales grew to $58.9 million by 1967 and nearly $76 million by 1973. Having held onto a controlling interest in the firm, Siegel took the company private again in 1976.

The Siegels' conservative management style, which included a spartan headquarters and lean manufacturing, were a corporate hallmark that outlasted the era of direct family management. For instance, the firm utilized computerized production and inventorying as early as the mid-1960s. As Robert F. Luehrs, president of the company in the late 1980s and early 1990s, told *Crain's New York Business,* ''We make a basic product, we make it good and we make it cheap.''

Rising imports hit the market for less expensive men's and boys' clothing especially hard in the 1970s. As a result, Jesse Siegel decided to suspend the men's line late in the decade to concentrate on the more profitable women's wear then being offered under the Chic label. In 1975, the company launched ''proportioned to fit'' jeans for women. This new sizing scheme took height as well as waist size into consideration, offering each waist size in a range of inseam lengths for a more tailored and comfortable fit. Later, Siegel added other fitting styles including relaxed fit, slim fit, and classic fit. By the mid-1980s, Chic was America's third-largest manufacturer of women's jeans, behind Levi Strauss and H.D. Lee.

Chief financial officer Burton M. Rosenberg, who had joined the company in 1969, spearheaded a management-led leveraged buyout in 1984. The reorganization piled on hundreds of millions in debt, making profitable cash flow an even greater imperative than ever before in the years to come. At the same time heavy competition surfaced, especially from rival Gitano, which was lowering its prices to gain market share. Rosenberg, who succeeded Jesse Siegel as chairman and chief executive officer in 1986, reduced retail prices to just under $20 in order to meet the competitive challenge and retain market share. The company also reintroduced its h.i.s men's line to the budget jeans market during this period. By 1988, the Henry I. Siegel Co.'s sales totaled $233 million.

1990s Range from Dynamic to Difficult

Rosenberg's fiscal control helped increase Chic's sales from $233 million in 1989 to $304 million in 1993, by which time the brand surpassed now-bankrupt Gitano to become the top brand of women's jeans sold in mass merchandising chains. With orders increasing and profits rising to nearly $5 million in the latter year, Rosenberg made an uncharacteristically bold move, raising $69 million in a public stock offering that February. The proceeds were used to reduce the renamed Chic by H.I.S, Inc.'s $114 million debt remaining from the 1984 LBO and to boost capacity by one-fourth in anticipation of continued growth. It was no small hazard, for as Phyllis Furman of *Crain's New York Business* pointed out in a July 1994 article, the company risked extending itself beyond the selling capacity of its customers.

Unbeknownst to Rosenberg, the expansion came just as the retail clothing industry was entering a marked downturn. Heavy dependence on debt-ridden mass marketer KMart, which contributed over one-fourth of sales in the early 1990s, proved particularly troublesome. Several of Chic's retail customers went out of business, in part because of pressure from mass discounters like Wal-Mart, to whom Chic refused to sell because of its reputation for squeezing the profit margins of its suppliers. With domestic plants operating at less than 40 percent of capacity late in 1995, Chic's officers quickly ran out of options.

Chairman and CEO Burton M. Rosenberg warned attendees at the company's March 1996 annual meeting that ''it's going to be a very, very difficult year . . . the type of year where you hunker down and strengthen your balance sheet in order to be there when the turn comes. If you have a good brand, it will eventually pay off.'' Rosenberg's ''hunker down'' strategy included the closure of several factories in Tennessee and Kentucky and the elimination of over one-fifth of Chic's workforce. And in a striking departure from its longstanding devotion to domestic manufacturing, the company took a $30 million charge to move production to Mexico. Chic hoped to return its North American operations to profitability in 1997 by expanding its foothold in the men's and boys' segment and by launching distribution into Canada.

Chic's European operations remained a particularly bright spot, generating operating profits of $10.4 million on sales of $106.7 million in 1996, up from $2.4 million and $51.8 million, respectively, in 1992. The company's h.i.s brand was positioned as a designer label there, earning profit margins of over 40 percent, compared to the domestic mass market brands' less than 15 percent gross margin. The label ranked second only to Levi's among adult jeans brands in Germany, Switzerland, Austria, the Czech Republic, and Slovakia by the mid-1990s. The parent company hoped to raise additional funds to help it weather its mid-decade difficulties by selling a minority stake in its German subsidiary to the public in 1997.

Principal Divisions

HIS Sportswear GmbH (Germany).

Further Reading

Bloomfield, Judy, "HIS Gives Retailers a Price Break," *WWD,* January 27, 1988, p. 13.

"Chic by HIS Is Paying Bills, Says President," *WWD,* January 22, 1996, p. 13.

"Chic by HIS Restructuring, Planning to Cut 1,100 Jobs," *WWD,* March 12, 1996, p. 16.

"Europe Is Key to Profits at Chic by His," *WWD,* March 6, 1997, p. 14.

Furman, Phyllis, "Conservative Chic Ducks Jeans Blues," *Crain's New York Business,* July 25, 1994, pp. 1–25.

Gordon, Maryellen, "Jeans: Marketing Jeans Is Not for the Faint-of-Heart," *WWD,* October 11, 1993, p. F26.

Heady, Robert, "H.I.S Move into Teen Consumer Clothing Market Hikes Sales Tenfold," *Advertising Age,* May 24, 1965, pp. 4, 26.

"Henry I. Siegel Racks Up Handsome Rise in Profits," *Barron's,* October 25, 1965, p. 26.

"Hola, Chic," *WWD,* January 2, 1997, p. 7.

"Jesse Made the Pants Just Right," *Forbes,* April 15, 1966, p. 23.

Lippert, Barbara, "Funky But Chic," *ADWEEK Eastern Edition,* November 11, 1991, p. 41.

Lloyd, Brenda, "H.I.S Exec Cites QR for Sharp Cuts in Production Time," *Daily News Record,* February 8, 1988, p. 24.

——, "Fights h.i.s Jeans War," *Daily News Record,* September 18, 1992, p. 3.

Maum, Emmett, "It May Be Called H.I.S., But It Was S.H.E. Who Brought It Back to Life," *Memphis Business Journal,* August 25, 1986, pp. 34–35.

Mhlambiso, Thembi, "Jeans Ads Focus on Young Men's," *Daily News Record,* August 4, 1992, pp. 1–3.

Ryan, Thomas J., "Chic's New Mexican Plant Will Let Firm Cut Prices," *Daily News Record,* January 3, 1997, p. 4.

Spevack, Rachel, "Henry I. Siegel Back in Men's with Line of H.I.S Jeans," *Daily News Record,* January 5, 1989, p. 3.

Williamson, Mickey, "The Perfect Fit," *CIO,* May 1, 1996, p. 38.

Woodyard, Chris, "Shoppers Get KMart's Attention," *USA Today,* April 9, 1997, pp. 1B.

—April Dougal Gasbarre

The Circle K Company

3003 North Central Avenue, Suite 1600
Phoenix, Arizona 85012
U.S.A.
(602) 530-5001
Fax: (602) 530-5278

Division of Tosco Corporation
Incorporated: 1951 as Circle K Food Stores, Inc.
Employees: 20,566
Sales: $3.57 billion (1995)
SICs: 5499 Miscellaneous Food Stores; 5989 Fuel
    Dealers, Not Elsewhere Classified; 5999
    Miscellaneous Retail Stores, Not Elsewhere Classified

The Circle K Company, which became a division of Tosco Corporation in 1996, is the third-largest convenience store chain in the United States and the largest operator of company-owned convenience stores. It is also a major marketer of gasoline, through the 85 percent of Circle K stores that offer gasoline and the more than 1,000 Tosco gasoline stations merged into Circle K following its purchase by Tosco. Overall, Circle K operates a retail system of more than 4,000 outlets in 34 states. There are also about 900 Circle K stores—operated via joint ventures or licensing agreements—in more than 50 other countries, notably Canada, Taiwan, Korea, Hong Kong, New Zealand, Mexico, and Argentina. Through a 1993 agreement, Uny Company of Japan operates 1,750 Circle K stores in Japan, from which The Circle K Company derives no royalties or other income.

Founded as Three-Store Chain in 1951

In 1951, Fred Hervey, a self-made businessman, bought three Kay's Food Stores in El Paso, Texas, and began operating them under the name of Kay's Drive-In Food Service. Hervey, who was born in 1909, began his business career in childhood by selling magazine subscriptions and by setting up a soda pop stand outside his father's outdoor theater. During the 1930s, Hervey and his brother started a profitable root beer stand. Hervey then went on to other business enterprises and even

served two terms as mayor of El Paso before he founded Circle K.

By 1957 Hervey had a 10-store chain in the El Paso area, and he decided to expand his operation to Arizona. The company adopted a new logo and corporate trademark: an encircled K to create a western image. By 1959 the Circle K Food Store chain had 15 units in Arizona in addition to the 10 in Texas. In those days, convenience stores were still a new idea—there were only 500 such stores in the country (in 1988, there were 80,000). In 1965 Circle K developed its contract store concept, individual owner-operated stores to serve remote areas.

In the early 1960s, the company doubled in size and moved its corporate headquarters to Phoenix, Arizona. In 1963 Circle K went public, issuing 96,000 shares of common stock. From this original stock offering to the late 1980s, Circle K's stock split eight times.

Began Selling Gasoline in the Mid-1960s

In 1964 Circle K celebrated the opening of its 100th store. That same year, the board of directors began to think about expanding into nonfood activities, and so changed the name of the corporation, eliminating the words ''Food Stores.'' The Circle K Corporation soon began selling gasoline as well as food products—the first convenience store to do so. In 1964 the company also test-marketed manufactured ice under the brand name Crystal Clear Circle K.

By the late 1960s, the company was able to devote more of its resources to technology: in 1967, business operations were computerized, and in 1968, a chemist was hired to develop food products, which eventually led to the Hi Spark'l line and Circle K Freezes. These products, along with others in the Polar Beverage division, such as Del Sol fruit punches and Just Orange juice, developed in the 1970s, continued to be sold until the mid-1980s. At that time, the trend in convenience stores was to enter into joint ventures with brand name companies to sell fast foods such as ice cream, juices, or doughnuts. For example, a Dunkin' Donuts brand program was successful in many Circle K stores.

138

In 1971, with the establishment of the foodservice division, the company began to sell sandwiches. In 1972, the company was operating in eight western states: Arizona, California, Colorado, Idaho, Montana, Oregon, New Mexico, and Texas. By the mid-1970s Circle K had acquired 26 Quick-Shop stores, thus expanding its base of operation into Oklahoma and Kansas.

Under the leadership of president John Gillet, Circle K began to expand overseas in the early 1970s. In 1972, businessmen from Japan came to the United States to study the convenience store concept; their visit to Circle K in Phoenix led to Circle K's first foreign licensing agreement, in 1979, with the Uny Company of Japan to establish Circle K stores there. Further overseas expansion in Asia, Europe, and Australia occurred in the 1980s. By 1989, Circle K convenience stores existed in 13 foreign countries.

Aggressive Growth in the Early 1980s

The early 1980s were a period of aggressive growth. Karl Eller, CEO and chairman of the board—with the help of his long-time associate, Carl H. Linder, a director—was given credit for Circle K's ambitious posture during this time. Eller, who previously founded Combined Communications Corporation and served as president of Columbia Pictures, had a reputation as an acute dealmaker and business opportunist. (An anecdote reported by *Business Week* claims Eller was once able to strike a good deal buying several television stations by reading about their owner's death in the obituaries.) And, indeed, under Eller's leadership sales soared and the number of Circle K stores nearly tripled, mostly through acquisitions from other chains. During the early 1980s, due to changing consumer needs and the growth of the industry, competition in the convenience food industry was fierce, and Eller's strategy was to buy up units from rivals hurt by this vigorous competition. In 1983 Circle K nearly doubled its size with its acquisition of 960 UtoteM units. Other acquisitions included 435 Little General stores and 21 Day-N-Nite stores in 1984, 449 Shop & Go stores in 1985, and 473 7-Eleven stores and 538 stores from Charter Oil in 1988. Circle K expanded from its base in the Southwest aggressively into the South and Northwest and to a lesser extent into the East and Midwest, as well as internationally.

In addition to expansion, the early 1980s also brought a number of innovations to Circle K stores. In 1983, stores in the Phoenix area installed automatic teller machines, while commissary operations developed the Deli-Fresh sandwich concept to serve company stores as well as some supermarket and military accounts. A third innovation that year was a redesigning project to establish a unique corporate identity for Circle K. Stores were remodeled in orange, red, and purple.

In fiscal 1984, Circle K passed the $1 billion sales mark, and the next year it constructed a new corporate headquarters in Phoenix—an elegant four-story building housing a Circle K store in its front section. But the fast growth and creative innovation of the 1980s were not without difficulty and controversy. Circle K's 1980 acquisition of 13.2 percent of Nucorp Energy, Inc., a petroleum corporation, brought with it a lawsuit by a group of shareholders and officers of companies acquired by Nucorp in 1981. The lawsuit, filed in 1983, questioned the integrity of Nucorp's accounting practices, and threatened the

financial stability and ratings of Circle K for five years. It was settled in 1988, when a jury ruled in Circle K's favor. Meanwhile, Nucorp filed for bankruptcy in 1982, then Circle K sold its interest at a loss the following year.

Controversies and Financial Problems in the Late 1980s

In 1988, however, there were other problems. Early in that year, Circle K triggered a gasoline price war in Alabama by cutting prices as much as seven cents a gallon. The state's attorney and a group of retailers claimed that Circle K's action violated the state's Motor Fuel Marketing Act and threatened to file a suit. The impetus for legal action was stifled when Circle K raised its gas prices once again. A spokesperson for Circle K told *National Petroleum News*, "As a convenience store chain, we give our customers the best possible convenience and value in pricing, but we don't sell below cost."

Circle K generated further controversy in 1988 when it instituted a new health insurance plan for its employees which sought to exclude "lifestyle-related" health care problems such as drug or alcohol abuse. This policy would also have excluded AIDS victims, except ones who contracted the disease through blood transfusions. It would not have excluded drug and alcohol rehabilitation, however. The plan created a furor among civil libertarians and gay-rights groups, who feared that other self-insured companies would rush to institute similar policies. Brent Nance, insurance case manager for AIDS Project Los Angeles, told *Business Insurance*, "It's almost as if Circle K says there are innocent victims and guilty victims, and they will cover only innocent victims." Criticism also came from less expected quarters such as the insurance industry and the convenience store industry. Circle K eventually withdrew the lifestyle exclusions from its policy.

Circle K's fast growth brought with it a number of personnel problems that the company had to address. Numerous acquisitions meant that uniformity of procedures and training simply did not exist. It also led to rapid turnover and a lack of company loyalty on the part of employees who often felt an allegiance to their original employer. Circle K instituted a number of communication and training improvements. Newsletters and a toll-free telephone number were designed to allay fears among employees whose stores were in the process of being acquired by Circle K. The No. 1 Club rewarded sales effort with cash and recognition; the Management Development Candidate program and the Professional Retail Operator program provided comprehensive training for managers.

All of these difficulties paled, however, in comparison to Circle K's mounting financial problems, which stemmed from the company's rapid expansion throughout the 1980s. In 1989, the company began to have serious financial problems, coincidentally or not the year after founder Hervey left the board of directors. From 1983 to 1989, Circle K had nearly quadrupled its number of outlets, going from 1,200 in 12 states to 4,500 in 32 states. To finance the expansion, long-term debt increased from $40.5 million to $1.1 billion over the same period. By 1989, Circle K was paying nearly $100 million annually simply to service its debt. Although sales reached a record $3.5 billion in 1989, net income was only $15 million, a minuscule 0.4

percent of sales. During the year, Circle K put itself on the block, but there were no takers.

In early 1990 Circle K brought in Robert Dearth from Chiquita Brands to be president, with Eller soon resigning. Dearth moved to cut costs, but it was too little, too late. Circle K declared bankruptcy in May 1990, in the midst of a year in which the company would post a $773 million loss.

Fortunes Turned Around in Early 1990s

Dearth resigned in June 1991. Bart Brown, an attorney from Ohio, was chosen as CEO and chairman and John Antioco became president and COO, leaving rival Southland Corp. to do so. Brown and Antioco began to slowly revive Circle K under bankruptcy protection, closing or selling stores to cut costs and renovating those that remained in the chain. No less than 45 percent of the stores would be jettisoned by mid-1993, when there were 2,800 stores chainwide. The renovation program ultimately led to Circle K's Shoppers Express format, which organized each store into six distinct departments: Sales and Service, Beverage Depot, Grocery Express, Food Court, Snack World, and Car Care. The company also began to add such enhancements to its stores as pay-at-the-pump credit card readers, safety lighting, and improved canopies.

By July 1993 Circle K's finances had improved to the point where Investcorp S.A., a Bahrain-based investment company, offered to buy the chain out of bankruptcy for $399.5 million. Following the purchase, Antioco took over the CEO position, with Brown remaining chairman. That same year, Circle K reached the first of several agreements with federal courts and state governments regarding the cleanup of sites contaminated by leaking underground gasoline storage tanks. In 1995, the company estimated that it would have to spend approximately $100 million through the year 2000 to clean up all the sites.

In 1994 Circle K returned to profitability, posting a modest profit of $18.4 million on sales of $3.32 billion. Early in 1995 Circle K became a public company again, when Investcorp sold 30 percent of Circle K to the public. The resulting capital was earmarked for a cautious program of growth. The company spent $24.6 million to purchase 16 Kwik-Stop stores in the Phoenix metro area. More significantly, Circle K entered the franchising arena for the first time through a deal with Gibbs Oil Co., based in Massachusetts, which soon thereafter ran 82 Circle K units in New England. A second franchising deal followed through a joint venture with Southgard Corporation which created 164 Circle K franchises in Texas and Oklahoma. These deals involved secondary markets, which was where Circle K intended to look for future franchising opportunities.

Circle K seemed to throw some of its caution to the wind later in 1995, however, when it made an unsolicited bid for National Convenience Stores Inc. and its 661 stores. But Diamond Shamrock Inc. outbid Circle K, purchasing National Convenience for $190 million. Also in 1995, Antioco succeeded Brown as chairman.

Began New Era with Purchase by Tosco Corporation

The following year, Tosco Corporation, a Stamford, Connecticut-based petroleum refiner and marketer, purchased Circle K for $750 million. Tosco merged its marketing arm, Tosco Marketing Company, with The Circle K Corporation to create The Circle K Company, a division of Tosco with more than 4,000 retail locations in 34 states. Brought together were one of the country's largest independent oil companies and one of the largest convenience store chains. Antioco soon resigned his position (quickly landing at Taco Bell as president and CEO), and Robert Lavinia, who had headed up Tosco Marketing, became the new Circle K's president and CEO.

Also in 1996, a jury awarded four former Circle K managers of Vietnamese heritage more than $20 million in damages in a discrimination case. The company planned to appeal the verdict. Later in 1996, Coca-Cola Co. and Circle K settled another suit, this one stemming from Circle K's decision to terminate an exclusive agreement to sell only Coke fountain products. Although terms were not announced, the two firms stated that they had signed a new agreement involving the sale of Coke products in Circle K stores.

In late 1996, Tosco signed a letter of intent to acquire the assets of 76 Products Company, the West Coast refining and marketing division of Unocal. Although it was not immediately clear how the acquisition would be integrated into Tosco, the deal brought 1,350 76-branded gasoline stations to the Tosco fold. Along with Tosco's existing deals to sell the British Petroleum "BP" brand in 20 states and the Exxon brand in Arizona, the Unocal deal added to the potential ways that Circle K could sell branded gasoline at its units. The power of the combination of the well-known Circle K convenience store brand with well-known gasoline brands was a main attraction for Tosco when it was considering the Circle K purchase.

Circle K approached the turn of the century seemingly at the beginning of another period of rapid growth. In addition to its move into franchising and the addition of Tosco outlets, Circle K had begun to experiment with a home-meal replacement store called Emily's Market, whose take-home meals might eventually be offered at Circle Ks as well. It had also been testing in-store Blimpie and Taco Bell franchises. Such experiments and the deep pockets of its parent boded well for Circle K's future.

Further Reading

Auerbach, Jonathan, and Louise Lee, "Marriage of Convenience: Tosco Gets Fuel Injection by Acquiring Circle K," *Wall Street Journal*, February 20, 1996, p. A4.
Francella, Barbara Grondin, "Circle K: Into the Selling Zone," *Convenience Store News*, November 18, 1996, pp. 23–30.
Smyth, Jeff, "Key to Circle K's Rebirth Is Changing People's Perception," *Advertising Age*, August 9, 1993, p. 3.

—Joyce Goldenstern
—updated by David E. Salamie

CLOTHESTIME

The Clothestime, Inc.

5325 East Hunter Avenue
Anaheim, California 92807
U.S.A.
(714) 779-5881
Fax: (714) 779-0512
Web site: http://www.clothestime.com;
   http://www.ctme.com

Public Company
Incorporated: 1974
Employees: 4,666
Sales: $308.20 million (1996)
Stock Exchanges: NASDAQ
SICs: 5621 Women's Clothing Stores; 5632 Women's
   Accessory & Specialty Stores

The Clothestime, Inc. is a retailer of discount sportswear, dresses, and accessories for junior-sized women ages 15 through 35. The chain sells quality merchandise at the lowest possible prices, typically offering branded merchandise at 30 to 70 percent less than the retail prices suggested by manufacturers. The company's subsidiary—Lingerie Time—sells off-price intimate apparel in companion stores next to selected Clothestime establishments. Clothestime stores in some outlet malls operate under the name Trend Club.

From Flea Markets to a Chain of Stores

During the early 1970s, a group of business partners visited flea markets and bought interesting items to resell to retailers in southern California. By 1974 the partnership—which included Ray DeAngelo and John Ortega II—settled into conventional retailing and opened their own store called Clothesline. Shortly after starting out, however, the partners changed the store's name to Clothestime when another retailer filed a lawsuit, claiming ownership of the rights to the Clothesline name. Undeterred, DeAngelo and Ortega developed their retail concept into a chain of stores under a different name.

With a motto of "always in fashion, never full price," Clothestime attracted enough fashion-conscious but financially conservative women to establish stores throughout the West Coast, particularly in California. Each store averaged about 4,000 square feet in size and stocked a variety of in-season sportswear, dresses, career wear, and accessories for women. Approximately 50 percent of the items carried were fashion merchandise, while the remaining 50 percent was comprised of basic wardrobe items. A typical sales transaction totaled about $28.00.

Unlike competing discount stores, Clothestime appealed not only to teens and college students but also to women up to 35 or 40 years old. So the company strategically located its retail establishments in low-rent strip centers anchored by food stores or giant discounters for accessibility to women interested in fashionable—not trendy—merchandise at discount prices. "Our customer is definitely value-driven," DeAngelo explained in *WWD*. "She still looks at the fashion aspects of clothes before the price tag, but she can't afford to pay a lot."

In 1983, DeAngelo and Ortega made Clothestime a public company, after which rapid growth of the retailer followed. In 1984, for example, Clothestime operated 155 stores. Within three years the chain grew to 338 establishments. Profits in 1987 totaled $12 million.

Merchandising Mistakes

As the decade closed, Clothestime re-approached its merchandising mix. In 1989, the company moved beyond name brands and off-pricing by introducing its own private-label items in addition to higher-priced career wear. The company lost $2.2 million that year and barely balanced profits with expenses in 1990 and 1991. Nevertheless, Clothestime reclaimed its customers by 1992 through a variety of strategies, including commercials on MTV. The chain's efforts resulted in $260.3 million in sales and $5.6 million in profits for the year.

In January 1993 Clothestime reported a 55.4 percent increase in profits—about $8.7 million. The company's performance exceeded Wall Street's expectations, and analysts heralded the chain as the up-and-coming retailer for apparel. Bolstered by this success, Clothestime began improving and expanding its operations.

The Private-Label Program

In order to offer customers more quality merchandise at lower prices, the company enhanced its internal product development operations. The company broadened its private-label program. In 1993, 30 percent of the chain's merchandise came from national junior brands. The remaining 70 percent originated from Clothestime's private-label program. The company purchased about two-thirds of the items in the private-label program from manufacturers, then attached a Clothestime label to the merchandise; for example, CIME, Viamax, Star Cody, Best World Brand, or Spoiled Girls. Clothestime's internal product development group generated the remaining one-third of the private-label merchandise. During this time—as Melanie Cox, assistant general merchandise manager, explained in *Chain Store Age Executive and Shopping Center Age*—the private-label program became "increasingly important to our image."

To ensure the success of the private-label program, Clothestime purchased a state-of-the-art computer-aided design system to increase the amount of merchandise generated from its internal product development. Though expensive, the new system was quickly cost justified. It improved the number and quality of in-house designs. The system created and revised designs faster than artists could conceive and draw them. Altering the color of a design, for instance, took only the click of a mouse. In addition, electronic versions of the designs could be transmitted quickly via phone lines. The computer's designs also were truer to actual garments than those of artists. (Artists often added flourishes to designs that could not be recreated for the physical garments.)

Clothestime's computer-aided design system also gave exclusivity to its private-label merchandise. It greatly increased the company's capabilities in re-coloring prints, assigning stitches or shades, or simulating weaves. The system could render two- and three-dimensional designs, as well as download images from its computer to automatic knitting machines in order to transfer an image—such as a painting—from the computer to a garment.

Other Technological Advancements

In addition to the new computer-aided design system, other technological advancements were added by the company in 1993. Clothestime upgraded its point-of-sale system by replacing its NCR terminals with IBM 4683 and 4684 equipment and Dataserv software. The company also instituted improved financial management and merchandise tracking systems. In particular, the chain inaugurated its Clothestime Retail Information System (CRIS) for monitoring merchandise and for automating its buying, distribution, and store operations. This system also utilized IBM equipment.

Expansion on the East Coast and Elsewhere

With advanced technology in place, Clothestime embarked upon a store expansion program. In 1993, the company was one of the more healthy junior apparel chains on the West Coast. Despite the economically depressed market in California, the company's 220 stores there did well owing to Clothestime's competitive pricing practices. The company easily assumed market share from other retailers failing in the state's poor economy. With $30 million in cash and no long-term debt, Clothestime decided to branch out, placing 83 percent of its new units outside of California.

In April 1993, the company launched the first of six stores in the metropolitan New York market. According to DeAngelo's comments in *WWD*, the first store in East Hackensack, New Jersey, did better than Clothestime expected. By May, six stores opened in central and northern New Jersey, Long Island, and Westchester County, New York. These new stores reflected 10 percent of the company's expansion goal of 65 stores for 1993. Expansion at this time was financed through internally generated funds; the company issued no secondary stock offerings. Clothestime planned 100 stores for the New York market by 1998, expanding in clusters in specific areas. "It will probably be about three or four years before we have the name recognition on the East Coast that we have on the West," DeAngelo explained to a *WWD* writer in 1993, "but we'll get there. We're very optimistic that our format will be successful in New York. We've seen whatever competition is out there, so we know what we're getting into." Clothestime also entered markets in Hawaii and Puerto Rico in 1993.

The overall corporate plan for 1993 called for Clothestime to achieve $1 billion in sales from 1,000 stores by the year 2000. Nevertheless, operations showed signs of slowing just as expansion got underway in 1993.

Advertising Schemes and Dreams

In March 1993, same-store sales increased as they had for the past 29 months, but the very next month same-store sales dropped 3 percent. By the Christmas season, same-store sales dropped 4 percent. At the time, Clothestime attributed the dip to low-profile marketing. The chain depended on word of mouth, radio ads, direct marketing, and print ads in national fashion magazines such as *Elle, Glamour, Cosmopolitan, Seventeen,* and *YM*. So, as a company spokesperson told *WWD*, "We're changing our ads to put more of a focus on our affordable pricing, in addition to fashion."

After three years, Clothestime ended its relationship with the Kresser/Craig of Santa Monica, California, advertising agency and started doing more things to be visible. For instance, Clothestime served as one of the sponsors for "VH-1 Honors," the first live concert televised by the VH-1 television network. (The concert showcased charitable organizations supported by celebrities such as Garth Brooks, Al Green, and Kenny G.) The chain also became a retail client of Muzak Limited Partnership's ZTV Video Services Division. This service exposed the chain's customers to in-store videos, with Clothestime ads and promotions incorporated into the programming.

Other Improvements

In addition to revamping its marketing style, Clothestime also initiated chain-wide improvements to its 549 stores in 1994. The retailer redid lighting in 69 stores during the first phase of store improvements that also saved money. For example, a $6,000 retrofit of lighting in store number 584 in Cathedral City, California, yielded close to $7,000 in electricity savings, plus a $1,400 utility rebate. Clothestime changed the four-lamp fixtures in phase-one stores to three T8 lamps and added electronic ballasts and aluminum reflectors. Phase two affected 480 stores, replacing their varied fixtures with standard models. The chain expected completion of the project in December 1995. As Adolph Garcia, manager of store development, construction services, told *Energy User News:* "This chainwide project comes after seven years of research. We were looking for ways to save money, and the estimated savings from a nationwide renovation were very attractive."

Lingerie Time

Clothestime also initiated a chain of off-price intimate apparel stores in 1994. The retailer opened five Lingerie Time stores in May 1994 in Placentia, Dana Point, Huntington Beach, and Anaheim, California, and in Pearl City, Oahu, Hawaii. These stores were situated next to existing Clothestime outlets; in fact, the stores shared connected interiors. Each Lingerie Time was between 2,000 and 5,000 square feet, with expected sales of $200 to $400 per square foot. Lingerie Time carried almost exclusively national brands rather than Clothestime's private labels. Merchandise—sold at 30 to 60 percent off retail prices—included innerwear, foundations, lingerie, and sleepwear by Natori, Bali, Vanity Fair, Christian Dior, Maidenform, Lilyette, and Lily of France. Ortega explained Clothestime's strategy to *Discount Store News:* "Unlike the women's junior business, intimate apparel has been traditionally dominated by brand names. We believe our customers will appreciate finding the brand names they have enjoyed wearing over the years at discount prices." The average age of Lingerie Time customers also differed from those of Clothestime. Women ages 24 through 45 were the chain's target customers.

At the first store's opening, Lingerie Time showed potential for becoming the first national off-price intimate apparel store chain. Twenty-five additional sites had been identified for Lingerie Time stores in 1994. Still, cautious expansion was planned for the chain in 1995—just nine stores in two states.

Steep and Swift Decline

Despite all its efforts, Clothestime continued to decline in 1994. Comparable store sales fell throughout the year, as did operating profits. Merchandise became too trendy and youthful, so the chain lost its 20- and 30-year-old customers. Clothestime again worked to attract customers in the 25- to 28-year-old age group. The company changed its buying staff, added more

dresses, and featured more career clothes that doubled as casual wear—for instance, blazers. While these efforts raised quality standards, they did not satisfy the store's customer base. The chain's decline continued.

In December 1995, Clothestime began reorganization under Chapter 11 bankruptcy proceedings. During the beginning of 1996, the company's sales dropped 36.2 percent to $103.2 million. Clothestime closed 170 stores, leaving 360 in the chain. Despite a net loss of $10 million, the company still cut its operating losses from $7.5 million to $4.4 million and hoped to emerge as a stand-alone company. Nevertheless, losses grew to $13.8 million, and more stores closed. During the fourth quarter of 1996, Financo, a New York-based investment banking firm, was hired to sell the chain.

Reorganizing the Company

With no firm buyers since hiring Financo and with creditors anxious for the company's sale or liquidation, chairman and chief executive officer Ortega resigned in 1997, as did chief operating officer and president Norman Abramson. Chief financial officer and vice president David A. Sejpal assumed leadership of Clothestime and initiated a reorganization plan.

The company's 10-K claimed that many of its losses were due to a failed advertising campaign that it now considered "sensational, controversial, and aggressive." (In 1996, Clothestime hired its first spokesperson—Gina Lee Nolan from the *Baywatch* television series. Television, radio, and print media spots featuring Nolan were supposed to show Clothestime as "a 'cool' place to shop.") The company document also reported the closing of 75 additional stores. In March 1997 Clothestime and its creditors reached an agreement on the terms of a plan for reorganization.

Clothestime intended to pay its creditors $.07 on the dollar in cash plus 75 percent of the reorganized company's stock. The company believed that this arrangement would allow it to emerge from bankruptcy in the summer of 1997. "The filing of our reorganization plan is a tremendous achievement," commented Sejpal in a press release, "and represents the culmination of months of extremely hard work and sacrifice by our associates, vendors, and creditors. We are delighted to be taking this first step toward Clothestime's emergence from bankruptcy with our creditors' committee fully committed to the company's reorganization." In June 1996, Clothestime operated 322 stores in 17 states and Puerto Rico.

Principal Subsidiaries

Lingerie Time.

Further Reading

"Clothestime Debuts Five-Store Test of Intimate Apparel Concept," *Discount Store News,* June 6, 1994, p. 3.

"Clothestime Engages Financo to Assist in Selling Company," *WWD,* November 18, 1996, p. 27.

"Clothestime Goes into Review," *ADWEEK* (eastern edition), May 30, 1994, p. 5.

"Clothestime to Be Sold or Closed," *WWD,* January 31, 1997, p. 4.

"Computer-Aided Clothes," *Chain Store Age Executive and Shopping Center Age,* October 1993, p. 117.

Macintosh, Jeane, "Prime Time for Clothestime," *WWD,* May 26, 1993, p. 10.

Nelson, Kessel L., "Enhanced Rebate Quickens Payback of Retail Store's Lighting Retrofit," *Energy User News,* May 1994, p. 18.

Owens, Jennifer, and Thomas J. Ryan, "Clothestime Aims to Shut Seventy-Five More Stores," *WWD,* May 2, 1997, p. 11.

Pogoda, Dianne M., "Lingerie Time Bows," *WWD,* May 11, 1994, p. 6.

Russell, Deborah, "Artists, Charities Will Co-Star in VH-1 Concert," *Billboard,* May 7, 1994, p. 12.

Russell, Deborah, "Muzak Delving into Video; Christian Music Award Set," *Billboard,* July 16, 1994, p. 46.

—Charity Anne Dorgan

CNS, Inc.

4400 West 78th Street
Minneapolis, Minnesota 55435
U.S.A.
(612) 820-6696
Fax: (612) 835-5229
Web site: http://www.breathright.com

Public Company
Founded: 1982
Stock Exchanges: NASDAQ
Employees: 40
Sales: $85.9 million (1996)
SICs: 3842 Surgical Appliances And Supplies

Formed as a medical equipment company, CNS, Inc. achieved rapid growth and profitability with the Breathe Right nasal dilator, an adhesive strip worn across the bridge of the nose. Breathe Right, a leading seller among products in the domestic cough and cold market, is an alternative to decongestant drugs and nasal sprays. By reducing airway resistance the strip also has been shown to eliminate or reduce snoring—perhaps the largest potential market for Breathe Right. CNS introduced an analgesic patch for temporary pain relief in 1997 and is developing other medical consumer products.

First Product Line: Brain Wave Monitors

Dr. Daniel Cohen and Dr. Frederick Strobl founded CNS, Inc. in 1982 in order to develop equipment for brain wave analysis. The men met while residents in the neurology department at the University of Minnesota Hospitals and discovered each wanted to use their medical training in a nontraditional capacity. Strobl, also an electrical engineer, was interested in biomedical engineering, and Cohen leaned toward using his medical knowledge in a business context.

Lawrence Sutin wrote in the October 1985 *Minnesota Business Journal*, "In their initial 1978 talks, the two doctors agreed

that the state of the art in monitoring equipment for brain activity was, in Strobl's words, 'in a relatively primitive state.' " Standard electroencephalograph (EEG) machines printed out the brain's electrical signals as marks on a continuous stream of paper and were difficult to read and analyze quickly. Strobl and Cohen wanted to develop a machine which could be easily used in the operating room—monitoring brain activity during procedures such as open heart surgery could reduce the incidents of brain damage through early detection of dangerously diminished blood supply to the brain.

The men initially formed a partnership and worked independently. In late 1982, they had advanced far enough in their research to hire an engineer and incorporate the business. A private stock offering to friends and fellow physicians raised nearly $350,000. In 1983, with more engineers and research personnel on board, Strobl and Cohen narrowed the scope of their activities in order to focus on product development. Additional rounds of stock offerings were made through financial institutions. And their first outside manager was hired in early 1984; but he left the company within a year over marketing strategy differences.

CNS's first product, the CNS-16 Tracer—a personal computer with a circuit board to receive brain wave signals via electrodes and software to measure electrical changes—was approved by the Food and Drug Administration (FDA) in December 1984. Strobl led the marketing efforts for the $75,000 machine. Cohen handled the general management of the company. They quickly found that changes in Medicare and Medicaid treatment reimbursements that were made in the early 1980s had tightened hospital budgets for new equipment. In 1985, CNS began to modify the system and software for use in sleep disorder clinics while they continued to try to build the surgical market.

The Mayo Clinic in Rochester, Minnesota, Twin Cities Hospitals, and other users of the CNS equipment had responded favorably to the product, but sales continued to be slow. To generate interest among the general public, CNS loaned a piece of equipment to a daytime soap opera and two years later to the television medical drama "St. Elsewhere." The tactic generated interest but no sales.

CNS Goes Public

CNS made its initial public offering (IPO) in June 1987 and generated $3.2 million. But Diane Beulke wrote in a November 1987 *Minneapolis/St. Paul CityBusiness*, "Five-year-old CNS, Inc. of Eden Prairie has been fighting an uphill battle to convince Medicare rule makers and heart surgeons that its brain wave monitors are an operating room necessity."

In 1987, the company's sleep lab monitoring equipment brought in nearly 60 percent of the $1.75 million in sales. CNS's computer-aided EEGs reduced the amount of time required to read and analyze the data gathered on factors such as eye movement, muscle activity, and oxygen level, which were used to diagnosis sleep disorders. Cost-effectiveness proved to be more readily measured in the sleep lab than in the operating room.

The company lost nearly $5 million from 1985 through 1987. Only 60 of the operating room monitors had been sold since 1984. CNS appointed Fred Brooks, a professional manager with experience in medical devise companies, to the position of president in July 1990. Cohen continued to serve as CEO.

The company reported profits for the first time in 1990 on revenues of $7.5 million. The number of sleep clinics had risen from 300 in 1985 to about 2000 by 1991. CNS's equipment ranged from $50,000 to $120,000, but most clinics needed one or two machines; in contrast, hospitals needed a brain monitor for each operating room. The company was pumping 12 percent of sales into product development in order to expand into areas such as home-use sleep monitors.

A New Direction

In October 1991, Cohen met with Bruce Johnson, who was seeking help to scientifically test the effectiveness of an external nasal dilator he had invented. Johnson, a mechanical designer in the electronics industry, formed his own consulting business, Creative Integration and Design Inc., in 1988, after being laid off by his employer of 10 years during the prior year. About the same time he was inspired to try a new approach to relieve his on-going allergy-related breathing problems.

Johnson had used a variety of methods to dilate his nasal passages internally, but they were uncomfortable. A building with an architectural design using external supports triggered an idea: he could dilate the nostrils externally. Eric J. Wieffering wrote in a September 1995 *Corporate Report* article, "For the next three years, he worked on a spring-loaded adhesive strip that would stretch across the outside of his nose, lift his nostrils gently, and allow him to sleep. He wore prototypes to bed and around the neighborhood. He endured the good-natured taunts of his son and neighborhood children, who asked, 'What happened to your face, Mr. Johnson?' " He applied for a patent on the device in 1990.

Cohen tried the strip and came to the same conclusion as Johnson: the potential market for a product that provided non-medicinal relief of nasal congestion was huge. Instead of agreeing to test the prototype, Cohen offered to buy the rights to manufacture and sell the nasal strip. CNS would pay for the testing and clinical trials necessary for FDA approval of the product. Johnson would receive warrants for shares of CNS, a

percentage of gross sales for the life of the patent, and work with CNS to further refine the strip. In February 1992, CNS announced the licensing agreement with Creative Integration and Design for the nasal dilator and the resignation of Brooks as president of CNS. Cohen assumed his duties.

Domestic sales of the larger lab-based diagnostic equipment fell in 1992 due to the uncertainty surrounding rules regulating third-party reimbursement for sleep testing. The company continued clinical studies on the benefits of the external nasal dilator and planned to begin marketing the product to hospitals and home care providers when cleared by the FDA. A secondary stock offering brought in additional funds in 1992. After a profitable 1990, CNS had reported losses in 1991 and then again in 1992.

A new president and chief operating officer, Richard E. Jahnke, came on board in March 1993. He had 20 years experience in marketing and general management with large corporations including 3M. In October, the FDA approved marketing of the Breathe Right strip as a medical device. CNS had shown it improved nasal breathing by reducing air resistance an average of 31 percent. CNS stock per share price climbed from about $4 to $14 within a month. According to Tony Carideo in a November *Star Tribune* article, "One thing clearly driving the issue is the enormous amount of publicity the product is receiving."

To build consumer demand for the Breathe Right strip, Cohen had been giving 10 to 20 interviews a week, blanketing radio, television, newspapers, and magazines. Although CNS had commitments from five of the top ten pharmaceutical wholesalers to supply the strips, customers had to request them before drugstores would create shelf space for the new product, a 10-count box selling for about $5. Breathe Right sales for 1993 were primarily in the Twin Cities area and other cities where they had received media coverage. The lengthy FDA approval process for Breathe Right plus continuing uncertainty in the U.S. sleep disorder market contributed to losses of $1.4 million for 1993.

Another stock offering brought in $8.6 million in April 1994. Breathe Right strips gained shelf space in Minneapolis-based Snyder's Drug Stores Inc. and then in two of the country's largest drug store chains, Walgreen's and Eckerd Drug Stores, in the beginning of the year. With the product now available in some stores, CNS began making plans for more traditional advertising and promotion. But the company continued to pursue creative low-cost promotional ideas.

In October 1994, Cohen sent a letter and case of Breathe Right strips to all of the National Football League (NFL) trainers. The Philadelphia Eagle trainer gave Herschel Walker a strip when he complained of cold symptoms. San Francisco 49er Jerry Rice, who had chronic nasal congestion, heard that Walker had worn the strip during a game and then donned a Breathe Right himself on a nationally-televised Monday Night Football. *Wall Street Journal's* "Heard on the street" column featured CNS a few days later. Fourth quarter sales of Breathe Right doubled and produced about one-half the year's total sales of $2.8 million.

Super Sales

The Breathe Right received more national exposure in January 1995, when about eight Super Bowl XXIX players wore the strip. Additional publicity came in February when Rush Limbaugh told his radio and television audiences that he and his wife had used and liked Breathe Right. National media attention sent sales skyrocketing. First quarter sales were $7.5 million. CNS could not keep up with demand. In order to finance the backlog of orders, CNS sold its diagnostic equipment business—which had annual sales of about $7 million—for about $6 million. CNS stock was on the ascent as well. Per share price reached the $30 range prior to a two-for-one stock split in June 1995. In August, CNS announced an agreement with 3M to distribute Breathe Right internationally.

CNS rounded out its spectacular year with two significant events. The FDA approved the marketing of Breathe Right for the reduction or elimination of snoring: clinical studies had shown that 75 percent of participants snored less often and less loudly when using the strip. With about 40 million chronic snorers in the United States, CNS saw snorers as the largest potential market for its product. And one day after receiving the FDA approval, the patent on Breathe Right was granted. "The timing of this event was crucial as knock-off products were increasing in number and retailers were considering offering private label products," said Cohen and Jahnke in the 1995 annual report.

Revenues for 1995 were $48.5 million, and net income on continuing operations was $13.3 million or 72 cents per share. By the end of the year the Breathe Right strip was in 98 percent of all drugstores and mass merchants and estimated to be in 70 percent of all grocery stores. The 30-count box, introduced mid-year, had grown to 25 percent of sales.

CNS placed its first network television ad in 1996: the two 30-second Super Bowl XXX spots, which targeted snorers, cost $1.6 million. Also in 1996, the company received additional FDA approvals for marketing the Breathe Right strip. One for relief of nasal congestion and stuffy nose and another for the temporary relief of breathing difficulties due to a deviated nasal septum—a bend in the cartilage and/or bone which divides the nostrils.

Building Markets

In 1996, CNS accelerated its advertising with network television ads during the NFL season and year-round radio, cable television, and print ads which were bumped up during the cough and cold season. CNS raised $35 million in a public offering to finance future growth and captured the number four spot on *Fortune* magazine's list of the nation's fastest-growing companies.

Clinical studies in support of additional uses for Breathe Right continued in 1996. Benefits related to athletic endurance and performance, asthma- and emphysema-related breathing problems, and sleep quality were under investigation. International sales climbed to 30 percent of revenues in 1996 as 3M built inventory and introduced the product in 30 foreign countries. Net sales for the year were $85.9 million or an increase of 77 percent. Net income was $15.5 million.

In 1997, CNS was the smallest company to buy ad time for Super Bowl XXXI. Joint promotions with Tylenol PM and the Universal Pictures movie *Leave It To Beaver* were also slated for later in the year. TheraPatch, an external analgesic product test-marketed in 1996 was distributed nationally beginning in 1997—the medicated patch market had climbed from $134 million in 1985 to $262 million in 1996. But, Pollen Guard Gel, a product being developed to reduce inhalation of airborne allergens, was found to be ineffective and was dropped. CNS hoped to introduce an appetite suppressant or smoking cessation product in the form of a lozenge and gum in 1998.

An estimated 10.5 percent of households of potential domestic customers used CNS products in the beginning of 1997. Piper Jaffray concluded in a first quarter analysis of CNS that "Breathe Right will be a very successful product over time due to its large potential markets, its effective relief of nasal congestion and snoring, and its relatively high rate of repeat users."

Further Reading

Begley, Laura, "He Wants Solid Bed for Sleep Device Firm's Future," *Star Tribune* (Minneapolis), July 30, 1990, p. 2D.

Beulke, Diane, "CNS Says Its Monitors Are the Wave of the Future," *Minneapolis/St. Paul CityBusiness*, November 4, 1987.

"Brooks Resigns As President Of CNS," *Star Tribune* (Minneapolis), February 6, 1992, p. 3D.

Carideo, Tony, "CNS Breathing Easy with New Product, Stock Rise," *Star Tribune* (Minneapolis), November 13, 1993, p. 3D.

"CNS Builds Breathe Right Brand," *MMR*, February 10, 1997.

"CNS, Inc.," John G. Kinnard & Co. Update, April 14, 1997.

"CNS, Inc." Piper Jaffray Equity Research Notes, April 15, 1997.

"CNS Inc. Testing An Appetite Suppressant," *Star Tribune* (Minneapolis), June 20, 1997, p. 3D.

DePass, Dee, "Sales of Adhesive Nose Strips Are Booming at Breathe Right," *Star Tribune* (Minneapolis), May 10, 1995, p. 1D.

Gross, Steve, "Makers of EEG Machine Made Waves in a New Market Niche," *Star Tribune* (Minneapolis), April 28, 1988, p. 1D.

Howatt, Glenn, "Publicity from NFL Sends Breathe Right Sales Soaring," *Star Tribune* (Minneapolis), April 4, 1995, p. 1D.

——, "More Than Words: Analyst's Predictions, Praise for CNS Inc. Boost Stock 15 Percent," *Star Tribune* (Minneapolis), June 13, 1995, p. 1D.

——, "FDA Tells CNS That Breathe Right Can Be Advertised As Way to Stop Snoring," *Star Tribune* (Minneapolis), November 9, 1995, p. 3D.

Judge, Gillian, "Sleeping Giant?" *Twin Cities Business Monthly*, February 1994, pp. 30–33.

Marsh, Ann, "Nose Jobs," *Forbes*, March 13, 1995, p. 140.

"Minnesota's Fastest Growing Small Public Companies," *Minneapolis/St. Paul CityBusiness*, May 30, 1988, p. 17.

Nelson, Wayne, "Neurologist Turns to Technology to Reduce Brain Damage in Surgery," *Minneapolis/St. Paul CityBusiness*, February 19, 1986, p. 7.

Sutin, Lawrence, "Diagnosis: Entrepreneurial Fever," *Minnesota Business Journal*, October 1985, pp. 52–57.

"The Talk," *Format*, February 1997, p. 8.

Wascoe, Jr., Dan, "There Are Reasons Why Advertising Seems Familiar," *Star Tribune* (Minneapolis), November 30, 1987, p. 3M.

Wieffering, Eric J., "Ace Bandage," *Corporate Report Minnesota*, September 1995, pp. 30–35.

Youngblood, Dick, "Neurologists Now Realize Their Dream," *Star Tribune* (Minneapolis), April 28, 1991, p. 1D.

——, "Breathe Right Nasal Strip Has Clear Potential," *Star Tribune* (Minneapolis), January 9, 1995.

—Kathleen Peippo

Coeur d'Alene Mines Corporation

505 Front Avenue, P.O. Box 1
Coeur d'Alene, Idaho 83816-0316
U.S.A.
(208) 667-3511
Fax: (208) 667-3617

Public Company
Incorporated: 1928
Employees: 1,217 (1997)
Sales: $105.8 million (1996)
Stock Exchanges: New York
SICs: 1044 Silver Ores; 1041 Gold Ores

Coeur d'Alene Mines Corporation (Coeur) is a global precious metals producer, specializing in the exploration, extraction, and development of both gold and silver resources in its seven active gold and/or silver mines. Directly and through its subsidiaries, the company operates primarily within North and South America, Australia, and New Zealand. Coeur silver is used in film, jewelry, medicine, batteries, electrical appliances, in high technology defense and scientific applications (where instant bursts of electric power are required), and as a bacteria killer in water—reusable laundry discs using silver can eliminate the need for detergents. Due to its ability to bind specialized superconductive materials together, silver is expected to play a significant role in a new era of high temperature superconductors—materials that conduct electricity with little or no electrical resistance. Silver and gold are being used to remove frost from automobile and airplane windows, by conducting heat through a nearly invisible layer of silver embedded in the glass. Due to its high reflectivity, gold is used in spacecraft to resist radiation and heat. It is used in all parts of the Internet to ensure static-free, reliable, and seamless connections; and gold circuitry within microchips is standard in all brand name microcircuitry. The brilliance and intrinsic value of gold and silver continues to recommend them for use in jewelry fabrication and ornamentation.

Coeur announced a gold production record of 214,130 ounces for 1996, and having established itself as North Amer-

ica's leading producer of silver, figures for that year show Coeur d'Alene's silver production at 9.5 million ounces. The world consumed 162 million more ounces of silver than was produced in 1995, and according to Erick Schonfeld, writing for *Fortune*, "Each 25-cent rise in the price of silver contributes about a dime to the bottom line of Coeur d'Alene Mines."

Coeur d'Alene Mining District Developed in the 1890s

The Coeur d'Alene district of Idaho has been an important producer of lead, silver, and zinc since the 19th century. Idaho and Utah were the great silver-lead producing states, accounting for over 40 percent of the country's total output during the period 1907–30, with most of Idaho's output coming from the Coeur d'Alene district of Shoshone County. The district extended over an area of only 200 square miles and was first developed for large scale mining in the 1890s, becoming one of the world's premier fields. According to a *Business History* article by Roger Burt, "Two developments were essential for the beginnings of large-scale mining in the district: the provision of reasonably inexpensive transport facilities to connect the mines with outside processing and consuming districts; and sufficient capital to meet the heavy investment necessary to exploit the rich hidden lodes." Railroad connections branched into the district from the Northern Pacific and Union Pacific Railroad lines, providing access to smelting areas and consumers on both coasts. Capital was supplied due to the promise of rich rewards—a high silver content in Coeur ores was attractive to investors—and because the Coeur d'Alene was one of the last American mining fields to be developed. The production of zinc, a supplement to the relatively low grade of lead ores, was also rapidly developed in the area. The new technologies of electric power and the combustion engine were large consumers of non-ferrous metals, establishing the strong links between technical progress, national economic growth, and the non-ferrous metals industry.

World War I Era: Rapid Change

Following expanded production in the area during World War I conditions rapidly began to deteriorate. Prices fell dramatically and production costs were elevated until concentration and separation techniques—which enabled more metal to be extracted from the same grade ores—were improved. By the late 1920s record levels of production again encouraged expansion. Inspired by this climate of optimism the Coeur d'Alene Mines Corporation was formed. Unfortunately, by the early 1930s, the overall economic depression began to be felt within the industry, forcing several mines to close. In Idaho, however, the silver production levels were sustained better than in most other states, and the company's share of production grew from 16 percent of the country's output to 30 percent in 1933. Coeur's flagship, the Coeur d'Alene Silver Mine, provided income until the 1950s when the mine was shut down due to poor metal prices.

In the following decade, the Silver Standard Mining Company and Rainbow Mining and Milling, Inc. merged into Coeur d'Alene Mines in a stock-swap basis, and negotiations between Asarco and Coeur resulted in an agreement between the two companies which would allow Asarco exploration rights in the Silver Belt of the Coeur d'Alene mining district. According to *Equity Research*, an Everen Securities bulletin, "If exploration results had warranted, Asarco proposed construction of a mine in exchange for a proceeds-and-cost-sharing arrangement with Coeur d'Alene Mines. Construction of the Coeur mine—the newest mine in the 100-year-old-plus mining district—began in the 1970s, costing $20 million for the mine and mill, with commercial production beginning in 1976. The company began stockpiling ore in that year when silver sustained a yearly average of $4.63 per ounce, before rising to a high of $5.34 per ounce in 1980. The Coeur mine maintained steady and consistent production. In 1979 four Idaho silver mining companies had formed a joint venture agreeing to rehabilitate and reopen Consolidated Silver Corporation's Silver Summit mine and to begin an extensive exploration program on that company's mining properties. The four joint venture partners included Hecla Mining Company (operating in the area since before the turn of the century), Silver Dollar Mining Company, Sunshine Mining Company, and the Coeur d'Alene Mines Corporation. The four companies were major shareholders in Consolidated Silver, a company formed in 1967 to consolidate several mining properties near the Silver Summit mine.

The 1980s: Turning Dollars into Gold

In 1983 $18 million was raised in Coeur's first stock offering through a major national firm. The capital was used to develop its Thunder Mountain gold property in central Idaho where completion of their drilling operation revealed ore reserves at 2.4 million tons, containing 0.09 ounces of gold per ton. Diamond drilling, mapping, geochemical analysis, and other technical work was carried out by the staff of Coeur's subsidiary, Coeur Explorations, Inc. Coeur had used funds accumulated when silver prices climbed to finance the purchase of Thunder Mountain, in addition to purchasing Asarco's operating lease on the Rochester mine, a silver and gold surface mine—the largest primary silver mine in the United States—located in Pershing County, Nevada. Both Thunder Mountain and the Rochester mines entered production phases in 1986. The Rochester site consisted of 16 patented and 544 unpatented contiguous mining claims and 74 mill-site claims, totaling approximately 9,370 acres. After completing their first full year of operations in 1987, both mines exceeded production goals. The Rochester mine became the company's largest revenue source, with overall revenues growing from a low $5.5 million in 1985 to $56.4 million in 1987. Representing an environmental success, Thunder Mountain received the Pacific Northwest Pollution Control Association's first place award for the protection of Idaho's natural resources.

One of the company's primary objectives was to increase Coeur's income from gold. In an effort toward accomplishing this goal the company added the purchase of the Alaskan Kensington mine from Placid Oil Company. Echo Bay Mines, Ltd. of Canada bought into the operation, making it a 50/50 joint venture partner and mine operator. An estimated $197 million would be required before placing the property into commercial production, with the expectation of producing up to 200,000 ounces of gold per year. Coeur's primary task was to drive a tunnel, intersect, and crosscut the major target—the Kensington vein. According to company reports, a "5,200-foot tunnel, driven into a mountain 800 feet above sea level, was completed in December 1988, substantially ahead of schedule." In 1995, Echo Bay Mines Ltd. won a temporary restraining order blocking Coeur d'Alene Mines from taking operating control of their Kensington joint venture. The Alaskan Superior Court ruled in favor of the Echo Bay injunction. Coeur charged "that Echo Bay's resources were stretched in Alaska and that it had dragged its feet obtaining permits for Kensington," according to Frank Haflich writing in *American Metal Market*. Coeur offered to buy out Echo Bay's 50 percent, which was agreed upon in mid-1995.

The Alaskan acquisition was followed by the merging of Royal Apex Silver, giving Coeur sole ownership of the Rochester mine. Reserves are an important measure of a mining company's value which prompted Coeur's maintenance of new silver and gold ore reserves at Rochester and Thunder Mountain as a strategy for future growth. In order to reduce the effects of metals' price fluctuations, the company continued to maximize the value of the gold and silver it sold by selling forward a portion of its products in times of higher prices. The policy limited sales forward to not more than 50 percent of production. In 1987, for example, the company sold forward 1.7 million ounces of silver at an average price of $9.03 per ounce and 22,500 ounces of gold at an average price of $505.09 per ounce. In the same year, Coeur redeemed its $25 million principal amount of convertible subordinated debentures. The company then issued $50 million principal amount of convertible subordinated debentures in the Eurodollar market, giving the company the largest supplement to its capital base in its 59-year history at highly favorable rates.

Headed by president and CEO Dennis E. Wheeler, the company proceeded with its aggressive expansion efforts. Two million common shares of stock were sold in 1990, raising approximately $50 million, which the company used to buy seven Chilean precious metals exploration properties from Freeport Minerals (costing $5 million). Shareholders approved the merger of Callahan Mining Corporation on a stock exchange basis into Coeur d'Alene Mines as a wholly owned subsidiary of the company, giving Coeur $22 million in cash and legal ownership of the Galena mine, the Caladay project, and the Flexaust Company, a manufacturer of flexible hose, ducting, and metal tubing (which the company sold in 1995). Silver prices declined to $3.93 per ounce in 1992, forcing the company to place the Coeur and Galena mines on standby. In late 1994, Coeur, Callahan, and Asarco formed Silver Valley, a Delaware corporation, and transferred certain assets, including their interests in the Coeur, Galena, and Caladay mines, to Silver Valley. Six directors sit on the Silver Valley Board, consisting of three appointed by Asarco, and three appointed by Coeur.

1993: Doubling Gold Production

The company acquired the New Zealand assets of Golden Cross mine for $54 million, giving Coeur its first operating mine overseas. New Zealand underwent major economic reform in an effort to encourage development, including deregulation, lowering of compliance costs, and removal of impediments to business. In the area of exploration, New Zealand companies are not favored over international investors. One hundred percent foreign ownership of mineral resources is possible provided the investment makes a significant contribution to New Zealand's growth and development. All expenditure on mineral exploration can be written off against tax commitment in the year of expenditure. The subsidiary of a New Zealand corporation, The Todd Company, Ltd., owns a 20 percent joint venture interest in the 961-acre Golden Cross property. The mine property includes open-pit and underground mine facilities, process plant, tailings pond, water treatment plant, and mine offices. An independent consulting firm estimates open-pit and underground proven and probable ore reserves totaling 2.989 million tons, averaging 0.086 ounces per ton gold. Total contained silver ounces are estimated at 1.112 million ounces, with an average grade of 0.37 ounces of silver per ton.

A 1995 investigation by the company revealed that the Golden Cross tailings impoundment was situated on a block of geologically unstable land that was moving down slope, actuated by heavy rainfall. Coeur was forced to construct a drain tunnel, horizontal and vertical drain holes, and buttressing with waste rock in an attempt to stabilize the tailings dam. Additional rainfall complicated the project and engineers determined that remedial measures would cost the company at least $11 million. Coeur announced a $53 million write-down of its interest in the Golden Cross Mine and nearby property when production was decreased and operating costs were increasing due to its inability to stabilize the dam. The company asserted legal claims against Cyprus Amax Minerals Company for an unspecified amount, alleging that the seller failed to make certain required disclosures relating to ground movement when Coeur had purchased the property. In August 1996, Cyprus filed a counterclaim for an unspecified amount of damages, alleging libel by Coeur in its press release announcing the write-off of the Golden Cross Mine. Coeur eventually raised the tailings dam crest, after fighting and winning a legal injunction filed by environmentalists to stop such action. Following the hearing the court determined that the crest raising posed no danger to the environment, and the company hopes to implement the previously planned mill optimization and to continue operating the mine at least through 1997.

By October 1995, construction of the Fachinal Mine facilities (located south of Coihaique, Chile) were completed, costing the company approximately $41 million. The property is known to contain multiple epithermal veins containing gold and silver. The milling process uses conventional crush/grind/flotation methods to produce a gold/silver concentrate, which is then sent to off-site smelters for further processing. For the year ending December 31, 1996, the mine's operations produced more than 25,000 ounces of gold and over 2 million ounces of silver. Coeur estimates that cash operating costs at the Fachinal Mine will approximate $272 per gold equivalent ounce in 1997, at a production level of 1,600 tons of ore per day. Precious metals bearing mineralization at the Fachinal Mine occur in an extensive epithermal, quartz-veins system hosted in Jurassic volcanic rocks. The total remaining, mineable reserves at the mine amount to approximately 3.653 million tons averaging 0.069 ounces per ton gold and 2.78 ounces per ton silver. Other developments in that country were announced in 1994 when Coeur's Chilean subsidiary signed an agreement to assume operating control of the El Bronce, a producing Chilean gold-silver mine, located on approximately 34,000 acres in the Andean foothills north of Santiago, Chile. Coeur is investing in exploratory and developmental activities designed to increase ore reserves to 65,000 ounces by the end of 1997.

In early 1997 Coeur acquired 36 percent of the Australian company Gasgoyne Gold Mines, Ltd., in partnership with one of the country's major gold producers, Sons of Gwalia Ltd. The company recognized the low costs and excellent growth potential of the Yilgarn Star Mine, a young mine which sits in the Marvel Loch region of Western Australia, one of the most active gold mining regions in the country. Southern Star and Navoria gold mines of Australia, and a 45 percent interest in the Awak Mas Gold Project in Indonesia were included in the deal. Probable reserves at Yilgarn Star approximate 721,000 ounces of gold.

Coeur began 1997 operations holding high reserve levels of 3.4 million ounces of gold and 109 million ounces of silver, making it an industry leader in terms of the level of reserves underlying its common stock. It holds cash and equivalents of $168 million. The company plans to continue targeting opportunities in "politically stable countries with historic mining traditions and ample opportunity for developing production and reserves."

Principal Subsidiaries

Coeur Australia, Inc.; Coeur Rochester, Inc.; Coeur Bullion Corporation; Coeur Explorations, Inc.; Coeur Alaska, Inc.;

CDE Chilean Mining Corporation; Gasgoyne Gold Mines NL (Australia; 50%); Silver Valley Resources Corporation; Compania Minera CDE Fachinal Limitada (Chile); Compania Minera CDE El Bronce (Chile).

Further Reading

Burt, Roger, "Mineral Production, Organization and Technological Change: The Coeur d'Alene District of Idaho, 1890–1933," *Business History*, July, 1990, pp. 49–74.

"Coeur d'Alene Mines Corporation," *Wall Street Journal*, December 19, 1986, p. 32.

"Coeur d'Alene Mines Corporation: Review of Chilean Operations," Equity Research, *(Everen Securities)*, September 16, 1996, pp. 1–22.

"Coeur d'Alene Mines in Red; Blames Loss on Callahan Link," *American Metal Market*, March 18, 1992, p. 5.

"Coeur d'Alene Mines," *Wall Street Journal*, September 12, 1983, p. 23.

"Four Concerns Agree On Venture to Reopen a Silver Mine in Idaho," *Wall Street Journal*, December 26, 1979, p. 14.

Haflich, Frank, "Cyprus, Coeur in Court for Claims Countersuit," *American Metal Market*, July 18, 1996, p. 2.

Kletter, Melanie, "Silver Demand Rises," *National Jeweler*, April 1, 1997, p. 4.

Knickerbocker, Brad, "Old Mines Pose New Hazards in Cleanup," The *Christian Science Monitor*, May 21, 1996.

Schonfeld, Erick, "A Silver Lining," *Fortune*, April 1, 1996, p. 161.

Trainor, Kenny, "Coeur d'Alene Approves 'Poison Pill' As Shield Against Hostile Takeover," *American Metal Market*, May 31, 1989, p. 5.

—Terri Mozzone-Burgman

Coinmach Laundry Corporation

55 Lumber Road
Roslyn, New York 11576
U.S.A.
(516) 484-2300
Fax: (516) 484-0905

Public Company
Founded: 1946
Employees: 1,180
Sales: $206.9 million (fiscal 1997)
Stock Exchanges: NASDAQ
SICs: 5063 Electrical Apparatus and Equipment, Wiring
    Supplies and Construction Materials; 5087 Service
    Establishment Equipment and Supplies; 7215 Coin-
    Operated Laundries and Dry Cleaning

Coinmach Laundry Corporation was, in the opinion of its management in 1997, the leading national supplier of coin-operated laundry-equipment services for multifamily housing properties in the United States. It owned and operated about 386,000 coin-operated washers and dryers in more than 38,000 multifamily housing properties in 31 states, the District of Columbia, and Mexico, and in 150 retail laundromats in Texas. Through a subsidiary, Coinmach was also a distributor of construction and laundromat equipment.

Growth and Development to 1990

The business was founded in 1946 in Long Island City, a community in New York City's borough of Queens, by the grandfather and father of Jan Sussman. They started with a single coin-operated washing machine and dryer in one apartment building, collecting the money in an old sock. The business grew by convincing owners and managers of apartment buildings that it was more cost-effective and less stressful to let the company service the laundry room than to do the job themselves.

Jan Sussman, an MBA graduate of the University of Pennsylvania's Wharton School of Business, assumed control of Coinmach Industries Co. in 1980, on his father's retirement, taking out a loan from NatWest to buy part ownership. The younger Sussman had worked for Solon Automated Services, Inc.—one of the largest coin-operated laundry-service companies—and had managed a race track for Rapid American Corp. Coinmach had only 75 employees, 14,000 customers, and annual sales of $12 million at this time, but Sussman's ambition was to stand atop the Empire State building and be able to say he owned all the coin-operated washers and dryers in all the buildings in sight.

With the rapid increase in the New York area of conversions from rental apartment buildings to condominiums and cooperatives, Sussman's first challenge was to persuade owners of condo and co-op units to continue using the central laundry room rather than install their own washers and dryers. Part of his strategy was to install larger washers and dryers, allowing residents to wash and dry fewer loads than if they had their own machines. Coinmach also provided amenities such as folding tables, drying racks, and seating areas.

Coinmach also needed better operations because, Sussman later told *LI Business News*, "At that time, there were no computers, they were doing business the same way they had for 40 years." Working with General Electric, Coinmach developed exclusive improvements to its washers and dryers to give them better rinse cycles and longer agitation periods. The company guaranteed a nine-hour repair response time and formed 20 five-person service teams, with five vans in operation to bring the machine parts to the repair personnel. Coinmach earmarked $3 million for computers and software and hired three programmers to assemble a database with information on every company washer and dryer. Eventually, said Sussman, Coinmach could dispatch a service call in 12 seconds, where it used to take three hours.

To motivate his employees, Sussman offered repair teams as much as $100 per person each month in bonuses, depending on the number of times they completed repairs in less than nine hours. Managers won the right to a share in the company in 1984, and the number of management personnel who became part owners in the firm grew from 28 that year to 52 in 1994. By the mid-1980s Coinmach had the largest coin-operated laundry business in the metropolitan New York area, with 60,000 washers and dryers in 7,000 locations and annual sales of $55 million.

Coinmach entered the pay phone business in 1986, installing more than 200 Northwestern Bell telephones in a joint venture with a group of small telephone companies. Linked to a central computer at Coinmach corporate headquarters, each of the coin-operated phones had a special two-digit number that, when pressed, automatically generated a service call through the computer. Another two-digit number allowed customers to call Coinmach for refunds if the money was lost. State-of-the-art features of the system included voice-synthesis messages, detailed record-keeping, problem diagnosis, and data updates. In addition, each phone was capable of initiating a service call on its own if in need of repair or tampered with, or if the coinbox needed to be emptied. This venture proved a disaster. "The phones didn't work," Sussman later told a *Wall Street Journal* reporter. "They were terrible." After 18 months, he said, "I got out. It was the worst period of my life."

A new-parts division was added in 1987 to sell other businesses some of the systems and programs Coinmach had developed. Sussman told *Vending Times,* "We realized our experience with collecting and handling coins, our superior maintenance and security systems, our computer software packages, our parts purchasing capability, and our expertise in facility-design layout and installation techniques are items that other companies would be interested in utilizing."

A 1989 leveraged buyout of Coinmach raised $15 million for future acquisitions and left Sussman's family with a 30 percent share in Coinmach, enough for him to continue control of the company with a small group of investment partners.

Coinmach in the Early 1990s

Coinmach's sales reached an estimated $85 million in 1990, when the company had 340 employees. Sussman had programmed its computer to predict when each of the 75,000 machines it was servicing in 7,000 buildings had taken in the $40 necessary to justify a collection, and a system enabling the company to handle 1,500 daily telephone complaints within 10 seconds each, guarantee repair calls within nine hours, and achieve a 98-percent rate in getting the right parts from storage to repair personnel.

Coinmach also had broadened the scope of its activities. One division was selling ready-to-operate laundromats and dry-cleaning establishments to investors, and a subsidiary was lending money to prospective store owners. The company also had established about 200 on-premise laundries in restaurants, hotels, health clubs, and similar businesses. It was selling commercial laundry parts at discount prices and remanufacturing its own old machines at the rate of 125 a week.

Sussman also was motivating Coinmach's employees by offering bonuses as they moved along a "growth path." This involved attending classes, demonstrating their skills, and undergoing performance reviews. As the workers moved forward, they were given the right to wear shirts of progressively lighter shades, starting with blue and advancing to white. Sussman claimed he was saving money by giving the ordinary worker more incentives and responsibilities, because it enabled the company to cut back on supervisors.

Also during 1990, Coinmach established American Laundry Systems, a joint venture with the government of Hungary to found the first self-service laundromats in Eastern Europe. These outlets, formed from converted state-run establishments, were to be equipped with video games and television sets. That year Sussman was named one of Long Island's five "entrepreneurs of the year."

By 1993 Coinmach had installed, in two apartment buildings, a computer system that allowed residents to call in to find out if the washers and dryers in the laundry room were occupied, thereby preventing needless elevator trips to the room. The company also was developing a feature allowing residents to call up and enter the number of washing machines and dryers needed. The computer then would call back to notify when that number of machines would be available. "The computer will even call you before the end of your dry cycle," Sussman said, "so your clothes won't wrinkle." The system not only notified company technicians when a machine had broken down but also reduced repair time by diagnosing the problem.

Coinmach Industries had flat annual revenues between 1992 and 1994, ranging between $71.9 million and $73.9 million. The company lost $13 million in 1992 and $12.3 million in 1993, mostly because of heavy interest expenses. It lost $5.7 million in 1994 before consideration of an extraordinary gain of $20.4 million stemming from early extinguishment of debt.

Emphasis on Acquisitions, 1995–97

In January 1995 management, with its equity sponsor, Golder, Thoma, Cressey, Rauner Fund IV, L.P., acquired Coinmach Industries Co., and initiated a strategy of growth through acquisitions. This strategy was designed to increase its installed machine base of about 54,000 in the Northeast and to provide the company with a strong market presence in other regions. Sussman's role in the company ended at this time, with Stephen Kerrigan, who had been chief financial officer, becoming chief executive officer.

Coinmach Industries became The Coinmach Corp. in April 1995, at which time it acquired Solon Automated Services, which had about 174,000 washers and dryers in 18 states. Although Solon had lost money in every year since 1987, it received an offer of about $12.5 million from Coinmach for its stock. One consultant explained that Solon had heavy depreciation expenses but a positive cash flow to help pay for the capital to run the company and service its debt. He also suggested that Coinmach might be acquiring Solon to prevent a competitor from purchasing it. Solon lost $6.9 million in fiscal 1994 on revenues of $104.6 million. It was merged into Coinmach in November 1995.

The Coinmach Corp. became a public company, Coinmach Laundry Corp., in July 1996, when it sold more than 4 million shares of common stock at $14 a share. After redemption of $19.2 million worth of preferred stock, net proceeds from the offering came to about $35.3 million, before expenses. Following the offering Golder, Thoma, Cressey, Rauner Fund IV, L.P. retained 45.5 percent of the shares of common stock.

Coinmach purchased Allied Laundry Equipment Co. of St. Louis in April 1996 for $15.5 million in cash, adding about 24,000 machines in the Midwest to its market presence. In November 1996 Coinmach agreed to buy Kwik Wash Laundries L.P. for $140 million in cash and notes. Based in Dallas, Kwik Wash was serving multifamily housing properties primarily in Texas, Louisiana, Arkansas, and Oklahoma, and also was operating about 150 laundromats in Texas. The acquisition added about 74,000 machines to Coinmach's roster. Coinmach took out $200 million in loans and revolving credit concurrent to this purchase.

Coinmach acquired Atlanta Washer & Dryer Leasing, Inc. (doing business as Appliance Warehouse) in March 1997 for $6.3 million in cash and notes, thereby increasing its presence in the South by about 14,000 machines. This purchase also put Coinmach into the business of leasing laundry equipment and other household appliances to property owners or managers, corporate-relocation companies, and individuals. And in April 1997 the company acquired Reliable Holding Corp. of Glendale, California, for about $44 million in cash, thereby adding about 49,000 machines in California and the Tijuana, Mexico, metropolitan area to its base. In June 1997 Coinmach increased its previous $130-million term-loan facility by $60 million.

Coinmach had revenues of $178.8 million and a net loss of $17.6 million—half of it from early extinguishment of debt—in fiscal 1996 (ending March 29, 1996). During fiscal 1997 (ending March 28, 1997) it had revenues of $206.9 million and a net loss of $10.5 million. Its long-term debt was $345.5 million at the end of fiscal 1997, compared to $42.2 million at the end of 1994, before the adoption of its acquisition program.

Coinmach in 1997

Coinmach's core business continued to involve the leasing of laundry rooms from building owners and management companies, installing and servicing laundry equipment, and collecting revenues generated from laundry machines. The owner or property manager maintained the premises and provided utilities such as gas, electricity, and water. In return for the exclusive right to provide laundry-equipment services, most of Coinmach's leases stipulated monthly commission payments to the location owners, usually based on a percentage of the cash collected from the laundry machines. Many of the leases required Coinmach also to make advance rental payments to the location owners.

Coinmach was meeting about one-third of its anticipated machine-installation requirements by rebuilding and reinstalling some of its machines at about one-third the cost of buying new ones. A fleet of 314 radio-operated vehicles allowed the quick dispatch of service technicians in response to the approximately 2,200 service calls a day.

Through its Super Laundry Equipment Corp. subsidiary, Coinmach was constructing complete turnkey retail laundromats, retrofitting existing retail laundromats, distributing exclusive lines of commercial coin and non-coin machines and parts, and selling service contracts. The construction of laundromats and related equipment sales constituted about 90 percent of its revenues.

With the Kwik Wash acquisition, Coinmach became the operator of 150 retail laundromats throughout Texas, providing laundromat services at all such locations. As a result of the Atlanta Washer & Dryer Leasing acquisition, Coinmach became a lessor of laundry equipment and other household appliances to corporate relocation entities, individuals, property owners, and managers of multifamily housing properties.

Coinmach was leasing 26 regional offices and its executive offices in Roslyn, New York, in 1997. It also was maintaining three regional remanufacturing facilities. Of its revenues in fiscal 1997, the Northeast (New York, New Jersey, and Connecticut) accounted for 39 percent; the South-Central region for 30 percent; the Mid-Atlantic for 14 percent; the Southeast for 12 percent; and the Midwest for 5 percent.

Principal Subsidiaries

Automática SA de CV (Mexico); Coinmach Corporation; Coinmach Laundromat GP Corp.; Coinmach Laundromat LP Corp.; Coinmach Laundromat Holding, LP; Grand Wash & Dry Launderette, Inc.; Maquilados Automáticos SA de CV (Mexico); Super Laundry Equipment Corp.

Further Reading

Aregood, Chris, ''Laundry Business May Be Spinning Toward Buyer,'' *Philadelphia Business Journal,* March 3, 1995, p. 7.

Bowers, Brent, ''Jan Sussman Coins Way to Clean Up in Laundry Business,'' *Wall Street Journal,* July 9, 1990, p. B2.

''Clean Profits,'' *Success,* March 1994, p. 32.

''Coinmach to Acquire Kwik Wash for $140 Million,'' *New York Times,* November 26, 1996, p. D4.

''Coinmach Launches New Parts and Services Division, Offering Systems, Programs Operation Has Developed,'' *Vending Times,* November 1987, p. 13.

''Coinmach Tel Begins to Install Northwestern Bell Payphones in NY Area, Linked to Central Computer,'' *Vending Times,* June 1986, p. 13.

''Jan Sussman: Cleaning Up with High Technology,'' *LI Business News,* February 28, 1994, p. S25.

Mason-Draffen, Carrie, ''A Tale of Dirty Duds and Soapy Suds,'' *Newsday,* November 12, 1990, Sec. III, p. 5.

Peters, D.J., ''Dial Away Laundry Hassles,'' *New York Daily News,* August 30, 1993, Sec. 1, p. 22.

—Robert Halasz

Coles Myer Ltd.

800 Toorak Road
Tooronga
Victoria 3146
Australia
(03) 9829 3111
Fax: (03) 9829 6787
Web site: http://www.colesmyer.com.au

Public Company
Incorporated: 1921 as G.J. Coles and Coy. Pty. Ltd.
Employees: 150,000
Sales: A$18.18 billion (US$14.58 billion) (1996)
Stock Exchanges: London New York Australia New
    Zealand
SICs: 5311 Department Stores; 5399 Miscellaneous
    General Merchandise Stores; 5411 Grocery Stores;
    5621 Women's Clothing Stores; 5921 Liquor Stores;
    5945 Hobby, Toy & Game Stores; 5999
    Miscellaneous Retail Stores, Not Elsewhere Classified

Coles Myer Ltd. is Australia's leading retailer in terms of number of stores—more than 1,800—and selling area. The company owns and operates stores in most sectors of the Australian and New Zealand retail markets. Coles Myer operates a wide range of supermarkets (Coles, Bi-Lo), discount department stores (Kmart, Target, Fosseys), department stores (Myer, Grace Bros.), women's clothing stores (Katies), toy stores (World 4 Kids), liquor stores (Liquorland, Vintage Cellars), fast-food outlets (Red Rooster), and office supplies superstores (Officeworks). The company, Australia's largest private employer, holds the exclusive rights to the Kmart and Target names in Australia and New Zealand.

Founded as "3d., 6d., and 1/-" Variety Store

The origins of Coles Myer can be traced to the first G.J. Coles & Coy. Ltd. (Coles) discount store, opened in the working-class suburb of Collingwood, Victoria, on April 9, 1914.

The "3d., 6d., and 1/-" variety store was founded by George James Coles, who had studied U.S. and U.K. chainstore retailing methods.

In 1919 a much larger store was opened, again in Collingwood, with the slogan "Nothing over 2/6d." In 1921 the proprietary company G.J. Coles & Coy. Pty. Ltd. was formed, and in 1924 the company opened its first city store in Bourke Street, Melbourne. With eight stores to its name, G.J. Coles & Coy. Ltd. was floated on the Melbourne Stock Exchange in 1927. One year later the first out-of-state store was opened in Pitt Street, Sydney.

The 1930s were years of rapid expansion for the company, with Coles's variety stores being represented in all states of Australia by 1933. A strong commitment to offering affordable goods to all sectors of the community meant that Coles continued to expand despite the Great Depression. Managing director A. W. Coles wrote at this time, "A store has no right to success just because it is open for business and has a bright display. The goods must reflect the wishes of the community in which the store is located." In 1938 inflation forced the "Nothing over 2/6" policy to be abandoned. A promise of "Satisfaction Guaranteed or Money Cheerfully Refunded" was instituted and continues today.

The outbreak of war in 1939 led to severe merchandise shortages, and 95 percent of Coles's male staff enlisted. Despite problems, the company survived with the assistance of newly promoted female managers under the leadership of A. W. Coles, who acted as managing director until 1944. His successor and brother, E. B. Coles, then led the company into another period of expansion that would earn him the title "The Takeover King." Major retailers acquired in this phase included Selfridges Ltd. in New South Wales in 1950, F&G Stores Ltd. in Victoria in 1951, and the Queensland chain of Penneys Ltd. in 1956.

Entered Food Retailing in Late 1950s

Food retailing was the next significant area to be explored by the company. This began in 1958 with the acquisition of the John Connell Dickins Pty. Ltd. group of 54 grocery stores. The link with supermarket retailing was reinforced in 1959 by the purchase of Beilby's in South Australia and again in 1960 by the acquisition of the Matthews Thompson chain of 265 grocery stores in New South Wales.

In 1962 customers were treated to a "New World of Shopping" with the opening of the first New World supermarket in Frankston, Victoria. This was a new concept in food retailing for Australia—selling groceries, fresh meat, fruit and vegetables, dairy goods, produce, and frozen foods all within one store. Coles New World Supermarkets offered customers more choice, greater savings, and a consistently higher standard of quality than ever before. Coles, in fact, was one of the first Australian retailers to take advantage of the customer trend toward supermarkets—a move that would earn the company a net profit increase of 30.7 percent and a jump in annual sales of £83 million in the first year.

Discount Stores Added in Late 1960s

Following this success, the company then ventured into discount stores. This began in 1968 with the opening of Colmart in Whyalla, South Australia—Coles's first major discount store. That same year, the company entered a joint venture with the U.S. company S.S. Kresge—now Kmart Corporation—to open Kmart discount stores in Australia, with Coles holding a 49 percent interest. The first Kmart store was opened in April 1969 at East Burwood, Victoria, introducing the concept of U.S. discount department stores to Australia. The sales performance of these stores surpassed those of many established retailers and Kmart soon became a significant force in Australian retailing. In the same year as Kmart's launch, the Coles New World Supermarket chain opened its 100th store and became Australia-wide with the unveiling of a store in Freemantle, Western Australia.

In 1977 Sir George Coles, the company's founder, died at the age of 92, having served the company for over 62 years. Continuing a long tradition of positive employee relations, Coles introduced equal benefits for male and female staff in the company's medical scheme and staff superannuation fund. The retirement age for females was extended to 60 years, and the number of staff members who had served the company for more than 25 years exceeded 1,000. The balance of the Kmart joint venture was acquired by the company in December 1978, making it a wholly owned subsidiary of Coles and making the company the second-largest employer in Australia, with more than 50,000 employees.

Further Diversification in the Early 1980s

The 1980s saw Coles diversify still further. In July 1981, 54 liquor stores operating as Claude Fay Cellars were acquired for cash. In August of the same year, 14 Liquorland stores and the Mac the Slasher liquor chain were purchased. The following year the name Liquorland was extended to cover all company liquor stores around Australia. These comprised Australia's largest nonbrewery chain. Coles entered the footwear business when Edward Fay Pty. Ltd. and Ezywalkin were purchased in 1981. Due to unsatisfactory results, however, the company divested itself of these in 1988.

In 1982 Coles opened Australia's first hypermarket, Super Kmart, the name used for combined Kmart and grocery stores until 1989, using the pooled resources and skills of the established Kmart business and Coles supermarkets. Many of the Super Kmarts that opened included automotive sections under the name K Auto, which were first established in 1961. They sold an extensive range of automotive accessories and parts, and offered full servicing and maintenance to fleet and private vehicle operators.

Women's clothing retailing was the next area of investment for Coles with the acquisition of the Katies Fashion (Australia) Pty. Ltd. (Katies) national chain of 117 specialty stores in November 1984 for A$47 million. At the time of purchase, Katies had an established reputation for quality women's fashions at competitive prices. Contrary to the usually high level of imported merchandise in the Australian clothing and textile area, Katies consistently offered a large proportion of domestically produced goods, with over 90 percent of garments for the 1987 summer season being made in Australia. In the same year, the 100th Kmart store opened in Campbelltown, New South Wales, and net profit for the company exceeded A$100 million for the first time.

Merged with Myer Emporium in 1985 to Form Coles Myer Ltd.

In 1985 the Coles Myer Ltd. organization was born, after a merger proposal was accepted by Myer Emporium Ltd. (Myer), a Melbourne-based retailer. Myer, the third largest retail group in Australia, was acquired through an agreed bid for a total cash offer of A$918 million.

Myer Emporium Ltd., which had been operating since 1901, strengthened its position in 1983 as the major department store retailer in Australia by purchasing Grace Bros., the largest department store retailer in New South Wales, for A$213 million. This was bought along with Boans, the largest Western Australian department store operator, for A$39.2 million. Prior to the merger, Myer was Australia's number one department store chain and the country's third-largest retailer.

The 1985 Myer merger brought in 56 department stores, 68 Target discount stores, 122 Fosseys discount variety stores, the Country Road chain of 45 stores which was subsequently sold for a profit of A$33.27 million, and the Red Rooster chain of fast-food chicken outlets. The name of the company was changed to Coles Myer Ltd. on January 27, 1986, and a new corporate symbol was adopted. In addition, a new company structure consisting of five divisions—Discount Stores; Supermarkets, Food and Liquor; Grace Bros.; Myer Stores; and Specialty Stores—was introduced at this time.

Coles Myer continued to grow and consolidate existing interests. In May 1986, 52 stores were added to the Red Rooster chain, making it the second largest take-out chicken restaurant chain and the largest Australian-owned fast-food group. In the same year the administrative structures of Coles and Fosseys amalgamated into a single business to become a market leader in the discount variety store segment. The ranges in both stores were rationalized to concentrate on their strong positions in budget clothing, toiletries, toys, fancy goods, and confectionery.

In 1987 the company's shares were listed on the London Stock Exchange, and a new corporate headquarters was officially opened at Tooronga, Victoria, by Prime Minister R. J. L. Hawke. A revised management structure requiring group managers to report to the managing director of retail operations led to strong growth during the year. Also in 1987 the company entered the discount food retailing field with the purchase of the Bi-Lo Supermarket chain. Originally from South Australia, Bi-Lo stores were known for doing business in relatively small sites with discount prices and cut-case displays, whereby goods are stacked in supermarket aisles in cardboard boxes that can be cut open for customers to help themselves directly. This keeps store overheads to a minimum. The company's expansion into discount food retailing continued the following year with the A$31.55 million acquisition of the Shoey's chain of budget food markets in New South Wales, adding 40 stores to the group. The company's discount food division, which was managed independently from the New World chain, now included both the Bi-Lo chain and the Shoey's group as well as a number of converted former New World stores.

In July 1987 Coles Myer acquired Charlton Feedlot Pty Ltd., a dairy and beef producing operation that supplied premium produce to Coles Myer's supermarket business.

Coles Myer made its first move overseas with the acquisition of Progressive Enterprises Limited in New Zealand in May 1988. This included 27 Foodtown premium supermarkets, 22 3 Guys discount supermarkets, and Georgie Pie family restaurants. The first Kmart discount store opened in New Zealand in October of the same year.

In October 1988 Coles Myer was listed on the New York Stock Exchange. During 1987–88, the company established Coles Myer/Ansett Travel Pty. Ltd. (CMAT), a joint venture

with Ansett Transport Industries Ltd., to manage retail travel centers located in company stores. In 1990 CMAT acquired the travel business of the ANZ Bank Ltd. Electronic funds transfer at the point of sale was introduced to all Coles Myer stores as part of the development of electronic scanning cash registers and other point-of-sale register systems to improve efficiency in 1989. In mid-1989, as part of a decision to concentrate on core businesses, the company sold its 25 percent minority stake in Bank of America Australia Ltd. to the bank's U.S. parent, BankAmerica Corporation. Also in 1989, Myer Stores launched Myer Direct, a mail order business. That same year, use of the Super Kmart name was discontinued.

Troubled Times in the 1990s

The 1990s were a difficult period for Coles Myer, as sales and profits stagnated as a result of a recession which hit nonfood sectors particularly hard. The company subsequently endured battles with institutional investors over corporate governance, specifically relating to Solomon Lew and Brian Quinn.

In November 1991 Lew, who held a more than 10 percent stake in Coles Myer, was elected chairman of the board, following Quinn's decision to relinquish the chairmanship and concentrate on his role as chief executive officer. Quinn then retired as CEO the following year, with Peter Bartels replacing him. In 1994 Quinn was charged with defrauding Coles of A$4.46 million (US$3.5 million), alleging that he had billed the company for work done to revamp his private home. Quinn was found guilty in 1997 and sentenced to four years in jail.

Lew came into the spotlight following accusations that companies associated with him had benefited from his board positions with Coles Myer. When institutional investor opposition to the board's composition came to a head in 1995, Lew stepped down to become vice-chairman and Nobby Clark, who had overseen the restructuring of Foster's Brewing Company, was brought in as new chairman. Additional changes followed, including the January 1997 appointment of Dennis Eck as CEO, replacing Bartels, and the July 1997 appointment of Stan Wallis as chairman, replacing Clark.

As these management controversies and changes were playing themselves out, Coles Myer made a number of significant changes to its corporate structure and mix of operations. As of August 1, 1990, the administrative and buying functions of the Myer Stores and Grace Bros. businesses were merged to form the Department Stores Group. While each group continued to operate under the separate Myer and Grace Bros. names, the move resulted in significant gains from overhead reductions and economies in buying and sales promotion.

In April 1991 Coles New World Supermarkets changed their name to Coles Supermarkets, together with the launch of a new visual identity and customer service programs. Later that year Coles reduced the prices of 6,000 product lines as part of a new pricing and advertising policy.

In 1992, the company spun off Progressive Enterprises onto the New Zealand stock exchange, significantly reducing its foreign operations. That same year, Coles Myer acquired 98 Big Rooster fast-food outlets and bolstered its liquor store holdings with the purchase of the Vintage Cellars chain from Magnum

Australia Pty. Ltd. The following year, Grocery Holdings Pty. Ltd. was established as a grocery wholesaling service for the Coles and Bi-Lo supermarket chains. Coles Myer added two more concepts to its assortment of retail outlets with the 1993 launches of World 4 Kids toy and leisure superstores and Officeworks, a discount warehouse-style office supplies superstore. In August 1993 Coles Myer announced that it would launch a A$4.15 billion (US$2.8 billion), five-year investment program, which would include 421 new stores, 1,136 store remodelings, and the expansion or construction of more than 12 major shopping centers.

In November 1994 the company bought back from Kmart Corporation the 147.8 million shares of Coles Myer stock that Kmart held. That same month, Coles Myer began a multiyear divestment program in relation to the company's property portfolio. Through early 1997, A$1.25 billion worth of property had been disposed of, allowing the company to concentrate more closely on its core business of retailing. Meanwhile, the retail businesses were reorganized into three groups: Basic Needs, which included the supermarkets, liquor stores, Red Rooster, Kmart, World 4 Kids, and Officeworks; Apparel Group, which consisted of Target, Fosseys, and Katies; and Department Stores. Under the new structure, the company hoped to better integrate groupwide services, thereby eliminating duplication and cutting costs.

The Coles Myer of the late 1990s was a much more streamlined and focused company than that of just a few years previous. Though still considered by some observers as too large for the relatively small Australian market, the company had rejected the idea of breaking up into separately listed operating units after an early 1996 investigation. With corporate governance controversies seemingly put to rest, Coles Myer seemed well-positioned for a significant turnaround in its fortunes.

Principal Subsidiaries

Amalgamated Food and Poultry Pty. Ltd.; Bi-Lo Pty. Ltd.; Coles Myer Finance Ltd.; Coles Myer International Pty. Ltd.; Coles Myer Properties Holdings Ltd.; Fosseys (Australia) Pty. Ltd.; Grocery Holdings Pty. Ltd.; Katies Fashions (Aust.) Pty. Ltd; Kmart Australia Ltd.; Liquorland (Australia) Pty. Ltd.; Myer Stores Ltd.; Officeworks Superstores Pty. Ltd.; Target Australia Pty. Ltd.; Tyremaster Pty. Ltd.; W4K.World 4 Kids Ltd.

Principal Operating Units

Basic Needs Group; Apparel Group; Department Stores; Coles Myer Properties.

Further Reading

"Coles Myer Ltd.: A Brief History of the Company," Victoria: Coles Myer Ltd., 1997.

McLaughlin, Judith, *Nothing over Half a Crown: A Personal History of the Founder of the G. J. Coles Stores,* Victoria: Loch Haven Books, 1991.

"Myer Chronology," Victoria: Coles Myer Ltd., 1996.

"The Story So Far—Coles Myer Ltd.," Victoria: Coles Myer Ltd., 1989.

Tait, Nikki, "Coles Myer Saga Enters Its Final Throes," *Financial Times,* October 18, 1995, p. 30.

——, "Coles Myer Rejects Break-Up Idea," *Financial Times,* March 6, 1996, p. 26.

—Julia Roberts
—updated by David E. Salamie

The Cooker Restaurant Corporation

5500 Village Blvd.
West Palm Beach, Florida 33407
U.S.A.
(407) 615-6000
Fax: (407) 615-6001

Public Company
Incorporated: 1986 as Cooker Bar and Grille
Employees: 4950
Sales: $110.3 million (1996)
Stock Exchanges: New York
SICs: 5812 Eating Places

The Cooker Restaurant Corporation is a 52-unit casual dining restaurant chain, with locations in Florida, Indiana, Kentucky, Maryland, Michigan, North Carolina, Ohio, Tennessee, and Virginia. Revenues per restaurant average almost $3 million annually, which establishes it among the highest for casual full-service restaurants. In 1996 the company served over ten million meals and net income reached a $100 million-plus milestone, gaining 52 percent over the previous year's revenues. Competing with chains such as T.G.I. Friday's, Chili's, and Applebee's, Cooker has grown from two to 52 locations in just 12 years, despite the economic recession of the early 1990s. The company has plans for further expansion into new market areas.

Traditional Fare in the Mid-1980s

In 1984, The Cooker Restaurant Corporation was founded in Nashville, Tennessee, by chairman and CEO G. Arthur Seelbinder, a former Wendy's franchisee, along with three others, Phil Hickey, Jerry Hornbeck, and trained chef Glenn Cockburn. Cockburn, a graduate of the Culinary Institute of America, who became director and senior vice president of operations for the company, created most of the items on the Cooker menu. Cockburn developed the home-style recipes including pot roast, lasagna, soups, meatloaf, fish, steaks, sandwiches, hamburgers, ribs, and chicken—all made from scratch—for their restaurants. Cooker varied its menu with a wide assortment of salads and

vegetables, but originally set its sites on offering heartier fare with the intention of competing with the leaner menus served in trendier restaurants. They began by offering traditional dining at a moderate price, averaging $8.75 per meal, with items on the children's menu for $2.50.

In the spring of 1989, an initial public offering raised over $12 million which was earmarked for paying off bank debt, with the balance intended for expansion costs. Within months of the offering, Seelbinder assumed the duties of Cooker President after a failed buyout attempt by then-president Philip J. Hickey Jr. (who held a 5 percent stake in the company), and an outside group. Rajan Chaudhry reported in *Restaurant News* that "the buy-out proposal called for the resignations of Seelbinder and all other company directors, except Hickey .... In June, Cooker [had begun] trading over the counter, and analysts [were] puzzled by the timing of the bid." The *Wall Street Journal* quoted Seelbinder (who owned 16 percent of the company), saying that there were "differences over control of the company," and long-term strategy. Hickey resigned from the company's board after a severance agreement was completed wherein Cooker's employee stock ownership plan bought out 1.1 million shares of the company's stock at $3.25 per share. Half of the shares were purchased from Hickey, with the remaining shares purchased from Gerald A. Hornbeck, who then resigned as Cooker vice president of development and became a company consultant. Both agreed to a five-year relinquishment of interest in Cooker, and entered into non competition agreements including the stipulation that they not participate in any proxy fight for the company. Speculation over the "management void" led to uncertainty concerning the future of the company, and analysts downgraded investment opinions. Cooker argued that despite the loss of its operations director, they maintained a strong management team capable of competent leadership.

Under New Leadership—The Early 1990s

New restaurant openings and lower pricing accounted for a 17 percent increase in 1991 sales, attracting notice from Wall Street. The company's stock price increased more than 300 percent, followed by two splits. Management attributed acceler-

---

Company Perspectives:

Our mission is to be a consistently profitable, fast growing, full services restaurant company offering guests a superior dining experience.

---

ated earnings on efforts to trim labor expenses and the savings gained in efficiency afforded by the chain's expansion. Cooker experimented with scheduling and profit margins, and concluded that by cutting labor in non-peak hours, service was not compromised. With labor costs at 34 percent of profits, they were considered high for the industry, but remained committed for the time to its strategy of providing exemplary service. At the administrative level, they found that with new stores opening, no new corporate staffers were needed to handle the higher percentage of sales.

In an effort to increase customer frequency, several value-priced items were added to the menu, including Caesar salad, grilled tuna Caesar salad, and an assortment of sandwiches. Obtaining a full liquor license resulted in boosted earnings that accounted for 14 percent of sales. Cooker's policy was to offer a money-back, satisfaction guarantee, or to give away free meals if customers were dissatisfied. In 1992 Cooker gave away $750,000 in free meals to back up the guarantee, and justified that expense as a positive advertising strategy.

By 1993, despite sluggish same-store sales trends, the company optimistically moved ahead with its restaurant expansion drive, concentrating six new locations in its already established regions, with plans for an additional 25 to 35 openings within the following five years. Eight to ten new restaurants were scheduled to open the next year in the cities of Ann Arbor, Cincinnati, and Columbus. Cooker decided that it needed to aggressively compete with other casual dining restaurants such as Applebee's, Chili's, and Lone Star Steakhouse that were moving into the upper Midwestern region. By the fourth quarter, company officials admitted that the timing of the new stores was off, and the corporation had stretched itself too thin. In its haste to expand, Cooker purchased some unprofitable real estate. Officials admitted that the goal of 50 percent growth was unreasonable, determining that 20 to 25 percent would have been more realistic. The company completed a $23 million convertible debenture offering to finance the openings and to make improvements in existing locations. A company official told Rebecca Walters of *Business First* that "The combined effects of lower sales and higher operating expense related to Cooker's expansion program caused the decline in earnings." But another official told Walters that the new units were placed in new market areas that were not performing to expectations. Walters reported that also affecting earnings was the "one-time, non-cash charge of between $800,000 and $900,000 to cover operating expenses for new store openings from 1991 through 1993." With approximately $200,000 needed to open a new store the company planned to pay off future store openings in 12 rather than 36 months. Walters explained that costs that remained from 1991 and 1992 would be paid off concurrently with 1993's pre-opening costs, effecting a write-off that would

help future earnings. The short-term effect of the company's too-rapid expansion into untried regions was reflected in decreased earnings, causing its stock to sink to a new low. The company then began buying back Cooker stock, paying about $6 million for 500,000 common shares, feeling that the lower stock price did not reflect the company's actual value. Officials reasoned that by decreasing the available stock, earnings per share would increase as profits were spread over a smaller number of shares, and confidence would be restored. The company also blamed the decline in earnings on higher labor costs and severe weather in the majority of its markets, which caused several units to close due to power outages.

Glen Cockburn explained to Marjorie Coeyman of *Restaurant Business*, that the company "started as a mom-and-pop kind of place. It was casual and homey, but it wasn't attracting the kind of clientele we wanted. It wasn't profitable enough." Pricing was too low, management thought, and its valued servers were leaving because their tips were based on checks averaging less than $9. The company instituted a more upscale menu and interior appearance. Explained Cockburn, "Low-voltage lighting replaced the warmer, pink lights of earlier units. Old-fashioned black-and-white photos aimed at evoking a cheerful, nostalgic tone gave way to starker art photos of, for instance, a lone tomato. Customers didn't like it. They looked at it and said, 'That looks too expensive,' " he said. As a result Cooker got burned by going too upscale, which alienated former customers.

New Recipes For Mid-1990s Growth

The company made changes in its 1994 development schedule, following a 52 percent plunge in profits, and targeted only six new sites for the year from its previous target of 12 stores. Cooker began a retraining effort for management and serving staff in an attempt to restore service standards and levels of ambiance which had faltered following cost cuts. "We've had to retool a bit," Glenn Cockburn told Bill Carlino of *Nation's Restaurant News*. He continued, "But we've had tough times before. You can say we've recommitted ourselves to the basics." The marketing team spent more than $100,000 on a radio and print campaign, deviating from the previous word-of-mouth-only promotional strategy, and introduced a new menu. Then in November, Cooker began organizing a new management team beginning with the selection of General Mills's China Coast Division operations vice president, Philip L. Pritchard, as the new company president, a newly created position. He had been a Dardon's Red Lobster Restaurant Executive VP from 1986 to 1992, and was credited with successfully implementing their rapid growth before moving to General Mills where he worked until taking the Cooker position. His strengths earned him a reputation as a manager who could handle aggressive expansion. A new human resources director, Jeff Karla, was recruited from McDonald's, and Dave Sevig became CFO, leaving his controller's post at Red Lobster. A new director of real estate was also hired to seek out new Cooker sites, relieving Seelbinder from that additional responsibility. The year 1995 also marked Cooker's move from Ohio to its new headquarters in Palm Beach, Florida, home to many of Cooker's executives—a southeastern region targeted for new expansion. The company continues to operate its headquarters in the areas it wishes to penetrate. Cooker bought the 32,000-square-foot building out of foreclosure for $1.9 million, a considerable bargain price for the area.

The company continued in its efforts to refinance its debt in order to strengthen existing operations. Finally, by the second quarter of 1995, Cooker managed to increase net revenues 8.9 percent over that earned in the previous comparable quarter, despite rising general and administrative costs. The company's reliance on attentive service and fresh ingredients came at a high price and Pritchard trimmed food costs through pre-portioning with vendors, and encouraged servers to promote appetizers and desserts, which provided healthier profit margins. He maintained that Cooker should still set itself apart from other casual dining restaurants by staffing for heavier traffic than the competition might employ, justifying the tactic of one-on-one advertising to increase the customer base by impressing diners with heightened service and quality levels. Cooker cut managers, who can earn over $85,000 including bonuses, from 8.3 per store down to 5.8, basing numbers of managers on store volume, which led to an average reduction of three managers per unit.

Cooker concentrated efforts on selecting sites in close proximity to office and retail centers. The company's expansion plans also continued to involve the opening of new restaurants in regions where Cooker restaurants already existed. The new operational strategy soon paid off. The company acquired six former China Coast Restaurants from Darden Restaurants, Inc. (owners of Olive Garden Italian Restaurants) with the intention of converting them to the Cooker concept in the areas of Saginaw and Grand Rapids, Michigan; Cincinnati, Chesapeake, Virginia; and Tampa, Florida. Eleven new Cooker restaurants opened in 1996—showing strong performance—and plans were implemented for the opening of another dozen or so by the end of fiscal 1997. According to an interview in *Financial News* with Nashville analyst Jonathan Ruykhaver, "Not only have they [Cooker] gotten preopening expenses and labor costs down, but they're continuing to improve unit volumes, and every extra sales dollar on top helps those margins." Net income for 1995 rose 49 percent from the previous year's performance and grew another 52 percent in 1996. That performance attracted investors to Cooker's secondary offering, which raised $34.7 million for the chain. After paying off its $29 million credit line (leaving approximately $15 million in outstanding debt), the remainder would fund further unit develop-

ment, along with another $10 million or so from cash flow. The company entered two new markets: Johnson City, Tennessee, and Boardman Township (Youngstown), Ohio, and closed one underperforming unit. Cooker Restaurants felt the impact of decreased sales for awhile, which were blamed in part on consumer focus on the Olympics. Dinner-oriented businesses were mainly affected, although successes at new Cooker unit openings offset its losses.

In July 1996, with restaurant stocks again slipping, Cooker president Pritchard increased his stock holdings to approximately 2 percent of Cooker's outstanding stock, indicating an insider vote of confidence in the company, and a move inconsistent with the trend away from investing in the consumer product sector. Mr. Pritchard told a *Wall Street Journal* reporter: "I put my money where my mouth is." With Cooker's steady growth commitment—and gains of over 20 percent in sales over 1995 figures, his diet appears more than ample.

Further Reading

Carlino, Bill, "Cooker Targets Unit-Level Basics to Rejuvenate Sales," *Nation's Restaurant News*, August 29, 1994, p. 3.

Chaudhry, Rajan, "Cooker President Exists After Failed Buyout Try," *Nation's Restaurant News*, October 2, 1989, p. 4.

Coeyman, Marjorie, "Slow Down," *Restaurant Business*, November 1, 1995, p. 28.

"Cooker Restaurant Corporation," *Business First—Columbus,* July 13, 1992, p. 27.

"Cooker Restaurant's President Is Replaced After Fight for Control," *The Wall Street Journal*, September 19, 1989, p. B18.

Hayes, Jack, "Cooker Uses Backfilling Strategy to Step Up Expansion," *Financial News*, June 3, 1996, p. 11.

Keegan, Peter O., "Cooker Trims the Fat, Boosts Earnings Growth," *Nation's Restaurant News*, August 12, 1991, p. 14.

Labate, John, "Cooker Restaurants," *Fortune*, June 28, 1993, p. 107.

Tippett, Karen L., "This Time Around, Cooker's Plans for Growth Look More Palatable," *The Wall Street Journal*, September 4, 1996.

Walkup, Carolyn, "Cooker Eyes Regional Push After Strong Second Quarter," *Nation's Restaurant News,* September 20, 1993, p. 18.

Walters, Rebecca, "Cooker Will Keep Growing, But More Cautiously, *Business First—Columbus,* January 24, 1994, p. 12.

Waresh, Julie, "Cooking Up Expansion," *Palm Beach Post,* April 6, 1997, p. 1F & 3F.

"When More Is More," *Restaurant Business*, March 1, 1997, p. 10.

—Terri Mozzone-Burgman

Cooper Cameron Corporation

515 Post Oak Boulevard
Suite 1200
Houston, Texas 77027
U.S.A.
(713) 513-3300
Web site: www.coopercameron.com

Public Company
Incorporated: 1895 as the C. & G. Cooper Company
Employees: 8,500
Sales: $1.4 billion (1996)
Stock Exchanges: New York
SICs: 1381 Drilling Oil and Gas Wells; 4925 Gas
    Production

Cooper Cameron Corporation is a diversified, international manufacturing company divided into two main segments: compression/power equipment and petroleum production equipment. To protect itself from the highly cyclical nature of the energy industry, Cooper Cameron, then operating as the privately held Cooper Industries, embarked in the mid-1960s on an aggressive program of acquiring manufacturing companies with high growth potential and reputations for high quality. In 1995, the company held its initial public offering and reorganized. While the company has proved itself expert at acquiring and managing low-technology companies, it does not hesitate to use high-technology equipment and production methods as well as sophisticated accounting, inventory, and quality-control techniques to streamline operations and maximize earnings.

Ohio Origins

Brothers Charles and Elias Cooper built a foundry in their hometown of Mount Vernon, Ohio, and called it the Mt. Vernon Iron Works. Soon better known as C. & E. Cooper Company, their first products were plows, maple syrup kettles, hog troughs, sorghum grinders, and wagon boxes. Charles Cooper was the stronger leader. Aggressively anti-slavery and a dedicated prohibitionist, he became a respected community leader, even though many of his views differed greatly from those of his neighbors. When Elias Cooper died in 1848, Charles Cooper

took a succession of partners, and with each the company name changed accordingly.

Mount Vernon was linked to the rest of the nation by the railroad in 1851 and the following year Cooper was able to ship its first steam-powered compressors for blast furnaces. Cooper's relationship with the railroad had its difficulties, however. When the Sandusky, Mansfield, and Newark Railway was delinquent in paying for woodburning locomotives from the company, Charles Cooper was driven to chain the wheels of a locomotive to the track, padlock it, and stand sentry until he was paid in full.

By the time of the Civil War, Cooper products included wood-burning steam locomotives and steam-powered blowing machines for charcoal blast furnaces. After Charles Gray Cooper, son of Elias, served in the Union army and attended Rensselaer Institute, he became a partner with his uncle.

Post-Civil War Development

In 1869 Cooper became the first company in what was then the West to produce the new, highly efficient Corliss engine. Six years later, it offered the Cooper traction engine, America's first farm tractor. Throughout the rest of the century, the Corliss engine was Cooper's principal product.

The company was incorporated as the C. & G. Cooper Company in 1895, and Frank L. Fairchild, a respected salesman of the Cooper-Corliss engine, was named its first president. Fairchild so enjoyed selling that throughout his 17-year presidency he continued to serve as sales manager.

By 1900 gas was being discovered in new fields and shipped more than 100 miles through primitive pipelines. At the same time, the oil industry was also beginning to develop. Not long after Charles Cooper's death in 1901, it became clear that steam turbine engines were destined to replace the Corliss engine. Cooper management recognized the necessity of focusing on a small segment of the market, and in 1908 it wisely chose to make a gradual change to natural-gas internal-combustion engines, which were being used successfully at the compression stage of pipeline transmission.

162

Fairchild died suddenly in 1912 and Charles Gray (C. G.) Cooper, took his place. One story describes C. G.'s famous bluntness particularly well: C. G. once visited a procrastinating client and without any preliminary niceties asked, "Do you want to buy a steam engine?" The man said he did not want one just then. "All right, then you can go to hell," C. G. said and stormed out abruptly.

From Steam to Gas, Transition Following World War I

During World War I, Cooper built high-speed steam-hydraulic forging presses for government arsenals, munitions plants, and shipyards, as well as giant gas engines and compressors and triple-expansion marine engines. The company's wartime production demands slowed its transformation from a producer of steam to gas engines, since steam engines were needed for the war effort. But after the war, it became clear that the company had chosen its direction wisely when it set its sights on developing gas internal-combustion engines. The old Corliss was quickly becoming outmoded by competition from steam turbines and gas-powered engines.

In 1919 C. G. Cooper became chairman and Desault B. Kirk, the company's treasurer, became president. Just a year later, Cooper began a long-range program for growth, and the directors elected Beatty B. Williams president. Although he'd married the boss's daughter, few credited Williams's rise to simply marrying into the family. Serving as vice president and general manager during the war years, Williams was singleminded in his dedication to the company's success and directed Cooper (and subsequently Cooper-Bessemer) with great energy and foresight for 22 years. Always mindful of what he called "an aloofness" that could develop between office and factory workers, Williams held conferences in which factory workers were invited to air their views and offered evening courses in production and management in which any employee could enroll.

Natural gas was gaining growing importance in the manufacture of steel and glass and in the emerging petrochemical industry. Cooper field service engineers were often on hand for months at a time to oversee the installation of huge four-cycle Cooper engines and compressors in compressor stations as new pipelines were routed through West Virginia, Louisiana, Arkansas, Oklahoma, and Texas.

Within just a few years, Cooper became the country's leading producer of pipeline compression engines. Although Cooper also produced smaller two-cylinder engines used in natural-gas fields to extract gas as it came from the well, the Bessemer Gas Engine Company of Grove City, Pennsylvania, dominated that field.

Founded in 1897, Bessemer had produced oil-pumping engines for most of its existence and had invested heavily in diesel engine development during the 1920s. While Cooper and Bessemer had some product overlap, their major strengths were in different areas.

By 1929 Cooper needed additional production facilities to meet the mounting orders for large natural-gas engine compressor units. Bessemer, after its lengthy period of diesel development, badly needed new capital. Both companies had posted nearly identical average earnings for the previous three years. The companies negotiated a merger for several months, and the Cooper-Bessemer Corporation came into being in April 1929. The merger made the company the largest builder of gas engines and compressors in the United States. Soon afterward it was listed on the American Stock Exchange.

Cooper-Bessemer's business boom was brief. The company continued the Bessemer line of diesel marine engines, and since most ships were built or converted on the East Coast, Cooper-Bessemer soon decided to open a sales office in New York. The office was opened on October 23, 1929, however, at the very beginning of the Great Depression.

Depression and Recovery, the 1930s

Two years later, annual sales had dropped more than 90 percent, reflecting the almost total halt of construction on long-distance pipelines and in American shipyards. Half of all sales that year were for repair parts. Along with thousands of other American companies, Cooper-Bessemer was forced to lay off workers.

Cooper-Bessemer slowly revived in the middle and late 1930s by continuing to improve products and by entering new markets. The company was convinced that the diesel would replace steam-powered railroad engines and it developed one for the new market.

World War II Production Spurs Growth

Charles B. Jahnke was elected president in 1940 and Williams moved to chairman of the board, but Jahnke died a year later and Williams returned to the presidency for two more years. Only when Cooper-Bessemer embarked on a wartime production schedule in 1941 did its sales figures surpass their pre-Depression level. The company had sold engines to several branches of the military before the war and was thus in a favored position to receive large orders during World War II. It became a major producer of diesel engines for military vessels of all kinds and also increased production of locomotive engines. At the peak of its wartime production, Cooper-Bessemer had 4,337 employees working in round-the-clock shifts.

In 1941 Cooper-Bessemer's net sales jumped to an all-time high, and just two years later they had more than tripled. The company was listed for the first time on the New York Stock Exchange in 1944.

Gordon Lefebvre was elected company president in 1943. He had previously served as vice-president and general manager. Formerly the head of General Motors's Pontiac division, he had a background in engineering and was energetic, likable, and a tough negotiator.

After World War II, Cooper-Bessemer became increasingly interested in selling its products worldwide. It formed an international sales office and announced its first sales-service branch outside the United States, in Caracas, Venezuela, in 1945. Later in the decade, it expanded warehouse facilities in Canada and established a subsidiary sales unit, Cooper-Bessemer of Canada, with three offices, and received its first postwar orders from the Soviet Union.

Cooper-Bessemer had developed its innovative "turbo flow" high-compression gas-diesel engine in 1945, and two years later it introduced the GMW engine, which delivered 2,500 horsepower and could be shipped in one assembled unit. In these postwar years Cooper officials began to discuss diversification, which Lefebvre defined as "finding new markets for old products and new products for old markets, rather than moving into fields with which we are not familiar."

In 1951 Cooper-Bessemer's sales of $52 million surpassed its wartime high by nearly $10 million. Business that year was boosted by the Korean War; company shipments were almost solely to markets supported by the war effort, such as the petroleum, aluminum, chemical, and railroad industries.

Strike—Takeover Attempt— New Leadership, the 1950s

A combination of internal and external circumstances in 1954 led to a startling 38 percent decrease in net sales and Cooper-Bessemer's first net loss since 1938. The company's problems included a seven-week strike at the Grove City plant and a nationwide recession, but the main difficulty was the U.S. Supreme Court's decision in the Phillips Petroleum case, which ruled that producers selling gas to interstate pipelines had to submit to the Federal Power Commission's jurisdiction. This decision produced upheaval and uncertainty among pipeline operators, and therefore for Cooper-Bessemer.

While the company was rebuffing a 1955 takeover attempt by a private investor named Robert New, Lefebvre resigned unexpectedly, and Lawrence Williams, Beatty Williams's son, became president. He served beside his father, who was chairman of the board. Lawrence Williams had already served the company in many capacities and had taken early retirement to pursue other interests; he considered his return a temporary one. The takeover attempt had shaken management. In an attempt to bring an infusion of young talent to the company, Williams made a number of top management changes, including elevating Eugene L. Miller to chief operating officer. Due to revitalized demand, sales bounced back in 1956 to a record high of $61.2 million, but it was becoming increasingly clear that Cooper-Bessemer needed to diversify in order to avoid the cyclical pitfalls of energy-related manufacturing.

In 1957 Gene Miller was elected president. At 38, he was the youngest man to hold the position since the company's original founder. Miller had begun at Cooper-Bessemer in 1946. A year

after he became president, the company acquired Rotor Tool Company of Cleveland, the makers of pneumatic and high-cycle electric portable tools.

Over the next few years Cooper-Bessemer struggled to develop an engine to meet the challenge of General Electric's new combustion gas turbine engine, which threatened to supplant several of Cooper's engines in the pipeline transmission market. Its efforts resulted in the world's first industrial jet-powered gas turbine, introduced in 1960.

Under Miller's leadership, the distinction between Cooper-Bessemer administrative and operational management grew more pronounced, as was happening in companies throughout the country. Innovations such as computerization, fluctuations in worldwide monetary exchanges, increased government controls, and changing tax structures had made operating a large business increasingly complicated. In recognition of this, Miller moved the corporate offices from the Mount Vernon plant to offices on the city square to "establish a corporate group capable of administering many relatively independent divisions."

Meanwhile, Cooper-Bessemer's international division was also growing. By the end of the 1950s Cooper had sales agents in 10 countries, licensees in three, and franchises in two. In 1964 it opened an office in Beirut and also formed a wholly owned British subsidiary, Cooper-Bessemer (U.K.), Ltd.

Cooper-Bessemer was no exception to the trend toward large conglomerates during the 1960s, but it did try to limit its acquisitions to those that could be mutually beneficial. In the early 1960s, it acquired Kline Manufacturing, a producer of high-pressure hydraulic pumps; Ajax Iron Works, which built gas engine compressors and a water flood vertical pump for oil and gas production; and the Pennsylvania Pump and Compressor Company. Between 1960 and 1965, the company's sales grew from $68 million to $117 million.

Cooper had grown into a large, diverse company. To better reflect its nature, it changed its name to Cooper, Inc. in December 1965. Two years later it moved its corporate headquarters to Houston, to be more in the geographic mainstream of American business.

Cooper acquired Lufkin Rule Company of Saginaw, Michigan, in 1967. It was the first of many acquisitions for what Lufkin president William G. Rector called a "tool basket"—a high-quality hand tools manufacturing group. Subsequent hand tool-related acquisitions included Crescent Niagara Corporation (wrenches) in 1968, Weller Electric Corporation (soldering tools) in 1970, Nicholson File Company (rasps and files) in 1972, Xcelite (small tools for the electronics industry) in 1973, J. Wiss & Sons Company (scissors) in 1976, McDonough Company's Plumb Tool subsidiary (striking tools) in 1980, and Kirsch Company (drapery hardware) in 1981.

Charles Cooper, the last Cooper family member to be associated with the company, retired in 1968. The grandson of Elias, he had served as a vice-president and board member.

The company branched out into aircraft services in 1970 by acquiring Dallas Airmotive, and later acquired Southwest Airmotive Company in 1973 and Standard Aircraft Equipment in 1975. While these acquisitions performed satisfactorily, the company sold its airmotive segment to Aviation Power Supply in 1981 because it did not see much potential for further growth.

The 1973 oil embargo threw many industrialized nations into an uproar. Cooper's Ajax division struggled to keep up with orders from domestic crude-oil producers and Cooper received a large order for its Coberra gas turbines for the Alaskan pipeline.

After having served as president and chief operating officer since 1973, Robert Cizik was named chief executive officer in 1975. Lured to the company from Standard Oil New Jersey (now Exxon) in 1961, Cizik started his career at Cooper as executive assistant for corporate development.

Cizik stepped up the company's acquisition program. After satisfying a Justice Department challenge, Cooper acquired the White Superior engine division, a heavy-duty engine maker, from the White Motor Company in 1976, and in 1979 Cooper realized a dream of acquiring the Dallas-based Gardner-Denver Company, a company roughly the same size as Cooper. Although *Forbes* described Gardner-Denver as "a company notorious for lack of planning or cost controls," Cooper was confident the company's three energy-related business segments could be successfully merged into its own energy-related manufacturing operations. *Forbes* reported at the time that the merger was one of the 10 largest in U.S. history. That year the company passed the $1 billion sales milestone, only three years after it had reached a half a billion dollars in sales.

Cooper has been criticized for handling acquisitions coldheartedly. After acquiring Gardner-Denver, it closed the company's corporate headquarters, decentralized it, reduced employment, and cut benefits. But many analysts defended these actions, noting that Gardner-Denver had been full of operational problems and very poorly managed.

Cooper is known for its manufacturing efficiency and willingness to make capital investments to improve production or market position. For instance, when the last domestic producer of the very hard steel needed to manufacture files stopped making it, Cooper developed a process for making its own steel that was different from the traditional method but still suitable for making files, at half the cost.

In 1981, Cooper acquired the highly respected Crouse-Hinds Company of Syracuse, New York, makers of electrical products, after a long battle in which Cooper played white knight, rescuing Crouse-Hinds from Inter-North Corporation. Cooper also acquired the Belden Corporation, a wire and cable manufacturer that Crouse-Hinds had been in the process of purchasing. This acquisition expanded Cooper's size by 50 percent. Shortly after the merger, Cizik explained to *Business Week* that he had entered the electrical components business because "we needed to be in a business that looked beyond the 1980s and even the year 2000 for growth." When demand for gas and oil began to slump in 1981, Cooper's diversification paid off. Sales of the company's energy-related products dropped by 60 percent but its other two divisions were hurt far less.

Acquisitions Culminate in 1985 Merger

Cizik continued to look for new acquisitions. Cooper's next bold move was a 1985 merger with McGraw-Edison Company, a manufacturer of electrical energy-related products for industrial, commercial, and utility use. The merger nearly doubled Cooper's size and made the company one of the largest lighting manufacturers in the world. Cooper's 1985 sales passed $3 billion.

Since the McGraw-Edison acquisition, most Cooper acquisitions have been on a somewhat smaller scale. In 1987 they included the molded rubber products division and the petroleum equipment and products group from Joy Technologies. In 1988, Cooper acquired RTE Corporation, a Wisconsin-based manufacturer of electrical distribution equipment, and Beswick, a manufacturer of fuses and related products in the United Kingdom. But in 1989, Cooper made yet another major acquisition, of the Champion Spark Plug Company, the world's leading manufacturer of spark plugs for combustion engines. Champion, based in Toledo, Ohio, was also known as a major producer of windshield-wiper blades. And in late November 1989, Cooper also acquired Cameron Iron Works, a Houston-based maker of oil tools, ball valves, and forged products with annual sales of $611 million.

Reorganization and Public Offering, 1995

Cooper, before its initial public offering in 1995, manufactured more than a million products in 145 plants, 41 of them in foreign countries. Its annual revenues exceeded $4 billion. But the company had divisions that were performing badly, resulting in a backlog of debt that ate away at the impressive figures. In early 1995, the company faced a net loss for the year of $500.1 million. It was time for a reorganization and, that July, with its initial public offering, the corporation became the publicly traded Cooper Cameron Corporation.

The new corporation took dramatic steps in its first months. It sold the Wheeling Machine Products division for $14 million and used that to help pay down the company debt. It also sold its foundry in Richmond, Texas. Plants and facilities were combined in the United States, Mexico, the UK, and France, and employees were offered severance packages. The number of employees plummeted from 43,300 to 8,500.

The new corporation poured itself into a new mold and created three divisions: Cameron, Cooper Energy Services, and Cooper Turbocompressor. Cameron, headquartered in Houston, was the petroleum production equipment side of the house, and was organized into 4 business units, each reporting to a vice president. The first three units were geographical: Eastern (Europe, Africa, former Soviet Union), Western (U.S., Canada, Mexico, Central and South America), and Asia-Pacific-Middle East. The fourth group was established to interface with valve customers, and was called Cooper Cameron Valves. Cooper Energy Services, headquartered in Mt. Vernon, Ohio, concentrated on compression and power equipment for the energy industry. Cooper Turbocompressor, headquartered in Buffalo, New York, sold specialized compressors. In 1996, Cooper Cameron cleared a profit of $64.2 million on earnings of $1.4 billion. Nearly 60 percent of its business was conducted overseas.

In June 1996, the company acquired Ingram Cactus Corporation, a manufacturer of oil and gas production valves and actuators. The $100 million company was folded into the Cameron division and retained its brand name. Tundra Valve & Wellhead, a Canadian firm, was also acquired, along with some of the assets of ENOX Technologies, for a sum of $13,431,000. The company's revenue was up 21 percent over 1995 levels, with the Cameron segment individually seeing a 23 percent increase. The Cooper Energy Services/Cooper Turbocompressor segments were up 19 percent over 1995.

A Look to the Future

In the future, Cooper Cameron foresees establishing itself even more firmly in the profitable and hazardous oil platforms of the North Sea. The company competes against industry giants such as General Electric, and other well-established firms such as European Gas Turbines, Caterpillar Inc., and Vetco Gray Inc. The company intends to push strongly into turbine and compressor markets in Canada, Europe, the Middle East, and the Far East. After declaring a two-for-one stock split in May 1997 and seeing its stock price rise from $20 to $70 per share in two years, the company was confident of a profitable future.

Further Reading

Keller, David N. *Cooper: 1833–1983,* Athens, Ohio, Ohio University Press, 1983.

—updated by Lisa Calhoun

Corporación Internacional de Aviación, S.A. de C.V. (Cintra)

Xola 535
03100 Mexico, D.F.
Mexico
(525) 448-8022
Fax: (525) 448-8042

Public Company
Founded: 1921 as Compañia Mexicana de Transportación Aérea
Employees: 15,540
Sales: $1.69 billion (1996)
Stock Exchanges: Mexico City
SICs: 4512 Air Transportation, Scheduled; 6719 Offices of Holding Companies, Not Elsewhere Classified

Corporación Internacional de Aviación, S.A. de C.V. (Cintra) is the holding company for Aerovias de México and Corporación Mexicana de Aviación, whose holdings include Aeroméxico and Mexicana, respectively—Mexico's two largest airlines. It was established in 1996 by four creditor Mexican banks, which took 70 percent of the shares in exchange for airline debt they converted into equity. The Mexican government took a 21 percent stake. Cintra controlled 78 percent of the market for domestic flights in 1996 and 39 percent of the Mexico-U.S. market.

Mexicana and Aéronaves to 1945

The history of Cintra's holdings is a virtual history of commercial aviation in Mexico. Founded in 1921, Compañia Mexicana de Transportación Aérea was the first commercial-aviation company in Latin America. It catered to oil executives, flying them between Mexico City and Tampico—then the center of the Mexican petroleum industry—for $100 each, or $50 if a passenger flew more than 100 hours a month. George Rihl founded Compañia Mexicana de Aviación in 1924 with 50,000 pesos ($25,000) in capital, teaming with William "Slim" Mallory, a pilot. Operating three Lincoln Standard airplanes, it was a specialty payroll-delivery service dropping sacks of currency at the Tampico oilfields to avoid banditry on the roads. Rihl then eliminated rival Compañia Mexicana de Transportación Aérea by purchasing it.

In 1925 Sherman Fairchild bought a 20-percent interest in Mexicana, which began flying Fairchild airplanes in 1927 and obtained landing rights in Brownsville, Texas, the following year. By this time Mexicana had won its first mail contract, to carry mail between Mexico City and Tampico for 10 years, and it also flew to Tejería, Veracruz, Tapichula, and Guatemala City. Around 1930 the carrier introduced a flight to Mérida with five improvised stops. That year Pan American Airways bought Mexicana for 300,000 pesos ($150,000). Mexico City's airport opened in 1934, but air travel remained very primitive. Planes skidded on wet runways and cattle wandered onto the field, despite barbed wire, forcing pilots to buzz them in order to scare them away. Cabins were neither pressurized nor heated.

Antónío Díaz Lombardo, a banker, founded Compañia Aeronaves de México, S.A. (predecessor of Aerovias) in 1934 with capital of 100,000 pesos ($50,000). Its first airplane was a Stinson SR, purchased in Kansas City and then flown to Mexico City, where it was put into service flying to Acapulco, with stops (if needed) in Iguala and Chilpancingo. Aeronaves received a government mail contract for the route in 1935 and bought Transportes Aéreas del Pacífico in that year. It adopted the Boeing 247, carrying 10 passengers, for its fleet in 1940 or 1941. Also in 1940 or 1941, Pan American acquired a large minority stake in Aéronaves. Later that year the airline won permission to open a Baja California route and one flying between Acapulco and Oaxaca.

Mexicana acquired the routes of Aerovias Centrales, S.A., a dissolved Pan American subsidiary that served the Pacific coast, in 1935. It began to operate Douglas DC-2 aircraft, which could carry 14 passengers, in 1937. The airline began flying to Havana in 1941 and in that year started direct service from Mexico City to Monterrey and also to the U.S. border at Nuevo Laredo, from where Braniff linked the flights to the U.S. Midwest.

World War II established better conditions for commercial aviation. The beefed-up Mexican air force built airfields with concrete runways in strategic locations, and the meteorological service added personnel for the 28 radiocommunications stations maintained by the air force. During this period both Mexicana and Aéronaves adopted the Douglas DC-3, carrying 21 passengers, for the majority of their routes. The DC-4, with room for 54 passengers, was in service before 1950, but it was not until that year that the first airplanes with pressurized cabins became available (the DC-6 for Mexicana, the Convair 340 for Aéronaves).

Mixed Fortunes, 1945–90

Mexican shareholders had taken a 36 percent stake in Mexicana at the end of 1944. Following the requirements of a postwar law, Pan Am reduced its share of the company to 45 percent, and later to 35 percent. Its interest in Aéronaves fell to less than 11 percent in 1958. When a strike hit both airlines in 1959, the Mexican government purchased Aéronaves. At this time Aéronaves was serving more routes, but Mexicana had the best intercity ones, including nonstop rights between Mexico's three largest cities. Beyond Mexico's borders, Mexicana had service from Mexico City to Chicago, Los Angeles, and San Antonio, while Aéronaves held routes from Mexico City to New York City and Washington, D.C., and from Acapulco to Los Angeles.

Aéronaves received its first jet aircraft, the Douglas DC-8, in 1960 or 1961. In 1967 it became the first Latin American carrier with all jets, its fleet then being based on the DC-9. Aéronaves was offering regular service to 32 Mexican cities in 1964, and also to Detroit, Los Angeles, Miami, New York, and Tucson, Montreal and Toronto, and Caracas and Panama City. The airline was renamed Aeroméxico in 1971. It began service to Paris in 1973 and to Buenos Aires, Rio de Janeiro, Sao Paulo, and Central America during 1974–76. Aeroméxico ranked 24th in sales among Mexico-based companies in 1977. (Mexicana was 21st).

Mexicana, without government financing, was traveling a rockier road. There were many aviation strikes during 1960–62, but Mexicana was hardest hit, losing 74.1 million pesos ($5.9 million). It lost $4.6 million in fiscal 1966 and $3.2 million in fiscal 1967 and had outstanding debt of about $14 million at this time. Pan American sold its stock to Crescencio Ballesteros, a Mexican industrialist, and the company sold 10 airports for cash. In 1968 Mexicana earned a profit, in spite of two fatal crashes of its new Boeing 727 aircraft. By contrast, no Aéronaves passenger lost his life between 1959 and 1971.

Mexicana's financial turnaround continued through the 1970s. By 1978 it had recorded 10 years of continuous annual profits. In 1977, with a fleet of 31 Boeing 727s, it became the largest passenger airline in Latin America in terms of total flights. That year it had revenues of 4.27 billion pesos ($208 million). It was the first Latin American airline to carry 5 million passengers a year in 1978. During the national economic crisis of 1982, however, it failed to make a profit, and the Mexican government raised its stake in the company from 14 to 54 percent. Mexicana had $350 million in outstanding loans at the time and was having difficulties in making payments.

Aeroméxico, carrying 40 percent of Mexico's domestic air passengers, had revenues of 11.74 billion pesos ($479 million)

and profits of $7.5 million in 1981. In 1987 it had a fleet of 45 jets and 39 destinations on three continents. However, in April 1988 the government declared Aéronaves, its parent, bankrupt, saying it was inefficient and was absorbing a subsidy of more than $100 million a year. In October a group of private investors led by Gerardo de Prevoisin bought between 65 and 75 percent of the company for about $330 million. It was renamed Aerovias de México.

Mexicana had a fleet of 44 jets in 1987, when it was serving 30 Mexican and 14 foreign destinations. In 1989 the government reduced its stake in the airline to 40.5 percent, and a consortium including Chase Manhattan Bank purchased a 25 percent share for $140 million. Mexicana made a profit of 307.6 billion pesos ($136.3 million) in 1988 but had $235.4 million outstanding in foreign loans. The company acquired Aerocaribe, a regional carrier serving the Yucatan Peninsula and other parts of southeastern Mexico in 1990, when it reached a peak of 9,058,498 passenger boardings.

Bumpy Ride in the 1990s

The private consortium, Corporación Falcón, which subsequently raised its stake in Mexicana to over 50 percent, also assumed management control of the airline and planned to invest more than $3 billion by 2000, increasing the airline's fleet from 48 to 85 aircraft and cargo traffic nearly tenfold. It established new destinations, created a new business class, and contracted for 38 Airbus A320s to replace 42 aging Boeing 727–200 jets. But its campaign faltered. It lost $70 million in the first nine months of 1992 alone and fell behind Aeroméxico in domestic passengers carried in 1993.

To restore financial solvency, Aerovias slashed Aeroméxico's fleet by more than a third and reduced its work force of 12,000 by two-thirds. It then launched an aggressive promotional and modernization campaign that included Mexico's first frequent-flier program, the extensive use of electronic-information technology, and a 96-percent on-time rating, one of the best in the world. Aeroméxico's market share climbed from 27 to 40 percent.

Aerovias de Mexico acquired 11 percent of Mexicana in 1992 and exchanged 15 percent of its own shares for a 55-percent stake in Corporación Falcón in 1993. The transaction, which in effect gave Aerovias a controlling interest in Mexicana, was valued at $110 million in cash and stock. The two companies maintained different executive staffs and public identities and images despite their close ties in ownership. In international services, Mexicana targeted ethnic traffic and gave priority to the United States, Central America, and the Caribbean. Aeroméxico aimed at business travelers and placed great emphasis on its routes to Europe, the United States, and South America. Aerovias also bought 47 percent of Aeroperú, a struggling state-run airline, for $15 million in 1993.

Aerovias's expansion moves soon proved a disaster. In 1992 the company lost $52.3 million, mainly because the Mexican government had deregulated the Mexican airline industry, forcing Aeroméxico to wage a price war in order to maintain its market share. Aerovias now also had to contend with Mexicana's problems. The company lost about $37 million in 1993, while Aerovias lost almost as much.

The economic slump that followed the peso devaluation of late 1994 created new problems for both airlines. Aerovias was taken over by its creditors, who were owed 2.6 billion pesos (about $380 million) in current liabilities alone. De Prevoisin, its chairman, fled the country amid charges of having embezzled more than $70 million in airline funds. A restructuring by creditor banks who exchanged debt for equity roughly halved the carrier's liability, to 3.2 billion pesos (about $470 million). Aerovias's outstanding long-term debt was 1.49 billion pesos ($220 million) at the end of 1995. Its net loss in 1995 of 136 million pesos ($20 million) on revenues of 6.17 billion pesos ($907 million) was, however, trivial compared to its net loss of 3.4 billion pesos (about $500 million) in 1994.

Mexicana, still 34 percent owned by the Mexican government, had a net loss for 1995 of 1.64 billion pesos ($241 million) on operating income of 5.32 billion pesos ($783 million), on top of a net loss of 2.84 billion pesos ($417 million) in 1994. Its outstanding long-term debt at the end of 1995 was 4.94 billion pesos ($727 million).

Cintra, the Corporación Internacional de Aviación, was created in June 1996 as the holding company for Aerovias and Mexicana, whose stockholders swapped their shares for stock in Cintra. The two airlines were required to maintain competition, however, keeping separate accounts and independent management. Aeroméxico had 39 percent of the domestic market in 1996, while Mexicana had 31 percent. Mexicana had 21 percent of the U.S.-Mexico market, while Aeroméxico had 18 percent. Aeroméxico flew 6,789,989 passengers in 1995, while Mexicana flew 6,562,278. In 1996 Mexicana had a fleet of 45 Boeing 727s, Airbus A320s, and Fokker 100s, some of them leased. Aeroméxico had a fleet of 51 MD-80s, DC-9s, Boeing 757s, and Boeing 767s.

Aeroméxico was believed to be more capable than its partner of combating competition from rivals such as Taesa and Aerocalifornia in the domestic market and foreign airlines on international routes. It installed a sophisticated computer system in 1995 to manage internal operations and had a strategic alliance with Delta Air Lines that included codesharing on a growing number of Mexico-U.S. routes. Mexicana had cut its work force, disposed of its DC-10s, and halved its number of Boeing 727s. Its number of Airbus A320s was to be increased to 28. It had codesharing arrangements with the Dutch airline KLM and Japan Airlines and joint-venture agreements with the Russian airline Aeroflot and the Venezuelan airline Avensa. Both Aeroméxico and Mexicana jointly offered, with Aeroperú, connecting services from the United States through Mexico to Peru, Chile, and Argentina.

Principal Subsidiaries

Of Aerovias de México, S.A. de C.V.: Aeromexpress, S.A. de C.V. (99 percent); Corporación Mexicana de Aviación, S.A. de C.V. (55 percent); Servicios Aéreos Litoral, S.A. de C.V. (99 percent). Of Corporación Mexicana de Aviación, S.A. de C.V.: Aerocozumel, S.A. de C.V.; Aeromonterrey, S.A. de C.V.; Aeropuertos y Terrenos, S.A. de C.V.; Aerovias Caribe, S.A. de C.V.; Servicios Operativos Aéreos, S.A. de C.V.; Turborreactores, S.A. de C.V.

Further Reading

"Aeroméxico on Firmer Footing," *Flight International,* March 27–April 2, 1996, p. 20.
"Aeroméxico to Obtain Control of Mexicana," *Journal of Commerce,* February 19, 1993, p. 2B.
Armbruster, William, "Aeroméxico Takes 11% Stake in Rival Airline Mexicana," *Journal of Commerce,* November 2, 1992, p. 4B.
Conger, Lucy, "Mexican Airline in $330m Sell-Off," *Financial Times,* October 25, 1988, p. 28.
Davies, R.E.G. *Airlines of Latin America Since 1919.* Washington, D.C.: Smithsonian Institution Press, 1984, pp. 1–85.
Dillon, Sam, "A Miracle Worker Turned Fugitive," *New York Times,* August 15, 1995, pp. D1, D5.
Dombey, Daniel, "Aeroméxico's Skies Starting to Clear," *Financial Times,* August 15, 1995, p. 19.
"A Free-Market Failure in Mexico," *Business Week,* August 2, 1982, p. 55.
Johns, Richard, and Doulton, Rebecca, "Mexicana Wins $140m in Step to Sell-Off," *Financial Times,* August 24, 1989, p. 23.
Jones, Geoffrey, "Turnaround in Mexico," *Flight International,* August 7, 1996, p. 55.
Knibb, David, "Mexican Standoff," *Airline Business,* December 1996, p. 26.
Malkin, Elisabeth, "Wanted: Buyer to Pull Airline Out of Deep Dive," *Business Week,* July 24, 1995, p. 50.
Pereira Lima, Edvaldo, "Mexican Roller Coaster," *Air Transport World,* June 1994, pp. 160–63.
Ruíz Romero, Manuel. *Historia de Aeroméxico.* Mexico City: Aéronaves de México, 1984.
Vargas Solis, Beatriz, "Breve historia de la aviación en México," *El Nacional,* October 23, 1987, special supplement, pp. 1–2.

—Robert Halasz

Corrpro
Companies
Incorporated

Corrpro Companies, Inc.

1055 W. Smith Road
Medina, Ohio 44256
U.S.A.
(330) 723-5082
Fax: (330) 723-0694
Web Site: http://www.corrpro.com

Public Company
Incorporated: 1984
Employees: 849
Sales: $139.6 million (1997)
Stock Exchanges: New York
SICs: 8711 Engineering Services; 8731 Commercial
Physical & Bio Research; 7389 Business Services,
Not Elsewhere Classified; 1796 Installation Erection
of Building Equipment 3599 Industrial Machinery,
Not Elsewhere Classified; 1389 Oil & Gas Field
Services, Not Elsewhere Classified; 3629 Electrical
Industrial Apparatus, Not Elsewhere Classified; 3679
Electronic Components, Not Elsewhere Classified

Corrpro Companies, Inc. is a world leader in corrosion control technology and innovation. Headquartered in Medina, Ohio, and located in more than 50 strategically placed offices worldwide, Corrpro provides a broad range and comprehensive line of quality corrosion control engineering services, systems, equipment and monitoring services, and products to highly diverse markets such as the infrastructure, environmental, and energy markets located throughout the world. Some other markets include defense equipment, marine vessels, marine piers, offshore rigs, crude oil lines, gas processing facilities, tank farms, power stations, airports, reinforced concrete bridges, water treatment plants, pulp and paper mills, parking garages, natural gas distribution facilities, service stations, oil refineries, petrochemical plants, transit systems, and water distribution systems. The company's corrosion control products and services include cathodic protection system design, chemical in-

jection system design, contract research, corrosion control materials, corrosion engineering, corrosion monitoring system design, corrosion surveys, customized monitoring and testing software, electrochemical testing, environmental studies, failure analyses, infrastructure condition surveys, internal corrosion monitoring equipment and services, laboratory simulation testing, leak detection surveys, material selection, non-intrusive ultrasonic monitoring, protective coating evaluation, natural marine testing, pre-construction surveys, process safety management program design, turnkey installation, ultrasonic B-Scan inspection, and water quality testing.

A U.S. Department of Commerce study estimated that, in the U.S. alone, the total cost of corrosion-related degradation exceeds $230 billion annually. Unlike many of its competitors, who concentrate on discrete segments of the corrosion protection business, the company offers a broad spectrum of services to the corrosion protection market. Corrpro's overall strategy is to build a worldwide integrated corrosion control company with a technological base. In addition to providing engineering, research and analytical services that assist customers in assessing corrosion problems and developing appropriate methods of corrosion control, the company designs, manufactures, installs and services cathodic protection systems and equipment. The company pursued that strategy aggressively in the late 1990s, building a staff of highly trained corrosion control professionals and over 130 corrosion engineers.

Corrpro began acquiring companies in 1987. The acquisitions included D. Foley Pipeline Services Limited, Corrosion Engineering and Research Company (CERCO) and, in 1988, PSG Corrosion Engineering Inc. and its subsidiary Ocean City Research Corp. Prior to 1990, the company's operations focused primarily on corrosion engineering and construction services. Around that time, the company reexamined its strategy and began focusing on the continued expansion of its presence in the domestic and international corrosion control markets through internal growth and selected acquisitions of companies or product lines that provide complementary products, services, or technologies and that can be effectively integrated into its operations, especially those with an emphasis on engineering

Company Perspectives:

Corrpro Companies, Inc.'s mission is to provide innovative, quality and cost-effective solutions to its customers for the preservation of the world's energy resources, infrastructure and environment. The company provides a complete corrosion protection source for all types of structures found in diverse environments throughout the world. Comprised of the largest group of dedicated corrosion control professionals, state-of-the-art research and testing laboratories, along with materials production facilities, the company has the strength to meet virtually any corrosion-related need. Using this strength, the company accomplishes its goals through progressive engineering, advanced research and a broad range of products and services.

and construction. In 1990, the company acquired Harco Technologies Corporation. This acquisition enabled the company to expand its operations in the manufacture and supply of products used in cathodic protection systems and helped contribute to the 98 percent increase in the company's revenues for that year. However, Corrpro experienced considerable difficulties integrating Harco's operations with its own, running into duplication of staffing, services, and office locations, as well as incompatible operating philosophies and organizational structures. In 1992, the company restructured its operations, closing overlapping offices, eliminating redundant staff positions, and improving management and control systems in order to more effectively assess the company's performance and improve accounts receivable collection and inventory level assessments, as well as establish minimum pricing policies. This allowed the full incorporation of Harco and contributed to a substantial improvement of the company's operating results.

In 1993, more changes were made as the company redesigned its organizational structure to provide for enhanced management reporting and accountability. Some of the changes included monthly budgeting and forecasting with weekly updates, daily cash monitoring, monthly individual productivity reporting, "on-time" material shipment tracking, daily monitoring of inventory purchasing cost variances, improved employee performance reviews and implementation of customer-centered quality programs and evaluation questionnaires which allowed the company to identify problems and take prompt corrective actions. In April of the same year, the company acquired Commonwealth Seager Holdings Limited, an Alberta, Canada-based corporation and provider of a wide range of corrosion control products, engineering services, and equipment doing business as Commonwealth Seager Group. Because Commonwealth Seager manufactures products such as rectifiers for cathodic protection systems and certain types of anodes which Corrpro did not previously manufacture, this acquisition enhanced the company's ability to provide a wider range of products and services to pipelines and expanded manufacturing capabilities, as well as increasing its Canadian customer base.

In 1994, Corrpro acquired a number of companies. The first was in January. Good-All Electric Inc., a wholly owned subsidiary of Valmont Industries Inc. located in Fort Collins, Colorado, which manufactures power supplies for cathodic protection systems and battery chargers, was acquired for $3.1 million in cash. The company acquired, in March, for $4 million, UCC Corporation, another Alberta, Canada-based company and provider of corrosion engineering and coating services and equipment. In addition to providing cathodic protection consulting engineering to customers in the oil, gas, and petrochemical industries, UCC also developed significant experience in the use of coatings in corrosion control applications and provided in-situ coating of storage tanks and other containment vessels. Also in March, Corrpro acquired, for $14.6 million, The Wilson Walton Group Limited, a United Kingdom-based provider of cathodic protection products and services for the international marine, offshore, and industrial markets, with six other offices located throughout Europe, Asia, and the Middle East. Wilson Walton also developed tank venting, electrolytic descaling, and remote monitoring systems for sale to customers in the marine market. Rohrback Cosasco Systems Inc., a Santa Fe Springs, California-based company, was also acquired in 1994 for approximately $8.5 million.

These and other acquisitions expanded Corrpro's customer base and the range of its services. CERCO and Ocean City enhanced Corrpro's specialization in corrosion control services for municipal water and transit authorities. Harco provided manufacturing capabilities for corrosion control materials and equipment. Good-All's established presence in the rectifier market further expanded Corrpro's Canadian customer base and increased its manufacturing capabilities. UCC's experience with protective coatings helped expand the company's presence in the overall market of corrosion control products and services. Wilson Walton's specialization in corrosion protection in the marine and offshore markets expanded Corrpro's customer base and increased its presence in a significant segment of the worldwide corrosion control market and furthered its manufacturing capabilities due to Wilson Walton's presence in the markets of zinc, aluminum, and cast iron anodes, antifouling systems and tank venting systems.

Within the corrosion control market, Corrpro has a specialty in the design, manufacture, and application of concrete cathodic protection systems. Cathodic protection is an electrochemical process designed to prevent corrosion problems in new steel-reinforced concrete structures and mitigate the corrosion process in existing structures. The major cause of corrosion in such structures is the presence of salt resulting from the application of de-icing salts, exposure to sea water, or the use of salt-contaminated sand in the original concrete mix. When steel bars in concrete corrode, the formation of rust causes high internal pressures. Tensile stresses are exerted on the surrounding concrete and cracks develop, leading to subsurface fractures and delaminations. Cathodic protection has been determined by the U.S. Federal Highway Administration to be the only rehabilitation technique able to prevent further corrosion in such structures regardless of the salt content in the concrete. Cathodic protection of reinforced concrete structures has also been endorsed by the American Concrete Institute, AASHTO-AGC-ARTBA Task Force 29, and the National Association of Corrosion Engineers (NACE). Structures commonly protected against corrosion by the cathodic protection process include above- and underground storage tanks, offshore platforms, ships, electric power plants, bridges, oil and gas pipelines, parking garages, transit systems, and water and wastewater treatment equipment. However, since the cathodic protection process is only effective in certain applications, the cathodic protection market is a relatively small component of the overall market for corrosion protection products and services.

The company believes that its ability to provide corrosion engineering and research significantly enhances its cathodic protection business, since involvement in the engineering process allows Corrpro to make customers, consultants, engineers, and governmental entities involved in a project aware of the applications and benefits of cathodic protection. Corrpro also plans to pursue its global marketing efforts in order to increase the awareness of the benefits of cathodic protection among potential customers.

In June 1997, the company entered into a definitive purchase agreement to acquire Cathodic Protection Services Company (CPSC) from Offshore Logistics Inc. and Curran Holdings Inc. for $15 million in cash. CPSC, headquartered in Houston, Texas, provides materials and services for the evaluation, design, installation, and maintenance of cathodic protection systems. Operating primarily in the energy industry, CPSC also provides extensive field service operations and construction experience. With 10 offices located primarily in the Southwestern United States and with annual revenues of $30 million in 1997, the acquisition strengthens Corrpro's full turnkey construction area. With little overlapping of CPSC and Corrpro customers, the acquisition also allows the company the opportunity to introduce its extensive engineering-related capabilities to a batch of new customers. Offshore owned 75 percent of CPSC; Curran held the remaining 25 percent.

As part of Corrpro's changing objectives and strategies in the 1990s, the company reviewed each of its operations in order to determine how each fit in with the company overall. As a result of the process, the company decided in 1997 to divest itself of substantially all of the assets of its noncore business units. In March, the company sold some of these assets from an operation it maintained in Lafayette, Louisiana, for approximately $2.5 million and, despite "significant operational improvements" in 1995 and 1996, the company also decided to put up for sale its CorrTherm foundry operation located in Belle Chase, Louisiana, due to lack of volume and revenue levels. CorrTherm was formed in November 1994 through the combination of the operations of Thermal Reduction Company (TRC) and American Corrosion Services Inc. (ACS). The company had purchased substantially all of the assets of TRC for approximately $10 million in October 1994 and purchased ACS in November of the same year for approximately $5 million. By 1996, the company was considered the U.S. market share leader in rectifiers, a key power supply component in cathodic protection systems and the worldwide leader in the maritime cathodic protection market, corrosion monitoring systems, and the manufacturing of anodes for cathodic protection systems.

Some of the projects the company has completed include the design and installation of cathodic protection for the submerged interior of 17 waste purification units at the Occoquan Treatment Plant of the Fairfax County Water Authority at Annandale, Virginia, and for 16 condenser water boxes at the Morgantown Generating Station for Potomac Electric Power Company at Newburg, Maryland; developed plantwide cathodic protection standards for all underground piping and tank bottoms at the Marathon Refinery at Garyville, Louisiana; and conducted an engineering study for corrosion control of four million square feet of concrete parking deck surface at the World Trade Center for the Port Authority of New York and New Jersey.

Fiscal 1997 marked a year of change for Corrpro as the company reevaluated itself and set the objective to better utilize the company's engineering strength and focus its efforts on growing the engineering, and construction portion of the business. Five areas considered "hot" markets on which the company will focus its engineering and construction segments include underground and aboveground tanks, reinforced concrete structures, ultrasonic inspection services, coatings engineering and inspection and pipeline integrity services.

The company's primary objective, however, in the late 1990s, was the enhancement of profitability through gross profit improvements, operating expense reductions, and better working capital management. In line with this objective, the company showed good growth over a three-year period, moving from $118 million to $127 million to $139 million from 1995 through 1997, respectively, providing an annual growth rate of approximately 10 percent. Several minor setbacks included lawsuits in which PSG Corrosion Engineering, a subsidiary of the company, was a codefendant. One, in 1992 with two other parties in California, regarded liability for a water pipeline rupture in January 1990; a second, in 1994 with 100 unnamed parties in California, regarded a fire service pipeline rupture which occurred in 1992 and a third, in 1997, was a shareholder class-action lawsuit settlement in the amount of $6.1 million which was filed after the company announced its earnings for fiscal 1995.

The company intends to continue pursuing the development of new corrosion protection technologies and new applications for existing technologies, meeting its financial objectives and streamlining and focusing its product lines and services. With increasing global awareness of infrastructure issues and the need to protect existing and new capital assets from deterioration and as more and more companies continue to realize that it is more cost-effective to protect a structure from corrosion than it is to replace one that has failed, the company, as the worldwide leader in corrosion control and with a well-developed international reputation for engineering and technical expertise, believes it will be provided with significant opportunities to expand its presence in existing markets and to enter new markets.

Principal Subsidiaries

Cathodic Protection Services Company; Corrpro Canada; D. Foley Pipeline Services Ltd.; Alcoke Distributors Ltd.; Commonwealth Pipeline Services Ltd.; Engineered Ceramic Products Inc.; General Castings Inc.; RTS Electronics Manufacturing Ltd.; Corrosion Engineering and Research Company;

CorrTherm Inc.; American Corrosion Services Inc.; Thermal Reduction Company; Durichlor 51 Anode Company; Good-All Electric Inc.; Harco Arabia; Harco de Mexico; Harco Europe; Harco Pacific; Harco Technologies Corporation; Harco Waterworks CP; PSG Corrosion Engineering Inc.; Rohrback Cosasco Systems Inc.; UCC Corporation; CSI Coating Systems Inc.; United Corrosion Consultants Ltd.; Wayne Broyles Cathodic Systems Inc.; The Wilson Walton Group Limited (U.K.).

Further Reading

"Accord Is Set to Acquire Cathodic Protection Services," *Wall Street Journal,* June 6, 1997, p. B4(W)/B4(E).

"Corrpro Companies, Inc.," *Wall Street Journal,* December 31, 1996, p. 10(W)/12(E).

"Corrpro Cos.," *Wall Street Journal,* August 1, 1996, p. B10(W)/B9(E).

"Corrpro Cos. to Buy Back Shares," *Wall Street Journal,* November 26, 1996, p. C22(W)/C22(E).

"Corrpro Cos. to Settle Class-Action Lawsuit Brought by Holders," *Wall Street Journal,* October 18, 1996, p. B16(A).

—Daryl F. Mallett

Cypress Semiconductor Corporation

3901 N. First St.
San Jose, California 95134-1599
U.S.A.
(408) 943-2600
Fax: 943-2796
Web site: http://www.cypress.com

Public Company
Incorporated: 1982
Employees: 2,000
Sales: $528.4 million (1996)
Stock Exchanges: New York
SICs: 3674 Semiconductors & Related Devices

Cypress Semiconductor Corporation designs, manufactures, and distributes a broad range of integrated circuits for the worldwide data communications, telecommunications, personal computer, and military systems markets. Cypress operates three wafer fabrication facilities, one in Round Rock, Texas, and two in Bloomington, Minnesota, with a fourth Round Rock facility scheduled to come online in 1998. A fifth facility, the company's original manufacturing facility in San Jose, was converted exclusively to research and development activities in late 1996. Cypress also operates design center facilities in Colorado, Minnesota, Mississippi, Oregon, Texas, and Washington, and in England, India, Germany, and the Philippines, and is preparing to open an additional design facility in Ireland. Assembly and testing of the company's products are performed at Cypress facilities in the Philippines and in Bangkok, Thailand.

After starting up as a producer for the niche semiconductor products markets, Cypress has turned its focus to mainstream, high-commodity chip markets in the 1990s. Cypress targets five primary product categories: memory products, with its flagship static RAM (SRAM) chips and multichip modules for personal computers, workstations, telecommunications systems, networking products, and other markets; programmable products, including programmable logic devices (PLDs) such as the UltraLogic family, including the high-performance Flash370i; nonvolatile memory division, including programmable read-only memory (PROM) chips for computers, peripherals, and communications products; data communications, including ATM and fibre channel devices, ethernet support transceivers, RoboClock clock buffers, and a range of specialty memory products; and computer products, including microcontrollers for Universal Serial Bus (USB) products, chipsets for personal computers, fast CMOS technology devices, and frequency synthesizers and programmable clock generators for computer systems.

Cypress is led by founder, president, and CEO Thurman John (T. J.) Rodgers, who also serves as a company director. In 1996, a difficult year for the semiconductor industry, Cypress posted revenues of $528 million and pretax profits of $83.5 million, down from $596 million in sales the previous year. The company, however, projects sales approaching $1 billion for 1997 and hopes to top $2 billion by the turn of the century.

The General Patton of the Semiconductor Industry

Rodgers, who was named "America's Toughest Boss" by *Fortune* magazine in 1993, quickly gained a reputation in the semiconductor industry for his visionary management, entrepreneurial and manufacturing techniques, and outspoken criticism of the U.S. semiconductor industry. Born and raised in Oshkosh, Wisconsin, his father a car salesman, his mother a schoolteacher, Rodgers displayed a talent for entrepreneurship at an early age. As a child, Rodgers learned electronics from his mother, who had taught basic electronics during World War II. In his high school chemistry lab, Rodgers created his first "product," a smoke bomb dubbed the "Thurm-O-Flare," a project which ended when Rodgers blew up the lab and put himself in the hospital. Rodgers was recruited to play football at Dartmouth University, where he earned bachelor's degrees in physics and chemistry, graduating second in his class, and first in both majors. Accepted into Stanford University's physics program, Rodgers instead decided to study electrical engineering—despite having taken only a single semester of electrical engineering at Dartmouth—earning his master's and Ph.D. degrees by 1975.

At Stanford, Rodgers studied under William B. Shockley, whose Shockley Electronics became the breeding ground of the famed Fairfield Eight (including Robert Noyce and Gordon Moore of Intel Corp.). While at Stanford, Rodgers invented a wafer etching technology called VMOS; he patented the technology, then sold it for cash and royalties to American Microsystems, Inc., where he worked until he was fired—when the VMOS process was eclipsed by new technology—in 1979. In that year, the 31-year-old Rodgers attempted to start his own company—a goal he had set himself to achieve by age 35—but was unable to find financial backing. Instead, he accepted a position with Advanced Micro Devices (AMD), where he worked until leaving to found Cypress in November 1982.

Rodgers faced the daunting task of starting up—and arranging venture capital for—a new company during the recession of the early 1980s. Nonetheless, Rodgers attracted the interest of L. J. Sevin, founder of Mostek Inc., during the 1970s. After preparing a business plan for his proposed company, Rodgers, with Sevin's backing, began raising the $7.5 million in start-up funds envisaged in his business plan. Rodgers quickly found offers totalling $13.5 million—enabling him to choose his investors. As he told *Santa Clara County Business*: "We were therefore in the position of picking backers as opposed to begging for backers. Only the best! We picked backers that had 'value-added.' " Initial backers included Sevin, Sequoia's Don Valentine and Pierre Lamond, J. H. Whitney of New York, and Kleiner, Perkins, Caulfield, and Byers. In exchange for this backing of Cypress, Rodgers gave up 75 percent of control over the company. Cypress continued to attract venture capital in the years leading to its initial public offering in 1986, raising some $48 million. Cypress was underway by April 1983.

Cypress debuted its first product, a CMOS (complementary metal oxide silicon) memory chip, by the beginning of 1984. The chip contained the world's smallest and fastest CMOS transistors, which were 1.2 microns wide (compared to a human hair at approximately 100 microns wide), operating three times faster than competing semiconductors, while using 80 percent less energy. The company immediately set to work on a new round of CMOS transistors, shrinking them to 0.9 microns. By 1985, the company was profitable and posting revenues of $17 million. Following Rodgers original business plan—and hitting the targets envisaged therein—the company sought to operate solely within niche markets, those with sales of no more than $40 million. In this way, the company could avoid head-on competition with the semiconductor industry's U.S. and Japanese giants, which had neither the flexibility nor the interest in producing for such small markets. By 1987, the company was producing more than 70 types of chips, all targeted at high-end, sophisticated markets. By then, sales had already tripled, to $55 million in 1986. In that year, the company's initial public offering raised $73 million, one of the largest public debuts for the time. By then, the company had added a second wafer fab, in Round Rock, Texas.

Cypress's extraordinary growth—by 1990 sales would reach $225 million, and net earnings of $33 million—was credited to an unusually intense corporate culture, beginning with its hiring process, a daunting marathon of some 10 interviews. Rodgers quickly earned a reputation as the "General Patton" of the semiconductor industry, demanding that employees create weekly task lists, and putting into place a computerized system for tracking completion of the tasks employees set for themselves—and those who did not meet their targets could expect a withering dressing down from Rodgers. The company's manufacturing processes were equally as strict, enabling the company

the flexibility to turn production quickly from one product to the next. As Rodgers explained to *Business Month*: "A semiconductor is a very unforgiving entity. If it takes 1,000 tasks to make one and you do 999 right but then forget one or do one wrong, the semiconductor won't work. Our system forces management to stick its nose in a big book every single week and find out what is going on. We can't afford surprises." In exchange for the high-pressure environment, Cypress employees received stock in the company. And Rodgers, unlike many high-flying Silicon Valley CEOs, gave himself the same benefits—and demands—as every other Cypress employee.

As Cypress grew, Rodgers also blossomed as an outspoken critic of the U.S. semiconductor, and particularly its quest, through Sematech and U.S. Memories, for U.S. government backing and intervention to help it compete against the rising Japanese power in the industry. Rodgers, a self-described Libertarian, instead demanded that the industry remain true to free market principles, a position that earned him little love among CEOs of his industry. Critics at the time pointed out that Cypress's focus on the niche markets—by 1990 the company was producing 159 products, generating as little as $1.6 million in sales each—enabled it to avoid the bruising head-to-head competition of the mainstream commodity markets. Nonetheless, Rodgers could hardly be faulted for the company's strong growth and its industry-leading productivity and profitability. At the end of 1990, the company bought its Bloomington, Minnesota wafer fab from Control Data VTC, paying just $14.7 million. The company also opened the first two of its design centers, in Mississippi and Texas.

A Mid-Life Crisis in the 1990s

SRAMs continued to provide the bulk of Cypress's revenues. But the company began branching out into other territories, including PROMs and RISC processors, featured in, among others, Sparc processors for Sun workstations—a market that Rodgers predicted would eclipse the Intel-dominated personal computer market. As Cypress grew during the 1980s, Rodgers fought hard to maintain its entrepreneurial spirit. Rather than creating subsidiaries, Cypress instead began acting as a venture capitalist, spinning off divisions into separate start-up companies, wholly owned by Cypress, each with its own CEO, and administrative and financial departments. Cypress's three subsidiary companies, which included Ross Technologies, created to produce high-performance RISC processors, contributed 10 percent of Cypress's sales by 1990; by 1991, these subsidiaries accounted for 28 percent of the company's revenues.

As sales continued to rise, reaching $286 million and record profits of $34 million in 1991, Rodgers strove to maintain the company's entrepreneurial origins. But the company was headed for trouble: the SRAM markets had developed enough to attract the interest of the larger semiconductor companies, including Motorola, Micron Technology, Toshiba, Fujitsu, and Hitachi, sparking a price war that saw prices for SRAMs cut in half. With SRAMs moving into the mainstream, prices falling with the increasing supply, and a shrinking market facing a worldwide recession, Cypress stumbled into a mid-life crisis. Adding to its woes, Cypress had hitched its wagon to Sun's workstations. But that market never developed into the Intel-killer Rodgers had hoped; worse, in 1992, Sun began reducing its inventories, cutting back on its orders to Cypress. Meanwhile, Cypress's Ross

Technologies subsidiary was developing a new Sparc processor, with no guarantees that Sun would purchase it. Indeed, when Ross was late in delivering the new chip, Sun turned to Texas Instruments for supplies instead. Meanwhile, the personal computer market was moving into a new explosion in growth, and Cypress found itself on the outside of this crucial market. Rodgers's style of micromanagement was also criticized, particularly as the company was late with another important product, a one-megabyte SRAM chip, allowing his competitors to beat Cypress to the market. On top of all of this, Rodgers insisted on maintaining the company's assembling and testing facilities at its San Jose plant, despite the fact that keeping these activities in the U.S. cost the company some $17 million per year over what it would cost to move them overseas.

In 1992—to the delight of Rodgers's enemies, who had long chafed under his criticism—Cypress tripped up. Revenues shrunk to $272 million, and the company posted its first loss in its history as a public company, to the tune of $21 million. Chastened, Rodgers was forced to reorganize the company and adapt himself to Cypress's new conditions. Long pressured by his board of directors to move the testing and assembly facilities to Asia (although actual manufacturing would remain in the United States), Rodgers agreed, slashing some 700 jobs. It took Cypress only three weeks to move these operations. Rodgers also agreed to tone down his micromanagement of the company's activities, in order to give focus instead on its long-term growth. As part of the reorganization, Cypress brought its subsidiaries back into the company as divisions, while selling off the Ross subsidiary to Fujitsu for $23 million in 1993.

The glee with which Rodgers's detractors greeted the company's difficulties proved short-lived. By 1993, the company was back on course, raising revenues to nearly $305 million, and regaining profitability, with net earnings of $8 million. The following year, with an aggressive push into new product territories, including the personal computer market, Rodgers—who had taken the lessons learned over the last years to heart—once again led the company to new heights. For the year ended 1994, Cypress posted sales of $406 million, and a net profit of $50.5 million. Aiding the companies return to growth were a series of acquisitions made between 1993 and 1994. The first, of IC Designs, Inc. for $16 million, brought that company's programmable clock oscillators for the personal computers; next, the company acquired Performance Semiconductor Corp.'s line of FCT-T high-speed logic chips, paying $5 million. In 1994, Cypress also acquired CONTAQ Microsystems Inc., and its line of personal computer chipsets, for $1.7 million.

Cypress arrived in the personal computer market to ride the surge in PC sales of the mid-1990s, spurred in particular by the introduction of the new Pentium processor, the first new PC chip since the introduction of the 486 at the beginning of the decade. The new computer market presented a double opportunity for Cypress—which began designing chipsets for the Pentiums—as the high-performance nature of the emerging technology opened a fresh demand for Cypress's core SRAM products. Where only 40 percent of personal computers contained SRAM in 1993, it was estimated that 80 percent would contain SRAM by 1997. Yet the company saw even greater benefits from the booming networking and telecommunications

industries. By the end of 1995, the company's revenues neared $600 million, and the company began making plans to become a $1 billion company, joining the industry's top ten, by the end of 1997.

In April 1996, the company began building a second wafer fab in Round Rock to meet the surge in demand. That project was delayed as the industry went through a worldwide slump in memory sales. Meanwhile, Rodgers's writing talents—he had also published a book, called *No Excuses Management* outlining his management philosophy in 1992—made the headlines in the summer of 1996. After receiving a letter from a Catholic nun criticizing Cypress for not having any women or minorities on its board of directors, Rodgers wrote a six-page letter attacking such "political correctness" and the election-year hot potato of corporate responsibility, and asserting that hiring on the basis of race or gender was immoral and "a lousy way to run a company." For this position, Rodgers was widely applauded among the executive and investor communities.

In October 1996, Cypress shut down its manufacturing facilities at its San Jose headquarters, converting the facility solely to research and development activities. Picking up the production was a second Minnesota wafer fab, and the start of construction on the new wafer fab in Round Rock, expected to be completed by 1998. At the end of 1996, however, Cypress found that its revenues had slipped back to $528 million in the face of the industry-wide slowdown. The company continued to plan, however, to become a $1 billion company as early as 1997. With a wiser, more experienced Rodgers at the lead, Cypress was poised to become one of the nation's—and the world's—premier semiconductor companies.

Principal Subsidiaries

Cypress Semiconductor Philippines, Inc. (Philippines).

Further Reading

Bottoms, David, "Roaring Back," *Industry Week*, November 4, 1996, p. 20.

Brandt, Richard, "The Bad Boy of Silicon Valley," *Business Week*, December 9, 1991, p. 64.

——, "Humble Pie for T.J. Rodgers," *Business Week*, November 23, 1992, p. 81.

Daszko, Marcia, "Venture Upstart: A Conversation with T.J. Rodgers," *Santa Clara County Business*, June 1986, p. 22.

Jones, Stephen, "T.J. Rodgers: A Patton-Like General Whose Weapon Is Cypress," *The Business Journal—San Jose*, February 9, 1987, p. 12.

Pitta, Julie, "Silicon Valley's (Profitable) Gadfly," *Forbes*, November 26, 1990, p. 56.

Rodgers, T. J.; William Taylor; and Rick Foreman, *No Excuses Management*, New York: Doubleday Currency, 1992.

Schniedawind, John, "Cypress' All-American CEO Survives Tough Market," *USA Today*, July 14, 1993, p. 4B.

Spiegelman, Lisa, "A Mea Culpa from Cypress' T.J. Rodgers," *Investor's Business Daily*, February 15, 1995, p. A4.

Stroud, Michael, "Cypress' T.J. Rodgers Will Bad-Mouth Almost Anyone," *Investor's Daily*, May 17, 1991, p. 6.

Wrubel, Robert, "Captain America," *Financial World*, May 29, 1990, p. 25.

—M. L. Cohen

DEP Corporation

2101 E. Via Arado
Rancho Dominguez, California 90220-6189
U.S.A.
(310) 604-0777
Fax: (310) 537-4098

Public Company
Incorporated: 1983
Employees: 300
Sales: $119.1 million (1996)
Stock Exchanges: NASDAQ
SICs: 2844 Toilet Preparations

DEP Corporation is a California-based company that develops, manufactures, distributes, and markets hair, oral, and skin care products. In addition to its leading trademark Dep styling gel, the company manufactures L.A. Looks, Halsa and Agree haircare products; Lilt home perms; Topol toothpaste; Lavoris mouthwash; and Porcelana and Cuticura specialty skin care products. Each DEP product line is supported by a team from finance, R & D, manufacturing, and other areas, and each brand is run as an independent business. DEP's products are marketed in over 40 countries worldwide, and are sold in every major drug, food, and mass merchandise store in the United States. DEP is also the exclusive U.S. distributor for Jordan toothbrushes, and the distributor for Molinard perfume and Unilever fragrances, Nino Cerruti men's products, and Pear's soap.

DEP began operations as a private company in 1955, marketing one product: Dep hair gel. The company and its hair gel were christened by warehouse workers, who nicknamed an ingredient called deprovinyllol that was used in the original hair gel. In the 1970s, DEP launched a children's toiletries line, but the new product coincided with the recession and did not take off.

After 27 years in business, the company went public in 1983, with an initial public offering of 1 million common shares. The company finished its first public year with sales of $15 million.

The next year, DEP entered the skin care market and added $6 million in sales when it acquired the Nature's Family line.

By 1986, chairman and president Robert Berglass wanted to initiate growth for DEP through acquisitions and internal expansion. A college graduate who started out in business by selling typewriters door-to-door, Berglass was a self-taught entrepreneur with big ideas. Lacking the capital to support his vision, Berglass approached investment bankers but was put off by long waits for available cash. Finally, now-deposed "junk-bond king" Michael Milken of Drexel Burnham Lambert's Beverly Hill's office came through with financing in three weeks. The deal featured a $16.5 million high-yield bond offering, and paved the way for DEP's successful—if often uneven—growth in the 1980s, growth that would include the creation of over 100 new jobs, the addition of a wing to the Rancho Dominguez plant, and a sales increase from $18 million to over $100 million by 1990.

The company began to expand its product line in 1987, purchasing 85 percent of Jeffrey Martin, Inc.'s shares in an acquisition valued around $73 to $75 million. With the acquisition, DEP inherited big-name products including Lavoris mouthwash, Topol toothpaste, and Porcelana Fade Cream. Other less promising product lines which came with the transaction included Bantron smoking deterrent tablets, Compoz sleeping pills, Doan's backache pills, and Ayds appetite suppressant candies. DEP sold the Doan's line, which it had bought for $14 million, and received an impressive $35 million. The company placed several other lines on the market block. In April 1987, the company further reduced the bank debt incurred in the acquisition, successfully selling Compoz and Bantron.

A delicate situation was presented by the Ayds candy line. New awareness of the AIDS epidemic created a name problem for the candy, which in turn presented a marketing dilemma to DEP as its new distributor. On the one hand, the name Ayds sounded exactly like that of the deadly virus. On the other, weight-conscious Americans had been purchasing Ayds candies for 48 years. Marketing campaigns to introduce a brand new name for the candy would throw away the rewards of almost a half-century of marketing and name-recognition. With Ayds sales dropping by 50 percent, and no prospective buyers for the line, DEP tackled the problem on a number of fronts: boosting the calcium level in the candies and marketing them to the health-conscious as well as dieters; redesigning the package; and test-marketing a new name (Aydslim) and new flavors (apple and black currant) in Britain. For the first time in years, broadcast advertising was used to support the new name. By 1988, DEP concluded that the candy required a second name change for the U.S. market, christening it Diet Ayds. In all, the company spent about $250,000 on the image campaign for Ayds—a candy priced at $5 per box.

However, with Ayds candies' $7 million sales accounting for a fraction of DEP's annual sales of $66.8 million, the name problem was not the company's top priority. To help design new product strategies, the company had hired ad agency Lowe Marschalk, Inc. With the advice of the ad agency, DEP set to work on the redesign and freshening of each product line, one at a time. To update the image of Dep styling gel, the company traded the tube container for a pump, redesigned the package, and invested in advertising stressing the ease of usage. The changes paid off, with Dep gel posting annual sales of $25 million in the $250 million hair-styling products market in 1987. A new mint flavor and updated image were introduced for Lavoris—one of the nation's oldest mouthwash products. Since the 1960s, the mouthwash's market share had dropped from 14 percent to 3 percent. The Lavoris campaign targeted younger mouthwash users, aged 18 to 24, in an effort to chase the market leader, Scope. The bottle was enlarged by 33 percent and television ads marketed Lavoris as a value brand. By 1993, market share for the mouthwash would double. New packaging and ad campaigns were also designed for Topol, and the ad agency set to work on the new campaign for Ayds.

In addition to its product marketing strategies, the company received recognition for the institutional imaging promoted by its annual reports. In 1987, DEP's annual report—which featured grainy black-and-white photographs of a female nude—received a design award. The company was encouraged to step out further on the same limb, and its 1988 annual report featured a cover photo of a nude in three-quarter's profile (with strategic shadowing), in full color. Scattered between financial reports and news inside the report were other nude photographs. Judith Berglass, vice president of corporate development and wife of chairman Robert Berglass, told the *Wall Street Journal* that the nude shots promoted an image of DEP as a young and aggressive company. While the design was suggested by an outside firm, Besser Joseph Partners, Robert Berglass's preference had always been to present the company flamboyantly, and earlier annual reports had sported spiky hairdoed models on the covers.

Aside from the presentational design, DEP's 1988 annual report had good news inside. The company's earnings had peaked at 71 cents a share, and its stock had peaked at $12. The next year, however, earnings dropped to 26 cents a share, rising again in 1990 to 32 cents. Such erratic earnings were the result of operating expenses that were rising faster than sales, with the introduction of the L.A. Looks hair care line, the expansion of the DEP line, and other product introductions. Berglass launched a major campaign to trim expenses.

In 1990, DEP surpassed the $100 million mark in sales, and employed 400 people. When smoking was banned on airplanes that year, DEP took advantage of the new market potential. The company began negotiating a deal with airlines to offer its Bantron stop-smoking pills to customers. Overall, 1990 was a year of conservative management for the company. Defaults on junk bonds had led to disastrous results, and the savings and loan crisis had spilled over to commercial banks, who had stiffened their requirements for business loans.

Notwithstanding profitability, the company shelved acquisition plans due to the difficulty of raising capital without losing equity.

DEP surprised the analysts and shareholders with a major success in 1991. DEP's three-year-old L.A. Looks hair care product, marketed at teenagers, suddenly took off with surging sales. A jump in quarterly earnings triggered an 87.5 cent stock price increase to a new 1991 high of $7 in June. The sweetest part of the success, though, was that DEP had spent nothing on advertising L.A. Looks. With no cash on hand for advertising, the company had resorted to what Berglass termed "guerrilla marketing." For the L.A. Looks line, the strategy consisted of no ads, a flashy package, and an affordable price (under $2), to attract young shoppers looking for a stylish hair care solution without a high price. By 1992, L.A. Looks had surpassed Dep in unit sales. The company had more than doubled its total sales since 1986, and it finally appeared that the spotty earnings record would catch up with sales.

Continuing to develop new hair care products and broaden markets for existing ones, DEP introduced two new spritzing formulas, designed to work together, in 1991. The company marketed the spritzers in magazines with teenaged and health and beauty conscious reading markets. In 1992, the company launched a major campaign targeting younger women with its DEP gel line and Lilt home permanent products. DEP had acquired the Lilt line—which had a customer base of older women—from Proctor & Gamble Co. in 1990. DEP used television commercials to target professional women and young mothers in their 20s and 30s. Appealing to the health conscious, DEP stressed the natural ingredients in its Nature's Family body lotion, with aloe vera, vitamin E, and extra strength products.

Nineteen ninety-three was the year of the toothbrush. Once an ordinary bathroom item, the toothbrush was acquiring a stylish new function, and sales were expected to increase by 13 percent that year. DEP jumped into the fray with its first toothbrush product: the Jordan Magic Color Changing toothbrush. Like the 1970s mood ring, the Jordan toothbrush changed colors after being held in the hand for two minutes—the amount of time dentists recommend for thorough brushing. Through a $10 million advertising campaign, DEP targeted both consumers and dentists with the new product. The company's 1993 sales reached approximately $123.7 million, but income fell 80 percent to $1.2 million due to slow core product sales and high promotion costs. By the next year, L.A. Looks and Dep gel together held 40 percent of the styling gel market, as the two leading products.

A major turning point for the company occurred in the summer of 1993, when DEP acquired the Agree and Halsa hair care brands from S.C. Johnson & Son Inc. for $45 million. Berglass's strategy was to increase DEP's presence in the shampoo market through this major acquisition. The company promoted several executives to integrate the new brands into the company, and hired E. Michael McNamara to fill the newly created position of senior vice president of marketing. In all, the transaction left the company owing over $60 million, with the bulk lent by Citicorp.

All too quickly, the deal went sour. DEP discovered that sales for Agree and Halsa totaled far less than the company had believed: only around $48 million. In March 1994, DEP filed a lawsuit against S.C. Johnson & Sons, alleging that the company misled DEP regarding the sales condition of the hair care brands prior to their sale. The lawsuit was not easily or quickly settled, and DEP began losing money due to declining sales for Agree and Halsa and increasing interest expenses related to their purchase. In the six months following the acquisition, DEP saw only $12 million in sales from Agree and Halsa. Total sales for the company were $138 million in 1994, but earnings continued to fluctuate, and a $3.6 million loss was incurred that year. By the second quarter of 1995, a loss placed the company in technical default of a bank loan, and stock prices fell from $15 a share in 1993 to $2.13 a share in 1995. The company received a bank loan waiver from its lenders.

In 1995, the company publicly admitted it needed a life preserver. Taking a first step toward a solution, DEP hired Donaldson, Lufkin & Jenrette Securities Corp. as its financial adviser, to formulate a strategic business plan. Layoffs of about 50 people were made, shrinking the work force, and executive salaries were cut. The company also wrote off $25.2 million in assets. After announcing that it was considering options such as a business combination, sale of assets, strategic investment, or refinancing, DEP saw its Class A shares fall $1 to $1⅛ on the market, and closed fiscal 1995 with a loss of $27 million on revenues of $127.7 million.

By April 1996, having explored its options, the company filed for bankruptcy-court protection. The company listed liabilities of $77.3 million and assets of $83.9 million. The filing to restructure the company's long-term debt provided for payment in full, with interest, to the company's lenders and creditors, allowing the company to continue operations while it worked out a repayment plan. Having reduced overhead and expenses by more than $3 million annually, the company believed that its goals were achievable. Under an amended reorganization plan, finalized in August, DEP's two classes of shares were reclassified into one class and the company obtained $62 million in long-term financing. Subsequently, the company's Class A shares rose 12.5 cents to $1.75.

New product development continued after the bankruptcy filing in 1996, including a mousse and a department store skin care line called Basique. Problems continued, however, and DEP was sued by Estée Lauder Cosmetics, who claimed that Basique was a repackaged look-alike of Lauder's Clinique line. The Basique line was recalled at a cost of $600,000. The company's new promotions included sponsorship of "Melrose Place on E!" on cable television, reaching 55 million homes. Purchasers of L.A. Looks hair care products received a special promotional opportunity to play a walk-on part in "Melrose Place." Fiscally, 1996 ended better than the company had projected in its court filings, with $3.1 million in operating income on net sales of $119.1 million, an increase over 1995 operating income of $1.5 million. Net loss for 1996 was $8 million, a considerable improvement over the previous year's $27 million loss.

In December 1996, DEP's executives decided to stop putting money and resources into the lawsuit against S.C. Johnson, which had been pending since 1994. The company reached an out-of-court settlement with S.C. Johnson, receiving $3.9 million, and set its sights on the future.

At the end of the 1990s, DEP strategized to strengthen sales by increasing advertising aimed at stabilizing and reinvigorating its brands, and by pursuing new contract packaging customers. The company's cash situation, despite the bankruptcy, continues to be positive. If the reorganization is successful, and if the company is not again plagued by unfortunate acquisitions, DEP will continue to achieve quiet success as the name behind stylish, value-priced brands with large market share.

Further Reading

"All That's Missing Is a Centerfold," *Wall Street Journal*, October 11, 1988, p. B1.

Brooks, Nancy Rivera, "DEP's Bottom Line Takes a Real Lather," *Los Angeles Times*, March 6, 1995, p. D1.

Brooks, Nancy Rivera, "DEP Corp. Ready to Put a New Face on Things," *Los Angeles Times*, November 5, 1996, p. D1.

Cuneo, Alice Z., "Lavoris Unveils New Flavor, Color," *Advertising Age*, February 8, 1988, p. 36.

"DEP Agrees to Buy Jeffrey Martin Inc.," *Wall Street Journal*, January 5, 1987, p. 12.

"DEP Corp," *Drug & Cosmetic Industry*, May, 1996, p. 8.

"DEP Files for Bankruptcy, Citing Purchase of Brands," *Los Angeles Times*, April 2, 1996, p. D2.

"DEP: Hair Today, a Lot More Tomorrow," *Business Week*, June 9, 1986, p. 97.

"DEP Initial Offering," *Wall Street Journal*, September 22, 1983, p. 44.

"DEP to Pay $45 Million for Hair Care Brands," *Los Angeles Times*, July 13, 1993, p. D2.

"Financial Markets," *Los Angeles Times*, July 12, 1995, p. D2.

Horovitz, Bruce, "Diet Product Firm in Dilemma," *Los Angeles Times*, June 24, 1987, p. 4.

——, "Ayds Considers Changing Its Name to Aydslim," *Los Angeles Times*, March 3, 1988, pp. 4–5.

——, "Where Have All the Yuppies Gone? Ads Have Dropped Them, Every One," *Los Angeles Times*, March 8, 1988, pp. 4–6.

——, "Familiar, Trusted Brand Names Are Lure for Grand Met," *Los Angeles Times*, October 5, 1988, p. 4.

——, "Thinning Sales Prompt Diet Candy to Change Name—Again," *Los Angeles Times*, December 27, 1988, p. 4.

Magiera, Marcy, "DEP Targets Younger Women," *Advertising Age*, March 30, 1992, p. 48.

Matzer, Marla, "E! Jumps Aboard DEP's *Melrose*-Manic Fall," *Brandweek*, July 15, 1996, p. 5.

Paltrow, Scott J., "Grieving Over Junk Bonds: Some Firms Sure Miss Them," *Los Angeles Times*, April 22, 1990, p. D1.

Petruno, Tom, "DEP's Stock Soars After Hair-Care Lines Get Restyled," *Los Angeles Times,* June 5, 1991, p. D3.

Rosendahl, Iris, "Hair-Raising Sales for Hair-Styling Products," *Drug Topics*, February 18, 1991, pp. 61–63.

Rosendahl, Iris, "Hand and Body Lotions Targeting Special Niches; Integrate Hand, Body Lotions for Best Results," *Drug Topics*, September 21, 1992, pp. 105–07.

Sanchez, Kimberly, "DEP Settles for $3.9 Million in Trademark Suit," *Los Angeles Times*, December 21, 1996, p. D2.

Sing, Bill, "The Milken Indictment," *Los Angeles Times*, March 30, 1989, p. 4.

Sloan, Pat, "DEP Joins Toothbrush Rush with Grip That Changes Color," *Advertising Age*, June 7, 1993.

——, "DEP Sues Over Halsa, Agree Deal," *Advertising Age*, March 14, 1994, p. 43.

Teitelbaum, Richard S., "DEP Corp.," *Fortune*, February 8, 1993, p. 127.

Woodyard, Chris, "Stop-Smoking Firm Ready to Cash in on Ban," *Los Angeles Times*, February 24, 1990, p. D1.

—Heidi Feldman

Designer Holdings Ltd.

1385 Broadway
New York, New York 10018
U.S.A.
(212) 556-9600
Fax: (212) 391-3882

Public Company
Incorporated: 1984 as Rio Sportswear, Inc.
Employees: 1,250
Sales: $480.4 million (1996)
Stock Exchanges: New York
SICs: 2329 Men's and Boys Clothing, Not Elsewhere
    Classified; 2339 Women's, Misses' and Juniors'
    Outerwear, Not Elsewhere Classified; 5136 Men's and
    Boys' Clothing and Furnishings; 5137 Women's,
    Children's and Infants' Clothing and Accessories;
    5611 Men's and Boys' Clothing and Accessory
    Stores; 5621 Women's Clothing Stores

Designer Holdings Ltd. develops, sources, and markets designer sportswear lines for men, juniors, and women under the Calvin Klein Jeans, CK/Calvin Klein Jeans, and CK/Calvin Klein Khakis labels, collaborating with the in-house design teams of Calvin Klein, Inc. to create a broad line of products that includes outerwear, knit and woven tops and bottoms, T-shirts, shorts, fleece shirts and pants, and caps and related accessories as well as jeans and khakis. Designer Holdings also owns and operates Calvin Klein Outlet Stores in North America and markets sportswear under the Bill Blass and Rio labels. After becoming a Calvin Klein licensee in 1994, the company quickly became a major player in the $20-billion-a-year denim market, boosting sales of Calvin Klein jeans sixfold in two years. Designer Holdings became a public company in 1996.

Rio Sportswear, 1984–93

Arnold H. Simon, Designer Holdings' cofounder, president, and chief executive officer, started out in children's apparel and underwear in the mid-1970s. Through a series of acquaintances he entered the denim business, founding Rio Sportswear, Inc. in 1984 with Stephen Huang to produce the material and market girls' and juniors' jeans under the Rio name. Simon was based in New York City, Huang in southern California. The company acquired the license to manufacture Bill Blass Jeans in 1987 and also obtained the manufacturing rights for Rifle jeans from Rifle Jeans Co. of Europe. Rio's extensive sourcing overseas included locations in Italy, Taiwan, Hong Kong, and Central and South America. Its products were distributed mainly through department and specialty stores. Company revenues were estimated at $30 million in 1989 and $60 million in 1990 and 1991.

Rio Sportswear added another line in 1992, when it signed a licensing agreement with L.A. Gear Inc. to produce under license women's and girls' jeans and a full line of woven tops and bottoms, including coordinated jackets for sale in department, chain, and specialty stores. "We're very excited to have Rio as our newest licensee," announced L.A. Gear's president. "They are known as one of the premier jeans manufacturers in the country and produce a well-designed, quality garment at a very competitive price." Rio had net revenues of $145 million in 1992 and $173.6 million in 1993. Net income was $3.6 million in 1992 and $2.1 million in 1993.

The Calvin Klein Deal, 1994

In February 1994 Rio and Calvin Klein entered into a letter of intent for Rio to buy Calvin Klein's men's and women's jeans divisions for $35 million plus ongoing royalty payments. Rio would acquire the assets of the Calvin Klein jeans business, which included a laundering facility in Nasquehoning, Pennsylvania, and a sewing plant in Abbeville, South Carolina. The agreement also called for Rio to receive the license to manufacture and sell Calvin Klein jeans and jeans-related products under the Calvin Klein label and to launch a children's jeans business in the future. The design studios and a showroom were to be maintained in Calvin Klein's offices in Manhattan's Seventh Avenue garment district.

Negotiations were impelled by Calvin Klein's decision to get out of manufacturing in order to focus on licensing and design. The Calvin Klein jeans business had been started in 1978 and by 1983 had reached a level of about $220 million a year. Soon after, however, sales dropped precipitously, and in 1992 all Calvin Klein casual clothes—mostly jeans—brought in only about $150 million. The company lost about $7.7 million in both 1991 and 1992 on this sector of its business. Retailers said the clothes—$60 or higher for a pair of jeans—were too expensive for the younger shoppers for whom they were targeted. Rio was expected to use its sourcing options to lower prices. Interviewed by *Women's Wear Daily (WWD)*, Klein said, "A designer's name on a product is not enough anymore. It has to be well-designed, made, and priced. We were not able to lower the price on our own."

At this time Simon also was engaged in negotiations with Oshkosh B'Gosh Inc., one of the largest producers of children's wear in the United States. The talks involved the possible acquisition by Oshkosh of all of Rio's businesses for $65 million, although Simon intended to remain in control of the Calvin Klein jeans business. No agreement was reached, however. On the breakup of their talks, Oshkosh's chief financial officer said that his company and Rio "couldn't reach an agreement on the strategic direction of the Rio business," while Simon blamed "Oshkosh's unwillingness to deal with Calvin Klein" and later told a *Crain's New York Business* reporter that Calvin Klein "was too racy for them . . . so I walked away."

But Simon's deal with Calvin Klein was also in jeopardy. Klein backed off from the deal in March, reportedly because of Rio's inability to finance it, and began talking to Fruit of the Loom. However, negotiations between these two companies ended in June, reportedly because Fruit of the Loom wanted rights to Calvin Klein's knit and woven casual sportswear pieces as well as jeans. Rio then raised its offer and came up with additional financing in the form of a partner, Charterhouse Group International, Inc., a closely held investment and buyout firm led by financier Merril Halpern.

Under their agreement, in August, Charterhouse (through Charter House Equity Partners II LP) acquired a 49.9 percent share in Rio, buying out Huang. In an earlier separate transaction Charterhouse and Simon had formed Calvin Klein Jeanswear Co., which completed the deal with Calvin Klein for around $50 million, exclusive of ongoing royalties and variables such as inventories. Designer Holdings Ltd. was created in March 1995 as the merged form of Rio Sportswear Inc. and Jeanswear Holdings Inc., which was the original holder of the Calvin Klein Jeans license.

Marketing CK Jeans and Khakis, 1995–96

Following the completion of the transaction, Designer Holdings implemented a number of initiatives to increase market share and improve the profitability of products under the Calvin Klein Jeans label. These included broadening the target market by reengineering the garments to provide a comfortable fit for a greater number of potential consumers so that, in Simon's words, "somebody other than Kate Moss could get into them." It also included increasing the value offered to consumers by lowering the price to between $45 and $52; targeting juniors', petites', and childrens' lines with a specific marketing strategy and product offering; expanding the core of basic styles for each line; and establishing an inventory replenishment plan to meet the requirements of retailers.

Calvin Klein Inc. created a youth-oriented advertising campaign for the jeans in 1995 that quickly incited controversy for showing young men and women in what the *Wall Street Journal* described as "suggestive poses." Amid outrage from a wide range of groups who were planning boycotts and picketing of stores carrying the designers' products, Klein called off the campaign, which was also criticized by President Clinton and made the subject of a federal investigation to determine if the models were under 18 years old. Klein later said he would reserve his racier ads for the European market.

According to Designer Holdings' 1996 description of its business, before it obtained the license Calvin Klein jeans were targeted primarily to the 30-to-50-year-old age group, and tailored to fit only a limited range of the consumer population. The company said it had subsequently designed, tailored, and targeted the products to both older and younger customers, including the teen market, thereby substantially increasing the potential market. Basic items, which change seasonally, accounted for 65 percent of Calvin Klein Jeans sales in 1995, while fashion items, continually updated, made up the other 35 percent. Denim Holdings contracted its manufacturing mostly to domestic companies, thereby allowing it to respond to trends quickly.

An amendment to the Calvin Klein licensing agreement in February 1995 added khaki pants, skirts, shorts, and related items to the Calvin Klein Jeanswear line, and a second amendment added caps. An aggressive advertising campaign ushered in the Calvin Klein Khakis Collection in March 1996, featuring narrow-hipped models—including Kate Moss—displaying, according to the *New York Times,* "equal measures of attitude and skin." The *Times* article added, however, that these advertisements were "much less provocative" than the jeans ads, and the full line included the popular baggy, oversized look. The khaki collection quickly became a $45 million business. A license for children's wear was acquired by Designer Holdings in early 1996.

The company had net revenues of $196 million in 1994 (including revenues as Rio Sportswear) and net income of $1.7 million. With the Calvin Klein business in operation throughout 1995, revenues shot up to $462 million and net income to $11 million. Licensee-generated revenues from the Calvin Klein Jeans line came to $361.4 million (with net income of $19.7 million), compared to only $59 million in 1993, when these products were controlled by Calvin Klein Inc. During 1995 KaiJay Pants Co., a subsidiary of Designer Holdings, was making Calvin Klein, Bill Blass, and Rifle jeans at the company's Pennsylvania plant.

At the beginning of 1996 Designer Holdings licensed the Rio label and sublicensed the Bill Blass labels to Commerce Clothing (25 percent owned by Designer Holdings), allowing the company to concentrate on high-end designer merchandise. The Rio and Bill Blass businesses generated about $101 million for Denim Holdings in 1995. Designer Holdings continued to market the products under the license and sublicense, receiving royalties from Commerce Clothing. In July 1995 Designer Holdings began distributing men's, women's, juniors', and petites' lines of Calvin Klein Jeans in Canada as well as in the United States.

Going Public and Further Developments, 1996–97

Designer Holdings made its initial public offering of stock in April 1996, selling 12 million shares of common stock at $18 a share and thereby raising, before expenses, $216 million. Some $34.7 million was earmarked to pay off a subordinated loan taken out in April 1995, with about the same amount to be used to retire an April 1995 loan from The CIT Group and other lenders. About half the stock was sold by existing shareholders instead of the firm. These included Simon, who held 46 percent of the company's shares subsequent to the public offering. Following the offering, New Rio L.L.C., whose controlling stockholders were Simon and Charterhouse Equity Partners II, held about 58 percent of the shares.

Investors not only snapped up Designer Holdings' offering of shares; within a few days they had bid the stock as high as $32.50 a share. One market observer told *Investment Dealers' Digest,* "A few years ago, the idea of a licensing operation going public would have been very odd. The market would have said it's a very nice brand name, but fashion is dangerous." Nineteen ninety-six was proving the year of the designer, however, with initial public offering of Donna Karan, Calvin Klein, and Mossimo also being grabbed by investors. Morgan Stanley & Co. Inc. and Merrill Lynch & Co., which co-managed Designer Holdings' IPO, forecast annual growth of 20 percent in the company's sales and 25 percent in earnings over the next three years and set target share prices in the mid-$30s.

In November 1996 Designer Holdings acquired 14 of the 15 existing Calvin Klein Outlet Stores owned by Calvin Klein Inc. in the United States and obtained the right to open additional outlets in the United States, Canada, and Mexico, together with the right to sell certain Calvin Klein-label goods in these stores. Simon said his company expected to open 50 more outlet stores in 1997.

Designer Holdings entered into a 30-year licensing agreement with a subsidiary of Donna Karan International Inc. in September 1996 for the exclusive production, sale, and distribution of men's, women's and, with certain exceptions, children's jeanswear under the DKNY Jeans label. The company saw DKNY jeans as supplemental to rather than competitive with Calvin Klein jeans, with the former directed to a more mature customer. The transaction dissolved, however, in March 1997. According to Simon, the major problem was Donna Karan's failure to deliver designs in time for his company to manufacture them. "They classically do things at the last minute and we don't do that," he told a *Wall Street Journal* reporter, adding that Donna Karan was late delivering designs for both fall and spring. Donna Karan International returned to Designer Holdings its initial $6 million payment and $1.26 million prepaid royalty.

Designer Holdings raised its net revenues to $480.4 million and its net income to $25.2 million in 1996, more than double the 1995 level. Nevertheless, investors expressed disappointment over the rupture of the Donna Karan deal and a statement by Designer Holdings that it expected revenues and profits to rise only slightly in 1997. The company's share price dropped as low as $6.62 in early April. Designer Holdings was reported to be looking for two licensing deals with nationally prominent designers—one for jeans and the other for lingerie or accessories.

Interviewed in 1996 by a *Women's Wear Daily* reporter in his garment district office, whose focus was a 300-gallon fish tank housing brilliant exotic species, Simon said he wanted to develop nonjeans businesses. "We'll look to two areas in the future—activewear, and underwear, which is where my background is." A *Crain's New York Business* reporter who interviewed him in 1997 described him as having a "stern meg and demeanor [that] make him a dead ringer for Marlon Brando." He retained about one-third of the company's stock.

Designer Holdings in 1996

Basic products, consisting of items such as jeans, T-shirts, shorts, shirts, vests, jackets, fleece shirts, and pants and caps, accounted for 60 percent of Designer Holdings' net sales in 1996. Fashion items, consisting of about 130 styles of bottoms and woven tops in the men's, women's, and juniors' lines, accounted for the other 40 percent. Men's products came to 41 percent of the total, juniors' for 36 percent, and women's for 23 percent. Seventy-eight percent of the company's goods were produced by U.S. vendors in 1996, 17.5 percent by overseas vendors, and 4.5 percent in the company's own production facilities in Nesquehonig, Pennsylvania, and Abbeville, South Carolina.

The Calvin Klein Jeans Label men's line was carried in 1,170 department stores and about 900 chain stores at the end of 1996. The juniors line was carried in about 1,120 department stores and about 650 chain stores, and the women's line, including petites in about 1,300 department stores and 250 chain stores. These lines were also available through smaller specialty stores and in about 150 shops within the stores of its major retailing customers. Federated Department Stores was the company's chief customer in 1996, accounting for 16.5 percent of sales, while May Department Stores accounted for 9.7 percent. Designer Holdings paid Calvin Klein Inc. $32.6 million in design and royalty fees in 1996 and received $2.2 million in royalties, primarily from the Rio and Bill Blass label products.

Principal Subsidiaries

Abbeville Acquisition Company; AEI Management Corporation; Broadway Jeanswear Company, Inc.; Broadway Jeanswear Holdings, Inc.; Broadway Jeanswear Sourcing, Inc.; Calvin Klein Jeanswear Company; CKJ Holdings, Inc.; CKJ Sourcing, Inc.; Jeanswear Holdings, Inc.; Kaijay Acquisition Company; New Bedford Shippers Corp.; Outlet Holdings, Inc.; Outlet Stores, Inc.; Rio Sportswear, Inc.

Further Reading

Bounds, Wendy, "Donna Karan Ends Designer Holdings Pact on Its Jeans," *Wall Street Journal,* March 6, 1997, p. B7.

Croghan, Lore, "Street Fears Designer Holdings Is Following Fashion IPO Pattern," *Crain's New York Business,* April 10, 1997, p. 4.

"Denim Dish," *WWD,* June 20, 1996, p. 13.

Elliott, Stuart, "Advertising," *New York Times,* March 14, 1996, p. D4.

Emert, Carol, "Calvin Klein's Jeans Licensee Files Initial Public Offering," *DNR*, March 14, 1996, p. 10.

Gault, Ylonda, "Stone-Washed Deal," *Crain's New York Business,* February 17, 1997, pp. 3, 21.

Goldman, Kevin, "Calvin Klein Halts Jeans Ad Campaign," *Wall Street Journal,* August 29, 1995, p. B14.

Gordon, Maryellen, "Calvin in Pact to Sell CK Jeans to Rio for $35M," *WWD,* February 11, 1994, pp. 1–2.

Lockwood, Lisa, "Charterhouse Group Buys 50 Percent Stake in Rio," *WWD,* August 29, 1994, p. 14.

——, "Hear Calvin Klein, Rio Sportswear Back in Talks for CK Jeanswear," *WWD,* June 24, 1994, pp. 2, 16.

Ozzard, Janet, Simon: Big Names, Big Plans," *WWD,* November 21, 1996, p. 8.

Ryan, Thomas J., "Jeans License Nets $32.6M for Calvin Klein in '96," *WWD,* April 10, 1997, p. 10.

"Warnaco in Stock Deal for Designer Holdings," *New York Times,* September 18, 1997, p. D4.

—Robert Halasz

Discreet Logic Inc.

5505, Boulevard St. Laurent
Suite 5200
Montreal, Quebec H2T 1S6
Canada
(514) 272-0525
Fax: (514) 272-0585
Web site: http://www.discreet.com

Public Company
Incorporated: 1991
Employees: 275
Sales: $83.99 million (1996)
Stock Exchanges: NASDAQ
SICs: 3577 Computer Peripheral Equipment, Not
    Elsewhere Classified; 3571 Electronic Computers;
    7372 Prepackaged Software; 7819 Services Allied to
    Motion Pictures

Montreal-based Discreet Logic Inc. is a leading developer and distributor of open-platform digital imaging processing software. The company's programs, designed to run on Silicon Graphics workstations and often packaged as turnkey systems including SGI workstations, scaleable disk arrays, and other peripherals, enable the nonlinear, online creation, editing, and compositing of visual imagery and special effects for film, video, and broadcast productions. Under the names Flame, Flint, Fire, Inferno, Frost, Vapour, Riot, Stone, Sparks, and others, the company's software systems have provided the special effects wizardry to such films as *Jurassic Park, Star Trek: First Contact, Independence Day, Speed, Mission: Impossible, Dragonheart, The Nutty Professor,* and *Twister*; television programs such as ''Star Trek: Voyager'' and ''Lois and Clark: The New Adventures of Superman''; commercials for clients including Coca-Cola, Pepsi, Budweiser, and Honda; music videos for the Rolling Stones, the Spice Girls, the Beatles, Michael Jackson, and others; and live broadcast productions such as coverage of the 1996 Presidential Election, the Eurovision Song Contest, the NCAA basketball tournament, and the 1996 Olym-

pic Games, as well as daily television news programming around the world. Sales of Discreet Logic's systems reached $84 million in 1996; approximately 57 percent of the company's sales were recorded outside of North America. Discreet Logic cofounder Richard Szalwinski serves as the company's chairman and CEO, and holds some 21 percent of the company's stock.

Discreet Logic systems support three principal segments of the film, video, and entertainment industry: visual effects, editing, and broadcast production. In visual effects, the company's products offer artists a wide-ranging set of image manipulation features such as perspective matching; image warping; simultaneous, multilevel animation tools; shadowing, lighting, skewing, and scaling and other 2D and 3D effects; paint, filter, and animation effects; color manipulation; and blue screen and compositing tools. Using Discreet Logic systems, artists are able to integrate special effects into film, video, and other projects to the extent where the effects seem ''real.'' Discreet Logic systems were at work, for example, in creating the dinosaurs of *Jurassic Park,* and in the handshake between actor Tom Hanks and President Kennedy in *Forrest Gump.*

Flame, the company's flagship program and chief revenue-generator, offers real-time, online, resolution-independent digital production capabilities for creating visual effects, compositing, editing, and advanced image processing. Because Flame processes film and video in a digital environment, artists are able to work in a nonlinear fashion, achieving greater flexibility over former analog or tape and film-based editing systems, while working online, that is, receiving near-immediate image processing. As an open-ended application, Flame often functions at the center of digital processing software suites supporting additional Discreet Logic and third-party programs. In mid-1996, the purchase price for the Flame software package was $175,000; as part of a turnkey system including a four-processor Silicon Graphics workstation, the purchase price was $450,000. Flame users typically rent time on Flame systems owned by production studios and others, with hourly rates ranging from $800 per hour to $1000 per hour or more. Similar to Flame is Flint, which provides an offline digital compositing and special effects environment with most of Flame's capabili-

Company Perspectives:

Discreet Logic is committed to independence: in ideas, expression and action. We develop high quality creative tools to empower the imagination and solve creative challenges. We're listening, evolving the technology to fit our clients' needs, and together, we're changing visual entertainment.

ties. Effects created with Flint can be fed into Flame for real-time viewing and manipulation.

The youngest member of the Discreet Logic visual effects family is Inferno, introduced in late 1995. The Inferno system is a fully integrated suite of image enhancement, motion tracking, and effects tools incorporating the capabilities of Flame while providing enhanced resolution and color processing capabilities. A turnkey Inferno system lists at $700,000; software-only Inferno systems sell for $225,000. Also among Discreet Logic's visual effects offerings is the company's Riot system, which provides film image scanning, image processing, and set-up, calibration, and control capacity for peripherals including monitors, film scanners and recorders, and tape drives.

While visual effects have been the core of Discreet Logic's sales, the company has branched out to offer editing and broadcast production systems as well. Fire, which began beta testing in 1996, offers online, non-compressed digital video editing capabilities, as well as professional audio features and limited special effects features. The company's Stone offers disk-based storage systems for video and film applications, while Wire offers networking and data transport capabilities. Discreet Logic has also entered broadcast production with the acquisition of Vapour, a system for creating the "virtual sets" used in live news, sports and other broadcasts, and Frost, which provides broadcasters with 3D modeling, animation, and rendering tools.

Growth Pains in the 1990s

Discreet Logic was founded in 1991 by Richard Szalwinski, former director of sales for Montreal-based Softimage, along with two Softimage coworkers, Simon Mowbray, and Diana Shearwood. Discreet Logic's first business was as a licensed distributor and developer for Eddie, a two-dimensional software program developed by Animal Logic Pty. Ltd. At the end of 1992, however, the company abandoned Eddie, reassigning the rights to that product to Animal Logic and Softimage. Instead, the company hitched its wagon to a new product, called Flame, bringing the company into the booming visual effects field. Flame, which took advantage of the advances being made in computer processing power, digital transfer techniques, and increases in storage and memory capacity, had been developed by Gary G. Tregaskis; as part of the rights assignment agreement with Discreet Logic, Tregaskis became a company shareholder and joined Discreet Logic as director of advanced products.

New technology made it possible not only to reduce the time and cost of producing special effects, but also introduced a whole new range of effects possibilities. Discreet Logic also looked to the rise of sophisticated, powerful computer workstations and related peripherals for its products. Where other visual effects systems producers, such as chief competitor Quantex, were developing proprietary hardware-based systems, Discreet Logic began designing its products for Silicon Graphics workstations. The open-ended nature of Discreet Logic's software meant that its customers could incorporate in-house and third-party programs into an integrated studio system based around Discreet Logic's products. Discreet Logic also developed more intuitive, graphical interfaces for its products, enabling artists to concentrate on the creative aspects, rather than the technical basis, of their work.

Sales neared $900,000 by the company's year-end in July 1992, although these sales were generated almost entirely by the Eddie package. By November 1992, however, the company began shipping a beta version of Flame; the full commercial release followed in January 1993. In July of that year, the company introduced the beta of Flint, shipping the full commercial release of this offline version of the Flame system by December 1993. Sales for that year reached $2.6 million.

Flame, and Flint, soon began to capture the attention of the film and video industry. Sales began to take off, aided by the success of such films as *The Mask, True Lies, Interview with a Vampire, Clear and Present Danger,* and others incorporating special effects generated on the Flame system. By year-end in 1994, revenues had jumped past $15 million. Soon after, the company brought in David Macrae, former director of the Softimage division, which had been acquired by Microsoft Advanced Technology, to serve as its president and CEO. Szalwinski was named the company's chairman, overseeing long-term strategy and new product development, while Macrae concentrated on the Discreet Logic's day-to-day activities, and particularly on expanding its sales and distribution systems.

The film and video industry's designers were quickly sold on the power and flexibility of the Flame and Flint systems. Use of Discreet Logic's products spread through the advertising, television, and film and video industries. Sales were further driven by audience demand: wowed by the effects in films such as *Apollo 13* and *Batman Forever,* audiences were bowled over by the near-lifelike dinosaurs of *Jurassic Park,* and the film industry raced to provide newer, more daring special effects to satisfy public demand. But it was the blockbuster hit *Forrest Gump,* perhaps more than any other film, that took the demand for Flame to new heights. By mid-1995, Flame had become the market leader among special effects applications. In June 1995, Discreet Logic went public, and the graphics designers' excitement spread to the investment community, which boosted the company stock from an opening price of $21 per share to $33 on the first day of trading. By year-end 1995 Discreet Logic's sales had more than quadrupled over the previous year, reaching $64.5 million and generating a net income of nearly $8 million.

With the market for its Flame and Flint systems inherently small—there were only some 2,500 production studios in the world—Discreet Logic began looking to expand its product line. In August 1995 the company unveiled its high-end Inferno system, and readied the launch of Fire to the video post-production community for the following month. Then in October 1995, Discreet Logic acquired Innsbruck, Austria-based Computer-und-Serviceverwaltungs AG (COSS) and assets of IMP Innovative Medientechnik-und-Planungs-GmbH, which was based in Gletendork/Kaltenberg, Germany, bringing in these companies' Vapour and Frost real-time broadcast production technologies; this acquisition followed up on the May 1995 acquisition of Brughetti Corporation, which added a number of software products initially marketed by Discreet Logic under the names Air, Pure, Slice, and Diplomat.

By the beginning of 1996, however, Discreet Logic began to show signs of growing pains. Macrae left the company, without explanation, and Szalwinski took over as interim and then permanent CEO and president. Next, the company faced the fickleness of the investment community, as the love affair with so-called high technology stocks turned sour. Despite continued growth of Discreet Logic's sales, the company's stock plunged as its earnings projections fell. The chief cause for this was the announcement of a new Silicon Graphics workstation, dubbed InfiniteReality, which in turn caused customers to hold off on purchases of Discreet Logic turnkey and software systems. Discreet Logic was forced to discount its Flame and Flint sales. While demand for Flame slumped, customers shied away from the company's new Fire program, which had proven to be "buggy" in its initial release. By year-end 1996, sales growth had slowed, to $84 million, while the company posted a net loss of $44 million, including a $15 million charge for a restructuring begun late in that fiscal year.

The company announced an even more extensive restructuring for its 1997 fiscal year. Discreet Logic reorganized its activities into three major areas: product development, sales and marketing, and finance. Staff was cut by some 28 percent, or 105 employees, as the company shut down a number of its offices, including its Cambridge, Massachusetts office, sales offices in New York and Boca Raton, Florida, and a manufacturing and integration facility in Ireland. The company's research and development activities, which represented nearly $17 million of the company's operating expenses, were consolidated at its Montreal base. The company also stopped development of the products added through its Brughetti acquisition.

Despite its growth pains, the young company remained a key player in the post-production industry. The incorporation of Vapour and Frost allowed it to extend its product range—and customer base—into the live broadcast production arena, while new product announcements, for the Stone, Wire, Sparks, and other software systems enhanced its capabilities in the video and film industries. Adapting its products to the Silicon Graphics InfiniteReality workstations, Discreet Logic unveiled the newest versions of its Inferno, Flame, and Flint systems in May 1997. In the face of increased competition from Quantex and Avid Technology, the upgraded systems were greeted enthusiastically by the post-production design community. With the loyal support of graphics artists, and consumer demand for larger and ever more exciting special effects, Discreet Logic was poised to retain its position as the industry's market leader.

Principal Divisions

Discreet Logic France; Discreet Logic Germany; Discreet Logic UK; Discreet Logic Asia.

Further Reading

Deck, Stewart, "Discreet Effects," *Computerworld*, November 27, 1995, p. 123.

Dickson, Glen, "Discreet Logic Stock Nosedives," *Broadcasting & Cable*, February 19, 1996, p. 68.

Higgins, Steve, "Discreet Logic Inc.," *Investor's Business Daily*, August 2, 1995, p. A6.

Lowry, Tom, "Discreet Suffers Growing Pains," *USA Today*, May 2, 1996, p. 3B.

Sanders, Lisa, "Life Is Like a Lousy Box of Chocolates," *Business Week*, July 15, 1996, p. 8.

Soter, Tom, "Some Like It Hot," *Shoot*, February 3, 1995, p. 19.

Stalter, Katherine, "Discreet Logic Confirms Revamp," *Daily Variety*, July 31, 1996, p. 19.

—M. L. Cohen

The Dixie Group, Inc.

1100 S. Watkins St.
Chattanooga, Tennessee 37404
U.S.A.
(423) 689-2501
Fax: (423) 493-7353

Public Company
Founded: 1920 as Dixie Mercerizing Co.
Employees: 5,900
Sales: $615.1 million (1996)
Stock Exchanges: NASDAQ
SICs: 2200 Textile Mill Products

The Dixie Group, Inc., previously Dixie Yarns, Inc., manufactures floorcovering and textiles. One of the largest floorcovering companies in the United States, Dixie operates four distinct floorcovering businesses. Masland Carpets produces high-end residential and commercial carpets and rugs. Carriage Industries makes tufted broadloom carpet for modular homes and recreation vehicles. Bretlin Needlebond makes indoor/outdoor carpet and floor mats for home centers and mass marketers, and Candlewick Yarns produces proprietary yarn for the tufting industry. Floorcovering accounted for two-thirds of the company's sales in 1996.

The rest of the company's sales came from its three textile and apparel businesses. Dixie Yarns is one of the largest spinners and dyers of cotton and high performance yarns in the world. Caro Knit, the company's fabric manufacturer, produces fine quality 100 percent cotton knit fabrics. C-Knit Apparel makes men's and boys' knit sports apparel. The company changed its name to The Dixie Group in May 1997.

Early Years, 1920–50

In 1920, several Chattanooga hosiery mill owners and other business leaders founded the Dixie Mercerizing Company to specially treat cotton yarn which was then used to make ladies' stockings. Two of the investors were J. T. Lupton and Cartter Lupton who became, respectively, president and treasurer of the company. In its first year Dixie had sales of $1.8 million and a profit of $56,784.

Named for a British calico printer, the mercerizing process used sodium hydroxide to shrink cotton yarn. This gave the yarn a silklike luster, popular for stockings, and also made it better able to hold dye. The company's biggest problem was finding an adequate supply of quality yarn that could stand up under the high tension required for mercerizing.

The owners of the nearby Dixie Spinning Mills, including the Luptons, decided to build a modern spinning plant to meet that need. According to Dixie's 75th Anniversary publication, "a 'model town with 72 artistically designed homes' along with playgrounds and a school were part of the plans for what would become known as Lupton City." The venture eventually cost $9 million. In 1925, Dixie Spinning Mills merged with Dixie Mercerizing Company. During the mid-20s, J. Burton Frierson became treasurer of Dixie.

The company remained profitable during the Depression, and in 1936, added to its production capability with the purchase of the Durham Hosiery Mills in North Carolina. During World War II, Dixie supplied the military and, experimenting with the "miracle fibers" developed during the war, was among the first spinners in the world to make synthetic yarn for military shoe laces.

After the war, J. Burton Frierson was named president and started expanding the company again. The company purchased two plants in North Carolina and in 1950 built a new spinning plant at Lupton to produce synthetic yarn.

Diversification, 1951–79

In 1951, Dixie began to diversify, moving into the making of carpet yarn with the purchase of Dalton Candlewick, spinners of cotton yarn for the high-volume tufting industry. In 1963, Frierson retired as president, becoming chairman of the board.

The Candlewick business grew quickly in the 1960s and 70s, taking up to a 10 percent share in the commodity nylon carpet yarn market. The company's core business had steady growth as well, producing yarns and threads for knitting, sewing, lace, braid, and related apparel uses. During this period Dixie commanded about 5 percent of the commodity apparel yarn market. Recognizing that the term mercerizing no longer reflected the scope of its operations, Dixie Mercerizing Company changed its name to Dixie Yarns, Inc. in December 1964.

To meet the demand for its yarns, the company built new plants for both Candlewick and the Apparel Yarn and Thread Division. It also bought Yarn Crafters, in 1968, and Southern Stretch Yarns, in 1969. Acquisitions continued during the 1970s, with the purchase of Sellers Manufacturing Co. & Sellers Dyeing Co. and the Jordan Spinning Co.

During this period, Don Frierson was named president of Candlewick. In 1979 he became Dixie's president and CEO when his father stepped down as chairman of the board. The senior Frierson had run the company for more than 40 years and the Frierson family had controlled the stock for nearly that long.

The Specialty Yarn Niche, 1980s

In 1980, Dixie Yarns operated 17 plants in five states and had a workforce of some 5,000 employees. Revenues that year came to $217 million, with nearly 40 percent of sales coming from commodity apparel and carpet yarns. Those two markets were to prove vulnerable for the company. The surge of cheap, imported textiles from Taiwan, Hong Kong, and China severely reduced the demand among Dixie's clients for apparel yarn. At the same time, carpet manufacturers in the U.S. found they could save 10 to 15 percent on the cost of carpet yarn by spinning their own.

Rather than try to compete for those markets, Frierson's strategy was to switch to high-margin specialty yarns, essentially returning Dixie to its roots. As Ayssa Lappen explained in a 1988 *Forbes* article, "Cotton apparel yarn with a stretchable Lycra core costs more to manufacture than traditional, undyed commodity cotton yarn, but it also sells for about one-and-a-half times the price."

To carry out his plans, Frierson had to close plants, lay off 30 percent of the workforce, and change a 60-year corporate culture. He implemented profit sharing and quality circles and set a goal for managers of 20 percent pretax return on capital, backing it up with stock options and a cash bonus. Sales, service, and quality were the focus of staff training, augmented by $50 million spent on new equipment and product development labs.

Frierson also spent money on acquisitions. In 1986 he bought China Grove Cotton Mills Co., which gave Dixie entry into more specialty yarn markets with Nomex, a synthetic fiber used in fire-retardant clothing, and Kevlar, for bulletproof vests and uncuttable safety gloves. Late in the year he took Dixie public. The public offering involved complex stock transactions that enabled Frierson and other members of the management team to retain majority control of the stock and "keep Dixie beyond the reach of predators," according to a 1988 *Textile World* article.

Acquisitions and complex stock deals continued with the $78 million purchase in 1987 of Ti-Caro, Inc. The addition of Ti-Caro involved Dixie in the making of knit fabrics for the first time through its Caro Knit division which produced 100 percent cotton knit fabrics. It also opened more than 15 new specialty yarn markets and made Dixie the country's leader in three major specialty markets: specialty yarns, knit fabrics, and carpet yarns. Dixie also became the largest supplier of industrial sewing thread used in items ranging from tea bags to baseballs. The two acquisitions doubled the size of the company and moved it to number seven among publicly held U.S. textile companies.

The industry recognized Frierson's talents and vision. He served as president of the American Yarn Spinners Association and chaired the American Textile Manufacturers Institute (ATMI) International Trade Committee. During 1988 alone, he was president of ATMI, chairman of the Fiber, Fabric and Apparel Coalition, and vice president of the National Cotton Council. That year, the editors of *Textile World* chose Frierson as the Textile Leader of the Year. In an interview with the magazine, Frierson described his business strategy: "Our basic markets are knit fabrics, threads, carpet yarns, and fine-count and specialty yarns. What we've tried to do is enhance our position in those four areas through increased productivity or plant improvement, through developing new processes or products, or through acquisitions." Dixie's revenue in 1988 was $606 million, with the company employing almost 10,000 people in 36 plants. Those sale figures proved to be a peak for the company, however, as sales fell for the next four years.

Floor Coverings and Consumer Products, 1990s

Frierson continued to consolidate facilities, cut payroll costs, and modernize the company's equipment, spending over $154 million on capital improvements between 1988 and 1993. Frierson's goal was fairly straightforward: to shift the company's emphasis from producing yarn and textiles for manufacturers to making consumer products with its own yarn and textiles itself. The most reasonable area to focus on was carpets since the company's Candlewick Yarns already was one of the country's largest producers of high-quality yarn used to make carpets for homes and businesses, bath and accent rugs, and floorcoverings for cars.

The carpet industry was going through a period of major consolidations during the early part of the decade, and Frierson made his move in 1993. He began with the acquisition of Carriage Industries. That 24-year-old company was based in

Georgia and made carpets for modular homes, recreational vehicles, and trade show industries. Major clients included Fleetwood Enterprises and Homes by Oakwood. The purchase included Carriage's subsidiary, Bretlin, Inc., which specialized in making durable indoor/outdoor needlebond carpets and runners, floor mats, and decorative accent rugs. The Bretlin Broadloom products were sold at home centers, mass marketers, and independent retailers including Home Depot, Lowe's, and Payless.

Dixie already owned shares in Masland Carpets, a manufacturer of high-end, designer-oriented carpets and rugs for the residential and commercial markets, and bought the entire company later that year. In 1994, Dixie bought California-based Patrick Carpet Mills and incorporated it into Masland, marketing its product line under the name Patrick Carpet. Masland customers included Nordstroms, Hilton Hotels, and Applebee's International, and the company was a partner in the DuPont Commercial Flooring Systems Network. At the end of 1996 Dixie bought Danube Carpet Mills, Inc., from Shelter Components Corporation for approximately $25 million. Danube made carpets for the same markets as Carriage Industries and its carpet manufacturing operations were consolidated into Carriage's facilities. Its carpet yarn plant became part of Dixie's Candlewick division.

Between 30 to 40 percent of Candlewick's yarns went to the companies in Dixie's floorcovering business. Other customers included Magee Automotive Products, Bentley Mills, Regal Rugs, and Fieldcrest. Frierson's research and development efforts at Candlewick led to the development of Weave-Tech, a spun yarn with a spandex core, and Naturesse, a heatset cotton yarn designed for bathroom rugs, which combines the aesthetics of cotton with the durability of synthetics. Three years after the purchase of Carriage Industries, the floorcovering business accounted for two-thirds of Dixie's sales.

The other part of the business, yarns and fabric, also underwent changes during the decade. Frierson's strategy in this area was to continue building on Dixie's niche of cotton and high performance specialty synthetic yarns while growing its own apparel business. As with floorcoverings, his goal was to manufacture consumer products.

Dixie Yarns continued to be the foundation for the company's textile/apparel business. While it still produced mercerized high-luster cotton, it also manufactured and marketed Supima and Pima cottons, combed and carded ring spun yarns, and Corespun yarns containing Lycra. Its spinning facilities produced DuPont's Thermastat and Coolmax polyester fibers and Courtauld's Tencel, a Lyocell fiber. By the mid-90s, Dixie Yarns was providing yarn to seven different markets in addition to various specialty markets: high-end upholstery, home furnishings, sportswear, hosiery, sweaters, underwear, and automotive body cloth.

Caro Knit, which was part of the Ti-Caro acquisition in 1987, continued to produce 100 percent cotton knit fabrics for retailers such as J.C. Penney and Brooks Brothers, catalogue retailers including Land's End and L.L. Bean, as well as sportswear manufacturer Polo. But as part of Dixie's customer product focus, Caro Knit began operating as a vertical company, using yarn from Dixie Yarns to make its fabric which was then turned into knit sports apparel by C-Knit, the third company in Dixie's textile and apparel business.

C-Knit began operating in 1995, providing cutting operations in South Carolina to prepare components that were shipped to plants controlled by Dixie in Central America where they were sewn into garments. The finished pieces were then shipped back to C-Knit warehouses in the U.S. ready to be sent to customers. Most of the garments were shirts—polo, henley, crew neck, and fleece—for customers including Ashworth, Coca Cola, and Cumberland Bay by Fruit of the Loom.

In 1996, Dixie sold its Threads USA division to American & Efird, Inc., a subsidiary of Ruddick Corporation, further honing its concentration on floorcovering and textile/apparel. More than half of Dixie's sales for the year were for consumer products, and the company redesigned its administrative and operating procedures and created a new management structure to respond more quickly and flexibly to changes in the markets.

In May 1997, shareholders voted to change the company's name to The Dixie Group, Inc. With increased sales for the first quarter of 1997 in both its business segments, it appeared that the years of restructuring had served their purpose. But Frierson did not rule out additional, "strategically appropriate acquisitions" to augment Dixie's growth.

Principal Subsidiaries

Carriage Industries, Inc.; Candlewick-Ringgold, Inc.; Candlewick-Lemoore, Inc.; Dixie Experts, Inc.; Dixie Funding, Inc.; Masland Carpets, Inc.; Patrick Carpet Mills, Inc.; T-C Threads, Inc.; Threads of Puerto Rico, Inc.

Further Reading

Christiansen, Larry, and Jan Sheehy, "Dixie's Dan Frierson Accentuates the Positive," *Textile World*, October 1988, p. 47.
"Dixie Yarns Capitalizes on Auto Yarn Quality," *Textile World*, February 1989, p. 48.
Dixie Yarns Inc., "Dixie Yarns: Seventy-Five Years of Workin' Together," Chattanooga, TN, 1995.
Jaffee, Thomas, "Whistling Dixie," *Forbes*, August 30, 1993, p. 240.
Lappan, Alyssa A., "Number One in Niches," *Forbes*, February 8, 1988, p. 45.
"Shelter Components Corporation Completes the Sale of Its Carpet Operations," *PRNewswire*, Elkhart, Inc., January 2, 1997.

—Ellen D. Wernick

Dolby Laboratories Inc.

100 Potrero Avenue
San Francisco, California 94103
U.S.A.
(415) 558-0200
Fax: (415) 863-1373
Web site: http://www.dolby.com

Private Company
Founded: 1964
Employees: 300
Sales: $60 million (1995)
SICs: 3679 Electronic Components, Not Elsewhere
    Classified

Dolby Laboratories Inc. made "dolby" a household word when it developed the first commercially feasible noise-reduction device for magnetic tape. Now providing noise-reduction products for film, fax, and the Internet as well as music, Dolby remains a private company owned by its founder and namesake. The company is a leader in both analog and digital markets.

The inventor and owner behind Dolby, Ray Dolby, worked his way through high school and later Stanford University, at Ampex (a tape company). There, he was part of the six-member team that developed the first videotape recorder in 1957. He then attended Cambridge University in England, where he received a Ph.D. in physics before joining UNESCO in 1963. It was during his professional tenure at UNESCO that Dolby developed his namesake noise reduction process, visiting an ashram in India in 1964. While recording sitar music with a reel-to-reel Ampex tape recorder, Dolby was bothered by the hiss on his tapes, which drowned the subtleties of the Indian musical instruments. After meditating on the problem, he invented electronic circuits that eliminate this hiss, and made his fortune on the product. Further, he remained in complete control of his invention and his private company through the changing technological times to come. While Dolby controls the patents and trademark for his product, he made the invention attractive by claiming very little in early royalties: sometimes only 7½ cents per tape player.

Dolby was the first to create such a noise-reduction system for tape, although phonograph records had previously contained frequency adjustments that suppressed needle noise. Creating a noise-suppression circuit for the high-frequency static (or hiss) on magnetic tape was a slightly different procedure. With Dolby sound, circuits artificially boost the loudness of the highest frequencies of music while it is being recorded, and then the playback circuit reverses the process, shrinking high-frequency loudness back to its original levels. The shrinkage process is what makes the tape hiss less audible. The process only takes place during quiet musical passages, for two reasons. First, magnetic tape is not capable of increasing the high frequency of loud music, since it is already at its limit. Second, the process is unnecessary in loud passages, as the ear is unable to hear static over high volume.

A capable inventor, Dolby proved to be a shrewd businessman as well. In the 1960s, he faced several problems in launching his sound-reduction device. First, he had to persuade manufacturers of tape players to use Dolby circuits before many music tapes were released in Dolby format. However, he was seemingly caught in a Catch-22 situation, for there was no reason for music publishers to release Dolby tapes before consumers owned Dolby players.

To penetrate the market, Dolby enlisted professional recording studios first, and then pursued manufacturers of high-end consumer electronics. Once these sectors were on board, Dolby was able to convince mass market manufacturers that Dolby sound was a seemingly "high-end" product that they could integrate at low cost. To ease the compatibility transition (allowing consumers to continue playing non-Dolby tapes), the new recorders were issued with switches that turned the noise-suppression circuit on and off. When the mass market electronics makers began issuing Dolby players, Dolby's first problem was solved: audio cassettes with Dolby sound quickly followed.

The digitalization process came to music recording in the 1970s, threatening to make Dolby noise reduction a dinosaur. Responding to change by diversifying his product, Dolby

Company Perspectives:

Dolby Labs seeks to provide the highest quality sound-reduction processes for music, film, television, the Internet, fax, and other recorded applications. Owned and operated by inventor Ray Dolby, the company has been at the vanguard of both digital and analog recording technology since 1965.

branched into movie theater sound systems, perfecting Dolby Stereo sound around 1975. He quickly followed this innovation by penetrating the home video market with Dolby Surround Sound for videorecorder stereo systems.

By 1982, the company was receiving $6 million annually in licensing fees from approximately 125 audio equipment manufacturers. With circuits in about 70 million different consumer products, Dolby had a monopoly in the consumer noise-reduction field. In the 1980s, virtually all prerecorded cassettes used Dolby B. The first major threat to Dolby's positioning began quietly in 1980, when dbx—a Newton, Massachusetts company—sold its system to several audio manufacturers, including the major Japanese company Matsushita Electric. In April 1982, the competition began to look more serious. Dbx pulled ahead of Dolby, developing the first miniature noise-reduction circuit for Walkmen, which at this time represented the fastest-growing consumer audio segment. Dbx, which had been developed in 1971, was a serious threat to Dolby because it reduced background noise by 40 decibels, a considerable improvement over Dolby's 10. Initially, high prices had made dbx unfamiliar to consumers, but the system was favored by recording professionals. By 1982, dbx had already far overtaken Dolby and held 70 percent of the commercial recording equipment market. In response to the threat posed by dbx's competition, Dolby introduced an upgraded version of its system, Dolby C, as well as a portable product.

The 1980s brought Dolby to Hollywood, with the beginning of film applications. As the movie *Tommy*, with its quadraphonic sound had shown, Dolby A could be incorporated into the optical soundtrack of film, improving the dynamic range and sound quality of that medium. Dolby Spectral Recording (or SR), which was introduced in 1986, worked on magnetic sound tracks for film as well as music cassettes, producing digital clarity from an analog sound system. Dolby SR used the same basic principle as Dolby's original circuit, monitoring the sound signal and adjusting frequency boost to suit the loudness level, with different signal levels boosted at different amounts. The result was a system that was dynamic and almost infinitely flexible. The system was used by many professional studios instead of digital recording, and in 1988 Dolby SR was in use at movie theaters showing the films *Robocop* and *Space*.

In 1989, Dolby covered all bases by simultaneously advancing in the digital and analog markets. Thus, the company worked to keep analog sound competitive in the age of digital recording, while placing a foot firmly in the digital era at the same time. First, a modified version of Dolby SR was introduced: Dolby S-Type. S-Type differed from Dolby SR in that it was compatible with the Dolby B system, which was the standard system used with domestic cassettes. While Dolby B reduced hiss by 10 decibels, Dolby S-Type improved noise-reduction to 24 decibels, using a bank of variable filters. At 24 decibels, noise is virtually inaudible by the human listener. Dolby C, which was present in high-quality tape decks, already provided more or less the same amount of noise reduction as Dolby S; however, Dolby S added 10 decibels of noise reduction in the lower midrange, which was vulnerable to "grunge" sounds. In short, Dolby S presented a threat to digital sound by making analog tapes sound just as good. Further, Dolby ensured that tapes using S-type sound reduction sounded good when played on the 270 million consumer-owned tape players with B-type sound reduction facilities. Meanwhile, Sony developed a set of microchips that could be built into recorders to provide S-type capabilities.

At the same time, Dolby came forward with a new digital recording system: Adaptive Transform Coding (ATC), which reduced the number of bits of information needed to record high-fidelity sound, allowing digital recordings to store six times as much sound as existing CDs, and thus making digital recording a cheaper process. The company had already experimented with digital coding, circulating its Delta Link system in satellite broadcasting markets in Australia, where it also was used to archive music recordings.

In 1992, Dolby achieved $40 million in revenues, with a third from royalty payments that headed straight to the bottom line. Dolby sound reduction was now featured on approximately 380 million tape players, boom boxes, headphones, and car stereos, as well as a few billion audio-cassette packages.

Dolby won a technological coup over competitors at Eastman Kodak and Optical Radiation Corp. in June of 1992, when the company premiered its new digitally encoded Dolby Stereo soundtrack process for movies with the release of the film *Batman Returns*. While competitors had released digital soundtracks, Dolby's was more attractive to distributors. A previous digital system, released by Dolby's competitors, forced distributors to stock both digital and analog film prints due to compatibility issues. Dolby, on the other hand, innovated SRD—a six-track digital soundtrack that was squeezed into the empty spaces between the holes of a traditional 35 millimeter movie print, allowing distributors to work with just one print for both digital and analog sound. In fact, this was the first successful combination of digital and analog sound on a single print. The cost to theaters for playback equipment that could produce SRD sound was about $20,000, which was a major savings over dual-system alternatives. The quality of SRD was comparable to a CD, professional digital formats, and Dolby Stereo 70mm magnetic releases.

The home movie-watcher was Dolby's next target. The company adapted SRD sound to the consumer video market, creating AC-3, its digital surround sound system for the home. The AC-3 system recorded five audio channels and an extra subwoofer channel as digital code. Separate left and right surround channels were provided. Through an agreement with a Santa Clara, California-based chipmaker, Zoran Corp., Dolby promoted this six channel digital signal processing chip as a new consumer product priced at $20 in 1993. Dolby aggressively marketed its surround sound, creating a presence through a Dolby Audio/Video Forum on America Online's Internet service. Subsequently, Bartelmann Music Group began to release music in the Dolby surround format.

As the United States prepared to adopt high-definition television as a standard in the early 1990s, two of the corporate teams involved in the nationwide competition adopted Dolby audio coding systems. When the "HDTV Grand Alliance" was formed to create technical specifications for a digital prototype system of President Clinton's plan for national information superhighways, the Alliance chose Dolby's AC-3 audio system as the audio technology. Dolby was selected based on critical listening tests at Lucasfilms' Skywalker Ranch in California.

The mid- to late-1990s brought Dolby to the world with telecommunications applications. In 1995, Dolby Fax technology brought Dolby sound to global transmissions by dubbing studios. Invented to solve the problem of transmitting high-quality audio for local storage or over satellites, Dolby Fax was used in remote past-production dubbing for movies, remote audio feeds for radio shows, and remote digital distribution of Hollywood movies to theaters with Dolby sound. The next year, Dolby made its first Internet audio deal. Liquid Audio, a San Francisco company, launched Dolby's Liquifier audio mastering tool for World Wide Web developers.

Invented at an Indian ashram in the age of analog, Dolby has proved to be a resilient and versatile company, able to ride the technological waves into the digital age and the era of high-definition TV. While the company has been presented with challenges by dbx and others, its noise-reduction products are now so enormously widespread that the name "dolby" is almost synonymous with sound recording.

Further Reading

Atwood, Brett, "Liquid Audio Gets Dolby License," *Billboard,* August 31, 1996, pp. 6–7.

Coghlan, Andy, "Plot to Remove Gunpowder from Fireworks," *New Scientist,* November 6, 1993, p. 22.

"Dolby Fights Back Against the Digital Wave," *New Scientist,* April 29, 1989, p. 32.

Fox, Barry, "Dolby Doubles Trouble for Competitors," *New Scientist,* November 25, 1989, p. 36.

——, "Squeezed Sound for the Silver Screen," *New Scientist,* July 13, 1981, p. 26.

——, "Video Viewers to Surround Themselves with Sound," *New Scientist,* May 2, 1992, p. 20.

Howard, Niles, "Dolby Labs' Pesky Rival," *Dun's Business Month,* July, 1982, pp. 60–61.

Hodges, Ralph, "Seizing the Day," *Stereo Review,* June, 1992, p. 112.

Krause, Reinhardt, "HDTV Alliance Polishes Spec on Prototype," *Electronic News,* October 25, 1993, pp. 1–2.

Mitchell, Peter W., "The Sound of Dolby AC-3," *Stereo Review,* July, 1995, p. 100.

Nunziata, Susan, "'Batman' 1st Feature to Fly with Dolby Digital Sound," *Billboard,* June 6, 1992, pp. 10–11.

Nunziata, Susan, "Dolby Digital May Be Heard on Home Vid, Audio Products," *Billboard,* September 5, 1992, pp. 57–58.

Phillips, Barry, "Carriers and Dolby jam on Remote Audio," *Telecommunications,* May, 1995, p. 14.

Stark, Craig, "Dolby S: A New Standard for Cassette Recording?", *Stereo Review,* May, 1990, pp. 77–79.

Straley, Karl, "The Sound of Movies: An Inside Look at Modern Cinema and What It Means for Home Theater," *Stereo Review,* January, 1995, pp. 114–18.

"The Sound of Silence on Film," *New Scientist,* March 3, 1988, p. 69.

Young, Jeffrey, "The Inventor from the Ashram," *Forbes,* August 3, 1992, pp. 90–91.

—Heidi Feldman

Dorling Kindersley Holdings plc

9 Henrietta Street
Covent Garden
London WC2E 8PS
United Kingdom
44 171 836 5411
Fax: 44 171 836 7570
Web site: http://www.dk.com

Public Company
Founded: 1974
Employees: 1,157
Sales: £174.4 million (US$270.9 million)
Stock Exchanges: London
SICs: 2741 Miscellaneous Publishing; 7812 Motion
    Picture & Video Production; 2721 Periodicals; 2731
    Book Publishing

For nearly a quarter-century, Dorling Kindersley Holdings plc (DK) has focused on creating an enduring catalog of over 900 reference and nonfiction titles. By the mid-1990s, it ranked as the most prolific publisher of multimedia products in Europe. Its reference and nonfiction books are sold in more than 80 nations worldwide and have been translated into three dozen languages. In fiscal 1996 alone, the company sold 40 million books. Other products include CD-ROMS, calendars, stickers, and videos. While other publishing houses might float more titles per year than DK has in its entire history, few can boast, as DK can, that 90 percent of its catalog—including the first book produced under its own imprint—is still in print. The company has also enjoyed constancy of ownership and leadership; co-founder, chairman, and CEO Peter Kindersley and his family retained a 35.5 percent stake in the house through the mid-1990s.

By 1996, operations included DK Adult books, constituting 48 percent of sales; DK Children's books, generating 33 percent of revenues; DK Multimedia products, with 12 percent of revenues; DK Direct sales, at five percent of revenues, and DK Vision (television and video production), with two percent of sales. Widely recognized titles—many of which have been produced in multiple formats (book, CD-ROM, video)—include: *Ultimate Sex Guide, Incredible Cross Sections, Royal Horticultural Society Encyclopedia of Gardening, The Children's Illustrated Encyclopedia,* and the *Eyewitness Series.*

Home-Based Business Founded in 1970s

The publisher is named for its two founders, Christopher Dorling and Peter Kindersley, both of whom were working for British publisher Mitchell Beazley in the early 1970s. Dorling was a cartographer-turned-salesman, while Kindersley had abandoned a career in painting to become art director at Mitchell Beazley. It was there that Kindersley first envisioned his unique brand of reference works: top-quality books that combined copious graphics with concise text to convey universally popular subject areas like arts and crafts, health, and nature. When Kindersley's managers at Mitchell Beazley balked at the costly concept, he decided to strike out on his own, inviting Dorling to handle the day-to-day operations while he worked on the creative side. Pooling £10,000 in savings between them, the duo founded their business in 1974 in Kindersley's London home.

Realizing that the publishing business required a much larger initial investment than they were prepared to risk, Dorling and Kindersley started out as "book packagers," creating, laying out, and editing works, then licensing them to larger publishers in exchange for royalties on sales. Though this strategy reduced the partners' profit potential, it also reduced the risk of printing thousands of books that could go unsold. Their first contract went to America's Alfred A. Knopf Inc., which purchased a license for three references. Two of these sold just enough to break even, but John Hedgecoe's *The Book of Photography,* published in 1976, would go on to sell a million copies and was still in print in the late 1990s. Other well-known DK titles from the 1970s include *Baby & Child* (1976) and *Success with Houseplants* (1979), selling a combined total of 4.5 million copies by the mid-1990s.

Company Perspectives:

We believe that more and more people around the world are rediscovering learning, and that being a self-educator can bring great benefits. To meet this growing market, DK is making relevant learning tools for people at all stages of their lives—from early childhood, through the school years, to work, hobbies, and retirement. By providing such quality learning tools, we believe that DK can really make a difference in people's lives.

Launch of DK Imprint in Early 1980s

By the early 1980s, the design formula that would become Dorling Kindersley's hallmark was well-established. Unlike most British publishers, who compiled a large, rather scattershot list of books each year, DK concentrated exclusively on reference and nonfiction, initially targeted solely toward the adult market. The house's easily-recognized style—dubbed "lexigraphic" by creator Kindersley—included bright, full-color, sharply defined photos, drawings, and graphics on a white background with "extended captions" as text. As Kindersley told *Business Week's* Heidi Dawley in 1996, "the information leaps off the pages." Extensive use of color illustrations and high-quality papers often pushed per-page costs to an average of over £1,000. Besides being visually attractive, DK's use of minimal text and widely popular subject matter also facilitated easy translation into languages other than the core English. By the mid-1990s, over 40 percent of the publisher's sales were made outside the U.S. and U.K. This global reach—initially achieved through licensing—helped mitigate the publishing house's high design costs through efficiencies of scale.

To further ensure sales, the editors often commissioned a well-known expert on a subject to act as author or garnered endorsements from trusted authorities. DK's first self-published work, *The First Aid Manual* (1982), carried the imprimatur of the British Red Cross. That year also saw the launch of DK's all-time-bestselling *Family Medical Guide* under an endorsement from The American Medical Association. By the mid-1990s, successive editions of this title had sold a cumulative six million copies and had been translated into 15 languages.

Late 1980s Expansion Into Children's Reference

When Christopher Dorling elected to retire in 1987, he sold his 50 percent stake in the venture that bore his name back to the company. With a view to forging an alliance with a major publisher and generating growth funds, DK sold the half interest to the Readers Digest Association Inc. for £1.3 million that same year. This cash infusion was invested in the development of a children's division, launched in 1987 with the *Windows on the World* series. The publisher inaugurated its most successful children's series in 1988 with the first edition of David Macaulay's *The Way Things Work*. DK also formed a 50/50 joint venture with France's Editions Gallimard to publish the first book in the *Eyewitness* series that same year. *Eyewitness Bird* and 54 other volumes in the ongoing series would go on to sell a cumulative 18 million copies in 39 languages in just eight years.

These new references were not only big sellers, but also made a major splash in publishing circles. According to a 1996 *Publishers Weekly* article by Sally Lodge, "no fewer than six children's publishers discussing the course the genre has run in the '90s refer to the 'DK revolution' as a milestone that changed the orientation and design of children's reference." The addition of the children's division also had a tremendous impact on DK's bottom line. Sales compounded 60 percent each year from 1988 to 1992, and profits multiplied 124 percent annually during that period.

Diversifications Continue in the 1990s

Though DK would continue to produce works in cooperation with Reader's Digest, the latter company sold back its stake in the former for £5 million in 1991. Seeking a new corporate partner—and some fresh growth funds—Peter Kindersley approached Microsoft founder Bill Gates with a proposal to form a joint multimedia venture wherein DK would furnish the content and Microsoft would contribute the software know-how. After a face-to-face meeting in Seattle, Gates agreed to purchase a 26 percent share of DK for £2.3 million. Bolstered by an additional £2 million loan, the British publisher established DK Multimedia in 1991 and soon launched its first CD-ROM, *Musical Instruments*.

While some industry observers surmised that Microsoft's stake in DK was a precursor to acquisition, that theory was blown out of the water in 1992. DK went public that year, raising £23.5 million on the sale of 19 million shares. At that time, Microsoft took the opportunity to reduce its stake to 18 percent, selling its remaining shares to institutional investors in 1995. The investment performed well over the period, rising from 165p to 213p in its first day, then multiplying to more than 500p per share by the time of the Microsoft divestment.

In the meantime, DK also embarked on several new ventures. DK Inc. (later renamed DK Publishing Inc.) was created to bring U.S. publishing in-house, marking an ongoing shift in strategy from licensing international book rights to other publishers to self-publishing, a move that would retain more profits in-house. The DK Vision division was founded to create complimentary video and television programs. Some of these were produced in cooperation with the BBC and aired on public television in the U.S. and Great Britain, including an "Eyewitness" spin-off, "Dig and Dug," and "Hullabaloo." A cartography division was established in the early 1990s to parlay DK's travel guide and atlas operations into a larger competitor. A foray into educational publishing was aborted after 18 months due to shrinking public school budgets in the U.S. and U.K.

DK launched a direct sales division in 1989 under the moniker DK Family Library (since changed to DK Family Learning). This operation used Tupperware-style home parties to sell books on a strict commission basis. Though items sold at a substantial discount to retail, this division had the potential to generate significantly higher profit margins than wholesale sales and helped to reduce the company's reliance on retail chains. By the end of 1996, DK had 20,000 sales representatives—

dubbed "presenters" by the company—in the U.K., U.S., Russia, and Australia, and plans to launch the operation in a new nation each year, likely starting with South Africa and India in 1997. DK Family Learning contributed £16.5 million (US$26.4 million), or nine percent, of the publisher's total revenues in fiscal 1996 (ended June 30).

This new marketing scheme was not welcomed by some of DK's retailing clients, however. Some bookstore owners took offense upon finding their territories invaded by DK presenters, fearing that they would lose customers to sales parties, noting especially the 10 percent to 30 percent discounts offered at the home-based events. DK attempted to reassure retailers that the new marketing method would not cannibalize sales by developing a separate catalog of direct sale books and by noting that most potential customers who attended party sales were not traditional bookstore shoppers. John Sargent, CEO of DK's U.S. subsidiary, told *Publishers Weekly's* M.P. Dunleavey that "This is not a competitive thing. In fact, bookstore sales are going up because we're creating new customers." *Management Today's* Anita van de Vliet concurred, noting in a December 1996 piece that "Encouragingly, DKFL turnover in 1996 of £16.5 million (up 76 percent) was achieved without hitting trade sales, thus genuinely widening the market."

Strategies for the Mid-1990s and Beyond

The multimedia market was expected to be a key to DK's growth in the mid- to late-1990s. The company launched its first generation of multimedia versions of the now-classic *The Way Things Work* series in 1994 and introduced CD-ROMS featuring links to "members-only" web sites. By the end of 1997, DK expected to have a total of 20 CD-ROMS on the market. In fiscal 1996, the division contributed 12 percent of sales, amounting to £21.2 million, up from £13.1 million in the previous fiscal year. Though fruitful, the multimedia industry was fraught with hazards, including heavy competition. Some industry observers predicted that leading companies, among which DK did not rank, would sacrifice profits to maintain market share. Peter Kindersley addressed this issue in the company's 1996 annual report, noting that "Although the U.S. retail environment for multimedia is currently in a state of flux and more challenging than in the past, we believe that a stable market will emerge in due course. The Directors remain confident of the strength of DK's various businesses."

Acquisitions in the mid- to late-1990s allowed DK to buy into specialty segments of the publishing business. In 1995, it acquired the U.K.'s Henderson Publishing for £5.4 million. The new subsidiary specialized in low-priced, mass market books for children known in the field as "pester purchase" or "pocket-money" books. The following year saw the £1.2 million cash acquisition of Hugo Language Books.

Dorling Kindersley's sales mushroomed from £70.9 million in fiscal 1992 to £174.4 million (US$279 million) in fiscal 1996, while pretax net income ballooned from £7.5 million to £17.4 million during the period. In his 1996 statement, Chairman and CEO Peter Kindersley assured shareholders that growth would continue for the publisher that was "poised to raise its profile to brand-name status."

Principal Divisions

DK Adult; DK Children's; DK Multimedia; DK Direct; DK Vision.

Further Reading

Barclays de Zoete Wedd Securities, "Dorling Kindersley—Company Report," The Investext Group, November 24, 1992.

Dawley, Heidi, "A British Publisher's Dreams of Empire," *Business Week,* November 18, 1996, p. 66.

Dunleavey, M.P., "Playing Party Game: Publishers' Home Party Plans That Offer Books at a Discount Have Some Booksellers Up in Arms," *Publishers Weekly,* May 8, 1995, pp. 48–49.

HSBC James Capel, "Dorling Kindersley—Company Report," The Investext Group, September 17, 1996.

Hilts, Paul, and Jim Milliot, "Dorling Kindersley Launches U.S. Multimedia Venture with 5 Titles," *Publishers Weekly,* March 7, 1994, p. 11.

Lodge, Sally, "Giving Kids' Reference a Fresh Look," *Publishers Weekly,* April 29, 1996, pp. 42–43.

Milliot, Jim, "Renamed DK Posts Sales of $64M in Fiscal '95,' *Publishers Weekly,* September 25, 1995, pp. 12–13.

Panmure Gordon & Co., Limited, "Dorling Kindersley—Company Report," The Investext Group, March 19, 1996.

van de Vliet, Anita, "Dorling Kindersley's Limitless Vision," *Management Today,* December 1996, pp. 50–54.

Wheeler, Sara, "Profits Down at DK; Lawsuit Pending Against Tiptree," *Publishers Weekly,* March 28, 1994, p. 18.

——, "Microsoft Sells Off Stake in DK," *Publishers Weekly,* December 4, 1995, p. 15.

—April Dougal Gasbarre

DTE Energy

DTE Energy Company

2000 Second Avenue
Detroit, Michigan 48226-1279
U.S.A.
(313) 235-4000
Fax: (313) 235-8055
Web site: http://www.detroitedison.com

Public Company
Incorporated: 1903 as Detroit Edison Company
Employees: 8,526
Sales: $3.65 billion (1996)
Stock Exchanges: New York Midwest
SICs: 4911 Electrical Services; 4931 Electrical and Other
Services; 6719 Holding Company, Not Elsewhere
Classified

DTE Energy Company serves roughly 2 million electrical customers in southeastern Michigan. While the company's market territory only covers 13 percent of Michigan's total area, it accounts for half of Michigan's total population, energy consumption, and industrial capacity. Electricity accounts for almost all the revenues of DTE's Detroit Edison subsidiary, although the company also sells a small amount of steam.

Electric companies sprang up throughout the United States after Thomas Edison's development of electric lighting in 1879. In Detroit alone Brush Electric Light Company, Fort Wayne Electric Company, Commercial Electric Light Company, Detroit Electric Light and Power Company, Edison Illuminating Company of Detroit, and Peninsular Electric Light Company all simultaneously existed. Edison Illuminating had been formed on April 15, 1886, to supply alternating current to homes and businesses; and Peninsular Electric Light Company had been formed on June 16, 1891, to operate Detroit's street lights. It was not long before competition became so fierce that the less successful companies were swallowed up, and Peninsular Electric Light Company and Edison Illuminating were all that remained.

Setting the Stage to Power the Motor City; the early decades

On January 1, 1903, Detroit Edison's founders purchased the securities of the Edison Illuminating Company and the Peninsular Electric Light Company and on January 17 The Detroit Edison Company was incorporated with Edison Illuminating as a subsidiary. For financial reasons, incorporation took place in New York rather than Michigan. Charles W. Wetmore became the company's first president and remained in that position until 1912. Detroit Edison's first general manager, Alex Dow, came to the company from its predecessor Edison Illuminating.

At that time the customer base it had acquired through Edison Illuminating had already outgrown its power supply, so one of the company's first objectives was to create additional generating capacity. In 1903 Detroit Edison began to construct the Delray power house. By 1904 this plant's two turbine generators were producing 3,000 kilowatts of electricity each, yet the city of Detroit was growing so rapidly that in 1905 another two turbine generators had to be added to the plant, and one more the next year.

In 1905 Detroit Edison began to expand through acquisition, in addition to construction. Among its purchases were Washtenaw Light and Power Company, Michigan Milling Company, and Ann Arbor Agricultural Company, making Detroit Edison the owner of the Argo, Barton, Geddes, and Superior generating dams on the Huron River. On July 24, 1906, the company formed a wholly owned subsidiary, Eastern Michigan Edison Company, and transferred all the Huron River companies to it as subsidiaries.

By 1907 it had become obvious that the company had to add more turbines, and construction began on a second power station at Delray to house a turbine capable of generating 14,000 kilowatts of energy. In 1910 and 1911 two more 14,000-kilowatt turbines were put on line.

In 1912 Dow became president of Detroit Edison. During his tenure Detroit Edison grew substantially. In 1913 a 15,000-kilowatt turbine was added to the new power house at Delray, and Detroit Edison began to construct a power plant at Conners Creek.

For roughly the first decade of Detroit Edison's existence—the period ranging from 1903 until 1915—the company's subsidiary Edison Illuminating Company distributed, sold, billed for, and collected on, the energy produced by its parent, Detroit Edison. In 1915, under Dow, Detroit Edison began to serve its customers directly. Edison Illuminating survived as a company handling the parent company's real estate. Also in 1915, the company put two of the Conners Creek facility's three 20,000-kilowatt units into service, with the third becoming operational in 1917.

The Detroit Edison Company's generating capacity continued to grow under Dow, and in 1919 the company bought Port Huron Gas and Electric. In 1920 a 30,000-kilowatt generator was added to the plant at Delray. In 1922 Detroit Edison completed its first in suburban Marysville. Detroit Edison put its second at Trenton Channel in Trenton in July 1924. The Trenton Channel plant burned powdered coal, a technical innovation at the time, but also a process that tended to pollute the air because powdered coal is burned while suspended. Detroit Edison was aware of this fact and consequently equipped the plant—the first of its kind to use these pollution control devices—with electrostatic precipitators.

In addition to expanding its generating capacity, Detroit Edison expanded its service area. By 1929 the company supplied more than 4,582 square miles. In 1936 Detroit Edison purchased the Michigan Electric Power Company and acquired the entire "thumb" territory of southeastern Michigan, to increase its service area to 7,587 square miles.

In 1940 Alex Dow retired as company president; two years later he withdrew from the company's board of directors. Under Dow's leadership, not only had generating capacity and service area expanded, but Detroit Edison had developed its own engineering research department, founded in 1913, and improved customer service. This included instituting free light bulb service, financing the connection of electricity to customers previously using gas, and lending electrical motors.

From 1944 to 1954 former U.S. Senator Prentiss M. Brown held the post of first chairman of the board, while James W.

Parker served as president and general manager. Walker Cisler, who joined Detroit Edison in 1943, became the company's first executive vice-president in 1948 and, in addition, worked with the U.S. government on the Marshall Plan, developing the economic and electric power of other nations.

When Parker retired in 1951, Cisler took over as president and general manager. Cisler's primary objectives for the company involved expanding generating capacity and improving transmission to the farthest reaches of Detroit Edison's service area, as well as exploring research opportunities. By 1954 the St. Clair Power Plant was completely operational, with a total capacity of 624,000 kilowatts. That year Cisler became senior officer of Detroit Edison, which by then was looking into nuclear energy.

In 1952 Cisler assumed the leadership responsibilities for organizing electric utilities to explore the possibilities of nuclear energy, a development he named the Enrico Fermi Breeder Reactor Project. Among the companies he persuaded to join the project was the Public Service Electric and Gas Co. of Newark, New Jersey, and he convinced that company to assign one of its nuclear engineers, Walter J. McCarthy, to join the project as head of the nuclear and analytical division in October 1952. The project was headquartered at Detroit Edison. It was formally organized in 1955, with 34 companies participating, as the Power Reactor Development Company (PRDC). This consortium would eventually own and operate the Enrico Fermi Power Plant. Ground was broken on Fermi's first unit that year with Cisler as president and principal organizer of the PRDC.

As the possibilities of atomic energy were explored by the PRDC, Cisler continued to build conventional generating capacity. The River Rouge plant was completed in 1956, and by 1958 it had a capacity of 841,500 kilowatts. In 1961 St. Clair's capacity was upped to 1.35 million kilowatts when its sixth turbine generator went into operation. With its assets growing so rapidly, Detroit Edison authorized a two-for-one common stock split in December 1962.

Company Attempts to Harness Nuclear Power, 1960s

In 1963 Walter McCarthy became general manager of the PRDC, with Cisler continuing as president. McCarthy also formally joined the Detroit Edison staff at this time, while continuing on loan to PRDC. On August 23 of that year, Fermi 1, the first commercial-sized fast breeder nuclear reactor, finally went into operation, beginning its first self-sustaining chain reaction. The plant used uranium to generate steam to produce electricity, and as part of the reaction process it produced plutonium, which was also an atomic fuel. In October 1966 a metal device that had been attached to the reactor's inside wall after it was built broke away. The device, whose purpose was to direct the flow of liquid sodium—used to transfer heat—through the nuclear core, ended up blocking the flow and caused the fuel to overheat and begin melting, damaging both the reactor and the fuel assemblies. After the partial core meltdown, Fermi I was taken off-line.

In spite of Walker Cisler's campaign for constant generating plant growth, demand still threatened to outstrip supply, and so, in 1966, peaking units were introduced into the generating system. Peaking generators burn gas and oil, are mobile, and can be brought on-line in 10 minutes. The first peaking units were installed at the company's generating facility near Monroe, Michigan.

In the midst of repairs at Fermi 1 and the company's efforts to continue building generating capacity, Detroit Edison was reincorporated in Michigan on April 17, 1967. By the time Detroit Edison's Harbor Beach Power Plant went on-line in 1968, nine peaking units were being used.

In that same year Detroit Edison requested its first electric rate increase in 20 years from the Michigan Public Service Commission (MPSC). The company sought the increase to help meet the expenses of building generating capacity.

In 1970 the first of the Monroe power plant's coal-fired units went on-line. At the time, the four-unit Monroe plant was the largest in the world, and the company planned to add five more units: the two-unit Belle River coal-burning plant, the Greenwood Energy Center with its oil-burning plant, and two nuclear reactors, Fermi 2 and 3.

In November 1971 William G. Meese took over Cisler's position as chief executive officer while Cisler remained chairman. Meanwhile, the company was burdened with huge plant costs: it had taken four years to repair the reactor and fuel assemblies at Fermi 1, and when the repairs were finally completed the problem-plagued reactor remained operational only sporadically before being shut down again on September 22, 1972. In November of that year the PRDC executive committee decided to decommission the plant as of December 31, 1975.

OPEC Oil Embargo Causes
Drop in Demand; the 1970s

By 1973 the Monroe power plant's four units had a total capacity of 3 million kilowatts. The Ludington pumped storage plant then began to operate commercially, supplying 49 percent of its generating capacity to Detroit Edison, with the remainder going to Consumers Power, which supplied the area with natural gas. Then the Middle East oil embargo hit, striking the southeastern Michigan auto industry hard, and the demand for energy dropped as automobile production slumped and inflation and environmental protection costs continued to rise.

William Meese began to look for ways to cut Detroit Edison's overhead costs. The energy-efficient Ludington plant was part of this effort. In 1974 Meese began to implement other important practices, such as the increased hiring of minorities and women, as well as establishing a strategic planning procedure designed to help management anticipate future conditions. To deal with the new difficulties brought about by southeastern Michigan's economic recession, Meese also temporarily suspended all power plant construction and environmental modifications.

In 1975 Cisler retired and Meese assumed Cisler's position as chairman of the board. The company reorganized, setting up six divisions within Detroit Edison's service area, each headed by managers responsible for their division's business. That year, Walter McCarthy became executive vice-president of operations.

In 1976 another Meese cost-efficient measure was implemented when the Superior Midwest Energy Terminal was opened by a subsidiary of Detroit Edison. All of Detroit Edison's major power plants consumed coal, but the company did not mine or transport the coal itself. Realizing the company's dependence on reliable transport and supply of coal, Meese created the energy terminal at Superior, Wisconsin, to provide rail and water shipment of western low-sulfur coal. He also negotiated a 26-year contract for the purchase of coal from Montana, and had the company purchase its own coal cars to ensure shipment.

In 1977 Walter McCarthy became executive vice-president of divisions. That year the temporary suspension on power plant construction was lifted, the Greenwood power plant was set into operation, and construction was started on the Belle River power plant.

In 1979, McCarthy became president and chief operating officer of Detroit Edison and John R. Hamann was elected to the newly created position of vice-chairman of the board. That was also the year that the company's Greenwood Power Plant became fully operational.

Federal Regulations Slow
Nuclear Expansion; the 1980s

In 1979, as Fermi 2 was in the midst of construction, the disaster at Three Mile Island hit. Two weeks later Detroit Edison had formed a 24-member safety review task force to review Fermi 2 again and recheck all its operating systems and safety features. Although the task force found everything to be entirely operational at Fermi 2, it took Detroit Edison several years of readjustments before the reactor could meet the new regulations that arose in response to the Three Mile Island incident. In fact, the added cost of meeting these new standards spun Detroit Edison into financial crisis.

The company began taking steps to help revive southeastern Michigan's economy. In 1979 it began the Energy Plus advertising campaign on a national and international level to interest companies in bringing their manufacturing facilities to Metro Detroit. With the Greater Detroit Chamber of Commerce, Michigan's Department of Commerce, and the Southeastern Michigan Council of Governments, Detroit Edison founded the Greater Detroit-Southeastern Michigan Business Attraction and Expansion Council. Detroit Edison also helped develop the Economic Alliance for Business, an organization aimed at improving Michigan's business climate. In September 1981 Meese retired and was succeeded by McCarthy as chairman and chief executive officer.

In April 1983, in order to consolidate the company, which was operating under dual incorporation in the states of New York and Michigan, Detroit Edison stockholders agreed to a merger plan. This plan was put into effect on June 30, 1983, when both the New York and the Michigan corporations merged with Detroit Edison's wholly owned inoperative subsidiary, Peninsular Electric Light Company. The Detroit Edison Company was the merger's sole surviving company, and retained only its Michigan incorporation. All liabilities, capital, assets, and operations remained unchanged.

In 1985 Fermi 2 was completed, and low-power testing began. McCarthy, having been general manager of Fermi 1 during its early stages, felt experienced operating management was needed. With the delays involved in bringing in new plant management and in receiving approval of the Nuclear Regulatory Commission, Fermi 2 resumed low-power testing in July 1986.

In 1987 Detroit Edison's wholly owned subsidiary, Washtenaw Energy Corporation, was merged into the company. Later that year, the company bought the electric business and properties serving the city of Pontiac from Consumers Power and began to supply the people of Pontiac directly, increasing the company's total service area to 7,598 square miles. Consumers Power had served Pontiac with electricity bought from Detroit Edison.

On January 15, 1988, Fermi 2 began full-power operation. By November Fermi 2 had passed its warranty run and was on its way to long-term operation. However, after-tax write-offs of $968 million—resulting partially from the MPSC's disallowances of costs connected with the unit, dating from a 1986 rate case—caused Detroit Edison to post a net loss of $378.8 million in 1988.

McCarthy began to implement programs designed to increase sales and cut costs, keeping close watch on operating and maintenance expenses, capital expenditures, and the size of the company's staff, reducing it to its smallest size in 12 years—9,669 at the end of 1990. Perhaps most important was the resolution of rate-making issues involving Fermi 2. In December 1988 the MPSC had increased Detroit Edison's base rates by adding $29.5 million to a previously authorized $404.2 million—for a total of $433.7 million—to partly cover the cost of building Fermi 2. This increase was to be phased in over five years beginning January 1, 1989. That year Fermi 2 was taken off the Nuclear Regulatory Commission's list of plants requiring special attention. It completed its first scheduled shutdown for refueling in December 1989, and it produced more than 5 billion kilowatt-hours of electricity during the year. By June 1989 The Detroit Edison Company stock had risen to its highest price in 17 years, positioning Detroit Edison as one of the top-performing U.S. utilities.

In 1989 Fermi 2 had represented 31 percent of Detroit Edison's assets. In 1990 this grew to 33 percent as the company purchased the minority share of Fermi 2 from Wolverine Power Supply Cooperative, Inc. for $539.6 million, giving the company total ownership of the plant. On May 1, 1990, McCarthy retired as chairman and chief executive officer of Detroit Edison and John E. Lobbia was elected to replace him. As a result of strong lobbying in Washington, D.C., Detroit Edison was already in compliance with the first phase of the requirements of the 1990 Clean Air Act amendments, scheduled to take effect in 1995.

A Decade of Transition, the 1990s

By keeping ahead of Federal regulations, in 1990 the company achieved record revenues as well as record earnings for its common stock. Detroit Edison's common stock hit its highest point in 23 years, when it reached $30.25, closing at $28.25, a full 11 percent higher than 1989's close. Sales during the year were reported at $3.31 billion, $104 million over 1989 levels.

However, things were soon to change. The recessionary economy of the early 1990s hit southeastern Michigan hard, slowing production at many automotive and steel plants and reducing demand for electricity from these industries. In response, Detroit Edison aggressively marketed its services to other industries, so much so that it had record sales to the commercial segment. In 1991, with record sales reaching $3.59 billion, the company received the "Electric Utility of the Year" award from the trade magazine *Electric Light & Power*. Based on the company's record revenues and earnings, in mid-December 1991 its common stock reached $35 per share, the highest price in 25 years.

1996 Deregulation Sparks Reorganization

Into the mid-1990s, Michigan's economy and state policy continued to be uncertain as its basic industries struggled to compete with foreign manufacturers. In addition, a new governor was redefining state goals. For these reasons, Detroit Edison continued to minimize staff levels, reduce its use of foreign crude, and cut its dependence on industrial sales, thereby maximizing the company's flexibility. Net income in 1993 reflected these efforts: $588 million, a jump of 14 percent over 1990's record levels.

As the decade advanced, it became increasingly clear that the utility industry was on the brink of major changes. In late 1992 Congress passed the Energy Policy Act, which allowed competition in the utility industry's wholesale sector by mandating existing utilities to transmit electricity generated by other producers through their lines. The company received yet another setback on Christmas Day 1993, when a turbine generator fire at Fermi 2 caused the high-production plant to close while repairs were made. The plant returned to partial service in 1995, as the company posted sales of $3.64 billion against net income of $406 million.

The Federal Energy Regulatory Commission issued a new set of rules in April 1996 that affected transmission capacity, wholesale and retail competition, and other issues. The following year the industry was deregulated when Congress repealed the Public Utility Holding Company Act of 1935, which had allowed utility companies such as Detroit Edison to operate as monopolies. Under the new federal law, the shift to a fully competitive industry could be phased in over a period of as little as two years. Where its primary concern had been to produce power and expand and maintain its plants and equipment, Detroit Edison now looked to its economic structure, further streamlining costs in preparation for battling competition on a level playing field.

To supplement the new federal legislation, the MPSC designed a framework for the gradual restructuring of Michigan's electricity business. Beginning July 1, 1997, the state's utility load would be gradually opened to competition through a bidding process, with all customers able to select their energy supplier by January 1, 2002. Technical, environmental, and business-related issues would also be addressed and responded to during this five-year period.

In response to these industry-wide changes, Detroit Edison was reorganized in late 1995. On January 1, 1996, DTE Energy Company became the holding company for subsidiaries that included Detroit Edison and several non-utility assets, among them Biomass Energy Systems, Edison Energy Services, and Midwest Energy Resources. The new structure allowed the company greater financial flexibility in creating new energy-related businesses and separated regulated subsidiaries from those not under state or federal regulations.

The biggest challenge facing DTE and CEO John E. Lobbia in a competitive market was the company's high cost of production, as well as the huge investment the company had made in its Fermi 2 plant. With deregulation and competition from other providers, electrical rates would be sure to drop drastically, and DTE feared it would be priced out of the market it had controlled for decades. In preparation for full-scale deregulation in 2002, DTE strong-armed its major commercial and industrial electricity customers—including the Big Three automakers— into 10-year contracts in order to help recover the company's high capital equipment costs. These capital costs would also diminish as a result of debt refinancing through the Michigan Legislature's approval of the issuance rate-reduction bonds in mid-1997.

DTE also began to leverage its extensive expertise in energy-related systems' engineering and installation. In an effort to increase consumption and attract new residential customers, new programs were developed, including an interruptible air conditioning program that promised to improve system management and also lower electricity rates by up to 20 percent. Over 250,000 customers were enrolled in the system in its first years of operation.

Continuing Its Commitment to Consumers in a Changing Climate

In addition to navigating in a changing business climate, DTE has continued its support of the communities that it serves, providing funding and other support to over 30 schools in the metropolitan Detroit area in tandem with other business and community leaders. Educational programs are aimed at teaching younger children how to use electricity safely, and DTE's The Heat and Warmth Fund (THAW) helps low-income families and the elderly pay their winter utility bills by matching company funds with those donated by generous electricity customers.

In addressing its portion of the upcoming statewide rate decrease to electric customers—predicted at $300 million— DTE remained guardedly optimistic. "The challenge will be for all of us to work together constructively to create a competitive utility environment in a way that meets the needs of all interests—our customers, our communities, our company and our state," president and chief operating officer Anthony F. Earley Jr. told the MPSC in early 1997. "The effort will require courage, foresight and trust." By continuing to implement its four-tiered strategy—debt reduction, investment recovery, divestiture of underperforming holdings, and broadening investment in non-utilities—DTE Energy intends to reward both its customers and shareholders in a deregulated industry.

Principal Subsidiaries

Detroit Edison; DE Energy Services, Inc.; Midwest Energy Resources Company; St. Clair Energy Corporation; Edison Illuminating Company; SYNDECO, Incorporated; UTS Systems, Inc.

Further Reading

Electric Utility Industry Overview: Introduction to the Restructuring Debate, Detroit Edison, 1996.
McCarthy, Walter J., Jr., *Detroit Edison Generates More Than Electricity,* New York, The Newcomen Society in North America, 1983.
Serju, Tricia, "The Light on Utilities," *Detroit News,* December 2, 1996, p. 6F.
"A Short History of Detroit Edison," Detroit Edison corporate typescript, 1990.

—Maya Sahafi
—updated by Pamela L. Shelton

Elscint Ltd.

P.O. Box 550
Haifa, 31004
Israel
(972) 4-831-0390
Fax: (972) 4-855-1216
Web site: http://www.elscint.co.il

Public Subsidiary
Incorporated: 1969
Employees: 1,950
Sales: US $311.42 million
Stock Exchanges: New York
SICs: 3845 Electromedical Equipment

Haifa-based Elscint Ltd. is a world leader in the advanced medical imaging equipment, successfully competing against such industry giants as General Electric and others to capture a strong share of this market. Elscint, one of the oldest of Israel's high-technology companies, is a vertically integrated designer, manufacturer, and distributor of computerized tomography (CT), nuclear medicine (NMI), mammography, and magnetic resonance (MRI) imaging systems. The company also supplies multi-modality workstations and connectivity systems to support its imaging products.

Elscint operates five manufacturing facilities, at its Haifa headquarters and in Tirat Hacarmel and Ma'alot in Israel, in Fort Collins, Colorado, and in Oxfordshire, England, as well as an assembly facility in Hackensack, New Jersey. Elscint's 13 subsidiaries are based around the world, governing the activities of its network of sales offices and representatives in dozens of countries. Also, since 1996, Elscint has engaged in cooperative development and manufacturing agreements, including a development and manufacturing agreement with Siemens, and a distribution agreement with Philips. In 1997, the company announced an agreement with General Electric to launch a joint-venture company, based in Israel, for the engineering, manufacturing, and distribution of products for nuclear medicine imaging systems.

After the company's "de-merger" from former parent and sister company Elbit Computers Ltd., Elscint remains a publicly traded subsidiary of Elron Electronics Industries Ltd., an Israel-based, multinational high-technology holding company. Shares in Elscint have been traded on the New York Stock Exchange since the early 1980s. With approximately 97 percent of the company's annual sales generated by imports, Elscint conducts its business and reports its sales in U.S. dollars. In 1996, Elscint's revenues reached $311 million. Approximately 10 percent of the company's sales are earmarked for its leading-edge research and development activities.

Leading Israel's High-Tech Boom in the 1970s

Elscint—a contraction of the words "electronic" and "scientific"—was founded in 1969 by a team of graduates, led by Avraham Suhami, from the Israel Institute of Technology, also known as the Technion, with the purpose of using advanced scientific research to develop and market products. Born in Izmir, in western Turkey, in 1935, Suhami immigrated by himself to Israel when he was 14 years old. Suhami spent two years on a kibbutz, then worked for a textile factory, before joining the Israeli army. In 1956, after three years of military service, Suhami went to Hebrew University in Jerusalem, earning degrees in physics and mathematics, then transferred to the Technion in 1960, where he completed a doctorate in nuclear physics and was appointed to the faculty.

In 1969, Suhami and a group of fellow researchers left the Technion after receiving encouragement to apply his scientific and technical knowledge to commercial uses from another former Technion professor, Uzia Galil, who had recently founded Elron Electronic Industries, and from Dan Tolkowsky, then managing director of the Israeli investment firm Discount Investment Corporation. Galil and Tolkowsky staked Suhami to the $250,000 needed to start Elscint, which would be grouped as a subsidiary under Elron. Tolkowsky—a Spitfire pilot for the British Royal Air Force in World War II and later the commander of the Israeli Air Force, was appointed chairman, while Suhami, as CEO, led the company's operations.

Elscint initially eyed markets based on the core nuclear physics expertise of Suhami and colleagues, producing equipment for recording measurements in nuclear experiments at laboratories including Argonne and Brookhaven. But, as Suhami explained to the *New York Times*, "the whole world market was a few hundred units, which we sold for $800. You soon find out that you just cannot make enough profit per unit." The company quickly moved into medical imaging equipment. Its first product in this area was a nuclear camera designed to detect cancer. That product, however, proved unsuccessful. Next, the company developed the VDP1, a rectrolinear gamma scanner used for tracking radioactive isotopes in the body. The VDP1, which was priced at $25,000, was the first in the industry to feature digital image processing and display.

This product proved the company's first success, helping the company to sales of $1 million, with a loss of just $25,000, for its first year of operations. Then, when the VDP1 was displayed at a Los Angeles trade show, it attracted the attention of General Electric, the world leader in medical imaging equipment. In 1971, Elscint and General Electric entered a distribution agreement that made GE the VDP1's exclusive North American sales agent. Placing its name on the product, GE insisted that the product match its own quality standards, forcing the young company to expand its technical and manufacturing capabilities, a process Tolkowsky described to *Fortune* as "absolute hell." For Suhami, the GE agreement would provide the learning experience for the company's future success. As he told *Fortune*: "GE taught me that the paint job on the outside was just as important as the electronics on the inside." Suhami took the marketing lessons learned from GE to heart, and soon began establishing international sales and marketing subsidiaries, beginning in Belgium in 1972, to bring the company's products to the world market.

Elscint's agreement with GE was to last three years, with neither party envisaging a permanent relationship. By 1972, Suhami began searching for a new partner, hoping to find a larger corporation to invest in the company. Instead, Suhami met Frederick Adler, a New York investor specializing in small scientific companies. Adler convinced Suhami that the better course was to take Elscint public—and thereby allow the company to remain independent. Suhami agreed, and Adler arranged the sale of 400,000 shares, trading on the over-the-counter market. Adler also proved to be a mentor for Suhami, whom Adler described as initially a "rotten manager," but

telling *Fortune*, "I saw Suhami develop into one of the world's finest scientific managers."

By the mid-1970s, however, sales of Elscint's gamma scanners and other measuring devices barely generated $12 million, while profits lingered under $400,000. In 1975, Suhami abruptly decided to move the company into a new product market altogether. Computer tomography, invented by EMI Ltd. of Britain and developed in the early 1970s, represented a major breakthrough in medical imaging techniques. The process, which used computers to record and reconstruct images from thousands of x-rays, enabling the more accurate and refined imaging of bones and organs than conventional x-ray techniques, represented not only an important advancement in medical diagnostics, but also a vast—and extremely valuable—new market. By leading Elscint into CT, Suhami was taking the tiny company into head-to-head competition with dozens of other companies, including Pfizer, Siemens, Hitachi, Toshiba, Philips, and former partner GE. As Suhami admitted to *Fortune*: "My friends used to tell me, 'Avraham, you must be mad.'"

The cost of developing its own CT scanner, which the company placed on the market in 1977, cut deeply into Elscint's financial health. Between 1975 and 1978, the company's capital dropped from $100 million to $2 million, while the company struggled to remain profitable. By then, too, the CT industry was undergoing a shakeout that was forcing many of Elscint's competitors—including the industry's founder EMI—out of the scanner market, and many out of business altogether. By the start of the 1980s, the final throes of the shakeout had produced a narrowed field of winners. GE led the market, followed by—to the surprise of many—Elscint.

The company's sales began a steady growth, from $21 million in 1979 to $42.6 million in 1981. In that year, Elscint, which had placed more than 100 of its CT scanners in hospitals and other medical and research facilities around the world, received an added boost when it acquired the servicing operations of Pfizer Inc.'s CT scanners, as that company, which until then had held the number two sales spot, announced it was exiting the CT market. Elscint, which would see its three percent market share rise to 10 percent by the middle of the decade, was content to allow GE to maintain its market leadership position. "We have no desire to overtake GE," Suhami told *Fortune*, "We prefer to live under their price umbrella and let them educate the market."

A High-Tech Wreck in the 1980s

Elscint continued to improve its CT scanner—bringing out a sixth version by the beginning of 1981, while also expanding the company's operations. In 1980, the company acquired Cambridge Advanced Research Laboratories in Cambridge, Massachusetts, and opened a plant in Brookline, Massachusetts, the following year, for its Elscint Inc. subsidiary. Elscint had also expanded its product offerings, adding nuclear cameras and ultrasound imagers to its line of CT scanners, digital radiography, and conventional x-ray equipment, making it the only small company in the world to produce equipment for all of the advanced imaging technologies. As the 1980s began, the company also launched into developing its own equipment for the latest breakthrough in medical imaging, the magnetic resonance imaging system. Meanwhile, the company had been extending its manufacturing capacity, becoming a vertically integrated manufacturer and distributor, with more than 3,000 employees at plants and research facilities in Oxford, England, Paris, Milan, Jerusalem, as well as in Haifa and Boston. In 1983, the company added a Chicago plant, when it purchased the x-ray sales and services operations from the failing Elgin, Illinois-based Xonics Inc. for $10 million. By then, sales had reached $132 million, and the company announced a net profit of $12.6 million.

While corporate sales were indeed strong, Elscint's profits proved an illusion. In fact, the company had been covering up a growing financial crisis that would cause the company nearly to collapse by the mid-1980s. Part of Elscint's difficulties were beyond its control. In 1983, the U.S. government tightened restrictions on Medicaid spending, a prime source of funding for expensive advanced imaging procedures, leading to a slump in new purchases from the crucial U.S. hospital market. Yet, much of Elscint's problems were self-generated. Entering the MRI market had cost the company dearly, with research and development costs of some $60 million per year, while the high price tag on the MRI scanners—of $1.5 million or more—and the earlier entry of larger competitors such as Johnson & Johnson helped to limit the market, despite the technology's future promise. More critical to Elscint's financial crisis, however, had been its rapid expansion in the early 1980s. The addition of too many new plants and research facilities, and the Xonics acquisition, helped sink the company deeply into debt, just as Israeli government restrictions on foreign borrowing were causing Elscint's creditors to apply pressure. Heavily dependent on exports—with only 3 percent of sales in its home country—the company had been pouring money into sales and marketing overseas. But Elscint's projections for revenue growth—with expectations of topping $220 million in 1985—failed to materialize. In 1985, with sales rising only to $142 million, the company posted a $33 million loss, a loss which was later adjusted, when the full scope of the crisis was revealed, upward to a loss of $50.3 million.

This loss, however, was only a taste of what was to come. In the meantime, Shuhami, who had taken over as president of the company's U.S. subsidiary in March 1985, resigned from Elscint—and fled Israel altogether—in June of that year, stating, as reported by the *Financial Times*, that he was resigning because "the loss resulted from the business strategy of which I was the author and executor, and I must take responsibility." Elron chairman Uzia Galil stepped in as Elscint's chairman, and began searching for a way to rescue the company. In 1986, the company cut more than a third of its workforce, and reorganized management, bringing in Benjamin Paled, formerly head of Israel's Air Force, to lead Elscint's operations. But in March 1986, the company's true financial position was finally revealed. As revenues for the year fell to $120 million, Elscint posted a loss of $115 million, the largest in Israeli corporate history.

The rescue of Israel's flagship high-technology company was ordered by a commission chaired by then Prime Minister Shimon Peres. In exchange for stock options in Elscint and

exemptions from the foreign borrowing restrictions, Elscint's bank creditors, including Bank Leumi, Bank Hapoalim, Israel Discount Bank, United Mizrahi Bank, and the First International Bank of Israel, agreed to write off some $80 million of Elscint's $150 million in debt. Elron, which held a 29 percent controlling interest in the company, also wrote off some $10 million in debt.

Rebounding in the 1990s

These steps rescued Elscint from immediate bankruptcy. But it would not be until the end of the decade that the company would again see a profit. The company reorganized, shutting its Paris, Milan, and Chicago plants, as well as other research facilities, and eliminated some of its product lines, including conventional x-ray equipment and ultrasound systems (which was eventually sold to Elbit Computers). Elscint also found its customers' confidence in the company's long-term survival shaken, and sales regained only slowly, to $133 million in 1987. In that year, the company's losses continued, reaching $51 million, in part because of the company's reluctance to implement its proposed workforce reduction. While extraordinary gains from restructuring charges enabled Elscint to post net gains in 1988, it was not until the following year that the company returned to profitability, with net earnings of $3 million on sales of $147 million.

At the end of 1989, Elron, which had written off its interest in Elscint in 1988 in order to enable the holding company to restore its own profitability, announced a shuffling of shares that gave Elscint's sister company, Elbit Computers, controlling interest (of 73 percent) in Elscint. The deal would also give Elscint access to its profitable new parent's strong cash reserves. With this brightening outlook for its next decade, Elscint could refocus on its advanced medical imaging products in its core CT, MRI, and NMI systems markets. Despite the company's financial difficulties, Elscint retained its worldwide reputation for quality and leading-edge technology, a position further enhanced with an announcement of an exclusive marketing agreement with JEOL Trading Co. to bring Elscint's products to Japan, the world's largest market for medical imaging systems. This agreement proved significant as well, as it marked an end to Japan's long acquiescence to the Arab-led embargo against Israel.

Elscint posted steady gains through the first half of the 1990s. Revenues rose from $191 million in 1991 to $221 million in 1992; by 1995, the sales, led by new generations of CT and MRI systems, as well as the introduction of advanced mammography systems, multimodal workstations, and connectivity and telephony products—which, for example, enabled a hospital in California to view the real-time MRI images of a procedure in New York—to $282 million. The company seemed to put its losses behind it as well, while continuing to invest heavily in research and development. And in January 1997, Elscint recorded another significant moment among Israel's high-technology industries, when it announced the sale of an MRI to Jordan's Al-Basheer Hospital, the first major Israeli high-technology product to be sold in that country.

Principal Subsidiaries

Elscint Inc. (U.S.A.); Elscint France S.A.; Elscint Central and Eastern Europe (Austria); Elscint Canada Ltd.

Further Reading

Balnerman, Joel H., "Israel 3: Sudden Plunge into Losses," *Financial Times*, June 1, 1987, p. 21.

Ellis, Walter, "Israel's Electronics Innovators Show Signs of Vulnerability," *Financial Times*, December 3, 1985, p. 22.

"Elscint: Scanner, Scan Thyself," *The Economist*, September 20, 1986, p. 74.

Friedlin, Jennifer, "Elscint Wins Tender in Jordan," *Jerusalem Post*, January 28, 1997, p. 8.

Landau, Pinhas, "New Look for Group: Everyone Benefits in Elron Deal," *Jerusalem Post*, November 14, 1989.

Lennon, David, "Elscint Chairman Resigns After Slide into Losses," *Financial Times*, June 27, 1985, p. 16.

Lipkis, Galit, "Elscint Profit Soars," *Jerusalem Post*, March 13, 1991.

Nash, Nathaniel C., "Israel's Apostle of High Technology," *New York Times*, July 8, 1984, Sec. 3, p. 6.

Ozanne, Julian, "High-Tech Horizons," *Financial Times*, February 25, 1995, p. 20.

Taub, Stephen, "Spotlight on Israel's High-Tech," *Financial World*, August 15, 1983, p. 36.

Tinnin, David, "How Elscint Profits from Inside Information," *Fortune*, March 23, 1981, p. 127.

—M. L. Cohen

E*Trade Group, Inc.

4 Embarcadero Place
2400 Geng Rd.
Palo Alto, California 94303
U.S.A.
(415) 842-2500
Fax: (415) 842-2575
Web site: http://www.etrade.com

Public Company
Incorporated: 1982 as TradePlus Inc.
Employees: 347
Sales: $51.6 million (1996)
Stock Exchanges: NASDAQ
SICs: 6211 Security Brokers & Dealers

E*Trade Group, Inc., through its subsidiary E*Trade Securities, is leading the investment services revolution of the digital age. E*Trade, one of the pioneers of electronic investment services, is also one of the top online and Internet-based brokerage firms. Unlike traditional "brick and mortar" houses, such as Merrill Lynch and Smith Barney Shearson, and discount brokers such as Charles Schwab Corp., E*Trade operates only online, without the overhead of the extended sales offices networks and large employee base of full-service brokerages. E*Trade offers its customers 24-hours-per-day, seven-days-per-week stock and options trading and access to real-time market information, company research, market analysis, and other investment information services. E*Trade's services are available through online services such as America Online, Compuserve, and the Microsoft Financial Network, through the World Wide Web at the company's web site, through Internet-based "push" services such as the PointCast Network, and through direct-modem access and the touchtone telephone Telemaster system. E*Trade has broken the paradigm of traditional investing by giving its customers—typically computer-savvy, individual investors—access to the information previously available only to brokerage professionals. E*Trade does not act as an adviser, but rather gives its customers the tools to make their own invest-ment decisions. As such, E*Trade has slashed the cost of trading, charging as low as $14.95 per 100-share transaction, compared to $150 or more at a full-service broker, or even the $70 or more per transaction charged by discount brokerage houses. The company, which operates a second "hot" facility in Sacramento, California, which duplicates the company's Palo Alto facility's equipment and customer service staff as backup protection, employs only around 350 people, compared to the many thousands at full-service brokers.

E*Trade customers subscribe to the service by establishing a minimum $1,000 account with the company. To discourage hackers, cash accounts are maintained offline—leaving the customer vulnerable only to the threat of unauthorized trading, which itself is discouraged by the company's secure online site. Customers are issued a password with which they can access their portfolio through the company's full web site. There they can choose among a variety of information, research, and portfolio management features, including personalizing the site for their own interests, and buy and sell stock and perform other investment transactions on the AMEX, NYSE, and NASDAQ exchanges. Based in Palo Alto, California, E*Trade's services are not limited to U.S. customers; indeed, the company's electronic services are accessed by private investors from more than 60 countries. At the same time, E*Trade, through its E*Trade Ventures subsidiary, has been establishing a presence on international exchanges, operating in Canada under the E*Trade brand name through a joint venture with Versus Brokerage Services, Inc. In June 1997, the company announced that it had reached a similar agreement to bring its services to Australia, through an alliance with that country's Nova Pacific Capital Limited.

Founder William Porter, E*Trade's chairman, owns a 20 percent stake in the company and serves on the board of directors. Leading the company's growth, however, is Christos Cotsakos, also a director with a 5 percent stake in the company, as president and CEO. E*Trade's growth has been dramatic: its nearly $52 million in revenues for 1996 is more than double its sales for the previous year, and estimates for 1997 expect revenues to double again. Meanwhile, the company adds 500 new customers and as much as $10 million in new assets daily.

E*Trade's more than 150,000 customers have also been steadily increasing the company's trading volume. In April 1997, the company reported a daily transaction volume of more than 14,000.

Fomenting the Brokerage Revolution in the 1980s

When William Porter formed TradePlus with $15,000 in startup capital in 1982, the online investment revolution was already underway. The first online service, called Tickerscreen, was initiated in May 1982 by Max Ule, as a division of Rosenkrantz, Ehrenkrants, Lyon & Ross, Inc. A bulletin-board system, Tickerscreen enabled customers to place orders after the markets were closed, which would then be transacted by the brokerage house when the markets opened again the next day. Porter, who had held management positions with General Electric and Textron, after earning an M.A. in physics at Kansas State College and an M.B.A. in management from the Massachusetts Institute of Technology, saw an opportunity to take online investment services further—by automating the full transaction process.

Porter's TradePlus "vision" combined two emerging trends. Already trading under his own account, Porter also looked at cutting the cost of trading. By then, a new breed of discount brokers, such as Charles Schwab, had arisen to challenge the full-service brokerage houses. By the mid-1980s, discount brokers amounted to nine percent—up from two percent at the start of the decade and rising—of all stock transaction commissions. Porter, however, believed that he could cut the cost of trading even deeper than the discount brokers, who still charged as high as $100 per transaction. The second trend was the appearance of the first personal computers in the early 1980s. Porter immediately recognized the potential of this new electronic market, foreseeing that personal computers—equipped with their own modems—would soon become commonplace office and home equipment.

In 1982, TradePlus contracted with C.D. Andersen & Co. to create a computerized order entry system. That system went online in July 1983. TradePlus enabled its customers to access market information, and conduct trades during market hours, while offering 24-hour-per-day portfolio management capability. By paying a premium on the basic service charge, customers could also receive real-time stock pricing and portfolio updates; otherwise, they received information after a 20-minute delay. Customers paid a signup fee, ranging up to $195, and monthly subscription fees of $15, which gave them one-hour of connect time per month. Use of the service beyond that cost $24 per hour during market hours, and $6 per hour when the markets closed. For the premium, real-time service, nonprofessional customers paid $75 per month and professional investors paid $135 per month, fees established by the National Association of Securities Dealers.

By 1984, C.D. Anderson counted some 500 TradePlus customers, who contributed as much as 12 percent of the firm's commissions. In that year, the Anderson's exclusive agreement with TradePlus ended, and Porter began marketing the company to other discount brokers, signing on Fidelity Brokerage Services, of Boston, and Texas Securities, Inc., of Fort Worth, by the middle of the year. By then, TradePlus was not alone: several other discount brokers had begun to offer their own online services. But TradePlus continued to build, in 1985 signing Quick & Reilly, then the nation's third-largest discount broker, to offer TradePlus through the Compuserve Information Network. The following year, TradePlus services were also added to another large database service of the time, Dialog Information Retrieval Service. The concept of online investment transactions was catching on, although individual investors were still burdened by monthly subscription charges. Toward the late 1980s, that changed when Donaldson, Lufkin & Jenrette introduced its PC Financial Network, which was incorporated into the standard services of such online businesses as America Online and Prodigy. TradePlus's primary customers, meanwhile, included a growing number of discount brokerage houses, conducting their activities via the TradePlus system.

Online trading continued to build momentum. By the summer of 1987, TradePlus reported that its servers were in use nearly every minute, often by several people at once, 24-hours per day, including a large number of international customers as well as domestic customers. By then, in addition to Quick & Reilly and C.D. Anderson, two banks began offering TradePlus as a brokerage gateway. Bank of America's Home Banking service gave customers access to Charles Schwab & Co. using TradePlus's computers, while Chemical Bank's Pronto customers could place orders through TradePlus to Quick & Reilly. Electronic trading seemed on its way to becoming a competitive force in the investment community. But then, in October 1987, the market crashed. Trade volume contracted, and the online trading services, TradePlus included, withered.

Reborn in the 1990s

Trading picked up only slowly as the 1990s began, crippled by a national recession, and then by the U.S. entry into the Gulf War. But in 1991, Porter, still active with TradePlus, again showed his visionary side. With several hundred thousand dollars of startup capital from TradePlus, Porter established a new company, E*Trade Securities, Inc., providing deep-discount brokerage services. Instead of the monthly fees charged by TradePlus, E*Trade offered flat-rate trading and free information services via the online services, including America Online and Compuserve. By the following year, Wall Street had recovered from its slump, entering the bull market of the 1990s. At the same time, interest in the online services began to build, while advances in modem technology and falling prices among computer equipment in general, were providing faster access to a widening range of people.

E*Trade quickly dominated this new investors market. As trade volumes continued to build, interest in investing—particularly among the Baby Boom generation—was also rising. By the mid-1990s, more than 20 percent of the nation's population was investing in stock, compared with less than 5 percent the decade before. By 1992, combined revenues at TradePlus and E*Trade neared $850,000. The following year, revenues—based on E*Trade's $40 per transaction charge—topped $2 million. The company also turned profitable, posting $100,000 in net earnings. The new availability of investment information, accessible by the online services' customers 24 hours per day, added to the popularity of investing, and particularly self-directed investing by the growing numbers of computer-literate customers. Both America Online and Compuserve were undergoing their own growth boom during this period. By 1994, the two companies counted some two million customers between them. In less than three years, America Online alone would count more than eight million customers.

Nineteen ninety-four proved significant for E*Trade as well: revenues exploded, nearing $11 million, making TradePlus and its E*Trade subsidiary the fastest-growing private company in the country. E*Trade quickly outpaced its parent, and the company would eventually be reorganized as the E*Trade Group, with E*Trade Securities remaining its principal subsidiary. The company, which counted 44 employees in 1994, scrambled to keep up with its own growth, adding more than 200 employees in one year, and expanding its office space from 4,800 square feet to more than 20,000 square feet in 1994. By the end of 1995, however, E*Trade was forced to move again, to new quarters with some 48,000 square feet.

By 1995, the new American information revolution was firmly underway. The appearance of so-called multimedia PCs, which bundled sound, video, and—particularly important for E*Trade—modems into relatively inexpensive and easy to install packages, brought a whole new wave of people to computers and online services. E*Trade soon found itself joined by competing online investment services, forcing it to drop its transaction rate to $19.95. But the company had already taken the lead among the growing home investors community—which was also served by such popular online services as America Online's Motley Fool investment information area. E*Trade found its system overloaded with customer calls, and in the summer of 1995 was forced to quadruple its systems. By the end of that year the company's revenues had doubled again, reaching $22.3 million and generating a net income of $2.6 million.

The online services proved merely a taste of things to come. By the end of 1995, the Internet—and more specifically its graphical World Wide Web interface—had become the buzzword of the country. A new range of service providers sprang up, countering the hourly charges of the online services with unlimited access at flat-rate monthly fees. E*Trade quickly set up shop on the World Wide Web as well. Within weeks after the company's entry on the Web, the Internet accounted for more than 13 percent of the company's sales.

In early 1996, E*Trade began preparing its own initial public offering. Porter stepped aside, bringing in Christos Costakos to lead the company. Costakos, a son of Greek immigrants from Paterson, New Jersey, had been a decorated Vietnam veteran—a volunteer awarded the Congressional Medal of Honor for his actions during the Tet Offensive—before joining the early 1970s startup Federal Express. Beginning at an hourly wage of $3.50, Costakos worked his way up the Federal Express ranks over nearly 19 years, before becoming president and CEO of Nielsen. With Porter as chairman, Costakos was named president and CEO in April 1996 and led E*Trade into its IPO that summer.

E*Trade was adding some 500 customers and as much as $10 million in assets per day; by May 1996, the huge increase in trading volume—in the first half of that year alone volume had tripled, from 50 million shares traded to more than 170 million—proved too much for the company's system, crashing the company's computers and leaving its customers stranded for some two hours. For that two-hour period, the company paid out $1.7 million to cover its customers' losses. A second, more limited glitch occurred in July. But the company had already begun to prepare for such an event, having leased a 53,000-square-foot space in Sacramento, California, to install a redundant hardware and customer service facility. The growth of its competitors, including the arrival of Schwabs' e.schwab service, forced E*Trade to cut its transaction rate again, to as low as $14.95.

E*Trade's growth pace continued, seeing revenues more than doubling again to near $52 million for 1996. The company also began expanding its services, offering investors the opportunity to buy shares in IPOs and purchase equity in private offerings. Trade volume continued to grow, reaching 8,000 transactions per day—with the Internet accounting for more than a quarter of all transactions. The company also formed a subsidiary, E*Trade Online Ventures, to search for other directions in which the company could expand. One such expansion was the company's agreement with Versus Brokerage to extend the E*Trade brand name to Canada's financial market. A similar agreement would bring the company to Australia in May 1997. In June 1997, E*Trade and leading World Wide Web search engine Yahoo!, which recorded some 10 million "hits" per day, announced an agreement which added a direct link to E*Trade's web site from the Yahoo! site.

With an estimated 40 million Americans online by mid-1997, and a total online community of some 60 million worldwide, E*Trade's future appeared electric. Analysts expected the online investment market to grow from 1.5 million in 1997 to 10 million or more by the turn of the century. E*Trade looked forward to becoming the top brand name of this new investment era.

Principal Subsidiaries

E*Trade Securities, Inc.; E*Trade Online Ventures, Inc.

Further Reading

Byron, Christopher, "Money Talks: Flame Your Broker!" *Esquire*, May 5, 1997.

Hoffman, Thomas, "Online Brokers Drive Industry Changes," *Computerworld*, April 14, 1997, p. 77.

Iwata, Edward, "Trading Up," *The San Francisco Examiner*, March 17, 997, p. C1.

Kerr, Deborah, "Number One: A Second-Thought Success," *The Business Journal*, October 23, 1995, p. S8.

McCarroll, Thomas, "Investors Rush the Net," *Time*, June 3, 1996, p. 54.

Tyson, David O., "The TradePlus Innovation: Latest Prices and Automated Orders in Market Hours," *The American Banker*, August 16, 1984, p. 1.

Wyatt, John, "Etrade: Is This Investing's Future?" *Fortune*, March 3, 1997, p. 190.

—M. L. Cohen

Euro Disneyland SCA

12 rue du Centre
93160 Noisy Grand
France
(33) 1 64 74 40 00
Fax: (33) 1 64 74 60 35
Web site: http://www.disneylandparis.com

Public Company
Incorporated: 1988
Employees: 10,000
Sales: FFr 4.97 billion
Stock Exchanges: Paris London
SICs: 7996 Amusement Parks; 7999 Amusement &
Recreation, Not Elsewhere Classified

Opened for just five years by 1997, Disneyland Paris (officially conducting business as Euro Disneyland SCA) has already made its mark on the French landscape—physically, culturally, and financially. Operating on part of a total 1,943-hectare (4,400-acre) site roughly one-fifth the size of Paris, the Phase I development of Disneyland Paris features a theme park, nearly 5,800 rooms among seven hotels, the Disney Village entertainment center, which includes a Planet Hollywood and an eight-screen Gaumont multiplex theater, a convention center, and a 27-hole golf course—all within 32 kilometers (20 miles) of the center of Paris. Linked to the world by its own high-speed TGV train station, with direct connections to London, Brussels, the west of France, and the Paris region's international airport, as well as with its own station for the Paris intercity RER train line and access ramps to the A4 autoroute, Disneyland Paris hosted 11.7 million visitors in 1996, making it Europe's largest entry fee-based, short-stay tourist destination. With a workforce, called "Cast Members," of more than 10,000 directly employed by Euro Disneyland, and supporting indirect employment of some 40,000 in the theme park's Marne-la-Vallée region and throughout France, Disneyland Paris has had a significant impact on a French economy troubled through much of the 1990s by a lingering economic recession and high unemployment levels.

Yet Disneyland Paris has experienced a mixed welcome through much of the years of its operation. Beset by low attendance levels, lower visitor spending levels, a withering debt brought on, in part, by Euro Disneyland's own overly optimistic financial projections, as well as labor problems and cultural miscalculations in adapting Disney's decidedly American theme park concept to a European market, the theme park—the fourth after the original Disneyland, Walt Disney World in Florida, and the Tokyo Disneyland—has already teetered on the brink of bankruptcy, and remains far behind its initial targets. Much of the site—approximately 1,300 hectares (3,300 acres)—remains undeveloped, although the company has finally reached agreements with the French authorities to begin its long-delayed Phase II development plan. After a staggering first-year (1992) loss of more than FFr 5 billion, the company has crept into profitability, posting a FFr 114 million gain on FFr 4.57 billion in 1995 and a FFr 202 million gain on FFr 4.97 billion in 1996. Meanwhile, Euro Disneyland continues to bear a FFr 15.1 billion debt load.

Principal shareholders in Euro Disneyland SCA are the Walt Disney Company, with 39 percent, Saudi Arabian Prince al-Waleed bin Talal bin Abudaziz, with 24 percent, and a collection of more than 60 banks, principally French, as well as individual shareholders, primarily from the European Community, holding the remaining 37 percent. Full development of the Disneyland site, originally projected to be completed in the year 2017, calls for the addition of 700,000 square feet of office space, a 750,000-square-foot corporate park, a 95,000-square-meter shopping mall, 2,500 single-family homes, 2,400 apartments, and 3,000 time-share apartments.

Mickey Goes to Europe, the 1980s

Flush with the huge and instant success of the Tokyo Disneyland, which opened in 1983, the Disney company immediately began looking for a site to build a European version of the popular tourist destination. On the one hand, Disney sought to capitalize on their first experience gained from operating a theme park in a foreign market—and, given the long-established European embrace of Disney's products, especially its films, which found even larger audiences in Europe than in America, Europe, with a population of 320 million within airplane distances of less than three hours, seemed a logical choice. On the other hand, Disney looked to correct what it saw as mistakes made with its previous parks. The Tokyo Disneyland was not owned by the Disney company, which meant that Disney was forced to content itself with only royalties on that theme park's massive revenues. At Walt Disney World in Florida, the company had not foreseen the mushrooming development of hotels and other theme parks and recreation centers outside of the relatively limited confines of the park, reducing Disney's hotel room take to merely 14 percent of the area's total.

Between 1983 and 1987, Disney considered sites in various countries, including the United Kingdom, Germany, and Italy, but by 1985 the choice had been narrowed down to the Costa del Sol in Spain and the suburban area around Paris. In 1987, the choice fell to Paris—despite the fairer Spanish climate—in part because of Paris's larger population, its well-developed transportation system, and its role as one of the primary tourism destinations in the world, but also because of a number of important concessions made by the French government, eager to secure the plum job- and revenue-generating theme park, including: using the government's right of eminent domain to sell the large, principally farmland Marne-de-Vallée site at the cut-rate price of $7,500 per acre; the French guarantee of some FFr 1.5 billion for new road construction, including access to the nearby autoroute; the extension of the RER train system to the theme park, as well as the building of a rail link and station for the TGV train line; an agreement to drop the value-added tax rate on ticket sales from 18.6 percent to just seven percent; and, finally, the French agreement to provide water, sewage, gas, electricity, and other services. Signing the contract with Jacques Chirac in March 1987, Disney head Michael Eisner was confident that the Paris theme park would be a success, despite France's winter climate—indeed, the Tokyo Disneyland experienced much the same weather conditions, but remained a year-round tourist draw for an eager and freely spending Japanese public.

The 4,400-acre site purchased by Disney was far larger than the company—now operating through a wholly owned development subsidiary, Euro Disney Associés SNC, which in turn would give way to theme park operator and publicly held company Euro Disneyland SCA—needed to build its theme park. But, remembering the experience of the Orlando-area Disney World, the company proposed to develop the site in several phases, excluding "mosquitoes" from the area. In addition, with the booming French real estate market of the 1980s, the company expected easily to recoup much of its development costs—initially slated at FFr 15 billion for the Phase I construction—by selling off the properties it developed, while retaining ownership of the land, and maintaining control of both the commercial use and design of the properties surrounding the theme park. These real estate sales were projected to supply 22 percent of Euro Disneyland SCA's revenues in 1992, when the park was scheduled to be opened, and rise to 45 percent of revenues by 1995.

The Disney Company itself would limit itself to a 49 percent stake (satisfying the French government's requirement that at least 51 percent of the company would be owned by Europeans); with the backing of the powerful Disney brand name and financial clout, the initial financing for the venture, completed in 1989, took two primary forms. The first was a loan package covering much of the projected Phase I cost raised among seven French banks. The second was a public offering of 51 percent of Euro Disneyland SCA, which raised US$1 billion to complete the financing. Disney was determined to build a state-of-the art theme park, "perfecting" the concept of its other theme parks, which in turn led to a number of so-called "budget breakers," that is, last-minute design changes, many of which were inspired by Disney chief Eisner himself. As the Phase I project neared completion two years later, Euro Disneyland, in order to cover construction cost overruns was forced to arrange additional capitalization of US$144 million and added loans of US$522 million, raised from a collection of what eventually became more than 60 banks. Confidence in the venture ran high, with Euro Disneyland forecasting an attendance figure of 11 million visitors in the park's first year, rising past 16 million annual visitors soon after the turn of the century.

Disney's French Folly of the Early 1990s

Euro Disneyland opened on schedule in April 1992—and from there its fortunes quickly dwindled. By the end of 1993 the company was facing bankruptcy—with a first-year loss of more than FFr 5 billion and a rise in its debt load to over FFr 21 billion—and Eisner was publicly suggesting his willingness to close the park altogether. A variety of factors had brought the company to this point.

Euro Disneyland had severely miscalculated the health of the French real estate market. When this collapsed in the early 1990s, the company's hoped-for property development sales failed to materialize. Indeed, the company was forced to abandon its planned 1994 start of the Phase II development of the theme park, from which the company had expected to pay down much of its debt load. At the same time, interest rates on the company's vast loans were rising rapidly.

Meanwhile, the company had underestimated the impact of the recession of the early 1990s, by then already taking hold in Europe, and refused to postpone the opening of the theme park, or to reduce its risk by allowing outside investors into the park's hotels and other properties, reasoning that it could weather the course of the economic downturn. But the recession slashed severely at consumer spending budgets—while Euro Disneyland nearly reached its first-year goal of 11 million, visitor rates swiftly declined, dipping to a low of just 8.8 million. Worse for the company, visitors proved reluctant to provide the company with important concession revenues, including gift sales, and restaurant and hotel revenues. As sales slumped and visitor attendance fell, and virtually stalled through much of the winter season, the company was confronted with another serious miscalculation: Its pre-opening calculations had projected labor costs would demand just 13 percent of total revenues; instead, labor costs drained 24 percent of revenues in 1992 and rose to 40 percent of revenues by 1993.

While the recession—and the company's delay in recognizing its effects—bore responsibility for many of Euro Disneyland's startup pains, the company itself had to be held accountable for a series of cross-cultural gaffes that reduced much of the consumer goodwill the company had expected. Chief among these was the company's seeming ignorance of the fact that its

European audience was very much unlike its American and Japanese audiences. Trouble started in the theme parks marketing efforts, which emphasized the grand size and scope of the project, an issue which may play well to an American or Japanese visitor, but which left the Europeans largely indifferent. High admission costs—running some 30 percent higher than a Disney World ticket—and a refusal to offer discounted prices for winter admission helped discourage the European visitors, who, unlike their American and Japanese counterparts, were less likely to take frequent short vacation trips, particularly during the school year, but preferred instead to spend their vacation budget on fewer, long vacations. Euro Disneyland hotels, which had geared up for receiving guests for average four-day stays, were surprised to find that the majority of their room bookings were only for overnight stays.

Inside the park, visitors found other oversights. Euro Disneyland's restaurants, geared toward the American feeding style of eating snacks at various times of the day, were not prepared for the more fixed schedules of France—projected to account for as much as 50 percent of all visitors—where the country all but shuts down at 12:30 every day to allow a leisurely lunch. But the park's restaurants had not been provided with the seating or staffing to accommodate the sudden influx of diners, resulting in long lines. Worse—and most famous—Euro Disneyland maintained the alcohol-free policy of its other parks, arousing the ire of a country where wine is an integral part of the culture. The company proved no more popular with its employees. Largely French and highly jealous of their individualism, the park's cast members chafed at the strict and elaborate dress and behavior codes imposed on its employees. Even at the corporate level, the Disney culture found itself at odds with its French hosts, which found the company's manner to be overbearing and patronizing—a manner which seemed to reach its peak when Eisner all but threatened to shut down the park in December 1993, arousing the ire of Euro Disneyland's creditors. But by then, with its losses mounting to FFr 5 billion and its debt load nearing FFr 22 billion, Euro Disneyland was in desperate need of its bankers' goodwill.

A Princely Rescue in 1994

By the end of 1993, Euro Disneyland had run out of cash. The Disney Company agreed to keep the company afloat, but only until the end of March 1994, when it required Euro Disneyland to have completed a restructuring of its finances. Euro Disneyland hoped to convince its creditors to waive up to half of its debt load; in return, the banks, concerned that the Disney Company should bear its share of the liability, sought concessions from Disney as well, particularly a waiver of the company's management fees of three percent of revenues, and a reduction in the Disney Company's royalty fees of 10 percent on ticket sales and five percent on concession sales. Negotiations faltered, however, in part because of Eisner's suggestion that he allow the park to close—seen as a bullying tactic by the banks—and in part because the Disney Company refused to reduce its royalty fees.

Less than a month before the deadline, the parties reached an agreement to rescue Euro Disneyland. The restructuring plan featured a rights issue, jointly subscribed by the banks and the Walt Disney Company, which raised some US$1 billion in cash. The Walt Disney Company also agreed to pay FFr 1.4 billion to purchase some of the Euro Disneyland assets in a sale-leaseback agreement; in addition, Disney waived its management and royalty fees for five years—worth some US$450 million per year—and thereafter to halve its royalty fees. The banks also agreed to waive interest payments for 18 months, and then to defer subsequent payments for three years, adding additional yearly savings of nearly FFr 2 billion to Euro Disneyland's relief.

With its debt load cut in half, Euro Disneyland next found help from a surprise rescuer: Prince al-Waleed, nephew of King Fahd of Saudi Arabia and a businessman who had built up a personal fortune estimated at over US$4 billion in just a decade, announced his intention to buy into Euro Disneyland, eventually spending over US$500 million to take a 24 percent stake in the company.

On with the Business of Fun in the Mid-1990s

With its refinancing completed, and with new management in place—American Robert Fitzpatrick, who had overseen the Phase I construction was replaced by Frenchman Phillippe Bourguignon in 1993—Euro Disneyland began addressing its internal problems. In 1994, the park's name was changed to Disneyland Paris, emphasizing its proximity to the Paris capital. The company made concessions toward resolving its poor labor and press relations. The no-alcohol policy was changed, allowing wine and beer to be served at the park's restaurants, while the company lowered its admission prices, some of its hotel room rates, introduced lower-priced menu choices, and instituted discount pricing for winter admission. In addition, the TGV link to the theme park was completed in 1994, complete with a direct linkup with the Eurostar Chunnel train service.

After narrowing its losses to FFr 1.8 billion on FFr 4.1 billion in revenues in 1994, Euro Disneyland turned profitable in 1995. The company also began moving forward on its Phase II development, attracting a Planet Hollywood restaurant and an eight-screen, state-of-the-art movie complex, owned by Gaumont, to the company's free-admission Festival Disney (renamed Disney Village in June 1997) entertainment complex located next to the theme park. The company also started construction on a second convention center, and began eyeing plans to open a Disney-MGM Studios theme park on the site. Meanwhile, the passing European recession and stronger marketing campaigns were spurring increasing attendance, rising from 10.7 million visitors in 1995 to 11.7 million in 1996. Posting its second year of profits in 1996, Euro Disneyland seemed finally to be rousing from its European nightmare and moving into the dreamland Disneyland Paris should have been all along.

Principal Subsidiaries

EDL Hôtels S.C.A.

Further Reading

Borden, Lark, ''Eurodisneyland: In Paris, When It Drizzles, It Sizzles,'' *Gannett News Service*, March 11, 1992.
Graves, Nelson, ''Euro Disney Attendance in Upturn but Woes Persist, *Reuter European Business Report*, September 4, 1992.

Kleege, Stephen, "Magic of Disney Wins Backers for Paris Theme Hotels," *American Banker*, March 26, 1991, p. 11.

McGrath, John, "The Lawyers Who Rebuilt EuroDisney," *International Financial Law Review*, May 1994, p. 10.

Rawsthorn, Alice, and Michael Skapinker, "Empty Pockets Hit Imported Dream," *Financial Times*, July 9, 1993, p. 23.

Rawsthorn, Alice, "Poisoned Apple Within the Magic Kingdom," *Financial Times*, November 25, 1993, p. 23.

Taylor, Charles Foster, and Stephen Richardson, "Focus on Leisure—Eurodisneyland," *Estates Gazette*, April 7, 1990, p. 85.

Webster, Paul, "Red Carpet Rolled Out for Eurodisney," *Guardian*, May 3, 1991, p. 27.

Wise, Deborah, "Will Eurodisneyland Be Able To Overcome Two Main Obstacles?" *Guardian*, March 1, 1991, p. 26.

—M. L. Cohen

Exide Electronics Group, Inc.

8609 Six Forks Road
Raleigh, North Carolina 27615
U.S.A.
(919) 872-3020
Fax: (919) 870-3100
Web Site: http://www.exide.com

Public Company
Incorporated: 19
Employees: 2,500
Sales: $459.9 million (1996)
Stock Exchanges: NASDAQ
SICs: 3629 Electrical Industrial Apparatus, Not
Elsewhere Classified; 7629 Electrical Repair Shops,
Not Elsewhere Classified

Exide Electronics Group, Inc. is the world's only provider of Strategic Power Management. Billing itself as "the global force for the preservation of uptime," the company is a leading maker of a full range of uninterruptible power systems (UPS) and leads the industry with a broad spectrum of intelligent power management hardware and software solutions.

The company began more than 33 years ago with a singular focus, to meet customer needs at every application level. By maintaining that focus, the company has produced a robust annual growth rate, expanding from $192 million in revenue in 1991 to $459.9 million in 1996. The company has innovative technologies and has brought UPS protection from the power room to the computer room to the desktop with a host of major industry innovations, some of which include digital UPS, super-redundant UPS, monitoring and remote control software, seamless Novell/UNIX integration, and virtual-battery UPS. The company also offers a comprehensive range of products and services that supply an extensive variety of hardware, software, and connectivity devices for enterprise-wide power conditioning, protection, and management solutions. Some of the products it produces include the Powerware Prestige family of online UPSs to provide clean, uninterrupted power to mission-critical networks. Those

products and services have been honored with numerous awards for their products and services. Powerware Prestige has won the June 1994 *LAN Recommended* Magazine Award, the December 1994 *Computer Reseller* News Editors' Choice Award, and the July 1995 *Network Computing* Magazine Choice Award, while Powerware Prestige EXT won the September 1994 Best Buy What PC? Award, the November 1994 *LAN Recommended* Magazine Award, and the March 1995 *Personal Computer* Magazine Reviewer's Choice Award. The company was incorporated as a Delaware corporation in 1979.

The company has traveled all over the world to maintain its customers' equipment. From aircraft carriers in the Mediterranean Sea to oil platforms in the Gulf of Mexico, from facilities on the nearly deserted island of Attu, Alaska, to the arid desert of Kabul, Afghanistan, the company has customers worldwide. One such has been the U.S. Federal Aviation Administration, which has relied on Exide's power consulting expertise to ensure mission-critical uptime for communications and radar systems at 21 Air Route Traffic Control Centers. This is one of the world's largest networks, vital to the operation of more than 82,000 flights transporting more than 1.5 million passengers throughout the U.S. each day. Another was the 1996 Summer Olympic Games in which timing systems, computers, and communications systems in 31 widespread venues were required to operate continuously. The system Exide supplied for the Olympics included 12,000 integrated power protection and management components, including UPSs ranging from 800VA to 80KVA to protect data centers and multiple networks. Other clients Exide serves include Canon, Digital Equipment Corporation, Ericsson, IBM, Seiko Instruments, and SITA.

The company's continued revenue growth has been a result of a slow but steady acquisition policy. In April 1990, the company acquired France-based Saft-Exide Electronics S.A. for approximately $440,000. November 1991 saw the company purchase London, England-based MPL Powerware Systems Ltd. Certain assets of DataTrax Systems Corporation were purchased in September 1993. Late in 1994, the company acquired two companies in Canada and one in the United Kingdom. These companies were involved in the sales and service of UPS products. In February 1995, the company com-

---

Company Perspectives:

Exide Electronics Group, Inc. is a leading developer, manufacturer and marketer of a full range of uninterruptible power systems (UPS) whose mission is to provide power protection solutions for customers worldwide in order to create enterprise value and achieve the common goals of superior financial performance, customer satisfaction, associate satisfaction and quality, to provide solutions that exceed customers' expectations and create value and whose vision is to become "the worldwide leader in strategic power management."

---

pleted its merger of International Power Machines Inc. (IPM), a developer, manufacturer, seller, and servicer of UPS products located in Dallas, Texas, with and into a newly formed subsidiary of the company. The acquisition included IPM's LorTec Systems Inc. subsidiary. Later that same year, in August, the company acquired Lectro Products Inc., a broadband industry leader specializing in power protection and other transmission enhancement devices for the converging cable television and communications networks, for approximately $12.4 million. Also in 1995, the company introduced new selling and marketing programs, including the realignment of the North American sales and support operation along customer groups, the launching of an integrated marketing campaign introducing the concept of SPM and the opening of an area sales office, Exide Electronics-Latin America, in Miami, Florida, to service markets in Latin America. The company was also negotiating to acquire the UPS business of Group Schneider S.A., but those negotiations fell through.

That same year, 1995, saw the company begin a strategy called Vision 2000. With the 21st century rapidly approaching, the company eagerly anticipates the new borderless world and swift advancement of internetworking technologies. Vision 2000 began in August 1995 with a meeting of a team of 40 people, representing the company's customers, suppliers, board of directors and associates, who gathered to form a blueprint for the company as it moved into the next century. Seven key strategies were defined which will guide the company's direction: customer obsession, a pervasive management system designed to enable and empower all associates at all levels with the quality process, tools, and environment to focus on continuous improvement, customer satisfaction and loyalty; continued corporate development; international expansion; increased presence in small systems; leadership in large systems and services; government business expansion and pursuit of emerging market opportunities.

In 1996, the company expanded product lines, strengthened the company's OEM partnerships, added manufacturing capabilities and developed its Emerging Technologies Group. New products in 1996 included NetUPS and Powerware Prestige UPS by Exide Electronics, PowerRite Max UPS by Deltec, and Internet UPS by Fiskars Power Systems. To accommodate the special installation requirements of contemporary computing, such as network racks and wiring closets, the company introduced new rackmount and stackable UPS. In addition to these hardware introductions, the company announced a new power management software family called Strategic Power Management (SPM), that supports the widest range of UPS in the industry.

The company believes that, in order to run a business, power must be managed. In the distributed environment of businesses in the late 20th century, with more and more corporate data residing in power-vulnerable devices, the need for one all-inclusive power management resource is critical. As the company's technology developed, Exide Electronics created a shift in thinking in the UPS industry from passive to proactive power management and stayed consistently one generation ahead of the power needs of critical electronic systems. One of its concepts is Strategic Power Management. SPM was created as a unique, enterprise-wide approach that will safeguard the integrity of electronic assets and the availability of information-on-demand. SPM ensures the availability of mission-critical information systems by mobilizing technologies, products, services, and partnerships which far exceed the conventional uninterrupted power sources (UPS).

Through its Emerging Technologies Group (ETG), the company is broadening its capabilities in specialized markets such as cable telecommunications and the information superhighway. The company also continues developing new power protection solutions for applications that never existed before. In its first full year of operations the ETG consolidated its manufacturing of communications-related power protection systems into a new facility in Raleigh, North Carolina. Working closely with leading cable companies, the ETG is also contributing to the deployment of broadband networks and, in 1996, introduced a new centralized power node for advanced cable network systems.

The company's Small Systems Group (SSG), located in Wilmington, North Carolina, is Exide Electronics' fastest-growing and most rapidly evolving business unit. In March 1996, the company acquired Deltec Power Systems Inc., one of the world's largest manufacturer's and marketers of offline and line-interactive small UPS, from Fiskars Oy Ab and an affiliated company, for approximately $197.6 million, mostly in cash. The purchase of the San Diego, California-based Deltec brought the company several complimentary networking products and an opportunity to expand its OEM business, in addition to increasing its low-cost manufacturing capacity. With Deltec's strong OEM relationships, Exide Electronics, already a leading supplier to most of the computer industry's top manufacturers, now becomes the industry leader in meeting the needs of emerging internetworking and vertical market OEM customers. With an expansion at the Wilmington facility and the addition of Deltec S.A. de C.V., a facility located in Tijuana, Mexico, the company's capacity to manufacture SSG products nearly doubled.

The company's Large Systems Group (LSG) also grew in 1996, targeting commercial business opportunities, especially in international markets, enhancing the performance of large systems products and leveraging longstanding relationships with federal government customers. The LSG formed two new subsidiaries to address significant large and small systems market opportunities in Brazil and India, partnering with Grupo Microlite S.A. and Crompton Greaves, respectively, which adds longstanding relationships and strong regional presence. In Europe, the LSG benefited from the acquisition of Finland-based Fiskars Power Systems as part of the Deltec acquisition. The Scandinavian market share leader adds strong presence for the company in Europe and in the emerging Eastern European and Russian markets.

The company's Worldwide Services Group (WSG) is a force of over 1,100 factory-trained service representatives around the world that focuses on preventing downtime as well as correcting it. Services at the WSG are available 24 hours a day and include a full range of powertrain services as well as UPS maintenance and upgrading. This division of the company also turnkey installs systems; designs power systems from the ground up; tests, replaces, monitors and consults on battery-related problems; and performs comprehensive audits of customers' power systems. The WSG also develops sophisticated software for onsite or remote monitoring and analyzation of data on the status of UPS equipment and batteries or on the entire facility environment. Some of the products in the WSG division include Powerware UPS, OnliNet Power Management Software, LorTec UPS, LecTro UPS, OneUPS UPS, ConnectUPS Network Adapters, and PowerPass Surge Protection.

Also in 1996, the company was awarded a follow-on contract of two years with the U.S. Air Force Air Logistics Center, received the European Community Declaration of Conformity "CE Mark" on its Powerware Systems and Series 3000M and 5000M UPS products, and the company additionally became the first in the power protection industry to achieve ISO 9001 quality status from the International Standards Office. Two patents applications were also filed for new technologies that utilize special control algorithms to connect UPS in parallel, removing a potential point of failure related to connecting wires which are traditionally used for communications between parallel UPS. The new technology allows each UPS module the intelligence to govern themselves independently.

The company continues to develop new technologies as the computer industry speeds into the 21st century, forging strategic alliances with customers, suppliers, and sales partners all around the world, enabling the company to share critical knowledge to create comprehensive, efficient, and cost-effective business solutions. One of the strategic partnerships the company has formed is with Data General in order to enhance the latter's system to provide easier, more efficient ways to order, install, and help maintain Data General's reliable, single-source business solutions for its customers.

Uptime—when computer screens burn phosphor tracks through the day and night, when networks talk to each other at the speed of light, when business transactions flow back and forth. Uptime is mission-critical because, without it, business stops moving, productivity decreases, customer confidence erodes, and revenue losses climb ever higher. The quality and availability of electrical power poses one of the biggest threats to the creation of downtime. Exide Electronics has grown into a company of more than 2,500 representatives in more than 100 countries, a company which is committed to exceeding customers' expectations through experience, dedication, and teamwork, a company which is equipped with leading-edge power management technologies, products, services, and partnerships, serving clientele and a company preserving uptime from a single PC to global information networks and everything in between. Maximizing the human potential worldwide is a major component of the company's Vision 2000 strategy. Exide Electronics will continue to benchmark and implement products and services throughout the world so it can attain worldwide leadership in Strategic Power Management.

Principal Subsidiaries

Advanced Technology Center; DataTrax Systems Corporation; Deltec Electronics Corporation; Deltec S.A. de C.V. (Mexico); Exide Electronics-Crompton Greaves (India); Exide Electronics-Grupo Microlite S.A. (Brazil); Exide Electronics-Latin America; Exide Electronics Canada Inc.; Exide Electronics de Mexico; Exide Electronics International-Australia; Exide Electronics International/IPM (China); Exide Electronics International/IPM (Singapore); Exide Electronics International Corp. (U.K.); Exide Electronics International Corp. (Middle East/Africa); Exide Electronics International GmbH (Germany); Exide Electronics S.A. (France); Fiskars Power Systems (Finland); GS-EE Co. Ltd. (Japan); GS-EE Co. Ltd. (Japan); MPL Powerware Systems Ltd. (U.K.).

Principal Operating Units

Large Systems Group; Small Systems Group; Emerging Technologies Group; Worldwide Services Group.

—Daryl F. Mallett

Fila Holding S.p.A.

Viale Cesare Battisti 26
Biella
Italy
39 15 34141
Fax: 33 15 350 6297
Web site: http://www.fila.com

Public Company
Founded: 1926 as Societa Anonima Fratelli Fila
Employees: 1,985
Sales: L2.1 trillion (US$1.4 billion) (1996)
Stock Exchanges: New York
SICs: 3149 Footwear, Except Rubber, Not Elsewhere
    Classified; 2329 Men's and Boys' Clothing, Not
    Elsewhere Classified; 2339 Women's, Misses' and
    Juniors' Outerwear, Not Elsewhere Classified; 5651
    Family Clothing Stores; 6794 Patent Owners and
    Lessors; 6719 Offices of Holding Companies, Not
    Elsewhere Classified

Fila Holding S.p.A. is the world's third-largest manufacturer and marketer of athletic footwear, behind Nike and Reebok. The company's product line includes more than 100 models of men's, women's, and children's shoes; a broad line of athletic apparel embracing sports from running to skateboarding; and high fashion sportswear. Though it had been active in the athletic apparel and footwear industry since the mid-1970s, Fila did not truly make its mark in this market until the mid-1990s, when the brand was embraced by trend-setting urbanites. Savvy endorsement contracts with the likes of basketball stars Grant Hill and Jerry Stackhouse helped push the brand from an eighth-place ranking worldwide to number three by 1996. In acknowledgment of the fact that America is its largest and most important market, Fila moved its global operations center to its U.S. headquarters mid-decade. Italian investment firm Gemina S.p.A. owned a majority interest in Fila in 1996, but that ownership structure appeared subject to change in 1997. Ongoing negotiations between Italian apparel giant Marzotto S.p.A. and Gemina could portend a merger or acquisition among the businesses.

Early History and Development of Apparel Emphasis in 1970s

Fila was established in 1923 by eponymous brothers to manufacture knitwear, specifically underwear. The company operated in this field for nearly a half-century, enduring the Great Depression, political upheavals, and high inflation throughout the ensuing decades. It was not until the 1970s and the arrival of managing director Enrico Frachey that the company began to take its present shape. Frachey, who served the company from 1974 to 1979, has been credited with transforming Fila into a manufacturer of athletic apparel. An endorsement contract with tennis star Bjorn Borg proved particularly important to the company's successful penetration of high-end markets for tennis and skiwear. Over the course of the decade, Fila rode a rising tide of popularity into country clubs and onto the ski slopes of Europe and the United States. Though it did not become a runaway hit, Fila and its trademark "F" logo were widely recognized throughout the world of sports apparel and footwear by the end of the 1970s. Frachey left the company late in the decade.

Acquisition by SNIA in 1980s

During the 1980s, Italian fiber company SNIA BPD S.p.A. acquired an 80.5 percent stake in Fila, while the remaining 19.5 percent was owned by Unione Manifatture, a holding company. Fila built a global network of licensees over the course of the decade and concurrently switched from backing athletes to sponsoring athletic events. The most important of the licensees proved to be America's H. Altice Marketing Inc., which was established in 1984 and was selling 75,000 pairs of Fila shoes annually by its second year in business. Altice targeted his product at Fila's traditional upper-crust constituency, restricting distribution to such high-end retailers as Macy's, Nordstrom, and Neiman-Marcus and such specialty shops as Foot Locker. By 1987, the U.S. licensee's sales totaled US$55 million. However, the brand went into a tailspin in the 1980s following a serious misstep. According to a 1988 piece in *WWD*, US$15

Company Perspectives:

FILA's new mission has been well identified: To offer an exclusive lifestyle, not only to those who practice sport to compete, test their own skills and overcome their limits, but also to those people who live the sport as an opportunity to play and have fun or, simply, as a firm point of reference in their free time and their every day life. Sport means psycho-physical balance and, at the same time, an important occasion to socialize. Remember that athletic shoes and apparel are mostly used "off the court," for "streetwear purposes," which implies relaxation, non-competition, but still a strong emphasis on the sportive image. FILA's lifestyle is what we will be focused on in the coming years, to take FILA to the next level.

million in Italian overstocks sold to a British liquidator ended up in America. The heavily discounted shoes undercut Fila's top-shelf image and flattened U.S. sales.

In the meantime, tennis, ski, and swimwear had continued to be Fila Holding's mainstays; footwear was little more than an afterthought, generating only seven percent of revenues in 1988. Though the parent company's sales had increased from L150 billion (US$78.5 million) in 1984 to L180 billion (US$138 million) in 1988, Fila suffered several annual losses mid-decade, culminating in a L7.8 billion (US$6 million) shortfall in 1987. SNIA re-hired Frachey that year, and the "new" managing director immediately undertook a L10 billion (US$7.6 million) restructuring that included an endorsement contract with tennis luminary Boris Becker, a revamp of the company's design team, and ongoing management shakeups. In 1988, SNIA sold its controlling interest in Fila to Gemina, a holding company that was in turn controlled by Italian automaker Fiat S.p.A., for L62 billion (US$47 million).

Fila Finds Success in 1990s

Fila completed a buyout of its U.S. license in 1991, thereby acquiring that company's US$70 million in annual sales. The move signaled a shift in geographic emphasis to the all-important American market and a focus on athletic footwear, particularly basketball shoes. Though Fila had long targeted upper-middle class whites, the company found that young urban blacks had by the early 1990s become its core constituency. According to apparel industry observers, Fila had become an "aspirational brand," a label that represented the dreams of inner-city kids whose reality was far removed from the tennis courts and golf courses where the brand had earned its early fame. Like many other of the decade's biggest marketers, Fila embraced its accidental positioning and the tough, gritty image that came with it. Ironically, the strategy was pivotal to helping the brand win over suburban youths increasingly enamored with urban culture. A revival of fashions from Fila's heyday in the 1970s did not hurt the brand's prospects, either.

As they had been in the 1970s, sponsorships were vital to Fila's success 20 years later. In 1994, the company inked an

endorsement contract with Grant Hill of the NBA's Detroit Pistons. After he won 1995's Rookie of the Year award, sales of his namesake shoe skyrocketed to over 1.5 million pairs. The brand continued its youth appeal with the 1995 addition of NBA rookie Jerry Stackhouse to its roster. From 1990 to 1995, U.S. sales as a percentage of overall Fila revenues went from 22 percent to 60 percent. Frachey also turned past growth strategies upside down. In 1990, footwear only constituted 14 percent of annual sales, with the remainder coming from clothing. By 1995 athletic shoes contributed more than 60 percent of revenues.

This combination of strategies helped make Fila America's fastest-growing footwear brand mid-decade, with U.S. sales burgeoning from US$70 million in 1991 to almost US$386 million, for a six percent share of this all-important market in 1995. The brand leapfrogged its second-tier competitors, growing from an eighth-place ranking among the world's athletic shoe makers to number three by 1996. Fila Holding's overall revenues mushroomed from L151 billion in 1990 to L2.1 trillion in 1996, while net increased to L177.7 billion. The parent company's profitability zoomed from 5.8 percent of sales to 8.3 percent over the period. Holders of the Fila's American Depository Shares (ADRs) rejoiced as their value shot up from US$18 each at issue in 1993 to nearly $66 at the end of 1996.

WWD called Fila's 1996 showing "breathtaking," but warned that the future was not free of challenges. For instance, the brand's emphasis on fashion left it vulnerable to competition from designer brands like Tommy Hilfiger, Donna Karan, and Ralph Lauren, all of whom were introducing stylish athletic shoes mid-decade.

Strategies for the Future

Having established itself in the number-three spot in the key footwear segment, Fila focused on parlaying its shoe success into continued growth by refocusing on apparel and accessories, diversifying into new sports, targeting women, emphasizing technology, and pursuing geographic expansion. Backed by the L90 billion (US$56 million) raised in a 1995 stock offering, the company invested in a variety of initiatives with a view to achieving L2 trillion (US$1.4 billion) in revenues in 1997.

Fila developed clothing for skiers, snowboarders, skateboarders, and baseball players, and concentrated on building its presence in specialized footwear for basketball, cross-training, running, hiking, volleyball, soccer, and tennis. It also established a joint venture with Italian eyewear manufacturer De Rigo S.p.A. to produce a branded line of sunglasses. Fila even created a skin care line including sun lotions and bath products. The company hired a slew of endorsers to support its new sports lines, including beach volleyball player Randy Stoklos, marathon runner German Silva, soccer players Claudio Reyna and Franco Baresi, and tennis player Marc Philippoussis.

The diversification also re-emphasized high-end sportswear and casual footwear with a particular focus on the long-neglected women's market. In 1995, Fila bought market share and expertise in women's and children's clothing via the acquisition of French sportswear manufacturer Dorotennis SA. The parent company hoped to expand this new subsidiary from its European base into America and Asia. New endorsement contracts with top-ranked female athletes, including tennis player Gabriela Sabatini and skier Deborah Compagnoni, supported the drive for the female consumer.

Fila fought the perception that it was a "fashionable but low tech" brand by establishing a research and development center in Portland, Oregon, and staffing it with engineers hired away from Nike. Fila's 1996 annual report stressed the strategic shift, asserting "Style is our heritage. Creativity is our strength. Technology is our future." The company also established new research and design centers in the key geographic markets of Italy and Korea. Efforts at geographic diversification were so successful that by 1995, Korea had grown to become Fila's second-largest market, behind the U.S. but exceeding Italy.

Controlled by Gemina S.p.A. since 1988, Fila's corporate ownership came under question in the mid-1990s. Stock offerings from 1993 on had reduced Gemina's stake in Fila to just over 50 percent by 1997. Following an aborted attempt to merge Gemina's ultimate parent company, HPI, with Italian textile and apparel giant Marzotto S.p.A. in 1996, many analysts speculated that a union between Gemina and Marzotto could yet occur. If completed, the deal stood to form a multibillion-dollar amalgamation of upscale clothing and footwear brands.

Principal Subsidiaries

Fila Sport S.p.A.; Ciesse Piumini S.r.l.; Fila Diffusion S.r.l.; Fila Shoes Italy S.r.l.; Fila U.S.A. Inc.; Fila Caribbean Inc. (Puerto Rico); Fila Korea Ltd.; Fila France S.A.; Elegam S.a.r.l.; Fila Philippines Inc.; Fila Boutique GmbH (Germany); Fila Far East Ltd.; Fila Nederland B.V.; Fila Do Brasil Ltda.; Fila U.K. Ltd; Fila Mexico S.A.; Fila Sports Inc. (United States); Fila Trading Inc. (United States); Fila Japan Ltd.; Fila Manufacturing Ltd.; Fila Canada Inc.; Fila Sport Taiwan Ltd.; Fila Marketing (Hong Kong) Ltd.; Fila Sport (Malaysia) Sdn. Bhd.; Fila Deutschland GmbH; Fila Sport (Hong Kong) Ltd.; Fila China Ltd.; ABCD S.A. (France); F.D.F. S.r.l.; Multutu International S.A. (France); Dorotennis S.A. (France); Doroten-nis Portugal Ltda.; Fila Sport (Asia) Pte Ltd.; Fila Marketing (Singapore) Pte Ltd.; Fila South Africa Pty Ltd.; Fila Argentina S.A.; Trademart S.A. Uruguay; Enyce Inc. (United States); Fila Morin S.A.S. (France).

Further Reading

Bannon, Lisa, "Fila Sees '89 Sales in U.S. Even With '88," *Footwear News,* November 21, 1988, pp. 2–3.

Chirls, Stuart B., "Activewear's Italian-American Exchange," *Daily News Record,* July 10, 1989, pp. 25–26.

Feitelberg, Rosemary, "Fila: Success, American-Style," *WWD,* July 20, 1995, p. 11.

"Fila Forward," *WWD,* May 18, 1995, p. 9.

Forden, Sara Gay, "Fila Planning Expansion in Apparel, Sportswear," *Daily News Record,* January 1, 1996, pp. 12–13.

Forden, Sara Gay; Samantha Conti; Stan Gellers; and Miles Socha, "Gemina Said to Ask Marzotto To Take Over GFT, Fila," *Daily News Record,* February 28, 1997, p. 1.

Forden, Sara Gay, and Samantha Conti, "New Scenario Emerges in the Gemina, Marzotto Talks on GFT," *Daily News Record,* March 3, 1997.

Gelsi, Steve, "Sneaking into Third," *BrandWeek,* December 4, 1995, pp. 24–25.

"Gemina Obtains Control of Fila for $47 Million," *WWD,* November 15, 1988, p. 23.

Hartlein, Robert, "Fila Sports Inc.," *WWD,* February 5, 1992, p. 10.

Levine, Joshua, "Badass Sells," *Forbes,* April 21, 1997, pp. 142–47.

MacDonald, Laurie, "The Battle for #3 ... Still Raging," *Footwear News,* July 11, 1994, pp. S18–S20.

Pereira, Joseph, "Nike's Rivals Hope Buyers Want Bargains," *Wall Street Journal,* June 2, 1997, pp. B1, B3.

Schroder Securities UK Ltd., "Fila-Company Report," *Investext,* August 8, 1996.

Seckler, Valerie, "Fila Maps Apparel Game," *WWD,* August 10, 1995, p. 8.

"U.S. Apparel Sales Strong As Fila Earnings Skyrocket," *Daily News Record,* November 9, 1993, p. 4.

Waxler, Caroline, "Fleeing Fila," *Forbes,* December 30, 1996, p. 162.

—April Dougal Gasbarre

Ford Motor Company, S.A. de C.V.

Paseo de la Reforma 333
06500 Mexico, D.F.
Mexico
(525) 326-6000
Fax: (525) 326-6274

Wholly Owned Subsidiary of Ford Motor Company
Incorporated: 1925
Employees: 9,700
Sales: 9.21 billion pesos (US$2.63 billion) (1994)
SICs: 3711 Motor Vehicles and Passenger Car Bodies

Ford Motor Company, S.A. de C.V. is the Mexican subsidiary of the Detroit-based parent corporation. This subsidiary was the first automaker to establish production in Mexico, in 1925, and it remained the only automaker in Mexico until 1938. Although the Mexican market has remained relatively small, Ford Mexico's production of motor vehicles increased greatly in the 1980s, when it began turning out vehicles for export to the United States.

Ford Mexico to 1960

Ford Motor Company, S.A. was incorporated in 1925 with capital of 500,000 pesos ($250,000). Adrian Rene Lajous, a Mexican of aristocratic parentage who was appointed managing director of the firm, knew President Plutarco Elías Calles personally and negotiated customs, tax, and railway freight-rate concessions from the government. Ford obtained a 50 percent rebate on duties for materials imported into Mexico. The company also was promised by the government that there would be no problems with the unions; however, a union was formed at the Ford factory as early as 1932. With regard to wages, Lajous suggested to Ford that it pay workers no more than $3 a day—a substantial sum at the time, since wages averaged only $1.25 a day.

Ford's first plant was located in a rented warehouse in the San Lazaro neighborhood of Mexico City. It had a total of 250 employees but assembled only 50 vehicles, using U.S.-made parts. Many of these were Model As, which replaced the Model T in 1928. In 1932 the company built a new assembly plant in the La Villa neighborhood. This factory had the capacity to turn out 100 autos a day—far beyond the realities of the Mexican market, even though Ford established a credit company to finance sales. The factory operated only two to three days a week, and a second daily shift was not added until nearly the end of the decade. Ford was the only auto manufacturer in Mexico until 1938, when General Motors opened a plant.

World War II was a prosperous period for Mexico, and Ford's Mexican subsidiary made a profit in each war year, ranging from $112,000 in 1939 to $851,000 in 1945. The La Villa plant was expanded in 1949. The postwar period, however, ushered in a mood of economic nationalism. In 1947, when there were seven automobile producers in Mexico, the government reduced customs duties on the import of auto parts and components but for the first time imposed quotas on the amount of material to be used for assembly that could be imported. In 1951 it introduced price controls on automobiles and trucks, and these, in one form or another, continued until 1977.

Even with price controls, an automobile bought in Mexico was 50 to 100 percent more expensive than in the United States, mainly because of the lack of automation in Mexican factories and the cost of importing parts. This confined sales to the well-to-do. The government, considering auto purchases a dangerous drain on the nation's dollar reserves, held the industry's production to about 15,000 cars in the mid-1950s. Since each company could easily sell every car it was allowed to produce, the quota set for each producer in the industry was the object of impassioned lobbying campaigns. In 1955 General Motors was allotted 33 percent of the market, Ford 28 percent, and Chrysler 20 percent, with American independents and European automakers holding the remainder.

Within each production quota at this time was a subquota. Of total production, 70 percent was mandated for low-priced cars, 25 percent for medium-priced ones, and not more than 5 percent for high-priced vehicles. There was also a requirement that the industry as a whole produce 55 trucks for every 45 passenger cars. Since price increases required government permission, an automobile company that earned more than 5 percent on sales before taxes, or more than 2 percent after taxes, was beating the industry average, according to a *Fortune* article.

Widening Its Scope in the 1960s and 1970s

In 1962 Ford purchased the Studebaker Packard plant at Tlalnepantla in the state of Mexico and made it a foundry for chassis and tools. The company was receiving parts from U.S., West German, and British Ford plants for assembly into nine different models. But instead of Detroit-style tooling for each car model, Ford Mexico had developed tools that could be used for several models, and also for use in several other Ford plants around the world. One observer told *Business Week,* "Mexican production technicians—born and raised in Mexico—have invented something that Detroit engineers might never have thought of. This is because Detroiters haven't had to live with the problems of low-volume, hand-to-mouth production the way the Mexicans have."

This form of production essentially came to an end after the Mexican government decreed, in 1962, that by September 1, 1964, 60 percent of the production cost of each Mexican-made automobile must consist of Mexican-made parts. All drive-train components—engine, transmission, and rear axle—had to be made in Mexico.

The measure was intended to close the $80-million-a-year deficit in trade because of imports of automobile components. The government also used production quotas to weed out some of the 11 companies that were manufacturing 34 models, and it even created its own firm. Of the 19 factories in Mexico engaged in auto assembly, 11 closed their doors.

Ford responded by finding local sources for 1,200 of the 1,800 new parts it needed and brought eight U.S. auto-parts manufacturers together with a Mexican refrigerator manufacturer to build a complex window regulator. It dropped its Lincoln, Mercury, Taurus, Anglia, and Consul models, retaining the Galaxie, Mustang, and Falcon. Most importantly, it opened a plant in 1964 at Cuautitlán in the state of Mexico for auto assembly and the manufacture of V8 engines. The company's employment rose from 1,209 in 1960 to 3,291 in 1965. Sales increased to 21,207 in 1969, when Ford had 29 percent of the market. It also sold 9,821 trucks and utility vehicles, 21 percent of the total. In 1970 Ford Mexico turned out its 500,000th vehicle.

Sales of Mexican-produced automobiles were barely exceeding 100,000 a year at this time, mainly because cars were still selling for up to twice as much as in the United States. The Mexican government contended that exporting was the only way the industry could break out of its low-volume, high-cost operations, and so it decreed that the automakers must increase exports to get higher production quotas, or to retain existing ones. Although already exporting parts to 23 countries, including the United States, Ford Mexico was unwilling to compete with its Detroit counterpart by exporting fully assembled vehicles.

The 1976 devaluation of the peso sharply increased the price of imported auto parts, raising Ford's costs. Anti-inflationary measures then made car loans more difficult to obtain, and Ford claimed that as a result of declining sales its profit margins were falling. Nevertheless, automobile sales continued to rise because Mexicans turned to cheaper compacts. In 1977 Ford was the ninth-largest company in Mexico, with sales of 7.88 billion pesos (about $358 million). Some 350,000 cars and trucks were sold in Mexico in 1978, of which 19 percent were Fords.

During this period Ford established a joint venture with Grupo Alfa to produce aluminum cylinder heads for its engines, with Grupo Vitro to make glass for its vehicles, and with Grupo Visa to make plastic components. The millionth Ford was produced in 1980. This was the last LTD assembled at La Villa, which ceased to be a production facility in 1984. Its assembly operations were transferred to Cuautitlán. An engine-manufacturing factory was opened in Chihuahua in 1983.

Turning to Exporting in the 1980s and 1990s

Mexico's 1982 economic crisis was much more severe than that of 1976, and the peso was devalued by a much greater amount. Mexico Ford's auto sales slumped from 78,947 to 62,821, and the company's president said its gross profit margin had been reduced by 50 to 75 percent. Ford now turned its attention to manufacturing cars in Mexico for export to the United States. In 1984 it announced that it would invest $500 million to build subcompacts at a new plant in Hermosillo, 150 miles south of the Texas border.

When the Hermosillo plant opened in November 1986, it had capacity to produce 130,000 cars a year and began turning out the new, Japanese-designed Mercury Tracer for the U.S. and Canadian markets. The factory featured a "just-in-time" system for this model's 2,400 components and 96 Kawasaki robots to do 95 percent of the welding. Another $300 million in funds raised the number of robots to 128, introduced personal computers, increased the plant's capacity to 170,000 autos a year, and retooled it to produce the Ford Escort. In 1990 the plant turned out 47,702 Tracers and 40,902 Ford Escorts.

A six-week strike by about 800 workers in Hermosillo ended in April 1987, when they received an average wage increase of 34.5 percent, plus a 20-percent inflation adjustment mandated by the government. They had been averaging $1.09 an hour for a 45-hour week. In September of that year Ford dismissed 3,200 workers at the Cuautitlán plant as part of a settlement ending a nine-week strike there. The company's Mexican sales had fallen 45 percent the previous year.

Labor trouble erupted again at Cuautitlán in 1990, when members of the Mexican Workers' Confederation (CTM) stormed into the plant, wearing company uniforms. They killed one and seriously wounded seven dissidents. A work stoppage of nearly a month ensued. About 1,300 returned to work, but Ford sent dismissal notices to another 2,400 and asked the CTM to provide replacements. The following year Ford announced it would invest more than $700 million to modernize the Chihuahua plant to manufacture a new four-cylinder passenger-car engine, the Zetec. Production of this engine began in 1993. The Ford Contour and Mystique automobiles were introduced in 1994.

Ford's Mexican sales reached a record 126,000 in 1992 but fell by one-fourth in 1993. Sales stabilized in 1994 but dropped another two-thirds, to only 32,000 in 1995, in the wake of the December 1994 peso devaluation, the ensuing recession, and the imposition of a tax on new autos to raise income for the government. Because of the export of vehicles to the United States, overall sales performance was better. Ford Mexico produced 235,000 vehicles in 1996 and sold 66,000 cars and trucks in Mexico, 20 percent of the total.

Ford had three plants in Mexico in 1997. Cuautitlán, which began turning out pickup trucks in 1996 for export for the first time, had capacity to produce 159,000 vehicles and produced 85,000 in 1996. Besides the Lobo pickup it produced the Contour and Mystique. Its foundry produced 36 tons daily of auto parts, and it was gearing up to produce as many as 120,000 engines a year. Hermosillo, which turned out its millionth vehicle in 1996, had capacity to produce 168,000 vehicles and produced 110,000 in 1996. These were Mercury Tracers and Ford Escorts. Chihuahua had the capacity to produce 435,000 engines and produced 215,000 Zetec engines in 1996.

Other facilities of Ford in Mexico in 1997 included Carplastics, a wholly owned subsidiary, and four *maquiladora* plants at Ciudad Juarez, just south of the Texas border, for export assembly. These were Coclisa (radiators, heaters, and air-conditioning components), Altec (radios and electronic components), Autovidrio (automotive glass), and Lamosa (catalytic converters). Additionally, Ford Mexico held a minority interest in three joint-venture companies: Nemak (aluminum casting), Vitroflex (glass), and Climate Systems Mexicana (air conditioning, refrigerant lines, and couplings).

Ford invested more than $250 million in its Mexican subsidiary in 1995–96 and pledged to invest $1 billion before the year 2000. On the sales side, Ford Mexico had a network of 123 dealers selling not only vehicles made by Ford in Mexico but also in North American plants. During this period Ford became the first Mexican auto company to establish satellite communications with all its dealers. The Mystique was named 1995 car of the year and the Lobo pickup 1997 car of the year by the magazine *Motor y Volante*. Exclusive production of the new Escort coupe ZXR, for the U.S. and Canadian markets, began at Hermosillo in 1997 with an investment of $125 million.

Further Reading

Carillo Viveras, Jorge, "La Ford en Mexico: Restructuración Industrial y Cambio en las Relaciones Sociales." Ph. D. dissertation, El Colegio de Mexico, 1993.

Cook, Carol, "Mexico Takes Action to Aid Auto Industry," *Journal of Commerce,* July 23, 1976, p. 3.

"Ford Sacks 2,400 Workers in Mexico," *Financial Times,* February 8, 1990, p. 6.

González López, Sergio, *Proceso de Configuración Territorial de la Industria Automotriz Terminal en México, 1964–1989.* Mexico City: Universidad Autonoma del Estado de Mexico, 1992.

"Hasta el 2000 Se Recuperará el Mercado Automotor: Philippe Mellier," *El Financiero,* January 27, 1997, p. 24.

"Mexico's Auto Makers Switch to Home Brew," *Business Week,* July 31, 1965, pp. 68, 70.

Nag, Amal, and Frazier, Steve, "Despite Ford Venture, Mexico Faces Struggle to Be Competitive," *Wall Street Journal,* January 11, 1984, pp. 1, 25.

Seligman, Daniel, "The Maddening, Promising Mexican Market," *Fortune,* January 1956, pp. 106–08.

Tanner, James C., "Mexican Officials Prod Local Auto Companies to Export to the U.S.," *Wall Street Journal,* April 12, 1968, p. 1.

"Versatile Tooling Aids Overseas Car Assembly," *Business Week,* July 22, 1961, pp. 48–50.

Wilkins, Mira, and Hill, Frank Ernest, *American Business Abroad: Ford on Six Continents.* Detroit: Wayne State University Press, 1964.

—Robert Halasz

Fred Meyer

Fred Meyer, Inc.

3800 Southeast 22nd Avenue
Portland, Oregon 97202
U.S.A.
(503) 232-8844
Fax: (503) 797-3469
. Web site: http://www.fredmeyer.com

Public Company
Incorporated: 1923
Employees: 48,000
Sales: $3.72 billion (1996)
Stock Exchanges: New York
SICs: 5122 Drugs, Drug Proprietaries & Sundries; 5311
    Department Stores; 5331 Variety Stores; 5411
    Grocery Stores; 5499 Miscellaneous Food Stores;
    5719 Miscellaneous Homefurnishing Stores; 5944
    Jewelry Stores

Operating primarily in the western United States, Fred Meyer, Inc. is a major regional retailer of food, apparel, general merchandise, home electronics, home improvement, and fine jewelry products. The company operates more than 110 Fred Meyer one-stop shopping supercenters, which average 145,000 square feet and include more than 225,000 food and nonfood products arranged within dozens of departments (e.g., grocery, housewares, domestics, apparel, shoes, toys, sporting goods, gardening products). These flagship stores are located in six western states: Oregon, Washington, Utah, Alaska, Idaho, and Montana. Through a 1997 merger, Fred Meyer owns Smith's Food & Drug Centers Inc., which runs more than 150 full-line supermarkets (which include drug and pharmacy departments) in seven southwestern and mountain states: Utah, Arizona, Nevada, New Mexico, Idaho, Wyoming, and Texas. Another subsidiary, Fred Meyer Jewelers, Inc., specializes in fine jewelry and—in addition to handling more than 100 Fred Meyer Jewelers located within Fred Meyer stores—consists of more than 150 fine jewelry stores operating in malls in 18 states under the names Fred Meyer Jewelers, Merksamer Jewelers, and Fox Jewelry; through these operations, Fred Meyer owns the fourth-largest fine jewelry chain in the United States.

Entrepreneurial Beginnings

The history of Fred Meyer, Inc. revolves around its founder, Fred G. Meyer, who guided the company until his death in 1978. In 1908, 22-year-old Frederick Grubmeyer, son of a Brooklyn grocer, moved to Portland and began selling coffee to workers at the farms and lumber camps that surrounded the burgeoning town of Portland. The horse-drawn route prospered, but young Grubmeyer, who eventually changed his name to Fred G. Meyer, wanted more. In a few years he moved to Alaska to seek other business opportunities. Alaska was overrun with would-be entrepreneurs, however, and Meyer returned to Portland and founded the Java Coffee Company, selling coffee, tea, and spices from a storefront in the market district.

The Java Coffee Company, later renamed the Mission Tea Company, prospered, but many neighboring businesses succumbed to the uncertain economics of the time. Meyer snapped up their properties and soon was landlord and sometimes operator of several specialty food operations.

In the early 1920s, the center of commercial activity moved uptown, and Meyer moved with it, consolidating his several specialty businesses into a single location that became the flagship store for the Fred Meyer chain. The store, which opened in 1922, had 20 employees, with Meyer serving as buyer and manager. Its seven departments included meat, delicatessen, coffee, lunch, homemade mayonnaise, grocery, and tobacco.

The next year Fred Meyer, Inc. was incorporated in Oregon, and a second store was opened that featured grocery and dairy products.

Fred Meyer continued expanding throughout the 1920s. Across the street from the parent store, he opened a packaged food store selling sugar, dry beans, rice, macaroni, spaghetti, coffee, and dried fruits. Then in 1928, he opened what many regard as the world's first self-service drugstore. The store's lower labor costs meant lower prices, and Meyer's reputation as a value merchandiser was established.

The company prospered despite the stock market crash of 1929 and the ensuing Great Depression. Meyer opened four new stores between 1929 and 1932: a toiletry store, a department store in the outlying Portland neighborhood of Holly-

Company Perspectives:

At Fred Meyer we are governed by beliefs that: Customers are essential, for without them we would have no business. Customers shop where they believe their wants and needs will be satisfied best. Satisfactory profits are essential, for without profits our business can neither grow nor satisfy the wants and needs of our customers, employees, suppliers, shareholders or the community. Skilled, capable, dedicated employees are essential, for the overall success of our business is determined by the combined ideas, work and effort of all Fred Meyer employees.

Based on these beliefs, we are committed to: Serving customers so well that after shopping with us they are satisfied and want to shop with us again. Operating our business efficiently and effectively, so we earn a satisfactory profit today and in the future. Providing an environment that encourages employees to develop their abilities, use their full potential and share ideas that further the success of the business, so they gain a sense of pride in their accomplishments and confidence in their capabilities.

We believe that by following this philosophy we will satisfy customers and earn their patronage, provide for the profitable growth of our company, and enrich the lives of Fred Meyer employees and their families.

wood, and his first stores outside Portland, in the towns of Salem and Astoria, Oregon.

The Hollywood, Oregon, store marked Meyer's recognition of the growing importance of the car in retailing. Finding that customers were often double-parking in front of his downtown stores and getting ticketed in the process—Meyer would pay the tickets—Meyer did an informal survey and found that many customers lived in the Hollywood section of Portland, about five miles from downtown. This led to the opening of the Hollywood store, which included an automobile lubrication and oil service and an off-street parking lot.

Throughout the 1930s, Meyer ran a series of aggressive promotions that highlighted the company's low prices. Meyer saw these entertaining promotions as ways of getting customers into stores during cash-starved times. He rented movie theaters and gave children free admission if they brought three My-Te-Fine store-brand labels. He had newspapers add peppermint to their ink, giving his candy ads a special sweet smell.

These and other promotions helped make Fred Meyer a major player in Portland, but the company was not without competition. Drugstores banded together to stop the company from obtaining a prescription license. Retailers threatened to drop lines if manufacturers sold to Fred Meyer. An anonymously sponsored radio show spent all its time lambasting the quality of Fred Meyer goods—all to no avail.

Started to Expand Product Line in 1930s

Fred Meyer began adding new products in the early 1930s, and the stores began selling men's and women's wear in 1933.

Automotive departments, housewares, and other nonfood products followed in succeeding years. The middle of the decade saw the opening of a central bakery, a candy kitchen, an ice cream plant, and a photofinishing plant. These facilities paved the way for house brands such as Vita Bee bread, Hocus Pocus desserts, and Fifth Avenue candies. Fred Meyer capped the decade with large new stores in northeast and southeast Portland.

As with other retailers, Fred Meyer was challenged by World War II. Demand was high but supplies were low, and many employees were called to service. After the war, a more modern Fred Meyer began to emerge. Old stores were renovated and standardized, and new Fred Meyer stores were built from the ground up—instead of being housed in existing space. A new management team still working under Meyer himself, began adding departments such as home improvement, nutrition centers, fine jewelry, and photo and audio. Some experiments, such as carpet and draperies, major appliances, furniture, and automotive service did not meet expectations and were eventually dropped.

The 1950s saw Fred Meyer opening a stream of successful outlets in suburban Portland. These stores were larger than previous Fred Meyer outlets, at 45,000 to 70,000 square feet. Meyer often led or kept pace with developers and was able to spot prime retail space on major suburban thoroughfares before suburban traffic patterns were apparent.

Made Series of Major Acquisitions in the Late 1950s to Mid-1960s

The mid-1950s also saw the construction of Fred Meyer's first modern distribution facility at Swan Island, Oregon. Also located at Swan Island was a new dairy plant and a central kitchen for the company's in-house food operation, Eve's Buffet Restaurant. In 1959 the company made its first major acquisition. For stock worth close to $1 million, Fred Meyer acquired four Marketime drug stores in Seattle, Washington.

In 1960, when there were 20 Fred Meyer stores with combined annual sales of $56 million, the company went public. Meyer then made a series of large acquisitions. In 1964 the company acquired Roundup Wholesale Grocery Company of Spokane, Washington, including 14 Sigman supermarkets in Washington and Oregon and three B & B Stores in Montana. The following year Fred Meyer purchased seven Market Basket stores in Seattle and one in Yakima, Washington.

In 1966 management again upgraded the look of Fred Meyer stores. Tiled aisles and carpeted apparel departments replaced concrete floors. Displays were made more colorful, and new marketing ideas were introduced throughout the store. By year's end, earnings had reached $1.56 million on sales of $170.8 million.

Fred Meyer also continued to develop a vertical management organization. The heads of each of up to 11 departments per store would eventually report to corporate vice presidents in charge of those departments rather than to an individual store manager. Individual departments became as strong as specialty stores and operated as such, complete with their own checkouts.

Although business was booming, not every venture went as planned. In 1968 Fred Meyer sold the Market Basket stores it had bought three years earlier, as the small stores did not fit in with other operations. This move meant a $225,000 writeoff against 1968 profits. Nevertheless, sales and income continued to grow.

Meyer, by now in his early 80s, continued to rule the company. A younger management team was beginning to take at least some of the reins of power, however. In 1969 Jack Crocker, a 20-year employee of the company, became president of Fred Meyer, Inc., with Meyer as chairman. Crocker's presidency coincided with Fred Meyer's opening of its Levi jeans centers.

Difficult 1970s Highlighted by Purchase of S&L

While profits continued to increase, the early 1970s were a difficult time for Fred Meyer's management. In 1971 Meyer suffered a stroke that left him weakened but still alert. In November of the same year Crocker tendered his resignation, effective January 1, 1972. In March 1972, the Fred Meyer board elected Cyril K. Green to replace Crocker as president and Oran W. Robertson as first vice president of the company.

The new management team continued relentless expansion. The main focus was on additions to existing stores, but plans also called for three new stores in 1972 and one in 1973. Acquisitions were also part of the plan. In 1973, Fred Meyer acquired five Valu-Mart stores in Oregon from Seattle-based Weisfield's Inc., ending the year with 52 stores and a thriving business in the Pacific Northwest.

In 1975 the company ventured into finance, buying a local savings and loan with deposits of $3.8 million. The idea was to install S&Ls in each of his full-service stores. The S&Ls would make money through banking and by bringing more customers and money into the stores. Although many in the banking industry were skeptical, Fred Meyer Savings and Loan Association grew rapidly, bringing in small depositors who probably had not saved at all before opening their Fred Meyer accounts. The company drew on its retailing experience to build the bank, offering free loaves of bread and steaks for customers opening accounts. The Fred Meyer Savings and Loans also stayed open longer hours than their competitors.

In 1975 Fred Meyer bought three Baza'r outlets and nine more department stores from Weisfield's Inc. of Seattle, including two Valu-Mart stores and six Leslie's stores located in Seattle, Spokane, and Yakima, Washington, and Anchorage, Alaska. All were to be merged into Fred Meyer operations.

In 1976 Fred Meyer retired from the day-to-day affairs of the company and became chairman of the executive committee. Oran B. Robertson was named chairman of the board and chief executive officer. Cyril K. Green remained president, and Virgil Campbell became executive vice president.

In 1978 Meyer died. The success of Fred Meyer, Inc. was a testament to his hard work, intuition, and intelligence. His stores dominated the Northwest and continued to expand. Their net profit margin of 1.9 percent was better than those of big national chains, such as Winn-Dixie Stores (1.7 percent), Lucky Stores (1.5 percent), and Safeway (0.9 percent).

Meyer's death inspired many testimonials, but it also set the stage for a power struggle among the four executors of his will; Meyer owned 29.1 percent of the company's outstanding stock. On one side was Oran B. Robertson, chairman and CEO. Opposing him was G. Gerry Pratt, a Meyer protegé, and chairman and chief executive of Fred Meyer Savings and Loan. Other executors included a Fred Meyer vice president, and Warne H. Nunn, Pratt's friend and longtime local power company executive.

The struggle over the will was further complicated by Pratt's troubles at Fred Meyer S&L. Pratt, a former journalist and talk-show host, was hired by Meyer in 1972. Two years later he was made head of Fred Meyer S&L. With Pratt's innovative flair, the Fred Meyer S&L grew fast, but when the cost of money skyrocketed in 1979, the S&L was overextended and lost $1 million. The savings and loan's loss ended nearly 20 years of quarterly profit increases. In May 1980 chairman and CEO Oran B. Robertson fired Pratt and replaced the Fred Meyer S&L board with Fred Meyer executives. Pratt responded with a lawsuit that was later settled. Fred Meyer sold its savings and loan.

Privatized Then Became Public Company Once Again During the 1980s

With the death of Meyer, outside investors began showing an interest in the company. In September 1980, the investment firm of Kohlberg Kravis Roberts & Co. (KKR) offered to buy the entire organization for $45 a share—more than $300 million. Ultimately KKR successfully negotiated a leveraged buyout in December 1981 with the Fred Meyer management as equity participants for $55 per share, or $435 million. This took Fred Meyer stock out of circulation and made the company private once again. In the meantime, the company had sold Roundup Wholesale to West Coast Grocery. The leveraged buyout split Fred Meyer into two companies. The retail operations continued as Fred Meyer, Inc., and the real estate assets were transferred to a separate partnership, Fred Meyer Real Estate Properties Ltd., which leased properties back to Fred Meyer, Inc. Occupancy expenses rose dramatically due to the spinoff of real estate holdings, and initially the company operated in the red.

Despite higher occupancy expenses and the cost of debt normally associated with leveraged buyouts, Fred Meyer continued to expand aggressively. Over the next five years it built 11 new stores and acquired the Grand Central chain, which had stores in several Rocky Mountain states. The company sold Grand Central's New Mexico and Nevada stores but kept its 21 stores in Utah and Idaho, remodeling 15 of them. Furthermore, it cut costs by consolidating departmental checkouts.

Overall, during the time the company was private, Fred Meyer grew from 64 to 93 stores. Net income increased from $5.2 million in fiscal 1982 to $22.5 million in fiscal 1986. Sales jumped from $1.1 billion to $1.7 billion over the same period.

Management attempted and failed to bring Fred Meyer public again in 1983. By 1986 management felt investors were ready to buy Fred Meyer stock. In the fall of 1986, the company issued 6.75 million shares of common stock, 4.5 million new shares and 2.25 million from existing shareholders, at $14.25 per share.

Through the late 1980s, Fred Meyer continued its expansion, adding several new stores yearly as well as replacing and expanding existing stores. The Pacific Northwest had become a more competitive market with the entrance of discounters—such as Dayton Hudson's Target stores and the grocery chains Food 4 Less and Cub Foods—but most analysts believed Fred Meyer's one-stop shopping centers gave it a unique niche in the market.

In 1988, under the leadership of newly hired CEO Frederick Stevens, the company began a major overhaul of its stores and management organization. Fred Meyer also unveiled a new prototype store with a flexible design to facilitate layout changes without expensive remodeling; the first store in the new format opened in 1989. In 1990 and 1991 the company opened eight large new stores, closed 10 small stores, and remodeled several other stores. The closings and remodelings led the company to take a $49.3 million restructuring charge in 1990 ($8.3 million of which was reversed in 1991); consequently, Fred Meyer posted a loss of $6.8 million in 1990. In January 1991 Stevens resigned unexpectedly; in August of that same year, Robert G. Miller took over the CEO spot, after most recently serving as executive vice president of retail operations for the Albertson's supermarket chain.

Expanded Fine Jewelry Operations and Acquired Smith's Food & Drug in Mid-1990s

As the 1990s progressed, Fred Meyer continued to fine-tune its store formats and locations in order to fend off increasing competition that cut into sales and earnings. The rise of category-killers was particularly troubling, especially in the areas of hardware and home electronics. In response, Fred Meyer reduced the amount of space devoted to lumber and building materials and began to phase out computer hardware. In 1993 Fred Meyer altered its growth strategy, deciding to concentrate on adding stores in areas where the chain was already strong; in some cases smaller-than-typical Fred Meyer stores were subsequently opened in smaller markets within these areas. A byproduct of this strategy was the chain's 1994 exit from the northern California market, into which it had only just begun to expand. The company incurred a $15.98 million charge as a result, leading to a profit of only $7.2 million for the fiscal year. Results for 1994 were also affected by an 88-day strike which centered around the number of part-time employees at the company.

Sales increased at a more healthy rate in fiscal 1995 and 1996, buoyed by a surge in sales in Fred Meyer's nonfood departments. But the mid-1990s saw the company make its most dramatic moves outside the realm of one-stop shopping supercenters.

Fred Meyer had entered the fine jewelry business in 1973. Over the next two decades it had built up a chain of about three dozen Fred Meyer Jewelers standalone stores which were located within malls and it had also included Fred Meyer Jewelers departments in nearly 100 of its supercenters. In 1995 the company acquired 22 mall jewelry stores located on the West Coast, then the following year purchased 49 Merksamer Jew-

elers mall stores spread throughout 11 states. In the summer of 1997, Fred Meyer further bolstered its jewelry operations with the acquisition of Fox Jewelry Company and its 44 Fox Jewelry stores located in malls in six Midwestern states—Michigan, Wisconsin, Indiana, Illinois, Iowa, and Ohio. With the addition of Fox Jewelry, which had been founded in 1917 with a store in Grand Rapids, Michigan, Fred Meyer became the fourth-largest fine jewelry chain in the country.

An even larger acquisition that same summer brought Fred Meyer an enhanced presence in food retailing. In a $2 billion deal, Fred Meyer purchased Smith's Food & Drug Centers, Inc., a leading regional supermarket and drug store chain with more than 150 stores in the southwestern and mountain states of Arizona, Idaho, New Mexico, Nevada, Texas, Utah, and Wyoming—making for an ideal geographic fit. Founded in 1948 and headquartered in Salt Lake City, Smith's large stores combined full-line supermarkets with drug and pharmacy departments and operated under the names Smith's, Smitty's Supermarket, and PriceRite Grocery Warehouse. Smith's reported sales of $2.89 billion for 1996.

With these acquisitions, Fred Meyer's 1997 sales would exceed $7 billion. During the remainder of the 1990s, it was expected that the company would need to concentrate on issues of integration, including administrative, purchasing, information systems, distribution, and manufacturing functions. The management team charged with this responsibility was Ronald W. Burkle, CEO of Smith's who was named chairman of Fred Meyer, and Miller, who would remain president and CEO. Fred Meyer's 11-member board included seven representatives from Fred Meyer and four from Smith's.

Principal Subsidiaries

Roundup Co.; B & B Stores, Inc.; B & B Pharmacy, Inc.; Fred Meyer of Alaska, Inc.; Fred Meyer of California, Inc.; Distribution Trucking Company; CB&S Advertising Agency, Inc.; FM Holding Corporation; Grand Central, Inc.; FM Retail Services, Inc.; Fred Meyer Jewelers, Inc.; FM Inc.; Merksamer Jewelers, Inc.; Smith's Food & Drug Centers Inc.

Further Reading

Dubashi, Jagannath, "Fred Meyer: One-Stop Shopping, One-Stop Investing," *Financial World*, September 28, 1993, p. 18.

Duff, Mike, "Fred Meyer: New Standard for One-Stop Shopping?," *Supermarket Business*, December 1990, pp. 43–46, 48, 77.

"Hypermarket Concept Is Old Hat in Pacific NW," *Discount Store News*, December 19, 1988, p. 99.

Lipin, Steven, "Fred Meyer Agrees to Buy Smith's Food," *Wall Street Journal*, May 12, 1997, p. A3.

Orgel, David, "Fred Meyer's Food Focus," *Supermarket News*, April 18, 1994, pp. 1, 10, 12.

Rose, Michael, "Fred Meyer's New Profile," *Business Journal-Portland*, January 3, 1997, pp. 11–12.

Schwartz, Donna Boyle, "Grand Design," *HFN—The Weekly Newspaper for the Home Furnishing Network*, December 4, 1995, p. 1.

Zwiebach, Elliot, "Fred Meyer Fuels Five-Year Plan," *Supermarket News*, July 25, 1994, p. 12.

—Jordan Wankoff
—updated by David E. Salamie

FRESH
AMERICA
Fresh America Corporation

One Lincoln Centre
5400 LBJ Freeway, Suite 1025
Dallas, Texas 75240
U.S.A.
(972) 774-0575
Fax: (972) 774-0515
Web site: email: investor.relations@fresham.com

Public Company
Incorporated: 1989
Employees: 476
Sales: $239.2 million (1996)
Stock Exchanges: NASDAQ
SICS: 5431 Fruit and Vegetable Markets; 5148 Fresh
   Fruits and Vegetables

Fresh America Corporation is a growing national force in the procurement, processing, warehousing, and distribution of fresh produce and other refrigerated perishable products. The company provides items such as apples, bananas, oranges, onions, potatoes, seasonal berries, high-end specialty produce, pre-cut fruits and vegetables, packaged salads, and fruit juices to marketers. Working with hundreds of growers and suppliers nationwide, Fresh America has dedicated itself to sustaining strict quality and performance standards, while maintaining strong vendor relationships, volume purchasing, and provision of products even in times of short supply. The company operates in 39 states through 14 distribution centers and processing plants. Fresh America competes with food service companies, produce distribution companies, and wholesale food distribution companies. The company's business is seasonal, with its greatest quarterly sales volume occurring in the fourth quarter. Factors such as adverse weather conditions, unavailability of quality produce, and heightened product cost are among the uncertainties of the industry.

1989: First Major Contract

Fresh America was incorporated in Texas in May 1989 as a successor to Gourmet Packing, Inc. Their core business, begin-

ning with the company's inception, involved providing fresh produce and other perishable products to Sam's Club membership warehouse clubs (a division of Wal-Mart Stores, Inc.) under a special agreement with that company. Mass merchandising through the 187 Sam's Club outlets that Fresh America had contracted to supply, provided accelerating revenues for Fresh America, largely accounting for growth from $22.5 million in fiscal 1993 to almost $32 million by the end of 1994. In an effort to purchase additional transportation equipment and other fixed assets, repay indebtedness, improve their management information systems, and fund working capital, among other things, the company went public in May 1994, with an offering of approximately 1.5 million shares at $9 per share. In that same month a staff writer for the *Wall Street Journal* stated that Fresh America reported a "first quarter loss of $43,000 or a penny a share, down from a profit of $266,000, or 11 cents a share a year earlier." Fresh America claimed that its first quarter revenue actually grew 6.6 percent and challenged whether its primary customer, Wal-Mart Stores, Inc., had underreported the revenue it was owed, spurring negotiations between the two companies in an attempt to settle the matter. Under their licensing agreement, Sam's Clubs' employees rang up all Fresh America purchases at store check-out counters, and then Sam's Club paid Fresh America, less a licensing fee, on a weekly basis. Since nearly all of Fresh America's revenue came from Sam's Club, resolution of the discrepancy was significant for the company. By August the company announced that an agreement had been reached regarding a new five-year contract with Sam's Club. The renegotiated agreement with Sam's Club included the stipulation that the warehouse retailer pick up costs that Fresh America had been responsible for in the past. The announcement precipitated an 11.6 percent rise in Fresh America's stock for that week. The company restated that its first quarter net was $182,000, or a gain of five cents a share. By the second quarter of the following year revenue more than doubled to $64.7 million. The company continued to have strong ties with Sam's Club, and the number of Sam's Clubs served by Fresh America nearly doubled in 1996, which accounted for about 90 percent of Fresh America's revenues. The company proceeded with maximizing system efficiencies, and added the distribution of fresh Florida orange juice to its Sam's Club cargo.

Selective Acquisitions in the Mid-1990s

Acting on management's intention to diversify the company's customer base through selected acquisitions, Fresh America entered the central Texas foodservice market at the end of 1995, when the company acquired Lone Star Produce of Austin, Texas, and demonstrated strong growth in the Austin to San Antonio region. In the Houston area, Fresh America supplied roughly 250 new retail customers following the purchase of Produce Plus, suppliers of fresh fruit and vegetables. The company began planning the construction of an 80,000-square-foot facility in Houston to accommodate Produce Plus and their value-added tomato operation.

In a further move toward developing and streamlining its system, Fresh America signed a 1996 agreement with DoleFresh Vegetables, Inc., agreeing to provide forward distribution of packaged salads and other fresh-cut produce through its Chicago distribution center. Product offerings nearly doubled by the end of the year, and Dole authorized additional distribution to 12 of its southeastern customers, serviced from Fresh America's Atlanta center. According to the company, "Under the forward availability concept, Dole ships products to Fresh America for warehousing prior to receiving firm customer orders. Fresh America then distributes the product as needed. This arrangement has enabled Dole to compete more effectively with local processors without having to build or maintain its own facilities in these regions."

Following a strategy of negotiating agreements with organizations willing to commit to volume produce sales, Fresh America began servicing Alliant Foodservice (formerly Kraft Foodservice), the second largest broadline foodservice distributor in the United States. Alliant benefits by saving on costs by using Fresh America to more efficiently purchase, warehouse, and distribute their fresh products. The original agreement allowed for the company's servicing of 10 Alliant districts in the Northeast, which soon grew to 16 additional districts, and should encompass Alliant's remaining 13 districts by the end of 1997, with the size of deliveries in each district steadily increasing.

The company also added to its purchasing power, and strengthened its national position in the fast foodservice sector when it entered into a long-term exclusive agreement with Fast Food Merchandiser's Inc. (FFM), a wholly owned subsidiary of Hardee's Food Systems, Inc., a nationwide restaurant chain and subsidiary of IMASCO, Ltd. and other customers through FFM's 12 distribution centers. Continuing to expand on processing capabilities, Fresh America acquired FFM's production center in Richmond, Indiana. The company provided a wide range of value-added products for FFM, including salad bar items, lettuce, tomatoes, and other sliced vegetables to top sandwiches, and intended to use the facility to produce items for other customers as well.

Buying One More Tomato: Acquisitions in the Late 1990s

Furthering its value-added capabilities, Fresh America also acquired the assets and business of One More Tomato, Inc., a tomato ripening and repacking company based in Houston, Texas. The company reported that revenues rose to $10 million in the first full year of operating within this higher-margin business segment. Fresh America executed a five-year exclusive distribution agreement with Delray Farms, Inc., a privately-held specialty grocery company based in Chicago, Illinois. In regard to the deal, company Chairman and Chief Executive Officer, David I. Sheinfeld commented in a press release that "We are very excited and pleased to form this new long-term affiliation with a dynamic and rapidly expanding company. The combination of Delray's focus on providing high-quality produce to the customer, and Fresh America's emphasis on delivering the best service available, enables us to provide value in the marketplace." He continued, "This agreement is part of our plan to develop new programs which build upon Fresh America's infrastructure and expertise."

Preparing for an era of rapid expansion, Edward Sabin, who previously held executive positions at both Del Monte Foods and Chiquita Brands, respectively, was named executive vice president of the company. Next in the lineup of company acquisitions was the 1997 purchase of Fresh America California, a company specializing in procuring and distributing high-margin specialty produce, such as white asparagus, Japanese baby eggplant and European salad greens. The company name was changed to Fresh America The Chefs' Produce Team and would specialize in items typically purchased in smaller quantities, including those that require special handling. At the time of the purchase the company catered to fine restaurants and higher-end hotels throughout California, and to places as distant as Las Vegas. The company has moved into a distribution center in San Francisco, and established satellite distribution facilities in San Diego and Las Vegas, and supplies approximately 100 customers. In May 1997 Fresh America announced the formation of Fresh America Orlando, serving fresh produce and foodservice to customers in the greater Orlando metropolitan area.

By purchasing a minority interest in Henri Morris & Associates, a software and systems provider to the produce and grocery industry, Fresh America is incorporating communications systems which will allow the company to better place and receive orders, communicate with customers, and manage logistics and product delivery in the most timely way possible—a crucial factor in the perishable items industry.

Due to the expansion of the company's operating territory under the revised 1995 agreement with Sam's Club, and the resulting addition of 184 Sam's Club locations within Fresh America's operation regions, and including the acquisitions of Lone Star Produce and Produce Plus—and the commencement of contracts with Alliant and Dole in January 1996, net sales for the company increased $114. million, or $91.6 percent, from $124 million in fiscal 1995 to $239 million in fiscal 1996. In regard to the Sam's Club agreement, the company became a wholesale distributor, whereas under the previous agreement the company was selling at retail to the Sam's Club members. In essence, Sam's Club took ownership of the product as it entered the clubs and resold the product to Sam's Club members, and assumed all costs and liabilities related to the operation of the departments, including personnel, merchandising and sales costs, product shrink, etc. Previously, Fresh America had been responsible for these costs and maintained ownership of the product until sold to Sam's Club members.

In February 1997 the company announced that Sam's Club exercised an option under its agreement to distribute to 40 clubs directly, in effect beginning in May of the same year, meaning that Sam's would take over the produce business for 40 clubs previously supplied by Fresh America. Under the contract, Fresh America received partial remuneration perpetually through the life of the agreement with Sam's so as not to feel the full financial impact of such a loss. The expectation is that the company will lose revenues of between $17 million and $20 million for 1997. The agreement stipulated that Sam's could exercise its option to take back up to 10 percent of its clubs in a given year if Wal-Mart opened a distribution center that operated at less than full capacity. The clubs being reclaimed by Sam's represented some of the longer-haul distances for Fresh America, and are not as profitable to the company as many other clubs. Now that Sam's has exercised this option for the first time, and has the legal right to take back up to 40 clubs per year for three years, it is expected that Fresh America will accelerate the pursuit of new non-Sam's Club agreements and acquisitions.

Although the company is a growing force in the $10 billion fresh produce market, its future, according to at least one analyst, depends on two major factors. Writing about Fresh America in *Produce Industry*, Mark Speeks addressed the challenge the company faces of increasing its operating margin while remaining competitive, and of convincing Wall Street to grant the type of earnings multiple common for the broadline companies. Speeks reported that "While welcoming the continuing diversification of the business, the increasing proportion of Fresh America's volume paid for by commission raises the question of how much Fresh America can increase its operating margin. While the nine months prior to September 1996 show an increase in operating margin to 2.2 percent from 1.8 percent for the same period in 1995, it is still comparatively low compared with distribution giants Sysco Corporation and JP Foodservice, Inc." With the underlying cost of items being paid for by the customer, Speeks speculates that the calculation of commission paid for distribution may not be elastic enough to reproduce a Sysco-type operating margin. Programs with Alliant and Dole showed an increase of 35 percent, while their specialty food service companies increased revenues 47 percent over the fourth quarter of 1996. Considering the company's commitment to growth and diversification, it remains to be seen what Fresh America will produce.

Principal Subsidiaries

Lone Star Produce Acquisition Corporation; Lone Star Produce, Inc.; Fresh America California; Produce Plus.

Further Reading

"Five-Year Accord Reached with Wal-Mart Division," *The Wall Street Journal*, August 4, 1995, p. B7.

"Fresh America Corp.," *Wall Street Journal*, August 8, 1996, p. A2.

"Results of the First Period Are Restated to a Profit," *Wall Street Journal*, August 10, 1995, p. B4.

"Fresh America Posts First Quarter Loss; Wal-Mart Is Cited," *Wall Street Journal*, May 12, 1995, p. B5.

"Fresh America Receives Job," *Wall Street Journal*, January 23, 1997, p. A6.

Speeks, Mark, "Fresh America on Target," *ID: The Voice of Foodservice Distribution*, February, 1997, p. 29.

—Terri Mozzone-Burgman

Fresh Choice, Inc.

2901 Tasman Drive, Suite 109
Santa Clara, California 95054-1169
U.S.A.
(408) 986-8661
Fax: (408) 986-8334

Public Company
Incorporated: 1986 as Gourmet California, Inc.
Employees: 2,200
Sales: $76.7 million (1996)
Stock Exchanges: NASDAQ
SICs: 5812 Eating Places

Now entering its second decade, California-based Fresh Choice, Inc. is a chain of comfortable but casual self-service restaurants which offer a selection of food stations and serve freshly prepared Sizzlin' Pan Pastas, soups, and baked goods along with a signature salad bar containing more than 40 make-your-own-salad ingredients. The Fresh Choice all-you-can-eat buffet includes over 50 recipes, including salads, soups, pasta dishes, and muffins, as well as a fresh fruit and specialty dessert area. Fresh Choice aims for tasty and satisfying—yet healthy—food choices, as an economical way to get the five to nine daily servings of fruit and vegetables recommended by the U.S. Department of Agriculture. Fresh produce is delivered four times a week, all foods are prepared from scratch each day, and many menu items are prepared in exhibition cooking areas, stressing the emphasis on freshness. In 1997, Fresh Choice operated and owned 48 restaurants in three states, with a concentration in northern California and other sites in Washington and Texas. At most Fresh Choice restaurants, lunch costs $5.99 and dinner is $7.49 per person for an all-you-can-eat buffet, not including beverages. The company's target market includes families, business professionals, students, and senior citizens, and it depends on a high rate of repeat business. The company also makes its food available for take out, catering, and retail.

Beginnings in Sunnyvale

With no experience in the restaurant business beyond dishwashing, Martin Culver and Brad Wells purchased a failing restaurant in Sunnyvale, California, in 1986. The first two years of operation were a learning period for Culver and Wells, who named their new restaurant Gourmet California. In 1988, they began an expansion program, merging with Moffett Partners, Inc., adding a second location in Sunnyvale, California, and renaming the restaurant Fresh Choice. Guiding its geographic decisions for new restaurant openings, Fresh Choice employed a plan of clustering restaurants in areas with highly educated and nutrition-minded residents. Education demographics were of primary importance in site selection, for Fresh Choice's staff believed that educated customers paid more attention to personal health. Income and population density are two other factors which come into play. The philosophy of clustering restaurants allows each market area to take advantage of operating and advertising grouping, as well as brand-name recognition and the discouragement of competition. This philosophy resulted in the opening of new restaurants in California in 1989.

In addition to clustered openings, Fresh Choice invested about 1.8 percent of sales on marketing, most notably, humorous radio commercials. Customer loyalty in its home communities was also generated through community service efforts, including fundraisers for local schools, employee volunteerism, donation of food, and sponsorship of local sports teams. School fund raisers served as new store promotions, whereby students sold dinner tickets to pre-opening parties for Fresh Choice restaurants to raise $2,000 to $3,000 for their school. Volume discounts were achieved through dependence on one national supplier for all non-produce business, and produce costs were kept low by contracting with growers for a full year.

Sales in 1990 were $15.1 million, with net income of $500,000. Expansion continued, with new California restaurant openings. The following year, revenues increased to $23.6 million, and net income jumped accordingly to $800,000. Continuing to look to the health-conscious California consumer, Fresh Choice introduced a line of foods called Healthier Choice in 1991, featuring no fat or cholesterol content.

Company Perspectives:

Fresh Choice's goal is to create a distinct dining experience that combines the selection, quality, and ambiance of full-service, casual restaurants with the convenience and low-price appeal of traditional buffet restaurants.

Public Offering in 1992

In December 1992, the company went public with 22 restaurants. Its initial offering was underwritten by Montgomery Securities and Alex. Brown & Sons Inc., with 1,112,500 shares of stock and net offering proceeds of $12.7 million. Shares were priced at 13 when the company went public, and they surged to 24½ quickly, astonishing the analysts. Sales for that fiscal year were $37.1 million, a 57 percent increase over the previous year. Net income also rose to $1.4 million. Stock prices that year closed at 22. Overall, the company now employed slightly over 1,000 people. In 1993, expansion continued to drive sales, with revenues rising to $53.6 million and net income surging to almost three times the previous year's achievements at $3.1 million. The company sold 850,000 shares at $25 per share, with net proceeds of $19.6 million.

Expansion began in new markets, with 14 restaurant openings in southern California, Texas, and Seattle, Washington, in 1993. The company now operated a total of 36 restaurants, and had a track record of generating profits at new restaurant sites after only 30 days. Specifically, that profit comprised about $330,000 annually at each site, on just under $2 million in sales. An exception to this rule were two restaurants opened in Fresno, California.

The Dallas, Texas site—the first inland restaurant—was opened in that city's Restaurant Row. Psychographic research, purchased from PepsiCo, indicated that Dallas would be an ideal location for Fresh Choice. The company was optimistic about the Dallas opening, since the area displayed lower taxes and housing prices than the San Francisco Bay Area. Menu changes were implemented to appeal to the Texas market, including hotter chilis and rice dishes and a baked potato and steamed vegetable stand. However, the company's executives held their breath, admitting publicly that they had never faced as much competition as that presented by the other stores on Restaurant Row.

Entry into East Coast Market

In 1994, the company opened 15 restaurants to bring its grand total to 43 sites, including its first East Coast breakthrough in Washington, D.C. The Washington, D.C., store was considered to be a vital entry to the East Coast market, with Fresh Choice looking for an area where it might quickly cluster 20 to 25 restaurants. Sales for that year increased to $77 million, but net income remained just slightly above the previous year's figure, at $3.2 million. Fresh Choice was named one of the 100 Best-Performing Companies in America by the *Los Angeles Times*. Since going public, Fresh Choice had been a favored

Wall Street pick and a seemingly unstoppable chain. However, at the end of 1994, Fresh Choice said goodbye to the smooth sailing expansion that characterized its first eight years of existence.

Early in 1995, Fresh Choice announced a plan to open 8 new restaurants, and seven were in fact opened. Revenue that year continued to increase, reaching $84.3 million, but for the first time, the company incurred a loss. In the second half of 1994, profitability had begun a steady decline, and a 1995 $27.8 million deficit was recorded in the net income category. Stock price had declined sharply, from $32.50 to $19.87, along with earnings per share, and the company's chief financial officer Sam Petersen left ship. After a brief interlude, a new CFO from outside the company, David Anderson, was hired in 1994. Anderson, former executive vice president and CFO of Pacific Western Bancshares, Inc., was teamed up with Carol Nolan, who had been promoted from director of finance to CFO when Sam Petersen left the position. Nolan was reassigned to the new position of vice president of finance.

Increasing competition, as well as the cannibalization of its existing restaurants, partially drove the loss. The company's key competitors are family restaurants and all-you-can-eat chains, including Bertucci's, General Mills, Hometown Buffet, Sizzler, and Soup and Salad. Many of these competitors have been in business longer than Fresh Choice, therefore possessing a larger market presence and more resources. Other problems included declining same-store sales (especially at lunch), the perception that the restaurant did not offer a value, and patron dissatisfaction with lines. In addition, costs outside California were a quarter to a half percent higher, due to the expense of shipping California produce. California restaurants were also hurt by the economy and the rains.

A further problem was pricing; in 1993, Fresh Choice had tried raising its dinner price from $6.99 to $7.25 with disastrous results. It seems that customers were not willing to pay over $7 for a meal without a "real" entree. The restaurants rolled back their prices to regain a following. In 1995, the company returned to a dual price structure, which it had used until 1990. Under dual pricing, customers pay $4.95 (lunch) to select salad, bakery, and dessert items; and $5.95 (lunch) for soup or pasta with baked goods. A third, combo price was offered for unlimited access to all choices. Entrees began to feature more meat, nuts, and cheeses, including gourmet pizzas and hearth-style breads stuffed with herbs, walnuts, and vegetables.

A major change implemented in 1994 was the introduction of scatter bars, allowing customers to select their items from several locations around the restaurant, eliminating bottlenecks, long lines, and the unpleasantness associated with waiting. Other methods instituted to bring the company back to its previous Wall Street status included the addition of a server to the operation, as well as baked potatoes and more filled pastas on the menu. By changing building materials, the company also cut its per unit investment by 10 percent.

Lynch In, Culver Out: 1995

Fresh Choice had been criticized by Wall Street analysts for its lack of seasoned executives appointed from outside the company, and in March 1995 the company brought in Charles Lynch, former Saga Corp. and Greyhound Corp. chairman, as chairman of the board. Lynch succeeded cofounder Martin Culver, who was to remain as president and CEO of the company, which now comprised 53 restaurants. Investor Richard Rainwater of Texas acquired 9 percent of the company's stock, telling the *San Francisco Chronicle* that he believed the company could be turned around. Two months later, Culver severed all professional ties with the company he had cofounded, stating publicly that it was time for a managerial change. Culver remained Fresh Choice's largest shareholder. One day later, marketing director Steve Pieters, a longtime associate of Culver's, followed suit and left the company. Charles Lynch was given the additional title of chief executive. Stock prices rose by a cumulative 20.8 percent, to $11.63, in the two days after Culver's announcement.

Lynch's first action was to disclose the $1.3 million shortfall incurred during the first quarter of 1995. Immediately, he pulled the reins in on expansion, and ordered a review of the 55 restaurants in operation. Lynch publicly addressed the confusion caused by price increases and rapidly rotating menu items in restaurant operations, and turned efforts toward major regrouping. However, in October, Fresh Choice stock was trading at between $6.50 and $7.50—down from the previous year's high of $20.25—and average unit volumes had fallen from $1.99 million in 1994 to a projected 1995 figure of $1.55 million. Lynch responded by bringing previously subcontracted janitorial services in-house, reducing the frequency of food rotation, and cutting corporate staff by 30 percent. He began work on a new restaurant prototype with lower development costs. The company's takeout business was also expanded in order to achieve better profits. Advertising costs were raised from 2.5 percent of sales to 3 percent. Finally, Lynch launched initiatives to endow general managers with entrepreneurial interests, tying bonuses to the bottom line more than they had been in the past.

Significantly, leadership continued to turn over amid these financial struggles. In December 1995, Fresh Choice hired former Bennigan's leader Robert Ferngren as president and chief executive, essentially filling the position vacated by Culver. In addition to serving as president of Bennigan's, Ferngren had worked at America's Clubhouse Grill, a folded chain. A new vice president of marketing, Tim O'Shea, was also hired. A 1995 net loss of $27.8 million was realized on $84.28 million in sales (a 9.5 percent revenue increase over the previous year).

The company continued to struggle in 1996, with steady operating losses between the end of 1994 and the first quarter of 1996. A profit was achieved in the second and third quarters of 1996, but the fourth quarter returned to loss status. Fiscal 1996 net sales decreased to $76.7 million, and the net loss was just under $2 million.

In a major restructuring with the goal of returning to profitability, Fresh Choice had spent $23.9 million on closing 11 restaurants and partially writing down assets to estimated fair value in some remaining stores. Business was ended in the Washington, D.C., area, through the sale of restaurants in Maryland and Virginia to Fresh Fare Enterprises, with an agreement not to compete in the Baltimore and Washington, D.C., area for

four years. At the end of 1996, Fresh Choice operated 48 restaurants, down from 55 the year before. Menu expansion took place in the form of Sizzlin' Pan Pasta, a line of pan-sauteed pasta recipes prepared continually through the day. Only one new restaurant was opened in 1996—a prototype located in Roseville, California, which cost the company $763,000 in cash, a considerable savings over the previous costs of over $1 million. The Roseville store featured a warmer, more inviting decor and a more efficient layout. Menu changes included new items such as Madras chicken salad, reggae chicken salad, and smokehouse cheddar soup, and new uniforms with fruit and vegetable graphics were implemented, along with the expansion of beverage offerings to include espresso and fruit smoothie stations. Comparable store sales decreased 5.9 percent, leading the company to focus, once again, on rebuilding the bottom line.

Amidst Struggles, Company Prepares for the Future

A plan for profitability, implemented in 1997, included the reduction of general and administrative costs by store closings and efficiency measures, a private offering with Crescent Real Estate Equities Limited Partnership of Dallas with net proceeds of approximately $5.2 million, new menu items, the incorporation of design concepts from the new Roseville location in five remodeled stores, the redesigning of training programs to enhance customer service and satisfaction, and the strengthening of the company's management and board of directors. Significantly, a new president and CEO, Everett Jefferson, and a new CFO, David Pertl, were brought on board to lead the new campaign. Robert Ferngren had resigned to become vice president of Rare Hospitality, Inc. in Atlanta, after only a little more than a year in office. Jefferson was previously chairman of Cucina Holdings, Inc., the Sacramento-based operator of Java City coffee-roasting company and 40 cafes. Jefferson announced plans to examine new options for the company, including: the return of the frequent-diner punch card; positioning of cash registers at the end of the line to eliminate the perception of long waits; the addition of protein items such as rotisserie chicken as an "add-on" selection at an additional price; and an increase in advertising expenses.

In addition to these measures, the company began to thoroughly examine other opportunities for building business, including a marketing campaign aimed at converting first-time customers into repeat diners, new openings and acquisitions in California and Texas, take-out business, catering, morning meals, and the addition of more protein to the menu (in response to results of customer surveys). The aggressive marketing campaign included an advertising blitz with the company's first television commercials.

In April 1997, the company purchased three Zoopa restaurants in the Puget Sound area of Washington state, which it would operate under the Zoopa name. Charles Lynch announced that the purchase would broaden Fresh Choice's market position, as the first step in the current return to growth strategy.

The Zoopa purchase was another step forward, but the question remained whether Fresh Choice would ever regain the profitable status it realized prior to its overambitious expansion.

Problems over the years included the fluctuation of stock prices (ranging from a high of $32 to a 1997 level of $3), the departure of key senior staff, susceptibility to adverse economic conditions in the San Francisco Bay Area, and the lower level of response to healthy eating options outside the state of California. The company, it seems, will only return to long-term profitability with the implementation of a thoroughly researched long-term plan by a committed senior staff who will ride the ship through the storm.

Further Reading

Brokaw, Leslie, "The First Day of the Rest of Your Life," *Inc.*, May, 1993, pp. 144–52.

Carlino, Bill, "Dressing for Success: Salad Buffet Rivals Toss New Ingredients into Growth Recipes," *Nation's Restaurant News*, April 28, 1997, pp. 45–50.

"4th-Q Charge Widens Loss at Fresh Choice for 1995," *Nation's Restaurant News*, April 1, 1996, p. 12.

"Financial Markets," *Los Angeles Times*, December 10, 1992, p. D3.

Greco, Susan, "Cause-Related Marketing: What works," *Inc.*, August 1994, p. 102.

Liddle, Alan, "As Same-Store Sales Falter, Fresh Choice Eyes Pricing," *Nation's Restaurant News*, January 16, 1995, pp. 3, 14.

Liddle, Alan, "Fresh Choice Board Elects Director Lynch Chairman, *Nation's Restaurant News*, March 27, 1995, p. 2.

Liddle, Alan, "Fresh Choice CEO Culver Resigns," *Nation's Restaurant News*, May 29, 1995, pp. 1, 59.

Liddle, Alan, "Fresh Choice: 'Execution Is Everything,'" *Nation's Restaurant News*, May 16, 1994, pp. 68–72.

Liddle, Alan, "Fresh Choice, High Tech Burrito, Chevys Shake Up Expansion Race Among California Chains," *Nation's Restaurant News*, August 19, 1996.

Liddle, Alan, "Fresh Choice Names Industry Vet Jefferson to Top Posts," *Nation's Restaurant News*, March 3, 1997, pp. 7, 59.

Liddle, Alan, "Fresh Choice Taps Anderson, Rolls Scatter Bars," *Nation's Restaurant News*, October 17, 1994, p. 7.

Liddle, Alan, "Fresh Choice Taps Ferngren for Prexy Post," *Nation's Restaurant News*, December 4, 1995, pp. 3, 72.

Liddle, Alan, "Prexy Jefferson Puts Improving Service Above Profit—for Now," *Nation's Restaurant News*, March 3, 1997, pp. 7, 59.

McLaughlin, John, "Wall Street Doesn't Always Like the Long-Term View," *Restaurant Business*, September 20, 1994, pp. 24–28.

Papiernik, Richard L., "Fresh Choice Searches In-House for Comeback Plan of Action," *Nation's Restaurant News*, October 23, 1995, pp. 11, 15.

Petruno, Tom, "Boom in Restaurant Stocks Starts Getting Stale," *Los Angeles Times*, December 21, 1992.

Romano, Michael, "Can You Raise Prices This Year?" *Restaurant Business*, January 1, 1994, pp. 56–62.

Romeo, Peter, "Will It Play in Peoria," *Restaurant Business*, December 10, 1993, pp. 54–58.

Sullivan, Janet, "Starting Fresh," *Restaurant Business*, June 10, 1995, pp. 60–62.

Weber, Jonathan, "The Times 100/The Best Performing Companies in America," *Los Angeles Times*, April 26, 1994, pp. D2–21.

—Heidi Feldman

Frozen Food Express Industries, Inc.

1145 Empire Central Place
Dallas, Texas 75247-4309
U.S.A.
(214) 630-8090
Fax: (214) 819-5625

Public Company
Founded: 1945
Employees: 2,604
Sales: $311.4 million (1996)
Stock Exchanges: NASDAQ
SICs: 4213 Trucking, Except Local; 5078 Refrigeration
Equipment and Supplies

Frozen Food Express Industries, Inc. was, in the mid-1990s, the largest temperature-controlled trucking company in North America. The company's temperature-controlled less-than-truckload (LTL) operation was the largest in the United States and the only one offering regularly scheduled nationwide service, including multicompartment refrigerated trailers to carry goods requiring different temperatures. Frozen Food Express also was believed to be one of the five largest temperature-controlled, full-truckload carriers in North America. More than 80 percent of its cargo, such as food products, pharmaceuticals, medical supplies, and film, consisted of temperature-sensitive perishables. The company turned a profit in every year of its first half-century in business.

Frozen Food Express Before 1980

Frozen Food Express was founded in 1945 by two uncles of Stoney M. Stubbs, Jr., joined shortly thereafter by his father. Its main assets were operating rights in Texas and a handful of trucks. Revenues for the first year's operations were less than $100,000. From the beginning the company was a specialist in transporting products requiring refrigeration. Because refrigerated tractor-trailers or "reefers," cost nearly three times as much as regular trailers and burned a good deal more fuel as well, big trucking companies were willing to leave this niche

market to smaller operators. The junior Stubbs washed and loaded trucks in high school and earned a business degree from Texas A&M in 1959. He then went back to work for the family enterprise, becoming president in 1979. Eugene O. Weller, his uncle, remained chairman and CEO of the company until 1984, when Stubbs assumed these positions as well.

Frozen Food Express Industries was formed in 1969, at which time the prior Frozen Food Express became its subsidiary. In 1971 Frozen Food Express Industries (hereafter called Frozen Food Express for short) became publicly held through an offering of 350,000 shares of common stock at $15 a share. Half of these shares were sold by existing shareholders. The $2.3 million in net proceeds from the shares sold by the company were applied in full against long-term debt. Revenues increased from $10.8 million in 1966 to $23.7 million in 1971. Net income rose from $232,000 to $1.2 million during this period.

Frozen Food Express expanded rapidly in the late 1960s by taking advantage of the decentralization of the meat-processing industry and the growth in the popularity of frozen convenience foods and fresh produce. By the end of 1971 the company was operating in 23 states, mostly in the Midwest and Southwest but stretching as far west as California and as far east as Ohio and Kentucky. Of 100 motor carriers classified as solid refrigerated carriers filing reports with the Interstate Commerce Commission in 1971, the company was the third largest, based on operating revenue. In that year the company acquired W & B Refrigeration Service Co., a franchised distributor for truck and trailer refrigeration equipment bearing the Carrier-Transicold brand. Made a subsidiary, W & B specialized in keeping refrigerated units, including the parent company's own, in top condition.

At this time large-volume shippers normally used Frozen Food Express's full-truckload (at least 10,000 pounds) service to transport their products to their destinations. This service, almost all under agreements with independent contractors, was nonscheduled and operated over irregular routes within the company's route authority. Small-volume shippers used the company's less-than-truckload service, which consisted of 240 weekly scheduled routes between specified points of origin and termination. LTL service was available between major metropolitan areas within the company's operating territory, including Chicago, Dallas, Houston, Kansas City, Little Rock, Los Angeles, Lubbock, Memphis, Minneapolis, New Orleans, Oklahoma City, Omaha, San Francisco, and St. Louis. Frozen Food Express's main terminal, in Lancaster, Texas, was completed in 1970. The company's full-truckload operations accounted for 58 percent of carrier revenue and 40 percent of net operating profit in 1971; LTL operations for 42 percent of carrier revenue and 60 percent of net operating profit. In all, the company was serving more than 3,000 shippers.

Frozen Food Express was a pioneer in its method of handling full-truckload shipments. The company had established independent contractors from the ranks of its employees, offering to sell them a tractor and the means of financing it. The company provided the trailer and the customers; the contractor provided the second driver and the power unit. Compensation was in the form of a percentage of the revenue generated by the shipments carried. The company founded a driver-training school in 1967 that offered a four-week course. LTL service featured compartmentalized trailers, capable of hauling multiple shipments requiring differing temperature levels.

Frozen Food Express's main truckload routes were from Texas northward carrying frozen foods, meats, meat byproducts, margarine, fresh produce, and bakery products; from Chicago and the surrounding Midwest to the southwestern states and California carrying meats, meat products, yeast, bakery products, dairy products, and frozen foods; and from the Gulf Coast-area ports to the Midwest carrying imported bananas and other fruits. The company also carried most of these products and biscuits, milk-chocolate drinks, and salad dressing on short or intermediate hauls between points in Arkansas, Louisiana, New Mexico, Oklahoma, and Texas. Nonfood items such as blood plasma were transported to California, and resin was transported from California into the Midwestern states.

The number of shippers using Frozen Food Express passed 4,000 in 1974 and 5,000 in 1977. By the end of 1977 the number of weekly LTL runs had reached 390. Revenues increased from $30.6 million in 1973 to $54 million in 1977. Net income rose from $1.4 million in 1973 to nearly $2 million in 1976, then slumped to $1.9 million in 1977. Revenue from full-truckload shipments grew faster than that from LTL shipments during this period, accounting for 66 percent of the total in 1977.

Deregulation in the 1980s

Prior to 1980, interstate trucking was tightly regulated by the federal government. Along with regulated rates, companies were issued permits by the Interstate Commerce Commission for specific routes. A permit almost guaranteed profits for the average trucking company. But the deregulation of the industry created price wars that, even during this period of high inflation, cut freight rates almost in half. Of the 45 publicly owned trucking companies listed before deregulation in the industry's leading trade journal, 33 were gone by 1987.

Full-truckload operations were particularly vulnerable to rate cutting, and so, although 60 percent of Frozen Food Express's annual revenue still was being generated by its full-

truckload fleet in 1979, the company sold its full-truckload equipment between 1980 and 1982 and used the proceeds to repay about $7.1 million in debt. In 1982 the company began offering to transport nonperishable cargo, with the exception of explosives, household goods, and commodities in bulk. Between 1983 and 1986 it acquired the operations of four regional less-than-truckload companies and thereby began providing service in all 48 contiguous states. Since all four were losing money at the time, Frozen Food Express's net income (before extraordinary items) fell from $1.7 million in 1983 to $1,000 in 1985. But in 1986 the company reported $1.1 million in net income, with revenue from the LTL operation reaching $59.9 million—more than the company's total revenue in 1983.

Frozen Food Express began 1988 with only 22 company-operated, full-truckload units, supplemented by about 200 owner-operators, but it had begun an ambitious program to field a new fleet of company-owned trucks. Some 109 such trucks were operating by the end of 1988, 440 by the end of 1989, and 660 by the end of 1990. Another 300 trucks were independently contracted in 1989. About 70 percent of the company's LTL operations were still being conducted by independent contractors in 1990.

In 1988 Frozen Food Express acquired certain assets from Lisa Motor Lines, Inc. of Fort Worth, Texas, for $4.6 million. These included operating rights, 32 tractors, 132 refrigerated trailers, and a tank trailer. Company revenues reached $102 million that year, compared to $56.7 million in 1982, and net income was $3.7 million, compared to $1 million in 1982.

Further Growth in the 1990s

By 1991 Frozen Food Express was the nation's largest publicly owned, nationwide full-service motor carrier of perishable commodities in the United States. In 1992 the firm made *Forbes*'s list of the 200 best small companies in America and for the first time attracted serious interest from Wall Street investors.

That year Frozen Food Express purchased the less-than-truckload division of Temperature Controlled Carriage Inc., a refrigerated-truck company based in Nashville, Tennessee, thereby gaining a $12-million-a-year business with 60 trailers, 15 tractors, and terminals in Nashville and Cincinnati. Consolidating this division's freight with Frozen Food Express's terminals in Chicago, Atlanta, and Memphis was "another way we can capture new revenue with very little incremental cost," Stubbs told a *Nashville Business Journal* reporter.

Stubbs added that Frozen Food Express was planning to expand its distributions to area grocery stores, food brokers, and drugstores from the newly acquired terminals. "The food business is moving to just-in-time inventory control faster each year," he said. "For the customer, it means less warehousing expense and inventory carrying costs." Frozen Food Express confirmed that its primary cargo was prepared foods and meats. By 1992 revenues—only $84.6 million in 1987—had risen in excess of 18 percent annually for the last five years. The company had sales of $195 million and net income of $7.1 million, both records for the third consecutive year.

Frozen Food Express credited a company efficiency program for sharply higher profits since 1990. This effort called for scheduling more loads per week per truck, with schedulers trying to arrange that trucks would have loads to pick up near the site of their most recent delivery. For 1993 the company had net income of $9.4 million on revenues of $227.4 million, both records.

Frozen Food Express began full-truckload, refrigerated service to and from Mexico in 1990, in alliance with a Mexican trucker who picked up goods at the company's new Laredo, Texas, terminal. This business grew at an annual rate of more than 30 percent and, in 1993, the company began offering less-than-truckload refrigerated service to Mexico as well. One special reason for Frozen Food Express to seek this two-way business was that western Mexico's growing season begins in November, during the trucking company's slack season. Full truckloads of Mexican-produced frozen vegetables were being hauled by Frozen Food Express drivers to U.S. processing and packaging plants.

By the spring of 1994 Frozen Food Express's trailers were making regularly scheduled stops every week in more than 7,000 cities and towns. The firm was picking up business from companies like RJR Nabisco and Coors Brewing that were choosing to eliminate their own refrigerated vehicles in order to save on capital and overhead. Frozen Food Express was converting its mainframe computer to a PC-based system, allowing customers to place orders and pay bills electronically. It was installing a satellite tracking system in its trucks at $4,000 per unit to allow dispatchers and customers to find the exact location of a shipment and to relay pickup and delivery times, weather and road information, route and fueling directions to truckers, who could communicate shipment status and other information electronically to dispatchers by means of a keypad.

Frozen Food Express had record sales and profits in 1994 for the fourth straight year, with revenues of $274.6 million and net income of $11.9 million. In 1995 it entered a comprehensive sales and marketing arrangement with Alliance Shippers, a railroad-based intermodal transportation-service company, for temperature-sensitive shipments through the United States, Canada, and Mexico. "Alliance has the high-volume agreements with the railroads and the intermodal expertise," Stubbs told *Distribution*. Alliance, with about 400 refrigerated containers and trailers, gained access to Frozen Food Express's 2,100 reefers. In return, Stubbs' company gained access to Alliance's extensive sales force.

In 1995 Frozen Food Express's net income dipped to $9.3 million on revenues of $292.3 million, but it eliminated its long-term debt of $9 million. In 1996 net income dipped again, to $8.5 million, on revenues of $311.4 million, of which full truckloads accounted for 60 percent. Management blamed industrywide trucking overcapacity for decreased productivity and downward pressure on full-truckload freight rates. The devaluation of the Mexican peso in December 1994 significantly reduced the flow of consumer products from the United States to Mexico because they became more expensive. And

fuel costs, though relatively stable during 1995, increased by 11 percent in 1996.

Frozen Food Express in 1996

At the end of 1996 Frozen Food Express had a fleet of 1,202 tractors that were company-owned and 703 provided by owner-operators. There were 2,998 company-owned trailers and 20 provided by owner-operators. Owner-operators normally provided both tractor and driver to pull the company's loaded trailer, receiving a percentage of the revenue from each load. The company had contractors for 443 owner-operated tractors in its full-truckload divisions and 266 in its less-than-truckload operations.

Frozen Food Express, through a subsidiary, was a franchised distributor in 1996 for Wabash trailers and Carrier Transicold-brand truck-and-trailer refrigeration equipment. This subsidiary was engaged in the sales, service, and rental of trailers and a variety of refrigeration and air-conditioning equipment. Such operations accounted for 7.5 percent of the parent company's revenues in 1996.

Frozen Food Express owned corporate offices in Dallas and its primary terminal and maintenance facility near Dallas, on about 60 acres in Lancaster, Texas. Lisa Motor Lines and its divisions, Middle Transportation Co. and Great Western Express, were using a terminal, offices, and a repair shop owned by the parent company in Fort Worth, Texas. Frozen Food Express also owned a cold-storage LTL terminal in Bridgeview, Illinois, near Chicago, and terminals near Orlando, Florida, and Avenel, New Jersey. The company was leasing a terminal or office facility at 26 locations. Some 27 percent of the company's shares of common stock were held by employees. The daughters of Edgar O. Weller held 17 percent and Stubbs 8.35 percent. The company had no long-term debt.

Principal Subsidiaries

Compressors Plus, Inc. (inactive); Conwell Cartage, Inc. (inactive); Conwell Corporation; FFE, Inc.; FFE Transportation Services, Inc.; Frozen Food Express, Inc.; Lisa Motor Lines, Inc.; Middleton Transportation Company (inactive); W & B Refrigeration Service Company.

Further Reading

"Current Corporate Reports," *Barron's*, February 15, 1993, p. 66.
"Food for Thought," *Distribution*, March 1995, p. 22.
"Frozen Food Express Shows Gains Without Increases in Rates," *Investment Dealers' Digest*, October 7, 1975, p. 20.
Hobbs, Bill, "Frozen Food Express to Expand After TCC Buy," *Nashville Business Journal*, November 2, 1992, p. 8.
Legg, William M., "Frozen Food Express Industries, Inc.," *Wall Street Transcript*, April 10, 1972, p. 27,967.
Nethery, Ross, "Frozen Food Express Is on a Roll," *Dallas Business Journal*, August 27, 1993, p. 33.
Palmeri, Christopher, "Reefer Man," *Forbes*, April 25, 1994, p. 82.
Wood, Sean, "FFE Stock Price, Earnings Keep on Truckin'," *Dallas Business Journal*, October 30, 1992, p. 41.

—Robert Halasz

FTP Software, Inc.

100 Brickstone Square, Fifth Floor
Andover, Massachusetts 01810
U.S.A.
(508) 685-4000
Fax: (508) 684-6978
Web Site: http://www.ftp.com

Public Company
Incorporated: 1986
Employees: 740
Sales: $158 million (1996)
Stock Exchanges: NASDAQ
SICs: 7372 Prepackaged Software; 7373 Computer
    Integrated Systems Design; 5045 Computers,
    Peripherals & Software

FTP Software, Inc. is a technology leader in the development of infrastructure software for electronic commerce and exchange of information across public and private networks. The company also provides applications and services that allow customers to create VIP Networks. Based on the premise that organizations manage people and their access privileges, the VIP Network enables customers to extend their network beyond traditional boundaries in a secure and manageable manner to encompass employees or associates anywhere, and to build enterprises to enable electronic commerce and virtual workgroups.

Named after the Internet term "File Transfer Protocol," the company is engaged in the design, development, marketing, and support of client networking software products based upon the industry standard Transmission Control Protocol/Internet Protocol (TCP/IP), data communications protocol suite, enabling personal computer (PC) users to find, access, and use heterogeneous hardware, information, and applications resources across local area networks (LANs), enterprise-wide and global networks, and a variety of operating systems, computing platforms and network environments. The company was incorporated in January 1986 in Massachusetts and is headquartered in Ando-

ver, Massachusetts, with offices in California, Virginia, England, France, Germany, Japan, Singapore, and Sweden. It went public in 1993.

Origins at MIT

The company had its beginnings, however, at Massachusetts Institute of Technology in the mid-1980s when five students wrote a version of networking language TCP/IP that allowed DOS-based IBM PCs to communicate with mainframe computers. Seeing the potential profit to be gained if their language was adapted to work with other systems, those five graduates founded FTP. By the time companies began replacing mainframe systems with personal desktop computers, FTP was ready to link the two.

With its VIP Network architecture, FTP Software is laying the groundwork for a transparent, software-based "virtual network" that connects users regardless of location, hardware or network protocol. The company develops, markets, and supports software products in three areas: Client networking for fast and intuitive user network interfaces; server networking for linking and extending enterprise networks; and agent applications that enable network administrators to manage, diagnose, and reconfigure IP network clients from a central site. Some key software products created and/or developed by the company include InterDrive networking applications; LANCatch, a network utility; LANWatch, a network analyzer; PC/Bind, a DOS-based domain name server; PC/SNMP Tools, a network management program; and PC/TCP, an internetworking system. Products under development in the late 1990s included Esplanade, a Web server; Explore and Explore Anywhere for Windows, Internet access programs; and FrontPage, a Web page development program.

The Nature of the Industry and the Competition

The software industry is one of the fastest-growing markets in the world. Since the late 1970s, computers have become more and more commonplace. Therefore, the computer industry is extremely competitive and is characterized by ever-evolving industry standards, the frequent introduction of new products and constant product enhancements. Continuous improvement in product reliability, compatibility, memory use, and performance make computer hardware and software practically obsolete from the moment they are released into the marketplace. The company's networking software products compete with major computer and communications vendors, including large competitors such as Adobe, Artisoft, DEC, IBM, Microsoft Corporation, Netscape, Novell Inc., Sun Microsystems Inc., and Wang, as well as smaller companies like Attachmate, Banyan Systems, Bay Networks, Cheyenne Software, Cisco Systems, Computer Network, Digi International, DIGICON, Gandalf Technologies, Inso, Microcom, Microtest, NetManage Inc., ON Technology, Retix, Spry, Sterling Software, TGV Software, VMARK Software, Wollongong, and WRQL. Some of the company's competitors have larger financial, technical, sales, and marketing resources than FTP, as well as greater name recognition and a larger customer base. Several of the company's competitors have also developed proprietary networking applications and provide a TCP/IP protocol suite in their products for little or no additional cost. Terminal emulation software makers such as Attachmate Corporation and Wall Data Inc. are also beginning to implement their own versions of TCP/IP. Because FTP's core product lines are based upon the TCP/IP, the introduction of such protocol suites by the larger companies makes the competition very fierce.

The company also manufactures networking, agent, directory services, and security software products, a new, but still rapidly changing market. And, again, the company competes against such corporate giants as Sun, Adobe, and Microsoft.

The Mid-1990s and the Future

The company has grown slowly but steadily. In 1994, the company acquired technology licensed from Spyglass Inc. and Unipalm Ltd. for approximately $4.9 million. March 1995 saw the company acquiring substantially all of the assets of Keyword Office Technologies Ltd., a developer of document viewer and conversion software products, for approximately $2.4 million. In August of the same year, the company entered into a multiyear joint marketing and development agreement with Open Market Inc. under which the company has the right to sell certain server products and to develop the server technology for use in future software platforms.

In February 1996, the company acquired the Mariner Internet searching software product line from Network Computing Devices Inc. for approximately $7.4 million in cash. The fol-

lowing month, the company acquired first the GroupWorks project team management utility software product of, and then all of the assets of, HyperDesk Corporation for approximately $6.3 million in cash. In April, the company acquired all of the outstanding shares of Campbell Services Inc., the developer of OnTime, a scheduling software product, for approximately $15 million in cash. July saw the company acquire Firefox Communications Inc., a supplier of server-centric departmental and LAN-based IP solutions and services, for a net purchase price of $61 million through the merger of Firefox with a wholly owned subsidiary of the company.

In September 1996, the company decided to completely realign itself. FTP Software announced the unveiling of its VIP Network strategy, developed to entirely focus the company on a new strategic vision of developing and marketing a software architecture concept designed to enable organizations to secure, manage, and transparently extend their networks beyond traditional boundaries. This software architecture concept is to be developed with the intent of helping the company's customers to support mobile personal computer users and remote sites, to build virtual collaborative workgroups within and across the organization, and to facilitate electronic commerce by building federated networks between and among the organization and its customers, suppliers and other business partners. The concept is threefold: client networking products; server networking products; and agent applications.

Part of the strategy involves streamlining the company over a period of years, spinning off, through the sale to third parties, the company's collaborative lines of business and to discontinue other selected non-material product lines. One sale occurred in June 1997, when the company sold its KEYview, KEYview Pro, and KEYpak email utility product line to Verity Inc. for approximately $1.5 million. The product line allows users to view, convert, compress, and secure most file types, whether encountered on the Internet, corporate intranets, received as email attachments or found on a hard drive or network and can be used as a stand-alone application or integrated with email or groupware applications or act as a plug-in to Web browsers.

Another part of the strategy involves strengthening the company through new leadership, greater operational discipline, and new corporate alliances. Also under this strategy, the company released products such as InterDrive(r) Client 2.1 NFS for Windows 95 and Windows NT; Internet Gateway for Windows NT; OnNet(r) 32 v2.0, an internetworking program, as well as related products, Services OnNet, a configuration management package and X OnNet, an applications access program; and Secure Client v3.0 for Windows 95.

The company also won numerous awards in 1996 and 1997 and received widespread industry recognition for its products and services, including the 1996 Internet Excellence Award from Network World & Intranet; Best TCP/IP Application Suite from Internetwork; a New Product Achievement Award from ComNet '96; Data Communications' Tester's Choice Awards for Secure Client v3.0 for Windows 95, a replacement TCP/IP stack, and a beta version of the Network Access Suite v3.0 for Windows 95 and NT 4.0, a collection of TCP/IP applications and utilities, the only two products chosen for this distinction;

and a STAR Award from the Software Support Professional Association. The company also achieved two industry firsts with client networking products when it released Support for WinSock 2.0 and Support for IPv6 and IPSec.

In July 1997, in line with the new Network strategy, the company restructured its business into three strategic business units: the Agent/Directory Management Business Unit, an advanced technology business unit to develop and market next generation network administration and management applications based on the company's leading-edge Java agent and directory technologies such as IP Auditor and IP Distributor, both released in May 1997; the IP Technology Business Unit, to develop and market the company's established client and server-based Gateway technologies, product solutions and networking products, as well as its other IP technology components; and the VIP Network Applications Business Unit, to develop and market the company's desktop and web-based network applications solutions, including its award-winning 32-bit Network Access Suite applications, along with its OnNet family of products and network application products which address the client and network computing markets, Internet Gateway products, as well as its other IP technology components.

Also in 1997, FTP Software began working in conjunction with other companies such as IBM, Lotus, Check Point Software Technologies Ltd., Cisco, Entrust Technologies, IRE, Raptor, Timestep Corporation, Trusted Information Systems, Chrysler Corporation, EDS, I-NET, MCI, Netrex, Precision Guesswork, and Netscape to develop new and improved computer programs. One such program released in 1997 was Network Communications Suite, a package which obtains multiple desktop software packages to solve a user's enterprise communications need.

As the software industry continues to grow, FTP Software is in a good position to continue operating as an industry leader.

Principal Subsidiaries

Campbell Services Inc.; Firefox Communications Inc.; Firefox (U.S.) Inc.; FTP Software Asia Inc.; FTP Software (Asia Pacific) Pte Ltd. (Singapore); FTP Software Canada Ltd. (Canada); FTP Software Export Inc. (Bahamas); FTP Software Kabushiki Kaisha (Japan); FTP Software GmbH (Germany); FTP Software Limited (U.K.); FTP Software Security Corp. Inc.; FTP Software Worldwide Inc.

—Daryl F. Mallett

FuncoLand
America's Place to Shop for Video Games

Funco, Inc.

10120 West 76th Street
Minneapolis, Minnesota, 55344
U.S.A.
(612) 946-8883
Fax: (612) 946-7251

Public Company
Incorporated: 1988
Employees: 486
Sales: $120.6 million (1997)
Stock Exchanges: NASDAQ
SICs: 5945 Hobby, Toy, & Game Shops

Funco, Inc. is a leading specialty retailer of new and used interactive entertainment products. At the end of March 1997 the company operated 188 FuncoLand stores in 12 major American markets. Funco, Inc. has weathered rapid growth, bust-and-boom cycles in the video game industry, the dynamics of consumer preference for particular games, game systems, and game categories (sports, adventure, action, role playing, and family games), as well as increased marketplace competition.

Learning the Hard Way, Early 80s

David R. Pomije had two failed business attempts to draw on as he began to build Funco, Inc. First was a travel-package company established in 1980, when he was 23 years old. According to Dick Youngblood, "It took him 18 months to put the business together—and less than a year to blow through the $100,000 he'd borrowed from friends and family before closing the doors in 1983." The next time the entrepreneurial bug bit was in 1985, when his employer rejected his idea to buy liquidated Commodore computers for resale through the mail-order business. He left his position as marketing director and purchased the equipment himself, with a loan cosigned by his father, a New Prague, Minnesota, high school teacher.

Protechtronics, Inc. sold $2 million in computers the first year and $10 million in year two. When his supply of computers deteriorated Pomije sold a hodge-podge of consumer goods ranging from Rambo knives to radar detectors. The company not only lacked focus but was burdened by heavy debt, an inadequate information management system, and Pomije's personal expenditures. Protechtronics moved into Chapter 11 reorganization in 1987 and then Chapter 7 liquidation in 1988. But out of the ruin Pomije salvaged the beginnings of a new business venture.

A New Start, 1988

Nintendo video games were just entering the U.S. market, and Pomije picked up two of the game systems. They sold quickly, and Pomije began purchasing more of the games. When Protechtronics was liquidated, he borrowed the money to buy back 1,100 game machines which he resold. But he had 1,100 game cartridges on his hands. Pomije approached video stores with the idea of renting the games, and with the help of his wife, uncle, and father, he was back in business.

Funco, Inc. grossed $24,000 in 1988, its first year of business. Pomije supplemented the original supply of video games with games purchased on sale from discount stores. Demand on games dwindled when kids tired of playing them, so Pomije began contacting used video game buyers/sellers listed in magazine ads. His experience with the mail-order businesses led him to believe he could do a better job, and he placed his first ad in September 1989. The home-based mail-order business took off. So many kids arrived on his doorstep wanting to buy or sell games neighbors suspected something illegal and called the police. Gross sales for the year were about $120,000.

Pomije moved the operation to a warehouse in 1990. Newspaper and video magazine ads drew mail orders from around the country and overseas. Funco's will-call window operation generated $15,000 in business in the first six months without any advertising. When Pomije tested his first retail ad in August 1990, it drew people from the five-state area. The first two FuncoLand retail stores opened in late 1990 and brought in $200,000 in sales by the end of the year. Funco, Inc. had grown from a family enterprise to a 40-employee operation in its first two years.

Funco managed its inventory by balancing the buy and sell prices of the used games. Dan Wascoe, Jr., wrote, "The company's nerve center in New Hope is a room whose grease-board walls are marked with the names of hundreds of games. Prices and supply symbols next to the names change frequently, making the place look a bit like the trading floor of a primitive commodity exchange." Popular out-of-production titles demanded higher prices, but paying too much for a less-in-demand game resulted in excess supply. With over 500 to choose from, Funcoland claimed to have the most titles of any company selling used games. In addition to buying used games from the public, Funco purchased discounted overstocked titles from manufacturer licensees.

At the time, 90 percent of sales came from used games—or as Funco referred to them, previously played games. The majority of titles, about 85 percent, were by Nintendo licensees: Nintendo controlled 80 percent of the $5.1 billion video game market.

Rapid Expansion

Funco continued to operate its mail-order and video game lease businesses, but the success of the FuncoLand stores fueled dreams of expanding the retail segment. But in order to manage the growth, Pomije needed a professional management team and an effective information management system. Pomije said in an August 8, 1994 *Fortune* magazine article, "This time I said, 'Time out! We need to have more than a cigar box and little bell for a cash register before we go forward.' " Pomije began by bringing in the former head of B. Dalton Bookseller's MIS department, as well as, a former senior vice president of Haagen-Daz, who had opened the company's stores in Europe and Japan.

The company employed more than 100 people and operated 10 Minneapolis-area stores when it announced its initial public stock (IPO) offering in July 1992. Funco stock sold at $5 per share and generated $5 million for a national store expansion. The company began with multiple-store openings in the Chicago and Dallas areas. The strategy both pushed aside independent used-video game businesses and kept individual store opening costs down through economies of scale in leasing, distribution, and advertising.

By February 1993, Funco owned more than 50 retail stores and its stock had climbed to nearly $18 per share. Pomije still held 71 percent of the company. The interactive video game industry had skyrocketed in 1992: game software sales climbed 60 to 80 percent and hardware sales climbed 20 percent. Sophisticated new games were drawing adults into the market. Funco stock was hot, but not for long.

The shares, which had been selling well above corporate earnings, had already begun to come down. But when Sega of America announced in April that it would offer subscribers the opportunity to download and sample its new video games on an interactive cable channel, Funco stock dropped to $8 per share. As Tony Carideo wrote, "Some investors interpreted the news as the distant death knell of the retail outlet concept." Revenues for Funco's 1993 fiscal year—which ended in April—were

$20.5 million, but the company lost $520,000 due to the addition of management and control systems.

A secondary stock offering, in June 1993, yielded $13 million at $11 per share. Funco, already the largest national seller of used videos, planned to move into the suburban New York metropolitan market with 30 stores.

Funcoland stores drew customers with video games selling for about half the original retail price, opportunities to try before buying both used and new games, and three times the number of titles as most specialty retailers. Funco was buying about 3000 games per day and offering store credit or cash for the used games. The top 10 bestselling games were more than five years old. New merchandise accounted for just 25 percent of total sales.

The rapid growth of the past two years boosted the number of Funcoland stores past the 100 mark and landed Funco the number 11 spot on *Fortune* magazine's fastest growing company list in 1994. The stores averaged about 1,600 square feet and were generally located in strip malls near busy retail areas. The company chose sites with little used game competition but showing high potential according to mail-order sales. New stores typically became profitable after six months. Funco published 250,000 mail-order catalogs on a quarterly basis, and its bimonthly video magazine, *Game Informer*, established in fiscal 1992, exceeded 100,000 subscriptions in 1994.

Funco Falters, 1994

Competition heated up for FuncoLand stores in 1994 when superstores and discounters entered into a price war. Funco had been building its new game sales, but could not compete when the big retailers slashed prices to or below cost. The company was also forced to cut prices on used video games. When Funco announced third quarter earnings would fall below the expectations of financial analysts, the stock fell by 46.5 percent, back to about its IPO level.

The delay in release of the next generation of video games made matters worse. Sales slowed during the important Christmas season as customers waited for the new video game technology. Game manufacturers dumped inventories of their existing games to mass merchandisers compounding the pricing problem.

Funco lost $1.3 million or 22 cents per share on $80.4 million in sales in fiscal 1995. The company turned its attention to improving sales in its 182 existing stores and improving expense controls and margins. Stanley A. Bodine, the Haagen-Daz executive who came aboard with the new management team, was promoted to president and COO; Pomije continued on in his positions as chairman and CEO.

Funco lost an additional $2 million or 35 cents per share in the first half of fiscal 1996. The company responded with salary cuts for the two top officials; freezes on other senior staff salaries; a 20 percent reduction in headquarters staff; tightening of store staffing; and cancellation of most of the 50 store openings scheduled for fiscal 1996—72 stores had been added in fiscal 1995.

The market outlook brightened with the release of new video game technology by Sony and Sega, but the industry slump had driven some used video game sellers out of business and hurt others. Video Game Exchange Inc., based in Cleveland, filed for bankruptcy protection in February 1995. When the company reorganized it reduced the number of its stores by half.

Funco cut its capital expenditure budget to $1 million for fiscal 1996, down from $8 million in 1995. The company also began to experiment with some new concepts. A FuncoLand outlet was opened in a super Kmart store, and Funco joined with Supercenter Entertainment Corp. in Dallas to test the used movie market. In a *Corporate Report* by Kelly O'Hara, Pomije predicted a video game industry comeback saying the cyclical industry was moving out of the transition period from the old to new technology.

The industry had changed somewhat since Funco first began selling used video games. More manufacturers were producing video games machines making it more difficult to read the used game market—the majority of Funco revenue continued to come from used games and equipment. And in February 1996, the $9 billion, 653-store Toys R Us began purchasing used video games from their customers.

The Game Continues

Seven new stores were opened but 16 were closed during the 1996 fiscal year, leaving 173 stores in operation in 11 major metro areas on the East Coast and central regions of the United States. The new Sony PlayStation and Sega Saturn systems had slowly begun to help lagging sales. Funco returned to profitability for fiscal 1996, but sales for the year were flat.

With the addition of Nintendo 64 to the market, Funco revenues recovered. In fiscal 1997, net sales were $120.6 million up 48 percent, and earnings were $5.34 million, the highest level ever posted by the company. New game sales were 47 percent of sales, also at their highest level. With business booming again, Funco elevated planned store openings to 40 for the remainder of calendar year 1997—the expansion included stores on the West Coast.

Funco's future held some of the same obstacles it had faced in the past: changing technology, a cyclical industry, and dynamic consumer preferences. Pomije had negotiated the company through the danger before and reached a higher level. It will be interesting to see if he continues to win the game.

Further Reading

Apgar, Sally, "Funco Inc. Stock Plunges 46.5% on News of Expected Lower Earnings," *Star Tribune* (Minneapolis), December 17, 1994, p 1D.

——, "Investors Bail Out of Funco in Wake of Woeful 4th Quarter," *Star Tribune* (Minneapolis), April 8, 1995, p. 1D.

Bradley, Peter, "Game Master," *Twin Cities Business Monthly*, October 1993, pp. 46–48.

Bunker, Ted, "Fun and Games," *Investor's Business Daily*, April 22, 1994.

Carideo, Tony, "Analyst Sees Selloff in Video-Game Retailer Funco As a Buying Opportunity," April 24, 1993, p. 2D.

Carlson, Scott, "Funco Stock Zooms Because of Strategy, Teamwork, Timing," *St. Paul Pioneer Press*, February 15, 1993.

Earley, Sandra, "Funco Economizes Amid Industry Flux," *Minneapolis/St. Paul CityBusiness*, October 27, 1995, p. 13.

Kafka, Peter, "A New Generation of Killers Boosts Funco," *Minneapolis/St. Paul CityBusiness*, May 23, 1997, p. 4.

Kaplan, Steve, "Second-Time Charm," *Minnesota Ventures*, May/June 1992, pp. 68–70.

Kratz, Vikki, "FuncoLand 1; Corporate Report 0," *Corporate Report Minnesota*, March 1997, p. 12.

Marksjarvis, Gail, "Video Game Retailer Plans $5 Million Stock Offering," *St. Paul Pioneer Press*, July 2, 1992, p. 1F.

——, "Analysts Like Funco for Its Niche, Outlook," *St. Paul Pioneer Press*, August 16, 1993.

Nissen, Todd, "He's Cashing in on Fun And Games," *Minneapolis/St. Paul CityBusiness*, February 12, 1993.

O'Hara, Kelly, "Mortal Kombat?" *Corporate Report Minnesota*, March 1996 pp. 48–54.

Phelps, David, "Funco Bounces Back with New Generation of Games," January 20, 1997.

Serwer, Andrew, "Lessons from America's Fastest-Growing Companies," *Fortune*, August 8, 1994, pp. 48–49.

Wascoe, Dan, Jr., "Electronic-Game Whiz Deals in Used Fun," *Star Tribune* (Minneapolis), December 2, 1990, p. 1D.

Waters, Jennifer, "Funco Fights to Stay in the Game," *Minneapolis/St. Paul CityBusiness*, May 26–June 1, 1995, p. 1.

Youngblood, Dick, "Funco Toys with Turnaround," *Star Tribune* (Minneapolis), December 4, 1995, p. 2D.

——, "Third Time Is the Charm As Funco Chief Succeeds After 2 Business Failures," *Star Tribune* (Minneapolis), September 13, 1993, p. 2D.

—Kathleen Peippo

Galey&Lord

Galey & Lord, Inc.

980 Avenue of the Americas
New York, New York 10018
U.S.A.
(212) 465-3000
Fax: (212) 465-3025

Public Company
Incorporated: 1988
Employees: 5,451 (1996)
Sales: $411.50 million (1996)
Stock Exchanges: New York
SICs: 2211 Broad Woven Fabric Mills, Cotton; 2221
Broad Woven Fabric Mills, Manmade Fiber and Silk;
2262 Finishers of Broad Woven Manmade Fiber

Galey & Lord, Inc. develops, manufactures, and markets fabrics for the apparel and home furnishings industries, particularly high-quality woven cotton and cotton-blended apparel fabrics and printed fabrics. As a leading producer of apparel fabrics, Galey & Lord sells to uniform and sportswear manufacturers of men's, women's, and children's wrinkle-free slacks, pants, and shorts. Known for innovative fabric dyeing and finishing techniques, this long-established company may be the world's largest producer of khaki, corduroy, and wrinkle-free fabrics, allowing Galey & Lord to survive even upheavals in the printed apparel fabrics business.

Nineteenth-Century Origins

Partners William Galey and Charles Lord founded Galey & Lord in 1886 to market fabrics to the apparel industry. The pair established the company as a selling agent for their other business, Aberfoyle, a mill in Pennsylvania. The firm grew steadily, and by 1922 it also functioned as sales agent for Camerton Mills. During the Great Depression, Galey & Lord manufactured a fabric common for civilian work wear—khaki. Though expensive, khaki earned its place as a conventional apparel fabric at this time.

Khaki Fabric Makes a Name for Itself

World War II marked a turning point for the company's khaki fabric. During the war, Galey & Lord began selling khaki to the U.S. military. The trademark Camerton Army Cloth became the standard issue for uniforms. Thus, the company gained a reputation as the "King of Khaki," and Galey & Lord maintained its position as a leader in the khaki market into the 1990s. The company sold 75 million yards of the fabric in 1996. Manufacturers used 70 percent of that khaki for men's wear. In the past, only consumers 45 years old and older wore khaki. By 1996, though, 15- through 20-year-olds sported khaki, too.

Khaki itself changed a lot through the decades, especially with the advent of business casual wear. Modern khaki fabrics came in a variety of colors such as tan, putty, olive, black, navy, sage, and chocolate, and Galey & Lord manufactured about 70 percent of its khaki with special sueded or napped finishes in 1996. One thing about khaki that remained constant, however, was the fabric's competitive pricing. "Khaki is a category," explained Galey & Lord vice president Cheryl Blanchette in the *Daily News Record.* "It has staying power, and the fashion influence is driving it. It is really being driven by consumers looking for an alternative to denim. The overall popularity of khaki is in the casualization of America. The young generation has always liked denim and now is looking for an alternative. The fashion influence of khaki is big. There are a lot of new players in khaki apparel." Some of Galey & Lord's khaki customers in 1996 included Calvin Klein, Ralph Lauren, Tommy Hilfiger, Guess, Polo Jeans, Liz Claiborne, the Gap, Banana Republic, L.L. Bean, and Land's End.

Galey & Lord as a Part of Burlington Industries

Shortly after the end of World War II, J. Spencer Love, creator of Burlington Industries, purchased Camerton Mills— and Galey & Lord as part of the acquisition. Burlington manufactured fine cotton and cotton-blended fabrics under the Galey & Lord name, so blended fabrics became synonymous with Galey & Lord. The company remained a division of Burlington Industries until 1987 when Asher Edelman threatened a takeover of the company. Burlington management engineered a leveraged buyout of Galey & Lord to fend off the attempt. The

Company Perspectives:

Galey & Lord, Inc., is a leading developer, manufacturer, and marketer of fabrics for apparel and home furnishings. The company is a major producer of woven 100-percent cotton fabrics as well as cotton-blended fabrics used in the apparel sportswear market and has been a leader in producing and marketing value-added fabrics. The company principally sells fabrics to well-known manufacturers of sportswear for use in the production of men's, women's, and children's pants and shorts and to manufacturers of commercial uniforms. . . . The company is the only vertical producer of corduroy in the United States and also produces fabrics for the uniform trade. Galey & Lord Home Fashion Fabrics manufactures and markets fabrics used in home furnishings, including comforters, bedspreads, and curtains. The company's products are produced at six manufacturing facilities located in North Carolina, South Carolina, and Georgia and six manufacturing facilities located in Piedras Negras, Mexico. Its principal sales location is New York City, and it has branch offices in Los Angeles, San Francisco, and Dallas. The company's dedication to developing and producing high-quality, value-added fabrics and garments has earned it a reputation for being a premier supplier to the apparel and home furnishings marketplace.

division was spun off to a Burlington executive—Arthur Wiener—for $150 million. Citicorp Venture Capital financed the spinoff and retained 39 percent of the new company's shares. Wiener became chief executive officer of the now independent Galey & Lord, headquartered in New York City and Greensboro, North Carolina. The company's strategy for the future involved manufacturing fabrics that were made differently than those of competitors by experimenting with dyeing and finishing. Wiener eventually made Galey & Lord a public company in 1992.

That year the company also created a new synthetic fabrics division. A converting operation under the direction of Edward Delfoe, the division supplied dyed and printed synthetic fabrics to Galey & Lord customers. The company established a batch dyeing facility at its Society Hill, South Carolina, plant to print and dye polyester/rayon, acrylic, and wool blends, mainly for two-piece dressing.

Corduroy Makes a Comeback, 1990s

In 1993 Galey & Lord once again saw a trend emerging in corduroy. The fabric once popular in the 1970s began to regain acceptance after falling from favor with consumers in the 1980s. Corduroy sales for the company rose 7 percent in 1993 and remained strong in 1994 when clothing manufacturers began offering more five-pocket jeans in corduroy. By 1996 more and more consumers considered the fabric another good alternative to denim, causing a resurgence in its prominence.

At this time Galey & Lord was the only vertically integrated corduroy manufacturer in the United States, and the company

produced a very different corduroy than in the past. For example, the fabric became available in a wider range of colors and textures. Softness became a priority for corduroy. Consumer tastes dictated that eight-wale corduroy replace 14-wale corduroy (unless the 14-wale fabric was really soft), and four- or six-wale corduroy became the fabric of choice for fashion items. Alternate ribbing also varied the look of the fabric now, and the wearing season of corduroy lengthened as well. Although corduroy pants remained a staple throughout the fall and winter seasons, corduroy shorts became popular as an item for spring wardrobes.

Galey & Lord received substantial business in the United States and Europe from the sale of its corduroy. In 1996 the company saw a 30 percent increase in its corduroy business. As Bob McCormack, president of apparel fabric marketing for Galey & Lord told the *Daily News* in early 1997: "We see a very optimistic future for corduroy. . . . The biggest growth is in the men's area." Buyers of Galey & Lord corduroy included Levi, Lee, Wrangler, Guess Mossimo, Penney, and the Gap.

Printed Fabrics

In 1994, Galey & Lord purchased the decorative prints division of Burlington Industries. This acquisition marked the company's entry into the non-apparel fabric market. Renamed Galey & Lord Home Fashion Fabrics, the new subsidiary supplied home decorator fabrics for bedspreads, comforters, and curtains. The company also launched Group II, a second printed apparel fabrics division. Galey & Lord Prints, the company's first such unit, printed on polyester and rayon blends or on 100-percent rayon. This new division printed on 100-percent cotton—and limited rayon challis—for the women's, men's, and children's wear markets. Galey & Lord executives appointed Leon Hecht and Joe Richards, both from Cranston Apparel Fabrics Company (a division of Galey & Lord's competitor Cranston Print Works) as heads of Group II. Galey & Lord located both the first division and Group II at its specialty plant in Society Hill, South Carolina. Late in 1994, Wiener explained to *WWD* that "we feel the print market is beginning to turn around, and the new division gives us additional products with which to address the market and pick up some additional."

Despite Wiener's optimism, printed fabrics did poorly for the year. In the middle of 1995, industry analysts predicted a "violent shakeout" in the printed fabrics industry, but they also anticipated an upswing the following year. Nevertheless, by the fourth quarter of 1995, Galey & Lord announced the closing of its printed apparel fabrics business. Conditions in this segment of the industry had been deteriorating since 1992. Raw material costs rose consistently during this time; the market remained soft, and low-price imports heightened existing competition.

Ironically, sales volumes for printed fabrics increased during this time; however, weak operating results ate away Galey & Lord's profit margins. Sales in 1994, for example, totaled $30.1 million for printed fabrics—6.7 percent of net sales. Yet the company sustained $9.4 million in operating losses that year. Likewise in 1995 sales in this area again amounted to 6.7 percent of sales—$33.8 million—but operating losses reached $13.4 million. In fact, losses for printed apparel in the first nine months ending in June 1995 showed losses of $9.7 million compared to an operating profit of $37.3 million for the apparel, woven apparel, and home furnishings divisions. As Wiener explained in the *Daily News Record,* "The losses had become too large to justify continuing the businesses without a firm belief that a turnaround could be completed near-term."

In addition to the operating losses, Galey & Lord expended $14 or $15 million more to close the divisions. The company also laid off 450 workers, most from the Society Hill plant in South Carolina .and some from the sales office in Greensboro, North Carolina. Executives from the printed apparel divisions—Hecht, Richards, and Maria Damiano—left the company.

Ron Loeser, a partner with the converter Omega Textiles, summed up the situation in *WWD:* "It's really scary what's happening. When a company with the resources like Galey & Lord decides it can't make it in the print business, there are some serious problems with it, the overall business." David Caplan, chief executive officer of another converter Metro Fabrics, agreed: "I hate to see any of the competition go out of business. Good healthy competition is important. Arthur Wiener is a tremendously bright man who runs a fantastic company. . . . This is a step backward for the industry."

At the heart of these concerns was the need for better margins among manufacturers. Demand for prints remained strong during this time as was evidenced by Galey & Lord's sales figures, but the business itself shifted. Operating costs grew as the prices of raw materials rose domestically, which encouraged the purchase of imported goods. The implementation of GATT further cultivated import use since access to U.S. markets expanded with the elimination of textile and apparel import quotas for several countries by the year 2005.

Wrinkle-Free Fabrics

However disappointing the performance of printed apparel, the showing by Galey & Lord's wrinkle-free fabrics compensated at least to a small degree. In 1995 Galey & Lord dominated this market with 100-percent cotton fabrics. Wrinkle-free fabrics accounted for 75 percent of Galey & Lord's men's wear sales and 14 percent of women's wear sales. One of Wiener's goals became expanding this area. As he revealed to *WWD:* "Developing more wrinkle-free products to fit into women's wear manufacturing and women's wear garments is one of the key challenges we've given to our merchants and product development people." Customers for wrinkle-free fabrics included Hagar, Levi Strauss, and Farah.

Mid-1990s Acquisitions

In 1995 Galey & Lord also signed a letter of agreement to purchase the South Carolina textile firm Graniteville Company, a subsidiary of Triarc Companies, Inc. Though this would have doubled the size of Galey & Lord, the company canceled the merger due to undesirable conditions within the retail, textile, and apparel sectors. Fees and expenses associated with the aborted venture totaled $1.6 million.

Nevertheless, Galey & Lord would successfully acquire Dimmit Industries the following year. Dimmit Industries sewed and finished pants and shorts for the casual wear market. Galey & Lord purchased the company from Farah for $22.8 million and acquired six manufacturing facilities in Piedras Negras, Mexico, in the process. These plants were to produce men's slacks and shorts from Galey & Lord fabrics, launching the company into the business of apparel manufacturing. Galey & Lord, in effect, became a full-service supplier to its established customer base after the acquisition. The company used its fabrics to make garments—apparel made in North American Free Trade Alliance (NAFTA) countries as opposed to the Far East—for its established customer base, thereby increasing its business at its six manufacturing plants in North Carolina, South Carolina, and Georgia. Bob McCormack, a Galey & Lord executive vice president, explained the company's rationale in *WWD:* "We are trying to protect the business we have in the United States by better servicing our customer base. As competition from overseas intensifies, we will be able to offer them a complete package."

The company established a new subsidiary—G & L Service Company, North America, Inc.—to run operations in Mexico. In 1996, the six Mexican plants operated at full capacity. Galey & Lord planned expansions to the facilities in 1996 and 1997.

Innovations in Finishing

Galey & Lord had long been associated with innovations in fabric. The company historically dyed and finished fabrics to differentiate items that it produced from its competitors' goods. In 1996 Galey & Lord purchase special wet and face finishing equipment to further its reputation in quality yarn-dyed fabrics despite the expense. "It's not a question of whether we can afford this development work," said Wiener in the *Daily News Record.* "We can't afford not to do it."

The company's strategy for the future in 1997 was to continue to develop its practice of unique dyeing and finishing. It also planned to produce better and different fabrics of world-class quality and to change fabrics as dictated by market demands. Above all, Galey & Lord intended to grow. "We have four internal goals to execute," Wiener told the *Daily News Record.* "We will continue to grow our core fabric business in the Carolinas and Georgia, with product development, to supply apparel yard goods to domestic, NAFTA, and international customers. We will expand our garment business to use those fabrics. . . . [W]e are constantly looking at . . . acquisitions. If we see the right one, we will do it. We will be in the Pacific Rim in a joint venture. There are 4.5 billion people in Asia, and 700 million can buy our products. We must find a way to participate in this market. . . . We will be larger through acquisition and growth. G&L's good growth pattern won't be reversed. How big we will be depends on what comes along that is right."

Principal Subsidiaries

G & L Service Company, North America, Inc.; Galey & Lord Home Fashion Fabrics; Galey & Lord Synthetic Fabrics Division.

Further Reading

Eliot, Edward, ''Galey & Lord Raises Effluent Treatment to a Higher Level,'' *Textile World,* May 1995, p. 73.

''G & L to Buy Six Factories from Farah,'' *WWD,* May 21, 1996, p. 15.

''Galey & Lord Forms Division,'' *Daily News Record,* July 14, 1992, p. 10.

''Galey & Lord Launches Its Second Unit for Prints,'' *WWD,* September 13, 1994, p. 18.

''Galey & Lord to Close Two Apparel Print Units in the Fourth Quarter; Will Take $14–$15 Million Charge in September Quarter,'' *Daily News Record,* July 21, 1995, p. 3.

Maycumber, S. Gray, ''King of Khaki and Court of Corduroy,'' *Daily News Record,* February 17, 1997, p. 58.

McNamara, Michael, ''Galey & Lord's Strategy: More Wrinkle-Free,'' *WWD,* February 9, 1994, p. 22.

——, ''Converters: Girding for a Fallout,'' *WWD,* July 25, 1995, p. 10.

—Charity Anne Dorgan

Gander Mountain, Inc.

P.O. Box 128
Highway W
Wilmot, Wisconsin 53129
U.S.A.
(414) 862-2331
. Fax: (414) 862-2330

Public Company
Incorporated: 1960
Employees: 1,378
Sales: $180 million (1996)
Stock Exchanges: NASDAQ
SICs: 5961 Catalog & Mail Order Houses; 5941 Sporting
Goods & Bicycle Shops

Gander Mountain, Inc. has been one of America's leading specialty companies in the hunting, camping, and fishing equipment industry. From 1960 until 1995, the firm was the leading catalog vendor of hunting accessories and supplies, and was one of the premier suppliers of hiking and outerwear clothing. Operating 17 retail stores, mostly located in the Midwestern United States, Gander Mountain reported sales of $246 million in 1994. Unfortunately, the company has fallen on hard times and has been forced to file for reorganization under Chapter 11 of the federal bankruptcy law. Having sold most of its catalog division and its retail stores, Gander Mountain management reached a joint reorganization plan with Holiday Companies, a privately-owned Bloomington, Minnesota-based wholesale and retail supplier of camping and sporting goods, to continue operating its retail stores under the auspices of Holiday until Gander Mountain can re-establish itself as a viable, independently operating company.

Early History

Gander Mountain, Inc. was founded in 1960 by Robert Sturgis, an avid outdoorsman and lifelong resident of the state of Wisconsin. Living in the town of Wilmot, a rather isolated community within the state, Sturgis, along with his fellow hunters, was unhappy with his inability to get high-quality hunting accessories and equipment without having to drive a hundred miles to the nearest sportsman retail store. As a result, Sturgis decided to open a small store in the center of Wilmot that would market shooting supplies to gun owners and dealers by mail order. Not surprised by the response to his simple marketing techniques, Sturgis soon began to mail catalogs directly to consumers. By 1965, the budding entrepreneur had built an impressive reputation as a supplier of high-quality shooting equipment to hunters across the Midwest.

Sturgis discovered that his mail catalog business was an overwhelming success. He marketed a wide range of products for the serious sportsman, including shotguns, an impressive array of unusual cartridges for high-powered hunting rifles, sophisticated archery equipment, and much more. As Gander Mountain's image grew, sportsmen from as far away as Montana and upstate New York began to order from the company's catalogs. In fact, nothing seemed like it would prevent the continued growth of his business. By 1968, Sturgis had opened a retail store in Wilmot to sell hard-to-get items to local hunters.

Unfortunately, in 1968 legislation passed by the United States Congress prohibited the sale of firearms through a mail order or catalog business. Both senators and representatives were responding to the assassinations of the 1960s, including President John F. Kennedy, Robert Kennedy, and Martin Luther King, Jr., and the public's perception that obtaining a gun was easily done, and that individuals who were unstable might be able to procure a firearm through a mail-order catalog if a retail store had refused to sell them one. As a result, Gander Mountain's catalog sale of hunting weapons, including shotguns, high-powered deer hunting rifles, and small arms used for target sport, was discontinued. Sales of firearms from the catalog were one of the fastest-growing sources of revenue for the company. As it happened, the company was forced to expand and re-orient its product line to include more items for fishing and camping.

From the late 1960s onward, primarily due to the federal curtailment of the sale of firearms through mail-order catalogs, Gander Mountain began to experience the volatility of the outdoor recreational equipment market. The company had been slow to adapt to the changes required by the 1968 federal legislation, and had turned initially to the sale of fishing rods, reels, bait, nets, lures, and other sundry items to replace the lost catalog market for firearms. But management soon discovered that the sale of fishing equipment was seasonal, with high revenues during the spring and summer months, and low revenues during the autumn and winter. To augment the cyclical nature of its sales, the company then decided to expand its catalog sales to include a wide variety of camping equipment and outerwear, including tents, lanterns, portable stoves, sleeping bags, and clothing such as shirts, woolen pants, boots, coats, and socks. But the demand for camping equipment was also seasonal, mostly from the latter spring to the early days of autumn, and management began to fear that the company needed an even greater expansion of its product line to garner a steady cash flow for its operations.

The entire decade of the 1970s was dedicated to finding the right mix of products by the Gander Mountain management. Small variations in fishing equipment, camping equipment, and clothing did not, however, raise the volume of catalog sales. The expansion of the store in Wilmot, Wisconsin, to provide a larger selection of items for local customers did not seem to help either, since the company had based its reputation as a supplier of firearms through catalog sales. As the decade drew to a close, Gander Mountain found itself growing deeper in debt.

Transition and Growth During the 1980s

Earnings and sales continued to fall during the early part of the 1980s, and before long Gander Mountain was unable to pay its growing debts. Management had no other recourse but to file for reorganization in the U.S. Bankruptcy Court. In 1984, an entrepreneur named Ralph Freitag, who had lengthy experience in the outdoor retail market, along with some of the individuals within the company's management, decided to purchase Gander Mountain and revive its fortunes.

The new owners had conceived a concerted strategy to develop Gander Mountain into one of the premier outdoor recreational equipment suppliers. Their first move was to take the company public in order to raise capital for both expansion activities and the pursuit of acquisition candidates. Almost immediately, the initial public offering on the over-the-counter (OTC) market raised $9.2 million. Unexpectedly, however, Gander Mountain executives were approached by several buyers within the year. The reason for the unsolicited approaches was a pair of highly unprofitable acquisitions made earlier by Gander Mountain. Master Animal Care, a pet care products company, and Western Ranchman Outfitters, a western clothing retailer, were not adding any earnings to Gander Mountain's coffers. But potential buyers saw the potential profit of selling these holdings separately, along with Gander Mountain.

In order to ward off any future hostile takeovers of the company, management decided to divest itself of both Western Ranchman and Master Animal Care, and concentrate more on its core business of hunting, fishing, and camping. The second move made by management, therefore, was to expand beyond its mail-order catalog business. Having operated one lone retail outlet at its headquarters location in Wilmot, Wisconsin, management was convinced that more retail stores based on the same format would not only be successful, but lead to greater opportunities for expansion. In 1987, the company opened its first offsite retail store in Brookfield, Wisconsin, and shortly thereafter new stores were also opened in Appleton, Eau Claire, and Madison. The company's overall plan included the opening of a string of retail stores within a 300-mile radius that stretched from western Wisconsin to north central Illinois.

Gander Mountain management believed it had discovered a market with hardly any competition. Executives within the company, including Freitag, thought that the only possible competitors within the outdoor recreational equipment market were Bass Pro Shops, located in Springfield, Missouri, and Cabela's Inc., a catalog company with only one retail shop. Although Cabela was the largest of the three companies, management at Gander Mountain remained confident that they could soon dominate the growing retail market.

The strategy behind Gander Mountain's expansion into the retail store market was simple to understand. Less than 10 percent of the market had been tapped during the mid- and late 1980s, including 31 million Americans who had fishing licenses, 16 million who described themselves as avid hunters, and nearly 50 million who went camping on a regular basis. The average customer was a male between 40 and 45 years of age, who had an above average income and was considered a hard-core outdoor sportsman. Gander Mountain had no intention of catering to the person who was buying fuchsia jogging suits or Nike running shoes, but wanted to focus on the avid outdoorsman who was knowledgeable about hunting or fishing equipment, and who took his hobby to the extreme. The strategy implemented by Gander Mountain management worked—from 1986 to 1989 sales increased from $41 million to $112 million.

The 1990s and Beyond

The early years of the new decade went well for Gander Mountain; in fact, some analysts would say that these few years were the best the company ever experienced. The solid growth in sales and increase in net income enabled management to arrange an impressive $50 million financing package. The arrangement, which included such high-profile and prestigious banks as Bank One Milwaukee, Firstar Bank Milwaukee, and LaSalle National Bank of Chicago, involved $30 million for working capital and $20 million for capital expenditures. Part of this money was used to expand the company's warehouse space in Wilmot, and also to expand its nearby office facility.

In 1992, Gander Mountain reported that just over 82 percent of its total sales volume was due to catalog sales. During the same year, the company mailed 35 million catalogs to customers in the United States, Canada, and other countries, primarily in Western Europe. The average customer sale from its catalog amounted to $80. Yet management was determined to increase its catalog sales, and to this end more specialized catalogs were mailed to prospective customers who favored particular sports, such as archery. According to Freitag and his executive team, carving out more specialized markets was considered crucial to the growth of the company.

The $50 million financing package also helped to create more jobs. The peak season for Gander Mountain sales, in both retail stores and the catalog, was the months of November and

December. During those two months, the company increased the number of its employees to approximately 1,200, including between 60 and 65 people working in each of its retail stores. With the infusion of new capital, management decided to retain some of the employees hired during the holiday season, in order to augment its 600 person staff during the offseason. One of the largest employers in Kenosha County, Wisconsin, Gander Mountain management thought that an increase in the number of employees at its retail stores would help increase sales during the offseason. Dollar for dollar, in-store sales were more profitable than catalog sales during 1991 and 1992, and a staff that knew the details of outdoor sportsman activities was believed to help create even more sales.

In the fall of 1992, with every indicator pointing toward continuing success, Gander Mountain decided to raise prices in its general catalogs while at the same time offering fewer reduced-price products such as hunting and fishing equipment in its sales catalogs. The reasoning behind the price increase was that profit margins had been stagnant for a number of years. More importantly, however, management did not think that its customers were price-sensitive due to the high quality of Gander Mountain merchandise. The strategy was a complete catastrophe from which the company never recovered. By the time management was able to correct its mistake, a significant amount of damage had been done. Net income for fiscal 1993 was reported at a mere $63,000, in contrast to $2.44 million at the end of fiscal 1992. To compensate for the debacle, management reached an agreement with Goldman Sachs & Company to sell a 27 percent interest in Gander Mountain for $20 million. The investment was used to expand the company's retail stores, the most recent having been built in Wausau, Wisconsin, and St. Cloud, Minnesota.

Even with the new investment, however, Gander Mountain could not regain its lost catalog-based revenues. Catalog sales continued to drop, with no sign of a resurgence on the horizon. In addition, the company's catalog operation began to suffer from special cost pressures, including a rise in postal rates. Gander Mountain responded by automating its catalog operation, sharpening its catalog marketing techniques, and focusing more on specialty catalogs for particular outdoor sports, but all to no avail. Catalog sales were not coming back, and the company began to lose money on the operation.

In early 1995, with sales decreasing, and Gander Mountain cash needs exceeding the amount of money both from sales and its credit arrangements with banks, the company decided to sell selected catalog assets to Cabela, Inc., a large catalog marketer of hunting, fishing, and camping equipment located in Sidney, Nebraska. For $35 million, Cabela purchased Gander Mountain's customer list and selected inventory. Still, the company was losing money and unable to meet its debts. As a result, after lengthy negotiations throughout 1996, Gander Mountain management decided to file a joint plan of reorganization under chapter 11 of the Federal Bankruptcy Court. This plan included the sale of 12 of the company's 17 stores to Holiday Companies, a retail sports store operator, and the agreement to pay Holiday back for the stores when Gander regained its financial health and resumed operations. Until that time, the stores acquired by Holiday would operate under the Gander Mountain name.

At the beginning of 1997, Gander Mountain management, in close cooperation with the executive team from Holiday Companies, were working to bring Gander Mountain back to operation. Whether or not this could be done depended on Gander Mountain management's ability to recapture the highly specialized niche market that it so carelessly had squandered away.

Principal Subsidiaries

GMO, Inc.; GRS, Inc.

Further Reading

Byrne, Harlan S., "Gander Mountain," *Barrons,* June 8, 1992, pp. 40–41.

"Catalog Business Is Sold to Cabela's for $35 Million," *The Wall Street Journal,* May 22, 1996, p. A12(E).

"Default Waiver Extended, But Stock Price Falls 24%," *The Wall Street Journal,* April 2, 1996, p. C19(E).

"Gander Mountain Inc., with Net Down 45%, Ends Talks to Sell Unit," *The Wall Street Journal,* February 12, 1996, p. B10A(E).

"Gander Mountain to Sell Its Catalogue Operation," *The New York Times,* p. C3(N).

Kaderabek, Denise, "With $50 Million in Hand, Gander Mountain Heads Up the Growth Trail," *Business Journal of Milwaukee,* January 1, 1993, pp. 14–15.

Kass, Mark, "Gander Mountain, Inc.," *Business Journal of Milwaukee,* January 9, 1993, p. 11.

——, "Gander Mountain, Inc.," *Business Journal of Milwaukee,* January 8, 1994, p. 11.

—Thomas Derdak

The Gillette Company

Prudential Tower Building
Boston, Massachusetts 02199
U.S.A.
(617) 421-7000
Fax: (617) 421-7123

Public Company
Incorporated: 1901 as American Safety Razor Company
Employees: 44,100
Sales: $9.70 billion (1996)
Stock Exchanges: New York Boston Midwest Pacific
London Frankfurt Zürich
SICs: 2844 Perfumes, Cosmetics & Other Toilet
Preparations; 2899 Chemicals & Chemical
Preparations, Not Elsewhere Classified; 3421 Cutlery;
3634 Electric Housewares & Fans; 3843 Dental
Equipment & Supplies; 3951 Pens, Mechanical
Pencils & Parts; 3952 Lead Pencils, Crayons &
Artists' Materials; 5064 Electrical Appliances,
Television & Radio Sets

The Gillette Company is the world leader in the men's grooming product category as well as in certain women's grooming products. Although more than half of company profits are still derived from shaving equipment—the area in which the company started—Gillette has also attained the top spots worldwide in writing instruments (Paper Mate, Parker, and Waterman brands) and correction products (Liquid Paper), toothbrushes and other oral care products (Oral-B), and alkaline batteries (Duracell products, which generate almost one-fourth of company profits). Gillette maintains 64 manufacturing facilities in 27 countries, and its products are sold in more than 200 countries and territories, with more than 60 percent of sales occurring outside the United States.

Entrepreneurial Beginnings

One summer morning in 1895, an ambitious traveling salesman found that the edge of his straight razor had dulled. King

Gillette later said that the idea for an entirely new kind of razor, with a disposable blade, flashed into his mind as he looked in irritation at his dull blade.

King Gillette had been searching for the right product, one that had to be used—and replaced—regularly, around which to build a business. His innovation in shaving technology was just such a product. Another safety razor, the Star, was already on the market at the time but, like the straight razor it was meant to replace, its blade needed stropping before each use and eventually had to be professionally honed. Gillette envisioned an inexpensive, double-edged blade that could be clamped over a handle, used until it was dull, and then discarded.

Gillette spent the next six years trying to perfect his safety razor. Scientists and toolmakers he consulted were pessimistic, and thought the idea impractical. Gillette, 40 years old at the time and a successful salesman, inventor, and writer, did not give up. In 1901 he joined forces with William Nickerson, a Massachusetts Institute of Technology-educated machinist. Nickerson developed production processes to make Gillette's idea a reality, while Gillette formed the American Safety Razor Company to raise the estimated $5,000 they needed to begin manufacturing the razor. Gillette became president of the company and head of a three-man directorate. Production of the razor began early in 1903.

The renamed Gillette Safety Razor Company began advertising its product in October 1903, with the first ad appearing in *Systems Magazine*. The company sold 51 razor sets at $5 each and an additional 168 blades—originally at 20 for $1—that first year.

In 1904 Gillette received a patent on the safety razor; sales rose to 90,884 razors and 123,648 blades that year. The following year the company bought a six-story building in South Boston. By 1906 the company had paid its first cash dividend. During the years before World War I Gillette steadily increased earnings through print advertisements, emphasizing that with his razor men could shave themselves under any conditions without cutting or irritation.

At the same time, Gillette was expanding abroad. He opened his first foreign office, a London sales branch, in 1905. By 1909

Company Perspectives:

The Gillette Company is a globally focused consumer products company which seeks competitive advantage in quality, value-added personal care and personal use products. We compete in three large, worldwide businesses: personal grooming products, stationery products, and small electrical appliances. As a company, we share skills and resources among business units to optimize performance. We are committed to a plan of sustained sales and profit growth which recognizes and balances both short- and long-term objectives.

he had established manufacturing plants in Paris, Montreal, Berlin, and Leicester, England, and offices in France and Hamburg, Germany. By 1923, foreign business accounted for about 30 percent of Gillette's sales.

In 1910 King Gillette decided to sell a substantial portion of his controlling share of the company to the company's major investor, John Joyce. Gillette had succeeded in fighting off challenges for control of the company from Joyce in the past, but this time he took approximately $900,000 and bowed out. Gillette retained the title of president and frequently visited foreign branches, but he no longer played an active role in company management. Joyce was made vice-president, a position he used to manage day-to-day operations. When Joyce died in 1916, his longtime friend, Edward Aldred, a New York investment banker, bought out the Gillette shares left to Joyce's estate and took control of the company. Aldred remained on Joyce's management team.

Razors Supplied to Soldiers in World War I Increased Customer Base

During World War I the U.S. government ordered 3.5 million razors and 36 million blades to supply all its troops. In order to meet military supply schedules, shifts worked around the clock and Gillette hired over 500 new employees. Gillette thus introduced a huge pool of potential customers to the still-new idea of self-shaving with a safety razor. After the war, ex-servicemen needed blades to fit the razors they had been issued in the service.

In 1921 Gillette's patent on the safety razor expired, but the company was ready for the change. It introduced the ''new improved'' Gillette razor, which sold at the old price, and entered the low-priced end of the market with the old-style razor, renamed the Silver Brownie razor, priced at only $1. Gillette also gave away razor handles as premiums with other products, developing customers for the more profitable blades. Expansion and growth continued.

The company also continued to expand abroad. In 1922 Gillette became royal purveyor to the prince of Wales and in 1924 to King Gustav V of Sweden. More favorable publicity followed when the Paris office gave Charles Lindbergh a Gillette Gold Traveler set the day after he completed the first transatlantic flight.

By the end of the decade, Gillette faced its first major setback. Auto Strop Safety Razor Company, owned by Henry J. Gaisman, filed suit for patent infringement after Gillette produced a new blade using a continuous-strip process similar to one originally presented to Gillette by Gaisman.

Gillette resolved the suit by merging with Auto Strop, only to face another problem. When Gaisman checked the company's financial records, he found that Gillette had over-reported its earnings for the past five years by about $3 million. Confidence in Gillette fell, as did its stock. From a high of $125 early in 1929, the stock bottomed out after the disclosure, at $18.

The crisis led to management reorganization. King Gillette resigned as nominal president, and died 14 months later at age 77. Gaisman became the new chairman of Gillette and Gerard B. Lambert, son of the founder of the Lambert Pharmacal Company—makers of Listerine—and a former manager there, came out of retirement to become president of Gillette. Lambert agreed to work for no salary with the guarantee of company stock if he could bring earnings up $5 per share.

Under Lambert, the Gillette Company made a bold advertising move: it admitted that the new blade it had brought out in 1930 was of poor quality. The company then announced what became its most recognizable product, the Gillette Blue Blade. Made under Gaisman's strip-processing method, the Blue Blade promised uniformly high quality.

The Blue Blade kept Gillette the leader in the field, but profits remained disappointing throughout the Great Depression, as men increasingly turned to bargain blades. Lambert resigned in 1934 without meeting his goal of improving earnings and without receiving compensation from the company. He was replaced by a former Auto Strop executive, Samuel C. Stampleman, who had no more success. With profits at their lowest since 1915, the board of directors appointed Joseph P. Spang Jr. president in December 1938 in an effort to invigorate the company.

Sports Advertising Boosted Sales Beginning in the Late 1930s

Spang immediately restored the company's advertising budget, which had been cut to save money. Under this policy, Gillette's trademark sports advertising developed. Spang purchased radio broadcast rights to the 1939 World Series for $100,000. Despite a short series, in which the Cincinnati Reds lost four straight games to the New York Yankees, sales of Gillette's World Series Special razor sets were more than four times company estimates.

This success encouraged more sports advertising. By 1942 the events Gillette sponsored were grouped together as the ''Gillette Cavalcade of Sports.'' Although it eventually included the Orange Bowl, the Sugar Bowl, and the Kentucky Derby, in addition to the World Series and the All-Star game, the ''Cavalcade of Sports'' became best known for bringing boxing to American men. Spang attributed Gillette's continuing success to the sports advertising program, and sports programs remained an important vehicle for Gillette advertising.

During World War II foreign production and sales declined, but domestic production more than made up for those losses.

Almost the entire production of razors and blades went to the military. In addition, Gillette manufactured fuel-control units for military-plane carburetors. The backlog of civilian demand after the war led to consecutive record sales until 1957.

Diversification Began Following World War II

During the profitable postwar period Spang began to broaden Gillette's product line. The company had introduced Gillette Brushless shaving cream, its first, nonrazor, nonblade product, in 1936. In 1948 Spang began to diversify by acquiring other companies when he bought the Toni Company, a firm that made home permanents. In 1955 Spang purchased Paper Mate Company, a manufacturer of ballpoint pens.

When Spang retired in 1956, Carl Gilbert became CEO. During the 1960s Gillette faced a threat to its bread-and-butter product, the double-edged blade. In 1962, the English Wilkinson Sword Company began to export stainless-steel blades to the United States. Wilkinson had developed a polymer coating that made it possible to put an edge on stainless steel, which resists corrosion, increasing the number of shaves from a blade.

Two of Gillette's domestic competitors—Eversharp, which made Schick blades, and American Safety Razor—rushed versions of the stainless-steel blade onto the market. Gillette, the market leader, was left behind without a stainless-steel blade of its own to compete, and profits slumped in 1963 and 1964. Gillette recovered much of its market share through a simple strategy: developing a better blade and initiating an aggressive advertising campaign that emphasized quality. After its own blade hit the market, Gillette's market share stabilized at 60–65 percent, compared to 70–75 percent before the challenge.

Vincent C. Ziegler, head of the company's North American razor operation, had developed the razor-marketing strategy, and when Gillette reorganized on a product line basis in July 1964, Ziegler was named president. He took over as chairman of the board in 1965. The stainless-steel blade controversy taught Ziegler not to rely on one product. He saw Gillette as "a diversified consumer products company," and promoted both internal development of new product lines and acquisition of other companies.

During the later 1960s Gillette pursued this strategy actively, but with mixed results. A new line of Toni hair-coloring products failed, as did Earth Born shampoos, luxury perfumes, and a line of small electronic items such as digital watches, calculators, smoke alarms, and fire extinguishers. Many of the companies Gillette acquired, such as Eve of Roma high-fashion perfume, Buxton leather goods, Welcome Wagon, and Hydroponic Chemical Company—which produced Hyponex plant foods—never found the fit with Gillette comfortable. The acquisitions led to shrinking profit margins.

Gillette did have some successes. The Trac II twin-blade shaving system introduced in 1971 was a success, and the 1970 acquisition of the French S.T. Dupont gave Gillette the disposable Cricket lighter, which Gillette introduced to the U.S. market. By 1971 Gillette had four domestic divisions: the Safety Razor Division; the Toiletries Division, which featured Right Guard deodorant and antiperspirant; the Personal Care Division; and the Paper Mate division.

By the mid-1970s Ziegler was ready to retire, and began to groom outsider Edward Gelsthorpe to succeed him, but Gelsthorpe left Gillette to join United Brands, now Chiquita Brands, 15 months after his appointment as president. Ziegler next tapped Colman M. Mockler Jr. to replace him when he retired in 1975. Mockler had been at Gillette since 1957 and had an entirely different background and style than Ziegler. He had come up from the financial end of the business rather than through sales.

Diversification Moderated Starting in the Mid-1970s

Mockler moderated Ziegler's diversification policy. He concentrated on a limited number of promising markets, particularly high-volume, repeat-purchase consumer items, selling Ziegler's least successful acquisitions—including Buxton in 1977, Welcome Wagon in 1978, and Hyponex and the Autopoint mechanical pencil business in 1979—and pumping money into promising companies compatible with already-existing manufacturing or distribution capabilities. Mockler stuck with the Cricket disposable lighter even though high introductory marketing costs and a costly price war with the Bic Pen Corporation, owned by the French Société Bic, kept it from showing a profit.

Mockler also held on to the West German Braun company. Ziegler had bought the family-owned business in 1967 to gain entry to the European electric-shaver market and for the quality and style of its small-appliance designs. Mockler pared Braun's less profitable lines and rode out a Justice Department antitrust suit against the acquisition. The suit eventually prevented Gillette from introducing Braun shavers in the U.S. market before 1984. Mockler also increased Gillette's advertising budget and undertook companywide cost-cutting measures in all other divisions. Before the results of those policies could be seen, Mockler faced other problems. Growing fear of fluorocarbons, which deplete the earth's ozone layer, affected sales of products in aerosol cans during the 1970s.

Gillette eventually developed new product-delivery systems to replace aerosol cans, such as nonaerosol pumps and roll-ons, for Gillette's already-established product line, and he put advertising dollars behind the products, which included Right Guard and Soft & Dri deodorants and Adorn and White Rain hair sprays. He also started development of a new deodorant product, Dry Idea, which feels dry when applied. Dry Idea was launched in 1978 after two years of development at a cost of $118 million. It quickly recovered a quarter of the deodorant market for Gillette.

Gillette faced a more serious threat from Bic. In the 1960s Bic came to the United States with a 19¢ disposable pen, which made dramatic cuts into sales of Gillette's 98¢ Paper Mate pens. In the 1970s Bic attacked Gillette's Cricket disposable lighter with its own disposable lighter. Since the Cricket was more expensive to make—it had more moving parts than the Bic—Gillette was losing the price war. Lighters and pens, however, produced only 15 percent of Gillette's pretax profits; razor blades accounted for 71 percent of profits. When Bic began producing disposable razors and purchased American Safety Razor, with its 13 percent of the blade market, from Personna and Gem blades, Gillette had to respond. Gillette countered by competing with Bic on price while emphasizing the higher quality of its products. Gillette brought out the Eraser Mate pen despite marketing studies that questioned demand for an erasable pen, and sales soared. By 1980 Gillette had improved profitability despite the attack by Bic.

Takeover Threats Dominated 1980s

Mockler's policies led to a higher profit margin and a surplus of cash. Some of this cash was used in 1984 when Gillette added oral care products to its product mix with the $188.5 million purchase of Oral-B Laboratories, Inc.—the leading maker of toothbrushes in the United States—from Cooper Laboratories, Inc. The excess cash, however, also led to a new threat in the mid-1980s: the threat of takeover. In 1986 Ronald O. Perelman, head of Revlon, offered $4.1 billion for Gillette. He was attracted by Gillette's well-known personal-care brands, the possibility of combining the sales and distribution systems of the two companies, and Gillette's expertise in marketing abroad.

Gillette rejected Revlon's offer of $65 a share and bought back stock from Perelman at $59.50 a share and paid some expenses, for a total of $558 million. Revlon made two other unsolicited requests to buy the company in 1987, both of which were refused by the Gillette board of directors.

In response to the takeover threats, Gillette reorganized top management; thinned out its workforce through layoffs; modernized its plants while shifting some production capacity to lower-cost locations; and sold many smaller and less profitable divisions.

That was not the end of the takeover threats. In early 1988 Coniston Partners announced that it had acquired approximately 6 percent of the company and was determined to replace four members of Gillette's 12-member board so it could influence company policy. Members of the partnership said they would actively seek offers to sell or dismantle Gillette if they managed to get representation on the board. Coniston Partners' battle to get shareholders' proxy rights was intense, but in 1988 Gillette came out on top with 52 percent of the votes for directors to Coniston's 48 percent. The matter was finally resolved when Gillette instituted a stock repurchase for all shareholders, which included 16 million of Coniston's 112 million shares at $45 a share.

Finally, in August 1989, Warren Buffett's Berkshire Hathaway bought $600 million of Gillette convertible preferred shares. The deal potentially placed 11 percent of Gillette's stock with Buffett, who had agreed to give the company the right of first refusal on the block, should he wish to sell it. The friendly agreement decreased the threat of takeover, though it tightened up cash flow at the company. Buffett's dividend was $52.5 million a year.

With takeover threats behind it and restructuring completed, Gillette returned to emphasizing its powerful brand names and its bread and butter, shaving products. While toiletries and cosmetics represented low-margin items and profitable stationery products accounted for only 9 percent of the company's total profits, razors and blades still accounted for a little over 70 percent of profits. Gillette brought in a new head of shaving operations, John W. Symons, formerly head of European opera-

tions, and developed new ad campaigns to emphasize the more profitable shaving systems over disposable shavers such as its own Good News.

In October 1989, Gillette unveiled the Sensor shaving system, which featured thinner blades mounted on springs by lasers so they could follow contours. The blades, to be used in a permanent shaving system, cost close to $200 million to develop and were launched simultaneously in the United States and Europe, backed by a $100 million advertising budget. Sensor's touted superior shave was a huge success with consumers, and the product garnered several awards. The Lady Sensor soon followed in 1992, with sales for both products exceeding $500 million that year.

1990s and Beyond

Gillette made another effort to expand its presence in shaving when it attempted to buy the U.S. and non-European operations of its old competitor, Wilkinson Sword, early in 1990. The Justice Department blocked the sale of Wilkinson's U.S. interests since Gillette controlled about half the U.S. market and Wilkinson was number-four in the market with about 3 percent. Also in 1990, as part of a realignment of its shaving and personal-care units in North America and Europe, Gillette sold its European skin and hair care operations to Nobel Consumer Goods AB, a division of Nobel Industries of Sweden, for $107 million.

Despite the Wilkinson setback, the 1990s proved to be extremely fruitful years for Gillette thanks to an aggressive program of new product development coupled with the pursuit of targeted acquisitions. Mockler, who had had a very successful term as CEO and chairman and who planned to retire at the end of 1991, died unexpectedly in January of that year. Alfred M. Zeien, Mockler's heir apparent who was president and chief operating officer, replaced Mockler in both of his positions. Also in 1991 Gillette launched another award-winning product, the Oral-B Indicator toothbrush, which had bristles that change color to show when a new toothbrush is needed. This popular feature was added to all Oral-B toothbrushes the following year.

Significant new product introductions and a major acquisition highlighted 1992. Gillette's personal-care product division launched the Gillette Series line of men's toiletries, which included 14 "high-performance" products in the deodorant/antiperspirant, shaving cream, and aftershave categories. The company announced the acquisition of Parker Pen Holdings Limited for £285 million ($484 million), with the deal being consummated in May 1993. The addition of the Parker brand to Gillette's Paper Mate and Waterman brands moved the company into the top position worldwide in writing instruments.

Late in 1993 Gillette took an after-tax charge of $164 million for a reorganization of its overseas operations, including the integration of Parker Pen facilities into Gillette's structure. About 2,000 jobs were eliminated as a result of the reorganization.

Just four years after the debut of Sensor, Gillette in late 1993 launched in continental Europe and Canada its next-generation shaving system, SensorExcel, which promised even closer and more comfortable shaving based on its skin guard made of "five soft, flexible microfins." After its successful debut, Sensor-

Excel was rolled out in Japan, England, and the United States in 1994. Other 1993 and 1994 product introductions included Braun's FlavorSelect coffeemaker; the Oral-B Advantage toothbrush, which was designed to remove plaque better than other toothbrushes; and Custom Plus men's and women's disposable razors with pivoting heads.

Gillette returned to acquisition mode in 1995 and 1996. In late 1995 Oral-B's position in Latin America was bolstered with the purchase of the Pro oral care line. Near the end of the year Gillette acquired Thermoscan Inc., a leader in infrared ear thermometers. Thermoscan promised to provide a base for Gillette to expand into the rapidly growing personal home diagnostic products area. Then in late 1996 the company made its largest acquisition ever when it paid $7.1 billion for Duracell International Inc., the world leader in alkaline batteries. Gillette thus added its first major product line since the purchase of Oral-B; in fact, batteries immediately became the company's second-leading product line in terms of sales, trailing only razors and blades. Duracell batteries had been underdistributed outside the United States, so Gillette planned to achieve sales growth by leveraging its existing marketing channels, which reached more than 200 countries by the mid-1990s. More immediately, the Duracell merger led Gillette to record a fourth quarter 1996 charge to operating expenses of $413 million to eliminate overlap between Gillette and Duracell operations.

In 1996 the company also launched more than 20 new products, including SensorExcel for Women. That year, a whopping 41 percent of Gillette sales came from products that debuted during the previous five years, a testament to the company's new product development strength. And an improvement on the SensorExcel was already in the works. Sales neared the $10 billion mark, as 1996 revenues were $9.7 billion, and net income—despite the Duracell charge—was a healthy $949 million. The company's commitment to developing innovative new products, to supporting those products through heavy ad-

vertising, and to seeking out appropriate acquisitions, all seemed certain to keep Gillette on the cutting edge of consumer products.

Principal Operating Units

Gillette North Atlantic Group; International Group; Duracell North Atlantic Group; Diversified Group.

Further Reading

Adams, Russell B. Jr., *King C. Gillette: The Man and His Wonderful Shaving Device,* Boston: Little, Brown, 1978.

Bulkeley, William M., "Duracell Pact Gives Gillette an Added Source of Power," *Wall Street Journal,* September 13, 1996, pp. A3, A4.

Chakravarty, Subrata N., " 'We Had to Change the Playing Field,' " *Forbes,* February 4, 1991, p. 82.

Donlon, J. P., "An Iconoclast in a Cutthroat World," *Chief Executive,* March 1996, pp. 34–38.

"The Gillette Company, 1901–1976," Gillette News, 1977.

Grant, Linda, "Gillette Knows Shaving—and How to Turn out Hot New Products," *Fortune,* October 14, 1996, pp. 207–208, 210.

Koselka, Rita, " 'It's My Favorite Statistic,' " *Forbes,* September 12, 1994, pp. 162–72.

Levine, Joshua, "Global Lather," *Forbes,* February 5, 1990, p. 146.

Maremont, Mark, "How Gillette Is Honing Its Edge," *Business Week,* September 28, 1992, pp. 60–61.

——, "How Gillette Wowed Wall Street: It Structured the Duracell Buy to Juice Up Earnings Immediately," *Business Week,* September 30, 1996, pp. 36–37.

Miller, William H., "Gillette's Secret to Sharpness," *Industry Week,* January 3, 1994, pp. 25–26, 28, 30.

Newport, John Paul Jr., "The Stalking of Gillette," *Fortune,* May 23, 1988, p. 99.

Ricardo-Campbell, Rita, *Resisting Hostile Takeovers: The Case of Gillette,* Westport, Conn.: Praeger, 1997.

—Ginger G. Rodriguez
—updated by David E. Salamie

Goldman, Sachs & Co.

85 Broad Street
New York, New York 10004
U.S.A.
(212) 902-1000
Fax: (212) 902-1512
· **Web site: http://www.gs.com**

Private Company
Founded: 1885
Employees: 7,200
Assets: $110 billion (1997)
SICs: 6211 Security Broker and Dealer

Goldman, Sachs & Co. has been a respected player in world finance for more than 100 years. While proving itself something of a cautious follower in an age of daring leveraged buyouts and corporate raids, Goldman, Sachs has moved aggressively into the asset management arena, where it has become the third largest investment firm. What Goldman lacks in bravado and innovation, it makes up for in prudence and surety.

The company was founded by Marcus Goldman, a Bavarian school teacher who immigrated to the United States in 1848. After supporting himself for some years as a salesman in New Jersey, Goldman moved to Philadelphia, where he operated a small clothing store. After the Civil War he moved to New York City, where he began trading in promissory notes. In the morning, Goldman would purchase customers' promissory notes from jewelers on Maiden Lane, in lower Manhattan, and from leather merchants in an area of the city called "the swamp." Then, in the afternoon, Goldman visited commercial banks, where he sold the notes at a small profit.

Goldman's son-in-law, Samuel Sachs, joined the business in 1882. The firm expanded into a general partnership in 1885 as Goldman, Sachs & Company when Goldman's son Henry and son-in-law Ludwig Dreyfus joined the group.

Henry Goldman led the firm in new directions by soliciting business from a broader range of interests located in Providence, Hartford, Boston, and Philadelphia. In 1887 Goldman, Sachs began a relationship with the British merchant bank Kleinwort Sons, which provided an entry into international commercial finance, foreign-exchange services, and currency arbitrage.

On the strength of this growing exposure, Goldman, Sachs won business from several Midwestern companies, including Sears Roebuck, Cluett Peabody, and Rice-Stix Dry Goods. With the establishment of Goldman, Sachs offices in St. Louis and Chicago, Henry Goldman became responsible for the firm's domestic expansion.

Railroads—indispensable to the opening of the American West—were the preferred investment of Eastern financiers at this time. But Goldman, Sachs, committed to a diversified portfolio, saw great potential in a number of other developing industries. At first difficult to market, these investments became profitable ventures only after Goldman, Sachs persuaded companies to adopt stricter accounting and audit procedures.

In 1896, soon after Samuel Sachs's brother Harry joined the company, Goldman, Sachs joined the New York Stock Exchange. With Harry Sachs in the company and with the New York operations firmly under control, Samuel Sachs took special responsibility for Goldman, Sachs's overseas expansion. Through Kleinwort, he gained important new contacts within the British and European banking establishments.

In 1906 one of the firm's clients, United Cigar Manufacturers, announced its intention to expand. Goldman, Sachs, which had previously provided the company with short-term financing to maintain inventories, advised United Cigar that its capital requirements could best be met by selling shares to the public. Although Goldman, Sachs had never before managed a share offering, it succeeded in marketing $4.5 million worth of United Cigar stock; within one year United Cigar qualified for trading on the New York Stock Exchange.

On the strength of this success, Goldman, Sachs next co-managed Sears Roebuck's initial public offering that same year.

Henry Goldman was subsequently invited to join the boards of directors of both United Cigar and Sears. The practice of maintaining a Goldman partner on the boards of major clients became a tradition that continues today.

During the 1910s, a time of feverish industrial activity, Goldman, Sachs instituted a number of innovative financial practices which today are common, including share buyback and retirement options. The firm managed public offerings for a number of small companies which, in part due to Goldman, Sachs's activities, later grew into large corporations. Some of the firm's clients at this time included May Department Stores, F.W. Woolworth, Continental Can, B.F. Goodrich, and Merck.

Henry Goldman retired in 1917 and shortly afterward Samuel and Harry Sachs became limited partners. The company was still a family business, and a third generation consisting of Arthur, Henry E., and Howard J. Sachs were promoted to directorships.

World War I depressed financial activity until 1919. In its aftermath, however, came a strong economic expansion. Built primarily on large war-related capital investments, the expansion led many of the firm's clients—H.J. Heinz, Pillsbury, and General Foods among them—to return to Goldman, Sachs for additional financing.

The expansion continued well into the 1920s and created great demand for investment services. Goldman, Sachs, eager to take advantage of this new and promising market, formed an investment subsidiary called the Goldman Sachs Trading Corporation. The new company expanded rapidly. But in the fall of 1929, Goldman Sachs Trading, like many other companies, fell victim to a crisis of confidence that forced the stock market into a devastating crash. By 1933 the investment subsidiary was worth only a fraction of its initial $10 million capitalization.

The company's recovery from the Depression was slow, but by the mid-1930s, the commercial-paper and securities businesses again were highly profitable. During this period Sidney J. Weinberg, an "outsider" in the family business, assumed a leading position within the firm.

Starting out in 1907 as a porter's assistant making $2 per week, Weinberg rose quickly at Goldman, Sachs. In 1927, at the age of 35, Weinberg became only the second outsider to be made a partner. Weinberg was known for his diligence and for his attention to detail.

In the aftermath of the 1929 stock market crash, Congress passed the Securities Act of 1933. This act created the Securities and Exchange Commission, which required that every investment be accompanied by a detailed prospectus, often containing confusing small-print passages. As a conservative and practical securities dealer, Goldman, Sachs worked to reduce investor confusion by providing concise information in common language.

Goldman, Sachs also began a securities-arbitrage business in the 1930s under the direction of Edgar Baruch and, later, Gustave Levy. Meanwhile, the firm continued to expand by taking over other commercial-paper firms in New York, Boston, Chicago, and St. Louis. The firm subsequently engaged in a broad variety of investment activities, including new domestic and international share offerings, private securities sales, corporate mergers and acquisitions, real estate financing and sales, municipal finance, investment research, block trading, equity and fixed-rate investment portfolios, and options trading.

During World War II, Sidney Weinberg was placed on leave to serve on the government's War Production Board. With virtually all U.S. industry under special government supervision, many of Goldman, Sachs's activities were supplanted by government agencies; investment capital was raised through instruments such as war bonds, which were sold to individuals.

Goldman, Sachs did not fully regain its prewar momentum until several years after the war ended. During that time, however, American industry and the economy in general experienced unprecedented growth. Intimately involved in this economic expansion, Goldman, Sachs recruited hundreds of new employees from leading business schools and launched many new activities in finance and investment.

Sidney Weinberg was called into government service again during the Korean War, serving with the Office of Defense Mobilization. His absence, in part, precipitated the creation of a management committee, intended to decentralize the decision-making process. Gus Levy, who later became president of the New York Stock Exchange, was its first chairman.

Postwar Investment Strategies Prove Pioneering

Goldman, Sachs's most important management of a new share issue occurred in November 1956, when shares of the Ford Motor Company were sold to the public for the first time. As co-manager, Goldman, Sachs helped market 10.2 million shares, worth $700 million. The firm set another record in October 1967, when it handled the floor trade of a single block of Alcan Aluminum stock consisting of 1.15 million shares, worth $26.5 million, at the time the largest block trade ever made.

Sidney Weinberg died in November 1969 and was succeeded as senior partner by Gus Levy. Goldman, Sachs began to attain its current position as a highly influential financial institution during the 1960s, but that position was solidified during the 1970s, as commodities such as oil grew to dominate the economy. Large new investments in domestic petroleum projects placed the company at a critical juncture; to some degree it was able to determine the complexion of the industry by channeling investment funds. Goldman, Sachs's expertise in this area resulted in its management of several large energy-industry share offerings.

John L. Weinberg and John Whitehead were promoted to senior partners upon the death of Gus Levy in 1976. Some years later, Whitehead left the firm to become assistant secretary of state in the Reagan administration and Weinberg became chief partner and chairman of the management committee.

Goldman, Sachs diversified late in 1981 by absorbing the commodities-trading firm of J. Aron & Company, which dealt mainly in precious metals, coffee, and foreign exchange. The company's acquisition of Aron would give it a strong footing in South American markets, an area of later growth for the firm. In

May 1982, under the leadership of co-partner John Weinberg—son of Sidney Weinberg—the firm took over the London-based merchant bank First Dallas, Ltd., which it later renamed Goldman, Sachs, Ltd.

Beginning in 1984, however, a new craze erupted on Wall Street in which investment companies engineered leveraged buyouts (LBOs) of entire firms. These buyouts were financed with junk bond debt, which was paid off with operating profits from the purchased firm or from the piecemeal break-up and sale of the firm's assets. At the time, the practice could be highly profitable for firms willing to assume the associated risks.

Goldman, Sachs, however, preferred to stress its transaction work rather than to undertake higher risk LBOs. But the market crash of October 1987, reduced the profitability of transaction work. In addition, Goldman, Sachs began to lose clients to more aggressive investment firms, forcing it to begin efforts at downsizing and reducing overhead. Several hundred employees would be laid off through the end of the decade.

In early 1989, in an effort to retain its partnership status in the face of growing corporate competition, Goldman, Sachs elected to seek capital to expand its merchant-banking activities. With seven insurance companies, it formed a 10-year consortium that infused the firm with $225 million in new capital. Structured like a preferred stock, the expanded partnership was similar to that undertaken in 1986 with Japan's Sumitomo Bank when the bank purchased a 12.5 percent share of the brokerage house for upwards of $500 million. While entitled to 12.5 percent of Goldman, Sachs's profits, Sumitomo, like the newer partners, would be prevented by federal law from having voting rights within the firm. Goldman, Sachs would continue to accept such equity investments into the next decade.

The company also created a holding company, Goldman Sachs Group, which, technically, was not subject to the capital requirements of the New York Stock Exchange. The firm also began to spin off several subsidiaries. Engaging in bridge loans, mortgage insurance, and LBOs—as well as the creation of the Water Street Corporate Recovery Funds, a $500 million fund dedicated to investing in financially troubled companies—the firm's subsidiaries bolstered the company's profits, but also caused lower bond ratings from Moody's and Standard & Poor's. Other changes in the company included the 1990 introduction of the GS Capital Growth Fund, a mutual fund targeted for the moderate-income investor through a minimum investment of $1,200. The introduction of this fund signalled the company's efforts to stretch its market beyond the rich client base it had previously catered to.

International Expansion in the 1990s

Goldman, Sachs began the 1990s with a boom, reporting a record pre-tax profit of $1.1 billion in 1991, and paying out end-of-1992 bonuses of 25 percent annual salaries to employees. By 1993, the company had become one of the most profitable companies in the world, with pre-tax earnings of $2.7 billion. Some of this gain could be attributed to its successful offering of Japanese securities to U.S. investors as other than foreign exchange instruments, as well as the investment banking firm's expansion of its markets overseas. The firm experienced rapid growth in several overseas investment projects, including as a global coordinator in Finland's Neste Oy oil company in 1992, although some markets, such as China, remained volatile due to differing political and cultural climates. And in a venture in the former U.S.S.R., the company worked with a government official who unfortunately lost his political influence during the changes in the Russian government. The company closed its Russian office in 1995, although interest in rekindling its involvement in that country's fluctuating financial markets would resume in mid-1997.

Despite Goldman, Sachs's record profits between 1991 and 1993, the company would find the decade contained its setbacks as well. In 1993 a federal appeals court ruled that an investment banking firm could no longer advise a company with whom it had a business relationship in bankruptcy proceedings. This decision, issued as a result of Goldman, Sachs's representation of client Eagle-Picher Industries in Chapter 11 proceedings, signalled the end to a lucrative area for large investment banking—the advising of corporate clients in bankruptcy reorganization—that netted Goldman and similar firms over $100 million a year.

The crash in the market price of Treasury and other bonds in 1994, as well as the drop of the U.S. dollar in foreign markets, found Goldman, Sachs laying off more employees by mid-decade. More serious, however, was a mass wave of "retirements" by almost 50 of the firm's veteran partners, including firm chairman Stephen Friedman. Due to Goldman, Sachs's rapid expansion in the early 1990s, partner relationships had become strained. As discontented partners left the company, they were expected to take their much-needed equity with them, forcing the firm to find $250 million worth of new capital. By mid-1994, the company had named 58 new general partners, a record for the company; announcements of a new wave of layoffs quickly followed.

Fortunately, the bull market that had been in place on Wall Street since August 1982, as well as a stronger bond market, helped to stabilize the firm, growing its profits to replace the capital lost due to departing partners. Cost cuts and an internal restructuring further buoyed the firm.

Firm Pursues More Aggressive Strategy

By 1996 the company was back on track, posting a pre-tax profit of $565 million for the first quarter. By mid-March, Goldman, Sachs had led an investor group in the successful but much-contested purchase of New York City's Rockefeller Center—dubbed the "greatest urban complex of the 20th century"—for $306 million. In further efforts to expand its roster of small-scale investors, the firm also began to aggressively acquire other firms, including Liberty Investment Management, the U.K.-based pension fund manager CIN Management from British Coal, and Stockton Holdings' Commodities Corp, located in New Jersey. The acquisition of such fee-based asset management firms helped to stabilize the company's unpredictable trading business both in the U.S. and on international markets, allowing Goldman, Sachs to retain its leadership role in the securities and banking industry.

Nineteen ninety-six was also a year notable for several internal changes. A new class of "junior partners" was created in

September—dubbed "partnership extension" by the company—in the hopes that such promotions would stem the tide of partner defections and retirements that characterized the beginning of the decade. The firm also voted to adopt a limited liability structure, effective in November. The conversion, while significant in that it changed the company's 127-year structure as a partnership, was expected to have little impact on the way the company conducted its business. This prediction was borne out by the company's year-end pre-tax profits of $2.7 billion—the second highest in company history.

Principal Subsidiaries

Goldman Sachs International Limited (U.K.); Goldman Sachs (Japan) Corp.; Goldman Sachs (Asia) Limited (Hong Kong); Goldman Sachs (Singapore) Pte. Ltd.; Goldman Sachs (Australia) Limited; Goldman Sachs Canada; Goldman Sachs Finanz A.G. (Switzerland); Goldman Sachs Money Markets Inc.; Liberty Investment Management; CIN Management (U.K.); Stockton Holding Ltd. Commodities Group.

Further Reading

Lowenstein, Roger, "Goldman Sets Fund for Firms in Distress," Wall Street Journal, April 16, 1990.

Raghavan, Anita, "Goldman Sachs Moves to Stem Staff Defections," *Wall Street Journal,* September 24, 1996.

Swartz, Steve, "Goldman Sachs Gets $225 Million as an Investment from 7 Insurers," *Wall Street Journal,* March 30, 1989.

—updated by Pamela Shelton

GOODYEAR

The Goodyear Tire & Rubber Company

1144 East Market Street
Akron, Ohio 44316-0001
U.S.A.
(330) 796-2121
Fax: (330) 796-2222

Public Company
Incorporated: 1898
Employees: 91,310
Sales: $13.11 billion (1996)
Stock Exchanges: New York Midwest Pacific
SICs: 2819 Industrial Inorganic Chemicals, Not Elsewhere
Classified; 2821 Plastics Materials, Nonvulcanizable
Elastomers & Synthetic Resins; 2822 Synthetic Rubber
(Vulcanizable Elastomers); 2891 Adhesives & Sealants;
2899 Chemicals & Chemical Preparations; 3011 Tires
& Inner Tubes; 3021 Rubber & Plastics Footwear;
3052 Rubber & Plastics Hose & Belting; 3069
Fabricated Rubber Products, Not Elsewhere Classified;
5531 Auto & Home Supply Stores

The Goodyear Tire & Rubber Company (Goodyear) is a major manufacturer, distributor, and seller of tires worldwide and holds the top position in tires in North America. It manufactures and sells other rubber products, including belts and hoses, and synthetic rubber chemicals for the transportation industry and a number of industrial and consumer markets. Goodyear operates 80 plants, of which 31 are in the United States, the balance being in 27 other countries. The company also provides auto repair and other services at retail and commercial outlets. Goodyear's Celeron subsidiaries maintain a 1,225-mile crude oil pipeline system, stretching from the California coast to central Texas.

After Founding in Late 19th Century, Goodyear Quickly Became Household Name

Without the discovery by U.S. inventor Charles Goodyear of vulcanization—the process by which extreme heat renders rubber flexible and strong—the modern rubber industry would not exist. Goodyear had nothing to do with the company that bears his name. He died insolvent in 1860, 38 years before Frank A. Seiberling founded Goodyear in Akron, Ohio, destined to be the world's first rubber concern to post $1 billion in sales. It reigned as the world's largest tire maker for seven decades.

Bicycle and carriage tires were the company's major products until the start of automobile tire production in 1901. Seiberling's 1899 application to make carriage tires under Consolidated Tire Company's patent was refused, so he started manufacturing a similar tire without a license, claiming it was monopolistic for Consolidated to grant patent licenses selectively. The ensuing legal battle meant that Goodyear's first- and second-year profits from the sale of carriage tires were held in escrow until the court decided, in Goodyear's favor, in 1902.

Goodyear introduced its straight-side tire under the Wingfoot trademark adopted in 1900, with a full-scale national magazine advertising campaign in 1905. The tire was quickly detachable from its rim, and this popular tire made Goodyear a household name.

Seiberling followed David Hill to the presidency in 1906, with Paul W. Litchfield, George M. Stadelman, and Frank Seiberling's brother Charles Seiberling composing the formative management team. In 1907 Goodyear opened its Detroit shop, providing 1,200 tires to equip Henry Ford's new Model T. By 1909 auto tire production jumped to 36,000, and Goodyear's sales reached $4.25 million, double that of the previous year. By 1910 Goodyear provided one-third of all original tires on U.S. cars. In 1909 Goodyear started production of airplane tires.

In 1910 Litchfield acquired a method for bonding rubber over fabric from North British Rubber Company in Edinburgh, Scotland. Goodyear's rubberized fabric, soon used for planes, including the Wright brothers', also formed the shell of early dirigibles, the production of which commenced in 1910.

Goodyear's tire production rose from 250 per day in 1916 to nearly 4,000 per day by the end of World War I. The company made 1,000 balloons and 60 airships during the war, as well as 715,000 gas masks and some 4.75 million other military supply parts, such as tire valves. It also provided many of the tires used on aircraft. Wages rose, and both the company and its employees ended the war years in prosperity. Sales had jumped from $110 million in 1916–1917 to $172 million in 1918–1919, and to $223 million in 1920.

Neared Bankruptcy in Early 1920s

Only two days after the November 1918 armistice, the government canceled its contracts and decontrolled prices. The economy swelled as industry rushed to meet postwar demand, but sales fell in late 1920 as unemployment and bankruptcy soared. Goodyear felt the squeeze as early as 1918, when it made its first attempt to recapitalize by a direct sale of stock to customers and employees.

As the recession deepened, Goodyear was forced to turn to bankers, a position Frank Seiberling in particular was loathe to assume. In 1920, nonetheless, the company accepted temporary refinancing of $18 million from a banking syndicate headed by Goldman, Sachs & Co. of New York and A.G. Becker of Chicago. The effort was not sufficient, and bankruptcy loomed imminent as the book value of its common stock, at $75 million in early 1920, was reduced to zero. By 1921 sales had fallen to $105 million with a $5 million loss.

In early 1921 the New York law firm of Cravath, Henderson, Liffingwell & De Gersdorff connected Goodyear with an investment bank, Dillon, Read, & Co., that agreed to manage Goodyear's refinancing and reorganization. Of the original officers, only Litchfield and Stadelman remained with the company. Frank Seiberling left and soon thereafter incorporated Seiberling Rubber Company, later acquired by Firestone. President E. G. Wilmer and a new management team were brought in. Wilmer focused on creating financial vigor at Goodyear, making few changes, if any, in the production and sales realms. One month after his appointment, in June 1921, he had reduced debt from $66 million to $26.5 million. Of 469 creditor claims in 1921, all but seven were settled. Sales picked up to $123 million in 1923, from $103.5 million in 1921. In 1923 Stadelman moved into the presidency, Wilmer assumed the board chairmanship, and Litchfield moved into the first vice-presidency. Wilmer would resign from Goodyear to head up Dodge Brothers, the forerunner of the Dodge Motor Company, in 1926.

The world's largest tire producer since 1916, Goodyear became the world's largest rubber producer by 1926. By 1928 the company operated in 145 countries and sales reached $250 million. Stadelman did not live to see the company reach that point, as he died in January 1926. Litchfield assumed the presidency,

commencing a 30-year tenure as chief executive officer. He spent his first year resolving litigation begun in 1922 by Goodyear common stockholders to increase their power and improve the position of common and preferred stock. The battle was concluded in 1927, on terms satisfactory to the stockholders.

Goodyear had produced all of the significant U.S. dirigibles since 1911, and it was commissioned in 1928 to build two huge dirigibles for the U.S. Navy. The enormous Goodyear airdock, then the world's largest building without internal supports, was erected to accommodate the project. Despite Litchfield's personal interest in the field of lighter-than-air craft, the industry came to an end in 1937 with the crash of the *Hindenburg.* Goodyear's famous fleet of smaller, nonrigid blimps continued to enjoy recognition at outdoor events since they were first floated as a friendly company trademark in the 1930s.

Goodyear was the defendant in one of the most famous antitrust cases of all time beginning in 1933 when the Federal Trade Commission (FTC) charged that its cost-plus-six-percent purchasing contract with Sears discriminated against independent dealers in violation of the Clayton Act, a U.S. antitrust law. The FTC issued a cease-and-desist order March 1936, and Goodyear appealed to the courts. Later that year, however, the Clayton Act was stringently amended, in large part due to the Goodyear case. In light of the stricter law, Goodyear voluntarily terminated its Sears contract. The federal Circuit Court of Appeals planned to drop the case, but Goodyear wanted its name cleared and the commission wanted a precedent set for other cases, so the court was pushed to make a firm decision. In 1939 it came out for Goodyear, relieving any threat of future damage claims by dealers. Goodyear's one-time loyal buyer, Sears, became a serious competitor as it took its business to manufacturers selling only to mass distributors.

Prior to the 1930s Goodyear's labor conflicts had been limited. In 1913 some Goodyear workers joined 15,000 other rubber workers in a strike against Akron's other rubber companies organized by the Industrial Workers of the World (IWW). The strike was terminated after 48 days by worker vote, but it did mark the beginning of employee-initiated gains in Akron. The following year Goodyear instituted the eight-hour work day and a paid vacation plan for workers of five to nine years' tenure. A number of employee benefit programs were established, including an in-factory hospital, a worker-oriented company newspaper called *Wingfoot Clan,* and athletic leagues that attracted many a sports-minded employee. In 1915 Litchfield donated an amount equal to his first 15 years' salary, about $100,000, to the factory workers to be used at their discretion. In the early 1990s the fund provided scholarships to children of Goodyear employees or retirees.

Labor Strife Marked 1930s

In 1919 under Litchfield's direction, Goodyear formed the industrial assembly, a representative body of 60 employees that voiced worker interests to management. The assembly existed for 16 years, until its place was challenged by newly organized chapters of the American Federation of Labor (AFL). Coleman Claherty, a major force in the AFL, began organizing in Akron in 1933 and, within the year, won 20,000 members throughout the city, 1,000 of whom formed Goodyear's Local 2. The first international convention of the United Rubber Workers (URW) was held in September 1935.

In 1935 the local union chapters demanded that the companies recognize them as bargaining representatives for all employees. The companies refused, and the unions threatened to strike. At Goodyear a companywide vote carried out by the industrial assembly voted down a strike 11,516 to 891. The unions threatened to strike based solely on member vote, and the federal government resolved tensions by establishing the Perkins agreement, which essentially required management to consult the unions on all wage and scheduling issues.

Goodyear had established a six-hour work day in 1932 to lessen the effects of the Great Depression among workers, by reducing layoffs and distributing work as evenly as possible among remaining employees. When national price controls were removed in 1935, however, Goodyear reestablished the eight-hour work day to increase productivity, decrease its prices, and make its products more competitive. The industrial assembly requested a return to the six-hour shift, and when this was denied it appealed to the board of directors. Local 2, encouraged by the industrial assembly's tenacity, appealed to the secretary of labor, who ruled in January 1936 that Goodyear was unjustified in its reversion to the eight-hour shift because it had voluntarily established a shorter day. The government also charged Goodyear with discriminating between industrial assembly and union workers. At the time, union membership was at ten percent.

Goodyear returned to the six-hour day as suggested, but layoffs became necessary as tire sales decreased, and the union struck in February 1936. Goodyear's strikers were supported by union sympathizers from other rubber companies and by Ohio and West Virginia coal miners from John L. Lewis's Committee for Industrial Organization (CIO). Within two days, thousands were picketing Goodyear's three major Akron plants. More than 1,000 employees, including Litchfield, moved into the factories to maintain as much production as possible. The union strategy was to break Goodyear, the largest rubber factory, so that the other companies would be more compliant. After 34 days the strike was settled by direct negotiations.

With a three-month stock of goods, Goodyear did not suffer financially from the strike, but the show of union muscle upped URW membership throughout Akron and increased Goodyear union members to 5,000. The Wagner Act, or National Labor Relations Act, was affirmed by the U.S. Supreme Court in April 1937. The industrial assembly was categorized as a company union and had to be disbanded. Workers supported the move to URW representation by a ratio of more than two to one.

Sitdowns and interworker violence frequently disrupted production after the 1935 strike, culminating in a May 1938 sitdown that attracted picketers even though none were formally requested. Police were summoned to disperse the demonstrators, and in an ensuing riot 100 people were injured. The company and union negotiated three days later and sitdowns decreased. Goodyear had decreased employees in Akron from 58,316 in 1929 to 33,285 in 1939. In 1941, after three years of cooperation, Goodyear signed its first formal contract with Local 2.

Despite labor and litigation difficulties during the 1930s, Goodyear continued its expansion. An Alabama plant and two textile mills were built in 1929, followed by another textile mill in 1933. In 1935 the company acquired a bankrupted company, Kelly-Springfield Tire. Another plant was acquired in Akron in 1936, and a Vermont factory was purchased to centralize shoe sole-and-heel production.

Goodyear's foreign expansion, begun in 1910 with its first of two Canadian plants, continued during the 1930s. In addition to its London and Australian plants, operative since 1912, Goodyear had distributors located throughout northern Europe, Russia, Central and South America, and the Caribbean. In 1931 a tire plant was opened just outside Buenos Aires, Argentina. The sixth foreign factory went up in Bogor, on Java in Indonesia in 1935, and the seventh was built in 1938 in Sao Paolo, Brazil. A Swedish plant was opened in 1939. Rubber plantations were established during the 1930s in Indonesia, Costa Rica, and the Philippines. Goodyear Foreign Operations was created to manage the company's 18 foreign subsidiaries, seven factories, seven plantations, 37 branches, 28 depots, and hundreds of distributors located outside of the United States.

Goodyear patented its first synthetic rubber, Chemigum, in 1927. It was first mass produced in 1935, and tires were made of it in 1937. In 1934 the company introduced Pliolite, a compound that cemented rubber to metal, and Pliofilm, a packaging material. Other popular Goodyear products were rubber floor tiles; many new models of tires; Airfoam, a cushioning material for seats and mattresses; and Neolite, a synthetic heel-and-sole material.

Returned to Military Contracting During World War II

Goodyear began producing 200,000 gas masks a month for the U.S. Army after Adolf Hitler's April 1939 invasion of Poland. The same year, Goodyear Aircraft (GAC) was established, and the Goodyear airdock, unused since the demise of the giant airships, housed wartime airplane and parts production, as well as the construction of 132 blimps for coastal submarine defense. In 1941 Goodyear joined other manufacturers to produce parts for 100 B-26 bombers a month. In 1943 some of GAC's 32,000 employees worked on the plane that dropped A-bombs on Hiroshima and Nagasaki in 1945, a B-29 Superfortress. GAC also produced 4,008 Vought Corsair FG1 fighter planes, beginning in 1943.

In 1940 Edwin J. Thomas, who began as Litchfield's secretary and assistant in the 1920s, ascended to the presidency as Litchfield continued as chairman of the board. The company took on management of a government-owned factory producing propellant charges for 600 types of artillery shells in 1940. In 1941 the U.S. government required each of the "big four" rubber producers—Goodyear, General Tire, Firestone, and Goodrich—to construct plants that would produce 400,000 tons a year of GRS, or government rubber, a synthetic compound including styrene and butadiene. Goodyear supervised the construction of three synthetic rubber plants for the government. Two of the plants became owned and operated by the company. Goodyear sales increased 52 percent over 1940.

Goodyear also produced the top-secret phantom fleet, used to confuse Nazi reconnaissance before the D-Day invasion of Normandy. The "fleet" was made of rubberized material, from which Goodyear constructed life-sized inflatable replicas of amphibious invasion craft, PT boats, tanks, combat vehicles, and heavy artillery. These impostors were blown up and set in one coastal English base, then rapidly deflated and moved by night to another. To Axis surveillance, the apparent serial establishment and abandonment of fighting bases was inexplicable and may have contributed to their unstable coastal defense.

Extraordinary Growth Followed World War II

When the war concluded, the government canceled $432 million in Goodyear contracts. GAC released almost 27,000 employees, reducing its payroll to 2,000 by 1946. Demobilization increased demand for consumer tires, and sales increased to 25 million in 1946–1947. Goodyear established factories in Colombia and Venezuela in 1945, in Cuba in 1946, and in South Africa in 1947. A Japanese-occupied factory in Indonesia was regained in 1945, as well as a rubber plantation in 1949. In its 50th year, 1948, Goodyear reached a peacetime sales record of $705 million. It employed 72,000 workers worldwide and was poised to expand its international presence.

In its first 50 years, Goodyear total sales had been $9 billion; in the decade from 1949 to 1958, sales would top $11.5 billion. In 1951 Goodyear became the first rubber company to exceed $1 billion in sales in one year. Goodyear's World War II production record garnered it several government contracts associated with the Korean War in 1950. A subsidiary, Goodyear Atomic Corp., was founded in 1952 when the government selected the company to operate a $1.2 billion atomic plant under construction in Pike County, Ohio. The facility opened in 1954.

In 1954 Goodyear acquired its first new plantation in 20 years in Belem, Brazil. The following year it acquired two government-owned rubber factories it had operated during the war. That same year, at Goodyear's Gadsden, Alabama plant, an $11.5 million investment elevated it to the largest tire-making facility in the United States. In 1957 it also built a 7,200-acre tire testing site with 18.5 miles of multisurface roads.

Rubber consumption after World War II was double that of prewar production. Much of the increase was due to new rubber products such as foam rubber, film, and plastics, and growth was fueled by newly developing synthetic rubbers such as polyisoprene, introduced by Goodyear in 1955 and called Natsyn, for commercial purposes. In 1960 Goodyear built a $20 million synthetic rubber plant in Beaumont, Texas; its annual production of 40,000 tons of Natsyn equaled the annual generation of 15,000 acres of rubber trees.

In 1958 Thomas became chairman of the board, and Litchfield moved to honorary chairman. Russell DeYoung became Goodyear's ninth president; his first full-time Goodyear position had been that of a tire inspector. DeYoung appointed Robert H. Lane as public relations director in 1958. Lane was largely responsible for the makeover of Goodyear's public profile from a somewhat stodgy, though quality, tire maker, to a contemporary innovator. The key to this image update was Goodyear's re-entry into racing. Once it overcame Firestone's domination of the field, Goodyear was able to equip winning cars in the Daytona 500 and other popular U.S. and European races. Lane also clearly defined the role of the Goodyear blimp as a corporate goodwill ambassador, capitalizing on the company's historic association with airships.

Foreign operations were consolidated in February 1957 under Goodyear International Corporation (GIC). In 1959 GIC initiated its European expansion program with construction of a plant in Amiens, France. Tire plants were built in 1965 at Cisterna di Latina, Italy, and in 1967 in Phillipsburg, Germany, giving Goodyear production sites in Europe's three major markets within ten years.

In the United States, Goodyear's expansion was partly by acquisition. In 1959 the company added a $3 million aeronautics research and development laboratory in Litchfield Park, Arizona, to supplement GAC's activities. The subsidiary received a $65 million contract in 1958 to produce Subroc, an antisubmarine missile. Goodyear would continue to derive much of its business from U.S. military and space program contracts, including production of equipment for several of the Apollo moon missions. In 1961 the company bought Geneva Metal Wheel Company, a maker of specialty wheels, and in 1964 acquired Motor Wheel Corporation, the world's largest maker of styled auto wheels. That same year, it was the first rubber corporation to exceed $2 billion in annual sales. Its profits were in excess of $100 million, with foreign subsidiaries contributing more than one-third.

In 1966, two years after Victor Holt assumed the presidency, Goodyear opened its tenth U.S. tire plant, in Danville, Virginia. This was followed in 1967 by a $73 million facility at its 593-acre site in Union City, Tennessee. Goodyear's sales doubled during the 1960s, topping $3 million in 1969. Net income rose from $71 million to $155 million. In 1969 it became the first rubber company to exceed $3 million in annual sales.

Became World's Leading Radial Tire Producer in the 1970s

Goodyear's biggest challenge in the 1970s was overhauling its factories to produce radial tires. The radial, with its excellent reinforcement system and extra belt of steel, was introduced by France's Michelin in 1948, and by 1972 it equipped eight percent of U.S. cars. Recognizing the superiority of the radial, Goodyear introduced a transitional fiberglass reinforced tire in 1967, and by 1972, 50 percent of U.S. cars rode on them. When Charles J. Pilliod assumed the presidency in 1972, he insisted that Goodyear bear the expense of adapting to full radial technology. The radial tire equipped 45 percent of U.S. cars by 1976, and Goodyear was the world's largest radial producer. In 1977, with a media blitz extolling its all-season tread, Goodyear introduced its Tiempo radial, the company's most successful tire to that time.

Goodyear's 75th anniversary year—1973—was marred by the debilitating Middle East oil crisis. In 1974, Pilliod became chairman and chief executive officer and John H. Gerstenmaier assumed the presidency, and Goodyear, prompted by the government, formed a joint project to stimulate domestic propagation of guayale, a native North American bush that provided 50 percent of U.S. rubber until 1910. As oil prices declined, however, the project slowed. In 1975 Mark Donohue, a well-known car racer, was killed when a tire blew out during prerace preparations. In 1984 his estate was awarded a $9.6 million settlement from Goodyear, one of the largest wrongful death payments in history.

In 1976 Goodyear suffered its longest strike ever when URW workers walked out on Goodyear, Goodrich, Uniroyal, and Firestone after talks at Firestone, the target company, failed. Goodyear's 22,000 strikers and their cohorts at the other companies returned to work some 130 days later, having obtained an agreement that wages and benefits would be increased 36 percent over the following three years.

In 1979 Goodyear fought hard and succeeded in avoiding the "neutrality" clause accepted by the other three rubber companies, which guaranteed that companies would not interfere with URW organizing. This was motivated by its desire to create a nonunion shop at its newly built Lawton, Oklahoma facility. Pilliod's new labor relations policies required individual workers, rather than supervisors, to be responsible for quality control. The new policies also provided regular and ongoing communications between management and laborers as well as worker involvement in problem solving. The factory was considered 50 percent more efficient than older facilities, and, by 1983, factory worker turnover was down to less than one-third of one percent.

In 1977 the Securities and Exchange Commission (SEC) accused Goodyear of maintaining a clandestine fund of $1.5 million to make foreign and domestic political contributions and government and labor bribes. The SEC charged that the company had made $500,000 in dubious payments since 1970 in 20 foreign countries. Goodyear agreed, without admitting guilt, to a permanent court injunction against violations of federal securities laws, providing a report of its activities in the countries in question. Two years prior, in 1975, Goodyear said it made political contributions of at least $242,000 between 1964 and 1972.

Robert E. Mercer assumed the presidency in 1978, when Gerstenmaier retired. That year Goodyear tire production was terminated in Akron, but the company began building Goodyear Technical Center, a $750 million research and design complex located on 3,000 acres in Akron. By 1980 despite national and global recession, Goodyear had record earnings of $264.8 million and had reduced debt to its lowest level in 17 years. By 1984 it supplied one-third of the U.S. tire market and one-fifth of the world tire market. In 1983 Pilliod retired, Mercer became chief executive officer, and Tom H. Barrett was voted president.

Briefly Focused on Diversification in the 1980s

Having won the ten-year battle to remain leader of the tire market, Goodyear entered the 1980s planning to scale some other peaks. Its diversification goal was to reduce tire revenues to one-half of corporate earnings and generate the other half through its GAC subsidiary and Celeron, a Louisiana oil and gas concern purchased in 1983. GAC had expanded at a com-

pound annual rate of 17 percent from 1973 to 1983, providing a 20 percent return on investment. In 1983 its annual sales were $617 million, despite a questionable $50 million investment in the production of centrifuges to enrich uranium for nuclear power plants. Celeron, although its sales slipped the year after it was purchased, began construction of the then-promising $750 million All-American Pipeline, a 1,200-mile tube used to transport 300,000 barrels per day of offshore California crude oil to Texas refineries.

The diversification came to an abrupt end in 1986, when takeover specialist Sir James Goldsmith made a bid for Goodyear. The company was able to beat off this takeover, but only by selling most of its nontire concerns, including GAC, which went to Loral Company for $588 million, and parts of Celeron, which went to Exxon for $650 million. Barrett became chief executive officer in 1988 and remained president. Hoyt M. Wells was voted president in 1991. In 1989 the company divested its South African operations, which it had maintained despite the social protest against apartheid during the 1980s.

Aquatread and Global Expansion Sparked 1990s Rebound

In 1990 Goodyear took its first loss since 1932 and surrendered its position as the world's largest tire maker to Michelin, when the French company bought out Goodrich's tire business, which had been merged with Uniroyal's. Firestone and General, weakened by Goodyear's dominance in the radial market, were absorbed, respectively, by Japan's Bridgestone and Germany's Continental, forcing upon Goodyear competition of its own size. Its All-American Pipeline, prevented from operating at full capacity by environmental restrictions, continued to produce losses; the company's $3.3 billion long-term debt, largely incurred by the Goldsmith battle, was also a weakness. Analysts pointed to Goodyear's sluggish internal efficiency as a major problem. For the first time since 1921, Goodyear went outside company ranks to choose a chairman and chief executive officer, as Stanley C. Gault succeeded Barrett in June 1991. Gault had been chairman and chief executive of Rubbermaid, Incorporated, while serving on Goodyear's board.

Between 1989 and 1991, Goodyear eliminated 12,000 jobs, or ten percent of its work force, with more than one-half of that coming from the salaried sector. In combination with the $1.4 billion investment in modernization and consolidation of factories, these cuts added up to an estimated savings of $250 million annually. Yet Goodyear remained committed to its annual research and development budget of more than $300 million a year, confident in this as a source of quality tires, such as 1990's Eagle GA and Eagle GT+4, successful luxury car models. By restructuring its U.S. marketing tactics, the company regained its lost market share and was holding its own in the tougher international market. Goodyear was also able by 1992 to reduce its long-term debt to a much healthier $1.47 billion.

More important, however, were the new tires rolling out of the company's research and development department. In 1991 alone four new Goodyear tires for the replacement market were introduced, the flagship of which was the Aquatread, an all-season passenger tire specially designed to provide better traction on rain-slickened roads. The tire proved to be a huge and immediate success. More troubling was Gault's 1992 decision to sell, once again, Goodyear-brand tires at Sears, more than half a century after it had stopped doing so. The following year the company began to sell its name-brand tires through Wal-Mart Stores and the Discount Tire chain. These moves angered Goodyear dealers, especially since some of their new competitors undercut their prices on Goodyear tires.

From 1993 to 1995, Goodyear enjoyed healthy profits, which increased from $387.8 million in 1993 to $567 million in 1994 to $611 million in 1995, and sales that increased from $11.64 billion in 1993 to $12.29 billion in 1994 to $13.17 billion in 1995. Some of this growth was fueled by global expansion through acquisitions and joint ventures. In 1993 the company entered into a joint venture in India with Ceat Ltd. to form South Asia Tyres and build a $150 million tire plant in India. The following year Goodyear purchased a 60 percent stake in Gold Lion, an automotive hose factory based in Qingdao, China, as well as a 75 percent stake in Dalian International Nordic Tire Co. (later known as Goodyear Dalian) based in Dalian, China.

In 1996 the Egyptian-born Samir F. Gibara, who had been president and chief operating officer, replaced Gault as chairman and CEO. That year, Goodyear acquired majority control of TC Debica, the leading passenger tire maker in Poland; the company planned to take advantage of Debica's central location and lower-wage environment as it expanded in Europe. This acquisition also meant that Goodyear now had manufacturing facilities in four of the world's most important developing areas: eastern Europe, India, China, and Latin America. Late in 1996, Goodyear reentered South Africa with the $121 million purchase of 60 percent of Contred Ltd., a unit of Anglovaal Industries Ltd. and a maker of tires, power transmissions, and conveyor belts.

The company's global spending spree continued in 1997. Early that year Goodyear entered into a manufacturing agreement with Sumitomo Rubber Industries Ltd. of Japan, through which the companies would manufacture tires for each other in Asia and North America. Goodyear's presence in eastern Europe was bolstered in May 1997 when Goodyear signed agreements with the Sava Group, based in Kranj, Slovenia, to form two joint ventures through which Goodyear would acquire a 60 percent interest in Sava's tire business and a 75 percent interest in its engineered products business.

Goodyear was not idle at home either. In 1995 the company's retail tire presence was beefed up through the purchase of 860 Penske Auto Centers and more than 300 Montgomery Ward-operated auto centers. The following year Goodyear unveiled the Infinitred, the first passenger tire with a manufacturer's lifetime treadwear limited warranty. In the spring of 1997 Goodyear had to endure its first strike in more than 20 years, when 12,500 United Steelworkers of America members went out on strike. This proved to be a brief setback as a contract agreement (an unusually long six-year contract) was reached after only 18 days of picketing. In June of that year Goodyear's Kelly-Springfield Tire unit entered into a long-term supply agreement with Lincolnton, North Carolina-based J. H. Heafner Co., whereby Kelly-Springfield would make at least one million Winston tires annually to be sold through Heafner's

network of tire distributors, one of the country's largest. Goodyear in July 1997 unveiled a line of "run-flat" tires called EMT ("extended mobility tire" or "empty"), which enabled a car to be driven between 50 and 200 miles at speeds up to 55 miles per hour on a deflated—even punctured—tire. Such tires also eliminated the need for a spare tire.

Gibara predicted that, by the early 21st century, 75 percent of Goodyear tires would feature EMT technology. Time would tell on that prediction (the tires' higher price tags could prove to be a major obstacle to widespread acceptance), but the company neared the turn of the century continuing to develop innovative new products and with a much enhanced presence outside North America. Goodyear also appeared ready to divest itself of its noncore Celeron oil pipeline subsidiaries as it took a $572.2 million fourth-quarter 1996 charge, most of which was a write-down of Celeron assets in advance of a sell-off. Divesting of Celeron would likely make a very strong company that much stronger.

Principal Subsidiaries

All American Pipeline Company; Belt Concepts of America, Inc.; Brad Ragan, Inc.; Celeron Corporation; Cosmoflex, Inc.; The Kelly-Springfield Tire Corporation; Goodyear International Corporation; The Goodyear Rubber Plantations Company; Goodyear Western Hemisphere Corporation; Murphy's Inc., Sales and Service; Wingfoot Corporation; Compania Anonima Goodyear de Venezuela; Compania Goodyear del Peru, S.A.; Compania Hulera Goodyear—Oxo, S.A. de C.V. (Mexico); Contred (Proprietary) Limited (South Africa); Corporacion Industriales Mercurio, S.A. de C.V. (Mexico); Deutsche Goodyear Holdings GmbH (Germany); Deutsche Goodyear GmbH (Germany); Goodyear Australia Limited; Goodyear Canada Inc.; Goodyear Chemicals, Europe S.A. (France); Goodyear Dalian Ltd. (China); Goodyear de Chile S.A.I.C.; Goodyear de Colombia S.A.; Goodyear do Brasil Produtos de Borracha Ltda (Brazil); Goodyear Broker's Limited (Bermuda); Goodyear Espanola S.A. (Spain); Goodyear Export, S.A. (Bermuda); Goodyear Export Sales Corporation (Barbados); Goodyear France (Pneumatiques) S.A.; Goodyear Finance Holding S.A. (Luxembourg); Goodyear Great Britain Limited (U.K.); Goodyear Hellas S.A.I.C. (Greece); Goodyear Holding Co. (Venezuela); Goodyear India Limited; Goodyear Italiana S.p.A. (Italy); Goodyear Jamaica Limited; Goodyear Lastikleri Turk Anonim Sirketi (Turkey); Goodyear Malaysia Berhad; Goodyear Maroc S.A. (Morocco); Goodyear (Nederland) B.V. (Netherlands); Goodyear New Zealand, Ltd.; The Goodyear Orient Company Pte Limited (Singapore); Goodyear Portuguesa, Limited (Portugal); Goodyear Philippines Inc.; Goodyear Qingdao Engineered Elastomers Company Ltd. (China); Goodyear S.A. (France); Goodyear S.A. (Luxembourg); Goodyear Singapore Pte Limited; Goodyear South Africa (Proprietary) Limited; Goodyear (Suisse), S.A. (Switzerland); Goodyear Taiwan Limited; Goodyear (Thailand) Limited; Goodyear Zimbabwe (Private) Limited; Gran Industria de Neumaticos Centroamericana, S.A. (Guatemala); Granford Manufacturing, Inc. (Canada); Gummiwerke Fulda GmbH (Germany); Neumaticos Goodyear S.A. (Argentina); Nippon Goodyear Kabushiki Kaisha (Japan); Philippine Rubber Project Company, Inc. (Philippines); P.T. Goodyear Indonesia; P.T.

Goodyear Sumatra Plantations (Indonesia); S.A. Goodyear N.V. (Belgium); Svenska Goodyear Aktiebolag (Sweden); TC Debica S.A. (Poland); Tredcor (Proprietary) Limited (South Africa); Wingfoot Insurance Company Limited (Bermuda).

Further Reading

Allen, Hugh, *The House of Goodyear: A Story of Rubber and of Modern Business,* Cleveland: Corday & Gross, 1943, reprinted, Arno Press, 1976.

Donlon, J. P., "A New Spin for Goodyear," *Chief Executive,* December 1995, pp. 34–35, 38–40.

Labich, Kenneth, "The King of Tires Is Discontented," *Fortune,* May 28, 1984.

Lubove, Seth, "The Last Bastion," *Forbes,* February 14, 1994, pp. 56, 58.

Magnet, Myron, "The Marvels of High Margins," *Fortune,* May 2, 1994, pp. 73–74.

Narisetti, Raju, "For Two Tire Makers, a Flat-Out Pitch for Safer Wheels," *Wall Street Journal,* July 3, 1997, p. B4.

Neely, William, *Tire Wars: Racing with Goodyear,* Tucson, Arizona: Aztex Corp., 1993.

O'Reilly, Maurice, *The Goodyear Story,* Elmsford, New York: The Benjamin Company, 1983.

Schiller, Zachary, "After a Year of Spinning Its Wheels, Goodyear Gets a Retread," *Business Week,* March 26, 1990.

——, "And Fix That Flat Before You Go, Stanley," *Business Week,* January 16, 1995, p. 35.

——, "Goodyear May Be Getting Some Traction at Last," *Business Week,* October 7, 1991, p. 38.

——, "Stan Gault's Designated Driver," *Business Week,* April 8, 1996, pp. 128, 130.

—Elaine Belsito
—updated by David E. Salamie

Goody's Family Clothing, Inc.

400 Goody's Lane
Knoxville, Tennessee 37922
U.S.A.
(423) 966-2000
Fax: (423) 675-1029

Public Company
Incorporated: 1954
Employees: 6,100
Sales: $819.1 million (1996)
Stock Exchanges: NASDAQ
SICs: 5651 Family Clothing Stores

Goody's Family Clothing, Inc. started as a 2,000-square-foot Ma-'n'-Pa apparel store opened in 1954 by Mike Goodfriend and his family. It developed into a value-priced chain with over 200 locations throughout Alabama, Arkansas, Florida, Georgia, Illinois, Indiana, Kentucky, Mississippi, North Carolina, Ohio, South Carolina, Tennessee, Virginia, and West Virginia. The first "Goodfriend" store, located in Athens, Tennessee, was modest and family-oriented. A big "G" over the door was the simple logo, and that remains the company's image today. The merchandise consisted of irregulars, last year's styles, and closeouts piled on tables and packed onto hanging racks. The lighting was poor, the customer service sketchy, but the lure of good clothes at great prices kept people coming.

The bargain store grew slowly over the next 20 years. When outlet and factory stores began to come into their own in the mid-70s, Goodfriend was in a very competitive niche, but stores continued offering seconds and discontinueds at discount prices. The chain had expanded to 12 stores by 1972 and had annual revenue of $12 million. Goodfriend was squeezed by the proliferation of national outlet stores and discounters and knew something had to change to keep his stores in the game. He looked to his son, Bob, for help.

Founder's Son Joins in 1972

In 1972, Bob—Robert M. Goodfriend—joined the team. With a background in retailing, Bob brought outside experience to the family-run operation. He considered the market and decided to take a middle road, a path different from that of discounters or department stores. He redirected the company to offer well-recognized, fashion names and up-to-the-minute trends at moderate prices. Everything re-oriented not around the family seeking a discount, but around the average family looking for today's stylish clothes at good prices. The store no longer purchased closeouts, irregulars, last year's goods, or factory seconds.

Acknowledging this adjustment of direction, the store was renamed "Goody's," after a college nickname of Bob's. By 1979, the chain had 21 stores, and Bob took over the reins of leadership completely as president and CEO.

New corporate headquarters were designed in 1990, when the company left the small town of Athens to relocate to Knoxville. Designed by award-winning architectural firm McCarty Holsaple McCarty, Inc., the headquarters not only contained an office complex but a completely customized 344,000-square-foot clothing distribution center. The state-of-the-art center made it possible to receive new fashions in one day and have them on trucks and out to stores the next, making for a minimal time lag in getting the latest fashions to the consumer. The distribution center could process 350,000 garments safely in one day and it is computer-linked to each of the chains. Whatever was going on out in the stores—sellouts, poor movers, runs on special items—is reported back to the main office. Acquisition strategy as well as distribution timelines can be adjusted. Clothes sales are also tracked by color and size, for a very precise measure of how business is running from day to day.

Success Leads to Public Offering in 1991

By 1991, prospering under a reign of technological advantage, Goody's had seen a decade of meteoric growth. The company closed the year with 91 stores and $273 million in annual sales. It was time to make a public launch. Goody's held

265

its initial public offering in October of that year. It elected a very conservative board of directors and successfully expanded its base of capital.

Three years later, the company had doubled its 1990 sales figures and growth to 171 stores. Goody's was also gradually remodeling its interiors, doing away with "tables" and updating to clean, brightly-lit interiors with wide aisles and clearly marked departments. The image went from discount house to department store, and the prices stayed 10 to 30 percent down from regular department store prices.

Boardroom Battles

Just when things were looking their best, the conservative board of directors began to clash with Goody's management, which wanted to pursue a more aggressive purchasing policy and keep the stores more up to date and more full of stock. In a bitter feud, chief operating officer Henry Call and the merchandising executive Tom Kelly left the store in 1992. Bob Goodfriend, despite the fact that his dream had developed much of what Goody's had become and that he was one of the members of the original family who started the chain, was forcibly ousted from the board. His departure lasted for three months, during which he sued the company and eventually won $1.24 million in legal settlement and fees. The store's margin of pre-tax earnings dropped from 5.6 percent of sales. Although Henry Call and Tom Kelly came back on board in 1995 as president and executive vice-president, respectively, and Goodfriend was accepted back on the board as chairman, the store has not yet returned to its pre-schism profitability margin. In 1996, it stood at only 3.4 percent. Climbing back up to 5.6 percent profitability and better is a continuing goal for the company and is reiterated in much of its internal literature.

Part of Goody's strategy to improve that profit percentage began in 1993, when it was decided to create Goody's own private label merchandise. The creating of a private label was seen to give Goody's long-range control over its inventory. Brand name fashions manufactured by other companies were always "outside" variables. But by developing its own fashions, Goody's management felt that it could more directly please and serve its customers. The first of these private labels was Ivy Crew for men, a stylish, golf-inspired collection, which became a popular suite of apparel for the store. Estimates in the late 90s saw that the Ivy Crew label accounted for 18 percent of the total sales in the men's department.

New Help and a New Slogan for 1995

Contracting year by year with overseas manufacturers in southeast Asia and Central America, Goody's has expanded its private labels into all of its clothing departments. It hired John Okvath in 1995, an old hand with the Asian rag market, to oversee product development. It also hired people away from The Limited and BIKE Athletic who were well-seasoned in overseas garment development. The expansion of the private label program is viewed by senior management as Goody's "ace in the hole" for future profit creation. While maintaining a commitment to national brand name fashions, Goody's is encouraging in its customers a taste for its own house labels.

One of the re-occurring elements in the story of Goody's is the store's striving to keep a friendly, family look and compete with the slick finish-outs of its department store competitors. As a part of this effort to stay in tune with its market, in the spring of 1995 Goody's came out with a new slogan—"Goody's feels like you." The logo was redesigned and the whole atmosphere of the stores was redone in shades of upbeat, feel-good, country casual. An in-house brochure recaps the marketing policy like this: "Customers like the prices, and they like the selection. But most important, they feel good about themselves when they wear the clothing they buy at Goody's." The "Customer First" training initiative helps carry out the theme by teaching store associates to smile, please, and respond to customers immediately. Goody's also follows up on its progress by bringing people from the sales floor to headquarters periodically for "roundtable" meetings that debrief associates on the customer experience and gather grassroots comments about improvement.

In 1995, the company opened 13 new stores and saw gross sales of $696.7 million. With better sales, aggressive promotion, remodeled looks, and Goodfriend, Call, and Kelly firmly back on board, Goody's stock rose 150 percent.

Enjoying a calmer political atmosphere, Goody's headed into 1996 full steam. The company opened 20 new stores and closed one. Now with a newly picked management team, the corporation redirected its policies away from slashing prices quickly on slow-moving apparel and more towards holding a stable, mid-priced lineup. The company also began to invest more heavily in inventory. The new corporate policy also encouraged a move out of the "country"—the suburbs where many of the chains were located—and into metropolitan areas. In 1996 Goody's opened six stores in Atlanta and three in Charlotte. Sales were up 17 percent over 1995, to $819.1 million, and the stores ended the year with no long-term debt.

Goody's business is seasonal in nature, with the peak seasons being traditional family-oriented times. Goody's makes its money during Christmas, back-to-school, and Easter—these few weeks accounting for 35 percent of the company's annual sales from 1993–1996, a trend expected to continue. In late 1996 the company also took a new direction by offering gifts and accessories, an approach which was evaluated as profitable and successful.

With the addition of non-clothing items, Goody's standard merchandise now fits in nine carefully tracked categories, and the labels in each category fluctuate slightly from year to year as the corporation determines which popular brands will fit into its pricing structure.

In 1997, Goody's planned to improve its profit margin by reducing "dependence" on denim, a low-cost leader for the store that brings in almost a quarter of all sales across all departments, and increasing its stock of house-label merchandise and high-margin garments, such as women's career clothing. It will also continue to lease, not own or build, its stores, in order to avoid long-term debt. Goody's looks for a very specific sort of location—nice strip centers with popular anchor stores in areas where its customers, the $30K–$50K annual income families, live. It plans a minimum of 20 new stores to open in 1997 and its goal is to reach $1 billion in sales by the close of 1998.

Part of the strategy to increase sales is sharp advertising. Goody's slogans "take a good look" and "Goody's feels like you" are splashed across all of their materials. Goody's advertising is headed by Mary Beth Fox, who joined the company in 1992 as a graphic designer. The company's point-of-sale, sign, print ads, and other sales materials are all designed and distributed in-house.

Not only does Goody's aggressively promote itself through ads in the local paper and direct mail, but the company also has strong corporate giving and community service programs. Local stores are often the drop-off points for canned goods and clothing to benefit the needy. Goody's also supports the Children's Miracle Network and mobile medical clinics in its communities. The store strives to foster a friendly, family image.

Poised for the Future

"We're in a position today not to keep pace, but to set the pace for our competitors," said chairman of the board Bob Goodfriend in 1997. "We have the right products, we have a great group of associates, and we have good locations. If we stay focused on our customers and concentrate hard on the day-to-day basics of the business, it's a winning combination."

Goody's rising stock figures seem to suggest that outside analysts also take this point of view. The stock has been bought by several large brokers to season mutual fund markets. Nevertheless, Goody's is in keen competition with a host of rivals that are larger and more established. Department store chains and factory outlet stores provide ongoing competition for the mid-priced family apparel chain.

Principal Subsidiaries

SYDOOG; GOFAMCLO, Inc.; Trebor of TN, Inc.

Further Reading

Blackmon, Douglas A., "Lower-Scale Chains May Be Worth a Look as Retail Stocks Slump," *Wall Street Journal* (southeast), June 25, 1997, p. S1.
Geisel, Amy, "Goody's Said to Be 'Clicking on All Cylinders.'" *Knoxville News Sentinel,* June 15, 1997, pp. D1–D3.
G.F.C. Fact Sheet, Knoxville: Goody's Family Clothing, 1996.
Owens, Jennifer, "Goody's Net Soars to $5M in 1st Quarter," *Women's Wear Daily,* June 19, 1997.
"Retailers' Earnings Exceed Expectations," 14 May 1997, Reuters, http://www.pathfinder.com.
Williams, Pam, "Record Year for Goody's," *Clothes Line,* Goody's Family Clothing, Spring 1997.

—Lisa Calhoun

Grand Casinos, Inc.

130 Cheshire Lane
Minnetonka, Minnesota 55305-1062
U.S.A.
(612) 449-9092
Fax: (612) 449-9353
Web site: http://www.grandcasinos.com

Public Company
Incorporated: 1991
Employees: 7,300
Sales: $490.0 million (1996)
Stock Exchanges: New York
SICs: 7011 Hotels And Motels; 7993 Coin-operated
     Amusement Devices

Grand Casinos, Inc., one of the largest gaming companies in the United States, develops, constructs, and manages casinos and related hotel and entertainment facilities. The company parlayed early success as one of the first companies in the country to manage and develop Indian-owned casinos into company-owned dockside casinos on the Mississippi Gulf Coast, but larger ventures proved more troublesome.

Indian Casino Management Group

In 1989, the chairman of the Mille Lacs Band of Ojibwe in Minnesota asked David W. Anderson, a member of two Indian tribes and of the first national task force on Indian gaming, to help find a manager for their bingo operation. Anderson contacted Stanley M. Taube, a one-time Minneapolis developer who managed Indian bingo concerns in the South. Taube and Anderson began to develop a proposal for the Mille Lacs Band about the same time the state of Minnesota entered into negotiations with the tribes in regard to the 1988 National Indian Gaming Regulatory Act which allowed Indian bands to open casino-style gambling in states which had other forms of gambling. The men broadened their plans to include a casino and drew Lyle Berman, a high-stakes championship-level poker player and successful leather goods retailer, into the management end of the gaming business.

The men initially formed a limited partnership through which Berman, who had recently sold the Bermans The Leather Experts chain, loaned the Mille Lacs Band $3 million to expand their gaming operation located in a popular fishing and resort area north of Minneapolis/St. Paul. Grand Casino Mille Lacs opened in April 1991 to a flood of business. Under the management contract Berman's group would receive 40 percent of the profits.

Grand Casinos, Inc. Established

Berman, Taube, and Anderson incorporated the management group in 1991. Grand Casinos, Inc. made its initial public offering (IPO) in October and brought in $12.4 million: the management contract with the Mille Lacs Band was their only significant source of income at the time. Berman recouped his $3 million investment, and the initial group retained more than 7 million shares or about 75 percent of the company at a cost of $15,000, or less than one cent a share. The Mille Lacs Band received approximately 100,000 shares, 1.2 percent of the company, and transferred the construction debt to their books.

Grand Casinos helped finance a second, much larger casino in Hinckley, Minnesota, the halfway point between the Twin Cities and Duluth on a route that saw millions of travelers during the busy tourist season. The Mille Lacs Band sought additional funding through government-guaranteed loans and banking institutions. The new casino, complete with child care center, video arcade, RV park, as well as a number of restaurants, opened in May 1992.

A secondary stock offering in May 1992 reaped $41 million at about $15 per share. The ownership share of the original three players was reduced to less than 50 percent—Berman held 26 percent and Taube and Anderson each held about 10 percent of the company. Grand Casinos expanded its operations to the South in 1992. The company received contracts to build and manage casinos for the Coushatta and Tunica-Biloxi Tribes in Louisiana. And with the legalization of dockside gambling in the state of Mississippi, Grand Casinos made plans to build its first company-owned casino in that state—the area was expected to become the third major gambling center in the U.S. after Atlantic City and Las Vegas.

Back in Minnesota, Indian-owned casinos helped reduce notoriously high unemployment rates among Indian people living on reservations, and the tribes became some of the largest employers in their areas for non-Indian people. The gaming profits helped improve education, health and public services, and housing on the reservations. Sixteen Indian-owned gaming facilities were in operation in the state by late 1992. The influx of competition cut into traffic to Grand Casino Mille Lacs, but together the two Mille Lacs Band casinos attracted 100,000 people a week and brought in over $74 million in revenues for fiscal 1992.

Chief operating officer Thomas Brosig, a key employee since the company's founding, succeeded Berman as president in May 1993; Berman continued as chairman of the board and chief executive officer. Grand Casino Gulfport, a three-story structure on four connecting barges, with restaurants and entertainment lounges, opened in May, and Grand Casinos stock climbed above the $50 per share mark by June.

Bets Placed on Larger Ventures

With an eye toward future growth, Grand Casinos, Inc. entered into a joint venture with Minneapolis-based Gaming Corp. of America to develop the Buck Lake Gaming Resort on a 2,000-acre site in Tunica County, Mississippi, about 20 miles south of Memphis. The company also invested in its first Las Vegas gambling concern.

The Stratosphere Tower project had been conceived by Robert E. Stupak, a Las Vegas legend and owner of the 932-room Vegas World Hotel and Casino. Stupak knew Berman from poker tournaments and asked him to invest in what would be the highest observation tower in the U.S. But Berman was interested in renovating and expanding the casino and hotel as well as completing the 1,149-foot tower, and Grand Casinos eventually gained controlling interest in Stratosphere Corp.

Grand Casinos raised $134.4 million through a stock offering of 5 million shares in September 1993 to help finance new projects. But its relationship with the Mille Lacs Band had become unsettled. The tribe wanted to renegotiate the terms of its contract with Grand Casinos, but the company resisted. In a December 18, 1994, *Star Tribune* article, Berman defended the agreement on grounds of the risk involved in the initial investment with the asset-poor tribes. The company also provided employee training and development as well as its professional gambling expertise. In November, an Inspector General audit listed Grand Casinos among management companies said to be charging excessive fees to Indian tribes.

Grand Casinos became the major gaming operator in Mississippi when it opened Grand Casino Biloxi, the world's largest floating casino, in January 1994. But the $600-million Buck Lake project being developed through the Mississippi Casino Development Corp. (MCDC) faced a challenging business climate. Attendance figures had been falling off in three of five casinos operating in Tunica County, and more competitors were in line to open in the area. The company said Buck Lake was closer to the main north/south highway out of Memphis than its competitors and would be a resort facility with amenities such as a theme park, theaters, and golf course, as well as gambling site.

Bill Dorn wrote in a May 1994 *Corporate Report Minnesota* article, "Grand Casinos has come this far this fast by using Lyle Berman's disciplines from chain retailing—centralized management to provide continuity and consistency of product." Dorn also mentioned management talent, casino location, and facilities as additional ingredients to the company's success.

Changes on the Horizon

Citing personal reasons, Brosig cut back his level of involvement with the company and was succeeded as president by Pat Cruzen, a former Las Vegas executive with experience in the gambling and hospitality industries. Josephine Marcotty, in an August 17, 1994 *Star Tribune* article, said, "Cruzen is assuming responsibility at a critical time for Grand." Its two casinos on the Mississippi Gulf Coast and the casino-resort complex being developed in Tunica County were facing very competitive markets. The Stratosphere Tower, located off the main strip and away from downtown Las Vegas, had been viewed as controversial from its conception. In addition, the company was in the midst of building hotels next to a number of its existing casinos at a time when financing for gambling concerns was tight.

In September, Grand Casinos announced that both the Buck Lake and the Stratosphere projects would be delayed. And while Grand Casino Avoyelles opened in 1994, negotiations to develop and manage casinos for tribes in California and Canada had fallen through. Stock was trading in the low teens at year-end.

Grand Casinos, Inc. ranked sixth in the gaming industry by total gaming footage, approximately 365,000 square feet, and by number of gaming devices, about 9,000 slot machines and nearly 400 game tables; the company was larger than Mirage Resorts, Inc., the Trump organization, and Bally Entertainment Corp. Net revenue for 1994 rose to $285.8 million, a 144 percent increase over the previous year; net earnings were $29 million or $1.30 per share.

Grand Casinos, Inc., which topped *Fortune* magazine's list of "America's 100 Fastest Growing Companies" in April 1995, held interest in related concerns including: Casino Data Systems, which developed player tracker and marketing systems; New Horizon Kids Quest, Inc., which operated child care centers at casinos; Innovative Gaming Corporation, which developed interactive video games for casinos; and Casino Hospitality Corp., which ran hotels at casinos.

Indian-owned casinos brought in a significant portion of operating income in 1994, but the Indian-gaming situation was changing. In addition to increased competition for contracts, the best locations and situations had already been developed and federal guidelines were tightening. Grand Casino Coushatta opened in January 1995, drawing guests from Houston and the surrounding area. The Indian-owned casino generated $12 to $14 million a month in revenue in its first two months of operation.

In mid-1995, Grand Casinos moved to jumpstart the Tunica County casino-resort project—renamed Diamond Lake—by infusing it with new loans and investments. The company then acquired full ownership of the project by merging with the other two players, Gaming Corp. of America and Grand Gaming Corp. (formerly known as MCDC). Other activity for the year included new financing for the Stratosphere Corporation, refinancing of Grand Casinos, Inc., and a three-for-two stock split. Grand Casinos, Inc. was named one of the best small companies in America by *Forbes* magazine in November and ended the year with net revenues of $372.9 million, but profit margins had been shrinking.

Stratosphere tower and casino complex opened in April 1996. The tower itself quickly became a top paid tourist attraction, but gambling revenue was lower than expected. In a September 1996 *Business Week* article Richard A. Melcher wrote, "Unless Berman can win a sharp reduction in Stratosphere's debt—talks with bond holders began in late August—he may put the company into bankruptcy." Stratosphere Corp. stock plummeted and shareholders filed law suits. Grand Casinos, Inc. stock was hurt by the fallout.

Grand Casino Tunica, the third largest casino in the U.S. behind MGM Grand in Las Vegas and Foxwoods Casino in Connecticut, opened in June 1996 to slower than expected traffic. Brosig, who had been working part time in investor relations, replaced Cruzen and returned the position of president in September 1996. To lure in more gamblers, the Grand Casino implemented new marketing strategies, such as more favorable odds, first at Stratosphere and later in Tunica.

The Mississippi Gulf Coast floating casinos, located 15 miles apart, had gained more than 40 percent of its market with 30 percent of the gaming capacity, but Mirage and Circus Circus had casinos under construction. Net revenues for 1996 reached $490 million, but earnings were hurt by nearly $150 million in writeoffs of investments in the Stratosphere Corporation. Stockholders lost $2.43 per share on the year.

Future Uncertainties

The Stratosphere Corp. filed for Chapter 11 bankruptcy in January 1997; Grand Casinos, Inc. held about 42 percent of the stock. Berman and two other Grand Casinos board members resigned from the Stratosphere board in July. Jim McCartney wrote in an August 1, 1997, *St. Paul Pioneer Press* article, "The move was prompted by Stratosphere Corp.'s independent directors statement a week ago that they now prefer a reorganization plan proposed by corporate raider Carl Icahn to a competing proposal from Minnetonka-based Grand Casinos." The company said the resignations were made to avoid potential conflicts of interest.

On the up side, the Clinton administration recognized Grand Casinos in May 1997 for its efforts in hiring and training unemployed and underemployed people, and gaming grew at Grand Casino Tunica with the addition of a 568-room hotel and helped boost the company's second quarter revenues. Grand

Casinos remained among the top Indian-owned casino management companies, but the lucrative contracts were set to begin expiring beginning in 1998.

Further Reading

Dorn, Bill, "Berman Maps Out A Gambling Strategy," *Corporate Report Minnesota*, May 1994, p. 30.
Fiedler, Terry, "Cruzen Out, Brosig Back As President of Grand Casinos," *Star Tribune* (Minneapolis), September 11, 1996, p. 1D.
——, "Tunica Resort Boosts Grand Casinos' Net," *Star Tribune* (Minneapolis), July 23, 1997, p. 3D.
Fiedler, Terry, and David Phelps, "Grand Plans, Harsh Reality," *Star Tribune* (Minneapolis), September 23, 1996, p. 1D.
"Grand Casinos, Inc.: Its Rise to Prominence," *Star Tribune* (Minneapolis), December 18, 1994, p. 25A.
Ison, Chris, and Lou Kilzer, "Outside Managers Are Big Winners In Indian Gaming," *Star Tribune* (Minneapolis), December 18, 1994, p. 1A.
Kennedy, Patrick, "Viva Mille Lacs!" *Corporate Report Minnesota*, April 1992, pp. 48–49.
Kurschner, Dale, "Tribes Get Fraction of Action, While Vegas Execs, Lots of Others Cash In," *Minneapolis/St. Paul CityBusiness*, December 11–17, 1992, p. 1.
——, "Gaming Trio Ups Ante with Huge Casino Deal," *Minneapolis/St. Paul CityBusiness*, April 22–28, 1994, p. 1.
——, "Grand's Full House of Projects Hits Delay," *Minneapolis/St. Paul CityBusiness*, September 23–29, 1994, p. 1.
Marcotty, Josephine, "Hinckley, Mille Lacs Casinos Roll Up Profits of $17.8 Million for Fiscal '92," *Star Tribune* (Minneapolis), October 27, 1992, p. 1D.
——, "Man Who Helped Fuel Grand Casinos' Growth to Quit As President; Cites Personal Reasons," *Star Tribune* (Minneapolis), May 10, 1994, p. 1D.
——, "Grand Casinos Executive Pat Cruzen Selected to Succeed Tom Brosig As Company President," *Star Tribune* (Minneapolis), August 17, 1994, p. 1D.
——, "Grand Casinos to Acquire Two Gambling Companies," *Star Tribune* (Minneapolis), July 7, 1995, p. 1D.
McCartney, Jim, "Leaving Las Vegas?" *St. Paul Pioneer Press*, March 12, 1997.
——, "Grand Directors Quit Stratosphere Board," *St. Paul Pioneer Press*, August 1, 1997.
Melcher, Richard, with Dale Kurschner and Ronald Grover, "You Gotta Know When To Hold 'Em," *Business Week*, September 9, 1996, p. 66.
Moylan, Martin J., "Grand Casinos Good Gamble, Analysts Say," *St. Paul Pioneer Press*, October 26, 1992.
Palmeri, Christopher, "Now the Public Takes the Risk," *Forbes*, August 17, 1992, p. 108.
Schafer, Lee, "What's in the Cards," *Corporate Report Minnesota*, May 1995, pp. 40–45.
St. Anthony, Neal, "Original Investors Could Win Big in Casinos Offering," *Star Tribune* (Minneapolis), September 19, 1991, p. 1D.
——, "Berman Bet on Casino Paying Off," *Star Tribune* (Minneapolis), February 17, 1992, p. 1D.
Stych, Ed, "Grand Casino's Chairman Plans to Expand Outside of Minnesota," *St. Paul Pioneer Press*, August 16, 1992.

—Kathleen Peippo

Groupe Vidéotron Ltée.

2000 Berri St.
Montreal, PQ H2L 4V7
Canada
(514) 281-1232
Fax: (514) 985-8425
Web site: http://gvl.videotron.com

Public Company
Incorporated: 1964
Employees: 4,000
Sales: C$846.93 (1996)
Stock Exchanges: Montreal
SICs: 4830 Radio & Television Advertising; 4841 Cable
   & Other Pay TV Services

Groupe Vidéotron Ltée. is a diversified telecommunications company providing cable television services, broadcast television programming, and interactive multimedia services, including Internet access. Vidéotron's primary market is French-speaking Canada, where the company holds a leadership position in both the cable and broadcast television markets. In Canada overall, Vidéotron is that country's second-largest cable television operator, behind Rogers Cablevision Ltd. The company's broadcast television holdings include the French-speaking TVA Network, and Tele-Metropole, a programming production group that includes Quebec's CFTM in Montreal, the leading private television station of French-speaking Canada. Vidéotron's June 1996 acquisition of CFCF Inc. added that company's 900,000-subscriber cable TV operations, CF Cable TV, and top-rated television station CFCF-12, extending Vidéotron's reach into English-speaking Quebec as well. Vidéotron also owns a chain of video rental stores, called Superclub Vidéotron, with some 40 stores in Quebec, making it the largest video rental chain in that province.

Long led by founder, CEO, and chairman André Chagnon, Vidéotron has built a cable system with some 1,500 kilometers of fiber optic cable and more than 1.5 million subscribers—and a penetration of more than 66 percent—primarily in the Quebec region of Canada. The cable subsidiary provides more than half of the parent company's 1996 C$847 million revenues. But Vidéotron's cable system offers more than the standard package of cable television networks and programs. While the rest of the world has dragged its feet, Chagnon has led Vidéotron firmly into the untested waters of interactive television. After creating the world's first interactive television service, Videoway, in the first half of the 1990s, Vidéotron is now looking to expand the company's interactive programming. Under the moniker "Universality, Bidirectionaltiy, and Interactivity," or UBI (pronounced "you-bee"), Vidéotron has joined with Canada Post, the National Bank of Canada, Loto-Quebec, Hydro-Quebec, and the United States' Hearst Corporation to launch a true two-way interactive television technology. By mid-1997, UBI has been placed in more than 10,000 homes, with plans calling for more than 80 percent penetration of Vidéotron's subscriber base within five years. Vidéotron's investment represents 30 percent of the UBI system.

Vidéotron has been less successful in developing its international operations. In 1996 the company began pulling out of the UK, where it provided cable television and other telecommunications services to the greater London area through its 55 percent ownership of Vidéotron Holdings Plc. Vidéotron also provides wireless cable and private cable television services to the United States, through two joint ventures, Wireless Holdings Inc. and OpTel Inc., primarily in the Florida and California markets. Vidéotron, however, has been attempting to exit these markets as well.

Founding a Cable Empire in the 1960s

Chagnon, a graduate of French Canada's vocational school system, built his first business, an electrical contracting service, in the late 1950s and early 1960s. A large share of that company's business was in laying coaxial cable for the still-emerging cable television industry. In 1964, however, Chagnon—after reading an article claiming that cable television would become a recession-resistant industry—decided to sell his business and enter this new industry. At the age of 32 and with $1 million from the sale of his electrical contracting company, Chagnon established his own cable television operations, called

Le Groupe Vidéotron Ltée, in Montreal, Canada. While building his new business, Chagnon also went back to school, attending night classes and earning a business degree from the University of Montreal.

Until 1980, Vidéotron remained a relatively modest operation, reaching revenues of C$15 million on a subscriber base of just 80,000. But Chagnon determined to expand the company. Reaching an agreement for financial backing from Le Caisse de Dépôt et Placement du Quebec, which gave the Quebecois government's official fund manger a 27 percent voting stake in Vidéotron, Chagnon purchased a far larger competitor, National Cablevision, for $14 million. The purchase paved the way for the company to expand rapidly through the 1980s—and by the end of the decade the company had acquired some 35 cable companies, building a network of more than one million subscribers with more than C$421 million in revenues. Meanwhile, Canada itself had become one of the most-cabled countries in the world, with a penetration of some seven million of the total 9.6 million Canadian households.

By then, too, Vidéotron had gone international. Chagnon first attempted to bring his French-speaking services to France. But legislative impediments in that country—cable operators were required to offer services through third parties—thwarted Vidéotron's 1985 French entry; cable television's penetration in France would remain stalled until well into the 1990s. Instead, Chagnon looked to Great Britain, where legislation enacted in 1987 at last opened the potential for offering television programming services beyond that country's four channel (the two public, fee-based BBC channels and two privately owned channels) television system. In 1989, the company's 61 percent-owned joint-venture with Bell Canada Enterprises Inc., Vidéotron Holdings Plc., was awarded franchises in London and in Southampton-Winchester, with a potential reach of more than one million subscribers. The company began building a cable infrastructure, and by 1990 had already connected some 1,000 subscribers to its 30-channel cable offerings.

An Interactive Vision for the 1990s

Chagnon was not content merely to provide traditional television programming. As early as 1980, he reasoned that television could offer a variety of multimedia services, and, particularly through cable, held the potential of providing an interactive experience to viewers. Vidéotron started out by offering services such as entertainment listings, a dating service, and real estate and employment advertising. A person trying to sell their home, for example, paid $350 to place an ad consisting of 10 or more slides of the house, along with text and voice descriptions of the property. If the property sold, the homeowner paid Vidéotron an additional $2,000. The dating service also proved popular, attracting some 3,500 members by the end of the decade.

Chagnon's vision, however, looked beyond such relatively passive services toward a richer interactive television environment. In 1986, Vidéotron purchased Tele-Metropole, a Quebec-based broadcaster with an eye on producing the programming it needed for future interactive services. And by the middle of the decade, Chagnon had found the technology to support his vision. Vidéotron obtained Canadian and European licenses for an interactive television technology developed by ACTV Domestic Corp. in 1987, and the following year purchased shares in that company. Vidéotron itself worked with ACTV's technology, investing some $43 million to develop its Videoway terminal.

Consisting of a set-top unit, which incorporated a cable converter and a small computer processor, a keyboard, and a remote control, the Videoway service would offer as many as 120 services, ranging from on-screen caption and subtitling to weather reports and other information services. But the true thrust of the service was in its interactive programming. Using four buttons on the remote control, a subscriber could choose from among four channels broadcasting simultaneously. During a sports event, for example, the subscriber had the ability to choose from several camera angles from which to view the event, or from a channel offering continuous instant replays. Subscribers, who paid a fee for the service on top of their regular cable bill, could also tailor a news broadcast to their interests, bypassing the sports reports, for example, in favor of more business news. Viewers were also able to participate in game shows, competing against players in the studio. Viewers would also be able to download and play a range of video games. While the service was still limited to one-way communication—the route back was made through the telephone, the Videoway terminal was able to switch instantaneously among the four channels, giving the viewer a feeling of interactivity.

Vidéotron was not the only one interested in interactive television. Other companies were testing interactive technologies, including the ACTV and Videoway systems in the United States. But Vidéotron was the first to go beyond testing and actually roll out the service to its subscribers. Videoway was launched in September 1989, and by September 1990 the service had been placed in 25,000 homes in Canada. That number more than doubled by the beginning of 1991. By 1995, the service had penetrated some 26 percent of Vidéotron's Canadian subscriber base, representing nearly 320,000 homes. The service had also been introduced into England, reaching some 100,000 of Vidéotron's 500,000 UK cable customers. By the mid-1990s, Videoway represented approximately 10 percent of the company's revenues, which gained steadily, nearing C$580 million by 1993.

While Videoway represented a breakthrough in television programming, it remained essentially a one-way transmission, and not the two-way, truly interactive experience that had captured the industry's attention. And as early as 1993, Vidéotron seemed under threat to be passed by in what was still believed to be the coming interactive television age. Other companies, including Time Warner and AT&T, were developing true two-way television technologies. Vidéotron, in order to upgrade its own system, was faced with an investment of some $250 million. Chagnon went in search of partners, lining up some 50 companies, such as Sears Canada and Quaker Oats, to provide direct marketing services, and attracting interactive services from the Canada Post and Banque National du Canada.

A year later, however, Vidéotron switched tracks. Instead of upgrading Videoway, which the company now dubbed its "Phase I" interactive system, the company instead eyed developing an entirely new interactive system. Forming a consortium, dubbed Universality, Bidirectionality, Interactivity, or UBI, with Canada Post, Banque National du Canada, Hearst Corp., Sociétés des Loteries du Quebec, and the Hydro-Quebec, the government-owned utility, Vidéotron announced its intention to develop a new set-top interactive television device. The "Phase II" device, based on a PowerPC processor, would operate through a 750 Mhz bandwidth along fiber optic cabling, using both analog and digital signals, and the newly developing MPEG II video compression standard. Set-top units would be equipped with smart card readers to enable secure financial transactions. Unlike the fee-based Videoway service, UBI was to be provided free to Vidéotron's cable subscribers, with the devices and services paid for by advertising and revenues generated through use of the interactive services.

UBI attracted strong interest among service providers, which saw the ability to incorporate interactive services as part of marketing and advertising promotions. Among the services to be included were yellow pages listings provided by Hearst Corp., email messaging service provided by Canada Post, and online banking provided by Banque National du Canada. In March 1994, UBI took a step forward when Vidéotron and IBM reached agreement to develop the set-top box technology. IBM later withdrew from the partnership, leaving Vidéotron to complete the development of the UBI system. Rollout of UBI was initially planned for January 1995 in the small northern Quebec city of Chicoutimi, with plans to reach an 80 percent penetration rate of the company's subscriber base by the year 2002. The cost for implementing the service to this extent was estimated at C$750 million.

While Vidéotron was developing UBI, the company was also extending its range. In August 1994, the company's Wireless Holdings joint venture with Transworld Telecommunications Inc., of Salt Lake City, acquired wireless cable licenses in California and South Carolina, adding to its wireless cable franchises in San Francisco, San Jose, Spokane, and Tampa. Later that year, the company's Superclub video store subsidiary acquired Video Supreme, a Quebec-based chain of 15 stores. In the U.K., the deregulation of the telecommunications industry enabled Vidéotron to begin offering telephone services to its subscriber area, which included the Westminster financial district of London. By then, Vidéotron had built the largest fiber optic network in England, and its cable service was the largest in London, with a potential reach of more than 1.2 million households. Its actual subscriber base, however, totalled only slightly more than 105,000 cable subscribers and just under 90,000 telephone customers.

UBI missed its targeted start date. Meanwhile, the company was preparing a new move to build its cable television group. In November 1995, Vidéotron reached an agreement with CFCF to swap assets in a deal worth some C$530. Under the deal, Vidéotron would acquire CFCF's 900,000 cable subscribers in exchange for Vidéotron's 10-station Tele-Metropole holdings.

That deal quickly hit a snag when a third cable company, Cogeco Inc. launched a takeover bid for all of CFCF, forcing Vidéotron to make its own takeover offer. In June 1996, Vidéotron won the takeover battle, and acquired CFCF for C$367 million in cash. The takeover agreement also provided for Vidéotron to assume CFCF's debt of more than $220 million.

The addition of CFCF's holdings boosted Vidéotron to its position as the number two cable operator in Canada, while giving it a lock on cable and broadcast services to the country's French-speaking population. Included in the deal was CFCF's Quatre Saisons television network, which Vidéotron sold off in April 1997 to satisfy Canada's television regulating body. Meanwhile, the unforeseen purchase put a strain on the company's finances. In order to absorb the CFCF acquisition, Vidéotron decided to exit the U.K. cable market. After spending some $800 million building its U.K. infrastructure, while achieving only a 21 percent penetration, the company sold its 55 percent stake in Vidéotron Holdings to Bell Cablemedia for $600 million in October 1996. Vidéotron also began looking to sell off its U.S. wireless cable holdings.

The UBI launch was finally readied for September 1996. The success of interactive television remained to be seen, particularly with the promised advent of increased Internet-based video and data technologies. But Vidéotron had not neglected that market. In April 1996, the company joined with several leading Canadian cable companies, including Rogers Communications, Moffat Communications, Cogeco Cable Inc., Access Cable, and Regina Cable, to form Vison.com with an eye on developing the nationwide, standardized cable network providing Internet, telephony, and interactive television services. As the technology prepared to advance, André Chagnon's vision of interactive television seemed more than a possibility—and Vidéotron was prepared to see it through to reality.

Further Reading

Enchin, Harvey, "Groupe Vidéotron Ltée, "*Variety*, August 26, 1996, p. 65.
Ingrassia, Joanne, "Canadian Firm Leads Two-Way Interactive Push," *Electronic Media*, p. 13.
Jenish, D'Arcy, "Wiring the World," *MacLean's*, July 17, 1989, p. 32.
Moshavi, Sharon, "Canada's Chagnon Bullish on Interactive TV," *Broadcasting*, September 3, 1990.
——, "A Pioneer's Lot Is Not a Happy One," *Forbes*, October 11, 1993, p. 80.
Snyder, Adam, "Videoway Pioneers Testing Ground for Interactive Ads," *Multichannel News*, April 11, 1994, p. 32A.
Stilson, Janet, "Vidéotron Unveils Grand Interactive Alliance," *Multichannel News*, January 24, 1994, p. 1.
"Vidéotron Builds a Dual Carriageway to Fulfill Founder's Interactive Vision," *New Media Age*, October 19, 1995, p. 8.

—M. L. Cohen

Gruntal & Co., L.L.C.

14 Wall Street
New York, New York 10005
U.S.A.
(212) 267-8800
Fax: (212) 962-1810
Web site: http://www.gruntal.com

Private Company
Founded: 1880 as Sternberger & Fuld
Employees: 2,000
Sales: $441 million (1996)
SICs: 6211 Security Brokers, Dealers and Flotation
Companies; 6289 Services Allied with the Exchange
of Securities or Commodities, Not Elsewhere
Classified

Gruntal & Co., L.L.C. is a brokerage house whose principal activity is trading stocks, bonds, and options. Its activities also include the underwriting and distribution of stocks and bonds, corporate and municipal finance, transactions in all types of tax-advantage investments, government securities and commodities, the underwriting and sale of mutual fund unit trust securities, investment banking, financial planning, life insurance and annuities, and other related services. Given the bull market of the 1990s, a series of scandals did not keep the firm from expanding and prospering during this period.

Private Partnership, 1880–1983

The company was founded as Sternberger & Fuld in 1880 by Maurice Sternberger, who entered a partnership with Ludwig Fuld. Sternberger bought a seat on the New York Stock Exchange in 1881 for $20,000. They were joined in 1884 by a third partner, Samuel Sinn, and the firm became Sternberger, Fuld & Sinn, with an office at 52 Broadway in lower Manhattan. There is little documentation to tell the exact nature of the firm's business, but Wall Street men of the time were known as merchant bankers. They would visit the city's merchants and businessmen in the morning to purchase IOUs, which they would stick under their hats. About noon they would walk uptown to the large banks to sell them. Hundreds, perhaps thousands, of similar small partnerships were formed, each specializing in certain kinds of investments.

Benedict H. Gruntal joined the firm in 1890 as a clerk at the age of 17 and worked his way up to cashier. He became a partner in 1900, shortly after obtaining a seat on the New York Stock Exchange—likely a wedding gift from Sternberger for marrying one of his daughters. Gruntal's net worth was only $5,000 when he paid $40,500 for the seat. Soon after, the firm moved to 60 Broadway and was renamed Sternberger & Sinn.

During Gruntal's early years as a partner, he developed a friendship and business relationship with a young stockbroker named Albert M. Lilienthal. Sponsored by Sternberger, Lilienthal purchased a seat on the New York Stock Exchange in 1908 for between $51,000 and $80,000. Since he was only 23, the seat was probably a gift from his father. When Sternberger & Sinn closed in 1918—its eponymous partners having retired—the firm immediately reopened as Gruntal, Lilienthal & Co. Benedict Gruntal's brother, Edwin A. Gruntal, bought Lilienthal's seat for $300,000 in 1928.

The firm became Gruntal & Co. in 1931, with the Gruntal brothers, Morris Hartig, and Samuel Wechsler as partners and offices still at 60 Broadway. It was one of the oldest houses with membership on the New York Stock Exchange when it acquired the bond-trading firm Speyer, Alexander & Co. in 1933. Benedict Gruntal sold his seat on the exchange in 1937 but remained a general partner until his death in 1968 at the age of 95. Hartig became the managing partner. In 1938 Gruntal & Co, opened its first branch office, in the Hotel McAlpin at Herald Square. During the early 1940s the firm opened several other branches, including one on West 47th Street in Manhattan's diamond district. By 1955 Gruntal had 10 general partners and had added a branch office in New Haven, Connecticut. The firm, now at 50 Broadway, merged with Stearns & Co. in 1963. Its net worth exceeded $3 million, and it had its own clearing operation.

A *New York Times* feature in 1970 on Harold T. Warshay, president of Gruntal's institutional department, indicated that a broker's life is anything but glamorous. Warshay had made large-block stock trades a significant part of the company's total trading, but only by a tedious daily telephone canvass to find prospective buyers of poor-performing "distress merchandise." "On a typical situation," he said, "we'll check out a dozen banks in New York, half a dozen in other parts of the country, and 50 to 60 insurance companies as well as our mutual fund contacts." He calculated that fewer than 5 percent of the calls were successful.

Gruntal doubled in size by purchasing the assets of the investment/brokerage firm Steiner, Rouse & Co. in 1974. Howard Silverman, who became managing partner that year, pursued a strategy of further growth through acquisition of other regional brokerages. After the acquisition of Philadelphia-based E.W. Smith & Co. in 1982, Gruntal had 23 offices in 7 Atlantic Seaboard states. Its revenues came to $102.1 million in fiscal 1983 (the year ended August 26, 1983), and net income was $7.4 million.

Expansion in the 1980s

In December 1983 the company went public as Gruntal Financial Corp., offering about 30 percent of its outstanding stock at $8.50 per share. The $23.3 million raised by this sale was used to finance acquisitions intended to make Gruntal & Co., a subsidiary, a full-service investment organization. At this time Gruntal primarily provided securities brokerage and trading services and related financial services in support of its broker-dealer activities. It also participated in the underwriting of corporate and municipal securities and the sale of tax-advantaged investments. Regional Clearing Corp., also a subsidiary and member of the New York Stock Exchange, provided securities execution and clearing services to Gruntal and other broker-dealers.

Gruntal added seven new offices to its 11 existing ones in fiscal 1984, in Pennsylvania, Florida, and Washington, D.C. It established a full-service division for futures trading in commodities and a proprietary index futures fund. The firm also added insurance products with specific tax and investment advantages to its financial planning activities and expanded its company-sponsored real estate syndication program. In addition, Gruntal increased the size of its corporate-finance department in an effort to expand its abilities to manage underwritings, render financial opinions, and advise clients with respect to mergers and acquisitions. Sterling Capital Management was a new money management division formed in September 1984 to direct both pension fund and individual accounts.

Gruntal nearly doubled its revenues by paying $3.1 million in notes and warrants to acquire the Herzfeld & Stern securities and investment banking unit of Josephson International Inc. in 1985. This unit had been losing $8 million a year, but two months after the purchase it was turning a profit. One of Gruntal's first steps was to farm out Herzfeld & Stern's clearing operation to an independent firm, a move that resulted in $4 million in savings. The acquisition strengthened Gruntal in the field of corporate finance, although retail brokerage remained its biggest revenue producer, with the trading department a strong second.

In fiscal 1987 Gruntal had net income of $8.4 million on revenue of $218.8 million and had more than 600 account executives operating out of 32 offices stretching from Maine to Florida. Brokerage transactions with retail customers continued to account for the greatest percentage of the firm's revenues.

Gruntal Financial Corp. was acquired by Home Insurance Co. in 1987 for about $145 million. Home Group Inc., the parent of Home Insurance, had a $4 billion investment portfolio and said it wanted to move into money management, planning to develop mutual funds for Gruntal to sell. It also expected Gruntal to sell insurance and planned to steer corporate finance business in Gruntal's direction. Silverman, president and chief executive officer of Gruntal, said the purchase would allow his firm to focus on the areas of managed money, mutual fund, and fixed income products, investment banking, and underwriting. Gruntal established a coast-to-coast presence during 1988–89 with the opening of offices in the Midwest and California. In 1990 it founded The GMS Group, L.L.C., a fixed income investment firm servicing both individuals and institutions.

Challenges of the 1990s

Home Group, subsequently renamed AmBase Corp., sold its Home Insurance subsidiary, including Gruntal, in 1991 for $970 million to an investment group led by Swedish-based Trygg-Hansa SPP Group Inc., the largest insurance company in Scandinavia. Home Insurance, with Gruntal, then became part of Home Holdings Inc., a consortium directed by Trygg-Hansa. Home Holdings later became a private company in which the Swiss insurance firm Zurich American took a large stake. By this time Gruntal had become the nation's 14th largest full-service brokerage firm, with more than 1,800 employees and capital of over $170 million—a tenfold increase in 10 years. The company also had established its own small institutional equity shop—a "research boutique." By mid-1994 Gruntal had $2.5 billion in assets and 35 offices in 10 states.

Unfortunately, Gruntal also accumulated heaps of publicity because of a succession of scandals. In 1994 the company fired two managers whom it accused of stealing at least $3 million. The alleged scheme involved the wire transfer of funds to fictitious accounts, according to the company, and to various accounts established by co-conspirators. The two suspects fled to Ireland but returned and pleaded guilty the following year. The scandal widened still further in 1996, when Edward Bao, formerly executive vice-president of the firm, was indicted by a grand jury in connection with the scheme. The Securities and Exchange Commission charged that $14 million had been embezzled. Gruntal agreed to pay $6.2 million in fines and $5.5 million in customer restitution, among the biggest penalties ever imposed on a Wall Street firm. Some of the money went to settle other improprieties in the firm's trading and managed account divisions. Bao pleaded guilty in 1997 to falsifying the firm's books and records.

Gruntal also reaped embarrassing publicity in 1995, when a synagogue in New York's suburban Westchester County said it had lost $650,000 from its capital campaign through investments in highly speculative securities. The Jewish center contended that it was misled by Gruntal into thinking the securities were virtually risk free and that it had been charged more than $100,000 in commissions. A spokesman for the company said the accusations were "completely unfounded," but six months later an arbitration panel of the New York Stock Exchange upheld the synagogue's complaint and ordered Gruntal to refund the money lost.

In a less publicized case, Ted H. Westerfield, a former Gruntal & Co. account executive, was convicted in 1996 of paying $35,000 in kickbacks to a bond analyst who sent junk-bond business his way. In 1997 a federal judge ordered Wester-field, who was sent to prison, to pay nearly $345,000 in restitution.

In still another embarrassing incident, the Equal Employment Opportunity Commission in 1997 upheld charges of sexual harassment by six current and former Gruntal female employees. According to the allegations, two branch managers at a company office in Manhattan had harassed the women with sexual gestures, groping, and lurid suggestions between 1993 and 1996. Gruntal agreed to pay each woman $125,000 but did not admit guilt. One of the managers had resigned in 1996 when he learned he was to be fired; the other was assigned to nonsupervisory work.

Silverman was ousted as CEO in 1995 after allegations of improper personal trading emerged in a wrongful dismissal lawsuit filed by a former Gruntal manager. He accused Silverman of cheating retail customers by having his own traders buy municipal bonds below the market and then selling them to the accounts of Silverman and another Gruntal executive. Silverman was replaced by Robert Rittereiser, formerly head of another brokerage firm, E.F. Hutton & Co. One of his first acts was to implement a policy forbidding traders and brokers from capturing for themselves, without disclosure, the spread in the trades they were doing for their customers. He was also said to be putting restraints on some of the company's more aggressive cold calling brokers.

Rittereiser indicated that Gruntal would go back to basics. Interviewed by *Investment Dealers' Digest* in 1996, he said, "The idea is not to be corporate-finance-driven, but investor-driven. The idea will be to keep simple, stay liquid, and trade traditional products. . . . Build a retail trading and institutional business without having to concentrate on manufacturing product on the advice and distribution side." Rittereiser acknowledged that by not creating and marketing its own mutual funds and other offerings Gruntal would lose income, but he said the company would also cut its costs.

In February 1997 Gruntal was sold to a management group led by Rittereiser in a leveraged buyout valued at about $235 million in securities. The company's parent Home Insurance

Co. received preferred stock valued at $225 million and the management group preferred stock valued at $10 million. The eight managers, who did not put up any of the cash for the buyout, would take an eventual 60 percent stake in the underlying equity of the new company as they retired the preferred stock, while Home Insurance would get the remaining 40 percent. Gruntal, which was said to have earned more than $20 million in 1996 on revenue topping $400 million, was restructured as a limited liability company, Gruntal & Co., L.L.C. Executives said the buyout could pave the way to eventually taking the firm public or merging it with another company.

Rittereiser said Gruntal planned to add 100 to 200 account executives in about a year and would build up its corporate financing operations while continuing to focus on research and stock trading. The company had some $2.8 billion in assets and capital of about $195 million.

Further Reading

Abele, John J., "Hard Work Pays Off for Gruntal," *New York Times,* May 17, 1970, Sec. 3, p. 2.

Brief History of Gruntal. New York: Gruntal & Co., rev. ed., 1997.

"Ex-Gruntal Employee to Pay About $345,000," *Wall Street Journal,* May 27, 1997, p. B2.

Lueck, Thomas J., "Brokerage Pays $750,000 in Harassment Case," *New York Times,* May 7, 1997, p. B7.

Morrow, David J., "Gruntal Agrees to Fraud Fine As U.S. Indicts Former Official," *New York Times,* April 10, 1996, pp. D1, D3.

Narod, Susan, "Home Strikes Merger Deal with Gruntal Fin. Corp.," *National Underwriter (Property & Casualty/Employee Benefits* edition), July 6, 1987, pp. 2, 7.

Pae, Peter, "AmBase Says Holders Clear Sale of Unit," *Wall Street Journal,* February 13, 1991, p. A4.

Raghavan, Anita, "Gruntal Agrees to Leveraged Buyout by Managers for $235 Million in Stock," *Wall Street Journal,* February 25, 1997, p. C21.

Sachar, Laura, "Growth Strategy," *Barron's,* July 28, 1986, pp. 42–43.

Salpukas, Agis, "Gruntal Executives to Lead Leveraged Buyout of Firm," *New York Times,* February 26, 1997, p. D21.

Steinberg, Jacques, "Synagogue Says Misleading Advice by a Brokerage Firm Resulted in a $650,000 Loss," *New York Times,* January 16, 1995, p. B5.

Willoughby, Jack, "Gruntal Senior Executives Accused in Back Office Scam," *Investment Dealers' Digest,* February 13, 1995, pp. 6–7.

——, "Gruntal Hires Fensterstock As It Moves to Clean House," *Investment Dealers' Digest,* February 12, 1996, p. 4.

——, "Gruntal Reorganizes Reporting in Anticipation of Major Fine," *Investment Dealers' Digest,* April 1, 1996, p. 5.

——, "Rittereiser Outlines Strategy for Gruntal's Rehabilitation," *Investment Dealers' Digest,* April 15, 1996, pp. 7–8.

—Robert Halasz

HAEMONETICS®

Haemonetics Corporation

400 Wood Road
Braintree, Massachusetts 02184
U.S.A.
(617) 848-7100
Web site: www.haemonetics.com

Public Company
Founded: 1971
Employees: 1,526
Sales: $309.8 million (fiscal year ended March 29, 1997)
Stock Exchanges: New York
SICs: 3841 Surgical and Medical Instruments

Haemonetics Corporation is the world leader in automated blood processing, developing and manufacturing equipment that automatically collects and processes blood and blood products. In 1997, it was the only company in the world with clearances from the U.S. Food and Drug Administration to market devices which collect whole blood and separate out the individual blood components (red cells, platelets, and plasma) at the same time. It also owns blood banks in Arizona, Kansas, and California and provides management services to blood centers throughout the United States. Its corporate headquarters are in Braintree, Massachusetts, with international headquarters in Nyon, Switzerland, and Far Eastern headquarters in Tokyo, Japan.

The company's primary products are used to collect and process blood from donors and from patients in operating rooms. In the surgical blood salvage market, involving the collection and reinfusion of an individual's own blood for use during surgery, the company had a worldwide market share of 60–65 percent in 1997. It held an even larger share (65–70 percent) of the worldwide market for collecting plasma, and had nearly 40 percent of the blood component therapy market—collecting blood components for therapeutic use.

Haemonetics' fourth market area is automated red cell collection. Technology developed by Haemonetics and approved in 1997 makes it possible for blood banks to collect two units (pints) of red blood cells from a donor, twice the amount that could be collected manually, the only alternative technology.

The company markets its products to hospitals, blood banks and centers, national health organizations, and plasma fractionators in over 50 countries, with 60 percent of its business coming from outside the United States.

Early Years

Allan "Jack" Latham, Jr. founded Haemonetics in 1971 and the company opened for business in 1972. Its first product was a blood processing machine called the Model 10, which it sold to blood banks and hospitals. Latham developed the Model 10 in the mid-1960s, while working as a scientist for Arthur D. Little Company, and Abbott Laboratories marketed it for a short time. When Abbott decided to stop selling the machine, Latham raised about $1 million from some private investors and created Haemonetics.

The Model 10 made use of a technology Latham had developed working with scientists and doctors from Harvard University to solve the problem of removing glycerol, a kind of antifreeze, from stored, frozen blood. His solution was a plastic, disposable bowl, which could be spun at high speeds to separate the glycerol from the denser red blood cells. His blood centrifuge, called the Latham bowl, made the development of large-scale blood freezing possible.

Haemonetics combined the chamber with a set of plastic tubing that could also be thrown away after being used. Because the plastic chamber was relatively inexpensive, and could be discarded after each donor, the Latham bowl revolutionized the way blood was collected and processed. No longer was it necessary to use stainless steel chambers that had to be taken apart carefully, sterilized, then put back together after each use.

These disposable sets served as the foundation for the company's future products and development. With Haemonetics' technology, the donor or patient blood was first mixed with a sterile solution to avoid clotting. The treated blood was then pumped between the person giving the blood and the Latham bowl chamber through disposable plastic tubing by pumps on the equipment. The blood flow was controlled by microprocessors and the blood was separated into its components by density, with red blood cells (the heaviest component) moving to the outside and the lighter cells and plasma moving to the inside.

In the mid-1970s, Haemonetics expanded on this technology to automate the collection of platelets, needed to help cancer patients whose own bone marrow could not produce enough platelets. Called bone marrow suppression, this condition usually occurred as a side effect of chemotherapy. Platelets made up a very small portion of a person's 10 pints of blood; a single pint of whole blood contained only one-sixth to one-eighth the number of platelets required for a therapeutic dose. Therefore, before Haemonetics introduced its system, platelets from as many as eight donors had to be pooled or merged to get enough for a treatment.

What Haemonetics did was to take the plasma out of the chamber once it was separated and collect it in a special bag. The remaining blood components (still in the chamber) were then returned to the donor. This apheresis technology meant that donors were not limited to donating whole blood, which could only be done every eight weeks. Instead, a donor could give plasma as often as twice a week. A blood bank thus could reduce the number of donors needed for pooling and provide a safer product. In 1979, the company went public.

The 1980s—More Innovations and a New Company

In the early 80s, Haemonetics introduced Cell Saver. This system automated the salvage and cleaning of a patient's blood during surgery. During the procedure, the red blood cells remained in the chamber and were washed clean of other blood components before being routed to a bag for reinfusion.

The timing was advantageous as the fear of contracting HIV infection or hepatitis from blood transfusions became a major health concern in the mid-1980s. To reduce that risk, the industry instituted what was known as autologous blood transfusions. That procedure involved a patient donating a pint or two of his or her own blood that was then given back to them after surgery. The CellSaver went even further, often eliminating the need for banked blood, since it recovered the patient's own blood in the operating room and reinfused it during and after surgery. Between 1984 and 1988, Haemonetics' sales tripled to over $90 million and net income skyrocketed, reaching $10 million. No only did the systems become more popular, the fact that they were disposable meant that hospitals and blood centers kept buying replacement tubes, chambers, and other supplies to use with the centrifuge, pumps, and other original equipment.

During this time, the company was sold, spun off, then taken private. In August 1983, American Hospital Supply Corporation bought Haemonetics for $70 million. Two years later Baxter Traneol Laboratories (Baxter International, Inc.) acquired

American Hospital Supply and then divested Haemonetics because of antitrust concerns since the two companies competed in certain areas. In December 1985, a group of private investors purchased Haemonetics. The investors were primarily present and former employees of Haemonetics, including John F. White, who became chairman, president, and CEO, and James L. Peterson, who became vice-chairman and president of international operations, and E.I. duPont de Nemours and Company (Du Pont).

The company introduced its first Automated Plasma Collection System (PCS) soon afterwards. Traditionally, plasma was collected manually as part of whole blood collection. In the United States, commercial firms collected the plasma from donors and then processed or fractionated it themselves to derive various products including gamma globulins used in preventing such diseases as tetanus, rabies, and measles; hepatitis vaccine; and albumin used with burn and shock victims.

Haemonetics' new system significantly cut the time needed to collect plasma, so that an individual spent only 40 minutes donating plasma instead of the 90 minutes required for manual collection. It also yielded a higher-quality plasma than manual methods because a smaller amount of anticoagulant was needed, and increased donor safety—since the donor was never separated from his or her own blood, there was no risk of having the wrong red cells returned.

To encourage commercial firms such as Alpha Therapeutics, Bayer, and Centeon to convert from manual procedures to the automated system, Haemonetics established a program under which it installed and serviced its plasma collection systems free of charge to certain plasma collection centers. Those centers, in turn, agreed to purchase at least a minimum number of the disposable chambers from the company.

By the end of the decade, fiscal 1990, Haemonetics had sales of over $124 million and net profits of over $11 million.

Improving the Systems, 1990–93

In May 1991, the company was taken public again, with Du Pont selling all of its 47 percent interest during the initial public offering. That same year Haemonetics acquired direct distribution rights for their blood component therapy and plasma collection products in Japan from Labo Science Co., Ltd. of Tokyo. The company, which had over 900 employees, ended fiscal 1992 with sales of $216.3 million and net income of $18 million. A few years later, the company acquired the direct distribution rights for their surgical blood salvage products in Japan from Kuraray, Co., Ltd.

Over the years, the company introduced various improvements on its systems. Building on its years of experience with automated platelet collection, the company developed the MCS and MCS+ apheresis systems which put the equipment on wheels, making it possible to collect blood components and provide blood component therapy to cancer patients or those with blood disorders at a blood bank or other outpatient location. Blood component therapy involved treating people who needed only specific blood components, not whole blood. The same system was also used for therapeutic plasma exchange, in which a patient's plasma was replaced with either frozen plasma or albumin. Because patients received treatments over weeks or months, convenience was a major consideration for them as well as for the hospitals and other groups providing the treatment. The company's major competitors in the blood component therapy market were COBE Laboratories, Inc. (a subsidiary of Gamboro AB) and Baxter International.

The company also expanded its Cell Saver line of products used to salvage blood during and after surgery. In situations such as organ transplants or open heart surgery, requiring transfusion of large volumes of blood and fluids, the Rapid Infusion System (RIS) incorporated a proprietary heating element that warmed the blood products before they were infused, eliminating the threat of hypothermia. The CollectFirst system could be used either for direct reinfusion or with the Cell Saver system for washing the collected red blood cells. The HaemoLite product line provided a portable automated system useful for procedures where there was less blood loss. The company sold these systems to surgeons, primarily cardiovascular, orthopedic, and trauma specialists. In this market, Haemonetics competed with Medtronics, Inc., COBE Laboratories, Inc., and Sorin Biomedica.

In the area of plasma collection, the company's PS and PS + systems competed with Baxter International and with manual collection systems. In the red cell market, Haemonetics had no competition other than traditional collection and separation methods.

New Ventures: 1994 to the Present

In 1994, the company began augmenting its traditional manufacturing activities. First was the establishment of Haemonetics Blood Services and Training Institute. Located in Arizona, the institute provided Haemonetics' customers with courses lasting three to five days in which they learned apheresis theory, regulatory requirements, and program management, and gained first-hand experience with the company's equipment in noncritical situations. HBSTI also maintained an extensive library in the field of transfusion medicine.

The following year the company acquired DHL Laboratories Corporation, a contract pharmaceutical manufacturer. DHL made solutions, including anticoagulants, storage liquids, and similar products. Haemonetics' products now included the solutions as well as the equipment and disposables used during blood and plasma collection.

In 1996, Haemonetics made a strategic move into the blood bank service business and created Haemonetics Management Services to manage blood collection agencies. It signed its first agreements with New England Medical Center, a major hospital in Boston, and the Oklahoma Blood Institute. Services included recruitment of donors and collection and distribution of blood components, with the new division receiving a fee for each blood component collected. To attract more donors to the centers, the company made telephone calls to people who had never donated blood before, opened easy-to-reach centers, and decorated the locations in bright, cheery colors with a play area for donors' children.

As part of this new strategy, the company also formed Pacific Blood Services, a 50/50 joint venture with the San Diego Blood Bank, to open apheresis centers in Orange County and other counties surrounding Los Angeles.

During 1997, Haemonetics continued to expand the number of blood centers it owned. In April it acquired the Santa Barbara-based Tri-Counties Blood Bank. That blood bank annually collected and distributed more than 24,000 red cell units and over 3,500 apheresis platelet components in Santa Barbara, San Luis Obispo, Santa Maria, and Salinas, California. In conjunction with Pacific Blood Services, Haemonetics was now able to provide blood products and services from Orange County in southern California to San Mateo in the north. In July, the company purchased Kansas Blood Services, a Topeka-based blood center collecting and distributing some 20,000 units of red cells and over 1,000 apheresis platelet products.

Both of these blood centers were not-for-profit entities, and the proceeds from each sale were distributed to a local foundation, to be used in medical education and research activities. All regulatory licenses owned by the centers transferred to Haemonetics with the purchases, making the company fully licensed to collect and distribute blood components. Through its owned and managed centers, Haemonetics was now a vertically integrated company, providing products and services as the company expressed it, "vein to vein."

While the growth of the service business was undoubtedly important to the company, more significant to the nation's blood supply was FDA approval to market Haemonetics' proprietary technology that made it possible for donors to give two pints of blood at one sitting. FDA gave its approval in 1996 to use the system with people donating their own blood, and then gave clearance in 1997 to use it with voluntary donors at blood banks.

Most of the 12 to 13 million units of blood collected by banks in the United States were collected and processed manually. The same held for the approximately 36 million units collected worldwide. Even if used only to collect the blood types in shortest supply, it was a big market. Haemonetics' challenge was to convince cost-conscious hospitals and other users that their systems were cost-effective and less than the additional recruitment and testing expenses needed with the cheaper manual procedure.

Principal Subsidiaries

Kansas Blood Services; Tri-Counties Blood Bank; Haemonetics S.A. International (Switzerland); Haemonetics Scandinavia AB (Sweden); Haemonetics GmbH (Germany); Haemonetics France; Haemonetics U.K. Ltd.; Haemonetics Japan Co., Ltd.; Haemonetics Ventures Corp.; Haemonetics Foreign Sales Corp. (Virgin Island); Haemonetics Services, Inc.; Nayon Associates Corp.; Haemonetics Blood Services and Training Institute; Haemonetics Belgium S.A./N.V.; Haemonetics Italia Srl (80%).

Further Reading

Alpert, Bill, "Cash Transfusion?" *Barron's*, April 29, 1996, p. 18.
Angrist, Stanley W., "Blood Money," *Forbes*, June 27, 1988, p. 139.
"Squeezing Higher Profits from a Pint of Blood," *Money*, September 1994, p. 65.

—Ellen D. Wernick

HAMPTON Industries, Inc.

Hampton Industries, Inc.

2000 Greenville Highway
P.O. Box 614
Kinston, North Carolina 28502-0614
U.S.A.
(919) 527-8011
Fax: (919) 527-3538

Public Company
Incorporated: 1925 as the Hampton Shirt Company
Employees: 960
Sales: $160 million (1996)
Stock Exchanges: American
SICs: 2321 Men's & Boys' Shirts Except Work Shirts;
2331 Women's, Misses' & Jr. Blouses & Shirts; 2254
Knit Underwear & Nightwear Mills; 2329 Men's &
Boys' Clothing, Not Elsewhere Classified

Hampton Industries, Inc. is one of the oldest companies in the United States engaged in the manufacturing and selling of wearing apparel for men, women and children. The company manufactures men's and boy's shirts, men's and women's sleepwear, sweaters, sportswear, swimtrunks and other items. While manufacturing and selling its own apparel under the company's tradenames "Le Tigre," "Campus," and "Kaynee," Hampton Industries also manufactures and sells apparel under the "Rawlings" and "Nautica for Boy's" trademarks as licensees, and has recently reached new license agreement with such prestigious apparel lines as "Ron Chereskin," "Bugle Boy," "Apex," and "Dickies." Hampton's products are sold across the United States in many of the nation's leading retail chains, including such stores as Wal-Mart and J.C. Penney Company. A majority of the company's apparel is manufactured domestically within the United States, but during the 1990s Hampton has made arrangements to produce more of its products in Central America and Asia. Under the auspices of the Caribbean Incentive Program, the company has entered into two joint ventures for apparel manufacturing in Central America,

and numerous agreements have been made with firms in Asia for the same purpose.

Early History

The founder of the Hampton Shirt Company was L. Hampton, a lifelong resident of North Carolina who believed in the value of a well-made man's shirt. Hampton was a successful businessman in Kinston who had always wanted to establish his own apparel company. The need for high-quality dress shirts was a priority in North Carolina, because a southern gentleman who was engaged in business during the 1920s was expected to dress appropriately. What this meant was that every man working in a bank, insurance agency, hospital, or government office was expected to wear a high, stiff-collar, white cotton dress shirt with a suit and tie. Recognizing the need for a regional manufacturer of high-quality dress shirts, Hampton decided to start his own company in 1925. By the end of the decade, the Hampton Shirt Company had garnered a reputation for low-cost, durable yet comfortable, cotton dress shirts that a man could wear to work. Business boomed, and soon the company had approximately 200 employees with an ever-increasing number of satisfied customers.

From the beginning, the company sold its shirts to local retail stores under its own brand name. At the same time, Hampton began to manufacture shirts under license to the brand name of retail stores in the region. This idea of licensing enabled the company to take advantage of the desire many small retailers had in selling their own brand name dress shirt. One of the obvious reasons was to instill of sense of customer loyalty so that the retailer would have a fairly regular customer list over a period of time. Another reason, not any less important, was for advertising the name of the retail store.

With the stock market crash of 1929, and the coming of the Great Depression, Hampton Shirt Company was especially hit hard. Although the effects of the economic downturn left no business in the United States untouched, Hampton Shirt Company not only lost a good many of its customers but was also forced to lay off many of its employees. Most businessmen, instead of purchasing newly-made, white cotton dress shirts, continued to wear their old shirts until they became frayed around the collar and cuffs. As revenues decreased, so did the fortunes of the company. When the Great Depression deepened in its economic severity, management at the company decided to reduce the workforce to a skeleton crew, and keep its operating expenditures to the absolute minimum. These draconian measures were effective to the extent that the company continued in business, but just barely.

World War II and the Postwar Era

With the U.S. entry into World War II after the Japanese bombed the American Naval Base at Pearl Harbor, Hawaii, the Hampton Shirt Company's fortunes changed dramatically. Suddenly, the company was contracted by the United States Armed Forces to manufacture millions of khaki cotton shirts in regular Army green, and numerous other regulation colors. Hampton shirts were worn by generals, privates, ensigns, fighter pilots, cooks, mechanics, and drill sergeants. The company expanded its workforce almost overnight, and added evening and night shifts in order to meet the deadlines established by the government contracts. Revenues increased, and the company continued to expand throughout the remainder of the war.

After World War II ended with the formal surrenders of Germany and Japan in April and August 1945, respectively, Hampton Shirt Company resumed the volume of business it had created for itself during the 1920s. Sales continued to increase as the postwar boom brought new business and activity to the region around Kinston, North Carolina. The company's customer list began to grow rapidly, as retail stores throughout the area contracted Hampton Shirts to manufacture dress shirts under their own label. As previously, Hampton Shirts still made products under their own brand name, and sold them in major retail stores throughout the South, but the licensing agreements were just as lucrative for the company.

The Hampton Shirt Company continued its success throughout the decade of the 1950s. In fact, the 1950s were much like the previous 20 years of the company's business; businessmen still wore white cotton dress shirts to work and were expected to do so in light of the social conventions of the time. Although the company began to expand into other kinds of shirts, including sports shirts and work shirts, the mainstay of the business was the ubiquitous white dress shirt. By the end of the decade, the Hampton Shirt Company had doubled its number of employees, while revenues had also increased significantly.

The 1960s saw Hampton Shirt Company grow slowly but steadily in product lines, revenues, and employees. At the beginning of the 1960s, men were still adhering to the time-honored, traditional dress code of white shirt and dark suit when conducting business. Yet as the social milieu of the United States began to change, and an attitude of skepticism and rebellion towards all that had been previously accepted, most evidently regarding government policies but also including social and behavior norms, swept through the younger generation of the country, people began to dress differently. The white cotton shirt and dark business suit was no longer thought of as the only appropriate manner of dress in which to conduct business. With this more casual approach to business attire came the colored dress shirt in hues of blue, pink, yellow, and beige. The Hamp-

ton Shirt Company thus began to manufacture many more lines of shirts and, as the demand for their products grew, so too did the need to expand the firm's facilities. As the 1960s came to a close, the company had designed a number of new product lines, expanded its facilities from one plant to three plants in order to accommodate the rising demand for its products, and had offered a public sale of its stock on the American Exchange.

Growth and Expansion

During the 1970s and 1980s, the company continued its uninterrupted period of postwar growth. New facilities were constructed in Virginia and North Carolina, with a brand-new, state-of-the-art executive headquarters built in Kinston, North Carolina. Having changed its name from the Hampton Shirt Company to Hampton Industries, Inc., to reflect its diverse product lines, the company employed approximately 2,000 by 1979. Recognizing that the company needed an office close to the center of the nation's retail activities, management decided to open a sales and merchandising office in New York City near the heart of the clothing district. Within a few years, Hampton Industries had expanded its operations to include seven plants and three distribution centers in Virginia and North Carolina, while the New York office continued to buzz with the excitement of procuring new contracts and licensing agreements.

The two factors that enable Hampton Industries to garner such success within the highly competitive apparel industry were the quickness of its manufacturing methods and the use of the latest technology for garment production. From the early 1980s on, management at Hampton Industries was committed to a capital improvement strategy that would increase the firm's production capacity while lowering costs at the same time. Over $10 million was apportioned during the 1980s for the company to take advantage of the latest technology within the apparel industry. One of the first installments made by management was the Amdahl 5860 computer, which was programmed to control all of the company's inventory, payroll, accounting, budgeting, order entry and shipping, purchasing, telephone systems for all company locations, cutting tickets, plant scheduling, and electronic mail.

Yet the most instructive example of the company's ability to reduce costs through the use of new technology was clearly evident in its collar constructions for shirts. Employing highly advanced fusing equipment, the lining of a shirt is fused to the top ply of a collar and then made on a state-of-the-art automatic collar-running machine. One Hampton employee was therefore able to combine collar clip-and-turn, press and topstitch into one operation. By using a Lunapress machine, one employee could accomplish the first three stages of this process on two collars at the same time. Additional technology that Hampton brought to its workrooms included a Gartech Teva servo cutting system, custom built spreading equipment, Necchi pocketsetters, mechanized sewing and indexing equipment, hemmers and cuff running machines, buttonhole indexers, Tajima embroidery machines, banding machines and collar runners, and automatic collar topstitchers.

All of this automation paid off handsomely for the company. From 1984 to 1989, sales rose steadily, and by 1989 sales totaled $181 million, up nearly $9 million from the previous year. At the same time, Hampton Industries became more cost effective, with its workforce reduced from 3,000 employees in 1986 to just under 2,500 by 1990. In both 1986 and 1990, the company was awarded the highly prestigious AIM Gold Star Award. Organized by the editors at the *Apparel Industry Magazine,* the AIM Gold Star Award was given to a company within the apparel industry that had been nominated and then chosen by over 100 industry suppliers, consultants, and research institutions as the "Best of the Brightest."

The 1990s and Beyond

In 1992, Hampton Industries reported its highest ever annual sales figure—$203 million. Yet even at that time the apparel industry was experiencing a dramatic transformation. Intense competition had led many clothing manufacturers to seek out and establish themselves in niche markets, such as work clothing or sportswear. Unfortunately, Hampton Industries had recently expanded its product line to include a host of new items such as ladies sleepwear, activewear, men's shirts and sportswear, and boy's shirts and sportswear. As the competition for customers grew fiercer, Hampton was gradually squeezed out of many of its traditional and sustaining markets. By 1994, annual sales for the company had fallen to $172 million.

Astutely recognizing the trends within the industry, management at Hampton Industries began to implement a comprehensive restructuring strategy that would help the company regain its competitive edge. One of the first steps management took was to immediately discontinue those product lines which were unprofitable and, more importantly, reduce excess domestic production capacity. Accordingly, the company decided to close a number of its plants in Virginia, thereby reducing its operating costs, but also began to increase its imports from overseas. Agreements were made with companies in the Far East, Central America, and the Caribbean to manufacture shirts and sportswear under the brand name of Hampton, and then ship them to the United States for distribution and sale. By the mid-1990s, Hampton Industries was importing approximately 40 percent of all its products from overseas manufacturers.

In addition, each of the company's eight divisions had clarified and established marketing goals and strategies to attain them. Narrower segments of each market were identified, and management pursued a niche in each market where Hampton's product line could be sustained over a period of five to 10 years. Licensing also played a significant role in the company's re-

structuring strategy, with Hampton Industries reaching agreements with Dickies to manufacture casual and rugged sportswear, and with Apex for men's activewear. Management hoped that Dickies' position as leader in the retail workwear apparel market, and Apex's spot as the premier sports apparel brand name, would provide exposure for the company's own brand name products and enable Hampton Industries to attain a similar position in the sportswear market.

The strategy to revive the company's fortunes is still awaiting a final verdict. Although sales rose in 1995 to $184 million, the 1996 sales figures were somewhat disappointing, having dropped to $160 million for the fiscal year. Yet Hampton Industries continues its restructuring strategy, with more and more products manufactured overseas and shipped to the United States.

Principal Subsidiaries

Production Link, Ltd.; Samsons Inc.; Samsons Manufacturing Corporation; Kinston Shirt Company; Samsons Apparel Corporation; Kinston Paper Box Co., Inc.; Kinston Die Cutting Corporation; Hampco Apparel, Inc.; Hampton Shirt Co., Inc.; Snow Hill Apparel Co., Inc.; Hamptex Inc.; IGM Corp., S.A. de C.V. (El Salvador).

Further Reading

D'Innocenzio, Anne, "Nautica: A New Approach," *Women's Wear Daily,* November 13, 1996, p. 7.
Feitelberg, Rosemary, and Ozzard, Janet, "Designers Eye a New Step," *Women's Wear Daily,* April 18, 1996, p. 7.
"Hampton Industries Has Been Making Children's Clothes for Nautica Since 1994," *Daily News Record,* May 21, 1996, p. 2.
Kulers, G. Brian, "Hampton Industries," *Apparel Industry Magazine,* December 1990, pp. 30–35.
Lloyd, Brenda, "Status Brands Gobbling Up Space in Southeast," *Daily News Record,* August 19, 1996, p. 28.
"The Lowdown on the '97 Licensed Label Lineup," *Daily News Record,* January 27, 1997, p. 10.
Parr, Karen, and Ellis, Kristi, "Key Issues: Price, Quick Turns," *Women's Wear Daily,* December 5, 1996, pp. 10–18.
Petersen, Anrea, "What's Cool For School?," *The Wall Street Journal,* August 30 ,1996, p. B1(E).
Socha, Miles, "Some 'Little Guys' Manage to Battle the Red, White and Blue; Secrets for Surviving in the World of Ralph, Tommy, Nautica," *Daily News Record,* March 31, 1997, pp. 6–7.

—Thomas Derdak

HARCOURT GENERAL

Harcourt General, Inc.

27 Boylston St.
Chestnut Hill, Massachusetts 02167
U.S.A.
(617) 232-8200
Fax: (617) 278-5397
Web site: http://www.irin.com/h

Public Company
Incorporated: 1919 as Harcourt, Brace and Company
Employees: 20,080
Sales: $3.29 billion (1996)
Stock Exchanges: New York
SICs: 5311 Department Stores; 2731 Book Publishing;
8742 Management Consultant Services

Through its core publishing arm, Harcourt General, Inc. remains one of the world's largest publishers of scholarly books and other printed and electronic educational materials. Its focus on educational, scientific, technical, medical, and other professional fields has made it a leader in both domestic and international markets. With publishing operations based in Sydney, Tokyo, London, Toronto, and Montreal, as well as its domestic offices, the company's Harcourt Brace publishing revenues accounted for over 34 percent of Harcourt General's total sales revenues in the mid-1990s. The company's retail division, composed of a majority share of The Neiman Marcus Group retailer, produced the balance, 62 percent.

Harcourt Brace (HB) publishes about 3,000 new book titles each year for the trade and textbook markets. While the company's publishing endeavors are diverse, its greatest activity centers around elementary school, secondary school, and college textbooks, and related educational materials. In the elementary and secondary school textbook market, HB is recognized as one of the nation's leading publishers and one of the nation's top five in the college textbook market. It is the largest publisher of journals for the scientific and medical communities, publishing hundreds of scholarly journals each year.

Company Gets Its Start During the Interwar Years

At the close of World War I, two former classmates from Columbia University, Alfred Harcourt and Donald C. Brace, left their positions at Henry Holt & Company and started their own trade publishing house in New York. The year was 1919, and the firm was known as Harcourt, Brace, and Howe. Harcourt had served as acquisitions editor and salesman in his 15 years with Holt; Brace, in manufacturing and production. Will D. Howe, an author and editor, had headed the English department at Indiana University. He left the new firm less than a year after its founding, and the name was changed to Harcourt, Brace and Company.

Three months after incorporation, Harcourt, Brace and Company published its first book, *Organizing for Work* by H. L. Gantt. In the months and years that followed, the company had one success after another. John Maynard Keynes's *The Economic Consequences of Peace* was considered a milestone in publishing history. Other notable works included Sinclair Lewis's *Free Air, Main Street*, and *Arrowsmith*, the latter winning a Pulitzer Prize. Lewis had followed his editor, Harcourt, from Henry Holt.

In its first decade, Harcourt, Brace and Company diversified into a number of genres, including religious works and college and high school textbooks. The house also published some of the nation's most outstanding trade books and best-known authors. Throughout its history, Harcourt, Brace and Company would be recognized as an innovator in the publishing industry. In the 1920s the company offered women employees equal career opportunities, a practice virtually nonexistent in the trade at that time. This philosophy was attributed in part to Ellen Knowles Eayres, the firm's first employee, who later married Alfred Harcourt.

Company Posts Publishing Milestones, 1940s–50s

First published in 1941, the company's ubiquitous *Harbrace College Handbook* would grow to 12 editions by the early 1990s to become the bestselling college textbook of all time. The head of the first children's book department, from 1946 to 1972, was Harcourt's Margaret McElderry. Well-known and

Company Perspectives:

Harcourt General continues to rank among the world's largest publishing houses, while also expanding its core business in the areas of electronic publishing and educational software. Publishing revenues are enhanced by company holdings in both specialty retailing and professional management services.

well-liked, she is credited with the discovery of many famous children's authors, Joan Walsh Anglund and Eleanor Estes among them.

During World War II Harcourt, Brace and Company published *Men Must Act,* an anti-fascist book by Lewis Mumford. It was offered free, in an advertisement in the *New York Times,* to the first 500 New Yorkers to respond. The response was unexpected: all 500 copies were given away by noon, and it was estimated that another 2,000 people were turned away.

The house retained many famous authors throughout the years, but in 1955 several of them followed a well-respected Harcourt editor, Robert Giroux, who left to become a partner in Farrar, Straus & Giroux. Among the more than 17 authors who left with him were T. S. Eliot, Flannery O'Connor, John Berryman, and Bernard Malamud.

In 1942 Alfred Harcourt resigned as president, leaving control of the company's operations in the hands of Donald Brace. In 1955, one year after Harcourt's death, William Jovanovich was elected president of Harcourt, Brace and Company. Donald Brace died in September of that year at the age of 74. Jovanovich, a Colorado native, had joined the company in 1947 as a textbook salesman with a salary of $50 per week. Six years later he headed the school department, and in 1955 had become president of the company. While Jovanovich, at the time, was the youngest director with the company and owned no stock, he was the strong leader that the families of the two founders desired.

Jovanovich Steers Company into the 1960s

Once at the helm, Jovanovich set a clear path for turning the company into a conglomerate. Two of his first goals were to take the company public and to merge with World Book Company, incorporated in 1905. Both moves were accomplished in 1960. Harcourt, Brace & World, Inc. was formed as a result, and took its position as the largest publisher of elementary, secondary, and college materials in the nation. Until 1990 the company would be led by aggressive and determined Jovanovich. The company would diversify into dozens of publishing markets as well as into businesses totally unrelated to publishing by acquiring more than 40 companies.

The late 1960s saw the acquisition of two educational film-strip production companies; several farm and trade publications; and Academic Press, Inc., an international concern that published physical and applied science books and journals.

Each year during the 1970s, except 1975, the company acquired at least one publishing or education-related firm.

In 1970 Jovanovich became chairman of the company, and its name was changed from Harcourt, Brace & World, Inc. to Harcourt Brace Jovanovich, Inc. (HBJ). Among the most notable acquisitions made during the 1970s were: The Psychological Corporation, in 1970, publishers of aptitude, diagnostic, achievement, and psychological tests; Beckley-Cardy Company, in 1972, a school-supply house; Bay Area Review Course, Inc. and BRI Bar Review Institute, Inc. in 1974, the two being among the nation's best bar exam review courses; and Pyramid Communications, Inc. in 1974, renamed Jove Publications, Inc., a mass-market paperback publisher of romance, inspirational, sports, and health books. Also in 1984 Drake-Beam & Associates, now Drake Beam Morin, Inc., an outplacement counseling firm, was acquired. By 1978 HBJ was publishing about 2,300 titles—from newsletters to romances—and 75 magazines, with revenues hovering around $360 million.

1970s Characterized by Obstacles to Expansion

The 1970s were not without their drawbacks. In 1974 operations at four German publishing houses purchased in 1970 were terminated because of poor profits. Price controls affected profits at Academic Press for a number of years. Jove/HBJ, an experimental imprint, was failing, and it was sold in 1979. HBJ's trade division operated at a deficit beginning early in the decade. In 1977 HBJ lost $1.6 million on its general-interest books alone.

In early 1978 Jovanovich cut the company's budget, firing six of the trade division's top personnel; he put himself in charge of hardcover adult and juvenile works. The discharge came several days after HBJ regrouped its operations and created an office of the president. Jovanovich claimed the firings had nothing to do with this reorganization.

Restructuring Followed by Acquisitions, the 1980s

Three executive vice-presidents were elected to fill the office of the president—Robert L. Edgell, Robert R. Hillebrecht, and Jack O. Snyder. HBJ was reorganized into five operational groups: university and scholarly publishing, school materials and assessment, periodicals and insurance, business publications and broadcasting, and popular enterprises. This latter group, headed by Hillebrecht, included the marine parks known as Sea World, an acquisition of 1976.

To acquire Sea World, Inc., HBJ had borrowed $46.7 million. Sea World was composed of three marine parks, located in San Diego, California; Cleveland, Ohio; and Orlando, Florida; and was considered to represent some of the world's finest living museums. In 1977 Sea World helped push the company's gross sales to $281.7 million.

In 1980 Jovanovich told the *New York Times* that he was again looking for new acquisitions, and the decade would see HBJ's attention turn to theme parks, insurance, and more publishing. In 1980 the company purchased a commercial insurance broker for the dental profession, and in 1982 bought three publishing concerns, acquiring business periodicals serving a number of specialized industries. Acquisitions made in 1984 and 1985 diversified HBJ into 11 new periodical markets. Also in 1985, HBJ acquired three insurance operations. The two largest, purchased for a total of $130 million, were Federal Home Life Insurance Company and PHF Life Insurance Company of Battle Creek, Michigan.

In 1982 HBJ made the startling announcement it would move the company's headquarters from New York City to Orlando, Florida, and the trade department to San Diego, California. The March 31 issue of *Business Week* quoted Jovanovich as saying "We're moving because the continued profitability of publishing is in jeopardy." A projected annual savings in rent and operation expenses of $20 million topped Jovanovich's reasons for the move. "Too much time is spent lunching, and not enough is spent reading. Many of our writers don't live in New York anyway," Jovanovich noted.

HBJ planned to use the employee pension fund, which, the company stated, was "hugely overfunded," to finance the new corporate headquarters. The investment, according to Jovanovich, would yield a considerable return—15 percent of the building's cost in annual rent. In September 1983, the U.S. Labor Department prohibited the use of the fund, and HBJ was required to return all monies to the fund. The move, complete in 1984, included the construction of an eight-story, 385,000-square-foot office building across from Sea World. The new HBJ headquarters cost the company $20 million. The move, as of 1986, cost the company a total of $35 million.

Once established in its new home, HBJ went on another theme-park buying spree, spending a total of $67.7 million. In September 1974 the company bought Stars Hall of Fame in Orlando, which was soon converted to Places of Learning. In 1985 HBJ acquired Florida Cypress Gardens, Inc., a botanical garden and entertainment park near Winter Haven, Florida, paying $22.6 million in stock for the opportunity. In December 1986 HBJ acquired Marineland Amusements Corporation in Rancho Palos Verdes, California.

Near the end of 1986 HBJ made the biggest purchase in its history. For $500 million it acquired the educational and professional publishing division of CBS Inc. The division's primary subsidiaries included W.B. Saunders, the world's largest publisher of medical and health science textbooks and materials; and Holt, Rinehart, and Winston, Inc. (HRW), one of the nation's top textbook publishers. HRW was the evolutionary product of Henry Holt & Company—the firm from which Harcourt, Brace, and Howe had started. The purchase made HBJ the largest publisher of elementary school and high school textbooks.

In 1987 Robert Maxwell, the chairman of British Printing and Communications Corporation (BPCC), set his sights on acquiring Harcourt Brace Jovanovich. Maxwell was looking for a U.S. publishing house, and offered more than $2 billion for the company. HBJ was not interested. Twice in HBJ's history takeover attempts had prompted Jovanovich into action—once in 1978 by Marvin Josephson, and again in 1981 by Warner Communications. Neither the action nor the results in either case had been far-reaching.

In a press release dated May 26, 1987, HBJ announced its plan to fight the BPPC proposal, a recapitalization distribution. The plan included a $40-per-share special dividend and the issuance of new preferred stock.

Two days later, Maxwell announced he had withdrawn his offer, but HBJ had paid a hefty price. To fend off the takeover, the company had more than tripled its debt, from $837 million to $2.9 billion, requiring bank loans for a substantial portion of that figure. The withdrawal of his offer notwithstanding, on June 1 Maxwell tried to block the reorganization plan. At the close of business June 2, more than 3.3 million HBJ shares had changed hands, with the price skyrocketing to $63.75. A number of companies, along with Maxwell's BPCC, opposed HBJ's reorganization. After an Orange County, Florida judge ruled in HBJ's favor in late June, Maxwell withdrew.

In August 1987 HBJ began its attempt to cover the cost of the takeover defense by selling assets. Among the first to go were HBJ's two VHF television stations and three corporate jets, the sales of which brought in about $20 million. Also to go were two book clubs. In November HBJ announced the sale of its 110 trade magazines and Beckley-Cardy, which it sold for $334 million. The buyer was Edgell Communications Inc., a new, private corporation formed in part by Robert Edgell, a former HBJ executive.

By year-end HBJ had met its performing-asset sale requirement under its credit agreements. The company had sold more than $370 million in assets. Speculation continued, however, as did the rumors as to which property HBJ would sell next and to whom. On January 1, 1988, William Jovanovich announced that the HBJ theme parks were not for sale.

Several months later, HBJ eliminated 729 jobs from its theme park operations. While neither the HBJ publishing or insurance divisions were affected, the layoff included more than 343 positions at Florida-based theme parks, and 17 percent of the work force at Sea World in San Antonio, Texas.

On March 30, 1988, the appointment of Ralph D. Caulo, age 53, was announced as HBJ's newly elected president and chief operating officer. Caulo, who joined HBJ in 1967 as a textbook sales manager, served as an executive vice-president in Orlando, heading the school publishing division. Since 1970 William Jovanovich had been chief executive, president, and chairman. On December 17, 1988, at age 68, Jovanovich resigned his position as president and chief executive officer of Harcourt Brace Jovanovich, retaining only his position as chairman.

During the late 1980s some analysts believed the company's financial situation to be anything but hopeful. Forced to sell revenue-generating assets to repay debt, HBJ was threatening its long-range solvency. William Jovanovich claimed that "HBJ could repay its obligations without now selling major assets."

Divestiture Followed by New Leadership in 1980s

In November 1989, HBJ sold all six of its theme parks and related land holdings to Anheuser-Busch Companies. The price was $1.1 billion, which went to retire the bank loans. The year also saw significant structural changes within HBJ operations.

menutary and secondary textbook divisions were divided.
HBJ would now publish kindergarten through eighth-grade
textbooks, while subsidiary Holt, Rinehart and Winston would
publish those for grades seven through 12. HBJ and HRW
school department heads resigned, as did six executives in the
elementary and secondary divisions. Ralph Caulo resigned as
president, and William Jovanovich's son, Peter Jovanovich,
was elected in his place.

Peter William Jovanovich was born in New York City in
1949 and joined the HBJ trade department in 1980. He inherited
the company's $1.6 billion debt, causing Wall Street analysts
and institutional investors to openly express concern regarding
his ability to pull the company from its troubles. HBJ's operating loss for 1989 reached $242 million, with interest payments
on its debt at $350.8 million, and its share price at around $3.

In April 1990 HBJ confirmed its intentions to sell additional
assets. Speculation by analysts targeted the company's professional publishing division, including W. B. Saunders as one
possibility, estimating a sale price at around $600 million.
Another option would be the company's insurance operations,
which in 1989 had generated $456.3 million in revenues. Still
other sources disclosed the possibility of a renewed interest in
HBJ by BPCC chairman Robert Maxwell.

On May 29, 1990, William Jovanovich retired from his
36-year tenure as chairman of HBJ, naming John S. Herrington
as his successor. The *New York Times*, May 30, 1990, quoted
Roger Straus, chairman of Farrar, Straus & Giroux: "It is very
sad. Bill was a great publisher in his time, but he went too far in
resisting Maxwell. Now I suspect that he does not want to be
there for the dismemberment." A lawyer, Herrington had
joined the HBJ board of directors in 1989 before serving as
secretary of energy to U.S. president Ronald Reagan.

In September 1990 vice-chairman and COO J. William
Brandner, HBJ's second in command, resigned. The company
announced that his resignation was part of a budget cut that was
expected to help curb operating expenses without hindering
operations. In the same month, HBJ hired a spokesman—a first
in its 71-year history. C. Anson Franklin had served as assistant
energy secretary under Herrington and as assistant press secretary in the Reagan administration. Franklin's job, in addition to
serving as liaison between the company, its shareholders, and
the press, was to improve HBJ's community and company
communications.

In October 1990 speculation continued as to HBJ's next
strategy for deferring its debt burden. With the company's stock
hovering at $1.25 per share and its long-term debt at $1.76
billion, analysts projected another large asset sale. This news
was offset by the announcement, in October 1990, that HBJ
author Octavio Paz had been awarded the Nobel Prize for
Literature. The poet, age 76, was the first Mexican writer to
receive literature's highest recognition, awarded by the Swedish
Academy of Letters.

As HBJ's 1993 obligation to pay dividends and interest to its
bond holders drew near, the company continued to consider its
alternatives, one of which was a merger offer from General
Cinema. The offer would wipe the debt slate clean, and prove
beneficial to all associated with the company except its bond

holders, who would collect less than they expected. After a
protracted offer to those bondholders, during which General
Cinema was forced to sweeten the offer, it was accepted by the
90 percent necessary.

Merger Gives New Name and Signals New Direction, the 1990s

In January 1991, after announcing it would sell its Orlando
book warehouse, the board of HBJ approved the merger with
General Cinema. The $1.5 billion deal made HBJ a subsidiary
of General Cinema, a movie theater giant founded in 1922 as
Philip Smith Theatrical Enterprise that retained a 53 percent
interest in upscale and innovative retailer Neiman Marcus
through its 37 percent interest in Carter Hawley Hale. Neiman
Marcus operated 28 stores in 25 cities throughout the United
States, as well as two Bergdorf Goodman stores in Manhattan.
In 1995 Harcourt would expand its interest in Neiman Marcus
to 58.6 percent through a privately negotiated stock transaction.

In 1992 the now enlarged company consolidated its publishing operations under the name Harcourt Brace and Company,
intending to incorporate the new name and logo in its many
imprints to integrate its publishing identity. Through a renewed
commitment to invest in the elementary and secondary textbook
programs offered through its Harcourt Brace School (grades
K–8) and Holt, Rinehart and Winston (grades 7–12) divisions,
as well as the introduction of the popular *Mathematics Plus*
instructional program for elementary grades, the company was
able to post profitable returns in these divisions on top of several
years of decline in the late 1980s. From 1992 revenues of
$223.4 million, combined elementary and secondary publishing
revenues would reach $313.7 million by 1995.

CEO Peter Jovanovich left the company in 1992, moving to
head a joint venture between textbook publishers Macmillan
Inc. and McGraw-Hill. He was replaced by Robert J. Tarr, who
would remain CEO of the company until January 1997, when he
was succeeded by Robert A. Smith, chairman and "patriarch"
of the family-based core of HBJ. Despite the shift in leadership,
the company's focus remained consistent: as Tarr stated in the
Wall Street Journal in 1993, "Publishing is going to be our core
business for a long, long time. It's going to be our growth
industry for the '90s."

The fall of 1993 saw a streamlining of General Cinema's
long-term holdings as the company spun off its 1,351-exhibi-
tion screen General Cinema theatre chain, plus $64 million in
cash, as GC Companies, giving each Harcourt shareholders one
GC share for every 10 shares of the company's common stock
held. The company also laid the groundwork for divesting itself
of HBJ's British affiliate through a deal with the company-
owned consulting firm Drake Beam Morin. Continuing its move
to focus on publishing, General Cinema also paved the way for
the 1994 sale of HBJ's insurance division to GE Capital-
affiliate GNA Corp. for $410 million. The changes begun in
1993 were symbolized by the company's change in name from
General Cinema to Harcourt General on March 12. The company ended the fiscal year by posting revenues of $3.65 billion,
$944.5 million of which were generated by its publishing arm.
By year-end 1994 publishing would account for 29 percent of
total revenue.

The Future of Publishing in the Electronic Age

In 1995, with sales of over $3 billion and net income of $166 million, Harcourt General announced that its Academic Press unit would be making all of its scientific and technical journals available on the Internet. This move followed the lead of Harcourt Brace College, a company branch that had formed a multimedia product unit called Harcourt Interactive the previous year.

On the international front, Harcourt Brace International moved its main offices from Orlando, Florida, to London, thereby increasing its international presence. The company also responded to the increased globalization of the scientific and medical marketplace by beginning to develop new products in these areas, creating another opportunity to expand the already strong markets for both its Academic Press and W.B. Saunders imprints internationally. Harcourt General also exhibited foresight in responding to changes in worldwide demographics as it approached the millennium. In 1995 Harcourt began expanding its markets in Asia and purchased Mosby-Year Book, a Spanish-language medical publisher marketing products in Spain, Mexico, and major cities in Latin America, from Times Mirror, which complemented the company's W.B. Saunders subsidiary, the world's leading publisher of medical books and journals focusing on the health sciences. Among the company's 300 scholarly journals and 2,600 titles released in 1995 was *View with a Grain of Sand,* by 1996 Nobel Prize-winning poet Wislawa Szymborska.

In addition to recognizing and responding to the changes in the publishing industry, Harcourt General streamlined its specialty retailing operations, focusing on the adult upscale clothing market by negotiating the exchange of its youth-oriented Contempo Casuals with Wet Seal for stock and cash in 1995. It also grew revenues in Drake Beam Morin, which by the early 1990s could claim preeminence as the world's leading human resources consulting/management firm. By the close of 1996, the company could boast revenues of $3.28 billion, and net earnings of $1.38 billion.

Companywide efforts to redeploy cash from sales of subsidiaries and more fully utilize debt capacity, as well as its intention to expand Asian and Latin American markets and search for acquisitions capable of generating high returns relative to those standard in the publishing industry boded well for the future. The 1995 acquisition of both Mosby-Year Book and Assessment Systems Inc., a computerized licensing and credentialing testing system used nationwide, signalled Harcourt General's belief that its future will reside in the worldwide merger of people and a far-ranging electronic technology.

Principal Subsidiaries

Academic Press, Inc.; Harcourt Brace and Company; Harcourt Brace Jovanovich International Corporation; Harcourt Brace Jovanovich Japan, Inc. (99.17%); HBJ Holding Corporation; Holt, Rinehart and Winston, Inc.; Drake Beam Morin; The Psychological Corporation; W.B. Saunders Company; Neiman Marcus Group Inc.

Further Reading

Putka, Gary, ''General Cinema's Makeover Seems a Textbook Case,'' *Wall Street Journal,* March 12, 1993, p. B4.
Tebbel, John, *A History of Book Publishing in the United States,* 4 vols., New York, R.R. Bowker Company, 1972–1981.

—Janie Pritchett
—updated by Pamela L. Shelton

Harris Corporation

1025 West NASA Boulevard
Melbourne, Florida 32919
U.S.A.
(407) 727-9100
Fax: (407) 727-9344
Web site: http://www.harris.com

Public Company
Incorporated: 1926 as Harris-Seybold-Potter Company
Employees: 27,600
Sales: $3.62 billion (1996)
Stock Exchanges: New York Midwest Pacific
  Philadelphia Boston
SICs: 3679 Electronic Switches; 3571 Computer
  Manufacturing; 3579 Office Machines; 3661
  Telephone Equipment; 3663 Radio and Television
  Broadcasting; 3669 Communications Equipment; 3674
  Semiconductor Devices; 3812 Search & Navigation
  Equipment; 3823 Industrial Process Control
  Instruments; 5045 Computers & Software, Wholesale;
  6719 Holding Companies; 7372 Prepackaged
  Computer Software; 8731 Commercial Research &
  Development

The origin of the Harris Corporation, a leading American electronics company, is actually to be found in the printing business. What began as a minor manufacturer of printing press machinery has evolved during this century into an important developer of cutting-edge electronics technology. In fact, Harris's role in the American electronics industry is so important that in 1987 the Pentagon stepped in to prevent its acquisition by a foreign company.

E Pluribus Unum: 1895–1950

In 1895 the Harris Automatic Press Company was founded in Cleveland, Ohio. This company manufactured the large multicolor presses that are used to print books and newspapers. In the early decades of the 20th century, the Harris Automatic Press acquired the properties of two other companies involved in the printing business—Seybold Machine Company of Dayton, Ohio, and Premier & Potter Printing Press Company, Inc. of New York. The name of the company was then changed to Harris-Seybold-Potter Company. In June, 1957 the company merged with the Intertype Corporation of Brooklyn, New York, and its name was again changed, this time to Harris-Intertype Corporation. Intertype was a manufacturer of hot metal typesetting machines and operated a plant in England in addition to the plant in New York.

Throughout these acquisitions the company's business remained essentially unchanged: it built and marketed printing and broadcasting machinery. Such machinery included offset lithographic presses, envelope presses, paper cutting machines, and bindery equipment, and at Intertype, hot metal typesetting machines. Later acquisitions, in particular the Gates Radio Company, gave the company the capacity to manufacture broadcasting transmitters and microwave equipment.

Radiation, Inc.: 1950–67

The boom in the aerospace industry that began in the 1950s gave rise to many companies that produced components for government projects. One of the earliest of these businesses was Radiation, Inc., established in 1950 by Homer Denius and George Shaw, both of whom were electronics engineers. At first Radiation employed a staff of only 12 and was housed in space rented from the Naval Air Station in Melbourne, Florida. The site was convenient because it was located only a few miles south of the Cape Canaveral (now Kennedy) Space Center. From the start, the company produced miniaturized electronics, tracking, and pulse-code-modulation technologies, all of which are crucial to aerospace programs. Radiation's involvement with the aerospace program included equipment for the Telstar and Courier communication satellites and the Nimbus and Tiros weather satellites. Military systems that relied upon Radiation equipment included the Atlas, Polaris, and Minuteman missiles.

Radiation's initial success was due in part to the high quality of its staff. Many of the highest-level managers held advanced

Company Perspectives:

We intend to be a much bigger player in areas such as communication and telecommunications markets worldwide, and we have the technological strength and marketing capabilities to do that. We also have a long history of providing products and services that substantially exceed customer expectations. The combination of technical excellence and customer satisfaction speak well for Harris being around to celebrate its second 100 years.

degrees in engineering. John Hartley, the CEO of the firm until 1995, joined Radiation after serving on the faculty of Auburn University. Hartley joined the firm in 1956, the same year that Radiation stock was first sold to the public. Another person who left academia to join the staff at Radiation was Joseph Boyd. In the late 1950s and early 1960s Boyd taught electrical engineering at the University of Michigan. At the same time he was also director of the Willow Laboratories, a prestigious science and technology research institute with a staff of more than 1,000 scientists and engineers. Boyd joined Radiation in 1962 and within a year was made president of the firm. His first significant action as president was to set up a microelectronics plant to develop and produce integrated circuits. The following year, Hartley was named as director of this division of Radiation.

During the early 1960s, Radiation devoted itself to improving its market position in the interconnected fields of digital communication, space communication, data management, and computer-based control systems. The company was also successful with satellite tracking systems and alphanumeric data processing. By 1967 the company was one of Florida's largest employers (at 3,000 employees) and sales passed $50 million a year. The company was well-established as a government contractor for both military and nonmilitary projects. But Radiation's management wanted to expand the company's business activity in the commercial sector. To do this, they decided to merge with a commercial company.

At roughly the same time, the Harris-Intertype Corporation was seeking to expand its operations into the electronics field. George Dively, the chairman of Harris-Intertype, had succeeded in building up the company's business from $10 million in annual sales to almost $200 million. But Harris-Intertype's printing machines were still mechanical, and Dively realized that future technological developments would require electronics. Radiation seemed a perfect candidate for acquisition. Dively and Harris-Intertype's president, Richard Tullis, paid $56 million for Radiation. The purchase price was considered quite steep—Harris shares were traded for Radiation's in a ratio that valued Radiation's earnings at twice those of Harris. However, Harris's management wanted Radiation's electronics talent, and not just its earning power. The two companies merged in 1967 under the Harris-Intertype name. Dively remained chairman of the company; Homer Denius, one of the founders of Radiation, became vice-chairman; and Boyd became an executive vice-president for electronics. After the merger, annual

sales surpassed the $250 million mark and the combined number of employees exceeded 12,000.

Growth through Acquisitions: 1968–79

The Harris-Radiation hybrid proved to be a success and innovations began to flow from the company almost immediately. Electronic newsroom technology, for example, was the direct result of a study made by Radiation of how to update Harris's mechanical presses. Most importantly however, the merger gave birth to an essential management strategy known as "technology transfer"—developing commercial applications of technology originally developed for the government.

Two years later, RF Communications, Inc. of Rochester, New York, was purchased through an exchange of shares. By the time of its purchase, RF was well established as a manufacturer of point-to-point radio equipment. Even after this rapid expansion, the company's electronics business remained primarily with the government, especially in the aerospace field. Harris-Intertype was responsible for the production and development of the data-handling systems for the preflight check of the Apollo spacecraft and for the digital command-and-control computer of the Gemini spacecraft.

At the beginning of the 1970s, the company made several other major acquisitions. In 1972, Harris-Intertype purchased General Electric's product line of TV broadcasting cameras, transmitters, studio equipment, and antennas for $5.5 million in cash, adding greatly to its original broadcasting product line. In addition, UCC-Communications Systems, Inc. of Dallas, Texas, was purchased from the University Computing Company for $20 million in cash. This company was a leading producer of computer terminals and communications subsystems for the data processing industry in general. Two years later, in 1974, Harris-Intertype acquired Datacraft Corporation and also divested itself of its corrugated paper machinery business. Datacraft was a producer of superminicomputers. During the same year the company changed its name to the Harris Corporation.

These acquisitions, made under the leadership of Richard Tullis, were integral to Harris's evolution from a company which was 84 percent mechanical into a company which was 70 percent electronic. However, the integration of the purchases and the continual introduction of new product lines took its toll on the company's earnings. From the late 1960s to the late 1970s earnings growth was not outstanding and investors largely ignored the company. But by 1976 things began to change for Harris; over the following three years its stock rose more than 100 percent. Meanwhile, the acquisitions campaign did not slow down even during the fallow period.

Subsequent acquisitions were all in the field of data processing and handling. Purchases were made every year throughout the remainder of the decade and well into the 1980s. By 1977 Harris's sales were more than $646 million and earnings were greater than $40 million. Boyd was appointed chairman and CEO two years later, in 1979.

That year Harris reached a significant agreement with Matra, a French state-owned electronics company. Under this agreement, which was to provide the French with a factory to manufacture integrated circuits, all of the $40 million funding was supplied by Matra and the French government; Harris provided only technology and management. The French retained 51 percent of the company, leaving Harris with the remaining 49 percent.

Technology Transfer: 1980–89

Since Harris had begun to deal predominantly in electronics, the company found itself in a market with extremely powerful competition. By this time the concept of technology transfer was the central element of the company's management policies. Though defense contracts accounted for only around 20 percent of Harris's business, military projects were its most advanced production efforts. In general government contracts are for custom products instead of standard items, which helps to push the state of a technological art to its limit. In addition, these projects tend to be motivated more by technology than by cost considerations.

Harris's challenge was to translate work on customized, ultra-high technology products into profitable commercial projects. Among the problems Harris faced in doing this was military secrecy—an obstacle which would eventually stymie attempts to take over Harris. In order to overcome problems such as these, Harris instituted managerial policies which made promotion and demotion dependent upon the successful development of commercial products from defense projects. Harris also adopted a more general strategy of competing for government work only in those areas in which the company anticipated the ready development of commercial products. The development of a video terminal for electronic newsrooms, derived from the company's Vietnam-era work on an Army battlefield message sender, was a successful example of this technology-transfer policy.

Throughout Harris's history its acquisitions program has been well planned. In 1980 Harris made another important purchase, of the Farinon Corporation, a manufacturer of microwave transmitters, electronic switchboards, and other sophisticated telephone products. At the time of its purchase, Farinon was a small company, with sales of only $100 million. Outside observers believed that the purchase price of four million Harris shares, worth around $125 million, was much too high. However, management at Harris justified the price on the grounds that it had to beat out other bids (GTE, RCA, Siemens, and Loral Corporation had all expressed interest in Farinon) and that Harris was buying technology and market position, not earnings or revenues.

Harris passed the billion dollar mark in annual revenues in 1981, and went on to weather the recession of the early 1980s quite well; earnings per share grew roughly 15 percent a year during this period. New plants were in operation 30 miles south of the Kennedy Space Center in Florida and the company had become the largest industrial employer in Florida. In 1983 Harris marked another turning point in its history. Harris had risen from the sixth largest supplier of printing machines to the number one position in the country, but in the spring of that year, Harris sold its printing business to concentrate exclusively on electronics. In the autumn of that year, Lanier Business Products, Inc. was merged into Harris on a $276 million stock purchase. Lanier was involved primarily in office automation

and was noted for its business computers, dictating systems, copying machines, and word processing systems. Lanier brought Harris greater strength in the commercial sector since it boasted 350 sales offices throughout the United States and a sales force of over 2,000 people, 700 of them marketing Lanier's copying machines (which were manufactured by the 3M Corporation).

Later in the year the Federal Communications Commission (FCC) ordered Harris to stop production and marketing of a system that allowed AM radio stations to broadcast in stereo. The FCC also ordered the stations which had already purchased the units to cease broadcasting using the units. According to the FCC, the unit actually marketed by Harris differed significantly from one that the agency had approved the preceding year. Management at Harris claimed that the order had little effect on the company's overall business performance since Harris had a backlog of only $2 million for the system, out of a total of $430 million for the communications sector that year.

But massive layoffs and a major reorganization began in the same year and continued for about three years. The company's government communications systems group was dissolved and employees from that group were reassigned to other divisions in the government systems sector. As other divisions were also consolidated, the workforce at Harris was reduced by several thousand employees. At the end of this period of adjustment, Harris and 3M entered into a joint venture to market and service copiers and facsimile machines as a result of their earlier connection through Lanier. The new company, named Harris/3M Document Products, Inc., was headquartered in Atlanta, Georgia, and owned equally by 3M and Harris.

Harris had a spate of problems with government contracts. In June 1987 the company agreed to settle out of court, for $1.3 million, a claim that Harris had overcharged NASA to upgrade the security system for a ground tracking station. Later in the year the company pleaded guilty to making false claims relating to a contract with the United States Army. The settlement in this case came to more than $2 million refunded as excess profits and another $2 million in penalties.

That same year the Pentagon stopped a takeover of Harris by the British communications company Plessey. Plessey, roughly the same size as Harris and one of Britain's largest electronics manufacturers, was itself acquired by Britain's General Electric Co. PLC and Germany's Siemens in 1989. The takeover was apparently blocked because of the security-sensitive nature of much of Harris's activities. For instance, the company is the major supplier of electrical components that are hardened against damage from the electromagnetic pulse generated by nuclear weapons. It is reported that Harris also manufactures top-secret equipment for the National Security Agency, which operates the government's spy satellites and communication-interception equipment.

In addition to being well protected against takeover, Harris is well-established in custom electronic systems, office automation, communications, and microelectronic products. Company revenues more than doubled in the 1980s, from $850 million to more than $2 billion. The largest growth in both sales and profits came in the semiconductor and government systems sectors. By 1989 Harris had become the largest U.S. supplier of radio and television broadcasting equipment and dictating equipment and the largest producer of low- and medium-capacity microwave radio equipment. It was the largest supplier of integrated circuits to the U.S. government and the sixth largest producer of integrated circuits in the country. It was also the largest producer of satellite communications earth stations, a major supplier to NATO armed forces, and sold commercial products in over 100 countries.

Centennial Decade: 1990–97

By the early 1990s the future of the Harris Corporation seemed difficult to assess. Competition with the Japanese continued to be fierce, growth was slowing in the communications industry, and office automation had been a more competitive field than Harris anticipated. But cutbacks in personnel and the major reorganization of divisions at Harris streamlined the company. In late 1988 Harris bought GE Solid State, General Electric's semiconductor company, for more than $200 million, and in 1989 Harris purchased 3M's 50 percent interest in Harris/3M and renamed the company Lanier Worldwide, Inc. after adding Lanier Voice Products to that business.

Harris's corporate strategy in the 1990s was marked by four emphases: it would continue to transfer the technology expertise of its Electronic Systems Sector to nondefense markets, it would build on the growth of Harris Semiconductor following the purchase of GE Solid State, its Communications Sector would lead the company into international markets, and it would continue to promote the products, services, and globalization of Lanier Worldwide. In January 1991 Harris learned that it had won a $1.7 billion Federal Aviation Administration contract to develop the voice switching and control system of the nation's air traffic control (ATC) communications systems. The contract—the largest in the company's history—demonstrated that Harris's strategy of diversification into nondefense work was bearing fruit and led to other major ATC projects in Alaska, the airports of Washington, D.C., and in Malaysia.

Harris's push into another nondefense high-tech sector—advanced energy management systems for electric utilities—was strengthened in 1992 when Harris acquired Westronic Inc. of Canada. And a year later Harris won a major contract to upgrade the FBI's National Crime Information Center database records using its specialized information processing technology. By the mid-1990s Harris added two new nondefense markets to its technology transfer strategy: healthcare and railroads. Harris developed information processing and communication technologies to improve diagnostic capabilities and cost efficiencies in the healthcare field, and in a joint venture with General Electric, Harris designed and manufactured an advanced electronic system for managing railroad traffic. Although the U.S. defense budget was reduced by two-thirds between 1984 and 1995, Harris continued to pursue—and win—major defense projects, primarily in defense communications and aerospace, most notably the Air Force's F-22 Advanced Tactical Fighter and the Army's Comanche helicopter.

Because of unexpected problems integrating Harris Semiconductor with GE's much larger semiconductor business fol-

lowing the merger in 1988 as well as a downturn in the semiconductor market in the late 1980s, Hartley reassigned Electronic Systems director Phil Farmer to Harris's semiconductor operations in 1991. Farmer immediately began flattening the unit's management structure, reducing costs and expenses, and rationalizing its plant capacity. By the end of 1992 Harris Semiconductor was profitable again and by 1995 it was introducing more than 200 new products a year, particularly for the automotive, communication, and power-control circuits industries.

Harris's Communications Sector meanwhile established itself as one of the company's fastest-growing businesses by moving aggressively to fill the communication infrastructure needs of the world's developing countries. Between 1990 and 1994, international sales in its communications division grew from one-third to one-half of its total business. It upgraded television stations in Mexico, sold digital microwave radio systems to emerging countries, and supplied telephone equipment to remote regions of China and India. It also moved quickly into the promising new markets of high-definition television and cell phone-based personal communications services (PCS).

Harris's 1989 formation of Lanier Worldwide was also paying off. By 1995 Lanier's global sales had climbed to $1 billion and with 1,600 international sales and service centers it had become the largest independent office equipment distributor in the world. Lanier enjoyed two important firsts in 1994: it introduced a line of multifunctional printer/fax/copy machines and began offering facilities management services to major corporations, in which Lanier not only provided clients with all the office machines and supplies they needed but brought in Lanier employees to perform the copying. In 1995, Phil Farmer, a 13-year veteran with Harris, succeeded Hartley as Harris's chairman and CEO.

In 1996 Harris acquired the wireless products business of NovAtel Communications, formed a joint venture to provide telecommunications and broadcast equipment to China, demonstrated the first HDTV transmitter, announced the construction of a semiconductor plant in China and a new U.S. facility to make power metal oxide semiconductors, and won a $73 million contract from the FAA for weather and radar processor systems.

In 1997, Harris announced the construction of a $5 million new space antenna facility, a $10 million digital television center in Cincinnati, a joint venture with GE to develop a new generation of digital information management systems for electric utilities in developing countries, and the acquisition of Northeast Broadcast Lab, a maker of radio broadcast equipment. It also strengthened Lanier's corporate office services business by acquiring American Legal Copy Services, a copying service for the legal profession; Quorum Group, an information services business for lawyers; and Trans-Comp, a provider of medical transcription services.

Principal Subsidiaries

Harris Data Services Corporation; Harris Far East Ltd.; Harris International Sales Corporation; Harris Investments of Delaware, Inc.; Harris Semiconductor, Inc.; Harris Semiconductor (Florida), Inc.; Harris Semiconductor (Ohio), Inc.; Harris Semiconductor Patents, Inc.; Harris Semiconductor (Pennsylvania), Inc.; Harris Southwest Properties, Inc.; Harris Space Systems Corporation; Harris Technical Services Corporation; Allied Broadcast Equipment Corporation (Canada); Lanier Worldwide, Inc.; Harris Publishing Systems Corporation; GE-Harris Railway Electronics, LLC (49%); Lanier Professional Services, Inc.; Lanier Leasing, Inc.; RF Communications, Inc.

Further Reading

"1895–1995," *FYI: The Harris Magazine of Technology at Work* (special centennial historical issue), Fall 1995, Melbourne, Florida, Harris Corporation; also available at http://www.harris.com.

—updated by Paul S. Bodine

Hecla Mining Company

6500 Mineral Drive
Coeur d'Alene, Idaho 83814
U.S.A.
(208) 769-4100
Fax: (208) 769-4107
Web site: http://www.hecla-mining.com

Public Company
Incorporated: 1891 as Hecla Mining Company
Employees: 1,259
Sales: $166.8 million (1996)
Stock Exchanges: New York Vancouver American
SICs: 3339 Primary Nonferrous Metals, Not Elsewhere
    Classified; 1031 Lead & Zinc Ores; 1044 Silver Ores;
    1041 Gold Ores

The oldest of Idaho's pioneer mining companies, Hecla Mining Company mines and processes silver, gold, and industrial minerals in the United States and Mexico. Hecla Mining earned the bulk of its income initially from its namesake Hecla mine, which yielded substantial ores of lead for four decades. Following the closure of its mainstay Hecla mine in the mid-1940s, the company subsisted on zinc before dabbling in uranium and securing its second mainstay mine, a silver-lead mine named Lucky Friday. Hecla Mining ran into trouble during the 1970s with copper production, but strong silver prices revived the company and fueled an aggressive growth program during the early 1980s that included two important acquisitions, Day Mines, Inc. in 1981 and Ranchers Exploration and Development Corporation in 1984. These acquisitions significantly strengthened Hecla Mining's silver holdings and brought it into the production of industrial minerals. During the late 1990s, the company derived nearly half of its sales from industrial minerals, more than 40 percent from gold, and 10 percent from silver and lead.

19th-Century Origins

The cause for Hecla Mining's formation occurred six years before the company's incorporation, when James Toner claimed the Hecla mine on May 5, 1885. At the time, Hecla was an unremarkable, 20-acre claim situated on a hillside, representing one hope among thousands of others in the Coeur d'Alenes of Idaho. The region was alive with activity during the late 19th century, inundated by wave after wave of prospectors who scoured the countryside in search of fortune, each bounding their respective plots of land with hastily scribbled claim notices and each hoping to find the vein of Idaho's mother lode. The rush was on, but for many of the fortune-seekers who flocked to the area, rich veins of ore never materialized, and once-promising plots became worthless tracts of scrubland. Such was the case with the Hecla claim, at least in the mind of Toner, who held onto the rights for a few short years before selling it to another hopeful prospector. The claim passed from hand to hand following Toner's ownership, the land on the hillside neglected, as the promise of Hecla was lost amid the frenzy for silver, lead, and gold.

Six years passed before anyone gave any serious thought to developing the Hecla claim, but by the beginning of the 1890s the Hecla mine was regarded as a "full-fledged lead prospect," according to the area's local newspaper, the *Wallace Press*. Ownership of the Hecla mine by this point had passed from Toner to an Idaho miner and subsequently to a local merchant before falling into the hands of an agent for Montana investors, its final sales price a modest $150. Other investors soon secured an interest in the mine, and by the fall of 1891 plans were being developed to form an operating company for the promising Hecla mine. On October 14, 1891, Hecla Mining Company was incorporated and capitalized for $500,000 by seven businessmen, some local and others from the East, primarily Chicago and Milwaukee. Once formed, Hecla Mining limped from the starting gate, but the company's inaugural year of business marked an historic occasion. Hecla Mining, despite its hesitant start, became the longest-surviving member of the pioneer mining companies dotting the Coeur d'Alenes.

The long legacy of mining conducted under the auspices of Hecla Mining began with a nine-year span much like the first six years of its namesake mine. Inactivity characterized much of the 1890s for Hecla Mining, as the company joined ranks with the dozens of other infant mining companies in Idaho, doing little to distinguish it from its brethren. Throughout the bulk of

Company Perspectives:

Hecla Mining Company is a precious metals company with an important industrial minerals component. Our business is to create value for our shareholders by discovering, acquiring, developing, producing and marketing mineral resources at a profit. To achieve our mission we will: Manage all business activities in a safe, environmentally responsible and cost-effective manner; Give preference to projects where Hecla can be the operator; Provide an environment for achieving personal excellence and growth for all our people; Willingly accept our responsibility to be a good corporate citizen by contributing to the well-being of the communities where we work and live; Conduct our business with integrity and honesty.

the 1890s, the company's directors invested only a modicum of resources and energy into Hecla, opting instead to lease the mine or raise money through assessments and forego serious exploration into the depths below the 20-acre site first staked by Toner. Hecla, as it had during the latter half of the 1880s, waited in the wings while other mining properties basked in the limelight. According to one estimate, Hecla produced ores worth no more than $14,000 during its first seven years under Hecla Mining's operation, a period that saw the area surrounding the mine fall under martial law on two occasions. While the territory embracing Wallace, Idaho, fought fitfully through its growing pains, Hecla Mining's management resolved to start anew after the company's lackluster start and reorganized the company in 1898, by which time more than half of the original founders had either died, moved elsewhere, or divested their interests.

The new version of the company emerged with a much greater capitalization—twice the amount of 1891—and exuded decidedly more vigor. Eight additional claims were purchased for $36,000, and Hecla Mining, after years of languishing in the background, moved resolutely forward, its directors intent on shaping the company into a regional force. As the new century began, and the promise of substantial growth neared, work was underway to bolster the infrastructure of the Hecla mine so the property could begin producing ore and the company could begin paying dividends. Roughly $40,000 was earmarked for tunnel building, tunnel renovation, and for the rental of a mill, enabling the company to pay its first dividend by the summer of 1900. By the end of the year, Hecla had sold $229,550 worth of ore and paid $100,000 in dividends, signalling the beginning of Hecla Mining's existence as a going, thriving enterprise.

Hecla prospered in the years to follow, its mining activities flourishing as the nation's consumption of lead increased. The demand for lead was stimulated by strong demand for sheeting from the chemical industry, sheathing for cable, and paint production, but in 1907 a nationwide financial panic brought the encouraging growth in the lead market to a screeching halt. Lead prices picked up again during World War I, only to collapse at the war's conclusion, as Hecla Mining's management was introduced to the capriciousness of fluctuating market prices.

Roller coaster lead prices was not the only problem executives in Wallace had to contend with, for the first decades of the 20th century were pocked with labor strife, pitting the company's miners against those at the company's headquarters, where those in charge were already involved in a heated battle. Inside the corporate offices, there was enough rancor without the added enmity stemming from labor problems because the directors of the company were waging a contentious debate against each other over the development of a zinc mine named Star. For years, those opposed to sinking money into the Star mine fought those in favor of branching out into zinc, with the outcome ultimately settled in court. The pro-Star faction won, and in 1922 Hecla Mining and another premier mining company in the Coeur d'Alenes called Bunker Hill & Sullivan agreed to develop the Star mine for zinc, a multimillion dollar project that signalled a turning point for Hecla Mining.

In reference to the Star deal, one chronicler of Hecla Mining's past noted that the decision to go ahead into zinc "changed Hecla from a company with a mine to a company bent on extending its operating life indefinitely," but however symbolic the move may have been the reality of the project was far less meaningful. By the time the mine was ready to begin producing, a point reached after considerable investment, the Great Depression had begun to exercise its stifling grip on the nation's economy. Metals prices began to plummet, and Hecla Mining's directors chose to shut down the Star mine in 1930, resolving to keep it closed until, in their words, "the metal situation justifies resumption." The mine remained closed for five-and-a-half years, eating through nearly $4 million before its subsidiary company, Sullivan Mining Company, paid its first dividend in 1936. As it did to the Star project, the crippled economy affected other aspects of Hecla Mining's business, engendering tough financial times for the mining concern, but although beaten, the company never succumbed to the deleterious economic conditions. The 1930s were spent further developing mines and searching for new ones, a search that was becoming increasingly important to the company's survival as the 1940s neared.

1944: The Hecla Is Lost

Entering the 1940s, the Hecla mine had been producing substantial yields of ore for four decades, proving to be an invaluable, sustaining force for Hecla Mining. Time, however, was running out, and the company's directors knew it. In the foreseeable future, they realized they would reach a point when they could no longer count on their mainstay mine to support the company and consequently would have to face the daunting challenge of operating Hecla Mining without the Hecla mine. That dreaded moment of uncertainty arrived in 1944, when the Hecla mine was closed at a depth of 3,600 feet, after yielding more than nine million tons of ore and realizing $81 million in net smelter returns. There were other, smaller mines operating in Hecla Mining's fold, and the Star mine had at last begun to produce appreciable income, but from 1944 on Hecla Mining was without a large mine, operating in one sense like a ship adrift without a keel to guide its course. The search was on for something to compensate for the loss of the Hecla, but until that something was found Hecla Mining operated much like a holding company, a corporate shell with partial stakes in various ventures but without a discernible, defining force inside.

During the immediate postwar years, Hecla Mining's financial position was tenuous, made unsteady by the lack of a large mine from which the company could regulate production according to market prices. Every effort was expended to find a new golden goose but nothing turned up immediately. The company lived of the income derived from its zinc production at Star during this period while the search continued. In one notable failure, Hecla Mining invested in a silver mine named Rock Creek, pouring in roughly $500,000 to develop the mine before divesting the property at a loss in 1955. Other attempts to find a reliable, revenue-generating engine brought Hecla Mining far afield and out of the mining industry altogether, such as the company's diversification in the late 1950s. Hecla Mining acquired a Seattle-based manufacturer of movable ceiling panels called Accesso Systems, Inc. and Ace Concrete Company in Spokane, but diversification never delivered great profits, underscoring the need for a second large mine.

Part of the solution to the company's problem had already been found by the time diversification had started, when Hecla Mining followed a trend in the mining industry and began looking for opportunities in uranium production. The company concentrated its search on Utah's uranium fields, and in 1954 struck an agreement with U & I Uranium, Inc., a coalition of six companies with uranium prospects. At the time U & I was in need of financial help and Hecla Mining presented itself as a savior, funnelling money into the company and gaining ownership of two bright uranium prospects, Radon, a group of ten claims and Hot Rocks, both located approximately 30 miles south of Moab, Utah. Of the two properties, Radon proved to be the most valuable, paying back Hecla Mining's development money after its first year, an $880,000 reward that was followed by successive years of substantial profits. It was the realization of this income that enabled Hecla Mining to finance its next important purchase, the long-awaited keel of stability.

Silver in the 1950s

With the proceeds generated by Radon, Hecla Mining began to invest in a silver-lead mine named Lucky Friday, a group of six claims staked between 1899 and 1906. In 1959, Hecla Mining purchased Lucky Friday, a milestone acquisition that represented the company's second Hecla mine, if such comparisons can be made. The acquisition of Lucky Friday was momentous, "the fulcrum that restored Hecla as an operating company with prolonged life," according to a company historian. With the income derived from Radon and Lucky Friday, management financed the company's next important moves, part of a long-range plan to accumulate a reserve that would allow Hecla Mining to pay dividends in recessive years as well as robust years and to expand the company on all fronts. By the mid-1960s, riding high on the shoulders of Lucky Friday, Hecla Mining was once again a thriving enterprise, earning nearly $6 million a year and with exploration offices in strategic locations such as Tucson, Reno, Salt Lake City, and Vancouver and Toronto, Canada. Its first big move with the resources stemming from Lucky Friday occurred during the 1970s, and it was a regretful misstep.

In Arizona, exploratory drilling on a copper claim jointly owned by El Paso Natural Gas and Transarizona Resources, Inc. had revealed a hefty deposit of ore, larger than El Paso cared to handle. The natural gas company began to look for a partner experienced in hard-rock drilling to take the remaining half belonging to Transarizona and operate a mine. The mine was christened Lakeshore and stood atop what was regarded as one of the largest copper deposits in the United States, capable, according to some estimates, of producing ores worth $3.7 billion. Hecla Mining, a septuagenarian as far as hard-rock drilling was concerned, neatly fit El Paso's description for a partner, and had its own reasons to bid for a stake in Lakeshore. Involvement in a copper property as large as Lakeshore would free the company from sole dependence on lead and silver and extend the company's productive life indefinitely, while tripling its assets and income in one daring move. There were massive profits to be made by Hecla Mining, to be sure, but there was an equally large risk associated with taking on Lakeshore, the exposure to which touched off a debate among the company's directors as intense and divisive as the battle over whether or not to develop the Star mine roughly a half century earlier. Those opposed to developing Lakeshore railed against those in favor of a bold move into copper, and vice versa, with the faction intent on development winning once again. This time, however, the winning side did not have the opportunity to gloat over their victory. Commercial production at Lakeshore began in 1976 when copper prices were severely depressed, mired in the worst market conditions since the 1930s. One year after production began, losses in Arizona reached a staggering $46 million, leading to Hecla Mining's worst financial year since the reorganization in 1898. By the end of the year, the embattled Lakeshore mine was closed, ending a disagreeable chapter and decade in Hecla Mining's history.

Early 1980s Acquisitions

Desperate attempts were made to sell the Lakeshore property, but given the market conditions there were no takers. The property was eventually sold at a greatly discounted price, and management moved quickly to put the stain of Lakeshore behind it. A major reorganization ensued, contemporaneous with a strong rise in silver prices that provided the company with much-needed relief at its bleakest point in the century. From the sweeping reorganization and the succor of swelling silver prices, a new corporate philosophy was born that focused on diversification and aggressive growth. Hecla Mining was "too small to be truly viable in the corporate world," according to its president in the company's annual report, and the diagnosis was quickly given an antidote. In 1981, Hecla Mining made good on the words of its president, merging with Day Mines, Inc., which along with Hecla Mining represented one of the two pioneer mining companies in Idaho. The consolidation of the two veterans, now made less vulnerable to hostile takeover, spawned record financial highs during the early 1980s, at a time when Hecla Mining was responsible for producing 15 percent of the newly mined silver in the United States.

A greater infusion of stature followed the Day Mines acquisition, one that provided much of the might that characterized the company during the 1990s. In 1984, Hecla Mining acquired Ranchers Exploration and Development Corporation, a New Mexico mining company involved in copper, gold, silver, clay, and volcanic rock production. The effect of the acquisition was large. It doubled Hecla Mining's size, diversified it, and gave it a silver mine, the Escalante, that produced more than two million ounces a year at the lowest production cost of any large-scale silver mine in the nation. Gold and copper were added to Hecla Mining's portfolio. Clay, provided by Ranchers' subsidiary, Kentucky-Tennessee Clay Company, joined the fold, adding ceramic manufacturers to Hecla Mining's roster of customers. Through another Ranchers' subsidiary, Colorado Aggregate Company, the company absorbed volcanic rock quarry operations. Following the incorporation of Ranchers into Hecla Mining, the company relocated to a more populous community, moving from Wallace to Coeur d'Alene in 1986, and enjoyed years of steady growth, as it realized the surge of vibrancy added by the two acquisitions completed early in the decade.

Though meaningful growth occurred following the early 1980s acquisitions, the remainder of the 1980s were not without their problems. The Lucky Friday mine was closed in 1986, its operation deemed to be too costly, but opened again in 1987. On the brighter side, the company delved into gold production in earnest, acquiring properties in the United States and Mexico that provided a substantial percentage of revenue during the 1990s. Further, the addition of the industrial minerals businesses gained through the purchase of Ranchers proved to be a boon, developing into a nearly 50 percent contributor to the company's total revenue volume and recording annual leaps in sales for more than a decade. By the late 1990s, after a 10-year stretch that saw the company's financial totals fluctuate widely, Hecla Mining's management was intent on increasing the company's gold and silver production and altering the composition of its business so that precious metals would account for 70 percent of total revenues. With this as its goal at the dawn of its second century of business, Hecla Mining rallied forward, a far cry from the $150 hillside claim that gave birth to one of the country's preeminent mining companies.

Principal Subsidiaries

Kentucky-Tennessee Clay; Mountain West Colorado Aggregate (MWCA); Industrial Minerals Exploration.

Further Reading

Bradley, Hassell, "Hecla Gets New Canada Base," *American Metal Market,* August 27, 1990, p. 5.

Fahey, John, *Hecla: A Century of Western Mining,* Seattle: University of Washington Press, 1990.

Knights, Mikell, "Hecla Mine Halts Operations; Cause of Mine Shaft Accident Is Under Investigation," *American Metal Market,"* September 1, 1994, p. 12.

LaRue, Gloria T., "Hecla to Up Gold, Silver Output," *American Metal Market,* March 7, 1997, p. 4.

Munford, Christopher, "Hecla's Largest Silver Mine Down on Luck; Firm Shuts Stopes, Lays Off Workers," *American Metal Market,* December 6, 1990, p. 2.

Schiffer, Craig, "Hecla Workers Return to Lucky Friday Mine," *American Metal Market,* December 8, 1994, p. 6.

Stavro, Barry, "Long Shot," *Forbes,* October 20. 1986, p. 127.

Stovall, Robert H., "Tarnished Trophies," *Financial World,* August 8, 1989, p. 96.

—Jeffrey L. Covell

Hollywood Park, Inc.

1050 S. Prairie Ave.
Inglewood, California 90301
U.S.A.
(310) 419-1500
Fax: (310) 671-4460

Public Company
Incorporated: 1981 as Hollywood Park Realty
    Enterprises, Inc.
Employees: 1,500
Sales: $143.2 million (1996)
Stock Exchanges: NASDAQ
SICs: 7948 Racing, Including Track Operation; 7993
    Coin Operated Amusement Devices

Hollywood Park, Inc. is a gaming, sports, and entertainment company that owns and operates card clubs, casinos, and thoroughbred tracks, including the famous Hollywood Park race track in Inglewood, a suburb of Los Angeles. For nearly half a century, Hollywood Park, and its precursor company, the Hollywood Turf Club, concentrated solely on running the Inglewood facility. But when attendance began declining in the early 1980s, Hollywood Park began to diversify, initially with card clubs and, in 1997, into full-service casinos with the acquisition of Boomtown, Inc.

Hollywood Turf Club

The Hollywood Turf Club was formed in 1938 with several legendary actors and Hollywood moviemakers among its original 600 shareholders, including Joan Blondell, Ronald Colman, Walt Disney, Bing Crosby, Sam Goldwyn, Darryl Zanuck, George Jessel, Ralph Bellamy, Wallace Beery, and Irene Dunne. Al Jolson and Raoul Walsh were on the original board of directors and Jack L. Warner, of Warner Brothers, was the first chairman.

Hollywood Park quickly became known as The Track of the Lakes and Flowers because of its landscaped infield. After being used as a storage facility during World War II, the track reopened in 1945 and became one of the most popular tracks in the world, leading all U.S. tracks in attendance from 1950 to 1959. The original Hollywood Park Turf Club incorporated as Hollywood Park Realty Enterprises, Inc. in 1981, with Hollywood Park Operating Co. managing the track as a paired-share with the real estate enterprise.

By 1984, revenues had reached $64.7 million, with net income of $8.3 million. During this stretch run, Hollywood Park was dominated by Marjorie L. Everett, whose father had owned two small horse tracks in the Chicago area. After her father died, Everett sold the tracks to Charles Bludhorn, then chief executive of Gulf & Western Industries. She continued to manage the race tracks until Bludhorn swapped them for a 10 percent stake in Hollywood Park. With Bludhorn's backing, Everett was named chief executive at Hollywood Park in 1972.

Everett's acknowledged strength lay in cultivating friends in high places, including Ronald Reagan, then governor of California, and actors Cary Grant and John Forsythe, whom she added to the board of directors. The grand dame of horse racing also had a grand design for Hollywood Park that included buying the 300-acre Los Alamitos harness-racing complex in Cypress, California, in 1984 for $58 million. Hollywood Park also spent another $40 million in 1984 to create luxury boxes at Hollywood Park, where attendance had started to suffer. Both investments proved disastrous.

Less than two years later, in 1986, Hollywood Park revenues had climbed to nearly $74 million, but net income had fallen to $3.5 million. In the 1987 annual report, Everett blamed the problems on heavy traffic in the Los Angeles area, but as *California Business* later noted, "there were signs that the trouble lay deeper than a freeway on-ramp."

For one, the magazine reported, the empty luxury boxes had become the butt of Hollywood jokes. Hollywood Park also bulldozed a popular golf course at the Los Alamitos track, which angered local residents. When the company applied to the City of Cypress for a zoning change to build condominiums, the plan was "enthusiastically rejected."

| Company Perspectives: |

Hollywood Park's strategic plan is to diversify its gaming, sports and entertainment businesses through the development, acquisition, ownership and/or operation of casinos, race tracks and other gaming, sports and entertainment attractions.

Takeover Challenges

In 1989, the deteriorating financial condition had become so serious that a headline in *Business Week* magazine asked, ''Is Hollywood Park on the way to the glue factory?'' The article noted that attendance at the famous track, although it still attracted Hollywood celebrities, had fallen sharply since the introduction of off-track betting and a California state lottery. As a result, Hollywood Park lost $16 million between 1987 and 1989, a $98 million loan from Wells Fargo Bank was coming due, and its stock was at a six-year low. A deal to sell the Los Alamitos track also fell through in early 1989.

But the more immediate challenge facing Everett was a takeover bid by Thomas W. Gamel, the wealthy owner of a Denver-based tractor-trailer manufacturing firm, who had started buying up Hollywood Park stock in 1987 and then held a 5.6 percent share.

Gamel accused the iron-willed Everett, who owned nearly 15 percent of Hollywood Park herself, of ''running a first-class track into the ground.'' In a proposal considered heresy by many, Gamel recommended converting the 10,000-seat Hollywood Park grandstand into an off-track betting facility and selling the rest of the 340 acres for residential and commercial development, raising as much as $150 million to be distributed to stockholders. That, said Robert Forgnone, a Hollywood Park lawyer, was ''like suggesting that General Motors give up the manufacture of automobiles.''

Gamel, who had resigned as a director at the crosstown Santa Anita racetrack to pursue Hollywood Park, threatened a proxy fight if Everett failed to act on his plan and sued to obtain a list of shareholders. However, in a deal engineered by oil and real estate billionaire Marvin Davis, a Hollywood Park board member, Gamel yielded in exchange for a seat on the board. He also agreed not to acquire any more stock in Hollywood Park. That fall, Hollywood Park eased its financial woes by selling the Los Alamitos track for $54 million, $4 million less than it had paid.

By early 1990, another challenge was brewing, this time from Davis himself. *Forbes* reported that Davis, with the support of television hitmakers and fellow board members Merv Griffin and Aaron Spelling, had ''taken the reins'' from Everett. *Forbes* also speculated that Davis wanted to take the company private. Then, just as suddenly, Davis announced that he was resigning from the board of directors. The *Los Angeles Business Journal* reported that Everett, described as the ''doyenne of the California horsy set,'' had mustered her forces and rebuffed Davis's bid to become chairman. In a letter to the board, Davis said he had ''reluctantly concluded that I am unable to devote the time required to my duties as a director of Hollywood Park.''

R. D. Hubbard

The final, and successful challenge, to Everett's control of Hollywood Park came in 1991 from Randall Dee Hubbard. Hubbard, known in the business world as R. D. Hubbard, became a salesman for a Wichita glass-installation company in 1959, rose to president nine years later, and eventually turned the firm into the largest autoglass replacement business in the United States. In 1978, Hubbard formed his own specialty glass manufacturer, AFG Industries, Inc., by buying and merging two failing businesses. In 1980, Hubbard bought into two horse breeding operations, Crystal Springs Farms in Lexington, Kentucky, and Frontera Farms in Sunland Park, New Mexico. In 1988, he and a partner bought Ruidoso Downs, a small horse track in New Mexico, where he introduced simulcasting—beaming closed-circuit telecasts of the races to other tracks to stimulate betting.

In the fall of 1990, Hubbard announced that he had acquired nearly 10 percent of Hollywood Park's stock, which was then languishing at about $20 a share. He also announced that he would seek the ouster of all current board members and filed a lawsuit alleging that Everett had made false claims to the SEC.

Outside the lawsuit, Hubbard also accused Everett of taking company equipment for personal use. Everett admitted having several televisions and a generator belonging to Hollywood Park, but claimed that it was an oversight that she had not been billed for them. Everett countersued, alleging that Hubbard was illegally manipulating Hollywood Park stock. The tension was so great that two board members, actor John Forsythe and Harry Ornest, a Beverly Hills financier in the Hubbard camp, got into a fist fight in one of the luxury boxes during a race.

In the closing days of 1990, Hubbard started a ''consent solicitation,'' a type of mini-proxy fight in which large shareholders are asked to support a non-board member's plan. Early in 1991, Hollywood Park announced that Hubbard had failed to received consent from shareholders representing a majority of the company's shares, but only by the narrowest of margins. Everett, realizing that Hubbard would win a full proxy fight, announced that Steven A. Wynn, then chairman of the Mirage Casino in Los Vegas, would join the board of directors at the annual meeting in February and succeed her as chairman and chief executive officer.

Actually, the announcement was a sham to keep Everett in control. As *California Business* later explained: ''. . . Wynn himself was never enthused about getting involved. Sources close to him say he was doing a favor for (former board member) Davis and (financier David) Batchelder, and that he saw an outside chance to make some money on a quick corporate restructuring. Besides, his role wouldn't be so tough: He'd simply buy some stock, make some noise and scare Hubbard away. Everett would still be involved, day-to-day.''

In the end, however, it was Everett who was derailed. Wynn, under pressure from his board of directors at the Mirage, backed out of the agreement. Everett was forced to negotiate with

Hubbard, who demanded that she resign from the board. In April, Hubbard was named chief executive officer, backed by an expanded board of directors that included 11 new members and six holdovers from the Everett regime.

Diversification

Of his plans for Hollywood Park, Hubbard announced, "Once we get this squared away, we'll be looking to sell some non-core real estate to raise capital for improvements on the track. But the biggest improvement won't cost so much. We're going to concentrate on raising the quality of service that people see when they come out to the (track) . . . Hollywood Park, like all horse racing, has a strong client base. We need to win back its trust and approval."

Hollywood Park spent $20 million that year to spruce up the track. The payoff was immediate: Hollywood Park earned $1.6 million in 1991, its first profit in five years. The financial results were even better in 1992, with earnings of $5.4 million, despite rioting in central Los Angeles that broke out on the track's opening day. Hollywood Park was forced to close for a week, including the profitable weekend of the Kentucky Derby, costing the track an estimated $35 million in parimutuel betting. The lingering effects of the riots held down attendance throughout the race season, despite full-page newspaper ads pointing out that Inglewood escaped relatively unscathed.

Regardless, in mid-1992 Hubbard announced plans for a $100 million expansion at Hollywood Park, including a 14,000-seat music center, renovated recreational facilities, including an 18-hole putting course and a two-deck driving range for golfers, and a retail and gambling complex. A key component of the expansion was converting the Cary Grant Pavilion, an off-track betting facility, into a "card club" with an upscale restaurant and legalized gambling. Inglewood also announced that it would build a police substation at the track.

Hollywood Park also dropped its status as a "paired share," with one company operating the race track and another owning the real estate, in 1992, and reorganized as a single entity, Hollywood Park, Inc.

The Hollywood Park Casino opened in July 1994. Under then-existing California law, publicly traded companies were prohibited from operating card clubs, so while Hollywood Park owned the facility, the club was managed by Pacific Casino Management Inc. Hollywood Park and Santa Anita Companies, another race track operator, lobbied California lawmakers to change the law, and in 1995, a measure passed that allowed Hollywood Park to manage the card club. However, along with the bill was a three-year ban on card club referendums that effectively halted expansion until 1999, although Hollywood Park was allowed to proceed with construction of a card club in Compton that had already been approved by the voters.

In 1995, Everett launched a last-ditch effort to regain control of Hollywood Park. In filings with the Delaware Chancery Court, she questioned the company's purchase of Sunflower Racing, which operated the Woodlands, a thoroughbred and greyhound racetrack in Kansas City, Kansas. Hubbard, who then owned 60 percent of Sunflower, convinced his board of directors to buy the company in 1994 for $20 million, with the

expectation that Kansas would approve casino-style gambling. But that never happened and poor attendance at the Woodlands, hurt by the opening of riverboat gambling in Missouri, dragged down Hollywood Park's financial results.

Everett also questioned a 1991 venture in which Hubbard and Hollywood Park each invested $243,000 in Midpointe Racing Inc., and agreed to finance the start-up company's application to build a race track in Texas. When Texas denied the application, approving a proposal from the Lone Star Jockey Club instead, Hollywood Park wrote off its entire $703,000 investment. Hubbard, however, maintained his personal share of Midpointe Racing, which later merged with the Lone Star Jockey Club. Finally, Everett challenged Hollywood Park's payment of $139,000 for "company use" of a jet owned by R. D. Hubbard Enterprises, Inc.

Although Everett's attempt to regain control of Hollywood Park fizzled, several of her concerns continued to plague the company.

In 1995, Hollywood Park had to fend off several shareholder suits alleging that executives inflated revenue and earnings projections to enable the company to acquire Turf Paradise, a thoroughbred track in Phoenix it bought for $34 million in stock in 1994, six months after acquiring Sunflower Racing. Then early in 1996, Sunflower Racing shut down the Woodlands track and filed for reorganization; Hollywood Park was forced to write off its entire $11.4 million investment. That fall, Hubbard's loudest critic on the board of directors, John Brunetti, also chief executive officer at Hialeah in Florida, quit the board in disgust. Brunetti told the *Los Angeles Times*: "I've tried to understand Mr. Hubbard's strategy, but all I see is a series of initiatives that go nowhere." Hollywood Park ended 1996 with a loss of $4.2 million on revenues that had fallen 15 percent in two years.

Despite the financial problems, Hollywood Park opened its second card club, the Crystal Park Hotel and Casino in Compton, California, in the fall of 1996.

California law continued to prohibit publicly traded companies from operating card clubs, except in conjunction with a race track, so Hollywood Park, an 88 percent owner of Crystal Park, leased actual operations of the club to Compton Entertainment Inc. Hollywood Park had a five-year option to purchase the gaming license from Compton Entertainment. Likewise, Compton Entertainment held an option to buy the hotel and casino if the California legislature failed to change the law before Hollywood Park's option expired.

As 1996 came to a close, Hubbard also announced perhaps his biggest gamble ever. Hollywood Park, whose efforts to use card clubs as an entree to full-fledged casino gambling had so far failed, agreed to buy Boomtown Inc., which owned and operated Western-themed casinos in Las Vegas, Reno, and Biloxi, Mississippi, and a riverboat casino in New Orleans, for $188 million—$58.5 million in stock plus the assumption of nearly $130 million in debt. The merger, which cleared its last regulatory hurdle in mid-1997, was expected to more than double Hollywood Park revenues to an estimated $330 million.

In its annual report for 1996, Hollywood Park, a company that consisted solely of a single thoroughbred track for most of its history, described itself as a "gaming, sports and entertainment company" whose strategic plan was to "pursue opportunities in the gaming business." Significantly, casinos were first in a list of the company's interests.

Principal Subsidiaries

Hollywood Park Operating Company; Hollywood Park Casino; Turf Paradise, Inc.; Sunflower Racing, Inc.; HP/Compton, Inc.

Further Reading

Bancroft, Thomas, "Long Shot," *Forbes,* August 3, 1992, p. 57.

Cornel, Laura, "Marvin Davis' New Wager," *Forbes,* February 19, 1990, p. 14.

Deady, Tim, "New Casino Plans Put on Hold," *Los Angeles Business Journal,* April 14, 1995, p. 1.

Grover, Ronald, "A Fast Mover Among Fast Horses," *Business Week,* July 20, 1992, p. 84.

Kerwin, Kathleen, "Is Hollywood Park on the Way to the Glue Factory?" *Business Week,* May 29, 1989, p. 36.

Moshavi, Sharon, "If You Can't Beat 'Em . . ." *Forbes,* May 9, 1994, p. 58.

Mullen, Liz, and Tim Deady, "Hollywood Park Buffeted by Financial Loss, Layoffs, Lawsuits," *Los Angeles Business Journal,* October 24, 1994, p. 1.

Mulligan, Thomas S., "Management of Track Challenged by Everett," *Los Angeles Times,* October 7, 1995, p. D1.

——, "Hollywood Park Goes for a Piece of the Action," *Los Angeles Times,* March 21, 1996, p. D1.

Mulligan, Thomas S., and George White, "Hollywood Park Plans $100-Million Renovation," *Los Angeles Times,* June 12, 1992, p. A1.

Peltz, James, "Hollywood Park Raises Its Bet on Gaming Ventures," *Los Angeles Times,* October 25, 1996, p. D1.

Walsh, James, "A Bloody Day at the Races," *California Business,* April 1991, p. 21.

—Dean Boyer

IMATION

Borne of 3M Innovation

Imation Corporation

One Imation Place
Oakdale, Minnesota 55128-3414
U.S.A.
(612) 704-4000
Fax: (800) 537-4675
Web site: http://www.imation.com

Public Company
Incorporated: 1996
Employees: 9,700
Sales: $2.3 billion (1996)
Stock Exchanges: New York
SICs: 3679 Data Storage & Imaging Systems; 3695
  Magnetic & Optical Recording Media; 3695
  Computer Software Tape & Disks, Blank: Rigid &
  Floppy; 3555 Printing Machines & Equipment; 3861
  Photographic Equipment & Accessories, Camera &
  X-ray Film; 3844 X-ray Apparatus & Tubes: Medical,
  Industrial, Research, & Control

In the closing months of 1995, Minnesota's 3M Corporation, one of the bluest of America's blue-chip companies, announced that five of its businesses would be spun off the following year to form a new data storage and medical imaging company named Imation Corporation (from the words imaging, information, and imagination). Little mystery surrounded the reasons for the $2.3 billion divestiture: since January 1994, 3M's data storage and imaging operations had been posting stagnant revenue growth year after year. 3M management decided a spinoff would not only remove the drag on its own balance sheet but might give its flagging businesses the capital and operational independence they needed to grow their way out of their earnings funk. Thus, as 1995 drew to a close, 12,700 of 3M's 70,000 employees received a letter informing them of their reassignment to the new company. Those "Imation designees" who agreed to the transfer would retain their 3M salaries and be relocated to a former 3M office complex in Oakdale, a suburb of St. Paul. Those who opted out—there were more than 3,000—

would be given early retirement packages and 3M's gratitude. On July 1, 1996, Imation would officially begin business as a public corporation.

Born of 3M Innovation: 1902–81

3M's penchant for creating (if rarely spinning off) new businesses had begun within a few years of its founding in 1902 as the Minnesota Mining & Manufacturing Company. Transparent Scotch tape, the dry-printing photocopy process, and the ubiquitous "Post-It" adhesive note pad were only the most prominent of the tens of thousands of new products it introduced over the next 90 years. Through strong management, an unusual research- and innovation-driven corporate culture, and an unbroken string of successful new product launches, 3M had grown by the mid-1990s into one of the 100 largest and most profitable companies in the United States. Its first foray into the businesses that would comprise Imation began in 1947 when its engineers unveiled the first magnetic recording tape, the forerunner of the cassette tape. With the marketing help of singer Bing Crosby, 3M's branded "Sound Recording Tape" transformed the music industry and by the 1950s had evolved into a new product, Scotch Commercial Videotape, just in time to supply the blossoming U.S. television industry.

In the 1950s and 1960s, 3M ventured into the related fields of dry-silver microfilm and photographic products. The medical imaging products that (with photo color products) would comprise 29.5 percent of Imation's revenues in 1996 were outgrowths of 3M's first forays into radiology and medical X-ray technology in the 1970s. Likewise, Imation's printing and publishing technologies (23 percent of 1996 revenues) grew out of such early printing-related 3M innovations as the Matchprint color proofing system for commercial printers, first introduced in 1972. The mainframe computer began to become an indispensable tool of U.S. industry in the 1950s and 1960s, following IBM's introduction of the first computer memory in 1956. That year, "Big Blue" unveiled a random access disk drive (one capable of accessing data anywhere on a computer's disk) with a capacity of 5,000 bytes (5 megabytes [MBs]). By the 1970s IBM's head start in computer memory had spawned the "Winchester" hard drive for mainframe computers (so named because it featured two 30-MB disks, echoing the famous ''30–30'' Winchester rifle). When Seagate Technology adapted the Winchester standard for a smaller 5.25 hard disk drive in the late 1970s and early 1980s, the stage was set for the personal computer revolution that erupted with IBM's introduction of the first PC in 1982.

Meanwhile, at 3M Lewis Lehr had been named CEO in 1981 and among his first acts was the reorganization of the company into 40 divisions divided into four major sectors—industrial and consumer products, life sciences, electronic and information technologies, and graphic technologies. The businesses that would become Imation were now distributed between 3M's Graphic Technologies and Electronic and Information Technologies divisions. Lehr linked them even closer when he eventually renamed the Graphic Technologies segment ''Imaging'' and combined it with the Electronic and Information Technologies operation.

Enter Removable Data Storage: 1982–94

In late 1982 an upstart California company named SyQuest Technology introduced the first removable PC hard disk drive (with a storage capacity of 6.38 MBs), giving computer users the ability to handily back up their important data in removable cartridges. Mission-critical data was now safe from disastrous system crashes and could be preserved on an infinitely expandable series of cartridges—regardless of the size of users' hard drives. The computer drive industry began a period of uninterrupted growth in which more than one hundred firms entered the fray, including Iomega, DMA, Eastman Kodak, and Data Technology Corporation, and drive capacity tended to double every year and a half. Over the next 10 years, the vast majority of these firms failed or were merged with other companies. And by 1986 the capacity of a typical removable data cartridge had grown to 15 MB and then by 1987 to 44.5 MB (when most PC hard drives themselves could still only hold 80 MBs of data). By the mid-1990s more than 150 million computers contained removable data storage (RDS) systems.

In the mid-1980s 3M had launched another of its future Imation businesses—CD-ROM manufacture—and by 1989 had appointed Imation's future CEO, Bill Monahan, to head its data storage products division. (Within three years, Monahan was transferred to 3M Italy where the specialized photographic chemicals used in 3M's photographic, medical imaging, and information printing products were developed and manufactured.) As 3M's diskette manufacturing business met intensified competition from price-cutting foreign makers like Sony it moved increasingly into the data storage products business, which was enjoying enormous sales growth and would eventually comprise more than 40 percent of Imation's total revenues.

In the early 1990s Iomega introduced its Bernoulli brand of removable data cartridges for the IBM compatible PC market, and Iomega and SyQuest waged ferocious price wars to claim the top spot in the RDS market.

In 1992, 3M introduced ''write-once'' optical media for multifunction PC drives, launched a huge 2 gigabyte (GB) data storage cartridge product, and unveiled data storage products for the common QIC data storage format. By 1993 it had rolled out data cartridges capable of holding a whopping 5 GB of data and by 1994 was proposing a 25 GB standard for the next generation of QIC data storage tapes as well as marketing data storage cards for laptop computers. By 1994 competitor SyQuest was offering data cartridges with a 110 MB to 270 MB capacity.

As new data storage media including optical (or ''floptical'') and magneto-optical disks began to vie for the data storage market, in 1995 3M unveiled its new Travan data storage line in a joint venture with a group of drive manufacturers. The Travan technology used minicartridges manufactured by 3M with a storage capacity of 400 MB to 4 GB—and eventually up to 15 GBs per disk by 1997. It quickly began to emerge as a new data storage standard, and 10 leading tape drive manufacturers, including Seagate and Hewlett-Packard, adopted the Travan format.

In the mid-1990s 3M and Iomega both conducted market research that showed that the typical PC user wanted an RDS product that could store at least 100 MBs of data, cost no more than $200, and use media priced at less than $20. But Iomega beat everyone to the punch with its new 100-MB Zip drive product, a technology that had originally been developed by Fuji. Because of its ease of use, reliability, $200 price, and Iomega's shrewd marketing campaign (''Because It's Your Stuff''), by mid-1995 the Zip drive had became the RDS leader, selling some 2 million units in its first year alone. By 1996 Iomega had expanded its lead over 3M and other competitors with the introduction of Zip's high-end successor, the 1 GB Jaz drive.

In its eagerness to capture the data storage market, however, Iomega marketed its drives as replacements for the standard 3.5-inch PC drive: users would have to purchase new high-capacity diskettes in order to use the drives, which were not backward-compatible with the longtime industry standard—the 1.44 MB, 3.5-inch floppy disk. For this reason, computer manufacturers did not rush to install Iomega's drives as original PC equipment and, though hugely popular, they remained aftermarket accessories.

Battling for Revenue Growth: 1995–96

Despite its successful efforts to remain at the forefront of the data storage and medical imaging industries the intensity of competition was keeping 3M's data storage and medical imaging divisions in the red. 3M's management decided to concentrate on its industrial, consumer, and life sciences product lines. By late 1995 3M was sending letters to 12,700 of its employees offering them a place in the new Imation spinoff. Gallup pollsters canvassing the ''Imation designees'' on their reaction to the plan were greeted with such responses as ''shocked,'' "betrayed," and "apprehensive," and only 75 percent of 3M's data storage and medical imaging workers eventually wound up in Imation cubicles. Two layers of management, five manufacturing plants, seven labs, and some 5,000 jobs had been jettisoned.

Why would Imation succeed where its businesses had failed under 3M? 3M's management pointed to the new company's streamline operations, which would enable Imation to move more nimbly in its competitive business segments through the "natural synergy" of its product groups, and a new management compensation program that would incentivize Imation executives by linking their pay to the company's fortunes. Finally, as an independent entity Imation would get the attention of Wall Street, enabling it to fuel its growth through public stock offerings. At its inception, Imation would be that rarity among newly minted corporations—a fully developed business enterprise with already-existing customers in 60 countries (most importantly, Italy, the United Kingdom, France, and Germany), no fewer than 10,000 products, an arsenal of 1,800 3M patents and hundreds of worldwide licensing agreements, and the right to market its products under the powerful 3M brand name for three years. 3M and Imation would not compete in each other's businesses for five years.

On Day One—July 1, 1996—Imation opened for business as the world's largest supplier of branded removable magnetic and optical media; the world's leading supplier of medical imaging systems for generating diagnostic images from magnetic resonance, computer timography, nuclear medicine, ultrasound, and other electronic imaging systems; one of the world's largest manufacturers of private-label 35-mm color film for the amateur photo market; and one of the world's largest suppliers of color proofing systems for the graphics arts industry. Its Matchprint and Rainbow printing industry products were industry standards, and it boasted an installed base of more than 7,000 thousand laser imagers for medical imaging applications. An enviable 50 percent of its sales went overseas, and its product lines covered four major markets: information processing, management, and storage (including computer diskettes, data cartridges and Travan cartridges, computer tapes, rewritable optical media, and CD-ROM replication services—41 percent of its 1996 revenues); information printing (including conventional color proofing, digital color proofing, printing plates, image setting and graphic arts products, and carbonless paper products); medical and photo imaging (laser imaging products, laser imagers, X-ray film, "dry" imaging products, film processors, and photographic film products); and information processing services (including technical field service support for equipment, customer service, documentation and training for equipment, engineering and office document systems).

Imation's presence in the competitive data storage industry had been given a major boost months before the spinoff took place. The Achilles' heel of Iomega's wildly successful Zip and Jaz backup storage drives was their lack of backward compatibility: they were designed to replace the 1.44-MB diskette drive whose diskettes would simply not work in Iomega drives. Spotting a potential market opening, in May 1995 Japan's Matsushuta-Kotobuki Electronics and Compaq Computer developed a 3.5-inch floppy disk drive for use with a diskette with 120 MBs of capacity the would one-up Iomega by offering

backward-compatibility: users could use both standard 1.44-MB and the new 120-MB disks in the Imation drive.

In March 1996 3M announced it would manufacture the diskettes for the new cross-format LS-120 drives in conjunction with OR Technologies. With one of the world's biggest PC makers already installing LS-120 drives on some of its new DeskPro computers, 3M/Imation seemed poised to steal some of Iomega's thunder. Moreover, a month before the spinoff, 3M announced the fifth generation of its Travan technology and the introduction of Tape-IT, a software program developed in conjunction with PGSoft Inc. that enabled users to use 3M's data cartridges in several new ways, including for large file transport and for the direct recording and playback of computer data, audio, video, and multimedia files. Joining them would be a new line of digital Rainbow color proofing systems, a new family of DryView imagers, and new medical imaging delivery systems developed with Cemax/Icon and Hewlett-Packard.

Wall Street greeted Imation's stock with less than unbridled enthusiasm. From an initial price of $33 a share it had fallen to $20 by the end of July 1996, and after regaining the $33 mark in December it began a slow but steady decline to under $24 by July 1997. Analysts and investors alike were clearly waiting to see signs that the businesses that had been unprofitable for so long with 3M had discovered the secret of success. Imation's management set a goal of achieving 15 percent annual growth in earnings per share by 1998 and in 1996–97 confidently added offices in the Philippines, Singapore, and Russia to its existing presence in such emerging markets as China, India, Indonesia, and Brazil. In July 1996 it sold off its Italian offset plate plant, reached an agreement with Israel's Scitex Corp. to create a new large-format digital proofing system, and in February 1997 won an agreement with Germany's Siemens Nixdorf Informationssysteme AG to integrate Imation's LS-120 drive technology into some of its European computers. In April, Imation convinced Samsung Electronics of Korea Co. to preinstall LS-120 drives in two of its multimedia PCs, and in August 1997 Imation and Norway's Tandberg Data ASA agreed to jointly design and manufacture new data cartridge technologies for the growing network server segment of the data storage market.

Although Imation managed in its first three months to break the 11-quarter string of stagnant revenue growth that stretched back to its 3M years, in its second quarter it posted a $37.8 million loss. While its hoped-for penetration of the RDS market continued to rest on the uncertain fortunes of the LS-120 diskette, Imation turned to acquisitions, partnerships, and new product launches to solidify its business. In August 1996 it bought Seattle-based Luminous Corporation, a developer of digital desktop publishing software, to strengthen its line of prepress printing products for the growing digital segment of the printing industry. In May 1997 it announced the acquisition of Cemax-Icon Inc., a developer of software and systems integrator for the medical imaging and information management industry, and in June it acquired Minnesota web developer Imaginet, which resulted in the creation of Imation Internet Services, Imation's bid to gain a foothold in the exploding Internet/intranet market. It partnered with Presstek in April 1997 to develop new digital halftone imaging solutions and with TeraStor Corporation to manufacture the latter's 20-GB "near field" data storage system. It also closed cooperative agreements with ECRM Corporation of Massachusetts to develop dry film imaging technology for the graphic arts industry and with ATL Ultrasound Inc. to provide its DryView Laser Imagers for use in ATL's mobile ultrasound demonstration vans.

It also stayed true to its 3M roots by unveiling a slew of new products and services, including winning its first non-3M patent in October 1996 (for a Travan RDS minicartridge design). In 1996 alone, Imation introduced a digital proofing system for the printing industry under its Matchprint brand, won a multimillion-dollar contract from the defense department for its medical imaging equipment and X-ray film, and launched a large-format color proofing system that promised to eliminate two hours from the prepress process used in the printing of posters and other oversize printed materials. In the fall of 1996 it announced a further advance in its continuing contributions to the digital revolution underway in the printing industry by announcing that its Rainbow digital color proofing system had been integrated within an automated prepress workflow environment created by Luminous. In a flurry of year-end product launches, it also introduced a Windows-compatible version of its printing workflow productivity software, Rainbow, which had previously been available only in a Macintosh version; installed its 1,000th DryView Laser Imager (only nine months after the product's introduction); unveiled an improved version of its single-use disposable camera; introduced its Image Acquisition Manager Plus system for transmitting medical images across computer networks; and began shipping a compact film handling and processing system.

In 1997 Imation continued to act like a miniature version of 3M by unleashing a new torrent of products and features. In March, technology giant Hewlett-Packard announced that Imation's DryView Laser Imager was its choice for hospital demonstrations of its new ultrasound system. In April, Imation unveiled a software product for monitoring and improving the productivity and security of backup tape libraries in client/server environments, which it developed in a joint arrangement with Sterling Software of California. Later that month it announced the expansion of its Rainbow color proofing software to work with Adobe's widely used PostScript language and through Luminous it unveiled a new software program that would allow printers to send proofs of their printing work to clients via a remote phone line connection for their approval. It also introduced new features for its Matchprint Laser Proof product line that would enable it to move closer to its goal of providing a "total customer solution" for the new age of digital printing technology. Its new Printers-Web software, for example, would enable printing firms to create an entire web site out of the box, which would allow them to offer clients job tracking, estimating, quotes, customer service, and even over-the-Internet transmission of completed printing jobs via the World Wide Web.

Though admitting that its earnings for the second quarter of 1997 would fall under analyst's estimates, Imation kept its new product juggernaut rolling with the introduction of a new family of RDS cartridges geared specifically to the business client/server and workstation environments, a tape library system that automates tape backup and data archiving for business computer networks, and a new generation of X-ray process films that use 50 percent less developer chemicals than existing products but with no loss of image quality.

Imation was meanwhile holding its own in its most visible and important product line: removable data storage for the business and consumer PC market. Although more and more vendors and computer manufacturers—including Hitachi-Maxell, Fujitsu, and Exabyte—were offering Imation's LS-120 backward-compatible disk drives, the pace of growth was slower than expected despite the fact that Iomega had partially fumbled its early market lead by being forced to recall thousands of its Jaz drives for defects. To jump start LS-120 sales, in June Imation renamed the product SuperDisk, wrapped it in a new snazzy package, and introduced a new external SuperDisk drive that would enable users to switch it from computer to computer. Major obstacles remained in Imation's path, however. It seemed unable to win Wall Street's confidence, and though Iomega had signally failed to make good on its claim that its Zip and Jaz drives would replace the tired-but-true 1.44-MB diskette, so too had the LS-120/SuperDisk. By the spring of 1997 only 15 percent of Compaq's computers came with the LS-120/SuperDisk preinstalled instead of the standard 1.44-MB 3.5-inch disk drive.

Principal Subsidiaries

Luminous Technology Inc.; Imation Australia New Zealand Pty. Ltd.; Imation Corp. Japan; Imation Hong Kong Ltd.; Imation Korea; Imation New Zealand; Imation Singapore Pte.

Further Reading

"A Superdisk That's Firing Up the Floppy Wars," *Business Week,* June 30, 1997, p. 80C.

Cook, Rick, "Explosion in Removable Storage," *VAR Business,* June 1, 1996.

Costlow, Terry, "3M's New Data Storage Spin-off Called Imation," *EE Times,* April 22, 1996.

Greenwald, John, "Spinning Away," *Time,* August 26, 1997.

Hachman, Mark, "LS-120 Getting Whipped by Zip," *Electronic Buyers' News,* April 28, 1997.

"Imation Opens Moscow Sales Office," *St. Paul Pioneer-Press,* April 9, 1997.

"Imation Puts Oomph in Disk'Drive Efforts," *St. Paul Pioneer-Press,* June 16, 1997.

"Imation, Samsung Team Up," *St. Paul Pioneer Press,* April 22, 1997.

"This Doesn't Look Like 3M Anymore," *St. Paul Pioneer Press,* June 30, 1996.

"3M Spin-off Imation Emerges," *CityBusiness* (Twin Cities), December 30, 1996.

"Zip Zapped?" *Forbes,* July 7, 1997, p. 426.

—Paul S. Bodine

Ingles Markets, Inc.

Post Office Box 6676
Asheville, North Carolina 28816
U.S.A.
(704)-669-2941
Fax: (704)-669-3668

Public Company
Incorporated: 1963
Employees: 11,000
Sales: $1.473 billion (fiscal 1996, ended September 28)
Stock exchanges: NASDAQ
SICs: 5411 Grocery Stores; 6512 Nonresidential Building
   Operators; 2026 Fluid Milk

Ingles Markets, Inc. is a regional supermarket chain with 188 stores in North Carolina, South Carolina, Georgia, Virginia, Tennessee, and Alabama. Most stores are located in rural areas, small towns, or suburban communities within 250 miles of the firm's headquarters/distribution center in Asheville, North Carolina. Ingles Markets also owns a milk processing plant which makes dairy products for sale in Ingles stores and other outlets. In addition, the firm owns 74 shopping centers and also 30 other properties, almost all of which contain an Ingles supermarket. Like its competitors, Ingles Markets in the 1990s offers much more than just canned, fresh, and frozen food. To provide one-stop convenience for busy consumers, Ingles also sells numerous nonfood items, from office supplies to cooking utensils, and includes services such as sit-down cafes, check cashing, take-out meals and deli items, floral shops, and video rentals. Ingles Markets sells national brands and also its generally lower-priced Laura Lynn private label items. All stores are open seven days a week and many operate 24 hours a day.

Origins

After working in the grocery business with his parents in Asheville, North Carolina, Robert P. Ingle started his first store in 1963 in his hometown. In that same year, the company began buying a significant part of its merchandise from Merchant

Distributors, Inc. (MDI), a wholesale grocery distributor based in Hickory, North Carolina. MDI continued into the 1990s to provide mainly frozen foods, produce, and slow selling items not stockpiled by Ingles.

Gradually Ingles opened new stores in the 1960s and 1970s. To support its expanded operations, Ingles Markets in 1978 built a new warehouse/distribution center in Asheville, North Carolina. From this 450,000-square-foot facility, the company shipped various items to its retail stores in North Carolina and neighboring states.

Growth in the 1980s

In September 1982 Ingles Markets acquired its own milk plant. Purchased from Sealtest, the plant operated as a wholly-owned Ingles subsidiary called Milkco, Inc. By 1996 it was North Carolina's second largest milk processing and packaging plant. Milkco supplied 90 percent of the fluid milk for Ingles supermarkets. It also sold citrus, dairy, and bottled water items to various customers such as other grocery stores and food distributors. These non-Ingles buyers represented about 58 percent of Milkco's business by 1996.

Milkco's corrugated boxes for shipping milk and other products were another important aspect of its business. They protected the bottled goods from damage and kept them cold. According to Ingles's 1996 annual report, Milkco was "the only dairy processing plant in the Southeast with this capability." Milkco also was committed to using packaging that could be completely recycled.

In 1982 Ingles gained a new president and chief operating officer. Landy B. Laney had been an executive officer and director of Ingles since 1972. He would serve in his new capacity until 1996.

In the late 1980s Ingles Markets took some important steps to expand its operations. In December 1986 it sold 23 shopping centers to Atlanta's IRT Property Company for $50 million, although the book value on those properties was only $33 million. In turn, Ingles leased the same centers from IRT and continued to operate them. At the same time, Ingles maintained ownership of 38 other shopping centers, a result of Robert Ingle's personal involvement in choosing properties.

The following year Ingles used another method to raise money for its expansion. In September 1987 Ingles became a public corporation by selling its stock under the symbol IMKTA on the NASDAQ exchange for $13 per share. Only Class A stock was offered to the public. Robert Ingle maintained control over the company by holding almost 75 percent of its Class B stock, which controlled company voting rights.

Using funds from the sale of its shopping centers and its stock offering, Ingles Markets opened new stores in the late 1980s. In 1989, for example, it opened 17 new stores to reach a total of 156 in North and South Carolina, Georgia, Tennessee, and Virginia.

According to *Food People* magazine, by 1990 Ingles enjoyed 45 percent of the grocery market in its Asheville, North Carolina base but had only 8 percent of the market in the state. All Ingles stores were west of Greensboro, leaving the eastern part of the state for other chains.

Food Lion, one of Ingles's main rivals, was a bigger chain. For example, it planned to open about 100 new stores in 1990, several times the number planned by Ingles. Jack Ferguson, Ingles's chief financial officer, said in the March 1990 *Business North Carolina,* "We try to find our niche in the market. We don't go head to head with Food Lion or Bi-Lo or Winn-Dixie or Kroger where they've got the market share. We say we're price competitive, but we don't say we're a price leader."

To avoid directly confronting such bigger chains, Ingles Markets concentrated on rural areas or small towns and suburbia, where there were fewer stores and thus less competition. In the late 1980s the company built its first stores in Atlanta's remote suburbs. Analysts pointed out that this strategy resulted in modest but consistent growth.

To differentiate itself from some of its competitors, Ingles used ads to remind consumers that it was owned entirely by Americans. Two competitors based in North Carolina, Food King and Bi-Lo, were owned largely by Europeans. Those ads probably were ineffective, since Food King and Bi-Lo gained more of the state's market share than did Ingles.

In any case, Ingles stock performance in the late 1980s reflected its relatively slow growth compared to its competitors. Its stock reached a high of $13.38 by the end of 1987 but then declined to about $9 per share by the end of the decade.

The 1990s

In early 1990 a persistent rumor concerning Ingles Markets surfaced again. Wall Street speculation that Ingles would be acquired by Publix Super Markets of Lakeland, Florida, resulted in Ingles's stock increasing to its highest point in 52 weeks. However, both Publix and Ingles representatives and analysts familiar with those firms discounted the rumor.

By the end of fiscal 1990, at the end of September, Ingles reached a new landmark in its history. For the first time in its 27-year history, the company had over $1 billion in annual sales. An increase of 11.4 percent from 1989 sales of $903.8 million resulted in 1990 sales of $1.007 billion. However, net income declined 37 percent from $15.9 million to $10 million due mainly to the firm's sale of marketable equity securities.

Corporate sales continued to increase in fiscal year 1991, reaching a company record of $1.044 billion; net income was $10.7 million. Based on that performance, one of Ingles's stock holders demonstrated its confidence in the grocery chain by buying more stock. Merchant Distributors, Inc. in November and December 1991 purchased 122,500 shares of Ingles Class A shares, giving it a total of 270,000 shares, 6.3 percent of all Class A stock. In addition, Merchants owned 150,150 shares of Ingles Class B stock.

In January 1992 Lloyd Kanev, the author of Smith Barney's Inefficient Market Series, raised his rating of Ingles's stock from "Hold" to "Buy." Kanev stated in *The Insiders' Chronicle* of January 27, 1992, "As a potential strategic acquisition by another supermarket chain, the company . . . would be worth a fair premium to book value."

Ingles Markets in 1992 took several steps to improve its competitiveness and appeal to its customers. It tried a new ad campaign pushing what it called the "Ingles Challenge," which encouraged customers to do their own price comparisons, instead of the company printing comparative price lists in the newspaper. The chain also added in 1992 the increasingly popular 12-pack option to its private-label sodas previously available only in 6-pack, two-, and three-liter sizes. Available by the Fourth of July weekend, the 12-pack was introduced to compete with discount and club stores.

By August 1992, 75 percent of the company's 160 in-store bakeries had changed their methods of preparing and presenting their baked goods. Instead of using premade frozen goods, it began using scratch/mix formulas for several items, including cookies and cakes. The frozen items were easy to order and then thaw at the store, but the quality improved when the store's own personnel prepared those items. To emphasize customers' desire to serve themselves, Ingles took its baked items from behind glass displays and placed them on flat tables.

Jim Owens, Ingles's new vice president over bakery-deli operations, began in 1992 special cake promotions which he had learned at his previous position at Safeway. By cutting prices during these sales, Ingles was able to increase its cake sales by as much as 30 percent.

In October 1992 Ingles announced it would reverse its 1986 deal with IRT by buying back the 23 shopping center properties it sold and then leased in 1986. It paid IRT $55.6 million for the 22 centers in North Carolina and one in Georgia.

In fiscal year 1992 Ingles's sales increased to $1.06 billion, but its net income dropped to $5.5 million, the lowest in several years. And the chain reduced the number of its stores to 170.

After a successful test in two stores, Ingles Markets in March 1993 announced it would introduce new drinkware sections in all of its 170 stores. It featured plastic glasses, tumblers, and bowls from April through September and then glass items from October through March. Prices on this merchandise were low enough to compete with the discount chains, particularly Kmart and Wal-Mart.

Also in March the company was fined $10,000 by the Georgia Department of Agriculture for repeated violations at 13 stores, including the presence of rodents and insects, outdated goods, and unsanitary equipment. State officials placed the 13 stores on probation for six months and said they would work with the firm to overcome those defects.

In fiscal year 1994 Ingles opened its first store in the state of Alabama. The Jackson, Georgia store, one of the chain's first to feature new video releases, began operations in October 1994. The following month the firm added a new store in Black Mountain, North Carolina, just a few miles east of the corporate headquarters in Asheville.

The opening of the Morristown, Tennessee store in summer 1995 illustrated an interesting trait of Ingles corporate culture. To gain firsthand knowledge of customers' opinions, Laney was there posing as a bagger. "The customer doesn't know me from you or anybody else," said Laney in the July 1995 *Progressive Grocer*. "So I know they're not trying to butter me up... The customers like the wide aisles in that store. I heard that more than anything." Chairman Robert Ingle also liked to participate in such store openings, a custom that employees liked because it gave them a sense of closeness to their leaders.

To deal with the challenge of growth, in 1995 Ingles created two new positions. Ed Kolodzieski, formerly with Tampa, Florida's Kash n' Karry for 18 years, became Ingles's first vice president of strategic planning. The company also created the new title of director of frozen foods.

The company took a major step forward in October 1995 when it opened its new produce warehouse in Asheville. In the December 11, 1995 *Supermarket News*, Robert Ingle stated, "We need this kind of facility to handle the needs imposed by our substantial and continuing growth." Vice president Ed Kolodzieski added, "We now have 100% control of the buying, warehousing and distributing process." Previously Ingles had purchased its fresh produce from Merchants Distributors. The new facility increased the company's ability to upgrade its quality control.

The new produce warehouse was part of an overall expansion of Ingles's warehouse/distribution center. The new 310,000-square-foot addition also contained sections for dry goods, meat, poultry, deli, and dairy products. The new warehouse sections brought the total size of the Asheville facility up to 760,000 square feet.

The Asheville warehouse/distribution center was managed and run by the Asheville firm of Thomas & Howard Company. Ingles used its fleet of 103 tractors and 438 trailers to ship merchandise to its retail stores, using truck drivers employed by Thomas & Howard.

In the 1990s many Americans emphasized eating more nutritious foods. Ingles Markets responded in several ways, including 1996 ads and special sales to encourage customers to eat frozen fruits and vegetables five times a day. In 1991 the Produce for Better Health Foundation, the National Cancer Institute, and the National Institutes of Health had started the Five-a-Day program. Following the suggestions of the American Frozen Food Institute, Ingles decided to stress the value of frozen foods which retain most of their vitamins and other nutrients. Ingles used quotes from the sponsors and the Five-a-Day logo in its promotionals.

The grocery chain in 1996 also used the National Frozen Foods Month of March to promote the consumption of all kinds of frozen foods. Ingles continued its past practice of running TV ads in the six states with at least one of its stores and also radio ads in North and South Carolina. The company also tried innovations such as a school sampling program and a kitchen-appliance sweepstakes to increase sales of frozen foods. The frozen-food hoopla even included inflated penguins floating in the air and little airplanes pulling balloons reminding consumers of Frozen Foods Month.

To provide more space for its goods and services, Ingles Markets on June 30, 1996, opened its first MegaStore, a 59,000-square-foot facility in the Atlanta suburb of Dacula. Soon other MegaStores were opened, including ones in Forsyth, Griffin, and Cleveland, Georgia; Hendersonville and Waynesville, North Carolina; Kingsport and Knoxville, Tennessee; and Boiling Springs, South Carolina.

Unlike the 42,000- and 52,000-square-foot stores opened several years earlier with two entrances, the new 54,000- and 59,000-square-foot MegaStores featured one major entrance to lead customers into a preferred shopping route. The first section they came to was a fresh foods section with three new Ingles offerings: freshly made pizzas, self-service rotisserie chicken, and chilled ready-to-eat prepackaged meals. Each new MegaStore also included a two-story sit-down cafe, a full-size bakery, a video section, a floral division, and various customer services such as check cashing, photocopying, gift certificates, and UPS and fax assistance.

The difference between these new stores and the older smaller format was "like night and day," said Neal Polaske, Ingles labor director in the September 2, 1996 *Supermarket News*. Robert Ingle added: "We are confident that our new look and schedule fits our program of continued growth and progressive changes to our stores. The go-ahead for any program is the response of our customers, and based on continuing sales increases, it is evident that our stores are being very well-received." The company's financial record for fiscal year 1996 confirmed Ingles's comment. Annual sales and income reached record highs of $1.473 billion and $20.7 million.

On December 28, 1996, president and COO Landy Laney voluntarily retired at age 65. He was replaced by Vaughn C. Fisher, the company's former vice-president for sales and marketing who had worked for Ingles for 24 years.

In 1997 Robert P. Ingle remained board chairman and CEO. His son Robert P. Ingle II served as vice-president of operations. As the chain approached the new millennium, it continued to focus on serving its customers in the Southeast. As Ingle stated in the July 1995 *Progressive Grocer*, "We're going to enhance our concentration where we already are," instead of moving into new areas.

Ingles Market's prospects in 1997 appeared positive. With modern stores featuring computerized inventory, checkout, and even computerized work scheduling, the firm appeared to have made the necessary investments to remain on the cutting edge of the grocery business. In April 1997 the chain received the "Retailer of the Year" award from McNeil Consumer Products, which gave it even more confidence in a bright future.

Principal Subsidiaries

Milkco, Inc.

Further Reading

Alaimo, Dan, "Ingles Video Rollout Stresses New Rentals," *Supermarket News*, December 5, 1994, p. 39.

Bennett, Stephen, "The Sweet Sound of the Big Ring," *Progressive Grocer*, July 1995, p. 88.

Boehning, Julie C., "Ingles Encourages Customers to Get 5 a Day from Frozens, *Supermarket News*, June 10, 1996, p. 31.

Brumbach, Nancy, "Ingles Markets Sales Climb with Single Margins on Beer," *Supermarket News*, August 9, 1993, p. 3A.

Elson, Joel, "Ingles Revamps HBC [Health and Beauty Care], Focuses on Low Pricing," *Supermarket News*, July 19, 1993, p. 27.

——, "Ingles Markets Boosts Sales by Tying into Fund-Raiser," *Supermarket News*, October 11, 1993, p. 27.

"Fisher Moves Up at Ingles Markets," *Supermarket News*, January 6, 1997, p. 6.

Harper, Roseanne, "Ingles Raises Size, Sales, Self-Service," *Supermarket News*, September 9, 1996, p. 56.

——, "Ingles' New Prototype Touts Deli, Food Service," *Supermarket News*, September 9, 1996, p. 23.

——, "'Meals to Go' Gets 'Go' Sign from Ingles Chainwide," *Supermarket News*, November 11, 1996, p. 29.

"Ingles Multifaceted Strategist," *Progressive Grocer*, November 1995, p. 12.

"Ingles Profit Falls on Record Sales," *Supermarket News*, December 31, 1990, p. 28.

"Jingo Jingles for Ingles," *Business North Carolina*, March 1990, p. 68.

Lenius, Pat, "Ingles Rolls Out Vacuum-Packed Meat," *Supermarket News*, May 24, 1993, p. 44.

Moore, Amity, "Ingles Generates Sales with New Program Emphasis," *Supermarket News*, March 25, 1996, p. 39.

Redman, Russell, "Ingles Ice Cream Ads Heat Frozens Volume," *Supermarket News*, August 21, 1995, p. 25.

Riddle, Judith S., "Ingles Revamps Merchandising Strategy," *Supermarket News*, August 3, 1992, p. 43.

Stickel, Amy I., "Ingles Opens Produce Warehouse," *Supermarket News*, December 11, 1995, p. 32.

Tibbits, Lisa A., "Ingles Extends Streak of Consecutive Gains," *Supermarket News*, January 2, 1995, p. 8.

Turcsik, Richard, "Ingles Stock Hits 52-Week High Amid Speculation of Takeover," *Supermarket News*, February 12, 1990, p. 41.

Zimmerman, Susan, "Breakfast Is Cooking; Low-Fat Entries and General Convenience Are Keeping Sales of Frozen Breakfasts Hot," *Supermarket News*, June 21, 1993, p. 8A.

—David M. Walden

Jardine Matheson Holdings Limited

Jardine House
33-35 Reid Street
Hamilton
Bermuda
292-0515
Fax: 292-4072
Web site: http://www.jardine-matheson.com

Public Company
Incorporated: 1984
Employees: 200,000
Sales: US $11.61 billion (1996)
Stock Exchanges: London Sydney Singapore Bermuda
SICs: 1796 Installation or Erection of Building
   Equipment; 4512 Air Transportation, Scheduled; 4581
   Airports, Flying Fields & Airport Terminal Services;
   5182 Wines & Distilled Alcoholic Beverages; 5411
   Grocery Stores; 5511 Motor Vehicle Dealers (New &
   Used Cars); 5712 Furniture Stores; 5812 Eating
   Places; 6282 Investment Advice; 6311 Life Insurance;
   6411 Insurance Agents, Brokers & Services; 6719
   Offices of Holding Companies, Not Elsewhere
   Classified; 7011 Hotels & Motels; 7349 Building
   Cleaning & Maintenance Services, Not Elsewhere
   Classified; 7381 Detective, Guard & Armored Car
   Services; 7382 Security Systems Services; 8611
   Business Associations; 8711 Engineering Services;
   8741 Management Services; 8742 Management
   Consulting Services

Jardine Matheson is one of the oldest names in East Asia, and Jardine Matheson Holdings Limited is an international group of companies with operations mainly in Asia, centered around Hong Kong and China. Of British origin, Jardine Matheson played a key, and rather dubious, role in the founding of Hong Kong, where the group was headquartered until 1984, when it relocated to Bermuda in anticipation of the July 1997 transfer of control of Hong Kong to China. Controlled through a complicated set of minority holdings by the Keswick family (descendants of cofounder William Jardine) Jardine Matheson is involved in a variety of activities, most prominently trading, financial services, and real estate. Other sectors include supermarkets, consumer marketing, engineering and construction, motor vehicles, insurance, and hotels. An increasingly multinational entity, Jardine Matheson derives about two-thirds of its revenues from Hong Kong and China, about 15 percent each from other areas of the Asia-Pacific region and from North America, and the remaining five percent or so from Europe.

Trading Company Founded in Canton, China, in 1832

William Jardine was born in 1784 in Dumfriesshire, Scotland. After studying medicine, Jardine went to work for the British East India Company as a ship's surgeon, but left the East India Company in 1832 to establish a trading company in Canton, China, with James Matheson, the son of a Scottish baronet, who had served for several years as Danish consul in China.

Trading with the Chinese was made extremely difficult by a xenophobic Manchu government, which believed that as the center of the universe, China already possessed everything in abundance and had no need for the products of "foreign barbarians." Among other things, Jardine Matheson & Company was restricted to a small plot of land on the banks of the Pearl River, near Canton, and was prevented from "keeping women" or dealing with Chinese merchants who were not officially sanctioned *cohongs.* On one occasion, Jardine was struck a blow to the head as he attempted to petition local authorities. Entirely unaffected by the attack, he earned the nickname "iron headed old rat" among the Chinese.

Unable to make money selling manufactured goods to the Chinese, Jardine Matheson began smuggling opium into China aboard ships chartered from Calcutta in British India. Opium clippers sailed under cover of darkness to forbidden ports, while company agents bribed harbormasters and watchmen to prevent being discovered by the authorities. The Chinese government declared the opium trade to be illegal, but was virtually powerless to stop it. Finally, Chinese authorities seized and destroyed 20,000 chests of opium worth $9 million.

Opium War Led to Founding of Hong Kong in 1842

Jardine persuaded the British Foreign Secretary Lord Palmerston to send warships to China to enforce a judgment for reparations and to preserve free trade. The hostilities that ensued became known as the First Opium War. The Chinese lost and were forced to sign a treaty on August 29, 1842, which awarded the British $6 million in reparations, opened the ports of Canton, Amoy, Foochow, Ningpo, and Shanghai, and ceded the island of Hong Kong to Britain.

Jardine Matheson purchased the first plot of land to be sold in Hong Kong and promptly moved its offices there. The colony's first governor, Sir Henry Pottinger, endorsed the opium trade (in defiance of Queen Victoria) and later won the support of Parliament, which viewed the opium trade as a method to reduce the British trade deficit with China. When the company's opium boats sailed into Hong Kong they were greeted by a cannon salute. Jardine Matheson profited greatly from its privileged position in Hong Kong, and through the strength of its opium trade, began to develop commercial interests throughout the region. Jardine Matheson became known among the local Chinese as a *hong* (the word implies "big company" but has no relation to the name Hong Kong), and its chairman became known as a *taipan,* literally a "big boss."

During this period Thomas Keswick, also from Dumfriesshire, married Jardine's niece and was subsequently taken into the Jardine family business. Their son William Keswick established a Jardine Matheson office in Yokohama, Japan in 1859 and later became a leading figure in company management. The Keswick family grew in influence within the company, largely displacing the Matheson interests.

Expanded Beyond Trading in Latter Half of 19th Century

Jardine Matheson established trading offices in major Chinese ports and helped to set up enterprises as diverse as brewing and milling cotton, in addition to trading tea and silk. The company introduced steamboats to China and, in 1876, constructed the first railroad in China, linking Shanghai with Jardine Matheson docks downriver at Woosung.

Continued hostilities between China and Britain resulted in a Second Opium War in 1860 and a war to protect colonial interests in 1898. As victors in both these wars, the British gained trade concessions and colonies throughout China and won virtually unrestricted commercial rights to conduct business in China. The opium trade, which China had been forced to recognize as legal, had become an extremely sensitive subject. Thousands of addicts (known as "hippies" because they would lie on their hips while smoking opium) had created a serious social problem. Elements in Parliament called for an end to commercial activities that perpetuated the pain and suffering of these addicts. The issue was seized by nationalists who argued for an end to the domination of colonial powers in China, and it eventually led to uprisings such as the Boxer Rebellion and the Republican Revolution. For its own protection and business interests, Jardine Matheson was forced to curtail trading opium.

By 1906, the year it incorporated in Hong Kong, Jardine Matheson had expanded into a wider range of operations, but experienced strong competition from another British trading house called Butterfield & Swire, which was also based in Shanghai and Hong Kong. The competition between Jardine Matheson and the Swires began in earnest in 1884 when Butterfield & Swire set up a rival sugar refinery in Hong Kong in an attempt to break Jardine Matheson's monopoly. The competition spread into shipping and trading, but remained on the whole civilized and constructive.

Jardine Matheson continued to operate in China relatively unobstructed by the Nationalist government, which had grown increasingly corrupt. The company continued to expand its interests in China and, with other foreign interests such as Swire and Mitsui, became one of the largest companies in the country.

Suffered Severely During World War II

In the summer of 1937 Japanese forces attacked China in an attempt to expand Japanese commercial and strategic interests on the Asian mainland. Jardine Matheson officials stationed in areas overrun by the Japanese were branded as agents of European imperialism and imprisoned. The company's compradores (Chinese intermediaries) were scattered, and its factories were looted; approximately 168,000 spindles were stripped from Jardine Matheson textile mills. Japanese military adventurism in China led to the occupation of several more Chinese ports, including Shanghai and Canton, where Jardine Matheson conducted a substantial portion of its business. Tony Keswick, a grandson of William Keswick, managed the company's affairs in Shanghai until 1941, when he moved to Hong Kong after having been shot by a Japanese. He was replaced by his brother John, who himself was forced to flee when the city came under siege. Jardine Matheson had been effectively prevented from doing any further business in China, but continued to operate in Hong Kong, which, as British territory, the Japanese were unwilling to invade.

As a member of the anti-Comintern pact, Japan was unofficially allied with Nazi Germany and Fascist Italy in the war in Europe. The increasingly belligerent military leaders in Japan pledged to evict European imperialists from Asia and to establish a trans-Asian "Co-Prosperity Sphere." On December 1, 1941, Japanese forces invaded British colonies in Asia, including Hong Kong. Jardine Matheson officials in the colony were imprisoned with other Europeans at Stanley Prison. John Keswick, however, managed to escape to Ceylon (Sri Lanka), where he served with Admiral Earl Mountbatten's staff.

Forced to Abandon China Following Postwar Communist Takeover

When the war ended in 1945, the British resumed control of Hong Kong and John Keswick returned to oversee the rebuilding of Jardine Matheson facilities damaged during the war. The company owned a small airline, textile mills, real estate, a brewery, wharves, godowns (warehouses), and cold-storage facilities. In 1949, however, after four years of civil war, Communist forces seized control of the Chinese mainland.

In Shanghai, John Keswick attempted to work with the Communists (who had invited capitalists to help rebuild the economy), in the belief that they would be more orderly and less corrupt than the Nationalists. Keswick argued for British recognition of the new government, and even attempted to run his company's ships past Nationalist blockades. By 1950, however, new government policies were enacted that increased taxes, restricted currency exchanges, and banned layoffs. Ewo Breweries, a Jardine Matheson subsidiary in Shanghai, was ordered to reduce its prices by 17 percent, despite heavy increases in the cost of raw materials. The government forced Ewo to remain open, despite a $4 million annual loss.

Companies based in Hong Kong were bound to observe a British trade embargo placed against China as a result of the Korean War. Conditions had deteriorated to a point where it was impossible to continue operating in China (on one occasion Keswick was arrested as he attempted to leave Shanghai). Compelled to close its operations in China, Jardine Matheson entered into negotiations with the government and, in 1954, settled the nationalization of its assets in China by writing off $20 million in losses.

Jardine Matheson continued to trade with the seven official Chinese state trading corporations and attended the biannual Canton Trade Fair, where Chinese companies negotiated approximately half their nation's foreign trade.

Many of Jardine Matheson's management traditions changed after the war. Although managers continued to be recruited primarily from Oxford and Cambridge, the company started placing younger men in higher positions. John Keswick, whose nephews Henry and Simon were too young to run the company, returned to Britain in 1956 to direct the family estate and appointed Michael Young-Herries to manage the operations in Hong Kong.

Became Public Company in 1961

In the late 1950s John and Tony Keswick enlisted support from three banks in London and purchased the last Jardine family interests in the company. Jardine Matheson became a publicly traded company in 1961 and, with additional capital provided by shareholders, acquired controlling interests in the Indo-China Steam Navigation Company and Henry Waugh Ltd. and established the Australian-based Dominion Far East Line shipping company.

In 1966 China embarked on its second campaign to form a nation of communes. During this campaign, called the "Cultural Revolution," China ceased virtually all trade with Hong Kong. Although Jardine Matheson lost a significant amount of trade with the Chinese, its association of textile companies in Hong Kong continued to generate large profits from exports to the United States. The company's greatest achievement during this period was the sale of six Vickers Viscount aircraft to the Chinese. By 1969 the Cultural Revolution had lost its momentum and Jardine Matheson was once again doing business with the Chinese.

In 1972 the Keswick family attempted to install Henry as the new *taipan,* but met considerable resistance from supporters of managing director David Newbigging, the son of a former director of Jardine Matheson. The Keswicks prevailed after winning the support of institutional shareholders in London, and Henry Keswick was named senior managing director, while his father John resumed the chairmanship to ensure that the Keswicks did not lose control of the company.

Three years later Henry stepped down and returned to London and was replaced by David Newbigging. Henry, remarked *Fortune,* lacked the "panache" of the elder Keswicks and made "more than a few enemies" through his bold financial maneuvers. Henry did, however, complete a buyout in 1973 of Reunion Properties, a large real estate firm based in London. Keswick financed the takeover by creating an additional seven percent of Jardine Matheson equity, but through the acquisition nearly doubled the company's assets. Henry Keswick also oversaw the acquisition of Theo H. Davies & Company that same year. Davies, a large trading company active in the Philippines and Hawaii, controlled 36,000 acres of sugar plantations. A few months after it was purchased by Jardine Matheson, world sugar prices rose dramatically.

Profits Suffered in the 1970s

At the time David Newbigging assumed the senior directorship of Jardine Matheson, a disturbing trend began to arise in Hong Kong. Throughout its history, Jardine Matheson had operated as a trading agent, or "middleman," arranging sales between producers in one location and consumers in another. Manufacturers in Hong Kong, however, discovered ways to sell their products directly to customers, bypassing agents such as Jardine Matheson. Even Hawker-Siddeley, a British company, managed to arrange the sale of six Trident jetliners to the Chinese without the negotiating expertise of Jardine Matheson.

Between 1975 and 1979, Jardine Matheson's profits grew at an annual rate of only ten percent (a poor record for Hong Kong). David Newbigging responded by disposing of underperforming Jardine Matheson subsidiaries outside Hong Kong. He redoubled efforts to increase trade with China (which had only invited the company back into China in 1979) and resumed investments in Hong Kong-based enterprises. Jardine Matheson, however, had little expertise in these enterprises and lost money in almost every venture.

During the 1970s British companies in Hong Kong such as Jardine Matheson, Swire, Hutchison, and Wheelock Marden, were consistently outperformed by local, ethnically Chinese *hongs*. Most of these *hongs* became public companies in the early 1970s and invested heavily in Hong Kong industries, which experienced strong growth during a decade-long bull market. These companies became serious competitors of the British establishment by the end of the decade.

Cheung Kong Holdings, a local *hong* run by an influential figure named Li Ka Shing, achieved a dominant position in the Hong Kong property market by 1980, threatening the business of Hongkong Land, a development company established in 1889 by William Keswick's brother James Johnstone Keswick which remained closely associated with Jardine Matheson. In addition, when the shipping magnate Sir Yue-Kong Pao decided to diversify from ships into property a year earlier, his first move was to outbid Jardine Matheson for the Hongkong & Kowloon Wharf & Godown Company, over which the two groups had previously shared control.

When it was discovered that a secret partner had begun acquiring shares of Jardine Matheson stock in late 1980, many observers suspected that either Li or Pao (or worse, both) were attempting to purchase a large enough share in Jardine Matheson to win control over Hongkong Land. Newbigging announced in early November that Jardine Matheson and Hongkong Land had agreed to increase their interests in each other, so as to make it impossible for any party to gain control of either company. The cross-ownership scheme, however, placed both companies deeply into debt.

Reorganized under Simon Keswick in the 1980s

The defensive actions required during 1980 forced Jardine Matheson to sell its interest in Reunion Properties to raise cash. Newbigging was criticized for being too conservative and placing too much emphasis on local and regional operations. Although members of the Keswick family attempted to have Newbigging removed, perhaps no one worked as tirelessly as John Keswick. Newbigging finally stepped down as senior managing director in June 1983, but retained the titular position of chairman. He was replaced as *taipan* by 40-year-old Simon Keswick, brother of Henry Keswick.

The election of Simon Keswick, who had not yet proved his business acumen, initially worried many investors of Jardine Matheson. Upon taking control, however, Simon moved decisively to reduce the company's debts and to place Hongkong Land on firmer financial ground. To raise cash, he authorized the sale of Jardine Matheson's majority stake in Rennies Consolidated Holdings, a South African hotel, travel, and industries group based in Johannesburg, for $180.1 million. Keswick also established a new decentralized system of managerial control,

which split operations into a Hong Kong and China division and an international division.

In early 1984 David Newbigging was replaced as chairman by Simon Keswick. With the company now thoroughly under Keswick family control, Simon announced on March 28 that Jardine Matheson & Company would establish a new holding company called Jardine Matheson Holdings Limited, incorporated in Bermuda. The announcement came at an extremely sensitive point in negotiations between the British and Chinese governments on the future of Hong Kong. Many observers regarded Keswick's plan as an attempt to remove Jardine Matheson from the uncertain business environment in Hong Kong, and as a solid display of no confidence in the Sino-British arrangement under which China would resume sovereignty over Hong Kong on July 1, 1997.

In defense of his actions, Simon Keswick admitted that Bermuda provided Jardine Matheson with a more stable operating environment than Hong Kong, but noted that the company was not abandoning its interests in Hong Kong, merely reducing its exposure there from 72 percent of total assets to a planned 50 percent. In addition, he pointed out that Bermuda (a British colony since 1612) permitted companies to purchase their own shares, a practice not allowed in Hong Kong.

In 1984 Jardine Matheson disposed of its sugar interests in Hawaii. The company also expanded into motor vehicles by investing in Mercedes-Benz distributorships, which eventually led to the formation of Jardine International Motors Management Ltd. The following year Keswick announced that, after 153 years, Jardine Matheson would leave the shipping business and that the company's fleet of 21 ships would be sold. By the end of the year many of the assets Jardine Matheson acquired during the 1970s had been sold, reducing holdings by 28 percent.

In 1986 Keswick dismantled much of Hongkong Land, selling the company's residential real estate portfolio and announcing that its Dairy Farm food subsidiary and Mandarin Oriental Hotels unit would become independent and be listed on the Hong Kong stock exchange. Keswick's plan to reduce Hongkong Land to real estate alone caused its managing director, David J. Davies, to resign in protest.

Renewed fears of a takeover attempt led to additional 1986 restructuring moves. Jardine Strategic Holdings Limited, placed on the Hong Kong stock exchange, was formed to hold stakes in Jardine Matheson Ltd. (the Hong Kong-based arm responsible for managing the activities of the group), Dairy Farm, Hongkong Land, and Mandarin Oriental. Jardine Pacific Ltd. was formed as the trading and services arm of the group.

Simon Keswick announced in June 1987 that he would relinquish the position of senior managing director to a 37-year-old American named Brian M. Powers. The nomination of Powers to become *taipan* caused great concern among members of the company's more traditional Scottish establishment. Keswick, who had reversed the company's decline with drastic and unpopular measures, and who had yet to demonstrate their success, defended his choice of Powers. He explained that Jardine Matheson was now an international company with

Hong Kong interests (rather than the other way around) and that, as such, Powers was best qualified to manage its affairs.

Moderately Successful International Expansion During the Late 1980s and 1990s

In any case, Powers's reign proved to be short-lived and well into the 1990s Simon and Henry Keswick essentially managed the group from London. Continuing to be wary of the fast-approaching return of Hong Kong to Chinese control Jardine Matheson during the late 1980s and early 1990s was determined to become more geographically diversified, subsequently meeting with middling success in its ventures in North America, Europe, and areas of Asia outside Hong Kong and China. In 1987 Jardine Matheson announced that it planned to buy a 20 percent stake in Bear Stearns but pulled out following that year's October stock market crash; following resulting shareholder lawsuits, it settled with shareholders of Bear Stearns four years later by agreeing to pay US $60 million in compensation.

In 1993 Jardine Matheson spent £300 million to acquire a 26 percent stake in Trafalgar House, a construction, engineering, and shipping conglomerate based in the United Kingdom. Trafalgar, a group more troubled than it was believed to be, became an albatross around Jardine's neck. After supporting its investment and attempting to turn it around for several years, Jardine Matheson decided to cut its losses in 1996, that year selling its stake to Kvaerner A/S, a Norwegian-based shipbuilder, at a loss of about £100 million.

During the early 1990s, Jardine Matheson also acquired a 23 percent stake in Cycle & Carriage Ltd., a Singapore-based company with motor vehicle operations in Singapore, Malaysia, Australia, and New Zealand and property investment and development activities in Singapore and Malaysia. India was another area of Jardine Matheson growth, most significantly with the 1996 purchase of a 20 percent stake in Tata Industries of India for 1.25 billion rupees (US $25 million). The privately held Tata boasted of numerous alliances with foreign companies—including AT&T, IBM, Singapore Airlines, and Mercedes-Benz, the last of which had connections with Jardine Matheson—but Jardine Matheson was the first outsider granted a stake in the group. Tata had several areas of interest in common with Jardine, including motor vehicle distribution, retailing, and property development. Jardine Matheson's Tata stake built on the group's previous investments in India, which included a number of joint ventures and a five percent stake in Housing Development Finance Corporation of Mumbai, a leading Indian financial institution. Overall, India had the potential to provide Jardine Matheson with the second beachhead it had sought—unsuccessfully—for so long.

Meanwhile, the group's rocky relationship with China continued in the early 1990s. Still concerned about possible takeover attempts, Jardine Matheson sought an exemption from Hong Kong's takeover code, which conflicted with takeover legislation enacted in Bermuda, but was refused. In response, the group in 1991 moved its primary stock exchange listing from Hong Kong to London, thereby enabling Jardine Matheson to remain under the British legal system. Chinese authorities were angered, feeling that the move reflected a lack of confidence in the post-transfer-of-control legal system. The

following year, perhaps in retaliation, China blocked a consortium led by Jardine Matheson that had gained development rights to Hong Kong's ninth container terminal. Then, in late 1994, Jardine Matheson moved its Asian stock listing from Hong Kong to Singapore, provoking further consternation among the Chinese.

Relations seemed to improve somewhat during 1995. Jardine Matheson's new managing director in Hong Kong, Alasdair Morrison, another Scot, issued a general apology to China in January 1995 over the group's actions in recent years. Morrison emphasized that Jardine Matheson intended to continue to do business in Hong Kong and China and to invest additional money there. By 1996 Jardine Matheson had about 70 joint ventures in China, a number that had been growing rapidly. And, that year, Jardine formed a consortium with Li Ka Shing's Hutchison Whampoa and Cosco Pacific, which was owned by China's largest shipping group, to develop and run a river trade terminal.

In early 1997, Jardine Matheson's insurance broking subsidiary, JIB Group plc, of which Jardine Matheson held 60 percent, merged with the insurance broking group Lloyd Thompson Group plc to form Jardine Lloyd Thompson Group plc. Jardine Matheson held an initial 34 percent interest in the new firm. In June 1997 takeover speculation arose once again when two companies owned by Li Ka Shing bought 3.03 percent of Jardine Matheson Holdings and 3.06 percent of Hongkong Land.

The Jardine Matheson of the transfer year of 1997 was still closely tied to Hong Kong, where more than half of its profits were generated, but had developed increasing interests elsewhere in China and outside the region, most notably in India. The group is likely to continue to seek opportunities for expansion outside Hong Kong and China, but the seemingly improved relations with China boded well for Jardine Matheson's numerous interests in that burgeoning state. Nevertheless, the recurrent takeover threats and rumors continued to hang over Jardine Matheson, clouding its future.

Principal Subsidiaries

Jardine Matheson Ltd. (Hong Kong); Jardine Strategic Holdings Limited (Hong Kong); Jardine Pacific Ltd. (Hong Kong); Jardine International Motors Management Ltd. (Hong Kong; 75%); Jardine Lloyd Thompson Group plc (U.K.; 34%); Jardine Fleming Holdings Ltd. (Hong Kong; 50%); Matheson & Co., Ltd. (U.K.); Dairy Farm Management Services Ltd. (Hong Kong; 52%); Hongkong Land Ltd. (Hong Kong; 32%); Mandarin Oriental Hotel Group International Ltd. (Hong Kong; 51%); Cycle & Carriage Ltd. (Singapore; 23%); Jardine Matheson (Australia) Ltd.; Jardine Matheson International Services Ltd. (Bermuda); Jardine Matheson Ltd. (India); Jardine Matheson Ltd. (Indonesia); Jardine Matheson K.K. (Japan); Jardine Matheson (Malaysia) Sdn. Bhd.; Jardine Matheson Europe B.V. (Netherlands); Jardine Matheson (China) Ltd.; Jardine Davies Inc. (Philippines); Jardine Matheson (Singapore) Ltd.; Jardine, Matheson & Co., Ltd. (Taiwan); Jardine Matheson (Thailand) Ltd.; Theo. H. Davies & Co., Ltd. (U.S.A.); Jardine Pacific (Vietnam).

Further Reading

Cheong, W. E., *Mandarins and Merchants: Jardine, Matheson, & Co., a China Agency of the Early Nineteenth Century,* London: Curzon Press, 1979.

Davies, Simon, and Ridding, John, "Taipans Who Missed the Boat," *Financial Times,* March 2/March 3, 1996, p. 7.

Edelstein, Michael, *Overseas Investment in the Age of High Imperialism: The United Kingdom 1850–1914,* New York: Columbia University Press, 1982.

Holberton, Simon, "The End of a Chapter at Jardine Matheson," *Financial Times,* December 21, 1994, p. 23.

"Jardine's Bolt Hole," *Economist,* April 6, 1996, p. 68.

Kennedy, Carol, "Can Two Hongs Get It Right?," *Director,* February 1996, pp. 34–40.

Keswick, Maggie, ed., *The Thistle and the Jade: A Celebration of 150 Years of Jardine, Matheson & Co.,* London: Octopus, 1982.

Morris, Kathleen, "There's No Place Like Home," *Financial World,* August 2, 1994, pp. 36–38.

"The Noble Houses Look Forward," *Economist,* October 1, 1994, p. 77.

Sender, Henny, "Fixed Assets: British Hongs Still Tied to the Colony," *Far Eastern Economic Review,* July 8, 1993, p. 22.

Smith, Craig S., "Jardine Lies Low in Colony's Handover: Firm That Helped Launch Hong Kong Can't Quite Escape It," *Wall Street Journal,* June 4, 1997, p. A15.

—updated by David E. Salamie

Kao Corporation

14-10, Nihonbashi Kayabacho 1-chome
Chuo-ku, Tokyo 103
Japan
(03) 3660-7111
Fax: (03) 3660-7044
Web site: http://www.kao.co.jp/index.html

Public Company
Incorporated: 1887 as Kao Soap Company, Ltd.
Employees: 6,994
Sales: ¥835.60 billion (US$7.86 billion) (1996)
Stock Exchanges: Tokyo Osaka
SICs: 2676 Sanitary Paper Products; 2819 Industrial
    Inorganic Chemicals, Not Elsewhere Classified; 2841
    Soap & Other Detergents, Except Specialty Cleaners;
    2844 Perfumes, Cosmetics & Other Toilet
    Preparations; 2869 Industrial Organic Chemicals, Not
    Elsewhere Classified; 2899 Chemicals & Chemical
    Preparations, Not Elsewhere Classified; 3695
    Magnetic & Optical Recording Media

Kao Corporation, often called the Procter & Gamble of Japan, is one of Japan's leaders in personal care products, cosmetics, laundry and cleaning products, hygiene products, and bath additives. Kao also manufactures and markets fatty chemicals, edible oils, and specialty chemicals, and is one of the world's leading suppliers of information technology products and services. The company has operations in 26 countries in Asia, North America, Europe, and elsewhere.

Early History

Founded in 1887 as Kao (face) Soap Company, Ltd. by the Nagase family, the company introduced its first soap product in 1890, selling it with the motto "A Clean Nation Prospers." That same year Kao adopted its crescent-moon logo, which was similar to Procter & Gamble Co.'s logo registered eight years earlier; thus began a longtime rivalry. By the end of the 1920s, Kao had developed coconut alcohol-based synthetic detergents, and after World War II, began manufacturing heavy-duty detergents.

From early on, Kao employed at least 25 percent of its workers in research, particularly in the field of surface technology. Early research in the properties of oils and fats, the basic elements in soap, allowed Kao to expand its product line quickly to include finishing products, polishing agents, waxes, insecticides, antiseptics, fungicides, and deodorants.

Kao's early success was made possible not only by its dedication to R&D but also by its unique network of proprietary wholesalers. In the early 1960s the company persuaded its wholesalers to establish jointly owned companies, called *hansha*, which would exclusively distribute Kao products. This system greatly simplified the usually complicated way that products moved from manufacturers to consumers in Japan, and provided Kao with competitive advantages, such as getting products onto store shelves faster and maintaining lighter inventories.

In 1971 Yoshio Maruta became president of Kao and continued the company's emphasis on R&D. Maruta, holder of a doctorate in chemical engineering and 16 patents, invented a process for producing aircraft lubricant from vegetable oil during World War II, when Japanese supplies of petroleum were low. An aggressive and charismatic leader, Maruta often was criticized for his domineering style that left little room for open discussion. He had a fierce respect for consumers, however. As one of his assistants told *Forbes*, July 25, 1988, "You can cheat housewives once, but not twice."

Series of Successful Product Launches in the 1980s

In the 1980s Kao's intense research operations paid off handsomely. In 1983 the company's Merries brand of disposable diapers far outsold Procter & Gamble's in Japan, because Kao had developed a highly absorbent polymer that reduced diaper rash. The following year Kao entered the cosmetics market for the first time with its Sofina line of cosmetics, and rapidly advanced to the number two position in the Japanese cosmetic market, trailing only Shiseido Co.

315

Kao's research in surface technology led the company into the electronics-software field as well. A research project on face powders resulted in the discovery of a dispersing system that was ideal for the management of magnetic particles spread over floppy discs, and Kao in 1985 established a U.S. subsidiary called Kao Infosystems Company to manufacture such discs. With the acquisition of West Coast Telecom in Portland, Oregon; Sentinel Technologies in Hyannis, Massachusetts; and the completion of a $60 million plant in Plymouth, Massachusetts, Kao Infosystems became in 1990 the largest North American maker of 3.5-inch floppy discs, although it was also consistently unprofitable. The company later branched out into CD-ROMs, hard disks, and digital audiotapes.

One of Kao's most successful introductions ever—Attack concentrated laundry detergent—came in 1987. Before Attack made its debut, Kao researchers collected dirt samples from around the world for four years in order to discover the bacteria that produces alkaline cellulose, an enzyme that cleans cotton. The researchers then spent two years synthesizing the enzyme through genetic engineering. The resultant detergent was four times as concentrated as cleaners that were then being sold—it was in fact the first concentrated laundry soap in Japan. Only six months after introduction, Attack commanded almost 50 percent of the Japanese detergent market. In spite of a price that was much higher than the competition, consumers appreciated the product's convenience—it was lighter to carry home and took up less space in the cabinet—and that it was better for the environment.

In 1990 Fumikatsu Tokiwa, who joined the company in 1965 in the research-and-development library, succeeded Yoshio Maruta as president. Around this time, Kao was the Japanese market leader in eight of its ten main product categories. It held more than half of the market in five categories: laundry detergents, fabric softeners, bleaches, skin cleansers, and household cleaners.

Aggressively Expanded Overseas in the Late 1980s and Early 1990s

Beginning in the early 1970s, when Procter & Gamble entered the Japanese market, Kao faced increasing competition at home from foreign companies. One of the company's responses to the encroachment of P&G, Unilever NV, and others into its home market was to turn the tables on the foreigners by aggressively expanding overseas itself. Kao began making seri-ous moves into the U.S., European, and non-Japanese Asian markets in the late 1980s. The company's timing seemed particularly fortuitous when the Japanese bubble economy of the 1980s gave way to the prolonged recession of the early 1990s. Nonetheless, Kao's overseas ventures met with only mixed results.

In 1988 Kao acquired the Andrew Jergens Company, headquartered in Cincinnati, Ohio, and placed it within its main U.S. subsidiary, Kao Corporation of America. High Point Chemical Corporation, a specialty chemical company based in North Carolina that was acquired in 1987, supplied the raw materials for the Jergens toiletry and skin-care products. A move into Germany was made in 1989 when Kao purchased a 75 percent interest in Goldwell GmbH, a manufacturer and marketer of hair-care and beauty products through professional hairdressers around the world.

These acquisitions greatly increased the amount of revenues Kao generated outside Japan (to about 20 percent by the mid-1990s), but the company encountered difficulty building upon the acquired firms' previous successes. Jergens, for instance, in 1989 introduced a line of bath tablets called ActiBath in an attempt to adapt for the U.S. market a Kao product extremely popular in Japan. ActiBath flopped in large part because Americans take fewer baths than the Japanese and take their baths less seriously. In addition to the challenge of understanding a new culture, Kao also faced fierce competition in the U.S. market from the already entrenched Procter & Gamble and Unilever. This competition was quite evident in the 1994 launch of Jergens Refreshing Body Shampoo, a line of liquid bath soaps. On the surface a product with more promise than ActiBath, the Body Shampoo—soon after its launch—had to contend with two rival products: Unilever's Caress Moisturizing Body Wash and P&G's Oil of Olay liquid soap. Overall, Kao's American and European operations were money-losing ventures into the mid-1990s.

Kao's forays elsewhere in Asia were more successful—and were as a whole profitable. By the early 1990s the company was holding its own alongside P&G and Unilever in Hong Kong, Malaysia, the Philippines, Singapore, Taiwan, and Thailand. As the decade progressed, Kao took an increasing interest in the newly opening markets of China and Vietnam. Overall revenue generated from the region increased at a 15 percent yearly clip from the early to mid-1990s. Nevertheless, Unilever and Procter & Gamble's deeper (R&D and marketing) pockets tended to place Kao at a decided disadvantage even this close to home. P&G, for instance, spent four times as much as Kao did on R&D in the mid-1990s, and was quickly able to capture 50 percent of the shampoo market in China and Taiwan. Meanwhile, Kao's market shares in these Asian countries ranged from 10 to 20 percent.

While the company's household products units defended their home turf from foreign invaders and attempted to gain beachheads overseas as vehicles for future growth, the information technology business continued to struggle thanks to fierce competition. By 1996 Kao Infosystems was still losing money. In response, a restructuring was initiated that year which initially involved the integration of operations in France and Germany into the subsidiary's facility in Ireland. In a second phase, facilities in the United States and Canada were to be restructured.

In June 1997 Takuya Goto moved into the Kao presidency, taking over for Fumikatsu Tokiwa who became chairman. Goto came from Kao's chemicals side—perhaps indicating that Kao's board wanted some fresh ideas from senior management. Goto, a chemical engineer, joined the company in November 1979 as a manager of a plant in Thailand. After moving up Kao's chemicals management ladder, Goto became general manager of the chemical business division and purchasing division in July 1994.

With its fiscal year 1996 results, Kao Corporation posted its 16th straight year of increased revenues *and* increased pretax profits. Heading into the new century, the company remained a dominant force in household products in Japan, but had to contend with the increasing price-consciousness of Japanese consumers, a portentous development for such high-priced products as Attack. Kao was likely to continue to improve its position outside its home market, but would probably concentrate more of its limited resources on Asia than Europe and North America. The company also faced the challenge of turning around its information technology business, although a divestment of this troublesome unit appeared possible as well.

Principal Subsidiaries

Kao Cosmetics Sales Co., Ltd.; Nivea-Kao Company Limited; Kao-Quaker Company Limited; Kao Corporation Shanghai (China); Kao Chemical Corporation Shanghai (China); Kao (Taiwan) Corporation; Kao (Hong Kong) Limited; Pilipinas Kao Incorporated (Philippines); Kao Industrial (Thailand) Co., Ltd.; Kao Commercial (Thailand) Co., Ltd.; Kao (Malaysia) Sdn. Bhd.; Kao Trading (Malaysia) Sdn. Bhd.; Fatty Chemical (Malaysia) Sdn. Bhd.; Kao Soap (Malaysia) Sdn. Bhd.; Kao Oleochemical (Malaysia) Sdn. Bhd.; Kao Plasticizer (Malaysia) Sdn. Bhd.; Kao (Southeast Asia) Pte. Ltd. (Singapore); Kao (Singapore) Private Limited; PT. Kao Indonesia Chemicals; PT. Dino Indonesia Industrial Ltd.; PT. Dinokao Indonesia; Kao Vietnam Co., Ltd.; Kao (Australia) Marketing Pty. Ltd.; Kao Corporation of America (U.S.A.); The Andrew Jergens Company (U.S.A.); High Point Chemical Corporation (U.S.A.); Jergens Canada Inc.; Quimi-Kao, S.A. de C.V. (Mexico); Bi-tumex S.A. de C.V. (Mexico); Chemische Fabrik Chem-Y GmbH (Germany); Guhl Ikebana GmbH (Germany); Kao Corporation (France) SARL; Guhl Ikebana Kosmetika GmbH (Austria); Guhl Ikebana AG (Switzerland); Kao Corporation S.A. (Spain); Kao Infosystems Company (U.S.A.); Kao Infosystems Canada Inc.; Kao Infosystems UK plc; Kao Infosystems (Ireland) Limited; Kao (Singapore) Private Limited; Goldwell GmbH (Germany); Goldwell Oy (Finland); Goldwell (Hair Cosmetics) Ltd. (U.K.); Goldwell Nederland B.V. (Netherlands); N.V. Goldwell Belgium S.A.; Goldwell Paris S.a.r.L. (France); Goldwell Handels Aktiengesellschaft (Austria); Goldwell AG (Switzerland); Goldwell Italia S.p.A. (Italy); Goldwell España S.A. (Spain); Goldwell Cosmetics (USA), Inc.; Goldwell Cosmetics (Canada) Ltd.; Goldwell South Africa (Pty.) Ltd.; Goldwell Cosmetics (Hong Kong) Ltd.; Goldwell Cosmetics (Australia) Pty. Ltd.

Further Reading

"Efficient Corporate Resources Enhance Kao's Group Strengths," *Cosmetics International*, October 25, 1996, p. 10.

Friedland, Jonathan, "Lean and Clean: Japan's Kao Defies Taboos and Recession," *Far Eastern Economic Review*, May 19, 1994, pp. 50–51.

Gray, James, "Turnarounds/United Appeal," *Canadian Business*, April 1988.

An Inexhaustible Spring: Research and Development Activities at Kao, Tokyo: Kao Corporation, 1988.

Johnstone, Bob, "Attacking a Mature Market: Technology and Marketing Help a Japanese Soap Maker Clean Up," *Far Eastern Economic Review*, March 17, 1988, p. 82.

Kanabayashi, Masayoshi, "Japan's Top Soap Firm, Kao, Hopes to Clean Up Abroad," *Wall Street Journal*, December 17, 1992, p. B4.

Merris, Kathleen, "The Tao of Kao," *Financial World*, April 26, 1994, pp. 42–46.

Ono, Yumiko, "Kao Tries to Sell Japanese Soap in U.S. Market," *Wall Street Journal*, August 8, 1994, pp. B1, B4.

"Should We Kow-Tow to Kao?," *Economist*, March 30, 1996, pp. 60–61.

Tanzer, Andrew, "High Noon in Cincinnati," *Forbes*, July 25, 1988, p. 38.

van Raalte, John A., "A Visit with Kao," *HAPPI*, July 1990.

—Mary F. Sworsky
—updated by David E. Salamie

Kash n' Karry

Fresh, Fast n' Friendly

Kash n' Karry Food Stores, Inc.

6422 Harney Road
Tampa, Florida 33610
U.S.A.
(813) 621-0200
Fax: (813) 621-0244

Public Subsidiary of Food Lion Inc.
Founded: 1947 as Big Barn
Employees: 8,800
Sales: $1.02 billion (fiscal 1996)
Stock Exchanges: NASDAQ
SICs: 5411 Grocery Stores; 5921 Liquor Stores

Kash n' Karry Food Stores, Inc. was, in 1996, one of the three largest food retailers in west-central Florida, operating 98 supermarkets, 35 liquor stores, and 2 super warehouse stores. More than half were in the Tampa-St. Petersburg area, Florida's largest retail-food sales market. Kash n' Karry was acquired by Food Lion Inc. in 1996.

Kash n' Karry to 1989

The history of the company dates back to 1947, when the Greco family founded its first Big Barn grocery store in Plant City, Florida. By 1962 the family-run business had expanded to nine stores and the Grecos opted for a new name, Kash n' Karry. Tampa Wholesale Co., whose principal shareholders were the Greco and Dominguez families, was operating Kash n' Karry in the 1970s. This firm had an estimated $32 million in annual sales and some 1,000 employees by 1968. The Kash n' Karry chain expanded in the 1970s partly through the acquisition at various times of about a dozen A&P stores. There were 46 Kash n' Karry supermarkets in a seven-county area on Florida's Gulf Coast in 1978. Kash n' Karry was believed to be in third place among supermarkets in the Tampa-St. Petersburg-Clearwater area, with about 9 percent of the market. In Hillsborough County, where it operated most of its stores and which includes Tampa, it held more than 50 percent of the market. The chain's annual sales were estimated at more than $150 million.

Most Kash n' Karry food stores were 20,000 to 23,000 square feet in size at this time. In 1974 the chain opened its first supermarket-drugstore combination in Tampa, in collaboration with Kare Drugs. Other such combination stores soon followed. They were about 43,000 square feet in size, with an area between 7,000 and 10,000 square feet operated by Kare.

Kash n' Karry was sold to Lucky Stores Inc. of Dublin, California, in 1979 for $26.8 million in cash and stock. The chain grew rapidly in the 1980s, both in size and market penetration. It competed aggressively for business, lowering prices on 3,000 items in 1985, when there were 84 stores, stretching from Fort Myers in the south to Gainesville in the north. "Kash n' Karry has managed to sell a total concept in the Tampa market," an observer told *Supermarket News,* "one that appeals to low-price-oriented shoppers and to more upscale shoppers alike."

The following year Kash n' Karry improved its service to handle the heavier flow of supermarket traffic between 5 and 7:30 P.M. by not allowing employee breaks and dinner hours during these times. The program called for stores to be cleaned and stocked again with a wide selection of frozen dinners and precooked meat before 5:30. A new checkout aisle was opened every time there were three people waiting in line. In 1988 there were 94 Kash n' Karry units, averaging 28,000 square feet in size. By now the chain had passed Winn-Dixie Stores to take second place in its field in the Tampa-St. Petersburg area, with market share of 29 percent. Annual sales came to about $900 million.

Having established a reputation for low prices, Kash n' Karry launched a television advertising campaign in 1988 emphasizing the quality of its services. The first phase of the campaign consisted of conversations with employees about the services Kash n' Karry workers provided, including fast checkout and help in product selection. The second phase used employees only as extras, hiring actors to portray the delicatessen, bakery, and produce people who described and discussed their work. In-store and newspaper advertising supported the TV campaign, featuring photos of as many as 100 of the chain's employees. Its vice president for advertising told *Supermarket Business,* "The customer really gets a kick out of coming to the store, and going to the register, and actually seeing the girl ring up her groceries whom she saw on TV the night before.''

In July 1988 Kash n' Karry opened a 40,000-square-foot prototype store in Largo with aisles wider than in older stores and many amenities. This store carried vast supplies of bulk produce, a huge frozen-food section, a wine-and-cheese island, and a ''nutritional information center'' offering brochures on healthful dining. The Largo store was among more than two dozen Kash n' Karry outlets with floral departments.

Independent Firm, 1989–96

Kash n' Karry was acquired by its management from American Stores—the parent of Lucky Stores—for $305 million in 1989, by means of a leveraged buyout in partnership with the New York City-based investment-banking firm of Gibbons, Green, van Armerongen Ltd. Fulcrum III Limited Partnerships, managed by Gibbons, Green, van Armerongen, emerged with a majority of the stock until November 1991, when Los Angeles-based Leonard Green & Partners invested $27.7 million to become the controlling shareholder. Green & Partners was acting as general partner for Green Equity Investors L.P. In 1994 Green Equity Investors L.P. held 60.9 percent of Kash n' Karry's common stock and Fulcrum III Ltd. 33.8 percent.

Even before the leveraged buyout was completed, Kash n' Karry purchased 24 Florida Choice Food & Drug units and 24 adjacent liquor stores from Kroger Co. for $55 million. The acquisition enabled Kash n' Karry to pass Publix Super Markets and take the No. 1 position in the Tampa-St. Petersburg area, where half of the acquired Florida Choice units were located. These units ranged in size between 25,000 and 54,000 square feet, while about two-thirds of Kash n' Karry's stores were about 40,000 square feet. Kroger's president said the Florida Choice stores had been unprofitable for some time.

Kash n' Karry opened full-service First Florida Banks branches in some of its 116 stores during 1989. In 1990 it launched a ''Nature Friendly'' shelf-tagging program that told customers whether an item was recyclable, recycled, reusable, or carried less packaging than it once did. Some 700 items were identified in this manner. The chain's own environmentally friendly agenda included a cardboard recycling program that it estimated saved 500,000 trees a year. Its point-of-purchase card-toppers won an award in 1991 for graphics to draw attention to delicatessen and bakery sale items.

In 1990 Kash n' Karry established, at a cost of more than $3 million, a prototype store in Tampa. One of its most distinctive features was the exterior, with redesigned signage and more glass for an airy look. All future stores were to have this basic design. National-brand sale items were promoted inside with highly visible front-end and in-aisle signage. The company was converting its Lady Lee store brand to the Kash n' Karry private label. Most locations began staying open 24 hours a day in 1991. Kash n' Karry began offering shopping and delivery services in Hillsborough County in 1993.

Kash n' Karry acquired from Wetterau Inc. three super warehouse stores—one of which was subsequently closed—in 1992, operating under the ''Save n' Pack'' name. Ranging in size between 76,000 and 88,000 square feet, these around-the-clock units featured among the lowest prices on basic items carried by supermarkets and were designed to meet the needs of low-income households. In its Kash n' Karry outlets, too, the company continued to emphasize its everyday low prices. ''Our prices are not based on cost, but on our competitors' prices,'' a marketing executive of the chain told *Progressive Grocer* in 1991.

By 1994 Kash n' Karry had annual sales of $1.2 billion. Same-store sales fell to a five-year low, however, during fiscal 1994 (the year ended July 31, 1994), and the company lost nearly $38 million in the face of intense competition from four major supermarket operators with greater financial resources. Kash n' Karry closed 17 stores but could not overcome the heavy debt load it had incurred, mainly in its leveraged buyout—$331 million in 1991, compared to only $12 million in 1988. The company filed for Chapter 11 bankruptcy in November 1994, listing assets of $389.9 million and liabilities of $446.3 million, of which $326.2 million was unsecured debt.

Shortly before the end of the year Kash n' Karry emerged from bankruptcy under a plan that was intended to reduce its debt burden by one-third and interest expenses by more than one-third, or $12 million a year. As part of the restructuring, Green Equity Investors traded its controlling interest in the company for a lesser stake of 15 percent. Shortly thereafter, however, Green Equity Investors bought $12.9 million worth of Kash n' Karry's common stock, raising its stake to more than 22 percent. In 1995 the company's stock began trading on the NASDAQ exchange.

Ronald E. Johnson was appointed in 1995 as Kash n' Karry's new chairman, president, and chief executive officer. He began a 16-store remodeling program that featured more perishables and more seasonal nonfood merchandise. ''We want to move toward a food court,'' Johnson told *Supermarket News* in an interview, ''with a power alley featuring a salad bar, soup bar, and a variety of prepared foods, plus enhanced and upgraded varieties in bakery-deli, service meat, and service seafood.'' The new system called for 3,500 square feet of space for a bakery, 3,000 square feet for the traditional deli, and 3,500 square feet for the food court and prepared-foods area. The latter included pizza and coffee shops and carving, salad, and sandwich stations, plus a sushi bar. A Slim Creations 18-item line of low-fat and no-fat prepared foods also was being added.

One economy measure the company adopted was to abandon a three-year-old, $1.5-million project in which it built its own object-oriented language, database, and development tools to make quicker, nimbler pricing and inventory changes and decisions. Instead the company decided to outsource its information-systems operations, including development of a new mainframe-based procurement system and store-based point-of-sales systems. It continued to use an object-based warehousing application and promotional pricing system already in production.

Food Lion Subsidiary in 1996

Kash n' Karry was purchased by Food Lion in late 1996 for $341 million, including assumption of $221 million in long-term debt. Food Lion thus added Kash n' Karry's 22.3 percent market share in the Tampa-St. Petersburg-Clearwater area to its own 4 percent. Food Lion closed Kash n' Karry's 625,000-square-foot distribution center in Tampa but announced it would remodel and expand almost all of Kash n' Karry's stores as a precursor to possible further expansion of the chain outside west-central Florida. It was not immediately decided whether the 10 or so Food Lion stores operating in the same area as Kash n' Karry would convert to the Kash n' Karry name.

Food Lion also said it would refinance Kash n' Karry's debt at lower rates, resulting in annual savings of about $9 million.

Kash n' Karry's stores, in 1996, continued to center on the Tampa-St. Petersburg area, ranging from Gainesville, about 130 miles to the north, to Bonita Springs, about 150 miles to the south. Fifty-one food stores had 40,000 to 57,000 square feet of space; 42 ranged in size between 25,000 and 40,000 square feet; and 5 were less than 25,000 square feet in size. Most of them were in shopping centers. All of them sold groceries, including fresh fruits and vegetables, bakery and dairy products, delicatessen items, frozen foods, and fresh meats. Some of the larger ones had a pharmacy and/or full-service floral department. Kash n' Karry food stores also offered such nonfood goods as health-and-beauty-care items, paper and tobacco products, soaps and detergents, drugs, sundries, and housewares. Each of the 35 liquor stores was adjacent to a company supermarket.

Kash n' Karry had net income of nearly $2 million on sales of $1.02 billion in fiscal 1996. Liquor-store sales accounted for only about 2 percent of the total. The company owned nine of its supermarkets and leased the remainder. It also owned its Tampa warehouse, distribution, and office facility on 53.6 acres of land, which the company also owned.

Principal Subsidiaries

KNK 702 Delaware Business Trust; KNK 886 Delaware Business Trust; KNK 891 Delaware Business Trust.

Further Reading

Beres, Glen A., "New Kash n' Karry Chief Lists Plans," *Supermarket News,* February 20, 1995, p. 4.

Buss, Dale, "Survival in the Fast Lane," *Florida Business—Tampa Bay,* August 1989, p. 30.

Clancy, Carole, "Buyout Firm Ups Its Stake in Kash n' Karry," *Tampa Bay Business Journal,* February 24, 1995, p. 1.

Duff, Mike, "People Power Key to Kash n' Karry Campaign," *Supermarket Business,* November 1988, pp. 68–69.

Fisher, John, "Eberhard in Talks to Acquire Kash n' Karry, Florida Chain," *Supermarket News,* April 10, 1978, pp. 1, 10.

"A Full-Scale Approach," *Progressive Grocer,* July 1996, pp. 102–04.

"Kash n' Karry Restructure Complete," *Supermarket News,* January 2, 1995, p. 4.

"Kash n' Karry Will Try In-Store Bank Branches," *Supermarket News,* July 24, 1989, p. 24.

King, Julia, "Back to Basics," *Computerworld,* March 20, 1995, pp. 1, 117.

Linsen, Mary Ann, "Price Isn't Everything at Kash n' Karry," *Progressive Grocer,* September 1991, pp. 95, 98, 100–01.

Malko, Constance, "Florida Chain Catering to After-Work Shoppers," *Supermarket News,* September 15, 1986, p. 10.

Merrefield, David, "Tampa: A Market in Transition," *Supermarket News,* December 9, 1985, Sec. 2, p. 28.

Ossorio, Sonio, "Chain Plans Debt Swap; Income Up," *Tampa Bay Business Journal,* May 1, 1992, p. 1.

Sansolo, Michael, "Going Green: 3 Ways to Build Trust," *Progressive Grocer,* February 1991, pp. 45–46, 50.

Zwiebach, Elliot, "American Stores Close to Kash n' Karry Sale," *Supermarket News,* August 8, 1988, p. 2.

——, "Kash n' Karry to Buy Block of Florida Choice Stores," *Supermarket News,* August 29, 1988, pp. 1, 38.

——, "Kash Investments," *Supermarket News,* April 24, 1995, pp. 1, 132–33.

——, "Remodels Set as Food Lion's First Step for Kash n' Karry," *Supermarket News,* November 11, 1996, p. 1.

—Robert Halasz

Kinetic Concepts, Inc. (KCI)

8023 Vantage Drive
San Antonio, Texas 78230
U.S.A.
(210) 524-9000
Fax: (210) 255-6993
Web site: http://www.kci1.com

Public Company
Incorporated: 1976
Employees: 2,106
Sales: $269.9 million (1996)
Stock Exchanges: NASDAQ
SICs: 8082 Home Health Care Services; 5047 Medical
and Hospital Equipment; 7352 Medical Equipment
Rental

Kinetic Concepts, Inc. (KCI), is a leading international provider of specialized hospital equipment to speed the recovery of immobilized patients. KCI has operations in Austria, Germany, the United Kingdom, Denmark, France, the Netherlands, Switzerland, Sweden, Italy, Canada, and Australia. Independent KCI equipment dealers penetrate 21 additional countries. With state of the art products ranging from surfaces that help burned skin heal, machines that speed wound recovery, and mattresses that turn patients automatically, KCI's products aid recovery for everyone from the unknown indigent to the likes of Christopher Reeve and Boris Yeltsin.

Not only a manufacturer of hospital equipment, KCI is also a top-notch contender in research to improve the healing process. The company has authored three proprietary software programs that track patient rate of recovery with different therapies and follow patient outcome plotted against cost of care. KCI uses these results to develop new products, publishes its findings, and advises facilities on how to improve care while maintaining reasonable cost. One of KCI's newest products, first introduced in Europe, is the V.A.C., which uses light suction and a sponge to help difficult wounds close. The new process has dramatic results, both for the patient and often for the hospital—Bowman

Gray Hospital in its 1996 annual report cited the product as saving them over $170,000 in cost of wound care. The company also pioneered the practice of renting equipment to healthcare providers, a $500 million dollar industry, and guarantees a two-hour delivery.

A Dream and a Beginning: KCI 1976–84

The founder of KCI, Dr. Jim Leininger, came home from his 24-hour shift in the ER one night in 1975 to tell his wife Cecilia about an amazing bed—the Roto Rest. It seemed to solve something that had always disturbed the sympathetic physician—the fact that many of the critically injured patients he stabilized in the emergency room would lose their lives strapped to immobile hospital beds. Burned skin would break down through the constant pressure of the prone patient, and damaged pulmonary systems were subject to fluid build-up that could literally drown a sick person.

The couple seized the promise of the new bed, which rocked 80 degrees to gently reposition the injured person several times a day. In a one-bedroom apartment, they founded Kinetic Concepts in 1976.

The company's first nine years were a constant struggle with bankruptcy. The fledgling enterprise moved into a 14,000-square-foot plant, acquired manufacturing rights and patent for the Roto Rest, and started production. But the demand did not seem to be there. Times were so tight, recalls long-time team member Terry Tejeda, that, "Everyone pitched in to help with what was needed. When I wasn't sewing, I learned how to work on the lathe and drill press. I remember cutting the foam for Roto Rest cushions with a device John Vrzalik created and an electric carving knife."

"We had to borrow money every year just to stay in business," remembers Dr. Leininger, who continued to work the emergency rooms of three Baptist hospitals in San Antonio, Texas. "Then finally one day, I called my Dad for more money and he said, 'There isn't any more. I've given you all I have.' It was so hard for me to realize I had not only bankrupted myself, but my family, too."

Company Perspectives:

Kinetic Concepts develops and markets innovative therapeutic healing systems that address skin breakdown, circulatory problems, and pulmonary complications associated with patient immobility. The company's healing systems include specialty beds, mattress replacement systems, and related medical devices. Kinetic Concepts services hospitals, long-term and home care settings both in the U.S. and abroad.

He prayed with his family and, miraculously, in the next few months more capital was raised and sales increased dramatically. The years 1979–84 marked a period of painstakingly slow growth, but the company was building a strong framework from which to rocket to success. In 1977, Kinetic Concepts made medical equipment history by renting—not selling—its product. In 1980, the first study on Kinetic Concepts' process, Kinetic Therapy, was completed by Dr. Barth Green at the University of Miami, where Dr. Leininger had earned his M.D. in 1969. In 1983, the Roto Rest bed was further publicized by an appearance on network television and five more articles in medical journals.

From Dreams to Dollars: 1984–88

In 1984 the company had its first big break—the release of a product designed completely in-house, the KinAir bed. Demand for this product was unprecedented, and the company grew fast to meet the market—over 100 percent in 1985. In 1986, Kinetic Concepts grew 250 percent over the previous boom year. In 1987, the company introduced another new product, the Bio-Dyne bed, and grew another 100 percent. Kinetic Concepts incorporated as Kinetic Concepts, Inc. (KCI) in 1988 and is traded as KNCI on the NASDAQ. A landmark year, 1988 also saw the company enter an international arena with its high-end products.

Developing the Corporation: 1989–93

The years 1989–93 marked a period of development for KCI. No longer a struggling, semi-bankrupt vehicle for a dream, as it was in the beginning, and with the explosive growth of the late 80s behind it, the company settled into consolidating its corporate identity. For the first time, a strong mission statement was defined—"healing patients through the delivery of therapies, not just providing equipment." The kind of culture the corporation wanted to foster was also established—"People with a Purpose."

KCI created a list of core values, reproduced not only in the office but also in the marketing material. The KCI Core Values "guide our decisions and everyday activities," the brochures state, and they include: the value of people; clear communication; teamwork; excellence in all endeavors; personal development; responsibility; stewardship; maintaining a servant's heart; and, integrity. KCI also elected to call its employees Team Members to further promote a caring corporate culture.

This period of companywide identity building also saw KCI's product expansion into lower-end, more affordable equipment. Hospitals and health care providers were beginning to feel the pinch of managed care, and cost containment became a priority. Under this onslaught, KCI made the strategic purchase of a company called Medirec, which became KCI Medical Services in 1990. In the next year, 1991, KCI continued acquisitions with Mediscus International, which brought KCI products into 10 countries and formed the KCI International (KCII) subsidiary.

Divisions

In the early 1990s, KCI began to detail its operations into what would become four divisions: KCI New Technologies, Inc. (Nutech), KCI Home Care, KCI Therapeutic Services, Inc. (KCTS), and KCI International (KCII). NuTech, organized in 1992, concentrates on lower-cost technologies and made its debut with PlexiPulse, a machine that improves circulation in the extremities. Immediately Novamedix Limited filed suit for patent infringement—Novamedix is the largest direct competitor for the PlexiPulse product. (By mid-1997, the lawsuit had not yet been resolved in favor of either party.) Nutech revenue accounts for approximately 6 percent of KCI's overall earnings.

KCI Home Care rents and sells products to the home health care market, primarily by selling wholesale to home medical equipment providers. Organized in 1995, this division contributes approximately 5 percent of KCI's total revenue.

KCTS accounted for 64 percent of the company's overall revenue in 1996 and almost half the company's workforce. This division rents specialty beds to patients or to hospitals and has a sales force of over 300. This arm of KCI provides continuous on-call service and delivers products within two hours, as well as picks up products when the patient is done with them, assists in product maintenance, and makes recommendations about the most effective use of KCI's special medical equipment.

KCII provides the services and products of KCI to foreign countries, including most of western Europe, Scandinavia, and Australia. Also, this division maintains relationships with independent distributors in the Middle East, Asia, and Eastern Europe. The international division accounted for 25 percent of KCI's total revenue in 1996.

Firmly established in the "big time," in 1992 KCI took a strategic leap and sued its main competitor, Hill-Rom, for patent infringement. The first major legal proceeding entered by the company, the law suit bore fruit—KCI was awarded $85 million in damages and the competitor was admonished to remove its rotating bed product from the market.

By the end of 1993, the company had indeed established itself on the forefront of medical equipment supplies. The corporate staff moved into a new setting—the crisp, elegant KCI Tower, sported a new, state-of-the-art show room, had organized into seven distinct operating units, and triumphed in its first major litigation. The company was poised to grow on a worldwide scale.

An Agile Competitor: KCI 1994–97

Ray Hannigan became CEO and president of KCI in 1994. Under his leadership, the Medical Services business was sold and the V.A.C. was brought into the fold, which is an innovative vacuum-assisted wound-closing device. In the late 1990s, KCI's complete suite of products for sale or for rent included several specialty beds that rotate the patient to prevent pulmonary problems, mattress overlays that promote good skin care, air-surface mattresses and pulsating mattresses that promote the healing of skin grafts and skin ulcers, versions of these hospital beds that will fit in a home, and a full line of beds, chairs, and equipment to facilitate the treatment of morbidly obese patients (weighing up to 850 pounds).

In 1995, KCI filed a civil antitrust lawsuit against Hillenbrand Industries, Inc. and its subsidiary Hill-Rom Company, Inc. for using its monopoly on the standard hospital bed to gain advantage in the specialty hospital bed market. Hill-Rom, which ranks as KCI's principal competitor, countersued, and then, in 1996, opened new litigation claiming that one of KCI's latest products, the TriaDyne critical care recovery bed, infringes on the Hill-Rom patent for a similar purpose. Discovery and resolution in these cases may continue for years.

What is not in contention, however, is that KCI is strongly positioned in the specialty medical care niche, competing only with Hill-Rom, Kendall, Inc., and Invacare, Inc. on a national level. The year 1996 brought record growth for the company, which had $60 million in cash, no debt, and an 11 percent increase over 1995 profits. In early 1997, KCI swallowed the California-based company H.F. Systems, which held assets of $7 million, the ACCESS Patient Care Device formerly held by Trac Medical, Inc., and the Ethos Medical Group of Athlone, Ireland.

And KCI is still hungry. CEO Ray Hannigan announced: "We are actively looking for opportunities to enhance and extend our product line and geographic reach." The company hired Boston-based financial advisor Alex, Brown, & Sons, Inc. in May 1997 to study the company's flexibility on strategic moves ranging from seeking a buyer to an increased pace of acquisitions.

A Healthy Future

KCI recognizes that changing trends in patient demographics will continue to motivate a demand for new kinds of services and new products. The number of elderly patients is on the rise and these patients tend to need care in a nursing home or a home care setting. Another trend to watch is the health care cost crunch that began in the late 1980s and continues to propel hospitals and health care providers to seek ways to cut costs.

Keeping these in mind, the company is setting a goal of tripling its earnings by the year 2000 and increasing shareholder value by an aggressive policy of buying back its own stock. The first quarter of 1997 saw a 13.5 percent increase over operating earnings in fiscal 1996 and represented an all-time three-month high for the company of $73.2 million in revenue. KCI is doing everything it can to make sure its record-breaking success is just that—one more record to break.

Further Reading

Fohn, Joe, "KCI Hires Financial Advisors," *San Antonio Express News*, May 30, 1997, p. E1.

"KCI: Twenty Years of Proven Therapy," KCI: San Antonio, Texas, 1996.

"KCI Founder Remembers Early Struggle and God's Faithfulness," KCI: *Turning Times*, November 1996. p. 1.

—Lisa Calhoun

Kingston Technology Corporation

17600 Newhope Street
Fountain Valley, California 92708
U.S.A.
(714) 435-2600
Fax: (714) 438-2720
Web site: http://www.kingston.com

Private Subsidiary
Founded: 1987
Employees: 450
Sales: $1.3 billion (1996)
SICs: 3572 Computer Storage Devices

Acknowledged as the world's leading provider of computer memory products, Kingston Technology Corporation also designs and manufactures portable products, processor upgrades, storage subsystems, and networking products for personal computers, workstations, and laser printers. With over 1,900 products and customers in over 60 countries, the company is the world's largest provider of enhancement products for PCs, laptops, notebooks, servers, workstations and printers. Domestic distribution channels include distributors, major reseller chains, and aggregators. This distribution, added to an international network, makes up 3,000 reseller locations across the world.

Kingston Technology Corporation was founded in 1987 by John Tu (originally from Shanghai) and David Sun (originally from Taiwan). Tu and Sun had met in 1982 and started Camintonn Corporation, a manufacturer of enhancement products for DEC systems. This fly-by-night company began in Tu's garage, with the two businessmen carrying computer memory chips in the back seats of their cars. By 1986, business took off with sales of $9 million. That year, they sold the company to AST Research for $6 million, investing their gains in the stock market.

When the stock market crashed in 1987, Tu and Sun lost almost everything. Then they saw an opportunity to recoup their losses. At that time, the computer industry was suffering from a shortage of memory modules for personal computers. Tu and Sun seized a simple solution to the problem, designing an industry standard Single In-Line Memory Module (SIMM) with an alternative chip that was readily available. This product and a mere $4,000 launched Kingston's operations, and the company soon began developing memory products for PCs.

A skeptical businessman, Tu found it difficult to believe that the simple solution the two had found to the memory crisis would result in a lasting company. He bet Sun a Jaguar that Kingston would not live past its first year. The PC market was beginning to produce computers that ran on separate proprietary systems, leaving the door open for Kingston to design and produce several unique memory upgrade devices for each individual market. In its first year, the company achieved $12.8 million in sales. Tu lost his bet, and Sun later bestowed the Jaguar upon an employee who had long dreamed of owning one.

By 1989, just two years after Kingston's emergence, the marketplace had changed. Chips were in ready supply once again, and as a result so were memory enhancement products. However, Kingston remained the clear leader in the memory market, and in 1989 the company earned $36.5 million in sales.

One of the ways in which Kingston quickly differentiated itself from its competition was the high level of customer services, including 100 percent testing of its products, comprehensive 5-year warranties, domestic 24-hour shipping, and free technical support. The company promised to immediately replace defective parts with no questions asked. Beyond customer service, Kingston established a holistic way of operating a family-style company. The company's philosophy places the customer third, after employees and suppliers. According to Kingston, if the company takes care of its employees and suppliers, the customers will be taken care of as well. Kingston employees are among the highest paid in the industry (as much as 30 percent above average), and an egalitarian work environment is demonstrated by the fact that Tu and Sun's working suites are cubicles among their staff family. Showing a generosity that is rare in corporate America, Kingston distributed 5 percent of pretax quarterly profits to employees as a bonus and matched employee contributions to 401(k) plans dollar for dollar. Further, managing the company conservatively, Tu and Sun ensured employees that should the company go out of business at any time, employees would be granted a full year's salary in order to find a suitable position elsewhere. Appreciative of such unusual treatment, Kingston employees tended to stay, with less than 2 percent annual attrition as of 1994.

Given such perquisites, one would imagine that job seekers clamor to work at Kingston. However, securing a position with the company is no easy task. Tu and Sun value experience over credentials, and seek employees who would be good members of the family. About 80 percent of new hires are the result of internal referrals. By hiring slowly, the company succeeds in implanting its family culture in each employee gradually. One of the most multicultural companies in the industry, Kingston employs a mix of whites, blacks, Chinese, Vietnamese, and Hispanic workers, with two-thirds of its workers in 1995 representing ethnic minorities.

Suppliers, the company's number two priority, are also treated well. The company never turns away shipments from chip vendors, nor does it renegotiate when market chip prices fall below contractual agreement levels. Kingston seeks to establish long-term relationships with vendors, working with them as partners over many years. Long-term relationships are also key management of currency risk, and Kingston has cultivated strong relationships with its foreign distributors based on mutual favors and support. When sterling fell against the dollar, for example, Kingston's U.K. vendor could not meet the cost of a more expensive dollar. At the expense of its profit margins, Kingston lowered its prices. However, the company, in such a situation, expects the vendor to return the favor when sterling's value again increases.

Kingston's early success was also due to the cutthroat computer market, where manufacturers customarily produced low-quality hardware products and made money on upgrades. With Kingston's upgrade products, these machines could handle the demands of word-processing and Internet software. Kingston soon became known for the speed with which it designed and delivered upgrades, sometimes producing the upgrade for a product before that product was even released to the consumer. Whereas most PC producers allow orders to pile up while they shop for the best bargains, shipping bulk orders every month or so, Kingston fills all purchase orders daily. The company places the quality of its relationship with suppliers and customers above any savings associated with waiting to fill orders. The result is that Kingston is the fastest company to meet its customers orders. Its reputation for speedy response is so strong

that original equipment manufacturers have been known to refer their own customers to Kingston when they cannot meet customer needs in a timely way. Filling orders quickly has another advantage: Kingston carries no inventory.

All of these qualities set Kingston apart from its first few years in business. In 1989, Kingston extended beyond memory products, entering the storage upgrade market. The next year, the company began offering processor upgrades, the company's first non-memory product line. The introduction of Windows 3.0 in 1990 gave sales a boost, as computers required more memory than what was contained within PCs. Revenues almost tripled in 1990, reaching $87.8 million, and in 1991 sales again surged to $140.7 million. The demand for memory was spurred in 1991 by the rise of the memory-intensive workstation market, and Kingston created a special department to serve this market in 1991. By this time, the company employed 110 people.

In 1992, Kingston was ranked the fastest-growing private company in America by *Inc. Magazine*. With no debt and no venture capital, revenues surged to $251 million (with about one-third coming from international markets) and the company grew to employ 175 people. Since 1987, sales had increased 368 percent compounded annually. Competing with about 15 companies, Kingston held a 45 percent share of the computer memory market in 1992. That year, the company continued to diversify its offerings, adding a line of Ethernet and Token Ring networking products. In 1993, new networking and storage product lines were introduced. That year, it became apparent that the company's innovative vendor relationships were working; demand for semiconductors exceeded supply, with suppliers shipping to Kingston when orders from other buyers were delayed. Sales for 1993 were $433 million, and the number of employees grew to 255.

By 1994, Kingston had developed nine separate processor upgrade products and a full line of portable products. The company entered the portable market with its introduction of DataTraveler, a portable hard disk drive, and DataPak, a portable PCMCIA hard disk drive. When ISO 9000 (International Organization for Standardization) became the worldwide quality standard, Kingston immediately passed the test, attaining certification in September 1994 and successfully completing its first audit. The billion-dollar mark began to feel reachable, as 1994 revenues climbed to $800 million due to the efforts of 310 employees. Kingston's competition had increased, with 70 companies in the $7.2 billion dynamic random-access memory (DRAM) module market, but Kingston was still number one. The company's growth was physically evident; the workstation memory group was moved to a different building, and Kingston purchased blue Huffy bikes to shuttle employees between the two worksites.

Yet, growth began to present questions for the company. In 1994, Kingston hired its first chief financial officer, a former Wall Street investment banker named Henry Tchen, and issued security badges to employees. Outsiders wondered if the company's family environment would be tossed aside when revenues reached the billion dollar mark.

When Microsoft introduced the Windows 95 operating system, in 1995, demand for Kingston's memory upgrades skyrocketed. Windows required more memory than most consumers had in their existing hardware. The company surpassed a billion dollars in sales that year, earning $1.3 billion with 450 employees.

International development became a major focus around this time. Expanding its worldwide distribution network, Kingston opened a branch office in Munich, Germany, in 1995. The next year, a branch office was opened in Paris. Kingston worked with Legend Technology Limited to develop computers for the Chinese market in 1996. Also in 1996, the company introduced the TurboChip 133 processor upgrade, which gave a 486 computer the power of a 75 megahertz Pentium chip, and three new plug-and-play Ethernet adapters.

By this time, Tu and Sun had become two of America's wealthiest entrepreneurs, occupying places on the *Forbes* list of America's 400 richest people. Leading the company, Tu focused on sales and marketing while Sun oversaw engineering. As a team, Tu and Sun were noted for their quick decision-making. The pair often decided to launch new products while walking from their cars to the Kingston headquarters, and the success rate for new products was an unheard-of 90 percent in 1992. Kingston's founders did not wish to take the company public, desiring to maintain the family environment they had built.

. In 1996, the price of DRAM dropped dramatically, forcing upgrade vendors to boost sales volume and enter new markets. Kingston responded by pursuing the OEM market, courting companies such as Compaq Computer Corp., IBM Corp, and Sun Microsystems, Inc.

Taking analysts by surprise, in 1996 Kingston was acquired by Softbank Corporation, the world's largest publisher of computer-related magazines and books and the world's largest producer of technology-related trade shows and expositions. Softbank was also the largest distributor of computer software, peripherals and systems in Japan. Softbank purchased 80 percent of the company for $1.5 billion, and Kingston characteristically shared $100 million with its employees as a holiday bonus (doling out approximately $75,000 to each employee). Softbank's revenues for fiscal year 1996 were $1.6 billion, and the company had 6,000 employees across the world. Under the terms of the acquisition, Tu and Sun remain in charge of the company's operations. What was surprising about the acquisition was that Tu and Sun, who had been extremely financially conservative from the outset (never even agreeing to take out a bank loan), had agreed to be purchased by a company that was in the process of a takeover spending spree with high financing. Why would Kingston agree to such an alliance?

The answer was that Softbank's strong distribution channels in Japan—where the company had virtually no presence—would be an asset to Kingston's expansion plans. The company's dominance of the distribution channels selling to America's *Fortune* 1000 had made it the largest memory module manufacturer, but outside markets remained unconquered. With Softbank's acquisition, the company began targeting international growth. In 1997, Kingston announced a $40 million expansion plan, involving the construction of production facilities in Europe and Asia and the expansion of its U.S. facility to include a new manufacturing center. The goal of the expansion was to achieve faster turnaround times and lower prices amid the plummeting price of memory, which had dropped 80 percent during 1996–97. Kingston opened a European Headquarters in the United Kingdom and announced plans to open a manufacturing site there as well.

In its first decade, Kingston has grown from a company that manufactured a single memory module to an international corporation with over a billion dollars in revenues. Astounding growth has been achieved through eschewing the cutthroat bargain-oriented mentality of the company's competitors, instead valuing long-term relationships and employee satisfaction. With the company's acquisition by Softbank and its expansion in Europe and Asia, a new phase of development has begun in the second decade. The lingering question about the company's future remains: can the family-style management that has secured Kingston's leadership place in the market continue to coexist with the demands of a billion dollar business?

Further Reading

Aragon, Lawrence, "Family Values," *PC Week*, September 19, 1994, p. A1.

Arterian, Susan, "Smooth Sailing Through Current Swings," *CFO: The Magazine for Senior Financial Executives*, January, 1993, pp. 53–55.

Burck, Charles, "The Real World of the Entrepreneur," *Fortune*, April 5, 1993, pp. 62–81.

Doebele, Justin, "Kingston: King of Retrofit," *Forbes*, December 19, 1994, pp. 312–13.

——, "Memory Gain," *Fortune*, September 9, 1996, p. 16.

"Face Value: Doing the Right Thing," *Economist*, May 20, 1995, p. 64.

"Kingston Technology—King of the Memory Module Hill," *Dataquest*, May 29, 1997.

Laabe, Jennifer J., "Kingston Employees Get Huge Bonuses," *Workforce*, February 1997, p. 11.

Lansner, Jonathon, "Fortune Smiles," *The Orange County Register*, May 25, 1997.

McKeefry, Hailey Lynne, "Kingston Plans Major Expansion: Memory Maker Will Add Two Overseas Facilities," *Electronic Buyers' News*, May 5, 1997, p. 74.

Pang, Albert, "DRAM Landscape on the Move," *Computer Reseller News*, July 29, 1996, p. 133.

The Ultimate Memory Guide, Fountain Valley, CA: Kingston Technology Corporation.

Welles, Edward G., "The 1992 Inc. 500: Built on Speed," *Inc.*, October, 1992, pp. 82–88.

"With the Fondest of Memories," *HP Professional*, June, 1996, p. 12.

—Heidi Feldman

Kiwi International Airlines Inc.

One Hemisphere Center
Newark, New Jersey 07114-0006
U.S.A.
(201) 645-8445
Fax: (210) 624-0537

Private Company
Incorporated: 1992
Employees: 550
Sales: $170.3 million (1995)
SICs: 4512 Air Transportation—Scheduled

Kiwi International Airlines Inc. was created from the ashes of Midway Airlines, Eastern Airlines, Pan Am, and other carriers which folded in the early 1990s. These closings left a slew of experienced and unemployed personnel in their wake, and put plenty of used equipment on the market. The New Jersey airline was named after the flightless bird from New Zealand which symbolized how the grounded flight crews felt after losing their wings. (The appropriation of the national symbol did result in both some ruffled feathers and some confusion later on.)

Taking Off in the Early 1990s

Employees started out by investing up to $50,000 each in the airline (at around $5 per share), making it employee-owned in a unique sense. Bob Iverson, formerly a pilot at Eastern Airlines, served as the company's first chief executive officer. Dave Bell, who also flew for Eastern, served as vice-president of strategic planning. His brother Codie, an Arthur Andersen consultant, helped plan the start-up and served as chief financial officer. The company's unique ownership joined the Airline Transport Association, the lobbying group that represents airline owners and sometimes takes a different regulatory stance than pilots' unions.

Iverson and the four other pilots who would control the company had originally set out to acquire an airline. However, the investment community proved too sluggish to accommodate them. They turned to displaced employees to raise $10 million to start a new airline: pilots invested $50,000 each, other types of employees $5,000.

Employee ownership benefited the airline with drastically lower labor costs as well as lower start-up capital. The maximum salary pilots and executives at Kiwi could command was $60,000, roughly half what other carriers allowed their most experienced pilots. It allowed pilots to retain their seniority, unlike the rest of the industry. The company started its flight attendants at $28,000 per year, nearly double the average.

Employees seemed to take a proprietary interest in their duties that resulted in high standards of service. Morale was high as the employees, who felt they had been treated as a burden by the owners of the airlines they had previously served, now felt they had a chance to demonstrate their value. The egalitarian spirit was represented in the newsroom-type layout of the company's headquarters, where all 200 administrative employees shared a large open office. In addition, employees were encouraged to help wherever needed when they could spare a moment, from helping load planes to volunteering in an auxiliary sales force.

Employee ownership was a popular trend in the airline industry at the time Kiwi International started. However, while Kiwi's employees provided the company's start-up capital, workers at other companies were granted shares either as a benefit or a concession for lower wages.

To much fanfare, Kiwi made its first flight from Newark International Airport to Midway Airport in Chicago. At the time, the company operated only two aircraft, Boeing 727-200s, which were relatively economical to purchase but were also less fuel efficient. Eventually, these older aircraft had to be upgraded to meet federal noise limitations.

The company's strategy was to offer low prices without the restrictions usually associated with discount fares, and superior amenities and levels of service. Its food costs, for example, were said to be twice ($6 per meal) the industry average. Lavatories were decorated with flowers. However, its costs per mile (6 cents) were well below the industry average of 9.5 cents. It could make a profit off half-empty airliners, which was fortunate, since the carrier always had some difficulty filling airplanes. Rather than operate on a hub system, the carrier offered simple nonstop flights, maintaining its flexibility. Travel agents fawned over Kiwi's attentive service. Kiwi's routes, which focused on major metropolitan areas, were typically boarded from smaller airports, which were often more convenient for travelers. In spite of the warm reception, Kiwi lost $6 million during its first year of operations.

In late 1994, Kiwi preemptively grounded its fleet of 13 leased planes in response to FAA scrutiny of its pilot training documentation procedures. The issue was quickly resolved, however. To placate potentially anxious passengers, the company touted its outstanding safety record, never having even "scratched a plane in 23,000 flights." Nevertheless, the grounding was estimated to have cost the company $2 million. Although the company initiated a new small package service in June and made $114.3 million in revenues in 1994, it failed to turn a profit as expected, instead losing $25 million.

Two Years of Travail: 1995–96

According to Bob Iverson, who lost his executive position in February 1995, the company's chief liability was its raison d'etre, its employee owners. He blamed the concept for a lack of discipline in spending and an atmosphere that paralyzed decision making. The resistance to centralized authority was endemic throughout the organization, including among the vice-presidents. Deals were lost as a result, and planning was futile in an organization more focused inside itself than on the market.

Other observers stated that employees had very little sway at the airline. They had no voting rights, which instead were reverted to a panel of five pilots. Its employees paid for stock after taxes. As the company did not have a formal employee stock ownership plan (ESOP), it did not make the same type of financial reporting to its shareholders, who bristled at subsequent cost-cutting measures. Some characterized the company's leaders as business novices in spite of their piloting experience. In addition, they criticized the abnormally high rate of pay some positions received in relation to industry norms; future CEO Jerry Murphy lamented "make-work" positions that overstaffed the airline.

Analysts also surmised that the company simply did not have the cash to make its low-cost/high-quality approach work. Quality invariably suffered; the airline reported on time performance of 65 percent in 1995. At the time, the company was leasing 16 planes and employing 1,000 workers.

The company's cashflow needs and the incident with the FAA prompted Iverson's dismissal, according to company sources. Iverson maintained that $7.5 million in financing he was attempting to secure was perceived as a threat to the directors' control of the company. He was initially replaced as chairman by Byron Hogue, one of the founders of Federal Express. Danny Wright, an aviation consultant, was named president. During this crisis period, employees' pay was cut by 17 percent. In May 1995, the company reported it owed $3 million to the Internal Revenue Service and $1 million (later

reduced) to the Port Authority of New York and New Jersey. In June 1995, Jerry Murphy, formerly co-president of the defunct MGM Grand Air, became the company's fourth CEO and Russell Thayer, formerly CEO at Braniff Airways, became its new chairman. His team implemented the company's first business plan early in 1996.

In August 1995, the airline began a marketing agreement with Air South, a discount airline based in Columbia, South Carolina. Nevertheless, marketing and sales efforts proved insufficient, and load factors (the percentage of seats booked on flights) were insupportably low, even for Kiwi. Ironically, in June 1995 *Consumer Reports* rated the carrier the third best airline in the United States. *Conde Nast Traveler* had rated it the best domestic airline in November 1994.

FAA scrutiny of its pilot training again interrupted the carrier's operations in mid-1996, when it grounded four of its 15 planes. The agency determined just over a tenth of Kiwi's 277 pilots were not sufficiently trained. Kiwi officials characterized the FAA's actions, which came after the disastrous May 1996 crash of a ValuJet airliner, as an overreaction, and took the unique step of touting their "perfect safety record" in advertising (specific safety claims are rare in airline advertising) rather than their low fares. Kiwi managed to hold on to a profit during this time, but not without pay cuts and layoffs.

Hope for Renewal in 1996–97?

Airlines typically do not advertise following catastrophes such as the explosion of TWA Flight 800 in July 1996. However, Kiwi did so; as one executive told *Advertising Age,* "we can't afford to have consumers afraid of flying." The airline was also able to obtain time on the Megavision screens at the Summer Olympics in Atlanta, site of the company's largest hub, due to the withdrawal of ValuJet.

In July 1996 Recovery Equity Investors of San Mateo, California, provided the company with $4 million to offset its constant cashflow problems. Ironically, concern over the safety of discount airlines following the ValuJet Everglades crash diluted the resolve of Kiwi's backers. Kiwi had proved perfectly safe throughout its four-year existence: no accidents, no injuries. Nevertheless, though the company's operating statistics showed a little improvement over the previous year, Recovery Equity Investors subsequently postponed a planned additional $6 million payment.

With liabilities totaling $55 million, Kiwi, valued at $35 million, entered Chapter 11 bankruptcy proceedings on September 30, 1996. (Oddly enough, Kiwi International Airlines of New Zealand—a younger, entirely separate company—had announced it was folding on September 9.) A couple of weeks later, on October 15, it suspended all scheduled flights, but continued to operate charter flights as it sought creditor backing. It resumed limited scheduled operations on January 20, 1997, recalling about half of its 1100-strong prior work force. These flights linked Newark, Chicago, Atlanta, and West Palm Beach with unrestricted one-way fares of $99 or less.

The Wall Street Journal reported that for the first time in history, a crash (ValuJet) had jeopardized the survival of an entire segment of the industry. Besides Kiwi's Chapter 11 filing,. several other carriers reported bleak news. JetTrain Corp., a new Pennsylvania airline, folded after less than a year. As reservations from cautious customers dwindled, others posted losses for the last quarter of 1996: Frontier Airlines, Western Pacific, Vanguard Airlines, AirTran, and ValuJet itself.

Dr. Charles Edwards, who had already invested more than $10 million in Kiwi, stepped up to provide further support in June 1997. Edwards-Wasatch Enterprises LLC (an affiliate of Wasatch International), led by Dr. Edwards, offered $16.5 million to buy the carrier, allowing the investment group more management control. Bankruptcy proceedings were expected to end in July 1997.

Kiwi International Airlines delighted many with its attention to detail and attempts to give customers more for less. Unfortunately, competitive pressures, untoward circumstances, and, some would say, an inherent flaw in its unique ownership and management structure, all threatened to keep this carrier on the ground. If Kiwi can learn to please investors as well as it has its customers in the past, it should find its most difficult flights behind it.

Further Reading

"Accounts in Review," *Adweek* (Eastern Ed., Southeast Ed.), February 19, 1996, p. 8.

"Ad Air Barrier," *Advertising Age,* August 5, 1996, p. 14.

Eckmann, Katy, and Jim Osterman, "Kiwi Touches Down," *Adweek* (Southeast Ed.), February 19, 1996, p. 6.

Fitzpatrick, Dan, "Kiwi Could Fly Pittsburgh Skies," *Pittsburgh Business Times,* July 8, 1996, pp. 1, 31.

Fron, Jennifer, "Kiwi International Waits for Bailout to Be Delivered," *The Wall Street Journal,* November 25, 1996, p. B10.

Ho, Rodney, "It's a Bird; It's a Fruit; and Now It's Also a Defunct Airline—Or Is It?" *Wall Street Journal,* September 17, 1996, p. B1.

"Kiwi Awaits Go-Ahead for Limited Service," *Aviation Week and Space Technology,* October 28, 1996, p. 34.

"Kiwi International Air Lines: Discount Carrier to Resume Some Flights This Month," *The Wall Street Journal,* January 3, 1997, p. B5.

"Kiwi's Ousted Chairman Sues the Airline, Directors," *The Wall Street Journal,* March 31, 1995, p. C15.

Lipowicz, Alice, "Kiwi's Frail Recovery Taxed by Levy, Slump," *Crain's New York Business,* August 28, 1995, p. 3.

——, "Kiwi Dogged By Questions About Its Safety," *Crain's New York Business,* July 29, 1996, pp. 1, 23.

Loro, Laura, "Kiwi Wings Through Some Growing Pains," *Advertising Age,* February 20, 1995, p. 4.

Lucas, Allison, "On a Wing and a Prayer," *Sales and Marketing Management,* May 1996, p. 22.

McCartney, Scott, "Air Pressure: Start-Ups Still Suffer From ValuJet Crash and FAA's Missteps," *The Wall Street Journal,* December 9, 1996, p. A1.

McCune, Jenny C., "Up and Away," *Management Review,* January 1995, pp. 20–25.

McDonald, Michele, "Groundings Leave Travel in a Tangle," *Travel Weekly,* December 22, 1994, pp. 1, 29.

Murphy, Anne, "Taking the Fall," *Inc,* September, 1995, pp. 81–86.

"On a Wing and a Prayer," *Sales & Marketing Management,* May 1996, p. 22.

Selwitz, Robert, "Niche Carriers Heat Up Small Package Competition," *Global Trade & Transportation,* June 1994, p. 32.

Underwood, Elaine, "Hutcheson to Pilot Kiwi Re-Branding," *Brandweek,* February 5, 1996, p. 33.

——, "Big Deal: Kiwi Airlines," *Mediaweek,* April 15, 1996, p. 58.

Underwood, Elaine, "New Kiwi Marketing Chief to Scrap 'Bird' Campaign for Quality Message," *Brandweek,* September 30, 1996, p. 14.

Velloci, Anthony L., Jr., "Concern for Kiwi Intensifies," *Aviation Week and Space Technology,* January 22, 1996, p. 33.

——,"Kiwi Strives to Minimize Impact of Partial Grounding, " *Aviation Week and Space Technology,* July 1, 1996, p. 32.

——, "Bankrupt Kiwi Seeks New Funds to Rebuild Route Structure," *Aviation Week and Space Technology,* October 7, 1996, pp. 23–24.

——, "Bankrupt Kiwi Seeks Quick Financial Rescue," *Aviation Week & Space Technology,* October 21, 1996, pp. 40–41.

——, "Financing May Provide Kiwi With Second Lease on Life," *Aviation Week and Space Technology,* December 16, 1996, p. 67.

Veverka, Mark, "Once-Green Kiwi Air Flying Into the Black," *Crain's Chicago Business,* October 3, 1994, p. 7.

Wilke, Michael, "Kiwi Airline Looks to New Agency for Lift," *Advertising Age,* January 22, 1996, p. 8.

——, "Kiwi Climbing Aboard High-Flying Promo Trend," *Advertising Age,* April 29, 1996, p. 21.

——, "Kiwi Gives Safety Them a Lift in Ads," *Advertising Age,* July 15, 1996, p. 4.

——, "Delta, Kiwi Forge On With $25 Million in Ads," *Advertising Age,* July 22, 1996, p. 4.

Zellner, Wendy, "The Startups Start to Stall," *Business Week,* December 9, 1996, pp. 64–66.

—Frederick C. Ingram

Koch Industries, Inc.

P.O. Box 2256
Wichita, Kansas 67201
U.S.A.
(316) 828-5500
Fax: (316) 828-5500
Web site: http://www.kochind.com

Private Company
Incorporated: 1942 as Rock Island Oil & Refining
Company
Employees: 13,000
Sales: $30 billion (1996 est.)
SICs: 1311 Crude Petroleum & Natural Gas; 2899
Chemicals & Chemical Preparations, Not Elsewhere
Classified; 2911 Petroleum Refining; 3089 Plastic
Products, Not Elsewhere Classified; 3443 Fabricated
Plate Work (Boiler Shops); 3599 Industrial &
Commercial Machinery & Equipment, Not Elsewhere
Classified; 4612 Crude Petroleum Pipe Lines; 4613
Refined Petroleum Pipe Lines; 5171 Petroleum Bulk
Stations & Terminals

Koch Industries, Inc., a diversified petrochemical company, is the second-largest privately held firm in the United States, trailing only Cargill. The bulk of Koch's revenue is derived from the transport of oil by pipeline, truck, and ship, but it also drills, refines, markets, and trades oil and gas products in the United States and around the world. In addition, the firm has substantial coal, chemical, and real estate interests, and raises many thousand head of cattle on ranches in Kansas, Montana, and Texas. About 80 percent of its multibillion-dollar assortment of assets is owned by two of the four sons of Fred C. Koch, founder of the company, while two other sons were bought out in 1983 after a bitter and continuing struggle among the brothers for money, corporate control, and pride. Traditionally a very secretive company, Koch has seen various lawsuits and investigations in the 1980s and 1990s pull away some of its veil.

Founder Battled Big Oil and Made Initial Fortune in the Soviet Union

The son of a Texas newspaperman, Fred C. Koch earned an engineering degree at Massachusetts Institute of Technology in the 1920s. Koch invented a new and more efficient method for the thermal cracking of crude oil, the process by which oil is heated to effect a recombination of molecules yielding higher proportions of usable compounds, especially gasoline. With the dramatic growth in the use of the automobile in the first quarter of the 20th century, refiners were constantly trying to improve their cracking technology, and Fred Koch's innovation was apparently good enough to draw upon him the wrath of the major oil companies. Protective of their tight control over every aspect of the oil business, the majors began a series of lawsuits against Fred Koch that would last 20 years and involve over 40 separate cases, eventually being resolved in 1952 when Koch won a $1.5 million settlement. Then as now, the international oil business was in the hands of only a few firms, which meant that Fred Koch would encounter the same obstacles wherever oil was bought and sold.

In the late 1920s there was at least one country in the world where oil was not bought and sold, in the usual sense—the Soviet Union. The Soviets had been trying to take advantage of their immense oil reserves since gaining power in 1917, and under Joseph Stalin the drive to industrial efficiency was pursued with ruthless speed but without the benefit of Western technology. Fred Koch offered to build oil refineries in the Soviet Union that would be more efficient than those in the West. The young engineer's ideas were welcomed, and he was awarded a large contract to coincide with Stalin's first five-year plan, beginning in 1929. The contract called for construction of 15 refineries for an initial fee of $5 million, from which Koch and his partner, L. E. Winkler, are said to have netted a $500,000 profit. Koch's work in the Soviet Union necessitated sojourns in that country, offering the Texas farmboy an intimate look at the Soviet system while providing the cash he would later need in building his U.S. empire.

By the late 1940s Koch had achieved a truce with his adversaries in the oil industry and begun assembling bits and pieces of business in the Midwestern United States. Having been burned severely by the majors the first time around, Koch carefully

Company Perspectives:

Koch Industries is the second largest privately held corporation in the U.S. with more than 13,000 employees worldwide. Koch embraces a market-based philosophy to grow its businesses worldwide in refined products, chemicals, gas liquids, crude oil services, mineral services, energy services, capital services, road and construction materials, chemical technology, and agriculture.

Our common vision is one of discovery. Charles Koch, chairman and chief executive officer, speaks of "a company where employees are motivated to look for and seize opportunities, a culture where our people can take initiative, challenge the past and apply their knowledge."

Together, we're working to become a "society of explorers," where everyone practices humility, intellectual honesty, teamwork, and an acceptance of risk in support of better satisfying customers' needs.

avoided head-to-head competition with the industry leaders, instead developing a knack for discovering unexploited niches and an ability to turn a profit on even the smallest orders. In an age of massive, worldwide integration in the oil industry, Koch concentrated on service businesses too small to interest the majors and too obscure to attract much competition. While the majors largely controlled oil at the wellhead, they still required an ever-growing network of pipelines and trucks to convey the oil to the refinery, thence to the mass of distributors, wholesalers, and retailers involved in its final sale. As the country's dependence on oil grew, so too did the need for more complete systems of oil distribution, and Fred Koch amassed a fortune in providing the equipment and expertise to meet that need.

Koch's main vehicle in the oil business was a company called Rock Island Oil & Refining Company, based in Wichita, Kansas. While busy picking up bargains in businesses from trucks to coal mines, Koch fiercely guarded the privacy of his company, ensuring that it would not only remain under family control but also stay far from the prying eyes of government and the media alike. It is reported that a number of Koch's good friends in the Soviet oil industry were liquidated during Stalin's purges of the 1930s, an experience that only confirmed his belief, perhaps originally instilled by the battering he took at the hands of big oil, that business is best conducted silently. Rock Island Oil & Refining had no public relations department, having no relations with the public, and the Koch family went out of its way to avoid doing business with the government. Fred Koch's particular aversion to Soviet communism took a more direct form in 1958 when he helped found the John Birch Society, an ultraconservative group soon to become notorious for its warnings about the threat of communists to U.S. society. Charles Koch, the second of Fred Koch's four sons, would later pour millions of dollars into the Libertarian Party, a proponent of minimal governmental interference in the affairs of business.

Charles Koch Diversified Company's Operations

Like his father, Charles Koch earned an engineering degree at Massachusetts Institute of Technology, and then spent several years working for a business consulting firm before joining Rock Island Oil in 1961. Fredcrick Koch, Fred Koch's eldest son, did not participate in the oil business. Charles Koch took over leadership of Koch Engineering, one of the family's many concerns, and helped make it into the world's largest manufacturer of mass transfer equipment for the chemical industry. By the time of Fred Koch's death in 1967, sales at Rock Island and the various Koch subsidiaries had reached about $400 million, presenting the 32-year-old Charles Koch with a weighty responsibility. Charles Koch was not only a capable leader in his own right but also enjoyed the continued presence of his father's top aide, Sterling Varner. Varner had already won a reputation as a shrewd buyer of what he referred to as "junk," the bankrupt or unwanted oil and gas properties that Rock Island habitually turned into profitable acquisitions. Under the ambitious administration of Charles Koch, Varner kept a low profile but was widely credited with supplying the savvy behind the company's rapid expansion.

Charles Koch brought a young man's energy to the company. From the new Wichita corporate headquarters of the renamed Koch Industries, Inc., Charles Koch oversaw his company's diversification into a number of new areas, including petrochemicals, oil trading services, and ownership of a refinery in St. Paul, Minnesota. In 1969 Koch Industries merged with Atlas Petroleum Limited of the Bahamas, a distributor of crude oil and petroleum products with about $100 million a year in sales. The next few years saw the arrival at Koch of Charles's twin younger brothers, William and David, both of whom took executive positions with the company. While sharing their father's basic preference for privacy, the brothers gradually let it be known that Koch Industries was a far larger concern than imagined. In 1974 the family admitted to owning some 10,000 miles of pipeline in the Midwestern United States and Canada, hundreds of tank trucks, barges, deepwater terminals, and storage facilities of every description. Through this system Koch distributed about 800,000 barrels of oil each day, some of it refined at its St. Paul refinery, some sold via the company's several hundred gas stations, but most of it transported to and from the major oil companies. Koch also participated in the rush to buy supertankers, owning a handful of the huge ships to complement its oil trading offices in eight countries. Finally, the company had begun its own program of oil exploration and drilling, and also owned around 60,000 head of cattle. Sales reached more than $2 billion in 1974, the first full year of post-OPEC price inflation in the oil business.

The OPEC price hikes of the early 1970s effectively killed the supertanker business, however, forcing Koch to sell all but one of its ships at salvage prices. Nevertheless, the dramatic run-up in oil prices during the 1970s helped Koch increase its revenue sevenfold in a matter of years. By 1981 its sales had reached $14 billion, 56 times their level in 1967, Charles Koch's first year as head of the company, and in some quarters Koch was beginning to be called an oil major in its own right. The company picked up a second refinery in 1981, paying $265 million for a Sun Company plant in Texas, and had greatly expanded its capacity in gas-liquids fractionating and asphalt production, to name only two of its myriad activities. While Koch had little luck in its exploration efforts, in 1979 the company moved decisively into the real estate business, joining Wichita businessman George Ablah in the formation of Abko Realty Inc. Abko was created specifically to buy Chrysler

Realty Corporation and its several hundred Chrysler dealership sites around the country. It is believed that the hard-pressed Chrysler sold the unit for less than $100 million in cash.

Family Feud in 1979 Culminated in First of Several Lawsuits

The year 1979 also marked the beginning of the feud that eventually would split the Koch family. William Koch, five years younger than Charles, grew restive with his secondary role at Koch and began pressing his brother for more power, freer access to information, and some means by which a fair market value could be assigned to the company's stock. As a private company, the only likely buyers of Koch stock were other stockholders, who, in the absence of an open market, would pay far less than the shares might otherwise fetch. William Koch gained the support of the oldest brother, Frederick, until then relatively uninvolved in company affairs, and the two of them launched a proxy fight in 1980 aimed at ousting Charles from his leadership. The attempt failed, and after a round of lawsuits and mudslinging, William and Frederick Koch were bought out in 1983 by Charles and David Koch for around $1.1 billion in cash. From that time well into the 1990s, William Koch has continued to wage legal and emotional warfare against Charles Koch, going so far as to hire private detectives to gather evidence of wrongdoing by Koch Industries that was subsequently handed over to federal investigators. In 1987 the Justice Department announced it was investigating several companies on price-fixing charges, a Koch unit among them.

Later in the 1980s a U.S. senate investigation forced Koch Industries further into the limelight. In 1989 the Senate looked into charges that Koch had been stealing oil from Native Americans in Oklahoma by deliberately mismeasuring the crude oil it was buying. A committee concluded that Koch had stolen $31 million in oil over a three-year period. Koch vigorously denied the charges, and hired public relations experts for the first time to fight the battle of public opinion. The committee submitted its findings to the Justice Department, which three years later dropped the case. William Koch did not let the matter drop, however, and subsequently filed yet another lawsuit—this one for $400 million—alleging that Koch Industries had defrauded the federal government by stealing oil on federal land.

The parade of litigation continued for Koch in April 1995 when the Justice Department, the Environmental Protection Agency, and the Coast Guard filed suit against the company for allegedly being responsible for more than 300 separate oil spills since 1990. The government claimed that 55,000 barrels of oil were spilled from Koch pipelines, some of which polluted wetlands and, in the biggest offense, Corpus Christi Bay on the coast of Texas. Koch, which faced a penalty as high as $55 million but was likely to pay only $5 or $6 million, claimed that more than half of the spills cited by the government had never happened.

Dealmaking Continued in the 1990s

Meanwhile, Charles Koch continued to build the company through wheeling and dealing in the 1990s. Among the deals were: the $21 million purchase of a marine terminal and other pipeline and oil gathering systems from Ashland Oil Inc.'s Scurlock Permian Corp. in 1991; the 1992 purchase of the 9,271-mile United Gas Pipe Line Co., with annual sales of $370 million and a valuation of $1.1 billion; the early-1995 acquisition of a second refinery in Corpus Christi, Texas, from Kerr-McGee Corp.; the formation of Koch Paper Technology Group in mid-1995 to consolidate Koch's activities in the pulp and paper industry; and the $250 million acquisition in mid-1997 of Glitsch International Inc., a supplier of products and services to the petroleum and chemical industries, from Foster Wheeler Corp.

By 1996 Koch Industries had revenues of about $30 billion, a 300-fold increase in the previous 30 years. It operated more than 40,000 miles of pipeline, refined about 540,000 barrels of crude oil a day, was the largest buyer and seller of asphalt in the country, ranked in the top 10 among U.S. calf producers, and was the country's 34th largest landowner (according to *Worth* magazine). These diverse operations—many of which were often overlooked businesses that Koch specialized in making money from—together formed one of the world's great private fortunes. As a private company, Koch had the advantage of being able to move fast to pick up undervalued assets as soon as they became available.

Notwithstanding the various unresolved lawsuits, when Koch looked to the future it planned to become more heavily involved overseas and wanted to beef up its capital services unit which was involved in oil, commodities, and currency trading through offices in Wichita, London, and Singapore. Not as publicity-shy as it once was—the company had even created a web site by 1997—Koch Industries promised to continue its position as one of the country's most diversified and important industrial corporations.

Principal Operating Units

Refined Products Group; Chemicals Group; International Group; Energy Services; Crude Oil Services Group; Chemical Technology Group; Operations; Mineral Services Group; Gas Liquids Group; Agriculture Group; Capital Services Group; Materials Group.

Further Reading

"High Profit, Low Profile," *Forbes,* July 15, 1974.
"Koch Industries, Inc.: Sons Make a Global Enterprise Flower in Kansas," *Nation's Business,* February 1970.
Kraar, Louis, "Family Feud at a Corporate Colossus," *Fortune,* July 26, 1982.
McMillin, Molly, "Koch Has Grown Quickly, Quietly," *Wichita Eagle,* March 23, 1997.
O'Reilly, Brian, "The Curse on the Koch Brothers," *Fortune,* February 17, 1997, pp. 78–84.
Petzinger, Thomas Jr., "Charles Koch Teaches Staff to Run a Firm Like a Free Nation," *Wall Street Journal,* April 18, 1997, p. B1.
Suber, Jim, "Koch Industries: 'The Kansas Business Connection,' " *Topeka Capital-Journal,* May 5, 1997.
Tomsho, Robert, "Blood Feud: Koch Family Is Roiled by Sibling Squabbling over Its Oil Empire," *Wall Street Journal,* August 9, 1989, pp. A1, A7.
Wayne, Leslie, "Pulling the Wraps Off Koch Industries," *New York Times,* November 20, 1994, pp. F1, F8, F9.

—Jonathan Martin
—updated by David E. Salamie

Kuhlman Corporation

3 Skidaway Village Square
Savannah, Georgia 31411
U.S.A.
(912) 598-7809
Fax: (912) 598-0737

Public Company
Incorporated: 1897 as Kuhlman Electric Co.
Employees: 2,782
Sales: $456.4 million (1996)
Stock Exchanges: New York
SICs: 3612 Transformers Except Electronic; 3357
    Nonferrous Wiredrawing & Insulating; 3714 Motor
    Vehicle Parts & Accessories

One of the fastest-growing companies in the United States, Kuhlman Corporation is an industrial manufacturing company with its business divided into two business segments: Electrical Products and Industrial Products. The Electrical Products half of Kuhlman represented its core, the company's greatest money-earner and the historical foundation of the Savannah, Georgia-based concern. Within the company's Electrical Products division were Kuhlman Electric and Coleman Cable, manufacturers of electric power transformers and electrical and electronic wire and cable, respectively. Kuhlman's Industrial Products segment comprised Schwitzer, Inc. and Emtec Products Corporation. Schwitzer, founded in 1918, manufactured turbochargers, cooling fans, fan drives, and crankshaft vibration dampeners for the automotive industry. Emtec produced a variety of spring and spring assembly products. During the mid-1990s, Kuhlman operated 17 facilities in 11 states and in two foreign countries (England and Brazil). Kuhlman products were sold in more than 60 countries worldwide.

Early History

Kuhlman Electric was formed in 1894 and incorporated three years later in Indiana as Kuhlman Electric Company. The company retained its name when another incorporation took place in Michigan in 1915. Kuhlman Electric from this point forward operated as a manufacturer of transformers for the electrical utility industry, its principal business for roughly a half-century and its exclusive business until the company acquired Detroit Electric Furnace Company in 1938 and began manufacturing small metal melting furnaces. The addition of Detroit Electric Furnace contributed only a small percentage to the company's total revenue volume, however, leaving Kuhlman Electric overwhelmingly dependent on the production of transformers for revenue. For decades the company remained in this state, doing little to distinguish itself from the scores of manufacturers in its industry and realizing little appreciable physical or financial growth. The company relied on a single manufacturing facility in Bay City, Michigan, during these years, and devoted itself nearly completely to manufacturing devices that regulated electrical currents.

The Kuhlman Electric of the first half of the 20th century was vastly different than the version operating during the latter half of the century. The company that exited the 20th century was a fast-growing, diversified, global competitor bent on expansion and acquisition to record significant growth. The turning point bridging these two distinct eras in the company's history occurred in 1952, when management resolved to extend Kuhlman Electric's geographic reach and enter new business areas. That watershed year divorced the company from its comparatively sleepy past and pointed it toward a future of steady growth, forever changing the character of Kuhlman Electric.

Diversification Begins in the 1950s

Management in the early 1950s first set itself the task of increasing Kuhlman Electric's manufacturing capacity and broadening its geographic scope, objectives that were intended to achieve greater penetration of the electrical transformer market. A second manufacturing plant was constructed in Crystal Springs, Mississippi, in 1952, followed by the establishment of a third manufacturing facility in Salinas, California, three years later. The erection of facilities in 1952 and 1955, and the extension of the company's presence out on the West Coast provided Kuhlman Electric with a newfound capability to serve the most important markets in the country, rather than serving

Company Perspectives:

We at Kuhlman have a clear vision of our corporate goals. We want to be a larger, more diversified company that continues to provide our shareholders with significant returns and consistent earnings growth over an extended period of time. We believe that through size and diversification, we can benefit from greater financial strength and avoid the cyclicality often associated with companies operating in a single industry or geography, with limited product offerings. Just as we are dedicated to serving our shareholders, we are similarly dedicated to the growth and development of all our employees worldwide. Their well-being and advancement not only improve their lives, but also enhance the progress of our Corporation.

just the middle portion of the country as the company previously had done. With the company's initial expansion plan completed, management next moved to complete its other objective, one that led to the multifaceted profile of the company during the 1990s.

In the strategic plan first implemented in 1952 there were two objectives. One was to strengthen the company's mainstay transformer business, which the construction of additional manufacturing facilities had accomplished, and the other was to lessen Kuhlman Electric's dependence on transformers, that is, to make the mainstay business less of a mainstay. Kuhlman Electric derived 95 percent of its revenue from transformer sales to electrical utilities, and management wanted that figure reduced. It did not intend to increase the five percent contributed by the company's involvement in manufacturing metal melting furnaces (Detroit Electric Furnace's contribution in fact would be reduced), so the quickest and most obvious method to reduce dependence on transformers was to add other business interests through acquisitions. This the company did in 1957 when it acquired California Export Processing Company, a processor of sheet metal parts for the automotive industry. The acquisition proved to be a boon to the company's bottom line. California Export, which rust-proofed, painted, and finished a large variety of car parts, including fenders, hoods, doors, panels, and tops, began contributing a significant percentage to Kuhlman Electric's total revenue volume as soon as it was assimilated into the company's corporate structure as a car-parts processing division.

Expansion and diversification drove annual sales up to $13.7 million by the beginning of the 1960s, in what would turn out to be Kuhlman Electric's most prolific decade of financial growth since its formation. Much of the growth realized during the 1960s was achieved through acquisitions, a means of expansion Kuhlman Electric's management did not abandon after the purchase of California Export. The company acquired Detroit-based U.S. Molding Fiberglass Corporation in 1963, renewing its efforts to diversify, but the foray into this business area proved to be only a dalliance. U.S. Molding was sold in 1964, by which point the company had seized a company whose tenure within Kuhlman Electric's fold would span two decades.

In 1964, at a juncture when the production of transformers accounted for a much reduced 48 percent of Kuhlman Electric's revenue volume, the company acquired Meier Brass & Aluminum Company, based in Hazel Park, Michigan. Meier Brass, which was christened Meier Metal Servicenters under the auspices of Kuhlman Electric, operated eight facilities that processed a wide range of metal products, such as rods, bars, coils, sheet, plate, tube, pipe, and wire for an equally wide variety of industries. The effect of the Meier acquisition ranked higher than the purchase of California Export in terms of the objectives pursued by Kuhlman Electric's management. One year after its acquisition, Meier was responsible for 35 percent of Kuhlman Electric's total revenue volume, by which point the company's car-parts processing division was contributing 12 percent to total revenue. By the mid-1960s, when annual sales stood at $36 million, or nearly three times their height at the beginning of the decade, the acquisitions completed since 1957 accounted for 50 percent of the increase in sales. In less than a decade the manufacturer of transformers had transformed itself, developing into a diversified manufacturer recording energetic leaps of financial growth instead of the measured steps realized during its first half-century of existence.

One more important acquisition was completed before the 1960s were concluded, and that was the purchase of Quality Spring Products, Inc., a manufacturer of a broad range of mechanical springs for the automotive, home appliance, building, and electric industries. By the end of the 1960s, after registering a robust 16 percent annually compounded growth rate in sales during the decade and after erecting a new transformer plant in Versailles, Kentucky, Kuhlman Electric was generating more than $50 million in sales a year and stood as a vastly different company than the one that had entered the 1950s. The company's management acknowledged as much in 1967 when the more general corporate title "Kuhlman Corporation" replaced "Kuhlman Electric Company." Kuhlman Electric subsequently became a subsidiary of Kuhlman Corporation.

Exiting the defining 1960s, Kuhlman comprised six divisions, three of which—Distribution Transformer, Power and Specialty Transformer, and Detroit Electric Furnace—were pre-1950s constituents. Together, Kuhlman's two transformer divisions accounted for 57 percent of the company's sales, with Detroit Electric Furnace contributing an additional one percent. The remaining half of the company comprised divisions created from the three acquisitions completed between 1957 and 1965. California Export had been organized as Kuhlman's Export Processing Division, one of the largest independent rust-proofing operations of its kind in the world and a contributor of seven percent to total sales. Quality Spring Products Division, the mechanical spring manufacturer, contributed another seven percent to total revenue volume. The third member of the new companies to join Kuhlman was the largest, the Meier Brass and Aluminum Division, which delivered nearly one-third of total revenue volume and helped greatly toward the fulfillment of the corporate objectives pursued since 1952.

Kuhlman Takes Shape for the 1990s

The achievements of the 1960s provided Kuhlman Electric a range of different business interests with which it would enter its second century of business, shaping the company into a diversified manufacturer of electrical and industrial products, but the composition of the company's businesses during the 1960s was not identical to the Kuhlman of the 1990s. Some subsidiaries would stay, others would be sold, and several key acquisitions remained to be completed in the decades ahead. One of the prominent subsidiaries supporting the company during the 1990s was acquired in 1973, when Kuhlman purchased Emtec, Inc. Emtec, which was organized into Kuhlman's industrial products segment, strengthened the company's involvement in the spring business, entrenching the business area entered into through the acquisition of Quality Spring Products.

The next pivotal transaction in the company's history occurred 12 years later, when Kuhlman executives chose to sell one of the company's important divisions. Offered on the auction block in 1985 was Kuhlman's metal distribution operations, the division operated under the purview of Meier Metal Servicenters. Meier, since being acquired in 1964, had served as a valuable aid in reducing Kuhlman's dependence on transformers, generating a sizeable percentage of the company's total revenue volume for two decades. With Meier's departure, Kuhlman leaned on its newly-acquired plastics business, which had been gained several months before the divestiture of Meier when Borse Plastic Products was acquired in March 1985. The company's involvement in plastics was relatively short-lived, however. In 1990, Kuhlman sold its plastic operations to Solvay America, Inc. for approximately $45 million.

Much was accomplished on the acquisition front during the first half of the 1990s to give the company its corporate structure during the late 1990s. In 1993, Kuhlman paid nearly $9 million for Coleman Cable Systems, Inc., a leading manufacturer and distributor of a broad variety of electrical and electronic wire and cable products. With operating facilities in Arkansas, Florida, Illinois, and North Carolina, Coleman Cable figured prominently among Kuhlman's operating companies during the late 1990s, composing, along with the company's flagship Kuhlman Electric subsidiary, its electrical products segment. The other half of the company, its industrial products segment comprising Emtec Products Corporation, was fleshed out with the acquisition of Schwitzer, Inc. in 1995. Schwitzer, a leading designer, manufacturer, and marketer of turbochargers, cooling fans, fan drives, and crankshaft vibration dampeners, added more than $150 million in annual revenue to Kuhlman and gave it operating facilities in North Carolina, Indiana, Georgia, and in two foreign countries, England and Brazil.

As these acquisitions were being organized into the company, Kuhlman recorded impressive gains in its revenue volume. Sales during the company's 100th anniversary year in 1994 shot up 64 percent to $396 million, swelling to $456 million by 1996. Net income also registered animated growth between 1994 and 1996, jumping from $9.9 million to $17.3 million. The continued increase of these figures was of great interest to the company's management as it entered the late 1990s and charted its future course.

During the late 1990s, the company was pursuing an aggressive growth strategy aimed at developing Kuhlman into a larger, more diversified company, and acquisitions figured largely in fulfilling this objective. In 1996, two acquisitions were completed, Communications Cable, Inc., and Web Wire Products, that bolstered the company's electrical products segment, specifically in the fastest-growing areas of the wire and cable industry: telecommunications and data transmission. In early 1997, the company completed another acquisition, purchasing the Transportation Products Group belonging to Kysor Industrial Corporation. Once combined with Kuhlman's Schwitzer subsidiary, the addition of Kysor's Transportation Products Group created one of the world's leading providers of proprietary products used in commercial and industrial transportation applications. Further acquisitions appeared to be in the offing as Kuhlman prepared for the turn of the century, its management wholly focused on increasing the company's stature as a diversified manufacturer of electrical and industrial products.

Principal Subsidiaries

Kuhlman Electric Corporation; Coleman Cable Systems, Inc.; Schwitzer, Inc.; Emtec Products Corporation.

Principal Divisions

Electrical Products Segment; Industrial Products Segment.

Further Reading

"Heavy Utility Demand, Acquisitions Brighten Kuhlman Electric Outlook," *Barron's,* September 26, 1966, p. 23.

Hoddeson, David, "The Pressure's On," *Barron's,* May 1, 1967, p. 3.

Kirsch, Sandra L., "Kuhlman Corp.," *Fortune,* December 18, 1989, p. 128.

"Kuhlman Corp.," *CDA-Investnet Insiders' Chronicle,* April 1, 1996, p. 1.

"Kuhlman Corporation," *Wall Street Transcript,* December 29, 1969, p. 19,038.

"Kuhlman Sees Increased Transformer Demand," *Investment Dealers' Digest,* December 22, 1970, p. 30.

Loehwing, David A., "Power Regeneration," *Barron's,* October 29, 1962, p. 3.

—Jeffrey L. Covell

Leo Burnett Company, Inc.

35 West Wacker Drive
Chicago, Illinois 60601
U.S.A.
(312) 220-5959
Fax: (312) 220-6533
Web site: http://www.leoburnett.com

Private Company
Incorporated: 1935
Employees: 6,950
Billings: $5.4 billion worldwide (1996)
SICs: 7311 Advertising Agency

No other advertising agency in the world has created so many memorable and marketable "product characters" as Leo Burnett Company, Inc. The Jolly Green Giant, Morris the Cat, and Charlie Tuna are all Burnett inventions. And that is only the beginning of the list. The near-unemployed Maytag repairman, the Pillsbury doughboy, Tony the Tiger, and the legendary Marlboro Man are also examples of the Leo Burnett agency's talent for giving a product an image that endears it to the consuming public.

The operating philosophy at Leo Burnett does not, however, involve instructing agency staff to merely foster recognizability for a client's product. Equally, if not more important, is the concept of "familiarity." In its advertising campaigns the Leo Burnett Company tries to establish a special rapport between producer and buyer and between agency and client. For this reason, Leo Burnett has been consistently more successful than its competitors in retaining customers for extended periods of time. Of its 31 accounts in the United States, half of them have been with the firm for 20 years or more.

Currently, the Chicago-based Leo Burnett Company is the 10th largest advertising agency in the world, the eighth largest in the United States, and one of only a handful of top-ten American agencies not headquartered in New York City. Ironically, the firm has never made growth one of its major goals or priorities. Rather than actively pursuing numerous, varied accounts, or increasing business by extending its services through diversification, it tends to take a more conservative approach to the business of advertising. It concentrates on winning a few "blue chip" accounts and keeping them for decades. Then, as the business and advertising expenditures of its clients expand, Leo Burnett also grows.

This approach to advertising is characteristic of the company's founder. Born in St. Johns, Michigan, on October 21, 1891, Leo Burnett attended the University of Michigan where he graduated with a degree in journalism. After college he obtained a position with Cadillac as the editor of an in-house publication and then became advertising manager in 1919. Later, he worked at Homer McKee Advertising in Indianapolis. In 1930 he was hired away from McKee by Erwin Wasey & Company of Chicago to assume the position of vice-president/creative head. Five years later Leo Burnett left Wasey & Company to form his own agency.

When Burnett first started his business in August 1935 he had one account, a staff of eight, and a bowl of apples on each desk in the reception lobby. The agency's only client was the Minnesota Valley Canning Company, which had formerly been with Leo Burnett's old firm. It had moved over to the fledgling Burnett agency because the management at Minnesota Valley liked Leo Burnett personally. "I want the little guy with dandruff and the rumpled suit," said the president of the company. To reward this display of confidence and loyalty, Burnett created the Jolly Green Giant.

In an industry centered in the high-fashion area of Madison Avenue in New York City, the Leo Burnett Company of Chicago was something of an oddity. Its ads tended to reflect a certain mid-American homeyness rather than eastern sophistication. The Green Giant and Kellogg campaigns typify this technique. Both have historically been aimed at the emotions of their respective audiences, portraying the products with a large degree of human warmth. Burnett used what he himself called "sodbusting corniness"—language and imagery that drive home a point by conveying a feeling of straightforward honesty. However, the "Chicago School" was more than just a creative philosophy. It was a commitment to a certain type of research and brand of workaholism.

Burnett was a firm believer in research but often felt that the questions traditionally asked in consumer surveys did not provide the advertising agency with enough information. Most surveys were conducted in order to determine which products and therefore which advertisements sold most effectively. While recognizing the importance of this type of investigation, Burnett wanted more. He wished to know whether his ads were "liked" by the consuming public. Always seeking a combination of image and language that would evoke the most positive emotional response, Burnett was one of the first to seriously use Motivational Research (MR) in advertising. This is not to say that the Burnett agency put advertising popularity above product sales. Burnett simply felt that if he could find out what people liked, he could more successfully create effective ads.

Motivational research became popular among a number of advertising firms in the late 1940s and 1950s, but the technique itself came under fire in the 1960s with the rising power of consumerism. Motivational Research was thought to be what gave advertising agencies the ability to influence buying patterns and behavior through psychological conditioning. That, of course, was not what Leo Burnett meant when he spoke of motivational research. He was constantly making public speeches imploring the advertising industry to be socially responsible and never to surrender the invaluable commodity of integrity. Nevertheless, motivational research was all but abandoned in the 1960s, although during the interim Leo Burnett had learned some of what he wanted to know about the American consumer's likes and dislikes.

During this time the atmosphere around the agency ranged from the hectic to the frenzied. Stories abound of Leo calling up his copywriters at various Chicago bars on Saturday nights to ask them to come in Sunday morning to rewrite still imperfect ad campaigns. What is more, the stories go, the writers were always eager to take Leo up on his "invitation." Leo Burnett either surrounded himself with like-minded, overly industrious people or his workaholism was contagious. He himself described the grueling creative review committee meetings as "being nibbled to death by ducks." The work, however, always paid off with ad campaigns that "stuck" in the mind of the consumer. Don Tennant, former worldwide chief creative officer, says of the agency, "They put their stamp on these brands and put a stamp on the American consciousness."

During the decade of the 1950s, the years of "I like Ike" and Pax Americana, the Leo Burnett Company was able to reflect the American values of strength, tradition, comfort, and family in its advertising campaigns. This talent won for the agency a number of new and profitable clients and secured those accounts already in the Burnett agency. A good example is the work the agency did for United Airlines. United, although it had a large market share of the passenger air travel business, was feeling the pressure of new carriers coming into the industry. For years United had been associated with the cold stainless steel of its airplanes and began for the first time to worry about its image. When it received the account, Burnett focused on the people who ran the airline rather than on the plane itself. This

gave rise to the "Fly the Friendly Skies" campaign. Similarly, the thematic catch phrases of "the best to you each morning" for Kellogg's and "you're in good hands" for Allstate carry with them a familial warmth and all-American appeal.

Marlboro Man Takes to the Trail in 1964

As successful as these campaign images were, none compares with the impact of the most famous Burnett creation, the Marlboro Man. In his book, *On Advertising,* David Ogilvy writes that, "Without any doubt, Leo's greatest monument is his campaign for Marlboro."

In the 1950s cigarette manufacturer Phillip Morris was having trouble selling its new filter-tipped Marlboros to an American public that had grown accustomed, during and after World War II, to smoking Lucky Strikes. Filtered cigarettes were viewed as unmasculine, and Marlboro could never claim more than 1% of the market share. So Burnett went to work creating a different image for it. He came up with a character that exuded masculinity and American heritage, namely, the cowboy. After the ad campaign's introduction in 1964, sales increased dramatically and Marlboro became and has remained the number one-selling cigarette brand in the world. What was particularly striking about the ad campaign was that it translated so well from television to magazine print and billboard advertising—an absolute necessity after cigarette commercials were banned from network television in the United States in 1970. The Marlboro brand was inducted into the Marketing Hall of Fame in 1994, due to its "enduring success in the marketplace," a success resulting from Burnett's work.

On the strength of its work for Phillip Morris, the Leo Burnett agency expanded to London by purchasing an interest in the firm of Legget Nicholson and Partners. In 1967 the company merged with Detroit-based D.P. Brother & Company, a move that added G.M.'s Oldsmobile to the company's list of accounts.

Continuing and Refining the Burnett Legacy: The 1970s

Leo Burnett died in 1971 at the age of 79. He left behind more than a successful advertising agency. He also left a personal legacy and a philosophy that encompassed both the business and creative aspects of advertising. The motto at the Leo Burnett Company was and remains, "Reach for the stars; you may not get one, but you won't come up with a handful of mud either." Nothing could possibly capture the homespun wisdom of Leo Burnett better. He kept a file called "Corny Language" and added entries to it whenever he overheard something in a passing conversation that struck him as honest and poignant. Most fundamental to the Burnett creative philosophy, however, was what Leo called "inherent drama." He thought every product possessed this quality and that it was up to him and his copywriters to uncover it. Inherent drama, he said, "has about it a feeling of naturalness which gives the reader an emotional reward. It is what the manufacturer had in mind in the first place when he conceived the product."

Yet the discovery and display of a product's inherent drama was not supposed to make the ad more striking than the product itself. The Burnett agency tried not to impose a "Burnett look" upon its customers. Instead, the specific client was given a "look" with Burnett's help. Also, the agency tended to measure the effectiveness of its creativity by way of sales rather than awards, an attitude that would occasionally draw criticism from the new breed of "idea" men in the industry. And the agency would sometimes be criticized for being overly cute, or for creating bland, homogenous advertising. The "Chicago School," some contended, was an antiquated concept that resulted in provincial, childlike campaigns. "Sod-busting" honesty, Burnett critics remarked, was passé.

New Directions, New Approaches Characterize 1980s and Beyond

Such criticism would not go unanswered. Both in the creative and business spheres, the Leo Burnett Company became increasingly more aggressive. It pursued and won the lucrative McDonald's account (stealing it away from Needham and Harper), began actively seeking foreign markets, and also ventured into the areas of service industries and high tech. From 1985 to 1988 the firm serviced computer peripherals giant Hewlett-Packard as a client, adding Noxell's Clarion cosmetic line, Proctor & Gamble's Bold detergent, and Hallmark Cards in 1988, and Pillsbury mixes in 1989. On the down side, accounts with candy giant Mars Inc. were lost to other agencies during the decade; in the face of declining profits, McDonald's would return part of its advertising business to Needham in 1990.

Industry-wide recognition for Leo Burnett's creativity also came to the firm during the 1980s. For instance, the Leo Burnett Company won more music awards at the 1985 *Advertising Age* magazine awards banquet than any other agency except J. Walter Thompson. The shift in posture and attitude symbolized by such increased recognition did not represent a change in fundamentals, however. The company had no intention of risking the "blue chip" clients among its 31 domestic accounts by altering the conservative campaigns that made those large, consumer-oriented accounts profitable. Agency heads did not wish to alter Leo Burnett in any way, just allow it greater latitude in dealing with changing industry trends. Said chairman and president John Kinsella, "I'm not against growth, but growing just to be bigger is not a goal at all."

During the 1990s the agency continued to experience a fluctuation in campaigns as well as clients. On the heels of a four-year slide in sales, long-time client G.M. dropped the "This is not your father's Oldsmobile" campaign and put its $125 million national account up for review in 1992. Noting that the Big Three automaker's action was the first client review that Burnett had ever participated in, *Wall Street Journal* reporter Joanne Lipman characterized the company as "a patriarchal empire which spawns devotion among employees and clients alike. . . known for coddling clients better than any other agency in the U.S." In what the *Wall Street Journal* characterized as a "stunning coup," Burnett ultimately retained the G.M. account. Equally symptomatic of the decade's fluctuating client base, Sony stayed with Burnett for three and a half years before placing its $40 million account in review; H.J. Heinz left the agency in 1994 after a long relationship, followed by Tropicana juice a year later.

However, Burnett gained votes of confidence from Phillip Morris and Miller Beer, who awarded the agency accounts for both the Benson & Hedges and Miller Lite products, respectively. In 1991 the Beef Industry Council chose the agency to handle its $25 million account, Fruit of the Loom joined the agency roster in 1992, and Seven-Up gave Leo Burnett the job of reviving its reformulated Diet Seven-Up brand soft drink, which Burnett continued until a conflict of interest forced the agency to resign in 1995.

Still Privately Owned, After All These Years

In an era of corporate giants, it had become unusual for a company with more than $2 billion in total billings to be privately owned. During the 1990s Burnett felt the pressure of such advertising conglomerates as the Interpublic and Omnicom groups, which could offer expanded services. When other major advertising agencies began to publicly trade shares, Leo Burnett was one of the few who did not. Instead, the company responded to the conglomerates by expanding its electronic services, producing online and Internet home pages through Giant Step Productions, which it acquired in 1996.

Leo Burnett also began to take its distinctly American approach to marketing overseas, gaining both the Vatican and Fiat motorcars among its several European clients, and exploring expansion opportunities in opening Asian markets, particularly for American cigarettes. In 1993, under the leadership of newly appointed CEO William Lynch and COO James Jenness, the company also began to streamline, cutting costs by trimming its work force through staff reductions and voluntary early retirement, and reorganizing its top managers into a six-member "global management group" led by Lynch.

The second half of the 1990s proved to be as unstable for Burnett as the first half had been, with Phillip Morris, under fire from President Clinton for its cigarette advertising, continuing to lose sales ground despite the agency's work for both Benson & Hedges and a revamped Marlboro campaign. In 1996 the company lost several of its blue chip accounts, including Miller Lite and United Airlines, whose announcement that it would be changing advertising agencies after 31 years with Burnett rocked the advertising world. Also in 1996 came the embarrassing news that Burnett had underestimated the McDonald's advertising budget to the tune of $20 million, forcing the firm to scramble to retain the fast-food king's confidence in the face of rising competition from other agencies.

On the plus side of the balance sheet, in 1995 Burnett won the account for Coca-Cola's Fruitopia, followed by the account for Surge, a new high-caffeine citrus beverage produced by the soft drink giant. Other clients gained during the second half of the 1990s included Reebok International, Rockport, Max Factor cosmetics, and United Distillers, who handed Burnett its global Johnnie Walker Black and Red Label Scotch whiskey accounts worth $80 million.

Due to the growth of worldwide billings during the decade, Burnett instituted a management shakeup in 1996 that created several new posts within the company in order to reapportion responsibility among an increased number of top-level executives. The following March, almost on the heels of the 1996 restructuring, the company ousted both its top management officials, and returned former chairman and chief creative officer Richard Fizdale to the CEO position he had held from 1991 to 1993. Calling the move a "coup" engineered by Fizdale, the *Wall Street Journal* noted that "morale at Burnett [had] slumped" due to the loss of United Airlines and Miller Brewing, and that the coup was in response to CEO William Lynch and COO James M. Jenness's efforts to "rein in lavish spending habits at the agency" at the request of the board of directors. While Lynch's cost-cutting measures led to three years of record profits, they also generated red tape and meetings, with morale dropping as more attention was spent "counting pennies" than pleasing clients.

Spirit of Company Founder Still Determining Factor in Future

Though Leo Burnett has been dead for several decades, his presence is still felt at the agency. Bowls of apples still grace office desks. His picture—a bald man with sloped shoulders, double chin, and a formidable lower lip, wearing a crumpled suit—hangs in every office, of which there are 38 in more than 32 countries. His words, "Steep yourself in your subject, work like hell, and love, honor and obey your hunches," still direct the work of the agency's many staff members. New CEO Richard B. Fizdale, a longtime Burnett veteran, as well as his vice-presidents and executive heads, remain dedicated to the Burnett method of advertising, where building long-term client relationships is primary. Nearly all of the chief officers at the firm began their careers with the Leo Burnett Company, which still rarely goes outside its own doors to hire its executives.

Despite the increasing competition by younger, leaner, aggressive firms, confidence in Burnett remains strong among the agency's many clients, inspired by the sales figures Burnett uses to gauge the effectiveness of its work. "Personality" and "warmth" are the two words which most accurately characterize the company's advertising campaigns, and clients know that such characteristics will not soon go out of style.

Principal Subsidiaries

Giant Step Productions.

Further Reading

Beatty, Sally Goll, "Leo Burnett Ousts CEO Who Cut Costs," *Wall Street Journal,* March 24, 1997, p. B1.

Cummings, Bart, *The Benevolent Dictators,* Crain Books, 1984.

Daniel, Draper, *Giants, Pigmies, and Other Advertising People,* Crain Communications, 1974.

Elsner, David M., "Leo Burnett: The Solid Sell," *Wall Street Journal,* January 12, 1977.

Hixon, Carl, "Leo," *Advertising Age,* February 8, 1982.

Lipman, Joanne, "GM's Oldsmobile Account Is Up for Review," *Wall Street Journal,* September 21, 1992, p. B4.

Yumiko Ono, "Eyes Turn to Management Change at Burnett, Imprint on Creativity," *Wall Street Journal,* July 22, 1996, p. B9.

—updated by Pamela Shelton

The Limited, Inc.

Three Limited Parkway
P.O. Box 16000
Columbus, Ohio 43216
U.S.A.
(614) 479 7000
Fax: (614) 479-7080

Public Company
Incorporated: 1963
Employees: 123,100
Sales: $8.64 billion (1996)
Stock Exchanges: New York
SICs: 5621 Women's Clothing Stores; 5632 Women's
Accessory and Specialty Stores; 5611 Men's and
Boy's Clothing Stores; 5641 Children's and Infant's
Wear Stores; 5961 Catalog and Mail-Order Houses

The Limited, Inc. is one of the largest corporate collections of specialty apparel retailers in the United States. The company owns and operates more than 5,300 stores throughout the United States and the United Kingdom, including big guns such as the Limited, Express, Structure, and Victoria's Secret. The Limited, Inc.'s holdings are separated into three main operating divisions: Women's Brands is composed of The Limited Stores, Express, Lerner New York, Lane Bryant, and Henri Bendel; the wholly owned subsidiary Intimate Brands, Inc. is made up of Victoria's Secret, Cacique, and Bath & Body Works; and Emerging Brands includes stores aimed at men and children, such as Structure, Abercrombie & Fitch, Limited Too, and Galyan's Trading Company.

The Early Years

The Limited, Inc.'s beginnings can be traced to 1961, when Leslie Wexner dropped out of law school and went to work in a women's clothing store owned by his father in Columbus, Ohio. After a short time there, Wexner suggested to his father that business would improve if the store concentrated on sportswear,

but his father, Harry Wexner, believed that a full product line was necessary to attract customers. Instead, he encouraged his son to try out the sportswear idea on his own, which Leslie Wexner soon did.

Two years later, in 1963, Wexner used a $5,000 loan from his aunt to open a 2,000-square-foot store in Columbus's Kingsdale shopping center. Wexner christened it The Limited, named after the limited line of merchandise it carried. Wexner's goal was to gross $100,000 the first year—a goal which was surpassed with sales of $162,000. This success soon prompted the opening of a second store.

By 1965, The Limited was so successful that Wexner's parents, Harry and Bella, closed their own store and joined him in running his new enterprise. Harry Wexner served as the company's chairman until his death in 1975. Bella remained on the board into the 1990s as corporate secretary, providing her son with advice on his business moves. One year after Wexner's parents closed up shop and joined him, The Limited opened its first corporate headquarters above its Eastland mall store in Columbus. The company's employee count had reached 100, and by 1968 The Limited's sales had surpassed the $1 million mark.

In 1969, with five stores in operation, Wexner issued The Limited's first public stock, traded over the counter. After going public, the company began to expand rapidly—too rapidly, in fact, causing earnings to collapse. Wexner responded by improving the efficiency of the company's manufacturing and distribution systems. In a brief period, what The Limited had done in order to survive became the company's distinctive strength.

Innovations and Growth Throughout the 1970s

After identifying The Limited's trouble spots, Wexner implemented a system of financial controls supported by electronic point-of-purchase terminals. These terminals allowed the company's Columbus headquarters to monitor inventory levels to see what was selling and where it was selling. This information helped the company aggressively mark down slow-selling items, which cleared shelf space for hot new items to be brought in. Although marking down slow-sellers was not necessarily a fresh idea, the speed at which The Limited's headquarters evaluated and authorized these markdowns was impressive. The computer lines that link The Limited's shops to corporate headquarters brought the company the flexibility and speed of a small privately run boutique. This became The Limited's competitive edge over department stores that were forced to stick to price adjustment budgets planned months in advance.

The Limited's 1970 annual report, produced with a common copy machine, was bold enough to predict that The Limited would become the largest and most profitable retailer of woman's specialty clothing in the nation, although, at the time, there were only six Limited stores in existence. Nonetheless, the company's confidence certainly paid off. By 1974, The Limited had more than 1,000 employees, and the company opened its 100th store two years later. In just over a decade, the company had carved out a niche for itself by selling to young, fashion-conscious women who could coordinate an entire wardrobe with one stop at a Limited store.

The Limited's purchase of Mast Industries in 1978 added to the company's efficiency and flexibility. Mast Industries, a supplier that contracted with more than 150 production facilities around the world, became The Limited's merchandise procurement arm. The acquisition of Mast, coupled with the electronic point-of-purchase terminals on line to headquarters, allowed The Limited to place orders, purchase, and restock shelves with its most popular merchandise within two to three weeks. In comparison, the company's department store competition required months to do the same. The Limited also added to its marketing strength when it opened its first distribution center, a 525,000-square-foot structure in Columbus.

Rapid Expansion in the 1980s

Meanwhile, on the retail end of things, The Limited did more than concentrate on a specific market segment; it segmented the segment. In 1980 it opened its first Limited Express store, which focused on the youngest of fashion-conscious women—teenagers—putting more trendiness into its designs than would go into its other women's sportswear. In 1982, The Limited Express was comprised of eight successful stores, and became a separate business that was later renamed simply Express.

The Limited's expansion and market segmentation did not stop there. In 1982 alone, The Limited acquired Lane Bryant, Victoria's Secret, and Roaman's, merging the latter with Sizes Unlimited. The Limited was also listed on the New York Stock Exchange that same year, and its employee count reached 10,000. Each of the 1982 acquisitions prompted the company to restructure portions of its existing business. The addition of Lane Bryant, which sold clothing for larger women, caused The Limited itself to drop its very largest sizes and restock shelves with lower-priced, more fashionable sportswear aimed at younger women. The company also signed a contract with Bonjour to produce jeans and other stylish sportswear in large sizes, giving the chain a new image. When The Limited purchased the Victoria's Secret stores and catalog enterprise, it legitimized women's purchase of sexy lingerie on a national scale. Victoria's Secret stores, full of floral and lace pillows, old English furniture, and classical music, projected a respectable image.

The Limited's procurement arm, Mast Industries, soon began to supply all of the Limited's subsidiaries. In 1984, when Limited buyers stocked stores with career clothes that no one would buy, the Limited was able to develop, place orders for, and receive the completely new and private Forenza line, all within a matter of months. This allowed the company to reverse a slump that could have been catastrophic.

Private-label goods such as the Forenza line, which The Limited manufactured specifically for its stores, were produced at low cost in other countries and sold domestically for whatever price the market would support. The private labels could support large markups because The Limited created a desirable image for each line. For example, the Forenza line sported a romantic Italian name, although most of it was produced in the Far East. Furthermore, garment tags bore the name of a fictitious designer, Maria Pia, a Limited production consultant whose name had appealed to Wexner.

By 1984 The Limited's sales had surpassed the $1 billion mark. That same year, the company was also listed on the London Stock Exchange. The Limited's growth showed little sign of slowing, and the company offered to buy the financially troubled Los Angeles-based retailer Carter Hawley Hale Stores for $1.1 billion, but the offer was rejected. The following year, The Limited acquired Lerner Stores, a chain of moderate-price shops that it made profitable within a year. Another purchase that year was that of Henri Bendel, a store chain which catered to upscale, fashion-conscious women. In 1985 the company also opened its second distribution center, a 1.07 million-square-foot facility.

Net sales rose past $3 billion in 1986. The first Lerner Woman store, carrying larger sizes, was opened in addition to existing Lane Bryant stores, in order to capitalize on The Limited's name recognition. Limited Credit Services was also formed. In partnership with Edward J. DeBartolo Corporation, the company again attempted to buy Carter Hawley Hale, offering as much as $60 per share. Once again, Carter Hawley Hale rejected the bid, instead selling more than 3.5 billion shares to White Knight General Cinema Corporation.

In 1987, the company continued to expand into new markets when it opened two Limited International Fashion ''superstores,'' and also introduced Limited Too, targeting children. It merged Sizes Unlimited and Lerner Woman, while Express unveiled its men's collection. At this point, the corporation was made up of over 50,000 employees.

The following year, The Limited acquired Abercrombie & Fitch, which was a somewhat upscale store chain featuring casual wear for men and women. Some tagged it as The Limited enterprise's answer to J. Crew and The Gap. The company also debuted its own private-label intimate apparel business, Lingerie Cacique, and a natural-toiletries store chain called Bath & Body Works. Another new entrance on the retail scene was that of Structure, a casual and trendy clothing store for men. The company also opened The Limited Building, a one million-square-foot distribution center and office. Then, to weather a slump in The Limited's fashion world, the company enlarged its specialty stores, giving them more expansive window displays in an attempt to attract customers. Sales for 1988 topped off at $4 billion.

The Limited sold Lerner Woman in 1989 to United Retail Group, Inc., in an agreement that gave The Limited a one-third interest in United Retail and its holdings. The company also obtained a charter for Limited Credit Services to become the World Financial Network National Bank, making it the first U.S. retailer to transform its credit division in that way. The company was ranked first in growth and profitability among specialty apparel merchandisers by *Forbes* in January 1989.

The 1990s and Beyond

Entering the new decade, The Limited continued its string of acquisitions and retail expansion with the mid-1990 purchase of Penhaligon's, a perfume and luxury gift marketer based in London that was formerly a division of Laura Ashley Holdings. Throughout the following two years, the company also completed the acquisition of Gryphon Development, L.P., a producer of bath and personal care products, for a total of approximately $79 million.

Some industry experts questioned how long The Limited could continue to grow at such a pace. Many wondered if The Limited might be losing its market advantage by leaving its original niche of small stores with limited lines of cost-conscious merchandise, and moving to larger groups of stores that were more department store-like in nature. Also, many U.S. manufacturers began refusing to produce The Limited's private labels and thus operate at the company's breakneck pace.

In part of 1990 and 1991, The Limited experienced organizational and distribution difficulties which resulted in the late delivery of new lines of merchandise to many of its Limited stores. Same-store sales at Limited and the budget-priced Lerner began to decline, and the company made moves to once again boost profits. The Forenza clothing line, which had formerly been a Limited exclusive, was introduced at Lerner in an attempt to attract new customers and increase sales. Many of the company's other predominantly mall-based store chains were either restructured, downsized, or closed if proving to be unprofitable. The company also dealt with quality problems that had surfaced in relation to some Victoria's Secret merchandise. Despite these problems, the company's efforts helped it increase 1992 sales almost 13 percent to $6.94 billion.

In late 1993, The Limited sold 60 percent of its stake in Brylane, an entity that had come to encompass and operate the Lane Bryant chain, as well as other catalog sales operations. The transaction brought in $285 million to The Limited, which maintained its control of the other 40 percent of Brylane. The Limited also reduced its stake in the United Retail Group, Inc. to 20 percent. The company continued to reevaluate each store unit's success, subsequently renovating or closing some stores based on their potential for growth.

In 1994, after having successfully introduced its own credit card, The Limited signed an agreement with Next plc to open Bath & Body Works stores in the United Kingdom, marking the company's first stray from the U.S. market. The decision to make Bath & Body Works the company's first entrance into the United Kingdom was an interesting one, given that the U.K. was the headquarters of The Body Shop, a huge rival in the natural-toiletries market.

The following year The Limited not only opened approximately 400 more stores, but also continued its string of acquisitions and expansion into new retail areas. In July 1995, the company purchased Galyan's Trading Company, an Indiana-based sporting goods store chain, for approximately $18 million. This addition added to the already diverse line of products for which The Limited was responsible, prompting the company to restructure its holdings into three main operating divisions. Women's Brands became responsible for the operation of all women's apparel holdings; Intimate Brands came to encompass the lingerie and toiletries holdings; and Emerging Brands was composed of the men's, children's, and sporting goods lines.

That same year, Intimate Brands was spun off and became a separate business entity, although listed as a wholly owned subsidiary of The Limited, Inc. Stock shares of the new company were offered to the public for purchase, and Intimate Brands was listed on the New York Stock Exchange. The company achieved first-year sales of $2.52 billion, which came from over 1,200 Victoria's Secret, Bath & Body Works, Cacique, and Penhaligon's store units, as well as from Victoria's Secret catalog sales. Intimate Brands was also made up of Gryphon Development, which was responsible for the creation of the company's personal care products.

Approaching the end of the century, The Limited was continuing efforts to position itself for further growth and increased earnings. In 1996, the company sold nearly 60 percent of its credit services to a New York-based investment firm, and also announced plans to close some 200 stores early the next year. These moves were not necessarily indicative of financial trouble, but instead of The Limited's experience in evaluating its weaker areas and then positioning itself for success. Even through its tougher years, The Limited had posted increased sales each year during the 1990s. In 1996 sales rose almost $800 million to $8.64 billion, from $7.88 billion in 1995. With an impressive portfolio of retail holdings, years of experience and proven success in the retail arena, and the international market still almost completely open, The Limited, Inc. approached the turn of the century with great potential for continued growth and expansion in the future.

Principal Subsidiaries

Abercrombie & Fitch, Inc.; Bath & Body Works, Inc.; Brylane, Inc. (40%); Cacique, Inc.; Express, Inc.; Galyan's Trading Company, Inc.; Gryphon Development, Inc.; Henri Bendel, Inc.; Lane Bryant, Inc. (40%); Lerner New York, Inc.; Limited

Distribution Services, Inc.; Limited London-Paris-New York, Inc.; Limited Too, Inc.; Limited Service Corporation; Mast Industries, Inc.; Mast Industries (Far East) Limited (Hong Kong); Penhaligon's Limited (U.K.); Structure, Inc.; Victoria's Secret Catalogue, Inc.; Victoria's Secret Stores, Inc.; World Financial Network National Bank.

Further Reading

Baumgold, Julie, "The Bachelor Billionaire: On Pins and Needles with Leslie Wexner," *New York,* August 5, 1985.
The Limited, Inc. Fact Book: 1989–1990, Columbus: The Limited, Inc., 1989.
Machan, Dyan, "Knowing Your Limits," *Forbes,* June 5, 1995, p. 128.
Sparks, Debra, "Limited Appeal," *Financial World,* August 12, 1996, p. 36.
Trachtenberg, Jeffrey A., "Merchant in a Rush: Leslie Wexner Pushes Limited's Fast Growth Despite Retailing's Ills," *Wall Street Journal,* August 15, 1990.
"The Unlimited Limited," *Forbes,* November 15, 1977.
Weiner, Steven B., "The Unlimited?" *Forbes,* April 6, 1987.
Zinn, Laura, "Did Leslie Wexner Take His Eye Off the Ball?" *Business Week,* May 24, 1993, p. 104.

—Maya Sahafi
—updated by Laura E. Whiteley

Lindsay Manufacturing Co.

East Highway 91
P.O. Box 156
Lindsay, Nebraska 68644
U.S.A.
(402) 428-2131
Fax: (402) 428-2795

Public Company
Incorporated: 1969
Employees: 542
Sales: $136.23 million (1996)
Stock Exchanges: NASDAQ
SICs: 3523 Farm Machinery and Equipment; 3317 Steel
Pipe and Tubes; 3479 Coating, Engraving and Allied
Services, Not Elsewhere Classified; 3443 Fabricated
Plate Work (Boiler Shops); 4213 Trucking, Except
Local; 4212 Local Trucking Without Storage; 3599
Industrial and Commercial Machinery and Equipment,
Not Elsewhere Classified

Lindsay Manufacturing Co. is one of the two largest makers of center pivot irrigation equipment in the United States, and America's largest exporter of such equipment. The company has weathered the storms of a changing marketplace and retained its position in a field where many of its competitors have gotten out of the business. Its ability to adapt and to deploy new strategies in the unpredictable world of agriculture has been a major factor in its success.

Beginnings

Lindsay Manufacturing Co. was founded as a farm equipment repair business in the small Nebraska town of Lindsay in 1955 by Paul Zimmerer. Over the next few years he was joined by his sons, Bernard and Arthur. In 1969, the company was incorporated and began to manufacture its first irrigation system, under the ''Zimmatic'' name. The so-called ''center pivot'' system, which involves a central tower 11 feet above the ground, attached to a quarter-mile-long pipe standing on motorized towers which slowly rotates to irrigate a large area, had first been patented (by a Nebraskan) in 1952. Compared to traditional flood plain irrigation, where water moves by gravity across a field from its higher end, a center pivot system can use as little as half as much water. By 1971, Lindsay was having enough success to bring in professional business and manufacturing managers. The following year, the Zimmerer sons bought the company from their father, selling it to DeKalb Corp. in 1974. In 1978, the Zimmerers left active involvement with the company, Bernard moving to California and becoming a Lindsay dealer. Arthur Zimmerer was killed in an automobile accident the day after he left his post as a Lindsay executive.

Gary Parker, who had started at Lindsay in 1971, was named CEO in 1984, when the steadily growing company reached a peak in employment of 1100 workers and annual sales hit a high of almost $40 million. At this time the company's sales were largely to the domestic market, which was to lead to near-disastrous consequences when the farm economy hit the skids over the next several years, at the same time that the company's growing exports also slipped. In 1985, Lindsay's annual sales plummeted to $1 million, sliding back up to $6 million the next year. The company's workforce bottomed out at 307 in 1986. The strength of farm equipment sales were dependent on many factors, a primary one being the size of the farmer's pocketbook. This could vary greatly, depending on the weather, the length of the growing season in a particular year, the prices in the national or international marketplace, etc. A company that produced expensive equipment exclusively for farmers was thus highly reliant upon the farmer's good fortune to have a successful year. With a Zimmatic system costing as much as $80,000 to purchase and install, it was easy for a company such as Lindsay to have widely varying annual sales figures.

But Lindsay was already laying the groundwork for the future. A new line of Zimmatic equipment, ''Generation 2,'' was ready to go, and the company had begun to establish itself in Saudi Arabia, soon to be a highly lucrative market. The company also was making efforts to find other ways to make money besides selling irrigation equipment. One approach was to do contract manufacturing for other businesses, making use

> ## Company Perspectives:
>
> *At Lindsay, we will continue to cultivate opportunities as we strive to further improve performance and shareholder value.*
>
> *While the farm economy is cyclical, long-term demand drivers, including farmers' need to conserve water, energy and labor while stabilizing yields, will be a constant. Pressures to protect the environment and conserve water will continue to mount as governments and consumer groups at the local, state and national levels increasingly press for policies designed to preserve resources. With the ability to reduce water usage by 40 to 60 percent over flood irrigation as well as decrease leaching and runoff of fertilizer and chemical inputs, center pivot and lateral move irrigation is the clear choice for efficient, environmentally responsible crop irrigation.*

of excess capacity at the company's 500,000 square foot plant. This has included work for Deere & Company and Caterpillar, for whom Lindsay has produced components. Other contract jobs included projects as small as manufacturing the invention of a Nebraska weightlifter—a machine which "spots" for people lifting weights, keeping the weight from falling if it slips. The company also made and sold large-diameter tubing which was used mainly in grain-handling equipment. In other efforts to improve the company's bottom line, manufacturing efficiency was continually being improved, with a reduction in the man-hours required to build a center pivot from 500 in the 1970s to less than 200 a decade later.

Sales to Saudi Arabia Boom in the Late 1980s

Lindsay's biggest success in the 1980s came through the company's relationship with Saudi Arabia. The company had pursued international sales since the early 1970s, with some success in South America, South Africa, Spain, France, and Iran. In 1976 Lindsay first sent sales representatives to the Middle East, but it was not until 1983 that the first significant sales were made. In that year, the Saudi government, flush with the huge amounts of cash flowing in from its oil fields, decided to become agriculturally self-sufficient, and began to subsidize the production of wheat in the desert. According to Lindsay CEO Gary Parker, the country also wanted to influence its Bedouin tribes, traditionally nomadic herders of livestock, to begin to settle down and convert to wheat farming, which would help stabilize the country's borders. This was initiated by setting the price of a bushel of wheat at approximately six times the going international rate. Soon, companies like Lindsay and its leading rival Valmont (also of Nebraska) were selling large numbers of irrigation systems to the Saudis, as well as to some of their oil-rich neighbors. The company's export sales, which had risen from five percent of its total business in 1978 to 32 percent in 1982, stood at over 80 percent by 1988, with sales to over 50 countries in all. Lindsay maintained sales offices in Riyadh, Saudi Arabia, employing Saudi natives as agents in order to most effectively do business in a way that respected the country's customs. Lindsay also sent a number of its employees

from different areas of the operation over, to get a feel for what the Saudis wanted from the company, and encouraged its foreign customers to visit the factory in Nebraska to see how the equipment was made.

At about the same time in the mid-1980s that Lindsay had experienced a precipitous drop in American sales, the Saudis, beginning to show grain surpluses due to the success of their wheat subsidy program, dropped their guaranteed price in half. However, while several competitors got out of the center pivot market at this point, Lindsay persevered, impressing the Saudis with their commitment to the business and successfully making the shift in sales from large project farms to individual farmers. The company also was working to find ways to spring back in the United States, seeking to increase sales of other products such as its "lateral move" irrigation devices. These were designed to better fit the needs of farmers who, as in California, could not afford to lose the revenues from the corners of expensive plots of land which were not irrigated by the circular reach of a center pivot.

In 1988 DeKalb Corp. divided itself into four companies, with Lindsay being spun off as a single entity. It was offered publicly on the NASDAQ market in October 1988. Lindsay's export sales had become the largest part of its business, and were driving the company's strong annual figures at the end of the 1980s. In 1990, Lindsay's sales had risen to $99 million, and its employment figures had also gone back up to over 500 from the low point of the mid-1980s. The company estimated it had manufactured over two-thirds of the irrigation systems in use in Saudi Arabia by that time. Lindsay was now appearing in annual rankings such as *Business Week* magazine's "Top 100 Small Businesses," where it was recognized for several years in a row.

Transitions in the 1990s

In 1991 Lindsay announced the introduction of a new computer controlling system for its irrigation equipment. The Automated Irrigation Management System, or AIMS, was available on Lindsay's center pivot and lateral move irrigation systems. The computer device allowed the user to program a week's worth of movement into the irrigation equipment, with options such as varying amounts of water, fertilizer, or chemicals that could be dispensed to different parts of a field. This enabled the farmer to make fewer trips to the field to adjust the equipment. Lindsay had previously introduced its Remote Monitoring and Control system, which was a radio-control device that performed some of the same functions. Also in 1991 the company lost a $7 million lawsuit against a well drilling contractor. Lindsay had claimed that in 1983, poorly drilled monitoring wells caused pollution from a waste pit to leach into the groundwater in the area, but the court ruled that Lindsay would have to pay for the cleanup itself. The company had prevailed the year before in a judgment against Warner Electric Brake and Clutch, being awarded $1.5 million in damages for faulty center pivot braking systems sold to Lindsay.

The invasion of Kuwait by Iraq in 1991 initially caused some concern at the company, which brought its staff in Saudi Arabia back to the United States out of fear for their safety. The Gulf War only slowed sales briefly, however, and actually generated some good publicity. American news gatherers, restricted by the Pentagon from reporting on much of the action, turned to writing stories about Saudi Arabia, and several articles appeared in the American media on the marvelous circles of grain growing in the desert. When the war ended, strong sales continued to the Saudis, until 1993 when the government suddenly cut back on its support for domestic agriculture. At this time the declining price of oil on the international market and the fact that Saudi Arabia was producing more wheat than the country needed led the government to put an end to its grain subsidies. Lindsay's annual sales to the Saudi kingdom fell from $44 million in 1991 to only $8 million three years later. However, while this was happening the United States farm economy was doing well enough for Lindsay's annual domestic sales to increase by 53 percent in 1994, for a record tally of $77 million. This, plus increasing sales to Latin America and Western Europe, effectively offset the losses in Saudi Arabia so that Lindsay maintained profitability with barely a dip in its year-end sales total of $112.7 million.

From the late 1980s onward, the company had been able to put away strong cash reserves. It was often announced that Lindsay was looking to acquire another company, but no acquisition materialized. Lindsay continued in the late 1990s to seek a compatible company to purchase, while its annual sales curve became relatively stable compared to the precipitous increases and decreases of the 1980s. Lindsay also continued to improve its manufacturing process, investing $3 million in robotics at its plant and offering employee incentives to improve productivity. Where there had once been as many as 75 American makers of center pivot irrigation equipment, by the 1990s only seven remained in business. Of those, Lindsay and Nebraska rival Valmont were the top two, Valmont the leader in domestic sales and Lindsay the top exporter.

Lindsay Manufacturing, while concentrating on the production of a highly specialized product, farm irrigation equipment, managed to ride out the vagaries of the marketplace in the 1980s and 1990s to emerge with strong cash reserves and steadily increasing annual sales. Through the introduction of product improvements, by continuing to develop new strategies to increase sales and operating efficiency, and by utilizing its large manufacturing plant for subcontracting work, the company has successfully found a path that should lead it to continued success through the end of the 1990s and beyond.

Principal Subsidiaries

Lindsay International Sales Corp.; Lindsay Transportation, Inc.

Further Reading

Browning, E. S., "Heard on the Street: Water, Water, Everywhere? The Bass Brothers Don't Seem to View That as a Likely Scenario," *Wall Street Journal*, December 15, 1995, p. C2.

Cook, James, "Making Every Drop Count," *Forbes*, April 29, 1991, pp. 103–04.

Flanery, James Allen, "Saudi Wheat Grower Gets $27.50 a Bushel: Nebraska Sprinklers Water Desert," *Omaha World-Herald*, October 21, 1984.

Garrett, Echo Montgomery, "Secrets of the Rainmaker," *World Trade*, April, 1993, pp. 52–55.

"Irrigation Firm Wins in Court," *Omaha World-Herald*, May 21, 1990, p. 16.

Jones, John A., "Lindsay Boosts Capacity with Demand for Irrigation Rigs," *Investor's Business Daily*, July 2, 1996, p. A18.

Jordon, Steve, "More Manufacturing Jobs for Nebraska—Independent Lindsay Plans Purchases," *Omaha World-Herald*, November 13, 1988, p. 1M.

"Lindsay Irrigation Firm Sprinkles Development in Saudi Arabia," *Omaha World-Herald*, December 25, 1990, p. 51.

"Lindsay Manufacturing Co. Wins Award for Export Sales," *Omaha World-Herald*, May 24, 1988.

McMorris, Robert, "Device Dreamed Up During Layoff—Man's Injury Aids Weight Lifters," *Omaha World-Herald*, November 10, 1990, p. 31.

"Owner Up the Creek Over Tainting of Aquifer," *ENR*, November 21, 1994, p. 72.

Rasmussen, Jim, "Lindsay Ranks 12th on Small-Firm List," *Omaha World-Herald*, October 30, 1990, p. 13.

——, " 'Most Dynamic' Lindsay Still Confident in Saudi Arabia Market," *Omaha World-Herald*, January 25, 1991, p. 20.

——, "Lindsay Offers Panel Computer Monitors Irrigation Systems," *Omaha World-Herald*, July 16, 1991, p. 11.

Samuelson, James, "Desert Storm," *Forbes*, March 27, 1995, p. 68.

—Frank Uhle

LIVE Entertainment Inc.

15400 Sherman Way, Suite 500
Van Nuys, California 91406
U.S.A.
(818) 988-5060
Fax: (818) 908-9539

Public Company
Incorporated: 1988
Employees: 119
Sales: $140.1 million (1996)
Stock Exchanges: NASDAQ
SICs: 7812 Motion Picture, Video Tape Production; 7822
   Motion Picture, Video Tape Distribution

LIVE Entertainment Inc. is one of the leaders in independent film production and videocassette distribution in the United States. Located in Los Angeles, California, LIVE was founded in February 1988 by former RCA employee Jose Menendez when he merged Lieberman Enterprises Inc. and International Video Entertainment. Growth began almost immediately when, in March, LIVE paid more than $6 million to acquire part of Vista Organization Home Video Corporation and then brought in nearly $25 million when they liquidated their Video Technology Services division.

Rough Waters, 1989–91

This film distribution leader has had its share of troubles during its history, however. Overambitious and attempting to expand too fast, LIVE floundered when, in headlines that would shock not just the film and music world, founder and CEO Menendez and his wife Kitty were murdered in their Los Angeles home by sons Lyle and Erik in August 1989.

In the next few years following Menendez's death, LIVE would fight an uphill battle to stay afloat. Running through capital at breakneck speed and operating at near debt capacity, the company continued to overreach itself with continued acquisitions through July 1991. LIVE, the parent company, picked up Straw-

berries Music, Movies & More (a chain of specialty retail stores) and Waxie Maxie Inc. (a specialty retailer of audio records and tapes, compact discs and video products) for approximately $54 million. The Lieberman subsidiary bought Navarre Corporation, a Minnesota-based company primarily engaged in the business of rackjobbing personal computer software, for $5 million, picked up over 80 percent of VCL, a distributor of home videos to the German-speaking worldwide market, for another $6 million in cash and $2.5 million promised, and acquired most of Vestron Inc. for another $21 million, leaving the subsidiary with debt of approximately $42 million. Some of that was recouped when LIVE sold most of Lieberman Enterprises Inc., including Navarre Corporation, to Handleman Co. for approximately $75 million. The bankruptcy of Ames Department Stores, a major account for LIVE, caused company writeoffs in 1990, hurting the company even more. And to top it all off, when Wal-Mart purchased Western Merchandisers in 1989, rackjobbers such as Lieberman were afraid that major disaffiliations would occur with outside rackjobbers.

Luckily, in what industry analysts would call "A Turtle Year," LIVE shipped almost nine million copies of *Teenage Mutant Ninja Turtles* on videocassette, bringing in sales of approximately $27 million. *Total Recall* was released late in 1990 and brought another $6 million. The sales from these two films, combined with another $34 million in sales from their home video catalog in 1990, helped LIVE manage to stay alive long enough to file for Chapter 11 Bankruptcy in California in 1992, which was approved in 1993.

Corporate Leadership Turnovers

Operating capital was not the only thing flying fast and furious at LIVE. Corporate leaders played musical chairs for many years. In an attempt to stabilize the management hierarchy after Menendez's death, Wayne Patterson, former chairman of Pace Membership Warehouse, was hired as CEO and Theodore Bean as CFO in 1990. It was hoped that the experience Patterson had in turning Pace around and selling it to Kmart would work for LIVE.

In what *Forbes*'s Lisa Gubernick would call "a revolving-door executive suite," two other CEOs and assorted other

Company Perspectives:

LIVE Entertainment Inc., headquartered in Los Angeles, California, is a diversified entertainment company organized to develop, produce, market and distribute pictures on a worldwide basis via distributors internationally and direct domestic distribution. LIVE acquires and finances the production of projects from independent producers as well as acquires distribution rights to projects in various stages of completion.

officers attempted to steer LIVE in the right direction before Iowa-born accountant Roger Burlage left competitor Trimark Pictures in 1994 to head LIVE as its new CEO. He decided to "get the company back to its core business" and began unloading dead weight. In August of that same year, Ivan R. Lipton, president of the Strawberries subsidiary of LIVE, along with 15 other subsidiary leaders and Castle Harlan Inc., purchased the Specialty Retail division of 155 stores for $35 million. Burlage also cleaned house, removing high-ranking officials such as LIVE Home Video's president David Bishop and vice president of sales and marketing Stuart Snyder and bringing in new figures such as Vision International's Elliott Slutzky and Epic Home Video's Jeff Fink to replace them. Other people such as Tim Landers and Ronald B. Cushey were brought in about this time, too, to take the positions of head of national sales for rental videos and CFO, respectively. Many of the people Burlage brought in have remained at LIVE to this day.

In what experts predicted could have been a financial disaster, LIVE, in 1991 in an effort to grow vertically, offered a merger with independent film production company Carolco, which already owned approximately half of LIVE in the early 1990s and with whom LIVE had been doing business for a number of years. Carolco, suffering from underperformance of its films, despite its success with *Total Recall*, had an operating debt of $230 million and would have benefitted greatly from the merger, but LIVE would have been hard-pressed to keep the ailing production company alive. In 1994, under Burlage's direction, the merger plans fell apart, an event which proved to be fortunate for LIVE since Carolco later filed for bankruptcy and was liquidated.

Better Times

Although the company's corporate headquarters suffered nearly a quarter million dollars in damage from the 1994 Los Angeles earthquake whose epicenter was a mere six miles from their building, LIVE bounced back under Burlage's guidance. LIVE Interactive was formed in October of that same year to produce CD-ROM titles, the first being *Angels: The Mysterious Messengers*, capitalizing on the sudden boom in popularity of angel merchandise and literature. The year 1995 saw LIVE Interactive entering into a partnership with Enteracktion for further development of CD-ROM projects. The LIVE International division was also created in 1994 for feature film financing and distribution around the world. The Avid Home Video division, in association with Ikegami, introduced a new video

camera the same year at the annual convention of the National Association of Broadcasters in Las Vegas. The camera did not use tape and had editing capabilities.

In addition to dropping many of their money-eating subsidiaries, Burlage also drove the company to buy the rights to films more selectively. Beginning in 1995, instead of buying "B"-rated films indiscriminately, LIVE purchased the rights to films such as *Wagons East*, a comedy-western which featured John Candy in his final appearance prior to his untimely death, and *Stargate*, the science fiction action film starring Kurt Russell, James Spader, and Oscar-nominee Jaye Davidson, which shipped one million units for sale and almost another half-million for rental. When LIVE obtained the rights to *The Terminator* from financially-distraught Hemdale Inc., they combined it with *Terminator 2*, which it already owned and had set a record with when it shipped 700,000 units, and created "Collector's Packs" and within a very short time sold a half-million copies at $24.98; the first three movies in the Rambo series sold a quarter-million copies at $29.94. Indeed, 1995 was the first year since Menendez's death that LIVE once again showed a profit, bringing in almost $9 million on sales of about $150 million from a loss of $180 million in 1994.

The following year, 1996, LIVE picked up *The Substitute*, starring Tom Berenger; *The Arrival*, starring Charlie Sheen; *Maybe . . . Maybe Not*; *Phat Beach*; and *Trees Lounge*, starring Steve Buscemi. LIVE Home Video distributed 240,000 copies of *Cutthroat Island*, directed by Renny Harlin and starring Geena Davis and Matthew Modine, which set a new record for video sales of features having earned $10 million or less at the box office. And in the first few months of 1997, LIVE had already acquired the rights to distribute *Critical Care*, starring James Spader, Kyra Sedgwick, Helen Mirren, Anne Bancroft and Albert Brooks, directed by Sydney Lumet; *Suicide Kings*, starring Christopher Walken, Henry Thomas, Sean Patrick Flannery, Jay Mohr and Johnny Galecki; Wes Craven's *Wishmaster*; *Gentlemen Don't Eat Poets*, starring Alan Bates, Theresa Russell, and Sting; *Dead Men Can't Dance*, starring Kathleen York, Michael Biehn, and Adrian Paul; and Australian film *Hotel de Love*.

LIVE Family Home Entertainment (FHE) has become one of the most successful distributors of high-quality family entertainment. In early 1997, FHE had already distributed an animated special called *The Littlest Angel* based on the bestselling children's book of the same name, LIVE International distributed *Washington Square* and LIVE Interactive released CD-ROMs *The Arrival*, based on the theatrical motion picture of the same name; *Speedracer*, a fast-paced game based on the classic animated television series broadcast in over 60 countries; *Radical Rick*, an interactive adventure based on the popular comic book character who goes everywhere on his bicycle, and *The Dream*. FHE also holds the rights to a musical animated feature based on Tom Sawyer, *Princess Gwenevere and the Jewel Riders*, the world-famous *Hello Kitty and Friends*, *Phantom 2040*, *Highlander: The Series*, *Littlest Pet Shop* and *Flash Gordon*. Christmas classics such as *Rudolph the Red-Nosed Reindeer*, *The Little Drummer Boy*, and *Frosty the Snowman* also top the charts every year and FHE has added *A Monster Christmas*, *The Moo Family Holiday Hoedown*, and *Santa's Christmas Crash*.

In late 1996 and early 1997, LIVE, along with longtime competitor Trimark Pictures and newcomers DreamWorks, Polygram, and a revitalized Orion Pictures, in a risky move, geared up for theatrical distribution of films. Such companies as New World, Savoy, National General, DEG, Hemdale, AFD, AIP, Hammer Films, and Interstar had already tried that route only to fall by the wayside and the three companies still operating in that market, New Line, TriStar, and Miramax, have all been purchased by the major studios.

Future Predictions

Despite its ups and downs, LIVE continues to hold the rights to an outstanding stable of films in addition to those already mentioned, including Academy Award-winning film *The Piano,* plus others such as *Dirty Dancing, L.A. Story, The Doors, Basic Instinct, Reservoir Dogs, Bad Lieutenant, The Crying Game, Light Sleeper, Air America, Mountains of the Moon, Narrow Margin, Jacob's Ladder, Johnny Handsome, Music Box, The Arrival,* and *Paula Abdul: Get Up and Dance.* At the time of this writing, LIVE was in negotiations with investor group Richland, Gordon & Co. to be acquired, ensuring its future as a leader in film production and distribution, although, perhaps, under another name.

Principal Subsidiaries

Chatter Inc.; Lieberman Enterprises Inc.; LIVE America Inc.; LIVE Film and Mediaworks Inc.; LIVE Ventures Inc.; Silent Development Corp.; Tongue-Tied Inc.; Vestron Inc.

Further Reading

Christman, Ed, ''Consolidations Quieter, Still Active: Strawberries' Move Was Biggest in a Busy Year,'' *Billboard,* December 24, 1994, p. 63.

''Executive Changes Fast & Furious in Video Industry,'' *Billboard,* February 12, 1994, p. 5.

Fitzpatrick, Eileen, ''LIVE Tunes *The Piano* for Video Release,'' *Billboard,* March 26, 1994, p. 71.

Giardina, Carolyn, ''Major Players Show Strong Hands as NAB Opens in Las Vegas,'' *SHOOT,* April 14, 1995, p. 1.

Gubernick, Lisa, ''A Survivor,'' *Forbes,* March 25, 1996, p. 81.

Hindes, Andrew, ''Distribution Debs Take Walk on the Wide Side,'' *Variety,* January 20, 1997, p. 1.

''Investment Group to Buy LIVE Entertainment,'' *New York Times,* April 19, 1997, p. 21(N)/35(L).

''Investor Group to Acquire Home-Video Distributor,'' *Wall Street Journal,* April 21, 1997, p. B7(W)/B5(E).

Lichtman, Irv, ''The Billboard Bulletin: LIVE Wants Out of Retail,'' *Billboard,* April 2, 1994, p. 82.

''LIVE Entertainment,'' *Television Digest,* May 22, 1995, p. 13.

''LIVE Entertainment,'' *Billboard,* August 31, 1996, p. 103.

''LIVE Entertainment Inc.,'' *Wall Street Journal,* April 15, 1997, p. B16(W)/C24(E).

Nichols, Peter M., ''Attention, Shoppers!'' *New York Times,* February 28, 1997, p. B4(N)/B15(L).

''Patti Bodner,'' *Television Digest,* February 21, 1994, p. 17.

''Paul Almond,'' *Television Digest,* January 31, 1994, p. 20.

Peers, Martin, and Rex Weiner, ''LIVE and Still Kicking: Investors Circle the Wagons While Burlage Sets Fiscal Plan,'' *Variety,* September 16, 1996, p. 11.

''Roger Burlage,'' *Television Digest,* January 3, 1994, p. 12.

Sharkey, Betsy, ''Designs on Women,'' *ADWEEK Eastern Edition,* October 10, 1994, p. 24.

Spring, Greg, ''Carolco, LIVE Entertainment Go Their Separate Ways As Merger Fails,'' *Los Angeles Business Journal,* October 24, 1994, p. 6.

Weiner, Rex, ''LIVE, Carolco Call Off Wedding,'' *Variety,* October 17, 1994, p. 30.

——, ''Product Floods Market,'' *Variety,* October 30, 1995, p. M14.

—Daryl F. Mallett

LOGICON

Logicon Inc.

3701 Skypark Drive
Torrance, California 90505-4794
U.S.A.
(310) 373-0200
Fax: (310) 373-0844

Division of Northrop Grumman Corporation
Incorporated: 1961
Employees: 4,896
Sales: $476.1 million (fiscal 1996)
Stock Exchanges: New York
SICs: 7371 Computer Programming Services; 8711
    Engineering Services

Logicon Inc. is one of the leaders in the information technology and defense electronics business. Not quite as large as giant competitors Lockheed Martin and Northrop Grumman Corporation, Logicon, with an annual growth rate of about 10 percent, nevertheless managed to carve a niche out for itself in the field, with customers including the U.S. Department of Defense (DoD), the U.S. Federal Aviation Administration, the U.S. Department of Justice, the U.S. Department of Agriculture, the U.S. Postal Service, the U.S. Internal Revenue Service, the U.S. Army, Navy, and Air Force, and the U.S. Defense Nuclear Agency. Incorporated in California on April 10, 1961, and reincorporated in Delaware on July 28, 1978, as a successor to the first company, it eventually merged in 1997 with industry giant Northrop Grumman.

In the late 1960s, Logicon began performing tests and analysis on software and systems for the Minuteman missile, a task continued on into the 1990s, when their "Weapons Systems" unit also began doing the same thing for the Peacekeeper Intercontinental Ballistic Missiles.

The company was contracted in the mid-1970s by the U.S. Defense Special Weapons Agency (DSWA) for scientific and engineering technical assistance. Over the next 25 years, Logicon would participate in a number of projects vital to national security. One such project developed in the 1990s, especially after the Gulf War, was for Logicon's "Science & Technology" (S&T) division to develop counterforce options for national leaders to use when dealing with nuclear, chemical, or biological weapons. Another project had the S&T unit working on DSWA's Data Archival and Retrieval Enhancement (DARE) system and "Project Graybeard" which, together, would preserve and archive precious data on nuclear testing acquired since the mid-1940s.

In the late 1970s, after purchasing International Computation (Cambridge, Massachusetts) for $549,000 in 1974, Logicon began developing sophisticated diagnostic systems to test interoperability of tactical data links for the military, including the Multiple Unit Link Test and Operator Training System (used to test and certify data link systems and train operators) and the LMS-11 and LMS-16 (used to troubleshoot actual operation of Link-11 and Link-16 systems respectively). By the late 1990s, the Command, Control, Communications & Intelligence (C3I) division had developed a digital communications system for the AEGIS Computer Center which enabled the center to network and test its systems over large geographical distances using standard dial-up telephone lines.

Beginning in 1980 and for over a decade, Logicon went through a spate of expansionism, acquiring Operating Systems Inc. (Woodland Hills, California) in a stock exchange; R&D Associates (Marina del Rey, California) in similar fashion in 1983; Chase, Rosen & Wallace Inc. the same way in 1985. Eagle Technology was purchased for $9.3 million in 1989 and became Logicon Eagle Technology. In 1990, Fourth Generation Technology Inc. (La Jolla, California) was bought for $2.7 million. Logicon Ultrasystems Inc. was created in 1991 when the company acquired part of the Ultrasystems Defense unit of Hadson Corporation and, the same year, Logicon established a wholly owned subsidiary called Logicon Canada Ltd. The only break in the expansion of Logicon came in 1982 when the company sold its newspaper text-processing system business and, in 1992, decided to focus on relocating three operating unit headquarters and consolidating administrative support functions in order to tighten up its growing operations.

From 1983, Logicon's S&T unit was a key in a number of remote sensing and spectral imagery projects for the DoD, which led to a wide range of commercial applications such as

Company Perspectives:

Logicon is a leader in providing advanced technology systems and services, hardware and software, to support national security, civil and industrial needs in the following areas: Command, Control, Communications & Intelligence; Weapons Systems; Information Systems; Science & Technology and Training & Simulation.

geological surveying, agricultural analysis, and disaster assessment. Logicon would eventually create the Spectral Imagery Training Center, complete with its own publication, the Multispectral Imagery Reference Guild, for training people in these commercial applications.

In the late 1980s, Logicon began providing technical support to human performance research at the U.S. Air Force's Armstrong Laboratory at Wright-Patterson Air Force Base in Ohio where engineering and human factors evaluations of crew stations, cockpits, pilot workloads, situation awareness, helmet-mounted displays, and night-vision goggles were performed. Logicon was also the systems integrator in the development of the Synthesized Immersion Research Environment (SIRE) Laboratory, a state-of-the-art virtual reality facility used for developing and evaluating crew-station technologies for future pilots and where experiments are conducted on brain-actuated control (similar to the movie *Firefox,* where Clint Eastwood's character merely had to think in Russian for the MiG to operate), bioacoustics (adding stereophonic, three-dimensional sound and surround-sound clues to aid pilots in target acquisition), tactile displays, and data gloves.

Logicon became an important player in the U.S. Navy's Battle Group Passive Horizon Extension System (BGPHES) in late 1994. BGPHES is a first-of-a-kind tactical surveillance and reconnaissance system that has the demonstrated capability to link U-2 aircraft to a Battle Group Commander embarked on a carrier. In 1995, the company was awarded a five-year contract to continue development support on this system.

In 1995, the defense electronics industry began to rapidly consolidate. The bigger companies in this industry had been going at it since 1992, with such giants as Martin Marietta and Lockheed and Raytheon and Litton Industries buying companies left and right. Logicon seemed to start the ball rolling among the smaller companies when, re-adopting what CS First Boston analysts would call its "activist acquisition strategy," Logicon began expanding quickly again. On February 16, 1995, Logicon purchased Syscon Corporation (a wholly owned subsidiary of Harnischfeger Industries, Inc. engaged principally in the business of providing systems development, systems integration, and systems services to the U.S. government and commercial enterprises) for $45.3 million. October 1 of the same year saw Logicon acquire the Space and Engineering Group of Applied Technology Associates Inc.

When the government shutdown occurred, analysts wondered if the company would suffer since most of Logicon's

business (like that of other information technology businesses such as BDM International, CACI International Inc., BTG Inc., Nichols Research Corporation, and Tracor Corporation) derives from contracts for government defense projects. But the shutdown did not affect the company adversely at all. The company's pursuit of new business in the "Information Technology" field resulted in Logicon being awarded a five-year, $200 million contract from the Internal Revenue Service for software and systems engineering services in support of the IRS's Tax Systems Modernization effort and a two-year, $20 million subcontract for information systems support to the Health Care Financing Administration. The company also continued its key support role at the U.S. Air Force's Phillips Laboratory under a four-year, $22 million contract award for support of laser research and development for high-energy laser applications and advanced imaging technology, giving the company the opportunity to model all aspects of the high-energy laser beam and design and conduct experiments using the artificial laser beacon, which allows for greatly improved imaging of objects in space. At the time, Logicon was the principal contractor for the U.S. Army's Battle Command Training Program (BCTP), which uses the Corps Battle Simulation (CBS) system, a computer-driven training and simulation system Logicon helped develop. In 1995, the Army decided to replace CBS with the next generation of computer-driven Command and Control training simulation environments, called Warfighter's Simulation (WARSIM) 2000, which Logicon also would develop.

In March 1996, Logicon acquired Geodynamics Corporation—a company specializing in remote sensing, geographic information systems, modeling and simulation, software development, and systems engineering and integration for the Department of Defense and other government agencies—for $31.7 million. This purchase extended Logicon's reach even further for, although Geodynamics' headquarters were located in Torrance, California, Geodynamics also had offices in Colorado Springs and Denver, Colorado; Fairfax, Virginia; Sunnyvale, California, and Gaithersburg, Maryland.

The same year saw Logicon developing the Force Level Execution (FLEX) system—specialized software which presents a time-oriented screen display of the status of all sorties flown in a specific theater—to help U.S. Air Force manage air operations. The C3I unit's Southwest Border States Anti-Drug Information System achieved full operational capability in 1996 after two years of engineering and development. The system provides an improved collection and sharing of criminal information among federal, regional, state, county, and city law enforcement agencies along the four southwestern states which border with Mexico (California, Arizona, New Mexico, and Texas), allowing rapid identification of law enforcement officials with similar investigative interests and rapid and secure exchange of sensitive intelligence and information between them.

In early 1997, the company was awarded a contract for Joint Interoperability and Engineering Organization (JIEO) Systems Engineering (JSE) by the Defense Information Systems Agency. On May 4, 1997, Northrop Grumman Corporation signed a definitive agreement to acquire Logicon in a merger with a $750 million stock swap. Northrop, whose corporate offices are located in Los Angeles, California, is a leading designer, systems integrator, and manufacturer of military surveillance and combat aircraft, defense electronics and systems, airspace management systems, information systems, marine systems, precision weapons, space systems, and commercial and military aerostructures, with sales of $8.1 billion in 1996. Northrop was to merge its information technology division with Logicon to create a "Logicon Information Technology Division" which, together, had an income of approximately $1 billion. Northrop chairman, president and CEO Kent Kresa said in a May 5, 1997 press release, the merger will give them "the technology, skills and business base to play a leading role in the continued development of highly integrated systems essential to meet the future warfighting requirements of our military services." At the time of this writing, sources at Logicon reported that Lockheed Martin, another industry giant, would be purchasing Northrop, continuing the consolidation of the marketplace in this industry.

Further Reading

Cole, Jeff, and Steve Lipin, "Northrop Agrees to Acquire Logicon in Stock Deal Valued at $750 Million," *Wall Street Journal,* May 6, 1997, p. A4(W)/B10(E).

Gilpin, Kenneth H., "Northrop to Purchase Logicon in a $750 Million Stock Swap," *New York Times,* May 6, 1997, p. D7.

Siegel, Morton L., et al, "Aerospace/Defense Industry," *Value Line Investment Survey,* April 4, 1997, p. 551.

—Daryl F. Mallett

maidenform

Maidenform Worldwide Inc.

90 Park Avenue
New York, New York 10016
U.S.A.
(212) 953-1400
Fax: (212) 983-5834

Private Company
Incorporated: 1923 as Maiden Form Brassiere Co., Inc.
Employees: 8,900
Sales: $420 million (est. 1996)
SICs: 2341 Women's, Misses', Children's and Infants'
    Underwear and Nightwear; 2342 Brassieres, Girdles
    and Allied Garments

Maidenform Worldwide Inc. is one of the nation's leading manufacturers of brassieres and other articles of women's intimate apparel. It was a pioneer in the development of brassieres and for many years produced and sold more bras than any other company. Still a family-run private company, Maidenform marked its 75th anniversary in 1997, but its future was uncertain because of a heavy debt load. The company filed for bankruptcy protection in July 1997.

Maidenform to 1950

Ida Cohen came to the United States from what is now Belarus in 1905. She established a small dressmaker's shop in Hoboken, New Jersey, the following year and married William Rosenthal, a dress wholesaler and manufacturer, in 1907. She moved her shop to New York City in 1919 and three years later relocated on Manhattan's fashionable 57th Street in partnership with an Englishwoman, Enid Bissett.

Mary Phelps Jacob (later known as Caresse Crosby) is credited with inventing the modern brassiere—free of bones and leaving the midriff bare—in 1913. The boyish silhouette favored in the 1920s required the bra to suppress, rather than enhance, the contours of the female bosom. Explaining the circumstances that led her into brassiere manufacturing, Mrs. Ro-

senthal later said, "In those [flapper-era] days—it was a very sad story—women wore those flat things like bandages, towels with hooks in the back. Now in those days the cheapest dress we made was $125, and it just didn't fit right. So we made a little bra with two pockets. Not too accentuated, of course."

William Rosenthal was an amateur sculptor. He improved his wife's brassiere, employing a fabric called swami, which was similar to soft nylon tricot. His bra also had an elastic center. Mrs. Rosenthal and Mrs. Bissett began to give away with each dress this simple brassiere, which proved so successful that they soon began manufacturing brassieres under the Maidenform (originally Maiden Form) name and within a few years left the dress business. Their company was incorporated with capital of $4,500 provided by Mrs. Rosenthal, her husband, and Mrs. Bissett. Maidenform established its manufacturing operations in Bayonne, New Jersey. William Rosenthal, who became president of the company in 1927, took out many patents on brassiere design, including nursing, long-line, and full-figure bras and the first seamed uplift bra. Maidenform was credited with being the first to offer a truly fitted bra cup. Rosenthal also organized a production line, with one seamstress sewing backs, another making straps, and a third sewing together bra cups. His wife assumed charge of sales and financing.

By 1928 Maidenform was making nearly 500,000 brassieres a year. Sales declined only in the Depression year of 1932. During World War II the company also made parachutes, head nets, mosquito bars, mattress covers, and a brassiere-like nylon vest for carrying courier pigeons when they traveled with the armed forces, but it always received an allotment of cotton gingham for bras because, in Mrs. Rosenthal's words, "women workers who wore an uplift were less fatigued than others."

Maidenform at midcentury was selling more brassieres than any other U.S. company, with about 10 percent of the market, annual revenue of $14 million, and net profit of nearly $1 million. The 12 million bras it produced in 1950 came in 15 styles, each with over 100 different combinations of size, cup size, color, and material. Even the simplest Maidenform brassiere consisted of at least 20 separate pieces, and a long-line model might have as many as 50. In addition to the Bayonne plant, Maidenform now was producing bras, bra pads, and garter belts at seven other factories in New Jersey and West Virginia. The company had 9,000 retail accounts selling its brassieres for between $1.25 and $5.

Adapting to the Marketplace, 1950–80

During the 1950s Maidenform's biggest seller became Chansonette, a pointy style. William Rosenthal died in 1958 and was succeeded by his widow as president, chairman, and chief executive officer of Maidenform. In 1960 she estimated that 30 percent of all U.S. women owned a Maidenform bra, and they were being sold in 115 other countries as well. That year the company, after taking in revenue of $34 million in 1959, continued to sell nearly 10 percent of all U.S. bras. By 1961 it also was selling swimsuits equipped with Maidenform bras.

Maidenform's profile in this period owed much to one of the most famous campaigns in advertising history, apparently prompted by the popularization of Freudian psychology in plays and movies of the 1940s. Between 1949 and 1969 the company launched 163 "dream sequence" print ads that showed a model wearing only a Maidenform bra above the waist. In the first one the copy read, "I dreamt I went shopping in my Maidenform bra," but from this prosaic start the campaign moved on to more adventurous activities, with the subject engaged in such dream pastimes as fighting a bull, hunting a tiger, addressing a jury, ascending a balloon, and floating down the Nile in a barge.

By the mid-1960s Maidenform's annual revenue had reached an estimated $50 million to $55 million, but its well-known name had not kept Playtex, and perhaps Warnaco as well, from surging to the front in bra and girdle sales. Maidenform even briefly had to face competition from designer Rudi Gernreich's No Bra bra, although Ida Rosenthal warned that "after 35 a woman hasn't got the figure to wear nothing." Analysts said the company's conservative styles and reluctance to move heavily into television advertising had cost it sales. After Mrs. Rosenthal suffered a stroke in 1966, her daughter, Beatrice Coleman, became chairman of the company. Dr. Joseph A. Coleman, her son-in-law, became president but died two years later, whereupon Mrs. Coleman also assumed the presidency. Ida Rosenthal died in 1973 at the age of 87.

By 1970 Maidenform was making sportswear and lingerie as well as foundation garments. Its girdles and brassieres now also came in stretch materials such as Lycra. Annual sales had reached $65 million to $70 million, with the company's products sold to some 12,000 department and specialty stores through its own sales force. But by the mid-1970s Maidenform had fallen farther behind Playtex in brassiere sales, although the firm maintained it held the top spot in the contemporary segment, which was accounting for about one-quarter of the total market. Maidenform's contemporary bra line includes No-Show Naturals, stretch-bra styles with a "softer, more natural frame than the traditional fortress-built bras," according to the company's vice president for advertising.

Maidenform had annual revenue of about $100 million in 1980, more than 60 percent from brassiere sales. The company now had 14 factories, some of them abroad, making bras, panties, girdles, sleepwear, and swimwear, with some 10 to 15 percent of its production exported. During the late 1970s it continued to shift emphasis not only from cotton and nylon to stretch materials but also from basic white to a variety of colors. Maidenform introduced three coordinated bra and panty lines: stretch-lace Private Affairs and satin-and-lace Chantilly and Sweet Nothings, and successfully agitated to place them in department-store lingerie departments. Ten million Sweet Nothing bras had been sold by 1987, making it the industry's best seller.

"Gradually we took a lesson from sportswear, and color and prettiness came in," Mrs. Coleman told a *New York Times* reporter in 1980. "Within the last five years, our production of white garments has shrunk to about half." She said the company had been profitable every year since its founding. Nevertheless, swimwear and sportswear, manufactured for Donald Brooks for about five years, proved unprofitable and eventually were dropped. The company also lost money on a short-lived jeans venture.

Advertising in the 1980s and 1990s

During the early 1970s Maidenform shifted 95 percent of its print-advertising dollars into television. Because TV stations would not show live models in their scanties, however, the company was reduced to unsatisfactory alternatives like the 1976 "chorus line" theme that clad the dancers in top hat, vest, cuffs, and bra over leotards.

Maidenform then returned to relying on print ads. The campaign adopted in 1979 harkened back to the exhibitionist "dream" concept. Women were depicted parading in their underwear in public places such as a theater lobby, an antiques shop, and a basketball court—even descending from a helicopter with attaché case. One ad showed the model as a physician in a hospital, another in a train station with fully clothed men. The caption read: "The Maidenform woman. You never know where she'll turn up." Times had changed, however, and in 1981 and 1982 Women Against Pornography awarded the company a plastic pig for sexist advertising. Maidenform toned down the campaign in 1983, continuing to display models in the company's intimate apparel, but doing their fantasizing at home, with no men present.

In 1987 Maidenform introduced a TV ad campaign that, instead of displaying women wearing the company's products, featured leading men such as Omar Sharif, Michael York, Christopher Reeve, and Pierce Brosnan discussing lingerie. Feminists objected to what they regarded as the implication that women wear undergarments mainly for men, so in 1991 the company, to deplore sexism, showed images of a chick, tomato, fox, cat, and dog in one TV ad and stereotyped women like schoolmarms and strippers in another. But feminists said the campaign was actually promoting what it affected to deplore.

In 1997 Maidenform introduced an expensive new print-advertising campaign carrying the theme "Maidenform Unhooked" to promote a less-formal, more contemporary image for the company's products. A number of women were to appear in brassieres, alongside copy such as "Most men don't notice my eyes are hazel" and "No one lays a hand on them without loving me first."

Maidenform in the 1990s

By 1989 Maidenform had dropped loungewear and sleepwear but was making such lingerie items as slips, petticoats, and camisoles. Garter belts had made a comeback, too. "They are a very hot item," Mrs. Coleman told a reporter. "I don't know what people do with them, but they are considered very sexy." The company also had introduced an Oscar de la Renta lingerie collection, consisting of about 30 daywear and foundation styles. In 1991 Maidenform acquired True Form Foundations Corp., a $40-million-a-year manufacturer of bodyshapers under the Flexees and Subtract names.

Mrs. Coleman died in 1990 and was succeeded as president and chief executive officer by son-in-law Robert Brawer. Maidenform's main factory remained in Bayonne, but there were five others in Puerto Rico, two each in Mexico and the Dominican Republic, one each in Costa Rica and Jamaica, and a cut-and-sew plant in Florida. A 250,000-square-foot distribution center was opened in Fayetteville, North Carolina, in 1992. Another distribution center was in Jacksonville, Florida. The company, which in 1985 also had opened a duty-free distribution and processing center in Shannon, Ireland, formed a European subsidiary in Hilden, Germany, in 1991. It closed a long-time production facility in Huntington, West Virginia, in 1992.

Maidenform began offering seamless bras in all its lines in 1994. That year it introduced a second Oscar de la Renta collection of bras and coordinated panties, aimed at younger customers. In 1995 the Maidenform name was added to a line of bras and coordinated panties under the Self Expressions label.

Brawer retired in 1995 and was succeeded by Elizabeth J. Coleman, an Atlanta lawyer and one of Beatrice Coleman's two daughters. She had been serving as chairman of the board since her mother's death. That year the company acquired 92 percent of NCC Industries, Inc. from NCC's largest shareholder, German underwear manufacturer Triumph International Overseas Ltd., for $9.8 million in cash and 28.2 percent of Maidenform's common stock. NCC manufactured the Lilyette full-figured bra, a licensed line of Bill Blass bras and panties, and merchandise under the Minimizer and Reflections names. "It was a strategic acquisition for Maidenform," the new CEO told a reporter. "Our market is mostly for average to smaller sizes. And 35 percent of the bra market is full-figure." The purchase also added $126 million to Maidenform's annual sales, which were running close to $300 million. However, NCC's sales came only to $99.8 million in 1996.

Coleman acknowledged in August 1996 that Maidenform had undergone "some cash-flow issues" earlier in the year. The company had, in 1995, entered into a revolving-credit facility for $120 million and had also taken out a $50-million term loan and issued $30 million in senior notes, pledging NCC's assets and stocks as collateral. At the end of 1996 its bank borrowings came to $171.2 million. A new agreement signed in December 1996 raised the revolving-credit line to $150 million. Maidenform lost money in 1996 and was reported to have defaulted from time to time on loan agreements during the year. It also sold inventory below cost during the year in order to raise cash. VF Corp., a $5-billion-a-year clothing manufacturer, signed a letter of intent in March 1997 to acquire Maidenform. Talks broke off, however, two weeks later.

Maidenform and NCC Industries announced in July 1997 that they were filing for Chapter 11 bankruptcy protection as they restructured their operation. Maidenform said it expected to receive $50 million in loans from its primary lending group as it cut costs and reduced its seven divisions into two.

Further Reading

Baltera, Lorraine, "Maidenform Goes on Stage for Dream Theme Revival," *Advertising Age,* April 26, 1976, p. 39.
Cook, Joan, "A Maidenform Dream Come True," *New York Times,* December 9, 1965, p. 62.
Detman, Art, Jr., "Survival of the Fittest," *Sales Management,* June 1, 1966, pp. 43–44, 46, 48.
Dougherty, Philip H., "Advertising: Years of Maidenform Dreams," *New York Times,* September 10, 1967, Sec. 3, p. 16.
Elliott, Stuart, "Maidenform Aims for Soccer Moms and Just About Everyone Else," *New York Times,* March 12, 1997, p. D2.
Ettorre, Barbara, "The Maidenform Woman Returns," *New York Times,* June 1, 1980, Sec. 3, p. 3.
"Ida Rosenthal," *Time,* October 24, 1960, p. 92.
"Ida Rosenthal, Co-Founder of Maidenform, Dies," *New York Times,* March 30, 1973, p. 42.
Kanner, Bernice, "The Bra's Not for Burning," *New York,* December 12, 1983, pp. 26, 29–30.
——, "Sending Up the Bra," *New York,* December 17, 1990, p. 19.
King, Thomas R., "Maidenform Ads Focus on Stereotypes," *Wall Street Journal,* December 10, 1990, p. B6.
"Maidenform's Mrs. R.," *Fortune,* July 1950, pp. 75–76, 130, 132.
Monget, Karen, "Coleman: Keeping Maidenform Fit," *WWD,* August 5, 1996, pp. 14, 16.
——, "Maidenform: Shaping Its Own Future," *Women's Wear Daily,* November 5, 1992, p. 8.
——, "Maidenform Clinches Deal with Triumph for 92% of NCC," *WWD,* April 27, 1995, p. 2.
Morris, Michele, "The Mother Figure of Maidenform," *Working Woman,* April 1987, pp. 82, 86, 88.
Palumbo, Sandra, "Maidenform, Looking Back, Moving Forward," *Women's Wear Daily,* January 5, 1987, p. 14.
Sacco, Joe, "Dreams for Sale: How the One for Maidenform Came True," *Advertising Age,* September 12, 1977, pp. 63–64.
Steinhauser, Jennifer, "Maidenform's Problems Reflect Industry Pitfalls," *New York Times,* July 24, 1997, pp. D1, D4.

—Robert Halasz

Marzotto S.p.A.

Largo S. Margherita, 1
36078 Valdagno
Vicenze
Italy
(39) 445 42 94 11
Fax: (39) 445 42 76 30
Web site: http://www.moda.italynet.com/
    www.modaonline.it/marchi/marzotto

Public Company
Founded: 1836
Employees: 9,741
Sales: L2.2 trillion (1996)
Stock Exchanges: Milan
SICs: 2310 Men's and Boys' Suits and Coats; 2330
    Women's and Misses' Outerwear; 2230 Broadwoven
    Fabric Mills, Not Elsewhere Classified; 2280 Yarn
    and Thread Mills; 2341 Women's and Children's
    Underwear

Italy's largest textile manufacturer, Marzotto S.p.A. is a vertically integrated producer of fabrics, yarns, and clothing with operations around the world. Though the company's origins are in fabric manufacture—it continued in the mid-1990s to be Europe's largest producer of wool and linen—its future success appeared to be pinned to its growing apparel operations, which ranked second among Europe's clothing companies. In addition to its own labels—Principe by Marzotto, Ciao, and Accento, among others—the company also produces apparel under license from such well-known designers as Gianfranco Ferrè and Missoni. The company's controlling stake in German menswear house Hugo Boss generated nearly half of global sales in the mid-1990s. Private-label clothing rounds out the line. Once the company's sole business, textile operations had by this time shrunk to about 36 percent of annual revenues. Over 70 percent of sales are made outside Italy. Throughout its more than 160 years in operation, the company has been led by five successive generations of Marzotto men, with Pietro Marzotto in the role of chairman in the late 1990s. The family continued to own a majority stake in the firm through this period as well.

Mid-19th-Century Origins and Early 20th-Century Development

The firm was founded in the town of Valdagno in 1836, before the collection of independent states later known as Italy had even achieved nationhood. Members of the nobility, the Marzottos were by no means poor; Luigi Marzotto established his woolens mill with a capital of 2,000 Venetian Lire, the equivalent of nearly $100,000 in the mid-1990s. He handed the business over to son Gaetano in 1842. The unification of the kingdom of Italy in 1861 opened new markets to the company, and its location in the northeastern region of the nation—which made the transition from an agrarian to an industrial economy more quickly than southern Italy—gave it an advantage over its competitors to the south. By 1866, 200 employees worked the company's carding, spinning, and dyeing machines and weaving looms. An 1880 expansion took the Marzottos to nearby Maglio, where Gaetano built a new spinning factory. The wool industry had by this time become one of Italy's largest, in terms of both employment and production, and enjoyed protective tariffs of up to 40 percent in the waning years of the nineteenth century.

By the turn of the century, Marzotto's payroll had risen to over 1,200. When Gaetano died in 1910, the company was split in two; son Vittorio Emanuele, who has been credited with leading the company into the export business, inherited the Valdagno operations, while Gaetano's grandsons took over the Maglio mill. Despite inflation, high unemployment, and rampant strikes in the period between the two world wars, the Marzotto group continued to grow. In fact, Vittorio was able to open another worsted wool mill during this period. By the time Gaetano Marzotto Jr. inherited the Valdagno mill from his father in 1921, the company employed over 2,000.

A company history characterizes Gaetano Jr. as "an authentic founder of the family business." His efforts at modernization and expansion during the fascist-dominated 1920s strength-

Company Perspectives:

Marzotto Group currently covers the full scope of yarn, fabric, and apparel sectors. The company does not have a vertically organized structure; rather, it is arranged in a network of companies that literally "mind their own business." The Marzotto network aims at satisfying its customers, creating lasting wealth, and gaining a competitive edge. Marzotto's success rests on the following factors: an efficient and exclusive clientele in leading world markets; continuous innovation of its products and services; "state of the art" technology; a solid financial structure.

ened the company to the extent that it not only survived the Great Depression without being nationalized, but also reacquired the family mill in Maglio. The leader capitalized on continental textile manufacturers' difficulties during this period, expanding exports to Eastern Europe, Latin America, and throughout the Mediterranean region. Experiencing difficulty in finding suitable lodgings during his nationwide travels, Gaetano Jr. also established the Jolly hotel chain, which the Marzotto family would continue to own and operate throughout the twentieth century.

Transformation Begins in 1950s, Accelerates in 1970s

Although the company came under government control during World War II, Gaetano resumed ownership at the conflict's end. He capitalized on Italy's "economic miracle"—a period of currency stabilization and exuberant industrial growth from the mid-1940s to the mid-1960s—by diversifying into the manufacture of traditionally-styled, private-label menswear during an early 1950s downturn in the core textile business. Though inflation and subsequent wage indexing (quarterly increases that corresponded to the rate of inflation) regularly increased hourly pay, worker unrest began in the late 1960s and continued throughout much of the 1970s. In 1969, striking laborers demolished a statue of patriarch Gaetano Marzotto in the middle of what had become the "company town" of Valdagno.

When Gaetano Jr. died in 1972, his son Giannino and grandson Pietro inherited an essentially healthy but outdated business. Modernization, both of production and management techniques, intensified under Marzotto's fifth generation of family management. "Stagflation"—slow economic growth combined with hyperinflation—brought a sense of urgency to these efforts. Whereas increases in employment levels had previously been a positive indication of the textile group's condition, high labor expenses made a fat payroll a distinct disadvantage in the 1970s and beyond. Pietro reduced employment from 9,000 in 1976 to 4,500 by 1986 and simultaneously managed to refurbish the company's plants without incurring excessive debt. Having gone public in 1961, the company issued voting shares in 1981. Marzotto started selling its private label apparel to retailers in the U.S. in 1973 and by 1985, when the parent company established an American subsidiary, two-fifths of its L402 billion sales were made outside Italy.

Geographic and Product Diversification Via Acquisition Begins in Mid-1980s

The gradual, yet cumulatively revolutionary strategy that unfolded at Marzotto over the decade from 1985 to 1995 incorporated three key goals: reduction of overheads, upmarket expansion in apparel, and elimination of non-core or loss-plagued operations. These objectives were achieved through acquisitions, divestments, restructuring, and internal development.

In a March 1988 interview with *WWD's* Mark Ganem, Pietro likened his corporate acquisition strategy to a moderate diet, noting that "Even after the best dinner, a big dessert can ruin everything." To illustrate, the company acquired the Fin-Bassetti Group, including its controlling interest in Linificio e Canapificio Nazionale, in 1985, but waited two years while integrating those operations before making a second purchase. The 1987 acquisition of Italy's Lanerossi increased Marzotto's total revenues by more than 72 percent, from L402 billion in 1985 to L691.5 billion in 1986. The L168 billion purchase, which catapulted Marzotto to the top of Italy's textile and apparel heap, was made over bids by competitors like Benetton, the Bertrand Group, and Cotonificio Cantoni. Furthermore, the addition of Lanerossi made Marzotto Europe's first fully integrated wool producer, incorporating everything "from the sheep to the suit," as Textiles General Manager Elio Lora Lamia told *Daily News Record's* Elizabeth Chute. Marzotto also acquired France's Le Blan & Fils, a yarn manufacturer, in 1989 and the Biella, Italy-based Guabello wool mill in 1991.

Internal growth was robust as well; even if acquisitions were excluded, revenue increases averaged more than 12 percent from 1983 to 1987. Sales flattened at about L1.5 trillion throughout the remainder of the decade, however, and net income actually declined from L59.7 billion in 1988 to L45.4 billion in 1990.

Marzotto also began to gradually shift its image upmarket in the mid-1980s by launching its own moderately priced men's fashion label, Principe by Marzotto. The company first penetrated the designer market with the 1986 launch of Missoni Uomo, later adding Laura Biagiotti and Gianfranco Ferre to its stable of licensed and house designers. A major turning point in this realm came in 1991, when Marzotto paid Japanese investor Akira Akagi L200 billion (US$165 million) for a controlling interest in Hugo Boss, Germany's largest manufacturer of menswear. The Hugo Boss purchase was considered a threefold success: it extended Marzotto's global reach, further strengthened its primary textiles business, and added a widely recognized, high-end brand.

Difficult trading conditions in the Italian economy as well as the global apparel market continued to depress Marzotto's fiscal results in the early years of the decade. Sales increased a cumulative 71 percent, from L1.4 trillion in 1990 to L2.4 trillion (US$1.5 billion) in 1995, but net income only rose about 25 percent, from L40.1 billion to L50.1 billion (US$32 million).

In response to this tough environment, Marzotto announced in 1992 that it would endeavor to transfer 40 percent of its clothing production overseas in order to reduce labor costs. The revelation that the company would relinquish the unique reputation enjoyed by luxury products "Made in Italy" came as a surprise to many observers. Marzotto cut about 600 jobs in its home country that year, closed a domestic clothing plant in 1993, and completed the purchase of a 90 percent stake in Czechoslovakia's Nuova Mosilana woolen mill in 1994.

Strategies for the Mid-1990s and Beyond

The company's grandest move to date came in the spring of 1997, when it announced that it would merge with compatriot HPI to form the world's largest designer clothing manufacturer, Gruppo Industriale Marzotto. The L8 trillion (US$4.7 billion) conglomerate would carry such names as Giorgio Armani, Valentino, Calvin Klein, Hugo Boss, and Gianfranco Ferré, and pose formidable competition to giants of the global luxury goods market like France's LVMH Moet Hennessy Louis Vuitton. Marzotto would have owned 12.4 percent of the new company, whose other leading stakeholders would have included Mediobanca (10.5 percent) and Fiat (17.3 percent). But by May 1997, Pietro Marzotto—who would have served as the new entity's chairman—abruptly pulled out of the deal, citing concerns over strategy, investment policies, and capitalization. Though the union with HPI fell apart, some analysts speculated that Marzotto might yet acquire HPI's GFT subsidiary, manager of the family of luxury brands.

Marzotto continued to evolve rapidly in the aftermath of the aborted HPI deal. Before the end of May, Pietro announced that he was turning day-to-day operations over to Jean de Jaeger, who two years previous had become the first non-Marzotto to be promoted to the chief executive office. With nearly 30 years at the company to his credit, the Belgian de Jaeger advanced to executive deputy chairman. Pietro Marzotto continued as chairman in charge of corporate strategy. The management troika envisioned continued acquisitions and joint ventures, further penetration of North America and Asia, and invigorated retail expansion.

Principal Subsidiaries

Marzotto International N.V. (Netherlands); Marzotto (U.S.A.) Corp.; Alicante S.p.A.; Marzotto France S.a.r.l.; Magnolia S.p.A. (99.81%); Larix S.p.A.; Lanificio Guabello S.p.A. (95.7%); Marzotto International Factor S.p.A. (80%); Nova Mosilana A.S. (Czech Republic). *Principal Affiliates:* Vincenzo Zucchi S.p.A. (25%); Mascioni S.p.A. (28.3%); Hugo Boss Australia Pty. (35.25%); Lininpianti S.p.A. (44.26%); Paul Le Blan et Fils S.A. (France) (44.26%); Filature de Lin Filin S.A. (Spain) (22.13%).

Further Reading

Bannon, Lisa, "Marzotto Planning to Buy U.S. Clothing Manufacturer," *Daily News Record,* December 7, 1988, pp. 2–3.

——, "Marzotto Automated Dyehouse Replaces 3," *Daily News Record,* June 7, 1989, p. 7.

Chute, Elizabeth, "Marzotto: 150; Lanerossi: 1; Ferre: 000.1," *Daily News Record,* January 4, 1988, pp. A50–A51.

Conti, Samantha, "For Marzotto's CEO: Timing Is Money," *Daily News Record,* November 19, 1996, p. 5.

——, "Italians Streamline for Harder Times," *WWD,* February 26, 1997, pp. S10–S11.

——, "Marzotto Plans to Hit Acquisition Trail," *Daily News Record,* May 28, 1997, p. COV.

Forden, Sara Gay, "More Italy Producers Look Offshore for Less-Expensive Manufacturing," *Daily News Record,* June 29, 1992, p. 6.

——, "Marzotto Makes a Move on Eastern Europe," *WWD,* October 21, 1992, p. 23.

——, "Marzotto to the Market and the Market to Marzotto," *Daily News Record,* June 20, 1994, pp. 16–17.

Forden, Sara Gay, and Samantha Conti, "End of the Affair: Marzotto-HPI Deal Suddenly Called Off," *WWD,* May 5, 1997, pp. 1–2.

Ganem, Mark, "Marzotto 'Designs' a Future," *WWD,* March 30, 1988, p. 50.

Gellers, Stan, "De Jaegher To Become CEO of Marzotto SPA on Jan. 1," *Daily News Record,* September 27, 1995, p. 2.

——, "Sighs of Relief in U.S. Market as Marzotto-HPI Merger Falters," *Daily News Record,* May 7, 1997, p. 1.

Gellers, Stan; Samantha Contin; and Miles Socha, "U.S. Retailers Give Marzotto, HPI Merger a Thumbs-Up," *Daily News Record,* March 12, 1997, pp. COV.

Morris, Nomi, "Marzotto Completes Purchase of Boss," *Daily News Record,* December 19, 1991, p. 3.

"A New Breed for the New Money," *The Economist,* March 15, 1986, pp. 71–72.

—April Dougal Gasbarre

Masco Corporation

21001 Van Born Road
Taylor, Michigan 48180
U.S.A.
(313) 274-7400
Fax: (313) 374-6135
Web site: http://www.masco.com/

Public Company
Incorporated: 1929 as Masco Screw Products Company
Employees: 22,800
Sales: $3.24 billion (1996)
Stock Exchanges: New York
SICs: 2434 Wood Kitchen Cabinets; 3089 Plastic
Products, Not Elsewhere Classified; 3429 Hardware,
Not Elsewhere Classified; 3432 Plumbing Fixture
Fittings & Trim

Masco Corporation is the world's largest faucet manufacturer as well as the leading U.S. cabinet manufacturer. The company manufactures hundreds of building specialty and home improvement products, including kitchen appliances, whirlpools and spas, bath and shower tubs and enclosures, residential and commercial locks and hardware, venting systems and ventilating products, electrical outlet boxes, and water pumps. Masco Corporation's best-known product is the single-handled Delta faucet, developed and promoted in the 1950s by the company's founder, Alex Manoogian. Masco's 20 lines and 250 styles of cabinets include stock, semi-custom, and custom cabinetry for the replacement/remodeling and new construction markets. Masco holds a 17 percent stake in MascoTech Inc. (formerly known as Masco Industries Inc.), a public company created by Masco and a major producer of metal and plastic products, primarily for the transportation industry. Another Masco spinoff, TriMas Corporation, in which Masco holds a four percent stake, is a public company that manufactures fasteners, towing systems, specialty containers, precision tools, and other products for commercial and industrial applications. As a result of the 1996 sale of its home furnishing unit to Furnishings International Inc., Masco also has a 15 percent stake in Furnishings International, an investment firm.

Founded as Screw Machine Business in 1929

In 1920 Alex Manoogian, at the age of 19, immigrated to the United States from Smyrna, Turkey, fleeing political persecution and danger that threatened him as a Christian Armenian in Moslem Turkey. After holding several odd jobs in Bridgeport, Connecticut, including brief employment in a screw machine business, Manoogian came in 1924 to Detroit, Michigan, where he worked in a screw machine business and learned about metalworking for automobile components. In 1929, six weeks after the stock market crash, he founded Masco Screw Products Company with two partners, Harry Adjemian and Charles Saunders, who left during the first year. They began with a few thousand dollars, several used screw machines, and a truck—less than $33,000 in assets. "Masco" was derived from the first letters of the partners' last names plus "co" for company.

The automobile industry was still young and largely untested, and Masco's initial years were difficult. Hudson Motor Car Company was the first customer, with a $7,000 contract, but Masco could not yet afford to pay salaries. Manoogian was sales manager, estimator, foreman, press operator, and repairman.

The first plant was located on the fifth floor of an old building, with a furniture manufacturer on the floor below. Soon after business began, oil from the Masco machines leaked through the floor, ruining newly upholstered furniture. Manoogian was able to remain in business by arranging extended payments for the furniture damage.

During the 1930s, Masco worked mainly with Chrysler and had contracts with Ford, Graham Page, Spicer Manufacturing, and Budd Wheel. Since Masco produced parts to the specifications of these firms, the company did not distinguish itself through product design and, instead, focused on providing excellent service.

In 1931 Manoogian brought his family to the United States and married Marie Tatian. In 1934 his brother Charles joined the company, followed a few years later by another brother, George. By 1936, all sales were to the automotive industry and had increased almost fourfold since the first year, to $234,000.

359

In 1937, Masco went public, its shares selling for $1 on the Detroit Stock Exchange.

Later in 1937, the plant caught fire. Fortunately, snow that had accumulated on the roof of the building melted and poured over the heavy machinery, reducing the fire's damage. Although Masco was in business again three months later, this was the one year in its history when the company lost money.

Like most U.S. metalworking companies during World War II, Masco worked exclusively for the defense industry. In 1942, its sales reached $1 million and continued to increase for two years. When the war ended in 1945, sales declined as Masco returned to manufacturing for the automotive industry.

In 1948, Masco offered more stock to the public. The sale of 13,000 shares generated the capital to buy the Ford Road Plant in Dearborn, Michigan, which then became the company headquarters.

In 1950, just after the Korean War began, Masco resumed production for the defense industry. Although sales increased, profits remained flat, due to the payment of wartime excess-profits taxes. Masco began work on a new kind of artillery-shell timing mechanism, a precision-made part that demonstrated the company's expertise in metalworking. Chrysler asked Masco to bid on a contract that required a new metalworking technique called cold extrusion, one unfamiliar to Masco engineers. Soon the company was producing satisfactory parts by cold extrusion. In 1953, when wartime contracts ended, Masco could not afford to continue developing the new technology and did not resume using cold extrusion until 1967.

Launch of Delta Faucet in 1954 Proved Pivotal

The year 1954 was a turning point for the company when Alex Manoogian won a small contract to manufacture parts for a new type of faucet being produced in California. At the time, Masco was still an automotive parts manufacturer with little experience in plumbing fixtures. The unusual design of this faucet was its single handle, which controlled both cold and hot water. Unfortunately, the faucet, nicknamed by plumbers "the one-armed bandit," did not operate properly, and orders for it ceased. Because of his metalworking expertise, Manoogian detected the deficiencies in the faucet and redesigned it. He paid the original owners for licensing rights to produce and market his own version. At first, he formed a separate company to protect Masco if the new faucet did not sell. He tried to interest plumbing manufacturers in marketing the faucet, but they claimed there was no market for it. Eventually, Manoogian transferred the rights to Masco, which produced and marketed the Delta faucet. Sales increased rapidly, topping $1 million by 1958. In 1959 Masco bought a separate plant in Greensburg,

Indiana for faucet manufacturing. That year also, Manoogian's son, Richard, graduated from Yale University and helped start the new faucet operation.

From the beginning of his career, Richard Manoogian led the company toward expansion. He engineered Masco's first major acquisition in 1961, that of Peerless Industries, Inc., a manufacturer of plumbing products, to widen Masco's production capabilities. In the same year, Masco closed its Dearborn plant and moved automotive parts production to Ypsilanti, Michigan. The faucet sector, which continued with steady success, offset the cyclical nature of the automotive industry. By 1962, Delta faucet sales reached $7 million and accounted for more than half of Masco's sales. By then, Masco Screw Products Company was an inappropriate name for a supplier to both the automotive and construction industries and the name was changed to Masco Corporation. In 1962, Masco acquired Mascon Toy Company, a manufacturer of toy telephones and play furniture, but Mascon was sold in the late 1960s, because of its low profit margins and its incompatibility with Masco's other interests.

Later in 1962, Masco was placed on the American Stock Exchange, and Smith Barney, the investment banking firm, accepted Masco as a client, opening new sources of financing. Masco began an aggressive plan of acquisition and diversification spearheaded by Richard Manoogian.

In 1962 Masco acquired Steel Stamping Company, and in 1964 it acquired Nile Faucet Corporation, broadening its capabilities in the automotive and plumbing parts sectors. Over the next few years, as the construction industry flourished, the company began to expand its product line, acquiring Auto-Flo Company and Auto-Flo Corporation, which produced air-handlers, such as ventilators, and furnaces, and Gibbs Automatic Molding Company, a plastics firm.

Masco headquarters moved in 1967 to new facilities in Taylor, Michigan. The company began using the technique of cold extrusion, a process that resulted in greater structural strength and improved energy efficiency. In 1968, Masco acquired the Burns Companies, which manufactured components by cold forging and by automatic screw machines, followed by a series of acquisitions in the metalworking industry throughout 1970, including Punchcraft, Inc., Molloy Manufacturing Company, Century Tool Company, Keo Cutters, Inc., and Commonwealth Industries.

In 1968 Richard Manoogian was made president of Masco, and Alex Manoogian became chairman of the board. Masco had become a major manufacturer of plumbing products for the kitchen and bathroom, with sales of $5.5 million. In 1969, Masco was listed on the New York Stock Exchange.

Acquisitions Continued in the 1970s and 1980s

During the 1970s, Masco's two main markets, the automobile industry and the construction industry, fared badly in the country's recession. American automobile companies faced increasing foreign competition. Inflation and high interest rates caused a 34 percent decline in the number of new homes by 1974.

Nevertheless, Masco earnings continued to grow at an average of 20 percent per year. Masco had become the leading supplier of many household items, and it continued to diversify. Plumbing products for do-it-yourself home improvement continued to do especially well, and renovation and replacement accounted for more than half of Masco's faucet sales by 1975. In 1972 Masco began to market a new faucet design, a double-handled faucet called the Delex, based on the same rotating-ball principle as the Delta. Masco continued to introduce new models in the next few years and by 1975 had increased its market share to 22 percent.

In 1971 Masco entered the communications business when it acquired Electra Corporation, which manufactured scanning monitor radios. That year Masco began to manufacture parts for trailers and other recreational vehicles with its purchase of Fulton Company in 1971 and Reese Products in 1973. In 1972 Masco bought several small manufacturing companies for its automobile sector, and in 1973 it bought American Metals Corporation.

In 1973 Masco made its first foreign acquisition with Holzer and Company, a West German manufacturer of air-handlers. That same year, Masco entered the petroleum equipment sector, acquiring 47 percent of Emco, a Canadian manufacturer of oil pipes and plumbing hardware. Foreign sales in 1973 accounted for four percent of the company's total, increasing one year later to seven percent.

Between 1973 and 1974, when the automobile and construction industries hit their worst slump of the decade, Masco's stock value plummeted from 46 times earnings to a multiple of 20, although sales were up 23 percent and earnings were up 22 percent.

In 1975, Manoogian took advantage of the growing market for citizens band (CB) radios and acquired Royce Electronics. CB sales continued to soar at the beginning of 1976, but, by the end of the year, the supply of CBs exceeded demand. When the federal government expanded the available channels from 23 to 40, the 23-channel radios became virtually obsolete. Royce's sales plummeted from $53 million to $17 million, and the company suffered $1 million in losses. Masco sold 51 percent of Royce in 1976 and its remaining shares in 1977.

Nevertheless, the company remained in the communications sector. Electra continued to make scanning monitor radios and other electronic products. In 1976 Masco sued RCA Corporation, Teaberry Electronics Corporation, and Sanyo Electric Company for infringing on Electra's patents for scanning radio receivers. Sanyo produced the radios in Japan for the other two companies, but Masco required that firms sign a licensing agreement to sell the scanners. The case was settled in court when Sanyo agreed to pay Electra royalties under a new licensing agreement.

Masco continued to penetrate the petroleum equipment market in 1976, acquiring A-Z International Companies and Grant Oil Tool Company, both manufacturers of drilling tools, as well as Dansk Metal and Armaturindistri of Denmark. Masco also created Forming Technology Company, a firm with technologically advanced equipment that produced larger metal components swiftly and economically. In 1977, Masco acquired Walker McDonald Manufacturing Company and R & B Manufacturing Company, producers of petroleum equipment, and, in 1978, Rieke Corporation, which made closures for oil drums and other large containers. In 1979 Masco purchased Jung-Pumpen, a West German maker of sump pumps, and Arrow Specialty Company, a maker of engines and engine repair parts.

During the late 1970s, Masco began to advertise its faucets on network television. In a March 16, 1981 interview with *Forbes,* Richard Manoogian stated, "Everybody thought we were crazy.... They told us that the only time you buy a faucet is when your old one leaks." Masco realized that there was a steady consumer demand for the product and continued to expand its line of faucets. By 1980, Masco had increased its market share to 28 percent.

In 1980, while automobile production slowed 24 percent, Masco worked with car manufacturers on design, to create additional car parts. In 1981, while the housing industry was in its worst state since the mid-1970s, Masco's sales in that sector continued to grow. Masco's products in the home improvement area were not subject to extreme economic swings, and the home improvement sector was growing faster than the industrial one.

Masco continued to expand in 1980, acquiring AlupKompressoren Pressorun, a West German maker of air-compressors; Lamons Metal Gasket Company; and Arrow Oil Tools, a manufacturer for the petroleum industry. In 1981 Masco introduced a nonceramic toilet, which used much less water and was insulated to muffle the sound of flushing.

Diversification continued in 1982. Masco acquired two small companies that made valves and related products for the oil industry, as well as Evans-Aristocrat Industries, which made steel measuring tapes; Baldwin Hardware Manufacturing Company, which made hardware for builders; and Marvel Metal Products, which made steel work stations for the office.

The year 1982 was the first since 1956 that earnings for operations did not increase, because of the effects of the recession. Masco's sales in the cold extrusion industry declined 17 percent, primarily because of the depressed automobile and construction industries.

In 1983 Masco acquired Brass Craft Manufacturing Company, a maker of plumbing supplies. Building and home improvement product sales were up more than 50 percent to $500 million, because of profitable acquisitions and steady faucet sales. At the same time, decline in oil prices spurred a drop in petroleum equipment sales.

Industrial Businesses Spun Off in 1984

For many years, the cyclical industrial sectors—petroleum and construction equipment and automobile parts—had lowered Masco's overall yearly results, even though total annual sales had continued to grow. In 1984 Richard Manoogian spun off Masco's industrial businesses into a separate, publicly held company, Masco Industries Inc. (MI). This change gave Masco Corporation a firmer identity as a home improvement and building products company, enabling it to focus on that sector. While the move allowed both companies to expand more quickly, it also gave Masco Corporation continued access to MI's metalworking technology. Richard Manoogian became CEO of the new company, and its headquarters remained in Taylor, Michigan, with Masco Corporation. Masco Corporation distributed 50 percent of MI stock to shareholders as a dividend and retained the other half, worth about $50 million. A year later, Masco ownership of MI decreased to 44 percent.

In the restructuring, the two companies formed Nimas Corporation as a vehicle to facilitate Masco's leveraged buyout of NI Industries, a large diversified company. NI Industries manufactured many building products, including Thermador cooking equipment, Weiser locks, Waste King appliances, Artistic Brass faucets, and Bowers electrical outlet boxes (Masco's first entry into the electrical equipment business). NI also produced several automobile and defense products. Masco paid $483 million for the company; using Nimas allowed Masco Corporation and MI to make an expensive acquisition without placing the debt on either company's balance sheet.

During the next few years, MI focused on developing its manufacturing technology and expanding through acquisitions, investing more than $1 billion. As a result, yearly earnings suffered, although sales increased from $545 million in 1984 to $1.7 billion in 1989.

Erwin H. Billig became president of Masco Industries in 1986. Between 1986 and 1989, MI diversified into architectural products, acquiring manufacturers of steel doors, door frames, metal office panels, security grills, sectional and rolling doors, and similar items. By 1989, it had become one of the largest U.S. producers of steel door products. MI also entered a new sector of automotive parts in 1986, acquiring several manufacturers of components such as windshield wiper blades, roof racks, brake hardware repair kits, and front-wheel-drive components. MI focused on establishing its own niches in the market, which continued to expand as the need for replacement parts for longer lasting automobiles increased. MI production of customized goods for the defense industry, including cartridge casings, projectiles, and casings for rocket motors and missiles, declined in the late 1980s, as the U.S. government began to decrease defense spending.

After the creation of MI, Masco Corporation continued its expansion, acquiring, in 1984, Trayco and Aqua Glass, both kitchen-and-bathroom-products manufacturers with sales of about $70 million. At the same time, Masco phased out its Electra personal communications products, a market no longer suited to the company's criteria for growth.

In 1985 Masco acquired Merillat Industries, a manufacturer of cabinets, and Flint and Walling Water Systems, which made water pumps. Masco also introduced the largest faucet selection in the history of the plumbing industry. Wayne B. Lyon became president of Masco in 1985, and Richard Manoogian served as chairman and CEO of both Masco Corporation and Masco Industries.

In the early 1980s, Richard Manoogian saw a great potential for growth abroad and acquired the Berglen group of companies, which distributed faucets in the United Kingdom, and 25 percent of Hans Grohe, the top European hand-shower manufacturer. Because of disadvantageous foreign currency rates, sales in dollars in Europe had remained stagnant for several years, but European sales in domestic currencies were thriving.

In 1986 Masco filed lawsuits against several plumbing suppliers—Waxman Industries, Keystone Franklin, and Radiator Specialty Company—for infringement on the Delta faucet trademark. The following year, Masco's competitors agreed to mark packages more clearly, following the trademark specifications. It was the first of several trademark infringement cases involving the Delta name.

Expanded into Furniture in the Late 1980s

Masco moved into the furniture industry in 1986, acquiring Henredon Furniture Industries and Drexel Heritage Furniture and, one year later, Lexington Furniture Industries. The three companies represented about $700 million in sales. Masco also acquired Walkins Manufacturing Corporation, a producer of spas, and Fieldstone Cabinetry.

In 1987 Masco purchased Marbro Lamp Company and Hueppe Duscha, a West German maker of shower equipment. Masco also issued 1.2 million shares to finance its acquisition of La Barge Mirrors; two new furniture companies, Hickorycraft and Alsons Corporation; and Marge Carson, Inc., a manufacturer of plumbing products. By 1988 furniture sales accounted for about 25 percent of the company's $2.9 billion sales, and Masco continued to expand, acquiring American Textile Company and the Robert Allen Companies.

In 1988, MI transferred nine of its smaller businesses to TriMas Corporation, a publicly traded spin-off, primarily a manufacturer of industrial fasteners. Two years later, Masco Corporation sold TriMas its recreational vehicle accessories and its insulation products businesses. Initially, Masco held a 19 percent (by the mid-1990s reduced to four percent) stake in TriMas, and MI held a 48 percent stake (by the mid-1990s 37 percent).

In 1989 earnings declined, and Masco Corporation's stock sold at discounted rates, due to investor uncertainty about the future of the home improvement sector. Consequently, the company repurchased four million of its common shares in 1989, and, in 1990, the board voted to repurchase up to ten million additional common shares.

Expansion continued in 1989, as Masco bought Universal Furniture of Hong Kong, its largest overseas acquisition. Foreign sales, mainly in Canada and Europe, accounted for about 13 percent of Masco's total revenues. In 1990 Masco bolstered its cabinetry operations through the acquisition of KraftMaid Cabinetry, Inc.

Returned Focus to Core Home Improvement and Building Products Businesses in 1990s

Masco's move into furniture turned out to be a major mistake. Part of the problem was bad timing, as the furniture industry in 1988 entered into a deep recession, which it did not pull out of until 1992. But furniture also simply turned out to be a bad fit for Masco, unlike the company's move into cabinetry, a product sector that was much more closely aligned to such Masco mainstays as faucets than furniture was. Following its move into cabinet making, Masco had been able to achieve manufacturing efficiencies, thus improving upon the businesses it acquired; furniture manufacturing, however, was less sophisticated and thus did not lend itself to the kinds of management techniques Masco typically used. Furthermore, Masco had great difficulty marketing its furniture lines, whereas it had been able to sell its cabinets through many of its existing channels.

By the early 1990s the company's furniture group was a major drag on company earnings. Despite this, Masco continued to increase its investment in furniture by making additional acquisitions, including the mid-1994 purchase of Berkline Corp., a Tennessee-based maker of recliners and upholstered family room furniture that had sales of $165 million in 1993.

Meanwhile, Masco also felt the effects from a troubled Masco Industries, which was suffering from the effects of the early 1990s recession, a downturn that hit the auto industry particularly hard. Prospects had improved by 1993 thanks to a restructuring and an improving economy and Masco took advantage of MI's stronger position by reducing its stake in its sister company that year to 35 percent. Also in 1993, MI changed its name to MascoTech Inc. By 1997 Masco Corporation had further simplified its holdings by reducing its Masco-Tech stake to 17 percent, with the prospect of completely eliminating this noncore holding by the turn of the century.

An even more important divestment occurred in 1996 when Masco sold its furniture unit. In June of the previous year, the company had decided to sell the unit, finally concluding that it would be unable to turn the unit around and that it would be best for Masco Corporation to return to an exclusive focus on home improvement and building products. Masco had been unable to increase the furniture unit's operating profits, which had ranged from three to six percent, nowhere near the 15 to 20 percent generated by the company's other operating units. In November 1995 Masco announced that Morgan Stanley Capital Partners would buy the furniture unit for nearly $1.2 billion, but in January of the following year the deal was abandoned without explanation. Then, in August 1996, Masco sold the troubled unit to an investment group, Furnishings International Inc., with proceeds exceeding $1 billion, $708 million of which was cash. As part of the agreement, Masco gained a 15 percent stake in Furnishings International. Masco soon used a large portion—about $550 million—of the cash it gained to reduce its long-term debt, which had been fairly high.

Following its abandonment of furniture, Masco made several acquisitions that extended its existing products lines in brand-name and geographic terms. In 1996 three European companies with combined 1995 sales of $140 million were acquired: The Moore Group Ltd., a leading U.K. maker of kitchen cabinets; Horst Breuer GmbH, a German manufacturer of shower enclosures for the do-it-yourself market; and E. Missel GmbH, a leading German manufacturer of proprietary specialty products for the new construction, remodeling, and renovation markets. In March 1997 Masco acquired Franklin Brass Manufacturing Company, a California-based maker of bath accessories and bath safety products, and LaGard Inc., another California company, which was an electronic lock manufacturer. Later in 1997 two more cabinetry companies were acquired: Liberty Hardware Manufacturing Corporation of Boca Raton, Florida, a maker of cabinet hardware; and Texwood Industries, Inc., a leading maker of kitchen and bath cabinetry based in Duncanville, Texas. Masco expanded further outside the United States in July 1997 when it acquired The Alvic Group, a leading Spanish manufacturer and distributor of kitchen and bath cabinetry, and The SKS Group, a

leading German maker and distributor of roller shutters and aluminum balcony railing systems.

As the new century approached—and with its ill-fated furniture adventure more or less behind it and its holding in Masco-Tech substantially reduced—Masco Corporation appeared ready to reclaim some of its past glory. Newly committed to its core home improvement and building products businesses, the company was likely to continue to seek out targeted acquisitions both at home and abroad to strengthen its already commanding position.

Principal Subsidiaries

Alsons Corporation; American Metal Products; Auto-Graph Computer Designing Systems, Inc.; Baldwin Hardware Corporation; Baldwin Hardware Manufacturing Corporation; Brass-Craft Manufacturing Corporation; Composite Products, Inc.; Computer Design, Inc.; Computerized Security Systems, Inc.; Fieldstone Cabinetry, Inc.; Flint & Walling Industries, Inc.; Franklin Brass Manufacturing Company; Gamco Products Co.; Kraftmaid Cabinetry, Inc.; Liberty Hardware Manufacturing Corporation; The Marvel Group, Inc.; Masco Building Products Corp.; Masco Corporation of Indiana; Delta Faucet Corporation; Merillat Industries Inc.; Morgantown Plastics Company; NI Industries, Inc.; Sherle Wagner International, Inc.; Starmark, Inc.; Texwood Industries, Inc.; Trayco, Inc.; Watkins Manufacturing Corp./Hot Springs Spas; Zenith Products Corp.; Weiser Lock Pty. Ltd. (Australia); N.V. Weiser Europe, B.V. (Belgium); Brass-Craft Canada, Ltd.; Gibralter Lock Co. Ltd. (Canada); Weiser Inc. (Canada); Weiser Lock Co. Ltd. (Canada); HTH Haustechnische Handels Ges m.b.H (Germany); Masco, GmbH (Germany); The SKS Group (Germany); Koema SRL (Italy); Rubinetterie Mariani S.p.A. (Italy); The Alvac Group (Spain); Weiser Thailand; Masco Corporation Limited (U.K.); Weiser (U.K.) Ltd.

Principal Divisions

Artistic Brass; Thermador; Waste King; Weiser Lock; Masco-Mex (Mexico).

Further Reading

Barkholz, David, "Masco's Furniture-Biz Pullout Could Be Costly," *Crain's Detroit Business,* June 26, 1995, pp. 1, 26.

Koselka, Rita, "Resetting the Table," *Forbes,* March 16, 1992, pp. 66–67.

Masco Corporation: A Tradition of Excellence for 65 Years, Taylor, Michigan: Masco Corporation, [1994].

Masco 50: The First Fifty Years 1929–79, Taylor, Michigan: Masco Corporation, [1979].

Palmeri, Christopher, "Keeping Good People," *Forbes,* May 24, 1993, pp. 50–51.

Reingold, Jennifer, "The Masco Fiasco: Masco Corp. Was Once One of America's Most Admired Companies. Not Anymore," *Financial World,* October 24, 1995, pp. 32–34.

Salomon, R. S., Jr., "Can an Old Boss Learn New Tricks?," *Forbes,* July 29, 1996, p. 102.

Stopa, Marsha, "Masco at Home in Mexico," *Crain's Detroit Business,* July 10, 1995, pp. 1, 24.

—René Steinke
—updated by David E. Salamie

McIlhenny Company

Highway 29
Avery Island, Louisiana 70513
U.S.A.
(318) 365-8175
Fax: (318) 369-6326
Web site: http://www.tabasco.com

Private Company
Incorporated: c. 1907
Employees: 230
Sales: $105 million (1996)
SICs: 2035 Pickled Fruits & Vegetables, Etc.

McIlhenny Company is a family-owned and operated manufacturer of Tabasco brand pepper sauce. Tabasco, perhaps the most famous of 150 pepper sauces available, actually started the pepper sauce industry. The company remains a leader in domestic pepper sauce with more than a 34 percent share of the market in the 1990s, as well as a longstanding provider of pepper sauce across the globe. As Mark Robichaux explained in the *Wall Street Journal,* the McIlhenny Company "still profits every day from developing the first widely sold hot sauce and, in essence, creating the market."

Early History of Avery Island

The history of the McIlhenny Company should begin with a discussion of Avery Island, since the Tabasco sauce recipe depended on the island's salt and peppers. Located 140 miles west of New Orleans and 150 feet above sea level, Avery Island—a 2,300-acre tract located in the bayou country of Louisiana—actually was the uppermost portion of a salt mountain. The largest of five such salt domes, Avery Island had rich soil, Cyprus-lined waterways, exotic flora, and ancient oaks. The earliest artifacts found on the island—stone weapons for hunting—dated back 12,000 years. Evidence of mastodons and mammoths, saber-toothed tigers, and tiny three-toed horses also had been discovered there. If interpretations surrounding the basket fragments, stone implements, and Indian pottery found

on the island are correct, a salt brining industry began there in 1300 A.D.

French explorers discovered the island sometime during the 18th century, and white settlers arrived in Avery Island by the century's end—when the Indians disappeared from the island. The salt brine springs, however, remained active, first distinguishing themselves during the War of 1812 when Andrew Jackson's troops used Avery Island salt in the Battle of New Orleans.

In 1818, Sarah Craig Marsh's father purchased some land on Avery Island, then known as Isle Petite Anse. Sarah Craig Marsh later married one Daniel Dudley Avery, and their descendants—through time and through marriage—came to control the whole island.

Mr. McIlhenny Visits 19th-Century Louisiana and Stays

During the mid-1800s, New Orleans was one of the largest, busiest cities in the United States. It was no surprise, then, that Edmund McIlhenny, an East Coast bank agent, should visit the city. A fifth-generation American of Scottish and Irish descent, McIlhenny was an accomplished marksman, yachtsman, and prize-winning horse breeder who loved good food. (Once at Antoine's restaurant he commented: "I enjoyed this so much. I feel like starting all over again." So he did: McIlhenny ate a second full-course dinner.)

In 1859 at the age of 43, McIlhenny married Mary Eliza Avery, the daughter of Sarah Craig Marsh and Daniel Dudley Avery. Avery, a lawyer and judge in Baton Rouge, Louisiana, also operated a sugar plantation on his land on Isle Petite Anse. In 1862, a massive rock salt deposit was discovered on the island, so the Averys moved from the city to the island to oversee the quarrying, which supplied salt to the blockaded Confederate states. The Avery family grew wealthy cultivating the island's rock salt and marketing the salt as a meat preservative.

McIlhenny enjoyed gardening as a hobby at the family's plantation on Isle Petite Anse. In 1848, a friend gave him some extra-spicy pepper seeds that the friend had come upon in

Mexico during the Mexican-American War. (Later these peppers were identified as *Capsicum frutescens*. Although about 20 wild species were known in the New World—mostly in South America—only about five species had been cultivated domestically. The Tabasco peppers were the only *Capsicum frutescens* cultivar in the United States.) McIlhenny planted the seeds and began experimenting with recipes for a pepper sauce with which to season local southern Louisiana dishes from Spanish, French, American Indian, and African traditions.

The Civil War, however, interrupted his work. In 1863, Union troops invaded Isle Petite Anse and captured the salt quarries. The McIlhennys and Averys fled to Texas. Upon their return, McIlhenny and his in-laws found a changed Louisiana. A career in banking in New Orleans was out of the question after the Civil War, so the Averys and McIlhenny relocated to Isle Petite Anse permanently and began to rebuild. The island, the salt quarry, the sugar cane all were in ruins—except for the pepper plants. McIlhenny learned that the humidity caused the plants to grow heartily on the island, so—motivated by dullness of Reconstruction food—he resumed his pepper sauce experiments until he perfected a recipe that everyone seemed to enjoy.

Post-Civil War Recipe for Success

McIlhenny's recipe was elegantly simple. He mashed the peppers the day he harvested them, mixed them with a little Avery Island salt (a half coffee cup of salt for each gallon of crushed peppers), aged the mixture for 30 days in wooden barrels, added the "best French wine vinegar," aged the mixture another 30 days—hand stirring to blend the flavors—and strained the naturally bright red sauce into old perfume bottles sealed with green wax and topped with shakers. Family and friends suggested selling "that famous sauce Mr. McIlhenny makes" for additional income, so McIlhenny began marketing his creation.

McIlhenny thought about naming his pepper sauce Petite Anse Sauce after his island home. Other family members, however, did not share McIlhenny's enthusiasm for using this name for a commercial product, so he called the sauce Tabasco—a Central American Indian word meaning "land where soil is hot and humid." McIlhenny's Tabasco sauce became the original hot sauce—now a trademark and service mark of the McIlhenny Company.

In 1868, McIlhenny sent 350 samples to wholesalers in New York—including the E.C. Hazard Grocery Company, owned by the cousin of a friend. By 1869 McIlhenny received thousands of orders for the sauce at $1.00 a bottle. The wholesalers even sent Tabasco sauce as far away as England. In 1870 McIlhenny received a U.S. Letters Patent for his Tabasco brand pepper sauce. He quit banking and began a full-time career in pepper sauce manufacturing.

In 1872, McIlhenny established a London office to meet the heavy demands of the European market for Tabasco sauce. Throughout its history, Tabasco sauce remained a favorite in England. For example, when the product's availability in Great Britain became threatened by the "Buy British" campaign of the isolationist British government in 1932, a crisis of national proportions erupted. Unhappy without their pepper sauce—a staple in the House of Commons dining room—Members of Parliament protested and, with support of the press, the "Buy British" motto became "Buy Tabasco."

John Avery McIlhenny Continues the Tradition, 1890s

When Edmund McIlhenny died in 1890, his son John Avery McIlhenny assumed control of making the Tabasco sauce. Immediately upon taking his new position, John McIlhenny visited established commercial Tabasco customers throughout the United States. He intended to familiarize himself with existing accounts and to court new business. Some of his marketing efforts included bill posters; large wooden signs in fields near cities; drummers canvassing house-to-house in selected cities; exhibits at food expositions; circulars and folders; and free trial-size samples. (Ironically, the company's marketing strategies changed little since John McIlhenny's plans. The McIlhenny Company relied heavily on print ads in trade and consumer periodicals to market Tabasco sauce throughout its history. It was many years from its establishment before the McIlhenny Company's first television commercial in 1985, although both print and TV ads were used widely in the 1990s.)

John McIlhenny also commissioned an opera company to perform the "Burlesque Opera of Tabasco." When in 1893 Harvard's Hasty Pudding Club asked permission to use Tabasco in one of its reviews, John McIlhenny bought the rights to the review and staged it in New York. Samples of Tabasco sauce were given away during the show's matinee performances. Other early marketing efforts included promotions such as a grocery store contest with a $3,000 prize and offers for famous painting reproductions in exchange for a Tabasco coupon and a 10 cents handling charge.

In 1898, John Avery McIlhenny joined the First Volunteer Calvary of the U.S. Army, serving as a Rough Rider with Teddy Roosevelt at San Juan Hill. McIlhenny traveled extensively after the Spanish-American War. In 1906 he left Louisiana to work for his friend President Roosevelt at the U.S. Civil Service Commission, eventually becoming the U.S. Minister Plenipotentiary to Haiti in 1922. Under John Avery McIlhenny's direction, the family's Tabasco business grew tenfold.

Mr. Ned

In 1907, Edmund Avery McIlhenny ("Mr. Ned"), the second son of the inventor of Tabasco sauce, became president of the just-formed McIlhenny Company, which was created to manufacture and market Tabasco sauce. Mr. Ned's brother, food authority Rufus Avery McIlhenny, served as the new company's production supervisor during this time. Rufus McIlhenny was also responsible for engineering and purchasing.

Mr. Ned grew the business both domestically and internationally, as well as successfully defended the company in several trademark infringement suits attempted by competing companies. Many competing pepper sauces were regional imitations of Tabasco sauce but, unlike competing brands, Tabasco contained no food colorings, stabilizers, garlic, or other ingredients. Tabasco also was the only national brand aged for three years in white-oak barrels. Other pepper sauces were made from cayenne peppers, which ranked between 1,000 and 3,000 on the Scoville Scale. (A pharmacist named Wilbur Scoville devised a scale by which to judge the intensity of hot peppers and related products. He reserved a zero rating for the mildest of peppers, i.e., an ordinary bell pepper. Mayan habanero peppers—the hottest of the hot—measured about 350,000 on the pharmacist's scale.) Tabasco sauce, however, was made from Capsicum peppers, so it rated higher on the scale than competing cayenne-pepper products: between 9,000 and 12,000. Tabasco sauce was "not just an old stand-by," revealed John Mariani in *Sports Afield*, "but a lovely, aromatic, beautifully balanced sauce with a true Louisiana vinegar tang to it."

Tabasco Sauce and the Environment

In addition to developing the McIlhenny Company, Mr. Ned preserved the natural environment of Avery Island through a variety of conservation efforts. Before becoming the company's president, Mr. Ned—a self-trained biologist—traveled the world on scientific expeditions. When Mr. Ned returned to Avery Island to run operations at the Tabasco factory, he realized that the snowy egret—a bird native to Louisiana—was all but extinct from plume hunters pillaging the species for feathers for ladies' hats. Mr. Ned captured eight snowy egrets and established a colony for them in which to multiply and live safely. Thousands of egrets and migratory birds have found homes since then in the Bird City rookery on Avery Island. In the 1990s, 20,000 snowy egrets and other water birds could be found on the island.

Mr. Ned also brought the nutria—fast-breeding, brown furry rodents with webbed feet and long, hairless tails—from South America to Louisiana in the 1930s. Plant life, too, was protected by Mr. Ned. When oil was found on Avery Island in 1942, Mr. Ned insisted that work crews bury pipelines or paint them green to blend with the surrounding Jungle Gardens.

Walter Stauffer McIlhenny and the 1940s

The son of John Avery McIlhenny succeeded Mr. Ned as the leader of McIlhenny Company. The great-great-grandson of President Zachary Taylor (on his mother's side), Walter Stauffer McIlhenny joined the family business during the 1940s. He built the brick Tabasco sauce plant and brought new management and marketing techniques to the company. Under his guidance, McIlhenny Company stayed true to its traditions. Walter McIlhenny refused offers to sell the business and recoiled from changing the recipe for Tabasco sauce. In fact, Walter McIlhenny's production process remained virtually unchanged from his ancestor's.

As others before him, Walter McIlhenny planted 75 acres of peppers on Avery Island. Workers hand-picked the hot peppers when they ripened. (He equipped each worker with *le petit baton rouge* (a red stick) by which to identify the correct shade of ripe peppers.) Walter McIlhenny himself hand weighed the day's harvest. Then the harvested peppers were chopped and packed with a little Avery Island salt in 50 gallon white-oak wooden barrels for three years. When properly aged, the pepper mash was inspected personally by McIlhenny. Then vinegar was added to the mixture, which was stirred by a mechanical arm for about four weeks (a rare modification of Edmund McIlhenny's hand stirring of the mixture with wooden paddles). Finally, the mixture was strained of seeds and pepper skins and bottled, but only the mixture went into the containers. No preservatives, additives, coloring, or flavoring ever went into a bottle of Tabasco sauce.

Tabasco Sauce Goes to War

Nicknamed "Tabasco Mac" by his fellow Marine Corps reservists, Walter McIlhenny served his country as well as his company with distinction. Stationed at Guadalcanal, he received the Navy Cross and a Silver Star during World War II before earning the rank of Brigadier General. He, too, was a distinguished marksman and a member of the President's One Hundred. Since soldiers were close to his heart, Walter McIlhenny created a C-ration cookbook for use by members of the U.S. Armed Forces during the Vietnam Conflict. Knowing that the U.S. Armed Forces used Tabasco sauce liberally on their C-rations, Walter McIlhenny produced the *Charley Ration Cookbook; or, No Food Is Too Good for the Man up Front.* Copies were sent to soldiers with bottles of Tabasco sauce. Walter McIlhenny even designed a Tabasco bottle holster that attached to a cartridge belt. This tradition continued into the Gulf War when every third MRE (Meals Ready to Eat) contained a small package of Tabasco sauce and a recipe booklet. Eventually every MRE included Tabasco sauce.

Those Hot Pepper Plants

Walter McIlhenny continued to select personally the pepper seeds for the next crop from the plants grown on Avery Island. The seeds were treated, dried, and stored on the island and in a bank vault until the next year's planting. Up until the 1960s, all plants used for Tabasco sauce were grown on Avery Island. When a shortage of harvesters caused concern, the company turned to the land and laborers of Mexico for planting and harvesting the pepper crops. (Mechanical harvesters proved less competitive than Latin American workers for the company.) Though all pepper plants start on the island, Avery Island peppers accounted for only a small amount of the peppers used in production since the 1960s. Peppers grown in Columbia, Honduras, Venezuela, or other countries eventually comprised about 90 percent of those used in manufacturing. In addition to the labor considerations, the company adopted this practice to ensure a constant supply of peppers since the Avery Island crop could be imperiled by disease or weather; for example, Hurricane Andrew threatened (but did no lasting damage to) the Avery Island pepper crop and Tabasco factory in 1992.

The growing cycle for the pepper plants remained unchanged over the years: workers planted seeds in greenhouses in January. In April, seedlings were moved to their respective fields on Avery Island or abroad. Workers harvested peppers by hand beginning in August.

Edward McIlhenny Simmons and the 1990s

Like his predecessors, Edward McIlhenny Simmons, the company's next president and a great-grandson of Tabasco's inventor, remained personally involved in the growing of peppers and making of Tabasco sauce. He continued the tradition of selecting 1,200 pepper plants annually for 70 pounds of seeds for future crops. Simmons stored 20 pounds of the seeds in a bank vault in New Iberia and 50 pounds at the company's headquarters as a safeguard against crop loss.

So Tabasco sauce production continued as it had for more than 100 years. As Robichaux wrote: "The shape of the bottle has changed little, as has the process of making the sauce." Nevertheless, the McIlhenny Company expanded the Tabasco line over the years to include chili powder, seasoned salt, and popcorn seasonings. The company also created a Bloody Mary mix, a Seven-Spice Chili recipe, and a picante sauce for Tabasco consumers. "We've been a one-product company long enough," said Edward McIlhenny Simmons in *Americana* magazine in 1991.

The year 1991 also brought the first acquisition for the company. McIlhenny Company purchased Trappey's Fine Foods, manufacturer of Red Devil pepper sauce and other seasoning-related items. The McIlhenny Company marketed these recently acquired products under a new name: McIlhenny Farms. The acquisition allowed the company to offer a wider variety of merchandise, including pepper jelly, ketchup, and molasses.

The amount of Tabasco sauce manufactured daily of course grew with demand. During the 1990s millions of bottles of the sauce had been sold throughout the world, with production requiring labels to be printed in no less than 15 languages. In 1996, for example, more than 50 million bottles of Tabasco sauce were sold in at least 105 countries. Canada alone used 250,000 bottles in one year. Japan, the largest consumer of Tabasco sauce abroad, imported the sauce for sushi, spaghetti, and pizza recipes.

By 1997, the factory on Avery Island operated four production lines. In total, 450,000 two-ounce bottles could be manufactured daily with all lines in operation. (Each two-ounce bottle typically contained about 720 drops of Tabasco sauce, so the factory had the potential to manufacture about 324 million drops of Tabasco sauce each day in 1997.)

On the Web

The company also launched an interesting and unusual interactive web site—PepperFest—in 1996 to reach the multitude of Tabasco consumers. "With users of Tabasco products located all over the world," explained executive vice president Paul C. P. McIlhenny in a press release, "it just makes sense to offer accessible information via the World Wide Web. We want people to have fun visiting our PepperFest, and at the same time we welcome their feedback and suggestions."

The Sauce with Universal Appeal

Indeed, Tabasco might be a household word throughout the world. McIlhenny's pepper sauce "traveled to Khartoum with Lord Kitchener," revealed Pat Mandell in *Americana*, "and was carried on Himalayan expeditions, in the mess kits of World War I doughboys, and aboard Skylab. It is the quintessential ingredient in Bloody Marys. Its pungent flavor enlivens gumbos, eggs, steaks and stews, salads, chicken a la king, French onion soup, and jambalaya." The pepper sauce even was approved for Kosher cooking. As the first commercial hot sauce ever, the elixir, its founder, and his descendants became known in legend, lore, and fact for creating a new product and a market. As Cal Garrett, a manager with rival Durkee's Red Hot sauce, said: "They've built a great niche."

Further Reading

Callahan, Maureen, "Fifteen Foods with Hidden Healing Power," *Redbook,* October 1991, p. 138.
Deveny, Kathleen, "Rival Hot Sauces Are Breathing Fire at Market Leader Tabasco," *Wall Street Journal,* January 7, 1993, p. B1.
Mandell, Pat, "Louisiana Hot," *Americana,* February 1991, pp. 26–32.
Mariani, John, "In Praise of (Very Hot) Sauces," *Sports Afield,* May 1996, p. 50.
"McIlhenny Company: Announcing the Tabasco Sauce 'Ultimate Summer Cookout' Online Sweepstakes," *M2 Presswire,* May 16, 1997.
McIlhenny Company, "Ask Mr. Broussard, the Tabasco Historian," *PepperFest: A Livin', Breathin' Festival on the World Wide Web* @ http://www.tabasco.com.
McIlhenny Company, "One Click Ahead," *PepperFest: A Livin', Breathin' Festival on the World Wide Web* @ http://www.tabasco.com.
"McIlhenny Company: McIlhenny Company Launches Tabasco PepperFest Website," *M2 Presswire,* August 27, 1996.
McIlhenny Company, *Recipes from the Land of Tabasco Pepper Sauce,* Avery Island, LA: McIlhenny Company.
Moore, Diane M., *The Treasures of Avery Island,* Lafayette, LA: Acadian House Publishing, 1990.
Morcos, Ann, "Wetlands Pest," *Boys' Life,* January 1996, p. 17.
Naj, Amal, *Peppers: A Story of Hot Pursuits,* New York, NY: Alfred A. Knopf, 1992.
"New on the Web: The McIlhenny Company," *Telecomworldwire,* May 20, 1997.
Reynolds, J. R., "L.A. House of Blues Is Foundation HQ," *Billboard,* July 30, 1994, p. 19.
Rice, William, "Tabasco Sauce Stands up to a Hurricane," *Detroit Free Press,* November 18, 1992.
Robichaux, Mark, "Tabasco Sauce Maker Remains Hot after 125 Years," *Wall Street Journal,* May 11, 1990.

—Charity Anne Dorgan

Mel Farr Automotive Group

24750 Greenfield
Oak Park, Michigan 48237
U.S.A.
(810) 967-3700
Web site: http://www.toyotadealer.com/mel_farr

Private Company
Incorporated: 1975 as Mel Farr Ford
Employees: 800
Sales: $492 million (1996)
SICs: 5511 Auto New and Used—Retail; 5531 Auto
   Parts Dealer—Retail

When it comes to auto dealerships in and around the Motor City, the name Mel Farr is ubiquitous. Under the umbrella of the Mel Farr Automotive Group, Fords, Lincolns, Mercuries, and Chevies, as well as import brands are marketed under the familiar "Mel Farr, Superstar" logo, both in the Detroit area and in other key markets across the United States. Hailed as one of the leading African American entrepreneurs in the nation, former Detroit Lions star running back Farr has spent over two decades building what has become one of the country's largest auto dealerships. Despite the scale of his auto empire, Farr continues to direct all facets of the Automotive Group that bears his name; in his role as sports hero-turned-successful businessman he has appeared on such television programs as the *CBS Evening News,* CNN's internationally aired *Moneyline,* and NBC's *Today Show,* and has been featured in business periodicals from the *Wall Street Journal* to *Black Enterprise* magazine.

Born in Beaumont, Texas, in 1944, Farr received a football scholarship to the University of California—Los Angeles, where he studied political science between 1963 and 1967 and played football for the UCLA Bruins. His success on the football field caused him to postpone college after his junior year, when the 22-year-old athlete was named Consensus All-American, joined the NFL draft, and became the number one draft choice for the Detroit Lions. Moving east to the Motor City, Farr earned rookie-of-the-year honors in 1967, and was a member of the NFL's All Pro Team in both 1967 and 1972. Equally ambitious and realistic about his post-Lions future, the running back got married and started a family, while also attending night classes. During the off-season he worked in various capacities at Detroit's Ford Motor Company, where he gained valuable job experience and, in 1970, helped Ford design a program to develop minority-owned dealerships. Farr completed his B.S. in political science at the University of Detroit, graduating in 1971; he retired from the Lions three years later due to extensive knee and shoulder injuries. Farr was inducted into the UCLA Sports Hall of Fame in 1988.

Opens First Dealership in 1975

Although in 1974 he ended the affiliation with the Lions that had originally brought him to Detroit, Farr now considered Motown to be his home. He wanted to transform his work experience with Ford into a lucrative career by purchasing an auto dealership, but Ford executives felt that the one-time football star needed more experience. So, in November 1975, Farr entered into a partnership with John Cook, one of his former trainers at Ford's, putting up $40,000 of his own money to purchase a dealership in Oak Park that had floundered under its two previous owners.

While Cook and Farr had been friends for several years, as business partners they rarely saw eye to eye. Growing increasingly frustrated, Farr finally bought out Cook's portion of the Oak Park dealership to form Mel Farr Ford in 1978, financing the purchase with money he had saved from his last three years as a running back for the Lions. While the purchase fulfilled one of Farr's dreams, it also brought him numerous headaches. As he would later admit in *Black Enterprise,* he was familiar with products and salesmanship but not with finance. "I thought I was buying a profitable business," Farr recalled. "Instead, I had bought a company that was on the verge of bankruptcy." Not only was the dealership on shaky financial ground to begin with, but the rug was pulled out from under it when the Organization of Petroleum Exporting Countries (OPEC) decided to begin their embargo of crude oil a year later, sending gasoline prices soaring and the U.S. economy into a nosedive. Sales of full- and mid-sized American cars plummeted, while inflation spiraled interest rates and the cost of living drastically upward.

1980s Prove to Be a Rollercoaster Ride for Auto Industry

By 1980, with auto sales fallen to half their 1979 level, Farr's Ford dealership in Oak Park was near collapse. His situation reflected the state of things around the nation: minority dealerships were closing in record numbers, down from almost 100 in the late 1970s to 16 by December 1980. The economic downturn across the United States continued to force car sales into a nosedive, and Farr feared he would be among the next casualties of the recession. Forced to lay off half of his work force—including his janitorial staff—the resilient Farr turned to the federal government for help. In 1978 Farr had been honored for his outstanding athletic achievements by President Jimmy Carter; he now turned to Carter for help, appealing directly to the president for loans for auto dealers. Carter responded by pledging to provide $400 million in low-interest Small Business Administration (SBA) loans to Farr and other minority business owners in 1981, allowing these entrepreneurs to avoid the fate of colleagues forced into bankruptcy due to prevailing double-digit interest rates. Farr obtained $200,000 from the SBA, and buoyed his business even more with a matching loan from Ford.

In June 1986, with the national economy stabilized and his Oak Park dealership now on solid financial footing, Farr purchased what he would grow into an award-winning Lincoln-Mercury Merkur franchise based near the city of Pontiac. Now with 78 employees, Mel Farr Automotive grossed $26.8 million in sales during the year. By 1989, with three dealerships—Farr opened another Lincoln-Mercury Merkur dealership in Aurora, Colorado—and the economy still on the fast track, Farr Automotive would earn $52.1 million in annual revenues through the efforts of its 160 employees.

Opportunities for Minorities Becomes Crusade

While there were still a handful of minority-owned Ford dealerships in place after the industry's tailspin in the early 1980s, most of them were located in struggling inner-city neighborhoods rather than in prime retail locations. "The general practice in the placement of the original black dealers was to place them in inner cities with deteriorating neighborhoods," Farr explained during a speech before the Automotive News World Congress in 1992. "These locations were without growth potential, with poor credit risks, and limited access to competent personnel. It should not surprise you that these dealerships failed."

Although continuing to expand his own business's market in the area of domestic car sales, Farr was also frustrated by the lack of minority-owned import car franchises in the United States. It was a situation that was also gaining the attention of state legislators. As early as 1983 Farr had recognized that the growing sales of Japanese cars among U.S. buyers was not a fad but a long-term trend; he applied for a Toyota dealership but was forced to wait almost eight years before receiving one. According to a report by Carol Cain in the *Detroit News,* gaining import franchises was a prime goal of large dealers in

an increasingly competitive auto market. "Under the wave of consolidation," noted Cain, "the survivors will most likely be the 'megadealers' which offer a variety of car lines under one roof." A savvy businessman, Farr intended to become one of these megadealers; in addition to Toyota, he pursued dealership opportunities with Mazda, Honda, and other import car companies, all without timely success. Finally, in July 1989, Farr's application for a Toyota dealership was approved. Deciding to close his Colorado Lincoln-Mercury dealership due to its distance from his Michigan home, Farr channeled those assets into building a foreign compact car market with Mel Farr Toyota. The dealership, which was the fifth African American-owned Toyota dealership in the country, would be expanded in 1993 and renamed Mel Farr Imports after franchises for Mazda and Volkswagen were added at its upscale Bloomfield Hills location. By 1997 the showroom would be staffed by over 50 employees.

Expands in Midwest and Beyond in Early 1990s

As a recessionary economy stagnated growth during the early 1990s, Farr was one of only 20 percent of minority dealers who managed to stay in business nationwide. In 1991, as 904 new-car dealerships went out of business across the country (70 of them minority-owned), Farr Automotive Group's collective sales were reported at $106 million, a 16 percent jump over the previous year, while the company's Oak Park store watched more than 300 new or used cars roll out of their sales lots each month. Mel Farr Automotive, which employed 240 men and women in 1991, ranked sixth highest in sales volume of any Ford dealer in the country and second in sales of the compact Festiva and Escort models.

Now director of the National Association of Minority Auto Dealers (NAMAD), Farr decided to approach the government regarding further SBA loans, this time to right what he saw as an uneven playing field, particularly in the foreign auto dealership sector. By 1992, minority dealers of Japanese and European import cars numbered only 60—scarcely 1 percent of the total import dealerships nationwide—according to NAMAD. In contrast, 43 percent of the cars purchased by African Americans were imports.

Farr continued to build upon his success throughout the decade. In May 1993 Mel Farr Automotive made its first move out of the metropolitan Detroit area, purchasing the Mel Farr Ford of Grand Blanc franchise. The year 1995 would find Farr crossing state lines for the first time; in April Mel Farr Lincoln-Mercury-Ohio opened its showroom in Dayton. The following year saw the opening of Mel Farr Ford-Texas in Houston and in January 1997 Farr opened a Ford dealership in Baltimore, Maryland, that employed 65 people.

One of the reasons for Farr's success was advertising. Whether or not you were in the market for a new car, chances were that if you lived in the Detroit area, Farr was a familiar sight. Beginning in 1979, his zany commercials—which he wrote, directed, videotaped, edited, and starred in—peppered the television airwaves. Calling himself "Mel Farr, Superstar" in reference to his moniker as a running back for the Lions, the auto dealer was pictured flying high above the competition by 1981, complete with a red cape à la Superman. Mid-1987 found the superstar dealer overseeing a giant "Wheel of Farr-tune" located in each of his Ford dealerships that new or used car-buyers could spin after a sale for a chance at $10,000. When the auto market turned sour, as it did in both the early 1980s and 1990s, Farr's ads became more wacky and more common; in fact, they had their genesis in the recession of 1979 when, as Farr later recalled, he thought to himself "things are so bad I might as well go for it. If I go out of business, I'm going to go out with a bang." In 1986 Farr would hire an advertising manager to take care of the production of his television spots, continuing his policy of frequent, high-visibility advertising.

Record-Breaking Sales Characterize Mid-1990s

Thanks to the work of an employee base that now numbered 495, company sales for 1995 climbed to $372 million, an 82 percent increase over 1994. Throughout the early 1990s Farr's dealerships continued to break records and receive praise both inside and outside of the industry. In 1995 alone, Mel Farr Ford would rank in the top 10 in new car sales in four car categories according to Ford Motor Company calculations, and its service department was cited for excellence as well.

The high sticker prices on new vehicles and the flood of late-model, preowned cars released onto the used car market during the mid-1990s after being turned in by leaseholders created both a strong demand and a steady supply in the used car market. Realizing that this was an ideal time to get into the market, in August 1996 Farr opened Mel Farr "Superstar" Used Cars in Ferndale, a suburb of Detroit. Staffed with 43 employees, the new dealership covered 13 acres with an inventory of between 400 and 500 used vehicles. The showroom for the new Farr location was a converted Midas Muffler Shop; in addition to serving as a used-car showroom it also housed a used car reconditioning center and a body shop.

During the same month, Farr also expanded in the foreign car market, supplementing his Toyota, Mazda, and Volkswagen franchise with Mel Farr Hyundai and Suzuki. By the end of 1996 Farr's nine franchises and his used car dealership reported combined annual gross sales of $492 million; the projection for the following year stood at over $700 million in new and used auto sales. In June 1997 he balanced these new import dealerships by acquiring a Chevrolet franchise in Metuchen, New Jersey.

Top Black Business-Owner in Michigan in 1997

Beginning in 1982 with only 52 employees at his flagship store, Farr would watch his payroll roster grow to 197 by 1997.

Regularly positioned at or near the top of annual rankings of state-operated businesses, Mel Farr Automotive Group was cited as the #1 Black Owned Business in Michigan by *Crain's Detroit Business* in 1997, an honor that followed its ranking as #24 of the top 200 privately owned companies in the state the year before. The network of 10 franchises, taken together, employed over 800, most of them in the metro-Detroit area.

In addition to his many area dealerships, Farr remained committed to the city of Detroit and to improving the opportunities for blacks and other minorities in the auto industry. Active in city and regional affairs, he served as a board member to numerous organizations, including the Better Business Bureau of Detroit and Southeast Michigan, the Metropolitan Detroit YMCA, the Oak Park, Michigan, Chamber of Commerce, and others.

In 1996 Farr was recognized by President Bill Clinton as one of the Top African American Businessmen in the United States. The father of three grown children with his wife, Mae, Farr has watched as sons Mel Jr. and Mike have followed in his footsteps, both as managers of Mel Farr Automotive Group and Mel Farr Ford, respectively, and as football players for the NFL. "I have always been a dreamer," Farr told Tedra Butler-Dudley of *African American on Wheels.* "You just need to set goals when you dream. My goal is to become the largest merchandiser of automobiles both new and used for urban dwellers." By 1997 Farr could claim to be fast approaching his goal, and expressed the possibility of going public with his business to further both Mel Farr Automotive Group and the industry.

Principal Subsidiaries

Mel Farr Ford; Mel Farr Lincoln-Mercury; Mel Far Imports; Mel Farr Ford—Ohio; Mel Farr Ford—Texas; Mel Farr "Superstar" Used Cars; Mel Farr Chevrolet.

Further Reading

Bray, Hiawatha, "Mr. Touchdown," *Black Enterprise,* June 1992.

Butler-Dudley, Tedra, "Flying High with Mel Far," *African Americans on Wheels,* Spring 1997.

Cain, Carol, "Import Carmakers Accused of Bias," *Detroit News,* May 2, 1987.

Gruley, Bryan, "Minority Dealers Seek Aid, Import Franchises," *Detroit News,* June 5, 1992.

Legette, Cynthia, "Nobody Does It Better," *Black Enterprise,* December 1988.

Yung, Katherine, "Farr to Open Used-Car Superstore," *Detroit News,* February 7, 1996.

—Pamela L. Shelton

MERCURY AIR GROUP, INC.

Mercury Air Group, Inc.

5456 McConnell Avenue
Los Angeles, California 90066
U.S.A.
(310) 827-2737
Fax: (310) 827-5510
Web site: http://www.mercuryairgroup.com

Public Company
Incorporated: 1956
Employees: 1,152
Sales: $225 million (1996)
Stock Exchanges: American
SICs: 4581 Air Freight and Ground Handling

Mercury Air Group, Inc. is one of the fastest-growing companies in the air services industry. The firm provides fuel, fueling, and maintenance services, and air cargo services to airline companies and airports around the globe, and aviation services to the United States Government. In 1996, total revenues grew by over 23 percent, and projections for the financial future of the company seem just as promising. Mercury Air Group's international aviation fuel services business provides fuel to more than 100 airlines throughout the world, and prides itself on being the largest independent supplier of fuel and fueling services at Los Angeles International Airport (LAX). Mercury Air Cargo, one of the company's subsidiaries, provides air cargo services for many of the largest airlines in the world, and handles such diverse items as perishable food and flowers to 50-ton generators. Maytag Aircraft Corporation, the other primary subsidiary of the company, provides aviation fuel storage, transportation, refueling and maintenance services to U.S. military bases throughout the world. Due to its reputation as one of the most trustworthy and reliable aviation services contractors, Maytag Aircraft had been entrusted to provide fueling services at the Blue Angels flying team base in Pensacola, Florida, and the Top Gun fighter-pilot training base in Fallon, Nevada.

Early History

Mercury Air Group, Inc. was founded by three of the original pilots of the "Flying Tigers," the legendary American Volunteer Group that fought against the Japanese during World War II. Even before the Japanese attack on Pearl Harbor in December 1941, and America's formal declaration of war against Japan, a group of adventurous pilots under the leadership of Claire Chennault formed a volunteer group to defend China from the Japanese. The "Flying Tigers," as the American Volunteer Group became known, was renowned for its fearlessness and courage under fire. The Flying Tigers fought the Japanese over an extensive front ranging from Rangoon, Burma, to Kweilin, China, and flew dangerous missions deep into enemy territory. It has been documented that the Flying Tigers actually prevented an entire Japanese division from invading a Chinese city in the southwest region of the country. As the war continued, the Flying Tigers heaped one victory upon another until, when World War II came to a close, the American group of volunteers had assured a place for themselves in the history of aerial combat.

After the war had ended, 12 members of the Flying Tigers pooled their resources and established the Flying Tigers Airline. This airline, mostly transporting cargo and passengers to remote destinations in the South Pacific and Asia, was immediately successful due to its association with the legendary World War II fighter pilot group. As the airline grew, with more and more passengers, and more cargo routes to Asia, the company established itself as a genuine competitor to the other nascent commercial airline companies such as Pan Am and Trans World Airlines.

Throughout the late 1940s and early 1950s, Flying Tigers Airline continued to focus on the transportation of both passengers and cargo. As the airline industry grew, however, a few of the men associated with the airline recognized that aviation support services, such as providing fuel and fueling services for commercial aircraft, could lead to huge revenues. Three of these men, Robert J. "Catfish" Raine, Robert P. Hedman, and Thomas C. Haywood, Jr., proposed the idea that the airline expand its operations to include aviation services. Unfortunately, the men were turned down by their colleagues.

Company Perspectives:

Our team of world class employees gives Mercury Air Group, Inc. the competitive edge in providing petroleum products, cargo and aviation services around the globe. Mercury Air Group was founded in 1956 by three original members of the legendary AVG Flying Tigers, whose focus on teamwork continues to guide our Company's core mission of service to the aviation industry today. Mercury Air Group's greatest asset is its people. By working together, we guarantee our customers an exceptional level of service and, in turn, we are able to build lasting values for our shareholders.

Undeterred by the refusal of their World War II chums, Raine, Hedman, and Haywood broke away from Flying Tigers Airline and formed their own company, Mercury Services, in 1956. With an initial investment of $80,000, and a fleet of 4 fuel trucks and one maintenance truck, the three men launched their business by attracting larger airlines to contract their services. By the end of the decade, Mercury Services had contracted a number of the airlines flying back and forth to Asia, as well as a growing client list of domestic airlines, to provide fueling and maintenance services. As Mercury Services grew, it garnered contracts for ground handling services, such as baggage loading and unloading, for Los Angeles International Airport. By the end of the decade, the company was growing slowly but steadily, and revenues were beginning to increase.

For the entire decade of the 1960s, Mercury Services provided fuel, fueling, and maintenance services, and ground handling services for a growing list of client airlines, mostly in the western region of the United States, particularly California. Not interested in expanding the company's operations, the three owners were content to procure contracts for Mercury's firmly established core businesses. Not surprisingly, the company continued to increase its revenues. By 1969, Mercury Services reported an annual sales volume of just under $2 million.

Transition and Expansion

Mercury Services was purchased in 1972 for approximately $750,000 by Seymour Kahn, the owner of an electrical manufacturing business on the West Coast. Kahn, a graduate of City College of New York and 47 years old at the time of the acquisition, recognized the need for expanding Mercury's operations to meet the burgeoning need of increased commercial and cargo aviation traffic. Kahn assumed control of the company from the three famous Flying Tigers as quickly as he could, and immediately initiated a comprehensive strategy to cut costs, increase profitability, eliminate redundant aviation services, and meet the needs of domestic and international commercial airline companies.

One of the most important moves Kahn made was to refocus the company's operations. He discontinued the company's contracts to clean domestic airline passenger cabins, and reduced Mercury's baggage handling services at Los Angeles Interna-

tional Airport. Instead, Kahn arranged for Mercury to concentrate on aircraft refueling at the airport, and many others along the coast of California. In addition, Kahn implemented Mercury's cargo handling operations, flying cargo from Asia to Los Angeles, and then arranging for its transportation by ship, rail, or air to the American East Coast, Europe, and South America. By the end of the 1970s, Mercury Services had changed its name to Mercury Air Group, Inc., and had increased its revenues to approximately $50 million annually.

During the 1980s, Kahn was diligent and unwavering in pursuing his strategy to build Mercury into one of the preeminent aviation service companies in the United States. Under Kahn's direction, Mercury Air Group was one of the first firms in the country to establish and operate a mechanized cargo-handling operation at LAX. Kahn also significantly expanded the company's aviation fuel services, especially at LAX where it developed into the largest independent provider of fuel and fueling services during the mid-1980s. By employing the latest computer technology, Mercury Air Group was able to monitor the flow of oil around the globe in order to get the best price per barrel on all petroleum products. This innovative system enabled the company to achieve an extremely high volume of sales, and ultimately resulted in partnerships with major oil companies and independent refiners. As a result, contracts for fuel and fueling services with the major airlines came fast and furious, including such well-known commercial and cargo airline companies as American, Aeroflot, Continental, Delta, Egypt Air, El Al Israel, Avianca, Federal Express, Burlington Air Express, DHL Airways, and many more.

Yet the most important decision Kahn made during the 1980s was to purchase Maytag Aircraft Corporation. With headquarters in Colorado Springs, Colorado, Maytag Aircraft was one of the premier contractors to the United States government and its military airbases throughout the world. Maytag Aircraft provided aviation fuel storage, transport, refueling, and maintenance services to American military bases in Okinawa, Colorado, and the Island of Crete in the Mediterranean, just to name a few. Besides providing support services to the Blue Angels flying team and the Air Force's Top Gun training facility, Maytag also provided ground handling services, air terminal operations, and base maintenance at military facilities both domestic and foreign. Having never defaulted on a government contract, the company had become widely known as one of the most reliable firms in the aviation services industry. With the acquisition of Maytag, and the continued expansion of its aviation services throughout the United States, Mercury Air Group reached approximately $70 million in revenue by the end of fiscal 1989.

The 1990s and Beyond

In the early 1990s, the company formed two subsidiaries, Mercury Air Cargo, Inc., which incorporated the wide variety of air cargo services it was already providing to major airlines around the world, and Hermes Aviation, Inc., an air cargo booking agency. As soon as it had been created and formally established operations, Mercury Air Cargo began to handle enormous amounts of domestic and international cargo for airlines by arranging space brokerage and logistical services for all types of air shipments, from flowers to 50-ton generators. Its list of clients soon included British Airways, Delta, Finnair, Virgin Atlantic, South African Airways, Swissair, Japan Airlines, Iberia Airlines, United, Aeromexico, and a host of other domestic and international carriers.

Perhaps even more importantly, however, was the formation of Hermes Aviation, Inc., the company's general cargo sales and marketing agent. International airline companies that only scheduled a few flights per week into Los Angeles soon discovered that, since they were already purchasing fuel from Mercury, they could reduce their operating expenses even more if they contracted Hermes Aviation to load, unload, and warehouse their cargo. Hermes bought large blocks of cargo space from the airline companies and then resold it to freight forwarders at a rate less than normally paid. This kind of outsourcing helped major airlines to significantly reduce their costs. In addition, the logistics experts at Hermes Aviation were in the forefront of arranging innovative sea-air shipments to Europe and South America. Cargo arriving by sea container at the port of Los Angeles was taken to the airport and repacked for cargo planes destined for Europe and South America. The greater availability of cargo space from California enabled Hermes to charge lower rates for shippers that did not require immediate delivery by air. All of this activity helped Kahn to achieve his goal of $100 million in revenues by the end of fiscal 1994.

During the early and mid-1990s, the company also expanded into what was dubbed "fixed air-base operation centers." This division of Mercury provided a full range of services to passenger and cargo airlines, including fuel sales, full ground support with heavy maintenance done on planes such as Boeing's 747-400s, hangar rentals, aircraft parking and tie down, catering, and weather reporting. Located near an airport's principal runways, the company soon established fixed air-base operation centers at Los Angeles International, Dallas, Atlanta, Ontario, Reno, and Santa Barbara airports.

In 1995, Mercury Air Group was included in the annual ranking by *Forbes* as one of America's top 200 small firms. Based on a five-year growth rate, sales, market share, and profitability, Mercury Air Group was ranked as the 115th best small company and the only aviation services firm included in the listing. The ranking was well justified. In 1996, Mercury Air Group reported total sales of $225 million, a 23 percent increase over the previous year.

By the end of fiscal 1996, the company was providing aviation fuel services to over 100 airlines around the globe, and had become the largest independent fuel and fueling services provider at Los Angeles International Airport. The company's

Mercury Air Cargo subsidiary acquired two air cargo firms to increase its presence at airports in Montreal and Toronto, Canada, as well as at airports in the Miami, Florida area. At the same time, the company received approval to build a new 170,000-square-foot warehouse at LAX, which would give Mercury Air the largest air cargo capacity at the airport.

In 1996, Maytag Aircraft Corporation won a major contract with Yokota Air Base in Japan to expand its military housing maintenance. The company was also involved in refueling operations at NSA Souda Bay, Crete, which provided military aircraft the ability to fly missions over Bosnia and northern Iraq. The company's fixed base air centers continued to expand their services, with major ground handling contracts awarded to the Reno, Nevada fixed base center, and record-breaking fuel sales at LAX. In August 1996, Mercury Air Group purchased the assets of five fixed base operations centers from Raytheon Aircraft Services, Inc. for $8.25 million, and came closer to its goal of creating a chain of fixed base centers across the United States.

Mercury Air Group is still headed by Seymour Kahn, whose goal is to double the company's sales figure to over $400 million by the end of the decade. As the demand for outsourcing airline ground services continues to increase at airports around the world, Kahn's goal is not unrealistic.

Principal Subsidiaries

Mercury Air Cargo, Inc.; Hermes Aviation, Inc.; Maytag Aircraft Corporation; Excel Cargo, Inc.

Further Reading

"Air Carriers Win Market Share, Lose Dollars," *Purchasing,* April 3, 1997, p. 51.

Davies, John, "Mercury's Success Fuels Growth," *Air Commerce,* January 27, 1997, pp. 14–16.

"Intra-Asia Still Dominates The Market," *Air Transport World,* January 1997, p. 63.

Malkin, Richard, "Facets of Competition," *Distribution,* January 1997, p. 62.

Nelms, Douglas W., "At The Crossroads," *Air Transport World,* January 1997, p. 57.

"New Air Regs Could Be Costly," *Purchasing,* March 20, 1997, p. 52.

Sullivan, Ben, "Air Merchant," *Los Angeles Business Journal,* March 10, 1997, p. 17.

Trunick, Perry A., "Continued Growth For Air Freight," *Transportation & Distribution,* April 1997, p. 52.

—Thomas Derdak

Montgomery Ward

Montgomery Ward & Co., Incorporated

Montgomery Ward Plaza
Chicago, Illinois 60671
U.S.A.
(312) 467-2000
Fax: (312) 467-3975
Web site: http://www.mward.com

Private Company
Incorporated: 1889
Employees: 60,000
Sales: $6.62 billion (1996)
SICs: 5311 Department Stores; 5722 Household
    Appliance Stores

Montgomery Ward & Co., Incorporated is a national retailer with more than 400 stores in 43 states. It is the ninth-largest U.S. retailer and the largest privately held retailer in the country. The company operates a number of retailing concepts, including the flagship Montgomery Ward stores, which contain up to five specialty departments: Electric Ave., major appliances and electronics; Rooms & More, home furnishings and accessories; Auto Express, tires, batteries, parts, and service; The Apparel Store, men's, women's, and children's apparel and accessories; and Gold 'N Gems, fine jewelry. Other concepts under the Montgomery Ward umbrella include Lechmere, a retailer of home products; Electric Ave. & More, which sells electronics, major appliances, and furniture; and HomeImage by Lechmere, touted as the first store in America to combine the areas of electronics, appliances, bed, bath, and housewares under one roof. The Signature Group subsidiary provides financial services and operates one of the largest auto clubs in the United States.

Early History

Montgomery Ward had its origins in the 1860s when young Chicagoan Aaron Montgomery Ward saw that he could undercut rural retailers by selling directly to farmers via mail-order without intermediaries and by delivering by rail. After a false start in October 1871—when the Great Chicago Fire destroyed his inventory—Ward and two minority partners sent out their first mailing in the spring of 1872.

Orders trickled in, and soon he bought out his partners, who were discouraged by the slow pace of business. Late in 1872 he got a break. The Illinois Grange, a farmers' organization, named Ward its purchasing agent. He began subtitling Montgomery Ward price lists with the phrase Original Grange Supply House. This gave Ward access to Grange mailing lists and meetings.

As the business grew, Ward needed more capital and more help. Late in 1873, his brother-in-law, George Thorne, put $500 into the firm and became an equal partner. While Ward had the inspiration for the business, George Thorne was a practical day-to-day manager.

Postal rates fell and Ward stepped up advertising in newly popular magazines. Through publications such as the *Prairie Farmer* he told farmers to query him for catalogs with penny postcards. His spring catalog for 1874 had 32 pages. That fall he expanded to 100 pages. By the end of 1874, sales topped $100,000.

Ward's primary customer was the farmer. City orders were a nuisance. His bestseller was the sewing machine, and the catalog was filled with pumps, feed cutters, cane mills, corn shellers, threshers, saws, grinders, and engines. Ward used buying power to cut prices, sometimes halving retail, but manufacturers formed trusts to keep prices high. Ward, in turn, found bargains in foreign markets and searched out small manufacturers willing to sell for less.

Increased sales—$300,000 in 1875—allowed Ward to increase service. He instituted a satisfaction-guaranteed-or-your-money-back policy; he carried three grades of merchandise, good, better, and best; and he counseled customers to band together and split fixed freight costs.

During the 1880s, competition in the form of major department stores began to enter the catalog field. Jordan Marsh & Co., John Wanamaker, Sears, and Carson, Pirie, Scott & Co. all began or resumed mail order operations. Still the biggest and most popular, Ward's 240-page 1883 catalog listed 10,000 items. In 1884 Ward bought the *Farmer's Voice* weekly newspaper to use as an advertising vehicle. In 1886 William C. Thorne, George Thorne's eldest son, increased the size and circulation of the catalog, leading to a boom in orders. By 1888 Ward's sales had reached $1.8 million. To cap off the decade, Ward and George Thorne turned their partnership into a corporation in 1889.

Heightened Competition with Sears Began in 1890s

In 1891 a depression hit. Aaron Ward and George Thorne responded by emphasizing value and quality. Their prices were low but not low enough for the poorest. Into that breach Richard Sears, founder of Sears, Roebuck & Co., walked with the slogan "we always undersell." By 1892, the Ward catalog contained 568 pages and 8,000 illustrations. Management had sold the *Farmer's Voice*, but kept advertising in it, and worked hard to beat trusts in twine, agricultural implements, sugar, and barbed wire. In 1893 Aaron Ward and George Thorne turned managing control over to Thorne's four sons. In the deal, the Thornes gained majority control of stock, but Ward remained president.

Thorne's sons believed that Montgomery Ward represented quality and Sears merchandise was inferior. Unwilling to compete for the bottom, they tried to convince the public that cheaply made goods were no bargain. As Sears grew, however, the Thornes began making exaggerated claims for Ward. Even with competition, Ward's sales were growing, and profits were good. In 1900 Ward built a new headquarters at Michigan Boulevard and Madison Street in Chicago. Sales that year, however, were $8.7 million, trailing Sears's $10 million. The Thornes's marketing approach was mixed. They did not emulate Richard Sears's outrageous copywriting, but they did compete on price. Like Sears they offered premiums as incentives for customers to buy more, and in 1906 they mailed out three million free catalogs, after having charged 15¢ per catalog for many years. Sales for 1906 were $18 million.

The Thornes wanted to increase profit margins by increasing quality and price. To sell higher-priced goods, James Thorne used advertising that compared Ward's and competing goods, and point for point explained why Ward's merchandise was better.

The business situation began to change. The U.S. Postal Service's initiation of a parcel post system in 1913 gave mail-order business a boost. Both Ward and Sears benefited, but the Thornes had trouble keeping profit levels high. In 1912 Ward made a 6.7 percent profit, and the following year it made 4.1 percent, while Sears made 9.1 percent. Ward, with fewer customers, spent proportionately more on advertising, was building branch warehouses, and made few of its own goods. Both Ward and Sears had become public companies but remained family-controlled.

Montgomery Ward made $3.4 million on 1915 sales of $49 million, as a boom period began. Already ahead in exports, it created a Spanish-language catalog for Latin America the following year. However, even with record profits—$6.4 million on 1918 sales of $76.2 million—the Thornes could see Montgomery Ward had fallen behind Sears. With the death of co-founder George Thorne in September—Aaron Ward had died in 1913—they sought new capital and new thinking. They sold a majority stake to a group fronted by United Cigar Stores's George Whelan and tobacco magnate James B. Duke and backed by financier J. P. Morgan. The Thorne brothers continued to run the business.

Post-World War I inflation pushed 1919 sales to $99.33 million, but profits were just $4.1 million. Former Quartermaster General of the Army Robert E. Wood was recruited to increase margins. In obtaining materials for the Panama Canal, Wood had instituted a bottom-up plan of buying. Bottom-up buying entailed working with manufacturers to lower prices while ensuring profits for both parties.

In September 1920 a financial panic hit, and prices began to fall. Caught with a high-priced inventory and a high-priced catalog, Ward sent out new circulars. Sales dropped to two-thirds of their 1919 level. Whelan and Duke sold their stock to J. P. Morgan and the First National Bank of New York. Losses for 1920 totaled $10 million.

To unload inventory, the Thornes set up retail outlets in big cities. As conditions worsened, Robert Thorne resigned from the presidency, and Silas Strawn became interim president. Ward's bankers then brought in their own president, Theodore Merseles, an engineer who had been vice president of the National Cloak and Suit Company.

In 1922 the economy rebounded. Merseles got back into contact with farmers and found a demand for medium-priced, quality goods. Wood used bottom-up pricing to acquire raw materials and get good deals on automotive supplies and radio kits, and Merseles, who had a feel for fashion, got bargains from cash-starved European manufacturers.

Even though 1922 marked a return to profitability, Wood sensed that the automobile would eventually render mail order obsolete. He pushed Merseles to get into retailing but Merseles refused. Ironically, car tires and batteries were then two of Ward's most profitable lines.

Frustrated by his inability to implement retailing, General Wood began negotiating with Sears. In 1924 Merseles heard of the negotiations and fired Wood. Wood soon joined Sears, which embraced his store program.

Retail Stores Opened in the Late 1920s

Through 1925, Merseles stuck with mail order but in 1926 he began to open catalog stores that exhibited merchandise. In the wake of a softening mail-order market, and after these exhibit stores began spontaneously selling merchandise, Merseles announced that Montgomery Ward would open stores in towns with populations of 10,000 to 15,000.

In 1927 Merseles left Montgomery Ward to run Johns-Manville. To replace him, the board picked George Everitt, Merseles's assistant. Everitt announced a crash plan for 1,500 rural stores by the end of 1929. Ward issued new stock in November 1928 and opened 208 stores that year. By early 1929 the economy and competition were heating up. Ward's sales for the first eight months of the year were up 31 percent. Sears began prepaying shipping. After many customers switched, Ward reluctantly followed suit in July.

The stock market crash came in October, but overall 1929 was not a bad year. Profits reached $13 million, and Ward had 531 stores operating. As the Great Depression began to set in, things disintegrated. The retailing business, which had expanded too fast, became unprofitable and disorganized. Executives resigned, catalog sales fell, and profits for 1930 were less than $500,000. Ward received a merger proposal from Sears.

Ward's situation worsened in 1931 with losses of $8.7 million on $198 million in sales. To save Ward, J.P. Morgan & Company representative Harry P. Davison recruited Sewell Avery. Avery was known for leading United States Gypsum (USG) to Depression-era profits.

Avery found cash-starved manufacturers to sell him goods cheaper than Sears could make them. He paid employees less than Sears was paying those it had hired before the crash. He recruited dissatisfied Sears people, who felt blocked from promotions, and talented executives who had lost their jobs with other retailers. Avery and Edwin G. Booz from USG evaluated Ward managers, promoted the good ones, and fired the bad ones. After closing 147 poorly performing stores, Montgomery Ward lost $5.7 million on 1932 sales of $176.4 million.

U.S. President Franklin D. Roosevelt's interventionist policy helped jump-start the economy and gave Ward and Sears an unintended benefit. Through the National Industrial Recovery Act he propped up prices, but Ward and Sears refused to cooperate and kept their prices low. Montgomery Ward returned to the black in 1933, making $2.9 million from store sales, but losing $630,000 on the catalog operation.

Avery continued to expand. Ward initiated telephone orders in 1934. Profits topped $13.5 million in 1935 and broke the $20 million mark in 1936. Credit terms became more generous, and stores were divided into classes ranging from department stores in cities to hard-goods stores in rural areas.

By 1937 Ward's sales were 76 percent of Sears's and well ahead of J.C. Penney's, but there were also problems. The federal Robinson-Patman Act, passed in 1936, prevented big stores like Wards from getting better deals than small stores. Fair trade laws stated that manufacturers could name retail prices. Ward tried to get around this by selling house brands.

The company made a public relations coup in 1939, when an in-house copywriter wrote a booklet about a little red-nosed reindeer named Rudolph, which became a Christmas classic. The booklet was included in millions of catalogs.

Avery's Mismanagement Led to Decline in 1940s and 1950s

With talk of war, Sewell Avery, who was not convinced that the Great Depression of the 1930s had run its course, was pessimistic. Profits for 1940 were a disappointing 4.5 percent of sales. As the United States entered World War II, imports from Europe virtually stopped. Shortages and substitutions became the rule. The government took even closer control of industry.

Avery, who detested interference, fought the government and the unions. In November 1942 he argued with President Roosevelt and the National War Labor Board over a closed shop for the United Mail Order, Warehouse, and Retail Employees' Union. Early in 1944, he refused to sign contracts with store employees. The War Labor Board ordered Avery to extend old contracts. Avery refused. On April 24 Roosevelt sent the National Guard to Montgomery Ward. They removed Avery bodily, got rid of several other top executives, and ran the company.

On May 9, 1944, the government returned Montgomery Ward to the management, but in December, labor problems struck again. The Congress of Industrial Organization (CIO) won an election in Ward's Chicago plant. Avery again refused a union shop. On December 28, 1944, the army seized Ward's Chicago catalog operations. The situation caused orders to pile up at the rate of 10,000 a day.

By 1944 Montgomery Ward's sales were just 62 percent of Sears's. As the war drew to a close Avery conserved cash for what he saw as an upcoming depression. The postwar boom—profits were $52 million in 1946—did little to change his mind as Sears and others expanded.

Three years later, Avery seemed increasingly out of touch. Disgruntled executives resigned, and others were fired in moments of pique. In 1950 Avery came down with pneumonia, but even on his sickbed he insisted on making decisions.

In 1954 dissident stockholder Louis E. Wolfson began a proxy fight to unseat Avery and take over Ward. The 42-year-old Florida financier had made a fortune during the war, first by selling odd lots to the army and then through moviehouses and real estate. The proxy fight culminated at the April meeting, during which the 81-year-old Avery gave disjointed answers to Wolfson and his group. Although Wolfson's bid failed, days after the meeting Avery resigned as chairman, and Edmund Krider, who led the counterattack against Wolfson, resigned as president. Three weeks later the board named John Barr president and chairman.

The Montgomery Ward that Avery left had fallen behind the times. Its 600 stores were smaller and located in less populous areas than Sears's 702 stores. It had 250 catalog offices compared to Sears's 605. Sales were one-third of Sears's $3 billion, and profits were just $35.4 million. Inflation had eroded Ward's cash position. J.C. Penney was moving up fast. Discount chains were undercutting traditional retailers.

Barr tried to reinfuse a positive spirit. He brought back Ward alumni, closed unsuccessful stores, and concentrated on modernizing existing ones. His program was basically the one Wolfson had originally proposed.

In 1957 Barr established a store research and development department that used demographic information to locate the first new stores since before the war. The following year, Barr began opening clusters of stores in key cities. He upgraded packaging, increased private brands, and announced an expansion plan. Ward opened 30 new full-line stores between 1958 and 1960.

Continuing Struggle for Profitability in 1960s and 1970s

The new stores did well, but by 1960, the old ones were doing poorly. Mail order was just a shadow of its former self. Sales for 1960 reached $1.2 billion, but profits were just $15 million, a trend that continued into 1961. Poor results at old downtown and rural stores were balanced to some degree by shiny new suburban and mall outlets. Strapped for cash, Barr stopped building new stores.

In his search for new management, Barr consulted Ward and Sears alumnus Theodore Houser, who recommended two other former Sears executives, Robert E. Brooker, president of Whirlpool Corporation, and Ed Gudeman, undersecretary of commerce in U.S. President John F. Kennedy's administration.

Brooker became president in November 1961 and by 1962 had brought in nearly 200 new executives. He conceived a strategy of encircling growing metropolitan areas, thereby cutting down on per-store costs for advertising. The strategy worked in such growing cities as San Diego and Dallas-Fort Worth, but was limited because of high start-up costs.

Working on the Sears model, Brooker cut the number of suppliers and increased private brands. He centralized management for procurement and promotion but decentralized it for retail operations. Like Wood, he established relationships with suppliers. He also increased loyal and profitable credit customers.

Throughout the 1960s Brooker and Gudeman—who became a director in 1963—pushed Montgomery Ward to greater sales and more efficient procurement. By 1966 long-term contracts with suppliers had increased to 75 percent from 30 percent in 1960. Profits still did not catch up to Sears's, however. In 1965 Barr retired and Brooker became chairman.

Ed Donnell, who became president in 1966, continued the expansion plans. Montgomery Ward, however, often had too few trained people to run the new stores properly. Profits for 1966 were just $16.5 million on sales of $1.7 billion.

In the late 1960s Brooker began to worry about hostile takeovers. To avoid this, Ward found a friendly acquirer, Container Corporation of America. To its advantage, Container Corporation could defer taxes on its profits because of Ward's tax-advantaged credit sales. The merger was announced in July 1968. Ward stockholders owned two-thirds of Marcor, the new holding company, but Container Corporation president Leo Schoenhofen was the largest stockholder and became chief executive officer of Marcor.

The joined companies retained separate offices. In May 1970 Robert Brooker retired. Leo Schoenhofen became chairman, and Ed Donnell was renamed president and CEO of Montgomery Ward. New stores continued to open at the rate of 25 a year, while old ones closed one by one. By 1972, Ward's 100th anniversary, the big retailer was adding a million square feet of store space a year, primarily in shopping centers.

While Montgomery Ward had been concentrating on its stores and catalogs, Ward executive Dick Cremer had been building a profitable direct-mail business within the company's billing operation, The Signature Group. In the late 1960s he began by inserting merchandise offers within bills sent to customers. In 1973 he began offering credit insurance through the mail, and in 1974 he started the hugely successful Montgomery Ward Auto Club, which became a Signature Group subsidiary.

Mobil Corporation secretly bought 4.5 percent of Marcor in 1973. Although Ward's profits remained low—just 2¢ on the dollar—the following summer Mobil paid $35 a share for 51 percent of Marcor. In 1975 Mobil bought the rest of Marcor and separated Ward and Container Corporation.

Montgomery Ward's new president under the Mobil regime, Sidney A. McKnight, continued to face disappointing profit levels. In an effort to cut catalog losses Ward began selling advertising space in the company's catalog in 1976.

McKnight's efforts and Mobil's money seemed to pay off at first. In 1978 sales reached $5.47 billion, and pretax profits hit $224 million. The following year was a disaster, however; Ward lost $133 million from operations and $30 million from closing old stores. Mobil, whose hopes had been high, lent the retailer $350 million interest-free and was trying to keep from lending more.

Since the end of the Avery regime Ward had been trying to remake itself. According to some analysts it was simultaneously bleeding cash and becoming extremely competitive with its new, modern stores. As losses mounted, Mobil lent Ward another $100 million. By the end of 1980, Montgomery Ward had lost $233 million on sales of $5.92 billion. On the bright side, both the Signature Group and the new Jefferson Ward discount chain made money.

Stores-Within-a-Store Concept Launched in 1980s

Searching for another savior, Mobil recruited Stephen Pistner, who had turned around Dayton Hudson's B. Dalton and Target chains. Pistner took another $50 million loan from Mobil and offered early retirement to hundreds of executives. He also squelched a plan to convert more than 100 Montgomery Wards to Jefferson Ward stores. He convinced Ward to accept more name brands, closed unprofitable stores, and eliminated unprofitable lines. Further, he experimented with the stores-within-a-store concept. Yet the losses continued. In 1981 Montgomery Ward lost $217 million on sales of $5.64 billion. The catalog was losing more than the stores.

Ward had another bad year in 1982, but in 1983 finally hit the black again with profits of $56 million. That same year Pistner centralized advertising and buying authority in Chicago and absorbed the fast-growing but sometimes chaotic Signature Group into the catalog and insurance division.

In 1984, after three years of experimentation, Pistner unveiled his seven-stores-within-a-store concept. In Pistner's vision, large stores might contain several smaller specialty stores. Those specialty stores also might stand alone. Before Pistner could implement his plans, however, he had a falling out with Mobil and left the company. Richard F. Tucker, president of Mobil Diversified Business, acted as president of Ward. In January 1985, Ward closed 300 catalog stores. What remained were 322 Montgomery Ward Stores, 44 Jefferson Ward stores, the catalog, and the Signature Group. A few months later the company sold 18 Jefferson Ward stores. Montgomery Ward was the sixth-largest retailer and the third-largest catalog house in the United States.

By then Mobil definitely wanted to sell Montgomery Ward. It also considered spinning Ward off as a dividend to stockholders. To make Ward more attractive it forgave $500 million in loans to Ward.

In June 1985 Mobil persuaded former Ward executive Bernard Brennan (who had previously worked as assistant national manager for furniture at Sears) to return as president and chief executive officer. Brennan had been coarchitect of the stores-within-a-store concept. Brennan closed the unprofitable catalog business and shuttered Jefferson Ward. He refined the seven-stores-within-a-store plan to four types of stores-within-a-store: apparel; home furnishings and accessories; electronics and appliances; and automotive goods. He experimented with stores with all four departments and some with fewer and leased store space to Toys "R" Us, Inc. and small specialty retailers. In another key move he bought 52 percent of the Clayton Bank and Trust of Clayton, Delaware. Through Clayton, which was later sold, Signature began offering credit cards, loans, and other financial services.

After another year of improved profits in 1987, Brennan oversaw what was then the largest management-led leveraged buyout in U.S. history, with the management group in partnership with General Electric Co.'s GE Capital Corp. paying $3.8 billion for Ward in 1988. Subsequently, GE Capital owned 49 percent of Ward, Brennan 35 percent, and other company managers the remaining 16 percent. Ward became the tenth-largest privately held company in the United States.

1990s Marked by Declining Profitability

The 1990s started on a promising note for Montgomery Ward as the company posted record earnings of $153 million in 1990. It appeared that the stores-within-a-store concept was working. In October 1991 Ward continued to expand in specialty markets by forming a 50–50 joint venture with Fingerhut Companies, Inc., the fourth-largest U.S. catalog marketing company. Known as Montgomery Ward Direct, the partnership was to pursue the same specialty marketing strategy in its catalogs that Montgomery Ward employed in its stores. This partnership proved to be less than a rousing success and Ward in June 1996 sold its interest in it to ValueVision International Inc.

Meanwhile the promise of 1990 quickly faded as profits fell in 1991 and 1992, remained level in 1993, rebounded slightly in 1994, then fell precipitously in 1995. Following 1990, the company's stores were adversely affected by a number of factors: increasing competition in the consumer electronics and appliances sectors, fueled by such category-killers as Circuit City and Best Buy, had a big impact on Ward's leading sector, Electric Ave.; the lack of brand name apparel became an even greater liability once Sears began to emphasize its "softer side" and Kmart added brand names to its racks; and the severe early 1990s recession in California hit Ward particularly hard, since the company had about 16 percent of its stores there. Compounding the situation was turmoil in the management ranks,

brought about—according to many observers—by tough boss Brennan, who ran through president after president; from 1992 to 1994, three people held the revolving door post of Ward president.

In the mid-1990s Montgomery Ward attempted to turn around its fortunes through expansion. In March the company acquired Lechmere, Inc., a Boston-based retailer of consumer electronics, appliances, and housewares with 28 stores in New England and $800 million in annual revenues. Lechmere originated as a Cambridge, Massachusetts, harness-making business in 1915, eventually emerging in 1948 as a retailer selling automobile tires, appliances, radios, and televisions, called Lechmere Tire and Sales Co. Lechmere became famous in New England for its low prices and was considered by many to be the first American discounter. Additional consumer items were added over the years, but by the late 1960s there were but two Lechmere stores. In 1969 the Dayton Company (soon called Dayton Hudson) bought Lechmere and quickly expanded it into a regional chain. In 1989 Berkshire Partners in conjunction with senior Lechmere managers purchased the company in a leveraged buyout. In 1994, Ward bought Lechmere from Berkshire for $113 million in cash and the assumption of $91 million of Lechmere debt. In order to improve Lechmere's profitability, Brennan decided to cut staff, a move that ran counter to the chain's emphasis on customer service. As a result, Lechmere lost customers. Although Brennan had expanded the chain soon after the acquisition, by early 1997 store closings had brought the number of Lechmere units down to 27.

Another 1994 expansion move was the launching of the Electric Ave. & More stores. Targeted at midsize markets, these Ward spinoffs carried electronics goods, major appliances, and furniture, sectors that remained the company's strongest. By early 1997 Ward had opened 11 Electric Ave. & More stores.

By mid-1996 any further growth of Lechmere or Electric Ave. & More was at least temporarily halted so that the company could concentrate on a new launch, HomeImage by Lechmere; six HomeImage stores opened in August 1996. These home superstores carried a full line of brand name, value-priced goods for the home, including home entertainment, home office, home wares (kitchen appliances, furniture, and cookware), and home comfort (tableware, bed and bath, and mattresses).

By mid-1997 it was too early to tell whether these expansion moves would bring Montgomery Ward back from the brink. After profits fell 90 percent in 1995, the company posted a $237 million loss in 1996. Results for 1997 were expected to be even more dismal. To make matters worse, 1996 sales of $6.62 billion represented a drop of 6 percent over the 1995 mark, after sales had increased each year since 1990. Same-store sales fell 11 percent in 1996.

In January 1997 GE Capital Services forced Brennan aside to allow an outsider to take over day-to-day responsibility for Montgomery Ward (Brennan did, however, retain his stake in the company). Roger Goddu, who had been president of U.S. merchandising for Toys "R" Us, was named the new chairman and CEO. Goddu began his attempt to turn around the beleaguered company by announcing a plan to shift focus to higher-margin merchandise, and to have Montgomery Ward occupy a narrow niche between discounters and department stores. Such a strategy would be similar to successful moves already made by Sears and Kmart.

In the first half of 1997 Goddu liquidated $500 million in unproductive inventory, leading to a first quarter loss of $144 million. Meanwhile, GE Capital Services provided a much needed infusion when it invested another $200 million in Montgomery Ward in May 1997. Then in June Goddu eliminated 400 of Ward's 1,800 corporate jobs. The company was also trying to sell The Signature Group to raise additional cash, hoping to realize more than $1 billion from the sale; in mid-1997 Ward was in negotiations with HFS Corp. about Signature. But before a deal could be consummated, Ward on July 1 went into default on $1.4 billion in loans, and after failing to reach an agreement with its lenders, filed for Chapter 11 bankruptcy protection from its creditors on July 7, 1997. Although GE Capital immediately provided Ward with $1 billion in financing to keep the company's stores stocked while it attempted to reorganize, the future of Montgomery Ward was very much in doubt.

Principal Subsidiaries

Lechmere, Inc.; The Signature Group.

Further Reading

Balu, Rekha, "Crunch Time at Montgomery Ward," *Crain's Chicago Business*, March 17, 1997, p. 1.

Berner, Robert, "Ward Files for Protection from Creditors," *Wall Street Journal*, July 8, 1997, pp. A3, A4.

Berss, Marcia, "Help Wanted, Retailing Exp. Req.," *Forbes*, May 6, 1996, p. 97.

——, "Temper Tantrums," *Forbes*, January 17, 1994, p. 47.

Chandler, Susan, "This LBO Could Be on Its Last Legs: Options at Montgomery Ward Are Dwindling, and It Needs Cash," *Business Week*, September 23, 1996, pp. 136, 138.

Collins, Lisa, "Shedding Siege Mentality Tough Test for Ward's," *Crain's Chicago Business*, October 29, 1990, p. 3.

Hoge, Cecil C. Sr., *The First Hundred Years Are the Toughest: What We Can Learn from the Century of Competition Between Sears and Wards*, Berkeley, California: Ten Speed Press, 1988.

Kelly, Kevin, and Greg Burns, "Is Peace Coming to Montgomery Ward?," *Business Week*, January 31, 1994, p. 34.

Latham, Frank Brown, *1872–1972 A Century of Serving Consumers: The Story of Montgomery Ward*, Chicago: Montgomery Ward & Co., Incorporated, 1972.

Mammarella, James, "HomeImage: Ward's Gamble for Growth," *Discount Store News*, October 7, 1996, pp. H5–H7.

Smart, Tim, and Susan Chandler, "The Monkey on GE's Back: Can Ward Map a Survival Plan before Welch Shuts Its Doors?," *Business Week*, May 19, 1997, p. 40.

Steinhauer, Jennifer, "Ward, Down and Struggling, Plans to Follow Revived Rivals," *New York Times*, May 3, 1997, pp. 21, 34.

—Jordan Wankoff
—updated by David E. Salamie

MYLAN LABORATORIES INC.

Mylan Laboratories Inc.

1030 Century Building
130 Seventh Street
Pittsburgh, Pennsylvania 15222
U.S.A.
(412) 232-0100
Fax: (412) 232-0123

Public Company
Incorporated: 1961 as Milan Laboratories Inc.
Employees: 1,300
Sales: $392.8 million (1996)
Stock Exchanges: New York
SICs: 2834 Pharmaceutical Preparations

One of the leading pharmaceutical manufacturers in the United States, Mylan Laboratories Inc. produces and markets numerous generic and proprietary drugs. Mylan made its mark in the pharmaceutical industry as a manufacturer of generic drugs, or those pharmaceutical products no longer protected by patents. From the manufacture of generic drugs, the company branched out into other areas of the pharmaceutical industry, introducing its first proprietary drug, Maxzide, in 1984 and a half-strength version in 1988. Acquisitions completed during the late 1980s and into the 1990s brought Mylan into other market niches, including anti-Parkinson's disease medications and transdermal drug delivery systems. During the late 1990s, the company's operations included high-technology research and development laboratories, manufacturing and packaging facilities in West Virginia, Puerto Rico, Texas, Vermont, Illinois, and Florida, and distribution centers in North Carolina and Nevada.

Origins

Industry stalwart Mylan began business as a small, privately-owned company in 1961. The company later earned accolades for its manufacturing speed and efficiency—two cornerstones of success in the generic drug business—but it began as an upstart distributor of pharmaceuticals based in the sleepy confines of White Sulphur Springs, West Virginia. Initially, the company operated under the name Milan, drawing its corporate title from the name of one of the company's two founders, Milan Puskar, who directed the company's fortunes during two distinct eras in its history. Puskar, in his mid-20s when he founded Milan, scored his greatest success as a manufacturer of drugs but early on he subsisted exclusively by reselling drugs manufactured by other companies to pharmacies and doctors. The foray into manufacturing occurred four years after the company began business, and after two relocations of the company's headquarters. In 1963, Puskar moved his operations to Princeton, West Virginia, and then moved again two years later, settling in Morgantown, West Virginia. The move to Morgantown in 1965 occurred the same year the company began producing vitamins, the first product manufactured under the Milan banner.

Manufacturing in Morgantown picked up speed quickly following the company's debut as a vitamin producer. In 1966, Milan received approval from the Food and Drug Administration (FDA) to start manufacturing Penicillin G tablets, the first in a long line of generic drugs the company would produce. Two years later, production activity in Morgantown was expanded when the FDA gave Milan the nod to produce the antibiotic Tetracycline. By the following year—in 1969—Parke-Davis had begun purchasing the company's manufactured drugs, becoming the first major drug company signed up as a Milan customer. Over the course of the next several years the number of major drug companies who purchased Milan's products under private label increased, as did the number of FDA-approved drugs Milan manufactured, such as the addition of Erythromycin in 1971 and Ampicillin in 1973. What looked good on the outside, however, was not necessarily positive in Morgantown. Milan's roster of major customers was growing and the number of approved drugs manufactured by the company was increasing, but Puskar was unhappy, frustrated by the direction the company was taking. In 1972, after a management dispute, Puskar left the company he had founded 11 years earlier, ending the first chapter in the company's history and marking the beginning of a near-disastrous period for the West Virginia pharmaceutical concern.

After Puskar's exit, Milan changed its name to Mylan and converted to public ownership, debuting on the OTC (over-the-counter) market in February 1973. The years immediately following Puskar's resignation were difficult ones for the small but rapidly growing pharmaceutical manufacturer, years that evinced Puskar's perception that the company was headed in the wrong direction. When Roy McKnight, president of a manufacturer's representative company, joined Mylan's board of directors in late 1975 he discovered precisely how errant the company's course had been, portending Mylan "was facing imminent bankruptcy." Despite the company's early success in gaining FDA approval to manufacture drugs and the growing number of major drug firms who had signed on as customers, Mylan was in dire need of help. Inventories were overstated by $2 million, more than $400,000 was owed in back taxes, 320 production workers were on strike, and the company had a negative net worth of $900,000. The situation was grave, but McKnight, who had no previous experience in the drug industry prior to joining Mylan's board, could not muster sufficient support in finding a solution to the company's problems. Discouraged, he wrested control of the company, naming himself chairman and chief executive officer, and fired Mylan's president. For a replacement to the company's presidential post, McKnight chose Puskar, reinstating the company's founder to his creation.

New Management in 1976

McKnight and Puskar took the helm in early 1976 and immediately began to effect sweeping changes, resolving to concentrate on the manufacture of generic drugs. McKnight persuaded Mylan's bankers to extend additional credit to the company, trimmed the company's workforce by one-third, and spearheaded more aggressive marketing campaigns, vowing at the same time to discontinue the production of any drug that was unprofitable. One year later, the measures enacted by McKnight had proven effective. By 1977, Mylan was once again a profitable company.

During the years following Puskar's return and McKnight's arrival, Mylan recorded steady and encouraging growth, its operations leaner and more cost-efficient as a result of the lessons learned from the mistakes during the first half of the 1970s. The company used only four salespeople to sell commodity generic pharmaceuticals under their chemical names, marketing the drugs to bulk buyers such as drugstore chains, mail-order houses, and distributors. The company also moved heavily into producing and selling branded generics that were no longer covered by patents. In the business of producing such generic drugs, foresight, manufacturing speed, and manufacturing efficiency were key attributes for success, attributes Mylan exuded as it developed from a small pharmaceutical concern into one of the nation's dominant forces. Being the first to market a branded drug once its patent expired meant exponentially higher profits for a generic drug manufacturer. Once a patent expired, the generic equivalent was generally introduced at 70 percent of the price of the brand. As more and more generic manufacturers entered the fray, typically marketing as many as twelve generic equivalents for each branded drug, the price for the generics dropped, eventually bottoming out at 10 percent of the brand price. Consequently, the first to market a generic response earned the highest profits, while the latecomers earned only a fraction of the original yield for their efforts. Mylan, with its operating costs down and its efforts sharply focused on being the first to market, began to flourish in the race for supremacy in the discount market, ascending to the top of the industry in less than a decade.

First Proprietary Drug in 1984

Annual sales by the beginning of the 1980s eclipsed $30 million, and Mylan began to steel itself for its entry into a new, potentially lucrative area of the multibillion-dollar pharmaceutical industry. Development plans were underway by the beginning of the 1980s for Mylan's first proprietary drug, its first pharmaceutical product developed, manufactured, and marketed in-house. In 1984, after five years of clinical tests and a $5 million investment, Mylan introduced an anti-hypertensive called Maxzide, an achievement McKnight hailed as the "single most important event in Mylan's history." Lederle Laboratories was licensed to distribute the drug, which was expected to generate $100 million in sales by 1988, and tests were immediately underway to introduce another version of Maxzide. In 1988, after three years of clinical tests, the FDA approved half-strength Maxzide-25, giving the company another powerful revenue-generating engine.

As these first steps into proprietary drug production were being made, progress was being achieved on other fronts, as Mylan reigned as the leading independent drug manufacturer in the United States, a number one position first achieved in 1985. Mylan's growing presence as a manufacturer necessitated the development of additional manufacturing facilities to complement its sole plant in Morgantown, which the company accomplished in 1987 when construction was completed for a new factory in Caguas, Puerto Rico. The company's first distribution center opened the following year in Greensboro, North Carolina.

As the 1980s drew to a close, McKnight and Puskar began an acquisition campaign aimed at developing a multifaceted Mylan with a greater, more well-rounded presence in the pharmaceutical industry. Much of the work toward this goal took place during the 1990s, when annual sales grew robustly, but before the 1980s were through Mylan completed a pivotal deal. In June 1989, the company acquired a 50 percent stake in Somerset Pharmaceuticals, Incorporated, the same month Somerset secured FDA approval to market a new medication for the treatment of Parkinson's disease called Eldepryl. Mylan's stock during the year provided an indication of the value of the acquisition, soaring 173 percent. Two years later, when annual sales topped the $100 million mark during the company's 30th anniversary year, Mylan completed another acquisition, merging with Sugar Land, Texas-based Dow B. Hickam Pharmaceuticals. A high-quality branded pharmaceutical company, Dow B. Hickam specialized in the manufacturing and marketing of wound and burn care pharmaceutical products, which added another quill to Mylan's quiver. The push to further broaden Mylan's arsenal of pharmaceutical goods continued in early 1993 when the company acquired Bertek, Incorporated, a manufacturer and innovator of transdermal (patch) drug delivery systems. The addition of Bertek gave Mylan five worldwide and seven domestic patents for transdermal drug delivery technology, the applications for which were expanding during the 1990s.

In late 1993, nine months after the Bertek acquisition was completed, Mylan employees were shocked to learn of the death of McKnight, who died suddenly of a heart attack on November 6th. Three days later, Puskar was named chairman and chief executive officer, assuming the posts vacated by McKnight and now wielding as much influence over the company as he had during its inaugural decade.

1990s Diversification Yields Growth

As the acquisitions were being completed during the early 1990s, annual sales rose sharply, leading to growth that quickly elevated Mylan's stature within the pharmaceutical industry. From $104 million in 1991, sales shot to $132 million in 1992, $212 million in 1993, and $252 million in 1994. Aside from broadening and deepening its involvement in the pharmaceutical industry through acquisitions, Mylan realized its animated growth by adhering to its philosophy of keeping manufacturing costs down and making sure to bring its products to market quickly. The company used just three manufacturing processes for all 79 of its pharmaceutical products, enabling it to meet any order within five days. Further, its focus on research and development of branded drugs well before their patents expired allowed the company to be the first on the market with the generic equivalent more often than not. In 1994, for instance, four of Mylan's six generic introductions were the first to market, giving the company hefty profit totals in comparison to the amount of revenue it generated. The company's introduction of cimetidine, a generic ulcer drug, in 1994, for example, held 39 percent of the market for all new cimetidine prescriptions in 1995.

As Puskar moved ahead with the strategy developed by McKnight and himself, he further penetrated the branded drug market, opting to fill niches deemed too small by the country's largest drug manufacturers. To give the company the manufac-

turing might to correspond to its growing presence, a third generic drug production facility was opened in Cidra, Puerto Rico, in late 1994, further bolstering the company's manufacturing capabilities in one of the havens of pharmaceutical production in the world. Sales recorded their most prolific leap during the first half of the decade in 1995, catapulting from $252 million to $396 million, from which the company registered an astounding $121 million in net earnings, nearly twice the total earned the previous year. The following year—in 1996—sales dipped to $393 million, but to compensate for the depressed revenue total the company completed another acquisition, purchasing UDL Laboratories Inc., a supplier of unit dose generic pharmaceuticals to the institutional and long-term care market.

As Mylan prepared to close out the decade and head into the 21st century, it occupied an enviable position in the pharmaceutical industry. Of all the pharmaceutical products produced by the company, 56 percent were ranked as the number one drug in their market and more than 70 percent were ranked either number one or number two. These percentage figures pointed to astute management and agile manufacturing abilities, qualities that promised to secure a leading market position in the future. The company's dedication to maintaining its position in the pharmaceutical industry was demonstrated in late 1996 when it opened a 150,000-square-foot research facility with bed space for 104 research subjects and two large laboratories. Such investment in the development of drugs, which was based on meeting goals rather than on a percentage of sales, pointed further to Mylan's bright prospects in the years ahead, as the company endeavored to make its future as successful as its past.

Principal Subsidiaries

Mylan Pharmaceuticals Inc.; Mylan Inc.; Dow B. Hickam Pharmaceuticals Inc.; Bertek, Inc.; UDL Laboratories Inc.; Somerset Pharmaceuticals, Inc. (50%).

Further Reading

Drahuschak, Greg, "Taking Stock: Mylan Labs Sets Pace for Local Market Index," *Pittsburgh Business Times,* January 8, 1990, p. 1.
"Drugs: Here Come the Sons of Valium," *Time,* September 16, 1985, p. 59.
Marano, Ray, "Roy McKnight Still Standard-Bearer for Mylan Labs," *Pittsburgh Business Times,* May 10, 1993, p. 11.
"Mylan Laboratories Inc.," *Pittsburgh Business Times,* March 26, 1990, p. 27.
"Mylan Laboratories Inc.," *Pittsburgh Business Times,* June 28, 1993, p. 23.
Oliver, Suzanne, "Make a Good Product," *Forbes,* August 14, 1995, p. 90.
Sabatini, Patricia, "Pittsburgh-Based Mylan, Heinz, Still Favorites of Investors," *Knight-Ridder/Tribune Business News,* April 8, 1997, p. 4.

—Jeffrey L. Covell

NATIONAL GRAPE CO-OPERATIVE ASSOCIATION INC.

National Grape Co-operative Association, Inc.

2 South Portage St.
Westfield, New York 14787
U.S.A.
(716) 326-3131
Fax: (716) 326-5494
Web site: http://www.welchs.com

Cooperative
Incorporated: 1897 as The Welch Grape Juice Company
Employees: 1,224
Sales: $550.8 million (1996)
SICs: 0172 Grapes; 2033 Canned Fruits, Vegetables etc.;
2037 Frozen Fruits, Fruit Juices, Vegetables; 6719
Holding Companies, Not Elsewhere Classified

Best known as the parent company of Welch Foods, Inc., National Grape Co-operative Association, Inc. is the world's largest producer and marketer of products made from Concord and Niagara grapes. National Grape encompasses an agricultural cooperative of nearly 1,500 fruit growers in New York, Pennsylvania, Ohio, Michigan, Arkansas, Missouri, and Washington. As America's first grape juice, Welch's became virtually synonymous with the beverage. Prohibition helped push the drink into the national spotlight in the early 20th century. The company's acquisition by National Grape mid-century effected vertical integration that stretched from the vineyard through to the finished bottle of juice. Welch's product line includes the core Concord grape juice, blended juices, fruit spreads, frozen fruit juice bars, frozen juice concentrate, sparkling juice drinks, and aseptically packaged juice concentrates.

Initial 19th-Century Launch Fails

National Grape's origins can be traced back to the 1860s, when Thomas Bramwell Welch, a Vineland, New Jersey dentist, was called upon by his Wesleyan Methodist church to serve bread and wine during Communion services. Thinking it duplicitous of the church to decry alcohol use yet serve wine, Welch took it upon himself to make an "unfermented wine."

Using home-grown grapes, he filtered fresh grape juice and bottled it, then boiled the bottles to kill the naturally-occurring yeast, thereby arresting the fermentation that would normally occur. Dubbing his product "Dr. Welch's Unfermented Wine," the dentist proudly took his product to local churchmen, certain that they would be happy to banish alcoholic wine from their sanctuaries in favor of his new product.

Welch was stunned to find that virtually all the pastors he approached turned him down flat. Anything other than wine would be heretical, they reasoned. After four unsuccessful years, Welch gave up on his unfermented wine in 1873. His disappointment over the whole project was so profound that he made no mention of it in his autobiography. Welch fell back on his former profession, inventing new dental alloys, selling dentistry tools, and later publishing one of America's largest dental trade magazines.

Second Generation Revives Business in Late 19th Century

An 1895 outbreak of black rot in Vineland forced Welch to move his operation to Westfield, New York, on the shore of Lake Erie, home of the dark Concord grape that would become Welch's signature juice. As the 20th century approached, advertising became a key factor in the product's success. Welch broadened his advertising from newspapers and trade magazines to national publications, later adding calendars and contests to the publicity drive. Using a theme that author Michael Gershman called "a masterstroke of suggestiveness" in his book *Getting It Right the Second Time*, Welch artfully paired prohibitionism with sex via a drawing of an attractive woman and the words, "Lips that touch Welch's are all that touch mine." Welch's annual advertising budget averaged half a million dollars, or nearly one-fourth of sales, from 1912 to 1926.

The company also got some free publicity from fellow prohibitionists William Jennings Bryan and Josephus Daniels in the 1910s. When Bryan, in his capacity as Secretary of State, substituted Welch's for wine at state dinners the switch was dubbed "grape juice diplomacy" in the press. Another high-ranking government official, Daniels was ridiculed as the Secretary of the ''Grape Juice Navy'' for prohibiting alcohol from ships and naval yards. Both incidents generated a flurry of political cartoons that, whether negative or positive, boosted nationwide awareness of Welch's signature product.

By 1909, Welch's was making one million gallons of juice per year, and within four years, its sales exceeded $2 million. The company acquired a Pennsylvania competitor in 1911 and set up production in Michigan in 1918 and Arkansas in 1922. The advent of Prohibition in 1919 pushed Welch's sales from $3 million to over $6 million in 1920. Charles Welch lived long enough to see two of his father's dreams—nationwide promulgation of both Prohibition and Welch's Grape Juice—to fruition before he died in 1926.

Third Generation Sells Business in Late 1920s

Three of Charles's sons—John, Edgar, and Paul—shared management of Welch's after their father's death. Within two years, however, disagreements among the brothers regarding the uncertainty of grape production spurred them to sell the firm. American National Company, a Nashville, Tennessee investment firm, acquired Welch's in 1928. The new owners hoped it would be a profitable short-term investment, but after achieving a net income of more than $500,000 in 1929, Welch's suffered successive losses in 1931, 1932, and 1933, as the Great Depression took its toll on the nation's businesses.

The new parent company acquired grape processing operations in Ohio, Michigan, and New York and expanded exports to more than three dozen countries worldwide during this period. Sales growth averaged 13 percent annually from 1928 to 1945, as Welch's added accounts with government agencies, the military, and international aid groups during World War II. By the war's end, sales had mushroomed to over $10 million.

But by many accounts, American National was less interested in building Welch's than in squeezing profits from the grape juice company. According to the company history *Welch's Grape Juice: From Corporation to Co-operative*, by William Chazanof, plant maintenance, product research and development, and grower relations all suffered during this period.

In the meantime, a competitor was gathering strength just seven miles from the Welch's headquarters. The rival was led by Jacob ''Jack'' Kaplan, a Russian Jewish immigrant who had garnered invaluable experience and a multimillion-dollar fortune in commodities trading and retailing in the early 20th century. In 1933, Kaplan and his brother Maurice put a piece of the family fortune to work by purchasing the grape processing operations of the Chautauqua and Erie Grape Growers Cooperative (C&E) in Brocton, New York, just west of Welch's Westfield headquarters. The repeal of Prohibition that same year allowed Kaplan to produce both wine and grape juice, but by 1939, when he changed the company name to National Grape Corporation, he elected to concentrate the company's efforts on juice. The new business was unprofitable until 1935 and operated at a breakeven level until 1939, but by 1945, it was selling about $3 million in private label and C&E brand grape juice, jams, and jellies.

In order to circumvent wartime restrictions on corporate profits and price controls, Jack Kaplan spearheaded the creation of a large grape growers' cooperative in 1945. The new organization would not only be immune from federal corporation taxes and pricing dictates, but would also guarantee his processing company a reliable supply of grapes. Promising that for ten years he would take a ten percent cut of the co-op's profits in lieu of a salary, Kaplan and his team convinced 900 growers to join the newly formed National Grape Co-operative.

Welch's Acquired by National Grape in Post-World War II Era

By the mid-1940s Welch's parent company, American National, was ready to divest its grape juice interests. Jack Kaplan purchased a controlling interest in the company in 1945 with the intention of quickly selling it to National Grape. First, however, he invested more than $5 million in plant modernization and consolidation, improved distribution, and increased grape production. He launched processing plants in Canada and California in 1948. Kaplan's strategies paid off well; Welch's sales more than tripled from $10.1 million in 1945 to $35.6 in 1956, and net income increased from $138,000 to $3.5 million. Perhaps most importantly, Kaplan had forged vital ties between National Grape and Welch. By the mid-1950s, National Grape farmers—whose numbers had swollen to over 4,000 in the meantime—were supplying 90 percent of the grapes processed by Welch.

Kaplan first offered to sell his stake in Welch to National Grape in 1949, but could not convince the rank and file to subscribe to the plan. In 1952, he devised a strategy whereby Welch's own profits would be diverted into a fund that would enable the cooperative to acquire the processor. In exchange, co-op members would commit their entire harvest to Welch, thereby ensuring a steady supply of grapes to the juice company. The final purchase price was $28.5 million, about $13.5

million of which was borrowed by the cooperative. Though the two companies were merged in 1956, they continued to operate autonomously, having separate boards of directors and management.

During this period, Welch's attached itself to two very popular children's television programs: "The Howdy Doody Show" and "The Mickey Mouse Club." New product launches in the late 1950s and throughout the 1960s included juice cocktails, frozen juice concentrates, jams, jellies, preserves, and reduced calorie products. In recognition of its expanded product line, National Grape changed the name of its sole subsidiary to Welch Foods, Inc. in 1969. Boosted by the creation of a formal marketing department and a multi-million dollar advertising budget, the merged companies' sales increased from $35.7 million in 1956 to $68 million in 1969.

Sales Flatten in Early 1980s, Are Rejuvenated Under New Management

By 1973, National Grape's sales had crossed the $100 million threshold. But most observers agree that management had overextended the brand to the detriment of the core Concord grape products. Though grape juice sales overall continued to grow modestly, Welch's sales plateaued from 1979 to 1982 as the brand's market share was eroded by competing brands and private-label juices. In 1982, Welch Foods hired Everett Baldwin as president and CEO to reposition and revitalize the brand. Bringing with him food marketing experience at Pillsbury and Land O'Lakes, Baldwin quickly recognized the company's and the brand's weaknesses and moved to correct them. Though National Grape remained headquartered in Westfield, New York, he moved Welch's corporate headquarters to Concord, Massachusetts. Recognizing that Welch needed to put its best efforts behind its most promising products—both new and old—he also launched a product development department, adopted convenient new packaging, and created a new logo.

Baldwin's strategies put Welch's back on the growth track, and by 1987 National Grape's annual revenues had reached nearly $300 million. In the late 1980s and early 1990s, the company expanded its international distribution to more than 30 countries via licensing agreements and the establishment of its own overseas operations. By the mid-1990s, Asia was proving a very important growth center. Welch's boosted domestic distribution by offering single-serve canned and bottled juices for vending machines.

Though grape juice ranked a distant third to orange and apple juices in popularity in the early 1990s, National Grape and Welch's benefited from a general trend toward increased consumption of fruit juice during the decade. The company's eagerness to adopt convenient new packaging designs ranked it among the first to adopt aseptic packaging for single-serve juices in drink boxes as well as aseptic canned concentrate. The advantage of aseptic packaging was that it did not require refrigeration until after opening, and could be shelved virtually indefinitely. The introduction of sparkling grape juices and ciders sold as alternatives to wine brought Welch's back full-circle to the teetotaling days of "unfermented wine."

By 1996, National Grape was selling 50 million cases of fruit products for over $550 million in annual revenues. That year, it processed a record-breaking 283,000 tons of grapes and distributed an all-time-high $63.9 million in net income to its grower-members. Management hoped to build sales to the $1 billion mark by the early 21st century by parlaying the company's strengths in Concord and white grape products.

Principal Subsidiaries

Welch Foods, Inc.

Further Reading

Chazanof, William, *Welch's Grape Juice: From Corporation to Cooperative,* New York: Syracuse University Press, 1977.

Cook, Jack, "The Legacy of Dr. Welch's Unfermented Wine," *Horticulture,* June 1980, pp. 42–51.

Damrau, Frederic, *Keep Fit and Slender: How to Take Off Seven Pounds Per Month the Welch Grape Juice Way,* New York: Welch Grape Juice Co., 1950.

Fucini, Joseph J., and Suzy Fucini, *Entrepreneurs: The Men and Women Behind Famous Brand Names and How They Made It,* Boston: G.K. Hall & Co., 1985.

Gelbert, Doug, *So Who The Heck Was Oscar Mayer?* New York: Barricade Books, Inc., 1996, pp. 75–76.

Gershman, Michael, *Getting It Right the Second Time,* Reading, PA: Addison-Wesley Publishing Company, Inc., 1990, pp. 84–88.

Jorgensen, Janice, ed. *The Encyclopedia of Consumer Brands, Vol. 1: Consumable Products,* Detroit, MI: Gale Research, Inc., 1994 pp. 629–31.

Welch's Centennial Year, 1869–1969, Westfield, NY: National Grape Co-operative Association, Inc., 1969.

Welch's, Since 1869: This Is Our Story, National Grape Co-operative Association, Inc. & Welch Foods Inc., A Cooperative, 1989.

—April Dougal Gasbarre

| cd international, inc.

Nimbus CD International, Inc.

State Route 629
Guildford Farm
Ruckersville, Virginia 22968
U.S.A.
(804) 985-1100
Fax: (804) 985-2893

Public Company
Founded: 1982
Sales: $118.2 million (1996)
Employees: 871
Stock Exchanges: NASDAQ
SICs: 3695 Blank Computer Software Tapes and Disks;
Blank Recording Compact Discs; Blank Optical Disks
and Digital Video Disks (DVDs); 3652 Prerecorded
Records and Tapes

In the mid-1990s Nimbus CD International, Inc. ranked as one of the largest independent manufacturers of compact discs (CDs) and CD-ROMs in the world. It was the fourth-largest independent CD-audio manufacturer in 1995 and the third-largest CD-ROM manufacturer in North America. With more than 1,500 customers and production facilities in Utah, Virginia, Wales (United Kingdom), and Luxembourg capable of producing about 200 million CDs a year, Nimbus's CDs were purchased primarily by independent record labels and by multimedia software developers in North America, the United Kingdom, and continental Europe.

In the 1990s, Nimbus—an offshoot of the classical recording label Nimbus Records Ltd.—diversified its product line by producing "Enhanced CDs" (CDs with both audio and video content) and by introducing holographic CD label imaging for antipiracy and specialized CD design uses. In addition to CDs, in the mid-1990s Nimbus was one of the first two companies in the world to manufacture digital video discs (DVDs), which were expected to begin replacing the CD and the VHS videocassette in the late 1990s. Besides manufacturing CDs and DVDs,

Nimbus also offers premastering and mastering services, disk replication, antipiracy holographic equipment, and complete "turnkey" services including packaging design consultation, materials procurement services, packaging assembly, and order fulfillment.

Records for the Count: 1957–69

The son of a Russian aristocrat who emigrated to France during the Russian Revolution, Count Alexander Numa Labinsky was raised in Birmingham, England, where his father had settled to run a jewelry business. When his twin brother died at age seven, Labinsky suddenly discovered he had a talent for singing and during the years of World War II he cultivated it by studying at the Birmingham Rep and giving evening recitals under the professional name Shura Gehrman. After the war, Labinsky briefly studied music in Paris, was regularly featured on the BBC, and performed with some of the major talents of his day. He also recorded songs by Schubert, Fauré, and other composers but soon concluded that the existing techniques for recording music were too crude to express the subtleties of his own voice.

In 1951 Labinsky thus formed a partnership with Michael and Gerald Reynolds that culminated in the establishment of Nimbus Records Ltd. in 1957. The company's mission, Labinsky declared, was to "record material of a specialist nature that was of excellent quality" and, moreover, was priced lower than the products of the major record labels. Labinsky decided to locate the company in a renovated 19th-century country house on the River Wye in Cwmbran, Wales. From this bucolic Welsh setting, Labinsky began recording the music he liked, and by the mid-1990s Nimbus's collection encompassed some five hundred recordings, from classical orchestral and chamber music pieces to "World Music" artists and a series of digital transfers of old 78-rpm vocal records and piano-roll music. The Nimbus stable would come to include the music of such artists as Shostakovich, Schubert, Haydn, and Shura Cherkassky as well as the Hanover Band, the Kansas City Chorale, native Brazilian musicians, Irish folk players, and many others.

''Ambisonics'' and the Nimbus Sound: 1970–82

Labinsky was a demanding, mercurial figure, and he ran Nimbus Records to suit his own tastes rather than the dictates of the bottom line. A colleague later recalled to *Forbes* magazine that ''Numa always wanted perfection. He drove everybody to achieve perfection and nearly drove them mad doing it.'' Part of this perfectionism was the conviction that Nimbus should design and build its own equipment and cut its own records. By relying on their own designs rather than the conventional technology of the day, Nimbus's engineers struck out in new technological directions, which at the same time helped hold down the company's equipment costs. Labinsky's perfectionism also manifested itself in his conviction that each Nimbus recording should recreate as closely as possible the distinctive essence of the musical performance it captured. The performances heard on Nimbus's records consequently displayed few signs of editing, and Nimbus's ''natural sound'' recording philosophy led it in the 1970s to embrace a new ''surround-sound'' recording technique known as ''Ambisonics.''

Developed by a group of British academics, Ambisonics sought to expand the two-dimensionality of stereo recordings to a three-dimensional level by eliminating the ''distortion'' that occurs when the human ear detects the difference between sound as it originates in real life—that is, from every direction—and the narrower experience of the audiophile listening to a symphony from the stereo system in his or her living room. Nimbus had made strides toward this ideal of ''sonic actuality'' by using direct-to-disc record mastering techniques, which eliminated the impurities introduced when a mastering tape was created during the transfer of recorded music to the vinyl disc. Ambisonics seemed to offer even greater possibilities for ''real-life'' recorded sound by overcoming stereo's ''directional distortion'' through the strategic placement of a variety of microphones, audio channels, and loudspeakers during the recording process.

Nimbus was among the first companies to embrace the new technology and over the years established itself as Ambisonics's principal licensee, producing hundreds of CDs employing the technique from the 1970s through the 1990s. The promise of Ambisonics as an industry standard faded, however, because no broad-based effort was made to market it to the entire recording industry. Nimbus thus eventually won the exclusive license for Ambisonics, which became a company trademark. A long-time supporter of the Ambisonics idea, Nimbus's company secretary, Stuart Garman, in turn marketed the technology to Japanese manufacturers who were seeking new ways to provide ''surround-sound'' audio effects. The first to bite was Mitsubishi, who declared their intention to record all their Home Theater System albums using a variation of Nimbus's single-microphone Ambisonic method.

By the late 1970s Nimbus had established itself not only as a premier independent record label but as an innovator of new recording technologies. In 1977 it established a vinyl record production plant at its Wales location, and in 1979 the Nimbus brain trust of Labinsky and the two Reynolds brothers was expanded to include Adrian Farmer, who joined the company as the company's director of music and deputy chairman. Two years later, Dr. Jonathan Halliday joined the four, eventually lending his name to Nimbus's proprietary mastering technology, the Nimbus-Halliday Laser Mastering System.

The Compact Disc and Robert Maxwell: 1982–91

Just as Count Labinsky had entered the recording business when the ''Long-Playing'' $33\frac{1}{3}$ vinyl record was cementing its place as the replacement for the prewar recording standard, the shellac 78-rpm record, in the early 1980s a new medium—the CD—emerged to consign the vinyl LP to oblivion. Originally developed by Philips and Sony, the CD made it possible to record music digitally by encoding the musical ''data'' in microscopic grooves, which were ''read'' by an infrared laser beam striking the disc. Able to hold 75 minutes of music (the length of Beethoven's *Ninth Symphony*—the designers' benchmark), the CD was not only more durable than the vinyl record (it was estimated to have a life span of eight years), it also offered crisper, brighter sound. Labinsky and his Nimbus brain trust saw the revolutionary potential of the medium and in 1982 Nimbus became one of only three companies in the world to produce CDs through a license granted by Philips Electronics. Nimbus refused to purchase Philips's CD mastering system, however, and to hold down costs Gerald Reynolds and Jonathan Halliday built Nimbus's own mastering lathe from scratch in 10 months' time. Incorporating a traditional analog design rather than a strictly digital approach, their CD mastering system allowed them to use smaller track pitches on their CDs than was common at the time. This innovation gave Nimbus the enviable potential of being able to make CDs with double and even quadruple the density, or data storage capacity, of other makers' CDs. From square one, then, Nimbus technology pointed the company toward the high-data-density CDs and DVDs it began to roll out in the 1990s. Despite the introduction of the first playable CD from Nimbus labs in May 1984 and the unveiling of a large-scale CD pressing operation the same year, by 1985 CD sales worldwide still amounted to only $3 million of the multimillion-dollar audio recording market. But in a little more than a decade, the number of audio CD players in the United States and Europe alone would grow from a few million to a staggering 250 million.

As the audio CD began its long assault on the LP-oriented habits of the music-buying public, however, Labinsky continued to channel Nimbus's CD manufacturing profits into his record label. As a Nimbus executive later recalled, Labinsky ''and his partners' great interest was in classical music, and they were quite happy to bleed everything else dry to get better classical records.'' In anticipation of the worldwide introduction of CD-ROM technology in 1987 (which enabled users to store large amounts of data on a single disc), Nimbus began pressing CD-ROMs in 1986. The demand for audio CDs grew sevenfold between 1984 and 1986 alone, and in March 1986 Nimbus's management closed its vinyl LP manufacturing operation and transferred those workers to its CD plants.

The CD-ROM was officially unveiled in 1987, opening another lucrative new niche for Nimbus's production lines. After searching the Eastern seaboard for a U.S. manufacturing site, in 1987 Labinsky opened a production facility on the grounds of an 18th-century manor in Ruckersville, Virginia, which became Nimbus CD's headquarters. Despite sales of $43 million in 1987, Nimbus managed to lose $8 million, largely because of Labinsky's preoccupation with developing Nimbus Records. Nimbus's board of directors grew increasingly anxious over Labinsky's apparent intention to drain the company's new CD cash cow and began casting about for a bottom-line-oriented executive to turn the company's fortunes around. They eventually recruited Peter Laister, an engineer and chairman of Britain's Thorn EMI recording company, who began looking for new sources of capital to keep Nimbus afloat. Laister had once been considered for an executive position by British media mogul Robert Maxwell, so he naturally turned to Maxwell as a potential investor in Nimbus's future.

Maxwell had turned raw ambition, native intellect, and a background in military intelligence into a position of great wealth and power in Britain's publishing industry. At Laister's urging he agreed to invest in Nimbus, acquiring 75 percent of the company in exchange for an influx of much needed cash and the assumption of Nimbus's debt. Through Laister's management and Maxwell's capital, by 1991 Nimbus had achieved profitability. While vacationing on his yacht off the Canary Islands in November 1991, however, Maxwell mysteriously drowned, throwing his company, Maxwell Communication Corporation, and Nimbus's future plans into disarray. While Maxwell's family suspected murder, experts later suggested he had committed suicide over the financial chaos that resulted from shady financial tactics he had employed to keep his empire afloat. When Maxwell's businesses came under government scrutiny after his death, Nimbus found itself facing the British equivalent of bankruptcy.

Nimbus U.S.A. and Nimbus CD International: 1992–94

As eager potential buyers lined up to stake their claim in the company's increasingly lucrative—and now available—CD business, Laister fought to keep Nimbus independent. In late 1992, however, Donaldson, Lufkin and Jenrette Securities Corp. (DLJ), a New York investment firm, bought Nimbus's disc manufacturing and distribution operations from Maxwell Communication for $13 million, gaining a 90 percent stake in Nimbus. The remaining 10 percent was given to Nimbus's former management, and Count Labinsky was allowed to keep Nimbus Records and Nimbus's technical business. "We were happy to let him keep his label," Thompson Dean, a DLJ managing partner, told reporters. The Nimbus CD manufacturing business was reincorporated in the United States as Nimbus U.S.A. and Lyndon Faulkner, a 31-year-old company executive, was made CEO.

DLJ began pumping money into its new business, paying down Nimbus USA's debt and priming it for future expansion through acquisitions. Nimbus ramped up its CD-ROM operations to meet the steady growth in demand. Rapid improvements in computer processing power had made it feasible for consumers to run data-heavy game programs like *Doom* or *Myst* from the CD-ROM drives of their PCs, and while only 25 million CD-ROMs were sold in the United States in 1992, by 1996 that number would explode to more than a half billion. Between 1991 and 1994 alone, Nimbus's CD-ROM sales grew from only 10 percent of total sales to 30 percent. By the end of its 1991–92 fiscal year, Nimbus was posting net sales of $63.59 million.

In 1992 electronics giants Sony and Philips began working on the compact disc's replacement—the DVD or digital video (or versatile) disc. The goal was a new medium that in one fell swoop would replace the video cassette tape and laser disc, the audio CD, the video game cassette, and the CD-ROM. First known as the "multimedia CD," this multipurpose mega-disk technology would allow a disc the size of a CD but with seven times its storage capacity to hold an entire movie without worry over rewinding, tape misfeeds, blurry images, or dull sound. Moreover, consumers would be able to play a DVD video game, a DVD audio disk, a DVD movie, or even an old-fashioned CD from multipurpose DVD players. As the electronics industry's major players developed and finalized the technology and began negotiating a single cross-industry double-sided DVD standard, Nimbus's annual production of CDs at its Virginia plant alone reached 30 million, and Nimbus's 1992–93 sales topped $69 million. In early 1994, Nimbus mourned the death of its founder, Count Labinsky, and officially changed its name to Nimbus CD International.

In April 1994 Nimbus acquired Damont Audio, a British record and CD producer and, more importantly, announced that Chicago-based R. R. Donnelley & Sons—the world's largest printer and a supplier of CD-ROMs to software giant Microsoft—would agree to order all its CD-ROMs (at least 23 million a year) from Nimbus in exchange for an equity stake in the CD maker. Part of the landmark alliance (christened Stream International) called for Donnelley and Nimbus to establish a CD-ROM manufacturing operation near Donnelley's software services facility in Provo, Utah. With a capacity of 37.5 million units a year, the Provo plant opened in early 1995, doubling Nimbus's U.S. CD manufacturing capacity.

Going Public and Launching DVD: 1995–97

The Donnelley deal enhanced Nimbus's cachet in the corporate mergers-and-acquisitions market, and beginning in March 1995 DLJ began to cash in on its Nimbus stake by selling 80 percent of its shares, for $69 million, to McCown De Leeuw & Co., a California-based venture capital firm. By the spring Nimbus was scouting for a site on the West Coast for its fourth CD manufacturing facility and in the summer it announced that a Sunnyvale, California, site had been chosen because of its proximity to Nimbus's Silicon Valley customers. Riding the continuing boom in CD-ROM-based software sales, Nimbus's net sales leapt nearly 23 percent between 1994 and 1995, to nearly $86 million.

In August 1995 Nimbus acquired HLS Duplication Inc., a vendor of turnkey software duplication services located in Nimbus's new Sunnyvale home and later rechristened Nimbus Software Services. In the summer of 1995 Nimbus also began offering mastering and replication of so-called Enhanced CDs, a CD hybrid that contained both audio and CD-ROM content and enabled Nimbus and its customers to offer consumers DVD-type performance using conventional CD players.

More good news followed. After expanding the production capacity of its Wales plant in the summer, in September 1995 Nimbus announced an agreement with Britain's Applied Holographics plc to license technology to produce CDs on which holographic images had been incorporated, which could be used to thwart copyright piracy and enhance CDs' visual design. The new holographic method, named 3-D I*D, enabled a "covert" or invisible holographic image to be integrated on one entire side of the CD-ROM rather than merely applied superficially to a small portion of the disk. Optical machine readers could then be used to read the encoded authentification data in the hologram and determine if the CD was counterfeit. Nimbus and Applied would profit both from leasing the holographic equipment to CD-ROM product makers and from the royalties from each disc made using the hologram-encoding technology.

On September 15, 1995, the major DVD-developing companies announced that an agreement had been reached on a common standard for the new technology. A major hurdle had been cleared on the DVD's path toward the consumer marketplace. Only Nimbus CD and megamedia firm Time-Warner announced unequivocally that they were ready to begin production of DVDs. While the DVD industry and Hollywood wrangled over the new encryption technologies that would make it as hard to copy a film from a DVD as from a videocassette, Nimbus began investing in DVD manufacturing equipment in earnest. To pay down the debt its conversion to DVD generated, in November 1995 McCown De Leeuw & Co. announced that Nimbus CD would become a public company through the sale of a third of its stake during a December initial public offering of stock.

Nimbus was now decisively committed to DVD. Robert Headrick, the president of Nimbus's Information Systems subsidiary, told *Tape/Disc Business*, "We are positioned to manufacture DVD from the get-go.... Usually, early adopters of a technology end up doing most of the volume work." Nimbus's R&D chief, John Town elaborated: "we feel that by getting in at this stage, we will be able to optimize production and learn all of the lessons in anticipation of early demand. At that time we will have removed enough costs from our process to become one of the manufacturing leaders." To gauge the viability of the DVD market, Headrick and Town visited nine companies in the Japanese DVD industry and came away with their instincts reinforced: Nimbus should strike while the iron was hot. On the cusp of news that Nimbus's 1995–96 net sales had grown a dizzying 33.5 percent to $118 million, company officials announced in March 1996 that Nimbus would be investing $25 million in DVD mastering, manufacturing, and packaging capacity and other improvements, sending Nimbus's stock price up twofold within a month of the news. In July 1996, the DVD industry and Hollywood finally agreed on an encryption method

for DVD movies, and in September 1996 Nimbus began manufacturing its first DVDs.

With Time Warner and Sony set to produce the DVDs for their own film studios, Nimbus focused on supplying DVDs to the remaining Big Six Hollywood studios—Disney, Fox, Universal, and Columbia. In late 1996 it expanded its Sunnyvale, California, plant and in January 1997 announced it would construct a new manufacturing plant in Luxembourg. DVD film titles hit video stores in seven U.S. markets in early 1997 and $500 dollar DVD players began appearing on electronics store shelves. Unexpectedly, Nimbus announced the closing of its two-year-old Sunnyvale site in early 1997, claiming that it had to consolidate its manufacturing operations to remain an efficient player in the DVD market, which was expected to begin in earnest in late 1997.

Although some observers argued that the hype surrounding DVD masked an abyss of consumer indifference, some industry analysts predicted that 900,000 DVD video players would be sold in 1997 alone and more than two million PCs with preinstalled DVD-ROM drives would reach consumers' homes and offices. By the year 2000, moreover, they estimated that the number of DVD video players sold would reach eight million and the number of DVD-ROM drives would climb to 43 to 63 million. As Nimbus faced the great unknown of the global consumer electronics market, it took comfort in analysts' predictions that its 1997 sales could climb as high as $150 to $160 million. Nimbus's future hopes were bluntly summed up by *Forbes* magazine: "Nimbus is poised to become a major player in the next great consumer electronics rollout, the DVD."

Principal Subsidiaries

Nimbus Manufacturing, Inc.; Nimbus Manufacturing (U.K.) Ltd.; Nimbus Information Systems, Inc.; Nimbus Software Services, Inc.; CD Manufacturing (UK) Ltd.

Further Reading

"Alexander Labinsky, Record Executive, 70" (obituary), *The New York Times*, February 3, 1994.

Barrett, Larry, "Cloud Hovers over Closing," *The Business Journal Serving San Jose and Silicon Valley*, April 7, 1997.

Burtner, Sydney, "Nimbus Stock Reacts as DVD Production Lines Form," *Charlottesville Observer*, May 30–June 5, 1996.

"Count Alexander Labinsky" (obituary), *Times (London)*, March 5, 1994.

"Donnelley, Quebecor Buy into CD-ROM," *Folio*, June 1, 1994, p. 13.

Galante Block, Debbie, "Nimbus Invests in the Future with Anti-Piracy Technology and DVD Research," *Tape/Disc Business*, May 1, 1996.

Gardner, Fran, "CD Maker Considers Two Sites in Oregon," *Oregonian*, June 23, 1995.

Goldfield, Robert, "Nimbus Scraps Tualatin, Still Considers Eugene," *Daily Journal of Commerce* (Portland, Oregon), June 21, 1995.

Gove, Alex, "DVD and Conquer," *Red Herring*, May 1997.

Griffiths, John, "In the Manor of Mastering," *Tape/Disc Business*, June 1, 1995.

——, *Nimbus: Technology Serving the Arts*, London: Nimbus Records, in association with Andre Deutsch Ltd., 1995.

Hinden, Stan, "Country Mouse, City Mouse Wage Record Battle," *Washington Post*, March 14, 1994.

Kidd, Joe, "Eugene Site a Finalist for CD Plant," *The Register Guard* (Eugene, Oregon), June 2, 1995.

"Nimbus Introduces Theft Protection Holographic Image," *CD-ROM Professional*, November 1995.

"Nimbus Invests in the Future with Anti-Piracy Technology and DVD Research," *Tape/Disc Business*, May 1, 1996.

"Nimbus Opens Provo Plant," *CD-ROM Professional*, February 1995, p. 89.

"Nimbus's Past Becomes a Whisp on the Horizon," *Buyouts*, August 7, 1995.

"Nimbus Shifts Emphasis to CD-ROM and DVD Manufacturing Capability," *Audio World*, September 24, 1996.

"Nimbus to Produce DVD, Holograph Technology," *Charlottesville Observer*, May 23–May 29, 1996.

"Nimbus to Set up In-House DVD Production," *Interactive Multimedia Association Show Daily*, September 19, 1996.

"Offerings in the Offing: Nimbus CD International," *Barron's*, May 16, 1994.

Renstrom, Roger, "Nimbus Trims Down to Beef up Capacity," *Plastics News*, March 31, 1997.

"Site for CD Plant," *Chicago Tribune*, June 18, 1995.

Speigel, Peter, "Sweet Music," *Forbes*, June 2, 1997, pp. 110–14.

"Three Companies Expand Their CD Production Capacities," *Information Today*, November 1996.

Verna, Paul, "Hologram Printing to Thwart Piracy," *Billboard*, September 30, 1995, p. 43.

"Whatever Happened to Ambisonics?" *AudioMedia*, November 1991.

—Paul S. Bodine

The energy to make things better.

Northern States Power Company

414 Nicollet Mall
Minneapolis, Minnesota 55401
U.S.A.
(612) 330-5500
Fax: (612) 330-6297
Web site: http://www.nspco.com

Public Company
Incorporated: 1909 as Washington County Light &
    Power Company
Employees: 6,470
Sales: $2.65 billion (1996)
Stock Exchanges: New York Chicago Pacific
SICs: 4931 Electric And Other Services Combined

Northern States Power Company (NSP) provides electricity and gas to customers in Minnesota, Wisconsin, North Dakota, South Dakota, and the upper peninsula of Michigan. In 1996 it had 1.4 million electricity customers and 400,000 natural gas customers. The bulk of its sales is direct to consumers, but it provides a small amount of energy for resale by other utilities.

Early Development of Electric Utilities

NSP's roots go back to 1881 when Henry Marison Byllesby, NSP's founder—then a 22-year-old dropout from engineering school—joined Thomas Edison as a draftsman to build a power plant in New York City. Byllesby went on to design plants for Edison in Chile and Montreal. In 1885 Edison's rival George Westinghouse offered Byllesby $10,000 a year to become vice president and general manager of Westinghouse Electric, and Byllesby accepted.

In his four years with Westinghouse, Byllesby invented and designed more than 40 electric lighting devices. In 1891 he received a job offer from another competitor, Charles A. Coffin, president of Thomson-Houston Electric Company. Coffin sent Byllesby to St. Paul, Minnesota, to run a subsidiary there. In St. Paul, Byllesby noted that most Midwestern electric compa-

nies had inadequate finances and other resources to meet customer demand. The weakest companies quickly went bankrupt or were swallowed by their competitors. Byllesby spent four years in St. Paul, until Thomson-Houston merged with Edison's General Electric Company. Unwilling to work for Edison again, Byllesby went to Oregon and became vice president of the Portland General Electric Company, where he designed, financed, and built four hydroelectric developments in four years.

In 1902 he put his years in St. Paul to use and organized his own engineering and operating firm in Chicago, with Samuel Insull and other backers, to buy and upgrade struggling midwestern utilities. Insull was a leading financier and acquirer of utilities. Financially troubled electric companies would approach Insull, and Insull would bail them out in exchange for stock in the company and an executive position. Byllesby bought companies in Illinois, Ohio, and Oklahoma, then in 1909 returned to Minnesota, where he organized the Washington County Light & Power Company in June 1909. In December 1909, the company's name was changed to Consumers Power Company. Byllesby and Insull also organized two utility holding companies: Northern States Power Company of Delaware in 1909 and Standard Gas and Electric in 1910.

Byllesby, like Insull, ended up acquiring many of the companies he helped. The companies for which Byllesby built steam and hydroelectric plants became insolvent. Byllesby's company would take over these troubled companies and provide engineering, management, and financial assistance. In 1912 Byllesby made his most important acquisition when he bought Minneapolis General Electric of Minnesota. That company was destined to become NSP's flagship company. Also in 1912 Byllesby and Insull parted ways.

World War I to the Depression: Expansion and Interconnection

On February 5, 1916, Byllesby changed his company's name to Northern States Power Company. The United States' entry into World War I in 1917 put a great strain on NSP's generating capabilities as wartime production and industrial customers' demands grew. After the war, the country experienced a brief

depression followed by a business boom that saw increased
demand for electricity and encouragement of merger activity.

In the company's first 20 years, NSP bought 25 more Upper
Midwest utility companies. It acquired the Northwest Light &
Power Company in 1917 and the Brainerd Gas & Electric
Company, St. Cloud Water Power Company, Hutchinson Light
& Manufacturing Company, and Ottumwa Railway & Light
Company in 1920. Ottumwa's electric and steam-heating busi-
ness was reorganized in 1923 as the Northern States Power
Company (New Jersey), while its railway business became the
Ottumwa Traction Company. All of the old Ottumwa properties
were sold in 1925, except transmission lines in northern Iowa.
NSP acquired the Wisconsin-Minnesota Light and Power Com-
pany in 1923; the Minnesota Valley Electric Company, Ren-
ville County Electric Company, and St. Cloud Public Service
Company in 1924; Glenwood Electric Light, Heat & Power
Company, Farmers Light & Power Company, and the St. Cloud
Electric Power Company in 1926; and the St. Paul Gas Light
Company, Sauk Rapids Water Power Company, South St. Paul
Gas & Electric Company, St. Croix Power Company, and the
Minnesota Power Company in 1927.

As NSP expanded its network of operating companies, it
interconnected them. Interconnection allowed massive power
production and brought customers lower rates and more reliable
service. NSP also replaced old plants with newer, more efficient
ones, constructing major hydroelectric units at Rapidan, Cannon Falls, and Coon Rapids, Minnesota, in addition to many
smaller installations all over the Midwest. The company put a
great deal of effort into improving its steam-generating plants,
focusing attention on the Riverside plant in Minneapolis. Riverside was huge by standards of the day, and its expansion illustrated Byllesby's belief that it was less expensive to generate
power at a favorable site and transmit it than to generate power
at the site where it is used. Byllesby died in 1924, but numerous
associates carried on his work, especially Robert F. Pack, general manager and later president of NSP.

1930s: Federal Action Brings Changes

Between 1921 and 1929, 3,744 U.S. public utility companies
were absorbed in mergers and acquisitions. This meant that 84
percent of all U.S. utility assets were in the hands of slightly
more than 1 percent of all utility corporations. During the Great
Depression, large holding companies such as NSP became the
subjects of much scrutiny.

The scrutiny resulted in the Public Utility Holding Company
Act of 1935, under which utilities had to simplify their structures. As a result of this law, NSP had to dissolve Standard Gas

and Electric, and NSP's Chicago-based financial backers had to
sell their stock back to the company.

During this period, NSP experienced major financial problems. The Securities and Exchange Commission (SEC) forced
the company to reevaluate assets it had overvalued for stock
issuing purposes in 1924, and NSP lost $75 million through this
readjustment. The SEC also ordered NSP to eliminate its Class
B voting stock, which had been created by Byllesby to guarantee him control of NSP, since the company could no longer pay
dividends.

Another part of U.S. President Franklin D. Roosevelt's New
Deal that affected NSP was the agency he developed to help
finance electrical lines for impoverished farmers, the Rural
Electrification Administration (REA). The REA encouraged
farmers to form electric cooperatives in order to borrow federal
funds for line extensions. These cooperatives competed directly
with private utilities.

The third blow the New Deal dealt power companies was
government sponsorship of municipal power company ownership. The government agreed to pay 45 percent of the cost for
any community willing to build, generate, and distribute its own
power. After an extensive battle and many town hall debates,
most communities ended up choosing NSP's service anyway,
for NSP had made voluntary rate reductions consistently since it
started operating.

Roosevelt's final implementation that affected NSP was his
National Recovery Act, which guaranteed employees the right
to organize, bargain collectively, and strike. This act, and the
safer working conditions encouraged by a union, was welcomed
by NSP linemen, who had lost nearly half their workers to
electrical accidents. On February 23, 1937, NSP suffered its
first labor strike. By the eighth day of the strike, Robert Pack
decided to cut his losses and agreed to recognize the workers'
union International Brotherhood of Electrical Workers. NSP
was one of the first utility companies in the United States to
become unionized.

1940s: War Years and Postwar Demand

In 1939 the company continued to expand in Wisconsin. On
August 29, 1941, NSP merged the wholly owned subsidiaries
Minneapolis General Electric Company, St. Croix Falls Minne-
sota Improvement Company, and Minnesota Brush Electric
Company into NSP. On December 27 NSP dissolved Northern
States Power Company (New Jersey) after selling certain assets
to South Dakota Public Service Company and transferring the
remainder to itself.

After the United States entered World War II in 1941,
demand for electricity rose rapidly, as industry contributed to
the war effort. NSP responded by adding a 50,000-kilowatt
steam turbine to its St. Paul High Bridge plant. NSP employees
were fingerprinted, as a precaution against sabotage and theft.
Most of NSP's advertising during the war focused on conservation and salvage programs. The electric-utility industry's car-
toon-character spokesperson, Reddy Kilowatt, regularly promoted victory gardens. More than 600 NSP employees served
in the war. In 1942 NSP's president, Robert Pack, retired,
turning over his office to his assistant, Ted Crocker.

While many utility companies saw demand slow after the war, NSP reported a record load on December 17, 1945, almost 10 percent higher than in 1944. Sales for 1945 were a record $53 million. NSP became heavily involved in a postwar planning program that helped businesses expand and convert their wartime production to peacetime needs. While NSP helped these businesses, the businesses' growth often helped NSP enlarge its customer base.

NSP's customer base grew so rapidly that when president Ted Crocker died unexpectedly on June 29, 1947, and B. F. Braheney took over, he was faced with a power shortage. Braheney quickly developed a demand-control system and called on customers to conserve. NSP also built new plants, many of them diesel-powered. During the 1950s the company launched its largest-ever construction program, investing nearly $400 million. After 1947 NSP's daily kilowatt-hour output surpassed that of the entire year 1916. Operating revenues doubled from 1941 to 1951.

1950s: Consolidation and Entry into the Nuclear Age

In 1950 NSP sold the utility properties of its Illinois-based subsidiary, Interstate Light & Power Company, and dissolved it. In 1955 NSP ranked among the top 10 utilities in the United States. In 1956 NSP consolidated three of its subsidiaries—St. Croix Falls Wisconsin Improvement Company, St. Croix Power Company, and Interstate Light & Power Company—into its already existing principal subsidiary, Northern States Power Company (Wisconsin) (NSP-Wisconsin). In October 1956 NSP sold its gas property in Brainerd, Minnesota, to Minnesota Valley Natural Gas Company and bought electrical distribution properties that served 13 Minnesota communities and surrounding rural areas, from Interstate Power Company.

In March 1957 NSP continued to consolidate, acquiring hydroelectric developments at St. Anthony Falls on the Mississippi River in Minneapolis from its wholly owned subsidiaries, St. Anthony Falls Water Power Company and the Minneapolis Mill Company. In August of that year NSP acquired an electrical distribution system in Farmington, Minnesota, from Central Electric & Gas Company. The following month NSP added more electrical distribution facilities in Delhi and North Redwood, Minnesota, from the city of Redwood Falls. In October 1957, NSP-Wisconsin acquired properties from Wisconsin Hydro Electric Company.

NSP had been interested in nuclear energy since 1945, and in the early 1950s it became one of the first utilities to receive access to information from the Atomic Energy Commission. In 1957 the company announced plans for its first full-scale atomic power plant, the Pathfinder, and chose a site on the Big Sioux River. Pathfinder began operating in 1964, but operating and safety costs were so high that in 1967 NSP substituted a gas-fired steam boiler for the nuclear reactor.

1960s: Environmental Concerns

In January 1960 NSP acquired NSP-Wisconsin's Minnesota properties, as well as the Wisconsin properties of Mississippi Valley Public Service Company. Later that year, NSP acquired NSP-Wisconsin's Minnesota gas properties, which were in the

Winona and Red Wing areas. In May 1961 NSP acquired Western Power and Gas Company's eastern business, which served the southeastern portion of South Dakota. In 1962 NSP sold its Tracy, Minnesota, water utility to the city of Tracy.

In March 1964 NSP acquired the properties and assets of Deichen Power, Inc. that had supplied southern Minnesota. In 1964 NSP began construction of the Allen S. King steam electric plant in Wisconsin on the St. Croix River and stirred up an environmental confrontation. The public outcry raised by the construction of this plant, which was perceived as a threat to the area's wildlife, was NSP's next real experience with public opposition and foreshadowed the controversy NSP's nuclear plant would raise. Despite an injunction—later lifted—brought by the Wisconsin attorney general, the company went ahead with the plant, which began production in 1968.

Around that time Allen King, NSP president until 1965, and his successor, Earl Ewald, created Mid-Continent Area Power Planners (MAPP), which brought 22 Upper Midwest power suppliers together to coordinate the planning, construction, and operation of new electrical plants throughout the region, in hopes of maximizing efficiency and minimizing duplication and waste. Through interconnection and coordination these companies were able to help each other supply the area.

All went smoothly for NSP through 1965. In June 1965 NSP acquired distribution facilities in Grand Forks, North Dakota, from the Nodak Rural Electric Cooperative. The tide turned in 1966, however, when NSP announced its plans for the Monticello nuclear plant. Demonstrators rose up in opposition. Although ground for the plant was broken in 1966, it took five years and $20 million in losses before the plant became operational. The controversy led NSP to create an environmental affairs department in 1969.

NSP continued expanding; in 1967 it acquired distribution facilities from Wright-Hennepin Cooperative Electric Association, as well as the electric distribution facilities of the village of Bayport, Minnesota. In 1968 NSP acquired the electric generating, transmission, and distribution facilities of the village of Mazeppa, Minnesota, and sold the electric distribution system of the village of Fischer, Minnesota, to the Otter Tail Power Company. In December 1969 NSP acquired several electric distribution facilities from Interstate Power Company.

1970s and 1980s: Rates and Resources

In 1971 NSP donated land skirting the Upper St. Croix River to the states of Minnesota and Wisconsin and to the National Park Service to be managed cooperatively. In 1973 as the OPEC oil embargo drove home the importance of conservation, NSP began researching solar energy, wind power, burning garbage as fuel, and even enormous underwater sea turbines. However, 94 percent of NSP's power still came from nuclear and coal-fired plants in 1978. It had added a second nuclear plant, Prairie Island, in 1973.

The 1970s were tough for NSP; as taxes and interest rates went up, NSP's earnings dropped, although revenues reached record highs. NSP, which had cut rates in earlier years, sought rate increases, but not all were approved by regulators. Near the end of the 1970s, NSP began to explore the possibilities of another nuclear power plant to produce low-cost energy. The company planned to participate in a plant called Tyrone, located in western Wisconsin. In early 1979, however, in the middle of NSP's battle with the Wisconsin Public Service Commission, came the nuclear accident at Three Mile Island, Pennsylvania. Soon after, NSP and other Tyrone owners voted to cancel the project.

NSP spent nearly $1 billion on pollution control from 1977 to 1987. The company also continued consolidating its principal subsidiaries. In 1987 NSP merged its subsidiary, Lake Superior District Power Company, into NSP-Wisconsin.

From 1980 to 1990, both NSP's sales and profits nearly doubled. It increased dividends for the 16th consecutive year in 1990. The company, however, contended that many of its costs, such as property taxes, were beyond its control and in 1989 had sought a $120 million electric rate increase from the Minnesota Public Utilities Commission. The commission rejected the request in 1990, and the Minnesota Court of Appeals upheld the commission's decision. In December 1991 the commission granted a smaller increase, $53.5 million. Also in 1991, NSP won rate increases in South Dakota and Wisconsin, although these, too, were smaller than initially requested. In North Dakota, a court case over a rate increase was pending. NSP also reported that its pollution control efforts of the 1970s and 1980s meant the company would not face great setbacks as a result of the restrictions of the Clean Air Act amendments passed in 1990.

The 1990s and Beyond

In 1992 the Minnesota Public Utilities Commission approved the storage of spent fuel rods in 17 above-ground casks outside the Prairie Island nuclear power plant. The Mdewakanton Sioux Indian tribe, whose reservation was adjacent to the site, and environmentalists were among those protesting the action. NSP said the 1,060 megawatt plant, which produced 20 percent of its total generating capacity, would have to be shut down by 1995 if additional storage space was not created. A planned permanent federal nuclear waste depository had yet to be established. Ruling that the above ground casks amounted to permanent storage, the Court of Appeals sent the issue to the Minnesota state legislature which gave final approval in 1994.

In 1995 NSP and Milwaukee-based Wisconsin Energy Corporation (WEC) announced a $6 billion merger plan which would create a new holding utility company, Primergy Corporation, based in Minneapolis and serving five states. The companies expected $2 billion in savings to come through consolidation over a 10-year period. Although market analysts and stockholders supported the merger, electric coops, industry groups, environmentalists, consumer organizations, and government regulators had reservations.

The merger plan was part of NSP's preparation for a future in which electric utilities would operate in a more competitive marketplace. In 1992, the federal government moved to allow the Federal Energy Regulatory Commission (FERC) to order electric companies to provide transmission service to other utilities and electric wholesalers, an action which supported the concept of increased competition among electric utilities. NSP

chairman and CEO James J. Howard, an executive in the telephone industry during deregulation, anticipated a time when the company would have to compete for business and pushed for streamlined operations. The company began to cut its work force, including corporate positions, and revamp inefficient operations.

By late 1996 the NSP-WEC merger was in limbo. Tom Meersman and Susan E. Peterson wrote in a November 19, 1996, *Star Tribune* article, "Much of the debate in Minnesota as well as in previous hearings in Wisconsin and Washington, D.C., focuses on four issues: rates, control, market domination and the environment." NSP stock, which had risen at the time of the announcement of the merger, fluctuated during the prolonged approval process.

In spite of difficulties related to the merger, NSP stayed on track. NSP Gas added 14,000 customers in 1996: the business was growing at twice the national average. And a new subsidiary, Seren Innovations, Inc., was created to provide services such as energy management, security control, and business information services by way of two-way communication networks.

Other nonregulated NSP subsidiaries included NRG Energy, Inc., the seventh fastest growing independent power producer in the world. The company built, managed, and operated power plants and was involved in projects using everything from coal to landfill gas. NRG Energy was expected to bring in 20 percent of NSP's earnings by the year 2000. Cenerprise, Inc., a gas and electric product and service company, operated nationwide, while Eloigne Company, which invested in affordable housing, operated primarily within NSP's service area.

In April 1997, Viking Gas Transmission Company, acquired by NSP in 1993, announced plans for an 800-mile pipeline to be built with TransCanada PipeLines Limited, one of North America's leading transporters of natural gas. The $1 billion gas transportation line was to begin in Emerson, Manitoba, and extend to Joliet, Illinois. NICOR Inc., a Naperville, Illinois-based holding company, also joined the partnership.

In May, NSP and WEC terminated their merger agreement. Approval had been granted by the state regulatory commissions in Michigan and North Dakota, but not in Minnesota or Wisconsin or by the FERC. Howard said in a press release, "What we encountered were regulatory agencies that were changing their merger policies as they were considering our filing." The two companies determined that changes in federal regulation would significantly reduce the benefits of the proposed merger.

NSP is one of the most efficiently run utilities in the country and provides some of the cheapest energy to its customers. The company's two nuclear plants, in particular, are considered some of the best-run in the nation. But growth in the electric utility industry is slow under the current system of regulation. Expansion of the company's nonregulated businesses, especially NRG Energy, is crucial to future growth. NSP's success in gaining natural gas customers—the gas business is regulated but not divided into designated territories—bodes well for NSP as it heads toward a less regulated future.

Principal Subsidiaries

Northern States Power Company (Wisconsin); NRG Energy, Inc.; Eloigne Company; Viking Gas Transmission Company; Seren Innovations, Inc.; Cenerprise, Inc.

Further Reading

Meersman, Tom, "Radioactive Waste," *Star Tribune* (Minneapolis), December 16, 1995, p. 3B.

Meersman, Tom, and Susan E. Peterson, "The NSP Merger," *Star Tribune* (Minneapolis), November 19, 1996, p. 1A.

Peterson, Susan E., "Two Executive Vice Presidents Are Leaving NSP As Part of a Reorganization of Top-Level Positions," *Star Tribune* (Minneapolis), December 2, 1992, p. 1D.

——, "NSP Shareholders Overwhelmingly Approve Merger of Equals with Wisconsin Energy," *Star Tribune* (Minneapolis), September 14, 1995, p. 1D.

——, "NSP: Wired for Change," *Star Tribune* (Minneapolis), June 23, 1997, p. 1D.

Pine, Carol, *NSP. Northern States People: The Past 70 Years*, Minneapolis: North Central Publishing, 1979.

Rebuffoni, Dean, "NSP Can Store Nuclear Waste," *Star Tribune* (Minneapolis), June 27, 1992, p. 1A.

Schafer, Lee, "Power Play," *Corporate Report Minnesota*, April 1996, pp. 36–41.

—Maya Sahafi
—updated by Kathleen Peippo

Oil-Dri Corporation of America

410 North Michigan Avenue, Suite 400
Chicago, Illinois 60611-4211
U.S.A.
(312) 321-1515
Fax: (312) 321-1271

Public Company
Incorporated: 1946
Employees: 670
Sales: $153.8 million (1996)
Stock Exchanges: New York
SICs: 3295 Minerals—Ground or Treated; 2899
    Chemical Preparations, Not Elsewhere Classified

Oil-Dri Corporation of America makes and markets leading sorbent products for use by individual, industrial, agricultural, and environmental customers. The company's main commodity, cat litter, accounted for 25 percent of all litter sold in the U.S. Its Cat's Pride is the only cat litter recommended by the American Humane Association. Oil-Dri absorbents which help clean up oil spills in garages and industrial sites have been a market leader ever since the company was founded in 1941. Oil-Dri's products in more recent years have become important in helping clean up environmental oil spills, making particulate carriers for agricultural fertilizers and pesticides, and aiding manufacturers of various kinds of cooking oils. Still a family firm, Oil-Dri operates eight manufacturing facilities in the U.S., Canada, and the United Kingdom and ships over 250 items worldwide.

Origins of the Family Business

This family enterprise began with the emigration of two individuals from Eastern Europe. Alex Jaffee and Rose Ganscoe both arrived in America through Ellis Island, met in Chicago, and got married there. Their second child, Nick Jaffee, later founded Oil-Dri.

Raised in Platteville, Wisconsin, Nick Jaffee as a teenager helped his father in his business of selling fur, hides, and junk.

When he was 15, Nick was sailing up and down the Mississippi River to buy furs and hides for his father's business. Thus Nick learned entrepreneurial values early in life.

In high school Nick Jaffee starred in basketball and was recruited by the Platteville School of Mining, which he attended before starting to work full-time for his father.

After the 1921 farmers' depression, Alex Jaffee moved to Chicago, while Nick remained in Platteville to run the family business. But in 1927, Nick sold the business and moved to Chicago, where he married Lucille Bloom, a University of Chicago graduate who taught school and, like her husband, was the child of immigrant parents. Nick and Lucille had two sons, Robert and Richard, born in 1933 and 1936.

Nick Jaffee during the Great Depression started his own business by selling car parts to garages, but in 1941 a wartime shortage of auto parts caused him to look for nonstrategic items to sell. Based on ideas he had learned while attending mining school, he soon thought that fuller's earth, a clay-like absorbent mineral substance used for thousands of years, could be used instead of sawdust to absorb oil spills. Unlike sawdust, fuller's earth was not flammable and thus would be a much safer alternative that would more effectively prevent slipping and job accidents.

With $3,000 borrowed from his mother, Nick Jaffee in 1941 started his sole proprietorship working out of his home, where he received 10 tons of fuller's earth in burlap bags. He first sold his product, Floor-Dri Oil and Grease Absorbent, to Sears car repair on Chicago's 79th Street.

Soon Jaffee formed a partnership with P. D. Jackson, the Motor Master owner whom Jaffee had met while selling auto parts. Jackson provided capital for investment and a trained sales force from his previous business. Jaffee changed the name of his first product from Floor-Dri to Oil-Dri. In 1941, Nick Jaffee also created the company's "slipping man" trademark, which shows a working man slipping on an oil spill. Oil-Dri Corporation has kept that image as part of its heritage and corporate culture.

Fuller's earth was not rationed during World War II, so the firm was able to obtain more raw material and expand. Oil-Dri in 1945 moved to its new office at 520 North Michigan Avenue, where it remained into the 1990s.

In 1946, the firm was incorporated under its present name, and three years later P. D. Jackson sold his share of the business to Nick Jaffee, who became the sole owner.

After Nick Jaffee's three brothers returned from military service, they joined the family business and helped start the Oil-Dri tradition of blending family and business. Woodrow Jaffee became sales manager, while Leo was the bookkeeper and Saul worked in accounting.

The Second Generation

Founder Nick Jaffee in the 1950s found a way to keep both his sons involved in the family business without fighting each other for control. With Robert, he started an Oil-Dri subsidiary called Amco Wire Corporation to make plastic and wire items for food-service use. The father and son by 1960 concentrated on building Amco.

Meanwhile, Richard Jaffee in 1952 had started working part-time for the Oil-Dri Corporation in the mailroom and office. After graduating from high school in 1953, he became a student at the University of Wisconsin, where he met his wife, Shirley Hanmaker. Jaffee earned his degree in accounting and went on to become a CPA. In 1958 he began working full-time for Oil-Dri and two years later became the firm's second president. Company sales in 1960 reached $1 million, while profits were $6,000 and the firm shipped 20,000 tons of its clay-based products.

In 1960, under Richard Jaffee's leadership, Oil-Dri introduced a new kind of product that would become its main source of income. It began marketing Cat's Pride Cat Litter to cat owners. By absorbing liquid from cat urine, this fuller's earth product slowed the growth of bacteria and the production of ammonia, the source of cat urine stench. Thus Oil-Dri helped consumers solve one of the main problems of owning a cat.

Actually, Oil-Dri was preceded by Edward Lowe Industries in introducing an absorbent clay-based cat litter. Ed Lowe started his company in the late 1940s when he controlled 100 percent of the market. Soon Oil-Dri and other firms competed in the growing market for cat litter.

Oil-Dri in the 1960s expanded in other ways. With cat litter and other new products and increasing costs of the firm's raw material, fuller's earth, Oil-Dri decided to invest in two clay mines in the South and become vertically integrated. Between 1960 and 1963, the firm acquired Cairo, Georgia Production

Company and Howell Southern Products in Ripley, Mississippi. Acquiring the two plants "set us on a course in which capital costs would ratchet up," said president Richard Jaffee in a 1995 issue of *Family Business*. "We converted from a wholesale distributor with almost all liquid assets to a capital-intensive business."

After the founder died in 1962 at age 56, Richard Jaffee struggled without the advice of his father to make sure the family business prospered. In 1962 Oil-Dri developed its Terra Green Soil Conditioner for maintaining lawns, golf greens, and playing fields. Three years later the company introduced its Agsorb Carriers, fullers earth-based products for delivering various pesticides and other crop chemicals.

Jaffee concluded that the growing capital needs of his firm required one of two solutions. Either Oil-Dri could borrow money or become a public firm. Jaffee decided to take the firm public in 1971. Its stock was bought and sold on the New York Stock Exchange under the symbol ODC.

Just before that major turning point in Oil-Dri's history, Jaffee sold his holdings in the Amco subsidiary to his brother and his nephew, which allowed Amco to become a completely separate firm under family leadership.

Also in 1971, Oil-Dri built its clay mining facility at Ochlocknee, Georgia. Like other clay mines, the Ochlocknee facility was a strip or open pit mine. Large machines simply scooped out 3.5 tons of earth and dumped it into waiting trucks, which carried the fuller's earth to the nearby plant. There the clay was ground into precise particles, dried, and sterilized.

In 1979 Oil-Dri expanded its West Coast operations by buying the facility and clay reserves of the American Fossil Company in Christmas Valley, Oregon. In the same year, the company moved its research and development to a facility it purchased in Prairie View, Illinois.

In 1981 the firm contracted with The Clorox Company to develop nationally sold Fresh Step and Control Cat Litters. That was a major agreement that was crucial in expanding sales of Oil-Dri's key cat litter products.

By 1988, the cat litter industry had expanded to the point where *Fortune* published a major article about the main players: Oil-Dri with 14 percent market share, Edward Lowe Industries with a little less than a third of the market, and Excel-Mineral with a 10 percent share based on its Jonny Cat and other brands. Several other smaller firms competed with the big three for the 27 million American families who owned at least one cat, which was 30 percent of all households in the nation.

Cat litter from Oil-Dri and its competitors, along with decreasing American family size, helped the cat replace the dog as the number one pet in America in 1985. By 1988, the nation's cats outnumbered dogs 58 million to 49 million. To meet the booming demand for cat litter, about 75 brands were offered to consumers, who purchased 245 million bags of cat litter in 1988. "Cat litter has done for the cat what air conditioning did for Houston," said William Moll, Oil-Dri Corporation's vice-president of research and development, in the *Fortune* article.

Oil-Dri developed some new agricultural products in the 1980s. It introduced Flo-Fre Flowability Aid to prevent soybean meal and other animal feeds from caking and also Pel-Unite, which helped manufacturers make stronger food pellets and also reduce wear on their machinery. Monsanto Agricultural Company awarded Oil-Dri its Supplier Quality Recognition Award in 1990.

Foreign operations enhanced Oil-Dri's competitiveness in the 1970s and 1980s. Using new patented synthetic technology, the firm in the 1970s constructed plants in the United Kingdom and Germany for making floor absorbents and cat litter, while establishing subsidiaries in the United Kingdom, Switzerland, and Germany. In the 1980s, the Cologne, Germany plant was sold, but sales began in Malaysia, Japan, and Australia.

Oil-Dri's Canadian operations commenced in the early 1980s with the acquisition of the assets of Favorite Products, Ltd., a company based in Laval, Quebec, that manufactured Saular cat litter products, Canada's market leader.

To support its growing domestic and international sales, Oil-Dri in the 1980s took several steps. In 1983 it created Oil-Dri Transportation Company to limit its distribution costs. Its large fleet of trucks took Oil-Dri products all over the U.S. and then contracted with other companies to haul their goods on return trips. The transportation subsidiary also used railroad shipping and leased storage facilities to provide economical and quicker delivery capabilities. Oil-Dri also started a customer service department in the 1980s and purchased a new IBM mainframe computer and added over 100 user terminals at sites across the nation.

The 1990s

When Oil-Dri Corporation celebrated its 50th anniversary in 1991, its sales were 100 times greater than 20 years before. Since 1971, Oil-Dri had doubled in size every five years. Oil-Dri in the 1990s introduced new products to meet the increasing need for environmental protection. In 1990 it acquired Industrial Environmental Products, Inc., the manufacturer of polypropylene absorbents. The new line of Oil-Dri Lite polypropylene products, including Oil-Dri Rugs, Rolls, Pads, Sweeps, and Booms, could be incinerated and in some cases recycled.

Oil-Dri Booms and Sweeps contained and absorbed maritime oil spills, such as the Exxon Valdez spill in Alaska's Prince William Sound, and also were used to keep marinas free of oil. Oil-Dri Corporation added over 100 specially trained distributors to meet the needs of users of its new Oil-Dri Lite products.

Strategic alliances were another source of Oil-Dri's success in the 1990s. For example, in February 1993 Wal-Mart contracted with Oil-Dri to make its Lasting Pride brand of scoopable cat litter. Scoopable litters clump up and thus small portions can be removed daily. Wal-Mart and other mass merchandisers attracted consumers who formerly could buy scoopable litter only at pet stores.

Agreements with Wal-Mart and also K-Mart ensured that Oil-Dri cat litter would be sold by national distributors, but that was a very competitive market. For example, the increasingly popular scoopable or clumping litters introduced in 1987 were sold in the early 1990s by Oil-Dri and nine other manufacturers, including Houston's A&M Pet Products, the maker of Ever Clean, Catsanova, and Scoop Away brands; South Bend, Indiana's Golden Cat Corporation; and Alfapet Inc. of St. Louis. However, by 1997 consolidation had reduced the cat litter industry to four major players, including Oil-Dri.

In 1995 Oil-Dri was honored when a Massachusetts Mutual Life Insurance-backed panel of five judges named it the "Family Business of the Year" in the category of firms with at least 250 employees. To promote family values at Oil-Dri, it emphasized the Ten Commandments and the Golden Rule, while encouraging different family members to work for the company under certain conditions. In the spring 1995 issue of *Family Business*, Richard Jaffee explained this aspect of his firm's corporate culture: "the value system established by my father and mother . . . was that if an employee had a good work ethic and values, chances were high his brother or uncle or kids did, too. . . We have modern business methods, but a folksy atmosphere."

The Jaffee family in 1995 maintained control over Oil-Dri by owning 30 percent of its stock and all its voting stock. In addition, Dan Jaffee, Richard Jaffee's son who had worked for the firm since 1987, on August 1, 1995 became the new company president and chief operating officer, while his father remained chairman and CEO. Richard Jaffee's three other children and two of his sons-in-law also worked for Oil-Dri in the 1990s.

Oil-Dri's revenues in 1997 came from three major sources. Cat litter brands, including Cats Pride, Lasting Pride, and Fresh Step, accounted for 60 percent of all sales. Agricultural products, sold to firms like Monsanto, Dow Elanco, and DuPont to provide the clay-based carriers for their insecticides, herbicides, and fungicides, brought in about 11 percent of all sales. Its fluids purification products, such as Pure-Flo to remove impurities from cooking oils and Ultra-Clear to help refine oil, represented about 12 percent of company sales. The rest of Oil-Dri's sales came from its industrial, environmental, and transportation segments.

One of Oil-Dri's major strengths in 1997 was its land used to mine the clay needed for several of its products. The firm owned or leased almost 11,300 acres of land with about 240 million tons of clay reserves in Mississippi, Georgia, Oregon, Florida, and Nevada. Another major asset was the firm's 19,100 square-foot research and pilot plant facility opened in 1991 in Vernon Hills, Illinois.

Oil-Dri continued to expand its international sales in the 1990s. For example, it sold Ultra-Clear to oil refineries and utilities in Saudi Arabia, Turkey, Germany, and Spain. By 1996, Oil-Dri sold mainly its fluids purification products to 60 nations. Its Latin American sales increased 32 percent in 1996.

With such advantages, Oil-Dri in 1997 nonetheless faced significant challenges. Due to investments in new computers, plant expansion, new products, and soft performance of its industrial commodities, Oil-Dri's stock declined from $25 per share in 1993 to about $16 per share in early 1997. Stiff competition in its primary cat litter market continued, and

Oil-Dri's management faced many uncertainties, such as changing agricultural markets and fluctuating mass merchandising practices.

Principal Subsidiaries

Oil-Dri Corporation of Georgia; Oil-Dri Production Company; Oil-Dri Transportation Company; Oil-Dri S.A. (Switzerland); Oil-Dri U.K. Limited; Blue Mountain Production Company; Favorite Products Company, Ltd. (Canada).

Further Reading

Fischetti, Mark, ''How Excellent Companies Do It,'' *Family Business*, Spring 1995, pp. 12–14.

McMath, Robert, ''Cat Litter: Myth and Reality,'' *Adweek's Marketing Week*, February 3, 1992, p. 24.

Moser, Penny W., ''Filler's the Name, Odor's the Game,'' *Fortune*, April 25, 1988, p. 107.

''Oil-Dri Corporation of America: Interview of Richard M. Jaffee,'' *Wall Street Corporate Reporter*, January 13–19, 1997.

''Oil-Dri Corporation of America: Celebrating 50 Years Together,'' company videotape, July 13, 1991.

''Oil-Dri Named Family Biz of the Year,'' *Industrial Distribution*, June 1995, p. 32.

''Oil-Dri Reports Third Quarter Results; Third Quarter Net Income Up 74 Percent, Nine Months Net Income Up 54 Percent,'' *PR Newswire*, May 20, 1997, p. 520DETU048.

''Scooping Up Pet Care Products; Chains Use New Cat and Dog Products to Defend Market Turf,'' *Discount Store News*, February 15, 1993, p. S21.

—David M. Walden

On Assignment

Employer of Knowledge Workers

On Assignment, Inc.

26651 W. Algonquin Road
Calabasas, California 91302
U.S.A.
(818) 878-7900
Fax: (408) 878-7930

Public Company
Incorporated: 1992
Employees: 6,750
Sales: $88.2 million (1996)
Stock Exchanges: NASDAQ
SICs: 7363 Help Supply Services

On Assignment, Inc. is an agency that places scientific and technical workers in temporary jobs with companies across the United States. While most temporary service agencies provide clerical and light industrial employees, On Assignment has maintained a unique market niche by providing scientific professionals to laboratories, including the biotechnology, environmental, chemical, pharmaceutical, food and beverage, and petrochemical industries. Since 1994, the company also provides temporary workers for finance needs, and since 1996, it services the environmental industries. On Assignment operates four divisions: Lab Support, Healthcare Financial Staffing, Envirostaff, and Advanced Science Professionals. The company maintains a telemarketing sales staff for client recruitment, and scientifically trained account managers make assignments from the pool of qualified jobseekers.

On Assignment began in 1986, when Bruce Culver and Raf Dahlquist founded a California company named Lab Support, Inc. Culver was an executive in the scientific instrument industry with Bausch & Lomb/ARI, Hach and Varian, and Dahlquist was a senior scientist at Bausch & Lomb. The two had also worked together at Applied Research Labs, a Valencia, California scientific instruments company. Their experience in the instrument industry convinced Culver and Dahlquist that there was a significant, unserviced market for temporary lab workers at companies across the country. Larger temporary personnel service companies were focused on the clerical and industrial markets, ignoring science companies and their needs.

To create a company that would occupy this special niche in temporary services, Culver and Dahlquist, with the help of their hairdresser wives, each contributed between $20,000 and $30,000 in personal funds to the startup of the business in 1985. Within 6 months, they were running short of funds, and embarked on a search for financing. Turned down by 20 different venture capital firms, they were at the point of closing the door on their attempt to start a successful company when the 21st capital firm, Sierra Ventures, agreed to support the company. Between Sierra Ventures and subsequent investors, Culver and Dahlquist raised $2.5 million of venture capital, and officially opened the doors of Lab Support, Inc. in 1986. That year, the company's revenues were $623,000, and they quickly surged to $2.9 million in 1987 and $7.4 million in 1988. In 1987, the company placed some 700 employees—including chemists, biologists, lab technicians, and other scientists—in temporary employment. Job-seekers received Lab Support placement services for free, but were promised no guaranteed placement. Over 6,000 resumes were stored in the company's computer system, and used to cross-reference employee qualifications with the needs of clients, including Chevron, Shell, Westinghouse, Monsanto, and Johnson & Johnson. Overall, company customers seemed to respond well to the temporary scientist solution, with over 75 percent of the company's revenue coming from repeat business from existing clients. When companies utilized Lab Support temporary workers, the employees technically worked for Lab Support, which provided them with a salary, insurance, a medical plan, and benefits. Lab Support then billed the company at a higher rate, keeping the profit. Although one reason job-seekers enlisted with Lab Support was in hopes of a full-time position, the company charged clients a fee for hiring workers who had been with Lab Support for less than six months. The fee, which did not apply when workers had been with the company for six months or more, amounted to as much as 25 percent of the worker's first-year salary. Typically, employment assignments for the company last about three months.

With its headquarters in Canoga Park, California, by 1987 the company also had opened five field offices, in Costa Mesa and Burlingame, California; Englewood, Colorado; Morristown, New Jersey; and Chicago. Such rapid growth, however, entailed a hefty investment in operating costs in an already slim-margin industry, and the company had not yet turned a profit. Expansion into new areas, including consulting and recruiting, was also hurting the bottom line. In 1989, the company's balance sheet looked pessimistic, with losses of $1.5 million on sales of only $7 million. This dilemma caused Culver and Dahlquist to invest in an experienced executive from the temporary personnel industry, to manage the next phase of the organization's development, expanding in the laboratory market and diversifying into other professional areas.

In March 1989, a new era of leadership began and the company was saved from near-extinction when H. Tom Buelter became Lab Support, Inc.'s president and CEO. Bavarian-born Buelter had a proven track record in the industry, having led Kelly Services, Inc.'s Assisted Living division through major growth in revenues between 1983 and 1988. He pulled in the reins on the consulting and recruiting businesses, and focused instead on client development. With the high number of companies that had downsized in the 1980s, Buelter had no trouble finding customers for temporary employees. Revenues continued to increase in 1989, and the company closed its first fiscal year without a loss, with earnings of $13.2 million and net income of $166,000. In fact, Buelter transformed Lab Support into a profitable company within a few months. That same year, both founders—Culver and Dahlquist—quit the company, leaving it in Buelter's more capable hands.

One of Buelter's restructuring brainstorms was the development of the account manager position in 1991. Under Buelter's plan, account managers must have scientific degrees and lab experience, so as to fully understand the technical needs of the company's clients. Account Managers were responsible for providing all client and employee services, including recruitment, training and coaching, business development, assignments, and followup.

Under Buelter's management, both revenues and net income continued to improve. In 1990, revenues increased 63 percent to $21.5 million and net income was $1.5 million—nine times that of the previous year. In 1991, revenues again increased to $26.2 million, with a decrease in net income to $1.1 million. The increase in revenues and profitability corresponded with more assignments made yearly. The average weekly number of temporary professionals on assignment went up from 392 in 1989 to 765 in 1991.

The background for the company's success was the rapid growth of the U.S. temporary services industry. Between 1975 and 1991, the industry's total payroll grew from $0.9 billion to $9.6 billion. The expansion of the temporary industry, in turn, was situated within the hiring of large numbers of white collar professionals, coupled with layoffs during the recession of the early 1980s. When the economy recovered, companies began to turn to temporary personnel, rather than replacing previous employees with permanent new workers. Companies using temporary personnel for a wide variety of needs were recognizing the benefits of nonpermanent employees, including decreased fixed overhead, increased staffing flexibility, elimination of expensive severance packages and low-risk, on-the-job evaluations of prospective employees.

The company took on its current name in 1992, in conjunction with its public offering. Operating under the new company name of On Assignment, Lab Support became the company's first operating division, with its specialization of industrial, pharmaceutical, and other laboratory positions. The company's intention, by establishing Lab Support as a division, was to soon expand into offering specialized services in other professional niches through additional divisions in the future. The public offering comprised 1.7 million shares at $7 per share.

At the time of its public offering, On Assignment was the only nationwide temporary services provider specializing exclusively in scientific laboratory personnel. By 1992, over 400 clients were served by 26 company branch offices in 24 metropolitan areas, and 1,000 scientific temporary workers were placed in assignments during the year. Some of the company's success may have been attributable to the booming medical and biotechnology businesses, which were receptive to On Assignment's temporary workers with special skills needed in medical laboratories, hospitals, and health care clinics. The company counted some of America's biggest drugmaking firms among its clients, including Abbott Laboratories, Hoffman-La Roche, and Bristol-Myers Squibb. In all, in 1992 On Assignment had a company client base of over 400 companies, including more than 30 *Fortune* 500 companies.

The first year as a public company set new records for On Assignment, with $32.7 million in revenues (a 25 percent increase over the previous year) and $1.76 million in net income (a 60 percent increase). The company attributed this success to two accomplishments: the restructuring and subsequent emphasis on the Account Manager position, and a 24 percent increase in the average number of employees in assignment, from 765 in 1991 to 945 in 1992. The temporary services industry continued to grow, with one in three Americans in the contingency worker category according to On Assignment's 1992 annual report.

By 1993, On Assignment was active in 32 cities with offices from Seattle to Miami, and clients included major companies such as Hewlett-Packard, Exxon, and Johnson & Johnson. An exclusive sales and marketing agreement was reached with Baxter International Inc., whereby the pharmaceutical company's scientific products division began to offer On Assignment's temporary services to its customers. During 1993 the company employed over 3,600 science professionals in assignments averaging between three-and-a-half and four months for 1,145 client firms. That year, the company was Number 22 on *Business Week* Magazine's Hot Growth list and Number 58 on *Forbes*'s list of the "Best Small Companies in America." Stock prices soared to a high of $15 in February 1993, and settled at $12 by May. Revenues grew 17 percent to $38.08 million, and net income surged 40 percent to $2.46 million. With no competitors on the national scale, the company was supplying 1,100 scientists with work, filling most customer orders within a

24-hour period. Typically, clients paid On Assignment wages from $10 an hour (for lab technicians) to $35 an hour (for experienced microbiologists), which left the company with a 30 percent profit after employment taxes. The company began to explore offering medical coverage to its workers in 1993.

Taking its first step toward diversification, On Assignment acquired the 11th fastest growing company in the San Francisco Bay Area in January 1994—1st Choice Mortgage Personnel Inc. This acquisition supported the opening of On Assignment's second division, Finance Support, which used the same methods as Lab Support to match finance professionals with the temporary needs of banking, lending, credit, and mortgage institutions. The acquisition quickly showed its merit in sales numbers; first-quarter revenues were up 23 percent from the same quarter of the previous year, second-quarter profit showed a 37 percent increase, and the third quarter was up by 36 percent. The success was attributed to the new division as well as expense controls, including decreased workers' compensation insurance. For the year as a whole, revenues increased 27 percent to $48.4 million, and net income saw a 36 percent growth to $3.35 million. During that year, 5,200 scientists were placed in jobs. The company was up to Number 36 on *Forbes*'s list of the "Best Small Companies in America," and the *Wall Street Journal* noted that On Assignment was changing personnel practices of U.S. businesses. Now billing up to 40 percent over worker wages, On Assignment had become a profitable business requiring very little capital; a transformation over its earlier incarnation with Culver and Dahlquist at the helm. Due to its market niche, On Assignment's 7 percent net profit margins greatly exceeded those of temporary agencies placing clerical workers, which typically earned around 2 percent profit.

A second acquisition at the end of 1994—of Sklar Resources Group, Inc.—was made to increase the size of the Finance Support division, and to expand its service by adding finance professionals in credit and collections. The company especially sought out businesses with serious collection problems, including health care, automotive leasing, and publishing. By July 1995, the company had 44 branch offices across the country. Credibility had been built based on the high quality of its temporary employees, with over 20 percent of its workers hired by clients into permanent positions.

In late 1995, On Assignment continued its rapid diversification with the creation of Advanced Science Professionals. Launched in New York, Pennsylvania, and New Jersey, this division was formed to serve the needs of biotechnology and pharmaceutical companies requiring employees with advanced science degrees and very specific skills for finite projects. For the company, Advanced Science Professionals marked its entry into the upper levels of the flexible staffing pyramid, and the resulting opportunity to secure higher wage levels. Revenues continued to grow, with a 28 percent increase to $62.04 million, and net income saw a corresponding jump of 29 percent to $4.33 million. By the end of 1995, 46 branch offices were operating in 41 markets, and 6,750 workers had been employed at over 2,000 client companies (including 800 new clients in 1995 alone). All employees were now offered benefits including access to group insurance, paid holidays, a 401(k) plan, an Employee Stock Purchase Plan, and an annual appreciation bonus.

Entering the environmental services industry, On Assignment acquired EnviroStaff, Inc. in 1996. This was the company's biggest acquisition by far, which involved the issuance of stocks valued at about $6.2 million to purchase the $10.6 million company. EnviroStaff became the name of On Assignment's third division, serving the environmental services, regulatory compliance and health and safety markets. Revenues in 1996 increased 21 percent to $88.2 million, with net income also healthy at $5.6 million (a 29 percent increase). The growth was attributed to the success of all three operating divisions. In addition to the new environmental division, in 1996 On Assignment initiated other new programs, including Assignment Ready (a service through which clients and prospects are notified of promising candidates through summaries and weekly reports), additional recruitment and training of Account Managers, and a new video-teleconferencing system allowing such interviews to be arranged faster and more efficiently.

As On Assignment looks toward the future, it plans to pursue the strategy that has worked so well since 1989: expanding in new and existing markets, providing highly valued services, and applying its assignment methods to a growing list of professional and technical job categories, through acquisitions or internal development. Since the company was made profitable when Buelter took over, its track record is glowing. Given consistent leadership and well-planned acquisitions and expansion projects, and with no major competitors in the nationwide market, On Assignment should continue to prosper.

Principal Divisions

Lab Support; Healthcare Financial Staffing; Envirostaff; Advanced Science Professionals.

Further Reading

Bettner, Jill, "Temporary Lab Help Is Formula for Success," *Los Angeles Times,* May 25, 1993, p. 3.

Block, Toddi Gutner, "Brains for Rent," *Forbes*, July 31, 1995, pp. 99–100.

Johnson, Becky M., "These Temps Don't Type, But They're Handy in the Lab," *Business Week*, May 24, 1993, p. 68.

Marcial, Gene G., "A Temp Agency's Expert Timing," *Business Week*, December 7, 1992, p. 115.

"On Assignment Completes Purchase of EnviroStaff," *Los Angeles Times*, April 9, 1996, p. D7.

"On Assignment Inc. Reports 27% Profit Gain," *Los Angeles Times*, January 30, 1996, p. D7.

"On Assignment Inc. to Sell Common Stock," *Los Angeles Times*, August 18, 1992, p. 9.

"On Assignment Plans Acquisition," *The Wall Street Journal*, January 21, 1994, p. A3.

"On Assignment Posts Profit in 1st Quarter," *Los Angeles Times*, April 26, 1994, p. 2.

"On Assignment Posts 38% Profit Increase," *Los Angeles Times*, April 25, 1995, p. 9.

"On Assignment Reports Doubling of Profits," *Los Angeles Times*, January 19, 1993, p. 17.

"On Assignment Reports 3rd-Quarter Income Up 8%," *Los Angeles Times*, October 19, 1993, p. 15.

Peltz, James F., "Lab Support Offers White Coats to Go," *Los Angeles Times*, January 5, 1988, pp. A4–9.

—Heidi Feldman

One Price Clothing Stores, Inc.

1875 East Main Street
Highway 290
Commerce Park
Duncan, South Carolina 29334
U.S.A.
(864) 433-8888
Fax: (864) 433-9784

Public Company
Incorporated: 1984 as J. K. Apparel, Inc.
Employees: 4,105
Sales: $298.99 million (1997)
Stock Exchanges: NASDAQ
SICs: 5621 Women's Clothing Stores; 5641 Children's and Infants' Wear Stores; 5632 Women's Accessories and Specialty Stores

Headquartered in South Carolina, One Price Clothing Stores, Inc., is a retailer of women's and children's clothing and accessories. This chain of stores sells only quality merchandise—no seconds or damaged goods—that is contemporary and in season. Most items are sold for a uniform price, typically below that of competing stores for similar merchandise. To achieve this advantage, One Price Clothing Stores stocks overproduced, canceled, odd-lot, and liquidated items. The chain also capitalizes on discounts for purchasing merchandise in large quantities. One Price Clothing Stores frequently locates its retail outlets in lower-income areas.

One Price Clothing Stores sells women's and children's apparel and accessories to consumers through company-owned retail stores in the continental United States, Puerto Rico, and the Virgin Islands. In order to succeed in the highly competitive world of retail apparel, the company sells its merchandise at lower prices than department stores, specialty retailers, discount stores, manufacturer-owned outlet stores, and other off-price retailers. One Price Clothing Stores generally purchases quality merchandise for its stores at discounted prices and at favorable terms from manufacturers, jobbers, importers, and other vendors. The company, which does not franchise its outlets, carefully plans its stores and maintains its flexibility to ensure profitable operations.

Mr. Jacobs Has an Idea: 1984

Henry D. Jacobs, Jr., founded the company in 1984 as a North Carolina corporation under the name J. K. Apparel, Inc. After changing the company to a South Carolina corporation named One Price Clothing Stores, Inc., Jacobs ultimately incorporated in Delaware in April 1987. In May of that year, the company issued its initial public offering of common stock.

One Price Clothing Stores headquartered its corporate offices and distribution center on 82 acres in Duncan, South Carolina. In 1993 the company expanded the corporate offices by 28,000 square feet. Two years later it expanded the distribution center to 500,000 square feet, an increase of about 90,000 square feet. Both expansions served to better support the company's future growth.

The One Price Concept

The company opened its first store in 1984. With merchandise for juniors, misses, and children, the store offered a variety of contemporary, in-season clothing. Fashionable sportswear comprised typically stocked items, namely knit tops, pants, blouses, shirts, skirts, sweaters, jackets, and shorts. Other items included dresses, swimsuits, lingerie, raincoats, and accessories such as scarves, socks, belts, handbags, jewelry, and fragrances. All merchandise was comparable to items carried by department and specialty stores, except each item in the One Price Clothing Store sold for seven dollars. Even two- and three-piece ensembles sold for seven dollars, less than half of the price of some competing merchandise elsewhere. The store was not dependent on any single group of customers, but the value- and fashion-conscious woman—usually from lower- or middle-income levels—became the average customer.

Company Perspectives:

One Price Clothing Stores, Inc., operates a chain of off-price specialty stores offering a wide variety of first quality, contemporary, in-season apparel and accessories for missy, junior, and plus-sized women and children. . . . We sell merchandise at substantially discounted prices by taking advantage of situations such as imbalances between supply and demand, order cancellations, and vendor needs for liquidity. Unlike most off-price retailers, One Price Clothing sells only first quality merchandise. Our commitment to fashion, quality, and exceptional value has earned us a loyal customer following in our markets.

Rapid Expansion During the 1980s and 90s

Rapid expansion followed that first store as the One Price concept was embraced by the company and its customers. "There's no sticker shock," Jacobs explained in *WWD*. "It simplifies inventory and operating procedures. The discipline required—in cost control, merchandise, real estate, expenses—is enormous. It's probably the reason why many who have tried it are now out of business." Yet Jacobs's stores were successful. Even the chain's more specialized areas held their own in sales. For example, in 1994 accessories accounted for 11 percent of One Price Clothing Stores' net sales, increasing to 12 percent the next year. Similarly, the company attributed 10 percent of its net sales to children's clothing in 1994 through 1996.

In 1990, the company registered "One Price" as a trademark with the U.S. Office of Patents and Trademarks. Awarded incontestable status, One Price Clothing Stores intended to renew the trademark as valuable and significant to its business. The company also registered "One Price" and its Spanish equivalent—"Un solo precio"—in Mexico; however, as of 1997, the company did not use the trademark there. Instead One Price Clothing Stores used "Ropa a un precio," a registered trademark in the United States, at stores with significant populations of Spanish-speaking customers. The company also received approval to register "One Price" and "One Price Plus" in Canada, but—as in Mexico—the company did not use the trademark in Canada as of 1997.

By 1993, the company operated more than 500 stores, each selling merchandise for seven dollars. Fifty stores were added in the Los Angeles market alone in 1994—five of them within two months.

One Price Clothing Stores established its first wholly owned subsidiary in February 1994, 10 years after the opening of its first store. Operations for One Price Clothing Store of Puerto Rico, Inc., began in May 1994. Within three years, 29 stores operated in Puerto Rico.

At the end of 1996 One Price Clothing Stores operated 645 stores in 27 states and Puerto Rico. The company opened 23 stores in 1996, relocated 11 others, and closed 66 underperforming stores. It planned to open 65 new stores in 1997, relocating 10 and closing 30 underperforming establishments.

The company further expanded the One Price concept by establishing One Price Clothing–U.S. Virgin Islands in 1997. This second wholly owned subsidiary began operations in March of that year. According to Jacobs's statement in the 1996 annual report, "This new store in St. Croix opened with extremely strong initial sales." Thus, One Price Clothing Stores expected similar ventures in the future. As Jacobs explained further: "We continue to search for new locations providing the right mix of demographics and market access needed to fuel future growth." In total, One Price Clothing Stores anticipated 680 stores in operation during 1997.

The Purchasing Strategy

In order to achieve the One Price concept, the company looked for vendors that needed excess capacity, import quotas, or liquidity. It also targeted suppliers unable to dispose of their merchandise through regular distribution channels. Essentially, One Price Clothing Stores bought merchandise discontinued because of color or style changes by manufacturers. It purchased overproduced merchandise, orders canceled by regular retailers, and unordered catalog merchandise. The company also bought odd-lot and broken-size assortments.

This strategy gave One Price Clothing Stores distinct purchasing advantages. For instance, it could buy merchandise in large quantities at greatly reduced prices. Such opportunistic buying allowed the company to purchase merchandise close to or during actual selling seasons—later than department stores or specialty retailers. One Price Clothing Stores then had the ability to react to trends that developed in each selling season. Often the company bought selected merchandise in advance of the selling season as well.

With a reputation for reliability in the industry, One Price Clothing Stores purchased merchandise inventories on credit. In all, the company dealt with nine hundred vendors, none supplying more than 10 percent of One Price Clothing Stores' annual total purchases. The chain maintained no long-term or exclusive agreements with vendors and easily added new vendors if they could provide quality merchandise at a low price.

The Stores

One Price Clothing Stores designed its outlet operations for customer convenience. The stores presented merchandise attractively, with all apparel on hangers and with much of the merchandise organized by classification, color, and style. The chain accepted cash, checks, and major credit cards as payment from customers and devised a liberal return and exchange policy. The company kept its stores open seven days each week from 10 a.m. to 9 p.m., although One Price Clothing Stores adhered to slightly shorter hours on Sundays. The company generally staffed each store with a full-time manager, one or two assistant managers, and up to ten sales associates. One Price Clothing Stores entrusted its senior vice president of stores with responsibility for its retail establishments and appointed two directors of store operations. Regional sales managers oversaw nine districts, with district sales managers assigned responsibility for 10 or 12 individual stores. District sales managers made regular site visits, promoted sales, trained staff, consulted about store layout and merchandise, and oversaw company operations and management policies.

Though One Price Clothing Stores maintained outlets throughout the continental United States and in selected U.S. territories, many of the company's stores were concentrated in certain areas. Texas, for example, had 87 One Price Clothing Stores at the beginning of 1997. Florida followed with 62, and 50 stores were located in California. Georgia was home to more than 40 One Price Clothing Stores.

Despite their locations, all of the company's stores shared a similar design in 1997. Each was about 3,300 square feet, with 2,400 square feet of selling space. The company leased all facilities at five- to 10-year initial terms, with one or two five-year renewal options. Seventy percent of the leases and renewal agreements were set to expire in 1997.

In 1997, 85 percent of the company's stores were located in strip shopping areas and 15 percent were situated in central business districts or malls. One Price Clothing Stores leased most of its facilities in or near communities with populations of 40,000 to 50,000 or in large metropolitan areas.

Weakness in Women's Apparel

Due to prolonged weakness in women's apparel, One Price Clothing Stores embarked on a program to address the critical situation in the retail environment in 1996. It began with customer surveys to re-identify its customer base, customer needs, and customer opinions of the chain. The company developed and tested new marketing and advertising campaigns, as well as adopted a new approach to markdowns.

One Price Clothing Stores reevaluated its stores, too. It remodeled 48 and re-fixtured about 400 stores. During 1995 and 1996, the company closed 89 underperforming stores and sought locations for new stores based on future demographics and market access.

Changing Seasons

Since sales in women's retail apparel are seasonal, One Price Clothing Stores changed its fiscal year in 1996 to better conform to seasonal patterns. The adjustment made comparing the company's quarterly and annual reports with those of its competitors easier. Prior to fiscal 1996, the company's financial year ran from January through December. Sales were lower in the first and third quarters—January through March and July through September—and higher in the second and fourth quarters—April through June and October through December. Sales, then, coincided with the transition of seasonal merchandise, so markdowns in transition times caused operating expenses as a percentage of sales to increase. After the change, however, the fiscal year ran from February through January. The first and second quarters—February through July—showed higher sales

and operating results than the third and fourth quarters—August through January. One Price Clothing Stores started to see greater absolute and relative sales performance in the second half of the year due to the greater selection of fall and winter merchandise.

One Price Clothing Stores also put a new merchandise replenishment system in place and continued its rigorous management of inventory levels and mix. The company instituted a sophisticated computerized inventory management system—including point-of-sale cash registers—that allowed the daily and weekly review of each store's sales and inventories. Armed with this information, decision makers could change the merchandise mix or purchasing strategies based on customer demand.

Now One Price in Name Only

One Price Clothing Stores even planned to expand its merchandising mix starting in 1997. The company added more categories and styles of merchandise; for example, jeans, silk jogging sets, sweats, heavy jackets, and plus sizes. It also initiated alternative price points instead of all merchandise at seven dollars. Though the majority of items reflected the standard price, up to 20 percent of a store's merchandise assortment could vary in price. Core inventory remained at seven dollars, but some items dropped to five or six dollars. Half of the chain's stores converted to the new format in May 1997, with the remainder of stores scheduled for August 1997.

The change in strategy resulted in improved sales and profitability. Customers responded positively to the new prices, and sales increased. "The sales increases and overwhelmingly positive customer survey responses generated during our testing of this new strategy led us to announce plans for a chain-wide roll out," Jacobs explained in the company's 1996 annual report. "We expect this new approach to our business . . . to generate improvement in sales and profitability."

Principal Subsidiaries

One Price Clothing Store of Puerto Rico, Inc.; One Price Clothing–U.S. Virgin Islands.

Further Reading

Berton, Brad, and Karen Glover, "One Price Clothing Stores Plans to Enter Southland Market in a Big Way," *Los Angeles Business Journal,* May 9, 1994, p. 24.
"Kelley Named President, CEO of One Price," *WWD,* April 2, 1997, p. 16.
Lee, Georgia, "One Price Clothing Stores: Big Profits from $7 Sales," *WWD,* November 17, 1993, p. 6.
"Shapiro Exits as President of One Price," *Daily News Record,* April 3, 196, p. 12.

—Charity Anne Dorgan

OREGON METALLURGICAL CORPORATION

Oregon Metallurgical Corporation

530 34th Ave. SW
Albany, Oregon 97321
U.S.A.
(541) 926-4281
Fax: (541) 967-8669

Public Company
Incorporated: 1955
Employees: 580
Sales: $146.9 million (1995)
Stock Exchanges: NASDAQ
SICs: 3339 Primary Nonferrous Metals, Not Elsewhere
    Classified

Oregon Metallurgical Company, known as Oremet, is one of only two companies in the United States that produce titanium sponge, the pure form of the rare metal used to produce titanium alloys for use in manufacturing. The company also forges titanium products for aerospace, medical, electronics, and other applications. Although nearly half of the company's sales in 1996 were for commercial or military aerospace applications, Oremet also was the leading provider of titanium for use in the manufacture of golf clubs, which accounted for 20 percent of sales. The Albany, Oregon-based company operates titanium metals service centers in the United States, United Kingdom, Germany, and Canada through Titanium Industries, Inc., an 80 percent-owned subsidiary. The only other U.S. producer of titanium sponge is Denver-based Titanium Metals Corporation, the industry leader.

U.S. Bureau of Mines

In 1942, with the United States at war in Europe and the Pacific Theater, Carl Curlee, then president of the Albany, Oregon, Chamber of Commerce, flagged down a passenger train heading from California to Washington State. On board was an agent for the now-defunct Bureau of Mines, then an agency of the U.S. Department of the Interior, who was on his way to inspect the proposed site of a new metals laboratory in Spokane, Washington. However, Curlee and other members of

the Albany Chamber of Commerce had an alternative site in mind—the 45-acre campus of buildings that had recently been abandoned by Albany College when it left the languishing Willamette Valley logging and farming community and moved to Portland to begin anew as Lewis & Clark College.

Curlee dumped aerial maps and brochures about the Albany area into the startled agent's lap and succeeded in convincing him to tour the former college campus. A few months later, the Albany business community sent Curlee to Washington, D.C., where he was able to present the city's proposal directly to the Bureau of Mines. As he wrote in January 1943, "My big moment had arrived. I did my best under pressure. What with Senators Wheeler, Murray, Cone and Walten, to say nothing of the score of 90 congressmen looking down my throat, I introduced our material. They immediately struck the fancy of the Bureau people." Not long afterwards, the Bureau of Mines designated the abandoned college campus as the site for the sought-after metals laboratory.

A decade later, Steve Shelton, then Northwest regional director for the Bureau of Mines, casually mentioned during an Albany Chamber of Commerce luncheon that perhaps the city should try to attract a titanium plant to boost the still-lagging local economy. The primary role of the Bureau of Mines, created in 1910, was to promote mine safety and develop more efficient mining methods. But during the war, it had assumed the added responsibility of assuring that the country had adequate supplies of critical raw materials. In the early 1950s, that was beginning to include titanium.

Titanium was discovered in 1791, but was not produced commercially until 1948, by the Du Pont Co., because it was difficult and expensive to refine. However, titanium is relatively light and has a higher strength-to-weight ratio than steel. It also resists rust and corrosion as well as platinum and better than stainless steel, and combines readily with nearly every other metal, except copper and aluminum, making it useful in creating strong, lightweight alloys for military and aerospace applications.

But in 1955, titanium was still an exotic, little-known material, and after the Chamber of Commerce luncheon, Charlie McCormack, then mayor of Albany, followed Shelton back to his office at the Bureau of Mines and asked, "What the hell is a titanium plant?'' Shelton explained and McCormack took on the project personally. He registered stock with the Oregon Corporation Commission for sale to Oregon residents and sold more than half a million shares at $1 each.

Founding of Oremet

The Oregon Metallurgical Company was incorporated on December 1, 1955, with Dale Fischer of Eugene, Oregon, as president. The company, known as Oremet for short, bought 56 acres about a mile south of Albany, and on March 15, 1956, hired its first employee, George Smith, as construction supervisor. Oremet broke ground the following day.

Shelton left the Bureau of Mines to became general manager at the end of March and hired Frank Caputo, a titanium and zirconium metallurgist for the Bureau of Mines, to design the refining plant. Several other employees also left the federal agency to join Oremet, which produced its first 60-pound ingot of titanium by Labor Day. Shelton was named president in 1959.

Despite the high cost of producing titanium, it was widely used by the military for ship propellers, armor plating, jet engines parts, steam-turbine blades in nuclear power plants, surgical instruments, and components in the U.S. space program. As a result, Oremet prospered during the 1960s, a period of rapid technological development in the United States, with revenues growing from $4.2 million in 1961 to $13.8 million in 1969, when it posted net earnings of $518,000. But sales began to slip in 1970, falling to about $12.4 million, with slowdowns in both the military and commercial aerospace industries and the U.S. space program. Oremet moved to reduce costs by producing its own titanium ''sponge''—the first stage in recovering metal from ore—completing a five-year, $9 million development program.

With a recession beginning, the market for titanium virtually disappeared the following year when Congress cut off funds to the Boeing Company, which was developing a U.S. version of the supersonic transport (SST), which was to have been a nearly all-titanium aircraft. Oremet was forced to mothball its new sponge plant. It also suspended research and development programs and cut its workforce by two-thirds, from more than 300 to barely more than 100 employees. Sales in 1971 fell to $8.3 million and Oremet posted its first loss, of nearly $2 million, in more than a decade.

Even with growing inflation, Oremet sales continued to fall in 1972, to $7.3 million, and the company posted its second consecutive loss of $1.7 million. With the slowdown in the aerospace industry, which had accounted for nearly 90 percent of all titanium orders, Oremet began exploring new markets. In

1974, both General Motors and Ford began to use a titanium-steel alloy in government-mandated antipollution equipment, adding about a half pound of titanium to every new automobile. Oremet also began selling titanium for use in seafood processing equipment because of its resistance to saltwater corrosion. In the company's annual report for 1973, then-President Henry F. Peters also noted that one of Oremet's customers ''has put considerable time and effort'' into experimenting with a titanium alloy for golf club shafts. By the mid-1990s, golf clubs would be the fastest-growing market for titanium.

Purchase by Armco

Government purchases of titanium for missile components and inflation above 10 percent pushed sales in 1974 to record levels of $22 million, although the sponge facility remained closed. That changed in 1976, when the company decided to reopen its moth-balled sponge plants in anticipation of the federal B-1 bomber development program. The board of directors decided the move was essential since the idled plants represented 70 percent of the company's fixed assets. But the decision came at a price. Oremet borrowed $3 million from the First National Bank of Oregon, with $2 million guaranteed by Armco Steel Corporation. Armco, which already owned about 1.6 million shares of Oremet stock, received an option for another 1.5 million shares at a par value of $1.

Only months after the three plants comprising Oremet's sponge facility were brought back on line, an explosion shut down operations in late 1977, injuring seven workers and causing $2.4 million in damage. The plant was back in operation by the end of the year, and Oremet finished fiscal 1978 with nearly $22 million in sales and a profit of $1.7 million. Sales and profits more than doubled the following year, and doubled again in 1980, with another resurgence in commercial aerospace.

Encouraged by the strong financial performance, Armco exercised its option to buy 1.5 million shares of Oremet stock. That gave Armco 62 percent of Oremet, and the titanium producer became a corporate subsidiary. Peters, in that year's annual report, noted, ''Armco management has stated its intent to encourage Oremet's on-going development as a growing, positive force in the titanium industry.''

Unfortunately for Armco, the boom in the titanium industry was short-lived. In 1982, *Business Week* reported, ''After three years of prosperity, the U.S. titanium industry is heading into a slump.'' The magazine noted that the ''big price boosts of the late 1970s was largely the result of misplaced optimism, particularly by commercial aircraft builders.'' The optimistic aerospace industry stockpiled titanium, creating the appearance of a shortage that turned into an overabundance of the metal when expectations failed to materialize.

After peaking at $111.5 million in 1981, sales at Oremet fell to $28.3 million in 1983. In 1985, Armco sold its Aerospace & Strategic Materials Group, including its share of Oremet, which had grown to 80 percent, to the Owens-Corning Fiberglas Corporation for $415 million. Owens-Corning, the worldwide leader in fiberglass products for industry and home insulation, was then expanding into high-tech composites and was interested primarily in Armco's Hitco Materials Division, which produced composites for the aerospace and defense industries.

Armco, however, made it clear that it would not sell the division piecemeal.

Owens-Corning announced it would sell its interest in Oremet, along with other parts of the former Armco aerospace division it did not want. But before the company could act, Owens-Corning found itself in a fight for survival. In 1986, the Wickes Companies, a California-based building materials retailer, launched a hostile bid to acquire Owens-Corning. Wickes, which already held about 10 percent of Owens-Corning's outstanding stock, offered shareholders $74 a share for shares that were then trading for about $35 on the New York Stock Exchange. To fight the takeover, Owens-Corning borrowed $2.5 billion to recapitalize, offering stockholders a package that included $52 a share plus one new share of stock for every old share the company repurchased. Wickes eventually withdrew its offer and walked away with a $30 million profit, while Owens-Corning was saddled with a massive debt.

Employee Ownership

In the late 1980s, Owens-Corning cut its payroll from a high of 29,000 in 1986 to less than 17,000. The company also sold several subsidiaries at fire-sale prices, including the entire aerospace division it had acquired from Armco. Rather than another corporate owner, however, the 280 workers at Oremet stepped in to buy the titanium producer. In a deal orchestrated by the United Steelworkers Union, the employees agreed to a 20 percent cut in hourly wages and borrowed $17 million from Owens-Corning in an employee stock ownership plan (ESOP). To provide the company with some stability, the ESOP placed strict limits on how much stock the employees could withdraw unless they quit their jobs.

Despite rising sales, Oremet struggled financially the next several years, accumulating more than $17 million in losses between 1990 and 1995. Caputo, the last remaining executive from the original Bureau of Mines group that launched the company in 1956, also retired in 1993. After serving as president for 13 years, Caputo took advantage of a brief financial upswing—Oremet's first profitable quarter in two years—to announce he was leaving while the company was the only profitable titanium producer in the world. He was succeeded by Carlos E. Aguirre, former president of Axel Johnson Metal, Inc., the U.S. subsidiary of Sweden's Axel Johnson Inc. Aguirre, a native of Argentina with a doctorate in metallurgy, told *American Metal Market,* "My role will be to develop a new strategic direction that results in consistent, profitable growth."

One of Aguirre's first accomplishments was a six-year agreement with the United Steelworkers, signed in 1994, that allowed the company to buy titanium sponge on the world market without paying laid-off employees the difference between their unemployment benefits and their regular wages, which the old contract required. At the time, titanium sponge could be purchased cheaper in foreign markets than it could be produced by Oremet because of "dumping" by former Soviet Union countries.

By 1996, sales had reached $236.9 million and Oremet seemingly had turned the corner on what the annual report that year called "one of the most severe downturns the industry has ever experienced." Oremet posted a net income of $22.3 million and the *Oregonian* reported that Oremet's employees were "reaping the rewards for a frightening risk they took nine years ago."

The *Oregonian* went on to note, "Today (the workers are) doing better than good. Many of these who spend their 12-hour shifts cutting, melting and pushing titanium around Oremet's dark and noisy plant buildings are wealthy. Some of them display it, many of them don't." When the ESOP purchased the company at the end of 1987, the stock was trading for about $3 a share. After fluctuating at about $12 a share through the early 1990s, it rocketed to $30 in late 1996, before settling back to the high $20s.

One reason for increasing sales was the purchase of 80 percent of the New Jersey-based Titanium Industries Distribution Group from Kamyr, Inc. in 1994 for $13.5 million. Titanium Industries operated Titanium Wire Corp. and metal service centers in the United States, United Kingdom, Germany, and Canada, which opened new markets for Oremet. In 1995, for the first time ever, more than half of Oremet sales were for non-aerospace applications, led by growth in recreational uses, including golf clubs and titanium lacrosse sticks. In the company's 1996 annual report, Aguirre declared, "New applications for titanium continue to arise and Oremet is well positioned to benefit in such a marketplace."

Principal Subsidiaries

Titanium Industries Inc. (80%); Oremet France.

Further Reading

Francis, Mike, "Patience Pays Off," *Oregonian,* September 8, 1996, p. G1.
Frye, Cory, "A Man, a Train, a Metals Empire," *Albany Democrat-Herald,* March 21, 1997, p. 19.
Haflich, Frank, "Oremet's Caputo Set to Retire at May's End," *American Metal Market,* May 27, 1993, p. 12.
——, "How Aguirre Sees Oremet; New President Examines Non-Aerospace Markets," *American Metal Market,* June 30, 1993, p. 5.
——, "Oremet-USW Pact Seen as Embracing Reality," *American Metal Market,* September 7, 1994, p. 5.
——, "Oremet Paves Path into Larger Market," *American Metal Market,* September 23, 1994, p. 1.
——, "Owens-Corning to Sell 80% Stake in Oremet," *American Metal Market,* February 12, 1986, p. 2.
——, "Oremet Price Plan Based on Stability," *American Metal Market,* April 29, 1997, p. 1.
Rogers, Jack, "Armco Companies Reported for Sale Only as a Package," *American Metal Market,* April 18, 1985, p. 2.
"The Titanium Market Falls Back to Earth," *Business Week,* July 12, 1982, p. 25.

—Dean Boyer

Outboard Marine Corporation

100 Sea-Horse Drive
Waukegan, Illinois 60085
U.S.A.
(847) 689-6200
Fax: (847) 689-7247

Incorporated: 1936 as Outboard Marine &
 Manufacturing Company
Employees: 8,283
Sales: $1.1 billion (1996)
Stock Exchanges: New York Boston Midwest Pacific
 Philadelphia
SICs: 3732 Boat Building and Repair; 3519 Internal
 Combustion Engines

Outboard Marine Corporation is the world's largest manufacturer and supplier of outboard motors and second largest producer of powerboats. Based in Waukegan, Illinois the company has become famous for its brand-name Johnson and Evinrude outboard motors, as well as its Chris-Craft and Grumman powerboats. Other products under the brand names of Four Winns, Seaswirl, Trade Winds, Sunbird, Stratos, and Hydra-Sports include fiberglass runabouts, cruisers, performance boats, and craft for offshore fishing. Outboard Marine also markets clothing for boating, and resort wear. Unfortunately, during the late 1980s and early 1990s, Outboard Marine has had a difficult time keeping up with the competition, notably archrival Brunswick Corporation, the world's largest manufacturer of powerboats.

Early History

Motorized transport was just becoming an everyday part of life in 1907, when Ole Evinrude invented the first practical outboard engine for boats. Evinrude placed an advertisement in a motor magazine to introduce his motor, drawing so many inquiries from U.S. and overseas readers that he decided to try large-scale production. Needing financial help with this undertaking, he found a backer and established the Evinrude Motor Company in 1910.

The business was an instant success—its market included not only recreational boaters but also the Scandinavian fishing fleets operating in the North Sea. Friction between the partners forced Evinrude to sell his share to his backer in 1914 and depart, after signing a guarantee restricting him from the outboard motor industry for five years. The company continued without him, becoming a subsidiary of the gasoline-engine manufacturer Briggs & Stratton Corporation in 1926.

By 1921 Evinrude was back in business, in a venture he called the ELTO Outboard Motor Company. His new offering was the Evinrude Light Twin Outboard, a motor partly made of aluminum, reducing its weight by a third. Popular with the fishing fleets, this revolutionary engine outstripped sales of Evinrude's original outboard motor within three years. It also attracted the attention of a competitor, Johnson Motor Company, which brought out its rival lightweight engine in 1922. Johnson gained market share, snatching the lead four years later with an updated model weighing a trim 100 pounds, costing a thrifty $190, and able to drive a boat at a zippy 16 miles per hour. Neither the Evinrude Company nor ELTO could match this. Now far ahead, Johnson produced a net profit of $433,000 in 1927, far outpacing Evinrude's $25,000 and ELTO's $30,000.

A new engine in 1928 restored the ELTO Company, whose annual net profit rose to $300,000. Evinrude merged ELTO with Briggs & Stratton the following year, becoming president of the brand-new Outboard Motors Corporation.

The Great Depression and World War II

Outboard scarcely had time to find its feet before the stock market crash of 1929 tested its staying power. Already responsible for $500,000 in bank loans as a result of the merger, the company had to increase its debt to $600,000 between 1930 and 1932, when operating deficits totaled $550,000. To keep the business afloat, the entire inventory was sold at bargain prices, and Evinrude sacrificed his salary until his death in 1934.

Johnson's fate was worse. A too-costly advertising campaign, as well as an ill-timed offering of matched motors and hulls, drained all cash reserves by 1930, when control of the company passed to its bankers. Next came an attempt to lessen its reliance on seasonal sales by entry into the refrigerator-compressor market. This last-ditch effort did not revive the business, and shortly thereafter Johnson was for sale.

In 1935, the Outboard Motors Corporation bought the Johnson Motor Company. Its $800,000 price tag brought Outboard a well-known line of outboards and plant and equipment worth $1.5 million. It also brought Outboard established overseas markets in China, Burma, Iran, and Albania, to broaden Evinrude's array of dealers in Europe, Australia, and New Zealand. Another plus was Johnson's niche in the refrigeration market; Outboard established the Gale Products Division at Galesburg, Illinois, to manufacture this new line.

Expansion brought changes. No longer devoted to purely marine interests, the company changed its name in 1936, to the Outboard Marine & Manufacturing Company. Stephen F. Briggs resigned his Outboard chairmanship temporarily—he had held this position since 1929—to take the Johnson helm. He instituted a rigorous cost-cutting regime, and by 1937 the Johnson division's gross sales were $4.3 million, as compared with Evinrude-ELTO's $2.5 million.

By now, Outboard Motors accounted for about 60 percent of U.S. outboard motor production. There were three engine lines, suiting most needs: the ELTO line for the buyer seeking thrift; Evinrude, the prestige line; and Johnson, offering special features. Though there was cooperation, operations were largely independent. This left each division to award contracts to outside bidders as well as those sharing a place under the Outboard umbrella. Even export sales operations were handled differently; although they were all routed through the Waukegan headquarters, Johnson tended to sell directly to its dealers, while most Evinrude sales were passed through distributors and then to the dealers.

In addition to the engines, selling mostly in seasonal markets, there were other items broadening the product lines. The Lawn-Boy lawnmower had been an Evinrude staple since 1932, along with pumps for drainage, firefighting, and lawn spraying. Offerings from Johnson included small generators, a gasoline engine for washing machines, and refrigerators. In combination with the motors, all these produced net sales of $6.8 million by 1937, generating profits of $945,000.

In the early 1940s, Outboard's facilities were all converted to the production of war materials. Bomb fuses, aircraft engines, and firefighting apparatus flowed from the Outboard factories, along with landing-boat motors for the Navy. Evinrude four-cylinder engines carried troops across the Rhine. Net sales for 1945 reached $1.8 million, topping $2.5 million the following year.

The personnel who steered the company through the hectic war years were Outboard oldtimers. In addition to Briggs, there was Joseph G. Rayniak, director of manufacturing research, whose career dated back to the Johnson brothers' 2 horsepower Light Twin, unveiled in 1922. There was Finn T. Irgens, holder of 92 patents, who had risen to be director of engineering from a start with Ole Evinrude, in 1929. There was Ralph Evinrude, who had succeeded to the company presidency after his father's death in 1934.

Expansion and Growth in the Postwar Years

These longtime staff members were all on hand with the return of peacetime, when the company converted its facilities back to the production of Johnson and Evinrude outboard motors. Spending $8 million on plant expansion and improvement by 1952, Outboard then offered models ranging from one-cylinder, 3 horsepower engines to two-cylinder, 25 horsepower models.

Several acquisitions broadened the Outboard product line during the 1950s. The first, in 1952, was RPM Manufacturing Company of Missouri, whose specialty was a rotary power mower that Outboard planned to sell under its familiar Lawn-Boy tradename. Featuring a detachable engine useful as an outboard, the mower was already a best-selling unbranded item in both the Sears and the Spiegel catalogs. Outboard coped with the huge volume of existing orders by completing entire units in one factory, rather than using the more time-consuming method of piecemeal assembly in several locations.

In 1956, the company changed its name to Outboard Marine Corporation (OMC). The same year, OMC purchased Industrial Engineering, Canada's largest chain-saw manufacturer, for C$2.55 million plus 40,000 shares. OMC moved this new subsidiary to Peterborough, Ontario, and changed its name to Pioneer Saws Ltd.

Cushman Motor Works of Nebraska joined the company subsidiary list in 1957. Well-known in the utility vehicle field, Cushman had manufactured the Airborne, a motor scooter dropped by parachute for ground transport of paratroopers. Later the company's lightweight vehicles became popular for agricultural, industrial, and recreational use. Costing 114,000 shares at 30¢ par, the new acquisition added three-wheel mail carriers, golf carts, and motor scooters to the OMC product line. Besides the Johnson and Evinrude motors then being sold by about 7,000 retail dealers, the swelling list of OMC offerings included Gale Buccaneer motors sold through hardware jobbers, as well as a number of unbranded models sold for retailers.

The company's most innovative engine appeared in 1958. The first mass-produced die-cast aluminum engine, it was a four-cylinder, 50 horsepower outboard, completely manufactured by OMC, its V-blocks came from Johnson, its steel parts from Evinrude, while the Gale division contributed its carburetors and ignition systems.

Export sales of all items surged ahead during the 1950s. Seeing a 215 percent gain in exports between 1949 and 1956, OMC expanded its export department in 1956, gaining a new subsidiary called Outboard Marine International S.A. By 1960, taking the next logical step of overseas production, the company was manufacturing and assembling motors in Brugge, Belgium. All these developments showed in the annual net sales, which soared from $27 million in 1950 to $171.5 million by 1959.

During the 1950s, OMC's main objective had been acquisitions to broaden basic product lines. In the 1960s, the company's aim was to improve all these products and find growing markets for them. Ensuring its industry leadership by constant innovation and improvement to existing products, OMC allocated more than $7 million annually to research and development.

As the 1960s began, the United States was in the trough of a recession. First-time buyers as well as those seeking bigger and better leisure-time equipment put their purchases on hold. Because its principal markets were tied to leisure-time activities mostly practiced on a seasonal basis, OMC sales sank to a 1961 low of $132.3 million.

The economic turndown did not, however, prevent the company from starting a five-year philanthropic program in 1961. In response to a request to benefit the United Nations Food and Agriculture Organization's freedom-from-hunger campaign, OMC contributed several hundred outboard engines each year to be used in fishing, part of a program to increase food production in underdeveloped countries. Also in 1961, the company established the OMC Boats Division to produce and market 16- to 19-foot boats featuring both outboard and the newer stern-drive engines. Production began the following year, helping to raise sales to $151.9 million by 1962.

The stern-drive, or inboard-outboard motors, were available both as separate units for boat-builders, or as components of boats produced by OMC. Built to give the fuel economy and dependability of inboard engines, they were nevertheless as versatile as outboards. By 1965 the company was selling only about 20,000 stern drives a year, however, and sales of the outboards were still outpacing them tenfold. The problem stemmed from the engine's state-of-the-art technology; many dealers did not know how to repair these motors, and owners were often ignorant of maintenance needs. OMC met this challenge by developing computerized week-long repair and maintenance classes for dealer training. Four schools, two permanently stationed in San Francisco, California, and Waukegan, Illinois, and two mobile units familiarized customers with the new engines.

During the 1960s, public interest in novel sports offered new market potential. Alert to novel trends, OMC entered the snowmobile industry with enthusiasm, introducing the Evinrude Skeeter and the Johnson Skee-Horse in 1964, each sure to thrill riders with speeds of more than 30 miles per hour. Another innovation was the Evinrude Aquanaut for skin diving, also sold under the Johnson tradename Air-Buoy. Consisting of a floating gasoline-powered compressor, the unit supplied air to two masked divers at the same time. Another breakthrough was the loop-charged outboard, devised after the company went back to powerboat racing for the first time since World War II.

By October 1967, OMC's fiscal year-end sales had reached $233.4 million. Of this amount, 10 percent came from power mowers, with golf carts and utility vehicles sharing second place at 7 percent, and with snowmobiles, the fastest-growing segment of the business, also at 7 percent. Chain saw sales accounted for 4 percent of the final figure, while a full 70 percent came from marine products. The only failure of the decade was the boat-building enterprise; initially small operating losses grew each year, until the line was sold to Chris-Craft in 1970. Otherwise, the 1960s had been lucrative, as the 1969 net sales figure of $327.1 million showed.

Retrenchment and Reorganization in the 1970s

The 1970s began with a dip to $304.5 million in net sales. This was partly due to the unprofitable boat line, and partly to a line of tent campers that had never fulfilled expectations after the 1967 acquisition of their manufacturer, Trade Winds Campers. The company discontinued the line in 1971, and immediately saw the improvement in their net sales figures, which soared to $394 million by 1972.

There were other disappointments. Golf cart sales sank to 2 percent of overall revenue by 1974, and were discontinued in 1975. Chain saw sales totaled $19.1 million in 1976, resulting in losses for the company and reflecting a flattening of future market potential. OMC discontinued them the following year. Snowmobiles, constituting about 4 percent of sales volume in 1972, were offered in 1973 with an optional Wankel engine costing about $235 more than the conventional motor. Though this was the United States's first introduction to the revolutionary rotary engine, OMC's hopes of success were dashed by heavy competition from other snowmobile brands, as well as by two winters of sparse snow. Snowmobile production came to an end in 1976, after a fiscal 1974 operating loss of $13.9 million.

Fuel shortages were another downside. Coming to an OPEC-inspired zenith in 1973, they brought fears of a buying slowdown in the peak spring quarter. An OMC environmental executive warned of possible gasoline rationing by the petroleum industry, and outlined steps for fuel conservation among boaters.

In the same year, OMC purchased a five-acre site in Hong Kong. Intended as a first step towards larger outboard motor markets in Asia, the move was also encouraged by a Hong Kong government program designed to attract specific, technologically advanced industries. Assembly operations began in the plant in 1975, with the manufacture of electronic outboard motor components following two years later.

In 1974 Charles D. Strang succeeded W. C. Scott as president. Strang's interest in powerboats, beginning in boyhood, had lasted through college and a post as a research associate at Massachusetts Institute of Technology. During a later period of employment with the makers of Mercury outboard motors, interest had deepened into vocation. In 1966 his experience in the powerboat industry had brought him to OMC. Eight years later he rose to the presidency.

An environmental question was one of his first challenges. It began in 1976, when OMC was cited by both the U.S. and Illinois environmental protection agencies for polluting a drainage ditch and Waukegan harbor with polychlorinated biphenyls (PCBs). The company filed suit against both agencies after lengthy negotiations, charging that the federal government had dragged its feet in spending funds authorized for pollution-control use. Company attorneys also stated that the PCB-contaminated pipes had been replaced in 1976, but the agencies likewise filed suit, asking that the company be ordered to remove the contaminants from the harbor, and to pay a maximum penalty of about $20 million, reflecting a $10,000 fine for each day the PCB sources had been in place. This suit was to dog OMC's footsteps throughout the 1980s.

Reorganizing his domestic operations was another Strang priority, with bringing together the Evinrude and Johnson divisions at the top of the list. Complete separation of the two since the company's beginnings had fostered an intense rivalry between them, along with disregard for competition by manufacturers outside the company. To unite the company against outside competitors, in 1978 Strang centralized all domestic manufacturing operations at the corporate headquarters in Waukegan, Illinois, charging vice president James C. Chapman with responsibility for their coordination, as well as for manufacturing policy.

Next came long-range plans for dealing with the competitors themselves. Chief among these were the Japanese firm Yamaha, eating into OMC's European market, and Brunswick Corporation, makers of premium-priced Mercury outboards. A joint venture between Yamaha and Brunswick had produced a low-cost engine called Mariner; thus Brunswick then had an engine at both high and low ends of the market, leaving OMC sandwiched in the middle. With his newly united company behind him, Strang cleared this hurdle by slashing prices by 25 percent and also by making sure that all products offered by competitors were available in the OMC lineup. In another move, he bought out independent distributors overseas, thus gaining greater control over foreign marketing operations.

Threatening OMC's competitiveness was a 1980 Department of Energy proposal that boating be banned on weekends. As a result of this suggestion, public concern about gasoline shortages caused OMC's net sales to plummet to $687.4 million in 1980, from $741.2 million just one year earlier. It was not easy to maintain the company's competitive edge against the Japanese at this time, but Strang slashed budgets, reducing his work force by one-third, to save an annual pretax amount of $47 million. The reward for this effort showed at the end of fiscal 1982, when net sales reached $778 million.

Transition in the 1980s and 1990s

OMC was now in a position to spend $100 million on the construction and tooling of nine new plants. Contrary to previous practice, each plant was designed to specialize in one manufacturing function. In addition, overseas plants were refined to reduce operations costs and provide more efficient handling and storage.

Streamlining made product innovation easier. Power steering, variable-ratio oiling—delivering exact mixtures of gasoline and oil to the engine—and saltwater protection were new features appreciated by powerboat buyers. Starting in 1983, OMC began to prepare the way for a new stern-drive engine, to supersede previous models. After reviewing the stern-drive market, the company sent interviewers to dealers and service department personnel, gathering information for the ideal stern-drive engine. The result was the OMC Cobra, introduced in 1985. Designed for both boat builders and consumers, its 7.5 liter engine delivered 340 horsepower.

In 1984, James Chapman stepped into the presidency of the company, succeeding Robert F. Wallace, whose short tenure had lasted from January 1982. Like his predecessors, Chapman grappled with the Waukegan Harbor question. This issue was finally laid to rest in April 1989, when the U.S. Department of Justice ordered OMC to fund a trust to remove the pollutants from Lake Michigan.

This was just the beginning of OMC's problems, however. In 1988, the boat market peaked and then went into a tailspin. Although Chapman decided to purchase 15 boatmakers to as-

sure OMC of captive customers for their outboard engines, the company did not develop a comprehensive or well-designed strategy to manage its growing operations efficiently. In the middle of the worst downturn in the industry's history, Chapman sold Lawnboy and Cushman for $235 million in 1989 to raise much-needed cash. In addition, he reduced staff, closed factories, and eliminated whole product lines, such as Chris-Craft engines and boat models—all to no avail. Between 1990 and 1993, OMC suffered losses totaling $440 million.

As OMC continued to lose money, Harry Bowman, the former CEO of Whirlpool Corporation, was hired to replace Chapman. When the boat industry finally rebounded from its economic downturn in 1994, OMC did not have enough of the right kind of product for its customers since much of it had been sold by Chapman. Bowman immediately formed a joint venture with Volvo to consolidate two engines into one brand name, finalized a contract with a German firm to bring in new technology for high-pressure fuel injectors so that OMC engines could be more fuel-efficient, initiated a thoroughgoing advertising campaign to strengthen its brand name Evinrude and Johnson outboard engines, and began to develop a new generation of outboard motors that were environmentally acceptable, fuel-efficient, and easily repaired. Bowman's strategy worked. By the middle of 1995, OMC's revenues were $1.1 billion.

As OMC regains its former position within the outboard engine and boat markets, Bowman is concentrating on developing strategies that will help his company weather the stormy cycles of the marine industry. With new technology, better marketing, and more astute management, OMC is better prepared to meet the future than at any previous time.

Principal Subsidiaries

Outboard Marine Asia, Ltd. (Hong Kong); Outboard Marine Australia Pty. Ltd.; OMC Europe (Belgium); Outboard Marine Corporation of Canada, Ltd.; Outboard Marine de Mexico, S.A. de C.V.; Bramco, Inc.; OMCCC Inc.; Ryds Batindustri AB (Sweden); Donzi Marine Corporation; Sea Nymph, Incorporated; Sunbird Boat Company, Incorporated; Adventurent, Inc.; Hydra-Sports, Inc.; Carl A. Lowe Industries, Inc.

Further Reading

"A 'Sudden' Superfund Liability," *Financial World,* April 27, 1993, p. 35.
David, Gregory E., "Sea Horses," *Financial World,* November 8, 1994, pp. 34–36.
DeGeorge, Gail, "Did Irv Jacobs Sandbag Outboard Marine?," *Business Week,* February 20, 1989, pp. 38–40.
——, "Men Overboard in Boatland," *Business Week,* August 22, 1994, pp. 30–31.
Golden Jubilee: Outboard Marine Corporation, 1936–1986, Waukegan, Illinois, Outboard Marine Corporation, [1986].
Jaffe, Thomas, "Hit It," *Forbes,* May 2, 1988, p. 146.
Rudolph, Barbara, "Why Putt-Putt Isn't Sputter-Sputter," *Forbes,* June 7, 1982.
Samuels, Gary, "After the Storm," *Forbes,* July 3, 1995, pp. 65–66.

—Gillian Wolf
—updated by Thomas Derdak

Owens Corning Corporation

One Owens Corning Parkway
Toledo, Ohio 43659
U.S.A.
(419) 248-8000
Fax: (419) 248-5337
Web site: http://www.owenscorning.com

Public Company
Incorporated: 1949
Employees: 18,900
Sales: $3.83 billion (1996)
Stock Exchanges: New York
SICs: 3229 Technical Glassware & Glass Products; 2821
Resins & Plastics; 3052 Plastic & Rubber Hoses;
3069 Rubber Products; 3087 Custom Compounding of
Plastic Resins; 3089 Plastic Products; 3275 Gypsum
Products; 3296 Fiberglass & Mineral Wool Products

Owens Corning Corporation is the undisputed world leader in fiberglass products for industry and insulation for homes, and one of the world's major producers of polyester resins. The company has sought to enter a number of technical and consumer-oriented markets and—through a combination of marketing techniques and technological leadership—to dominate those markets completely. Owens Corning enjoys commanding market share in the domestic market for home and industrial insulation; the domestic market for reinforced plastics, with applications such as automobiles, pleasure boats, and aerospace; and the domestic market for residential roofing.

Inventing Fiberglass: 1932–45

The genesis of Owens Corning, and of the production of modern fiberglass products, dates back to the Great Depression. Owens-Illinois, then a leader in the development and marketing of new glass products, transformed one of its idle bottle plants into a research facility to study the potential uses of fiberglass. O-I vice president Harold Boeschenstein named engineer Games Slayter to oversee the research and development effort. The project bore fruit quickly with the development of cheap, high-efficiency dust filters for home furnaces, manufactured from glass wool. These filters replaced the much more expensive, traditional steel filters. The truly dramatic breakthrough for O-I and for glass fibers came during a 1932 experiment at the small O-I laboratory in Columbus, Ohio. Dale Kleist was working on ways to melt glass rods. If his experiment worked, the molten glass would seal glass blocks together. The experiment produced, however, a very fine fiber—not what Kleist had in mind. As Kleist mused over how the experiment had backfired, his colleague John Thomas, according to legend, realized that Kleist had stumbled onto a new way to make glass fiber.

Slayter and Thomas predicted that very fine glass fibers would have myriad uses and urged the formation of a joint venture between Owens-Illinois and Corning Glass Works, the country's premier manufacturer of glass products, in 1935. Harold Boeschenstein agreed, and the joint venture began developing new products and technologies immediately, including the first continuous filament fibers in 1937.

In October 1938, a new company was formed from the joint venture. It was called Owens-Corning Fiberglass and its mission was to manufacture glass-fiber products, market them to homes and industry, and develop new related technologies. Some of the technologies were implemented during World War II, when Owens Corning manufactured insulation and fireproof materials for ships and aircraft. Harold Boeschenstein, Owens Corning's director, served on President Franklin D. Roosevelt's War Production Board. The most important use of glass fiber was, of course, in fiberglass, a glass-fiber-reinforced resin product.

Postwar Prosperity 1945–70

After the war business boomed. The company built two new plants and rehabilitated or converted four more from a war footing. Construction products—together with a technological leading edge that no other competitor could match—became a mainstay of its overall strategy. The company expanded into many aspects of new home construction with its distribution of Kaylo fiberglass pipes, and it developed a new process for manufacturing building insulation. Its "Comfort Conditioned Home" was a major national marketing effort in 1957, which promoted fiberglass insulation in homes. Owens Corning led the way with its involvement in the first glass-fiber-reinforced automobile body, Chevrolet's Corvette in 1953. The company also produced many new components for industry, including a wide array of acoustical materials and industrial and automotive insulation.

Owens Corning was so successful that in 1949 Owens-Illinois and Corning Glass works were accused of illegally monopolizing the fiberglass industry through their joint control of the company. Under a court-mandated consent decree in 1949, Owens Corning was required to license its patents to competitors, and both parent companies were forced to relinquish control of what had been their subsidiary for 14 years. As a separate entity, Owens Corning went public in 1952 when it put one-third of its shares on the New York Stock Exchange.

In the 1960s, Owens Corning expanded even more, building plants in Texas, at Waxahachie and Conroe; Indiana; and Georgia, as well as embarking on new construction for its subsidiary company in Bogota, Colombia. The company at this time was moving ahead in three broad areas: new products, new technology, and remarkably efficient marketing techniques.

Among the new products in the 1960s was a new glass-fiber yarn, called Beta, with superior flexing and handling characteristics, and the development of the glass-fiber-reinforced-plastic (FRP) underground storage tank. The development and marketing of this tank underscored the success of Owens Corning in developing new products and in getting them accepted in the marketplace. Indeed, Owens Corning has created markets for many of its innovative products. Until the late 1960s, steel underground storage tanks—such as those used by the oil industry—were the standard. Owens Corning developed the first FRP tank, which was lighter and stronger than steel, but they were also more expensive. The tank's noncorrosive properties would be the key selling point, long before government-mandated codes for such tanks, which today are utilized not only for petroleum storage, but for toxic chemicals and a wide variety of industrial and agricultural uses. By 1970, 10,000 FRP tanks were in use in the United States, and in the 1980s the company developed the first double-walled storage tanks. By 1985, Owens Corning had sold 100,000 fiberglass underground fuel storage tanks.

The company had pioneered the use of fiberglass in the recreation industry. By the late 1950s, more than 90 percent of all fishing rods in the United States were made of glass-fiber-reinforced materials, and by the late 1960s, FRP components were common in new cars. The company was also heavily involved in producing components for fiberglass pleasure-boat hulls.

Market Share, R&D, Divesification: 1971–86

In the 1970s and 1980s, the company enjoyed its market dominance and continued its diversification. It expanded into Europe, Asia, and South America, furthering its technological and marketing lead. New plants were opened in Bakersfield, California, and New York State, as well as in Texas, Pennsylvania, and Florida. The market, research, and product diversification was reflected in Owens Corning's complex organization. By the mid-1980s, the company was split into 11 different divisions, employing some 29,000 persons.

One of Owens Corning's hallmarks has been its intent to dominate any new market that it enters. To this end it uses innovative products, superb communications with retailers, and an overwhelming marketing presence. When successful, the company enjoys tremendous vertical integration in those areas in which it chooses to compete. Two examples illustrate this successful Owens Corning strategy in the 1970s and 1980s. As with FRP storage tanks, fiberglass roofing shingles were met initially with skepticism. Contractors, used to cheaper organically composed shingles, were reluctant to use the unfamiliar fiberglass products. An aggressive marketing campaign, however, stressed the much greater strength and longevity of the product. This campaign, together with the company's purchase of Lloyd A. Fry Roofing and its subsidiary, Trumball Asphalt in 1977, gave Owens Corning a commanding position in both new home roofing and reroofing of older homes. In 1980, only 20 percent of the domestic home roofing consisted of fiberglass shingles, but by 1986, the figure stood at 77 percent. The downside of this tremendous change was, as one analyst with Salomon Brothers pointed out, a resultant glut in the roof shingle market; because fiberglass shingles are easier and speedier to produce than felt shingles there was a consequent shutdown of many manufacturing facilities nationwide.

The second major example of its marketing genius was the four-to-one brand preference among consumers for Owens-Corning fiberglass blanket insulation over the nearest competitor. Owens Corning's 50 percent market share of domestic home insulation eclipsed its major competitors such as CertainTeed, Manville, Knauf, and Guardian. This brand preference, for an often-more-expensive product, was furthered in the 1986 by a U.S. Court of Appeals ruling that granted Owens-Corning a trademark on a color—pink—for its exclusive use in fiberglass insulation and advertising. The court ruling paralleled Owens Corning's exclusive rights to United Artists's Pink Panther cartoon character for its advertising and promotions. The word "Fiberglas" is also a company trademark. Through a sophisticated computer network, "Pink Link," it could keep track of inventory, and communicate with its retail dealers nationwide, thus diminishing the need for outlets to store large inventories of Fiberglas insulation. (Pink Link was replaced by an integrated enterprise management software program made by SAP of Germany in the 1990s.) Owens Corning's sales force is conceded to be among the best in the business. The company further enhanced its name recognition in 1981 by underwriting the TV program "This Old House."

The 1970s and 1980s saw not only the proliferation of Owens Corning products and an aggressive marketing strategy, but also heavy investment in research and development, forays into new and sometimes unproven technologies, and acquisition of subsidiaries. These activities emphasized the long-term, and saw the company develop expertise in a number of fields that had little resemblance to its core areas of construction products and industrial materials. Primary among these acquisitions was the aerospace and strategic-materials group from Armco, in 1985. The intent was primarily to take control of Armco's high-technology and composites subsidiary, Hitco. Hitco was responsible for research into visionary carbon-based composite materials used in such applications as missile nose cones and lightweight armored plating for army vehicles. Owens Corning was now on the cutting edge of future technologies and product applications that could not be foreseen. The consumer housing market was leveling off; the company was looking ahead to new areas for expansion. Just as in the early 1930s, when Owens-Illinois and Corning Glass delved into a highly speculative joint venture, Owens Corning was again placing its bets increasingly on long-term, costly research.

Fighting Takeover and Debt: 1986–91

The year 1986 brought the most significant—and traumatic—changes for Owens Corning in the company's history. In early August, Wickes Companies, a Santa Monica, California-based building materials retailer, announced a tender offer to buy up Owens Corning's public stock at $74 a share. Wickes chairman Sanford Sigoloff had already bought almost 10 percent of Owens Corning's shares earlier and now was out to capture the company to expand Wickes's operations into roofing and insulation. Wickes was on the rebound from bankruptcy proceedings and looking for acquisitions. At a tense meeting in Owens Corning's New York offices, chairman William Boeschenstein, son of the former chairman, rejected Sigoloff's offer and, according to affidavits filed later by Wickes, countered by threatening to "make a substantial financial investment in Wickes," which Wickes labeled the "Pac-man defense."

Owens Corning urged its shareholders not to accept the takeover bid of $74 a share, more than twice the New York Stock Exchange value prior to the bid, while it studied its options for survival. The company was also hoping for a buyout from a friendly suitor, but this was not forthcoming.

The company chose as its most viable strategy for survival as an independent company a leveraged buyout, borrowing huge sums of money to recapitalize. After borrowing $2.5 billion from Drexel Burnham Lambert and others, it was able to offer its shareholders a package including $52 a share on its stock plus a junior subordinated debenture, with a face value of $35, but which was valued at issue at half that amount, and one share of newly issued stock. Wickes was forced to withdraw its offer, and walked away with over $30 million in profit by selling its Owens Corning stock. Other shareholders were happy with the windfall. The company that emerged, however, was laden with debt and was almost unrecognizable in terms of organizational structure and goals.

In 1990, Owens Corning bore little resemblance to its former self. Its goal could be put succinctly: retire the debt. The company set about doing that in two ways. It had economized and instituted massive layoffs, early retirement, and mothballed or closed plants in several locations. From a mid-1986 employee roll of 29,000 the company in 1987 had only 17,000. The second strategy was to sell the company's many subsidiaries that were not immediate profit generators. Owens Corning thus sold 10 companies in very short order, including Hitco and the entire aerospace and strategic-materials group, Olympic Fastening Systems, the glass-fiber-reinforced-plastic-components division, and Performance Contracting, Inc., which was the largest specialty contracting firm in the United States. Four entire divisions, out of 11, were sold off, accounting for roughly $1 billion in annual sales.

There were enormous cutbacks in long-term research and development. Virtually overnight, Owens Corning transformed itself from a company known for its long-range research-and-development work—fiberglass itself had been 20 years in development before market applications bore fruit—to a "cash machine," spitting out profit to pay its creditors. In its research-and-development division, the company laid off nearly 50 percent of its work force or lost them through divestiture of assets. In 1986, before the takeover bid, Owens Corning spent $63 million on research and development. In 1987, this figure had been slashed to $29 million.

Long-term research projects with little hope of short-term profit or even markets are difficult to justify in publicly held corporations. Owens Corning had, for instance, been developing liquid crystal polymers, for which no application could be foreseen at the time. The cost and lead-time for such a project require a large research investment, patience, and creative vision, three areas in which the "new" Owens Corning could not afford to indulge. The project was sold to an Italian company after the recapitalization.

The company did a solid job of retiring the debt. By early 1990, total indebtedness had been reduced to less than $1.5 billion, and the company was generating profit beyond all expectations. Indeed, in the wake of several leveraged cash-outs in the late 1980s, the Owens Corning example had become a textbook example of how to survive. Earnings were solid enough in 1989 to allow it to buy up the 50 percent share of Fiberglass Canada that had been owned by PPG Industries, a major competitor. Costs were down and profits were generally up, but the company still had a negative book value, that is, its debt outweighed its assets.

After the restructuring, the company emerged as a leaner, more centralized concern with a profit and structural emphasis on its leading cash generators. Owens Corning had organized its remaining divisions into three major units: Construction-products division, industrial-materials division, and international division, which consisted of overseas operations exclusive of Europe. The cyclicality of the housing market and the overall slowdown in housing starts affected the company's profitability in 1989–90, although the industrial materials division accounted for more and more of Owens Corning's earnings. The "soft" nature of the housing market had affected sales and profitability in the wake of the restructuring, although reroofing, not affected by housing starts, accounted for 75 percent of the demand for shingles. Net income and operating profit were both down in 1989 compared with the previous year. Profit in 1988 was $477 million, with 1989 at $430 million. The economic slowdown in 1989 and 1990 especially had cut into the company's construction products, automotive, and pleasure boat components.

The former European divisions had been absorbed into the construction-products and industrial materials divisions, primarily due to the similar consumer and industrial purchasing patterns. The emphasis in the international division was on the smaller but growing markets in the developing world. The Asia-Pacific area was the fastest-growing, with automotive manufacturing and electronic equipment providing the largest markets. Owens Corning had affiliates—less than 50 percent ownership—or subsidiaries—more than 50 percent ownership—in Japan, South Korea, and Taiwan. Latin America was another area of expansion, with Owens Corning manufacturing auto component parts in Brazil, for example. Brazil's unstable fiscal condition, however, was eroding the viability of Owens Corning investments there.

By 1990 Owens Corning's future concerns included asbestos litigation and world petroleum prices. The threat of class-action litigation stemmed from large suits brought against manufacturers and distributors of asbestos products in the 1970s and 1980s. Prior to October 1988, all claims against various asbestos manufacturers were handled through a joint claims facility, set up by 55 corporations that contributed funds to its accounts. The funds were used to pay meritorious claims. On August 6, 1987, Owens Corning notified the joint Asbestos Claim Facility's trustees that it intended to withdraw from the organization. Most of the outstanding claims had been brought by litigants who had been employed by the tire and rubber industry and who worked with asbestos brake linings. The company maintained that it had little involvement in these industries, and would not contribute to the payment plan in the future. In 1990, Owens Corning had roughly 84,500 asbestos-related lawsuits pending against it, but it looked to its liability insurance to handle those matters.

At the beginning of the 1990s, Owens Corning was the dominant manufacturer of fiberglass products in the world. It was exerting tighter control over its foreign affiliates and subsidiaries, such as controlling 100 percent of Fiberglass Canada, and concentrating on retiring its still considerable debt. The company showed every indication that it would emerge debt-free and refocused on a profit-generating business. William Boeschenstein, chairman and CEO, stepped down in 1990, ending the family dynasty, which guided Owens Corning to its preeminent position in home and industrial fiberglass and polyester resins. Owens Corning President Max O. Weber became chairman and CEO. While cutting back its long-term research, the company could continue in its role as an innovator in products in its chief areas of competition.

The Hiner Years: 1992–97

In 1990 it formed alliances with BASF, Lucky-Goldstar, and Siam Cement to expand its global presence and in 1991 formed a new products division to make window products for the home building market. At the end of the year, however, Owens Corning's new CEO Weber became fatally ill and was forced to retire, leaving the company in the hands of Gregory Hiner, the head of GE's plastics operation under Jack Welch. With the company still buried in debt and its sales $74 million lower in 1991 than in 1986, Hiner had his work cut out for him. He immediately reinstated Owens Corning's long-term research budget and by 1993 announced that, debt or no, the company was going to begin growing again. By 2000 sales would reach $5 billion; Owens Corning would be manufacturing in virtually every home products niche, from insulation to siding to windows; and international sales—which accounted for 21 percent of 1993 sales—would rise to 40 percent by the turn of the century. To reach those dizzying heights it would use acquisitions and joint ventures to broaden its product line and enter new markets, and it would fundamentally change its vision of its business. It would shift from being a bulk manufacturer of building materials to an all-in-one supplier of the entire spectrum of home-building products, thereby benefiting from lower shipping costs, low inventory levels, and reduced exposure to the seasonality of the home-building market.

In 1993 Hiner established a new division, Asia/Pacific, and traded its commercial roofing line to Schuller International (formerly Johns-Manville) for the latter's residential roofing business. In 1994 Owens Corning made the first of a long line of small acquisitions that by mid-1997 would total 16 when it acquired UC Industries, a maker of rigid insulating foam. It followed it by adding the insulation and industrial supply business of Pilkington plc, doubling its European capacity. It also formed a joint venture with Alpha Corporation to create the largest polyester resin producer in North America, developed a new home sound insulation product called Quiet-Zone, and introduced its first new fiberglass in six decades, Miraflex. By the end of 1994, Hiner announced that Owens Corning's year 2000 goals could be achieved by 1999.

In 1995 Owens Corning made five more acquisitions, adding foam manufacture and vinyl windows to its home-products arsenal, formed two new Latin American companies, and established a joint venture in India. It also began offering its retail-store customers (Home Depot, Lowe's, and others) logistics support and product training services, adopted SAP's information management software to streamline and integrate its entire information structure, and launched System Thinking, a new marketing program to help customers better understand its home-building products, work with contractors, and arrange financing. With debt down $100 million from 1993, to $800 million, Owens Corning officially dropped Fiberglass from its corporate name to reflect the new diversity of its product line.

Seven more acquisitions followed in 1996 as well as the formation of a joint venture in China to build its fourth plant in that huge new market, and by May 1997 Owens Corning had built or acquired facilities on every continent save Australia. It had also adopted a tough new policy to reduce its outstanding asbestos litigation debt. In 1996 it announced it would be contesting one-third of its asbestos case backlog and filed suit against three southeastern U.S. labs that it charged had falsified asbestos testing reports to incriminate Owens Corning. By mid-1997 Owens Corning was still hampered by stagnant sales in Europe and the stock market seemed unimpressed by Hiner's reengineering feat. But with sales well past $3.8 billion and debt headed downward, in *Fortune* magazine's words Owens Corning appeared to have pulled off a "striking renewal" from an also-ran to a global leader.

Principal Subsidiaries

Barbcorp, Inc.; Crown Manufacturing Inc. (Canada); Eric Company; Falcon Foam Corporation; IPM, Inc.; Knytex Company, LLC; Matcorp, Inc.; N.V. Owens-Corning Capital L.L.C.; Owens-Corning S.A. (Belgium); Owens-Corning Fiberglas A.S. Limitada (Brazil); Owens-Corning Overseas Holdings, Inc.; O/C/FIRST CORPORATION; OCFOGO, Inc.; O/C/SECOND CORPORATION; Owens-Corning Cayman Limited; Owens-Corning Fiberglas Espana, S.A. (Spain); Owens-Corning Fiberglas Deutschland GmbH (Germany); Owens-Corning Fiberglas France, S.A.; Owens-Corning Fiberglas (Italy) S.r.l.; Owens Corning (Japan) Ltd.; Owens-Corning Veil Netherlands B.V.; Owens-Corning Fiberglas (U.K.), Ltd.; Owens-Corning Real Estate Corporation; Palmetto Products, Inc.; Roscorp, Inc.; Soltech, Inc.; UC Industries, Inc.; Western Fiberglass of Texas, Inc.; Willcorp, Inc. The company also maintains subsidiaries in Denmark, Norway, China, Uruguay, Sweden, Barbados, Cyprus, Zimbabwe, Singapore, and South Africa.

Further Reading

Focus, Toledo, Ohio, Owens-Corning Fiberglas Corporation, October 1988.
"A History of Innovation," http://www.owenscorning.com, 1997.
Stewart, Thomas A., "Owens-Corning: Back from the Dead," *Fortune,* May 26, 1997.

—Karl F. Rahder
—updated by Paul S. Bodine

Pennzoil Company

Pennzoil Place
Post Office Box 2967
Houston, Texas 77252-8200
U.S.A.
(713) 546-4000
Fax: (713) 546-6639
Web site: http://www.pzl.com

Public Company
Incorporated: 1968 as Pennzoil United, Inc.
Employees: 10,000
Sales: $2.49 billion (1996)
Stock Exchanges: New York Pacific Toronto London
  Basel Geneva Zürich
SICs: 1311 Crude Petroleum & Natural Gas; 1321
  Natural Gas Liquids; 2911 Petroleum Refining; 2992
  Lubricating Oils & Greases; 3569 General Industrial
  Machinery & Equipment, Not Elsewhere Classified;
  7549 Automobile Services, Except Repair & Washes

Pennzoil Company is a major energy company consisting of three main operating units: Pennzoil Exploration and Production Company, which has about 100 oil and gas fields in the Gulf of Mexico and the gulf coast, Texas, Arkansas, Louisiana, Canada, Azerbaijan, Egypt, Qatar, Australia, and Venezuela; Pennzoil Products Company, which operates two refineries in Shreveport, Louisiana, and Rouseville, Pennsylvania, and markets the bestselling motor oil in the United States; and Jiffy Lube International, Inc., the world's largest franchiser and operator of fast oil change service centers, with about 1,400 outlets. Pennzoil's history is one of mergers and takeovers. Though one of its earliest ancestors was a part of the vast Standard Oil interests until 1911, Pennzoil was not a major factor in the oil and gas industry until its 1965 takeover of United Gas Corporation, a company many times its size. In a high-profile corporate war, in 1988 Pennzoil accepted a settlement of $3 billion from Texaco after the latter was found guilty of interference in Pennzoil's failed merger with Getty Oil. The cash payment, larger than Pennzoil's total assets at the time, was a climax to Pennzoil's long and complex history of corporate gamesmanship, much of it engineered by the company's longtime chairman, J. Hugh Liedtke. Ironically, the Texaco settlement actually weakened Pennzoil, and the company was subsequently in danger of being taken over itself.

Early History Was Centered in Pennsylvania

The companies that originally came together to form Pennzoil were all involved in the oil industry's early history in Pennsylvania and the neighboring states. One of them, the South Penn Oil Company, was formed on May 27, 1889, by a unit of Standard Oil Company, John D. Rockefeller's enormous oil concern. Standard already controlled approximately 90 percent of the oil refining in the United States, but it had been slow to move into oil producing until the late 1880s, at which time it bought up a large number of ground leases in the Pennsylvania oil region and created South Penn to work them. Under first president Noah Clark, South Penn made rapid progress with its initial wells and was soon pushing across the border into the rich West Virginia fields. South Penn enjoyed all the benefits of membership in the Standard family of companies, including guaranteed sale of its crude to Standard distributors and refineries, ample provision of capital for expansion, and an absence of threatening competition. When Standard reorganized itself in 1892 into a closely interlocked trust of 20 operating companies, South Penn was capitalized at $2.5 million, a significant figure for the time, but among the smaller of Standard's holdings.

The reorganized South Penn received a new president as well. John D. Archbold had been a Pennsylvania oil man since the 1860s, and after joining Standard had rapidly risen to become one of the company's top five policy-makers and its director of all producing activity. As such, he became the president of South Penn upon its reorganization in 1892, when the Standard companies were responsible for over a quarter of all U.S. oil production. In the 1890s South Penn increased tenfold its annual production of crude, and by 1898 it was the leader among the Standard interests with 7.6 million barrels per year, most of it pumped from its West Virginia fields. The year before, it had bought the drilling rights to some 20,000 acres of land in the Pennsylvania oil region, paying $1.4 million in what was described as the largest deal in the history of U.S. oil production.

In 1899 Standard Oil was again reshuffled, all of the affiliated companies becoming subsidiaries of the newly enlarged Standard Oil Company (New Jersey). John Archbold remained head of South Penn and was now effective head of New Jersey Standard as well, John D. Rockefeller having largely retired from the scene. South Penn was thus well-positioned to grow into one of the giants of the American petroleum business, with unlimited financial backing, top management skills, and a healthy share of the existing crude market. It soon became apparent, however, that South Penn lacked the one indispensable ingredient of the oil industry: oil. By 1900 the Appalachian oil region had reached its all-time peak of production and its many thousands of wells began to run dry. South Penn production dropped by about 50 percent during the following decade and would never again provide more than small amounts of high-grade crude, in addition to useful quantities of the recently harnessed natural gas.

In 1911 the Supreme Court ordered the dissolution of Standard Oil Company (New Jersey). South Penn began life on its own as one of the leading drillers of crude oil in a region that was largely played out. About the time South Penn had been formed, two independent refineries were built in nearby Rouseville, Pennsylvania. The Pennsylvania Refining Company and Nonpareil Refining Company were both founded in 1886 to process the great stream of oil then produced by the region and bound for the eastern seaboard. The founders of Pennsylvania Refining (PRC), Henry Suhr, Samuel Justus, and Louis Walz, invested $40,000 in their new company and commenced production of kerosene, at that time the most valuable end product of petroleum. Nonpareil Refining, on the other hand, designed its facilities to make lubricating oil and enjoyed only mixed success from the beginning.

The early oil industry was volatile, in more ways than one. By 1893 Nonpareil had already changed hands once and was then bought out by PRC for $50,000 at auction. Nonpareil's name was changed to Germania Refining Company and its offices consolidated with those of PRC. In the meantime, PRC had suffered a catastrophic fire in 1892, which destroyed its barrel factory and much of the adjoining refinery, killing 50 workers and causing an estimated $1 million in damage. Fires were common in the early years of the petroleum industry, as safety regulations were almost nonexistent and the product naturally flammable. PRC rebuilt its facilities and within a few months had restored production to full capacity.

Pennzoil Name First Used in the 1910s

The growing use of the automobile and other internal-combustion engines gradually changed the relative value of oil's refined products. Use of kerosene began a slow decline, its illumination replaced by the cleaner and more-efficient electricity; while gasoline, previously an unwanted oil byproduct, was increasingly required by the new machines. Internal-combustion engines also depended on efficient lubricants, which PRC recognized in 1904 when it expanded its lube facilities and five years later formed a new company to market its lubricants, Oil

City Oil and Grease Company. Prevented by Pennsylvania's limited crude supplies from becoming a major refiner of gasoline, PRC shifted more of its production to lubricants and quickly developed a reputation for manufacturing high quality products. PRC's president and part owner was Charles Suhr, son of one of the company's founders, and in 1913 Suhr agreed to invest in a California company that wished to distribute Germania lubricants on the West Coast. A few years later, Suhr and his associates came up with the brand name Pennzoil, which would henceforth become the company's trademark and one of the country's more widely recognized logos. To capitalize on Pennzoil's growing popularity, Suhr changed the name of his two marketing companies in 1921 to the Pennzoil Company (California) and the Pennzoil Company (Pennsylvania).

In the meantime, Suhr had merged his refining outfits in 1914 into a single company called Germania Refining Company, soon changed for patriotic reasons to Penn-American Refining Company. In 1924 Penn-American and its marketing companies, now three in number with the addition a few years before of Pennzoil Company (New York), were merged into an umbrella corporation called Pennzoil Company. Pennzoil was not only refining and marketing about 3,000 barrels per day of crude oil; it also had bought gas stations in Detroit, Cleveland, and Pittsburgh. Having organized the refining and marketing aspects of the oil business, Pennzoil was still lacking crude-production capacity, and in the mid-1920s it began talks with South Penn Oil about a possible merger. South Penn, the former Standard Oil producer, had limited refining and marketing capacities, and in 1925 the two companies came together when South Penn bought 51 percent of Pennzoil's stock. Though not a merger, South Penn's purchase effectively united the two medium-sized Pennsylvania oil concerns. South Penn completed its purchase of Pennzoil in 1955.

While Pennzoil motor oils were racking up an impressive series of Indianapolis 500 automobile racing and transcontinental flight records, South Penn continued consolidating its holdings in the Appalachian oil and gas region, which though limited in scope remained a source of high-grade petroleum. The focus of U.S. oil production had shifted to the South, however, where the vast east Texas fields had begun pumping in the early 1930s, and initial efforts were underway to tap the offshore riches of the Gulf of Mexico. The immediate effect of this surge in production was to depress the price of Pennsylvania crude to an all-time low in 1933, but its long-term effect on Pennzoil's future history was to be much more profound.

Zapata Petroleum Founded in 1953

After World War II, as America developed its love of the automobile, investors continued to pour into the Texas oil regions in search of more spectacular finds. One such wildcatting firm, Zapata Petroleum Corporation, was founded in 1953 by two brothers, J. Hugh and William Liedtke, John Overbey, and a young man named George Bush, later to abandon oil for the richer field of politics. The Liedtkes had already formed a useful friendship with another future U.S. president, Lyndon Baines Johnson, at whose Austin, Texas, home they rented rooms while attending law school at the University of Texas. The four men all had some experience in oil, and in raising the $1 million to form Zapata planned to have a go at big-time oil gambling themselves. As it turned out, they were both lucky and talented: Zapata leased several thousand acres in Texas's West Jameson field and proceeded to drill 127 wells without once coming up dry.

Zapata soon moved offshore, creating Zapata Offshore Company and Zapata Drilling Company to pursue the oil fields then being uncovered in the gulf. In 1959 these two companies were spun off as independent concerns, with Bush remaining as Zapata offshore's head until his election to the House of Representatives in 1966. The so-called spinoff would become a favorite tactic of the resourceful Liedtke brothers, who were able time and again to realize substantial gains by relying on the willingness of shareholders to pay more for equity in a smaller, easily comprehended asset than they would for the same asset hidden in a large corporation. The Zapata partners were already wealthy men by the late 1950s, but the Liedtke brothers were eager to expand, and became interested in the fortunes of Pennzoil, whose corporate name had become South Penn Oil Company after the final merger of its partner companies in 1955. South Penn was well known as a producer of premium motor oil but its profits had never reached their potential. The company's largest shareholder was J. Paul Getty's Tidewater Oil, and the Liedtkes, who knew Getty through previous dealings, began buying large amounts of South Penn stock with Getty's approval. Convinced that South Penn's assets were not being fully exploited, the Liedtkes soon bought out Getty's position and in effect gained control of South Penn in the early 1960s. J. Hugh Liedtke became president of South Penn in 1962, and in the following year South Penn was merged with the Zapata companies in a new entity called Pennzoil Company. Pennzoil was still a relatively small player among the oil giants, with sales in 1963 of only $77 million and a net profit of about $7 million. The corporation was headquartered in Houston, with regional offices in Los Angeles and Oil City, Pennsylvania.

Acquired United Gas Corporation in 1965

The Liedtkes next set their sights on a much richer prize, United Gas Corporation. United was formed in 1930 as a holding company for some 40 gas and oil concerns in the Gulf of Mexico region and by the mid-1960s had become one of the largest distributors of natural gas in the country, its United Gas Pipe Line Company carrying approximately 8 percent of the nation's supply. United also produced and processed natural gas and owned an important mining company, Duval Corporation. As with his friendly takeover of South Penn, Hugh Liedtke saw in United a company unable to exploit its large resources and hence undervalued in the market. He offered to buy one million shares of United at $41 per share; five million shares were promptly tendered, and Pennzoil bought all of them in 1965 for a total purchase of 42 percent of United's stock, borrowing $215 million of the $225 million required. The move was an early example of corporate raiding, in which a much smaller company—in this case, one-eighth the size of its target—gained control of a vast but underperforming competitor. As he did with Zapata, Liedtke proceeded to sell off much of United's assets, first spinning off its retail business and then, in 1974, the huge United Gas Pipe Line Company. According to Pennzoil, the latter divestment was made necessary by government regulations which inhibited Pennzoil's operation of both producing

and distributing concerns, but the Liedtkes's handling of the affair resulted in a barrage of lawsuits and an investigation by the Federal Power Commission. In addition, the brothers agreed to pay $100,000 to former Pennzoil stockholders in settlement of insider trading charges brought at the time of the spinoff.

In any event, the absorption of the United companies turned Pennzoil into a large and diversified natural-resources company. Its 1970 sales hit $700 million, up tenfold from 1963, and its Duval Corporation mining subsidiary went on to make a series of quick strikes in sulfur, potash, copper, gold, and silver. To keep its natural gas production up, Pennzoil created two new companies in the early 1970s, Pennzoil Offshore Gas Operators (POGO) and Pennzoil Louisiana and Texas Off-shore, Inc. (PLATO), selling shares to the public in order to raise capital needed for further offshore drilling while also enjoying a sizable appreciation in the value of the stock it retained. By 1980 Pennzoil sales had passed $2 billion, the bulk of it generated by the company's traditional strength in the refining and sale of motor oil. Pennzoil had become the second-leading seller of motor oil, bolstered by its reputation for quality and by an increasing use of mass marketers instead of gas stations for its retail trade. Its assorted mining ventures brought in about 20 percent of corporate sales, while sulfur added another 10 percent. It was not surprising that Hugh Liedtke began pushing hard for more oil and gas production—though representing but one-fourth of sales, production accounted for fully 50 percent of net income, crude oil and gas always commanding a higher margin than refined products.

Legal Struggle with Texaco over Getty Oil Dominated 1980s

With that in mind, in the early 1980s Liedtke became interested in the squabbling heirs of J. Paul Getty. Liedtke calculated that Getty Oil Company stock was severely undervalued and began buying it up, and in January 1984 he reached an agreement with Gordon Getty to buy three-sevenths of the company's shares at $112.50 per share, well over their current trading price. The $3.9 billion purchase would vastly increase Pennzoil's reserves of oil and gas, and probably precipitate the dissolution of Getty Oil at prices even higher than Liedtke had paid. The agreement was duly approved by Getty's board of directors and announced at a press conference, but Getty's investment bankers and lawyers continued to solicit higher offers for Getty stock. They got one from Texaco, which several days later announced that it had agreed to buy all of Getty's stock at $128 per share, or about $10 billion. At that point, Hugh Liedtke sued Texaco for tortuous interference with Pennzoil's prior contract with Getty, and shortly afterward a Texas jury agreed with him, deciding that Texaco owed Pennzoil about $10.5 billion in real and punitive damages—the highest such award to date.

With the exception of Hugh Liedtke, the award seemed to stun everyone. Texaco had not taken the suit seriously, assuming that at worst it would be forced to pay off Pennzoil with a nominal settlement fee. Not only did the Texas jury express the general public's growing dislike for big-money takeovers; its verdict was upheld upon appeal though the award was lowered to $8.5 billion. Texaco threatened to declare bankruptcy if Liedtke did not accept a "reasonable" settlement, but the

Pennzoil chairman refused. In April 1987 Liedtke turned down an offer of $2 billion cash from Texaco, which promptly followed through on its promise and filed under Chapter 11 of the bankruptcy code. Upon that news the stock value of Pennzoil dropped $631 million overnight. Liedtke was aware, however, that Texaco was a wealthy company even for the oil business, able to sustain a huge cash loss, and by the end of 1987 Texaco agreed to pay Pennzoil $3 billion to have done with the case.

While this legal struggle was being waged, Pennzoil had decided to sell its various mining interests, with the exception of sulfur. Liedtke spun off the gold-mining subsidiary into an independent company, Battle Mountain Gold Company, whose stock tripled in a short time. The mining disposal left Pennzoil with a mix of motor oil refining and marketing, oil and gas production, and sulfur production, the last two far more profitable than the former; and about $3 billion in cash.

Based on a court ruling, Pennzoil management was led to believe that it could avoid paying taxes on the Texaco settlement if it invested the money in an asset similar to that of Getty. Liedtke, therefore, in 1989 spent the bulk of the money, $2.1 billion, for a big chunk of a larger oil concern, in this case 8.8 percent of Chevron. Anticipating the worst, Chevron immediately filed suit to prevent the purchase and readied itself for a hostile takeover bid. Nevertheless, Pennzoil, which was essentially making a tax-sheltered investment, did not follow through with a takeover bid. Meantime, money from the Texaco settlement also went into Pennzoil's purchase of Purolator, a maker of oil filters.

Restructurings and Threat of Takeover in the 1990s

Unfortunately, over the next several years, company management had to pay considerable attention to the Chevron investment and to haggling with the Internal Revenue Service over whether it owed taxes on the Texaco settlement, all of which led management to be somewhat neglectful of its core operations. A subsequently weakened Pennzoil was forced to restructure its operations throughout the 1990s and operated with the threat of a hostile takeover hanging over it.

Nevertheless, Pennzoil began the decade with a promising acquisition. In January 1990 Pennzoil bought more than 80 percent of Jiffy Lube International, Inc., a franchiser, owner, and operator of automotive lubrication and fluid-maintenance centers. Jiffy Lube had successfully found a niche as a speedy-service center, but was deeply in debt. Pennzoil's $43.5 million purchase price bought a company with assets of $237.3 million and liabilities of $239.5 million. Two months later, James L. Pate, who had been company treasurer, was named president and CEO, with Liedtke remaining chairman. In September 1991 Pennzoil paid $9.3 million for the remainder of Jiffy Lube, which then became a wholly owned subsidiary of Pennzoil.

Pennzoil began to reduce its Chevron holding in October 1992, when it exchanged 48 percent of its shares (worth about $1.2 billion) for Chevron PBC, which owned 240 million barrels of oil and gas reserves in and around the Gulf of Mexico. As part of the agreement, Pennzoil and Chevron also said they would not buy each other's stock for the next five years. In November 1993 Pennzoil sold 8.2 million shares of its remaining stake at $89 per share, gaining $171 million over what it paid for the stock. These deals left Pennzoil with just over 9 million shares of Chevron.

Continuing its 1980s sales of noncore assets, Pennzoil in December 1992 spun off Purolator in a public offering that generated $206 million. The following month, the company sold its Mt. Muro gold mine located near Kalimantan, Indonesia. In October 1994, after Pate had in May of that year succeeded the retiring Liedtke as chairman, Pennzoil sold the remaining U.S. assets of its sulphur division to Freeport-McMoRan Resource Partners LP.

Wanting to concentrate on rebuilding the company's long-neglected exploration operations, Pate moved quickly to close the chapter on the Texaco settlement by reaching an agreement with the IRS whereby in October 1994 Pennzoil made a $556 million payment in cash for back taxes, including $294.3 million in interest charges. That same month the company incurred a $500 million charge for the back taxes, a loss on its sale of its sulphur division, and bad real estate investments. Pennzoil was sufficiently weakened by this point that Pate feared the company was in danger of a hostile takeover. The company board therefore in early November adopted a "poison pill" defense to guard against any unwanted suitors.

For the year, Pennzoil posted a $288.7 million loss in 1994, which was followed by a 1995 loss of $305.1 million. The company was particularly hurt by a decline in the price of natural gas, which accounted for about two-thirds of the company's production, and continuing high debt. Pate subsequently restructured Pennzoil's operations, achieving savings in operating costs of more than $75 million a year, and reduced the company dividend in 1995 and 1996 to save cash. He was also able in 1996 to cut company debt by $300 million. With natural gas prices on the rise, 1996 showed a huge improvement—net income of $133.9 million.

By mid-1997 Pennzoil was looking forward to a bright future based on its improved financial picture and on long-awaited payoffs for its investments in exploration in Azerbaijan and the Gulf of Mexico. In June 1997, however, Union Pacific Resources Group Inc.—an energy exploration and production company based in Fort Worth, Texas—launched a $4 billion hostile takeover bid of Pennzoil (ironically, Pennzoil had been rebuffed in 1995 when it had approached Union Pacific's then parent about a Pennzoil takeover of Union Pacific). The company board soon announced their opposition to the bid, and their desire to have Pennzoil continue on its own, letting Pate's restructuring play itself out. Whether the company would have that opportunity was uncertain, although Pennzoil had some formidable defenses in place and seemed determined to stay independent.

Principal Subsidiaries

Jiffy Lube International, Inc.; Pennzoil Exploration and Production Company; Pennzoil Products Company.

Further Reading

Baldo, Anthony, "The Pennzoil Pickle: How Hugh Liedtke's Windfall from Texaco Could Be Torpedoed by the IRS," *Financial World,* November 26, 1991, pp. 30–31.

Barrett, William P., "Another Rabbit, Please," *Forbes,* December 10, 1990, p. 92.

Burrows, Peter, "Pennzoil Switches on Its Searchlight," *Business Week,* February 13, 1995, pp. 74–75.

Byrne, Harlan S., "Revving Up," *Barron's,* November 11, 1996, p. 20.

Chubb, Courtney, "Pennzoil Emerges Dry from Sea of Red Ink, Prepares for Growth," *Oil Daily,* May 15, 1997, p. 1.

Gentry, Mickey, and Kimberly Patrick, *Pennzoil Company: The First 100 Years,* Houston: Pennzoil Company, 1989.

Ivey Mark, "Pennzoil's Trip Down a Slippery Slope," *Business Week,* July 22, 1991, p. 53.

Ivey, Mark, and Maria Shao, "What Does Liedtke Want?," *Business Week,* December 25, 1989, p. 42.

Lipin, Steven; Allanna Sullivan; and Terzah Ewing, "In Fight for Pennzoil, Old Suitor Becomes the Pursued: Union Pacific Resources' $4 Billion Offer Faces an Arsenal of Defenses," *Wall Street Journal,* June 24, 1997, p. B4.

"Love Her and Leave Her," *Forbes,* September 15, 1974.

Nulty, Peter, "How a Foxy Deal Became a Dog," *Fortune,* November 2, 1992, pp. 82, 86.

Petzinger, Thomas, *Oil and Honor: The Texaco-Pennzoil Wars,* New York: Putnam, 1987.

Shannon, James, *Texaco and the $10 Billion Jury,* Englewood Cliffs, N.J.: Prentice Hall, 1988.

Sherman, Stratford P., "The Gambler Who Refused $2 Billion," *Fortune,* May 11, 1987, p. 50.

—Jonathan Martin
—updated by David E. Salamie

Pentland Group plc

The Pentland Centre
Lakeside
Squires Lane
Finchley
London, Greater London N3 2QL
United Kingdom
44 181 346 2600
Fax: 44 181 346 2700
Web sites: http://www.world-of-speedo.com
        http://www.ellesse.com

Public Company
Founded: 1936
Employees: 6,969
Sales: £889.6 million (US$1.3 billion)
Stock Exchanges: London
SICs: 5139 Footwear; 5136 Men's and Boy's Clothing;
    5137 Women's and Children's Clothing; 5112
    Stationery and Office Supplies; 5064 Electrical
    Appliances, TV & Radios

The Pentland Group plc owns and licenses some of the world's best-known shoe and sporting goods brands, including Speedo swimsuits; Ellesse and Berghaus sportswear; Mitre soccer balls; and Pony, Lacoste, Kickers, and KangaRoos footwear. The company also sells Red or Dead designer apparel, Grazia brand clothing, and several brands of fashion footwear. Throughout its first 50 years in business, Pentland was a relatively obscure manufacturer of mostly private-label shoes sold in Great Britain. The company catapulted onto the global stage in the early 1980s via its role in the development and success of Reebok brand athletic shoes. Pentland made a vital investment in the then-struggling U.S. licensee of the brand in the early 1980s and helped guide its explosive growth during the decade, later divesting its stake in the multibillion-dollar firm. A subsequent series of rapid-fire acquisitions in the early 1990s formed a family of prestige sporting goods labels. Chairman R. Stephen Rubin, who took Pentland's helm in 1969, continued to own a majority interest in the publicly-traded company into the late 1990s.

Founded in 1930s

Pentland's origins stretch back to 1932, when Berko and Minnie Rubin established the Liverpool Shoe Co. to sell footwear to Britain's retail chains. A 1973 article on the company credited the business's early success to its founders' "extraordinarily good sense of what would sell." From a base capital of £100, Liverpool Shoe incorporated in 1936 and purchased its first manufacturing operation, Merrywell Shoes, in 1946. Liverpool Shoe continued to grow via acquisition throughout the postwar era, purchasing both Dines Shoes Ltd. and Batson and Webster Ltd. in 1962 and John F. Kirby Ltd. in 1963 before going public in 1964. Though the shares were in high demand—the floatation was oversubscribed 97 times—the Rubin family retained a majority interest in the firm.

Liverpool Shoe was by this time manufacturing a wide variety of footwear, from formal to athletic, men's, ladies', and children's. The company's "Beatle boots" were a big hit in the 1960s, and the 1965 acquisitions of Wareings Ltd. and Wesco Footwear Ltd. continued to boost the company's domestic manufacturing capabilities. But the firm began to suffer under pressure from rising imports during the latter years of the decade, incurring losses from 1967 to 1971. These difficulties were exacerbated by the untimely death of the founder in 1969 at the age of 56. Thirty-one-year-old son R. Stephen Rubin took the helm that year and undertook a restructuring and diversification in the hopes of revitalizing the business.

Second Generation Brings Diversification in 1970s

Trained as a barrister, Rubin had started out at the family company in sales, but quickly proved himself a savvy investment manager. While continuing to support the shoe business, he began in the early 1970s to shape the company into something of a venture capital firm. Rubin acquired Pentland Maritime Shipbrokers Ltd. in 1971 and while the resulting amalgamation would never be known for its shipping interests, he changed the company name to Pentland Industries Ltd. two years later. In 1973, Rubin launched Pentland Shipping Services Ltd. and Pentland Insurance Brokers Ltd. The company made its first venture capital-type investment in 1974, when it bought a 51 percent interest in Unican for a meager £51. The home-brewing and wine-making business took off, and in 1978 Pentland sold its stake to Robertson for a handsome £1 million. Pentland used the proceeds to launch its own line of skateboards, shoes, handbags, luggage, and sportswear under the Airborne brand in 1978.

In the meantime, Rubin had maintained Liverpool Shoe as a holding company for the growing conglomerate's footwear interests. Faced with a flood of cheap shoes from the Far East, he reluctantly slashed domestic production to a single plant and set up his own Hong Kong manufacturing operation in 1969. Pentland acquired Amalgamated Shoe Company and Priestly Footwear Ltd. in 1972, and by the end of the decade had purchased the U.K. license to the Pony footwear brand as well. Over the course of his first decade in the role of chairman, Stephen Rubin had succeeded in turning his birthright from a loss-plagued shoemaker into a budding conglomerate that by 1979 had over £25 million in annual sales and more than £1 million in pre-tax profits. It was only the beginning of a string of stunning successes.

Reebok Acquisition Highlights 1980s

The most significant event of the 1980s, if not Pentland's entire history, started with the apparently inauspicious investment of £50,000 (US$77,500) in Reebok USA Ltd. Inc. in 1981. In exchange for the capital infusion, Pentland received a 55.5 percent interest in the firm. Reebok USA was then the struggling North American licensee of J.W. Foster & Sons Inc. Established in 1895, the family-owned J.W. Foster—the world's oldest shoe company—was then hand-making expensive running shoes for world-class athletes. American Paul Fireman had first taken note of the company's Reebok brand shoes—named for an African gazelle—at a 1979 trade show, and garnered the North American rights to the trademark that same year. Acting as chairman of Reebok USA from 1981 to 1984, Stephen Rubin taught the company the secrets of East Asian sourcing and helped formulate a fresh, new marketing plan.

Late in 1982, the company launched the world's first shoe designed specifically for aerobic exercise. The shoes' bright colors and fashionable styling took the U.S. footwear market by storm. A particularly innovative feature was the use of garment or glove leather, which eliminated the need for a breaking-in period. Sales rose from US$300,000 in 1980 to US$66 million in 1984, the same year that Fireman and Pentland acquired Reebok International (and the worldwide rights to the Reebok brand) from the founding Foster family for US$700,000. By 1986, Reebok's sales had rocketed to US$919 million, giving it a leading 34 percent share of the American athletic footwear market.

When Reebok International went public in 1985, Pentland made US$12.5 million on its sale of 14.8 percent of the company's total equity. The value of its remaining 40.7 percent stake continued to grow throughout the rest of the decade, exceeding a half billion US dollars by the end of the 1980s. In addition to this astounding return on its initial investment, Pentland was by the mid-1980s earning "dividends"—its share of Reebok's profits—amounting to 80 percent of Pentland's after-tax profits. By 1990, Pentland's sales had multiplied nearly 30 times from 1979, to £743.45 million ($1.3 billion), and its after-tax net amounted to £29.91 million (US$53.39 million).

Not content to simply sit back and enjoy the bountiful fruits of his Reebok investment, Rubin sought out new opportunities. Pentland used US$700,000 of the proceeds of the 1985 Reebok offering to acquire a 51 percent stake in Boston-based Holmes Products Corp., a manufacturer of household heating and air conditioning appliances. Aided by the launch of the "Heat Director"—promoted as "the first-ever oscillating fan heater"—Holmes's sales more than doubled to US$12 million in 1985 and jumped to US$30 million in 1986. Other late 1980s acquisitions added real estate management, ceramic tile distribution, and refrigeration interests to the group. In 1989, a reverse takeover joined Bertrams Investment Trust PLC as well as its stationery and greeting card business to the conglomerate.

Acquisitions Pace Early 1990s

In February 1991, Rubin began a two-stage divestment of Pentland's remaining 30.9 percent stake in Reebok, selling 18 percent of the equity back to Reebok for US$460 million. The remaining 12.9 percent went to an investment firm for US$310 million that December. Though he was rather tight-lipped at the time, Rubin would later acknowledge that "certain political differences" with Paul Fireman had helped motivate the sale. The divestment reduced Pentland's year-over-year sales by more than half, to £340.1 million in 1991.

Rubin was not about to let the resulting bankroll mold in a vault. Though he had—and would continue to—dabble in a variety of consumer products, the chairman increasingly targeted acquisitions in the sporting goods industry. In 1990, he purchased a significant stake in Authentic Fitness Corporation, the North American licensee of the Speedo brand. Before the year was out, he acquired an 80 percent stake in Speedo (Europe) Ltd., adding complete ownership of Speedo International and Speedo Australia early in 1991. One of the biggest names in swimwear, Speedo accounted for 65 percent of competitive (as opposed to the much larger fashion) swimsuits sold worldwide. In an effort to broaden the brand's appeal without losing its high-performance image, Pentland carefully expanded its scope to include gear for triathletes and beach wear. Speedo's status, and Pentland's piecemeal strategy of acquiring it, would become a model for the company's activities in the early 1990s.

Building upon more than a decade of ownership of the UK Pony distributorship, Pentland purchased Pony International Inc., the global shoe and sportswear subsidiary of Adidas AG, in July 1991. Two years later, Pentland took a controlling 80 percent stake in Pony USA, which was then generating about three-fourths of the brand's worldwide sales. (The remaining 20 percent was purchased in 1995.) Rubin worked Pentland's marketing and distribution magic on the struggling organization, repositioning the brand as a performance shoe and increasing its advertising budget. He also boosted research and development and transferred Pony's production to Pentland's own East Asian sources. Rubin even made a stab at acquiring former Pony parent Adidas AG in the ensuing year and a half, but abruptly pulled out of the deal with no comment late in 1992.

From 1992 through 1996, Pentland purchased controlling stakes in, or made outright purchases of, nine major sporting goods brands. In 1993, the company added UK's Berghaus mountaineering apparel, footwear and accessories; Brasher hiking boots; and Ellesse, an Italian line of tennis and downhill ski apparel. (Pentland had been the UK's Ellesse licensee since 1981.) Reusch, a German manufacturer of ski and goalkeeping gloves, was acquired in 1994, and another soccer-related company, ball maker Mitre International, came on board in 1995. Pentland also bought the global Lacoste license, with its famous crocodile; U.S. fashion footwear manufacturer Main Woods Inc.; and designer clothing labels Red or Dead and Moda Prima during this period.

Concentration on Sporting Goods in Mid-1990s and Beyond

In keeping with his 1997 self-characterization as "a long-term builder of brands," Rubin committed himself and his company to an emphasis on sporting goods, including apparel, equipment and footwear, as well as sporty clothing. The company divested all of its consumer products subsidiaries save Holmes Products, the air conditioning firm, but was merely waiting for "the right opportunity" to sell this company. Having assembled a group of "next generation" brands, Rubin began to set up the infrastructure necessary to support their continued expansion. From 1995 through mid-1997, he created joint ventures to distribute Pentland brand goods to South Korea, China, Vietnam, Singapore, Malaysia, Indonesia, Argentina, and India.

Known—and sometimes criticized—for his cautious fiscal management, Rubin could not hope to duplicate the unbelievable, Reebok-fueled growth in sales and profits recorded in the 1980s. While Pentland's revenues more than doubled, from £326.5 million in 1992 to £889.6 million in 1996, pretax net only increased by about nine percent, from £33.7 million to £36.6 million, during the period. As analyst Michael Costello had predicted to *Footwear News Magazine's* James Fallon in 1992, "The value of major brands like Reebok and Nike could peak in 1996 or 1997 as their markets mature. What Pentland is doing is putting itself in a position for the next group of brand names to develop." In 1997, it appeared that Rubin had positioned his company well. What remained to be seen was whether he would be able to capitalize on the situation.

Principal Subsidiaries

Pentland Industries Ltd.; Pentland USA Inc.; Pentland Ventures Ltd.; Berghaus Ltd.; Brasher Boot Company Ltd (75%); Ellesse International SPA (Italy); Ellesse (U.K.) Ltd.; Kangaroos International Ltd.; Kangaroos Ltd.; Mitre Sports International Ltd.; Olympico srl (Italy); Pentland Asia Pacific Ltd. (Hong Kong); Pentland Australia Pty. Ltd.; Pentland Brands Ltd; Pentland Canada Inc.; Pentland France sarl; Pentland Latin America Inc.; Pentland Sports Group Inc. (U.S.A.); Pentland Sports Group Ltd.; Pony International Inc. (U.S.A.); Pony International Ltd.; Pony Sports UK Ltd.; Reusch International GmbH & Co. (Germany); Speedo Holdings BV (Netherlands); Speedo International Ltd.; Speedo Australia Pty Ltd.; Airborne Footwear Ltd.; Airborne Leisure Ltd.; LJS Inc. (U.S.A.); Luc Berjen-Paris-Lte (70%); Maine Woods Inc. (U.S.A.); Medallion Shoe Corporation (U.S.A.); Morgan & Oates Ltd.; Pentland Shoe Company Ltd.; Red or Dead Ltd. (75%); Sportsflair Ltd.; H&H Refrigeration Ltd.; Holmes Products Corp. (U.S.A.); Asco General Supplies (Far East) Ltd. (Hong Kong); Asco-Eegim (Far East) Ltd. (51%) (Hong Kong); Pentland Management Services Ltd.; Asco General Supplies Ltd.; Pentland Shipping Services Ltd.

Principal Divisions

Sports and Outdoor; Footwear and Clothing; International Trading; Service Companies.

Further Reading

"Andrew Rubin," *Sporting Goods Business,* July 1994, p. 56.

Fallon, James, "Pentland Confirms Plan to Take Reebok Public," *Footwear News,* May 13, 1985, pp. 1–2.

——, "Pentland Is Filthy Rich But Will Avoid the Cleaners," *Footwear News,* May 16, 1988, pp. 8–9.

——, "Pentland Details Acquisition Strategy," *Footwear News,* May 28, 1990, p. 55.

——, "Pentland to Put 31.5% Reebok Stake on Block," *Footwear News,* June 18, 1990, pp. 2–3.

——, "Rubinesque: Pentland's Stephen Rubin Knows the Art of the Deal," *Footwear News Magazine,* January 27, 1992, pp. 36–37.

Forman, Ellen, "Pentland to Start Trading in U.S.," *Footwear News,* July 14, 1986, p. 35.

McEvoy, Christopher, "Stephen Rubin, Executive Chairman, Pentland Group," *Sporting Goods Business,* February 10, 1997, pp. 40–41.

"Political Football: Adidas," *The Economist,* April 11, 1992, pp. 69–70.

Seckler, Valerie, Reebok Looks at Possibility of Going Public," *Footwear News,* March 11, 1985, pp. 1–2.

——, "El Greco, Pentland Join Forces," Footwear News, August 3, 1987, pp. 1–2.

——, "El Greco Went for $24.5 Million," *Footwear News,* September 28, 1987, pp. 2–3.

——, "Pentland Net Up 13.2% on 41.6% Higher Sales," *Footwear News,* March 21, 1988, p. 27.

——, "Warnaco-Authentic: What Went Wrong with Wachner's Deal," *WWD,* July 31, 1996, pp. 1–3.

Tedeschi, Mark, "Reebok Will Buy Back Most of Pentland Shares," *Footwear News,* February 25, 1991, pp. 2–3.

Tosh, Mark, "Rubin Sketches Plans for Pentland," *Footwear News,* September 9, 1991, p. 22.

—April Dougal Gasbarre

Piaggio & C. S.p.A.

Viale R. Piaggio 25
I-56025 Pontedera, Pisa
Italy
(0587) 272576

Private Company
Founded: 1884
Employees: 12,000
Sales: L2.1 trillion (1995)
SICs: 3751 Motorcycles, Bicycles & Parts; 3711 Motor
    Vehicles and Passenger Car Bodies

Piaggio & C. S.p.A. is the holding company for a group of companies manufacturing light vehicles, principally two-wheeled motor scooters, motorcycles, and bicycles. The company's most important product is the "Vespa" motor scooter, a model that became extremely popular in Europe after World War II. Piaggio is the European leader for motor scooters, with a market share just over 50 percent. The company is ranked third worldwide, with growing sales in India, China, Indonesia, Vietnam, and Latin America. Annual production of Piaggio motor scooters exceeds 850,000 vehicles. Piaggio is also Italy's largest bicycle manufacturer, and makes bikes under the well-known trademarks Raleigh, Puch, and Bianchi. Annual output of bicycles is approximately 500,000. The company also manufactures a minivan, the Piaggio Porter, under a joint operating agreement with the Japanese manufacturer Daihatsu. Piaggio makes electric two- and three-wheeled vehicles, which are able to meet stringent anti-pollution regulations. The company operates subsidiaries in France, Spain, Argentina, Singapore, The Netherlands, Germany, Greece, Britain, and elsewhere, and markets its products through distributors in more than 60 other countries.

19th-Century Beginnings

Piaggio & C. dates back to 1884, when Rinaldo Piaggio, son of a Genoa joiner, expanded his family's old woodshop in the town of Sestri Ponente into a steam-driven sawmill. Rinaldo was only 20 years old, but he demonstrated precocious business acumen. He set his new factory to produce fittings and furniture for ships, and courted the accounts of the local shipyards. Within 15 years, Piaggio's naval fittings shop had won a virtual monopoly over the northwest coast of Italy. All the shipyards turned to Piaggio for furnishings. The business continued to expand as contracts came in from other parts of Italy, and then from international shipbuilders. When the century turned, Piaggio was a well-known name abroad as well as in Italy. The cabins and saloons of more than 70 shipping lines were outfitted with Piaggio furnishings.

Rinaldo Piaggio, on the lookout to expand his factory in a new direction, began to solicit business from railways to build and outfit railway cars. The work was not too different from the complex woodworking required for naval fittings, but the factory had to be altered to accommodate sheet steel work. Within a few years, Piaggio had more jobs for railway cars than for ship fittings, and the company opened a new factory in the town of Finale Ligure. With the opening of the new factory in 1906, Piaggio was able to take on even more railway car business, and began to make other wheeled vehicles as well. Piaggio made trucks, trams, freight cars, and even luxury automobiles.

Wartime Production

During World War I, the two Piaggio factories were refitted to manufacture weapons. The factories also began to make motor boats and airplanes. The new factory at Finale Ligure manufactured boats, including an anti-submarine boat known as the MAS, which was instrumental in destroying the Austro-Hungarian submarine fleet. The older factory at Sestri Ponente principally repaired and maintained war planes. But both factories were soon converted to mass-produce airplanes. In 1917 Rinaldo Piaggio bought a new factory in Pisa, and transferred the production of railway cars and wheeled vehicles there. Piaggio bought another factory, a car works in Pontedera, and began to build airplane engines there. Piaggio produced engines under license to more established manufacturers, and then began designing its own. Piaggio made the "P2," a single-engine fighter plane, beginning in 1923. Five years later, Piaggio equipped the Finale Ligure factory with a complete wind tunnel and hydrodynamic testing tank. Piaggio had turned from motorboats to "flying boats"—high-speed planes that could take off from and land in water. In the 1920s and into World War II, the various Piaggio factories were turning out some of the most advanced flying boats in the world, as well as airplane engines, small planes, bombers, passenger and cargo planes capable of transoceanic flights, as well as railway cars and stainless steel locomotives. All these products contributed greatly to Italy's war effort. And so the factories were bomb targets. The Pontedera factory was completely destroyed in World War II, having been not only bombed by the Allies but mined by the Germans as they retreated. When the war ended, Piaggio had virtually nothing left.

Postwar Success

Founder Rinaldo Piaggio had died in 1938, and the job of postwar renewal fell to his two sons, Armando and Enrico. They split responsibility for the company's four factories. Armando took over the two older ones, Sestri Ponente and Finale Ligure, and Enrico took Pontedera and Pisa. It was Enrico who came up with the idea of making motor scooters.

The scooter was not a new idea. Several manufacturers had made small, light motorcycles before, but they had not caught on. Enrico Piaggio decided that scooters would sell if they could be made right. A small, light, cheap vehicle might be all that many families could afford, so he envisioned a wide market for the scooter. He imagined it as something that women would ride, as well as men. He thought further that it needed room for a spare wheel, which should be easy to change. And if it was not to be just for sunny days, it should have some sort of mudguard to protect the rider's clothes from puddle splashes. With these general specifications, Enrico contacted one of the chief designers from Piaggio's prewar days, Corradino D'Ascanio. D'Ascanio was a brilliant engineer who had created the first fully functional helicopter. D'Ascanio drew up plans for a scooter that had a pressed steel body with a shield-shaped front and a wide back housing for the engine and spare wheel. There was no chain linking the front and back wheels, as the rear wheel was powered by a direct drive. The platform seat was built to be comfortable for women in skirts. It took only five months to move from plans to development. Piaggio rebuilt the demolished Pontedera factory to mass-produce the scooter, and in 1946 the first model was offered for sale. This was the Vespa, Italian for wasp, so named because of the thin-waisted shape of the vehicle.

The Vespa was an immediate success, and quickly became a symbol of postwar Italy. Enrico Piaggio had been correct in assuming that small, cheap transport would sell well, but he could not have guessed the chic appeal of the little machine. In 10 years, Piaggio had sold over one million Vespas. Audrey Hepburn and Gregory Peck rode one in the 1953 film *Roman Holiday,* and the Vespa was clearly the thing to have. Though celebrities rode them, so did workers using them to get to their jobs, and families piled on them for weekend vacations. By 1956, there were 4,000 Vespa sales outlets in Italy, 8,000 in the rest of Europe, and another 2,000 in other parts of the world.

The company also produced the Ape ("bee"), a three-wheeled version of the Vespa, and made Vespa models in a variety of engine sizes. Piaggio also briefly marketed a small car, but when Fiat came out with a similar one, Piaggio withdrew its model. The two factories under the control of brother Armando Piaggio were making airplanes and engines, as they had through the war. The airplane division eventually split off from the scooter division, and still exists today as a separate company, Rinaldo Piaggio. The scooter business continued to thrive into the 1960s. It was the bestselling scooter in over a hundred countries, and was being built under license in several European countries and in Brazil and India. The Vespa still had its movie star cachet, especially as seen in *La Dolce Vita,* ridden by Marcello Mastroianni.

A Changing Industry—1970s and 80s

Enrico Piaggio died suddenly in 1965, at the age of 60. His successor was his son-in-law, Umberto Agnelli. Agnelli's family ran Fiat, the Italian car manufacturer and conglomerate, and Umberto later became managing director of that company. The scooter industry had dipped somewhat in the late 1950s, as wages rose and many consumers spent their money on cars instead of two-wheelers. But the Vespa was still popular through the 1970s, especially among young people. Production remained high, though by the end of the 1970s the company was hampered by labor disputes. Strikes held down production to about three-quarters capacity in 1979, though sales were nevertheless close to $500 million, and Piaggio turned a profit. Costs increased, as the company spent more on developing new models, and also spent money on acquisitions such as Gilera, a leading Italian motorcycle manufacturer. Foreign sales still made up more than 40 percent of Piaggio's business.

One place the Vespa did not catch on was the United States. Piaggio sold its scooters there beginning in the 1950s under its own name and also through a Sears, Roebuck brand, the Allstate Crusaire. But sales were never high, and in 1982 Piaggio stopped its U.S. exports because it was unable to comply with strict pollution control standards. Meanwhile, Piaggio was shipping roughly 17,000 scooters a year to Japan in the early 1980s. By the mid-1980s, Japanese manufacturers were exporting their own scooters. Kawasaki, Yamaha, Honda, and Suzuki all made significant inroads into European motorcycle and scooter markets in the 1980s, with serious repercussions for some of the older brands. The Japanese models were in many cases cheaper, lighter, and better made than the European vehicles they had copied, and many European makers suffered. But the Italian government kept down the number of light motorcycles imported to Italy to protect its own industry, and the Japanese threat if anything solidified Piaggio. About half its sales were of its Vespa models, and half were mopeds. The company continued to invest heavily in its plants, and began to cooperate with other European companies to fight back against the Japanese imports. In 1981 Piaggio signed a deal with the French bicycle and moped maker Peugeot to develop a motorcycle, hoping to find a mid-range niche between the cheap Japanese models and the German luxury models.

Nevertheless, the shrinking European market for two-wheeled vehicles stalled Piaggio in the mid-1980s. The number of units sold in 1980 was 937,000 vehicles, while in 1984 it was only 553,000. Piaggio had a new managing director in 1984, Giorgio Brazzelli. Brazzelli took the view that the slump in sales was more or less permanent, and the company had to reduce its costs in order to make a profit. After barely breaking even for three years in a row, Piaggio finally had a decent profit of L17 billion ($11.05 million) on sales of L663 billion in 1986. Much of the jump was attributable to greatly increased sales of components and parts.

Reorganization in the Late 1980s

The company diversified further in the late 1980s, increasing its investments in automobile components and other industries related to vehicle manufacture. Piaggio also reorganized its corporate structure in 1988, forming a sub-holding company under the main umbrella of Piaggio & C. S.p.A., called Piaggio Veicoli Europei S.p.A. Piaggio Veicoli held all the core businesses related to the manufacture and sale of vehicles, including scooters, motorcycles, three-wheelers, and the light trucks the company was beginning to develop. Another division handled the manufacture of Piaggio's bicycle brands. A third major division was responsible for car and motorcycle components and the other miscellaneous ventures, such as industrial robots, that Piaggio had bought into.

Along with diversification and reorganization, Piaggio aimed to make its business more international in the late 1980s, increasing its joint ventures with foreign companies. In 1989, Piaggio joined a West German engine component manufacturer, Kolbenschmid, in a joint venture to produce water pumps and oil pumps at plants in Italy and France. Then in 1991, Piaggio entered a joint venture with the Japanese firm Daihatsu to develop light transport vehicles. Piaggio also attempted to expand its presence in mainland China by taking on a joint venture with a Hong Kong firm in 1993.

Despite all these changes, Piaggio had difficulty extricating itself from the troubles of its shrinking market. In the early 1990s, Piaggio's share of the European market for two-wheeled vehicles had fallen to about 28 percent, largely due to the success of Japanese imports. Piaggio still had almost half the market share where only low-priced scooters were concerned, but profits were low, and in 1993 the company lost L91 billion ($60 million). In that year Piaggio got a new chairman, 29-year-old Giovanni Agnelli, son of former chairman Umberto Agnelli. Agnelli was both the Piaggio heir and perhaps in line for a position at his father's company, Fiat. He had been raised and educated in the U.S., and had worked for I.B.M. and in a Fiat subsidiary before taking over Piaggio. He found the company in disarray. Diversification into components had taken away the focus on Piaggio's core product, motor scooters, and the company was not only limping along but losing money. Agnelli

quickly sold off unprofitable component businesses, and spent huge sums on the development of new scooter models. Agnelli guessed that the scooter might have a comeback in Europe, because auto traffic was getting more and more congested. Piaggio came out with plastic-body models, which the Japanese companies had long favored, gave them stronger engines, and tried to recapture the star appeal the Vespa had had in the 1950s and 60s. Whether due to transportation strikes, traffic jams, rising car and gas prices, or clever marketing, the scooter market indeed picked up. Between 1991 and 1996 sales of scooters in Europe more than doubled, and sales in Italy alone quadrupled. Piaggio's share of that growing market rose from about 25 percent to almost 50 percent.

Aware that the boom in Europe might soon peak, Piaggio also built up its presence in overseas markets, particularly in India and China. These countries were in a similar position to Italy's just after the war, with a large population in need of basic transportation, and not quite ready to afford a car. Piaggio's Indian subsidiary had sales of about $200 million annually in the mid-1990s, and a respectable market share of around 15 percent. In China, sales were about $36 million in 1995, and all Piaggio's Asian subsidiaries were accounting for more than 30 percent of the company's total sales. Chairman Agnelli aimed to increase the amount of Piaggio's business in Asia over the next five years, hoping to have half the company's sales come from there by the end of the century.

Piaggio's turnaround in the late 1990s demonstrated the strength of its basic product, the scooter. The company had lost considerable ground from the late 1970s on, when Japanese imports eroded its core European markets. Yet the Vespa had very strong brand recognition because of its past. It managed to be classic without being outmoded, due in large part to the improvements carried out after 1993. Piaggio's management was able to foresee a renewed need for the scooter in Europe, and to move on to growing markets abroad. Piaggio's Chairman Agnelli sees the future of the company in its overseas markets, where there is still room for considerable expansion. He has also speculated about bringing the company public. This would presumably spur the company to increase the amount of profit on its substantial sales.

Principal Subsidiaries

Piaggio International Holding B. V. (Netherlands); Piaggio Veicoli Europei S.p.A.; Piaggio Pro-Ind S.p.A.; Piaggio Italia S.p.A.; Altea S.r.l.; Piaggio France S.A.; Piaggio Espana S.A. (Spain); FIV E. Bianchi S.p.A. (75%); Piaggio Argentina S.p.A. (62%); Piaggio Lyman China Co., Ltd. (Hong Kong; 51%); Piaggio Asia Pacific PTE Ltd. (Singapore); Piaggio Indochina PTE Ltd. (Singapore); Almec S.p.A.; Sidca Srl; Intent S.p.A. (75%); Free Time Srl (75%); Reparto Cose Bianchi S.r.l. (75%); Bianchi U.S.A. Inc. (75%); Eudicycles S.A. (France); Piaggio Vespa B.V. (Netherlands); Piaggio Deutschland GmbH (Germany); Piaggio Ltd. (U.K.); Piaggio Portugal Ltda. (92.8%); Piaggio Hellas Epe (Greece); Findutch Service N.V. (Netherlands Antilles); Pro-Ind Brasil Ltda. (Brazil); Piaggio V.E. Poland sp. Zo.o (97.5%); Errebi S.r.l.

Further Reading

Blum, Patrick, "Steyr Sells Moped Division to Piaggio," *Financial Times,* February 25, 1987, p. 27.

"The Bottom-Pinchers' Chariot," *The Economist,* September 21, 1996, p. 64.

Buxton, James, "Piaggio Profits Trebled," *Financial Times,* May 22, 1981, p. 29.

Cornwell, Rupert, "Entering a Year of Promise," *Financial Times,* January 31, 1980, p. 23.

Dodsworth, Terry, "Peugeot and Piaggio to Co-operate on Motorcycles," *Financial Times,* September 13, 1980, p. 19.

Pollack, John, "Vespa Scooters Collide With Anti-Japan Charge," *Advertising Age,* June 22, 1992, p. I4.

"Significant Advance at Piaggio," *Financial Times,* June 23, 1986, p. 30.

Tagliabue, John, "Sometimes Two Wheels Are Better Than Four," *New York Times,* August 17, 1996, pp. 33–34.

Wallace, Charles P., "The Next Mr. Fiat?" *Fortune,* October 14, 1996, pp. 182–186.

Wyles, John, "Piaggio and Kolbenschmid in Venture," *Financial Times,* June 21, 1989, p. 33.

—A. Woodward

Placer Dome Inc.

Box 49330 Bentall Postal Station
Suite 1600, 1055 Dunsmuir St.
Vancouver, British Columbia
Canada V7X 1P1
(604) 682-7082
Fax: (604) 682-7092
Web site: http://www.placerdome.com

Public Company
Incorporated: 1910 as Dome Mines Limited; 1926 as
    Placer Development Limited; and 1944 as Campbell
    Red Lake Mines Limited
Employees: 8,300
Sales: $1.157 billion (1996)
Stock Exchanges: New York Toronto Montreal Paris
SICs: 1041 Gold Ores; 3341 Secondary Nonferrous
    Metals; 1021 Copper Ores

Placer Dome Inc. is an international gold mining company and North America's largest gold producer. In 1996, it operated 16 mines in 5 countries: Canada, the United States, Australia, Chile, and Papua New Guinea and produced 2.2 million ounces of gold. Placer Dome's share of this production amounted to 1.9 million ounces. The company also mined silver, copper, and molybdenum (used to make steel). In addition to its active mining operations, Placer Dome had exploration activities underway in 20 countries, spending on average more than $100 million each year searching for deposits.

The Creation of a New Company

Placer Dome Inc. was formed in 1987 by the amalgamation of three Canadian mining companies, creating the largest gold producer in North America with an annual output of more than 800,000 ounces of gold. Dome Mines Limited, the oldest of the three predecessors and one of Canada's most venerable gold producers, was incorporated in 1910, following the discovery of the Dome Mine, a hard-rock mine in northern Ontario, which

was still producing gold in 1997. The mine and the company got their name from the shape of the gold-studded rock structure a band of prospectors literally stumbled over in 1909.

Placer Development Limited was incorporated in British Columbia in 1926, and made its first earnings, during the 1930s, dredging gold from the gravel of a river in Papua New Guinea, then under Australian mandate. "Placer," which was Spanish for shoal, referred to water-borne deposits of sand or gravel containing particles of gold or silver. Mining that deposit was no easy task. Because there were no roads over the mountains from the coast to the interior, the dredges had to be disassembled and then flown in. This, according to the company, resulted in what was at that point the greatest peacetime airlift ever undertaken. The Bulolo project produced gold until 1965. Between then and 1984, when its next mine was developed, the company invested in coal mining, cattle ranching, timber production, and fishing. It even established a cattle company in Papua New Guinea to provide Bulolo workers with fresh meat. By the early 1980s, Placer Development had sold off most of these interests and was focused on developing the Kidston Mine in Queensland, Australia.

The third company, Campbell Red Lake Mines Limited, was incorporated in 1944 in Ontario, and eventually became a subsidiary of Dome Mines. Its Campbell Mine, one of the highest-grade and lowest-cost gold mines in the world, has produced continuously since 1949.

The merger itself came about because both Placer and Dome Mines were threatened with hostile takeovers by Australian-based companies. Placer arranged the merger to protect itself, raising its market value from $700 million to $4.3 billion.

1987–92: Separate Managements

The type of gold mining done by the companies was not their only difference. Dome Mines and Campbell Red Lake were considered conservative operations. They concentrated on their long-term operations and did not increase their output or acquire new mines despite rising gold prices and lower production costs. Placer, on the other hand, continued to bring new mines on-stream, increasing its gold production from 45,000

Company Perspectives:

Placer Dome is a global mining company whose primary emphasis is gold. We are committed to long-term profitable growth. The added value to our Company will be achieved by investing in our strategy, and in people whose combined skills will lead to successful exploration, property acquisition, mine development and mine operation.

We believe in integrating the efficient extraction of mineral resources with responsible environmental stewardship and providing a safe and healthy workplace for our employees.

ounces in 1982 to 331,000 ounces in 1986, the year before the merger.

During its first five years, Placer Dome kept the separate managements of the original companies in place, along with their conflicting business philosophies. The company did expand through acquisitions. Between 1988 and 1991, the company sold its Canadian and U.S. oil and gas operations as well as various mines, developed and constructed six new mines, and acquired several other mining properties. These acquisitions included shares in Consolidated TVX Mining Corp, which owned the La Coipa gold/silver property in Chile and the Kiena Gold Mines Limited and Sigma Mines in Canada. In 1989, Placer Dome acquired a 50 percent interest in the La Coipa gold/silver property in Chile as well as 50 percent of the shares of a newly-formed Chilean company that bought the La Coipa property from the TVX Group. In addition, the company expanded its interest in the 23-year-old Cortez Gold Mine Joint Venture in Nevada following the discovery of the Pipeline gold deposit in 1991, and in 1992, purchased 50 percent of Compania Minera Zladivar, the owner of the Zladivar copper property in Chile.

To finance its gold mines, Placer Dome often used a relatively new form of financing called a "gold loan." As the mine developer, the company borrowed actual gold deposits from its financing institutions, not their cash. The company sold the gold to pay for building the mine and then repaid the loan in gold from production. Because the gold deposits earned little or no interest, Placer Dome was usually able to negotiate a lower, more favorable rate than if it had borrowed cash. If the rates were too high, however, Placer Dome or another developer could incorporate a new company to hold the property and the mine when it was built, then sell shares to raise the money to develop the property.

Among its other activities during this period, the company and its partners were trying to come up with an acceptable feasibility plan for extracting the gold deposits along the shore of Lake Opapimiskan in northern Ontario. The problem was that the gold was collected within a convoluted iron foundation. The debate had been going on since the Musselwhite brothers discovered the gold in 1962. One thing that was finalized, even before the project was approved for mining, was an agreement between Placer Dome and the leaders of the four First Nations (aboriginal) communities in the area. The company agreed to hire one-quarter of the mine's workforce from the local communities, to provide other economic benefits, such as education, health care, communication, and transportation to the area during the life of the mine, and to respect both the land and the First Nations' culture.

The issue of complex community conditions was not limited to Canada. At the Porgera mine in Papua New Guinea, the joint venture was spending approximately $10 million a year on infrastructure improvements in the region. In 1991, to help the national government channel tax and royalty revenues from the mining back into the community, Placer Dome proposed a Tax Credit Infrastructure Scheme, under which the mine held back some of the taxes owed and directly invested that amount in local improvements.

During this period, sales revenues increased from $624 million in 1987 to $1.02 billion in 1992. Earnings, however, fluctuated, and the company ended 1992 with earnings of $105 million.

1993–94: Creating a Common Goal

In 1993, John M. Willson joined Placer Dome as president and CEO. Willson came to the mining industry "genetically"—his father was a mining engineer. Born in Sheffield, England, Willson graduated from the Royal School of Mines at the University of London in 1962 and immediately went to work at the Nsuta manganese mine in Ghana. Two years later he came to the United States where he took a job in Butte, Montana, at Anaconda's copper mine and learned "how mining should not be done," as he related in the Placer Dome company magazine. He moved on after two and a half years to Cominco Limited's Sullivan zinc-lead mine in Canada, "the first mine I worked at where they knew what they were doing." Four years later, in 1971, Cominco made Willson project manager for construction and operation of its Black Angel zinc-lead mine in Greenland. When that job was completed he left the mining industry for seven years, returning to Cominco in 1981. In 1989 he was appointed president and CEO of Pegasus Gold Inc. of Spokane, Washington, a middle-rank gold producer. He held that position until Placer Dome selected him to replace retiring Tony Petrina.

Willson set about uniting the Placer Dome companies into a single unit with a common goal: higher productivity and lower costs. His aim was to have the company produce 2.5 million ounces of gold by the year 2000 (an increase of nearly 40 percent) while cutting costs by a third.

He began by starting a companywide debate about how to meld the organization's three disparate cultures. The debate produced two strategic changes: concentrate on mining gold, reducing earnings from the company's other minerals to 25 percent of revenues; and decentralize management into four regional units, each responsible for the mining activities in its own area. It also reinforced the importance of the company's tradition of corporate responsibility and high ethical values.

The management reorganization established four subsidiaries: wholly-owned Placer Dome Canada, Placer Dome U.S. Inc., and Placer Dome Latin America; and publicly-owned Placer Pacific Limited, with the corporate headquarters in Vancouver overseeing strategic growth. Internally, the company flattened its structure and introduced team-building, career development, and succession planning and extended its stock option plan to retain its employees in a highly competitive industry. The concentration on gold saw the continued purchase of shares in gold companies, including all the shares of Sulphurets Gold Corp. and Continental Gold Corp. It also led to an increase in exploration costs, which by 1994 were around $100 million.

1995 to the Present

In 1995, the company completed construction of two more mines, the Zaldivar copper mine in Chile and the Osbourne gold mine in Australia, and had 85 exploration projects in 28 countries.

The year 1996 began well. The price of gold hit a six-year high of $414.80 during the first quarter, and in March, construction began on two new gold mines, the underground and open pit Musselwhite mine at Opap Lake, the first mine to be approved under Canada's stringent Environmental Assessment Act, and the Pipeline project in Nevada.

But that same month, in the Philippines, there was an accidental discharge of 4 million tons of mill tailing at the Marcopper Mine, and that mine was closed. Although Placer Dome owned only 40 percent of the corporation operating the mine, neither the joint venture nor the major shareholder had the resources nor the interest to contribute to the cleanup. Placer Dome assumed 100 percent of the financial responsibility. Cleanup involved re-sealing a drainage tunnel that had failed and clearing the spill itself and resulted in a $43 million after tax charge to earnings.

As if that were not trouble enough, the price of gold declined for the rest of the year. Contributing factors included the strength of the U.S. dollar, movement towards a single European currency (and the fear of sales from reserves by European central banks), and gains in stock markets around the world. The main problem was that with low inflation, people put their money in investments other than gold. On the other hand, demand for gold jewelry set a new record in 1996.

In order to reach its long-term corporate goals, the company decided it needed to focus its development and mining activities on a smaller number of larger, sustainable mines. During the year, Placer Dome acquired properties in Africa, Australia, Brazil, Canada, Ecuador, Mexico, the Philippines, and Russia for investigation. Mineral systems had been identified on these and additional work was planned to confirm known gold resources while searching for more. Total exploration expenditures for 1996 came to $117 million and was expected to increase slightly to $120 million in 1997.

In December the company announced it was selling the relatively small Sigma and Kiena gold mines in Quebec as well as the Enkado molybdenum mine in British Columbia. The company ended the year with revenues at an all-time high of $1.2 billion, but with an earnings loss of $65 million, arising from the after-tax charges reflecting the mine sales and the Marcopper cleanup.

The environmental accident at Marcopper caused the company to reevaluate its participation in joint ventures. As Willson stated in a 1997 speech, "In joint ventures, the rewards of success are shared in proportion to equity interest; but unless our partners share our principles of corporate responsibility and are willing to act accordingly, we will end up bearing the full cost of any untoward event. . . . It has made us more determined not to take on a minority partnership in the future, and to be more selective about the partners that we team up with."

In line with that thinking, the company initiated takeovers of Highlands Gold Limited, a Papua New Guinea company that owned 29 percent of the Porgera Mine, and the 24.8 percent publicly-owned interest of Placer Pacific Limited. By early 1997, Placer Dome owned 50 percent of the Porgera Mine and all of Placer Pacific Limited. The company hoped this would simplify its holdings in the Asia Pacific region and to give it a greater share of the exploration potential of the area. Placer Dome also announced plans to combine two of its wholly-owned subsidiaries, Placer Dome Canada and Placer Dome U.S. Inc., to form Placer Dome North America.

In January 1997, the company bid $6.2 billion for Bre-X Minerals Ltd. of Calgary, which owned 90 percent of the Busang gold deposit in Indonesia, "the richest gold find on earth," according to *Maclean's*, with an estimated holding of 100 million ounces of gold. However, the company withdrew its bid the following month. Investigators later reported evidence that gold had been salted at the deposit.

On March 6, 1997, the first gold doré bar was poured at the Pipeline plant, three months ahead of schedule and $70 million under budget. Four days later, the first bar was poured at the Musselwhite mine, one day less than a year after construction of the mine began. Placer Dome's Project Development Division had built two gold mines concurrently, one in Canada and one in the U.S., in a 12-month period. Production at the two mines began in April. Annual gold production at Musselwhite was expected to be 200,000 ounces, and 400,000 ounces at Pipeline.

But the year was not without controversy—over the ownership of the Las Cristinas mine in Venezuela. Crystallex International Corp., a small, Vancouver-based mining company claimed it had the rights, based on its claim to two of the deposit's richest blocks. According to the Venezuelan mining ministry, that ownership had expired in 1989, and belonged to Venezuela. That had certainly been Placer Dome's understanding when it formed a joint venture with a government agency earlier in the decade to develop the site. In July, the Venezuelan supreme court allowed Crystallex's copper rights to be reviewed by the court, but prohibited a trial regarding the gold rights. While Crystallex appealed, Placer Dome took the court's action as acknowledgement of its rights to the gold and began construction of the $576 million project in August, the 15th mine construction or expansion project since the company was formed 10 years earlier.

Whatever the legal outcome, Las Cristinas has been the site of innovative approaches to problems arising when a huge mining operation comes into an isolated, undeveloped area. At Las Cristinas the local population was a mixture of aboriginal communities and migrating, small-scale miners of mixed race and nationality. In 1995, the company instituted a program to help a group of the miners form a collective and work on a part of the project's construction concessions under controlled conditions. The World Bank recognized that effort as a new model for reducing problems between huge mining operations and small miners. Additionally, Placer Dome was exploring new ways to create "sustainable development" of the region around the mine. In a joint venture with the Industrial Co-operation Branch of the Canadian International Development Agency, the company was attempting to involve non-governmental and for-profit organizations in both Canada and Venezuela in community development projects, such as municipal water and sewer systems and agricultural diversification, at Las Cristinas.

In July, the company announced sales of $599 million for the first six months of the year, compared with $562 million for that period in 1996. Net earnings were in the black at $32 million. Gold production was 1.168 million ounces, 25 percent higher than the year before and the average cost of production dropped significantly to $214 per ounce, compared to $246 per ounce for the first two quarters in 1996.

While the technology of gold exploration and mining has changed dramatically since the Dome Mine began operating in 1910, the high level of risk involved has not. Placer Dome appeared to be able to move quickly, selling off older, less productive mines and taking advantage of low gold prices to acquire high-quality properties. Furthermore, its new mines were exceeding production expectations and it looked likely that production in 1997 would reach 2.4 million ounces, the highest yield in its 10 years of existence, and close to Willson's annual production goal of 2.5 million ounces by the year 2000.

Principal Subsidiaries

Placer Dome Latin America (Chile); Placer Dome North America; Placer Pacific Limited (Australia); Placer Dome Exploration, Inc.

Further Reading

Atlas, Riva, "All That Glitters . . . ," *Forbes*, July 29, 1996, p. 96.
"Brawling for Busang Gold," *Maclean's*, January 27, 1997, p. 55.
Crespo, Mariana, "All That Glitters," *Financial World*, September 13, 1994, p. 58.
Gibbon, Ann, "Firms Dig in for Battle Over Venezuelan Gold," *The Globe and Mail*, July 25, 1997, http://www.globeandmail.com.
"Highlands Set to Sell Porgera Mine Stake," *American Metal Market*, January 9, 1997, p. 5.
Jenish, D'Arcy, and Ann Shortwell, "Defence of a Gold Mine," *Maclean's*, August 17, 1987, p. 32.
Leggatt, Hugh, "Deep Roots Down Under," *Placer Dome Inc. Prospect*, March 1997, p. 2.
——, "Executive Profile: John M. Willson," *Placer Dome Inc. Prospect*, June 1997, p. 13.
McMurdy, Deirdre, "Chile's Copper Rush," *Maclean's*, November 1, 1993, p. 45.
"The Mine Development Process," Placer Dome Inc.: Vancouver, 1995.
Rathbone, John Paul, "Las Cristinas Mine Bogged Down in Legal War," *Focus*, July 18, 1997.
Terry, Edith, "Placer Dome: Will It Pan Out?" *Business Week*, September 7, 1987.
Werniuk, Jane, "Miracle at Opap Lake," *Placer Dome Inc. Prospect*, June 1997, p. 8.
——, "Pipeline to the 21st Century," *Placer Dome Inc. Prospect*, June 1997, p. 2.

—Ellen D. Wernick

"Justice For All"

Pre-Paid Legal Services, Inc.

321 East Main Street
Ada, Oklahoma 74820
U.S.A.
(405) 436-1234
Fax: (405) 436-7565
Web site: http://www.ppls.com

Public Company
Incorporated: 1976
Employees: 142
Sales: $59.9 million (1996)
Stock Exchanges: American
SICs: 7389 Business Services, Not Elsewhere Classified

Pre-Paid Legal Services, Inc. develops, underwrites, and markets various legal service plans for customers in all states and the District of Columbia. Because of the increasing need for legal services in many areas of life and the increasing costs for attorney consultations, Pre-Paid Legal makes available plans based on monthly payments similar to insurance for health care or car accidents. If needed, customers then can access a network of selected lawyers or in some cases choose any attorney they wish. Since this company was created in 1972, it has paid over $140 million to more than 100,000 lawyers who have aided Pre-Paid Legal customers. Pre-Paid Legal promotes its services in various ways, but network marketing has been one key to its success. One of the first firms in the U.S. to provide prepaid legal services, in 1997 Pre-Paid Legal remains a leader in a rapidly expanding industry. It is the nation's only public corporation devoted entirely to developing and marketing prepaid legal services.

Origins

Many individuals think you have to pay a fee directly to a lawyer for his or her services. However, options to that direct method of payment have existed since around the turn of the century. For example, the Physicians' Defense Company from 1899 to 1910 offered doctors prepaid legal protection against malpractice lawsuits. In the 1920s some auto clubs offered members free legal advice in car-related cases, a type of service the American Bar Association declared unethical.

Meanwhile, Europeans began offering early versions of prepaid legal insurance. Germany had such plans back in the 1930s. However, it was not until the 1960s that certain U.S. Supreme Court cases paved the way for American prepaid legal plans. Backed by the American Bar Association, the first prepaid plan in modern America began in 1971 in Shreveport, Louisiana, where the General Contractors Association provided limited legal services for union members.

These events set the stage for Harland C. Stonecipher to start Pre-Paid Legal Services. In the June 2, 1986 *Forbes*, he explained one of the reasons for his career choices. "When you grow up a sharecropper's son like I did, you make a list of things you don't want to do for the rest of your life. I didn't want to farm." Stonecipher was the only person in his family to finish high school and attend college. He went to East Central University in Ada, Oklahoma, near his hometown of Tupelo.

After he left college in 1961, Stonecipher began teaching English, debate, and drama. He loved teaching but not its low pay, so in 1966 he quit teaching and began selling life insurance. He did quite well in his new career, and by the early 1970s he considered starting his own life insurance company instead of working for someone else.

Then in 1972 Stonecipher, still a life insurance salesman, had a serious car accident that changed his life. He found his insurance covered both his car and medical bills but not his legal expenses of several thousand dollars. He thought why not have legal insurance, so he first approached the Oklahoma insurance commissioner to gain approval for his idea. He then started Pre-Paid Legal's predecessor company, an Oklahoma "motor service club" which offered reimbursement for legal expenses.

Stonecipher began his business in Ada, a farming and college community of about 17,000 located a couple hours drive southeast of Oklahoma City. Many at first laughed at his idea, and he had to rely on friends to help finance the new enterprise.

In the November 1987 *Nation's Business*, the founder reflected on the somewhat haphazard origins of Pre-Paid Legal.

434

Company Perspectives:

To provide middle America with affordable access to quality attorneys and to the legal system of the United States of America through exceptional customer service and rigorous screening of all Provider and Referral Law Firms.

"If I hadn't had the accident, I probably would have started a life-insurance company. If you wait until you know all the answers, you're not going to start. My theory is simple: ready, fire, aim. I think that's the story of anybody who makes a success. What that means is that you adjust your course as you go along. Looking back, it seems like everything I've done was like jumping off a cliff. But it seems like when I've jumped, things have come out fairly well."

In January 1976 Stonecipher incorporated Pre-Paid Legal Services and acquired its predecessor through a stock exchange. Stonecipher became the chairman, president, and CEO. In 1979 Pre-Paid Legal became a public corporation when its stock was traded on the NASDAQ exchange.

1980s: Expansion and Troubled Times

Pre-Paid Legal and its predecessor firm in its first 10 years used typical marketing strategies in the insurance industry to sell its legal insurance. In 1982 sales reached $4 million, then Harland Stonecipher decided to take the advice of an old friend named John Hail that multilevel marketing (MLM), also known as network marketing, was a legitimate and effective way to sell goods and services. Hail created the independent firm called TVC Marketing Associates to promote Pre-Paid Legal as an experiment in a few states.

Pre-Paid Legal's use of MLM started out great. In just one or two years Pre-Paid Legal sales had jumped to $8 million. The results were so favorable that Stonecipher in 1985 purchased TVC and began using network marketing as the sole means of selling its legal services contracts.

Pre-Paid Legal also used its distributors to market a small radio device called Companion Caller in 1985. Designed by Dr. R. Darryl Fisher, Companion Caller was available to automatically contact a central office in case of emergencies.

By 1987 Pre-Paid Legal had recruited over 200,000 sales associates, who were independent contractors, like distributors in other MLM firms. Each paid $55 to sign up. It also began using network marketing to sell a package of noninsurance services called TVC Advantage. For an annual fee of $120, members received a toll-free telephone number to receive the guaranteed lowest prices on some 250,000 brand-name items.

Not everyone thought multilevel marketing was a great way to sell legal insurance. In 1985 Christopher P. Nolan worked as a Pre-Paid Legal Services salesman, but he felt MLM was more suited for selling a tangible commodity. He left Pre-Paid Legal and worked for a competitor, but frustration at how its services were marketed caused him to start his own firm. Nolan founded Landmark Legal Plans Inc. in Denver and was profiled in *Inc.* in

September 1988, but three months later his firm had almost completely collapsed. Nolan's new firm had been supported by a Denver law firm that provided legal advice for Landmark's customers. However, that same law firm worked with several Landmark competitors, including Pre-Paid Legal. The law firm decided to drop Landmark.

Pre-Paid Legal of course continued to work with the Denver firm and other law firms around the nation. Its revenues jumped from $4.5 million and 39,836 policies sold in 1983 to $42 million and 229,632 policies in 1986. In spite of this rapid growth, Pre-Paid Legal in 1987 still maintained modest headquarters in Ada, Oklahoma. It remodeled a former car dealer's showroom instead of building new offices.

The reality was that Pre-Paid Legal suffered a severe cash shortage at the time. In an interview in the July/August *Success*, Stonecipher described this most serious crisis in his firm's history. "[We] didn't have the cash to keep growing. So in 1986, we basically shut down our marketing, laid off half our office staff, and just focused on maintaining the accounts we had. Our sales force went from 50,000 to 1,500. It was a terrible thing.

"When we started I was still supporting my family on my renewal commission income from my life insurance career. There were numerous weeks that to meet our payroll of $600 or $700 a week, I would go down to the bank to mortgage my house furniture. After 1986 we went eight years without recruiting. We were $23 million in debt. People thought we were dead."

Pre-Paid Legal in 1987 made a major change in its legal services. It no longer offered the type of contract called an open plan, where consumers could choose their own attorneys. The company began selling only closed plans in which clients had to choose from a network of attorneys created by Pre-Paid Legal. Usually, the company contracted with one law firm per state. Provider attorneys received a fee for each customer in their area. Of course, Pre-Paid Legal continued to honor the open plans signed before 1987, but those declined as time passed. By 1997 about 85 percent of Pre-Paid Legal's business concerned closed contracts. Meanwhile, Pre-Paid Legal in October 1986 changed from using NASDAQ to the American Stock Exchange. Its AMEX symbol was PPD.

While Pre-Paid Legal was barely surviving in the late 1980s, several other firms had entered the rapidly growing field of legal insurance. The National Resource Center for Consumers of Legal Services estimated that in 1987 about 30 million Americans were enrolled in a prepaid legal plan. From about 1985 to 1987, newcomers to this industry included the Montgomery Ward Signature Group, which sold its plan through direct mail. In just two-and-a-half years it sold 200,000 plans. Other firms using direct mail to promote legal insurance included Hyatt Legal Services and Jacoby & Meyers. Amway used its distributor network to sell 14,000 plans in just eight states within one year of starting its Ultimate Legal Network.

The American Bar Association conducted a 10-year study which concluded that in the late 1980s some 70 percent of Americans, mostly middle-class, seldom if ever used a lawyer's service. Pre-Paid Legal and other prepaid legal firms were encouraged by these statistics indicating many more people were potential customers.

1990s: Stable Growth and More Services

As the new decade began, Pre-Paid Legal Services found it was keeping enough customers to generate some cash to pay off part of its huge debt. To raise more money, Harland Stonecipher decided to offer additional stock, which resulted in gaining several million dollars from investors. That gave the firm the resources to expand in major ways in the 1990s and dramatically reverse its earlier poor showing.

Pre-Paid Legal in 1993 began seeking contracts with large businesses, defined as those companies with at least 1,000 employees.

In the 1990s Pre-Paid Legal offered several different prepaid plans. About 40 percent of its customers worked for a company with legal insurance as a benefit funded by payroll deductions. Some 60 percent of all Pre-Paid Legal customers chose one of five individual options.

In 1997 over 90 percent of individual Pre-Paid Legal customers chose the Family Plan, which allowed the customer to have preventive legal services such as unlimited toll-free phone consultations, correspondence, will preparation, and review of all legal documents. The Family Plan also covered trial defense, Internal Revenue Service audit assistance, and motor vehicle legal services. By 1997 the firm was offering its Family Plan in Spanish in states such as Florida, California, and Texas.

Since 1986, the company has offered its Commercial Driver Legal Plan designed for truck drivers and others who drove commercial vehicles. Underwritten by the Road America Motor Club, this plan's benefits included legal assistance in case of moving and nonmoving violations, arrest and bail bonds, tragic accident defense, car rental discounts, and ambulance services.

In 1991 Pre-Paid Legal began offering its Law Officers Legal Plan, which provided many benefits in the Family Plan, plus 24-hour emergency telephone access to attorneys and also legal assistance for any administrative and post-termination hearings.

The firm's Small Business Legal Plan was first developed and marketed in 1995. Small businesses with a maximum of 15 employees and no more than $250,000 net annual income received limited legal correspondence for debt collection or other business disputes, limited document reviews, certain trial defense benefits which increased each year the contract was renewed, and limited other legal consultations and services.

Pre-Paid Legal added two other plans for targeted groups in the 1990s. In 1993 it developed the School Teachers Legal Plan to help teachers facing administrative hearings. Two years later the company worked with a CPA firm to introduce its Tax and Financial Services Plan, designed to help Pre-Paid Legal sales associates receive the legal advice needed to prepare their state and federal income tax forms.

Regardless of the specific legal plan, Pre-Paid Legal customers were entitled to limited benefits. For additional services from a provider attorney, they received a discount, usually 25 percent off standard hourly fees. Average prices for new legal plans increased from $165 in 1993 to $215 in 1996.

In the 1990s Pre-Paid Legal added some new features to its multilevel marketing system. Beginning March 1, 1995, it introduced a level commission schedule where commissions of about 25 percent were paid during each year customers paid their premiums. Previously, Pre-Paid Legal had paid first-year commissions of around 70 percent, followed by commissions in later years of about 16 percent.

A second innovation to the MLM system was the creation of the regional vice president (RVP) program in July 1996. Pre-Paid Legal Services at that time promoted 14 of its top distributors to become regional vice presidents. This decentralization gave each RVP the responsibility to train sales associates within his or her area.

Third, Pre-Paid Legal began on January 4, 1997 a one-day classroom and field training program for sales associates. This optional program allowed new associates to pay $249 covering their regular $65 enrollment fee and also the enhanced training and opportunity to advance faster in the firm's MLM program. Current associates paid just $25 for this new Fast Start Program, which by 1997 already was helping to increase associate productivity.

By the end of 1996, Pre-Paid Legal had 110,350 active sales associates, an increase from 78,281 active associates in 1995. The company defined active associates as those who sold at least three new contracts per quarter or retained his or her personal contract. Similar to other companies using MLM, a significant number of sales associates or distributors worked part-time.

Pre-Paid Legal also was developing a cooperative marketing strategy where insurance companies and other service companies would use their established agents to offer the various Pre-Paid Legal plans in addition to their regular policies. In its 1996 annual report, Pre-Paid Legal stated it had "mixed success with cooperative marketing arrangements in the past and is unable to predict with certainty what success it will achieve, if any, under its current cooperative marketing arrangements."

Another marketing strategy used by Pre-Paid Legal in the 1990s took advantage of the fame of sports celebrities. In 1993 the company entered a marketing agreement to use the services of Roger Staubach, the former Dallas Cowboys quarterback. In 1996 Fran Tarkenton, another former National Football League quarterback, joined the Pre-Paid Legal Board of Directors. In May 1997 Pre-Paid Legal added membership in the Fran Tarkenton Small Business NETwork as one of the benefits of subscribing to its Small Business Legal Plan. This new benefit allowed small businesses to receive motivational audio tapes, newsletters, advice on setting up a web site, and various other aides. This was a good example of the joint operations characteristic of business life in the Information Age.

Like all businesses, Pre-Paid Legal was concerned about government laws and regulations. In 1997, according to a Salomon Brothers report, only 14 states regulated prepaid legal services companies as insurance businesses, while the American Bar Association monitored the interaction between Pre-Paid Legal and similar firms with their provider attorneys.

There appeared to be some confusion on regulation of this new industry. The situation in California, the leading state in social and economic trends, illustrated this disorder. A California Bar official in a July 9, 1996 *Los Angeles Times* article stated prepaid legal service firms were not required to register with the bar, but that the various plans came under state Insurance Department rules. However, representatives of the California Insurance Department said the bar, not the state agency, regulated the plans.

By 1997, Pre-Paid Legal had contracts with 35 law firms, ranging in size from 10 to 60 attorneys. For example, the Columbus law firm of Maguire, Vivyan and Schneider was the only firm in Ohio authorized to provide legal services for Pre-Paid Legal customers. Pre-Paid Legal began marketing its individual plans in Ohio in February 1995.

The nation's various plans were represented by a trade organization, Chicago-based American Prepaid Legal Services Institute. In 1996 the institute's executive director reported that 90 percent of all prepaid plan subscribers were satisfied with their plans, most state bars had approved prepaid plans, and that they were increasing by 10 percent annually. A 1997 Salomon Brothers report verified that last statistic. It reported that the industry grew 11 percent from 29.5 million consumers 1995 to 33 million in 1996.

Fueling this growth were several general trends in the 1990s. First, increasing litigation over all kinds of issues has increased the need for access to an attorney. The growth of the concept of individual rights unheard of in past years has helped create this litigation. Second, attorneys have become more aggressive in seeking work for themselves, influenced by a 1977 U.S. Supreme Court decision that lawyers have a right to advertise. With more lawyers graduating from law school, they needed ways to find work, even if it meant working under reduced fees through prepaid legal insurance plans. Third, an increasing number of Americans were starting home-based businesses, including those using multilevel marketing. Formerly often ridiculed, MLM gained respect for successfully marketing a wide range of goods and services, from MCI and Sprint long-distance services to Franklin Quest day planners. Salomon Brothers emphasized, "Network marketing is Not a Pyramid Scheme," in its report on Pre-Paid Legal on May 29, 1997.

With all these positive reasons for Pre-Paid Legal's future success, there was a major trend that would tend to damper those prospects. First, more individuals seemed to despise attorneys and thus sought other alternatives. The self-help movement has empowered such individuals to gain knowledge on their own and not rely on professionals. John Naisbett in *Megatrends*, Alvin Toffler in *The Third Wave*, and many others agreed that the computer revolution has given average persons the ability to access information and thus gain more control over their own decisions. Doctors, lawyers, and other professionals obviously had not disappeared, but their roles were changing as the new millennium approached.

In any case, Pre-Paid Legal's prospects in 1997 looked pretty good for the immediate future. With no debt and $18 million in cash, the firm was poised for major expansion. Founder Harland Stonecipher in the July/August 1997 *Success*

predicted that all the big insurance companies will soon offer legal insurance and that his own firm would have $1 billion in annual sales within just five years. That confidence was echoed by *Forbes* on November 4, 1996, including Pre-Paid Legal as one of the 200 best small companies in the U.S. And both Sovereign Equity and Salomon Brothers in 1997 rated Pre-Paid Legal stock as a "Strong Buy."

In 1997 Stonecipher remained at the Pre-Paid Legal helm after 25 years, but the transition to new leadership already was underway. In March 1996 the firm's directors elected Jack Mildren, the former Oklahoma lieutenant governor who in January 1995 was chosen as Pre-Paid Legal's president, to replace Stonecipher as CEO. At the same time the company appointed Randy Harp, its chief financial officer, to the new position of chief operating officer.

Then in February 1997 Mildren resigned as Pre-Paid Legal president, CEO, and director. Wilburn Smith was appointed to be the president and a new board member. Stonecipher re-assumed the position of CEO.

With this new management team in place, Pre-Paid Legal moved forward in 1997 to meet the challenges of a rapidly changing industry.

Principal Subsidiaries

Pre-Paid Legal Casualty, Inc.; Pre-Paid Legal Services, Inc., of Florida; National Pre-Paid Legal Services of Mississippi, Inc.; Legal Service Plans of Virginia, Inc.; Ohio Access to Justice, Inc.

Further Reading

Anderson, Duncan, "Toughness," *Success*, July/August 1997, pp. 27–28.

Brokaw, Leslie, "Autopsy of a Start-Up [Landmark Legal Plans]," *Inc.*, July 1989, p. 79.

Cadwallader, Bruce, "Prepaid Legal Representation a Boon for Average Joe," *Columbus [Ohio] Dispatch*, June 25, 1995, p. 5C.

Greene, Sheldon L., "Is 'Lawcare' Next?" *Nation*, December 11, 1972, pp. 591–93.

Gubernick, Lisa, "Pyramid Play," *Forbes*, June 2, 1986, p. 125.

Hanania, Joseph, "Who's Minding the Prepaid Legal Service Plans?" *Los Angeles Times*, July 9, 1996, p. E3.

Hyatt, Joshua, "Cheap Counsel," *Inc.*, September 1988, p. 102.

Kovach, Jeffrey L., "Will Clearer Tax Picture Boost Prepaid Legal?" *Industry Week*, June 10, 1985, p. 19.

McLinden, Steve, "The Future of Law May Be in 'LMOs' [legal maintenance organizations]," *The Business Press*, July 14, 1995, p. 14.

Moreland, Jonathan, "Lay-Away Lawyers," *Individual Investor*, December 1995, pp. 48, 50.

"Pre-Paid Legal Services, Inc.—Redefining the Legal Industry," *Salomon Brothers: United States Equity Research*, May 29, 1997.

"Pro's Pick: Legal Care," *USA Today*, August 20, 1996.

Reid, Jeanne, "Prepaid Legal Service: They Offer Advice Without Criminally High Prices," *Money*, April 1987, p. 43.

Thompson, Roger, "Ready, Fire, Aim," *Nation's Business*, November 1987, p. 77.

Urbanski, Al, "Lawyers Go Mass Market," *Sales & Marketing Management*, August 1987, p. 32.

—David M. Walden

Qualcomm Inc.

6455 Lusk Boulevard
San Diego, California 92121-2779
U.S.A.
(619) 587-1121
Fax: (619) 452-9096
Web site: http://www.qualcomm.com

Public Company
Incorporated: 1985
Sales: $813.9 million (1996)
Employees: 6,000
Stock Exchanges: NASDAQ
SICs: 3663 Mobile Communications Equipment

In 1959, two former engineering classmates at the Massachusetts Institute of Technology, Irwin Jacobs and Andrew Viterbi, reunited at an academic conference and resowed the seeds of a friendship that during the 1960s evolved into a consulting business and then, in 1968, into Linkabit, a San Diego-based manufacturer of digital communications equipment.

After graduating from MIT in 1959, Jacobs had become a professor of electrical engineering and in 1965 authored *Principles of Communication Engineering*, later described as "the first comprehensive textbook on digital communications." Viterbi had gone into research, helping to design the telemetry equipment of the first successful U.S. satellite, Explorer I, and playing a pioneering role in developing the potential of digital transmission technology for the telecommunications systems of space and satellite equipment.

At Linkabit, Jacobs and Viterbi applied their considerable talents to developing satellite communications applications for the television industry and by 1980 had transformed tiny Linkabit into a thriving communications enterprise with more than 1,000 employees and over $100 million in sales. In August 1980, Linkabit merged with M/A-COM, forming M/A-COM Linkabit, a developer of cable television, data transmission, and other electronics technologies. Though Jacobs had risen to M/A-COM's executive vice presidency by 1983, mobile satellite communications technology had developed to the point where both he and Viterbi saw a golden opportunity to create a new business with the potential to dominate its industry. If they could work out the as-yet-unsolved technical obstacles, Jacobs and Viterbi reasoned the wireless mobile communications (WMC) market was so young—and so complex—that they could grab an insurmountable three- to five-year headstart over any future competition.

Revolutionizing the Trucking Industry: 1985–88

In 1985 they therefore left M/A-COM (which was later sold and broken up) to form Qualcomm Inc., a provider of contract research and development services and which *Business Week* later described as a "tiny military house." Their real goal, however, was a full-fledged integrated research-to-manufacturing business, and they began to cast about for an application of digital satellite communications with commercial potential. Military uses were considered first but Jacobs soon decided that the transportation industry offered the best opportunity for building a WMC-based company.

If there was any segment of the U.S. transportation industry that needed the help of wireless, long-distance communications it was the trucking industry. Valuable shipping time was routinely lost as truckers pulled off the road to call into their dispatchers with updates on their location and expected arrival, and dispatchers' inability to precisely monitor and coordinate their fleets' schedules meant many "deadhead" miles as truckers wasted return trips with empty trucks that could have been used to haul more freight. Moreover, shippers themselves often had to act as ersatz dispatchers, continually checking in with trucking companies to see if their shipments would arrive on time. To solve these problems, between 1985 and 1988 Jacobs and Viterbi began developing a wireless, two-way messaging and positioning system that would enable trucking firms to closely track their drivers' progress across their routes while enabling drivers and dispatchers to send messages to each other.

Christened OmniTRACS, the system would lease the capability of existing communications satellites to create continent-wide coverage. Qualcomm's proprietary signal processing technology meant that OmniTRACS could operate without interfering with other satellite transmissions, and the position-reporting component would use either the federal government's Global Positioning System (GPS) satellites or a signal generated on a leased satellite using Qualcomm's own automatic satellite position-reporting system. Down on earth, a keyboard-and-terminal hardware and software package would be located next to the driver in the cab and a huge integrated network management facility in San Diego would route messages between truckers and dispatchers.

By 1988 Qualcomm was ready to unveil OmniTRACS to the public. Jacobs invited 300 trucking industry leaders to San Diego for a demonstration of the 30-pound device. It worked, and within months Qualcomm had signed up its first customer—Schneider National Inc. of Wisconsin, one of the largest long-haul truckers in the country. The Schneider contract alone was worth $20 million and involved 5,000 trucks, and by the end of 1989 Qualcomm's revenues had soared to $32 million. Qualcomm established OmniTRACS systems for Canada and Europe, and in August 1991 OmniTRACS enjoyed its first profitable month. On the eve of Qualcomm's initial public stock offering as a public corporation in the fall of 1991, it landed a deal to launch OmniTRACS for Brazil's and Japan's trucking industries, and by early 1992 more than 23,000 OmniTRACS terminals had been installed worldwide by some 150 transportation companies and 50,000 trucks and their dispatchers were generating 400,000 messages and position reports each day. By 1993 Jacobs was being anointed by *Fleet Owner* magazine as "The Man Who Changed Trucking."

Revolutionizing the Cell Phone Industry: 1989–91

In the late 1940s, AT&T's Bell Laboratories conducted the first test to determine the commercial feasibility of cellular communication technology. In 1970 the Federal Communications Commission (FCC) set aside radio frequencies for land mobile communications and by 1977 had announced the construction of two cellular development systems in Baltimore/Washington and Chicago. A U.S. cellular phone industry began to emerge in the 1980s, and by 1985 some 300,000 Americans were making cell phone calls from their car phones. It was clear to Jacobs and Viterbi that the analog transmission technology with which the cellular industry had started would eventually be replaced by digital signals (which transformed the electrical signals of the traditional phone into the zeros and ones of computer technology), and they began to develop a new standard that they hoped would become the sole medium by which all cell phone calls would eventually be made. In 1989, however, the Cellular Telecommunications Industries Association adopted a cell phone standard developed by Sweden's Ericsson called time division multiple access (TDMA), which divided phone conversations into blocks of digital data that were streamed one after the other over specific radio frequencies, allowing cell phone channels to carry three to six times as many callers as traditional analog systems.

Jacobs and Viterbi's own standard, called code division multiple access (CDMA), took a different approach. Instead of assigning an entire frequency channel to each cell phone call, CDMA tagged each conversation with a code that could be identified and retrieved only by the phone of the intended recipient. Once coded, the call was divided into 10 different digital pieces that were then transmitted across all available cell phone channels. By thus using the cellular frequencies more efficiently, voice quality could be sustained over greater distances, reducing the number of antennas needed to cover a given territory and cramming twice as many conversations onto the airwaves as TDMA phones—and 10 times as many as analog phones.

The catch was twofold: the cell phone industry had already adopted TDMA, and Qualcomm's CDMA was untested and, as far as the industry was concerned, thus only a theory. In 1989 Jacobs nevertheless pitched CDMA's advantages before the Cellular Telecommunications Industries Association. He was given a cool reception but resolved to rally the financial support of key industry firms to conduct a series of tests that would conclusively establish the superiority of CDMA over TDMA. The wireless division of Pacific Telesis agreed to commit $2 million toward a CDMA trial, and throughout 1989 Qualcomm lined up some $30 million to construct limited CDMA test networks in San Diego and New York City. While Qualcomm closed licensing or development agreements with such companies as Nokia, Motorola, Northern Telecom, and Sony; established international CDMA partnerships in Europe, Japan, and Canada; and convinced AT&T and Nynex to adopt the CDMA standard for their cellular service, it continued to test CDMA's call quality, coverage area, and call capacity.

In November 1991, 14 international and domestic cellular carriers and manufacturers conducted a large-scale field validation test of Qualcomm's CDMA technology. The tests were conclusive enough to convince the Cellular Telecommunications Industries Association to reopen the cellular standard debate. Buoyed by the news that its technology might indeed become the new cellular standard, Qualcomm nevertheless faced a daunting challenge. A national CDMA infrastructure simply did not exist, and to make CDMA cell phones a commercial reality a huge base station and network system had to be created—at Qualcomm's expense. To help raise the funds, Qualcomm went public in December 1991, generating $53 million.

While Jacobs and Viterbi were recasting Qualcomm into a cellular industry giant, they were also pursuing other cutting-edge technologies. In 1991, Qualcomm continued research on high-definition television signal processing components, data link systems, specialized modems, and custom VLSI (very large scale integrated) circuits, as well as a number of classified communications-related research projects for the U.S. government. It also formed a joint venture with satellite-maker Loral Corporation to develop a network of low earth orbit satellites called Globalstar that would use CDMA technology to provide—beginning in 1998—mobile communications service to regions of the world that could not be economically served by ground-based cellular systems. It also unveiled Eudora, a cross-platform email software program originally licensed from the University of Illinois that by 1997 claimed some 18 million Internet users.

CDMA Approaches Critical Mass: 1992–94

Though 1992 represented the third straight year in which Qualcomm suffered a net loss, its sales continued to climb and its future continued to brighten. In 1992 it prepared for the rollout of CDMA in 1993 by signing a technology agreement with Nokia and a licensing agreement with Northern Telecom; by promoting CDMA in Korea, Australia, Switzerland, and Germany; and by opening regional offices in Pittsburgh, Dallas, Atlanta, Salt Lake City, and Washington, D.C. It secured a license from the FCC to tailor CDMA technology for the new personal communications service (PCS) niche of the cellular industry and created a PCS corporate group to create applications for this market. By bundling traditional cellular phone service with paging, messaging, fax, and email service all from a single all-purpose "pocket communicator," PCS appeared to have become the future of CDMA and of the cell phone industry as a whole.

Sales of OmniTRACS meanwhile leaped 68 percent over 1991 to 36,000 installed units and 200 trucking customers in North America. In 1992, OmniTRACS's first and largest customer, Schneider National Inc., renewed its OmniTRACS contract; Qualcomm added Werner Enterprises, one of the five largest truckload carriers in the United States, to its stable; and Mexico, Japan, and Brazil committed to adopting the Omni-TRACS system in 1993.

The tidal shift toward the CDMA cellular standard began to snowball in 1993: the U.S. Telecommunications Industry Association adopted CDMA as a cellular standard; three Bell regional operating companies and Alltel Mobile Communications placed orders with Qualcomm and its partners for CDMA handsets and infrastructure equipment; and major telecommunications firms conducted tests of CDMA service. Internationally, companies in Korea and the Philippines placed orders with Qualcomm for CDMA systems, and Chile, China, India, Malaysia, Pakistan, and Russia signed memoranda edging them closer to the adoption of Qualcomm's CDMA technology for the wireless local loops (WLL) that would take the place of traditional copper wire for connecting telephone switching centers to homes in the developing world. OmniTRACS, however, re-

mained—for the time being—Qualcomm's money machine, and the company sold 62 percent more units in 1993 than it had the year before. Moreover, 50 new trucking firms adopted the system—including J.B. Hunt, the largest truckload carrier in the United States.

In 1994 the CDMA rollout anticipated for 1993 was delayed until 1995 while the FCC began auctioning off PCS licenses to potential service providers and Qualcomm battled off patent suits brought by competitors who claimed it had lifted its CDMA technology from their own research. A growing number of U.S. cellular carriers—now including AirTouch, GTE, Sprint, and Ameritech—prepared to deploy or test CDMA-based PCS service in major American markets, and the International Telecommunications Union adopted CDMA as one of four global wireless communications standards. Moreover, China and Argentina began testing CDMA cellular systems, and Qualcomm opened offices in Beijing, New Delhi, and Buenos Aires. With more and more companies signing onto the CDMA/PSC standard, Qualcomm moved to fill the void of manufacturers offering CDMA/PCS equipment by partnering with Sony Electronics to to create Qualcomm Personal Electronics, a joint venture to manufacture and market up to a million PCS cell phones a year.

OmniTRACS had meanwhile increased its customer base to 425 and by the end of 1994 was processing 2.5 million trucking messages and position reports every day on 13,000 Omni-TRACS units in 25 countries. Qualcomm augmented its Omni-TRACS software offerings by acquiring Integrated Transportation Software Inc. in 1994 and continued to integrate the 10,000 customers of Motorola's CoveragePLUS ground-based radio operation it had acquired in late 1993 into its OmniTRACS network. Qualcomm's long-planned Globalstar satellite communications system also got a welcome boost when Qualcomm signed the largest development contract in its history—valued at $266 million—to develop Globalstar's ground communications equipment and telephones.

Qualcomm Arrives: 1995–97

For all the billions spent on development, testing, equipment, and market by mid-1995 CDMA still remained a largely unknown quantity. In a feature article on Qualcomm's battle to establish CDMA as the cellular standard, Britain's *Economist* magazine described CDMA as a "clever—but fiendishly complicated and unproven—technology" that was still "a good year away from the market" and one that might never be made to work as well as the thoroughly operational TDMA standard. Moreover, despite 1995 earnings estimated at only about $30 million, Wall Street investors had hopefully driven Qualcomm's stock valuation to an atmospheric $2.4 billion. What is more, Qualcomm was entering a telephone equipment market in which it was dwarfed by such giants as AT&T, NEC, and Motorola.

Nevertheless, by July 1995 Qualcomm could claim that 11 of the 14 largest telephone carriers in the United States had committed to CDMA. In addition, 12 cell-phone suppliers, including Motorola, NEC, Mitsubishi, Matsushita, and Sony, had each paid Qualcomm $1 million for its CDMA technology, and six manufacturers—including AT&T, Northern Telecom, and Motorola—had each surrendered $5 million for the right to make CDMA network equipment. From its CDMA royalty fees and microchip sales alone Qualcomm stood to profit handsomely in the years to come. In August 1995, it raised $500 million in a public stock offering to fund its transformation from a cellular standard licenser to a cellular phone maker.

By partnering with virtually every major telecommunications carrier and manufacturer in as many markets as it could, Qualcomm sought to translate the CDMA PCS market from an idea into a foregone conclusion almost overnight. In late 1995 the first telephone calls on a commercially installed system using CDMA were made by Primeco customers, and AirTouch announced plans to launch the first commercial CDMA system in Los Angeles.

Qualcomm's equipment joint venture with Sony received an $850 million order for handheld phones in 1996, and by mid-year a Qualcomm/Sony truck departed from San Diego for the East Coast with thousands of PCS phones ready for delivery to Primeco customers. When it was discovered that a software bug rendered the phones' menu screens inoperable, however, a Qualcomm team was dispatched to the Primeco warehouse with the software fix. Four days later, the 40,000 handsets had been reprogrammed and overnighted to Primeco's anxious retail outlets. With a potentially damaging PR gaffe evaded, in March 1997 Qualcomm introduced its newest PCS handset, the Q phone. Motorola sued Qualcomm for stealing the Q phone design from Motorola's own StarTAC phone, but a San Diego court ruled in Qualcomm's favor a month later.

By mid-1997, 57 percent of all digital wireless systems under construction used Qualcomm's CDMA standard, which now boasted some 4 million users, and Primeco and Sprint had agreed to spend $850 million over the next two years to buy Qualcomm/Sony handsets. Handsets and equipment orders from China, Korea, Russia, and Chile were expected to add another $500 million to Qualcomm's coffers, and Qualcomm made plans for new equipment factories in Asia and Latin America. In June 1997, it opened a Moscow sales office and could claim that it had licensed CDMA to over 45 leading telecommunications manufacturers worldwide.

Because it was wedded to the CDMA standard, however, Qualcomm's fortunes as a cellular phone maker were threatened by its larger phone-making rivals, who had long offered handsets for every cellular standard. Nevertheless, by the end of its 1997 first quarter, Qualcomm's sales were a full 165 percent greater than a year earlier, and with the penetration of the U.S. wireless communications market expected to increase from 16 percent to 48 percent by 2006, Qualcomm appeared to have plenty of room to grow. Its one-time cash cow, OmniTRACS, had in the meantime grown to encompass 200,000 terminals at 800 transportation companies in 32 countries worldwide. When Qualcomm announced in May 1997 that San Diego's Jack Murphy sports facility had been officially renamed Qualcomm Stadium, Jacobs and Viterbi's dream of building a communications business that could dominate its industry appeared to have been fulfilled beyond anyone's rosiest expectations.

Further Reading

Aguilera, Mario, "CDMA Gets the Press While OmniTRACS Pulls the Qualcomm Wagon," *San Diego Transcript*, January 6, 1995.

Armstrong, Larry, "Qualcomm: Unproven, But Dazzling," *Business Week*, September 4, 1995.

Crawley, James, "Telecom Valley," *San Diego Union-Tribune*, March 1, 1994.

Douglass, Elizabeth, "Tracking Trucks Ia Big Business for Qualcomm," *San Diego Union-Tribune*, April 14, 1989.

Mele, Jim, "The Man Who Changed Trucking," *Fleet Owner*, October 1993.

"Qualcomm Spars with Motorola," *Business Week*, April 21, 1997.

"Satellite System Helps Trucks Stay in Touch," *New York Times*, June 5, 1991.

Schine, Eric, "Qualcomm: Not Exactly an Overnight Success," *Business Week*, June 2, 1997.

"Shorts Circuited," *Economist*, July 29, 1995, p. 45.

Therrien, Lois, "Cellular Phones: The Static Is Getting Louder," *Business Week*, January 28, 1991.

"Trucking Looks to the Sky for Its Future," *Industry Week*, April 3, 1989.

—Paul S. Bodine

QUICK&REILLY
MEMBER NEW YORK STOCK EXCHANGE

The Quick & Reilly Group, Inc.

230 South County Road
Palm Beach, Florida 33480
U.S.A.
(407) 655-8000
Fax: (212) 747-5651
Web site: http://www.quick-reilly.com

Public Company
Incorporated: 1974 as Quick & Reilly, Inc.
Employees: 1,169
Sales: $507 million (fiscal 1997)
Stock Exchanges: New York
SICs: 6211 Security Brokers, Dealers and Flotation
Companies; 6289 Services Allied with the Exchange
of Securities or Commodities, Not Elsewhere
Classified; 6719 Offices of Holding Companies, Not
Elsewhere Classified

The Quick & Reilly Group, Inc. is the holding company for Quick & Reilly, Inc., one of the three largest discount brokerage houses in the United States in the 1990s, with 13 percent of the market in 1996. Another subsidiary, U.S. Clearing Corp., was the third largest in its field, maintaining accounts and clearing securities transfers for hundreds of banks and brokerage firms. A third, JJC Specialist Corp., was engaged in softening price volatility for hundreds of stocks on the New York Stock Exchange. It was the second largest firm in this field. Quick & Reilly was an industry leader in efficiency and profitability; in 1995 it ranked second on a list of the 10 most profitable brokerage houses by profit per employee.

Private Company, 1974–83

Leslie Quick, Jr. ran an unsuccessful money-management firm before teaming with Kevin Reilly in 1974 to form a small New York City brokerage house, mainly with borrowed money. When the federal government eliminated fixed commission rates in 1975, Quick & Reilly, with a staff of only four, was the first company with a seat on the New York Stock Exchange to offer a significant discount to the public—40 percent below the standard rate—for its no-frills service. Like full-service houses, the company assigned each customer a particular broker, but these officers did not receive commissions nor offer investment advice.

Major Wall Street brokerage houses were already offering discounts to institutional investors, but they were so angered by Quick & Reilly's action that one threatened to withdraw new issues from a firm that was merely processing trades for Q&R. In a 1984 speech to the annual meeting of the Securities Industry Institute, Quick told brokers that they had "created the discounters" by "a lack of concern for your customers." He said clients who had come over to Quick & Reilly had spoken of "bad experiences" with other firms after stocks these companies recommended fell in value "and there is no one there to tell them what to do."

Although Quick & Reilly was first on the discount scene, the public did not immediately beat a path to its door, and before the year was out Reilly had left the firm. The situation changed after the company received a mention on television news. In Quick's words, "people walked in with shopping bags loaded with stock certificates." But vital to increased business, Quick found after taking a short-term lease on a Palm Beach, Florida, office, was an accessible place for customers. "You need branch offices," he told a *Forbes* reporter in 1982. "National 800 numbers don't bring in very big business. People want to feel they can walk right in." Establishing branch offices set Quick & Reilly (and Schwab & Co.) apart from run-of-the-mill discounters.

By 1979 Quick & Reilly was doing so much business that it had to assume processing trades itself under the newly formed subsidiary U.S. Clearing Corp. That fiscal year (the year ended February 28, 1979) the company earned $948,000 on revenues of $14 million—up from $6 million the previous fiscal year. Three years later the totals had swelled to $5.9 million and $40.5 million, respectively. By then the company had found a major revenue source—38 percent in fiscal 1982—in interest, mostly earned on margin accounts.

Quick & Reilly had 18 offices in nine Eastern seaboard states and the District of Columbia by 1980. That year it opened its first Midwest branches, in Chicago, Cincinnati, Cleveland, Detroit, and St. Louis. In 1983 the firm established itself west of the Mississippi River for the first time, opening five California offices as well as branches in Denver, Phoenix, and Seattle.

Quick & Reilly entered a new field when it bought the assets of Colin, Hochstin Co. for $2.8 million in 1982. Among its activities Colin, Hochstin functioned as a specialist—a market maker—for 27 stocks on the New York Stock Exchange. As a specialist, the company had an effective monopoly in the trading of these stocks, dampening price volatility and maintaining orderly markets by selling when the public was buying and buying when the public was selling. Quick & Reilly's new operation was named JJC Specialist Corp.

Growing in the 1980s

A holding company was established in 1981 for the Quick & Reilly brokerage subsidiary (which the following year began underwriting and dealing in tax-exempt bonds issued by states and their subdivisions), JJC Specialist, and U.S. Clearing (which in 1983 was clearing securities transactions for 18 brokerages besides its own and 9 banks and banking groups). In 1983 the parent company had 38 offices in 20 states and the District of Columbia. That year it became a public company, raising $16.8 million for the firm and about the same for its existing shareholders by offering common stock at $18 a share. Quick, his children, and a family trust retained about 62 percent of the shares.

Quick & Reilly began offering clients research reports by the firm's securities analysts in 1984, for an annual fee. The following year the company started taking orders by computer for subscribers to the CompuServe Information Service, months after it had become the broker for Citibank customers who had on-line accounts. It was only the second broker to allow customers to fill in an application electronically. "If he's cleared by Quick & Reilly, he can start trading the next day," said an executive of the company furnishing the link between the brokerage firm and CompuServe.

By 1986 Quick was presiding over a family empire. One son was chief operating officer, responsible for the holding company's day-to-day operations. Three other sons ran the three subsidiary units, and a daughter was editor of the company newsletter. The Quicks were known as cost-control obsessives, initialing each bill from each branch—roughly 500 a month—before payment. Quick & Reilly maintained a staff of only 15 at headquarters and bought all its office furniture used. Brokers started out making only $18,000 a year, but they—and other employees, including clerks—received bonuses allotted from 30 percent—later one-third—of each branch's profits. True to its founder's maxim, "We don't have to be the biggest, we just have to be the most profitable," the company was opening only five to six new branches a year. During fiscal 1986 Quick & Reilly had net earnings of $11.8 million on revenues of $73.3 million.

The stock market crash of October 1987 put an end to Quick & Reilly's unbroken string of annual record profits and earnings. Because of its reluctance to make acquisitions the firm had accumulated a $60 million cache, mostly invested in municipal

bonds. This enabled it to ride out a drop of 20 percent in sales and about 60 percent in earnings. Quick & Reilly's cash holdings also enabled it to acquire specialists undermined by the crash. After the firm acquired the specialist unit of Drexel Burnham Lambert in 1990, it was the market maker for 82 New York Stock Exchange stocks. Quick & Reilly also bought five discount brokerages during fiscal 1989 and 1990, bringing its total of branch offices to 64 in 27 states and the District of Columbia. And it was clearing trades for 81 banks and brokerages, an activity responsible for nearly half the holding company's revenue of $106 million in fiscal 1990.

Booming in the 1990s

Quick & Reilly held 12 percent of the discount brokerage market in 1992. That year a *New York Times* study found that it was charging less in commissions than Schwab or Fidelity Brokerage Services Inc., the two companies in the field larger than Q&R. However, the firm did not offer as many services as its two larger rivals. To narrow the gap, Quick & Reilly began making it possible for customers to call and get help researching financial information on publicly held companies, including Standard & Poor's latest earnings estimates. And the company announced, as part of a $5-million advertising campaign, that it would refund commissions to customers who complained in writing, within 45 days of a trade, about any aspect of the broker's service. The guarantee did not apply to declines in stock prices. Two years later the firm said only .01 percent of its trades had resulted in refunds.

Quick & Reilly moved its headquarters to Palm Beach in 1992 and acquired the specialist operations of Stokes, Hoyt & Co., bringing its roster to 123 companies listed on the New York Stock Exchange. Although a risky operation during selling panics, specialist-trading was yielding 40 percent pretax earnings for Quick & Reilly. The firm acquired the brokerage and specialist business of Spears Rees & Co. in 1993 and by late 1994 had the second largest specialist operation on the New York Stock Exchange. The firm's U.S. Clearing Corp. also was a major source of business, accounting for about 40 percent of revenues. By late 1994 it was the fourth largest clearing firm in the United States, and by 1997 it ranked third.

Quick & Reilly increased its marketing budget to as high as $8 million in 1994 in order to keep up with Schwab and Fidelity and fend off competition from dozens of discounters offering even lower rates than the Big Three. Its services now included 24-hour touch-tone access to account and stock information. The company had 825,000 clients in 1995. That year it opened its first office in a bank branch, in Palm Beach. Within a year this office had brought in over $20 million in business. Thomas Quick, president of Quick & Reilly, said, "This is allowing us to experiment in smaller communities where it might not make sense from an overhead point of view" to open a stand-alone office.

Quick & Reilly began clearing transactions in 1996 for institutional investors in Great Britain and Switzerland, establishing its first overseas branches in London and Zurich. In November of that year the company introduced QuickWay Net, its Internet trading service. In addition to offering stock, options, and mutual-fund transactions for $26.75 a trade, lower than its standard minimum fee of $37.50, QuickWay Net offered unlimited free quotes and portfolio management tools and was a marketing aid for U.S. Clearing, which offered banks and brokerages software to give their customers Internet access to portfolios, market and company news, and real-time stock quotes. Certain national publications called QuickWay Net the most user-friendly link of this type. In January 1997 Quick & Reilly greatly expanded the specialist segment of its business by agreeing to purchase Nash Weiss & Co., a specialist for 2,500 over-the-counter stocks on the NASDAQ exchange.

From 1992 through 1996 the revenues and profits of discount brokerages grew twice as fast as those of full-service brokers. Quick & Reilly's revenues and net income rose for the fifth consecutive year in fiscal 1994. The following year net income dipped slightly, a development the firm blamed on rising interest rates and adverse market conditions. In fiscal 1996 net income soared to $69.4 million on revenues of $443.9 million, for a pretax profit margin of 37.7 percent, compared to the industry average of 16.4 percent. In fiscal 1997 the company earned $82 million on revenues of $507 million. Quick & Reilly had no long-term debt in 1996. The Quick family held about 35 percent of the stock that year, with the senior Quick continuing as chairman and chief executive officer.

Quick & Reilly had 116 offices in 34 states and the District of Columbia at the end of fiscal 1997. It represented more than 2,100 mutual funds provided by outside vendors. U.S. Clearing was clearing all securities transactions for 330 correspondent firms. JJC Specialist was making markets in 278 New York Stock Exchange issues. Nash Weiss & Co. became a subsidiary for the firm's specialist activities in the over-the-counter market. Clearance commissions and income accounted for 48.6 percent of company revenue in fiscal 1997, while interest came to 36.8 percent and trading to 11.8 percent.

Principal Subsidiaries

JJC Specialist Corp.; Nash, Weiss & Co.; Q&R Capital Corp.; Q&R Charter, Inc.; Quick & Reilly, Inc.; Quick & Reilly Tara Corp.; U.S. Clearing Corp.

Further Reading

Bianco, Anthony, "Charles Schwab Vs. Lee Quick," *Business,* May 12, 1986, pp. 80–83.

Cassidy, Anne, "The Lean and Mean Way to Fat Profits," *Venture,* August 1988, pp. 74–75.

Friedman, Jon, "Like Father, Unlike Son at Quick & Reilly," *Business Week,* September 17, 1990, p. 132.

Hensley, Scott, "Quick & Reilly Opens Office in a Florida Bank Branch," *American Banker,* August 23, 1995, pp. 1, 13.

——, "For Quick Profit, Discount Broker Alliance," *American Banker,* April 9, 1996, p. 8A.

Kansas, Dave, "Fervor Grows in Discount Broker Battle," *Wall Street Journal,* February 7, 1994, pp. C2, C7.

Newman, A. Joseph, Jr., "Quick & Reilly Reveals Plan to Develop and Sell Research Reports," *American Banker,* March 14, 1984, pp. 3, 11.

Phalon, Richard, "We'll Come Out All Right," *Forbes,* November 9, 1992, pp. 162, 164.

Power, William, "Irreverence Doesn't Slow Quick & Reilly," *Wall Street Journal,* August 1, 1991, p. C1.

——, "Quick & Reilly, with Strings Attached, Offers Money-Back Guarantee on Trades," *Wall Street Journal,* March 16, 1992, p. C16.

"Quick & Reilly Buys Colin Hochstin Assets, But Won't Assume Ex-Partner's Liabilities," *Wall Street Journal,* August 25, 1982, p. 2.

Siwolop, Sana, "A Premium Buy Among Discount Brokers?," *New York Times,* January 26, 1997, Sec. 3, p. 3.

Stern, Richard L., "Next?," *Forbes,* January 18, 1982, pp. 38–39.

Tyson, David O., "Broker to Feature On-Line Application," *American Banker,* May 3, 1985, pp. 3, 5.

Van Allen, Peter, "Quick & Reilly Unit Targets Banks Through Internet Trading System," *American Banker,* February 5, 1997, p. 11.

——, "Quick & Reilly Targets Cable TV Audience in Advertisement for Its On-Line Service," *American Banker,* March 12, 1997, p. 8.

Willoughby, Jack, "Quick & Reilly Picks Through Mabon's Clearing Customers," *Investment Dealers' Digest,* January 9, 1995, pp. 6–7.

Zigas, David, "The Slow and Steady Success of Quick & Reilly," *Business Week,* February 1, 1988. p. 73.

—Robert Halasz

RailTex, Inc.

4040 Broadway, Suite 200
San Antonio, Texas 78209
U.S.A.
(210) 841-7600
Fax: (210) 741-7629

Public Company
Incorporated: 1993
Employees: 850
Sales: $121.1 million
Stock Exchanges: NASDAQ
SICs: 4011 Railroads, Line Haul Operating; 4741 Rental
    of Railcars; 6517 Railroad Property Lessors

RailTex, Inc. is the leading short line railroad operator in the United States. Short line railroads are created when large, main line railroads such as Union Pacific, Burlington Northern/Santa Fe, or Norfolk Southern decide to jettison a few hundred miles of unprofitable feeder rail to concentrate on core traffic. Most rail freight originates or terminates on feeder lines, so their upkeep is vital to the main line—yet the larger, Class I railroads no longer want to invest in running them. That is where companies like RailTex step in, purchasing the short line and then charge the main line a fee for every car that comes from that feeder line onto the main track.

According to Bill Loftus, president of the American Short Line Railroad Association, short line railroads account for 541 out of the nation's 550 railroads, 36 percent of the route miles, 11 percent of those employed on a railroad, and 9 percent of the rail industry's revenue. About 12 companies compete for short line acquisitions and, of those, RailTex has a clear lead.

In the late 1990s, Railtex managed approximately 3,800 miles of feeder track in the United States, Canada, and Mexico, and has interests in Kazakstan and Brazil. Its 897 profit-sharing employees are cross-trained and, unlike the average railroad, 96 percent of Railtex employees do not belong to unions. From 1990 to 1996, the company posted an average yearly growth of

33 percent and operating revenue rose from $21.4 million to $121.1 million.

RailTex, Inc. was founded in 1977 by entrepreneur Bruce Flohr, no stranger to the railroad business. After a tour with the Army Corps of Engineers in Alaska, he went to work with Southern Pacific as a train-crew brakeman in 1965. He rose to superintendent of Southern Pacific's San Antonio Division until, in 1975, he became deputy administrator of the Federal Railroad Administration. In 1977, he returned to San Antonio and started raising money from venture capitalists to start a new company—he had decided there was an untapped market for the leasing of railcars.

Tracking Tactics: RailTex 1977–88

RailTex got off to a slow-rolling start in San Antonio with Flohr's own $50,000 and another $50,000 from investors. The new enterprise almost derailed in the first five years because of poor economy and high inflation rates. RailTex was struggling, and by 1982, with revenues of $2 million, the company still was not profitable.

Always the entrepreneur, Flohr reorganized his small, hand-picked team of railroad veterans. He and his team began to seek consultancy contracts with small railroads. Many short lines were also having trouble being profitable, and Flohr figured if he and his team of experts could help the smaller companies back on their feet, he would diversify his revenue base.

The strategy was a stroke of luck and a turning point for the company. They discovered that the smaller lines were in desperate need of competent management and marketing. Never one to hold back on a hunch, Flohr decided to purchase the San Diego & Imperial Valley Railroad, owned by Kyle Railways, Inc. Although a Big Six accounting firm report to Kyle warned that the line would always operate at a loss and could only remain open by government subsidy, Flohr was unimpressed. "I didn't think the consultants understood the industry," he said, and made a successful bid on the property.

He then needed to acquire a locomotive. All of his leasing cars were just that—cars, not engines. A new locomotive cost

---

Company Perspectives:

RailTex, Inc., is North America's leading short line railroad organization, providing freight service over approximately 3,800 miles of track in the United States, Canada, and Mexico. The Company's strategy is to grow though additions to its portfolio of short line railroad and other properties, seeking overall diversification with respect to geography, customers, commodities, and connecting railroads; and improvement in the operating performance of newly added and currently operated properties. RailTex believes its expertise in adding railroad properties to its portfolio and its focus on customer service and operating efficiency positions it to effectively implement its strategy.

---

about $1 million, but older models sold for a tenth of that. RailTex acquired a remanufactured 1950s-era diesel, laid off the union employees that had worked the line, and put in place salaried, non-union workers that were paid a fraction of the union wage. According to *Inc. Magazine* writer Jay Finegan, unionized trains run with a crew of three to four that were each paid $23 dollars an hour on average—and are limited in the kinds of jobs they are contracted to do. Non-union employees can fix the track as well as run the train, can make sales calls when they are in the station, and can do maintenance work. Union contracts forbid that kind of multi-tasking.

RailTex is able to operate its trains with two multi-functional employees, called transportation specialists or "transpecs," paid on a salary that averages $10–$15 an hour. RailTex transpecs receive generous medical benefits and also profit-sharing bonuses. The principle of hiring non-union, flexible workers became one of the cornerstones of RailTex's profitability.

To complete the transformation of the San Diego & Imperial Valley Railroad, Flohr decided to hire three marketing managers for the line—an unprecedented approach, when much larger railroads tended to employ only one marketing person. The team of three sought business from alongside but also five and ten miles from the track. Traffic increased from 1,600 cars per year to 6,000 in three years.

With this taste of success, the leasing-car-company-cum-railroad-operator tried its hand at a second line in 1986, the Austin & Northwestern Railroad. In three years, the traffic had increased from 2,700 cars per year to 9,000, and RailTex was operating 325 miles of rail.

Choosing the Right Route: RailTex 1989–93

Meanwhile, the leasing car business was back on track and Flohr was defining his approach to what had become a two-pronged company. RailTex had its roots in the leased car business and operated a fleet of 600, with customers demanding he buy more. Simultaneously, short lines that Flohr was confident RailTex could turn around and make profitable were popping up for sale across the country. The company had limited

capital resources, and Flohr knew he could only choose one future. He sold the railcars to Chrysler Corp in 1989. "It was like throwing out the baby with the bathwater, because we took our original line of business and dumped the whole thing," he told *Inc. Magazine* in February 1993.

Since then, the company has never looked back. RailTex immediately launched a wholehearted acquisitions strategy and has not stopped. In 1989, RailTex revenues were at $16.6 million and leaped to $39.3 million in 1992. With over 100 locomotives and 2,400 miles of track, RailTex's combined assets were at $81 million and rising. *Railway Age* gave RailTex its prestigious "Short Line of the Year" award, unique that year because *Railway Age* honored not just one line, but the portfolio of 20 lines that comprised RailTex.

Pleased by accolades but undistracted, Flohr continued to refine his growth plan. Smart acquisitions policy and follow-up with smart management were the core of RailTex's success strategy. RailTex only sought out certain kinds of short lines to buy—those with a relatively small crew, comparatively small purchase price, and those with a strong likelihood of good business for years to come. Flohr liked to see clean, well-run factories next to his lines, not aging businesses in disrepair. Then, once a new line had been added to the fold, RailTex dispatched its "Go Team," a formalized group of RailTex employees that operates the line under its first several weeks of RailTex management. The Go Team hired, trained, and supervised until the RailTex culture and entrepreneurial spirit were ingrained in the new acquisition. Finally, the railroad was released to market itself and set its own policies, with guidance from headquarters on large purchases, accounting, sales strategy, technical policies, and little else. The general manager of each rail ran the business as an autonomous unit.

A Public Success Story: RailTex 1993–97

RailTex went public in November 1993. With a new supply of capital from its stock offering, the company plunged into its most aggressive purchases up until that time: the Central Oregon & Pacific Railroad and the New England Central Railroad (NECR). The line was a special challenge for RailTex. An offset of the then government-owned Canadian National (CN) rail, the unionized employees didn't want CN to accept the RailTex proposal. When CN did, there was bad feeling all around. Nevertheless, many of the workers chose to drop their union allegiance, accept less pay, and hire on as multi-capable RailTex employees. By the end of the year, *Railway Age* had given its "Short Line of the Year" distinction for 1995 to NECR for overcoming tremendous initial turmoil to become a highly profitable and well-organized team.

By the end of 1995, with over 3,300 miles, RailTex opted for a second public offering. Also in 1995, the company created a subsidiary, RailTex Distribution Services, Inc. (RDSI), to help companies find the best logistical means to transport their materials.

"We are transforming from a highly entrepreneurial company to a more structured, results-oriented company," said Flohr in 1995. Free of the day-to-day operations responsibilities of the company and with a talented management team in place,

Flohr questioned his own role as the head of RailTex. Entering his fifties, he wondered if he could perhaps hold the company back, if perhaps hiring "professional management" was not in order. Flohr studied company leadership and recrafted his role at RailTex to one of corporate visionary. This led him to eventually put in place railroad insider Henry M. Chidgey as president and COO and to place himself in the role of chairman of the board and CEO. Flohr decided to leverage his time in the acquisitions, shareholder relations, and the constant study of ways to improve and streamline RailTex processes.

"At the onset of 1996," Flohr wrote in his 1996 shareholder address, "we established clear goals and accountabilities for producing extraordinary results in every area . . . . One primary area targeted for improvement in 1996 was same store growth in operating revenue. Through a revitalization of our marketing team and improved processes to link field marketing personnel with the resources of our senior marketing staff in San Antonio, we exceeded our goal, bringing in new revenues of $5.5 million."

As one of the many results of Flohr's decision to put an accent on vision for the future, RailTex expanded its fleet of railcars almost 41 percent in 1996, from 2,694 to 3,085. In 1997, plans were to purchase another 3,000. This purchasing boom came about to increase RailTex's independence and ability to serve its customers. In the past, when customers needed a specialized railcar, RailTex would likely have to lease the car from one of the large railroads. Now, with a large and diverse fleet of boxcars, gondolas, covered grain hoppers, and "intermodal" cars that accept semi-truck trailers, RailTex can provide for its customers directly.

In 1996 RailTex also began to look outside of North America for acquisitions. In September of that year, RailTex International Holdings, Inc., a wholly owned subsidiary, purchased almost 13 percent equity in the 4,400-mile Brazilian Ferrovia Centro Atlantica S. A. (FCA) rail. Much larger than other RailTex properties, the FCA nevertheless had much in common with the much shorter lines RailTex was used to turning around. Like the NECR acquired from Canadian National, the FCA used to be a government-owned railroad, and was now making the transition, under RailTex, to a market-driven, capitalist enterprise. Late in the year RailTex also took on a 6 percent interest in a newly formed railroad named the Ferrovia Sul Atlantica, S.A. (FSA), which assumed operations for 4,200 miles of rail in southern Brazil.

Wholly owned subsidiary RailTex Distribution Services, Inc. (RDSI) took on the first privatization of rail in the former Soviet Union, providing consulting services to the new Tengizchevroil (TCO) rail, a limited liability partnership between a Kazakstani oil company and Chevron.

Despite expansion into international arenas, RailTex found that the 1995–96 period was generally slow in acquisitions for all short line operators. Mergers among the large railroads slowed down decision-making on casting off feeder rail. In 1997, RailTex stock was exposed to a jerky decline, falling to $14.25 on April 25, below its initial public offering price of $16 in 1993. Start-up of the company's largest acquisition to date, the Detroit, Toledo, & Ironton Railroad (DTI), and loss due to the collapse of a wall in a coal mine served by Railtex were considered factors in the loss of net income.

However, compared to the first quarter of 1996, carloadings increased by 27 percent to 109,698 in fiscal 1997, operating revenues increased by 19 percent to $34.2 million, and operating income increased by 2 percent to $5.1 million. As a part of an overall strategy to boost stock value for shareholders, the company hired a new vice president for development and acquisitions, Greg Petersen, whose background is similar in airline transportation.

Although the first half of 1997 may have been a little shaky from a stockholder's point of view, long-term prospects for continued RailTex growth remain excellent. Between 1990 and 1996 RailTex's compound annual growth per share was a healthy 19 percent. The voracious appetite of the short-line giant will have a smorgasbord of offerings to choose from in the next few years. Privatization of rail is a trend that will continue in Canada, which expects to free 10,000 miles of track in 1997 and 1998, and in the former Soviet Union. Closer to home, Mexico, with which RailTex has a long-term agreement, is set to shed miles of government rail. In the U.S., the Burlington Northern-Santa Fe merger should result in 4,000 miles of track up for grabs. The acquisition of Contrail by CSX and Norfolk Southern could result in divestures in two to three years. Union Pacific, which recently merged with Southern Pacific, will want to slim down to a trunk line, potentially offering several more thousands of miles. Flohr, who acknowledges a passion for acquisitions, is also eyeing tempting properties in Australia. RailTex keeps eight of its staff busy on acquisitions, and although 1995 and 1996 were slow by RailTex standards, 1997 promises to blow the boiler lid off.

Principal Subsidiaries

RailTex International Holdings, Inc.; RailTex Trac Co., Inc.; RailTex Distribution Services, Inc.

Further Reading

Allen, Margaret, "RailTex Will Benefit from Railroad Commission Grant," *San Antonio Business Journal,* June 20, 1997, p. 31.
Burke, Jack, "Mergers, Capital Concerns to Accelerate Spin-Offs of Shortline and Regional Railroads," *Traffic World,* June 19, 1995.
——, "Shortline Competition Heats Up," *TrafficWorld,* August 26, 1996.
Evert, Ed, "Short Line Marketing: How Old Ideas Create New Profits," *Progressive Railroading,* October 1992.
Finegan, Jay, "The Continuously Improving CEO," *Inc. Magazine,* February 1993.
Hendricks, David, "RailTex Seeks New Railroads," *San Antonio Express-News,* May 22, 1997, p. E1.
Weber, James, *RailTex, Inc.,* Harvard Business School: Boston, 1994.

—Lisa Calhoun

RemedyTemp, Inc.

32122 Camino Capistrano
San Juan Capistrano, California 92675
U.S.A.
(714) 661-1211
Fax: (714) 489-2940
Web site: http://www.remedystaff.com

Public Company
Incorporated: c. 1965
Employees: 51,400
Sales: $285.52 million (1996)
Stock Exchanges: NASDAQ
SICs: 7363 Help Supply Services

RemedyTemp, Inc. provides temporary staffing of a clerical or a light industrial nature to mid-sized industrial and service companies, professional organizations, and government agencies. The company utilizes technology and value-added services to provide clients with solutions to their staffing problems. RemedyTemp offers its clients temporary staff—called "associates"—for full-time, long-term temporary, short-term temporary, and part-time work assignments. The company also maintains a full-time placement service. Headquartered in San Juan Capistrano, California, RemedyTemp has franchises throughout the United States, in Mexico, and in Canada.

Jobs for Middle-Market Companies in Clerical and Light Industries

Historically, RemedyTemp targeted middle-market companies with 50 to 500 employees. These clients allowed the temporary-help supplier to expand its revenues and profitability in an environment with less price-cutting and competition than the national market. RemedyTemp earned a reputation for providing more personalized, value-added services and for building closer relationships with decision makers at client companies, thus promoting longer client relationships.

RemedyTemp offered the following types of jobs to clients: office/clerical; computer applications; call center and customer service; light industrial; manufacturing; technical; shipping and receiving; and distribution. Clerical positions, one of the larger job categories, included secretaries, word processors, receptionists, accountants, bookkeepers, telemarketers, computer operators, and other office staff. Light industrial work jobs—done by mechanical assemblers, machine operators, stock clerks, forklift operators, lab technicians, electronic engineers, and mechanical engineers—comprised the second large job category supplied by RemedyTemp.

RemedyTemp focused on clerical and light industries as core business segments. Since 1991, clerical and light industries contributed $12 billion in revenues to the temporary-help arena, growing at an annual rate of 18 percent. Staffing Industry Analysts, Inc., found that clerical and light industries were worth $25 billion combined and accounted for about 60 percent of the total payroll for temporaries in the United States during 1995 alone. Paul W. Mikos, president and chief executive officer, explained in a *Business Wire* press release: "Our focus on the rapidly growing clerical and light industrial markets places us in the two largest segments of the temporary staffing industry; and we have successfully targeted middle-market accounts which represent high growth areas in U.S. business."

Value-Added Work Force Support

RemedyTemp was among the first temporary-help suppliers to offer value-added work force support—such as human resources services—to clients, especially in the area of office technology. The company used proprietary information technology widely in obtaining and maintaining relationships with clients, placing associates, and managing temporary-help resources. RemedyTemp initiated technology programs that provided extra services for its client base. According to Mikos, quoted in a *Business Wire* news release, "Our proprietary information-based technology programs continue to differentiate RemedyTemp and provide us with a competitive advantage in the marketplace. Specifically, our HPT and EDGE Systems help to provide superior client services, positioning RemedyTemp as the 'intelligent staffing' provider in the industry."

Winning Attitudes and Intelligent Staffing

Studies long established that attitude was the primary criterion for employers when contracting temporary help. In his 1996 president's letter, Mikos explained: "We learned that employee attitude was the most critical factor. While clients expect temporary employees to have basic skills at a minimum, attributes such as attitude, work ethic, and fitting in with their corporate culture are the key criteria from their point of view." RemedyTemp, then, adopted the Human Performance Technology (HPT) evaluation system that predicts how employees will perform on the job. Based on a testing method developed by Detroit-based HRStrategies, HPT was similar to tests used by *Fortune* 500 companies such as General Motors, Chrysler, Ford, AT&T, Pepsi Cola, and Hewlett Packard. HPT's multimedia tests measured attitudes in varying work situations, as well as work habits, initiative, team work, and adaptability. An individual's scores allowed RemedyTemp to ascertain that person's attitude, work ethic, and flexibility. The company looked for people with "will do" attitudes: employees who demonstrated initiative, teamwork, dependability, and an ability to learn. (Employees who simply possessed acquired skills or technical knowledge might have "can do" abilities, but not the gumption or flexibility of someone with a "will do" attitude.) HPT test results profiled associates; then RemedyTemp matched associates to corporate profiles to ensure that its temporary workers would fit in well wherever they were placed. Using the HPT method, Remedy-Temp increased the productivity of its associates, as well as shortened training and orientation schedules for client companies, hence lowering costs—even worker's compensation costs.

RemedyTemp also developed technology to better match its associates with client companies. The company designed an Intellisearch database that held client and associate profiles, HPT results, skill test results, and associate recommendations. This technology allowed clients to search for specific associate qualifications that meshed with their specific needs. Extensive use of the Intellisearch database resulted in longer assignments for associates and improved perceived quality of the temporary-help service operations of RemedyTemp.

Giving Clients the EDGE

RemedyTemp created an automated time keeping and management program—Employee Data Gathering and Evaluation (EDGE) System—to facilitate the onsite management of temporary staff. The EDGE System offered clients online access to workforce hours, costs, attendance, and performance evaluations. The system easily tracked hours, monitored costs, showed labor costs, reported head count, projected costs, and forecasted future needs and costs. According to Mikos, quoted in a 1997 *Business Wire* release, "Our proprietary EDGE Systems remain a major marketing differentiator for RemedyTemp, and we now have 102 EDGE Systems installed throughout our customer base, with average annual sales of approximately $1 million per installation. During each week of our second fiscal quarter, one new EDGE System was installed and an average of 1.5 new EDGE Systems were sold, expanding our reach and enhancing our future growth potential."

The EDGE System operated simply: RemedyTemp associates electronically swiped cards when starting and ending their work days for online tracking of their work hours and productivity. The system required less paper and yielded more timely replacements for habitually late, absent, or unproductive associates. Some client companies also used the EDGE systems for tracking the work of staff hired through RemedyTemp's competitors as well.

A Major Industry Shift

Robert E. McDonough—chairman of the company in 1996—founded RemedyTemp in 1965. He opened the first office in Riverside, California, and followed that one with others located in the western United States. At this time, temporary employees used to be a one-time event for client companies; for instance, a client company might hire a temporary worker to fill in during vacations or sick leaves. Typically, lower-level staff at client companies worked with Remedy-Temp to hire for such positions.

Beginning in the 1980s, however, the role of temporary help changed dramatically. The help supply service industry experienced remarkable growth as the use of temporary workers became planned and purposeful. Client companies, for instance, utilized temporary workers for special projects or during peak seasons. Human resources and purchasing executives assumed responsibilities for hiring temporary help.

Franchisees and Licensees

RemedyTemp traditionally operated independently managed offices in addition to company-owned—direct sales—offices. In the late 1980s, however, RemedyTemp developed a strategy to expand beyond its locations in the western United States in order to play a larger role in the growing help supply service industry. At this time, the company initiated an expansion program that was successful in meeting client companies' demands for strong local offices. RemedyTemp concentrated on developing a growing network of local offices throughout the United States with a national resource base. Henceforth, RemedyTemp focused on opening new local offices—independently owned and operated by experienced business professionals with known records of achievement and entrepreneurial spirit—and new markets. As Mikos revealed in his 1996 president's letter: "We essentially harness the entrepreneurial energy of the new licensees who then build the business in new markets. Once our name has been established, we can then either invest or buy into these new mature markets."

Between 1987 and 1990, RemedyTemp operated independently managed offices as franchises. Franchisees paid RemedyTemp an initial franchise fee and royalties from their gross billings, as well as assumed financial responsibility for their leases and office-related working capital costs such as payrolls. Franchisees employed any management staff and all temporary personnel associated with their individual offices. RemedyTemp processed payroll and invoiced client companies for the franchised offices.

Beginning in 1990, RemedyTemp opened independently managed offices under licensing arrangements. According the RemedyTemp's 1996 management discussion, "The company switched from [a] franchise to [a] license format to exercise more control over the collection and tracking of the receivables of the independently managed offices and to allow the company to grow without being limited by the financial resources of franchisees." Nevertheless, licensed offices operated in a similar fashion to franchised ones. Licensees paid initial fees and assumed all lease and working capital costs. Licensees also employed any management staff for the office, but temporary personnel were employees of RemedyTemp. RemedyTemp also invoiced clients and collected on accounts. The company remitted a percentage of profits to the licensees, the size of which depended on the level of billed hours from the previous contract year.

A New Breed of Temporary Help

The 1990s brought more sophisticated clients and a more strategic use of temporary personnel, changing the role of contingent workers in U.S. businesses. As businesses increased outsourcing, temporary personnel became a significant component in the long-term workforce because they increased a client company's productivity, added flexibility, and contributed to cost efficiency.

Instead of being just transient workers, temporary personnel became more a part of the organizations for which they worked, receiving more perks and benefits. For example, companies allowed temporary personnel to work flexible schedules. Remedy-Temp began a generous benefit program for its associates, although particulars of the programs varied because Remedy/Temp offices were independently owned and operated. Still, Remedy-Temp workers typically received a wide range of benefits: Associates participated in 401(K) plans. An associate's contributions stayed in the plan when his or her assignment ended and resumed upon reassignment. Associates also received bonuses for longevity, holidays, referrals for new hires, and 40-hour-a-week drawings for free gifts or bonuses. In addition, RemedyTemp provided its temporary personnel with medical and dental insurance and a voucher-based child care program.

Most importantly, the company gave its associates on-the-job experience at client locations before actual assignments began and initiated an extensive training program for its associates. The company sponsored free instruction in personal computer software, as well as cross-training in word processing, spreadsheets, database programs, presentation packages, desktop publishing, and Windows and Macintosh operating systems. RemedyTemp also subsidized advanced PC workshops for its associates.

Growth and More Growth

From 1993 through 1995, RemedyTemp added 61 offices. The company's before-tax revenues increased at a compound growth rate of 30.6 percent, amounting to $209 million. Its before-tax income grew at a compound growth rate of 63.7 percent or $6.5 million. In 1995, RemedyTemp placed 93,000 temps at 13,000 client companies, totaling 24.4 million staffing hours.

Through 1995, RemedyTemp operated as an S corporation. In July 1996, though, the company became a public company and changed its status to that of a C corporation. RemedyTemp's initial public offering included 3.57 million shares at $13.00 per share: Company shareholders sold 1.47 million shares, and RemedyTemp issued the rest for net proceeds of $24 million. The company used the proceeds from the sale of stock for shareholder distribution, expansion, technology, and working capital.

More than 90 percent of businesses in the United States utilized temporary help in some capacity by 1996. This amounted to $41 billion in revenues annually for the temporary-help service industry, and about two million temporaries employed weekly in 1996. RemedyTemp placed 109,000 of those temporaries at 14,000 client businesses in 1996—more than 29.3 million staffing hours in the year ending September 29, 1996. In 1996 RemedyTemp added 19 offices, so the company comprised 158 offices in 32 states at this time: 65 offices were company-owned; 93 were independently managed offices (20 franchised and 73 licensed).

Before-tax revenues for the company from 1993 to 1996 increased to $285.5 million—a compound annual growth rate of 32 percent. Before-tax income grew at a compound annual growth rate of 69 percent or $12 million. By the first quarter of 1997, quarterly revenue rose 31 percent to $84.6 million. The company's net income for the quarter was $2.6 million.

Positioned for the Future

With a secure financial footing, RemedyTemp planned to expand market awareness in the future and to increase sales nationwide. The company intended to broaden its role as a national presence by opening additional offices. In a 1997 *Business Wire* release, Mikos commented: "We continued to experience robust sales growth in both our company-owned and independently managed offices. . . . We made significant progress on the expansion of our network of nationwide offices, opening ten new offices during the [first] quarter, eight of which were independently managed and two were company-owned offices." RemedyTemp also expected to market its proprietary data management technology and to develop client relationships further in the future.

Further Reading

"RemedyTemp Appoints John Swancoat Controller," *Business Wire*, September 27, 1996, p. 9270009.

"RemedyTemp, Inc.," *Going Public: The IPO Reporter*, June 24, 1996.

"RemedyTemp Names Two Additional Board Members," *Business Wire*, September 25, 1996, p. 9251003.

"RemedyTemp Reports 32 Percent First Quarter Net Income Growth," *Business Wire*, January 21, 1997, p. 1210013.

"RemedyTemp Reports 61 Percent Second Quarter Net Income Growth," *Business Wire*, April 23, 1997, p. 4231006.

"RemedyTemp Reports Record Results for Third Quarter and Nine Months," *Business Wire*, August 6, 1996, p. 8060216.

"RemedyTemp Reports Record Fourth Quarter; Operating Income up 67 Percent Proforma Net Income Rises 47 Percent," *Business Wire*, November 19, 1996, p. 11190344.

—Charity Anne Dorgan

REMY · COINTREAU

Rémy Cointreau S.A.

152, av. des Champs-Elysées
75008 Paris
France
01 44 13 44 13
Fax: 01 42 25 60 30
Web site: http://www.remy-cointreau.com

Public Company
Incorporated: 1724 (Rémy Martin), 1849 (Cointreau)
Employees: 3,700
Sales: FFr6.8 billion
Stock Exchanges: Paris Frankfurt London
SICs: 2084 Wines, Brandy & Brandy Spirits; 2085
    Distilled & Blended Liquors

Acclaimed the world over for its Rémy Martin cognacs, the group Rémy Cointreau S.A. is also a leading producer and distributor of liqueurs, spirits, wine, and champagne. The company's VSOP, XO Special, top-of-the-line Louis XIII, and other cognacs are enjoyed throughout the world; sales of more than nine million crates per year establish the company as the top-selling VSOP-grade and higher brand of cognac in the world. Cognac is also the company's largest source of revenue, generating approximately one-third of the group's nearly FFr7 billion in annual sales.

Rémy Cointreau produces and distributes fine champagnes under the Krug, Piper-Heidsieck, and Charles Heidsieck labels, and champagnes under the de Venogne, Bonnet, and other labels. Champagne sales reached FFr889 million in 1996. The company's wines, principally from the Bordeaux region, are grouped under the subsidiary Grands Vins de Gironde, and represent the entire range of wine grades, producing more than FFr732 million in sales.

Rémy Cointreau's family of liqueurs and spirits include the famed Cointreau, a white liqueur based on orange peels; the company distributes the Italian liqueur Galliano, rums under the Mount Gay, Barbade, and Saint James de la Martinique labels, the Scotch whiskeys The Famous Grouse and The Mac-allan, as well as the passion fruit-based Passoa, and others. The liqueurs and spirits segment of the group accounted for nearly FFr1.4 billion of Rémy Cointreau's 1996 revenues.

Rémy Cointreau has also built up a distribution network, Rémy Associés, placing the company among the top five alcohol-based beverage distributors in the world. Rémy Associés distributes not only the company's own labels, but also selected labels of other liqueur, wine, and spirits producers. The group is present in over 35 countries, and distributes its products to more than 130 countries worldwide. After more than 200 years, Rémy Cointreau remains one of the largest independent producers and distributors of alcoholic beverages; the group has also remained largely a family affair, led by president Andreé Hériard Dubreuil (from the Rémy Martin side) members of both the Cointreau and Hériard Dubreuil families feature among the company's principal shareholders and on the group's board of directors.

Marrying Traditions in the 1960s

Founded in 1724, Rémy Martin would hold a prominent place in the growth and definition of the cognac category. Established near the town of Cognac, in the Charentes region north of Bordeaux, Rémy Martin developed a reputation for the singularity of its brandy. This singularity would soon be recognized by law. In 1850, a direct correlation was made between the Cognac region's soil and the quality of the area's "eaux-de vie." This correlation would lead to the official delimitation of the Cognac region, into six zones surrounding the city of Cognac itself, in 1909. From there, the law fixed the various cognac appellations, beginning in 1936. Rémy Martin, purchasing from some 2,000 vineyards in the region, concentrated on the highest appellation of "fine champagne Cognac," which required that at least 50 percent of the cognac's contents came from the Grande Champagne zones immediately bordering Cognac.

Rémy Martin remained focused on its line of cognacs until well into the 1960s; the company had remained relatively small, however, ranking only 25th among the region's cognac houses. The death of André Renaud, inheritor of the Rémy Martin tradition, in 1965 would lead the company to the next phase in its growth, that of developing a worldwide distribution network. Renaud's will bequeathed the company to his daughters, with 51 percent going to oldest daughter Anne-Marie Hériard Dubreuil, and 49 percent going to her younger sister Geneviève Cointreau. This development would also represent a first step in the later merger between the Rémy Martin and Cointreau families—and set the stage for a long-running family feud: Geneviève Cointreau was married to Max Cointreau, one of the heirs of the popular French liqueur. André Hériard Dubreuil, husband of Anne-Marie and majority shareholder, was named president of the company, taking active control of operations, while Max Cointreau was named director-general.

The Cointreau company had been founded by Edouard Cointreau and his brother Adolphe near the town of Angers in 1849 to produce a white liqueur, flavored with orange peel, that would grow to become one of France's most popular specialty drinks, particularly with its ready status as a mixer in cocktails. Cointreau, too, would remain entirely a family-run operation. In 1948, a new generation of Cointreaus took over the company's leadership—brothers Robert and Max, and their cousin Pierre—dividing the running of the company among them, with Pierre overseeing the Angers factory, Robert in charge of developing international development, and Max in charge of the distribution network.

Max Cointreau's marriage to Rémy Martin heir Geneviève in 1946 would lead the two companies to a combining of forces in the late 1960s. Both companies were seeking to expand their operations, if only to maintain their independence in an industry that was beginning to show signs of consolidation. In 1969, Cointreau and Rémy Martin joined together to form a distribution network to develop both companies' brands worldwide. In the 1970s, both Cointreau and Rémy Martin would begin expanding their product offerings, acquiring brands and production and distribution agreements to offer a more extensive line of alcoholic beverages.

In 1973, Cointreau acquired Picon, an orange-peel and quinine-based aperitif invented in 1837, as well as the rums of Saint James de Martinique. In the early 1980s, Cointreau would also add the Scotch whiskey Glenturret and the Izarra and Clé des Ducs lines of liqueurs; the company was also preparing new products, including a peach-flavored liqueur Péché Mignon, introduced in 1983, and the passion fruit-flavored liqueur Passoa, launched in 1987. For its part, Rémy Martin focused on expanding its cognac distribution, while acquiring the first of its champagne labels, Krug, in 1977, and diversifying into Bordeaux wines, acquiring the De Luze wine purchasing and exportation firm in 1980. In the mid-1980s, Rémy Martin added two new champagne labels, Charles Heidsieck and Piper Heidsieck, and toward the end of the decade added the Italian liqueur Galliano and the Barbados-based Mount Gay brand of rum. By the late 1980s, Rémy Martin, under André Hériard Debreuil's leadership, had raised itself to the position of the third largest cognac house. By then, Rémy Martin's sales had topped FFr4 billion.

Feuding in the 1980s

Trouble was brewing in the Cointreau family, however. In 1973, Max Cointreau installed son André as head of the newly acquired Picon label. Yet André Cointreau's leadership was called into question by other members of the Cointreau family, in particular by Robert Cointreau. With 40 percent of the company's stock against the 20 percent each held by Max and Pierre, Robert Cointreau called for an audit of the company's operation in 1978, and restructured the company under a holding company—ending the three-member governance of the company—in which he took majority control. At the same time, Robert instituted an amendment in the company's charter restricting sales of the family-held shares to a third party. While Pierre was named president of the new holding company, Max Cointreau was named president of Cointreau S.A., which continued to represent some 70 percent of the company's sales of FFr1.6 billion.

Max Cointreau would not remain long as president of Cointreau—in 1982, Robert and Pierre joined together to relieve their relative of his position. Max Cointreau, in turn, threatened to sell off his 20 percent of the company to a third party, leading Robert and Pierre and the other family shareholders to harden the restrictions on stock sales to third parties. Max Cointreau was effectively forced out of all control of the company. The feuding within the family ranks was dampening the position of the otherwise healthy company. As the battle for control raged on, the company's distribution activities fell into disarray. In 1985, however, the company moved to improve its distribution position, forming a partnership with IDV and Cinzano.

Max Cointreau, meanwhile, was faring no better on the Rémy Martin side. Tensions between the two sisters—and their husbands—flared by the early 1970s. In the late 1960s, Max Cointreau was already suggesting a combination of the Cointreau and Rémy Martin operations—envisaging himself at the lead of the combined groups, a vision that undoubtedly ran counter to those of Robert and Pierre Cointreau on one side, and André Hériard Debreuil on the other. By 1973, Max Cointreau, running for local office, reportedly suspected his brother-in-law André Hériard Debreuil of backing an opposing candidate. Cointreau won the election, but the tension among the family was mounting. The death of Anne-Marie and Geneviève's mother added to the simmering battle for succession of the family operation, with Max and Geneviève chafing under their minority position. The tension finally erupted into an all-out feud in the early 1980s, when the Hériard Debreuils sought to increase the company's capitalization, a move opposed by the Cointreaus. A flurry of court battles—some 22 or more—ensued, lasting until the end of the decade.

Merging in the 1990s

The parallel feuds with Max Cointreau had, perhaps, another effect: forging closer relations between Cointreau, led by Robert and Pierre, and Rémy Martin, led by André Hériard Debreuil. Faced with the growing consolidation of the beverage distribution industry, and competition against such industry giants such as Guinness, Seagrams, and Grand Metropolitan, Cointreau and Rémy Martin reinforced their joint distribution activities, forming partnerships especially focused on the Far East and the U.S. markets. The agreement would provide a boost to Cointreau, which had had only limited success in these markets. For Rémy Martin, which had based much of its growth on conquering these markets—carrying the company to the number three position in cognac sales—the addition of the

Cointreau labels enabled it to present a full line of beverages. In 1988, the two companies further strengthened their links when Robert and Pierre Cointreau purchased 10 percent of Rémy Martin's stock.

That link proved to be a bridge in November 1989 when Rémy Martin and Cointreau announced their agreement—kept secret from Max Cointreau and sons—to merge the two companies. Effected in 1990, the merged operations soon adopted the new name of Rémy Cointreau. Soon after the merger, Max Cointreau and his family sold off their shares—19 percent of Cointreau and 49 percent of Rémy Martin—to competitor Grand Metropolitan.

The merger created a company with more than FFr6 billion in annual sales, and an extensive worldwide distribution network boasting many of the industry's most respected brands. The first half of the 1990s proved difficult years for the company: the recession of the early years of the decade, and its lingering effects on Europe, helped dampen sales of the company's luxury-oriented products. The slipping Japanese economy—an important market for Rémy Cointreau's cognacs—also hurt sales of the company's core revenue generator. Nevertheless, the company's overall revenues would post steady growth toward the middle of the decade, rising from FFr6.4 billion in 1994 to FFr6.8 billion in 1996.

Principal Subsidiaries

E. Rémy Martin & Cie. SA; Les Domanies Rémy Martin; Krug, Vins Fins de Champagne SA et Filiales; Rémy Distribution France; Cointreau SA; Champagnes P. & C. Heidsieck; Champagne F. Bonnet P. & F.; Piper-Heidsiecl Compagnie Champenoise SA; Rémy Associés; Grand Vignobles de l'Aube; Grands Vignobles de la Marne SA; Cointreau Holding GmbH (Germany); Hermann Joerss GmbH (Germany); Rémy Deutschland GmbH; SA Euromarques/Euromerken N.V. (Belgium); Commericial Rovirosa SA (Spain); Destilerias De Vilafranca SA (Spain); Rémy Hellas SA (Greece); Distillerie Riunite Di Liquori Spa (Italy); Acom SA (Luxembourg); Duty Free Distributors International BV (Netherlands); Jacobus Boelen BV (Netherlands); Lestada Multi—Brancch Enterprise Spolka Zoo (Poland); Rémy Calem Vinhos E Bebidas, LDA (Portugal); Denview Limited (Russia); Eurobrands Limited (U.K.); Topline DFD Limited (U.K.); Sainsbury & Company Ltd. (Canada); Vintage Consultants Ltd (Canada); Rémy de Mexico SA DE CV (Mexico); Krug Rémy Cointreau Amérique Inc. (U.S.A.); Piper Sonoma, Inc. (U.S.A.); Rémy Américas, Inc. (U.S.A.); RMS Vineyards Inc. (U.S.A.); Bodega Tres Blasones SA (Argentina); Mount Gay Distilleries Ltd. (Barbados); Cointreau Do Brasil (Licores) Ltda (Brazil); KRC Do Brasil Vinicola Ltd. (Brazil); Rémy Australia Ltd et Filales; Seguin Moreau, Australia Pty Ltd.; Rémy Corée Ltd. (Korea); Cavesde France Ltd. (Hong Kong); Remy China & Hong Kong Ltd. (Hong Kong); Rémy Japon KK (Japan); Rémy Malaisie Fine Wines & Spirits SDN Bhd. (Malaysia); Rémy Philippines Fine Wines & Spirits, Inc.; Rémy (Thailand) Ltd.

Further Reading

Barjonet, Claude, "Cointreau Contre Cointreau," *L'Expansion*, December 19, 1986, p. 71.
Gallois, Dominique, "Une Querelle 'Quinze Ans d'Age,' " *Le Monde*, November 11, 1989, p. 44.

—M. L. Cohen

Rubbermaid Incorporated

1147 Akron Road
Wooster, Ohio 44691-6000
U.S.A.
(303) 264-6464
Fax: (303) 287-2864
Web site: http://www.rubbermaid.com

Public Company
Incorporated: 1920 as The Wooster Rubber Company
Employees: 13,861
Sales: $2.35 billion (1996)
Stock Exchanges: New York
SICs: 2392 Housefurnishings, Except Curtains & Draperies;
   2675 Die-Cut Paper, Paperboard & Cardboard; 2679
   Converted Paper & Paperboard Products, Not Elsewhere
   Classified; 3069 Fabricated Rubber Products, Not
   Elsewhere Classified; 3085 Plastic Bottles; 3086 Plastic
   Foam Products; 3089 Plastic Products, Not Elsewhere
   Classified; 3991 Brooms & Brushes; 3944 Games, Toys
   & Children's Vehicles, Except Dolls & Bicycles; 3999
   Manufacturing Industries, Not Elsewhere Classified

Rubbermaid Incorporated is a leading U.S. manufacturer of housewares and other goods, with an emphasis on innovation, a record of steady growth throughout its history, and a sterling brand name. The firm is the top home products company in the United States and is number two in home products in Europe. Rubbermaid is organized around four core brand-driven units: home products and commercial products, both under the Rubbermaid brand; juvenile products, under the Little Tikes brand; and infant products, under the Graco brand. Started in a kitchen, the company—whose products are now primarily plastic rather than rubber—has been a household name in household products for most of the 20th century.

Began with Toy Balloons and a Better Dustpan

The Wooster Rubber Company got its start in May 1920, when nine Wooster, Ohio, investors pooled $26,800 to form a company to manufacture toy balloons, sold under the Sunshine brand name. The Wooster Rubber Company, contained in one building, was sold to Horatio B. Ebert and Errett M. Grable, two Aluminum Company of America executives, in 1927. Grable and Ebert retained the firm's management. By the late 1920s, a new factory and office building had been constructed to house the prosperous business, but the fortunes of The Wooster Rubber Company fell during the Great Depression. In 1934 Ebert spotted Rubbermaid products in a New England department store, and worked out a merger between the two firms.

Rubbermaid got its start in 1933, when a New England man named James R. Caldwell, who had first entered the rubber business as an employee of the Seamless Rubber Company in New Haven, Connecticut, looked around his kitchen during the depths of the Great Depression to see what he could improve. Caldwell and his wife conceived 29 products, among them a red rubber dustpan. Although the rubber dustpan, designed and manufactured by Caldwell and his wife, cost $1.00—much more than the 39¢ metal pans then available in stores—Caldwell "rang ten doorbells and sold nine dustpans," as he recalled in an interview published in the *New York Times* on May 19, 1974. Convinced there was a market for his products, Caldwell gave his enterprise a name—Rubbermaid—and expanded his line to include a soap dish, a sink plug, and a drainboard mat, selling these products in department stores throughout New England.

In July 1934 Caldwell's fledgling enterprise merged with The Wooster Rubber Company, located in a small town 50 miles from Cleveland, Ohio. Still called The Wooster Rubber Company, the new group began to produce rubber household goods under the Rubbermaid brand name. With the merger, under Caldwell's leadership, The Wooster Rubber Company had a happy reversal in fortunes, and sales rose from $80,000 in 1935 to $450,000 in 1941. Of the 29 new products Caldwell and his wife had thought up in their kitchen in 1933, the company had marketed 27 of them by 1941.

In 1942, however, U.S. involvement in World War II caused the government to cut back civilian use of rubber, so that raw materials would be available for products necessary to the war effort. This eliminated Rubbermaid's housewares business, but the company was able to convert to military manufacturing.

Beginning with rubber parts for a self-sealing fuel tank for warplanes, and moving on to other products such as life jackets and rubber tourniquets, the company manufactured military goods through the end of the war, in 1945. In 1944 Wooster Rubber introduced an employee profit-sharing plan.

Following the advent of peace, The Wooster Rubber Company picked up its prewar activities where it had left off, and resumed production of rubber housewares. Because wartime shortages had not yet been completely redressed, however, no coloring agents were available, and all Rubbermaid products were manufactured in black for several months. In 1947 the company introduced a line of rubber automotive accessories, including rubber floormats and cup-holders.

The company's first international operations commenced in 1950, when The Wooster Rubber Company began producing vinyl-coated wire goods at a plant in Ontario, Canada. By 1956 the plant was producing a complete line of Rubbermaid products.

Began Making Plastic Products in the Mid-1950s

In 1955 The Wooster Rubber Company went public, offering stock on the over-the-counter market. This capital infusion allowed the company to branch into plastic products, and in 1956 a plastic dishpan was introduced. This switch required significant retooling from the manufacture of exclusively rubber goods.

In 1957 The Wooster Rubber Company changed its name to Rubbermaid Incorporated to increase its association with its well-known brand name. The following year, the company began its first expansion beyond its traditional focus on household goods by broadening its targeted market to include restaurants, hotels, and other institutions. Rubbermaid initially produced bathtub mats and doormats for these customers. By 1974 industrial and commercial products provided 25 percent of the company's sales.

After James Caldwell's retirement and a one-year stint as president by Forrest B. Shaw, the company presidency was taken over by Donald E. Noble in 1959. Noble had joined The Wooster Rubber Company as a "temporary" associate in 1941. Also during 1959, Rubbermaid stock was sold for the first time on the New York Stock Exchange. The following year, Rubbermaid's management set a goal of doubling the company's earnings every six years, a goal which was consistently met throughout Noble's tenure. Noble also placed a heavy emphasis on new product development, evidenced by the objective he set

in 1968 that aimed to have 30 percent of total annual sales come from products introduced over the preceding five years.

In 1965 Rubbermaid made its first move outside North America, purchasing Dupol, a West German manufacturer of plastic housewares, whose products and operations were very similar to Rubbermaid's U.S. operations. "Our plan is to grow from within except when an acquisition can lead us into a market we already have an interest in," Noble told the *Wall Street Journal* on August 2, 1965, explaining the company's growth policy during this period.

In 1969 Rubbermaid added the sales party to its traditional marketing efforts, a sales technique first popularized by Tupperware. The party division had its own line of slightly more elaborate merchandise, accounting for around 10 percent of Rubbermaid's sales within five years. Nevertheless, the party plan was not profitable until 1976.

Difficult Years in the 1970s

In the early 1970s Rubbermaid marketed a line of recreational goods such as motorboats and snow sleds, but the company lacked the necessary distribution to support the products and abandoned the effort. "We bombed," the company's vice president of marketing told a *Wall Street Journal* reporter on June 9, 1982.

Rubbermaid continued to grow in the early 1970s, but the combination of government controls on prices and the shortage of petrochemical raw materials caused by the energy crisis of the early 1970s kept a lid on earnings. In 1971 Rubbermaid began to market its products through direct supermarket retail distribution. Although initially profitable, this practice resulted in the company running afoul of the Federal Trade Commission (FTC) in 1973. The FTC challenged the company's pricing policies in connection with its role as distributor, charging Rubbermaid with illegal price-fixing and violations of antitrust laws. The complaint alleged that Rubbermaid engaged in price-fixing between wholesalers because it sold its products directly to some retailers—acting as its own wholesaler—and also allowed other wholesalers to sell its products, while stipulating the price for the products. Rubbermaid discontinued its minimum price agreements with wholesalers and retailers in 1975, citing pending legislation and negative public opinion. In 1976 the FTC ruled unanimously that Rubbermaid had violated antitrust laws and issued a cease-and-desist order to prevent the company from renewing these practices.

As part of its continued growth, Rubbermaid opened a new plant in La Grange, Georgia, in 1974, to relieve demand on its main Ohio plant and to supply the automotive-products division. Despite rising earnings since 1968, a sharp increase in the price of raw materials, combined with a change in accounting practices, caused a large drop in Rubbermaid profits in 1974. By this time, Rubbermaid was selling 240 different items, of which about one-tenth were products introduced that year. The company continued to place strong emphasis on innovation and the introduction of new products, generated by a research-and-development staff of designers, engineers, and craftsmen. This staff built prototypes to be used and critiqued by thousands of consumers, resulting in an eight-month process from drawing board to store.

The company experienced labor unrest in 1976, when 1,100 members of the United Rubber Workers called a strike at Rubbermaid's only unionized plant, in Wooster, Ohio, after rejecting a proposed contract. Although the strike eventually was settled amicably, traditionally the company has sought to minimize union activity by building plants outside union strongholds, in places such as Arizona, where it began construction of a plant near Phoenix in 1987 to serve its western markets. In 1985 the company successfully negotiated a contract with its Ohio workers, providing a three-year wage freeze in return for guarantees against massive layoffs.

Streamlining and Acquisitions in the 1980s

Noble retired in 1980, and Stanley C. Gault took over as chairman. Gault, a former General Electric (GE) executive and a son of one of Wooster Rubber's founders, had grown up in Wooster and worked his way through college in a Rubbermaid plant. Despite the company's record of steady growth throughout the 1970s, caused in part by Rubbermaid's expansion from old-line department stores into discount and grocery stores, Gault felt that the company had become somewhat stodgy and complacent. In 1980 he set out to quadruple its sales (about $350 million in 1981) and earnings (about $25.6 million in 1982) by 1990. Anticipating a recession, Gault streamlined operations and introduced racy new products, such as the "Fun Functional" line of brightly colored containers. Gault's stress on growth through the introduction of new products was exemplified by his continuance of the company's campaign to reap 30 percent of each year's sales from products introduced during the last five years.

By 1983 Gault had eliminated four of Rubbermaid's eight divisions: the unstable party-plan business and the automotive division were each sold at a loss and the European industrial operations centered in the Netherlands, and the manufacture of containers for large-scale garbage hauling were also eliminated.

The remaining divisions were combined into two areas: home products—accounting for about 70 percent of the company's sales—and commercial products. The home-products division was further restructured into seven product groups: bathware, food preparation and "gadgets," containers, organizers, sinkware, shelf coverings, and bird feeders and home horticulture. Rubbermaid continued to advertise heavily in both magazines and on television, emphasizing consumer promotions to get customers into the store and offering rebates and coupons for its products for the first time.

In tandem with the product reorganization, about half of Rubbermaid's middle management was eliminated, and 11 percent of the company's management was fired. Many top spots were filled by former GE employees.

In 1981 Rubbermaid had made its first outright acquisition, buying privately held Carlan, owner of the Con-Tact plastic coverings brand name. In the 1980s Rubbermaid was able to move successfully beyond housewares and institutional customers, entering new industries through the strategic purchase of other companies. The company entered the toy industry in 1984 by buying the Little Tikes Company; went into the booming computer field in 1986, with MicroComputer Accessories; into floor-care products with Seco Industries in the same year; and into the brush industry with a Canadian company, Viking Brush, in 1987.

Following these and other acquisitions, Rubbermaid created additional divisions to accommodate its new product lines. In 1987 a seasonal products division was formed to produce and sell lawn and garden products, sporting goods, and automotive accessories. The following year the company created an office products division, which included MicroComputer Accessories and—eventually—Eldon Industries, acquired in 1990. Little Tikes became the core of a juvenile products division. The three new divisions gave the company five divisions, with the preexisting home products and commercial products divisions.

Rubbermaid formed a joint venture with a French company, Allibert, to manufacture plastic outdoor furniture in North Carolina in 1989. In addition, the company expanded its capacity in plastic and rubber products in 1985 with its purchase of the Gott Corporation, maker of insulated coolers and beverage holders. Rubbermaid formed a second joint venture—with the Curver Group, owned by Dutch chemical maker DSM—in 1990 to make and sell housewares and resin furniture in European, Middle Eastern, and north African markets through Curver-Rubbermaid. This diversification resulted in continued growth throughout the 1980s, despite the rising price of petrochemical resins, the raw materials for plastics. Rubbermaid ended the 1980s with 1989 sales of $1.45 billion.

Major Acquisitions and a Restructuring in the 1990s

Throughout the early and mid-1990s Rubbermaid continued to pump out new products at an amazing rate—about 400 a year—which along with several major acquisitions pushed sales higher every year. Net earnings grew as well, until a major restructuring in 1995–97 cut company profits. Management changes marked the early years of this period as Gault retired in 1991 and was succeeded by Walter W. Williams, who soon retired at the end of 1992. After a brief transition period during which Gault was brought back to the company, Wolfgang R. Schmitt, who had joined Rubbermaid in 1966 as a product manager, became chairman in 1993 after having attained the CEO spot the previous year and having served as co-chairman with Gault during the transition period.

In 1992 the company acquired Iron Mountain Forge Corporation, an America maker of commercial playground systems. Two years later Ausplay, the leader in commercial play structures in Australia, was purchased. Both Iron Mountain and Ausplay became part of the juvenile products division. Also brought into the Rubbermaid fold in 1994 were Empire Brushes, a leading U.S. maker of brooms, mops, and brushes; and Carex Inc., which made products for the burgeoning home health care market. Carex was placed in the company's commercial products division.

As of 1993, Rubbermaid generated only 11 percent of its sales outside the United States, and almost all of that went to Canada. Schmitt aimed to increase nondomestic sales to 25 percent by 2000 (later, this goal was boosted to 30 percent), and began to seek out acquisition and joint venture opportunities to help reach this goal. In 1994 the company entered into a joint venture with Richell Corporation, a leader of housewares in Japan, to form Rubbermaid Japan Inc. After abandoning its stake in Curver-Rubbermaid, a partnership that ended up being noncompatible, Rubbermaid reentered the European housewares market in 1995 when it bought Injectaplastic S.A., a French plastics manufacturer of such items as home and food storage products, camping articles, bathroom accessories, and garden products. Also in 1995 the company bought 75 percent of Dom-Plast S.A., the leading maker of plastic household products in Poland. By 1996 foreign sales were up to 16 percent of overall sales, a rate of increase which if continued would mean the company would fall well short of its 30 percent goal. Nevertheless, in early 1997 Rubbermaid announced that it had entered into a strategic alliance with Amway Corp. to develop and market in Japan a line of co-branded premium Rubbermaid products.

In addition to slow overseas growth, a number of other factors forced Rubbermaid to embark in the mid-1990s on its first major restructuring. In the spring of 1994 the prices of resins, used in nearly all of the company's products, began to rise and eventually doubled, increasing manufacturing costs. Rubbermaid also faced increasing competition in the 1990s as other housewares makers improved their products but kept their prices lower than Rubbermaid's premium prices, leading to customer defections and retailer dissatisfaction with the company's pricing policies.

In response to these difficulties, Rubbermaid began a two-year restructuring effort in late 1995. A charge of $158 million was taken in 1995 to cover such cost-cutting moves as closing nine factories and eliminating 1,170 jobs (the charge was the company's first-ever). An earlier effort to achieve $335 million in productivity savings reached fruition in 1996. That year also saw Rubbermaid streamline its product lines, by eliminating 45 percent of its stock-keeping units (SKUs), which when combined generated only 10 percent of overall sales. The company also added a new infant product division to its organizational chart with its 1996 acquisition of Graco Children's Products Inc., maker of strollers, play yards, and infant swings, for $320 million. But Rubbermaid also divested its office products division by selling it to Newell Co. for $246.5 million in May 1997. At the same time the company merged its seasonal products division into its home products division, combining these operations because they had similar distribution channels. As a result of these moves, Rubbermaid was left with four divisions: home products, commercial products, juvenile products, and infant products.

Despite its mid-1990s difficulties, Rubbermaid Incorporated remained one of the most admired corporations in America. Although management sometimes set goals that seemed unat-tainable, such lofty targets were in keeping with a company that possessed such a rich history of innovation. As the company neared the 21st century, it aimed to generate more than 10 percent of annual sales from new products, to enter a new product category every 12 to 18 months, and to have 30 percent of overall sales come from outside the United States.

Principal Subsidiaries

Rubbermaid Europe S.A. (Belgium).

Principal Divisions

Home Products; Commercial Products; Juvenile Products; Infant Products.

Further Reading

Braham, James, "The Billion-Dollar Dustpan," *Industry Week,* August 1, 1988, p. 46.

Campanella, Frank W., "Wide and Growing Line Spurs Rubbermaid Gains," *Barron's,* October 3, 1977.

Christensen, Jean, "How Rubbermaid Invites Profits," *New York Times,* May 19, 1974.

Deutsch, Claudia H., "A Giant Awakens, to Yawns: Is Rubbermaid Reacting Too Late?," *New York Times,* December 22, 1996, pp. F1, F13.

Farnham, Alan, "America's Most Admired Company," *Fortune,* February 7, 1994, pp. 50–54.

Narisetti, Raju, "Can Rubbermaid Crack Foreign Markets?," *Wall Street Journal,* June 20, 1996, pp. B1, B4.

Neiman, Janet, "New Structure Poured for Rubbermaid Push," *Advertising Age,* November 9, 1981.

Noble, Donald E., *Like Only Yesterday: The Memoirs of Donald E. Noble,* Wooster, Ohio: Wooster Book Co., 1996.

Nulty, Peter, "You Can Go Home Again," *Fortune,* June 15, 1981, p. 180.

Ozanian, Michael K., and Alexandra Ourusoff, "Never Let Them See You Sweat: Just Because Rubbermaid Is One of the Most Admired Companies in the Country Doesn't Mean Life Is Easy," *Financial World,* February 1, 1994, pp. 34–35, 38.

Schiller, Zachary, "The Revolving Door at Rubbermaid: Is CEO Schmitt's Tough Style Driving Executives Away?," *Business Week,* September 18, 1995, p. 80.

Smith, Lee, "Rubbermaid Goes Thump," *Fortune,* October 2, 1995, pp. 90–92, 96, 100, 104.

Stevens, Tim, "Where the Rubber Meets the Road," *Industry Week,* March 20, 1995, pp. 14–18.

Taylor, Alex III, "Why the Bounce at Rubbermaid?," *Fortune,* April 13, 1987, p. 77.

Yao, Margaret, "Rubbermaid Reaches for Greater Glamour in World Beyond Dustpans and Drainers," *Wall Street Journal,* June 9, 1982.

—Elizabeth Rourke
—updated by David E. Salamie

Salomon Worldwide

Metz-Tessy
74996 Annecy Cedex 9
France
04 50 65 41 41
Fax: 04 50 65 42 56
Web site: http://www.salomonsports.com

Public Company
Incorporated: 1947
Employees: 2,820
Sales: FFr4.42 billion (1996)
Stock Exchanges: Lyon Tokyo (through subsidiary)
SICs: 5091 Sporting & Recreational Goods

Salomon Worldwide is going downhill—and they could not be happier. From the foot of the French Alps, Salomon has long held a global leadership position in the design, manufacture, and distribution of ski bindings, with nearly 45 percent of that market; the company is also the world's second-largest designer, manufacturer, and distributor of ski boots (23 percent of the market), and is a prominent player in the high-end and professional alpine ski market. Together with longtime rival and neighbor Rossignol, the leading ski maker, Salomon has helped to make France the dominant force in the worldwide ski market.

While the alpine ski segment makes up the largest part of Salomon's winter sports sales, the company has launched itself into the booming snowboarding market, through the design, manufacture, and sale of boards and bindings, and, through its Bonfire subsidiary, acquired in 1995, in snowboarding and ski apparel and accessories. Salomon is also introducing the winter world to a brand new sport with its 1997 introduction of "snowblades," which the company describes as "on-snow skating."

After 50 years leading the winter sports business, Salomon has also actively diversified into other seasons, so that the company's non-winter products have grown to account for half of its annual sales. Salomon's oldest diversification effort is its Taylor Made subsidiary, the world's second largest designer, manufacturer, and distributor of golf clubs—woods, irons, and putters—and accessories. The introduction of the Taylor Made "Bubble" shaft line of golf clubs in 1995 has increased significantly Taylor Made's contribution to—and position in— Salomon Worldwide. By 1997, Taylor Made's products represented 41 percent of Salomon's group sales, equal to its alpine ski segment sales.

Through the company's MAVIC subsidiary, acquired in 1994, Salomon is also a world leader in top-of-the-line and professional bicycle rims. The company has also built a strong position in the hiking world, with a respected line of summer and winter boots. In 1997, Salomon ventured into the world of in-line skating for the first time, designing, manufacturing, and distributing a line of skates targeted at the high-end and amateur and professional racing markets.

In 1997, the company changed its name to Salomon Worldwide to emphasize its diversified, international status. With eight manufacturing plants in France, and 21 subsidiaries in North America, Europe, and Asia, more than 60 percent of Salomon's sales are made outside of Europe.

A public company, Salomon Worldwide remains controlled by the founding Salomon family, which holds some 39 percent of the company's stock and more than 56 percent of voting rights. While the Salomon family remains active in the company, leadership of the company's operations has been provided by president Jean-François Gautier since 1991.

Breakthrough Bindings in the 1950s

In 1947, François and Jeanne Salomon, of the French Savoy region, joined by son Georges, set up a 50-square-meter workshop in the town of Annecy, near the French Alps, and began manufacturing saw blades and ski edges. By 1952, using equipment developed by Georges, the company turned to automated manufacturing, boosting their output to some 700 kilometers of ski edges per year. During the same period, however, Georges had another idea that would propel the company into world-renown: attaching a spring to the binding of a ski. The new binding, the first quick-release system, uncoupled the ski from a skier's boot in the event of a fall. The spring-loaded cable release system provided a definite safety feature, boosting not only the Salomon company's fortunes, but the popularity of skiing worldwide.

By the early 1960s, Salomon took its bindings to the international export market, developing relationships with key wintersports importers in the major ski markets, while also making the rounds of the industry's trade fairs. While still a small operation, Salomon was already laying the foundation for its future market dominance. In 1967, the company debuted a new binding, with a cableless heel unit, sparking a revolution in the industry. By 1972, success of the units, under the "Competition" and "All Snow" names, had propelled the company to the leadership in the world ski binding market. With its cable-free binding system as a base, the company would hold its industry lead through the next 25 years. A key component of Salomon's success would be its intensive research and development efforts, as the company continually perfected its products and won a reputation for top quality.

By the late 1960s, the company was expanding. In 1969, it replaced its sales agents in Switzerland with a full subsidiary in that country. Over the next four years, Salomon would establish subsidiaries in Germany, Italy, Austria, and the United States as well, giving the company a local presence in most of the world's important ski markets. Scandinavia, another crucial market, soon followed, with Salomon subsidiaries appearing in Sweden, Norway, Finland, and Denmark.

Diversification in the 1980s

Until the end of the 1970s, Salomon remained a single-product company, placing itself in a precarious position. That changed in 1979, when the company introduced its first ski boot. The boot's design and features quickly captured the attention of the market, and by the mid-1980s the company had captured the second place in the world ski boot market, behind leader Nordica, of Italy. In 1980, Salomon unveiled another new product, further diversifying the company: a cross-country boot-binding system, marketed first in France and Sweden, and then to the rest of the world. Cross-country, while profitable, would not become a major Salomon market, however.

Salomon's early diversification moves had given the company a taste for expansion. In 1983, the company sold shares to the public for the first time, entering the unlisted market of the Lyon stock exchange, and joining the official market as a fully public company the following year. At the end of 1984, Salomon moved not just into a new market, but into a new season, when it acquired Taylor Made, a U.S.-based golf club manufac-

turer. Founded by golf pro Gary Adams in 1979, Taylor Made achieved early notoriety by being the first to design and manufacture its "woods" with metal heads. Joining Salomon gave Taylor Made the capital—and research and development culture—to continue to develop its golf clubs. And Salomon would benefit greatly from its new subsidiary: from its 1984 sales of US$12 million (worth FFr72 million in 1997 French francs), Taylor Made would grow to revenues of FFr1.8 billion and 41 percent of Salomon's combined group sales.

The mid-1980s would see a boom in the ski industry as the sport found a new popularity during the strong economy. The Asian market, particularly Japan, was also becoming an increasingly significant source of sales. From 5.6 million pairs of skis sold in the 1983–84 ski season, the worldwide market would peak past seven million pairs in the 1986–87 and 1987–88 seasons. Salomon's sales climbed strongly, topping FFr3 billion in 1988. The company had also continued to invest in its infrastructure, opening an 8,900-square-meter plant in Chavanod for its boot production in 1987, and an ultramodern, 35,000-square-meter plant in Rumilly for its bindings—and for the production of a new line of products.

Salomon's sales continued to climb in 1989, nearing FFr3.2 billion. In that year, Georges prepared a changing of the guard, naming Jean-François Gautier to succeed him upon his retirement in 1991. Control of the company would remain in the Salomon family, with its 39 percent of the company's stock and 55 percent of voting rights being placed in a new shareholder group, Sport Développement, led by Georges Salomon and son Bernard. Gautier, then 35, had spent his career in the electrical appliance division of Thomson S.A. He arrived at Salomon just in time to guide the company through an industrywide crisis.

The Slippery Slope of the 1990s

What could be worse for the ski industry than a year without snow? Three years without snow. In both Europe and North America, the last three winters of the 1980s had barely produced snow. Ski sales slipped dramatically, falling to just 5.5 million pairs in 1990. At the same time, retailers, overburdened with inventory, stopped placing new orders. Protected somewhat by its successful golf club subsidiary, Salomon watched the rest of the industry suffer, resulting in a shakeout that would see the collapse of many of its smaller competitors. Even Salomon's longtime archrival, Rossignol, based in nearby Grenoble, the world-leader in ski sales, was struggling, posting a loss of FFr15 million in the 1989 season. But by 1990 Salomon too saw red, to the tune of nearly FFr350 million over two years. In that year, Salomon's revenues plunged to FFr2.6 billion. Adding to Salomon's difficulties by then was the introduction of a rival golf club, dubbed the "Big Bertha," which stole much of Taylor Made's thunder and saw the subsidiary's sales sink by some 30 percent in one year.

Even as the snow returned, Salomon was confronted by a new crisis, this one of the economic variety, as the world slipped into a recession that not only cut deeply into ski and ski equipment sales—particularly in Japan—but also saw the drop in the dollar and the yen, doubling the impact of the crisis as Salomon's U.S. and Japanese sales had become important sources of revenue. Salomon was forced to cut back, laying off

600 of its 3,000 employees. But by 1993, the ski industry seemed to be on the rebound—aided by the U.S. economy's return to growth—and the worst was over.

Yet, even during these crisis years, Salomon had continued to invest heavily in its research and development as it prepared to diversify its operations still further: in 1990, the company, after spending some FFr350 million in development costs, launched its own line of high-performance skis. Produced in the Rumilly factory, Salomon's skis caught the attention of the skiing world. Selling some 75,000 pairs in their first year, Salomon's skis would top 300,000 pairs by 1993—still far behind Rossignol's 1.6 million pairs, but an impressive debut nonetheless.

In 1991, the company made a new diversification move, expanding its summer category with the addition of its line of hiking boots. Continuing Salomon's reputation for innovation and quality, Salomon's hiking boots would quickly establish a presence in the high-end categories, reaching some FFr75 million in sales within two years. Salomon moved to increase its hiking boot capacity by acquiring Italian boot manufacturer San Giorgio in 1993. The following year, Salomon moved further afield, purchasing the famed bicycle-rim manufacturer MAVIC (Manufacture d'Articles Vélocipèdiques Idoux et Chanel), a company founded in 1890, and the first to produce aluminum rims (in 1926). MAVIC would add some 200 employees and FFr200 million in sales to the Salomon group.

With ski and ski equipment sales back on track—and including a new line of skis for the rising "carving" market—and a strong diversification drive underway, Salomon's next leap in revenues would come from Taylor Made. Taking a lesson from the "Big Bertha" scare, Taylor Made had gone back to the drawing board and come up with its new "Bubble" shaft clubs—a product that found immediate success in the golfing community. From sales hovering around FFr700 million, Taylor Made's revenues climbed to FFr1.15 billion in 1995, and again to FFr1.8 billion in 1996.

Salomon was not quite finished with its diversification strategy. In 1995, the company acquired Bonfire, a US-based maker of apparel for the snowboard market, and announced its intention to enter the snowboard and snowboard boot segments—the wintersports industry's fastest-growing—in 1997. Salomon was also readying the launch of its own line of in-line skates, launched in 1996 and geared toward the amateur and professional racer. In 1997, Salomon also debuted its "Snowblades," announcing the creation of a brand-new sport. The company likened using Snowblades, which resembled shortened skis with a length of 90 centimeters (three feet), to "on-snow skating." The industry seemed to agree: in 1997 the Snowblade was named the most innovative product at the Salon International de Grenoble. In keeping with its diversification, in 1997 Salomon changed its name to Salomon Worldwide in order to give more emphasis to each of its brand names.

Principal Subsidiaries

Salomon SA; MAVIC SA; MAVIC Sports SAS; Catidom SAS; Salomon North America Inc. (U.S.A.); Taylor Made Golf Company Inc. (U.S.A.); Bonfire Snowboarding, Inc. (U.S.A.); Salomon Canada Sports Ltd; Salomon & Taylor Made Ltd. (U.K.); Salomon Sport AB (Sweden); Salomon Norge A/S (Norway); Salomon Sports Finland OY; Salomon & Taylor Made Co. Ltd. (Japan); Salomon KBO (Korea); Salomon Italia SPA; Salomon Sangiorgio SPA (Italy); Salomon Romania SRL; Salomon GmbH (Germany); Salomon Osterreich GmbH (Austria); Salomon Schweiz AG (Switzerland).

Further Reading

Delberghe, Michel, "Salomon: la Création Sans Précipitation," *Le Monde*, April 10, 1989, p. 43.
Mital, Christine, "La Glisse, La Gagne . . . Mais Chacun sur Ses Ski," *Nouvel Observateur*, February 3, 1994, p. 62.
Renard, François, "Le Discret du Ski Français," *Le Monde*, February 16, 1993, p. 29.
——, "L'Optimisme Retrouvé du Ski Français," *Le Monde*, February 15, 1994, p. V.
——, "Le Slalom Parallèle de Rossignol et de Salomon," *Le Monde*, February 20, 1995, p. 14.

—M. L. Cohen

Sanborn Hermanos, S.A.

Calvario, 100 Tlalpan
14000 Mexico, D.F.
Mexico
(525) 325-9800
Fax: (525) 573-2756

Public Subsidiary of Grupo Carso
Incorporated: 1907
Employees: 15,892
Sales: 2.28 billion pesos ($335.3 million, 1995)
Stock Exchanges: Bolsa de Valores
SICs: 2064 Candy and Other Confectionery Products;
    5735 Record and Prerecorded Tape Stores; 5812
    Eating Places; 5813 Drinking Places (Alcoholic
    Beverages); 5947 Gift, Novelty and Souvenir Shops

Best known in the United States as the American tourist's home away from home in Mexico, Sanborn Hermanos, S.A. (universally called Sanborns) is much more than that to Mexicans. The Sanborns units (86 in 1995) generally serve food and drink, and there also is a chain of Sanborn Café outlets (35 in 1995). Drugs, cosmetics, confections, sundries, gifts and toys, audio and visual equipment, and books, magazines, and newspapers are also found in Sanborns' upscale shops. Unlike many other enterprises, Sanborn Hermanos remained profitable despite the vicissitudes of the Mexican economy in the 1980s and 1990s.

Family Business, 1903–46

Walter Sanborn, a young American recently licensed as a pharmacist, wandered down to Mexico in 1898 and took a job in the Mexico City apothecary shop run by an old German named Schmidt. Four years later his brother Frank came down for a visit and was equally fascinated by the country. In 1903 the brothers opened their own drugstore in Mexico City. "We decided that Mexico couldn't be a land of manana and a land of opportunity at the same time," Frank recalled in an interview many years later. "We decided we'd have to work just as hard here as we would at home, and we decided we were here to stay, not to make a quick fortune, but to build our homes and lives. That makes a difference in the attitude of people here just as it would in our hometown."

The business, founded as Farmacía América, became Sanborn Hermanos in 1907 (*hermanos* is the Spanish word for brothers). One of the first decisions was to eliminate the 15 percent commission that doctors charged for directing prescriptions to a pharmacist. Most of Mexico City's doctors refused to deal with them, but a few agreed because, Walter said, he promised them "not only quality, but service you have never seen before." At the time, it took hours—and sometimes even days—for medicine to reach the patients from drugstores. Sanborns' bicycle messengers provided the city's first quick free delivery service. By the early 1940s the company estimated it had filled nearly 3 million prescriptions.

The Sanborn brothers not only had to overcome the reluctance of Mexico City's doctors to direct prescriptions to their pharmacy but also the virtual monopoly that three German firms held over the drug business in Mexico. Besides importing German and American brands, they produced cheap imitations of others and sold them at a discount. The Sanborn brothers brought in American brands and refused to discount but offered guarantees of quality. "We missed a lot of sales, but once we'd won a customer, we never lost him," Frank recalled.

One of the German firms then played its trump card: it placed an enormous order with an American manufacturer for a brand Sanborns' was importing, an order big enough to supply all Mexico for more than a year. Frank Sanborn took a train to New York and convinced the manufacturer that the Germans planned to divide the goods among themselves, then flood Mexico's pharmacies with them at discount prices until Sanborns was driven out of business, then return to their old practices, which favored German brands over American ones.

The Sanborns were not content to run a pharmacy. They started to serve lunch to their employees to keep them from going home for the siesta and soon began serving sandwiches to their customers as well. In 1910 they sent to the United States for a soda fountain, which was still a novelty even there. The needed milk supply for ice cream and malteds was unsafe, but the brothers found a few healthy cows and imported Mexico's first cream separator along with the soda fountain to serve what they claimed was the first scoop of ice cream south of the border. Sanborns did so well catering to the Mexican sweet tooth that the brothers brought in a herd of tested cattle, thereby becoming fathers of Mexico's modern dairy industry. They rented more space to accommodate trade, and the soda fountain grew into a restaurant.

Undoubtedly Sanborns most difficult period was the decade that followed the Mexican revolution of 1910, during which the country was plunged into bloodshed and anarchy. The store was smashed by soldiers in 1914, when the brothers evacuated their U.S. workers, but it survived as a kind of neutral zone in which Sanborn employees were forbidden to talk politics and the same ban was "tactfully impressed" on its patrons. In 1919 the brothers decided the political situation was stable enough to move into the House of Tiles—a stone palace, covered with blue tiles, in the heart of downtown, that had just been vacated by the Jockey Club. It had been built in 1596 for a Spanish aristocrat and had later served as the Russian and Japanese embassies and as a dormitory for homeless newsboys. A Mexican later recalled that the opening of the new Sanborns in 1921 "was like a rebirth of optimism in the city. Other businessmen, too, decided the revolutions were over, and money that had been hidden for 10 years began to circulate again."

The Sanborns restored the House of Tiles and commissioned the celebrated painter José Clemente Orozco to produce a mural facing the great stairway. Waitresses were dressed in the colorful costumes of the Tehuantepec Indians. Politicians, civil servants, journalists, and businessmen—the movers and shakers of Mexican society—gathered in the restaurant. Churchgoers began dropping in for breakfast after Mass, and Sanborns even became home for debutante teas. By the end of World War II almost 2 million people were visiting the two-story tiled palace each year.

Sanborns entered a new endeavor in the early 1920s, when Frank Sanborn found he could not locate a competent silversmith even though Mexico led the world in silver production. While another American, William Spratling, was reviving the art and craft of silverwork in Taxco, Sanborns stimulated the trade by using workmen to fashion silver to its own designs. By the early 1940s Sanborns annual sales volume from silverwork came to $250,000. Ten years later it was the biggest silver shop in Mexico.

By this time Walter Sanborn was long retired and Frank was administering the business with the help of his two sons, Frank, Jr. and Jack. The tile-clad patio restaurant served 3,500 customers a day, and there was a cocktail lounge, too. Besides silverwork, Sanborns, the biggest crafts shop in Mexico, was selling the output of some 1,300 native craftsmen in wood, wool, glass, pottery, stone, metal, leather, and feathers. The second floor offered furs, gowns, and furbelows, men's suitings, and household goods. There was a post office and information bureau for tourists. A second Sanborns had been opened in Monterrey.

Sanborns was a considerable wholesaling and manufacturing concern as well. The company was Mexico's largest drug

manufacturer, with a modern factory. There was also a toilet-goods plant. In addition, the company was serving as the Mexican wholesaler for nearly 30 U.S. manufacturers. Sanborns held the manufacturing and distribution rights to several major U.S. drug and cosmetic lines, including Hinds hand cream, Listerine, Pro-phy-lactic brushes, and the products of the American Safety Razor Corp. Its annual sales volume came to close to 20 million pesos ($4 million). The company had between 700 and 800 employees.

Under Walgreen Management, 1946–84

In 1946 the Sanborns sold their business, which now included a second Mexico City outlet in the Hotel Del Prado (a victim of the 1985 earthquake), to the Walgreen Co. drugstore chain for about $2.5 million. By Mexican law, the purchaser was required to form a Mexican corporation in which at least 51 percent of the stock was owned by Mexican citizens. In the mid-1960s this controlling interest was in the hands of a group headed by two of the nation's biggest industrial and financial tycoons, Carlos Trouyet and Julio Lacaud. Walgreen's received a share of the profits and ran the enterprise under a long-term management contract. It was the chain's only venture outside the United States. A Sanborns plant manufacturing chocolates, candy, and other comestibles was added around 1950.

Sanborns opened a four-story, $5 million store in 1953 on Mexico City's swank Paseo de la Reforma, next to the U.S. embassy. This virtual department store included, besides a restaurant and soda fountain, a big drug department, cosmetics, clothing and accessories, household goods, arts and crafts, photographic equipment and supplies, and a bakery. It also included a plush cocktail lounge. The structure, with 98,000 square feet of floor space, was leased to Sanborns on a rent-plus-profit-sharing basis.

In the ensuing 20 years Sanborns grew into a chain of eight stores, all of them in Mexico City except the Monterrey outlet. Three of the Sanborns stores now had cocktail lounges. About 45 percent of the chain's sales came from restaurants and lunch counters. Only four of the outlets maintained drug departments, because with prices controlled by the government and discount stores glutting the market, the company had decided the business was no longer profitable. Sanborns had displays of U.S. magazines, money-exchange booths, and the kind of trinkets and sombreros that attracted tourists, but the tourist trade only made up about 15 percent of the company's business.

More than 10 percent of Sanborns' income now came from wholesaling popular-priced Sanborns-labeled products to other stores. These consisted mainly of toiletries, coffee, ice cream, and candy, with candy the leading single item sold in all the stores. Sanborns was still making its own candy and selling more than 100 tons a month in its own stores and through the wholesaling operation. Sanborns' manufacturing line also included shampoo, cold cream, and cologne (Mexico's top seller), and it was licensed to produce four items under the Walgreen name: a henna hair rinse, a shampoo, a cleaning fluid, and an after-shave lotion. The company no longer was manufacturing and distributing U.S. products under other licenses except to bottle Eye-Gene, an eyewash, and to distribute Mentholatum and Tampax. "Most of the companies that once licensed us now have moved in with their own manufacturing operations after the market was developed for them,'' explained general manager James Mitchell.

Sanborns opened a store in Acapulco in 1966 and one in Puebla in 1969, when its number of outlets reached 12. Also in 1969, it completed construction of a large modern complex that included a laboratory, warehouse, commissary, and laundry. In 1971 its number of stores reached 17, including three new Mexico City outlets, one of them in the Plaza Satelite, a shopping mall. A second Acapulco store opened in 1973. By this time the company's arts-and-crafts offerings included sculpture and paintings. Sanborns acquired the 18 units in five Mexican cities of the Denny's fast-food chain in 1976. A year later the company ranked 71st in sales among Mexican-based companies, with 1.29 billion pesos (about $58 million) in revenues.

Sanborns had revenues of 2.98 billion pesos (about $130 million) and net income of 255.8 million pesos (about $11.3 million) in fiscal 1980 (the year ended June 30, 1980), when it operated 44 retail outlets (including the Denny's chain), of which 14 were outside Mexico City. But the 1982 Mexican economic crisis so reduced the value of the peso that Walgreen's lost faith in the chain's ability to return a significant profit in dollars. In 1984 the company sold its 46.9-percent share in Sanborns to a group of Mexican investors for $30 million. The company had been selling shares on the Bolsa de Valores, Mexico City's stock exchange, since 1956, and most of the shares not held by Walgreen's belonged to banks and mutual funds. The purchasers of Walgreen's stock were not disclosed, but by 1990 Carlos Slim Helú had a controlling share of the company through the firm Galas de México, in which he held majority control.

Sanborns in the 1990s

After Walgreen's sold out, James Mitchell was replaced as general manager of Sanborns by Juan Antonio Pérez Simón, who also assumed the title of president. Sanborns continued to turn a healthy profit. In 1991 it had net income of 81.04 billion pesos ($26.9 million) on net sales of 990.54 billion pesos ($328.4 million). By the early 1990s a large portion of Slim Helú's assets were in the holding company Grupo Carso, which owned a two-thirds share of Sanborns. Sanborns was now selling books as well as magazines (and was, or would soon become, the largest bookseller in Mexico) and audio products such as stereo systems. Some 90 percent of company sales were coming from the Sanborns chain, with the rest from Denny's. The company's assets now included a significant amount of real estate.

By 1995 Carlos Slim Domit, son of Carlos Slim Helú, had become general director of Sanborns, replacing Pérez Simón, who became chairman of the board of directors. Despite the devaluation of the peso in December 1994, resulting from a flight of capital abroad, and the devastating economic crisis that followed, Sanborns continued to be profitable. In 1995 it had net income of 158.1 million pesos ($23.2 million) on net sales of 2.28 billion pesos ($335.3 million). The long-term debt was 142.9 million pesos ($21 million) at the end of 1995. By then the Denny's units had been converted into more-upscale Sanborns Cafe coffee shops. The company also had taken a majority interest in the Mix-Up and Discolandia music-store chains. There were 86 Sanborns units and 35 Sanborns Cafe units at the end of 1995. During the first quarter of 1997 Sanborns accounted for 12.1 percent of the consolidated revenues of Grupo Carso and 7.4 percent of its operating profit.

Principal Subsidiaries

Acolman, S.A.; Administración Integral de Alimentos, S.A.; Bienes Raices de Acapulco, S.A.; Central Imobiliaria de México, S.A.; Fideicomiso de Administración 2393; Imobiliaria Buenavista, S.A.; Imobiliaria Ciudad del Sol, S.A. de C.V.; Imobiliaria Diana Victoria, S.A. de C.V.; Impulsora de Empresas y Exportaciones, S.A. de C.V.; Operaciones e Inversiones, S.A.; Pam Pam, S.A.; Productos Chase, S.A. de C.V.; Promotora Musical, S.A. de C.V.; Santepec, S.A.

Further Reading

''A Chain Plus Personality,'' *Business Week,* August 1, 1953, pp. 76–77.

''Mexican Venture,'' *Business Week,* June 8, 1946, pp. 80–81.

''Mexico's 'Drug Store' Changes Prescription,'' *Business Week,* May 15, 1965, pp. 72–73, 76.

Poole, Claire, ''El Conquistador,'' *Forbes,* September 16, 1991, pp. 68, 72.

Pozas, Ricardo, and Luna, Matilde, eds. *Empresas y las empresarios en Mexico.* Mexico City: Editorial Grijalbo, 1991, pp. 337–354.

Scully, Michael, ''Pan America's Crossroads Store,'' *Pan American,* January 1942, pp. 8–11.

''Walgreen Sells Stake in Sanborn of 46.9% for $30 Million Total,'' *Wall Street Journal,* September 18, 1984, p. 20.

—Robert Halasz

SCOR S.A.

1, avenue du Président Wilson
92074 Paris La Defense Cedex
France
(33) 1 46 98 70 00
Fax: (33) 1 47 67 04 09
Web site: http://www.scor.fr

Public Company
Incorporated: 1970
Employees: 1,164
Sales: FFr 13.81 billion (1996 gross written premiums)
Stock Exchanges: Paris New York
SICs: 6399 Insurance Carriers, Not Elsewhere Classified

Paris-based SCOR S.A. is France's leading reinsurance company and one of the world's top ten ''insurer's insurers.'' SCOR provides facultative and treaty reinsurance to property-casualty and life insurance companies. A global company, with operating units in the United States, Canada, Germany, the United Kingdom, Singapore, Japan, Hong Kong, Italy, Bermuda, and other major countries and cities throughout the world, SCOR's customers include leading primary insurance providers of property, casualty, marine, space and transportation, construction, credit risk, and life and health insurance policies. In 1996, SCOR's gross written premiums totaled FFr 13.8 billion, generating earnings of FFr 624 million. The company's claims-paying ability has been rated as A + by Standard & Poor and as A + (superior) by A.M. Best.

Reinsurance operates much like the traditional insurance industry; however, reinsurance companies such as SCOR do not directly underwrite insurance policies protecting property or casualty risk, but instead insure the primary insurance company, called the ceding company, writing the policy. The ceding company contracts with the reinsurer—and usually several reinsurance companies—in order to buffer itself against catastrophic losses such as those experienced during Hurricane Andrew and other natural disasters. While the ceding company retains the direct risk on its policies, and is responsible for paying out on claims, its reinsurers accept a contracted percentage of claims made against—and premiums paid for—a policy. Use of reinsurance companies helps protect primary insurers against extreme variations in their financial position caused by major losses, while reinsurance companies also allow ceding companies to underwrite more and larger risk policies. Reinsurance companies also provide ceding companies with the cash needed to pay out on major losses, protecting the ceding company's assets.

Reinsurance contracts, or treaties, generally take one of three forms. Under a proportional treaty, the reinsurer contracts for a specific percentage of a policy or portfolio of policies written by a ceding company; the reinsurance receives that percentage of the premiums generated by the ceding company, and becomes responsible for paying the same percentage on any claims against the policy or portfolio. The second form of treaty, becoming more common in the 1990s, is the non-proportional treaty, in which the reinsurance company contracts to pay out on claims exceeding a level provided for in the treaty. The ceding company may be responsible, for example, for paying out the first $1 million on losses claimed against a $5 million policy. After the ceding company has fulfilled its deductible, the reinsurer becomes responsible for the remaining losses, up to the policy's remaining $4 million limit. The reinsurance company's risk exposure is therefore limited only to claims for losses above the deductible level, while the ceding company's limited risk on the full claim enables it to offer the larger policy.

The third form of reinsurance treaty more directly involves the reinsurance company. In a facultative treaty, policies are written on an individual basis, often involving treaties above the ceding-company's claims paying ability or beyond its range of risks. Facultatives are generally written for large-scale industrial and civil engineering projects, and to a lesser extent for liability claims. The reinsurer is responsible for risk-assessment and for establishing policy limits, terms, and premiums. Among reinsurance companies, SCOR is one of the leading underwriters of facultative treaties. SCOR's portfolio of facultative treaties numbered some 10,000 in 1997, generating more than one-fourth of the company's total income.

SCOR's services also extend toward providing ceding companies with research, information, and support, especially in highly specialized areas such as marine insurance and major public works projects. The company deploys specialist underwriters with expertise in individual fields, such as life insurance, credit insurance, marine and aviation, as well as for specific sectors requiring facultative reinsurance coverage such as in the oil, gas, nuclear power, and chemical industries, or for specific projects including the construction of dams, high-rise buildings, or offshore drilling rigs, or the launching of satellites and other high-profile endeavors. SCOR provides on-site inspection and consultation on risk-management techniques, as well as establishing premium rates and, in the event of losses, damage assessment and claims adjustment services.

Founded in 1970

SCOR was founded in 1970 by the French government as the reinsurance arm for state-owned or controlled insurers. At the time, the reassurance industry was largely dominated by London and New York, while in France the reassurance industry remained underdeveloped. In 1972, the company began setting up foreign branches to expand its position in the worldwide market. The company remained capital-constrained through much of the decade, however, as the French government restricted SCOR from issuing shares to outside investors. At the same time the government was engaged in a massive effort to place a number of industries and major corporations under government control—including leading automaker Renault, steel makers Usinor and Sacilor, chemicals concern Saint Gobain, and others—leaving little capital to invest in SCOR.

In the early 1980s, SCOR underwent a diversification program, expanding its reinsurance offerings. The company also set up its foreign branches as subsidiaries, including those in the United States, Canada, and Singapore. These subsidiaries were taken public, enabling the company to raise the much-needed capital for its expansion. In 1983, Patrick Peugeot was named SCOR's president-director general, a position he would hold for 11 years. Peugeot led the company on an expansion and diversification program through the 1980s and early 1990s that saw the company grow not only to a leadership position in France's reinsurance industry, but to the number six position among reinsurers worldwide.

SCOR took several significant steps towards this position in the late 1980s. In 1988, the company acquired leading Italian reinsurance company La Vittoria Riassicurazioni. In that same year, SCOR also set up two new subsidiaries, SCOR Réassurance and SCOR Vie, increasing its portfolio of products. The following year, the company moved into Germany when it acquired that country's Deutsche Continental Rückversicherungs. But by then SCOR was already preparing a major reorganization that would carry the company through the mid-1990s.

Restructuring in the 1990s

The wave of corporate conversions to state control of the late 1970s was largely finished by the mid-1980s. Indeed, by 1984, the government was already engaged in a long process of re-privatization of much of its state-controlled businesses. SCOR, too, found its independence in the late 1980s. In 1989,

that process began when SCOR agreed to merge with UAP Ré, the reinsurance arm of the Union des Assurances de Paris (UAP). Under the merger agreement, UAP took some 40 percent control of SCOR. The company was then reorganized, with SCOR S.A. operating as a subsidiary of holding company HCS. Joining UAP in the venture were two other French insurance companies, Assurances Générales de Paris (AGF) and AXA S.A., which each took shares of approximately 20 percent in HCS. The following year, SCOR was taken public, selling the remaining 25 percent of shares—principally to Credit Agricole subsidiary Predica and to Swiss Re—and listing on the Paris stock exchange. HCS retained a controlling 53 percent share of SCOR S.A. Meanwhile, UAP, AGF, AXA, and SCOR entered a pact to maintain the level of their participation in SCOR, with each of the major shareholders guaranteeing not to sell their shares without the consent of the others, thereby protecting SCOR from the threat of a hostile takeover.

The early 1990s held a threat of a different sort, however. Beginning in 1991 and lasting through much of 1992, the insurance industry was rocked by a series of natural and other disasters, including Hurricane Andrew, which alone cost the insurance industry some US $16.5 billion. SCOR's share of that disaster mounted to FFr 300 million; meanwhile, the company was hit more directly by several industrial disasters, resulting in a loss of FFr 858 million on its technical results, and a net loss of FFr 135 million for 1992, on net sales of FFr 8.4 billion.

Yet, despite posting its first loss in nearly a decade, SCOR retained a solid foundation, with a capitalization of some FFr 5 billion, and a positive cash-flow of more than FFr 800 million. Elsewhere, the industry was not as healthy—the year of catastrophes proved disastrous to a number of prominent reinsurers, forcing the disappearance of such reinsurance companies as NRG, the Netherlands largest reinsurer, and NW Re and Royal Re, two of the top four reinsurance companies in London. Even Lloyds of London was eventually forced to shed its reinsurance operations. The industry underwent a wave of consolidation that reduced the number of reinsurance companies worldwide from more than 400 in the 1980s to approximately 200 by the mid-1990s.

The industry found some relief in 1993, as insurers and reinsurers saw more limited exposure to the year's major natural disasters –including the flooding of the Mississippi and Missouri Rivers, and the Los Angeles earthquake, as well as flooding in the south of France, most of the losses of which were picked up by governmental disaster assistance. Aided in part by a strong increase in reinsurance tariffs—of 20 percent and as much as 100 percent—SCOR returned to profitability by the end of 1993, posting net earnings of FFr 157 million. The following year saw SCOR continue to recover, with net income climbing some 80 percent to FFr 282 million, with revenues nearing FFr 10 billion. In September 1994, Patrick Peugeot stepped down from SCOR's leadership, replaced by Jacques Blondeau.

The shareholder's pact among SCOR, UAP, AGF, and AXA reached completion of its term at the end of 1994, setting in motion a new restructuring of SCOR. The company's major shareholders were looking for the freedom to decrease their participation in SCOR, and the company announced its intention to reorganize its structure, merging the HCS holding company into the SCOR S.A. subsidiary. Following upon the merger, AGF and AXA, and, to a more limited extent, UAP, planned to decrease their participation in SCOR. That move, however, was postponed temporarily, given the weak financial market at the beginning of 1995. At the same time, SCOR began buying up the minority shares in its U.S., Singapore, Canadian, and other public subsidiaries, removing them from the stock market.

By the end of 1995, SCOR's profits had rebounded fully, with net earnings of FFr 522 million on revenues of FFr 11.85 billion. AGF, in a portfolio-shedding drive to reduce its debt, began selling back its shares to SCOR, reducing its holding in the French reassurance leader to a symbolic 0.7 percent by September 1996. AXA also began selling its stake, dropping its participation to 7.5 percent by the middle of 1996 and then selling its remaining 2.75 percent by August of that year.

In July 1996, SCOR moved to double its U.S. activity when it acquired the US $400 million reinsurance premium portfolio of Allstate subsidiary Allstate Re. The US $500 million acquisition, which included Allstate Re's post-1985 risk portfolio, placed SCOR in the top 10 in the U.S. reinsurance market. It also set the stage for the next major development in the company's history: its listing on the New York Stock Exchange, making SCOR only the sixth French company to do so. The October 1996 listing allowed UAP to follow AXA and AGF, when it announced its intention to place 30 percent of SCOR on the international market, while retaining its remaining 10 per-

cent interest in SCOR as a long-term investment. The 9.2 million-share offering raised some US $350 million.

SCOR, in the meantime, continued its restructuring, with an eye on increasing its global presence in the major reinsurance markets. The company opened branch offices and divisions in Brazil and South Korea. In June 1997, SCOR reorganized its Italian subsidiary, transferring all of its Italian reinsurance activities to the newly renamed SCOR Italia. With revenues nearing FFr 14 billion and 1996 net earnings nearing FFr 625 million, SCOR continued to confront the ongoing consolidation of the reinsurance industry with its own global expansion plans.

Principal Subsidiaries

SCOR Vie; SCOR Réassurance; SCOR Italia; SCOR Deutschland; SCOR U.S.; SCOR Canada; Commercial Risk (Bermuda); SCOR U.K.; SCOR Asia Pacific (Singapore).

Further Reading

''French Reinsurer SCOR Lists on NYSE,'' *Euroweek*, October 11, 1996, p. 8.
''Keeping SCOR,'' *Reactions*, February 1, 1995.
Kielmas, Maria, ''Insurers Divest Shares of Reinsurer SCOR,'' *Business Insurance*, September 9, 1996, p. 23.
''SCOR,'' *World Corporate Insurance Report*, March 24, 1995.
''SCOR's Roadshow Rolls on with Global Strategy,'' *Financial Times*, October 1, 1996, p. 24.

—M. L. Cohen

Scotsman Industries, Inc.

775 Corporate Woods Parkway
Vernon Hills, Illinois 60061
U.S.A.
(847) 215-4500
Fax: (847) 913-9844
Web site: http://www.scotsman-ice.com

Public Company
Incorporated: 1989
Employees: 2,182
Sales: $356.4 million (1996)
Stock Exchanges: New York
SICs: 3585 Refrigeration & Heating Equipment; 3556
    Food Products Machinery; 3632 Household
    Refrigerators & House & Farm Freezers; 6719
    Holding Company

Scotsman Industries, Inc. is the world's largest manufacturer of commercial ice machines. With subsidiaries in the U.S., Germany, Italy, and the U.K., alliances with companies in the U.S., U.K., and China and with sales in over 100 countries, Scotsman truly is an international corporation. Among the other types of products Scotsman manufactures are food preparation and storage equipment, beverage dispensing equipment, refrigerated display cases, and insulated panels and doors. With its continuing quest to acquire new companies that build on its existing product line, Scotsman is sure to grow and expand through the end of the 1990s and beyond.

Company Beginnings

Scotsman traces its origins back to 1921, when the Queen Stove Works was founded in Albert Lea, Minnesota. This company originally produced camp stoves, later adding oil space heaters, kitchen stoves, and other products. In 1950 Queen purchased the American Gas Machine company, a manufacturer of lanterns, ice chests, heaters, and one model of commercial ice machine. Queen used the name ''Scotsman'' to market its commercial ice machines from this point forward. After being acquired by King-Seeley Corporation in 1957, which then merged with the American Thermos Products Company in 1960, Queen shifted its focus entirely to the manufacture of ice machines, then still a fairly new business.

In 1967 King-Seeley Thermos acquired Frimont S.p.A., a large Italian maker of commercial ice machines, and began to use the Scotsman name for the products produced by them as well. This immediately made Scotsman the largest-selling ice machine brand in the world, as Frimont products were sold in Europe, the Middle East, and the Far East. In 1968 Household Finance Corporation (later known as Household International) absorbed King-Seeley Thermos. Household created the Household Manufacturing subsidiary to house this new acquisition, in 1969 adding to it Halsey Taylor, makers of drinking fountains and water coolers.

Household Manufacturing added another Italian ice machine maker in 1985, Castel MAC, S.p.A. Castel, which also made commercial freezers, blast freezers, bakery dough retarders, and water coolers, had its own distribution network in Europe, Africa, the Middle East, and the Far East. Another acquisition came the following year, when Household purchased Glenco-Star, a maker of commercial refrigerators, freezers, and restaurant food preparation tables. Booth, Inc., a Dallas-based maker of fountain drink dispensing machines with its own subsidiary Call-Star, makers of ice cooled equipment, was added in 1987.

Scotsman Industries Created in 1989

In 1989, Household International divested itself of Household Manufacturing, which spun off three units as public companies, including its Refrigeration Products Group, headquartered in Vernon Hills, Illinois. Renamed Scotsman Industries, Inc., shares began trading on the New York Stock Exchange in April 1989. Though the first year as a new, public company saw Scotsman's stock value drop by about 40 percent, with flat annual sales, the company rapidly recovered its footing under CEO Richard Osborne through restructuring, consolidating manufacturing plants, improving cost-effectiveness, and sharpening its marketing focus.

The next several years saw further streamlining of operations, as Halsey Taylor and Glenco-Star were sold off. The former's line of drinking fountains and water coolers were not consistent with the main thrust of Scotsman's business, food preparation equipment, while it was felt by the company that the latter did not offer enough potential for growth. In 1992 subsidiary Booth Inc. brought Crystal Tips into the corporate family. Iowa-based Crystal Tips was also a manufacturer of commercial ice machines, which further increased Scotsman's share of this market. Following the purchase both Booth's and Crystal Tips's operations were merged in Booth's Dallas location for greater efficiency.

Other acquisitions ensued, including Simag, an Italian ice machine maker purchased by Frimont in 1993; Delfield Company and Whitlenge Drink Equipment Ltd., acquired by Scotsman in 1994; Hartek Beverage Handling GmbH, added in 1995; and Kysor Industrial Corp., which was purchased in 1997. Each of these companies brought something useful to Scotsman's overall profile. Simag further consolidated Scotsman's position of strength in the growing ice maker market in Europe. Delfield, based in Mount Pleasant, Michigan, was the largest maker of custom food preparation workstations in the world and also produced commercial refrigerators. Whitlenge was a United Kingdom-based maker of soft drink and beer dispensing equipment, with a strong presence in the U.K. and Europe, selling its products in over 30 countries. Hartek, based in Germany, was also a leading maker of soft drink dispensing equipment, in addition to producing beer coolers, with its line of products sold throughout Europe. The purchase of Hartek made Scotsman the second largest beverage dispenser manufacturer in Europe, and the third largest in the world. By 1995, half of Scotsman's revenues came from the companies it had purchased since going public.

Scotsman's purchase of Cadillac, Michigan-based Kysor in 1997 brought additional food preparation-related products into the fold. Kysor manufactured refrigerated display cases, commercial refrigeration systems, and insulated panels and doors at 14 locations in the U.S., Great Britain, and South Korea. It was the second largest maker of walk-in refrigerators and refrigerated display cases in the United States. Kysor's strong sales to supermarkets such as Winn-Dixie and Food Lion, as well as the superstores of Wal-Mart, helped Scotsman increase its presence in this area of the marketplace. Scotsman would also be able to market Kysor's products to the restaurant chains and institutional food service clients it had established ties to. The purchase of Kysor for approximately $300 million in cash and assumed debt would increase Scotsman's annual revenues by close to 70 percent (Kysor's Transportation Group was sold to a third party by Scotsman immediately after the acquisition).

The 1990s: Joint Ventures

Scotsman also entered into joint ventures with three companies. The first of these came in 1992, when an alliance was formed with Howe Corporation of Chicago to exclusively market Howe's Rapid Freeze line of industrial ice flakers worldwide. In 1995, Scotsman and Shenyang Xinle Precision Machinery Company agreed to a joint venture to produce ice machines in Shenyang, China. These were to be initially sold in China, but could later be produced for other markets as well. The formation of SAW Technologies Limited was announced in August 1996. This was a partnership with Aztec Developments Limited of the U.K., a maker of sophisticated beverage dispensing valves. These were to be incorporated into new lines of products from the three beverage dispenser manufacturing companies Scotsman owned. This was projected to give Scotsman a further edge in its important beverage dispensing business, which in 1996 accounted for almost 20 percent of the corporation's annual sales.

Scotsman's worldwide presence has been one of the company's strongest suits. Foreign sales accounted for over a third of the company's 1996 revenues, and were one of its fastest-growing sources of income. One reason for this trend could be seen by looking at the relative prevalence of ice machines in restaurants. According to William Blair & Co. analyst Chris Serra, by the mid-1990s about 90 percent of restaurants in the U.S. were estimated to have ice making machines, while only about 50 percent to 60 percent of those in Europe had them. Markets in less-developed countries had an even greater potential for expansion. Scotsman's position at or near the top in most of its product categories in Europe, and worldwide, positioned it strongly for continued growth.

Responding to New Challenges in the Early 1990s

Scotsman has also aggressively responded to changing demands of customers and government regulators to keep its products up to date. When the U.S. government decided to ban refrigerants that use chlorofluorocarbons (CFCs) after January 1, 1996, due to concerns that they contributed to the destruction of the Earth's ozone layer, the company decided to have a CFC-free ice machine model ready by the spring of 1993, in order to have a fully-tested product line in place by the deadline. With the design process beginning in early 1991, this required reducing the company's normal timeline for bringing a product to market from about 32 months to 18 months, including the development of a CFC-free refrigerant, which did not yet exist. At the same time, Scotsman had learned from recent customer surveys that its quality was not considered to be especially high, and it was determined to improve its ratings with the new products.

The company decided to design these new ice machines using a team approach, incorporating its parts suppliers directly into the design process. This way, before prototypes would be made, dialogue between suppliers could help eliminate problems before they occurred. For example, the refrigerant supplier tried several different formulas before settling on one that most closely matched the older CFC-containing coolant. The compressor maker then tested it to see how it would work in its machines. It was found that the new refrigerant interacted chemically with the mineral-based lubricant used in regular compressors. Ultimately, a usable synthetic lubricant was found, though this cost many times what the mineral type did, thus raising the cost of the end product. The company in turn adjusted the projected price of the machines, giving customers advance notice of what to expect. After several such problems were worked out, Scotsman met its deadline and was the first manufacturer to bring out a CFC-free ice machine. Reliability over Scotsman's previous models was doubled as well. For future product design challenges, the company projected reducing the time to market still further, using online communications systems to save even more time.

The Late 1990s: A Complementary Mix of Products

By 1997, Scotsman's product mix included ice machines, food preparation and storage equipment, beverage dispensing equipment, refrigerated food display cases, and insulated panels and doors. The types of ice machines made around the world under the Scotsman name included several different varieties. Cuber or nugget machines were used in hotels to supply ice to guests, or in fast food outlets, cafeterias, institutional settings, etc. to provide ice for beverages. In the late 1990s Scotsman added the CM^3 line of cubers to provide greater ice making capacity than previous models at roughly the same price, with reduced energy use and 40 percent fewer moving parts. Other Scotsman ice machines included flakers to make ice for food storage and display, and a line of consumer ice makers intended primarily for the luxury home market.

Food preparation and storage equipment, manufactured mainly by Scotsman subsidiary and U.S. market leader, The Delfield Company, included custom food preparation tables and serving line equipment, as well as mobile serving carts, self-contained kiosks, reach-in refrigerators and other products. Delfield had established strong relationships with a number of clients, including the Boston Market chain of restaurants. When Boston Market needed new serving line equipment, Delfield was able to develop prototypes in under six weeks, ultimately being named sole supplier of such equipment to the chain. Scotsman subsidiary Castel MAC in Italy also produced blast freezers, dough retarders, and other refrigeration and storage equipment for the bakery industry, giving Scotsman additional sources of components for the creation of custom food preparation workstations.

Beverage dispensing equipment was manufactured in the U.S. and Europe by Scotsman subsidiaries Booth, Whitlenge, and Hartek. Combined, these gave the company the position of third largest manufacturer and distributor of such products in the world. Types of products in this category included pre-mix and post-mix soft drink dispensing machines, combined drink dispenser/ice machines for self-service and fast food restaurant use, or bartender style dispensers with a single hose and control buttons for different beverages. The joint Scotsman/Aztec Developments venture, SAW Technologies, was created to manufacture and market the Aztec valve, a sophisticated type of electronically controlled beverage dispensing valve. It was capable of differentiating between different types of soft drink syrups, monitoring and regulating the mix of syrup and carbonated water, and handling beverages with other characteristics such as fruit juices, which may contain pulp that is problematic to the older types of mechanical valve systems.

The refrigerated display cases and insulated panels and doors manufactured by Kysor constituted the last major category of products made by Scotsman. Display cases included self-service models for use in stores selling refrigerated or frozen food products and refrigerated deli cases. Insulated panels and doors were used in walk-in cold storage rooms and larger refrigerated enclosures and warehouses. Kysor also manufactured mechanical refrigeration systems. As with other Scotsman product lines, the expansion of its major U.S. customers into foreign markets was expected to give Kysor continued growth in this area.

In 1997 Scotsman Industries, taken as a whole, was a thriving, well-integrated family of companies that was directed toward a common goal, that of being, in CEO and Chairman Richard Osborne's words, "Recognized as a premier supplier of equipment to any location where food and beverages are sold." It has continued to meet that goal by acquiring successful companies from around the world that produce complementary products.

Principal Subsidiaries

Booth, Inc.; Castel MAC, S.p.A. (Italy); The Delfield Company; Frimont, S.p.A. (Italy); Hartek Beverage Handling GmbH (Germany); Kysor Industrial Corp.; SAW Technologies Limited (U.K.; 50%); Scotsman Ice Systems; Whitlenge Drink Equipment Limited (U.K.); DFC Holding Corporation; Hartek Awagen Vertriebsges m.b.H. (Austria); Scotsman Drink Equipment, Limited (U.K.); Whitlenge Acquisition Limited (U.K.); Whitlenge Drink Equipment N.V. (Belgium).

Further Reading

Breskin, Ira, "Scotsman Grows by Acquiring Worldwide Food-Service Lines," *Investor's Business Daily*, April 3, 1997, p. B15.
Carbone, James, "How Scotsman Used Alliances to Solve a Design Problem," *Purchasing*, February 16, 1995, pp. 36–40.
"The History of Scotsman Industries, Inc.," Vernon Hills, Illinois: Scotsman Industries, Inc., 1996.
Lambert, Ron, "Icemaker Mfrs. Do Their Part; Techs Are Urged to Conserve Ice Machines' Refrigerant," *Air Conditioning, Heating & Refrigeration News*, June 3, 1991, p. 15.
"New Stock Listings," *The Wall Street Journal*, April 10, 1989.
"Scotsman Indus Backs 3Q Net View of 54c a Diluted Share," *Dow Jones News Service*, October 22, 1996.
"Scotsman Indus-Kysor-2: Merger to Be Completed in March," *Dow Jones News Service*, March 10, 1997.
"Scotsman Restructures, Reclaims Market Stake in Wake of Spin-off," *HFD-The Weekly Home Furnishings Newspaper*, May 21, 1990, p. 130.
"Scotsman to Acquire Kysor for $300m in Cash, Assumed Debt," *Nation's Restaurant News*, February 17, 1997, p. 56.
White, James A., "Heard on the Street: Investing in Spinoffs Grows Treacherous; Popularity of Issues Puts End to Bargains," *The Wall Street Journal*, June 1, 1990, p. C1.

—Frank Uhle

Sears Roebuck de México, S.A. de C.V.

San Luis Potosí 214
06700 Mexico, D.F.
Mexico
(525) 227-7500
Fax: (525) 584-9692 or 574-2268

Public Subsidiary of Grupo Carso
Incorporated: 1945
Employees: 50,122
Sales: 2.18 billion pesos (US$320.6 million) (1995)
SICs: 5311 Department Stores

Sears Roebuck de México, S.A. de C.V. was, in the mid-1990s, the only national full-line department-store chain in Mexico. A more upscale version than the U.S. Sears, it was long a subsidiary of the parent Chicago-based Sears, Roebuck & Co., which revolutionized merchandising in Latin America. The Mexican conglomerate Grupo Carso bought a majority share of the enterprise in 1997.

A Smash Hit, 1947–59

Sears, Roebuck & Co. was the first U.S. retailer with a presence in Latin America. In 1945 it paid $516,000 for a store in a quiet part of Mexico City on Avenida Insurgentes, close to a fashionable residential area and far from the main shopping district. When this store opened in 1947, the company had to issue passes to hold down the crowds, who on opening day numbered 123,000 and bought $600,000 worth of goods, all paid in cash. Sears Mexico sold practically all its stock within a week, requiring three airplanes to bring in more goods from the parent company's Texas warehouse.

Although Sears charged more than it did in the United States and so expected its clientele to be an upper-class one, its prices were still lower than that of local merchants, including the department stores that catered essentially to a wealthy, but small, upper class. Customers also liked Sears's fixed prices and prominently displayed price tags, which eliminated the need for

bargaining. A sophisticated formula was used to determine just what Sears would charge. Almost any appliance would have to be bought on credit since few Mexicans could be expected to pay full price.

Sears stimulated consumer interest by introducing window displays to Mexico. A "satisfaction guaranteed or your money back" promise was as popular here as in the United States. Household appliances like refrigerators and stoves were particularly popular, as were men's shirts and underwear, and cloth for dressmaking, since most Mexicans still wore clothing made by seamstresses or tailors working out of their homes. The Mexico City store did an estimated $16 million in business in its first year, exceeding the parent company's own expectations by 2½ times.

Within months of the store's opening, however, Mexico barred some nonessential imports and raised tariffs on others as much as threefold in order to prevent a drain on the nation's foreign-currency reserves. Sears Mexico, which had imported as much as 90 percent of its merchandise, adjusted to the situation by forming alliances with Mexican manufacturers. The company offered financial and technical help to its suppliers, some of whom were recruited from small-scale entrepreneurs, such as a woman with only two machines. Sears Mexico bought a half-interest in a factory making work clothes and another manufacturing sports shirts. It brought into being an enterprise producing radio and television goods. Some of these suppliers became subsidiaries of the company.

Sears also pioneered in and popularized installment buying, the use of cash registers, and large-scale display advertising in the press. By 1949 Sears Mexico had 2,500 Mexican suppliers furnishing some 80 percent of the goods in the Mexico City store. Prices had come down because of the greater use of Mexican suppliers and an increasing orientation toward the middle class. The store's profits were estimated at $2 million that year. A second Mexican Sears store opened in 1949 in Monterrey and a third the same year in Guadalajara.

By 1953 Sears had seven stores in Mexico and annual sales of more than $15 million. The company was credited with having helped 1,300 Mexican manufacturers get into business, expand, and diversify. It often lent money, making advance payments of up to 50 percent for merchandise. Of its 1,900 employees, all but 19 were Mexicans. They received overtime, merit raises, cost-of-living allowances, paid vacations, profit-sharing contributions to a retirement fund, access to company cafeterias serving lunch at cost, free medical treatment and medicines, and a discount on purchases. Salespeople received a commission on top of base salary.

By 1956 there were 17 Sears stores in Mexico, nine of which had opened the previous year. Their combined sales volume was around $25 million, and only 16 of 3,200 employees were U.S. citizens. About 90 percent of the merchandise sold was made in Mexico. Installment buying now constituted about half of all sales, indicating that Sears Mexico was reaching the emerging middle class. By 1959 it had over 40,000 items in stock. Of its 3,560 workers, only 22 were not Mexican. Of its 20 stores and sales offices, Mexicans were managing 16.

Losing Its Way in the 1980s

In 1969 Sears, in concert with a trust of the Mexican national bank, established Plaza Universidad, a shopping mall with 80 stores and parking for 1,100 vehicles. It was a partner in the creation of Plaza Satélite in 1971, with space for 3,600 cars. In 1980 it took part in the creation of Perisur, with parking for 6,000 automobiles.

Chosen from among 15,000 applicants, Jorge Lemus went to work as a warehouse checker in the first Sears store for 400 pesos ($US46) a month. In five years he worked his way up to become manager of the Puebla store in 1952. In 1973 he became the first Mexican to head the company, which was by then 80 percent owned by U.S. Sears. The rest was owned by a profit-sharing plan. There were now 38 Sears stores in Mexico, with 6,400 employees and some 3,000 suppliers. In that year the government passed a law by which the company was restricted to a minority interest in any new stores.

During the 1970s Sears Mexico's expansion slowed, but it had 43 stores in 1981 and remained the leading retailer in markets outside the capital, although it faced formidable native competition in Mexico City. The company was now 75 percent-owned by the parent firm and 25 percent by its employees. Sears Mexico responded poorly to the economic crisis of 1982, during which the peso went into free fall. "After the devaluation and the crisis that hit then," a Sears executive told *WWD* in 1995, "we basically cut off all investment and all costs. We instituted mandatory cost decreases in terms of operations. What we ended up doing was not operating the store intelligently. We lost market share."

Resurgence, 1987–94

It was only in 1987 that Sears decided again to adopt an aggressive marketing strategy in Mexico. "By the end of the 1980s Sears just wasn't living up to our Mexican customers' expectations," Thurman Williams, who became president of the chain in 1988, told the *Wall Street Journal* in 1993. "We had to choose between getting serious about Mexico or getting out of the market." The company had been in the red, but soon it was making money again.

Sears Mexico aimed for the affluent top tenth of the population in this period by upgrading its stores. A new one in Mexico City's suburb of Villa Coapa had marble floors, tastefully subdued lighting, and fashions by Nina Ricci, fragrances by Guerlain, and Bally shoes. The Sears private-label credit card gained the highest penetration in its market sector, with some 900,000 holders in 1993. Its average sales per store was still lower than its main competitors, but analysts were impressed by the credit-card operation and the fact that it was the only store chain with automotive centers.

In 1992 Sears Mexico had 37 stores and annual sales of $410 million. That year it went public, selling 25 percent of its stock for $144.7 million, with the money to be used to remodel existing stores and to open new ones. Also in 1992, Sears opened a 55,000-square-foot self-service discount test store in Pachuca. This outlet offered carpeting, furniture (both upholstered and ready-to-assemble), an auto service center and Craftsman tools center, a videocassette rental department, a basic assortment of soft goods, and candy and snack foods.

Sears Mexico opened a furniture store in Gómez Palacio in 1993 to sell primarily imported furniture. This was the first Homelife Sears store outside the United States, and the company followed with several more in 1994. Imports included products from Singer, Bassett, Guildcraft, Klaussner, Action, Pilliod, and Howard Miller Clock. Lower tariffs resulting from the North American Free Trade Agreement (NAFTA) were expected to have a significant impact on the Homelife format.

Sears had 45 stores in early 1994. Metropolitan-area stores ranged in size between 110,000 and 170,000 square feet while smaller communities had stores of 50,000 to 75,000 square feet but the same inventory, although in smaller quantities. The company was considering adding a third tier of stores for rural areas, with Sears's basic merchandise but a less upscale image, substituting, for example, carpeting for marble floors. New that year was its Santa Fe outlet in Mexico City, located in the largest mall in Latin America. This four-story emporium resembled a specialty store, with the emphasis on apparel and women's labels like Jones New York and Evan-Picone that were not carried in Sears' U.S. stores. Apparel was accounting for 40 percent of the chain's sales, with half of the merchandise being made in Mexico, including licensed designer labels like Oscar de la Renta and Christian Dior.

In 1993 Sears Mexico had net income of 237.4 million pesos ($US75.4 million) on sales of 1.71 billion pesos ($US542.9 million). Warren Flick, who succeeded Williams as chief executive officer of the chain in 1994, estimated that by the early part of the 21st century the company would have more than 100 stores, representing an increase of 20 percent per year in floor space. He told developers that Sears was searching for more space and was "willing to be a tenant, to go into a joint venture, or to do it on our own. We are not going to wait." The company was planning to open 22 stores in the next three years with a capital investment of $250 million.

Dealing with the Crisis, 1994–97

Following the economic crisis that descended on Mexico after a capital outflow resulted in the peso devaluation of December 1994, such U.S. competitors as J.C. Penney, Dillard Department Stores, and Wal-Mart Stores temporarily put their expansion plans on hold, but Sears intended to fortify its position as Mexico's only national department-store chain. To help keep costs in line, Flick emphasized a buy-Mexico-first strategy. "The customer is resorting to basics," he told *WWD* in 1995. "They still want fashion, they still want a label, but they are buying more moderate labels." Focus groups had indicated that Mexicans regarded Sears Mexico as generally overpriced for many of the country's middle class.

During the second half of 1994, before the full effects of devaluation, the company earned 37.7 million pesos (about $10.8 million) on sales of 898.1 million pesos (about $256.6 million), but in the first half of 1995 it lost 47.9 million pesos ($US7.9 million) on sales of 827.5 million pesos ($US135.7 million). For 1995 as a whole the company lost 647.4 million pesos ($US95.2 million) on sales of 2.18 billion pesos ($US320.6 million).

Under the impact of the economic crisis, Sears Mexico modified its merchandising program. It set aside part of each department for items priced under 200 pesos ($US33), which represented about one-fourth of its women's apparel. It increased the ratio of its domestic merchandise from 65 percent to 85 percent and the ratio of soft goods to hard goods from 50 percent to 70 percent. Some of the higher-end labels were replaced with lower-priced Mexican-made clothes that were similarly styled. The company also was turning to Mexican manufacturers to produce its private-label apparel.

In April 1997 parent Sears, Roebuck & Co. reduced its stake in Sears Mexico from 75 to 15 percent, selling the remainder to the giant Mexican conglomerate Grupo Carso for $103 million. Grupo Carso also made a tender offer for the remaining shares. Since the devaluation, Sears Mexico stock had been trading at less than half of book value. The company retained the right to use the Sears name in Mexico under an exclusive license with a five-year initial period.

In a conference call addressed to media and securities analysts immediately after the purchase, Fernando Chico Pardo, a managing director of Grupo Carso, declared, "We don't plan to change the Sears concept, or we wouldn't have asked to buy the brand." He endorsed the company's growing orientation to a lower-middle-class-to-middle-class consumer but went on to add that the chain had "an ambience and merchandise that look 40 years old." Chico Pardo revealed plans to implement point-of-sale technology similar to systems used in Sears's U.S. stores so that Grupo Carso could micromerchandise the Mexican units. One analyst told *WWD* that some Sears stores "need some heavy renovations. They also have a lot of work to do on merchandising."

In 1997 Sears Roebuck de México had 47 stores (of which 12 were in the Mexico City metropolitan area and 8 were wholly owned), ownership of a shopping mall, and part ownership of two other malls. Some 64 percent of its sales in 1996 were made through its credit card, and it had 1.9 million credit-card accounts.

Further Reading

Fusoni, Anna, "Sears Says It's Still Go in Mexico," *Home Furnishing News*, January 9, 1995, p. 11.
"How Sears Moved into Mexico," *Business Week*, May 9, 1953, p. 168.
James, Daniel, "Sears, Roebuck's Mexican Revolution," *Harper's*, June 1959, pp. 65–70.
Meyers, Harold Barton, "That Incredible Economy South of the Border," *Fortune*, September 1975, pp. 115–16.
Millman, Joel, "Sears Will Sell Most of Its Stake in Mexican Unit," *Wall Street Journal*, April 3, 1997, p. B9A.
Moffett, Matt, "Chic Star of Mexican Retailing: Sears Roebuck," *Wall Street Journal*, March 8, 1993, pp. B1, B6.
Ramey, Joanna, "Sears Says It'll Stick with Mexico Agenda," *WWD*, April 11, 1995, pp. 2, 19.
——, "Sears in Mexico: Policing Its Prices," *WWD*, August 2, 1995, p. 16.
"Sears de México Looks to Homelife," *Furniture Today*, February 14, 1994, p. 26.
Seckler, Valerie, and Ramey, Joanna, "Sears Mexico Maps Mission," *WWD*, April 9, 1997, p. 20.
"Selling More for Less in Latin America," *Business Week*, June 4, 1949, pp. 105–06.
"South of the Border," *Nation's Business*, May 1954, pp. 68, 70, 72–73.

—Robert Halasz

Seattle FilmWorks, Inc.

1260 16th Avenue West
Seattle, Washington 98119–3401
U.S.A.
(206) 281-1390
Fax: (206) 285-5357
Web site: http://www. filmworks.com

Public Company
Incorporated: 1976 as American Passage Marketing
Employees: 608
Sales: $84.15 million (1996)
Stock Exchanges: NASDAQ
SICs: 5961 Catalog and Mail Order Houses; 7384 Photo Finishing Laboratories

Seattle FilmWorks, Inc. markets film and photofinishing services to amateur photographers through the mail. The company maintains a photofinishing laboratory in Seattle, Washington. The lab has the potential to process 160,000 rolls of film weekly, with 24-hour turnaround from receipt of film to production of finished photos. In 1996, 450 employees worked at the lab in production areas; 70 held positions in administration; 23 held jobs in marketing; 53 in customer service; and 12 in research-and-development activities. Approximately 95 percent of Seattle FilmWorks's sales come from direct-mail activities, although the company also maintains 12 retail stores in the Seattle area. The company's imaginative leadership excels at adding value to its products and services through innovation and the adaptation of new technologies for computer-savvy customers.

In addition to its direct-mail photofinishing services, Seattle FilmWorks offers its customers photo reprint and enlargement services, as well as private-label photofinishing services on retail and wholesale basis. The company also wholesales 35 mm rolled film, single-use cameras, and photofinishing supplies to photofinishing mini-labs, retail stores, and commercial users. Such supplies are packaged by the Seattle FilmWorks and sold under the company's OptiColor Film and Photo brand name;

film and single-use cameras, however, are sold on private labels. Seattle FilmWorks also licenses digital technology to photo finishers outside of the United States. Seattle FilmWorks reorganized in 1996 when the company formed two subsidiaries: Seattle FilmWorks Manufacturing Company and Opti-Color, Inc.

Origins in Direct Marketing

The company known today as Seattle FilmWorks was founded in 1976 as American Passage Marketing by Gilbert Scherer. The company offered primarily media and marketing services, but also initiated photofinishing services as a secondary area of operation. The photofinishing services did well, so during the 1970s the company began offering innovative products and services to enhance this area of operation. It introduced its own brand of film and offered customers both prints and slides from the same roll of film.

American Passage Marketing became a public company in 1986. Two years later the photofinishing segment of the business accounted for 90 percent of the company's activities. In 1988, American Passage Marketing split into two distinct organizations. Scherer left the company, taking with him all operations not related to photofinishing. Gary Christopherson replaced Scherer as the leader of the photofinishing business.

A Visionary Leader

Formerly a public-policy researcher, Christopherson joined American Passage Marketing in 1982 as the director and vice-president of operations. In 1983, he was promoted to senior vice-president and general manager. As the manager of the company's film operations, Christopherson eventually assumed responsibility for refining its direct marketing operations. As Piper Jaffray analyst Robert Toomy told *Forbes:* "Gary is a marketing genius." During the 1980s Christopherson focused on customer service, encouraging innovations that ultimately would be copied by other photo finishers. When Seattle Film-Works established itself as a separate company from American Passage Marketing, Christopherson became the new company's chief executive officer and president. By 1990, Christopherson had created a steadily growing mail-order business in an industry known for little or no growth.

Innovation and Technological Advancements

Photo finishers traditionally competed fiercely for their shares of a stagnant market. For example, Photo Marketing International Association statistics from 1990 through 1997 showed that people took roughly the same number of pictures at the start of the decade as near its end. When supermarkets and drug stores began offering photo services—including services such as inexpensive onsite and one-hour photofinishing—competition in the industry increased further. But a strong plan, innovation, and value-added products and services were at the heart of Christopherson's operating strategy, which differentiated Seattle FilmWorks from its competitors. ''What separates us,'' explained Christopherson in *Chain Store Age Executive with Shopping Center Age,* ''is we're not a price cutter. We add value to photofinishing. We specialize in developing 35 mm photographs, and there are more and more people today who appreciate quality processing.''

Indeed, the company's dedication to innovation and technology secured its place in the photofinishing industry, for—as Smith Barney's Peter Enderlund told *Chain Store Executive Age with Shopping Center Age*— ''Seattle FilmWorks has been one of a few of its kind of business to have a solid growth plan that they meet year after year. The company has a commitment to research and development to bring forth innovations that separate it from the competition.''

At first, Seattle FilmWorks took modest steps toward innovation. In 1978, the company launched its own brand of film and offered customers photo prints and color-corrected slides from one roll of film. During the 1980s, the company initiated a special introductory offer to film-processing customers: Each received two rolls of Seattle FilmWorks film for $2.00 or less. Seattle FilmWorks advertised the offer in newspaper supplements, magazines, and package inserts.

A Decade of Changes

Mail-order turnaround time haunted Seattle FilmWorks throughout the 1980s. Average time from the customer sending film to receiving finished pictures took seven to 10 days—far longer than the one-hour service of some competitors. So in 1991, Seattle FilmWorks instituted Express Mail pick up and delivery services through the U.S. Postal Service for customers willing to pay an extra charge for more speedy processing. The company also shortened its lab processing time to one day.

That same year Seattle FilmWorks initiated an Easy-Order System for standing orders. This convenience eliminated repeat order forms for customers with standing orders. In 1992, the company began backprinting. The date, roll identification, and print number appeared on the reverse of each photo printed by the company. Such cross-referencing information was included on corresponding negative strips as well.

Seattle FilmWorks also began Professor FilmWorks in 1992. This service offered customers using a toll-free number brief prerecorded photography lessons over the telephone. Backprinting evolved into the Pictures Plus Index by 1993. This innovation allowed thumbnail images of each photo from a roll of film to appear on a single four-inch by six-inch print for easy duplication of prints and convenient indexing of stored photos.

Digital Imaging Technology

Seattle FilmWorks pioneered digital imaging technology beginning in 1994. Recognizing digital technology as a threat to conventional photography, the company took its first steps to compete in this new arena. The company first offered Pictures on Disk in 1994. This service provided customers with digital versions of the images on a roll of film on one floppy disk for use on home personal computers.

Also in 1994, Seattle FilmWorks introduced its PhotoWorks software for MS-DOS and Windows. This software created digitized photos for PC use. A customer could send his or her 35 mm film to the company and receive prints, picture files on a floppy disk, negatives, and a free roll of film for about $14.00 for 24 exposures. The customer could then create digital photo albums or incorporate his or her pictures as digital images into text, slide shows, or screen savers. Of the photo digitizing alternatives available, Seattle FilmWorks's held some distinct advantages: PhotoWorks found a market as the most affordable product of its nature. Competitors such as Kodak, for example, priced their CD-ROM photo software for the high end of the market.

Seattle FilmWorks also recognized digital cameras as an evolutionary leap from conventional photofinishing. Savvy PC users now could purchase digital cameras and ''develop'' their own pictures stored as bytes on computer chips, ready for downloading on their home computers. So Seattle FilmWorks gave customers PhotoWorks software with their first Pictures on Disk orders. Customers also could download the software from Seattle FilmWorks's web site without charge. PhotoWorks produced excellent thumbnail images for identifying pictures that the user might want, making it the easiest product through which to find images. Maarten Heilbron, writing in *Computing Canada,* noted: ''Whether you are creating graphics for a Web site, or storing interesting pictures from the Web, PhotoWorks is an ideal bitmap image companion.''

Seattle FilmWorks issued an upgrade to PhotoWorks for Windows—PhotoWorks Plus—in 1994. The company sold this version directly to customers or through selected software retailers. In 1995 a Mac version of the software became available. That same year, Compaq installed PhotoWorks software on its Presario personal computer models as a pre-loaded feature. In August 1996, Seattle FilmWorks published a 260-page reference guide to the software: *PhotoWorks Plus—How to Use Every Feature.*

To complement PhotoWorks and to speed turnaround time, Seattle FilmWorks launched PhotoMail in 1995. Basically, PhotoMail provided customers with the private delivery of digitized images over the Internet. The customer would mail his or her film to Seattle FilmWorks with a downloaded order form. The company then would send the customer an e-mail message alerting him or her when the pictures were ready for downloading, including a special access code to ensure privacy for downloading. Twenty-four exposures—about 1.3 MB of data—would take about seven or eight minutes to download with a 28,800 bps modem. The cost of 24 four-inch by six-inch prints was about $15.00.

Seattle FilmWorks also introduced multimedia e-mail in 1995. Like some of the company's other products and services, multimedia e-mail provided pictures from 35 mm film as digitized images and on floppy disk. Using PhotoPlus software, a customer could convert digitized photos to a common format for sending pictures online; for example, JPEG files. Then the customer could attach a photo and audio clip to an e-mail message in a Windows WAV file and transmit photo, text, and sound to friends and family through Prodigy's online network.

In 1996 Seattle FilmWorks made a related service—FilmWorks Net—available. This free service allowed customers to create photographic home pages uploaded to the company's web site. Guest passwords admitted family and friends to the customers' home pages.

Computer Users and Other Customers

As extensions of the Pictures on Disk service, these Internet-based services appealed greatly to PC devotees. Beginning in 1995, Seattle FilmWorks successfully targeted home computer users as a customer base. When announcing the company's eighth consecutive year of record revenues and earning in a 1996 news release, Christopherson noted that "we attribute these strong results to the continued expansion of our core business, largely by targeting users of home computers. Our Pictures on Disk, PhotoWorks, and Internet services and products give customers exciting new ways to use and share their photos."

Identifying customers with a common characteristic—such as personal computer users—had long been a tactic employed by Seattle FilmWorks, and the company proved to be very good at acquiring customers. "We're a direct marketing company

that happens to do photofinishing," explained Case Kuehn, chief financial officer of Seattle Film Works, in the *Puget Sound Business Journal.* "We're sort of tight-lipped about how we get our names. The industry has been scratching its head wondering how can it grow, but we've been able to figure out ways to increase market share." One method of adding customers included a referral program by established customers. In a 15-year period, the company managed to compile a massive database that profiled and identified existing and potential customers, as well as commanded 24 percent of the mail-order market share by 1994.

As one of *Consumer Reports* top-rated companies, Seattle FilmWorks worked for customer loyalty throughout its history. The company delivered 99.8 percent of its orders without loss or damage and attracted new customers when competitors' could not. For instance, Seattle FilmWorks's net revenues grew at an 18 percent compound annual rate from 1991 through 1996 when the rest of the industry saw little—if any—growth. In order to maintain this momentum, Seattle FilmWorks planned to increase its sales to customers through bigger average order sizes, by increasing the frequencies of orders, and by using more digital-imaging products and additional Internet-related services to attract new and keep established customers. As Christopherson explained in the 1996 annual report: "We have continued our company's growth by marketing differentiated products that represent added value to our customers. . . . These advances add further value to Seattle FilmWorks's photofinishing product, differentiating us from the competition. By creating products that combine the digitization of photographic images with traditional processing technology, we have strengthened our product line. That has helped us acquire a record number of new customers during the year as we have been able to focus our customer-acquisition efforts on computer users."

Principal Subsidiaries

Seattle FilmWorks Manufacturing Company; OptiColor, Inc.

Further Reading

Fryer, Alex P., "Seattle FilmWorks Finds New Customers in Computer Niche," *Puget Sound Business Journal,* August 4, 1995, p. 8.

"Gary Christopherson," *Chain Store Age Executive with Shopping Center Age,* December 1996, p. 74.

Heilbron, Maarten, "Ideal Bitmap Companion," *Computing Canada,* July 4, 1996, p. 29.

Henricks, Mark, "The Digital Family Album," *Popular Science,* July 1995, p. 45.

Kirschnet, Suzanne Kantra, "Photos by the Web," *Popular Science,* July 1996, p. 30.

"Say http://cheese," *PC Week,* December 18, 1995, p. E5.

Wooley, Scott, "An Unflattering Closeup," *Forbes,* January 13, 1997, p. 58.

—Charity Anne Dorgan

The Stanley Works

1000 Stanley Drive
New Britain, Connecticut 06053
U.S.A.
(860) 225-5111
Fax: (860) 827-3895
Web site: http://www.stanleyworks.com

Public Company
Incorporated: 1852
Employees: 18,903
Sales: $2.67 billion (1996)
Stock Exchanges: New York Pacific
SICs: 3421 Cutlery; 3423 Hand & Edge Tools, Except
 Machine Tools & Hand Saws; 3425 Hand Saws &
 Blades; 3429 Hardware, Not Elsewhere Classified;
 3496 Miscellaneous Fabricated Wire Products; 3541
 Machine Tools, Metal Cutting Types; 3546 Power
 Driven Hand Tools

The Stanley Works is a manufacturer of a broad range of tools and hardware for home improvement, consumer, industrial, and professional applications. Stanley is a global manufacturer, with production facilities in 18 countries, and is the world leader in hand tools, based on its 20 percent share of a $12 billion market. Stanley is an old and successful company in a hidebound industry—metalworking—that has proven extremely vulnerable to foreign competition since the 1960s.

Stanley Brothers Founded Company in Mid-19th Century

The company was founded in 1843 by Frederick T. Stanley, a 41-year-old merchant and manufacturer whose previous work experience included stints as a clerk on a Connecticut River steamboat and as an itinerant peddler in the South. In 1831, Stanley, in partnership with his younger brother William Stanley, had opened a small facility in New Britain, Connecticut, for the manufacture of house trimmings and door locks. Though the business failed to survive the Panic of 1837, it seemed to have served as the prototype for a second manufacturing venture in New Britain—Stanley's Bolt Manufactory—which Frederick Stanley, again in concert with his brother, established in 1843.

The establishment of this "manufactory" marks the official beginning of the Stanley story. The company's present name was adopted in 1852, when the Stanley brothers—along with five neighbors—were granted a charter of incorporation by the state of Connecticut for a newly organized firm, The Stanley Works. This corporation, initially capitalized at $30,000, was to be directed by Frederick T. Stanley, who was named its first president.

During its early years Stanley was one of hundreds of similar companies in antebellum America producing hardware and builders' goods. Frederick Stanley was not unique in perceiving an entrepreneurial opening for such goods in a nation growing and industrializing as rapidly as the United States. There were scores of shops similar to his in Connecticut alone.

If Frederick Stanley had an early competitive advantage, at least locally, it may have been in his manufactory's power source, a single-cylinder high-pressure steam engine, which he had purchased from the firm of William Burdon of Brooklyn. This relatively sophisticated engine enabled Stanley's Bolt Manufactory and, later, The Stanley Works, to produce goods—whether bolts, T-hinges, or wrought-iron straps—in a more capital-intensive and efficient way than was the case in less automated shops in the area.

Nevertheless, the firm's early growth was not exceptionally rapid. Total sales were $7,328 in 1853 and $21,371 in 1854, and rose to about $53,000 in 1860, on the eve of the Civil War. Only after that conflict ended would the dramatic rise of The Stanley Works begin.

To say that the firm's rise postdated the Civil War is not to imply that the war itself was directly or fundamentally responsible. More significant than any war-induced demand for Stanley's products were deep-seated economic forces related to industrialization and increased market size and integration. Productivity gains made possible through mechanization and the creation, via the railroad, of an embryonic national market transformed the U.S. business environment in the late 19th century, presenting new opportunities to—and posing new

476

Company Perspectives:

All Stanley employees share a common vision: To please our customers so well that our products are their first choice. *As a resource for customers around the globe, we are committed to providing: innovative products which are appropriately tailored to meet regional needs throughout the world; outstanding customer service and effective marketing support; specialized products to fulfill individual customer requirements; a company-wide commitment to rigid environmental and quality standards for our manufacturing—worldwide.*

problems for—most U.S. manufacturers. Alfred D. Chandler describes this transformation in his *The Visible Hand: The Managerial Revolution in American Business.*

In order to exploit new production and marketing possibilities and to overcome problems arising from oversupply and greater competition, Stanley developed new business strategies and structures. In so doing, it integrated and expanded its operations, and employed new productivity-enhancing and competition-dampening methods of production, marketing, and organization.

Such policies resulted in the dramatic growth of The Stanley Works. Frederick T. Stanley seems to have had little to do with the company's rapid postwar ascent; from the 1860s to the time of his death in 1883, he increasingly withdrew from active business operations, devoting more of his time to politics and civic affairs in New Britain. The animating spirit behind Stanley's rise was William H. Hart, whose career with the firm stretched from 1854 to 1918.

William H. Hart Led Company's Dramatic Early Growth

Prior to joining Stanley in 1854 at the age of 19, Hart, like a number of 19th-century industrialists, had worked in the railroad industry—as a freight agent and assistant station manager. Hart rose quickly at Stanley, assuming the position of secretary-treasurer a few months after joining the firm and in 1856, before he had reached the age of 21, winning election to the board of directors. From there, he gradually took on more direct managerial responsibility, eventually rising to the position of president, a post he held from May 1884 to February 1915.

Under Hart's leadership, the firm pursued a number of successful strategies that enabled Stanley to thrive even in the fiercely competitive business environment of the day. Hart expanded hardware production facilities in New Britain in 1866, for example, and in 1909 opened new facilities in Niles, Ohio—strategically located in the steel belt of northeastern Ohio—and in Canada in 1914. He helped to reduce Stanley's production costs by mechanizing operations to a greater degree and by repositioning equipment in his factories. Manufacturing technology improved dramatically under his helm—Stanley was particularly important in the development of a process for the cold rolling of wrought-iron strip—and the firm came to hold several

significant manufacturing patents, including one issued in 1889 for the development of the first hinge to use ball bearings.

At Hart's urging, the firm made several small but noteworthy innovations in the marketing of hardware, packing installation screws along with the firm's hinges and shipping hardware in labeled boxes. In 1870, when Stanley opened a sales office in New York City, the firm began to devote attention to developing export markets for its products, a precocious strategy for the time.

Hart also tried to diversify the company and to develop a fuller product line. By moving into the production of steel strapping at the turn of the century, for example, Stanley was able to not only diversify its operations but also vertically integrate to a degree. The move into steel strapping was to prove of major consequence to the company; Stanley was one of the nation's leading manufacturers of this product before moving out of the industry in 1987.

Stanley had an impressive record of expansion in the period between the beginning of the Civil War and the end of World War I. The company's net sales by 1872 had already reached $480,000, a ninefold increase over the figure for 1860. By 1919, the year after Hart stepped down as chairman of the board, net sales were over $11 million. Nor was Stanley's a case of growth at any cost; in 1877 the firm began an unbroken streak of yearly dividends. During World War I Stanley produced belt buckles, gas mask components, and ammunition tubes.

Although William H. Hart was the central figure in the rise of The Stanley Works—the company's trademark was heart-shaped for a time—Stanley survived his departure. By the time Hart retired as chairman in 1918, he had created a corporate culture and strategy conducive to continued growth.

Acquisitions Fueled 1920s Growth

Stanley's efforts to reduce costs, often through external integration, and to diversify did not abate with Hart's retirement. For example, after years of trying, the firm was able to cut energy costs by purchasing—and later rebuilding—a hydroelectric power plant on the Farmington River near New Britain. Even more important, however, was the firm's 1920 merger with its crosstown neighbor in that city, The Stanley Rule & Level Company, an old-line manufacturer of measuring devices and hand tools, which had been founded in 1857 by a cousin of Frederick Stanley. The acquisition of Stanley Rule & Level—at the time one of the largest and most respected companies in its field—allowed The Stanley Works to increase its labor force by some 1,200 workers, its capitalization by 50 percent, and its net sales by $6 million. In addition, it brought Stanley the benefits of diversification, without distancing the company from its historical roots or its areas of experience and expertise: hardware, hand tools, and measuring devices were naturally complementary.

Stanley Rule & Level had long been active in the merger and acquisition business itself. As early as 1863 the firm had acquired a competitor, the Brattleboro, Vermont, rule factory of E.A. Stearns & Company. Two later acquisitions, that of the Atha Tool Company of Newark, New Jersey, in 1913 and that of the Eagle Square Manufacturing Company—a maker of carpenters' steel squares, based in Shaftsbury, Vermont—in 1916 contributed significantly both to the company's growth and to its appeal.

Although similar strategies were being employed elsewhere as well, the consolidation of Stanley Rule & Level into The Stanley Works—and the success of this consolidation—clearly spurred the development of one of Stanley's principal growth strategies in the post-1920 period, the aggressive pursuit of competing or related companies through merger or acquisition. Other, less dramatic, growth strategies were also employed. During the interwar period, the company continued to expand operations into new geographical areas, both at home and abroad. Stanley opened a woodworking plant in 1923, for example, in Pulaski, Tennessee, near timberlands which the company had acquired previously. By 1926 Stanley was producing hardware in Germany, and in 1937 the firm opened a factory in Sheffield, England, for the manufacture of hand tools.

Technological innovations also continued under Hart's immediate successors, at times furthering the company's efforts to develop a fuller product line and to diversify. Perhaps the most impressive individual innovation during the interwar years was Stanley's introduction in 1931 of the first automated entranceway in the United States, a technology the company patented under the name Magic Eye. The Magic Eye, which opened doors through the activation of a photo-electric cell, and other devices based on similar technology became mainstays of Stanley's product line. A number of other products were also introduced during the period, most notably a line of electric tools, which were produced under a new division established in 1929.

Great Depression Brought on Decline

If Stanley's culture and strategy were still conducive to profits and growth, they were not enough to assure either. Between roughly 1930 and 1945, economic and political conditions were at work that minimized the difference corporate culture and strategy—good or bad—could make. Stanley's fortunes declined sharply during the Great Depression, which hit manufacturing and construction—and thus the tool and hardware industries—extremely hard. The company's net income was negative in 1932, for example, and, after paying out dividends, Stanley ran a deficit on its income account in 1934 as well.

Stanley's performance in the 15 years after 1930 was neither fundamentally shaped nor adversely affected by corporate decisionmaking. The four men who successively followed William Hart as president—his son, George P. Hart, who served from 1915 to 1918; E. Allen Moore, whose term began in 1918 and ended in 1923; Clarence F. Bennett, who was president from 1923 until 1941; and Richard E. Pritchard, who served between 1941 and 1950—each performed ably, but to little effect.

With the advent of World War II Stanley, of necessity, had been forced to retool, transforming itself for the most part into a manufacturer of military hardware. Annual sales rose significantly as a result, reaching $44 million in 1943. Yet wartime sales were just that; Stanley sold 460 million belt links for machine gun bullets and 36 million cartridge clips during World War II, but this contribution did not boost its postwar performance.

Struggled During Immediate Postwar Years

The same management strategy that had helped the firm to succeed earlier limited the company's performance in the dec-

ades after the war. In emphasizing manufacturing matters, key decisionmakers tended to neglect the marketing and financial dimensions of Stanley's operations. This situation was particularly true between 1945 and the early 1960s.

Despite the fact that Stanley—like many traditional New England manufacturers—continued to produce high-quality products during this period, the company's expansion was slow and its earnings erratic. For example, Stanley's annual net sales, already over $90 million in 1951, had grown only to $95.4 million by 1960; moreover, the company's earnings for 1948—$5.25 million—were surpassed only twice between that year and 1965.

Stanley's sluggish performance in this period was shaped in part by structural factors. Much of America's basic manufacturing sector—the principal market for Stanley's products—was not mature, which dampened opportunities for rapid growth. Even when opportunities did present themselves in basic manufacturing—some segments of the metal-working industry did, in fact, grow rapidly during this period—Stanley, entrenched in its traditional lines, could not always move quickly. Indeed, were it not for the postwar baby boom, which boosted the U.S. construction industry and thus the demand for builders' tools, Stanley's record might have been worse.

While Stanley's management neglected certain key business functions, they were not totally inert and their policies were not ineffectual. Under the leadership of John C. Cairns, chief executive officer from 1950 to 1966, the company made several important acquisitions and continued efforts to expand to modernize existing operations. During the 1950s Stanley acquired the Humason Manufacturing Company of Forestville, Connecticut, a maker of springs and screw machine parts; the H. L. Judd Company of Wallingford, Connecticut, a large producer of drapery hardware; and the Florida-based Denison Corporation, a manufacturer of aluminum window frames and doors. In addition, in 1957 Stanley opened a 115,000-square-foot, state-of-the-art steel-strapping plant in New Britain, which nearly doubled the firm's manufacturing capacity for this product.

Company Revitalized by Donald W. Davis Starting in Early 1960s

Nonetheless, as Stanley entered the decade of the 1960s, its management's recent performance had been disappointing. Fortunately for Stanley, a bright and energetic young executive, Donald W. Davis—the most important figure in the company's history since William H. Hart—was coming to the fore.

Born in Springfield, Massachusetts, in 1921, Davis joined The Stanley Works in 1948. He rose rapidly at Stanley and in 1962 was promoted from his position as general manager of the steel-strapping division to executive vice president of the firm. With this promotion Davis took de facto control of the company, functioning as Stanley's chief operating officer between 1962 and 1966, when he was named president and chief executive officer.

In the quarter century between 1962, when Davis assumed control, and 1987, when he turned over day-to-day managerial responsibilities to Richard H. Ayers, Davis was able not merely to rouse Stanley from its long postwar slumber, but to transform the company into an aggressive leader in the globally competitive tool and hardware industry.

Stanley's rejuvenation program under Davis can be broken down into several distinct parts. Each part of the program was shaped by his recognition that if Stanley was to remain a central player in the industry, the company would have to become more competitive and would have to assume a more aggressive, growth-oriented posture. Davis believed that as world markets became more integrated, Stanley—as well as The Black & Decker Corporation, Snap-On Tools Corporation, and other U.S. tool and hardware companies—would have to face the harsh reality of global competition for the first time.

Davis called for increased competitiveness and faster growth at The Stanley Works. Under his leadership the company rationalized production and modernized plant facilities; aggressively pursued mergers and acquisitions, while at the same time divesting itself of poorly performing or nonstrategic divisions and product lines; identified new markets and penetrated such markets once identified; devoted much more attention to marketing and advertising; and exploited more fully international manufacturing and marketing opportunities.

In order to see these policies through, Davis, along with Garth W. Edwards, vice president for finance, overturned company policy in the mid-1960s by taking Stanley into long-term debt. This gambit proved extraordinarily successful; over time, borrowed funds helped to accomplish Davis's goals without compromising Stanley's financial integrity through excessive leveraging.

Davis used retained earnings, equity capital, and borrowed funds to build a number of new plants—the hand-tool plant that Stanley opened in New Britain in 1964 was the largest in the world at the time—and to upgrade existing facilities. Between 1979 and 1983 the company spent about $55 million yearly on upgrades alone. In part as a result of such efforts, Stanley was able over time to improve substantially both its capital-labor ratio and its overall manufacturing productivity.

During Davis's tenure Stanley made more than 25 major acquisitions, including Berry Industries (maker of garage doors and operators; acquired in 1965); Volkert Stampings (stampings and components in the television, radio, spacecraft, and electronic equipment industries; 1966); Ackley Manufacturing Company (hydraulic tools; 1971); Compo-Cast ("dead blow" striking tools; 1980); Mac Tools (auto-repair tools; 1980); Taylor Rental Corporation (tool rental centers; 1983); Proto Industrial Tools (specialty industrial tools; 1984); National Hand Tool (mechanic's hand tools; 1986); and Textron's Bostich Division (fasteners and fastening tools; 1986). During the 1980s Davis streamlined the company by selling off its garden-tool and electric-tool businesses, its drapery-hardware business, and its steel and steel-strapping divisions. In 1986 Stanley sold its South African interests to local management.

Successful Pursuit of Do-It-Yourself Market Starting in Early 1970s

Stanley's modernization, acquisition, and rationalization strategies under Davis were impressive. More impressive still were the company's efforts during the same period to identify and penetrate new markets. In particular, Stanley's early and aggressive push during the early 1970s into the so-called do-it-yourself (DIY), or consumer, hand-tool market paid handsome returns. This market—propelled by such factors as inflationary building and repair costs, a shortage of skilled tradesmen, and the movement of upscale baby boomers into older homes—became one of Stanley's largest and most profitable markets and one of its most important in strategic terms. Because the DIY market, unlike Stanley's others, was countercyclical, the chances that a general economic downturn would spell disaster to the firm were now significantly reduced.

In order to establish itself in the DIY market, and for other strategic reasons as well, Stanley, formerly a production-driven company, committed itself under Davis to developing its marketing capabilities. By working more closely with wholesalers and retailers of its products, increasing its market research, and, perhaps most importantly, making a sizable investment in television advertising, the company over time did just that. The phrase "Stanley helps you do things right"—coined by Davis—became familiar in different languages around the world.

Stanley became a much more international company under Davis. Not only did the firm increase its commitment to exporting but it also expanded foreign production by acquiring facilities in Latin America, Canada, France, and Germany. Perhaps most significant of all, given geopolitical trends, was Stanley's 1986 move into the Pacific Rim with its acquisition of Taiwan-based Chiro Tool Manufacturing Corporation.

By the time Davis stepped down at Stanley—Richard H. Ayers, who had risen through the ranks since joining Stanley in 1972, succeeded him as president and chief executive officer in 1987 and as board chairman in 1989—the company bore little resemblance to the one Davis had taken over in the early 1960s. Stanley had not merely survived, but had flourished under his helm, with net income and earnings at all-time highs in 1989.

Difficult Years in the 1990s

Unfortunately for The Stanley Works (and Ayers) the optimistic ending of the 1980s was quickly succeeded by the dark days of the early 1990s. First weak economic conditions contributed to flat revenues in both 1990 and 1991 and earnings declines of 9 percent in 1990 and 11 percent in 1991. Then the very future of Stanley as an independent company came into serious doubt through the appearance of a hostile takeover bid.

Stanley had itself taken over numerous companies in its long history but always companies interested in a merger. So it was somewhat ironic that the Newell Company initiated a hostile takeover attempt of Stanley in mid-1991. After initial friendly talks between executives of the two firms led nowhere, Newell—desirous of the respected Stanley brand name—began buying Stanley stock, acquiring a less than 1 percent stake, then filing a notice that it intended to boost this stake. Stanley responded in June 1991 by filing a federal antitrust lawsuit against Newell. Subsequently the state of Connecticut's attorney general, Richard Blumenthal, filed a similar lawsuit, which served to persuade Newell to abandon its hostile bid. In October 1992 a court agreement was reached whereby Newell promised to sell its Stanley stock within one year and not to purchase any additional

Stanley securities or "seek to control or influence Stanley for 10 years." In return Stanley agreed to drop its lawsuit.

As he battled to keep Stanley independent, Ayers also sought out expansion opportunities through joint ventures and acquisitions, the most notable of which increased the company's overseas presence. A 1991 joint-venture agreement created Stanley Poland Ltd. to manufacture tools in the newly opened Eastern Europe. Among 1991 acquisitions were Mosley-Stone, a U.K. maker of paint brushes, rollers, and decorator tools; Nirva, a French manufacturer of closet systems; and Sidcrome Tools, the leading maker of mechanics tools in Australia. The following year brought Stanley a controlling interest in Tona a.s. Pecky, a major Czech manufacturer of mechanics tools. The domestic area was not neglected, however. In 1992 Stanley acquired American Brush Co., Inc., manufacturer of paint brushes and decorator tools; LaBounty Manufacturing, Inc., a maker of large hydraulic tools; Mail Media, a catalog marketer of precision tool kits consisting of Jensen Tools, Inc. and Direct Safety; and Goldblatt Tool Co., which manufactured masonry, tile, and drywall tools.

These acquisitions helped Stanley enter another period of sales growth, as revenues increased each year (to record levels each year) from 1992 through 1996, with the $2 billion sales mark reached for the first time in 1992 and $2.5 billion in 1994. Unfortunately, earnings did not keep pace with sales, and instead bounced up and down during this period.

Starting in 1993—the year Stanley celebrated its 150th anniversary—Ayers began making some restructuring moves in an effort to boost earnings. That year the company's 23 divisions were streamlined into 11. Ayers also sought to make selective divestments of units with low margins, and in 1993 sold the franchise operations of Taylor Rental, then sold the company-owned outlets the following year.

Ayers embarked upon a more aggressive divestment strategy in July 1995 as part of the "Four by Four" program. Over a four-year period Stanley sought, in addition to increasing revenues to $4 billion, to save $400 million by reducing operating costs by $150 million and assets by $250 million. In 1995 and 1996 Stanley exited from eight product categories; closed six factories, three distribution centers, and two support facilities; and eliminated about 550 jobs. In early 1997 the company completed the divestiture portion of "Four by Four" when it sold its garage-related operations—garage doors, garage door openers, and gate operators—to Whistler Corporation. Stanley incurred 1995 charges of $85.5 million and 1996 charges of $47.8 million related to these restructuring moves.

To reach $4 billion in sales by the year 2000, Stanley had to increase revenues 10 percent a year. 1996 sales, however, grew less than 2 percent, and Ayers decided early that year to retire at year-end. Analysts quoted in *Business Week* felt that Stanley needed to bring someone in from the outside to shake things up and reinvigorate the company. Stanley's board did just that when it hired John M. Trani as CEO and chairman at the beginning of 1997. Trani had led the turnaround at General Electric Co.'s GE Medical Systems and had a reputation as a cost-cutter and tough leader. He also had a great deal of experience in the acquisition of foreign companies; this background was likely to be put to use at Stanley, which needed to beef up and improve the profitability of its non-U.S. operations (as of 1996, 71.6 percent of sales were derived from domestic operations, and 84.6 percent of profits).

Trani wasted no time getting started on a possible Stanley turnaround. In April 1997 the company announced a reorganization into a product management structure, aimed at strengthening the Stanley brand, focusing more on customers, improving new product development, and enhancing efficiency. The plan called for the formation of eight new product groups, which would be supported by centralized manufacturing, engineering, sales, and service, and the creation of a new corporate marketing and brand development function.

Although the 1990s were rough years for Stanley, the company seemed poised for a renaissance as it approached a new century, which would be the third for the famous Stanley brand. Competition promised to remain fierce for the foreseeable future but the Trani-led Stanley appeared ready for the challenges ahead.

Principal Divisions

Stanley Tools; Stanley Mechanics Tools; Stanley Storage Systems; Stanley Mail Media; Stanley Fastening Systems; Stanley Hydraulic Tools; Stanley Air Tools; Stanley Hardware; Stanley Home Decor; Stanley Door Systems; Stanley Access Technologies.

Further Reading

Chandler, Alfred D., *The Visible Hand: The Managerial Revolution in American Business*, Cambridge, Mass.: Belknap Press, 1977.

Davis, Donald Walter, *The Stanley Works: A 125 Year Beginning*, New York: The Newcomen Society in North America, 1969, p. 24.

Green, Hardy, "Once a Company Town, Always a Company Town," *Business Week*, September 27, 1993, pp. 28D–28J.

Jackson, Susan, and Tim Smart, "Will the GE Magic Work at Stanley?," *Business Week*, April 21, 1997, pp. 144, 148.

Leavitt, Robert Keith, *Foundation for the Future: History of The Stanley Works*, New Britain, Connecticut: The Stanley Works, 1951.

"Proud of Our Past: 150 Years of Growth Through Excellence at The Stanley Works," New Britain, Connecticut: The Stanley Works, 1993.

Rodengen, Jeffrey L., *The Legend of Stanley: 150 Years of The Stanley Works*, Fort Lauderdale, Florida: Write Stuff Syndicate, 1996.

"Stanley Tries the Faster Track," *Business Week*, November 5, 1966.

Uchitelle, Louis, "The Stanley Works Goes Global," *New York Times*, July 23, 1989, p. F1.

——, "Only the Bosses Are American," *New York Times*, July 24, 1989, p. D1.

Weiner, Steve, "How Do You Say 'Tape Measure' in Chinese?," *Forbes*, June 25, 1990, pp. 96, 99.

Welsh, Jonathan, "Stanley Works Picks GE Official as Chief in Apparent Bid to Boost Overseas Sales," *Wall Street Journal*, January 3, 1997, p. B3.

—Peter A. Coclanis
—updated by David E. Salamie

Stewart Enterprises, Inc.

110 Veterans Memorial Boulevard
Metairie, Louisiana 70005-3027
U.S.A.
(504) 837-5880
Fax: (504) 849-2196
Web site: http://www.stei.com

Public Company
Incorporated: 1970
Employees: 7,500
Sales: $433.4 million (1996)
Stock Exchanges: NASDAQ
SICs: 7261 Funeral Service and Crematories

With over 300 funeral homes and more than 120 cemeteries, Stewart Enterprises, Inc. ranks among the largest and fastest-growing companies in the so-called ''death care'' industry. A program of growth through acquisition that began in the 1970s, gathered steam in the 1980s, and was running full-out in the 1990s built the company from a small Louisiana cemetery operator into a multinational funeral management firm. In the five fiscal years from 1992 through 1996, Stewart's sales increased at an average annual rate of more than 30 percent while net income growth, at nearly 38 percent, outran even that rapid pace. Furthermore, Stewart's stock price increased by a cumulative 334 percent from its initial offering in 1991 to October 31, 1996. Like many of its dozens of subsidiaries, Stewart Enterprises continued to be managed by descendants of the founding family. Chairman Frank B. Stewart Jr., a grandson of the founder, controls nearly 40 percent of the company's voting rights.

Early Twentieth-Century Origins

The company was founded in 1910, when Albert Stewart acquired three New Orleans-area cemeteries and embarked on a renovation program. The business grew modestly over its first two generations of management, diversifying into the construction of mausoleums, vaults, and crypts for its own use and later selling them to other cemetery operators. A major mausoleum first developed by the Stewarts in New Orleans in 1949 would expand over the ensuing four decades to serve as the final resting place for 31,000 of the city's citizens. Reflecting an industry-wide division between cemetery operators and funeral home managers, the Stewarts remained focused on cemetery ownership and management throughout their first 60 years in business. In 1969, the company was still chugging along with its original three cemeteries.

Although it remained a strictly local, family business, Stewart was an early innovator in the industry. For example, it beat many of its rivals into the ''pre-need'' side of the business in the 1950s, nearly two decades before its leading competitors got into the segment. Pre-arrangement of funerals and interment would prove mutually beneficial to the Stewarts and their customers. Clients could make their funerary preferences known to their loved ones in advance, thereby freeing relatives from difficult decisions during the mourning period. Furthermore, customers purchased their cemetery plots and memorials at current prices and could even avail themselves of installment payment plans, rather than leaving the expense to be settled by their estates. Stewart benefited by not only locking in future business and market share, but also by increasing current cash flow. By the mid-1990s, the company's backlog of pre-planned funeral and interment services totaled six times its 1995 volume.

Industry-wide Consolidation Begins in 1960s

The death care industry entered a period of transition in the 1960s, when Service Corp. International emerged as North America's first funeral home conglomerate. The consolidation—albeit gradual—of the industry echoed the evolution of several service industries from a multitude of fragmented ''mom and pop'' type operations into national organizations. Several industry-wide trends fostered the consolidation movement. Some owner-operators grew weary of complying with—or hiring attorneys to deal with—ever-increasing state and federal regulation. Others who found that none of their children were interested in learning and owning the family business began to seek out mergers.

Company Perspectives:

At Stewart Enterprises, we are committed to maintaining a total death care perspective of quality service to individual families in their own communities by offering funeral, cemetery, cremation and memorialization products and services. We intend to maintain and enhance the decentralized, autonomous management structure that remains sensitive to local customs and provides the incentive for so many top-quality professionals to join our ranks. We intend to maintain our leadership in sales of prearrangements and development of combination operations. We will continue our emphasis on enhancing profitability at the level of each individual business, while maintaining a global vision to our acquisition program. We always uphold the value of quality service to families set out by our founders. We will continue to grow globally while we serve locally. It is a formula that has worked quite well since 1910 and promises to work even better as we move into the next millennium.

Not surprisingly, the timing of Stewart's first major acquisition also reflected a generational shift in management. According to a 1993 investment analysis of Stewart by Johnson, Rise & Co., several founding members of the company passed away in the mid-1960s, making way for a new generation of young, aggressive managers led by Frank Stewart, who took the helm in 1967 at the age of 31. Under his leadership, the company acquired New Orleans's most reputable cemetery, Metairie Cemetery, in 1969. The purchase reflected what would become one of the company's most fundamental growth criterion, that acquisitions be "heritage properties." The incorporation of Stewart Enterprises, Inc. one year later integrated the family's holdings.

Stewart Hits Acquisition Trail in 1980s

Nearly a decade would pass before Stewart embarked on a major growth program. The company applied several simple, yet well-considered principles in pursuit of expansion. Realizing that it could not easily supplant the long-established reputations of local funeral homes and cemeteries with its own "brand," Stewart favored acquisitions over the establishment of new funeral homes and cemeteries. He described this particular dynamic to Joseph R. Mancuso of the Center for Entrepreneurial Management in a 1997 interview for *YourCompany.* "Our business is a community business. Owners of funeral homes and cemeteries often are respected individuals who have served families in their neighborhoods for years—sometimes for generations. That's why buying well-established, reputable, family-operated businesses, rather than building companies from scratch, has been a great way to expand into local markets." Stewart's strategy was to purchase the biggest and best facilities in a given metropolitan area, using clustering to effect marketing and administrative economies. Affiliates would, for example, share transportation fleets and crematorium and embalming facilities.

The company made its first foray outside the New Orleans market in 1979, when it acquired one of the industry's largest and most prestigious properties, Dallas's Restland Memorial Park and Funeral Home. Stewart expanded at a relatively moderate pace over the course of the ensuing decade, increasing from five cemeteries and one funeral home to 33 funeral homes and 26 cemeteries throughout the southeastern United States by 1989. At that time, annual revenues totaled $96.8 million. Consolidation paid off handsomely for the company, enabling it to earn pretax profit margins that nearly doubled the industry average.

Stewart did not rely on acquisitions alone to drive its growth during this period, however. The family's decades of experience in cemetery management proved significant. As noted in a 1996 report by Interstate/Johnson Lane, the Stewarts found that "customer loyalty is stronger with a cemetery where family members are buried than with a funeral home." Stewart parlayed this concept into increased market share by building funeral homes on its best cemetery properties in the 1980s. Besides offering "one-stop-shopping," the combinations helped both operations to grow more quickly. By the end of 1996, over two-fifths of Stewart's cemeteries had on-site funeral homes.

IPO Presages Exponential Growth in 1990s

Stewart made its initial public offering in October 1991 with shares starting at $17.75. The company used the proceeds to jump-start its acquisition program, multiplying the number of facilities in its portfolio sevenfold, from less than 60 in 1990 to 425 by the end of 1996. The program took Stewart international in 1993, when it purchased a Puerto Rican funeral home. The company bought the Gayosso group of six upscale funeral homes in Mexico in 1994, entered Australia in 1995, and penetrated New Zealand in 1996. Stewart's biggest single acquisition to date came in 1996, when it purchased Urgel Bourgie, a Canadian group of 77 funeral homes and five cemeteries with a particular concentration in the province of Quebec. On the domestic front, the company began to expand from its southeastern stronghold into the West and Midwest. By the end of 1996, the company had properties in 23 states, up from just six at the time of its IPO.

Notwithstanding the breakneck pace of acquisitions made by Stewart and its two primary rivals, the death care industry remained highly fragmented in 1997. According to the 1994 Survey of Funeral Home Operations quoted in Raymond James & Associates' early 1997 evaluation of Stewart, the Louisiana company and its top four publicly traded competitors only accounted for one-fifth of domestic industry revenues, while more than four-fifths of the nation's 22,000 funeral homes and 9,600 cemeteries remained privately and often family-owned.

These statistics were promising, in that they implied plenty of room for continued consolidation, but there was no question that competition for the choicest properties in each metropolitan area would intensify in the years to come. Those concerns grew somewhat more pressing in 1997, when Service Corp. International, the $2 billion leader of the death care industry, mounted a hostile takeover of second-ranking Loewen Group. If completed, the merger would place Stewart a far-distant No. 2, at less than half a billion in annual revenues, in comparison to Service Corp.'s $3 billion.

These modest caveats went largely unnoticed in the mid-to-late 1990s, however. The price of Stewart's stock increased to $34.25 per share by mid-1996, and when splits were taken into account, the shares had grown more than 300 percent from their offering price. Total revenues more than tripled, from $130.3 million in 1991 to $433.4 million in 1996, while net income quintupled, from $9.4 million to $51.3 million.

Principal Subsidiaries

Acme Mausoleum Corp.; Cemetery Management, Inc.; Griffin Leggett, Inc.; Highland Memorial Cemetery, Inc.; Holly Hill Memorial Park, Inc.; Holly Hills, Inc.; Hopson Mortuary, Inc.; International Stone & Erectors, Inc.; Investors Trust, Inc.; Kingsport Cemetery Corp.; Lake Lawn, Metairie Funeral Home, Inc.; Lake Lawn Metairie Funeral Home (Joint Venture); Lake Lawn Park, Inc. (94%); Lakewood Memorial Park, Inc.; Lassila Funeral Chapels, Inc.; Legacy One, Inc. (94%); Les Enterprises Stewart (Canada) Inc.; Metairie Cemetery Association; Montlawn Memorial Park, Inc.; Mount Olivet Cemetery, Inc.; Nashville Historic Cemetery Association, Inc.; Pasadena Funeral Home, Inc.; Restland Funeral Home, Inc.; Rocky Mount Memorial Park, Inc.; Rose Haven Funeral Home & Cemetery, Inc.; Royal Arms Apartments, Inc.; St. Bernard Memorial Gardens, Inc.; St. Vincent De Paul Cemetery Association; S.E. Acquisition of California, Inc.; S.E. Acquisition of Oregon, Inc.; S.E. Acquisition of Sacramento, California, Inc.; S.E. Australia, Inc.; S.E. Mid-Atlantic, Inc.; S.E. South-central, Inc.; Stewart Resource Center, Inc.; Stewart Services, Inc.; Victor V. Desrosier, Inc.

Further Reading

Byrne, Harlan S., "Stewart Enterprises: 'Death Care' Generates Lively Results," *Barron's,* October 11, 1993, pp. 52–53.

Fitch, Malcolm, "Five Local Favorites Ready to Surge 25% or More," *Money,* August 1996, pp. 39–41.

"Funeral Home Giant Bids for Chief Rival," *Times-Picayune,* September 18, 1996, p. C1.

Haman, John, "Death Becomes Them," *Arkansas Business,* November 29, 1993, pp. 1–3.

Interstate/Johnson Lane, "Stewart Enterprises, Inc.," *Investext,* November 21, 1996.

Johnson, Rice & Co., "Stewart Enterprises—Company Report," *Investext,* February 10, 1977.

Mancuso, Joseph R., "A Buy-Out Strategy to Die For," *YourCompany,* Forecast 1997, p. 68.

McClain, Randy, "The Rite Stuff," *Times Picayune,* June 5, 1994, p. F1.

McLean, Bethany, "An Urge to Merge," *Fortune,* January 13, 1997, pp. 158–59.

Meitrodt, Jeffrey, "Stewart Makes Big Buy Overseas," *Times-Picayune,* December 10, 1994, p. C1.

Pare, Terrence P., "Picking the Stars of Tomorrow from Today's New Stocks," *Fortune,* November 4, 1991, pp. 27–28.

Raymond James & Associates, Inc., "Stewart Enterprises, Inc.," *Investext,* January 2, 1997.

Selz, Michael, "How Big Business Is Shaking the Tradition-Bound Funeral Trade," *Florida Trend,* September 1985, pp. 43–46.

Tomsho, Robert, "Funeral Parlors Become Big Business," *The Wall Street Journal,* September 18, 1996, p. B1.

Welsh, James, "Cemeteries Feeling Recession's Squeeze," *Times-Picayune,* September 6, 1991, p. C1.

Zipser, Andy, "Grave Error?" *Barron's,* August 21, 1995, p. 15.

—April Dougal Gasbarre

Today's Man, Inc.

835 Lancer Drive
Moorestown, New Jersey 08057
U.S.A.
(609) 235-5656
Fax: (609) 235-9323
Web site: www.todaysman.com

Public Company
Incorporated: 1992
Employees: 1,670
Sales: $263.3 million (fiscal 1996, ended February 3)
Stock Exchanges: NASDAQ
SICs: 5611 Men's and Boy's Clothing Stores

Today's Man, Inc. is a chain of men's clothing stores that has a significant part of the market in the Philadelphia, New York City, and Washington, D.C. areas. Under its founder, chairman, and CEO David Feld, Today's Man operates 25 retail stores in New Jersey, Maryland, Connecticut, New York, Pennsylvania, and Virginia. It is well-known as a pioneer in offering good quality tailored suits at a 30 to 40 percent discount compared to typical retail prices. With about 25,000 square feet, each Today's Man superstore offers a wide selection of both brand name items and its own lower-cost private-brand labels, including Today's Man, Brookcraft, and Torriani. In addition to suits, each store sells dress shirts, sport coats, ties, shoes, casual slacks and shirts, and most other accessories for white-collar men. Each Today's Man store has its own staff of tailors.

Origins in the 1970s

In 1971 David Feld saw what he considered an unmet need in the men's market for tailored clothing. Some upscale stores featured high prices and good quality, but they lacked an adequate assortment. At the other end of the spectrum, discount stores carried clothing with lower prices and lower quality.

Feld thought he could fill the void in the middle range for a good selection of clothing at reduced prices, so at the age of 23 he opened his first store in Philadelphia. That first 2,000-square-foot store opened on Third and Market Street.

David Feld had little experience to begin that first men's clothing store. In 1950 his parents, survivors of the Jewish Holocaust, had brought their three-year-old son from West Germany to the United States. David grew up working in his parents' retail clothing store in the Berlin Farmers Market in southern New Jersey. Feld started his own chain with white-collar males aged 25 to 54 in mind. Such men wore suits to work. "Our customer is in the middle of his career," said Feld in a 1991 article in *Discount Store News*. "Ten years ago he was buying cheap suits because it was all he could afford. Now he is looking for better quality, but he still wants the value."

Although Today's Man often has been described as a discount store, Feld has rejected that term. In a 1991 issue of the *Daily News Record*, he argued that Today's Man defied traditional retail store labels. Because his chain was not large enough, it could not be called a mass merchandiser. And because top quality clothes were offered, the chain was not an off-pricer. Feld defined his chain as a "merchandise-dominant specialty retail store, carrying attractive, branded merchandise."

Regardless of labels, the chain's competitive prices were one reason for its success. By buying in bulk and well before items would be sold, Today's Man was able to offer considerable savings on its suits and accessories. Prices remained constant, except for a few clearance sales a year.

By 1974 Today's Man had annual sales of $8 million. In that year the firm expanded its men's suit selections and opened its second Philadelphia store, located at City Line Avenue and 54th Street.

Expansion in the 1980s

Gradually Today's Man opened larger stores. Thus in 1980 the company opened a 12,000-square-foot store at 1528 Chestnut Street in Philadelphia. Three years later the 18,000-square-foot store in the Lawrence Park Shopping Center in Broomall, Pennsylvania, was opened to the public. To make its merchandise more accessible, the Broomall store used a "race-track" floor plan which placed all items within a few steps of a continuous aisle. Today's Man's annual sales reached $13 million in 1983.

The firm considered its Broomall store to be its first "superstore," although the size of such operations gradually increased. By learning from superstores in other fields, such as Toys "R" Us, Home Depot, and Circuit City, Feld found he could apply those lessons to market men's attire.

In 1984 four additional superstores began in Cherry Hill and Deptford, New Jersey, and in Montgomeryville and Allentown, Pennsylvania. In 1986 the company decided that all new superstores would be at least 25,000 square feet.

To increase sales by giving men the opportunity to buy clothes by one-stop shopping, the firm in 1984 expanded its choice of furnishings, such as ties and shoes. It also began offering sportswear, including casual slacks, sweaters, and sport shirts.

In 1986 the company began selling its own private brand merchandise. Sold under the labels Today's Man, Brookcraft, Torriani, Lamerti, and Amherst and Brock, such items represented a company strategy to keep prices down. About one-third of all its clothing was private label. To keep up with expanding sales, in 1987 Today's Man built a new office complex and distribution center in Moorestown, New Jersey.

The firm entered the Washington, D.C., area market for the first time in 1988 when superstores were opened in Rockville, Maryland, and Bailey's Crossroads, Virginia. The same year, two other superstores began operating in King of Prussia, Pennsylvania, and in Langhorne, Pennsylvania. In 1988 Today's Man began promoting its own credit card, and at the end of the year the company celebrated reaching $50 million in sales.

This expansion was facilitated by computers. In 1985 the company bought a Honeywell minicomputer to hook up to the firm's electronic cash registers. That was a step in the right direction, but each transaction had to be keyed into the system. That very labor-intensive method resulted in pricing errors and other discrepancies. So in 1987 the company decided to modernize and purchase a point-of-sale (POS) system mainly from Post-Tron Systems of Providence, Rhode Island. The new system integrated the firm's Honeywell minicomputer and its electronic cash registers with a modified IBM AT computer at each store. This hardware coupled with customized software allowed clerks to use bar codes for automatic pricing and thus not have to type in so much sales data. The new technology also reduced time for training cashiers, an important factor because of the frequent turnover of cashiers.

Good and Bad Times in the 1990s

By 1990 Today's Man had converted all its existing stores to superstores and sales had reached $100 million. The firm entered its main market when it opened two new superstores in the New York City area in 1991. In March the Paramus, New Jersey store opened, the company's 13th store with 30,000 square feet. Later in the year, a similar size store in Carle Place on Long Island began greeting customers with great selections such as

20,000 ties and 50 sizes of men's suits. This expansion into the New York City market led to an increase in its Moorestown, New Jersey office/warehouse from 60,000 to 100,000 square feet.

To continue expanding, raise working capital, and pay some debts, Today's Man became a public corporation in 1992. Its stock prospectus described the average superstore as having about 25,000 square feet with the following merchandise: 8,000 men's suits, 3,000 sports coats, 15,000 ties, 15,000 dress shirts, and 10,000 pairs of casual or dress pants.

Underwritten by Paine Webber and Alex, Brown & Sons, the firm in June 1992 offered its stock (symbol TMAN) on the NASDAQ Exchange for $7.50 per share. The same month, Men's Warehouse, considered by Today's Man to be its main competitor, came out with its IPO (initial public offering). Both enjoyed a substantial rise in their stock prices by December.

In 1992 Today's Man opened three new stores. Its Wayne, New Jersey store was the second in that state. The Stony Brook store expanded the company's efforts in the New York City area. The company also added a Fairfax, Virginia store, its third in the Washington, D.C. area.

Today's Man welcomed the public to several new stores in the New York City area between 1993 and 1995. When asked about this concentration in or near the Big Apple, president David Feld in the August 27, 1993 issue of *Daily News Record* replied, "They asked Willie Sutton why he robs banks and he said, 'That's where the money is.' New York has the money and the biggest population [in] the country. Men who live there spend the most money spent on clothing." So in 1993 the company opened stores in Woodbridge, New Jersey; Staten Island; and Manhasset, New York.

In May 1993 Today's Man came out with its second stock offering of 2 million common shares, 1.38 million shares to be sold by the company and the remaining 620,000 shares to be sold by existing stockholders. Following the secondary offering, the firm had 10.7 million shares outstanding.

In March 1994 the company opened its first store in New York City: the 28,000-square-foot Chelsea store at 625 Sixth Avenue and 19th Street. The second New York City store opened in September at Broadway and 81st Street on Manhattan's Upper West Side.

The following spring Today's Man began operations at its flagship Manhattan store at 529 5th Avenue at the intersection of 44th Street. The company leased the two-story 25,000-square-foot building from Silverstein Properties. David Feld reported that this prime location was chosen because of the area's several hotels and other nearby men's clothing retailers, including upscale Brooks Brothers and Paul Stuart stores. Feld said the reputation and magic of 5th Avenue also attracted his firm's interest. In 1995, the chain added other new stores in Norwalk, Connecticut and Greenbelt, Maryland.

In the early 1990s, as Today's Man entered the New York City area, it did well financially. For example, its sales increased 26 percent from 1992 to reach $167.1 million in 1993. And Feld, the owner of about 51 percent of Today's Man stock, supported several charities and community endeavors, such as God's Love We Deliver, which provided meals to homebound individuals with AIDS. To honor some who had died from AIDS, Today's Man sponsored an exhibition of the Names Project AIDS Memorial Quilt at the Guggenheim Museum SoHo and also hung quilt panels in the display windows of the Chelsea and Upper West Side stores. In 1992 B'Nai B'rith honored Feld with its Distinguished Achievement Award. Feld also backed the Temple University Entrepreneurial Institute, Harvard Business School, Israel's Ben Gurion University, and the Holocaust Memorial Museum in Washington, D.C.

Although discount men's clothing stores in the early 1990s did quite well as they followed the footsteps of successful women's discount retailers a decade or so earlier, they did so in spite of an overall negative trend in men's apparel. Sales of men's tailored clothing were dropping, partly as a result of the increase in more casual attire. About 4,000 men's stores, 23 percent of the total, closed their doors between 1990 and 1994. At the same time, large department stores, including J.C. Penney and Sears, decreased their men's suits for sale. By fall 1994 Sears sold no men's suits, only separate pants and coats that could be sold without tailoring, and Penney's also emphasized this approach.

By the mid-1990s, Today's Man experienced some real setbacks. Management changes in July 1995 indicated troubled times. Howard Gross, the firm's president and chief operating officer since March 1994, resigned after a poor Christmas 1994 season and a 48 percent decline in earnings for the fourth quarter of fiscal year 1994. Chairman and CEO David Feld decided not to replace Gross and took over his responsibilities. At the same time, the company went forward with its very aggressive plans for expansion on the East Coast and also into the Chicago area.

However, by November 1995 the company had reversed its position and began retreating. It announced that six new store openings scheduled for 1996 would be postponed. Following a dismal third quarter in which the firm lost $4.1 million, due to increased advertising costs and a late merchandise shipment for a company promotion, Today's Man's stock declined to $5.25 per share.

Not surprisingly, the company by November 1995 also faced major debt problems. Today's Man reached "an understanding" with its bank lenders to relax some commitments under its $50 million line of revolving credit.

In early December 1995, Today's Man hired Dillon, Read & Company as an outside source of advice and options, but their downturn continued. On December 18, the company's stock dropped another 11 percent to just $3 a share, the lowest in 52 weeks on the NASDAQ market. At that point, Today's Man operated 35 stores.

The new year saw more troubled times at Today's Man. In early February 1996 the firm filed for Chapter 11 bankruptcy in the U.S. Bankruptcy Court in Delaware. At the end of the day the bankruptcy was filed, Today's Man stock declined to just $1.875 per share. Later in the month, the company announced the elimination of 235 jobs by closing its seven Illinois stores and an outlet in Sunrise, Florida.

In March 1996 the company gained approval from the bankruptcy court to secure $20 million in credit from CIT Group/ Business Credit Inc. That allowed Today's Man to continue purchasing new merchandise for its stores.

What accounted for the decline of Today's Man in 1995 and 1996? Some analysts argued the firm simply tried to do too much too quickly. That assessment seemed reasonable, especially in light of David Feld's goals or dreams in the early 1990s. "Our objective is to [be] the dominant men's wear retailer in every market we serve," said Feld in the September 2, 1992 *Daily News Record*. "We intend to achieve this through our three-point strategy, which focuses on obtaining prime store locations, providing superior inventory and achieving the dominant advertising voice."

At a 1993 Paine Webber retailing conference, Feld said the chain planned by 1997 to dominate the men's tailored retail market in Chicago. The reality was that they did open a few stores in Chicago, but none operated in 1997. Feld also predicted his chain could operate 100 stores by the end of the decade.

Some critics thought that this expansionist zeal was demonstrated when Today's Man opened its flagship store on 5th Avenue in Manhattan. After throwing a huge party for 1,000 guests to celebrate that opening, Today's Man's leaders no doubt felt they were sitting on top of the world. One American Express analyst in the January 25, 1996 *Wall Street Journal* said, "Some people think that when a retailer builds a flagship in New York, that is the point in time when their ego is largest and their fear of failure is smallest. It's also when they're most likely to trip up." Others in the same article pointed out how high rent was in the heart of Manhattan and how difficult it was to make a profit there.

Hiring too many top executives was one mistake, admitted Feld. And some analysts thought Today's Man's entry into the casual clothes field in fall 1993 was a little late and more difficult than the firm anticipated. In the December 19, 1995 issue of *The Wall Street Journal*, Bernard Sosnick of Oppenheimer & Company argued that Today's Man began selling those items "without having a strong franchise in the casual clothing business. They expected shoppers would buy private-label [casual] merchandise, but it's difficult to develop a franchise along those lines."

Another analyst in the same article pointed out that Today's Man's price-cutting strategy was used by other firms to undercut it. Although Today's Man by December 1995 had gained 10 percent of the tough New York City area market and hurt such competitors as NBO Stores and Syms Corporation, it faced constant challenges from competitors having going-out-of-business sales and other price slashings.

In summary, a combination of soft demand for men's business attire, management's overambitious plans and mistakes, money problems, and tough competition led to Today's Man decline.

In August 1997 the firm announced that the U.S. Bankruptcy Court had approved its disclosure statement detailing the company's reorganization plan to pay its creditors cash and $15 million in equity. David Feld said, "Approval of our disclosure statement will remove one of the final hurdles to our emergence from Chapter 11. I am pleased that our dramatic turnaround enables us to provide full recovery to our creditors. At the same time, the financing of our plan leaves the Company with a healthy balance sheet for a moderate expansion plan and ongoing operations."

Thus Today's Man in 1997 was close to overcoming its Chapter 11 bankruptcy, a fundamental step to continuing as a major player in its core areas in and near New York City, Philadelphia, and Washington, D.C.

Further Reading

Auerbach, Jonathan, "Bankruptcy Filing Is Being Readied by Today's Man," *Wall Street Journal*, February 2, 1996, p. A5B.

Bird, Laura, "Today's Man Stock Drops As President, Chief Operating Officer Gross Resigns," *Wall Street Journal*, July 14, 1995, p. B5.

——, "Some Factors Refuse to Guarantee Payment on Today's Man Goods," *Wall Street Journal*, December 19, 1995, p. B4.

Gellers, Stan E., "Today's Man Bites into the Big Apple," *Daily News Record*, August 27, 1993, p. 4.

Lettich, Jill, "Men's Off-pricer Expands to New Market," *Discount Store News*, September 23, 1991, p. 5.

MacIntosh, Jeane, "Two Category Killers Cash in on Clothing; in the East It's Today's Man," *Daily News Record*, October 29, 1992, p. 4.

——, "New Issues in Retail, Apparel Heat Up; Hilfiger, Today's Man, Men's Wearhouse Are Among Hottest Stocks," *Daily News Record*, December 9, 1992, p. 8.

Marsh, Lisa, "Today's Man: Expanding for Tomorrow," *Daily News Record*, March 26, 1991, p. 3.

Palmieri, Jean E., "Today's Man Projects Sales to Hit $1 Billion," *Daily News Record*, January 18, 1990, p. 2.

Patterson, Gregory A., "Nineties Men Want Cheap Suits, And These Three Chains Oblige," *Wall Street Journal*, October 19, 1994, pp. B1, B10.

Pulliam, Susan, "Retailers Find New York Opening's Flash Is Often Followed by Stock-Price Crash," *Wall Street Journal*, January 25, 1996, pp. C1, C2.

Rothstein, Mervyn, "A Banking Corner Tries on a New Wardrobe," *New York Times*, November 13, 1994, section 9, p. R15.

Ryan, Thomas J. "Today's Man to Dominate Chicago Market by '97: Feld; CEO Tells Paine Webber Gathering," *Daily News Record*, September 14, 1993, p. 10.

Shaw, Dan, "Doing Good, and Doing Well, Too," *New York Times*, December 11, 1994, section 1, p. 67.

"Today's Man Inc. Files for Bankruptcy Protection," *Wall Street Journal*, February 5, 1996, p. B8.

"Today's Man Sets Public Offering," *Daily News Record*, March 31, 1992, p. 10.

—David M. Walden

Tommy Hilfiger Corporation

6/F, Precious Industrial Centre
18 Cheung Yue Street
Cheung Sha Wan
Kowloon
Hong Kong
(852) 2745-7798

Public Company
Incorporated: 1992
Employees: 794
Sales: $661.7 million (1997)
Stock Exchanges: New York
SICs: 2321 Men's and Boys' Shirts; 2325 Men's and
    Boys' Separate Trousers and Slacks; 2329 Men's and
    Boys' Clothing, Not Elsewhere Classified; 2339
    Women's Misses/Juniors Outerwear, Not Elsewhere
    Classified; 5136 Apparel, Men's Wholesale; 5699
    Sportwear, Retail; 6794 Patent Owners and Lessors

Tommy Hilfiger Corporation primarily markets men's and boys' clothing designed by Tommy Hilfiger. Hilfiger sells a complete line of clothing from socks to shirts, swimwear, jackets, pants, belts, wallets and ties, as well as sleepwear, golf clothes, eyewear, shoes, and fragrances. The company also markets women's clothing, primarily sportswear. Some of these lines are produced under licensing agreements with other companies, who produce the items using Hilfiger designs. The corporation operates over a thousand shops inside established department store chains such as Bloomingdales, Macy's, Saks, Nieman-Marcus, Marshall Field's, Dillard Department Stores, May Department Stores, and Federated Department Stores. The company also operates several dozen freestanding Tommy Hilfiger stores, including huge flagship stores under construction in Beverly Hills and on New Bond Street, London. Though most of its market is in the United States, the company also markets its clothing in Japan, Europe, and in South and Central America.

Origins

Though the company was not incorporated until 1992, its history properly begins with the fortunes of its namesake, Thomas Jacob (Tommy) Hilfiger. Born in Elmira, New York, in 1951, Hilfiger started his first clothing business while still in high school. He and two friends invested $300 in used blue jeans and sold them out of an Elmira basement. Hilfiger never attended college, but built up the blue jean business into a chain of seven upstate New York stores called People's Place. People's Place sold jeans, bell bottom pants, and other clothing, as well as candles, incense, and posters. The stores were successful enough to afford Hilfiger a Porsche, but they were poorly managed. In 1977, People's Place was forced to declare bankruptcy. Hilfiger moved to Manhattan and tried to find work as a clothing designer. Though he had no formal training, he had designed and sold vests and sweaters for People's Place. He worked freelance, and then started a sportswear company that went out of business after only one year. He eventually found work designing jeans for Jordache.

In 1984, Hilfiger was contacted by Mohan Murjani, an Indian textile magnate. Murjani owned the license to Gloria Vanderbilt jeans, and had helped spark the craze for designer jeans in the 1970s. Murjani had an idea to update the popular "preppy" look associated with designer Ralph Lauren, and give it a younger and more mass appeal. He chose Hilfiger to design the line for his firm, Murjani International. But in the beginning, marketing was much more important than the actual clothes.

First Marketing Campaign, 1985

The line of Tommy Hilfiger clothing debuted in the fall of 1985 with an ad campaign that featured no clothes, but declared that Hilfiger was a designer on par with Ralph Lauren, Perry Ellis, and Calvin Klein. The ads did little more than insert Hilfiger's name in the pantheon. Yet this was somehow effective. The brashness of the strategy attracted attention in the fashion industry, and caused comment by Johnny Carson and other notables. The first ads were centered around New York City, using print and outdoor media. By 1987, the Hilfiger line was attracting more national attention with advertisements in

People, USA Today, Newsweek, GQ, Sports Illustrated, and others. The entire advertising budget for Hilfiger clothing was only $1.4 million, and ads appeared infrequently. But they made a splash with double-page spreads, and because they featured words, logos, or Hilfiger's face, and no images of clothes or models, they stood out from other fashion advertisements. George Lois, who helped create the ads for the firm Lois, Pitts, Gershon, Pon/GGK, claimed in a March 1988 *Marketing and Media Decisions* article that he could not make Hilfiger's clothes ''look any better than anyone else's,'' and therefore the ads sold ''an idea'' and not the particular fashion. According to one survey, after only two years of his ads Hilfiger had succeeded in convincing 68 percent of sampled New Yorkers to name him as one of the top four or five important designers. Sales also attested to the brilliance of the marketing strategy. In 1986, Hilfiger brand clothing was available in 60 department stores and 25 specialty shops, and brought in $32 million in retail sales. A year later, retail sales had more than doubled, to $70 million.

Though clever advertising turned Hilfiger from an unknown into a top-selling designer, it was not only the mystique of the ads that accomplished this. The clothing was for the most part casual—khaki pants and a big polo shirt being the quintessential Hilfiger outfit. There was a little more flippancy in the cut and colors than the more staid Ralph Lauren style that Murjani had set out to imitate, and the clothes retailed for a bit less than similar designer togs. Hilfiger clothes fit the trend towards more casual work clothes—many offices in the 1980s were just instituting casual Fridays—so this particular niche was expanding. Hilfiger clothes became staples of college men, and others in the 20- to 35-year-old age group. The clothes were well-made, well-priced, similar to an existing fashion but with enough difference to stand out, and the offbeat ad campaign ignited a craze for them.

Expanding the Label, Late 1980s

By the late 1980s, Murjani International was troubled financially. The company also licensed Gloria Vanderbilt and the Coca-Cola brand of clothing. The company seemed unable to focus adequately on the Hilfiger brand, which was growing enormously. In 1988, Tommy Hilfiger, Mohan Murjani, and two others formed a new company, called Tommy Hilfiger Co. Inc., buying out Murjani International. The deal was complicated, and it took the new company almost a year to finally purchase back from Murjani the rights to the Tommy Hilfiger name. In the meantime, the company found a new financial

backer in Hong Kong businessman Silas Chou. Chou's firm, Novel Enterprises, was one of the largest sweater manufacturers in Asia, and the company was willing to invest money in Tommy Hilfiger Company to allow it to expand. The new principles were Chou, Hilfiger, and two former Ralph Lauren executives, Lawrence Stroll and Joel Horowitz. Mohan Murjani was out. With Chou's extensive contacts in the Asian garment industry, the new company not only designed but manufactured Hilfiger clothing, using Asian factories that produced low-cost, high-quality goods.

Chou was eager to push the Hilfiger line to greater availability. Sales for the new company were only $25 million its first year, so they had fallen off quite a bit from the Murjani days. Yet Chou insisted on renting a luxurious midtown Manhattan office space as New York headquarters, surmising that things would quickly get better. And they did. In the fall of 1992, the company made an initial public offering on the New York Stock Exchange at $15 a share. Within a few months, the stock was selling at $25. Revenue for 1992 was $107 million, an astonishing increase that justified Chou's hopes. Hilfiger became a Wall Street darling, with steadily increasing earnings. In November 1993, a secondary stock offering brought in $70 million. The company used this cash to expand its in-store shops and to develop new outlet stores, which would sell past-season Hilfiger garments at reduced prices.

Mid-90s Successes

Hilfiger's sales went up and up, from $107 million in 1992, to $138 million in 1993, to $227 million in 1994. There were close to 500 Tommy Hilfiger sections within department stores by the mid-1990s. About half the company's revenues came from sales at three big department store chains: Dillard's, Federated, and May. Another 15 percent of sales came from the discount chains T.J. Maxx and Marshalls, which sold the outdated stock at lower prices. Hilfiger began opening its own freestanding shops as well, debuting in Stamford, Connecticut, and Columbus, Ohio.

By 1994, it seemed everyone knew who Hilfiger was. President Clinton wore Hilfiger designs, as did the Prince of Wales, rock stars Michael Jackson, Elton John, and Snoop Doggy Dogg. But perhaps the most fanatic fans of Hilfiger designs were urban youths who gave the ''preppy'' look a new twist. Hip ghetto kids began taking the essentially suburban Hilfiger clothes and wearing them in extra large sizes, in eclectic mixes with sports gear. Drooping pants from which Hilfiger logo underwear peeked out was one peculiar fashion. The designer noticed the street trend and responded by making extra extra extra large sizes (labelled ''giant''), brighter colors, and bigger and bolder logos. It was apparently what the people wanted, and sales soared. Hilfiger had achieved a remarkable level of mass appeal, with everyone from bike messengers to CEOs dressed in his designs.

Sales and earnings kept going up dramatically. The company used its profits to expand in various ways. Between 1994 and 1995 Hilfiger Corporation added over 200 in-store men's shops. The company had introduced boys' clothes in sizes 8 to 20, and when this line was successful, introduced a line for boys in sizes 4 to 7 in spring 1995. The company had close to 500 in-store boys' shops, and planned to add more. Hilfiger licensed its name to Cypress Apparel to make robes and sleepwear, and to other manufacturers licensed scarves, handkerchiefs, umbrellas, and a line of golfing clothes. Hilfiger had a presence in Japan, with 36 shops inside Japanese department stores by 1995. And in that year, the company launched 12 in-store shops across Central and South America. A new fragrance line, produced through a licensing agreement with Estée Lauder, also sold well.

Hilfiger slowly built more freestanding stores, with six full-price and 16 discount outlet stores open by 1995. The company had to move cautiously on its own stores, in order not to appear to compete with the Hilfiger shops operated by its best customers, the large department chains.

Plans to launch a line of women's clothing started and stopped. There had been an unsuccessful attempt to make women's wear when Hilfiger designs were backed by Murjani International. The designer acknowledged that he had taken on too much too soon, and women's wear was dropped. But it was a logical extension of the brand's popularity, and potentially enormously profitable. In March 1994, Tommy Hilfiger Corporation hired Jay Margolis as its new president and vice-chairman, with the specific task that he develop a women's wear line. But little over a year later, the company announced that it would not develop the women's line, and Margolis resigned. The company declared that bringing out its own women's wear would be prohibitively expensive, and the new plan was to find a competent licensee. The company eventually licensed women's wear to Pepe Jeans International. Hilfiger chairman Silas Chou owned the Pepe Jeans brand, and the company already produced a men's jeans line for Hilfiger. The women's line came out in the summer of 1996 at more than 400 major department store shops. Like Hilfiger menswear, the women's line was mostly sportswear, and aimed for the same casual wear-to-work niche. The company also put out a women's perfume, "Tommy Girl," through a licensing agreement with Estée Lauder. In other expansions, the line of boyswear was extended down into toddler and infant clothes.

Sales for 1996 were close to $500 million, and the company's earnings increased over 60 percent. Hilfiger stocks had at times been the highest traded apparel stocks on Wall Street, and investors seemed to love the company's strong growth. The danger to investors, of course, was that the enormously popular Hilfiger brand would suddenly turn stale. Fashion stocks tended to be unpredictable, because apparel's success was mostly dependent on a fickle public. But Tommy Hilfiger Corporation still seemed capable of continued expansion. Profit margins were widening, something investors looked at as an indicator of soundness. And the trend toward casual work clothing that Hilfiger had first taken advantage of was still running. One industry survey indicated that over 20 percent of offices were casual every day—not just Friday. Workers were spending money on nice casual clothes such as Hilfiger designs, and so there did not seem to be a looming end to the clothing's popularity. And though Hilfiger Corporation had brought out its women's line, its staple was still menswear, traditionally more stable than women's apparel. Hilfiger designs were also priced well. General consumers typically spent less than $50 on individual items of clothing, and most

Hilfiger apparel was in that range. Nevertheless, Hilfiger was perceived as high quality. The company had not watered down its appeal by making the brand available at lower-end chains such as Penney's and Sears. And by 1997 the company was just beginning to expand into European markets. A huge flagship store was under construction in London, and presumably there was much market potential overseas.

Tommy Hilfiger Corporation had taken a virtually unknown designer and declared him a dean of menswear on par with industry leaders Calvin Klein, Ralph Lauren, and Perry Ellis. Remarkably, consumers bought the idea, and bought the clothing. A dozen years after the company's brash inaugural ads, the clothing was selling more strongly than ever, not only in the United States but in Japan, Europe, and Central and South America. The combination of guileful advertising, shrewd management, and a truly appealing and useful product brought the company to this global level. The staying power of a fashion product is always doubtful, but this only makes Hilfiger's present level of success more extraordinary.

Principal Subsidiaries

Tommy Hilfiger U.S.A. Inc.; Tommy Hilfiger Licensing, Inc. (U.S.A.); Tommy Hilfiger Retail, Inc. (U.S.A.); Tommy Hilfiger (Eastern Hemisphere) Ltd. (Hong Kong); Tommy Hilfiger (HK) Ltd. (Hong Kong); Tommy Hilfiger Nippon Co., Ltd. (Japan; 90%); Tommy Hilfiger Japan Co., Ltd. (49%).

Further Reading

Alson, Amy, "7th Avenue's Bad Boy," *Marketing & Media Decisions*, March 1988, pp. 79–82.
Bradford, Stacey L., "Tommy Who?" *Financial World*, March 18, 1997, pp. 41–44.
Brady, Jennifer L., "Hilfiger Head Sees Huge Growth for Women's Line," *Women's Wear Daily*, October 3, 1996, p. 5.
Conant, Jennet, "A Flashy Upstart," *Newsweek*, October 6, 1986, p. 68.
Cropper, Carol, "Designing Earnings," *Forbes*, February 1, 1993, p. 105.
Doebele, Justin, "A Brand Is Born," *Forbes*, February 26, 1996, pp. 65–66.
Gibbons, William, "Confirm New Firm to Make, Market Tommy Hilfiger Apparel," *Daily News Record*, November 29, 1988, p. 7.
Green, Michelle, Johnson, Kristina, and Little, Benilda, "With Brash Advertising and a $20 Million Boost, Tommy Hilfiger Takes on Seventh Avenue Titans," *People*, July 7, 1986, pp. 89–90.
Hochswender, Woody, "Prep Urban," *Esquire*, March 1996, pp. 131–32.
"Margolis Resigns As Hilfiger Plans to License Women's," *Daily News Record*, June 2, 1995, p. 2.
Norton, Leslie P., "Hot Pants," *Barron's*, October 17, 1994, pp. 17–18.
Palmieri, Jean E., "Bergdorf's Santacroce Joining Hilfiger," *Daily News Record*, May 30, 1997, p. 2.
Ryan, Thomas J., "Tommy's Biz Still Playing Happy Tune," *Daily News Record*, May 25, 1995, pp. 1–2.
——, "Hilfiger Net Climbs 24.6% in 4th Quarter," *Daily News Record*, June 4, 1997, p. 1.
Tyrnauer, Matthew, "It's Tommy's World," *Vanity Fair*, February 1996, pp. 108–13, 150–51.

—A. Woodward

Tractebel S.A.

Place du Trône 1
1000 Brussels
Belgium
(322) 507 02 11
Fax: (322) 513 43 27
Web site: http://www.generale.be

Public Subsidiary
Incorporated: 1929
Employees: 36,900
Sales: BFr 340.69 billion (1996)
Stock Exchanges: Brussels
SICs: 4931 Electric & Other Services Combined; 4932
Gas & Other Services Combined; 6552 Subdividers &
Developers, Not Elsewhere Classified; 8711
Engineering Services; 4841 Cable & Other Pay
Television Services; 4899 Communications Services,
Not Elsewhere Classified

Tractebel S.A. is one of Belgium's leading industrial groups, with holdings ranging from utilities to engineering to real estate. A publicly traded company, Tractebel is controlled by principal shareholder Société Générale de Belgique (SGB), which holds 50.3 percent of Tractebel's stock. SGB, which is Belgium's largest holding company, is in turn controlled by France's Suez-Lyonnaise, the holding giant formed by the merger of Compagnie de Suez and Lyonnaise des Eaux in early 1997.

Through its holdings, Tractebel concentrates on seven specific sectors—electricity and gas utilities in Belgium; international electricity and gas utilities, communications, technical installations and services, real estate, and engineering—in both the Belgian and international markets. Tractebel's holdings in more than 140 subsidiaries worldwide are organized into seven primary operating units: Electricity in Belgium (EIB); Gas in Belgium (GIB); Electricity and Gas International (EGI); Communications; Technical Installations and Services to Communities; Real Estate; and Engineering. Active in more than 100 countries, with nearly 37,000 employees worldwide, Tractebel has worked steadily on reducing its traditional reliance on the Belgian market for its revenues and profits—by the mid-1990s, Belgium represented less than 72 percent of the company's profits, down from 90 percent or more during the 1980s. Nonetheless, Tractebel's Belgian utilities holdings remain the company's core activity.

With its controlling share of Electrabel, Tractebel's EIB unit supplies more than 93 percent of Belgium's electricity requirements, as well as more than 89 percent of gas distribution, nearly 55 percent of cable television distribution, and 5 percent of the country's water distribution. Through Electrabel and the company's nearly 80 percent ownership of CODITEL, Tractebel is also a primary supplier of cable television services in Belgium, and in Luxembourg, Switzerland, and the United States. The company's GIB unit, through Tractebel's Distrigas holdings, provides supply, transportation, and storage facilities for natural gas in the Belgium market, as well as an expanding presence in positioning Belgium as a hub for European natural gas distribution.

International utility distribution is conducted through Tractebel's EGI arm. From its beginning in the early 1990s, EGI has expanded Tractebel's utility presence in more than 100 countries. The company has invested some US $650 million into more than 17 electricity and gas installations beyond Belgium, adding some 10,000 megawatts of generating capacity and positioning Tractebel as one of the top utility suppliers worldwide. Through EGI, which includes subsidiaries Powerfin and CRSS, Tractebel has power projects under construction or already in operation in the United States, Canada, Germany, Italy, Northern Ireland, Portugal, Italy, Hungary, China, Thailand, Vietnam, Singapore, Kazakhstan, India, and Argentina.

The company's Technical Installations and Services segment, operating primarily through Tractebel's holdings in subsidiary Groupe Fabricom, provide international construction and management of industrial installations, as well as environmental services, particularly waste management collection and treatment, for some 11 countries. Tractebel Ingenerie, the company's long-established engineering arm, is one of the largest in Europe and the world, with more than 2,500 engineers,

491

Company Perspectives:

The Tractebel Group's strategy is to offer its shareholders a long-term return higher than the Belgian stock exchange average. To achieve this in an economy that is rapidly becoming global, with ever-fiercer competition, the Tractebel Group has adopted a double strategy: firstly, to attain sufficient overall size as a player to be reckoned with on the international scene, and secondly, to develop critical mass in each of its core activities, on a European or even worldwide scale.

draftsmen, and other staff providing engineering services for projects in the electricity, gas, hydraulics, construction, regional and urban, computer systems, and systems integration fields. Through Tractebel's 31 percent holding in Compagnie Immobilière de Belgique, the company is also a primary player in Belgium's real estate development, construction, and management markets.

Since the late 1980s, Tractebel has undergone a dramatic transformation in its activities. Chief architect of this development is Baron Philippe Bodson, who has served as the company's CEO since 1989. Tractebel's 1996 sales were approximately BFr 340 billion, equivalent to some US $11.6 billion. The company's 44 percent controlling stake in Electrabel contributed some BFr 241 billion to the company's total sales for the year.

Roots in the 19th Century

Tractebel celebrated its 100th anniversary in 1995, tracing its history back to the creation of two companies, Compagnie Mutuelle des Tramways and Société Générale Belge d'Entreprises Electriques in 1895 by long-time controlling shareholder Société Générale de Belgique, the Belgium holding company powerhouse. SGB's own history traced back to 1822 and before the official creation of the Belgian state, when it was established by William I of Orange. Charged with fostering the economic and industrial development of the southern provinces of the low countries, which had only recently emerged from under the rulership of the Austria-Hungary empire, the Société Générale de Pays Bas, as it was then called, was given the authority to issue bank notes and act as the state cashier, a role it continued to play after Belgium's independence from the Netherlands in 1830.

After the Banque Nationale de Belgique was formally established in 1850, SGB concentrated on its role as Belgium's primary joint-venture capital and development concern, playing a key role in developing the country's infrastructure. In this capacity, SGB provided capital for the building of Belgium rail and road infrastructure, major construction projects, coal and other mining activities, and the development of the country's gas and electrical utilities, as well as other industrial projects. In 1895, SGB established subsidiary companies for two of its primary activities, tram (streetcar) construction and operation, and electricity gas distribution. Both the Compagnie Mutuelle des Tramways and the Société Générale d'Entreprises Elec-

triques were active internationally, with the subsidiaries of the former supplying streetcar lines to cities around the world, and the latter becoming through its subsidiaries a global utility operator. By the start of World War I, these international efforts represented as much as 70 percent of both companies' activities.

The social and political upheaval following World War I, however, and the rise of new nation states, particularly with the break-up of the Austria-Hungary empire, saw the nationalization of many of the companies' foreign subsidiaries. In October 1929, the two companies were combined, forming Tractebel. The newly named company continued to lose its foreign utility and tramway concessions, especially during the Depression of the 1930s and the build-up to World War II. By 1945, Tractebel had been forced to give up its international operations entirely. For the next 40 years, the company would concentrate almost solely on its home market.

Following the Depression and especially World War II, SGB began consolidating the related activities of its many subsidiaries, giving rise to Electrobel, which served as Belgium's primary utility supplier, and Tractionel, which provided industrial engineering services, including playing a role in establishing the company's nuclear power industry. Electrobel and Tractionel also began operating a joint-venture subsidiary, Tractionel Electrobel Engineering, which grew to become the sixth largest international engineering design firm. Both Tractionel and Electrobel evolved into major Belgian holding companies, with Tractionel's holdings extending beyond its energy portfolio into the foods, chemicals, cable television, and property sectors. SGB remained principal shareholder of both companies.

Return to Global Focus in the 1990s

In 1986, Tractionel and Electrobel agreed to merge operations, forming the present-day Tractebel. Several factors were behind this move: the growing internationalization of the world industry, with the resulting heightening of international competition; the coming unification of the European market; and a rising trend toward the deregulation of many state-controlled industries. The newly combined companies' operations boasted a 1985 portfolio worth some BFr 56 billion, with combined net profits of BFr 5.7 billion. One year later, Tractebel's portfolio had grown to BFr 67.8 billion and the company's net profit reached BFr 6.15 billion (worth nearly US $164 million). Tractebel itself, however, remained a largely passive holding company. More than 90 percent of the company's business came from its utility holdings.

In 1987, with the breakup of Imperial Continental Gas into two companies, the Calor Group and Contibel, Tractebel and partner Groupe Bruxelles Lambert, launched a successful takeover bid for Contibel, which contained a strong portfolio of investments in Belgium's utilities. The bid, which cost the two holding companies nearly US $740 million, gave Tractebel tighter control of the Belgian utility sector. But the "Black Monday" stock market crash in October of that year cost the company dearly, and exposed it—and parent SGB—to new vulnerabilities.

These became particularly evident the following year, as parent SGB faced a new upheaval: In 1988 Carlo De Benedetti, the Italian industrialist, launched a hostile takeover bid for SGB. The company resisted for several months, and finally turned to the French Compagnie Financière de Suez as a "white knight." Suez's holding in SGB rose to 63 percent, while SGB's own holdings, previously spread out over a variety of industries, tightened to focus on several major Belgian players, including Tractebel. One year later, SGB increased its hold on Tractebel, after swapping part of its shares in Belgian oil and petrochemicals group Petrofina, the country's largest company, for a large part of the Tractebel shares held by rival Groupe Bruxelles Lambert, led by Albert Frere. The deal boosted SGB's participation in Tractebel to more than 40 percent. By then, Tractebel's net profits had risen to BFr 9.5 billion (US $271 million). More than 85 percent of the company's profits, however, continued to come from the Belgian energy market.

The attempted takeover of SGB and its subsequent rescue by Suez spurred Tractebel to make its own transformation. In 1989, faced with the inevitable loss of its near-monopoly on Belgium's utility sector with the looming unification of the European market, Tractebel adopted a new strategy calling for the company to return to the global industrial market of its early history. Leading the company's transformation was Baron Philippe Bodson, who had earned his title of nobility as the head of the Belgium Industrial Federation prior to joining Tractebel.

The U.S. market, where deregulation had progressed more rapidly than elsewhere, became one of Tractebel's primary expansion targets. Tractebel at first eyed building a media portfolio, beginning in 1989 with the US $30 million purchase of a 20 percent stake in Act III Communications, based in Los Angeles. The company's communications arm would increase its U.S. presence during the first half of the 1990s, adding, through its Coditel subsidiary and its financial and management participation in the Prime Cable Group, cable television operations in the Houston, Las Vegas, and other large U.S. city markets. Next, the company began building its U.S. energy portfolio, adding, through its American Tractebel Corporation subsidiary, 50 percent ownership of the construction and operation of an electrical plant in Quebec. The company also returned to Argentina's energy market—where the company has been active early in the century—after that country abandoned state control of the utility sector. In Europe, Tractebel, through its Fabricom subsidiary, purchased 70 percent of Hungary's PVV, focused on that country's electrical utility market. On the home front, the company's Electrabel and Distrigas subsidiaries reached agreement to build an electricity generating facility in Zeebrugge.

Posting a net profit of BFr 29.4 billion (US $835 million) in 1994, Tractebel's international expansion would continue into the mid-1990s. As Bodson explained to the *Houston Chronicle*, "The Belgian market is almost saturated and that is why we have decided to go abroad." The company's expansion drive was helped by its strong war chest, Bodson continued: "I think an acquisition of half a billion dollars would definitely be possible for us, even tomorrow." In May 1995, Tractebel,

through its Powerfin subsidiary, paid US $206 million for the friendly takeover of CRSS, based in Houston. This move brought Tractebel in the U.S. utility market, with several electric power generating stations, principally located in Vermont. Meanwhile, the company's energy utility interests had spread to include locations in Ireland, Hungary, Portugal, Oman, Italy, Chile, and other countries. After taking over the utility management of Kazakhstan, formed after the breakup of the Soviet Union, Tractebel company would also move into the Asian market, adding Thailand, Singapore, and India, among others. In the United States, Tractebel increased its energy capacity, when it announced a US $500 million joint-venture with Phillips Coal Co. to build a 400-megawatt lignite-burning power plant in Mississippi.

In September 1996, SGB reached agreement with Electrafina and Royale Belge, both controlled by Groupe Bruxelles Lambert, to buy those companies' combined 25 percent share of Tractebel. The purchase, worth some BFr 49 billion (US $1.6 billion), raised SGB's ownership position to more than 65 percent. Several months later, however, SGB prompted the merger between Tractebel and another subsidiary, Powerfin, in which Tractebel already had a strong interest. The merger, which involved a shares flotation in Tractebel, and the dissolving of Powerfin's shares into Tractebel, decreased SGB's direct participation in Tractebel to 50.3 percent. This move came in the light of major development in SGB's control: the merger of parent company Suez into French water company Lyonnaise des Eaux, a move that effectively placed the Belgian utility sector under a foreign utility operator's control for the first time. In this light, Tractebel's international expansion—which, by mid-1997 had placed the company in more than 100 countries, with power generating capacity of more than 32,000 megawatts—assured Tractebel of a prominent role in the future worldwide industrial market.

Principal Subsidiaries

Coditel (79.46%); Groupe Fabricom (73.38%); Electrabel (37%); Powerfin; Distrigas (57.53%); Tractebel Engineering; CRSS, Inc. (U.S.A.).

Further Reading

Banks, Howard, "Counterattack," *Forbes*, February 24, 1997, p. 70.
Buckley, Neil, "Tractebel and Powerfin Set for $8 billion Merger," *Financial Times*, March 18, 1997, p. 33.
——, "Alarm Sounds Over Tractebel," *Financial Times*, April 4, 1997, p. 26.
Gottschalk, Arthur, "Belgium's Tractebel Wants to Light up the US," *Journal of Commerce*, April 10, 1997, p. 7B.
Javetski, John, "Tractebel, Belgium's Centenarian, Takes up Globe-trotting—Again," *Electrical World*, March 1996, p. 26.
Minder, Ralph, "CRSS Suitor Still Searching," *Houston Chronicle*, May 28, 1995, p. 7.

—M. L. Cohen

Transmedia Network Inc.

11900 Biscayne Boulevard
North Miami, Florida 33181
U.S.A.
(305) 892-3300
Fax: (305) 892-3317
Web site: http://www.transmediacard.com

Public Company
Incorporated: 1987
Employees: 119
Sales: $78.6 million (1996)
Stock Exchanges: New York
SICs: 7389 Business Services, Not Elsewhere Classified;
6153 Credit Card and Other Credit Plans; 2171
Periodicals, Publishing, and Printing; 7311
Advertising Agencies and Counselors; 7319
Advertising, Not Elsewhere Classified

Transmedia Network Inc. is a Florida-based specialized consumer finance company that provides restaurants with interest-free loans (ranging from $1,000 to $25,000) in exchange for blocks of meals sold to Transmedia for half price. When customers with Transmedia charge cards dine at restaurants honoring the Transmedia card, they pay full price and charge the meal on their Transmedia card, which is linked to one of their credit cards. Transmedia takes the difference between the half-price meals it bought from the restaurant and the full price the customer pays and divides it two ways. Half is returned to the customer on his or her credit card statement in the form of a 25 percent credit on the meal and half is pocketed by Transmedia to cover overhead, other expenses, and its profit on the transaction.

In 1997, Transmedia's 1.2 million card members could choose from more than 7,000 restaurants and merchants honoring the Transmedia card in the United States, Europe, and the Pacific Rim. In addition to straight discounts on restaurant meals, Transmedia also allowed members to use the card for reduced hotel room rates and to accrue free airline miles with selected U.S. airlines as well as discounts on orders from a variety of mail-order businesses. Its main U.S. regions of operation were New York City (which alone accounted for 39 percent of its revenue in 1996) and southern Florida, but the Transmedia card was also honored in such areas as Chicago and Milwaukee; the New England states; Philadelphia, Baltimore, and Washington, D.C.; Phoenix, Denver, Dallas, and Houston; Georgia, eastern Tennessee, Virginia, and the Carolinas; and California.

From Security Alarms to Media Barter: 1963–84

Transmedia CEO Melvin Chasen took the long road to success. Beginning as a young entrepreneur in Colorado Chasen had experimented with everything from selling security alarms to running a mergers-and-acquisitions firm before he settled on the media barter concept that became Transmedia's business model. In 1963, while still in his early thirties, Chasen founded his first company, Midway Enterprises Inc., in Colorado, and within five years it had evolved into Pike's Peak Turf Club and then by 1974 Pike's Peak American Corporation. In the early 1980s, Chasen, with the help of ad agency executive Hank Seiden, entered the media barter industry. In media barter, companies such as Transmedia buy up blocks of advertising from media outlets (i.e., newspapers) and exchange them to companies for their excess merchandise or services. (Often such companies will get advertising equivalent to the wholesale price of their goods or services rather than having to settle for the heavily discounted price they would charge in a closeout sale.)

To capitalize on the media barter idea, in 1983 Chasen renamed his business Transmedia Network and located it in New York City where he began arranging advertising-for-services exchanges between radio stations and potential radio advertisers who needed ready cash. The majority of these companies were restaurants, which because of the dining industry's notoriously high turnover and thin profit margins were often unable to get loans from banks. Early on, Transmedia also operated as a media placement firm, earning 15 percent commissions on ad space purchased from such publications as *New York* magazine. In exchange for financing his new business Chasen's investors insisted that he run it, and in 1983 Chasen introduced the Transmedia card through which restaurant goers could receive 25 percent off meals at restaurants that had bartered meals for blocks of advertising. By lining up $500,000 in investment capital through the private placement market, Chasen financed Transmedia's early growth and merged the company into a public shell corporation in 1984. Chasen soon discovered, however, that restaurants much preferred cash to advertising space, and despite his own tight cash reserves he began offering pure cash advances to restaurants that agreed to accept the Transmedia card. The change in strategy paid off immediately and cash-strapped restaurants began lining up for Transmedia loans.

The amount of money Transmedia loaned restaurants was based on their reputation and capital needs as well as the amount of time Chasen estimated it would take Transmedia's cardholders to "pay off" the loan through restaurant visits. In exchange for a $5,000 interest-free loan to a restaurant (the standard amount Transmedia loaned to a new restaurant), Transmedia received $10,000 in meal credits, which Chasen anticipated would be used up by Transmedia cardholders within six months. Since restaurants' actual cost for food and beverages ranged from only 30 to 40 percent of the cost charged to customers, Chasen's major obstacle was not in finding restaurants willing to participate—or investors willing to loan Transmedia capital—but getting consumers to believe they could get 25 percent dining discounts without some "catch." When even ads offering to waive the $50 membership fee for new members failed to do the trick Chasen began hawking the Transmedia card to teachers' unions, law and accounting firms, police departments, and other professional groups to widen Transmedia's member base.

Working in Transmedia's favor were the features that made its card an improvement over earlier incarnations of the discount dining concept: no coupons had to be clipped and presented, maitre d's and waiters did not have to be forewarned that the customer intended to pay with the Transmedia card (though large parties had to make reservations in advance through

Transmedia), and there were no limits on dining times or menu choices. As a Transmedia executive later recalled to the *Los Angeles Times*, "we designed the card so that there would be no restrictions, no coupons, no negatives."

Building a Franchise: 1985–91

The first directory listing the restaurants that honored Transmedia's "Executive Savings Card"—41 in all—was issued to Transmedia's 225 New York City members in 1985, just as a new competitor, In Good Taste (IGT), entered the meal barter/discount card market. In 1986, with revenues approaching $1 million, Chasen issued Transmedia shares in a public stock offering that infused $1 million of much-needed expansion capital into the business. By 1987 Transmedia had posted revenues of $1.8 million but suffered a net loss of $422,000. In July Chasen reincorporated Transmedia (which, as an outgrowth of Chasen's earlier ventures, had been a Colorado corporation) in Delaware.

By painstakingly expanding consumer awareness of the card and marketing the Transmedia concept to the ever-growing pool of new cash-starved restaurants, Chasen realized a net income of $35,000 in 1988 on sales of $2.9 million. The Transmedia card generated traffic for restaurants, filling up empty seats and conferring an image of popularity on struggling restaurant startups. Despite the heavy two-for-one price of the Transmedia loan, restaurant owners began embracing the idea of cash-on-the-spot loans that never had to be repaid in cash and offered the prospect for increased word-of-mouth traffic as Transmedia card users brought in new business. Although the risk that a new restaurant would fold before customers used up its meal credits was unavoidable, in 1990 Transmedia wrote off only $109,000 in meal credit losses.

In its sixth year in business, Transmedia's sales vaulted to more than $4.4 million and net income nearly tripled to $99,000. To expand his business even further, Chasen began offering Transmedia franchises for sale in 1990, and by 1991 its first franchisee was offering the Transmedia card for restaurants throughout the New Jersey area. With 13 employees (nine of whom were independent sales staff under contract), 500 participating restaurants, and 25,000 cardholders in 1990 Chasen opened a Cardholder Service Center in North Miami and saw sales rise 70 percent to almost $7.5 million.

In 1991, the torrid pace of Transmedia's growth began to draw the attention of Wall Street and the national media. The *Wall Street Journal* boosted the company's profile with a favorable piece describing happy Transmedia cardholders pocketing $50 a month in savings and *Business Week* listed Transmedia as one of its top "Hot Growth Companies" in the spring. Not coincidentally, Transmedia's shares rose from $3 in February 1991 to $12 by late summer. By the end of 1991, Transmedia's staff had grown to 21, membership had risen to 50,000 cardholders, and sales had climbed to $13 million.

Competition and Growth: 1992–93

With his company now servicing New York, New Jersey, Connecticut, and Florida, Chasen offered 500,000 shares in a private placement stock offering in 1992 that generated close to $5 million in additional capital. In 1990–91 a new entrant in the discount dining market, The Signature Group of Chicago, began negotiating with Transmedia for a joint licensing agreement in which both companies would honor each other's cards. Chasen allowed the talks to collapse, however, and the stage was set for Signature's entrance as a new player in the industry in June 1993. Already, in 1992, a fourth discount card service, A la carte International Inc., had begun offering restaurant-goers a discount dining card plan. By 1993 the discount dining card market was ruled by Transmedia, Executive IGT (In Good Taste), and a new participant, Entertainment Publications. Each offered variations on the others' program, tweaking the discount card business model to strike the right balance with consumers.

In August 1991 Transmedia had optimistically predicted its membership would reach 100,000 by 1992. When 1992 closed, however, more than 112,000 members were actually toting Transmedia cards, which were now honored at 1,449 restaurants. With sales approaching $24 million, Transmedia moved its corporate headquarters from New York City to Miami and continued its national expansion. By the end of 1993 Transmedia was adding 200 new restaurants a month, had extended its program throughout most of the East Coast, and had established franchise beachheads in San Francisco and Chicago. To extend the Transmedia concept overseas, in late 1992 Chasen announced a $1.25 million deal with Boston-based merchant bankers Conestoga Partners Inc. to license Transmedia's service in the United Kingdom and Europe. In February 1993 Transmedia Europe—comprised of Transmedia Europe plc, Transmedia UK plc, and Transmedia UK Inc.—was incorporated to extend the Transmedia cards' reach from the British Isles to Turkey and the former states of the Soviet Union.

In late 1993 Chasen began a policy of partnering Transmedia with selected U.S. companies in order to broaden the company's offerings beyond restaurant dining. Among the first to sign on was the *New York Times*, which allowed Transmedia customers to take advantage of the benefits of its "Times Card" discount and membership program through a "cobranded" Transmedia/Times card. Transmedia also absorbed the restaurants honoring the Times card into its own network. The program had produced 64,000 new Transmedia cardholders by mid-1994 and spawned a series of cobranding, "retail loyalty" deals with such direct mail catalog merchants as The Sharper Image and Jos. A. Bank Clothiers and eventually even cruise lines like Carnival. Moreover, by the end of the year Chasen had announced plans to introduce the Transmedia program to Los Angeles, Texas, Georgia, Arizona, and Mississippi. With close to 200,000 cardholders and 2,300 participating restaurants, Transmedia's sales had swept past the $36 million mark by the end of its 1993 fiscal year, and its stock could boast two- and five-year total returns of 205 and 2,732 percent, respectively—placing it 14th on *Business Week*'s 1993 annual "Hot Growth Company" ranking.

Doubts and a Falling Stock: 1994–95

In March 1994 Transmedia struck a $1.25 million deal with Conestoga Partners II to allow them to license Transmedia's program in Australia and New Zealand and to sublicense it elsewhere on the Pacific Rim under the name Transmedia Asia-Pacific. With more than 222,000 cardholders and 2,467 participating restaurants, Transmedia struck agreements with Cellular One, the cell phone service provider; Prodigy Services, the commercial online service provider; Amtrak; credit card issuer MBNA America Bank; and cable company Comcast to market the Transmedia card to the four companies' customers. Transmedia picked up 4,500 new card members when Cellular One offered its San Francisco customers the card as a premium, and Comcast generated another 3,500 members through a similar program. Prodigy made a blanket offer of the Transmedia card to any of its 700,000 subscribers who lived within 20 miles of a Transmedia-affiliated restaurant, and in July 1994 Amtrak began binding the card into copies of its on-board magazine on its East Coast routes. Aided by a new federal tax law that reduced the allowable business meal deduction from 80 to 50 percent—which forced many business people to look for cheaper ways to wine and dine clients—Transmedia went ahead with plans to expand outside Los Angeles into Orange County and basked in the glow of a *Financial World* magazine article that ranked it as America's third-best growth company. As Chasen doubled his staff to 90 employees, Transmedia finished the year with a net income of $4.4 million on sales of $48.6 million.

The year 1995 marked a watershed in the company's history. On the one hand, it expanded its network to 5,330 restaurants and almost 600,000 cardholders, began trading on the New York Stock Exchange, established a literacy-promoting philanthropic program called "TransReadia," and continued to expand its offerings beyond restaurant discounts. In an agreement with GE Capital it offered cardholders substantial discounts on long distance phone calls and initiated a new program called Transmedia Dollars that allowed cardholders to forego the 25 percent discount on meals in exchange for credits toward the purchase of airline tickets. Members could now also use the Transmedia card for discounts at a growing number of hotels, ski resorts, and spas.

On the other hand, the shimmer was beginning to fade from Transmedia's growth story. Although Transmedia cardholders charged $85 million on their cards in 1995, 70 percent of that volume came from New York City members alone. Its attempt to franchise its license was also proving costly, and in July it repurchased its Chicago franchise and waited for its so far unprofitable Denver and Phoenix programs to turn the corner. What is more, two new competitors, CUC International's Premier card and the Florida-based Gusto card, were offering new competition, and in June Transmedia announced that its upcoming quarters would show earnings below Wall Street's estimates. Although revenues grew by 20 percent in 1995, that pace marked the slowest increase in the company's short history and net profits remained stagnant. In a telling feature article, *Forbes* magazine characterized Transmedia's business concept as a kind of restaurant-punishing sleight of hand and wondered aloud, "How far can Transmedia go on this marketing ploy?" Transmedia responded that its further expansion into the Midwest, the west coast of Florida, and the Southwest augured well for its future revenue growth and that its less than stellar performance in 1995 could be blamed on the late mailing of a marketing campaign that would have scared up even more new customers. The rarely spoken doubts behind four years of media hype seemed to come to a head all at once in late 1995, however, when Transmedia's stock began a harrowing decline that more than 18 months later it still had not recovered from.

The seeds of investors' concerns could perhaps be traced to worry over Transmedia's pell-mell expansion, but the media suggested that the company's trouble might involve the very core of its business scheme. By requiring restaurants to cough up meal credits valued at twice the amount of Transmedia's loans to them, the company was making it all but impossible for some of its restaurants to greet Transmedia customers with a welcoming smile. For every three new restaurants added to Transmedia's bimonthly directory, on average one would drop out or go out of business within a year. Although some restaurants found that as many as 40 percent of their first-time Transmedia customers came back, others complained that though the card attracted new customers it also encouraged existing full-paying customers to switch to the Transmedia card as well, cutting even deeper into margins. Still others groused that the typical Transmedia customer was rarely a big spender and that by buying into the Transmedia program restaurants were announcing to the community that they were in trouble, so desperate for cash that they were willing to sacrifice profits. As one of Transmedia's competitors frankly admitted, "The nature of the business is that successful restaurants don't need us."

Retrenching: 1996–97

Chasen and Transmedia fought back against Wall Street's doubts on multiple fronts. In January 1996 it struck a deal with Continental Airlines and United Airlines to allow cardholders to earn 10 free miles for every $1 charged (versus the 2 to 3 miles earned by other charge cards). Its two overseas units reached an agreement to gain access to the 6-million-member database of British discount service provider Countdown Holding, and Transmedia began offering some of its customers a "free-for-life" Transmedia card to bolster card holder retention. Chasen also reached an agreement with Western Transmedia, his franchisee in the western United States, to reacquire control of its unspectacular programs in California, Oregon, Washington, and Nevada. Transmedia also began to exploit the global marketing potential of the World Wide Web by creating its own web site and marketing itself through the web site of the "Diner's Grapevine" service. Moreover, Chasen announced plans to spend $2.6 million in 1997 on computer software to modernize Transmedia's transaction processing operations, thus enabling it to perform the transaction processing for major credit card companies in addition to its own programs. Finally, in December 1996 Transmedia sold $33 million of its restaurant meal credits (known as "rights to receive") as securities to a group of investors in a private placement offering that promised to generate needed capital. Describing the deal as "a major milestone" in the company's history, Chasen excitedly characterized the newly capitalized Transmedia as a "powerful cash machine" now able to fund its future growth without having to take on new debt or sell shares of stock to the public.

In a sign of Chasen's commitment to returning Transmedia to its glory days, in February 1997 he recruited Stephen Lerch, a financial specialist from accounting firm Coopers & Lybrand, to become his right-hand man under the title executive vice-president. The same month Transmedia's two overseas units, Transmedia Europe and Transmedia Asia Pacific, announced an agreement to combine forces, subject to shareholder approval. Despite Transmedia's failure to acquire the operations of its

competitor, Gusto, in June 1997, with more than 1.2 million cardholders worldwide and agreements with more than 7,000 restaurants and over 400 hotels, Transmedia remained a force to be reckoned with, and Chasen announced that Transmedia's belt-tightening measures would begin to bear financial fruit during the summer of 1997.

Principal Subsidiaries

TMNI International Inc., Transmedia Restaurant Co. Inc.; Transmedia Service Co. Inc.

Further Reading

Bongiorno, Lori, "The Class of '95: Where Are They Now?" *Business Week*, May 26, 1997, p. 104.

Coulton, Antoinette, "Transmedia, A Dining Card Firm, Expands Its Reach with U.K., Australia Deals," *American Banker*, September 19, 1996, p. 13.

——, "Card Exec Still Dining Out on His Discount Idea," *American Banker*, February 13, 1997, p. 26.

Fickenscher, Lisa, "Transmedia Network, Signature Group Offer Dining Programs for Frequent-Flier Customers," *American Banker*, January 23, 1996.

"Gusto-Transmedia Merger Discussion Ended," press release, North Miami, FL: Transmedia Network Inc., June 16, 1997.

Heimlich, Cheryl Kane, "Dining Cards: Will Work for Food," *South Florida Business Journal*, August 5, 1996.

Hutheesing, Nikhil, "Keeping the Seats Warm," *Forbes*, January 1, 1996, pp. 62–63.

Jenkins, Kathie, "Hollywood's New Calling Card Is Gray," *Los Angeles Times*, August 14, 1994, p. F16.

Knecht, G. Bruce, "A Charge Card That Buys a Cheap Meal and a Loophole," *Wall Street Journal*, February 9, 1994, p. B1.

Levin, Gary, "Discount Dining Card Makes Tasty Premium." *Advertising Age*, June 4, 1994.

Marcical, Gene G., "Queuing up for Deals on Meals," *Business Week*, August 26, 1991.

Mariani, John, "The Art of the Meal," *Worth*, February 1994.

"Plastics Tasty Trend," *Credit Card Management*, February 1994, p. 8.

Ring, Trudi, "The Quest for High-Calorie Perks," *Credit Card Management*, March 1997, p. 129.

Stern, Gary M., "A Guide through Discounting Minefield," *Restaurant Hospitality*, February 1993.

Swafford, David, "Dining Card Savings—From Hotels to Haircuts," *Business Week*, October 9, 1995, p. 159.

Tannenbaum, Jeffrey A., "Issuer of Restaurant Discount Cards Tastes Success," *Wall Street Journal*, April 23, 1991.

Teitelbaum, Richard S., "Good Food Cheap? Pick a Card!" *Fortune*, March 18, 1996, p. 133.

"Transmedia Acquires Spinoff's Operations," *American Banker*, January 13, 1997.

"Transmedia Adds Phone Call Feature," *American Banker*, March 28, 1995.

"Transmedia Program Going Down Under," *American Banker*, March 23, 1994, p. 15.

"Transmedia Network Agrees with Estimates on First-Period Net," *Wall Street Journal*, January 18, 1993.

"Transmedia Stock Listed on New York Exchange," *American Banker*, July 7, 1995.

"Up and Down Wall Street," *Barron's*, March 15, 1993, p. 43.

White, George, "Hungry for Bargains," *Los Angeles Times*, October 27, 1993, p. D1.

—Paul S. Bodine

Ugine S.A.

Immeuble Pacific
13, cours Valmy
92070 La Défense 7 Cedex
France
(33) 01 41 25 60 20
Fax: (33) 01 41 25 60 07
Web site: http://www.ugine.fr

Wholly Owned Subsidiary of Usinor S.A.
Incorporated: 1985
Employees: 12,055
Sales: FFr 16.33 billion (1996)
SICs: 331 Basic Steel Products; 3312 Blast Furnaces and
Steel Mills

Ugine S.A. is the stainless steel and special alloys division of French steel giant Usinor S.A. (formerly Usinor-Sacilor) and is one of the world's leading producers of specialty steels. Major manufacturing subsidiaries grouped under the Ugine branch and owned wholly or in part by the company include Ugine, Ugine-Savoie, and Imphy S.A., in France (all 100 percent owned); J&L, in the United States (53.6 percent); and Thainox, in Thailand (28 percent).

Ugine operates 31 manufacturing plants through 13 industrial subsidiaries in France, elsewhere in Europe, in the United States, and in Asia. The company also operates four research facilities in France: at Ugine, in the Savoie, concentrated on stainless steel; at Guegnon (stainless steel); at Isbergues (stainless steel and electrical steel); and at Imphy (stainless steel and special alloys). In addition to its production and research facilities, the company operates a worldwide network of sales, trading, and finishing units through nearly 30 marketing subsidiaries. In 1996, the company's payroll topped 12,000 employees. Ugine's FFr 16 billion in sales for that year represented nearly one-quarter of parent company Usinor's total sales.

Ugine's manufacturing concentration is on stainless steels—alloys of iron and chromium, with a chromium content of at least 10.5 percent. The chromium reacts with air and water during the manufacturing process, creating a thin layer of chromium oxide that acts as a protective film. This film provides resistance to rust and corrosion, and protection against other environmental exposures. The addition of other substances, such as nickel or molybdenum, provide additional resistant and protective properties, such as retaining form at extremely high temperatures, or maintaining ductility at extremely low temperatures. Ugine's stainless steel production falls into five major product categories: stainless steel flat products; stainless steel long products; special alloys; electrical steel; and welded stainless steel and carbon steel tubes.

Produced by Ugine in France, J&L in the United States, and Thainox in Thailand, each of which concentrates on a specific range of stainless steel grades, Ugine's stainless steel flat products include martenistic steels, which have high carbon and chromium content, but which contain no nickel. These steels are chiefly used for silverware and other cutlery products. The company's ferritic steels, which have a low carbon content and contain no nickel, are used for such diverse products as household appliances, automobile parts, heat exchangers, containers, and decorative trim products. The third type of stainless steel flat product produced by Ugine and its subsidiaries are its iron-rich austenitic steels, which contain nickel in addition to chromium and are used in the food, chemicals, nuclear power, and construction industries, as well as for sinks and cooking utensils. In addition, the company produces super ferritic, super-astenitic, and austeno-ferritic duplex or hardened steels. Ugine is the world's second-largest producer of stainless steel flat products. Sales of flat products represented 64 percent of Ugine's total sales in 1996.

Ugine is the world leader in stainless steel long products manufacturing. These are stainless steel grades formed into bars, wire rods, and billets, and which are further processed by Ugine customers into a wide range of products, including valves, faucets, pumps, tubes, turbine and reactor components, and fittings for ship superstructures. Long products produced 21 percent of Ugine's sales in 1996.

Through its Imphy S.A. subsidiary, Ugine is also a world leader in special alloy production. These alloys, which include such metals as nickel, molybdenum, chromium, cobalt, and others, are used for high-tech applications in the electronics, aerospace, telecommunications, and data processing industries. The company produces special alloys in various forms, such as wire, thin strips, and forged segments. Special alloys contribute more than 8.5 percent of Ugine's annual sales.

Ugine is also a leading European producer of electrical steels—which feature high magnetic properties and are used especially for the production of electrical transformers—for Usinor Aciers Electriques. Electrical steels formed more than six percent of Ugine's 1996 sales. The company's La Meusienne subsidiary also produces welded stainless steel and carbon steel tubes, put to a variety of uses, including automotive exhaust fittings, store and showroom fixtures, furniture, medical equipment, and in the construction, food, railroad, and chemicals industries.

Forged in the 1980s

With roots stretching back to the mid-19th century, Ugine, in one form or another, held a central place in France's steel industry, centered in the Savoy region. During the early part of the 20th century, Ugine combined with Kuhlmann, to form the chemicals and steel alloys concern Ugine-Kuhlmann. But the company's modern form began to take shape especially during the French government's industrial interventionist drives in the late 1960s and 1970s, leading toward the French Socialist government's nationalization policies of the early 1980s.

In the late 1960s, the French government, then led by Georges Pompidou, sought to boost the country's relatively small and disparate chemicals industry, encouraging the consolidation of France's smaller chemicals concerns. This process began in 1968 as Rhône-Poulenc, at the time a medium-size company focused on textiles and fine chemicals, rebuilt itself into one of the ten largest chemicals companies in the world. The same year saw the formation of another French chemicals giant, CdF Chimie, followed by the ATO Chimie joint plastics venture by oil companies Elf and Total. Ugine-Kuhlmann soon joined the government-inspired consolidation drive, when it was merged into Pechiney S.A., then Europe's leading aluminum producer, which itself had been founded in 1855, and which operated extensive mining activities both in France and around the world. The new company, called Pechiney Ugine Kuhlmann (PUK), became France's largest private company, employing some 104,000 workers worldwide, and posting US$4.7 billion in sales by 1974. In 1972, the chemicals operations of Ugine-Kuhlmann were reformed into a new division, called Produits Chimiques Ugine-Kuhlman (PCUK). By the mid-1970s, PCUK joined Rhône-Poulenc, ATO Chimie, CdF Chimie, and L'Air Liquide in France's top five chemicals producers. Ugine-Kuhlmann's specialty steels activities were re-

formed as a separate division of PUK as well, operating as Ugine Aciers, and completing PUK's production range in aluminum, chemicals, nuclear fuels, and specialty steels.

The PUK merger, however, quickly proved ill-inspired and ill-timed. The oil crisis of 1973 led to a worldwide economic slump, cutting into PUK's aluminum, chemicals, and steel activities. By 1975, PUK saw its sales shrink back to US$3.9 billion, and posted a loss of as much as US$144 million. While the company's aluminum arm recovered in the second half of the decade, its specialty steels division continued to struggle, as did PCUK, which, together with much of the French chemicals industry, found itself burdened by over-capacity, France's low level of domestic natural resources, and an underdeveloped investment program. Both PCUK and the Ugine Aciers specialty steels division would continue to drag on PUK's profits, with both divisions posting heavy losses through the end of the 1970s. Only PUK's U.S. aluminum operations, which included Howmet Corp. and its subsidiaries, and Intsel Corp., a metals trading and marketing arm set up by Pechiney in the 1920s, enabled PUK to eke return to profitability, accounting for some 98 percent of the company's 1978 net income of FFr 261 million (US$64 million), on sales of more than US$6 billion. In that year, the specialty steels division alone posted a loss of nearly FFr 524 million. By the late 1970s, the French government again began encouraging a reshuffling of the country's chemicals and steel industries. PUK began restructuring its chemicals and aluminum operations, selling off a number of its smaller divisions, and cutting back on its workforce. Meanwhile, it began eyeing exiting the specialty steels business altogether.

PUK's restructuring efforts became more urgent as the next decade began. Struggling with building losses in its aluminum division, as this industry began feeling the effects of a new worldwide recession, PUK faced a threat of a different sort: the French national elections of 1981. Led by François Mitterand, the Socialist Party had, since the early 1970s, made no secret of its desire to nationalize many of France's largest financial and industrial companies—with PUK featuring prominently on the list of proposed companies. The nationalization drive was inspired in part by a desire to boost employment levels—a mood which would restrict PUK's and other companies' flexibility in their restructuring and international expansion efforts. As the May 1981 election loomed, PUK began making plans to dissolve its already pared-down chemicals operations, which had managed to post profits in 1979, but had again slipped into the red by 1980. At the same time, the company had been working on finalizing the sale of Ugine Aciers to Sacilor S.A., then France's second-largest steelmaker and itself a primary target for nationalization.

The agreement to sell Ugine Aciers, which had been in the works since the late 1970s, nearly floundered by 1981, as the steel division, which had lost some FFr 855 million over the previous three years, was heading for fresh losses. By the end of 1981, the steels division accounted for much of PUK's total losses of FFr 1.75 billion on that year's revenues of FFr 41 billion. After continued government prodding—including the promise of financial support to absorb the costs of the acquisition—Sacilor agreed to take over Ugine Aciers. The move completed the consolidation of the French steel industry into just two companies: Sacilor and Usinor. In the late 1980s, these two companies themselves merged, forming Usinor-Sacilor. PCUK, meanwhile, was dissolved in 1983, when its assets and operations were divided up among Rhône-Poulenc, EdF Chimie, and Entreprise Miniere et Chimique (EMC).

Ugine Aciers now operated as a separate division of Usinor-Sacilor. In 1984, Ugine was combined with another Sacilor specialty steel subsidiary—and a longtime partner with Ugine—Forges de Guegnon. The new subsidiary, called Ugine-Guegnon, was placed on the Paris stock exchange, selling 47 percent of the company to private investors. Sacilor, through Ugine Aciers, retained 53 percent of the company. The combined company, which focused on the specialty 430 steel grades, boasted an annual production of some 200,000 tons. In 1985, Sacilor set up a new company, Ugine S.A., to combine all of its specialty steel subsidiaries into one centralized operation.

A Specialty Steel Leader for the 1990s

By then, the French nationalization drive had all but run out of steam, leading to a new period of "de-nationalization," which would continue into the mid-1990s. In the meantime, by the mid-1980s, and after a cost of some FFr 50 billion buying up 12 of the country's largest corporations—including Rhône-Poulenc, Saint Gobain, Usinor, Sacilor, PUK, Thomson-CSF, Dassault, Matra, Roussel Uclaf, and Cie Honeywell Bull—the government-owned sector's losses had only continued to grow—from FFr 1.9 billion in 1980 to FFr 39 billion in 1982 and FFr 36 billion in 1984. Chief among the state-owned sector's loss makers were its steel giants, Usinor and Sacilor, which were combined soon after to form Usinor-Sacilor.

By the beginning of the 1990s, the steel industry in general, and Usinor-Sacilor in particular, had recovered strongly from its mid-1980s slump. Led by Francis Mer, who would be given a larger share of the credit for Usinor-Sacilor's recovery, the parent company had also been engaged on a series of takeovers and cooperation agreements within the European steel industry, enhancing its value-added product lines, such as the specialty steels produced by Ugine. In 1990, Ugine received a fresh boost when Usinor-Sacilor announced the friendly takeover of Pittsburgh's Jones & Laughlin (J&L), then the second-largest stainless steel producer in the United States. Grouped under Ugine, J&L boosted the company's share of the stainless steel market to 15 percent, making it the world leader by a wide margin. The takeover agreement, with a purchase price of some US$400 million, also made Ugine the largest U.S. producer of stainless steels, with annual sales of some $2.5 billion.

In March 1990, Ugine added the grained electromagnetic sheet division of Belgium's Cockerill Sambre S.A., raising its output in that product to 140,000 tons per year. In November 1990, Ugine made a move to increasing its Far Eastern presence when it entered discussions to build a $200 million stainless steel sheet mill in Thailand. That agreement would lead to the formation of Thainox Steel Co., based in Bangkok. Ugine's participation in the venture, originally slated at 51 percent, would eventually be reduced to a 28 percent holding.

The J&L merger, which added complementary stainless steel grades to Ugine's line, proved successful enough that Usinor-Sacilor could use its U.S. arm as an investment vehicle (French government-owned companies were not allow to raise capital by selling shares in the parent company). In December 1993, Usinor-Sacilor, through S&L, sold 42 percent of Ugine, taking the subsidiary public by listing J&L on the New York Stock Exchange. By the end of the following year, Ugine's total sales had risen past FFr 19.9 billion.

Just 18 months after selling shares in its stainless steel subsidiary—and only two months after its own "de-nationalization"—Usinor-Sacilor announced its intention to buy back complete control of the subsidiary, for a purchase price of some FFr 3.7 billion in September 1995. Two months after completing the stock purchase, Usinor-Sacilor merged Ugine into Usinor, restructuring Ugine as the stainless steel division of the parent company. Usinor-Sacilor itself changed its name to simply Usinor in 1997. Meanwhile, Ugine began expanding its Asian presence, planning a stainless steel sheet plant in China, and beginning construction on a US$765 million steel plant in New Delhi, India, in a joint venture, to be called Jindal Uginox Ltd., with that country's Jindal Strips Ltd.

Principal Subsidiaries

Ugine; J&L (U.S.A.; 56.3%); Thainox (Thailand; 28%); Ugine-Savoie; Imphy S.A.; La Meusienne (99.91%); Mecachim; Sacem; IST (U.S.A.); Trafilierie Bedini (Italy); Sprint Metal (France and Germany); Techalloy (U.S.A.); Mecagis; Hood-Rahns (U.S.A.).

Further Reading

Collingwood, Harris, ed., "Birth of a Stainless Steel Colossus," *Business Week*, March 26, 1990, p. 44.

Dawkins, William, "Luck and Judgment in Stainless US Acquisition," *Financial Times*, March 16, 1990, p. 34.

Dodsworth, Terry, "Sacilor Takeover of Ugine Completes Steel Rationalization," *Financial Times*, January 21, 1982, p. 17.

"Pechiney Ugine Kuhlmann: In Every Fat Man There's . . ." *Economist*, April 18, 1981, p. 77.

Rao, N. Vauski, "Ugine Sets India Steel Joint Venture," *American Metal Market*, April 30, 1996, p. 2.

Ridding, John, "Planning to Bring Ugine Back Into the Fold," *Financial Times*, September 19, 1995, p. 25.

Semmler, Edward R., "J&L's Markets for Stainless Steel Expand," *Repository*, March 15, 1993.

Smosarski, Greg, "Ugine Planning China Steel Investment," *American Metal Market*, April 3, 1996, p. 66.

"Ugine Up 26% As Buy-in Intrigues Paris Bourse," *Financial Times*, October 3, 1995, p. 37.

—M. L. Cohen

U.S.FILTER

...taking care of the world's water.

United States Filter Corporation

40-004 Cook Street
Palm Desert, California 92211
U.S.A.
(760) 340-0098
Fax: (760) 341-9368
Web Site: http://www.usfilter.com

Public Company
Incorporated: 1953
Employees: 10,000
Sales: $1.367 billion (1997)
Stock Exchanges: New York
SICs: 3569 General Industrial Machinery, Not Elsewhere Classified; 8711 Engineering Services; 3589 Service Industry Machinery, Not Elsewhere Classified

United States Filter Corporation (USF) is the world's largest and fastest-growing water and wastewater treatment company. Founded in 1953, it was once a regional company with less than 500 employees in the United States and annual revenues of less than $30 million. USF has since grown into a worldwide industry leader with more than 10,000 employees, annualized revenues of $1.36 billion and operations on every continent with customers such as Coca-Cola, Chrysler, and 3M.

Since 1991, USF has acquired and integrated more than 100 companies worldwide including many of the oldest, most-respected names in the water and wastewater industry. These acquisitions have enabled USF to greatly increase its presence in those industries, to expand its worldwide service in all of the markets it serves, and to build its installed base, service network and range of products and technologies.

In 1991, USF obtained Lancy Environmental Systems, a leader in industrial wastewater treatment, metals removal and recovery, advanced biological treatment, and landfill leachate treatment systems. January 1992 brought USF Illinois Water Treatment, a Rockford, Illinois-based leading water treatment equipment manufacturer that specialized in high-purity technol-

ogies such as ion exchange (IE), reverse osmosis (RO), and ion exchange resin processing and Metro Recovery Systems, a Roseville, Minnesota-based RCRA Part B-permitted hazardous waste and recovery facility. In April of the same year, USF acquired Societé des Ceramiques Techniques, a Tarbes, France-based world leading fabricator of advanced ceramic materials and Membralox ceramic membranes.

In January 1993, USF acquired Permutit, a Warren, New Jersey-based pioneer in water and wastewater treatment technology with expertise in evaluating, designing, engineering, and building systems. In December of the same year, USF acquired Ionpure Technologies Corp., a Lowell, Massachusetts-based manufacturer and service provider of ultrapure water systems based on RO, ultrafiltration (UF) and "continuous deionization" technologies, as well as service deionization (SDI) services, laboratory water systems and replacement cartridges.

Speeding up Acquisitions, 1994–96

May 1994 took USF to Barcelona, Spain, where it acquired Sation S.A., a company which primarily services ultrapure water purification products, specializes in SDI and auto-deionization equipment for the general industrial market. In June, USF acquired Sanila S.A., an Amboise, France-based company specializing in SDI and auto-deionization equipment for the automotive, aeronautics, semiconductor, pharmaceutical, and power markets.

July brought USF a company called Continental Water Systems, a manufacturer of ultrapure water systems based on RO, UF, and IE cartridges that also provides SDI for laboratory and medical markets. Also acquired that same month were Penfield Corporation, a leading manufacturer of customized high-purity water systems for pharmaceutical applications; Ransbach-Baumbach, Germany-based Seral Erich Alhauser GmbH, the largest provider of SDI in Germany which also designs, manufactures, installs, and services water purification products and systems for laboratory and commercial markets; and Liquipure Technologies Inc., which provides SDI products and services through company-operated and franchised dealers and designs, manufactures, installs, and services ultrapure water purification products and systems primarily for the pharmaceutical and laboratory markets.

Company Perspectives:

The cycle of water—the conversion of moisture as it evapo-rates and rises to form clouds that release rain to Earth once again—brings infinite promise. Although nature's manage-ment system creates deserts and floods, it delivers one of Earth's most precious assets on a scale that defies imagina-tion. This cycle is an implicit warning that, as the population of Earth grows, change must occur in the way the world uses water. That change is U.S. Filter's mission.

In August, USF bought Ceraflo(r) Products, a part of Milli-pore Corporation, a leader in the manufacture of ceramic mem-brane filters used in the pharmaceutical and beverage markets; and Smogless S.p.A., a Milan, Italy-based provider of a broad range of services for wastewater treatment, including feasibility studies, process evaluation, plant design, construction, and commissioning and design of specialized machinery which also specializes in custom turnkey industrial treatment plants.

In December, the company acquired Group Crouzat, a Tou-louse, France-based developer and distributor of water purifica-tion products for industrial and laboratory customers and the French industry leader in SDI; and L'eau Claire, an industry leader for over 30 years in upflow media filtration for the petroleum, power, chemical and plastics markets.

April 1995 brought USF another Permutit holding, this time The Permutit Group, a Hertford, England-based pioneer in water and wastewater treatment technology with expertise in evaluating, designing, engineering, and building systems and a major provider of SDI services in the United Kingdom, Austra-lia, and New Zealand which produces custom and standard water treatment products for the pharmaceutical laboratory and chemical markets. In May, USF acquired Arrowhead Industrial Water Inc., a supplier of owned and operated onsite industrial water treatment systems in the United States and provides emergency and temporary mobile water treatment systems. USF, in August, acquired Interlake Water Systems, a Broad-view, Illinois-based provider of water treatment services, in-cluding SDI, in Illinois and Michigan that also sells and services a broad range of complex water treatment systems. In October, USF acquired Polymetrics Inc., a provider of treatment systems and services for the electronics, pharmaceutical, laboratory, power generation, and cogeneration industries and also pro-vides water treatment services, including SDI. November brought USF Home Waterbehandeling B.V., a Zoetermeer, Netherlands-based provider of SDI, IE, and wastewater treat-ment systems for metal finishing and general industry and Houseman B.V., a Bergen op Zoom, Netherlands-based pro-vider of water treatment systems for the power and petrochemi-cal markets. Bekox, a Madrid, Spain-based provider of large RO and biological wastewater treatment systems to the general industry market was obtained in December.

January 1996 saw USF acquiring Jet Tech, an Edwardsville, Kansas-based manufacturer of products which are used to en-hance the biological destruction of organic contaminants using high-efficiency air diffusion and mixing with sequencing batch reactors and aerobic digesters which treat sludge and biosolids for land applications or landfilling without restrictions; and Ponzini Acque Sd (Italy), a Soresina, Italy-based company which provides water treatment for pharmaceutical industry applications.

The next month, USF acquired KBS Pure Water Ltd. of Singapore and KBS Pure Water Sdn. Bhd. of Penang, Malaysia, both of which provide a variety of water treatment equipment and services including SDI, water purification equipment and wastewater equipment to microelectronics manufacturers and other industrial customers in Asia; Wastewater Treatment Sys-tems, a designer and assembler of wastewater treatment systems specializing in microelectronics, wastewater treatment, and re-cycle systems; and, continuing to eat away at the Permutit companies, USF acquired in the same month Permutit (Egypt) Ltd., a company which designs water treatment systems used primarily in the Middle East and whose facility also added seawater desalination and potable and wastewater treatment technologies to the company's product offerings.

In March, USF acquired Sagei Electropure, a provider of SDI and RO systems in the dialysis market. May brought USF Posey Pure Corporation, the Houston, Texas-based leading pro-vider of SDI in that city's market and Zimpro Environmental Inc. and Enviroscan Inc., Rothschild, Wisconsin-based manu-facturers of wastewater treatment equipment using proprietary technologies in wet oxidation, landfill leachate systems, groundwater remediation, filtration and sludge treatment sys-tems, and providing environmental analytical services for wa-ter, wastewater, soils, sludges, and air, including analyses re-quired for priority pollutants, safer drinking water, and landfill monitoring and remediation projects.

In July, USF acquired Coyanosa Product, a distinctive oil and water separation process by means of walnut shell filtration and Xentex Corporation, a provider of SDI, water purification systems, and regeneration services in Kansas and Missouri. August brought USF two businesses: Davis Water and Waste Industries, a leading distributor of water and wastewater distri-bution products and services to the industrial and municipal markets which also designs, engineers, manufactures and in-stalls water and wastewater treatment and pumping equipment; and Viking Water Systems, a leading provider of drinking water treatment and bottling equipment.

In September, USF acquired Kisco Water Treatment Com-pany, a Greendale, Wisconsin-based manufacturer of water treatment equipment for the industrial and commercial markets that offers a full range of standard and custom-engineered prod-ucts including softeners, filters, deionizers, dealkalizers, con-densate polishers, degasifiers and RO equipment; and Marga Chemical & Industrial Corporation, a Philippines-based manu-facturer of water treatment equipment for the industrial and commercial markets with a full range of softeners, filters, deion-izers, and dealkalizers and whose services include installation, maintenance, and SDI.

The following month saw USF obtaining Norris Environ-mental Service, an RCRA Part B-permitted hazardous waste treatment and recovery facility; The Utility Supply Group Inc., a Waco, Texas-based leading distributor of water and wastewater distribution products and services to the municipal market primarily in Texas, California, and Florida; and WaterPro Supplies Corporation, a leading distributor of water and wastewater distribution products and services to the industrial and municipal markets within the U.S. November brought USF Akvapur AB, a Stockholm, Sweden-based engineering firm specializing in power applications with technologies including flocculation, media filtration, softening, IE, and condensate polishing; and Perrier Equipment S.A., a company involved in sales, engineering, and manufacturing for industrial process water purification and effluent treatment, filtering screens, intake systems and flow control for dams, canals, and irrigation ditches and municipal wastewater treatment.

USF, in December, acquired the Water Systems and Manufacturing Group (WSMG) of Wheelabrator Technologies Inc. (WTI) for $369.6 million in cash. This acquisition strengthened USF's technological capabilities and product offerings, particularly in the municipal and industrial wastewater markets and expanded USF's engineering and manufacturing capabilities outside North America, especially in Europe and Asia, where WSMG generated approximately half of its 1995 revenues. WSMG products and systems include EVAP, IX/ER, Memclean, RMS, and Totaltreat.

As part of the WSMG package, USF ended up acquiring The Wheelabrator Corporation, a Naperville, Illinois-based designer and manufacturer of environmentally sound surface-cleaning and preparation equipment and supplies and a producer of metal screening and grating used in wastewater and organic and inorganic waste handling; USF CPC Engineering, a designer of water and wastewater treatment systems for municipalities on a standard or custom-engineered basis under the Microfloc brand name and a producer of solids screening, dewatering, conveying, and grinding equipment for municipal and industrial applications; Darchet Engineering, a specialist in water and wastewater needs of the microelectronics, metal finishing, and other industries in the Pacific Rim region and also a specialist in IE, RO, UF, and conventional technologies; HPD, a leader in evaporation and crystallization water treatment technologies serving the pulp and paper, chemical, petrochemical, mining, and power industries which enhanced USF's zero-discharge and product recovery techniques; Johnson Screens, a recognized leader in well screen design and development and screen installation with operations in Minnesota, France, India, and Australia; Memtek, a maker of sophisticated cross-flow membrane microfiltration products to remove inorganic solids and heavy metals from contaminated wastewater for the microelectronics, metal finishing and industrial laundry marketplace; PSS, a Spain-based provider of evaporation, crystallization and membrane separation technologies primarily in the chemical and pulp and paper industries; Sun Chi, a Taichung, Taiwan-based designer and installer of wastewater treatment systems primarily for municipal applications; and Westates Carbon, a full-service granular activated carbon company that provides USF with the ability to recycle and reuse spent carbon used in both water and wastewater treatment applications.

The same month, USF acquired Didier Gutling GmbH, a Stuttgart, Germany-based metal finishing sales and systems engineering company; Effimex, S.A. and Sitindustrie S.p.A.,

manufacturers of well screens; and RECON Verfahrenstechnik GmbH, a metal finishing company specializing in the galvanizing industry with IE and metal recovery capabilities.

First Billion-Dollar Water Treatment Company, 1997

In 1997, USF became the United States' first billion-dollar provider of industrial and municipal water and wastewater treatment systems, products and services. *Fortune* magazine ranked USF among the 100 fastest-growing companies in the world, with compound annual revenue growth of 66% between 1991–96.

In January, USF acquired the Process Equipment Division (PED) of United Utilities Plc for approximately $160 million in cash and over one million shares of USF common stock, providing USF with a significant manufacturing and distribution presence in the municipal wastewater treatment equipment and systems market, primarily in North America and Europe. Included in the acquisition were several PED units, among them Edwards & Jones, a designer, manufacturer, and installer of biosolids handling equipment primarily for municipal markets in Europe and the Pacific Rim region; Asdor, also a designer, manufacturer, and installer of biosolids handling equipment in North America; Envirex, a leading manufacturer of wastewater treatment equipment, including screening, grit removal, biological treatment, and solids collection equipment with particular strengths in the municipal treatment market, with one of the world's largest installed bases of municipal wastewater treatment equipment and broadest product lines; and Wallace & Tiernan, the Vineland, New Jersey-based world leader in the manufacture of water and wastewater disinfection systems and components and the inventor of the chlorine gas purification technologies in 1913.

Also as part of the PED purchase, USF acquired Consolidated Electric, a St. Paul, Minnesota-based supplier of automation and control systems for municipal water and wastewater treatment equipment using liquid level pressure and flow sensors, automatic pump controllers, and alternators and remote control technology; and General Filter/Acumen, leading providers of pretreatment equipment, granular media filtration systems, and microfiltration systems, primarily to the municipal water markets in North America. Acumen also sells microfiltration systems for the treatment of surface and ground water to potable water standards for industrial and municipal users in the U.S., U.K. and Australia.

Other acquisitions in January included Geopure Systems and Services Inc., a provider of SDI in Florida, Alabama, Texas and Virginia; and an SDI provider called Technipure Inc. The following month brought USF Lazers H2O Inc., a supplier of high-purity water systems to the medical, pharmaceutical, biotechnology, and electronics industries servicing Minneapolis (whose facility contains a high-purity water ion exchange resin regeneration plant which is registered with the U.S. Food and Drug Administration as a medical device manufacturer), as well as North Dakota, South Dakota, Iowa, and Wisconsin; and PORI International Inc., a Baltimore, Maryland-based company that designs, installs, operates and services wastewater treatment for large industrial customers, including steel and aluminum manufacturers.

USF, in March, acquired Cass Corporation, a manufacturer of mobile surface preparation equipment; a water distribution company called Lone Star Water Inc.; Sidener Supply Company, a leading distributor of waterworks equipment, supplies, and services with 15 facilities in Illinois, Indiana, Kansas, and Missouri; and a supplier of high-efficiency hydrocyclone oil/water separators called Trident Separation Technologies.

April brought a number of companies under the USF umbrella. Continuing to buy up Wheelabrator Technologies, USF acquired Wheelabrator EOS Inc., another Naperville, Illinois-based segment which was the contract operations and privatization businesses of WTI in exchange for over two million shares of common stock. WTI is a provider of water and wastewater treatment maintenance and operation services for over 130 clients. WTI also is developing privatization initiatives for municipal wastewater treatment facilities and, in 1995, became the first company in the United States to acquire a publicly owned wastewater treatment plant under Executive Order 12803.

During the same month, USF acquired United States Water Company Inc. (USW), a Cedar Rapids, Iowa-based network of 20 service branches that serve residential and commercial water treatment markets, mostly in the Midwestern U.S. and Florida, in exchange for approximately 500,000 shares of common stock. This acquisition gave USF a strong entry into the residential market of bottled water, water softeners, and whole-house and household point-of-use water treatment products and systems. However, the acquisition triggered a lawsuit by Culligan Water Technologies against USF when USW terminated all agreements with Culligan. Culligan alleged USW violated franchise agreements with Culligan and the possible passing of confidential Culligan information from USW to Culligan competitor USF.

April also saw the acquisition of Adaline Water Systems Inc. in Dallas and Bedford, Texas, a company which provided self-service bottled water and bottled water delivery as well as residential and commercial water softening products and drinking water treatment systems; Chester Engineers Inc., an engineering firm specializing in the metals, design-build, and automotive industries; Dan Little Water Marts #44 and #45, retail water stores located in Waco and Temple Texas, which provide self-service bottled water and bottled water delivery, as well as residential and commercial water softening products and drinking water treatments; Florida Springs Distribution Inc., a residential and commercial bottled water distribution company; and Pure H2O Inc., two West Palm Beach, Florida-based retail water stores offering self-service bottled water and bottled water delivery for the residential and commercial markets.

The following month, USF purchased Gene McVety Inc., a wastewater distribution company with operations in Phoenix, Arizona; J. Mortensen & Co. Limited, a manufacturer, distributor, and service provider of a broad range of water and wastewater equipment for the industrial, commercial, and municipal markets of Hong Kong, Taiwan, and China; Mobley, a Baytown, Texas-based company that specializes in the collection, treatment, recycling, and management of a wide range of non-hazardous oil/water and fuel/water mixtures, used oil filters, antifreeze, and other related materials; Southwest Abrasives & Equipment Co., a surface preparation sales, service, and distri-

bution company; and Trinity Coast Sales Incorporated, a distributor of residential and commercial bottled water located in Colleyville, Texas, that offers water in both natural spring and purified forms and distributed under the Coral Springs label. In June, USF acquired Fife, a wastewater distribution company with operations in Florida, South Carolina, and Mississippi.

Near the end of 1997, USF's owned or operated facilities processed nearly 600 million gallons of water per day and its products could be found in more than a quarter million customer facilities, making it the only company in the world with the ability to design, manufacture, install, service, maintain, operate, finance and own nearly every product, service, and technology required to process, treat or distribute industrial, municipal, or residential water and wastewater. With no sign of slowing its growth, USF far outstrips leading competitors in many industries, including Culligan, Sparkletts Water and Crystal Water, Osmonics Inc., Calgon Carbon, RainSoft Water Treatment Systems, and Air Sep Corporation.

Principal Subsidiaries

General Filter Company; Illinois Water Treatment Co.; Ionpure Technologies Corp.; Permutit Company Inc.; Polymetrics (France); Seral Erich Alhauser GmbH (Germany); Smogless SpA (Italy); U.S. Filter Asia (Singapore); U.S. Filter Europe (Spain); U.S. Filter Mexico (Mexico); Xentex Corporation.

Further Reading

"Absolute Control: Invest Where You Have the Knowledge and the Edge, In Yourself and Your Industry," *Success,*—June 1997, p. 17.

Ascenzi, Joseph, "U.S. Filter Continues Buying Binge," *Knight-Ridder/Tribune Business News,* May 5, 1997, p. 505B1013.

Bergstrom, Danna, "Largest Environmental Firms in Silicon Valley—Ranked by Number of Professionals Locally," *Business Journal,* March 17, 1997, p. 16.

Caldwell, Bert. "MPM Technologies, Spokane, Acquires Unit of U.S. Filter Corp.," *Knight-Ridder/Tribune Business News,*—May 7, 1997, p. 507B1270.

Caminiti, Susan, "Outsourcing Water," *Fortune,* December 11, 1995, p. 209.

Carrell, Romi E., "U.S. Filter Acquires U.S. Water; Culligan Files Suit," *Water Conditioning & Purification,* March 1997, pp. 60–61.

Conon, Bernard, "Waterfall: Richard Heckman Is Great at Selling Investors on His U.S. Filter Co., If Not Actually Producing Profits," *Forbes,* December 16, 1996, p. 42.

"$46 Million Stock-and-Debt Bid for Utility Supply," *New York Times* September 7, 1996, p. 21.

Holden, Benjamin A., "U.S. Filter Hopes Acquisitions Can Keep Profits Flowing; Water Concern Agrees to Deal with WMX Technologies; Stock Surges to 15%," *Wall Street Journal,* September 23, 1996, p. B4(E).

"Industrywise," *Beverage World,* January 1995, p. 22.

McDevitt, Kevin, "U.S. Filter, A Really Pure Play," *Financial World,* July 18, 1995, p. 20.

Palmeri, Christopher, "Good Water, Good Will," *Forbes,* February 13, 1995, p. 20.

"Waterpro to Be Acquired in a $95 Million Stock Deal," *Wall Street Journal,* September 12, 1996, p. B16(E).

"WMX Technologies to Sell Some Lines for $385 Million," *Wall Street Journal,* September 17, 1996, p. B4(E).

—Daryl F. Mallett

U.S. Satellite Broadcasting Company, Inc.

3415 University Ave.
St. Paul, Minnesota 55114
U.S.A.
(612) 645-4500
Fax: (612) 642-4578
Web site: http://www.ussbtv.com

Public Subsidiary of Hubbard Broadcasting Inc.
Incorporated: 1981 as United States Satellite
    Broadcasting Company, Inc.
Employees: 116
Sales: $191.99 million (1996)
Stock Exchanges: NASDAQ
SICs: 4841 Cable & Other Pay Television Services

U.S. Satellite Broadcasting Company (USSB), Inc., a publicly traded subsidiary of Hubbard Broadcasting, Inc., is a pioneer and leading provider of Direct Broadcast Satellite (DBS) subscription television services to the United States and to part of Canada and Mexico. From its National Broadcast Center located in Oakland, Minnesota, USSB broadcasts high-quality digital television signals to customers equipped with Digital Satellite System (DSS) equipment—consisting of an 18-inch satellite dish, digital receiver, and remote control—via five of the 16 transponders of a satellite transmitter owned by USSB and partner DirecTV, a subsidiary of the satellite's manufacturer, Hughes Corporation. USSB's satellite transmissions, which use MPEG-II digital compression technology, provide laser-disc quality video and CD-quality sound, with no degradation of quality regardless of customer location. Set-top receivers are also equipped with ports for eventual data transfer to customer computers.

Launched in June 1994, USSB already attracted more than a million subscribers by the beginning of 1997, compared to a total installed base of DSS home receiver systems of approximately two million. Industry analysts expect DSS penetration to reach more than 10 million households by the year 2000. USSB offers subscribers a choice of 10 programming packages, rang-ing from its $7.95 per month basic service to its premium $34.95 per month Entertainment Plus package, which features 25 channels, including MTV, Comedy Central, Lifetime, Nick at Nite's TV Land, and up to 16 channels of movie programming through multichannel services such as HBO, Showtime, and Cinemax. USSB broadcasts also feature pay-per-view programming and CD-quality radio broadcasts, as well as CNN-rival All News Channel, originally developed by Hubbard Broadcasting through a partnership with Viacom. DSS owners also have the option of subscribing to USSB partner DirecTV's 200-channel broadcast service. The partners, while operating as competitors, present largely complementary programming—DirecTV's programming emphasizes sports and pay-per-view in contrast to USSB's movie channels. More than two-thirds of customers subscribing to DirecTV also purchase USSB subscriptions. DirecTV investor AT&T has also agreed to promote USSB's services to its 90 million long-distance customers.

Led by the Hubbard family—Stanley S. Hubbard is chairman, and sons Stanley E. and Robert are, respectively, president and CEO and executive vice-president—USSB has posted strong gains in revenues since launching its satellite services. In the company's fiscal year ending July 1996 the company posted sales of $192 million. The company has yet to show a profit, with losses mounting to $95 million for the 1996 fiscal year. Nonetheless, the introduction of DSS has been considered one of the most successful electronics product launches in history and USSB hopes to reach its break-even point of 1.6 million subscribers by the end of 1997.

Looking to the Sky in 1981

The Hubbard family already had a long history as broadcast pioneers before the introduction of the DSS system. Company founder Stanley E. Hubbard started out in radio in 1923 with WAMD—Where All Minneapolis Dances—the first radio station in the country to generate revenues solely through advertising. In 1948, Hubbard turned his attention to the nascent television industry, purchasing a camera and forming the first independent NBC affiliate station. Hubbard also introduced what would become an industry mainstay—the 10 p.m. nightly news broadcast—before purchasing a color television camera and becoming the first television station in the country to broadcast entirely in color. The Hubbard television empire would eventually grow to include nine television stations, two radio stations, and affiliated companies including Conus Communications and the All News Channel.

Son Stanley S. Hubbard was named president of Hubbard Broadcasting in 1967 and was later named CEO in 1983. By then, the younger Hubbard—continuing the family tradition—had already recognized the potential of a new broadcasting technology, satellite transmission. In 1981, when the Federal Communications Commission announced its intention to offer licenses for the newly developed DBS spectrum of satellite transmission, Hubbard formed United States Satellite Broadcasting Company, Inc. and became one of the first, and the few, to apply for the new licenses. USSB was granted its DBS license in 1982. Hubbard proposed launching a three-channel broadcast service, which would be funded by advertising revenues and be received directly by homes or made available to other television stations for rebroadcast.

Home satellite reception was not entirely new. In the late 1970s, a number of people had discovered that they could tap into HBO and cable television satellite feeds using backyard satellite dishes. During the 1980s, a new business sprung up around sales of satellite dishes capable of receiving these transmissions. Because the satellites' power output was limited to 10 to 15 watts (compared to the 120 watts of the USSB and DirecTV satellite), early satellite reception required dishes ranging up to eight feet in diameter, for a cost of some $2,000 per dish. In the late 1980s, broadcasters began scrambling their transmissions and began selling subscription-based decoders to unscramble the signals. By the mid-1990s, an estimated 4.5 million households were receiving these satellite transmissions; about half of that installed base were subscribers, paying an average of $25 per month for the full range of cable television and other broadcasting services. An unknown number of satellite dish owners either contented themselves with only still-unscrambled transmissions or had outfitted themselves with decoders capable of pirating the scrambled transmissions.

Meanwhile, the cable television revolution took off firmly during the 1980s. The rise of cable—and the rush of investors to that industry—quickly eclipsed the proposed DBS system. Hubbard's USSB was greeted with skepticism from the cable and television broadcasting industry and, more importantly, from the investment community. In 1984, however, USSB appeared to be underway. Hubbard announced an agreement with RCA Astro-Electronics for the purchase of two direct broadcast satellites. The satellites, which were each to carry 240-watt amplifiers, would supply six channels of USSB programming. With a cost projected at $160 million, USSB's satellites would join the two satellites already contracted for by Comsat's Satellite Television Corp. Launch of the USSB satellites was projected for 1988. At the same time, Hubbard formed Conus Communications as a satellite-based news gathering service, which evolved into a 24-hour news network by the end of the decade.

The evolution of USSB, however, stalled through the 1980s. Raising investment capital proved difficult, with investors becoming wary after the failure of the Comsat and other satellite ventures, and it was not until 1990, with an investment by Chicago-based Pittway Corp., that USSB had procured the funding necessary to move forward. Other investors included Burt Harris, a Los Angeles-based cable operator and television broadcaster, and Nationwide Mutual Insurance and that company's broadcast subsidiary Nationwide Communications. The Hubbard family continued to hold the largest investment—as much as 60 percent—in USSB. By then, Hubbard, who had already spent as much as $20 million through USSB, planned to launch a five-transponder satellite. With newly developing digital compression technologies, the five transponders would be capable of transmitting as many as 20 channels of programming. The USSB satellite would join another proposed satellite, a 27-transponder system being developed in a partnership among Hughes Communications, NBC, Cablevision Systems, and News Corp. as Sky Cable.

The Sky Cable partnership never took off and was scuttled in early 1991. The high-power DBS technology itself seemed dead in the water. Broadcasters began looking toward other satellite technologies, such as the medium-power direct-to-home service being developed as PrimeStar by a consortium of cable operators. But in June 1991, USSB and Hughes Communications agreed to join together to build and launch a 16-transponder DBS satellite. Terms of the deal called for USSB to pay Hughes $50 million upfront and another $50 million in installments, for ownership of five of the satellite's transponders. The proposed satellite would broadcast at 120 watts, allowing households to receive the signal via small, windowsill-sized satellite dishes, initially projected to cost some $300 for the dish and receiver. Hughes would pick up the remaining $200 million of the estimated cost of $300 million to build two satellites and to launch at least one by 1994.

The Hughes-USSB deal established a common digital broadcast standard and revived DBS as a home entertainment technology. DBS quickly took steps to become a viable system. While Hughes began work on manufacturing the satellite itself, in 1992 USSB and Hughes reached an agreement with RCA/Thomson Consumer Electronics, Inc. to design the DBS satellite dish and receiver distribution system to be used by the Hughes-USSB satellite. That system, dubbed Digital Satellite System, or DSS, was established in the same year.

Hubbard's vision was at last coming to fruition. And that vision itself had expanded. With the Hughes-USSB satellite offering a proposed capacity of 120 channels, the DSS launch was seen as the world's first "broadcast supermarket." While DBS's initial consumer base was considered rural households that had been passed by cable television, Hubbard and others in the industry began envisaging the emergence of niche programming services. Because the DBS satellite's transmission could be received throughout the North American market with no degradation of signal quality, the potential arose for offering magazine-style stations, targeted at specific consumer interest groups. Niche programming remained financially unfeasible for the largely locally based cable television operators. But DBS's reach would be more universal. As Hubbard told *Success*: "Let's say we put on a program that appeals to 1 percent of the population. That's a million homes." DBS offered another advantage over cable. While DBS's launch had long been slowed by the capital intensive nature of its startup, expanding its customer base presented none of the costly cable-laying and trench-digging of the cable industry.

With the launch of the Hughes-USSB satellite slated for the end of 1993, the two companies—Hughes formed the DirecTV subsidiary to provide its DSB service—began negotiating for programming. Technically competitors, the two companies remained intertwined, sharing the same satellite and position. DirecTV, with a capacity of some 200 channels compared to USSB's potential 25, was seen as having the edge. However, in June 1993, USSB scored a coup when it reached agreements with both Time Warner, owner of HBO, and Viacom, owner of Showtime, for exclusive satellite broadcasting rights to these companies' movie channels. USSB had beaten out Hughes by promising to accept the two movie broadcasters' full multichannel offerings. In HBO's case, this meant eight channels of HBO and Cinemax. Viacom would provide its Showtime, Flix, and the Move Channel, as well as MTV, VH1, and Nickelodeon/Nick at Nite. In addition, USSB lined up Comedy Central, Lifetime, as well as its jointly owned All News Network. Meanwhile, with DirecTV focusing on pay-per-view programming, sports coverage—including exclusive deals with the National Football League and the National Basketball Association—and cable television networks such as the Disney Channel, the two companies developed complementary, rather than competing, programming packages. With the companies broadcasting from the same satellite and using a common technology, potential customers could be encouraged to subscribe to both satellite services.

DBS-1, the first high-power DBS satellite in the United States, was launched in November 1993. Satellite transmission was originally set to begin in April 1994. Hubbard, with much of USSB's programming already set, went in search of funding needed to complete the new station's launch—an additional $50 million earmarked for construction of USSB's National Broadcast Center command center, a $12 million, 20,500-square-foot facility, and another $20 to $40 million for marketing and promotion of the USSB service. By April 1994, however, Hubbard had raised some $140 million in equity investment—including $20 million from Microsoft cofounder Paul Allen, $42 million from George Soros, and $25 million from Dow Jones. The Hubbard's $50 million startup investment continued to give the family 60 percent control of USSB.

By May 1994, the company was at last ready to begin transmitting. The roll-out of the satellite dish and receiver packages—which included a free initial month of the full USSB program package—began in Albuquerque, New Mexico; Shreveport, Louisiana; Tulsa, Oklahoma; Jackson, Mississippi;

and Little Rock, Arkansas, all cities with low cable television penetration. Rollout to other states continued through the summer, with the DSS satellite package, initially priced at $700, available in most of the country by the autumn of 1994. By the end of that year, Thomson announced that it had shipped more than 300,000 DSS systems. That number has climbed to one million by mid-1995. USSB's subscriber base had by then reached 320,000, providing revenues of $42.3 million. The company, which had posted losses in 1993 and 1994, continued to lose money—some $74 million in 1995.

Nonetheless, the announcement of the company's initial public offering for the beginning of 1996 was greeted enthusiastically by the investment community. The DBS industry itself was picking up, adding a new service, EchoStar, in December 1995, and additional manufacturers, including Sony, GE, and ProScan, of DSS satellite dishes and receivers. Meanwhile, AT&T paid $137.5 million to purchase 2.5 percent of DirecTV, adding the long-distance company's massive marketing strength and its 90 million customer base to the future potential of DBS. Other companies, including MCI and News Corp., were preparing their own satellite television entries. USSB's IPO had been expected to raise about $174 million for the company; instead the stock offering, made on February 2, 1996, generated $224 million.

Through 1996, USSB continued to add customers, reaching 800,000 by its fiscal year end, with another 400,000 potential customers engaged in the initial free month trial. USSB's revenues gained strongly over the previous year, nearing $192 million. Its losses continued to mount, however, dipping to $95 million for the year. Yet, these losses were expected to fade, as forecasts called for USSB to reach its break-even point of 1.6 million subscribers, an event expected to occur in 1997.

Further Reading

Ezaki-Smith, Anna, and Michael Warshaw, ''Czar of the Airwaves,'' *Success*, January 1993, p. 31.

Fiedler, Terry ''USSB Reaches Marketing Agreement with AT&T on Satellite Broadcasting,'' *Star Tribune*, March 26, 1996, p. 3D.

Gross, Steve, ''Hubbard's TV Venture Via Satellite,'' *Star Tribune*, June 14, 1993, p. 1D.

Jessell, Harry A., and Peter D. Lambert, ''USSB Lines Up New Investors,'' *Broadcasting*, July 9, 1990, p. 28.

——, ''USSB, Hughes Revive DBS in $100 Million + Deal,'' *Broadcasting*, June 10, 1991, p. 35.

Kincaid, Mesa, ''In Focus: Stanley S. Hubbard,'' *Corporate Report Minnesota*, January 1991, p. 52.

—M. L. Cohen

Vornado Realty Trust

Park 80 West, Plaza II
Saddle Brook, New Jersey 07663
U.S.A.
(201) 587-1000
Fax: (201) 587-0600

Public Company
Incorporated: 1936 as Windsor-Fifth Ave., Inc.
Employees: 72
Sales: $116.9 million (1996)
Stock Exchanges: New York
SICs: 6512 Operators of Nonresidential Buildings

Vornado Realty Trust is a real-estate investment trust (REIT) that owns, leases, develops, and manages real-estate properties, primarily in the Northeast and Mid-Atlantic states. At the end of 1996 the company owned 57 shopping centers in 7 states. Vornado was a retailer until 1980, when Steven Roth wrested control of the firm and converted it into a developer of the properties occupied by its Two Guys store chain. In the 1990s Roth positioned Vornado to become a major developer of commercial real estate in midtown Manhattan.

Retail Operator, 1947–80

Vornado's corporate history dates back to Windsor-Fifth Ave., Inc., a Manhattan decorating company formed in 1936. In 1947 Herbert Hubschman and his brother Sidney opened a household-appliance store in a Harrison, New Jersey, converted diner. This was the first in a discount chain named Two Guys From Harrison, which originally sold major appliances, later adding other appliances and housewares. The Hubschmans were pioneers in the development of one-stop shopping centers in New Jersey, all under one roof and consisting chiefly of leased departments. Vital to their success was their policy of locating in outlying areas, where they could obtain cheaper land and offer customers larger parking lots than other retailers. Sales grew from $6.8 million in fiscal 1952 (the year ended August 31, 1952) to $38 million in fiscal 1957. Net income rose from $162,723 to $816,675 over this period.

Two Guys From Harrison was operating, through subsidiaries, 16 discount stores—14 of them in northern New Jersey—when it went public as Two Guys from Harrison, Inc. in 1957, offering one-fourth of its common stock at $9 a share. In 1959 Two Guys entered a new field by acquiring O.A. Sutton Corp., Inc. for stock. Incorporated in 1941, Sutton was in 1954 manufacturing Vornado electric fans and room air conditions, fuel tanks for the Air Force, and air conditioners under the Westinghouse, Hotpoint, and Kelvinator trade names in Wichita, Kansas. Auto air conditioners and dehumidifiers were later added to its products. Net sales rose from $3.1 million in fiscal 1949 (the year ended November 30, 1949) to $38 million in fiscal 1954, while net income grew from $282,859 to nearly $1.5 million over this period. In fiscal 1957, however, Sutton lost $1.7 million on sales of $37.9 million. The next year it suspended manufacturing and began liquidating its inventories to pay off bank notes.

The acquisition provided Two Guys with additional working capital as well as the Vornado line of appliances and an income-tax shelter later challenged by the Internal Revenue Service. Renamed Vornado, Inc., the consolidated company expanded the Vornado line of appliances to more than 50 in under three years, including ranges, freezers, hair dryers, and electronic can openers sold by the Two Guys chain as well as other dealers. Manufacturing operations were contracted out, however, rather than retained by the firm. Meanwhile, Two Guys continued to thrive. By the end of 1965 it was the nation's fifth-largest discount chain, with 25 stores in 5 states, stretching from Connecticut to Maryland, and sales in fiscal 1966 (the year ended January 31, 1966) of $247.2 million, with net income of $8 million.

Two Guys's units, which included seven company-owned properties, were among the largest in the discount industry, with average store size close to 146,000 square feet. All but seven included company-operated supermarkets. Food, appliances, and clothing and apparel contributed the most to sales volume, with other items including housewares, home furnishings, shoes, auto accessories, jewelry, cosmetics, toys, and seasonal merchandise. Leased departments now accounted for only 5 percent of sales. Vornado maintained a fleet of almost 200 trailers and trucks and had in-house advertising, service, and construction departments. Herbert Hubschman died in 1964; since his brother had previously left the company, an associate, Frederick Zissu, succeeded as chairman.

In 1967 Vornado acquired Food Giant Markets, Inc., a West Coast supermarket chain that also held a discount-store division and other retail enterprises, for an estimated $50 million of company stock. The purchase seemed to be a bargain: for its stock Vornado acquired a company doing $350 million worth of business a year, with 70 supermarkets, 241 Foster's Freeze franchised fast-food drive-ins, 14 Unimart general-merchandise discount stores, 5 package liquor stores, and a chain of more than 20 Builders Emporium stores selling do-it-yourself supplies. Vornado's sales immediately more than doubled, and its profits rose, although by a lesser amount.

Before long, however, security analysts were characterizing the acquisition as a serious drag on profits. Food Giant, still under its old management, instituted discounting but alienated shoppers by shortening hours and eliminating trading stamps. When managers from the East took over, they eliminated established California brands in favor of Vornado's own private labels, which were unknown out West. Unimart had a huge inventory of unsalable merchandise. Company debt had reached $97.2 million by 1971.

In fiscal 1972 the Vornado empire enjoyed record sales of $827.1 million and record net income of $12.1 million. There were 53 Two Guys stores (including 4 in California), 65 Food Giant stores, 240 Foster Freezes, and 31 Builders Emporium units. Most of the Unimarts had been phased out or were being converted to Two Guys outlets. In addition the company had purchased 12 Disco Fair stores in California from Beck Industries Inc. and also owned a bakery and a dairy-products company. The Food Giant chain was disposed of piecemeal in 1971 and 1972, but this failed to stem a steady decline in profits. In fiscal 1977 Vornado earned only $145,000 on sales of $946.5 million.

In 1978 Vornado sold 22 Two Guys stores in California and a Builders Emporium to Fed-Mart Corp. for $38.3 million and the assumption by the buyer of $27.3 million in mortgage debt. It sold the other 59 Builders Emporium stores to Wickes Corp. for $56.3 million in cash and the assumption of $10.7 million in mortgage debt. This left the company with 60 Two Guys stores and some $100 million in cash but also about $103 million in debt. By the fall of 1979 Interstate Properties Inc., a private partnership engaged in shopping-center development, had taken a 17-percent stake in Vornado. In fiscal 1980 the company reported a loss of $750,000 on sales of $733.4 million, and later that year Interstate Properties took control of the firm after winning a proxy struggle.

Shopping Center Landlord in the 1980s

Steven Roth, the active Interstate partner, regarded Vornado's real-estate holdings as more valuable than its declining retail operations. He liquidated Two Guys, which was doing $600 million a year in business but had an operating loss of more than $20 million in the first half of 1981, disposing of $196 million of inventory. Montgomery Ward & Co., Inc. had leased 12 Philadelphia-area locations from Vornado in 1980; in March 1982 The Stop & Shop Cos., Inc., agreed to lease 11 more Vornado shopping centers for its Bradlees discount department stores. While seeking tenants for its 34 other shopping centers and its eight warehouses, the company retained three Sutton Place catalog stores, which were subsequently phased out, and the Steinwurtzel finished-apparel wholesaling operation. Company revenues, $36.2 million in 1982, had reached $66.3 million in 1985, when real estate outstripped merchandising from Steinwurtzel (which was discontinued in 1991) as the chief source of sales. In 1989 Vornado had net income of $10.4 million on sales of $81.6 million.

Eyeing Manhattan in the 1990s

Roth, through Interstate Properties, entered the Manhattan real-estate market in 1985 by buying a small stake in Alexander's, a failing retailer whose land holdings included its flagship store, occupying the entire block between East 58th and 59th streets and Lexington and Third avenues. Interstate and developer Donald Trump raised their respective shares of Alexander's to 22 percent each in 1987 and agreed to expand or sell their interests in the firm jointly. In 1988 they each raised their stakes to 27 percent. The agreement lapsed in 1991, when Trump turned over his holdings in Alexander's to Citicorp, which had been holding them as collateral for a personal loan. The following year Roth and Alexander's creditors forced the firm into bankruptcy. They closed the remaining stores in operation and raised $120 million by leasing a half-dozen of its properties to Caldor.

Alexander's emerged from bankruptcy in 1993, but as a real-estate investment trust (REIT). Two years later Vornado, which already held a small portion of the retailer, bought Citicorp's share for $54.8 million—about 25 percent under market value. Roth, who now held majority control through Vornado and Interstate, became chief executive officer of the company. Vornado's plans for Alexander's East Side property—perhaps the most conspicuously unoccupied tract of prime Manhattan real estate in the 1990s—remained uncertain.

Vornado Inc. was converted to Vornado Realty Trust, a REIT, in 1993. By this time the company held $115 million in cash and $421 million in total assets. Its shares had increased in value by about 17 times since 1981, and Roth had realized $29.2 million the previous year by exercising options on 1.5 million shares of Vornado stock. The new equity offering raised $172 million and left Roth, through Interstate Properties and his personal holdings, with 38 percent of the outstanding shares. A special dividend of $54 million was distributed to shareholders.

At the end of fiscal 1995 Vornado had posted average 3-, 5-, and 10-year annual total returns of 27.4, 33.7, and 28.9 percent, respectively. The company suffered a blow when Bradlees, now the anchor store in 21 of Vornado's 56 shopping centers, filed for bankruptcy protection in 1995. Standard & Poor's concluded, however, that most of the leases would survive the bankruptcy because of the above-average sales of the stores involved, superior locations, and Bradlees' lease guarantees from its former owner, Stop & Shop. Bradlees held 17 leases from Vornado at the end of 1996. They were mostly in New Jersey but also included the location of its store near Manhattan's Union Square.

Michael Fascitelli, a Goldman, Sachs & Co. real-estate investment banker, was recruited to become president of Vornado in December 1996 by a compensation package valued at from $50 million to $100 million or more. The lucrative deal was seen as evidence that Vornado was ready to buy downtown office buildings and regional malls. Rumors about the company's intentions sent the price of the stock to $61 a share in March 1997, compared to $37 a share a year earlier. Shortly thereafter Vornado confirmed one source of speculation by purchasing Mendik Co. for $437 million in cash and securities from developer Bernard Mendik, who became co-chairman of Vornado. Vornado also assumed $217 million in debt. Mendik Co. held control of seven midtown Manhattan office buildings totaling 4 million square feet of space. Roth was said to have told friends privately that he intended "to become the largest owner of commercial real estate in New York."

One of Mendik's buildings was adjacent to Madison Square Garden, and another was across the street. A few months later Vornado agreed to buy another nearby building, the Hotel Pennsylvania, in a $160-million joint venture with Ong Beng Seng, a Singaporean hotel developer and financier. And in June 1997 Vornado purchased three small buildings a block north of the hotel, plus leases of retail spaces in two buildings previously acquired by Vornado, for about $75 million. These transactions aroused speculation that Vornado was contemplating a multilevel shopping and entertainment complex in the area, which included not only Madison Square Garden but also the Manhattan passenger terminals for Amtrak and the Long Island Rail Road.

At the end of 1996 Vornado owned 57 shopping centers in New Jersey New York, Pennsylvania, Maryland, Connecticut, Massachusetts, and Texas, containing 10 million square feet of space. They were generally located on major regional highways in densely populated areas. Shopping centers accounted for 92 percent of Vornado's rental revenues in 1996, and the occupancy rate was 90 percent. About 80 percent of the square footage was being leased to stores taking more than 20,000 square feet. Such stores included discount department stores, supermarkets, home-improvement stores, discount apparel stores, membership warehouse clubs, and "category killers": large stores that offered a complete selection of a category of items at low prices, often in a warehouse format. The company also owned eight warehouse/industrial properties in New Jersey, containing 2 million square feet of space, and two office buildings with 250,000 square feet of space. Vornado was leasing its executive headquarters in Saddle Brook, New Jersey.

Vornado had record income from continuing operations of $61.4 million in 1996 on record revenues of $116.9 million. Interstate Properties, a general partnership in which Roth was managing general partner, held 24.4 percent of its shares. Vornado held 29.3 percent of Alexander's common stock at this time and was managing, developing, and leasing Alexander's properties under a three-year agreement.

Principal Subsidiaries

Vornado, Inc.; Vornado Acquisition Corporation; Vornado Finance Corp.; Vornado Holding Corporation; Vornado Investments Corporation; and Vornado Lending Corp.

Further Reading

Allimadi, Milton G., "Vornado Nears Vote to Convert Firm to a REIT," *Wall Street Journal,* April 23, 1993, p. A7E.

Bagli, Charles V., "Big Realty Trust to Take Over 7 Manhattan Office Towers, Long a Family's Domain," *New York Times,* March 13, 1997, p. B7.

Barmash, Isadore, "Marriage at Vornado Is Mended," *New York Times,* September 22, 1968, Sec. 3, p. 15.

"Cash at a Discount?" *Forbes,* May 15, 1978, p. 192.

Feldman, Amy, "Roth Flashes Alexander's Trump Card," *Crain's New York Business,* August 20, 1990, pp. 3, 25.

Freeman, William, "Trading Stamps? Chain Takes All," *New York Times,* August 26, 1962, Sec. 3, p. 9.

Griffith, L. Timothy, "Vornado, Inc.," *Wall Street Transcript,* January 6, 1969, p. 15,392.

Gross, Daniel, "Building Expectations," *New York,* July 7, 1997, pp. 22–23, 87.

Halbfinger, David M., "A Developer Buys a Swath of Midtown with a Garden View," *New York Times,* June 28, 1997, p. 23.

"Herbert Hubschman Dies at 52; Chairman of Discount Chain," *New York Times,* September 22, 1964, p. 39.

"O.A. Sutton Says It's Liquidating Stocks to Pay Off Bank Debt," *Wall Street Journal,* September 17, 1958, p. 11.

Pacelle, Mitchell, "Control of Alexander's To Be Acquired by Real-Estate Developer Steven Roth," *Wall Street Journal,* February 7, 1995, p. A8.

"The Price of a White Elephant," *Forbes,* December 15, 1968, p. 19.

"Profits of Vornado Sweep Toward New Record High," *Barron's,* March 7, 1966, p. 26.

Rudnitsky, Howard, "No More Mr. Nice Guy," *Forbes,* September 13, 1993, pp. 100–01.

Vinocur, Barry, "Steve Roth's Property Company Takes Big Stake in Alexander's, the Old Store Chain," *Barron's,* February 13, 1995, p. 46.

——, "Deal Maker Leaves Goldman Sachs for Big-Buck Job at REIT," *Barron's,* December 9, 1996, pp. 46–47.

Winans, R. Foster, "Vornado Becomes Attractive to Institutions, But Buyers Advised Not to Expect Quick Payoff," *Wall Street Journal,* February 4, 1983, p. 43.

—Robert Halasz

The Pharmacy America Trusts

Walgreen Co.

200 Wilmot Road
Deerfield, Illinois 60015
U.S.A.
(847) 940-2500
Fax: (847) 940-2897
Web site: http://www.walgreens.com

Public Company
Incorporated: 1916
Employees: 77,000
Sales: $11.78 billion (1996)
Stock Exchanges: New York Midwest
SICs: 5912 Drug Stores & Proprietary Stores

Walgreen Co. is the largest drugstore chain in the United States in terms of sales, nearly half of which derives from retail prescriptions. Walgreen fills more than 8 percent of all retail prescriptions in the United States. It operates more than 2,200 Walgreens drugstores in 34 states and Puerto Rico. In addition to the flagship Walgreens, the company also manages Walgreens RxPress units, AdvanceCare institutional pharmacies, and Walgreens Home Medical Centers. As of 1996, Walgreen was the 16th-largest retailer in the United States.

Early Years of Rapid Growth

The company had its origin in 1901, when Charles R. Walgreen bought the drugstore, on the south side of Chicago, at which he had been working as a pharmacist. He bought a second store in 1909; by 1915, there were five Walgreen drugstores. He made numerous improvements and innovations in the stores, including the addition of soda fountains that also featured luncheon service. Walgreen also began to make his own line of drug products; by doing so, he was able to control the quality of these items and offer them at lower prices than competitors.

By 1916, there were nine Walgreen stores, all on Chicago's South Side, doing a business volume of $270,000 annually. That year, the stores were consolidated as Walgreen Co. with the aim of assuring economies of scale.

By 1919 there were 20 Walgreen stores, 19 of which were on Chicago's South Side while the other was on the near north side. Also in 1919, the company opened its first photofinishing studio; it promised faster service than most commercial studios.

The 1920s were a booming decade for Walgreen stores. In 1921, the company opened a store in Chicago's downtown, its first outside a residential area. Walgreen stores introduced the milkshake at their fountain counters in 1922. To meet the demand for ice cream and to assure its quality, Walgreen established its own ice cream manufacturing plants during the 1920s. The company continued to add to its number of stores, and by mid-1925, there were 65 stores with total annual sales of $1.2 million. Fifty-nine of the stores were in Chicago and its suburbs, with others in Milwaukee, Wisconsin, and St. Louis, Missouri. Before the year was out, the company had expanded into Minneapolis and St. Paul, Minnesota.

The company opened its first East Coast store, in New York's theater district, in 1927. That year, the company went public, listing its shares on the New York Stock Exchange. By the end of 1929, there were 397 Walgreen stores in 87 cities; annual sales were $47 million with net earnings of $4 million.

Great Depression Years

At first, the company suffered little from the 1929 stock market crash and the subsequent Great Depression. Sales actually rose in 1930, to $52 million. The same year, the company opened a 224,000-square-foot warehouse and laboratory on Chicago's southwest side. Early in the 1930s, the company expanded on a project begun in 1929 setting up an agency system by which independent drugstores could sell Walgreen products.

By 1934, 600 Walgreen agency stores were functioning in 33 states, mostly in Midwestern communities with populations of less than 20,000. By 1932, however, the company was feeling the Depression's pinch. Sales dipped to $47.6 million, and wage cuts were instituted; the company also set up a benefit fund to assist retirees and needy families inside and outside the company. The company continued promoting itself, however; in 1931, it had become the first drugstore chain in the United States to advertise on radio.

There were several major events for Walgreen in 1933. The company paid a dividend on its stock for the first time, its concessions at Chicago's Century of Progress exposition helped boost sales, and Charles Walgreen Jr. became a vice-president of the company. With the repeal of Prohibition late that year, Walgreen Co. acquired liquor licenses and soon was selling whisky and wine in 60 percent of its stores.

In 1934 the company opened its first Walgreen Super Store, in Tampa, Florida. At 4,000 square feet, the store was nearly double the size of the typical store, and it had a much larger fountain and more open displays of merchandise than an average store. Other Super Stores followed in Salt Lake City, Utah; Milwaukee, Wisconsin; Miami, Florida; and Rochester, New York.

Walgreen's business recovered in the mid-to-late 1930s; 1938 sales totaled $69 million. By 1939 the founder's health was failing; Charles Walgreen Sr. resigned the presidency of the company in August. His son was named to succeed him, and Justin Dart, who had been with the company in various capacities since 1929, was named general manager. Dart had been married to and divorced from Ruth Walgreen, the founder's daughter. Charles Walgreen Sr. died in December 1939 at the age of 66.

Continued Expansion in the 1940s

The company began the 1940s with the opening of a superstore in downtown Chicago. The store was the 489th in the chain and featured a two-way high-speed escalator to provide access between the two floors of the store, the first of its kind in any drugstore in the world. The store also contained a full-service restaurant-tea room. In April 1940 the Marvin Drug Co., which operated eight stores and a warehouse in Dallas, merged with Walgreen Co. At year-end, Walgreen Co. announced the establishment of a pension plan, with an initial contribution of more than $500,000 from the proceeds of Charles Walgreen Sr.'s life insurance policy.

In 1941 there was a split between Charles Walgreen Jr. and Justin Dart. Dart's unorthodox management style made others in the company uncomfortable; he was arbitrary in determining bonuses to store managers and critical of the company's conservative approach to business. Board members considered him erratic and extravagant. They called for his resignation in July

1941. In November of that year he resigned and joined United Drugs Inc., where he built a substantial career and diversified beyond the drug business.

Walgreen Co. put continued growth and expansion on hold with the United States's entry into World War II after the Pearl Harbor attack in December 1941. The company felt the war's impact in a variety of ways; certain foods became scarce, as did film and tobacco products. More than 2,500 Walgreen employees served in the armed forces; 48 did not survive. Walgreen stores sold war bonds and stamps. In 1943, the company opened a store in the Pentagon, in Washington, D.C.

After the war, expansion was once again possible. In 1946 the company acquired a 27 percent interest, later increased to 44 percent, in a major Mexican retail and restaurant company, Sanborns. More Walgreen Super Stores were opened in the late 1940s, including one on Chicago's Michigan Avenue, a street of elegant shops and restaurants. In 1948 the company expanded its corporate headquarters in Chicago. That year, sales were up to $163.6 million, and Walgreen began advertising on television.

Transition to Self-Service Begins in 1950s

The 1950s ushered in the era of self-service in drug retailing, a concept Walgreen had tried on an experimental basis at three stores in the 1940s. In 1949 the company canceled plans for a merger with Thrifty Drug Co., a California chain, largely because Thrifty's clerk-service style would hamper a conversion of the entire company to self-service. In the course of the merger negotiations, however, Charles Walgreen Jr. had researched Thrifty's competitors and had been impressed by the self-service Sav-On chain, which fueled his interest in taking his stores in that direction.

The first self-service Walgreens opened on Chicago's South Side in June 1952; the second followed in a few months at Evergreen Plaza, Chicago's first major shopping center. The self-service stores offered lower prices than traditional stores but often actually required more employees, because the stores were larger and carried more products. By the end of 1953, there were 22 self-service Walgreens. Self-service continued to grow throughout the 1950s; the company built many new self-service units and converted conventional ones. It also closed some older conventional stores because they were too small or in locations that had become undesirable. While the number of stores grew to only 451 in 1960—from 410 in 1950—sales grew from $163 million to $312 million over the course of that decade, thanks largely to the increased size and wider selection of the self-service stores.

With the opening of a self-service store in Louisville, Kentucky, at the end of 1960, self-service units outnumbered traditional ones. Another major event of 1960 was the opening of the first Walgreens in Puerto Rico.

Diversified Beyond Drugstores in 1960s and 1970s

In 1962 Walgreen Co. entered the discount department store field by paying about $3 million for the assets of United Mercantile Inc., which owned three large Globe Shopping Center stores and seven smaller Danburg department stores, all in the Houston, Texas, area. The company expanded the Globe chain throughout the South and Southwest; by 1966, there were 13 Globe stores generating annual sales of more than $120 million.

Operating Globe gave Walgreen Co. experience in running larger stores, and the company began to open ever-larger stores under the Walgreens name. The first Walgreens Super Center opened in 1964 in the Chicago suburb of Norridge. By 1969 there were 17 Super Centers around the country.

Walgreen Co. changed and diversified its restaurant operations in the 1960s. A detailed analysis early in the decade showed that the return on investment of Walgreen's fountains and grills was generally less than that of the rest of a store. Therefore, the company decided not to include fountains and grills in new stores and began closing them in others. Instead of getting out of food service altogether, however, the company went into full-scale restaurants; the first of these was the Villager Room, located within a Walgreens in Oak Park, a Chicago suburb. Also added during the 1960s were the fast-food chain Corky's and the medieval-decor Robin Hood restaurants. By the decade's end, there were 287 in-store restaurants, 14 Corky's and two Robin Hoods.

A third generation of Walgreens ascended to the company presidency in 1969. C. R. (Cork) Walgreen III was named president, succeeding Alvin Borg, who had become president when Charles Walgreen Jr. became chairman of the board during a 1963 corporate reorganization. This made Walgreen Co. one of the few companies headed by second- and third-generation descendants of the founder, though the Walgreen family no longer owned a controlling share of company stock. Also in 1963, the company elected its first outside directors to the board.

Several changes occurred in the mid-1970s. In 1974 the company opened its first Wag's restaurant; Wag's were freestanding family restaurants, many open 24 hours a day. That year it also acquired the Liggett chain of 29 Florida drugstores. In 1975 Walgreen Co. moved into a new corporate headquarters in Deerfield, a suburb of Chicago. The previous facility had become inadequate in size and outmoded. Also in 1975, the company completed the first phase of a new drug and cosmetics laboratory in Kalamazoo, Michigan; expanded its distribution center in Berkeley, Illinois; and, in Chicago, replaced its plastic container plant and photo processing studio with new ones. The company surpassed the $1 billion mark in sales in 1975.

In 1976 Charles R. Walgreen III succeeded his father as chairman of the board, and Robert L. Schmitt, who had been with the company since 1948, became president. Schmitt oversaw the liquidation of the Globe chain, which had been showing significant losses. He also was charged with forming a partnership with Schnuck's, a St. Louis grocery store operator, to establish combined supermarkets and drugstores, and with opening optical centers in Walgreen stores. Schmitt's tenure ended, however, when he died suddenly in October 1978. Fred F. Canning, a 32-year company veteran, succeeded him. In 1979 Walgreen Co. acquired 16 Stein drugstores in the Milwaukee area. It closed the 1970s with 688 drugstores, sales of $1.34 billion, and earnings of $30.2 million.

Refocused on Drugstores in 1980s

The company began the 1980s by refocusing on drugstores and eliminating certain businesses. In 1980 it ended the agency program, begun in 1929, which accounted for only 2 percent of sales. This step did not sit well with some former agency stores; a group of store operators in Wisconsin sued Walgreen Co., eventually winning a $431,000 judgment. The following year, Walgreen closed its 27 optical centers and ended the partnership with Schnuck's. The company also eliminated many in-store restaurants, concentrating on Wag's instead; in-store restaurants decreased in number from 231 in 1979 to 119 in 1984.

Expanding the drugstore business, Walgreen Co. brought the Rennehbohm chain, based in Madison, Wisconsin, in 1980. Rennehbohm had 17 drugstores, two clinic pharmacies, two health- and beauty-aid stores, a card shop, and six cafeterias. In 1981 Walgreen bought 21 Kroger SuperX drugstores in Houston. In 1982 the company added additional services to its drugstores: it made next-day photofinishing available chainwide and put grocery departments in some stores located in urban areas.

In 1983 Walgreen completed chainwide installation of its Intercom computerized pharmacy system. By the end of the decade Intercom connected each store in the chain via satellite to a mainframe computer in Des Plaines, Illinois. This system enabled customers to have their prescriptions filled at any Walgreens in the country.

Walgreen opened its 1,000th store, on the near north side of Chicago, in 1984. The company continued expanding in the drugstore area, while divesting itself of other businesses; also in 1984 it sold its interest in Sanborns, by then 46.9 percent, to Sanborns's other principals for about $30 million, a move spurred by Mexico's high inflation rate.

In 1986 Walgreen bought the 66 Medi Mart stores, located primarily in New England, in the company's largest single acquisition ever. That year, the company also bought 25 stores from the Indiana chain, Ribordy, and opened 102 new stores, making 1986 Walgreen's biggest year for expansion.

In 1988, continuing to trim non-drugstore businesses, Walgreen sold its 87 freestanding Wag's restaurants to Marriott Corporation. In 1988 the Haft family sought regulatory clearance to acquire a block of Walgreen stock—a move that company officials feared would lead to an unfriendly takeover bid, as the Hafts had tried to acquire other retailers. Walgreen responded with a move that was seen as an antitakeover device—the establishment of ''golden parachutes,'' payments to be made to executives if they left the firm after a takeover. No bid came through, however.

In 1989 the company opened four mini-drugstores called Walgreens RxPress, which offered a full-service pharmacy and popular non-prescription items in areas where full-sized store locations are difficult to find. By the mid-1990s, these 2,000-square-foot units, some of which offered one-hour photofinishing services, also featured convenient drive-through pharmacies. There were 25 RxPress locations by 1996.

Accelerated Expansion in the 1990s

For Walgreen, the 1990s were dominated by an unprecedented rate of expansion. Walgreen ended the 1980s with 1,484 units. By mid-1997 the company had more than 2,200 units (an increase of almost 50 percent) and was aiming for the 3,000 mark by the turn of the century. Although most of this growth was accomplished organically, the 1990s began with an acquisition, the 1990 purchase of Lee Drug, a nine-unit drugstore chain in New Hampshire and Massachusetts. That same year Fred Canning retired as president. L. Daniel Jorndt, who had been senior vice president and treasurer, succeeded him.

For the pharmacy industry as a whole, the 1990s were a decade of profound change. Demographically, there were more and more people over the age of 50; as a result, more prescriptions were being filled each year, making pharmacies a hot commodity. Consequently, competition became fiercer as aggressive chains such as Wal-Mart challenged Walgreen's leading position in prescription drugs. Additionally, managed care health plans grew increasingly important as the decade progressed putting pressure on drugstores to lower prices on prescriptions, thereby squeezing margins. Walgreen responded to these challenges by investing heavily in technology and by launching new initiatives aimed directly at taking advantage of the trend toward managed care.

On the technology side, the company improved its inventory management capabilities when it rolled out point-of-sale scanning equipment chainwide in late 1991, followed by the chainwide completion in 1994 of SIMS (Strategic Inventory Management System), which united all elements of the purchasing-distribution-sales cycle. By 1997 Walgreen was rolling out a second-generation Intercom Plus system, which performed more than 200 functions and enabled customers to order prescription refills using the keys on a touchtone phone. The system also cut in half the time customers had to wait to receive their prescriptions.

In response to the managed care boom, one byproduct of which was the growth in cost-effective mail-order pharmacies, Walgreen formed a subsidiary—Healthcare Plus—in 1991 to offer managed care providers a pharmacy mail service of its own. Launched with an Orlando, Florida, mail service facility capable of handling 5,000 prescriptions a day, Healthcare Plus added a second facility in late 1994 in Tempe, Arizona, with a capacity of 7,500 prescriptions per day. Mail service sales were expected to hit $500 million by 1998. In the fall of 1995 Walgreen expanded Healthcare Plus into WHP Health Initiatives, Inc.—a pharmacy benefits manager—in order to offer additional products and services to managed care providers, including long-term care pharmacies, durable medical equipment, and home infusion services. WHP was aimed at small and medium-sized employers and HMOs in Walgreens' top 28 retail markets.

Meanwhile the expansion of the Walgreens chain continued apace, supported by the opening of two more distribution centers—in Lehigh Valley, Pennsylvania, in June 1991 and in Woodland, California, in July 1995—bringing to eight the number of such centers. The Woodland center was particularly important as it supported an aggressive expansion in California, as well as the opening of the first Walgreens in Portland, Oregon. Walgreens also expanded into several other new mar-

kets in the mid-1990s, including Dallas/Fort Worth, Detroit, Kansas City, Las Vegas, and Philadelphia. Throughout the 1990s expansion, the chain concentrated on opening freestanding stores, which were considered more convenient than mall stores. By 1996 more than half of all Walgreens were freestanding. Drive-through prescription service at more than 700 Walgreens further enhanced the chain's image of convenience. In addition to all the store openings—210 in 1996 alone—the chain also remodeled or closed some of its older units; consequently, the average age of a Walgreens stood at 7.4 years in 1996, about half what it was 10 years earlier. Walgreen posted 1996 net sales of $11.78 billion, more than double that of 1989.

In May 1997 Walgreen entered foreign territory for the first time since the failed Sanborns venture. That month the company formed a joint venture—RX Network Inc. (RXN)—with Itochu Corp. and five other Japanese companies to set up a drugstore chain in Japan. RXN aimed to create a 500-unit chain by 2002. In January 1998 Charles R. Walgreen III retired as CEO (but remained chairman), with Jorndt taking over the CEO position.

Walgreen flourished during the challenging environment of the 1990s, turning such threats as managed care into opportunities for further growth. The company was well on the way to meeting its goal of 3,000 Walgreens by the year 2000 and was well-positioned to profit from the aging of the American population. Most remarkably the company grew dramatically without the benefit of a major acquisition. As a new century approached, Walgreen seemed likely to remain America's leading pharmacist for years to come.

Principal Subsidiaries

WHP Health Initiatives, Inc.

Further Reading

Block, Toddi Gutner, "We Need You, You Need Us: Drug Benefit Managers Have Grabbed Power in the Retail Pharmacy Industry. Walgreen Co. Is Grabbing It Back," *Forbes*, May 8, 1995, pp. 66–67, 70.

Brookman, Faye, "Innovative Chain Ranks No. 1," *Stores*, April 1993, pp. 21–23.

Byrne, Harlan S., "A Winning Prescription," *Barron's*, March 7, 1994, p. 21.

Clepper, Irene, "Walgreens: One of the Oldest and Still Growing," *Drug Topics*, April 8, 1996, pp. 116, 118.

Dubashi, Jagannath, "Walgreen: Just What the Doctor Ordered," *Financial World*, May 1, 1990, p. 20.

Henkoff, Ronald, "A High-Tech Rx for Profits," *Fortune*, March 23, 1992, pp. 106–107.

Kogan, Herman, and Rick Kogan, *Pharmacist to the Nation: A History of Walgreen Co., America's Leading Drug Store Chain*, Deerfield, Illinois: Walgreen Co., 1989.

Simon, Ruth, "Pills and Profits," *Forbes*, June 30, 1986, p. 33.

—Trudy Ring
—updated by David E. Salamie

The Washington Post Company

1150 15th Street, Northwest
Washington, D.C. 20071
U.S.A.
(202) 334-6000
Fax: (202) 334-4613
Web site: http://www.washpostco.com

Public Company
Incorporated: 1889
Employees: 7,300
Sales: $1.85 billion (1996)
Stock Exchanges: New York
SICs: 2711 Newspaper Publishing & Printing; 2721 Periodicals Publishing & Printing; 4833 Television Broadcasting; 4841 Cabke & Other Pay Television Services

The Washington Post Company and its subsidiaries are leaders in the news and communications media industry. *The Washington Post* has been a nationally respected and influential newspaper published daily to serve Washington, D.C., and the adjacent suburban area for over 120 years, and has consistently contributed a large share of the company's revenue. The company also published the politically-oriented *Washington Post National Weekly Edition*, a daily newspaper in Everett, Washington, and the increasingly popular *Newsweek* magazine. Other subsidiaries included six television stations, cable television systems in 16 states serving over 600,000 households, educational centers to prepare students for standardized college-admission tests and other professional exams, and an online legislative-information service. Through its ownership of all the company's class A common stock, the Graham family has maintained effective control over the company.

From a Democratic Slant to Mainstream Political Respect, 1877–1905

The Washington Post was first published on December 6, 1877, by Stilson Hutchins. Hutchins had come to the nation's capital from St. Louis, Missouri, where he had been associated with several newspapers. His goal in starting the *Post* was to establish a newspaper at the center of national affairs reflecting the views of the Democratic Party. At this time, the era of Reconstruction had just ended with the controversial presidential election of Rutherford B. Hayes, a Republican, over Samuel Tilden, a Democrat, by a special congressionally-appointed electoral commission. Hutchins did not approve of Hayes's victory and his paper rarely referred to the man as "president." Within a year, the *Post*'s circulation had reached more than 6,000 copies a day. The first Sunday edition was published on May 2, 1880, making it the first seven-day paper in Washington. By the late 1880s, Hutchins gave up his editorial allegiance to the Democrats and began to describe his paper as "independent." By 1888 Hutchins had bought out the *Post*'s only competitor (the *Republican National*) and, for a short time, published the *Evening Post*, an afternoon edition. The paper made a profit for most of its early existence, but Hutchins soon sold it to pursue other interests.

The paper was purchased in 1889 for $210,000 by Frank Hatton and Beriah Wilkins, $30,000 of which was raised by selling a press back to Hutchins. Hatton, who had a background in journalism, took care of the production of the paper, while Wilkins, who had served three terms in the House of Representatives, handled business matters. They incorporated their newspaper company as The Washington Post Company and the same year, at the request of the newspaper's new owners, noted bandleader John Philip Sousa wrote "The Washington Post March" to be played at the awards ceremony for winners in a *Post* essay contest. For the next several years, the company flourished under the guidance of Hatton and Wilkins, with profits averaging $100,000 a year between 1892 and 1894. Circulation was reported at about 16,000 daily and 20,000 on Sundays.

In 1903, however, with Hatton dead and Wilkins seriously ill, the paper was again for sale. Wilkins died before a sale could be made, but his son made a deal with John R. McLean, owner of the *Cincinnati Enquirer*, with McLean obtaining a minority share in the paper. By 1905, McLean had secured enough additional shares to place himself in control of the *Post*.

From the Ashes, A New *Post* Emerges, 1906–46

McLean adopted the style of journalism that had been so successful for William Randolph Hearst. He added sections to the *Post* for feature stories, comic strips, and sports. He gave less emphasis to political news, which had been the paper's

Company Perspectives:

The Washington Post Company has established six goals: 1) quality—to produce the best newspapers, magazines, television programs and other products we can; 2) to run an outstanding business, measured by the increase in intrinsic shareholder value over time; 3) to be not just a good, but an exceptional, place for people to work, and a leader in the hiring and promotion of minorities and women; 4) to be a company that provides outstanding customer service; 5) to be creative, adaptive, flexible and intelligent enough to adapt to the changes in our business environment; and 6) to be a respected part of the communities where we do business.

specialty. From 1905 to 1909, Sunday circulation was as high as 40,000, the best in the city, but daily circulation, while it averaged 30,000, began to decline. When McLean died in 1916, his son Edward McLean took over operations. The first years of the younger McLean's tenure were prosperous, with the *Post*'s Sunday circulation reaching 75,000, placing it second to the *Washington Star*, and profits reached a peak of $376,612 from 1921 to 1923. Edward McLean, however, became ensnared in the Teapot Dome scandal that rocked the presidency of Warren G. Harding during the early 1920s. At the center of the scandal was U.S. Secretary of the Interior Albert B. Fall, who had taken bribes to secretly lease oil-rich government lands without taking competitive bids. McLean became less able to handle the company's business affairs, and the editorial quality of the *Post* declined. From 1924 to 1932, the paper had only two profitable years. In 1933 it went through bankruptcy proceedings and was eventually sold for $825,000 at an auction held on June 1, 1933.

Eugene Meyer, a New York investment banker, was the new owner of the *Post*. With a sizeable fortune in investment banking, Meyer was willing to spend his money to make the *Post* both a quality newspaper and a profitable one. His task would not be easy, as circulation had fallen to about 50,000. He quickly began hiring a new staff of reporters and editors, and went to court to prevent several comic strips from being transferred to the *Washington Herald*. This was a period of great upheaval in Washington, as the New Deal policies of Democratic President Franklin D. Roosevelt were being implemented to pull the U.S. out of the Depression. One such aspect of the New Deal was the creation of the National Recovery Administration, which was supposed to spur industrial recovery and create jobs. Although Meyer was a staunch Republican, he did place the Blue Eagle, symbolic of the National Recovery Administration, on his paper. The paper was not as supportive, however, of other New Deal programs—particularly the Works Progress Administration (WPA), which funded construction of buildings, bridges, and roads to fight unemployment.

The New Deal period also saw one of the *Post*'s most comical typographical errors. At a time when Roosevelt was suffering from a cold, a *Post* headline read, "FDR in Bed with Coed." The president called the paper to ask for 100 copies of the first edition, but the error had been caught and copies of the issue had already been pulled from circulation. By 1938 circulation had climbed to 100,000 and its advertising volume was the second-highest in Washington. This performance was still well below that of the *Star*, the only profitable newspaper in the capital during the Great Depression. Annual losses at the *Post* were about $1 million from 1934 to 1937. Business improved during World War II, with profits for 1942 to 1945 totaling $249,451.

Eugene Meyer relinquished daily control of the *Post* in 1946 when President Harry S. Truman appointed him first president of the World Bank. Control of the paper stayed in the family, however, as Meyer transferred his voting stock to his daughter, Katharine Graham, and her husband, Philip Graham, on July 23, 1948. Philip Graham had already been installed as publisher of the paper, and the majority of the voting stock, 3,500 shares, was transferred to him, compared to 1,500 shares for Katharine. Under a modified incorporation of the company, the shares were put in a trust controlled by a five-member committee. The committee was authorized to decide on any future changes in the ownership of the voting stock in order to ensure that the company remained true to certain editorial standards (the committee remained in place until shares of the Washington Post Company were first offered to the public in 1971).

A Changing of the Guard Twice, 1947–65

When Graham became publisher of the paper he began instituting managerial changes. Within two years he had hired a new managing editor, business manager, and circulation manager. Following the lead of Meyer, who in 1944 had purchased a radio station, Graham acquired a radio station and a television station in Washington in 1949. In 1953 he bought another TV station in Jacksonville, Florida. The next year, 1954, The Washington Post Company made its most important corporate acquisition. After a period of negotiation, Meyer, who still acted as the company's chairman of the board, agreed to buy the *Washington Times-Herald* for $8.5 million. With the removal of the *Times-Herald* as a competitor, the *Post* was assured of a monopoly as Washington's only morning newspaper. The operations of the two papers were combined very quickly to counter any antitrust action the government might undertake, but no such action was pursued. Within four months, the combined papers had a daily circulation of 381,417 and 393,680 Sunday, and ranked as the ninth-largest morning paper in the country.

In March 1961, Philip Graham made another monumental acquisition—purchasing *Newsweek*, the general newsmagazine—from its stockholders for $15 million. *Newsweek* soon became an integral part of the company's operations. The following year Graham exhibited further foresight by forming a national news wire service in conjunction with the *Los Angeles Times* which would later serve upwards of 500 subscribers worldwide. In 1963, Philip Graham's tenure and years of manic-depressive illness ended when he took his own life. Upon his death, Katharine Meyer Graham took the reins of the company as president, to the chagrin of many who doubted her abilities to run the Washington Post Company in a man's world. She not only proved herself as more than up to the job— eventually earning the nickname of "the Iron Lady"—but basked in the glow of transforming the *Post* from a successful operation into a phenomenally profitable newspaper that put journalism first, whatever the price. Though she originally kept the same management team put in place by her husband, in 1965

Katharine ushered in a new era at the *Post* with the appointment of Benjamin Bradlee as managing editor.

A New Era of Responsibility and Recognition, 1966–75

In 1966 Graham continued her husband's acquisition program by buying a 45 percent interest in the Paris edition of the *New York Herald-Tribune*. The next year, through a partnership with the *New York Times*, The Washington Post Company began to publish the Paris paper as the *International Herald Tribune*. The end of the decade found Philip's last major acquisition, *Newsweek*, prospering, having exceeded the domestic advertising pages of its nearest rival, *Time*. Bradlee had also begun to make his mark on the *Post*, including the introduction of the "Style" section in 1969 as a way of combining all cultural news in one place. Bradlee was also to play a pivotal role in the two big stories of the 1970s that earned the *Post* its widest acclaim as an important national newspaper.

The first of these stories involved the publication of the Pentagon Papers. On June 13, 1971, the *New York Times* began to publish this secret, government version of the history of the Vietnam War in serial form, but within three days the administration of President Richard M. Nixon had secured an injunction forcing the *Times* to cease publication of the documents. A few days later, the *Post* secured a copy of the papers; in a meeting at Bradlee's home, reporters prepared the *Post*'s version of the Pentagon Papers for publication. Lawyers for the paper advised against publishing any story. The Post Company was in the process of going public; the stock had been issued but not yet sold. An indictment for criminal liability could easily place the transaction in jeopardy, threatening the very foundation of the company. Bradlee argued strongly in favor of publication and Katharine Graham made the final decision to publish. The government soon filed suit against the *Post* and the cases against both the *Times* and the *Post* were argued jointly. On July 1, 1971, the Supreme Court decided in favor of the newspapers by a six-to-three vote.

Soon after its success with the Pentagon Papers, the *Post* scored another major reporting coup with its handling of the Watergate affair. On June 27, 1972, there was a burglary at the Democratic Party headquarters in Washington. Because of its location, the *Post* was better equipped to go after the Watergate story than other newspapers. Two reporters specializing in the Washington city beat, Bob Woodward and Carl Bernstein, were assigned to the story, and with the help of several government officials, uncovered the link between the Watergate burglary and the Nixon Administration. Nixon and his aides retaliated by having Administration supporters challenge the broadcasting licenses of the company's Florida TV stations before the Federal Communications Commission. The company prevailed, though its share price suffered a decline during the Watergate period. Yet the *Post*'s reporting ultimately led to Nixon's resignation as president and in 1973 the paper was awarded a Pulitzer Prize for public service for its coverage of the Watergate affair.

While the Watergate and Pentagon Papers stories propelled the *Post* into the national limelight, several changes took place on the business side of the company. In 1971 the Washington Post Company completed its IPO of more than 1.35 million shares of Class B stock for $33 million. All of the Class A stock stayed within the Graham family; a capitalization that gave the Grahams a majority of the vote and the right to elect 70 percent of the directors, with Class B stockholders electing the remainder. In that same year the company also organized the Washington Post Writers Group to syndicate material produced by its staff writers, and moved into a new $25 million building in downtown Washington. It also purchased the *Trenton Times*, of Trenton, New Jersey, which proved to be a modestly successful operation.

By 1973, the *Post* had achieved the number-one position in Washington, accounting for 65.8 percent of advertising space, 56.6 percent of daily circulation, and 67.1 percent of Sunday circulation. The only other newspaper remaining to compete with it was the *Star*. The *Post* also encountered labor difficulties in the 1970s, facing strikes by its printers in 1973, by reporters and other members of the Newspaper Guild in 1974, and an especially brutal strike by the pressmen in 1975. Nevertheless, growth continued and the paper was able to emerge from all three strikes in a stronger position than before. The company, meanwhile, continued its media buying trend, acquiring TV stations (Miami in 1969, and Hartford in 1974). The Washington radio station purchased in 1949 was disposed of through the donation of its FM operations to Howard University in 1971 and the sale of its AM facility in 1977. In 1978, the company traded its TV station in Washington for a station in Detroit.

The Ascent of a Third Graham, 1976–95

During the heady 1970s, Donald Graham, son of Katharine and Philip, had begun working at the *Post*. By 1976 he had moved up the ranks to become general manager and in '79 he took charge of the paper as its publisher, with Katharine remaining in overall charge as chairman of the company. Meanwhile, *Newsweek*'s annual profits for 1977 were almost triple the price Philip Graham had paid in 1961; a year later, the company purchased the *Herald,* a daily newspaper located north of Seattle, in Everett, Washington.

The *Post* received a big boost in 1981 with the closing down of its last remaining competitor, the *Star*; circulation increased from 595,000 to 730,000 daily, and from 827,000 to 952,000 on Sundays. However, additional competition emerged in 1982 with the establishment of a new paper, the *Washington Times*, and further competition came from specialized suburban newspapers. Nevertheless, the company finished the year with solid operating revenues of $877.7 million and net income of $68.4 million. In 1983 came the launch of the *Washington Post Weekly,* a government-oriented paper specializing in politics, economics, and diplomatic matters; the following year, the *Post* was redesigned from top to bottom, for the first time in 50 years.

By 1988 when hostile takeover bids were becoming common in the corporate world and especially among newspapers, the Graham family took steps to protect its ownership of the *Post*. Because lawsuits at other newspapers had challenged the system of having two classes of stock by arguing that all stockholders should be entitled to vote on a merger plan, the charter of the *Post* was changed to make a majority vote of both classes of stock necessary to approve a merger. This year also marked a zenith for profit, when net income soared to $269.1 million on operating revenues of $1.37 billion and stock earnings leaping to $20.91 per share. The company's jubilation was somewhat short-lived, however, for both revenue and income began a downward trend after a modest increase in 1989, a year in which the company began the first of several ambitious stock repurchasing plans as both a good investment and to ward off potential takeovers. *Newsweek,* though, continued to shine brightly by achieving a subscriber base of 3 million and an estimated readership of nearly 20 million.

With the dawn of the 1990s, the company's growth slowed for the first time in years, and operating revenues and net income fell. Though revenues slipped just over $5.4 million, income plummeted by $23.3 million. Was this a chance occurrence due to a culmination of circumstance or the beginning of a trend? *Post*-watchers had seen their urban newspaper weather many a blight and survive when other newspapers had folded. Just four years earlier, in 1986, the 15 largest newspapers in the United States accounted for 21 percent of all newspapers sold. Along with this trend, however, came a decline in urban population and a sales drop for daily metropolitan newspapers. The *Post,* as a survivor, benefited from the elimination of its major competitors yet soon faced another difficulty with the emergence of more news-related television (especially 24-hour cable news services). Yet it was helped by the ever-growing population of the Washington metro area and capitalized on this boom by offering special sections geared to readers in suburban Maryland and Virginia, and the company purchased land to build additional production facilities nearer to its suburban readers.

In 1991 Donald Graham was named CEO of the company in addition to his responsibilities as the *Post*'s publisher. Katharine remained chairman of the board. Two years later, in 1993, Katharine was named chairman of the executive committee, while Donald became the company's chairman of the board. Another major transition was the retirement of Ben Bradlee, the *Post*'s charismatic guiding force. Replaced by Leonard Downie, the paper seemed to stumble and lose its edge while the *Washington Times* quickly filled the gap. Yet after a few years of dismal earnings (1991's $70.8 million, 1992's $127.8 million) managed a comeback to 1993's $165.4 million in net income on revenues of nearly $1.50 billion.

For 1994 and 1995, revenue continued to climb with $1.61 billion and $1.71 billion, respectively, and income corresponded with a modest step in 1994 to $170 million and a grander hike to $190 million in 1995. The latter year also marked the purchase of eight new top-of-the-line offset presses and groundbreaking on a new printing facility in College Park, Maryland. The new plant, which was to be operational by 1998, was designated along with another in Springfield, Virginia, to take over all printing for the region and replace two older facilities in the D.C. area. Circulation for the *Post* in 1995 had reached 834,641 for its daily paper (about 60 percent of the area's total circulation), and 1.14 million for its Sunday edition.

The Future of the *Post* and Its Parent Company, 1996 and Beyond

In 1996 the company continued to broaden its communications empire with the purchase of Columbus Television Cable Corp. of Mississippi, and Rural Missouri Cable T.V. of Branson,

Missouri. Over at the magazine division, trouble brewed with the "anonymous" publication of a Clinton presidential satire called *Primary Colors,* whose author turned out to be *Newsweek* columnist Joe Klein. The furor and controversy over Klein's identity and refusal to come forward led to his resignation from the magazine. In addition, two big names were added to the company's Board of Directors—Warren Buffett of Berkshire Hathaway, Inc. (which owned nearly 19 percent or over 1.7 million shares of the Post Company's Class B shares) and Daniel Burke, retired CEO and president of Capital Cities/ABC Inc. Operating revenues for the year hit a healthy $1.85 billion and net income soared to nearly $221 million, climbing over $100 million for the first time since 1988's spectacular $269.1 million.

The following year Katharine Graham was once again in the limelight with the publication of *Personal History,* a 642-page memoir detailing her rocky ride as the Iron Lady of the Washington Post Company. Candid about the effects of her husband's suicide, emerging from his and her father's imposing shadows, and mistakes in the early years trying to please everyone, Graham chronicled her journey from shaky newcomer to steely matriarch of one of the world's most respected newspapers.

In 1997 the company diversified further into communications by producing a weekly news magazine show with Maryland Public Television called *Healthweek,* to be anchored by CBS's Sharyl Attkinsson on PBS. As the Washington Post Company forged ahead into more TV and cable systems, the broadcast division's profits overtook those of the print media. The *Post,* once the dominant force behind the company in sales and earnings, accounted for only a third of operating income beaten by the broadcast division's 44 percent—a whopping figure given its 18 percent figure in revenue. Yet no matter how large the company's broadcast media became, the newspaper bearing its name would always represent the company. With 11 local news bureaus around D.C., five national (Austin, Chicago, Los Angeles, Miami, and New York) and 20 international bureaus, the *Post*'s professional edge was second to none—a feat Stilson Hutchins never imagined when he founded his politically-based newspaper in 1877.

Principal Subsidiaries

The Washington Post; The Washington Post National Weekly Edition; The Herald; Robinson Terminal Warehouse Corporation; Capitol Fiber, Inc.; the Gazette Newspapers, Inc.; Post-Newsweek Broadcast Division—WDIV-TV; KPRC-TV; WPLG-TV; WFSB-TV; KSAT-TV; WJXT-TV; Post Newsweek Cable; *Newsweek* International; *Newsweek* Japan; *Newsweek* Korea; Itogi; *Newsweek* en Espanol; Kaplan Educational Centers; Legi-Slate, Inc.; Moffet, Larson & Johnson, Inc.; PASS Sports; Digital Ink Co.; TechNews, Inc.

Further Reading

Graham, Katharine, *Personal History,* New York, Knopf, 1997.
Roberts, Chalmers M., *In the Shadow of Power: The Story of The Washington Post,* Washington, D.C., Seven Locks Press, 1989.

—Donald R. Stabile
—updated by Taryn Benbow-Pfalzgraf

WHITBREAD
Whitbread PLC

Chiswell Street
London EC1Y 4SD
England
(0171) 606-4455
Fax: (0171) 615-1000

Public Company
Incorporated: 1889 as Whitbread and Company PLC
Employees: 75,000
Sales: £2.75 billion (US$4.20 billion) (1995/96)
Stock Exchanges: London
SICs: 2082 Malt Beverages; 2083 Malt; 5181 Beer &
  Ale; 5812 Eating Places; 5813 Drinking Places
  (Alcoholic Beverages); 5921 Liquor Stores; 7011
  Hotels & Motels; 7991 Physical Fitness Facilities;
  8299 Schools & Educational Services, Not Elsewhere
  Classified

Whitbread PLC is one of the leaders in the leisure industries of the United Kingdom. Founded as a single brewery, the company grew to become one of the most prestigious of London's older breweries, with its history closely paralleling that of the Whitbread family, which retained continuous control of the company from 1742 to 1992. Whitbread began to diversify in the early 1960s, and by the mid-1990s only 31 percent of sales and 14 percent of total profits were derived from brewing operations, whose brands include Stella Artois, Murphy's Irish Stout, Boddingtons Bitter, Heineken, Wadworth 6X, and Labatt Ice. The remainder of the revenues and profits came from Whitbread's various retail sectors, which include pubs, restaurants, coffee shops, wine and liquor stores, hotels, health and fitness clubs, and children's nurseries.

Samuel Whitbread Established Brewery in 1742

Samuel Whitbread, at the age of 14, was sent to London by his mother in 1734 to become an apprentice to a brewer. Whitbread, raised as a Puritan, proved to be an extremely hard worker. In 1742, eight years after coming to London, he established his own brewery with a £2,000 inheritance and additional underwriting from John Howard, the renowned prison reformer. As the brewery became successful, Howard's investment became more lucrative—it even led to a reciprocation of financial support by Whitbread for Howard's reform movement.

By 1750 Whitbread had acquired an additional brewery located on Chiswell Street. At this time there were over 50 breweries in London, but, despite intense competition, the Whitbread brewery expanded rapidly. By 1760 its annual output had reached 64,000 barrels, second only to Calvert and Company.

Whitbread was enthusiastic about new brewing methods. He employed several well-known engineers who helped to improve the quality and increase the production volume of the company's stout and porter (a sweeter, weaker stout).

The Whitbread family had a long history of involvement in English politics. Samuel Whitbread's forefathers fought with Oliver Cromwell's Roundheads during the English Civil War and later developed a connection with the Bedfordshire preacher and author John Bunyan. Samuel Whitbread himself was elected to Parliament in 1768 as a representative of Bedford. His son, Samuel II, succeeded him in Parliament in 1790, and Whitbread descendants served in Parliament almost continuously until 1910.

Samuel Whitbread died in 1796. Samuel II assumed control of the brewery, but was so preoccupied with Parliament that by 1799 he was compelled to take on a partner. The partnership, however, was shortlived. The brewery entered into seven more partnerships over the next 70 years, only two of which were successful. Most notably, Whitbread's 1812 partnership with the Martineau and Bland brewery resulted in a full merger of the two companies' brewing operations. The Martineau and Bland facility at Lambeth, however, was later closed down and its equipment was moved to Chiswell Street.

During the early 19th century the bulk of Whitbread's business was conducted with "free houses," public houses—or pubs—neither owned by, nor bound to sell only the products of one brewer. These pubs numbered several hundred, and their business remained fairly stable. But when the Drury Lane Theatre burned down in 1809, Samuel II saw an opportunity to profit from its renovation. He led a committee to restore the theater, invested heavily in the project, and persuaded several friends to join him. The venture yielded only a small dividend when the theater was reopened, and cost Whitbread the friendship of many of his fellow investors. In Parliament, Whitbread opposed the resumption of war with Napoleon, a position that made him even more unpopular. In July 1815, shortly after Waterloo, Samuel Whitbread II committed suicide.

Whitbread's sons, William Henry and Samuel Charles, inherited their father's interest in the brewery. Whitbread family control, however, had been greatly diminished by the company's nine partners. It was not until 1819 that the Whitbread brothers were able to reestablish direct family control over the operation. The number of partners was reduced, and the brewery remained under Whitbread control for many years.

In 1834 Whitbread introduced ale to its product line. The ale gained immediate popularity and resulted in a substantial increase in turnover for the brewery. Whitbread expanded even more dramatically after 1869, when the family established its last partnership.

Went Public in 1889

During the 1880s, a sudden and significant decline in demand for beer caused many "free houses" to sell their leases to breweries (and thereby become "tied houses"). Breweries such as Whitbread, which had established numerous tied houses, were forced to extend loans to public house operators so that they could remain in business. The capital required to purchase free house leases and to extend loans could only be satisfied by the public through share flotations. Therefore, when Whitbread's partnership agreement expired in 1889, the partners decided to transform the brewery into a public company.

An attempt by brewers to raise the profitability of tied houses by reducing beer prices backfired; their tenants competed on price and went even further into debt. A recession in 1900 forced Whitbread to write down the value of its tied house properties—a move which may have saved the company. Demand for beer recovered steadily and permitted Whitbread to

increase its production every year from 1899 to 1912. Accordingly, the value of tied houses recovered as they became profitable. Just prior to World War I, however, the government raised its license duty on tied houses, rendering many of them financial liabilities. Whitbread stopped buying tied houses, and instead concentrated on expanding its bottled beer trade.

While Whitbread weathered this difficult period virtually intact, many competitors were forced to close. Whitbread's ability to survive was attributed to three factors: the maintenance of a harmonious relationship between the brewer and the publican (public house operator), sustaining a good public image of the brand, and keeping influence in government.

Francis Pelham Whitbread, the director of the brewery at the time, devoted his energies to maintaining a stable atmosphere for profitable brewing; as chairman of the Brewers Society, he promoted better brewer-vendor relations. Later, as chairman and treasurer of the politically active National Trade Defence Association, he lobbied against the temperance movement in Parliament. After World War I he played a major role in the formation of policies within the brewing industry, and was particularly opposed to the proliferation of tied houses.

During the interwar period Whitbread took over the Jude Hanbury brewery. As its situation with vendors remained unsettled, Whitbread concentrated further on the expansion of bottled beer sales. Whitbread beer had become available throughout the world. Francis Whitbread, however, became increasingly divorced from the everyday operation of the brewery; his position as a spokesman for the industry and his dedication to philanthropic activities occupied most of his time.

On December 29, 1940, German incendiary bombs landed in five separate areas of the brewery. Each of the fires was put out by the company fire brigade, with the exception of a malt fire which, like burning coal dust, is very difficult to extinguish. It was finally doused a week later. Damage to the brewery and the surrounding area was great. Nevertheless, Whitbread resumed brewing almost immediately.

Francis Pelham Whitbread died in 1941. His leadership of the brewery was highly conservative—especially when compared to the policies of his successors. Francis was in many ways a popular figurehead for the company. Much of the actual burden of management fell on the shoulders of Samuel Howard Whitbread, who served with the company from 1915 until his death in 1944. William Henry Whitbread assumed leadership of the company that year, but was forced to postpone his plans for the rehabilitation of the brewery until after the war.

Postwar Era Brought Wave of Amalgamations

Though the war ended less than a year later, the British economy continued to suffer from aftereffects for many years. Conditions were so grave that Whitbread was unable to begin its modernization until 1950. At that time Whitbread undertook a sweeping rationalization program which included the concentration of human resources and retooling of machinery.

Other smaller breweries were in less stable condition, and many were threatened with bankruptcy. Whitbread, however, offered an amalgamation scheme to these breweries. Under this formula, called the "Whitbread Umbrella," failing breweries agreed to coordinate their operations and distribution networks with Whitbread. Many of these arrangements resulted in Whitbread's eventual acquisition of the smaller brewers. In the period from 1951 to 1970 Whitbread took over 26 breweries and expanded its number of tied houses from less than 100 to 10,000.

Some of the breweries acquired by Whitbread were large well-established companies. Beginning with the Dutton brewery in 1964, Whitbread took over Rhymney in 1966, Threlfall and Fremlin in 1967, Strong in 1968, and Brickwood in 1971. These additions to Whitbread also gave the company greater geographical coverage—Threlfall's was located in the northwest port of Liverpool, and Brickwood's was in Portsmouth, on the south coast.

Streamlining and Beginnings of Diversification in the 1970s

The 1970s were characterized as a period of streamlining for Whitbread and also saw the beginning of a move toward diversification. The company disposed of many of its marginally profitable or outdated operations—even the Chiswell Street brewery was closed in 1976. Still, Whitbread suffered from the aftereffects of a serious economic recession during the mid-1970s, and the company came very close to bankruptcy. A gradual economic recovery led to improvements in the market which greatly strengthened Whitbread's financial position.

Meanwhile, however, as popular demand shifted from ale to lager, total beer consumption began to fall. Whitbread started to deemphasize certain brewing assets and began to diversify outside brewing. The company had already gained a chain of wine retail outlets when it acquired Thresher in 1962. Along the way, Whitbread built up a wines and spirits division that included Beefeater Gin, Long John Scotch Whiskey, and Cutty Sark Scotch Whiskey. Food was added in 1974 with the opening of the first Beefeater Restaurant & Pub, which was in the casual dining sector, and with the 1979 debut of Brewers Fayre, a chain of pub food outlets.

Notwithstanding these nonbeer ventures, Whitbread did not abandon the brewing industry but in fact became more active in licensing non-U.K. brewer's brands. In 1968 the company gained the right to brew Heineken lager under a license agreement and in 1976 the Stella Artois brand began to be brewed by Whitbread under a similar agreement.

Further Diversification in the 1980s

Whitbread continued to diversify in the 1980s under the guidance of new leadership. William Henry Whitbread had given up day-to-day control of the company during the 1970s, whereupon Samuel Whitbread (a fifth generation descendant of the company's founder) became chief executive and eventually chairman, in 1984. He initially sought to bolster his company's restaurant holdings. In 1982 a 50–50 joint venture with PepsiCo Inc. began, which went on to build a significant chain of Pizza Hut restaurants in the United Kingdom. T.G.I. Friday's joined the company's restaurant fold three years later, when Whitbread signed a franchise agreement to develop U.K.-based outlets of

this chain, also in the casual dining sector. By the 1995/96 fiscal year, beer operations accounted for only 43 percent of profits, with wine and spirits accounting for 20 percent and retail operations 37 percent.

Next, Whitbread entered the hotel industry. The year 1987 marked the debut of the Travel Inn chain, budget hotels which were usually located next to another Whitbread property such as a Brewers Fayre, Beefeater, or T.G.I. Friday's. Whitbread's diversification program gained further momentum in 1989 when management announced that the company would focus on the leisure retailing industries in general, with a particular emphasis on areas, such as travel and eating out, that were projected to grow rapidly through the end of the century. Brewing was still to be included in the mix but would continue to account for smaller percentages of company profits, notwithstanding the 1989 acquisition of Boddingtons brewery. Another sector to be retained was the Thresher unit, which specialized in retail outlets for alcoholic beverages; Thresher was subsequently bolstered with the opening of the first Wine Rack in 1989 and the 1991 acquisition of Bottoms Up, a chain of wine superstores. On the divestment side was the company's wine and spirits division, which included a distiller of such brands as Beefeater Gin and a U.S.-based importer and distributor of wines and spirits. The division was sold late in 1989 to Allied-Lyons PLC for £545 million (US$880.2 million).

Compliance with MMC Orders Dominated Early 1990s

Nineteen eighty-nine was also important because it was the year that Whitbread began to plan for its compliance with new rules on tied houses set down by the British government's Monopolies and Mergers Commission (MMC). After an investigation into the system of tied houses that had been created from the numerous mergers in the brewing industry in the 1960s and 1970s, in early 1990 the MMC ordered brewers with more than 2,000 pubs to sell or lease half of the number over 2,000, meaning that Whitbread would have to do so with about 2,300 pubs. And the MMC gave brewers a November 1, 1992, deadline to comply. Meanwhile, Peter Jarvis, who had joined Whitbread from Unilever in 1976, took over as chief executive in 1990. Later, in August 1992, Michael Angus, chairman of The Boots Company and former chairman of Unilever, became chairman of Whitbread as well. This management team—noticeably minus a Whitbread—led the company through the MMC compliance process.

Following the issue of the MMC orders, Whitbread first pulled its pubs out of its brewery division. It then sold about 1,300 of them by the deadline, and leased the remaining 1,000 on a short-term basis. At the time the United Kingdom had too many pubs, and property values had fallen sharply since the boom years of the early 1980s. Consequently, Whitbread's profits took a large hit from the forced sales and squeezed its plans to expand its retail activities. A plan for Whitbread to take the Pizza Hut chain into continental Europe fell apart when the company could not afford to commit the initial £100 million needed.

A further consequence of the MMC orders was that Whitbread had to untangle itself from its complicated system of cross-holdings in regional brewers—held through Whitbread

Investment Company—that it had developed during its acquisition spree. In November 1993 Whitbread acquired Whitbread Investment Company, then in March 1994 sold nearly all its regional brewery stakes, raising about £300 million in the process.

Renewed Spending Spree in Mid-1990s

Whitbread thus emerged from the MMC orders with some cash to spend on its retailing sectors. A new wave of activity began in 1994 with the acquisition of the Maredo steak restaurant chain located in Germany. In August 1995 Whitbread paid Canada-based Scott's Hospitality Inc. £180 million (US$288.2 million) for 16 Marriott hotels and also signed an agreement with Marriott International to develop the brand name in the United Kingdom. That same month, the company acquired David Lloyd Leisure (DLL) for £200.7 million (US$321.3 million). DLL, named after tennis champion David Lloyd, operated 20 private sports and fitness clubs as well as 24 nursery schools through its Gatehouse Nursery Services subsidiary. In March 1997 DLL bought Curzon Management Associates and its five London gym sites.

Whitbread's restaurant holdings received further boosts in 1995 and 1996. The Costa Coffee chain of coffee shops was acquired in October 1995. In July of the following year, £133 million (US$208.8 million) was spent to purchase Pelican Group and its 110 restaurants spread throughout several chains, most notably Café Rouge, a French bistro/cafe; Dôme, a bar/cafe emphasizing beer, drinks, coffee, and cafe-style food; and Mamma Amalfi, a family-style Italian restaurant. In November 1996 Whitbread bought the BrightReasons group for £46 million (US$72.2 million). The key chain acquired therein was Bella Pasta, with 55 outlets, while the Pizza Piazza chain was subsequently sold to Passion For Food for £11.25 million and 102 Pizzaland restaurants were converted to Pizza Huts and other Whitbread restaurant brands. The acquired pizza chains were jettisoned to avoid a conflict with Pizza Hut.

In the summer of 1997 Jarvis stepped down as chief executive and was replaced by David Thomas, who had joined Whitbread in 1984 as a regional director of the Inns division. Thomas took over a company that had seen sales and profits rise throughout the 1990s, thanks in large part to Whitbread's increasing emphasis on nonbeer activities. In the future, Whitbread was likely to aggressively grow the various leisure brands it had acquired in the 1980s and 1990s. Continuing to derive most of its revenue from its home market, Whitbread nonetheless seemed likely to pursue opportunities elsewhere in Europe as another channel for growth.

Principal Operating Units

Beefeater Restaurant & Pub; David Lloyd Leisure; Inns; Pub Partnerships; Restaurants; The Beer Company; The Hotel Company; Thresher.

Further Reading

Barrow, Martin, "Brewer to Spend £300m on Retail to Offset Decline," *Times* (London), November 2, 1995, p. 27.

"A Conundrum that Could Have Whitbread Crying in Its Beer," *Times* (London), May 13, 1992, p. 21.

"Losing a Beer Belly," *Economist*, August 12, 1995, p. 54.

Murray, Alasdair, "Whitbread to Seek Links with Regionals," *Times* (London), August 12, 1996, p. 40.

Parker-Pope, Tara, "Whitbread PLC Expands into Leisure as Traditional Beer Market Contracts," *Wall Street Journal*, August 9, 1995, p. A6.

—updated by David E. Salamie

Whole Foods Market, Inc.

601 North Lamar Boulevard, Suite 300
Austin, Texas 78703
U.S.A.
(512) 477-5566
Fax: (512) 477-1301
Web site: http://www.wholefoods.com

Public Company
Incorporated: 1980
Employees: 9,848
Sales: $892.01 million (1996)
Stock Exchanges: NASDAQ
SICs: 2833 Medicinal Chemical & Botanical Products;
5122 Drugs, Drug Proprietaries & Sundries; 5148
Fresh Fruits & Vegetables; 5499 Miscellaneous Food
Stores; 5961 Catalog & Mail Order Houses

Whole Foods Market, Inc. is the leading chain of natural food supermarkets in the United States. The company's stores average 22,000 square feet in size and feature foods organically grown, free of artificial ingredients, and that have not been irradiated; no product is sold that has been tested on animals. Many locations include in-store cafes and juice bars. Whole Foods has also developed a growing line of private label products such as organic pasta, freshly roasted nut butters, oak-aged wine vinegars, and aromatic teas. After the company was founded in 1980 with a single store, it grew dramatically—into a chain of more than 75 stores in 18 states and the District of Columbia, in less than two decades. Much of the growth has been fueled by acquisitions of other chains of natural food stores, so that the company's stores operate under five different names: Whole Foods Market, Bread & Circus, Fresh Fields, Wellspring Grocery, and Bread of Life. Whole Foods also manufactures and distributes vitamins and nutritional supplements through its Amrion Inc. subsidiary acquired in mid-1997.

Founded by Hippie and Partners in Austin, Texas, in 1980

The company was founded in Austin, Texas, in 1980 when the first Whole Foods Market opened on September 20. The company's founders were Craig Weller and Mark Skiles, owners of the Clarksville Natural Grocery, and John Mackey, owner of Safer Way Natural Foods. Mackey, a self-described hippie who had dropped out of the University of Texas a few credits shy of gaining a philosophy degree, had cajoled $45,000 out of family and friends to open Safer Way, a small health food store, in Austin in 1978. Age 25 at the time, Mackey had, as he described it, "had the natural foods conversion," and wanted to convert others.

Natural food stores first began to appear in the United States in the late 1960s as an outgrowth of the 1960s counterculture. Well into the 1970s, these stores were typically small, rather dingy and unattractive, and often poorly managed. The Whole Foods Market that Mackey, Weller, and Skiles opened in 1980 after they decided to merge their businesses was huge—12,500 square feet—by comparison; it was in fact a supermarket. This was not the first natural food supermarket but there were less than half a dozen others at the time, and the immediate success of Whole Foods Market showed that the founders had gotten the formula right.

That first store included but went well beyond the typical fare of natural food stores—organic fruits and vegetables, dried beans, and whole grains. Also available were fresh fish, all-natural beef, locally baked bread, and selections of cheese, beer, wine, and coffee that far exceeded that offered by conventional supermarkets. The store's selection, neat and clean appearance, and helpful staff of 19 attracted not only those already "converted" to natural foods but also people who had never stepped into one of the smaller health food stores. Mackey and his partners also found out early on that many people were willing to pay a premium price for food products considered more healthful, more nutritious, or simply devoid of artificial ingredients.

Unfortunately, on Memorial Day in 1981, Austin suffered from its worst flood in 70 years. The Whole Foods Market was

---

Company Perspectives:

Whole Foods Market is a dynamic leader in the quality food business. We aim to set the standards of excellence for grocers. We are building a business in which quality permeates all aspects of our company. Quality is a state of mind at Whole Foods Market.

We recognize that our success reaches far beyond the company by contributing to the quality of life renaissance occurring here on earth. We are willing to share our successes and failures, our hopes and fears, and our joys and sorrow with others in the quality food business. Moreover, we have a responsibility to encourage more people to join us in the quality food business, to adopt higher standards of excellence, and generally to contribute wherever and whenever it makes sense to the quality of life renaissance. The future we will experience tomorrow is created one step at a time today. The success of our business is measured by customer satisfaction, Team Member happiness, return on capital investment, improvement in the quality of the environment, and local and larger community support.

Our ability to instill a clear sense of interdependence among our various stakeholders (the people who are interested and benefit from the success of our company) is interconnected with our desire and efforts to communicate more often, more openly, and more compassionately. Better communication equals better understanding and more trust.

---

caught in the flood's path, with $400,000 in resulting uninsured losses; the entire store inventory was wiped out and much of the equipment was damaged. Nevertheless, the store was reopened only 28 days later thanks to the cooperation of creditors, investors, customers, and staff alike.

Expanded to Eight Stores by the End of the 1980s

By 1985, two more Whole Foods Markets had opened in Austin and another in Houston. The company suffered a setback, however, when it ventured beyond retailing by opening a restaurant in 1985 that subsequently failed, costing Whole Foods $880,000 in the process. In these early years, Mackey clearly emerged as the company leader; Skiles left the company in 1986, while Weller headed up Texas Health Distributors, the wholesale division of the company founded in 1980, which served both the company's stores and other natural food stores and restaurants.

In October 1986 Whole Foods made its first purchase of an existing store, when it bought the Bluebonnet Natural Foods Grocery in Dallas and converted it into a Whole Foods Market. From this point forward, the company expanded both by purchasing existing natural food stores or chains and by opening new stores. The expansion program was a gradual one, ensuring that Whole Foods did not grow too quickly. Typically, each year saw the addition of one new store in each existing region as well as the addition of a new region.

In May 1988 Whole Foods ventured outside Texas for the first time when it acquired the Whole Food Company, which

operated a large natural food supermarket in New Orleans. This store had opened in 1981, having replaced the Whole Food Company's first store which debuted in October 1974. Later in 1988 the seventh Whole Foods Market was opened in Richardson, Texas.

The president of the Whole Food Company, Peter Roy, stayed with Whole Foods following the purchase and in July 1988 moved to California to help launch a new region. In January of the following year, the first California store opened in Palo Alto.

Whole Foods next launched a private label, called Whole Foods, in January 1990. For the majority of the products in this line the company sought out smaller manufacturers located in the "right" region—a salsa maker in Texas, a producer of pasta in Marche, Italy—who were committed to producing quality organic products. The private label proved quite successful, generating healthy margins and brand loyalty that helped to encourage customers to return to Whole Foods Market despite an increasingly competitive market. In just a few years, the Whole Foods label included more than 500 stock-keeping units (SKUs) within 22 categories.

Team Approach Clashed with Union Advocates in Early 1990s

From the beginning Mackey espoused a team-oriented atmosphere at Whole Foods, believing that management and staff should work together to attain the company's goals. In such an environment he believed that workers did not need unions, that they were "beyond unions." Nonetheless, he and his company were at various times accused of being antiunion, a charge that first surfaced in 1990 when the company opened its second California store in Berkeley at the location of a Berkeley Co-Op that had closed. Starting on the day of the grand opening, the United Food and Commercial Workers local set up a picket line to protest that the store paid its workers from $1 to $5 less per hour than other supermarkets paid comparable employees and that Whole Foods had practiced discriminatory hiring in terms of age and race, the store having failed to hire a single person who had worked at the Co-Op. Picketing continued for the next 18 months to no avail. In the years that followed, similar union protests occurred at newly opened Whole Foods Markets in such union strongholds as Los Gatos, St. Paul, and Madison, Wisconsin.

During 1991 Texas Health Distributors (THD) moved into a new, 85,000-square-foot facility. As Whole Foods expanded, however, the company decided that it needed a warehouse and distribution center in each of its regions to better serve its increasingly far-flung stores. THD was eventually transformed into the central distribution center for the Southwest Region, serving stores in Texas and Louisiana.

In November 1991 the company acquired Wellspring Grocery, Inc. and its two natural food supermarkets in Durham and Chapel Hill, North Carolina. Wellspring had been founded in March 1981 by Lex and Anne Alexander. This buyout marked the beginning of Whole Foods' Southeast region. Unlike in previous purchases, this time Whole Foods decided to retain the Wellspring Grocery name, in order not to alienate existing customers. In October 1992, a third Wellspring opened its doors in Raleigh, along with Wellspring Distributors, which was launched to serve as the region's central distribution center. Lex Alexander stayed with Whole Foods, becoming director of private label products.

By the end of 1991 Whole Foods had 10 stores, more than 1,100 employees, sales of $92.5 million, and net profits of $1.6 million. It had quickly become the largest chain of natural food stores in the country. The company went public in January 1992 through an initial public offering, raising $23.4 million in the process. A secondary offering in 1993 raised an additional $35.4 million. Backed by this war chest, Whole Foods subsequently grew rapidly, moving in concert with a rapidly expanding industry. From 1990 to 1996, sales of natural products in the United States more than doubled, increasing from $4.22 billion to $9.14 billion, while organic sales grew from $1.0 billion to $2.8 billion during this same period.

Whole Foods' $26.2 million acquisition of Bread & Circus in October 1992 was the firm's largest to date, bringing with it six stores in Massachusetts and Rhode Island and a central distribution center in Boston which served Whole Foods' new Northeast region. Bread & Circus was founded by two students of macrobiotics, Anthony and Susan Harnett, when they purchased a store in Brookline, Massachusetts, in 1975. The name derived from the first store's unusual product line: natural foods and wooden toys. The Harnetts subsequently opened stores in Cambridge, Wellesley, Hadley, and Newton, all in Massachusetts; and in Providence, Rhode Island. They also in 1991 relocated the Brookline store to Brighton, Massachusetts. When acquired by Whole Foods, Bread & Circus was the northeast's largest retailer of natural foods and enjoyed an outstanding reputation for its produce, meat, and seafood departments. As with Wellspring Grocery, Whole Foods decided to keep the Bread & Circus name. Following the acquisition, two additional Bread & Circus stores opened in the Boston area. One other consequence of the buyout was that Mackey was accused of union busting, since the stores' employees had been unionized but voted against union representation following the takeover.

Minor and Major Acquisitions Marked the Mid-1990s

In February 1993 Whole Foods acquired a majority interest in The Sourdough: A European Bakery, which had been providing breads to the stores in Texas and Louisiana for a number of years. The move enabled the company to leverage the expertise of master bakers through an apprenticeship program. Whole Foods also went on to open bake houses in all of its operating regions.

Whole Foods launched a Midwest region in March 1993 with the debut of a Lincoln Park store in Chicago. Over the next few years additional stores were opened in the Chicago area, as well as in Ann Arbor, Michigan; St. Paul, Minnesota; and Madison, Wisconsin. Also in 1993, Peter Roy, who had been serving as president of the company's northern California region, was appointed president and chief operating officer in August. Mackey remained chairman and chief executive officer (he had also been president; the COO position was new). With the appointment, Whole Foods' regional presidents now re-

ported directly to Roy, who was also charged with coordinating national purchasing, distribution, and vendor programs.

In September 1993 Whole Foods made an even larger acquisition than Bread & Circus, when it paid $56 million for Mrs. Gooch's Natural Food Markets, a chain of seven stores in the Los Angeles area with 1992 sales of approximately $85 million. Mrs. Gooch's, which was the nation's number two retailer of natural foods at the time of the buyout, had been founded in 1977 by Sandy Gooch, a homemaker and former grade school teacher, and Dan Volland, who ran three health food stores in southern California. The two opened the first Mrs. Gooch's in west Los Angeles in January 1977, then added six more over the next decade. In 1987 the chain opened a distribution center, which following the takeover became Whole Foods' central distribution center for its new southern California region.

Mrs. Gooch's stores, which operated under the name Mrs. Gooch's Whole Foods following the acquisition, traditionally had a slightly different product mix than Whole Foods Markets. Sandy Gooch did not sell any product that contained white flour or sugar and did not offer beer or wine, either. Whole Foods subsequently added these products to the stores, as well as its Whole Foods private label items, although it did keep some Mrs. Gooch's brand products also.

During fiscal year 1995, Whole Foods made several small acquisitions. In February the company acquired Bread of Life and its two stores in the San Francisco Bay area, as well as the Unicorn Village Marketplace in North Miami Beach, Whole Foods' first location in Florida. In December, the Oak Street Market in Evanston, Illinois, was added to the company fold. All four of these stores subsequently operated under the Whole Foods Market name.

In July 1996, as part of a restructuring of the southern California operations, the company began to transform the Mrs. Gooch's stores so that they would completely resemble other Whole Foods stores, including having them adopt the Whole Foods Market name. The change in name apparently resulted in a 5 to 10 percent sales drop—in a testament to customer loyalty—but company officials were confident that this was a temporary phenomenon. Nevertheless, in the future Whole Foods was more cautious about changing the names of acquired stores.

By January 1996 the company had 43 stores in ten states, with plans for about a dozen more to be opened in 1996 and 1997. Many of the newer stores were much larger than the 22,000-square-foot company average. With 30,000 to 40,000 square feet, Whole Foods was finding that it could generate sales of $15 million a year from a single store. Company management, meanwhile, was setting aggressive expansion targets: 100 stores and $1.5 billion in sales by 2000 (fiscal 1995 sales were $496.4 million).

Whole Foods took a giant step toward achieving these goals in September 1996 when it acquired the 22-store Fresh Fields chain, its closest rival, for $135 million in stock. Fresh Fields had been founded only in May 1991 but had grown more rapidly than any other natural food chain. It had stores in four different market areas: Washington/Baltimore, Philadelphia, New York/New Jersey/Connecticut, and Chicago. One of Fresh

Fields founders was Leo Kahn, who had previously found retailing success by building the Purity Supreme and the Staples office supplies superstore chains.

Following the acquisition, Fresh Fields stores in Chicago and Washington, D.C., were closed, while three other Chicago stores became part of Whole Foods' Midwest region. Four stores in the greater New York City area were folded into the Northeast region, a store in Charlottesville was added to the Southeast region, and the remaining 12 Philadelphia and Baltimore area stores were combined with four Bread & Circus stores to create a new Mid-Atlantic region. The Chicago stores were converted to the Whole Foods Market name because the company was already established there, but name changes at other Fresh Fields stores were placed on the back burner for the time being.

In March 1997 Whole Foods bolstered its operations in Florida with the purchase of a two-store Bread of Life chain. Bread of Life had been founded in 1990 by James Oppenheimer and Richard Gerber with the opening of a 7,000-square-foot location in Fort Lauderdale. The cofounders then opened a 30,000-square-foot store in Plantation in 1995 and had in development a 33,000-square-foot store in Coral Springs scheduled for opening in fiscal 1998. At least initially these stores would retain the Bread of Life name, and along with the Whole Foods Market in North Miami Beach formed a newly created Florida region, headed up by Oppenheimer as regional president and Gerber as regional vice president.

In the spring of 1997, in a move designed to contain costs and improve productivity, Whole Foods began to roll out a centralized purchasing system. Installed systemwide by the end of 1997, the system enabled the company to track product movement and prices. Also that spring, Whole Foods launched a low-priced private label called 365, which was meant to denote value every day of the year. The 365 line differed from the Whole Foods line in that 365 did not feature organic products and the 365 products were priced about 20 percent cheaper. The new label was meant to attract more value-conscious customers, people who typically shopped at conventional supermarkets.

In June 1997 Whole Foods acquired Amrion Inc.—a manufacturer and marketer of nutritional supplements and natural medicinals based in Boulder, Colorado—in a stock swap that translated into about a $138 million purchase price. Amrion was formed in 1987 by Mark Crossen and his father, Henry Morgan Crossen. The father had read about a compound that was supposed to strengthen the heart muscle; the Crossens then ordered some and found that it relieved their genetically caused irregular heartbeats. Amrion was founded to market this compound to others and the company expanded into other nutritional supplements, eventually producing more than 200 such products. The Crossens took the company public in 1988 and by 1996 posted net income of $4.5 million on sales of $54 million, 85 percent of which was generated through direct mail and catalog orders.

In 1996 the Crossens decided that it was time to sell Amrion or merge it with another firm, since they wanted to reach a broader market and knew that they had to step up their retail presence to do so. By joining forces with Whole Foods, Amrion

would gain dozens of outlets at which its products could be sold. Amrion would take over the manufacture of the Whole Foods brand of nutritional supplements and further expand this line. Whole Foods would also gain Amrion's expertise in selling these items through catalogs and the World Wide Web. Following the acquisition, Amrion became an "autonomous subsidiary" of Whole Foods and Mark Crossen remained Amrion's CEO and also joined Whole Foods' board of directors.

Through the first half of fiscal 1997, overall sales for Whole Foods had increased 20 percent over the same period in 1996, and the company was well on its way to surpassing the $1 billion sales level for the year. The company set a new target of expanding to 140 stores by 2003, with most of the new stores coming through organic growth since Whole Foods had swallowed up most of its rivals. With Fresh Fields now in tow, the company's chief rival had become another Boulder-based company, Wild Oats Markets Inc., a 44-store chain of smaller (14,000-square-foot average) stores located primarily in the mountain states but also expanding into such Whole Foods' territories as Los Angeles and San Francisco. In response to this challenge from Wild Oats (which Whole Foods had tried to purchase prior to the Fresh Fields acquisition but had backed away because the price was too high), Whole Foods planned to enter several markets dominated by the competitor, including St. Louis, Salt Lake City, Denver, and even Boulder itself. The company also wanted to eventually enter the fast-growing Northwest region of the country. Additional pressure was being placed on Whole Foods from conventional grocers, who responded to the burgeoning natural food market by increasing shelf space allotted to organic and natural foods within conventional supermarkets and by experimenting with stand-alone natural food stores of their own. Nevertheless, with an aggressive yet not overreaching approach to growth and with expertise in the natural food arena matched by no one else, Whole Foods Market, Inc. seemed well-positioned to meet the challenges of the early 21st century.

Principal Subsidiaries

Amrion Inc.

Principal Operating Units

Private Label Products; Texas Health Distributors; Florida Region; Mid-Atlantic Region; Midwest Region; Northeast Region; Northern California Region; Southeast Region; Southern California Region; Southwest Region.

Further Reading

Algeo, David, "Whole Foods Buying Colo. Vitamin Maker," *Denver Post,* June 11, 1997, pp. 1C, 8C.

Breyer, R. Michelle, "Whole Foods Spells Out Recipe for Growth," *Supermarket News,* March 31, 1997, pp. 1, 7.

Brooks, Nancy Rivera, "From Gooch to High Gloss," *Los Angeles Times,* July 24, 1996, pp. D1, D7.

Gattuso, Greg, "Nature Trails: The Two Main Natural-Food Players Chart a Course for Rapid Growth," *Supermarket News,* March 24, 1997, pp. 1, 11, 14, 61.

Hammel, Frank, "Green Goes Gourmet," *Supermarket Business,* April 1996, pp. 103–107.

Lee, Louise, "Whole Foods Swallows Up Nearest Rival," *Wall Street Journal,* June 19, 1996, pp. B1, B6.

Locke, Tom, "Colorado Pharmaceutical Amrion Inc. at a Crossroads," *Daily Camera* (Boulder, Colo.), November 19, 1996.

Loro, Laura, "Doing What Comes Naturally: Whole Foods and Fresh Fields Grow Their Own Strategies," *Advertising Age,* August 6, 1994, p. 22.

Mack, Toni, "Good Food, Great Margins," *Forbes,* October 17, 1998, pp. 112–113, 115.

Mackey, John, "Beyond Unions: The CEO of Whole Foods Market Explains Why Workers Don't Need Unions," *Utne Reader,* March/April 1992, pp. 75–77.

Murphy, Kate, "Organic Food Makers Reap Green Yields of Revenuc," *New York Times,* October 26, 1996, pp. 37, 39.

Patoski, Joe Nick, "John Mackey: Winning the Food Fight," *Texas Monthly,* September 1996, pp. 119, 148.

Saxton, Lisa, "Leo Kahn's Fresh Start," *Supermarket News,* August 17, 1992, pp. 1, 40–41, 46–47.

Tosh, Mark, "Whole Foods' Natural Progression," *Supermarket News,* December 20, 1993, pp. 1, 44–45.

—David E. Salamie

Woolworth Corporation

Woolworth Building
233 Broadway
New York, New York 10279-0003
U.S.A.
(212) 553-2000
Fax: (212) 553-2018

Public Company
Incorporated: 1905 as F. W. Woolworth & Co.
Employees: 82,000
Sales: $8.09 billion (1996)
Stock Exchanges: New York Boston Cincinnati Midwest
    Pacific Philadelphia Toronto Amsterdam Lausanne
    Basel Geneva Zurich
SICs: 5331 Variety Stores; 5611 Men's & Boys'
    Clothing & Accessory Stores; 5621 Women's
    Clothing Stores; 5632 Women's Accessory &
    Specialty Stores; 5641 Children's & Infants' Wear
    Stores; 5943 Stationery Stores; 6719 Offices of
    Holding Companies, Not Elsewhere Classified

Woolworth Corporation, whose name is expected to be changed in late 1997, is a diversified multinational retailer with stores and support operations in North America, Europe, Australia, and Asia. The company runs more than 6,700 specialty units worldwide and about 700 general merchandise stores in Germany and Mexico. Woolworth's best-performing specialty chains are the various Foot Locker athletic footwear and apparel concepts and the Northern Reflections specialty apparel format and its spinoffs, while the general merchandise area is still headed by the venerable Woolworth's although that chain no longer exists in the United States where it—and the company— were founded.

Origins as First "5-and-10¢" Store

The company's founder, Frank Winfield Woolworth, parlayed the idea of the 5-and-10¢ store into an international retailing empire. Born in 1852 in Rodman, New York, and raised on a farm, he moved to Watertown, New York, in 1873 where he apprenticed and then clerked with Augsbury & Moore, a wholesaler and dry goods store. Wanting more money, Woolworth soon left Augsbury & Moore for A. Bushnell & Company, a local dry goods and carpet store. His new employer, however, found him a poor salesman and lowered his wages from $10 to $8 a week. In response Woolworth overworked himself, had a complete breakdown, and spent six months convalescing.

When Woolworth recovered in 1876, he returned to his former employer William Moore, whose business was now called Moore & Smith. There he concentrated on window displays. In 1878 Moore & Smith found itself with high debt and excess inventory. To raise money the store held a 5¢ sale. Smith and Woolworth laid a group of goods such as tin pans, washbasins, button-hooks, and dippers, along with surplus inventory, on a counter over which they hung a sign reading: "Any Article on This Counter, 5¢." After the sale Frank Woolworth was convinced a 5¢ strategy could work on a broader basis.

In 1879 Woolworth left Moore & Smith. On February 22 of that year he opened his first "Great 5¢ Store" in Utica, New York. At first business was good, but as the 5¢ novelty faded, the store's poor location became a handicap and he closed it in early June. Still, he had repaid Moore & Smith's loan of $315.41, which he had used for his initial inventory, and had made $252.44 in new capital.

On June 21, 1879, Woolworth opened his second Great 5¢ Store in Lancaster, Pennsylvania. This time he had three windows on a main street and $410 worth of goods. The store was a success. The first day he sold 31 percent of stock. In succeeding months he changed the store's name, first to Five-and-Ten, and later to Woolworth's. The increase to 10¢ allowed him to search out further bargains.

Woolworth soon began opening new outlets. Some stores succeeded, while others failed. By the mid-1880s, there were seven Woolworth's in New York and Pennsylvania. Most were run by partner-managers. These men—Woolworth's brother Charles Sumner Woolworth, cousin Seymour Horace Knox,

former employer W. H. Moore, and Fred M. Kirby—ran the
stores and held a 50 percent interest. Frank Woolworth ran the
initial store and took care of purchasing.

In succeeding years these partner-managers bought out
Frank Woolworth's shares and began opening chains on their
own. Woolworth continued opening stores. After 1888 he did so
completely with his own capital. In these new stores he entered
into a profit-sharing agreement with managers.

While Woolworth owed much of his success to low prices,
his treatment of the customer was also important. In the 1870s
and 1880s, patrons usually had to ask for goods held behind the
counter; prices varied according to the customer; and it was
considered impolite to enter a store without buying. Woolworth
changed all that. His merchandise sat on counters for everyone
to see. His price was the same for everyone. He encouraged
people to enter the store even if they were just looking.

Another reason for Woolworth's success was the decline in
wholesale prices during the first 12 years of Woolworth's existence. This led to wider availability of goods in the 5-and-10¢
price range, wider margins, and higher profits.

As operations grew, Woolworth found he needed a New
York City office from which he could govern his stores. In July
1886 he took an office on Chambers Street. Soon after, he began
writing a daily general letter that went out to all store managers.

In 1888 Frank Woolworth contracted typhoid. Until then he
had handled everything from accounting to ordering to inspecting stores; however, after two months in bed, he realized the
importance of delegating authority. With that in mind, he chose
Carson C. Peck to run day-to-day operations. Peck had been a
fellow clerk at A. Bushnell & Co. and a partner-manager in
Woolworth's Utica, New York, store. He became Woolworth's
first general manager.

Freed of day-to-day operations, Woolworth made his first
European buying trip in 1890. On his return, U.S. consumers
flocked to obtain pottery from England and Scotland, Christmas

decorations from Germany, and other goods from the great
commercial fairs of Europe.

The same year, Woolworth established the "approved list."
On the approved list were goods that Woolworth would reorder
for his managers. This system allowed managers the leeway to
adjust stock for local preferences while at the same time benefiting from the chain's buying power. In 1897 Woolworth
opened his first Canadian store, in Toronto, Ontario. Three
years later there were 59 Woolworth's with sales of $5 million.

Tremendous Growth in Early 20th Century

By 1904 Woolworth was opening stores at a fantastic rate.
He opened some stores from scratch. Others he converted from
small chains he had bought. In 1905 he incorporated as F. W.
Woolworth & Co. At this point Woolworth had $10 million in
sales and 120 stores.

In 1909 Woolworth sent three associates to open the first of
what was to be a hugely successful group of English stores,
known as "Three and Sixpence" stores. In 1910 he appointed
the first resident buyer in Germany, and in 1911 he opened his
first overseas warehouse at Fuerth, Germany.

At this point competition began to increase from such retailers as J. G. McCrory and S. S. Kresge Company. Also, many
former partner-managers had chains of their own. In 1912
Woolworth saw the opportunity to create a huge new entity. He
merged with five other retailers—W. H. Moore, C. S. Woolworth, F. M. Kirby, S. H. Knox, and E. P. Charlton. All were
former partner-managers except for Earle Perry Charlton, who
had built a chain west of the Rocky Mountains. F. W. Woolworth & Co. became the publicly traded F. W. Woolworth Co.,
a nationwide retailer with 596 stores and $52 million in sales.
Frank Woolworth was chief stockholder and president.

The new retailing behemoth took residence in the 60-story
neo-Gothic Woolworth building in New York City. Frank
Woolworth's office, within the $13.5 million "Skyline
Queen," was a replica of Napoleon Bonaparte's Empire Room.

In 1915 Carson Peck died. Peck had been supervising day-
to-day operations since 1888. Woolworth assumed Peck's
duties, but the strain proved to be too much. On April 8, 1919,
Woolworth himself died.

To succeed him as president the board named Hubert T.
Parson, Woolworth's first bookkeeper and later a company
director and secretary-treasurer. The board also named Charles
Sumner Woolworth, F. W. Woolworth's brother, chairman of
the board.

Expansion continued under Parson. The company sent its
first buyers to Japan in 1919. In 1924 it opened stores in Cuba.
Woolworth inaugurated a German operating subsidiary in 1926
and in 1927 opened its first German store. By the company's
50th anniversary in 1929, there were 2,247 Woolworth stores in
the United States, Canada, Cuba, England, and Germany. Sales
topped $303 million.

In the United States F. W. Woolworth was far and away the
biggest five-and-ten retailer. Its 2,100 U.S. stores had 1929

sales of $273 million. By comparison, J. G. McCrory had about 220 stores with $40 million in sales, and S. S. Kresge had about 500 stores with $147 million in sales.

The Great Depression caused the first decline in the company's sales since 1883, reaching a low of $250 million in 1932. In 1931 the company sold off part of its British operations, allowing that subsidiary to become a public company.

In 1932 Hubert Parsons retired and Byron D. Miller became the company's third president. Miller had worked his way up in the company and had helped start Woolworth's U.K. operations. Among Miller's first acts was to raise the 10¢ price ceiling to 20¢. Woolworth was the last five-and-ten chain to raise its prices.

After three years in office, Miller retired and Charles Deyo became president. On taking office in 1935, Deyo and the board of directors removed all arbitrary price limits.

Sales turned upward during the late 1930s, but World War II posed new problems. Nearly half of Woolworth's male employees entered the Armed Forces, as did many female employees. During the war, women managed 500 stores. Demand expanded. Supplies were limited, but consumers tolerated substitutions, and because the war meant labor shortages, consumers also tolerated less service.

Entered Prolonged Slump Following World War II

In 1946 Alfred Cornwell succeeded Deyo. Under Deyo and Cornwell, Woolworth had difficulties adapting to the postwar rush of discount houses, supermarkets, and shopping centers. According to a 1965 *Dun's Review* article, "Woolworth was mired in a depression mentality. It was keeping costs down and prices low at a time when customers wanted service and when prosperity made prices a secondary consideration."

The situation began to deteriorate, and in 1953 earnings hit a five-year low of $29.8 million. Concerned with what was happening, three board members—Allan P. Kirby, Seymour H. Knox, and Fremont C. Peck—forced Woolworth to create a new forward-looking finance and policy committee to combat what they saw as the management's overly conservative tendencies.

Woolworth's British operation was having similar problems. Consumers were abandoning the stores for supermarkets and rivals such as Marks & Spencer, British Home Stores, and Littlewoods. In response Woolworth increased the number of stores in England but did little to upgrade the existing outlets.

In 1954 James T. Leftwich became president. Leftwich addressed some of Woolworth's problems and spent $110 million to expand, modernize, and move stores. In 1956 Woolworth opened two stores in Mexico City and in 1957 began operations in Puerto Rico. Much was left to be done, however, under the leadership of Robert C. Kirkwood, who took over as president in 1958.

Under Kirkwood, Woolworth raised price limits and added profitable soft goods such as clothing and fabrics. Kirkwood also introduced self-service, opened hundreds of new stores, enlarged or relocated hundreds of others, and pushed Woolworth into shopping centers. Further, he increased advertising, instituted formal job training, and shortened hours and improved benefits for traditionally underpaid sales people, a move that reduced costly employee turnover from 43 percent to 19 percent.

Yet while Kirkwood was rejuvenating Woolworth, competitors such as Kresge and W. T. Grant had already overhauled their stores and were moving into new lines and new locations. Each was able to surpass Woolworth in earnings growth.

In fact, while Woolworth sales surpassed $1 billion for the first time in 1960, U.S. earnings dropped from $14 million in 1960 to $12.6 million in 1963. It was only the return from British Woolworth that enabled consolidated earnings to keep moving up. British stockholders later accused the U.S. board of milking the English operation without infusing the proper amount of capital.

Diversified in 1960s and 1970s

Woolworth and Kresge both sought new types of stores that would better fit the changing retail environment. In 1962 Woolworth opened the first Woolco, and S. S. Kresge opened the first Kmart. Each offered the services of a full-line department store and was very large, in some locations more than 100,00 square feet. Woolworth had 17 Woolco stores by 1965.

As the 1960s continued, Woolworth expanded, diversified, and modernized. In 1965 it acquired the G. R. Kinney Corporation for $39 million. Founded by George Romanta Kinney in 1894, Kinney had 584 family shoe stores in 45 states.

The same year, Lester A. Burcham became president. Under Burcham, Woolworth expanded operations into Spain and established a buying office in Tokyo. Two years later, it opened the first Woolco in England.

In 1968 sales topped $2 billion, and in 1969 Woolworth acquired Williams the Shoemen, an Australian shoe store chain that has since become a dominant force in Australian shoe retailing with more than 460 stores ranging from high fashion to athletic and family footwear. Also in 1969, Woolworth acquired Richman Brothers Company, a manufacturer and retailer of men's and boys' clothing. Finally, as part of a 90th anniversary celebration, Woolworth replaced the old "Diamond W" logo with a modern looking white "W" on a light blue field.

Yet Woolworth was still not growing at the rate of its competitors. By 1970 sales at Kresge were running essentially neck and neck with Woolworth. One problem was British Woolworth. In 1965 Woolworth's 52.7-percent-owned subsidiary, F. W. Woolworth Ltd., had contributed 50 percent of the parent company's profits, but during the late 1960s it began a steep decline. The reasons included a lack of investment, a devaluation of the pound, and an increase in employment taxes. By 1969 the British subsidiary was contributing just 30 percent of profits. In an effort to gain market share, British management cut prices. Sales grew, but profits fell.

John S. Roberts, who became Woolworth's president in 1970, also needed to address problems at Woolco, which was performing at nowhere near the rate of Kmart. His solution was to consolidate Woolworth and Woolco in one division in 1972. Rather than providing economies, however, the consolidation only blurred the identity of each chain. Woolworth's 1973 sales were $3.7 billion; Kresge's were $4.6 billion, 90 percent generated by Kmart. A positive event occurred, however, in 1974, when the Kinney shoe division opened the first two Foot Locker stores, athletic-shoe retailers that would later prove highly profitable.

With stock prices on the wane, the board recognized the need for change and in 1975 named outsider Edward F. Gibbons president. Gibbons in turn named W. Robert Harris the first president of the U.S. Woolworth and Woolco Division. In 1978 consolidated annual sales topped $6 billion, of which Kinney, growing at a rate of 18 to 20 percent a year, contributed $800 million. Also in 1978, Harris became president and Gibbons became chief executive officer.

Juggling of Store Lineup Continued in 1980s and Early 1990s

While Woolco continued its sluggish growth and Woolworth stores suffered neglect, F. W. Woolworth Co. continued diversifying. In 1979 Woolworth opened the first J. Brannam, a men's clothing store whose name stood for "just brand names." J. Brannam was a quick moneymaker and often stood within or beside otherwise lackluster Woolco department stores. No matter how much the management tinkered, the problems of Woolco refused to go away. After the stores lost $19 million in 1981, Harris and Gibbons hired Bruce G. Albright to revive the ailing chain. Albright, who had come from competitor Dayton Hudson's Target stores, had a plan to revive Woolco, but company projections still saw the stores losing money. After Woolco lost $21 million during the first six months of 1982, Gibbons decided to shut down all 336 Woolcos in the United States, shrinking the $7.2 billion company 30 percent and laying off 25,000 employees. Closing costs were estimated at $325 million.

In the fall of 1982, Woolworth disclosed plans to sell its interest in British Woolworth to a syndicate of English investors, for $279 million. One analyst, quoted in *Business Week*, October 11, 1982, blamed British Woolworth's failure on the U.S. parent, saying, "The American Woolworth has been milking the British unit for years, insisting on high dividend payout that has forced it to scrimp on investment and to take on more and more debt."

Analysts, however, were pleased with the company that remained. Left were the profitable, but shaky, 1,300 variety stores, Richman Brothers, and Kinney Shoe Corporation—a $1.1 billion division that had done well with Kinney, Foot Locker, a women's clothing store known as Susie's Casuals, and the newly created and profitable J. Brannam. Woolco's closing, however, left 28 of the 41 J. Brannam outlets homeless.

Edward F. Gibbons died suddenly in October 1982. Contrary to expectations and much to the chagrin of younger talent, the board named company veteran John W. (Bud) Lynn chief executive officer. As a variety-store man, Lynn paid close attention to Woolworth's. He changed merchandise, reducing the number of high-priced items such as appliances and dresses

and expanding basic lines like candy, and health and beauty aids. He arranged stores in arrow patterns to cut down on unprofitable corners.

Lynn pushed the company to adopt a set of strategic priorities that angled Woolworth away from money-losing businesses and toward specialty retailing. Kinney's Canadian operation had started the remarkably successful Lady Foot Locker in 1982, and in 1983 Woolworth paid $27 million for Holtzman's Little Folk Shop, a full-price children's clothing merchandiser and its subsidiary, Kids Mart, a discount operation.

Lynn retired in 1987, and the board named Harold Sells as the new chief executive officer. Sells continued to push Woolworth's profitable mall-based specialty operations. Managers sought out new ideas for stores and those that the company liked were tried. If the stores were profitable, it opened more. If they were not profitable, the company tried another idea at the same location.

In 1990 Woolworth opened 896 stores and closed 351. Many of the new ventures were specialty stores, such as Kinneys, Kids Marts, Foot Lockers, and Lady Foot Lockers. The latter two sold a full 20 percent of all brand-name athletic footwear in the United States in the late 1980s. The 40 types of specialty stores included After Thoughts, seller of costume jewelry and handbags; Champs, seller of athletic goods and apparel; and Woolworth Express, seller of the fastest-moving goods of a traditional Woolworth.

In 1993 Sells retired and was replaced as CEO by CFO William Lavin, who quickly proceeded to make additional moves pointing toward the elimination of the company's general merchandise stores in favor of an exclusive focus on specialty formats. Four hundred Woolworth's were closed in the United States and 122 Woolco stores in Canada were sold to Wal-Mart, terminating Woolco altogether. Woolworth also sold 300 underperforming Kinney outlets and liquidated the 286-store Richman Brothers/Anderson-Little men's and women's clothing stores. Along with the nearly 1,000 stores, about 13,000 jobs were also eliminated. As a result of these moves, the company recorded a $558 million charge resulting in a net 1993 loss of $495 million.

These radical moves had barely been made when an accounting scandal arose in early 1994, revolving around alleged false reporting of quarterly results during 1993. Several lawsuits were filed which were eventually combined into a class-action lawsuit. This suit had appeared to be settled by mid-1997 when Woolworth agreed to make undisclosed cash payments to affected shareholders. Later in 1994 Lavin was forced out and Roger Farah became chairman and CEO in December 1994.

Mid-1990s Rebuilding and Restructuring

Farah, a longtime department store manager who had most recently been president of R. H. Macy & Co., took over a Woolworth in shambles. Thanks to dwindling profits, by early 1995 the company was nearly out of cash and short-term debt had swelled to $853 million. Consequently, Farah's first task was to improve cash flow in 1995. To do so, he broke Woolworth's string of 83 straight years of dividends; restructured company debt, reducing total debt by $475 million and shifting

$290 million of short-term debt to longer-term financing; reduced operating spending by $100 million; wrote off $241 million of inventory; and began to sell off nonstrategic chains and real estate. Early in 1995 Woolworth sold the Rx Place chain of pharmacies for $37 million and the 331 Kids Mart/Little Folks children's clothing stores to the LFS Acquisition investor group for $15 million. Two other Canadian chains—Karuba and Canary Island—were also closed during the year. The various charges incurred as a result of these actions led to a net loss of $164 million.

In 1996 Woolworth continued to restructure. Short-term debt was eliminated altogether and total debt was reduced an additional $116 million. Another $100 million in operating spending was eliminated. And $222 million in cash was generated from the disposal of additional nonstrategic chains and real estate. Among the divestments were the Accessory Lady chain in the United States; the Silk & Satin lingerie chain in Canada; the Lady Plus apparel chain, the Rubin jewelry chain, the Moderna shoe store chain, and the New Yorker Süd jeans business, all in Germany; and the Gallery shoe store chain in Australia. All told, 1,443 unproductive stores were disposed of in 1995 and 1996.

In the midst of these moves, institutional investor Greenway Partners forced to a vote a shareholder proposal to spin off Woolworth's Athletic Group, which included the profitable and growing Foot Locker and Champs chains. In a boost to Farah's attempt at rebuilding the company, the plan was soundly defeated.

Unlike his predecessor, Farah was not ready to give up on the neglected Woolworth's chain. To better monitor and plan sales, point-of-sale equipment was installed at all locations in 1995 and purchasing, pricing policies, and promotional strategies were all centralized. In 1996 the chain began testing new formats featuring higher-quality (and higher-priced) merchandise, with more brand names. Based on customer surveys, the prototype stores were aimed at the time-pressed and budget-minded working woman looking for products for herself, her home, and her family. So, rather than carrying everything from hamsters to beach chairs, the product mix included more cosmetics and housewares. The antiquated lunch counters were replaced by small coffee bars. The three-store 1996 test was successful enough to justify an expansion of the test to 13 more stores in 1997.

Early in 1997 Woolworth spent $146 million to acquire Wausau, Wisconsin-based Eastbay Inc., a catalog company specializing in athletic footwear. Woolworth and Eastbay planned to develop catalogs for such Woolworth retail brands as Foot Locker and Champs. Also in 1997, in a telling psychological blow, Woolworth was replaced by Wal-Mart on the Dow Jones Industrial Average.

Overall, Woolworth's fortunes were improving in the late 1990s, as the company posted a net profit of $169 million in 1996. The company appeared to be on track with the paring back of its unwieldy portfolio of retail formats. Nevertheless, 1997 brought not only the company's ouster from the DJIA but also accelerating losses for the Woolworth's chain—a $24 mil-

lion operating loss for the first quarter as compared to a loss of $37 million for all of 1996. Unable to withstand such hemorrhaging long enough to turn the chain around, Woolworth announced on July 17, 1997, that it would close its more than 400 five-and-dime stores in the United States, lay off about 9,200 Woolworth's workers (about 11 percent of the company's workforce), and take a $223 million charge for the discontinued operations. The company planned to convert about 100 of the Woolworth's locations to Foot Locker, Champs Sports, and other specialty formats. Although the Woolworth's chain had seen the final chapter written on its history in the United States, the chain's saga would continue on in Mexico and Germany, where about 700 of the five-and-dimes still operated. The company also announced that it planned to change its name "to better reflect its global specialty retailing formats," though this change would not occur until later in 1997. In more ways than one, therefore, the Woolworth Corporation of the early 21st century would certainly be quite different from that of the 1980s and early 1990s.

Principal Subsidiaries

Cliftex; Eastbay Inc.; Kinney Shoe Corporation; Team Edition Apparel, Inc.; Woolworth Overseas Corp.; Woolworth World Trade Corp.; Foot Locker Europe B.V. (Netherlands); Kinney Shoes (Australia), Ltd.; Kinney Shoes of Canada, Ltd.; Retail Company of Germany, Inc.; Woolworth Canada Inc.; Woolworth Mexicana, S.A. de C.V. (Mexico).

Further Reading

Berman, Phyllis, and Caroline Waxler, "Woolworth's Woes," *Forbes*, August 14, 1995, pp. 47–48.
Biesada, Alexandra, "Dumping on the Dime Store," *Financial World*, October 30, 1990, p. 62.
Bird, Laura, "Hamsters Get Heave-Ho in New Five-and-Tens," *Wall Street Journal*, September 26, 1996, pp. B1, B10.
——, "Woolworth Is Hoping to Score in Sportswear," *Wall Street Journal*, March 12, 1997, pp. B1, B6.
——, "Woolworth Corp. to Post a Charge and Cut 9,200 Jobs," *Wall Street Journal*, July 18, 1997, p. C16.
Bongiorno, Lori, "Lost in the Aisles at Woolworth's," *Business Week*, October 30, 1995, pp. 76, 78.
Gill, Penny, "Sells: Key Player in Woolworth Renaissance," *Stores*, May 1991, p. 24.
Miller, Annetta, "A Dinosaur No More: Woolworth Corp. Leaves Dime Stores Far Behind," *Newsweek*, January 4, 1993, pp. 54–55.
Nichols, John P., *Skyline Queen and the Merchant Prince*, New York: Pocket Books, 1973.
100th Anniversary, 1879–1979, New York: F. W. Woolworth Co., 1979.
Saporito, Bill, "Woolworth to Rule the Malls," *Fortune*, June 5, 1989, p. 145.
Winkler, John K., *Five and Ten: The Fabulous Life of F. W. Woolworth*, Freeport, N.Y.: Books for Libraries Press, 1970 (reprint of 1940 ed.).
Woolworth's First 75 Years: The Story of Everybody's Store, New York: F. W. Woolworth Co., 1954.
Zinn, Laura, "Why 'Business Stinks' at Woolworth," *Business Week*, November 25, 1991, pp. 72, 76.

—Jordan Wankoff
—updated by David E. Salamie

WTD Industries, Inc.

10260 SW Greenburg Road
Portland, Oregon 97223
U.S.A.
(503) 246-3440
Fax: (503) 245-4229

Public Company
Incorporated: 1983
Employees: 1,100
Sales: $284.1 million (1997)
Stock Exchanges: NASDAQ
SICs: 2411 Logging; 2499 Wood Products, Not
   Elsewhere Classified

WTD Industries, Inc. is one of the largest producers of lumber products in the United States, operating mills in Oregon, Washington, and Vermont. The company markets its lumber in the United States, Canada, and other countries under the Tree-Source brand name through a wholly owned subsidiary, Tree-Source, Inc. Its top three customers in the United States are Georgia-Pacific Corporation, the Weyerhaeuser Company and HomeBase Inc. The company is also a major producer of wood chips for pulp and paper manufacturers in the Northwest. In 1996, WTD Industries produced more than 485 million board feet of lumber and 194,000 BDU (bone dry units) of wood chips.

Founding

WTD Industries got its start during one of the timber industry's cyclical downturns. In 1981, Bruce Engel, then a 41-year-old attorney in Portland, Oregon, purchased the bankrupt Little River Lumber Co. in Glide, Oregon, from one of his clients, the Johnson Lumber Co., for $3,000 and the assumption of $2 million in debt. Engel, who was raised on a farm in Oregon and graduated from the University of Chicago, had seldom seen the inside of a sawmill, but as he later told *Forbes,* "There's a fine line between legal and business advice that I think frustrates many lawyers."

Engel and a partner, William G. Williamson, incorporated WTD Industries in 1983, after acquiring sawmills in Silverton and Philomath, Oregon. They also established TreeSource Inc. as the company's lumber sales organization. Over the next few years, WTD Industries continued to buy bankrupt sawmills at favorable terms, a strategy that enabled the company to rid itself of burdensome union and long-term timber contracts. By one estimate, production costs at WTD Industries mills in the early 1980s were $65 per thousand board feet of lumber, compared to $100 for the Weyerhaeuser Company. Communities also offered Engel and Williamson substantial enticements to retain local timber jobs. For example, Sedro-Woolley, a small timber community north of Seattle, gave them a $500,000 economic development loan at 7 percent interest.

By 1986, when Engel announced that WTD Industries would become the first Pacific Northwest lumber company to go public since the 1960s, the company operated nine sawmills west of the Cascade Mountains, stretching from Bellingham, Washington, to Rosewood, Oregon. Sales had increased from less than $50 million in 1983 to nearly $100 million in 1986, and the company had become the 17th largest timber producer in the United States. Engel, who by then had bought out Williamson's 23 percent stake in the business for $606,000, sold 42 percent of the company in an initial public offering for $24 million, making him one of the richest men in Oregon. At one point, Engel and his wife, Teri, were worth an estimated $90 million. They used their fortune to buy bowling alleys, a weekly newspaper, several small manufacturers, and ranches in Oregon, British Columbia, and New Zealand. They also attempted to buy the Seattle Mariners baseball team for $37 million, and they contributed freely to charitable organizations, including the Oregon Symphony, underwriting the cost of producing three recordings.

WTD Industries continued to soar into 1987, its stock price doubling less than four months after going public. According to industry estimates, nearly 100 Pacific Northwest sawmills and plywood and veneer plants had closed between 1980 and 1987, but Engel, and his strategy of buying timber on the spot market instead of bidding on long-term contracts, was successfully bucking that trend. He told *Forbes,* which dubbed Engel "Paul

Bunyan in pinstripes," "We represent something of a slap in the face to the established industry. In the midst of all their woe, here we come operating successfully."

That fall, the U.S. stock market crashed and the value of WTD Industries shares fell by half, costing the Engels at least $40 million. But the company seemed unstoppable. In December, WTD Industries announced plans to acquire a plywood mill in Whitehall, New York, the company's first expansion east of the Rocky Mountains. G. Alan Guggenheim, then vice president, told the *Portland Business Journal* that WTD Industries did not have "an East Coast strategy." But, Guggenheim added, "We've never limited ourselves to the Northwest. The image of New York is that of an intensely urban state. But three-fifths of the state is forested. There are millions of acres of commercial forest land."

Collapse

WTD Industries' breakneck expansion slowed in 1988, and the company began investing more of its cash in the stock market instead of snatching up additional mills. After buying 16 small lumber companies in 1986–87, WTD Industries acquired just two more in 1988. Jerry Griffin, then vice president for corporate development, told the *Portland Business Journal*, "The market has been so strong that people have been over-valuing their mills. Our strategy has been to buy capacity at below value. That opportunity hasn't been available." The company also reported that nearly 15 percent of its income for the last quarter of 1988 came from its investments in the stock market, rather than lumber sales, where its profit margin was beginning to shrink.

Nevertheless, by 1989 WTD Industries had become the fourth largest lumber producer in the United States, operating more than two dozen sawmills and veneer plants in seven states and restoring more than 3,000 jobs in depressed Northwest timber communities. The company was also planning to expand into the pulp and paper industry with a $300 million plant on the Columbia River near Clatskanie, Oregon, and there were rumors that WTD Industries was interested in acquiring the much larger Longview Fibre Company, in Longview, Washington. Longview Fibre then operated 14 mills in seven states, but more importantly for "timber poor" WTD Industries, it owned more than 500,000 acres of harvestable forest. WTD Industries acquired 4.8 percent of Longview Fibre's stock in partnership with Mack Capital of New York. But Longview Fibre, with sales of $657.2 million in 1988, adopted several "poison-pill" anti-takeover measures, including changing the state of incorporation from New Jersey to Washington, which had more stringent shareholder rules. Richard P. Wollenberg, then chief executive at Longview Fibre, told the *Oregonian,* that WTD had "neither the capital nor the character" to take over Longview Fibre.

Then, as quickly as WTD Industries rose to prominence, it all began to fall apart. Most of WTD Industries lumber was softwoods for the construction industry. As the country slipped into a recession in the late 1980s, housing starts fell, along with lumber prices. At the same time, environmentalists were raising concerns over the spotted owl. The federal government restricted logging in national forests to protect the owls environ-

ment, which forced up the cost of timber on the spot market. Since the beginning, WTD Industries' business strategy had been predicated on the belief that the cost of timber and lumber would rise and fall in concert, but that was not happening. As *Forbes* had cautioned two years earlier, "Key to keeping WTD's costs down is Engel's policy of operating with timber inventories of only three weeks; industry convention used to require raw material supplies of three years. Buying spot is fine when, as now, tree owners are eager to sell. But timber prices could escalate again, especially if conservationists win a 20% reduction in the timber set for public auction. . . ."

In mid-1989, WTD Industries reported its first unprofitable quarter since 1982. Company officials also began talking about closing mills instead of expanding, which sent the stock plummeting to $3.50 a share. Engel told the *Oregonian*, "I don't believe the spotted owl will permanently reduce timber production in the Northwest (but) I don't think we know what the (cost) will be." Engel, who saw his personal wealth fall along with the price of WTD Industries' stock, was also having financial problems. He had borrowed heavily to acquire his other businesses, personally guaranteeing more than $7 million in loans. In a precursor of what faced WTD Industries, Kimber of Oregon, a rifle manufacturer owned by Engel in Clackamas County, filed for protection from creditors in U.S. Bankruptcy Court. The Engels also sold their radio stations for $9 million and mortgaged their home in Portland for $500,000.

At first, WTD Industries tried to work out its problems through business as usual. The company bought five more lumber-products companies in early 1990, including the Cornett Lumber Co. sawmill in Central Point, Oregon; Cascade Lumber Co. sawmill in Cottage Grove, Oregon; Yoncalla Timber Products Inc. veneer mill in Yoncalla, Oregon; McDougal-Meyers Inc. sawmill in Judith Gap, Montana; and Mountain View Lumber Inc. sawmill in West Burke, Vermont. But in April, the company announced that it would close, or delay reopening, eight sawmills—one fourth of the company—including all of the newly acquired sawmills except the one in Vermont. The *Oregonian* reported succinctly: "WTD Industries, Inc., the nation's fastest growing lumber manufacturer, has been sidetracked by the fight over the northern spotted owl." The company was also forced to write off losses from its proposed pulp mill on the Columbia River when it failed to get a wastewater permit from the Oregon Environmental Quality Commission.

Engel announced that the writeoff and the cost of closing the sawmills would wipe out virtually all of the company's earnings for fiscal 1990. Almost immediately, two stockholders filed suit in U.S. District Court in Portland, claiming that WTD Industries had misled them about the company's financial condition. The suit also alleged that Engel and his wife, Teri, a WTD Industries director, unfairly profited by selling 360,000 shares of stock between 1989 and 1990 at up to $16 a share. Other shareholder suits followed soon afterwards. The suits were settled out of court in 1991.

In May 1990, the Dow Jones News Service reported that WTD Industries would seek protection from its creditors in federal bankruptcy court. Engel denied the report. In a prepared statement, he said, "WTD has not and does not intend to file for bankruptcy protection. WTD continues to operate conservatively in response to an unanticipated and unusually depressed lumber market relative to high log costs by reducing capital expenditures significantly and reducing overhead.'' He told the *Oregonian*, ''It is more than a little frustrating that, even though WTD continues to operate sensibly, rumors of our demise by short sellers and other self-interested parties contribute to volatility in our stock price.'' Engel and his wife, who then owned 36 percent of WTD Industries compared to 43.8 percent a year earlier, also registered to sell another 200,000 shares of stock to hold off their mounting personal financial troubles.

In June, the company's dismal financial predictions were confirmed. WTD Industries reported a loss of $10.1 million for the quarter ending April 30, more than wiping out $8.6 million in earnings for the first three quarters of the fiscal year. The $1.5 million loss was WTD's first unprofitable year since 1982, despite record sales of $460 million. A month later, WTD Industries put into operation the $7 million Trask River sawmill near Tillamook, Oregon, the company's first all-new sawmill. WTD Industries hoped the modern, high-efficiency sawmill would revive the company. But the sawmill was forced to compete for limited timber supplies with the Tillamook Lumber Co., then owned by John Hampton, who was also chairman of the Northwest Forest Council. Hampton predicted only one mill would survive. He told the *Oregonian*: ''He's (Engel) looking right down the gun barrel, and I'm going to pull the trigger.'' That summer, WTD Industries reported its second straight quarterly loss—of $11 million. The stock price fell as low as 75 cents a share.

In January 1991, WTD Industries, once the fastest-growing company in the lumber industry, filed for Chapter 11 protection from its creditors in U.S. Bankruptcy Court in Seattle. Half of the company's mills had already been closed, and court records indicated WTD Industries owed more than $120 million, most of it to First Interstate Bank of Oregon and three of the nation's largest insurers, the Aetna Life Insurance Co., Principal Life Insurance Co., and Northwestern Mutual Life Insurance Co.

Emerging from Bankruptcy, 1992

The company continued to operate under the court's protection for the next two years, selling or liquidating 17 of its 31 sawmills and plywood and veneer plants. In November 1992, the bankruptcy court approved a plan of reorganization, and WTD Industries became the largest Oregon company to ever emerge from a Chapter 11 filing. Although considerably smaller, WTD Industries, which had entered bankruptcy proceedings as the fourth largest producer of lumber in the United States, was still the sixth largest. Engel told the *Oregonian*, ''We didn't doubt the validity of our company to reorganize.''

In a show of faith, WTD Industries' creditors allowed Engel to remain as chief executive officer under the plan of reorganization. Several of the largest creditors also accepted stock in the company, then worth about 20 cents a share with a four for 10 reverse split, in lieu of payment of nearly $60 million in debt. However, First Interstate Bank of Oregon, wanted nothing more to do with the company and agreed to take $2.4 million in cash to satisfy a debt of $9.2 million. Engel and his wife, who owned 34 percent of the company before filing Chapter 11, owned less than 5 percent after the reorganization.

By mid-1993, WTD Industries was again operating in the black, and recorded a net income of $23.8 million on sales of $246.9 million for its first full fiscal year following the reorganization. However, a volatile lumber market the next four years held down sales and cut into the company's profit margins. By 1996, when sales slipped to $192 million, WTD Industries was again losing money, posting a net loss of $6 million. In the company's annual report, Engel said the fiscal year ending April 30, 1996 ''was the apparent culmination of the longest and most unusual down period for solid wood manufacturing in the Pacific Northwest in recent history.'' Although there were encouraging numbers during the company's fourth quarter, Engel also noted that ''for the first time in our history we were unable to generate a profitable quarter the entire year.''

As anticipated, WTD Industries rebounded the following year, posting a profit of nearly $9 million on sales of $284.1 million for fiscal 1997. In an interview with the *Oregonian* during the worst of the most recent industry slump, Engel had also voiced his optimism. ''The Northwest is the largest wood basket in the U.S.,'' Engel said. ''There should be an industry in the Northwest because the raw material is not only here, but it regrows faster here than in any other part of the country.''

Principal Subsidiaries

TreeSource, Inc., Portland, Oregon.; Western Timber Co., Portland, Oregon; Burke Lumber Co., West Burke, Vermont; Central Point Lumber Co., Central Point, Oregon; Glide Lumber Products Co., Glide, Oregon; Morton Forest Products Co., Morton, Washington; North Powder Lumber Co., North Powder, Oregon; Pacific Hardwoods-South Bend Co., South Bend, Washington; Pacific Softwoods Co., Philomath, Oregon; Philomath Forest Products Co., Philomath, Oregon; Sedro-Woolley Lumber Co., Sedro-Woolley, Washington; Spanaway Lumber Co., Tacoma, Washington; Trask River Lumber Co., Tillamook, Oregon; Tumwater Lumber Co., Tumwater, Washington.

Further Reading

Colby, Richard, ''President of WTD Denies Report,'' *Oregonian*, May 14, 1990, p. D10.
Gauntt, Tom, ''WTD's Eastward Leap Illustrates a New Strategy,'' *(Portland) Business Journal*, Dec. 14, 1987, p. 9.
——, ''WTD Invests in Stocks Instead of Lumber Mills,'' *(Portland) Business Journal*, March 27, 1989, p. 2.
Hamburg, Ken, ''Company Puts Up Defenses,'' *Oregonian*, January 24, 1990.
Jones, Steven D., ''Bankruptcy Reshapes Big Lumber Producer WTD,'' *(Puget Sound) Business Journal*, June 12, 1992, p. 12.
——, ''Slimmer WTD Edging Out of Bankruptcy,'' *(Portland) Business Journal*, June 15, 1992, p. 1.
Kadera, Jim, ''WTD Exercising Caution in Slow Times, Chief Says,'' *Oregonian*, May 29, 1990, p. D8.
——, ''WTD Industries, Once Headed for Top of Timber Industry, Is Treading Water,'' *Oregonian*, June 24, 1990, p. C1.
——, ''Analysts Praise, Criticize Engel,'' *Oregonian*, September 23, 1990, p. D1.
——, ''WTD Industries Inc. Files for Protection,'' *Oregonian*, February 1, 1991, p. A1.
——, ''WTD Seeks Damages, 10 Years to Pay Debts,'' *Oregonian*, September 25, 1991, p. C1.

——, "WTD Hopes to Trim Mills Down to 14," *Oregonian*, September 27, 1991, p. C2.

——, "WTD Reorganization Disclosed As Company Seeks Clean Slate," *Oregonian*, October 6, 1992, p. C12.

——, "Court OK Lets WTD Emerge from Ch. 11," *Oregonian*, November 24, 1992, p. D11.

——, "WTD Faces Difficult Path Back to Financial Health After Chapter 11," *Oregonian*, December 6, 1992, p. K1.

——, "Stock Analyst Predicts Demise of Small Timber Companies," *Oregonian*, July 7, 1993, p. E9.

Klahn, Jim, "WTD's Engel Pleads Case in Bankruptcy Court," *Oregonian*, March 7, 1991, p. C1.

Nordquist, John C., "Timber Shootout Looms in Tillamook," *Oregonian*, July 12, 1990, p. E10.

Woodward, Steve, "Industrial Turn-Around Artist Faces Tough Time," *Oregonian*, September 23, 1990, D1.

—Dean Boyer

INDEX TO COMPANIES

Index to Companies

Listings in this index are arranged in alphabetical order under the company name. Company names beginning with a letter or proper name such as Eli Lilly & Co. will be found under the first letter of the company name. Definite articles (The, Le, La) are ignored for alphabetical purposes as are forms of incorporation that precede the company name (AB, NV). Company names printed in bold type have full, historical essays on the page numbers appearing in bold. Updates to entries that appeared in earlier volumes are signified by the notation (**upd.**). Company names in light type are references within an essay to that company, not full historical essays. This index is cumulative with volume numbers printed in bold type.

Grupo Zeta, **IV** 652–53; **7** 392
Gruppo IRI, **V** 325–27
GSG&T, **6** 495
GSI. *See* Geophysical Service, Inc.
GSI Acquisition Co. L.P., **17** 488
GSR, Inc., **17** 338
GSU. *See* Gulf States Utilities Company.
GT Interactive Software Corp., **19** 405
GTE Corporation, II 38, 47, 80; **III** 475;
    V 294–98; **9** 49, 171, 478–80; **10** 19,
    97, 431; **11** 500; **14** 259, 433; **15
    192–97 (upd.)**; **18** 74, 111, 543. *See
    also* British Columbia Telephone
    Company.
GTO. *See* Global Transport Organization.
GTS Duratek, Inc., **13** 367–68
Guangzhou M. C. Packaging, **10** 130
Guaranty Bank & Trust Company, **13** 440
Guaranty Federal Savings & Loan Assoc.,
    IV 343
Guaranty Properties Ltd., **11** 258
Guaranty Savings and Loan, **10** 339
Guaranty Trust, **16** 25
Guaranty Trust Co. of New York, **II**
    329–32, 428; **IV** 20
Guardian, **III** 721
Guardian Bank, **13** 468
Guardian Federal Savings and Loan
    Association, **10** 91
Guardian Mortgage Company, **8** 460
Guardian National Bank, **I** 165; **11** 137
Guardian Royal Exchange Plc, III 350;
    11 168–70
Gubor Schokoladen, **15** 221
Guccio Gucci, S.p.A., 12 281; **15
    198–200**
GUD Holdings, Ltd., **17** 106
Guelph Dolime, **IV** 74
Guernsey Banking Co., **II** 333
Guess, Inc., 15 201–03; **17** 466
Guest, Keen and Nettlefolds plc. *See* GKN
    plc.
Guest Supply, Inc., 18 215–17
Gueyraud et Fils Cadet, **III** 703
Guild Press, Inc., **13** 559
Guild Wineries, **13** 134
Guilford Industries, **8** 270–72
Guilford Mills Inc., 8 234–36
Guilford Transportation Industries, Inc., **16**
    348, 350
Guinness Peat, **10** 277
Guinness plc, I 239, 241, **250–52**, 268,
    272, 282; **II** 428–29, 610; **9** 100, 449;
    10 399; **13** 454; **18** 62, 501
Gujarat State Fertilizer Co., **III** 513
Gulco Industries, Inc., **11** 194
Güldner Aschaffenburg, **I** 582
Gulf + Western Inc., I 418, **451–53**,
    540; **II** 147, 154–56, 177; **III** 642, 745;
    IV 289, 672; **7** 64; **10** 482; **13** 121, 169,
    470
Gulf + Western Industries. *See* Paramount
    Communications.
Gulf Air, **6** 63
Gulf Canada Ltd., **I** 216, 262, 264; **IV** 495,
    721; **6** 478; **9** 391; **13** 557–58
Gulf Caribbean Marine Lines, **6** 383
Gulf Engineering Co. Ltd., **IV** 131
Gulf Exploration Co., **IV** 454
Gulf Mobile and Northern Railroad, **I** 456
Gulf Mobile and Ohio Railroad, **I** 456; **11**
    187
Gulf of Suez Petroleum Co., **IV** 412–14
Gulf Oil Chemical Co., **13** 502

Gulf Oil Corp., **I** 37, 584; **II** 315, 402,
    408, 448; **III** 225, 231, 259, 497; **IV**
    198, 287, 385–87, 392, 421, 450–51,
    466, 470, 472–73, 476, 484, 508, 510,
    512, 531, 538, 565, 570, 576; **17**
    121–22
Gulf Plains Corp., **III** 471
Gulf Public Service Company, **6** 580
Gulf Resources & Chemical Corp., **15** 464
Gulf States Paper, **IV** 345
Gulf States Steel, **I** 491
Gulf States Utilities Company, 6 495–97;
    12 99
Gulf United Corp., **III** 194
Gulfstream Aerospace Corp., 7 205–06;
    13 358
Gulfstream Banks, **II** 336
Gulton Industries Inc., **7** 297; **19** 31
Gummi Werke, **I** 208
Gump's, **7** 286
Gunder & Associates, **12** 553
Gunderson, Inc. *See* The Greenbrier
    Companies.
Gunfred Group, **I** 387
The Gunlocke Company, **12** 299; **13** 269
Gunns Ltd., **II** 482
Gunpowder Trust, **I** 379; **13** 379
Gunter Wulff Automaten, **III** 430
Gunther, S.A., **8** 477
Gupta, **15** 492
Gurneys, Birkbeck, Barclay & Buxton, **II**
    235
Gusswerk Paul Saalmann & Sohne, **I** 582
Gustav Schickendanz KG, **V** 165
Gustavus A. Pfeiffer & Co., **I** 710
Gustin-Bacon Group, **16** 8
Gutehoffnungshütte Aktienverein AG, **III**
    561, 563; **IV** 104, 201
Guthrie Balfour, **II** 499–500
Gutta Percha Co., **I** 428
Gutzeit. *See* W. Gutzeit & Co.
Guy Carpenter & Co., **III** 282
Guy Motors, **13** 286
Guy Salmon Service, Ltd., **6** 349
GW Utilities Ltd., **I** 264; **6** 478
Gwathmey & Co., **II** 424; **13** 340
Gymboree Corporation, 15 204–06
Gypsum, Lime, & Alabastine Canada Ltd.,
    IV 271

H & R Block, Incorporated, 9 268–70
H Curry & Sons. *See* Currys Group PLC.
H N Norton Co., **11** 208
H.A. Job, **II** 587
H&D. *See* Hinde & Dauch Paper
    Company.
H&H Craft & Floral, **17** 322
H.B. Claflin Company, **V** 139
H.B. Fuller Company, 8 237–40
H.B. Nickerson & Sons Ltd., **14** 339
H.B. Reese Candy Co., **II** 511
H.B. Tuttle and Company, **17** 355
H.B. Viney Company, Inc., **11** 211
H. Berlind Inc., **16** 388
H.C. Christians Co., **II** 536
H.C. Frick Coke Co., **IV** 573; **7** 550
H.C. Petersen & Co., **III** 417
H.C. Prange Co., **19** 511–12
H.D. Lee Company, Inc. *See* Lee Apparel
    Company, Inc.
H.D. Pochin & Co., **III** 690
H. Douglas Barclay, **8** 296
H.E. Butt Grocery Co., 13 251–53

H.F. Ahmanson & Company, II 181–82;
    10 342–44 (upd.)
H. Fairweather and Co., **I** 592
H.G. Anderson Equipment Corporation, **6**
    441
H.H. Brown Shoe Company, **18** 60, **18** 62
H.H. Cutler Company, **17** 513
H.H. Robertson, Inc., **19** 366
H. Hackfeld & Co., **I** 417
H. Hamilton Pty, Ltd., **III** 420
H.I. Rowntree and Co., **II** 568
H.J. Green, **II** 556
H.J. Heinz Company, I 30–31, 605, 612;
    II 414, 480, 450, **507–09**, 547; **III** 21; **7**
    382, 448, 576, 578; **8** 499; **10** 151; **11
    171–73 (upd.)**; **12** 411, 529, 531–32; **13**
    383
H.J. Justin & Sons. *See* Justin Industries,
    Inc.
H.K. Ferguson Company, **7** 355
H.K. Porter Company, Inc., **19** 152
H.L. Green Company, Inc., **9** 448
H.L. Judd Co., **III** 628
H.L. Yoh Company, **9** 163
H. Lewis and Sons, **14** 294
H.M. Byllesby & Company, Inc., **6** 539
H.M. Goush Co., **IV** 677–78
H.M. Spalding Electric Light Plant, **6** 592
H. Miller & Sons, Inc., **11** 258
H.O. Houghton & Company, **10** 355
H.P. Foods, **II** 475
H.P. Hood, **7** 17–18
H.P. Smith Paper Co., **IV** 290
H.R. MacMillan Export Co., **IV** 306–08
H. Reeve Angel & Co., **IV** 300
H. Salt Fish and Chips, **13** 320
H.T. Cherry Company, **12** 376
H.V. McKay Proprietary, **III** 651
H.W. Heidmann, **I** 542
H.W. Johns Manufacturing Co., **III** 663,
    706–08; **7** 291
H.W. Madison Co., **11** 211
H.W. Wilson Company, **17** 152
H. Williams and Co., Ltd., **II** 678
Häagen-Dazs, **II** 556–57, 631; **10** 147; **14**
    212, 214; **19** 116
Haake-Beck Brauerei AG, **9** 86
Haas, Baruch & Co. *See* Smart & Final,
    Inc.
Haas Corp., **I** 481
Haas Wheat & Partners, **15** 357
Habirshaw Cable and Wire Corp., **IV** 177
Habitat/Mothercare PLC. *See* Storehouse
    PLC.
Hach Co., 14 309; **18 218–21**
Hachette, IV 614–15, **617–19**, 675; **10**
    288; **11** 293; **12** 359; **16** 253–54; **17**
    399. *See also* Matra-Hachette S.A.
Hachmeister, Inc., **II** 508; **11** 172
Hacker-Pschorr Brau, **II** 242
Hadleigh-Crowther, **I** 715
Haemocell, **11** 476
Haemonetics Corporation, 20 277–79
Hafez Insurance Co., **III** 242
Hagemeyer, **18** 180–82
Haggar Corporation, 19 194–96
Haggie, **IV** 91
Hahn, Inc., **17** 9
Haile Mines, Inc., **12** 253
Hain Pure Food Co., **I** 514
Hainaut-Sambre, **IV** 52
A.B. Hakon Swenson, **II** 639
Hakuhodo, Inc., 6 29–31, 48–49; **16** 167
Hakunetsusha & Company, **12** 483

INDEX TO INDUSTRIES

Index to Industries

ELECTRICAL & ELECTRONICS

ENGINEERING & MANAGEMENT SERVICES

ENTERTAINMENT & LEISURE

FINANCIAL SERVICES: BANKS

FINANCIAL SERVICES: NON-BANKS

FOOD PRODUCTS

HEALTH CARE SERVICES

HOTELS

INFORMATION TECHNOLOGY

MATERIALS

MINING & METALS

PAPER & FORESTRY

PERSONAL SERVICES

PETROLEUM

PUBLISHING & PRINTING

RUBBER & TIRE

TELECOMMUNICATIONS

WASTE SERVICES

NOTES ON CONTRIBUTORS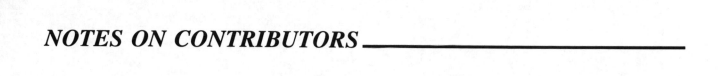

Notes on Contributors

AZZATA, Geraldine. Freelance writer, researcher, and editor based in Medford, Massachusetts; former academic reference librarian with graduate degrees in law and library science. She has published numerous materials in the areas of law, business, health, and online research.

BODINE, Paul S. Freelance writer, editor, and researcher in Milwaukee, specializing in business subjects; contributor to the *Encyclopedia of American Industries, Encyclopedia of Global Industries, DISCovering Authors, Contemporary Popular Writers,* the *Milwaukee Journal Sentinel,* and the *Baltimore Sun.*

BOYER, Dean. Newspaper reporter and freelance writer in the Seattle area.

CALHOUN, Lisa. San Antonio-based business and technical writer who has covered topics from the Russian mafia to refrigeration in China. She received her degree in professional writing from Baylor University.

COHEN, M. L. Novelist and freelance writer living in Paris.

COVELL, Jeffrey L. Freelance writer and corporate history contractor.

DERDAK, Thomas. Freelance writer and adjunct professor of philosophy at Loyola University of Chicago.

DORGAN, Charity Anne. Detroit-based freelance writer.

FELDMAN, Heidi. Los Angeles-based freelance writer.

GASBARRE, April Dougal. Archivist and freelance writer specializing in business and social history in Cleveland, Ohio.

HALASZ, Robert. Former editor in chief of *World Progress* and *Funk & Wagnalls New Encyclopedia Yearbook*; author, *The U.S. Marines* (Millbrook Press, 1993).

INGRAM, Frederick C. South Carolina-based business writer who has contributed to *GSA Business, Appalachian Trailway News,* the *Encyclopedia of Business,* the *Encyclopedia of Global Industries,* the *Encyclopedia of Consumer Brands,* and other regional and trade publications.

MALLETT, Daryl F. Freelance writer and editor; actor; contributing editor and series editor at The Borgo Press; series editor of SFRA Press's *Studies in Science Fiction, Fantasy and Horror*; associate editor of Gryphon Publications and for *Other Worlds Magazine*; founder and owner of Angel Enterprises, Jacob's Ladder Books, and Dustbunny Productions.

MOZZONE-BURGMAN, Terri. Iowa-based freelance writer specializing in corporate profiles.

PEIPPO, Kathleen. Minneapolis-based freelance writer.

PFALZGRAF, Taryn Benbow. Freelance editor, writer, and consultant in the Chicago area.

SALAMIE, David E. Part-owner of InfoWorks Development Group, a reference publication development and editorial services company.

SHELTON, Pamela L. Freelance writer and editor.

UHLE, Frank. Ann Arbor-based freelance writer; movie projectionist, disc jockey, and staff member of *Psychotronic Video* magazine.

WALDEN, David M. Freelance writer and historian in Salt Lake City; adjunct history instructor at Salt Lake Community College.

WERNICK, Ellen D. Freelance writer and editor.

WHITELEY, Laura E. Freelance writer based in Kalamazoo, Michigan.

WOODWARD, Angela. Freelance writer.

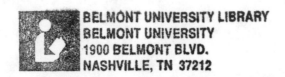